CW00522230

MACMILLAN
REEDS

YACHTSMAN'S HANDBOOK
for sail and power

EDITOR
Neville Featherstone

Consultant Editor
Edward Lee-Elliott

Published by Nautical Data Ltd

Editor: Neville Featherstone

Consultant editor: Edward Lee-Elliott

First published 1984 by Macmillan, London, Limited
This edition published by Nautical Data Limited

Copyright © Nautical Data Limited 2001

ISBN 0-333-90451-6

IMPORTANT NOTE

Whilst every care has been taken in compiling the information contained in this Handbook, the publisher, editors and their agents accept no responsibility for any errors or omissions, or for any accidents or mishaps which may arise from its use. They will be grateful for any information from readers to assist in the update and accuracy of the publication.

This Handbook is updated to Notice to Mariners No 43/2001 dated 25 October 2001

Correspondence on editorial and commercial matters should be addressed to:
Nautical Data Ltd, The Book Barn, Westbourne, Hampshire PO10 8RS

Production Control: Chris Stevens

Artwork: Jamie Russell, Garold West, Edward Lee-Elliott

Typesetting: Chris Stevens

Design: Slatter Associates

Printed and bound in Italy by Milanostampa

Foreword

This Handbook was first published by Macmillan in 1984 as a sister volume to the Macmillan Nautical Almanac. It was intended to contain all the information that changed rarely, if at all, from year to year. Thus the Almanac would be slimmer and handier than it might otherwise have been. Later editions of the Handbook grew in size and stature as new chapters were added so as to provide yet more knowledge in a variety of different fields. This new Edition has a new name, a wholly new layout and hugely updated material.

The original brief was to revise the 1995 edition, but it was soon apparent that the book needed to be almost totally re-written. It was also decided that the Handbook should be a reference work in its own right, no longer in thrall to the Almanac. Thus the decks were cleared for a more radical approach to re-organising material and chapters.

As the contents page indicates, the Handbook is now in three broad, and by no means watertight, parts which address the three essential ingredients of yachting, namely:

Part 1.   **The Human being** – you and me – as discussed in Chapters 1 to 6.
Part 2.   **The Environment** in which we go about our business (Chapters 7 to 14); and
Part 3.   **The Boat** which we sail and maintain (Chapters 15 to 21).

Before briefly considering these three ingredients, please accept that the Human being is both male and female and that 'He' (and its derivatives in this book) embraces all humankind. It is indeed one of the great pleasures of sailing that women and men participate on equal terms, whether changing the fuel filters, keeping a seamanlike watch at night, bargaining for *moules* on a French quayside or skippering a boat across the Southern Ocean.

The first six chapters deal with the business of acquiring a boat (whether or not you actually do so), training at sea and ashore, delighting in being at the helm, always conscious of the legislation which binds, yet also protects, us afloat. The former chapters on Food and Clothing have been combined into one, which might fittingly be called the Inner and Outer Man. The verbatim Collision Regulations and explanatory notes are now an important separate chapter.

The term Environment is used loosely. It encompasses, of course, the ancient elements of air and water and the disciplines of Navigation, both traditional and electronic. The Astro chapter has been retained in view of the resurgence of interest in it. Astro enshrines so much that is best in seafaring and represents a skill which has not died, despite the advent of GPS. The chapter on Safety at sea is reassuringly large, which may reflect an increasingly responsible attitude towards self-sufficiency and the art of planning and operating safely. But, despite huge advances in both Communications and GMDSS, safety must always lie first and foremost in our own hands. Knowledge, experience and sound judgement is one definition of good Seamanship. The Racing chapter neatly encapsulates the urge in most of us to sail our boats more efficiently – ergo faster.

Finally the Boat herself which for many is an enduring love affair: maintaining her yourself saves money, and could save your bacon. Here, as in other parts of the book, we have drawn on the expertise of those who design, build and equip yachts. In the course of many dialogues their depth of knowledge, quiet professionalism – and indeed understanding of their fellow humans – have been inspirational and reassuring. The important new chapter on Electrics illuminates those holes (in our knowledge) traditionally so black for so long for so many yachtsmen.

As Joseph Conrad put it in "Lord Jim": *There is nothing more enticing, disenchanting and enslaving than the life at sea.* I take it that you have already been enticed and enslaved;
I hope this book will alleviate any fleeting bouts of disenchantment.

Yachtsman's Handbook for Sail and Power

CONTENTS

Acknowledgements

A reference book of this scope and diversity owes a huge debt to the many contributors who have given so generously of their expertise and time. It is a great pleasure to thank them publicly and put their names on record.

But first I thank those who made it all possible: My wife Ann who tolerates with good humour my summers at sea and virtual absence at the keyboard during the long winter months – truly my sheet anchor (and cutter of grass).

Next my Publisher, Piers Mason, who initiated and master-minded the whole process of re-writing this sizeable tome – and who winced only slightly when I sailed around the UK on my own in the Millenium summer.

Within his publishing house I particularly pay tribute to Edward Lee-Elliott, whose unfailing good humour and patience have kept my head above water at difficult times. And within the engine room may I thank Chris Stevens, Jamie Russell and Garold West for their design excellence, artistic flair and computer skills which have happily graced the book.

To the founding fathers who first launched this Handbook into the world, the late Commander Dick Hewitt and the late Rear Admiral Tim Lees-Spalding, I pay tribute for having shown the way with such clarity of thought and expression.

May I next thank those major organisations which have kindly advised on their particular domains: The UK Hydrographic Office, the Royal Yachting Association, the British Marine Industries Federation, the Meteorological Office, the Maritime and Coastguard Agency, HM Customs & Excise, the Radiocommunications Agency, the Registry of Shipping and Seamen, the RNLI, Trinity House and Lloyd's.

Finally my personal thanks to all the individuals who helped to revise the book word by word and chapter by chapter, in whole or in part:

1. James Stevens and Kathryn Burnett (RYA); Clive Clifford (RYA Sailability); Tom Nighy (BMIF); Jane Gentry (YBDSA); Capt. Ian Wilkins (IIMS); Bill Bullimore (Patrick Boyd Multihulls Ltd); P. M. Slaughter (SMMT Ltd); and Michael Brown (YCA).

2. Annie Kettle, freelance cook and sailor; and Tim Jeffery (Daily Telegraph Sailing Correspondent).

3. Mary and Julian Ashby; Mike Balmforth.

4. Tim Bartlett and Edward Lee-Elliott.

5. João Filipe Galvão de Carvalho (Portugal); Lt Cdr Mal Tennant (UKHO).

6. Edmund Whelan and Natalie Campbell (RYA Legal).

7. Brian Goulder (NDL), Dag Pike, John Magraw and Catherine Hohenkerke (proof-reader).

8. Dr. Bernard Yallop, Tim Bartlett and Gavin McLaren.

9. Dr. Bernard Yallop and John Magraw.

10. Michael Faul (Flag Institute); Capt Richard Yeoward (Cdre Royal Dee YC); Macrocosm Ltd.

11. Frank Singleton (ex-UK Met. Office).

12. Cdr John Page (UKHO)

13. Penny Haire (RYA); Cdr Tony King (NCI); Linda Goulding (EPIRB Registry, Falmouth); John Scott (Chief Executive, Firemaster Extinguisher Ltd); Bob Wilkins (GMDSS); Martin Quaintance (Lightmaster Software); Lt Cdr D. Whitehead (CO 771 Naval Air Squadron); Roger Brydges (MAIB); Lt Cdr Les Snaith, Staff Officer (Publications), HM Coastguard; Surgeon Cdr H.L. Proctor, RD, RNR and Mrs J. Proctor (First Aid).

14. Trevor Lewis and Ken Kershaw.

15. Edward A. Burnett B.Eng (hons).

16. The late Patrick Boyd.

17. John Passmore (Selden Masts); BMIF and English Braids; Rob Kemp (Kemp Sails).

18. David Greening (Northshore Yachts).

19. David Greening (Northshore Yachts); and David Wickham (Penguin Engineering Ltd)

20. Cdr HE Manners.

21. Alistair Garrod (Practical Boat Owner).

Neville Featherstone
Trent, Dorset
November 2001

Chapter 1 Getting afloat

CONTENTS

1.1 TRAINING

1.1.1 A YACHTSMAN'S RESPONSIBILITIES

Being in charge of any boat at sea, even keeping a watch while the skipper is asleep, places real responsibility on the individuals concerned. The skipper's responsibility is total, since he alone is accountable for the safety of the yacht and her crew – even while he is asleep.

The Skipper must:

- be able to handle the boat under sail and/or power in all conditions (which may include winds of gale force);
- be totally familiar with every aspect of the boat and her equipment;
- be able to cope with whatever emergencies may arise, eg fire, man overboard, engine failure, dismasting etc;
- understand the Collision Regulations and be able to interpret and comply with them in a seamanlike way;
- be competent to navigate safely from place to place;
- be able to forecast the weather; and, very importantly,
- train his crew to play a full part in running the boat, without endangering themselves or others aboard.

All these requirements, and many others, are described in this and later chapters. They are based on considerable theoretical knowledge and practical experience, without which no skipper should go to sea. One of the delights of yachting is the apparent freedom which it offers from all the restrictions governing life ashore. But as well as being a pleasure, going to sea is something of a challenge. It also involves compliance with certain regulations, safeguarding the welfare of your crew, and possibly taking responsibility for the lives of people in other vessels or those manning the rescue services.

In Britain the authorities have so far generally adopted a policy of voluntary training and have tried to place the minimum restraints on the use of small pleasure craft. Safety standards on all yachts and power craft used for commercial purposes are now enforced by Department of Transport regulations. Yachts over 13.7m (45ft) LOA are required by law to carry certain safety equipment, but there are no such legal requirements for smaller craft. Nor are there (as yet) compulsory standards of competence for those who skipper or handle yachts. Such regulations would be difficult and expensive to enforce, but they do exist in other

countries and our authorities would not be slow to impose strict rules and expensive licencing if the situation should so require. The best safeguard against such moves is that all who go afloat for pleasure should have sufficient knowledge and practical experience to be able to cope with any problem that might reasonably be foreseen, and that their boats should be built, equipped and maintained to a proper standard.

It is however quite possible that safety regulations and standards of competence could be imposed on British yachtsmen by European legislation, which has already introduced common standards for items of safety equipment such as lifejackets.

1.1.2 RYA TRAINING SCHEMES

There is no requirement in the UK for anyone to hold a certificate of competence to use a yacht of less than 80 GRT, for sport or recreation. This freedom from regulation imposes a duty of self-sufficiency on all yachtsmen; it is up to them to ensure that they have the knowledge, skill and experience to handle their boat safely.

For over 50 years the Royal Yachting Association (see 6.6.1) has managed voluntary training schemes which encompass windsurfing, dinghy sailing, powerboating and cruising under power and sail. The schemes aim to provide appropriate training for all who want to learn to sail, to use a powerboat, or to improve their boathandling, seamanship and navigation.

The RYA training schemes are operated by more than a thousand recognised teaching establishments, which include clubs, local authority sailing centres, commercial sailing schools and night schools. To gain recognition schools must show that they have boats which are sound and suitably equipped for teaching, with qualified instructors and adequate shoreside teaching facilities. For a list of schools and the courses they offer contact the RYA at RYA House, Romsey Road, Eastleigh, Hants SO50 9YA. Tel 023 8062 7400; Fax 023 8062 9924. www.rya.org.uk admin@rya.org.uk

The RYA believes that its voluntary system of training is more effective in keeping the risks inherent in yachting down to an acceptable level than any system of compulsory 'driving licences' could possibly be. By its very nature, a compulsory system would have to be confined to a test of the lowest acceptable level of proficiency. The voluntary scheme, on the other hand, can encourage very much higher standards.

For those wishing to take up sailing there are

two Schemes, depending on age: The Youth Sailing Scheme is for young people (1.1.3) and the National Sailing Scheme (1.1.4) for adults. The difference between the two lies not so much in what is learned as in the way that it is learned.

1.1.3 YOUTH SAILING SCHEME

This Scheme attracts about 20,000 youngsters a year who first sail dinghies at RYA recognised schools. As shown in Fig. 1(1) the first module, "Start Sailing", progresses through three stages of competence, both on the water and in the classroom. After that there is the option of going on to the Advanced Sailing module or the Racing module or both. These also progress through Red, White and Blue levels of competence, both practical and theoretical. They also require one season of sailing experience between each of the three levels.

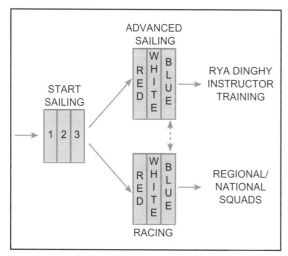

Fig. 1(1) The Youth Sailing Scheme.

By the time the Blue levels have been achieved, the young sailor is competent to take away a dinghy on a coastal cruise in tidal waters or be eligible for training as an RYA Dinghy Instructor. On the racing side, he/she has a wide knowledge and experience of racing techniques and tactics. From such beginnings an aspiring helm or crew may well elect to progress further into Regional and ultimately National Squads and beyond ...

The RYA booklet G11 *Dinghy Sailing* gives details of these schemes and a logbook for recording your sailing experience and retaining the various certificates.

The National School Sailing Association (NSSA) is a charitable trust which works with the RYA to promote youth sailing. For details contact the Secretary on Tel/Fax 01767 627370 or cmarch@nssa.softnet.co.uk

1.1.4 NATIONAL SAILING SCHEME

Most successful racing helmsmen/women started sailing in dinghies and anyone who wants to learn to sail, whatever boats they may eventually plan to own, can do no better than to begin with a dinghy sailing course. They must, however, not mind getting wet. Dinghies have no ballast; the weight of the crew keeps them upright and at some stage a capsize is virtually inevitable. An integral part of learning to sail dinghies is learning to right a capsized boat, which necessitates a short swim.

The structure and syllabus for the National Sailing Scheme is in RYA booklet G4 *National Sailing* which is also a logbook; a summary is in Figs. 1(2) and 1(3).

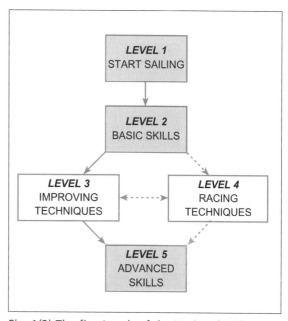

Fig. 1(2) The five Levels of the National Sailing Scheme.

Traditionally, dinghy sailing was taught in boats such as the Wayfarer, in which the instructor sailed with his students. While this system is still very effective, it is now just as common for students to go straight into single-handed dinghies such as Optimists, Toppers or Lasers, with the instructor in a powerboat accompanying up to six dinghies. The speed of learning is generally faster, with each student spending much more time at the tiller, thereby enhancing the satisfaction of achievement.

For those who want to learn in something larger and more stable than a dinghy (but do not plan to live aboard a boat), keelboats provide the appropriate training from Level 3 onwards. It is broadly similar to dinghy sailing, but excludes capsize recovery and places more emphasis on handling larger, heavier boats.

	LEVEL 1 Start Sailing	LEVEL 2 Basic Skills	LEVEL 3 Improving Techniques	LEVEL 4 Racing Techniques	LEVEL 5 Advanced Skills
Rigging	Wind awareness, rigging a single-hander or training dinghy.	Rigging a training dinghy or dayboat, reefing ashore, parts of the boat and sails.	As Level 2 (using all the boat's equipment)	Rigging a racing dinghy as appropriate, rig tuning controls.	Rigging any type of dinghy or dayboat, including spinnaker/trapeze.
Ropework	Figure of eight, round turn and two half-hitches.	Bowline.	Fisherman's bend, sheetbend, clove hitch, rolling hitch. Whipping, splicing.		
Launching/ Recovery	Wind awareness, use of trolley, launching, leaving the shore, coming ashore.	Storage ashore, paddling, rowing.	Leaving/returning to beach, jetty or mooring, Windward/ leeward shores. Use of anchor.		As Level 3. Sailing backwards.
Sailing techniques and manoeuvres	Wind awareness, reaching, stopping, tacking, getting out of irons, sailing upwind and downwind,	The five essentials. Man overboard recovery.	Anchoring, heaving to, reefing afloat, towing/being towed.	Advanced tacking/gybing, sailing to windward, mark rounding.	As Level 3, using all boat's equipment to best advantage, rudderless sailing, sailing without a centre board, sailing in a tight circle.
Capsize recovery	Stay with boat.	Righting - scoop, righting a single-hander.	Righting an inverted dinghy.		As Level 3 plus full bailing.
Racing	Clubs and classes.	The course, starting procedure.	Mark rounding.	Starting techniques, rules, tactics.	
Sailing theory and background	Basic rules: port/starboard, windward boat, overtaking boat.	Points of sailing, no go zone, basic aerodynamic theory, buoyage, sea/inland advice.	Sea terms, resuscitation and First Aid, IRPCS.	Handicap v. Class racing. Club racing, sailing instructions, insurance.	Navigation for dinghies and dayboats, construction and repair.
Meteorology	Onshore/offshore winds,	Sources of forecasts, when to reef.	Simple met. and interpretation of forecasts.	Local weather patterns, strategy.	Detailed interpretation, planning for day's journey.
Clothing/ equipment	Clothing, personal buoyancy.	Boat buoyancy, safety equipment.			Requirements for day's journey/ dinghy cruising.

Fig. 1(3) Outline Syllabus for the National Sailing Scheme

1.1.5 NATIONAL CRUISING SCHEME (SAIL AND POWER)

Separate schemes cater for Sailing yachtsmen and Motor yachtsmen, although the syllabi of the shorebased courses are virtually identical.

These schemes contain three complementary elements, each of which, plus written and practical examinations, must be satisfied in order to be awarded a Certificate of Competence at the Coastal Skipper, Yachtmaster Offshore or Yachtmaster Ocean levels:

1. *Shorebased courses.* These are usually taken as night school courses, over the two winter terms, although they are also available by correspondence or as full-time courses of about one week. They concentrate on navigation and meteorology.

2. *Practical courses.* These are five-day courses at sea, offered by RYA-recognised sailing schools around the UK coast and by a limited number of schools abroad.

3. *Practical experience.* Although the full syllabus for Yachtmaster Offshore can be covered in a winter of night school courses and three five-day practical courses, it is impossible to become a competent yacht skipper without spending a considerable amount of time putting the lessons learnt in the classroom

Course	Suggested minimum pre-course experience	Assumed experience	Course content knowledge	Ability after course	Minimum duration
Competent crew practical	None	None	Basic seamanship and helmsmanship.	Useful crew member.	5 days
*Day Skipper shorebased**	*Some practical experience desirable.*	*None*	*Basic seamanship and introduction to navigation and and meteorology.*		*40 hrs tuition & 4 hrs for exams*
Day Skipper practical†	5 days, 100 miles, 4 night hours.	Basic navigation and sailing ability.	Basic pilotage, boat handling, seamanship and navigation.	Skipper a small yacht in familiar waters by day.	5 days
Diesel engine	*None*	*None*	*Diesel engine operation, maintenance and simple defect rectification.*	*Operate a diesel engine effectively and carry out simple repairs.*	*6 hours*
*Coastal Skipper/ Yachtmaster Offshore shorebased**		*Navigation to Day Skipper shorebased standard.*	*Offshore and coastal navigation, pilotage and meteorology.*		*40 hrs tuition & 6 hrs for exams*
Coastal Skipper practical†	15 days (2 days as skipper). 300 miles, 8 night hours.	Navigation to Coastal Skipper shorebased standard. Sailing to Day Skipper practical standard.	Skippering techniques for coastal and offshore passages.	Skipper a yacht on coastal passages by day and night.	5 days
Yachtmaster Ocean shorebased	*Coastal and offshore sailing.*	*Navigation to Coastal Skipper and Yachtmaster Offshore shore-based standard.*	*Astro-navigation, ocean meteorology and passage planning.*		*40 hrs tuition & 2 hrs for exams*

*Fig. 1(4) Sail Cruising Courses. *Same syllabus for sailing and motor cruising yachtsmen. † Different courses for tidal and non-tidal waters.* Shorebased courses are shown in italics.

and in the sailing school into practice in a range of different locations and under different weather conditions at sea. Each practical course syllabus therefore specifies a minimum recommended level of pre-course experience and every candidate must have specified amounts of experience to be eligible to take a practical exam for a Coastal Skipper or Yachtmaster Certificate of Competence. Coastal Skipper and Yachtmaster candidates must also hold a First Aid certificate and a Radio Operator's Certificate (VHF only or SRC) before taking the practical examination. A one day Diesel Engine course is not a requirement, but is highly recommended as mechanical failure is the main reason why the RNLI are called to the aid of auxiliary cruising yachts.

The Yachtmaster training courses are outlined in Figs. 1(4) and 1(5).

The syllabi for the Coastal Skipper, Yachtmaster Offshore and Yachtmaster Ocean exams are set by the Yachtmaster Qualification Panel. The chairman and 2 members of the panel are appointed by the RYA; other members are appointed by the Marine Directorate of the Department of Transport, the Department of Education, the Association of Sea Training Organisations and the military sailing associations.

Details of the pre-exam requirements and the form of examination are shown in Fig. 1(6).

Coastal Skipper and Yachtmaster Offshore practical exams are, as far as possible, tests of effective competence at sea. Details are given in the RYA Cruising and Motor Cruising Logbooks, G15 and G18 respectively. Candidates must provide a cruising yacht, normally not less than 24ft LOA, in sound, seaworthy condition and equipped to the standards set out in RYA booklet C8, *Cruising Yacht Safety.* The yacht must be equipped with a full and up-to-date set of charts and navigational publications and be efficiently crewed, as the examiner will play no part in the management of the yacht during the exam. It is often convenient to take the exam in a sailing school boat at the end of a course.

Yachtmaster Ocean exams are oral, with questions based on the candidate's qualifying

Course	Suggested minimum pre-course experience	Assumed experience	Course content knowledge	Ability after course	Minimum duration
Helmsman's course	Some practical experience desirable.	None	Boating safety, helmsmanship, boat handling, Introduction to engine maintenance.	Competent to handle motor cruiser of specific type in sheltered waters.	2 days
*Day Skipper shorebased**	*Some practical experience desirable.*	*None*	*Basic seamanship and introduction to navigation and meteorology.*		*40 hrs tuition & 4 hrs for exams*
Day Skipper practical†	2 days	Basic navigation and helmsmanship.	Pilotage, boat handling, seamanship and navigation.	Skipper a motor cruiser in familiar waters by day.	4 days
Diesel engine	*None*	*None*	*Diesel engine operation, maintenance and simple defect rectification.*	*Operate a diesel engine effectively and carry out simple repairs.*	*6 hours*
Coastal Skipper/ Yachtmaster Offshore shorebased		*Navigation to Day Skipper shorebased standard.*	*Offshore and coastal navigation pilotage and meteorology.*		*40 hrs tuition & 6 hrs for exams*
Coastal Skipper practical†	15 days (2 days as skipper), 300 miles, 8 night hours.	Navigation to Coastal Skipper shorebased standard. Boat handling to Day Skipper practical standard.	Skippering techniques for coastal and offshore passages.	Skipper a motor cruiser on coastal passages by day and night.	5 days
Yachtmaster Ocean shorebased	*Coastal and offshore passages.*	*Navigation to Coastal Skipper and Yachtmaster Offshore shorebased standard.*	*Astro-navigation, ocean meteorology and passage planning.*		*40 hrs tuition & 2 hrs for exams*

Fig. 1(5) Motor Cruising Courses. *Same syllabus for sailing and motor cruising yachtsmen.
† Different courses for tidal and non-tidal waters. Shorebased courses are shown in italics.

Grade of examination	Minimum seatime (within 10 years of exam)	Form of examination	Certificates required before examination
Coastal Skipper	30 days, 2 days as skipper, 800 miles, 12 night hours*.	Practical. 6-10 hrs one person; 8-14 hrs for two people.	VHF or SRC Radio Operator's Certificate. First Aid Certificate.
Yachtmaster Offshore	50 days, 5 days as skipper, 2500M, 5 passages over 60M, including 2 overnight and 2 as skipper.	Practical 8-12 hrs one person; 10-18 hrs for two people.	VHF or SRC Radio Operator's Certificate. First Aid Certificate
Yachtmaster Ocean	Ocean passage as skipper or mate of watch.	Oral, and assessment of sights taken at sea. (Written exam in lieu of shore-based course completion certificate)	RYA/MCA Yachtmaster Offshore and Yachtmaster Ocean shorebased Course Completion Certificates.

Fig. 1(6) Practical Examinations – RYA/MCA Certificates of Competence.
*For holders of the Coastal Skipper Practical Course Completion Certificate the seatime requirement is reduced to: 20 days, 2 days as skipper, 400 miles, 12 night hours.

ocean passage; the examination includes an assessment of the results of the candidate's astro navigation carried out at sea.

To apply for certificates of competence obtain an application form from the RYA or any of the examination centres listed at the end of the G15 Log Book. Examination dates are arranged by these centres to suit the mutual convenience of candidates and examiners.

Other benefits of the Yachtmaster certificates
Although a certificate of competence is not required to skipper a British yacht of less than 80 GRT, yachts over this size are subject to the provisions of the Merchant Shipping (Certification of Deck Officers) Regulations. Holders of Yachtmaster certificates are exempted from these regulations (for passages appropriate to their level of Yachtmaster Certificate) in yachts up to 200 GRT, provided that they are not used for commercial purposes.

A Yachtmaster certificate may also be used as a qualification to skipper a yacht of up to 24 metres LOA, used for commercial purposes, subject to some additional provisions which do not apply to the amateur sailor. The certificate holder must pass a medical exam, have attended a survival course and revalidate his qualification five-yearly by showing that he has recent sea experience and continues to be medically fit.

1.1.6 POWERBOAT COURSES
The RYA Powerboating Scheme, Fig. 1(7), provides courses at RYA recognised schools for handling the many different types of small powerboat in a competent and responsible way. For further details see RYA booklet G20 "Powerboating Logbook".

Levels **1** (Introduction, 1 day) and **2** (2 days National Certificate) cover the basics of

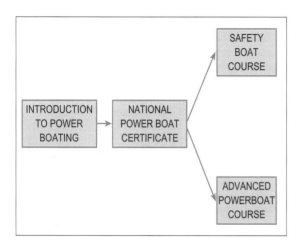

Fig. 1(7) National Powerboating Scheme.

boathandling, safety and good seamanship, both afloat and in the classroom. Having gained the National Certificate, the next stage is either the Safety Boat Course (2 days) or the Advanced Powerboat Course (2 days) or both. These courses are run in conjunction with the appropriate governing bodies of other water sports (ie the British Water Ski Federation, British Sub-Aqua Club, British Canoe Union and the Royal Life Saving Society).

1.1.7 INTERNATIONAL CERTIFICATE OF COMPETENCE
In October 1998 a new, now the current, version of the International Certificate of Competence (ICC) came into force under UN Resolution No 40. It superseded the old ICC and the former Helmsman's (Overseas) Certificate of Competence (HOCC). Any existing HOCCs remain valid until expiry, when they will be convertible to an ICC.

The main differences between old and new ICCs are:
  a. The latter can only be gained by practical tests of competence and knowledge at an RYA-recognised school or Club, unless you qualify as the holder of an RYA Day/Coastal Skipper or Yachtmaster Offshore Certificate; or have professional or military seagoing qualifications.
  b. If you intend navigating on inland waters, rivers and canals when abroad, you must pass a written test on CEVNI; see the final paragraph of this section.

The ICC is issued only by the RYA. It is valid for five years and needs a passport photograph. The fee for non-members of the RYA is £26.00, but it is free to members. CEVNI stands for *Code Européen des Voies de la Navigation Intérieure* (European Rules for inland water-ways), in effect an inland version of ColRegs. CEVNI includes a good many inland waterway signs which must be known for both test and practical reasons. The primary textbook for Britishers is *"The RYA book of EuroRegs"* by Marion Martin (Adlard Coles) at £5.99; also available as RYA booklet ZE 02. The *Vagnon Carte de Plaisance* in French, English and German should suffice in France. In addition to the ICC, certain countries require their own national rules for inland waterways to be held on board, eg in the Netherlands, the *Binnenvaart Politie Reglement* (BPR) in the Dutch language. See RYA booklets C1 and C2 for such national requirements.

The RYA website (www.rya.org.uk) gives further details about both ICC and CEVNI requirements.

1.2.1 CHOOSING A BOAT

There are so many boats of differing types and sizes on the market, both new and second-hand, that the choice can be quite bewildering even for a relatively experienced yachtsman. So sail in as many different types as possible. Listen to the opinions of other owners. Do not hesitate to seek advice. Read reviews of every boat that may interest you; study the For Sale and brokerage columns of the yachting magazines. Visit the major boat shows if you are in the new boat market, but be wary of the gloss and artificiality; however at the same time you may be able to negotiate worthwhile terms. Gradually a short list of say three or four different types should emerge. Be prepared to spend a lot of time viewing boats and getting frustrated in the process. You will see a lot of grossly neglected boats for sale, but the good ones are there too, although you may need to move fast to clinch a deal when the right one appears.

A bad choice could be both a nautical and financial disaster, which may put you and your family off boats for ever. The right choice can give you endless pride and pleasure – the pride of owning, cruising and maintaining a good boat is very lasting and tangible. You will develop an enormous bond with your boat, especially when she has seen you safely through bad weather.

1.2.2 ANALYSING YOUR NEEDS

To arrive at this happy state of affairs you need to ask yourself a lot of questions, and to be utterly objective and truthful in answering them:

a. Why do you want a boat at all? How often will she be used? Where will she be cruised? Who is likely to be on board? Will the boat take the place of holiday trips, or only be used for occasional weekends during the summer? Where will she be kept?

If you find it difficult to justify owning a boat because of the limited use she might have, do not ignore the very popular option of chartering which is described in 1.9.

If however you can satisfy yourself, and perhaps your wife, that a boat is justified, then continue the analysis:

b. Can you afford her (the boat), both now and in the longer term? Exactly how much money can you spare for the initial outlay? Have you drawn up an annual budget for running and maintaining the boat? The principal items of expenditure will be: berthing, maintenance and repair, new equipment, insurance and fuel – probably in that order. Maintenance and repair may appeal to a handyman if he can devote the time and thereby save money, but the others are inescapable.

c. Have you allowed for annual depreciation in the value of the boat, and for the capital locked up in her? If you need a marine mortgage or other financing (see 1.2.11), has the cost of servicing the loan been considered?

d. If buying a new boat, have you allowed quite a large sum to buy vital equipment which is not included in the price? For example, navigational gear, charts, safety equipment, a dinghy, galley and other domestic gear fall into this category. This is one attractive reason for buying a second-hand boat, as many such items may be included.

Taking all these figures into account gives an idea of the cost, and hence the size, of boat that can be afforded.

e. Then decide where you will keep her and at what cost. Will she be in a marina? Or at a mooring? How sheltered and accessible will the latter be?

f. Will she need to dry out, either when on the mooring or in her intended cruising area? Have you considered a small cruising boat (but only the smallest) which can be kept ashore on a trailer, and towed to different locations?

g. Do you intend to sail locally, or to cruise along the coast, or perhaps further offshore? What sort of crew will normally be available, and how strong are they both in physique and in experience? Is the boat to be sail or power, or a combination of the two?

By now a clearer idea of the type and size of boat should be emerging, and your short list may be narrowing down. Study the appropriate magazines in detail to see what is on offer, and visit the major boat shows.

h. Next consider some more detailed requirements which might include hull form and material, accommodation layout, rig, type of engine and deck plan. Unless you are an experienced yachtsman it may be advisable to seek advice on some of these points, although they are dealt with in more detail in later chapters.

i. Before starting to search in earnest, write out a detailed specification, based on your answers to the above questions, and decide on the priority of the various items. Ensure that the requirements are not mutually exclusive, or your hunt will be a waste of time and money. Travel is expensive, so try to cover boats in your locality before journeying to the other end of the country.

j. You may discover that your dream boat does not exist in production form, possibly for good reasons. But if you wish to persist the only solution would be to have a boat specifically designed and built for your needs. This would probably be an expensive project, but one likely to produce the best answer for unusual requirements.

k. Another possible approach is to take a stock hull (a large variety of GRP mouldings are readily available, for example) and have it completed to your specifications. If you have the necessary skills and plenty of spare time, you may be able to undertake some of this work yourself, with a consequent saving in cost.

l. There are two ways that an individual owner may be able to afford ownership of a more expensive boat:
   i. part ownership; and
   ii. time sharing.

The former is well established, even though it may pose practical difficulties. Partners must share common views on how the boat is operated and maintained. Problems may arise when one wishes to sell his share, unless some form of contract has been agreed.

Time sharing is relatively new, and you may wonder how it (and the boats concerned) will work in practice. If you are to avoid problems with shared usage and holiday times, again some form of contract is worth considering.

1.2.3 LEGAL ASPECTS

It helps to understand current consumer legislation, as described in *The Yachtsman's Lawyer* by Edmund Whelan and published by the RYA (G9). This booklet is also a comprehensive guide to other legal aspects of yachting.

New boats (1.2.4) are sold either by their builders or by distributors acting as agents for the builder; or, in the case of yachts built abroad, by importers acting as principals rather than as agents. Larger firms advertise prominently, and exhibit their products at the major boat shows, but there are many smaller yards which produce good boats and have lower overheads. In boat building, big is not necessarily beautiful. Excellent and detailed advice is provided in the RYA booklet *Buying a New Yacht* (G10, 3rd edition).

Second-hand boats (1.2.6) are sold either privately by the owner (sometimes in a boat auction), or through a yacht broker. For further information read RYA booklet G21 *Buying a Second-Hand Yacht.*

Standard forms of agreement for buying a new boat are available from the BMIF or RYA; likewise for buying a second-hand boat through an ABYA broker (Note: the ABYA agreement was revised in Spring 2001). For private purchase of a second-hand boat, a standard form of agreement is available from the RYA. It is highly advisable to use one of these agreements as they define the rights and liabilities of both seller and buyer at every stage of the contract. This is particularly important if problems arise, eg the builder going into receivership before delivery of the yacht. If a builder or agent offers another form of agreement, compare it carefully with the standard forms of agreement before committing yourself.

Where a boat is being sold by an agent on behalf of a UK builder, it is worthwhile obtaining an undertaking from the builder that he will honour any contractual obligations either before or after delivery of the boat, if the agent goes out of business. Get such an undertaking in writing before committing yourself. Do **NOT** pay all the money up front. At the very least retain a final instalment for the completion of the sale and transfer of ownership.

Consumer Legislation

Substantial consumer protection is afforded to the private buyer of a boat (and any boat owner who enters into transactions with chandlers, sailmakers, riggers, engineers or any supplier of goods) under the Sales of Goods Act 1979 (amended) and the Supply of Goods and Services Act 1982. The consumer's general concerns under the *Sale of Goods Act 1994* are limited to sections 12 to 14 of that Act – Section 12 (legal right of the seller to sell goods); Section 13 (goods to comply with the seller's description or sample); and Section 14 (terms as to quality and fitness: goods to be fit for the purpose for which they are required and to be of satisfactory quality).

Section 12 provides that the seller must have the right to sell the goods. If he is not the owner, or if a third party (eg a finance company) has an interest in the goods, the Act imposes a condition to protect the buyer whether or not the seller knew his title was defective (unless the parties have made a specific agreement to the contrary). In such a case the buyer may repudiate the contract and claim a full refund of the purchase price in addition to damages for any resulting loss.

Section 13 provides that goods sold by description must comply in all material particulars with that description, failing which the buyer may reject the goods or claim damages. This would be relevant where the agreed specification of a standard yacht was changed between the order and delivery without the buyer's agreement. Even if a yacht were able to be modified so as to comply, unless the difference in specification was minimal, the buyer would be entitled to reject it or claim damages.

If the buyer decides that he wishes to exercise his option to reject, this must be exercised promptly; a delay of even a few weeks can be fatal to the right to reject, although of course he can still claim damages.

Section 14 strictly applies to consumer sales and imposes an obligation, which cannot be excluded or restricted, that the goods sold must be of a standard that a reasonable person would regard as satisfactory, taking into account any description of the goods, the price and all other relevant circumstances. The quality of the goods will take into consideration: (a) the fitness of those goods for the purpose for which they are commonly supplied; (b) appearance and finish; (c) freedom from minor defects; (d) safety; and (e) durability.

In non-consumer sales, the obligation can be restricted or excluded only in so far as it is reasonable to do so.

The implied term of satisfactory quality will not extend to any matter making the goods unsatisfactory which has been drawn to the attention of the buyer, or where the buyer has examined the goods before negotiating a contract of sale, or on sale by sample when the buyer has had the opportunity to identify a defect which would have been apparent in the sample on reasonable examination of a sample.

Section 14 also provides that where goods are sold in the course of a business and the buyer makes known to the seller, expressly or implicitly, the purpose for which the goods are required, there is an implied condition that the goods will be reasonably fit for that purpose. This provision only applies where the buyer relied on the seller's skill and judgement in advising him on his requirements. The seller is not deemed to promise that the goods are absolutely suitable, rather that they are reasonably fit for the purpose. A boat may be reasonably fit for the purpose even though she is known to require repairs or modifications to be absolutely suitable for that purpose. On the other hand even a minor defect making her unfit will entitle the buyer to reject, provided his rejection is made as soon as possible after delivery of the boat. For example, the Environment Agency, British Waterways Board,

and the Broads Authority impose a set of precise construction and equipment standards on new craft coming onto their waterways. If the builder or dealer had been told that the boat was required to comply with those standards, and she failed to pass the scrutiny of an Authority's licensing inspector, the buyer may be entitled to reject the boat (or claim damages) unless the defects were really trivial.

In addition to the *Sales of Goods Acts*, the newest being 1994, there is an increasing range of legislation to protect the consumer, including the *Sale & Supply of Goods Act 1994, Supply of Goods and Services Act 1982*, and the *Unfair Contract Terms Act 1977*. You should pursue your rights as quickly as possible, as a court may decide that a delay implies acceptance of the goods with all their faults; or you may be deemed to have had enough use of the goods to endanger your rights to receive damages.It is also important to pursue any complaint against the seller rather than the manufacturer or builder, since the seller is the one with the obligation to remedy matters. You only need concern yourself with any additional warranty provided by the manufacturer if the seller is unable to meet his contractual obligations.

Be warned that if you buy a boat (or even an item of equipment) direct from an overseas supplier, you are unlikely to have any claim under English law if some problem should arise, but you may be able to pursue a claim in the country where the contract lies if it is within Europe. Unless stated otherwise, the contract jurisdiction will normally be where the transaction took place.

1.2.4 BUYING NEW

Agreement for the Construction of a New Boat is a standard form of agreement which can be obtained from the BMIF or the RYA. When a boat is being built to order instalment payments should be agreed, typically: 10% on signing the agreement; 30% on the hull being available at the builders; 40% on completion of interior joinery work, installation of the engine, or stepping of the mast; 20% on completion of the acceptance trial to the customer's satisfaction.

An important feature of the standard agreement form is the provision for the property (ie the right of ownership) in the yacht, her raw materials and other component parts and equipment to pass to the buyer as soon as they have been allocated to the job by the builder, subject only to the builder's lien in respect of incomplete stage payments. This provision gives valuable protection in the event of the builder going into liquidation, as the yacht herself will not be an asset of the company. The purchaser should ensure that valuable items, such as engines, sails, spars etc, received by the yard prior to completion of the yacht are clearly identified as being appropriated to his contract. Some form of insurance needs to be arranged for such items. The boat should also comply with the Recreational Craft Directive; see 1.2.5.

Where VAT is payable it forms part of the price, and the figures written into the contract should include VAT at the rate applicable on the date of the agreement. The form also sets out the expected dates for an acceptance trial, and for delivery. It may be appropriate to include an Agreed Damages Clause, as a time penalty against late delivery.

For stock production boats the above system of stage payments is usually modified to provide for a deposit of (say) 10% on order, and the balance on delivery. This would be stated in *Agreement for the Sale of a Stock Boat* another BMIF standard form of agreement.

A purchaser should insist on a proper sea trial for any boat (whether new or second-hand). Ideally such a trial should show not only that the boat is in working order but that she and all her equipment perform in accordance with the designed specification. But this takes a lot of time, and requires expensive instrumentation; so yacht owners have to be content with a purely functional trial. This, however, should demonstrate all aspects of the boat and her equipment. It should, for example, be shown that the engine runs satisfactorily for a reasonable time, without overheating and without undue noise or vibration, and that it propels the boat at the designed speed while operating within its designed rpm. Ahead and astern operation of the gearbox should be demonstrated. Engine instrumentation should be checked, together with any alarms that may be fitted (for example to indicate high cooling water temperature). Similar trials should be conducted for all other items of equipment: navigational instruments, anchor windlass, steering gear, autopilot, bilge pumps, refrigerator, cooker, lighting systems etc.

The purchaser may refuse to accept the boat until any faults exposed by the acceptance trial have been rectified. When this has been done, the buyer must sign the acceptance form and make the final payment. Ownership of the boat is then transferred to the purchaser, who should have arranged insurance cover from that moment (see 1.2.12).

Should any fault subsequently develop with the boat, the buyer still has redress as described above. The BMIF and the RYA may advise on arranging arbitration. This is certainly speedier and less formal than court proceedings, but it is more suitable for deciding questions of fact such as the value and standard of work done, rather than questions of law such as rights and liabilities arising out of a contract. Both parties must be agreeable to this procedure, which may be written into the original contract. Notes on arbitration are available from the BMIF, Meadlake Place, Thorpe Lea Road, Egham, Surrey TW20 8BF; Tel 01784 473377; Fax 01784 439678. ashepard@bmif.co.uk www.bmif.com

The possible bankruptcy of a boat builder has always been of concern to clients, but the problem has been somewhat reduced by the inclusion of a special clause in the agreement referred to above, which establishes that material or equipment obtained by the builder specifically for a certain contract becomes the property of the buyer of the boat on settlement of the first instalment payment. The purchaser should ensure that valuable items, such as an engine, received by the yard are clearly identified as being appropriated for his yacht.

1.2.5 THE RECREATIONAL CRAFT DIRECTIVE (RCD)

The RCD is a substantial document (94/25/EC) produced by the European Union. It has been in force since June 1996 and its requirements became mandatory two years later on 16 June 1998. It requires most new recreational craft, (and some secondhand craft), from 2·5m to 24m LOA, when first sold in the EU to comply with certain Essential Safety Requirements (ESR). It is these ESR which lie at the heart of the RCD and the emphasis throughout is on safety – just as the motor industry has to comply with legislation affecting seat belts, MoT tests, motorcycle crash helmets etc.

The effect of the RCD is to set a standard specification for the construction of boats within the EC. Prior to the RCD, different sets of rules applied in the various EU countries. Thus a significant barrier to trading within the EU is/will be removed.

It is up to boatbuilders to comply with the 29 ESR and failure to do so could result in a £5000 fine and/or three months imprisonment, and an inability to sell boats on the UK and European market. Trading Standards Officers are enforcing the RCD. However some of the ESR fall within the description of "good boatbuilding practices"; others require an Owner's Manual to be produced and a Technical File demonstrating how each ESR has been met. Compliance will result in the granting of the CE mark and this must be verified by prospective buyers.

They should also be aware of the four Design Categories which apply certain sea and wind criteria to craft:

Category	Significant wave height	Wind force
A - Ocean	> 4m	> F8
B - Offshore	4m and less	F8 & below
C - Inshore	2m and less	F6 & below
D - Sheltered waters.	0·5m and less	F4 & below

These categories do not determine how the craft is used, but may vary the relevant ESRs and their compliance. For further details on the RCD consult the BMIF Technical Service (Tel 01784 223634) or the DTI.

1.2.6 BUYING SECOND-HAND

Buying a second-hand Yacht – the legal aspects (RYA G21, 2nd edition) is a very useful booklet covering the whole process from survey to finding a mooring or berth. It includes draft contracts and a specimen Bill of Sale.

Second-hand boats are mainly bought through yacht brokers, or are advertised and sold privately. A few are sold at marine auctions, where you should note that a boat is sold 'as she lies', so that it is very important to find out all about her before bidding.

Unless the equipment, specification or condition of the yacht has been specifically misrepresented by the seller or his agent, a buyer is unlikely to have legal redress against a private individual who sells him a boat which proves to be unsatisfactory. The buyer is only automatically protected in this respect if he buys the boat from somebody who is selling her in connection with his trade or business. So, although there may be good bargains to be had, buying a second-hand boat can be chancy for an inexperienced yachtsman unless he is prepared to seek professional advice. A survey by a qualified surveyor is virtually essential; see 1.2.10.

The question of title must be investigated. With a Part I registered yacht contact the Registry of Shipping and Seamen (see 1.4.2) who can confirm the present owner(s) and whether the boat is subject to a marine mortgage. Otherwise check whatever documents are available (eg a Builder's Certificate and subsequent contracts or bills of sale). Note that Small Ships Registration (see 1.4.3) does not give clear proof of ownership.

Since an increasing number of finance houses are now offering customers unregistered mortgages, this is becoming a particular risk for subsequent buyers. Unfortunately there is no means (short of enquiring from each and every finance house in the marine market) of checking whether an unregistered mortgage is outstanding, should the seller choose to conceal the fact. In recent years a number of innocent private buyers have had their boats repossessed by finance houses where the sellers had failed to settle an outstanding mortgage on receipt of the purchase money. The purchaser should secure a letter of indemnity from the seller as part of the contract of sale. Then, if the yacht is repossessed by a finance house, the purchaser may seek the loss from the seller.

When buying direct from an individual a written agreement is strongly advised, to cover the following: The intending purchaser, having paid a deposit of 10% of the agreed price, is free to arrange a survey of the boat at his own expense within 14 days. On completion of the survey the purchaser may withdraw from the agreement, in which case he must restore the boat to her original condition before his deposit is refunded. If the purchaser wishes to proceed, any defects found on survey must be discussed between the two parties, so that the seller either agrees to make them good or to reduce the price accordingly, taking into consideration the age and value of the boat. If agreement cannot be reached, the contract is void.

The agreement should include statements to the effect that the boat is being sold free of all encumbrances or lien (ie that nobody else has any claim on the boat). There may be an outstanding marine mortgage (which will only be obvious if registered) or personal loan attached to the boat; or a boat yard, chandler, marina or salvage claimant may have a continuing lien. A declaration should also be obtained that there are no known defects other than those which have been shown to the purchaser. These points can be found in the RYA's *Agreement for the Sale of a Secondhand Yacht*, which is aimed at people selling their boat privately and not in the course of business.

If a yacht is registered under Part I of the Register, Merchant Shipping Act 1995, further formalities have to be completed. These include a Bill of Sale and a Declaration of Eligibility, which have to be forwarded with the Certificate of Registry and the appropriate fee to the Registry of Shipping and Seamen. For a yacht on the Small Ships Register, registration is automatically terminated on change of ownership, and the certificate should be surrendered by the previous owner. The new owner must make a fresh application. More information about registration appears in Section 1.4.

If you are buying a boat with a trailer and

are doubtful about the latter's condition or legality (section 1.10), it is advisable to consult one of the motoring organisations.

1.2.7 PART-EXCHANGE OF YACHTS

In recent years trading-in a secondhand yacht against the purchase of a new one has become more common, and several yacht builders and distributors now offer this facility. Some only accept their own make of boat in such transactions, while others will take any boat that is in good enough condition for re-sale, but may limit the value of the second-hand boat compared to the cost of the new one. Some builders and dealers operate their own brokerage firms to sell off boats taken in part exchange, while others sell them through normal brokers.

Inevitably the price offered for part-exchange is less than could be obtained by private sale or through a yacht broker, and sometimes it is well below that figure. But to offset this there are certain advantages: no commission to be paid; none of the costs such as advertising that are incurred in a private sale; plus the benefit of being able to make an immediate deal which in turn may attract a special discount on the price of the new boat.

But obviously there are no general rules governing such transactions (unlike sales brokered by members of the YBDSA), so anybody buying a boat on part-exchange should look into the deal very carefully.

1.2.8 YACHT BROKERS

Yacht brokers provide an important service for buying and selling boats. If you are buying a boat of any size, or are inexperienced in such matters, it is highly advisable to deal through a yacht broker. They can advise on the suitability of a boat for your particular purpose, and can track down those which are likely to meet your needs. They can help to arrange slipping and survey (very useful if you happen to live elsewhere), with a mortgage, if required (see 1.2.11) and with insurance (see 1.2.12). They can check details such as the inventory of the boat, and ensure that documentation is properly completed so that title is fully transferred.

The Yacht Brokers, Designers & Surveyors Association (YBDSA) is a Holding company which administers its two component bodies: the Yacht Designers & Surveyors Association (YDSA) and the Association of Brokers and Yacht Agents (ABYA). Contact the YBDSA at Wheel House, Petersfield Road, Whitehill, Bordon, Hants GU35 9BU; Tel 01420 473862; Fax 488328. info@ybdsa.co.uk.

The ABYA is the professional body for individual yacht brokers (as opposed to brokerage companies) and yacht agents. The distinction is a fine one: a broker buys and sells boats on behalf of clients. An agent, who could also be a broker, might be employed by a buyer to look after his interests when, for example, taking delivery abroad of a new yacht from a foreign builder.

To become a member a broker must show a record of continuous trading for a number of years, with a well established reputation, and proof that he or she has the necessary experience. An application must be proposed and seconded by members to whom he or she is known professionally, and names are circulated to the membership for approval. Members of ABYA operate under a *Code of Practice for the Sale of Used Boats,* obtainable from YBDSA, the BMIF or RYA.

A standard form of agreement is used, setting out the following terms:

The agreed purchase price; 10% of this is paid when the agreement is signed, allowing the purchaser to have the yacht lifted out and surveyed at his own expense; usually the survey should be completed within 14 days, although this can be longer, by agreement. Within a stated period from completion of the survey, if any material defects or deficiencies have been found, the purchaser may either reject the yacht (giving notice of the defects or deficiencies discovered), or ask the seller either to make good such shortcomings or to reduce the price accordingly. A broker is legally liable to divulge any known defects to a purchaser when acting in a sale.

If the sale proceeds, the agreement states that the yacht is considered to have been accepted by the buyer and the balance of the agreed price is due if:

a. A period of 14 days elapses, and no survey has been made; or
b. after an agreed time after the survey the purchaser has not acted; or
c. the seller remedies any specified defects to the satisfaction of the surveyor; or
d. an agreed reduction in price is made.

The form also includes other provisions concerning the obligations of the two parties, default by the purchaser, the transfer of risk, and arbitration procedure in the event of any dispute.

The buyer should be aware that if the seller is a private individual (not selling the boat in the course of trade or business), and if that fact is known to the buyer, there is no question of warranty on the sale of a second-hand boat because the buyer is quite at liberty to inspect the craft and to satisfy himself as to her condition – either personally or by employing a surveyor. Unquestionably a survey should always be made, except perhaps in the case of a very small and cheap boat where the buyer has enough experience to detect any serious faults. The work of surveyors is discussed below.

Buying and selling yachts can be a complex business, particularly when the boat, the seller and the buyer are all miles apart. Two brokers are often involved, and access must be provided by the yard or marina where the boat is lying. Consequently the Code of Practice provides for a fair split of the total commission between those involved. (See 1.3.3. for the broker's role in the sale of yachts). The seller of the boat pays an agreed commission based on the selling price. For guidance the normal rates (plus VAT) are: 8% of the selling price for vessels in the UK; 10% for vessels on inland waters. 10% also applies if the vessel, owner or buyer are abroad.

1.2.9 THE INTERNET

An increasing amount of work is being conducted and contracted by brokers via the Internet. This is true both locally and internationally in today's marketplace. A most important facet of 'displaying your wares' on the Internet is the strong visual impact that it has. A good photograph will advertise the boat and subsequent information such as specific photos, survey reports, inventory lists etc may be sent to prospective buyers as e-mail attachments. Or they may be downloaded from the broker's website. In effect the office is open 24 hours, 365 days. Moreover by the time the buyer starts talking to the broker, he is well primed with information and already has a good idea of what to expect from any particular boat. The whole process of buying a boat is thus dramatically speeded up.

A broker's website has another valuable function, the prior education of a client before he talks to the broker. Standard reference pages on such topics as "The steps involved in buying a boat"' "Why use a broker?"; and "VAT implications of boat purchase" all give excellent background knowledge to the client and more valuable telephone time to the broker who does not need to educate each client individually. Thus discussions with the client can start at a higher level.

The way in which brokers advertise in the yachting press is also moving away from listing particular boats, towards prominently displaying the website address and channelling information into this highly effective virtual shop window.

1.2.10 SURVEYORS

As already stated in 1.2.6, it is foolish to buy a second-hand boat without having a proper survey done, with the boat out of the water. To get a proper survey you need a proper surveyor, and sadly a small minority of surveyors lack the knowledge and experience required. Members of the Yacht Designers and Surveyors Association (YDSA), have to pass exams, satisfy a probationary period and hold Professional Indemnity insurance. For names of member surveyors near the boat's location, contact the YDSA, Wheel House, Petersfield Rd, Whitehill, Bordon, Hants, GU35 9BU. Tel 01420 473862; Fax 01420 488328.

Three other organisations, dealing partly with yachts and commercial vessels, are:

The International Institute of Marine Surveyors, Stone Lane, Gosport, Hants PO12 1SS. Tel 023 9258 8000; Fax 023 9258 8002. iims@compuserve.com www.iims.org.uk

The Society of Consulting Marine Engineers and Ships Surveyors, c/o 202 Lambeth Rd, London SE1 7LQ; Tel 020 7261 0869; Fax 020 7261 0871. scms@btinternet.com

The Institute of Marine Engineers, 80 Coleman Street, London EC2R 5BJ. Tel 020 7382 2600; Fax 020 7382 2670.

The purpose of a full survey is to determine the condition of the entire yacht: hull, machinery, gear and all the equipment relating to her operation. A competent surveyor should report on every aspect of the boat's structure, depending on the materials concerned. He should comment on whether the condition of the various items is attributable to fair wear and tear, or whether other factors such as poor design, inferior materials, bad workmanship or lack of maintenance are involved. His examination should include all items such as fastenings, chain plates, shafting, steering gear and rudder fittings. The engine itself may need to be surveyed separately, although the surveyor should certainly be able to assess its general condition and simialrly the rig. A hull condition survey is just that and is clearly more limited in scope.

Instruct the surveyor in writing; the details are important as they will form the basis of a contract with him. As well as full and hull condition surveys, surveyors assess accident damage for insurance purposes, and oversee repairs or modifications.

1.2.11 MARINE FINANCE

Many boat buyers need some degree of help when borrowing money so it pays to shop around for the best rates and most favourable repayment terms. You should also consider discussing your requirements with a company who have specialists in marine business for guidance on security and what the affect changes in Interest rates will have Tax relief on mortgages is not normally allowable, unless the boat is a business purchase.

Small boats and marine equipment can be financed by personal loans without security from various institutions, Banks, Building Societies and specialist marine finance companies.

Larger and more expensive craft can be purchased on a marine mortgage, where a mortgage on the boat or your house provides the necessary security. The precise details vary. The cost of the loan (ie the interest to be charged) may be added to the sum financed at the outset, and the total then repaid in equal instalments. But nowadays it is more usual for institutions to offer contracts where the interest varies with the money market, usually related to the Finance House Base Rate. This can be done either by altering the amount of the instalments from time to time, or by keeping the instalments the same and altering the number of payments (ie the time over which repayment is made). Normally the borrower is expected to put down 20% of the purchase price, but sometimes more. The repayment period ranges between five years and a maximum term of ten years for some special schemes. me over which repayment is made). A borrower may like to consider other options currently available, for example: "Low Start"" or "Residual Valuation".

Only a statutory mortgage provides the necessary legal security for a sea-going vessel, and this requires the yacht to be registered (see 1.4.1). More Finance Houses now provide loans against a non-statutory mortgage (not applicable under Scottish law) for which registration is not required. This is certainly an attractive option for a buyer keeping his boat in UK waters. Title must be established, ideally by original title documents provided from the time of first purchase.

A survey is not normally required for a new boat, but is needed for a second-hand one. The yacht must be insured against all normal risks, as described in 1.2.12.

Marine mortgages can be arranged to provide stage payments for a boat under construction, and also to finance major refits or improvements.

1.2.12   YACHT INSURANCE
Nothing is ever certain at sea and, however careful a skipper may be, a boat is always at risk of being seriously damaged, even becoming a total loss or causing damage to third parties.

Most yacht insurance policies are now issued by specialist yacht insurers who have there own policy wordings. These are based on the IYC (Institute Yacht Clauses), but often provide a wider basis of cover and should be easier to understand.

Owners should insure their boat for her full value, not necessarily the same as the purchase price. Since marine insurance is a contract for an agreed value rather than the market value of the boat, the owner can agree any sum he wishes with the insurer. Any appreciable discrepancy between price paid and proposed insured value should however be explained to the insurer and agreed with them as, in the event of a claim, they may repudiate on the grounds of mis-disclosure of material facts. A reasonable basis for the **insured** value is that being a willing seller how much would you get for the boat? Alternatively in normal market conditions how much would you have to pay for a boat that is the same and of similar age and in similar condition? Outboard Motors are usually subject to a Market value clause. In any case you should read the proposal form very carefully, and answer the various questions accurately and truthfully. Remember that answers to questions such as where is the boat normally kept? What fuel is used? etc, if altered, become a material fact. Otherwise insurers may subsequently be entitled to avoid liability in the event of a claim.

A policy normally covers the boat for a certain period in commission each year. If you need to extend the period, be sure to tell the company beforehand. Similarly cover is arranged for a certain cruising area. Make certain that the agreed limits are kept to, or make special arrangements when necessary. Many boats are now based or go abroad, maybe to the Mediterranean, and individual cruising ranges should be negotiated.

The policy contains a number of warranties and conditions, either implied or expressed. These can be identified by reading the various sections carefully, and usually include the following important points:
1. If any loss or damage occurs the owner must take all steps necessary to minimise further loss, and the underwriters will contribute to any charges properly incurred by the owner in taking such steps.
2. Charter or hire of the boat is not covered, except by special arrangement.
3. If an incident may give rise to a claim, prompt notice must be given to the underwriters. Alternative estimates may be required before repairs are undertaken.

4. The amount payable for a claim may be reduced for fair wear and tear of items such as sails, running rigging and protective covers.

5. Theft of equipment is only covered where forcible entry or removal can be shown. Outboards must be securely locked to the boat. Tenders must be clearly marked with the name of the parent vessel. Check that there is no exclusion of cover for dropping off and falling overboard of outboard motors.

6. Sails which are split by the wind or blown out are not generally insured, unless due to damage to spars or caused by the yacht being stranded or in collision. The exclusion applies equally to sails stowed on self-furling gear which are liable to unfurl and flog when the yacht is left unattended. Also excluded is damage to sails while racing, unless caused by the boat being stranded, sunk, on fire or in collision. Racing risks which provide much wider cover for sails may be covered as a separate item with extra premium.

7. Under the IYC, damage to or loss of engine or other mechanical or electrical items is only covered if caused by the yacht being flooded, sunk, stranded, burned or in collision; or while being moved to or from the yacht; or by theft of the entire boat; or by theft following forcible entry; or by fire in a store ashore; or by malicious acts. Many tailor-made policies also provide cover following sudden incursion of water.

8. Personal effects can be included, if specially arranged.

9. Boats with a maximum designed speed of 17 knots or more are subject to 'Speedboat Clauses' which specify certain conditions and generally attract higher premiums. These will also require either the Insured or another competent person to be on board and in charge. Note that if a young person took the boat out and was not able to establish competence, liability would not be accepted.

10. Clauses dealing with Third Party Liability deserve special attention. Cover for at least £1,000,000 is recommended. Normally somebody using the boat with the consent of the owner is covered, but this should be confirmed.

11. When in transit or trailing by road, a boat may be covered for accidental loss or damage, but the policy excludes all third party liabilities or offences against the current road traffic legislation. If your boat is over 16 feet long check that your policy covers Road Transit.

12. If no claim is made under the policy, most insurers will grant a no-claim bonus.

13. In the case of yachts over 15 years old, most underwriters require a recent survey on first insurance and after a change of ownership, followed by periodic surveys thereafter.

14. A Marine policy is not assignable. If you buy a boat you cannot take over the old owner's insurance without permission of the insurer, who will almost certainly require a new proposal form. If you sell your boat you cannot say 'Oh it's all right, it is covered under my policy'. The moment the ownership changes the old policy is dead and should be cancelled.

Marine Insurance policies contain 'conditions' (which have previously been referred to with the warranties).

These can include: that the owner shall keep the boat and its equipment in seaworthy, or for trailers roadworthy, condition and in a proper state of repair. It means an insurer can repudiate a claim where the design or condition of the yacht was such as to render the loss or damage inevitable in the normal course of navigation or use of the yacht. If the damage was 'fortuitous' it is recoverable; if 'inevitable' it is not.

The Marine Insurance Act 1906 specifically excludes wear and tear.

Some insurers will argue that single handed sailing infers under manning and therefore the boat is not seaworthy. A failure to disclose on the proposal form that the yacht is habitually to be sailed single or short-handed may be held as failure to disclose material facts and may be grounds for repudiation. If you do it, tell your insurer and get it agreed.

Marine insurance is a specialised business. Either deal with a broker or intermediary who is experienced in yacht insurance or get proposal forms from several established firms who advertise in the yachting press; it will be apparent that some insurers give wider cover than others. Return those forms which best seem to meet your needs, and then compare the quotations. However, firms with the lowest premiums are not necessarily the best at settling claims. Useful information is given in RYA booklet G9 *The Yachtsman's Lawyer* and *Marine Law for Boat Owners* by Edmund Whelan.

Information on Insurers and Finance Houses that are members of The Insurance, Financial & Legal Services Association of the BMIF, may be obtained from The Hon Sec, Richard Winter, 28 West Way, Worthing, W. Sussex BN13 3AY. Tel: 01903 261755. winter@mistral.co.uk

1.3 SELLING A BOAT

1.3.1 GENERAL
Many yachtsmen change their boat at least once in a sailing lifetime – most much more frequently – usually because they wish to trade up to something larger. This section deals with the transfer of ownership in general terms. There are basically two ways of selling a boat: privately or through a yacht broker. A third method is at a boat auction, which follows a procedure similar to any other kind of auction sale.

It is vital to decide the right price for the boat. This implies a good knowledge of the market and is where a yacht broker can advise. It is also important to present the boat in the best possible condition, clean and tidy, and with all outstanding defects attended to as far as possible.

1.3.2 SELLING PRIVATELY
On the face of it, selling a boat privately should give the maximum return. This, however, assumes that the owner can correctly judge what the asking price should be. This ought to be the most that can be obtained within whatever time limit is set for the sale, but few yachtsmen can have sufficient insight to the second-hand market unless they have a boat which is of a type that is numerically large and is regularly traded.

Most probably some advertising costs will be incurred, and these can soon build up at £5.75 per line for classified advertisements in most yachting journals, but a small photograph of the boat is often included free of charge. When drafting an advertisement it is perfectly fair to emphasise the particular merits of the boat, but important not to misrepresent her condition. In order to answer enquiries (which may conveniently be arranged at a price through a box number), it is useful to have a printed sheet which gives full particulars of the boat, where she is lying, and arrangements for inspection. One or two good photographs should be included. There needs to be an accurate inventory of equipment to be sold with the boat.

The seller will have to attend at the boat whenever potential buyers wish to inspect her. Apart from travelling costs, this can involve a good deal of waiting around – particularly for those who never show up. Some viewers will arrive without the slightest intention of buying.

Be sure that the boat is scrupulously clean, inside and out, and that all repairs have been made good before she is put on the market. If there are known defects or important examinations outstanding it is best to declare them honestly, rather than to have them exposed subsequently.

Naturally it creates a better impression if the boat can be inspected conveniently and in good surroundings, rather than in a mud berth a couple of miles from the nearest road.

Once an individual shows real interest in buying the boat, be prepared to start negotiating a price. Leave room for manoeuvre, but decide the lowest figure to accept; much will depend on how long the boat has been on the market, what other offers have been received and the urgency of the sale.

When a price has been agreed the sale can proceed in the way described in 1.2.6. As stated there, it is most advisable to have a written agreement. It is most important to make sure that the entire payment has been received before the boat is surrendered.

If the boat is registered on Part I of the Register, then a Bill of Sale must be completed from the Registrar (DoT Form ROS 20). The new owner should complete a declaration of eligibility and forward this with the Certificate of British Registry, Bill of Sale and a fee to the Registry of Shipping and Seamen.

If the boat is either unregistered or registered on the Small Ships Register, then DoT Form ROS 20 may not be used. The RYA Legal Department can supply a Bill of Lading suitable for such cases

The Radio Licensing Centre at Bristol (10.4.1) must be advised of the transfer of the boat to new ownership. Tell your insurance company that the boat has changed hands. Return any permit you may hold for a special ensign (10.8.3) to the club concerned, and make sure that such ensign is not transferred with the boat.

The CG66 (now the Voluntary Safety Identification Scheme) is a scheme for registering the identification of the yacht for the purposes of search and rescue. The details have to be re-registered with the Coastguard every two years. The purchaser should check whether the seller has registered the yacht on this scheme and should arrange to re-register the yacht with the new information if the purchaser wishes to continue with the scheme.

1.3.3 SELLING THROUGH A YACHT BROKER
Selling a yacht through a yacht broker may be a useful and appropriate course of action for a number of people. It eliminates most of the work and problems involved with a private sale, and because a broker has access to a wide market it may enable a higher price to be obtained or a quicker sale to be achieved. It is advisable to use a broker whose firm is affiliated to the YBDSA and operates under the *British Boating Industry Code of Practice*, a joint

RYA, ABYA and Yacht Harbours Association document. This is basically a trade agreement, but it ensures good business standards and affords protection to clients.

When instructing a broker to sell a boat, the owner will be asked to complete a form which requires full particulars of the boat and of her material condition. It is important that these are accurately stated. Agree with the broker whether or not he is to be the sole agent (see below) and whether the owner may at the same time try to obtain a private sale (not very popular with brokers). Confirm with the broker arrangements for viewers to inspect the boat, especially the need for a responsible person to accompany them; it is frustrating to view a boat in the company of a brokerage person who is unable to answer even the most basic questions.

A broker acts as a go-between for buyers and sellers of yachts all over the world. If a broker is appointed as sole agent he will pass full details of the boat to other selected brokers, who will receive half of the eventual commission if they produce a sale. Central listing facilities allow the interchange of information about boats for sale between all participating brokerage firms, so that the net is spread as wide as possible.

Very importantly, a broker is able to advise on the correct price at which a boat should be offered – a price that is likely to attract some response, but which will be fair to the seller. It is in the interest of the broker to obtain the best figure possible, because his commission is based on the selling price (see 1.2.8).

Any advertising material produced by the broker must be accurate because, being in business, he is liable under the Trade Descriptions Act. He will advertise the boat in whichever journal(s) he considers most appropriate, and will handle all enquiries and inspections. When a potential buyer appears the broker will prepare a Sale Agreement on a standard form of contract. If the sale proceeds after survey, he can advise the owner regarding any defects that may have been found, in order to negotiate a fair price. The general procedure is outlined in 1.2.4. Finally the broker prepares the Bill of Sale, and ensures that title is not transferred until the purchase money has been received.

1.4 REGISTRATION OF YACHTS

1.4.1 INTRODUCTION

It is not compulsory to register a ship or yacht on the Register of British Ships unless:
   a. you intend to leave UK waters;
   b. the vessel is more than 24m (79ft) LOA and you want to wear the Red Ensign; or

c. you want to register a mortgage on the vessel.

The Register of British Ships is in four Parts:
Part I   – merchant ships and pleasure vessels;
Part II   – fishing vessels;
Part III   – small ships;
Part IV   – bareboat charter ships.

A British owner may register his yacht on Part I or Part III of the Register; see 1.4.2 and 1.4.3 respectively.

Information Registration of British ships is covered by the Merchant Shipping Act 1995, available from TSO. For an informative booklet *"Registering British Ships in the UK"*, copies of Registry forms and advice on registration write to the Registry of Shipping and Seamen (RSS), PO Box 165, Cardiff, CF4 5FU; or apply in person (Mon-Fri, 0900-1600) to Anchor House, Cheviot Close, Parc Ty Glas, Llanishen, Cardiff CF4 5JA; or request the necessary forms on Answerphone 029 2074 7333; or call the RSS Helpline on 029 2076 8206.

Recent background Originally British owners wishing to register their yachts could do so only under Part I, a comparatively lengthy and expensive process, but the registration was valid for life. In 1983 a Small Ships Register (SSR) was established under which yachts less than 24m LOA could be registered more cheaply and simply for 5 years. In 1994 the SSR was transferred into Part III (Small Ships) of the Register.

Also in 1994, Part I registrations were transferred from HM Customs & Excise to RSS, computerised and made valid for only 5 years. The issue of new certificates is being staggered over the years 1999 to 2003, each year dealing with certain dates of build; see the end of 1.4.2.

1.4.2   PART I REGISTRATION

This bestows the following benefits:
   a. Proof of title;
   b. Enables a marine mortgage to be registered;
   c. Internationally acceptable documentation to ease passage to foreign ports;
   d. Protection by the Royal Navy;
   e. The services of British Consuls;
   e. Can enhance a vessel's re-sale value;
   f. Provides proof of date of build for exemption from the EU's recreational craft Directive; and
   g. Ensures that your ship's name is unique on Part I.

Applications. Apply well in advance of your sailing date, as processing can take time. Post the following completed forms and fees to RSS, PO Box 165, Cardiff CF4 5FU:

a. application to register a British ship; and
b. declaration of eligibility.

Other documents. For a new ship (yacht) you must provide the builder's certificate; if you are not named on the certificate you will need other papers such as bills of sale or receipts, which link you to the ship.

For an older ship, or one which has been registered before, you need to provide either a previous bill or bills of sale showing the owners of the ship for at least five years previously; or if the ship has been registered with Part I registration at any time within the last five years, a bill or bills of sale evidencing all transfers of ownership during the period since last registered.

Note: RSS do not accept copies of documents. Ensure the application is properly completed and accompanied by the correct fee; current rates are available from RSS and cheques are payable to 'Department of Transport'.

Survey. Before it can be registered, every ship must have a Tonnage Survey by an approved classification society for a fee. For yachts less than 13.7m (45ft) LOA contact: the RYA; the YDSA; or Lloyd's Register of Shipping (Yacht and Small Craft Department).

For ships more than 13.7m (45ft) LOA, contact: American Bureau of Shipping, Bureau Veritas, Det Norske Veritas, Germanischer Lloyd, or Lloyd's Register of Shipping.

Shares. For the purpose of Part I registration, ships are divided into 64 shares. You may be registered as the owner of all or any of the shares. A share may be owned by up to five people or companies (or a mix of both) as joint owners. Joint owners must act together in selling or mortgaging a vessel.

Ship's name. Choose a name that is different from any other ship on the Register. A name which might cause confusion in an emergency or which could be regarded as offensive may be refused, so have other names in mind. If your chosen name is available it will only be reserved for you for three months. Permission must be obtained to change the name of a registered ship.

Port of registration. You will be asked to choose a port with which you want your ship to be associated. The ports of choice available for Part I register include most of the main harbours in England, Scotland, Wales and Northern Ireland. A list is available from RSS.

A certificate of registry lasts for five years. If ownership changes during that period a new five year certificate will be issued. Registered owners or mortgagees must write to the Registry if their name or address changes. There is no fee for this.

Qualified persons eligible to register a vessel on Part I include:
1. British citizens
2. Persons who are nationals of an EU or European Economic Area (EEA) country other than the United Kingdom and who are 'established' in the UK. To be 'established' a person must make an economic contribution to the UK, eg have a job or business. In June 1996 the EEA countries were: Austria, Belgium, Denmark, Eire, Finland, France, Germany, Greece, Holland, Iceland, Italy, Luxembourg, Norway, Portugal, Spain, Sweden and the UK (including Gibraltar but not the Channel Islands and the Isle of Man).
3. British Dependent Territories citizens
4. British Overseas citizens
5. Persons who under the British Nationality Act 1981 are British subjects
6. Persons who under the Hong Kong (British Nationality) Order are British Nationals Overseas
7. Bodies corporate incorporated in one of the EEA countries
8. Bodies corporate incorporated in any relevant British possession and having their principal place of business in the UK or any such possession
9. European Economic Interest Groupings (for further information contact the Registry).

These individuals, companies, local authorities and groups eligible to register a vessel are called 'qualified persons'. At least 33 of the shares in the vessel must be owned by qualified persons to be eligible for registration.

When none of the qualified owners are resident in the UK a representative person must be appointed. He may be either an individual resident in the UK, or a company incorporated in one of the EEA countries with a place of business in the UK.

If the vessel is owned by more than one qualified person (and no representative person has been appointed), one of the qualified owners who lives in the UK must be appointed as the managing owner. All correspondence will be sent to that person unless another person, such as an agent, is so nominated.

An official number, which has to be carved into the ship, will be issued when the Registry is satisfied that all documents are correct. This number never changes and will stay with the vessel at all times. The Registry issues a 'carving and marking note' (C&M) showing the official number and other details to be marked on the vessel. For pleasure vessels less than 24m in length the owner may sign the C&M note. Otherwise it must be certified by a surveyor, or if abroad by a Consular Officer.

When the C&M note is returned and all fees have been paid the ship is formally registered and a certificate of registry is issued containing details of the ship and her owners. The certificate establishes the ship's nationality and tonnage. It does not prove ownership or show mortgages.

Death. When a joint owner (or joint mortgagee) dies his interest passes to the surviving joint owners (or mortgagees). Write to the Registry enclosing the certificate of registry and one of the following: death certificate, burial/cremation certificate, grant of probate, or letters of administration. These need to be an original or a copy certified by a court or solicitor.

On the death of a sole owner (or mortgagee) interest passes to the executors or administrators named on the proof of death. Inform the Registry and surrender the certificate of registry. New owners must apply promptly for the transmission to be registered, or registration may be cancelled.

Sale. If you sell a registered ship or shares to qualified owners you must complete a bill of sale (available from the Registry). Hand over the bill of sale to the buyer. You must also write and tell the Registry who the buyer is and send them your certificate of registry.

Purchase. If you buy a registered vessel the procedure is to obtain a bill of sale and to register the transfer by completing a declaration of eligibility on the form available from the Registry, forwarding both with the appropriate fee. You must apply within 30 days or registration may be cancelled and you will be faced with the more expensive business of applying for registration.

However when buying a registered boat it is wise to see if the seller has registered his ownership by inspecting the Register either personally or by a transcript, on payment of a fee. Then it can be seen if there is an outstanding mortgage on the boat but be aware that there is no means of reserving title, and in theory a vessel could be mortgaged the very next day. It is however now possible to record a 'Mortgage Intent', valid for 30 days but renewable. This registers the mortgage's priority, and details are available from RSS.

When the boat is already registered and therefore named, it is easier to transfer registration on change of ownership if the name remains with the vessel. This should be part of the deal, but sometimes the seller wishes to retain the name for his next boat. Then another name has to be given either before or after the change of ownership. Either way costs money and may take time to complete.

Where a purchaser finds that a yacht is registered in the name of a previous owner who cannot be traced, or who has not completed a bill of sale correctly, or who has some reason to refuse to sign a bill of sale, there is nothing the new owner can do to force him to sign a bill of sale, nor has the Registrar any discretion to shortcut the formalities on transfer (as he has on original registration). It will therefore be necessary to instruct a solicitor experienced in marine registration problems to prepare an application to the High Court for a direction to the Registrar to amend the record. This can be an expensive and time consuming business, and intending buyers of yachts on the Part I register can avoid these problems by ensuring that the documents are all in order before parting with their money.

Mortgage. To register a mortgage, the mortgagee (the person or company lending you the money) must complete a mortgage deed (available from the Registry) which you must sign and forward with the appropriate fee. It will then be registered and returned to the mortgagee.

A mortgage remains on the Register until the Registry are told that it has been discharged, even if the vessel is sold to another person or the loan repaid. The discharge section on the back of the deed must be completed by the lender and the deed sent to the Registry who will register the discharge and return the endorsed deed. There is no charge for this service.

Re-registration, due to the period of validity changing from life to 5 years, is being achieved over the following dates dependent on the year in which your yacht was built (only the remaining renewal dates are shown below):

Year of build	Dates for renewal
1976-1989	1 Jan – 31 Mar 2002
1990-20.3.94	1 Jan – 31 Mar 2003

If the year of build is unknown, apply as soon as possible. The cost of re-registration is £46. For further information call 02920 768215.

1.4.3 PART III REGISTRATION (SMALL SHIPS)

The Merchant Shipping Act 1983 set up a Small Ships Register for vessels less than 24m (79ft) in length. Instead of being measured under the tonnage regulations of the 1894 Act, such vessels are measured by LOA.

In March 1994 the Small Ships Register (SSR) was closed and all ships registered on it were transferred to Part III of the Register of British Ships. The Merchant Shipping (Registration of Ships) Regulations 1993, Part XI sets out the requirements for registering a Small Ship. A Small Ship may be registered if it is owned by one or more of the persons, ordinarily resident in the UK, listed on the previous page under **Qualified persons** 1 – 6, and Commonwealth citizens not within that list. 'Ordinarily resident' means living and sleeping in the UK for a significant part of the year, ie for periods of 186 days or more in a twelve month period.

Part III Registration is a cheap, simple registration which proves the boat's nationality, rather like a passport. It costs £10 and is valid for five years. It does not register 'title' or mortgages. It is accepted in most European countries, but is not valid if the boat is being used for 'commercial' purposes, eg diving or chartering. For a yacht which cruises extensively it is better to have Part I registration as in 1.4.2.

Apply to the Small Ships Register (Part III), PO Box 508, Cardiff, CF4 5FH. Tel: 01222 761911 or 01222 747333 ext 289.

For details of registering a bareboat charter craft under Part IV of the Register, apply to RSS.

1.4.4 LLOYD'S REGISTER

Lloyd's Register (LR) originated in 1691 at Lloyd's coffee house in the City of London. It is now the premier ship classification society, dealing with merchant ship design, surveys etc world-wide. But its Yacht and Small Craft Dept ceased to exist in 1996. Only large yachts are still included in the Passenger Ship and Special Service Craft Group.

Such yachts, if built under such supervision, can be classed ✠ 100A1. The Maltese cross shows that the boat was built under survey; the 100A implies that the best materials were used and that the workmanship conformed to good practice. The final digit 1 indicates that the yacht carries adequate anchors, cables and warps. To keep in class a yacht must be regularly inspected by LR surveyors.

Services no longer offered by LR, but which may still be evidenced in older yachts, include the following:

a. Glass Reinforced Plastics (GRP) Hull Moulding Note issued when the moulding of hull or deck components has been completed under survey, and documented to the satisfaction of the LR surveyor.

b. Hull Construction Certificate (HCC) issued to a builder when hull, deck and other components contributing to structural and watertight integrity have been completed under survey and documented to the satisfaction of the LR surveyor.

c. Machinery Installation Certificate (MIC) issued to a builder when main and auxiliary machinery, and associated systems, have been installed and tested under LR survey, and have been satisfactorily trialled.

d. Lloyd's Register Building Certificate (LRBC) issued when the attending surveyor's reports on hull and machinery surveys for HCC and MIC, plus successful trials, have been examined and verified.

For further details contact Passenger Ship and Special Service Craft Group, Lloyd's Register, 71 Fenchurch St, London EC3M 4BS. Tel 020 7423 2325; Fax 020 7423 2016. psg-general@lr.org www.lr.org

1.5 WHERE TO KEEP A BOAT

1.5.1 MARINAS

Although some yachtsmen positively dislike marinas, preferring a quiet berth up some secluded creek, most people who have sampled the convenience of a marina would not willingly return to a swinging mooring. It all depends on what you like, what you can afford, and also on the way that you use the boat. The RYA booklet G8 is an annual listing of marinas in the UK and North France.

Most marinas operate under the terms of business agreed by The Yacht Harbour Association (TYHA), Evegate Park Barn, Smeeth, Ashford, Kent TN25 6SX. sueheale@tyha.freeserve.co.uk Tel 01303 814434; Fax 01303 814364. You should read the small print of the agreement, which is likely to include various restrictions that might not have been expected.

The agreement may state that vessels are berthed entirely at the owner's risk, although it is doubtful that the marina could get away with denying liability for damage actually caused by their own employees. Except by written permission a boat in a marina cannot be used for a commercial purpose of any kind, and any owner chartering his yacht out will therefore need the consent of the marina.

In some cases the agreement will provide for a commission of 1% to be paid if the vessel is sold during the licence period (ie at any time the boat is permitted to be at the marina, even if not there at the moment of sale), and this will be enforceable if framed clearly and unambiguously. The contract will usually provide for the marina brokerage to have equal selling rights if the vessel is placed with another broker.

Most conditions prohibit work by outside contractors without the consent of the marina, but such consent should not be withheld for warranty work or for work which the marina cannot undertake from its own resources or within a necessary time. Usually a general lien is attached to a vessel and her gear while on the premises, in respect of outstanding work or storage charges. But this lien is broken when the yacht is taken away, which leaves the marina with only a personal claim against the owner for unpaid fees.

In most cases the agreement will provide that the marina has the right to move the yacht from one berth to another at their discretion. It is quite unusual for a customer to have more than a simple licence to occupy a marina berth. Marina companies are at pains not to create any relationship which could be construed as giving the owner the right of a leaseholder to hold over after the expiry of the contractual period.

Upon expiry of the licence period most marinas will be ready to offer a fresh term, but in areas of high demand some marinas will only offer renewal terms to owners who have provided a reasonable amount of maintenance and repair work to their yard in the course of the season. Distasteful as this may appear, it is quite lawful, and owners intending to change to a new marina should check whether such a policy is followed at the intended new base.

A further difficulty can arise where work is carried out at the marina yard, and a dispute arises over the standard of workmanship or the costs involved. In such cases the marina has very much the upper hand as they are liable to expel the owner at the end of the licence period irrespective of the merits of the case under dispute. Where a lot of work has to be done, get alternative quotations from other yards to avoid any such difficulty arising, unless the marina operates the closed shop policy described above.

TYHA, a group association within the BMIF, also produces a Code of Practice for the Construction and Operation of marinas and yacht harbours. This recommends a wide range of criteria from fairway widths to toilets to access for disabled persons. TYHA introduced the 'Golden Anchor Award Scheme', designed to improve the standard of marina facilities.

1.5.2 MOORINGS

Moorings are hard to get in most popular yachting centres, and if you want to keep a boat in such a centre the best advice is to explore every possible source (harbour master, boatyards, marinas, clubs) and to put your name on any waiting list(s) that may be open. Contrary to popular opinion, moorings do become available from time to time, but finding one invariably takes patience and perseverance. Every season some yachtsmen give up the sport for one reason or other – age, finance, change of family circumstances, or even moving house to a different area – so there is in fact a steady turnover. However in a number of harbours the

waiting time for a berth is unduly long, in which case look elsewhere in the short term.

Deep water moorings are naturally more difficult to come by than those in shallower water, but the latter are perfectly acceptable for boats which are able to take the ground for an hour or two near low water. Multihulls, bilge keelers and motor boats which have outdrive units can all use such moorings if the minor inconvenience of drying out is accepted. In fact this is not always a great disadvantage because it is a good chance to scrub or antifoul the hull, if the harbour bottom is hard enough to walk on.

Details of individual moorings vary with the weight of boat they are intended to take, but basically any mooring has a heavy sinker, a strong chain called the riser, plus a buoy rope and a buoy to take the weight of the mooring when it is unoccupied. Sometimes a number (or trot) of moorings are all secured to a ground chain lying along the sea bed with an anchor or a sinker at each end of it. Heavier moorings often have a separate pick-up buoy; where the rope for this is attached to the top of the riser, there is usually a strong rope strop which can be taken inboard and secured to the boat's mooring post or cleats, while the large mooring buoy remaining in the water.

1.5.3 LAYING A MOORING

In some remote places you can lay your own mooring. While this is a cheap approach to the problem, it also involves a lot of work – not just the original laying of the mooring, but the annual lifting to examine it which requires special gear.

The two distinct types of mooring – for deep water and drying out – have different requirements. For a deep water mooring there is more upward pull. For a drying mooring in normal tidal areas the pull is more horizontal, but the boat must not sit on the anchor(s) or sinkers, which demands the sort of layout shown in Fig. 1(8).

Consider the type of bottom: Mud or firm sand provide good holding, while at the other extreme rock must be avoided. Shingle, pebbles, shells or soft mud give only poor holding. Bear this in mind when deciding the type and weight of your sinker, and whether the site is sheltered or exposed, or subject to strong tidal streams. Heavy and efficient anchors with large flukes and heavy chain give the best holding power, but are costly. Cheaper but less efficient are concrete blocks or old truck engines. A concrete block will lose about a quarter of its weight when in water, so, for general guidance, a concrete block needs to be at least 5% of the weight of the boat, and much more for exposed locations or those with suspect holding.

Ideally a permanent mooring should have two special mooring anchors (or two heavy sinkers) which are laid in line with the tidal stream, and are connected together by a heavy ground chain, which should be about four times the length of the boat. A swivel is shackled to the centre of the ground chain, and above this is shackled the riser. Except in very shallow water, the riser should be divided into two lengths of chain, separated by another swivel. The lower riser is considerably heavier than the yacht's anchor cable, because the bottom end of it will be in regular contact with the bottom. The upper riser can be one size larger than the yacht's normal anchor chain. A sketch of the general layout is shown in Fig. 1(8). The total length of the two risers should be about twice the depth of water at MHWS. All shackles must be securely moused.

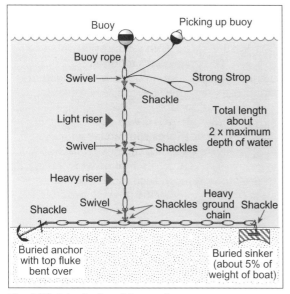

Fig. 1(8) A typical yacht mooring.

1.5.4 SECURITY

Wherever a boat is to be kept, it is sensible to think about security. Although most yachtsmen are familiar with the Police slogan 'Watch out! There's a thief about', many boat owners take no serious precautions to safeguard their craft. In creeks and harbours around the coast there are rich pickings for thieves – items such as outboard motors and liferafts worth several hundred pounds apiece, and even entire boats.

A basic precaution is to record the serial numbers of all items of equipment that are remotely portable – radios, navigational instruments, portable generators, outboards, binoculars and the like. This at least may help

recover any stolen property, but it is better to stop it disappearing in the first place.

If the boat is to be left for any length of time, items such as the liferaft should be taken below. The cabin door must be fitted with a really stout lock – not often seen in the average boat. Hatches must be firmly secured from inside, with some form of strongback if necessary. Windows in yachts are seldom big enough to gain access, but they too must be securely fastened.

Consider fitting a strong locker or safe down below in which all valuables can be placed and which can be fastened securely.

If an outboard engine cannot be locked away, it must be locked in place so that it cannot be unshipped, even by a determined thief with spanners and screwdrivers. Securing nuts can be fitted which need to be key operated to release them.

The smaller the boat, the harder it is to prevent her removal. Tenders, dinghies and runabouts are all very simple to remove unless they can be stored in a locked shed (or firmly chained to some solid object). Any boat which is kept on a trailer is simply asking to be stolen, unless the trailer is immobilised in some way. One possibility is a fixed point, strong and securely set in concrete or into a wall, to which the trailer hitch can be attached and very securely locked. Or the trailer can be jacked up and the wheels removed, or the wheels fitted with some form of clamp.

Larger boats can be fitted with anti-burglar devices, which safeguard equipment as well as the boat herself. Boat windows can be etched with the owner's postcode, in the same way as car windows are marked with the vehicle's registration number. As another form of deterrent, consider ways of immobilising the engine. A lock on the stop control of a diesel engine is one suggestion, and there are various simple ways of de-activating a petrol engine.

Get advice about the security of your boat from the local Crime Prevention Officer.

1.6 ORGANISATION

1.6.1 AN ORGANISED APPROACH TO OWNING A BOAT

Having taken the important step of buying a boat, a range of new problems arise about how to look after her. Proper maintenance of a boat is important for two reasons:

a. Unless she is kept in good order even a new boat will soon tend to become unreliable in various respects. An unreliable boat is unseaworthy and a possible danger; and

b. Unless a boat is well maintained she will start to depreciate in value much more quickly than one which is well looked after. Repairs of any kind are costly, so it is much more sensible to try to forestall any failures.

In the following chapters, much advice is offered on various aspects of running and looking after a boat, but the owner himself must get well organised from the outset – hence this subject recurs yet again.

Organisation is really the key word, because operating a modern yacht successfully requires administrative skill, a methodical approach towards her material preparation, and systematic maintenance. A boat is a substantial capital investment, which can deteriorate all too quickly unless properly serviced and maintained. A systematic approach to all this work is essential, particularly if an owner does not live near the boat and is therefore unable to maintain her during the week. At the weekend chores such as inspecting the rigging aloft may well be neglected in the rush to cast off the mooring and get away to sea.

A well organised boat – where the gear is reliable, and everything functions as it should – is generally a much happier affair for her owner and her crew than one where things are left to chance. She is also likely to be much safer.

So why not get organised? For a start an owner should find it useful to complete the Boat Details at Fig. 1(9) opposite, so that a record is kept of at least some of the more important facts that should be known. For a more detailed record of a boat and her gear, it is well worth keeping an alphabetically tabbed, hard-back notebook in which you can record when new equipment was bought, serial numbers and price; when certain servicing was carried out; how the anchor chain is marked .... and so on.

If that seems to be making rather a business of what is essentially a sporting activity, remember that a systematic approach to all the work and routine checks which are required to get a boat into good order and to keep her in that state is well worth the initial effort involved. Even in a fairly simple yacht there are many things which have to be memorised unless they are put down on paper – and the human memory can be notoriously unreliable.

In an age when more and more boats are berthed in marinas, and often spend a substantial proportion of their lives secured alongside, this Handbook will hopefully encourage owners and skippers to make worthwhile cruises to other ports, harbours and anchorages. Boats are for going places, and the satisfaction of successfully completing a well planned passage and of arriving in some

strange harbour – yet fully aware of the possible dangers it presents as well as the facilities which it offers – must be experienced to be believed.

Many people find the joys of cruising infectious and for a lucky few it becomes a way of life. But most of us lack either the time or the money, or both, to be able to make long and adventurous passages across the oceans. However, any coastal cruise can be something of a challenge, and there is plenty to be learned especially if you are new to the game – so please read on.

1.6.2 PLANNED MAINTENANCE
In later chapters some of the detailed considerations are covered – not just in handling and navigating a boat – but also in caring for and maintaining her equipment. These give a better idea of the many points which need regular attention if skipper and crew are to enjoy safe and trouble-free cruising.

Do not underestimate the number of items which need systematic attention in a boat of any size. Only a few require any degree of technical skill, but the main thing is that they should all be checked. This implies some kind of documentation, even just simple check lists, so as to be sure that nothing vital is overlooked.

The more that an owner can do himself, the more he will learn about his boat, and the less will be the cost. But many owners are busy people, and if unable to carry out routine inspections in person, then some system is needed to ensure that the work is completed satisfactorily by somebody else. In either case it is a matter of organisation. The question of maintenance is mentioned in several places throughout this book, when dealing with specific parts of the boat or different items of equipment. Some of this work can be progressed on a week to week basis, but there comes a time when arrangements must be made for the more major items to be undertaken. This entails making the boat available for whatever period is needed for the work to be done, arranging for somebody to do it, and making financial provision to pay for it! In other words, the more significant items on the maintenance list do not just happen, they have to be planned and arranged, or important things will get overlooked, probably affecting the boat's safety.

Traditionally yacht maintenance was conditioned by the fact that nearly all yachts had wooden hulls which needed extensive re-painting at the start of each season (both to preserve them and make them presentable), and this period was a convenient time to undertake the other essential work. Also in

Fig. 1(9) Boat details

OWNER's name		
Address		
Tel No	Fax No	e-mail

BOAT's name	Registration No	Port of Registry (Pt 1 only)	
Displacement	Thames tonnage	Register tonnage	
LOA	LWL	Beam	Draught
Designer	Builder	Date built	
Classification	Date and place of last survey		
Sail areas	Sail No	Mast height above WL	
Rating	Date of issue	TMF	
Insurance company	Policy No	Renewal date	

ENGINE make/type/serial No (s)			
H.P at	at	rpm.	Fuel cons rpm
Fuel capacity	Fresh water	Lub. oil type/grade	
Gearbox	Lub. oil type	Capacities	
Propeller diam	Pitch		
Battery capacity	Date new		

Radio call sign	Ship Licence No	Renewal due
Compass last swung	Liferaft serviced	Serial No
Flares renewed	Other safety equipment checked	
Serial Nos.		
Outboard	Radio	
Boat last slipped	Antifouling used	Coats
Anchor cable markings		

CG Form 66 held by		Shore contact	
Tel Nos:	Marina	Harbour Master	Boatyard
Yacht Club	Customs	Coastguard	Sailmaker
Weather			
Other information			

those days the sailing season was short for most yachts, probably only from May to September, when they were hauled out of the water or put in a mud berth for the winter.

Now for many owners the sailing season relates more closely to the duration of British Summer Time, late March to late October. Most yachts are built in GRP, needing only to be lifted out for antifouling, and otherwise they are kept in the water throughout the year. It is sensible to visit the boat during the winter, so that items such as engines and electrical equipment can be operated regularly and thereby are less likely to deteriorate; nor do they need the same degree of protection to withstand the rigours of the winter.

So work can now be spread more conveniently over the year, rather than concentrated into what were well defined periods for fitting out and laying up. A realistic plan is however still needed. Work that is done in the late autumn must include whatever is necessary to safeguard the boat during the winter. Similarly jobs undertaken in the spring should include all those important checks, without which the season might come to a premature end. Otherwise, within reason, maintenance work can be undertaken whenever it is convenient – or perhaps least inconvenient – but remember that certain jobs go hand in hand. For example, while the boat is out of the water for antifouling is the logical time to do all other underwater work; if the mast has to be unstepped for any reason, there is an opportunity to survey all the rigging and the mast fittings; if the engine has to be removed, be sure to clean and examine everything in that area and do any repainting.

1.6.3 DEALING WITH BOATYARDS

Many owners rely on a yard for doing at least part (and some most) of the annual maintenance work on their boats. This means facing up to a fairly hefty bill, but may be necessary because the owner does not have the necessary time, skill, or inclination to tackle the work himself. To get the right result you must instruct the yard precisely what is to be done, which means compiling a defects list. This should be in two parts: one for matters affecting seaworthiness and safety, and the other for items which are desirable for reasons of comfort or appearance.

Some of the items on the list will be routine jobs which need to be done every year – eg antifouling, examining underwater fittings, changing oil filters and lubricating oil, overhauling winches and checking all rigging fittings. Other important items may be defects which have arisen during the past season but

which have not received immediate attention.

Some items do not need annual attention but should be checked say, every three or four years. These might include withdrawing the propeller shaft(s), examining keel bolts and other important fastenings, looking at rudder bearings, and more major items of engine maintenance. It is best to plan these in advance, and to budget ahead for the work involved and for the probable replacement of expensive items such as batteries.

Lower priorities include cabin furnishings, interior paintwork or varnishing, joinery, and other matters of a more domestic nature which do not affect the boat's seagoing capability.

Having produced the list of work, inspect each job with the yard manager, and request an estimate for each one (not the total bill). The quotations should be broken down into costs for labour and material, which enables individual items to be queried if the estimate seems to be unduly high. Work priorities can then be assessed in order to keep within a budgeted figure, and perhaps arrange certain items differently. You may decide to tackle some yourself, or defer to a later date.

Then you must decide a programme for the work to be done. The sooner agreement can be reached on all these matters, the more likely it is that the boat will be ready when required. Boatyards are always very busy in the spring, when all their customers want to have their boats refitted and put back into the water.

If often happens that, whilst the yard is working on some item of equipment or part of the boat, certain additional work, not originally foreseen, needs doing. It is advisable to get a quotation for this, just as for the bulk of the work, even if this causes a little delay. This is another reason for making an early start. Boatyards are notoriously bad at meeting dates, but you can help by trying to anticipate your needs and by allowing a realistic time for the work to be completed.

Establish the exact terms upon which the boatyard is carrying out the work. If they are members of the British Marine Industries Federation and use standard BMIF/ RYA terms and conditions of business, you will have a degree of protection.

The standard agreement provides that: completion dates are not guaranteed (unless there is an express agreement to the contrary); the owner uses the yard premises at his own risk; and is responsible for any charges involved in moving other vessels to enable his to be launched or taken ashore for lay-up; quotations are subject to inflation and subject to acceptance within seven days; and the yard will have a lien on vessels and gear against unpaid bills.

The agreement also provides that: no work may be done on the vessel by outsiders, other than work under warranty or which the yard or its subcontractors cannot undertake, or minor work being carried out by the owner or his crew.

Although the standard form gives some protection, owners will be well advised to satisfy themselves on the following points:

1. In the event of liquidation, any new equipment paid for in whole or in part by the owner for the benefit of his yacht will be deemed to be the property of the customer and not that of the receiver or other creditors. Arrange to have a specific agreement from the yard to this effect.

2. That the yard has the facilities and manpower available to tackle the job in question. In many cases work has gone weeks or months beyond the target date as a result of a yard taking on work beyond its capability or capacity. A yard should be prepared to include a penalty clause in a substantial repair or conversion contract.

3. That the boatyard is adequately insured. It can happen that a substantial claim could be beyond the capacity of the company to settle, and the yacht's own policy may not cover certain causes of damage.

4. That there will be an adequate opportunity to inspect and test the work done before payment of the final instalment of the fees. In the case of a new yacht a 5% or 10% retention is normally allowed until the satisfactory completion of sea trials, and there is no reason why a yard should not agree to a similar proportion in respect of major repair or conversion work. If after taking delivery of the yacht after repair or conversion it is found that some aspect of the work is unsatisfactory, the yard is in the same legal position as if it had sold unsatisfactory goods. The Supply of Goods and Services Act 1982 provides very much the same sort of legal remedies as the Sale of Goods Act does for new yachts. In the event of a dispute it is important to know your legal rights, though it is always preferable to attempt a negotiated settlement rather than going straight to the lawyers.

In order to keep a proper record of the general state of the boat, get full details of what has been done by the yard at the end of a refit. For example, if an anchor windlass has been overhauled and put in working order, the owner really wants to know exactly what was wrong with it in the first instance and what has been done to rectify matters. If spare parts have been used, have these been replaced? Has a proper trial been carried out to ensure that the windlass is now working to its proper specification. If there is an overload trip does it function at the right loading? What caused the original problem, and what has been done to avoid a repetition? As the person paying the bill, you have a right to know the answers to all these questions, and often it is advisable to record them in some form of notebook for future reference, in case something similar occurs at a later date.

And, talking about bills, it is not a bad idea to file receipted invoices because these can help when budgeting for future refits.

1.6.4 BUDGETING
It used to be said of yachting that if you were worried about what it cost, you could not afford it. If that were true in an era when a young man could often afford to run a ten-tonner and have a paid hand to look after her, it is even more true today. Sadly, the costs of owning any kind of boat continue to escalate, and it is therefore vital to have some kind of financial plan to meet recurring expenses. If this depresses you, it is best to skip the next paragraph, but no attempt has been made to insert actual figures because these can vary so greatly, depending on the type and size of boat, where she is kept, and how she is run and used.

Marine mortgage payments, insurance premium, mooring/marina fee, hauling out and antifouling, fuel, sail repairs and replacement, club subscription, charts and publications, and travelling to and from the boat are likely to be the main items of expenditure. Most of these can be anticipated on certain dates. It is also sensible to provide for contingencies: miscellaneous costs for maintenance and repair, chandlery etc.

1.7 CREWS

1.7.1 ADVICE TO CREWS
Much of this book contains information or advice which applies equally to skippers and crews. But even in this informal age, a few guidelines for crews may not come amiss particularly for the inexperienced or those crewing in a strange boat. Knowing that a well-informed crew is most likely to be happy and efficient, some well-organised skippers offer a checklist along the following lines:

1. Clothes, shoes, equipment to be brought; see also Chapter 2. Any collar-&-tie functions expected? Gear to be in a soft bag; stowage

space may be limited. Stow gear tidily, including in the oilskin locker, bunk space and toilet gear in the heads.

2. Lifejackets and safety harnesses provided or not? Bring own foul-weather gear and boots.
3. Bring your own seasick pills, waterproof torch and a yachting knife on a lanyard.
4. Know how to work the heads, shower and the shower tray pump. Use fresh water sparingly.
5. Know how to work the cooker. Be aware of gas safety precautions.
6. Get briefed on where all safety and emergency equipment is stowed and how to use it, including fire extinguishers, lifejackets, safety harnesses, liferaft, man overboard gear, flares, First Aid kit, bilge pump, radio distress calls, seacocks and fuel.
7. Be very careful in dinghies or tenders which are the scene of many yachting accidents.
8. Be able to tie and use correctly the basic knots: reef knot, clove hitch, bowline, round turn and two half-hitches.
9. Know how to work all the gear on deck. In a sailing yacht, for example, check out halyards, winches, reefing gear and anchor gear, including windlass and chain markings.
10. Always return equipment to its correct stowage, eg winch handles, pencils from the chart table.
11. Do whatever the skipper tells you; ask tactfully afterwards, if need be.
12. Dress sensibly and warmly. In rough weather, at night or when told, wear a safety harness and clip on in the cockpit and on deck.
13. Alcohol is fine for a party in harbour, but go easy at sea. Don't smoke below, if at all, bearing in mind the fire risk.
14. Do your fair share of domestic chores without being asked. Do not throw rubbish overboard.
15. In harbour always cross the foredeck, not the cockpit, of an alongside yacht.
16. Do not make unnecessary noise, either in harbour to avoid disturbing neighbouring boats, or at sea, especially at night, out of consideration for those off watch.
17. Be punctual coming on watch.
18. If in doubt – ask.

1.7.2 WATCH KEEPING

Most owners of both cruising and racing yachts need crew to help them sail their boats. Remember that the crew of a typical cruising yacht, be they friends or family, are probably also on holiday and deserve to be involved when arrangements are being made or passages planned.

For safety, efficiency and enjoyment, the crew should be split into two watches, either of which can handle the boat under normal conditions unsupervised by the skipper. Obviously the skipper may want to be on deck, for example when making a landfall or piloting the boat in narrow waters. Sometimes all hands may be required on deck, but otherwise the watch on deck should be able to cope, so that those off watch can eat and rest in peace. On any passage of more than about 12 hours this is essential, lest the entire crew becomes exhausted. Offshore sailing makes big demands on stamina, and people who leave an office desk at the end of a tiring week can soon succumb to the effects of hard physical work and lack of sleep, especially if cold, wet and possibly seasick.

A proper watchkeeping system should start soon after leaving harbour, and the skipper must ensure that those off watch go below and get some rest. The watchkeeping system is a matter of personal choice and circumstances. The time-honoured four hours on and four hours off will be too long in some conditions.

TIME	Skipper	Wife	Son	Daughter	NOTES
1400	▓			▓	Sail Mudport
1500	▓			▓	
1600	▓				
1700			▓		
1800			▓		
1900			▓		
2000		▓			2040 Sunset
2100		▓			
2200		▓			
2300		▓			
2359	▓				
0100	▓				
0200	▓				
0300	▓				
0400	▓				
0500	▓			▓	0530 Sunrise
0600		▓			
0700			▓		
0800			▓		
0900	▓				Arrive Belle-Havre ?
1000					
1100					
1200					

Fig. 1(10) In a family crew the watchkeeping routine must make best use of the available experience. In this example the son is capable of standing watch alone by day, but the daughter is learning the ropes and does not keep watch on her own.

Unfortunately few family crews match up to the above requirements. Many are very inexperienced, so that the skipper has to do the lion's share of all the work. This may be acceptable on a short passage in fair weather, but it allows no margin for deteriorating weather or trouble with the boat – nor of course for any accident befalling the skipper.

If going to sea lightly-crewed is unavoidable, a skipper should arrange the passage very carefully, ie not pushing his luck with the weather, best utilising tidal streams, having a safe bolt-hole up his sleeve, and so on. The watch system should allow the skipper to be on deck at 'key' times, but otherwise he should hold himself in reserve. Less experienced crew should do the bulk of the watchkeeping, and if the skipper can first do a short spell with each of these in turn, he can give them guidance and confidence in the prevailing conditions, see Fig. 1(10).

Similarly, the overall plan for a family cruise needs to be most carefully considered. Key factors include: not going too far; enough rest days in harbour; opportunities for younger members to do their own thing; and a flexible programme which allows ample time for the passage home in the event of bad weather.

1.7.3   SHIP HUSBANDRY
There is truth in the old saying that if the corners are kept clean, the rest will look after itself – and everyone has a part to play in this. Cleanliness on board is good not only for health and aesthetic reasons, but because dirt harbours moisture and encourages deterioration.

Cleaning has become something of a science both in the home and in industrial applications, but once afloat these principles tend to get overlooked. Always use the right materials, not only to get the best results, but to avoid damage to the surfaces being cleaned. Use clean materials, cloths, brushes etc and change the water frequently. When washing down, do not use more water than necessary.

Proper care of a boat reduces the amount of cleaning that is needed, and minimises the number of minor repairs that have to be carried out. Remember that guests may not be familiar with practices afloat, so tactful instruction about not blocking the heads or the galley sink may not come amiss. Some owners may seem obsessed with tidiness, but in a small yacht gear which is left lying about collects damp and dirt, gets damaged or blocks bilge pumps. Galley spillages are not only dirty but dangerous, because they make the cabin sole slippery.

Crew members can contribute more

positively to the cleanliness of a boat if their efforts are properly directed. Painted surfaces or Formica should be wiped down with warm water, to which a small quantity of soap or detergent has been added, and then be lightly rinsed off. Glass (such as doghouse windows) should be washed with soap and fresh water, and then be polished with newspaper, unless a proprietary window-cleaning fluid is available. Perspex needs care to avoid scratches, and should be cleaned with a soft cloth. Dirty leather-cloth should be washed with soap and warm water, although normally it is sufficient to wipe it over daily with a damp cloth, not using too much water. Shower curtains need to be washed down with liquid soap and water, with the addition of a mild antiseptic to prevent mould or mildew and the possibility of permanent staining.

1.7.4   BEHAVIOUR AFLOAT
Our inshore waters are now painfully over-crowded. Once peaceful and empty anchorages have disappeared with the development of marinas and the pressing demand for moorings. Many harbours are severely congested or even closed to visitors in high season. In these circumstances only commonsense, courtesy and consideration for the interests of others can make life pleasant and tolerable.

The following are some items where a good standard of behaviour and code of conduct will contribute to the well-being of fellow yachtsmen and what they may reasonably expect from you, and vice versa:
1. Comply with harbour by-laws and regulations which invariably cater for the common good. They include:
    a. A speed limit, at least in certain areas, so as not to cause excessive wash, noise and inconvenience.
    b. An obligation to obey the Collision Regulations, by, for example, keeping clear of larger vessels navigating in the fairway.
    c. Obeying traffic signals which control entry to or exit from the harbour.
    d. Observing areas where anchoring, fishing, water skiing, board sailing and so on are prohibited.
    e. The payment of harbour dues.
    f. No mooring to navigational buoys, beacons.
    g. No unauthorised diving activity.
    h. Use of the correct Port VHF channel(s).
2. In any anchorage anchor clear of other boats already at anchor. Do not anchor amongst moored boats; keep clear of oyster beds etc. Take anchor bearings to check that your anchor is not dragging.

3. Never leave the boat unattended on somebody else's mooring, except with permission. Do not overload a mooring.
4. Avoid shouted orders or enquiries.
5. Before berthing rig clean warps and fenders.
6. Ask permission to berth alongside another boat.
7. Always take your own lines ashore or to a buoy or piles, even when lying alongside a larger vessel; it may need to move.
8. Do not run the engine or a generator or play loud music when others would be inconvenienced.
9. Keep halyards frapped so that they do not slap against the mast.
10. Keep the boat clean and tidy (eg sails properly furled, mainsail cover on, gear squared away). A neglected boat is an eyesore and possible hazard.
11. Pay attention to flag etiquette (see Chapter 10). Slack halyards, ensigns left flying overnight (except abroad) are sloppy.
12. If leaving a mooring trot, especially at an unsocial hour, forewarn neighbouring boat(s). If, for example, you are leaving early in the morning, consider shifting to the outer berth the previous evening, to avoid disturbing others.

No man will be a sailor who has contrivance enough to get himself into a jail; for being in a ship is being in a jail, with the chance of being drowned. ... A man in jail has more room, better food and commonly better company.
Dr Samuel Johnson

1.8 CLUBS AND ORGANISATIONS

1.8.1 CLUBS
Most owners find it beneficial to belong to one or more clubs or associations. Quite apart from the social contacts, clubs provide an excellent opportunity for members to exchange information.

A very good example is the Cruising Association, founded in 1908. At its purpose-built headquarters at Limehouse Basin alongside the River Thames, the Cruise Planning Section contains material which has been collected by members for members. There is a wealth of information for anyone planning a cruise to North-West Europe, the Baltic, the Mediterranean, or the eastern seaboard of North America. Apart from all the necessary publications (such as pilots and light lists) there are files which are compiled from information sent in by members who have cruised the different areas. There is also an excellent library

and a marina, with access to the Thames and to the inland waterways. For further details contact The Cruising Association, CA House, 1 Northey Street, Limehouse Basin, London, E14 8BT. Tel: 020 7537 2828. Fax: 020 7537 2266.

The Little Ship Club has a rather different slant, running a whole series of courses on navigation, seamanship and related subjects during the winter months. These are followed up by practical training afloat during the summer, organised from the club's centre at Yarmouth, Isle of Wight. The address is The Little Ship Club, Bell Wharf Lane, Upper Thames Street, London EC4R 3TB. Tel: 020 7236 7729.

The Royal Cruising Club has its headquarters at the Royal Thames Yacht Club, 60 Knightsbridge, London SW1X 7LF and is one of the foremost British cruising clubs. For over a century it has encouraged good seamanship, and its membership of genuine cruising yachtsmen is respected world-wide. It, too, provides port information, largely compiled by members, and currently produces pilot guides for yachtsmen through the RCC Pilotage Foundation.

In the context of clubs with a national interest, the Royal Ocean Racing Club (RORC) was founded in 1925 when ocean racing on this side of the Atlantic was in its infancy. It is no exaggeration to say that the RORC has greatly influenced the sport in Europe as a whole, while it still continues to administer British ocean racing activities from its pleasant clubhouse at 20 St James's Place, London SW1A 1NN. Tel: 020 7493 2248; Fax 020 7493 5252. rorc@compuserve.com http//rorc.org

Yachting affairs in Britain are co-ordinated by the Royal Yachting Association (RYA); see notes in 1.8.3.

1.8.2 YACHT CLUB VISITORS
Some yacht clubs are preoccupied by racing, or by domestic matters, but others actively encourage cruising and welcome visiting yachtsmen to their premises. Some offer useful facilities such as moorings or a club launch, and may have attached to them a small boatyard for repairs or hauling out.

Such hospitality and facilities should never be taken for granted. An owner or skipper should at the very least sign the Visitors' Book and additionally it is courteous to check in with the secretary, club steward or boatman. Ask to use the club's facilities (showers, bar, restaurant etc), and if staying for any length of time it is tactful to ask about temporary membership (which in any case may be needed to comply with licensing regulations).

Visitors should observe club rules on, for example, dress in certain public rooms and at stated times. Keep your yacht shipshape, particularly if she is lying on a club mooring or pontoon. Observe flag etiquette, especially about flying a courtesy flag in foreign harbours (10.8.5).

Tipping club staff is unusual, but a contribution to the club or staff funds may be appropriate for services received. Hospitality ashore can pleasantly be reciprocated on board. Behave in another yacht club as you would expect visitors to your own club to behave; it is very much an unwritten reciprocal arrangement.

1.8.3 ROYAL YACHTING ASSOCIATION (RYA)

When it started in 1875 the RYA was the body responsible for those involved in the 'gentlemanly' pursuit of yacht racing. Since then it has grown, like the increasingly popular sport it represents, into a national body which supports all forms of pleasure boating from sail and motor cruising to windsurfing, dinghy sailing and powerboat racing.

Its training courses from "Start Sailing" to Yachtmaster Ocean are respected and imitated the world over. Its racing division governs all forms of competitive sailing in Britain, from the ever-popular club activities through to the British Olympic Sailing Team who won three Gold medals at the 2000 Olympics. But the RYA's activities do not stop at its extensive training and racing departments. With a gross annual turnover of £5 million and nearly 100 staff, the RYA is a sizeable organisation looking after every aspect of recreational boating activity from lobbying Parliament to protecting the UK yachtsman's interests in Brussels.

Empowered by its 90,000 personal members, 1500 affiliated clubs and classes and 1000 recognised sea schools, the RYA's job has never been more important for those who enjoy cruising and racing than it is today. As the RYA's President, the Princess Royal, commented in a recent speech:

'It is a strong and active membership that strengthens our voice not just in the UK but in Europe and elsewhere.'

The freedom that yachtsmen now take for granted is coming under increasing pressure from outside bodies. Whether it is talk of compulsory licensing, a tax on boats or the European Commission proposing unnecessarily stringent rules and regulations in the construction and equipment of boats, the RYA always makes sure that the voice of the user is strongly represented.

The Association keeps a close eye on parliamentary bills, harbour revision orders, byelaws, planning applications and a mass of legislation which might affect the yachtsman. Whether it is a threat from a developer attempting to close down a local sailing club or a foreshore landowner trying to increase mooring rents exorbitantly – the RYA with its large membership and breadth of previous experience has a better chance of making the yachtsman's case heard and represented than any individual club or member.

Reacting to concerns from a large number of its members over the subject of rising berth fees, the RYA has set up a Marina Berth Holders' Initiative. The response has been very encouraging, with boat owners from all around the UK (not just the crowded South Coast) contacting the RYA's special coordinator with a view to creating a marina berth holders' association. Such associations enable the marina owner and the user to discuss not just berth fees, but also for example facilities, security and special rallies.

The RYA is also a prolific publisher, producing a wide range of reasonably priced and instructive booklets and videos giving detailed advice on subjects as varied as buying a new yacht, foreign cruising documentation or advanced windsurfing techniques such as 'cheese rolls' or 'forward loops'. Full RYA personal members can obtain a selection of these booklets free of charge as well as other individual benefits such as reduced insurance, free sail numbers, a special charge-free RYA Visa card, a quarterly magazine 'RYA', in addition to being able to draw on the pool of legal, training or racing expertise at RYA House.

For general enquiries contact the Royal Yachting Association, RYA House, Romsey Road, Eastleigh, Hants SO50 9YA. Tel 023 8062 7400; Fax 023 8062 9924. Web site www.rya.org.uk

The following direct dial telephone extensions (in lieu of 7400) and e-mail addresses apply to specific RYA departments:

International Cert of Competence	7467	icc@rya.org.uk
Legal	7499	legal@rya.org.uk
Membership	7419	member.services @rya.org.uk
Motor cruising	7462	motor.cruising @rya.org.uk
Power boat racing	7446	powerboat.racing @rya.org.uk
Publications	7412	orders@rya.org.uk
Public Relations	7416	public.relations @rya.org.uk
Sail cruising	7460	sail.cruising @rya.org.uk

Technical & Measurement	7409	technical@rya.org.uk
Training	7400	training@rya.org.uk
Windsurfing	7457	windsurfing @rya.org.uk
Yacht racing	7434	racing@rya.org.uk

1.8.4 RYA SAILABILITY (RYAS)

RYA Sailability is the UK Development Charity for Disabled Sailing, set up to integrate disabled people into the sailing community. Sailability grew out of the RYA Seamanship Foundation which originated in 1973. By 1986 the two organisations had merged. In 1995 RYA Sailability was launched in its own right as a registered charity. The RYA Seamanship Foundation ceased to exist.

RYAS is particularly involved in organising courses and providing boats or equipment to enable the disabled to learn to sail and afterwards participate on equal terms with the able-bodied. Every year RYAS organises courses on cruising yachts for visually handicapped people and, in addition, encourages and assists sailing clubs to run their own courses. It now has a national responsibility for everyone with special needs in boating, and acts as secretariat for the National Disabled Sailing Committee.

Although the RYAS operates as an independent charity it is very much part of the RYA and represents the interests of all disabled sailors, whether a novice or one aspiring to international competitive sailing.

In order to meet the needs of more and more people who are involved in disabled sailing, the Charity has taken the following steps:

a. Establishment of a National Development Board to attract major funding;
b. Incorporation of the Charity;
c. Establishment of the RYAS Foundation Entry Level scheme;
d. A National Awareness & Volunteer Training scheme;
e. More involvement in expanding opportunities for disabled sailors in offshore and competitive sailing.

These steps will allow many more disabled people, their family, helpers and friends to be introduced to the sport with obvious benefits for all.

RYAS is supported entirely by subscriptions and donations from the public, and its ability to assist the deprived and handicapped depends directly on the support received. Please contact: RYA Sailability, RYA House, Romsey Road, Eastleigh, Hants SO50 9YA. Tel 023 8062 7489. smyths@ryasailability.org.uk

1.8.5 ASSOCIATION OF SEA TRAINING ORGANISATIONS

This Association (ASTO) is an umbrella that exists to represent the major sail training schemes in Great Britain, where central representation is needed. For example it has played a large part in advising the MCA on Codes of Practice for sail training vessels. There are over forty members of ASTO, of which perhaps the better known include: The Sail Training Association, the Ocean Youth Trust, Jubilee Sailing Trust, London Sailing Project, the Sea Cadet Corps and Gordonstoun School. Between them they muster an amazing fleet of tall ships, sailing barges, old gaffers and modern offshore yachts.

By different methods they all provide an opportunity for young people to go to sea in a sailing vessel, thereby not only experiencing a unique and challenging adventure but also developing their initiative, sense of responsibility, discipline and team work.

A bursary scheme can help defray the cost of a cruise for those who cannot afford it. Some of the vessels have vacancies for adults and many of them welcome suitably experienced yachtsmen who can help take charge. From time to time ASTO vessels take part in the Tall Ship races together with sail training vessels from other countries.

The RYA acts as Secretary for ASTO and further details, including a booklet "Sail to Adventure" can be obtained from ASTO, c/o Royal Yachting Association, RYA House, Romsey Road, Eastleigh, Hants SO50 9YA.

There are many organisations which help individuals to get afloat. In many instances they provide boats and equipment, either for a charge or after paying a small subscription. The British Marine Industries Federation (BMIF) provides a free leaflet *Guide to starting boating* for young people; for a copy Fax 01784 439678; e-mail bmif@bmif.co.uk or visit www.bmif.co.uk

1.8.6 BRITISH MARINE INDUSTRIES FEDERATION (BMIF)

Established in 1913, the BMIF is the trade federation for businesses operating in the UK marine industry. With more than 1500 member companies representing over 75% of the industry's turnover, the BMIF is recognised by the government as the voice of the boating industry.

The BMIF aims to:

- serve the interests of all participants in the marine industry, both small businesses and very large concerns;
- help member companies pursue business opportunities that accrue from growing public interest in boating and watersports; and

- assist members to develop and realise their full potential.

The BMIF has 28 Regional and Group Associations which act as a communications forum for members. Group associations include the Yacht Designers, Brokers and Surveyors Association, the Marine Trades Association, the Yacht Harbours Association, the British Marine Electronics Association and the Marine Engine and Equipment Manufacturers Association, together with yacht charterers, sailing schools, moorings and marina operators, manufacturers and wholesalers of marine equipment, and pleasure craft operators. Services provided by the Federation are divided into eight sectors: Technical, Legal, Export, Training, Marketing, Government Relations, Finance and Environment.

Within its remit to protect and promote the boating industry, the BMIF actively works to increase boating participation in the UK under its "Big Blue" brand name.

The BMIF also operates a subsidiary company, National Boat Shows Ltd, which provides "shop windows" for boating and watersport products and services through the ownership and operation of the following major UK Boat Shows:

- London Boat Show, Earl's Court – one of the UK's largest public events and the world's best known boat show, with 600 exhibitors and around 173,000 visitors. 2002 dates are 3-13 Jan. In Jan 2004 the Show will take place at the ExCel exhibition centre near the Royal Victoria Dock, just north of the Thames Barrier.
- Southampton Boat Show, Western Esplanade, 14-23 September 2001 (Press and Preview Day 13 Sept). Europe's largest on-water boat show, with around 600 exhibitors and attracting 118,000 visitors (1999). 2002 dates are 13-22 September.
- Marine Trade Show, Windsor racecourse for two days in approx mid-October. The dedicated trade exhibition for the UK marine industry, hosting around 200 exhibitors from all sectors of the industry and buyers from all over the UK.

The BMIF is located at Meadlake Place, Thorpe Lea Road, Egham, Surrey TW20 8HE. Tel 01784 473377; Fax 01784 439678. e-mail: ashepard @bmif.co.uk. Websites: www.bmif.com and www.bigblue.org.uk

1.8.7 TRINITY HOUSE

The Corporation of Trinity House was constituted under a Royal Charter granted by Henry VIII in 1514, whereby Trinity House regulated pilotage on the River Thames. Today the Corporation has three roles as:

a. The General Lighthouse Authority (GLA) for England, Wales, the Channel Islands and Gibraltar;
b. A charitable oganisation caring for the safety, welfare and training of mariners; and
c. A deep sea pilotage authority.

As a GLA, Trinity House Lighthouse Service provides aids to general navigation around the coast from Berwick-upon-Tweed to the Solway Firth. Within this area it maintains 72 lighthouses, 11 lightvessels, 2 lightfloats, 18 beacons, 429 buoys, 47 radar beacons (Racons) and 6 DGPS stations.

In addition Trinity House:
d. inspects annually over 9000 local navigation aids;
e. approves or advises on marking requirements in Local Lighthouse Authority areas and for offshore installations; and
f. removes any dangers to navigation due to wrecks.

Trinity House constantly reviews the overall mix of aids to navigation to match the changing needs of all classes of mariners. The RYA is represented on the Trinity House Users Consultative Committee, together with other organisations such as the MCA and the RNLI. Requests from yachtsmen for alterations or additions to aids to navigation should be channelled through the RYA.

On the world stage Trinity House plays an important role in the International Association of Lighthouse Authorities (IALA).

Trinity House, Tower Hill, London EC3N 4DH. Tel: 020 7481 6900. Fax: 020 7480 7662. e-mail: hcooper@admin.thls.org Web: www.trinityhouse.co.uk

Specific points of contact in 2001 are:
Director of navigational requirements – Capt D Glass;
Media and Communication Officer – Mr H Cooper; and
General Manager, Corporate Dept (charitable activities) – Mr R Dobb.

Lighthouse services in Scotland and the Republic of Ireland/Northern Ireland are provided respectively by the Northern Lighthouse Board, 84 George Street, Edinburgh EH2 3DA; and by the Commissioners of Irish Lights, 16 Lower Pembroke Street, Dublin 2.

These two authorities, together with Trinity House, comprise the General Lighthouse Authorities (GLA).

Light dues

Lighthouse Services provided by the GLA are financed from Light dues, a system of user charges levied on commercial shipping calling at ports in the UK and the Republic of Ireland. Vessels are liable to a maximum payment of one voyage per month and a total of seven payments in a year. Payments, which are based on a vessel's net tonnage, were charged at 41p per ton in 2000/01. Fishing vessels, tugs and pleasure craft over 20 tons are liable for periodic payments; but the vast majority of yachts are not liable for Light dues.

Light dues are collected via Shipping Movement returns and receipts are paid into the General Lighthouse Fund which is under the stewardship of the Secretary of State for Transport. In a very few UK ports the local Customs Officer may check that light dues have been paid, but this is largely an historical throwback.

1.9 CHARTERING

1.9.1 THE CHARTER BUSINESS

After discussing yacht ownership, it is natural to consider chartering, which has become very big business in recent years. On one side of the coin a yachtsman can help to pay some of his running costs or the instalments on his marine mortgage by chartering his boat. On the other side, chartering allows a person who does not own a boat, for whatever reason, to get afloat and enjoy a holiday not necessarily in home waters but perhaps in more reliably sunny climes. In either case it is important to have a proper written agreement which covers every conceivable eventuality.

The Yacht Charter Association (YCA), which is a part of the BMIF, oversees the business. It exists to raise standards and protect the customer. UK charter companies which belong to the YCA, agree to abide by the YCA's standards and requirements in respect of service, operations and maintenance. The YCA provides: a list of member companies; advice on where and how to charter at home and abroad; a complaints service; advice to owners wishing to charter out their yacht; guidance to those wishing to set up their own charter business; a DTI-approved YCA Bond (all YCA members are required to be bonded) to protect charterers against loss of deposit or pre-payments if the charter company becomes insolvent, plus arrangements for replacement yachts – and much more advice on detailed practicalities.

Further information from the Secretary, Yacht Charter Association Ltd, Deacon's Boatyard, Bursledon Bridge, Southampton, Hants SO31 8AZ. Tel: 023 8040 7075; Fax: 023 8040 7076; e-mail charter@yca.co.uk Website www.yca.co.uk

A similar (except that there is no DTI-approved Bond) service for Scottish waters is available from the Secretary, Association of Scottish Yacht Charterers, 86 Fairhaven, Dunoon, Argyll PA23 8NS. Tel/Fax 01369 706727; e-mail info @asyc.co.uk. Website www.asyc.co.uk

Legal

Under the Merchant Shipping (Vessels in Commercial Use for Sport or Pleasure) Regulations 1993 (SI 1993/1072) all vessels proceeding more than 15 miles from the point of departure or more than 3 miles from land on a commercial basis must either comply with the Load Line Regulations or, if under 24m LOA, claim exemption by complying with one of the two Codes of Practice below:

a. The Blue Code, for the Safety of Small Commercial Sailing Vessels, ISBN 0-11-551184-9;
b. The Yellow Code, for the Safety of Small Commercial Motor Vessels, ISBN 0-11-551185-7.

Both Codes are sold by the Stationery Office or the RYA.

They cover nearly all the matters related to the safety of a yacht including construction, stability, machinery, equipment and manning. These were developed by the DOT in consultation with a working group representing the interested parties.

Certain chartering terms may be defined as follows:

Bareboat charter. This means that the yacht is supplied, but no crew or skipper. Bareboat charters are usually applicable to yachts up to about 12m (40ft) LOA. The owner or the charter company will need some evidence as to the competence of the charterer, or they may insist on providing a skipper (at extra cost) for the first few days until they are satisfied that the boat is in good hands. Less experienced charterers should either arrange for a skipper in advance, or consider one of the growing number of flotilla cruises which are now available (see 1.9.4).

Crewed charter. This implies that the yacht is supplied complete with skipper and crew, the number of which depends on the size and luxury of the yacht concerned. A crewed charter yacht of, say, 15m (50ft) might be crewed by a husband and wife team who live on board. Larger yachts come with larger crews (and possibly a larger bill for feeding them).

Headboat. A headboat is a yacht or similar craft which carries a number of passengers, not necessarily of the same party, at so much a head more like a floating hotel or a miniature cruise ship.

1.9.2 BAREBOAT CHARTERING

Many people prefer to charter a yacht for two or three weeks a year, rather than face the continuing responsibility and costs of looking after a boat throughout the year. There are plenty of charter boats on offer around the UK, with some of them in delightful areas such as the west coasts of Scotland and Ireland. Chartering in home waters is naturally cheaper, because travel costs are much reduced. Also, if required, it is feasible to change crews during the charter. The yachting magazines invariably contain advertisements for a wide range of charters, some of which are enhanced by excellent websites.

Whatever company or private owner you charter from, find out as much as possible about the firm or individual concerned, preferably from people who have had first-hand experience of the boats or boat. Chartering from a YCA member company will free you from a lot of the worries and potential problems which might otherwise detract from your holiday. Carefully check the equipment provided against a comprehensive list. Pay particular regard to navigational items and to safety equipment. What is the age of the boat, and is she the best type for your purpose? Does the accommodation really match your requirements? Look closely at insurance to see what excess is included, and check the third party cover, which should be for at least £1,000,000. What sort of service is provided in the event of some problem developing with the boat during the charter period (probably none, if you are chartering from a private individual). If the boat becomes unusable, what refund will be offered?

A proper form of written agreement is essential, covering such items as: the date, time and place to take over and hand back the boat; booking deposit; balance of the charter money (payable before the charter starts); arrangements for cancellation; a security deposit for loss or damage (returnable on completion of the charter); any insurance excess which the charterer may have to bear; cruising limits, where applicable; payment for items such as fuel, harbour dues, food, laundry etc; what penalty may be imposed for late return of the boat; and, if crew are carried, who pays for their food.

1.9.3 BAREBOAT CHARTERING ABROAD

Since air fares are now cheaper in real terms, it may make good economic sense to sail in established areas like the Mediterranean or Caribbean (including the British Virgin Islands, the Bahamas and Florida), where the weather is likely to be reliable. One of the attractions of chartering is to explore different places and these now extend as far afield as the Indian and Pacific Oceans, including the Great Barrier Reef in Australia.

All charter yachts are fitted with radiotelephones, allowing them to keep in touch with base, and invaluable should any problem arise with the boat. The company should have a service, which in a few hours can reach any yacht which has trouble with gear or engine, for example. With the larger companies the spares back-up is usually very impressive, with makes and types of equipment rationalised amongst their fleet, which may number 50 boats or more.

If bound for the Caribbean (say), travel becomes a major factor – certainly in cost. Most charter companies, or their agents in this country, will not only advise on route and timings but also the booking. Apply early, so as to take up any cheap fares on offer. Also remember that a three week holiday is more economical per week than a fortnight's holiday, both in terms of travel costs and particularly since a few charter companies make reductions for the third week of a charter.

Most companies will arrange for provisioning the boat in advance, to a scale agreed by the charterers. It is often wise to take advantage of such a scheme, since there may be no convenient shops on arrival. 'Split provisioning' provides enough food if three or four main meals are taken ashore each week.

The inventory is normally very comprehensive and the firm should provide a detailed list. Although items such as snorkel gear are included binoculars are usually not provided. It may be advisable to take your own pilot guide to the area concerned. The firm will almost certainly give a 'chart briefing' ashore, in which will be described the better anchorages and shore facilities, where to get items such as ice, and any areas which are 'off limits'. In some localities sailing is forbidden after dark, due to the absence of shore lights and the danger of reefs.

1.9.4 FLOTILLA SAILING

Flotilla sailing is a good opportunity for less experienced sailors to start cruising, with advice from the flotilla 'leader' always readily available. The boats will be fitted with VHF radiotelephones, so that help is readily on call.

Most flotilla operations are in relatively small yachts, sleeping four or six persons, and often ideal for a family holiday. The leader knows the area, the best anchorages, the more attractive harbours, and the places ashore where food and drink are good and cheap. He can also help, where necessary, with language problems, Customs formalities and the like.

Such a holiday will usually be offered as a complete 'package', including air travel and transfers. Greece is the most popular area, but in recent years there has been increasing charter activity in Turkey. The several firms which specialise in this operation advertise regularly in the yachting press.

1.9.5 LARGER CHARTER YACHTS

A fully-crewed charter yacht can provide an unequalled holiday, and at a cost per person which compares quite favourably with a cruise in a luxury passenger ship. But in a charter yacht you have complete freedom about the itinerary and about every aspect of life on board. And of course there's that added bonus – you choose your fellow passengers!

The range of yachts available is enormous from 12m (40ft) sailing yachts with perhaps a skipper and cook/stewardess, to 60m (200ft) motor yachts which can accommodate 20 guests and as many crew.

Certain standard terms are used to describe charter rates:

Western Mediterranean Terms include the hire of the yacht with her crew, and insurance of the yacht. Operating expenses such as food and fuel are borne by the charterer.

Greek Terms include the hire of the yacht and crew, and insurance of the yacht, and also the crews' food, fuel for five hours cruising per day, harbour dues, water and ship's laundry.

Caribbean Terms include hire and insurance of the yacht, the crews' salaries and food, all maintenance, fuel, laundry, harbour dues and three meals per day for the charterer's guests.

Operating expenses such as fuel and food for the crew vary considerably, depending on the area, while the charterer's food bill also depends on the sort of cuisine expected. Charter agents will give advice on these sorts of expenses, and also whether quoted charter rates may be subject to local taxes.

1.9.6 CHARTERING YOUR OWN BOAT

If sensibly managed, a yachtsman can recover at least some of the expense of running his yacht by chartering her (bareboat) for a few weeks each year. Should he have the time available, perhaps as a retired person, he can of course alternatively offer skippered charters. For the sort of person who uses his boat very regularly, and possibly keeps her in commission throughout the year, chartering is not such an attractive proposition as for the yachtsman who finds it difficult to make full use of his boat.

The main problem for the private owner with bareboat chartering is to find responsible people who will take good care of his yacht; moreover commercially he is in direct competition with charter companies and their fleets of boats. At best he should anticipate much more wear and tear on the boat and her gear (so higher maintenance costs), and some charterers may not leave the boat as clean and tidy as the owner might wish. If the yacht is based at her normal home port it may perhaps be possible for the owner to advertise and book the charters, to meet the charterers when they arrive and show them the boat, to check over the boat and her inventory on completion of the charter, and then to clean and service the boat before the next party arrives. But this is quite a tall order, and it is more than likely that somebody else will have to do some of these tasks. If time is short between charters there may well be problems with spares that are suddenly needed, since the private owner cannot afford the sort of spares back-up that is expected in a well-run charter company. If the yacht is based abroad, it will obviously be necessary to employ a reliable agent to look after the boat, so this will syphon off some of the profit.

Before chartering your boat – even to a friend for the weekend – you must inform your insurance company; and remember that the vessel must comply with the MCA Code of Practice.

Under Section 94 of the Public Health Act 1907 local authorities in England and Wales have power to grant licences for pleasure boats to be let for hire to the public or to be used for carrying passengers for hire. Under these powers a vessel let on charter can be controlled by her local authority in matters of equipment, insurance, competence of skipper, and even permissible cruising limits in specified weather conditions. These powers arise when a vessel is 'let for hire' or 'carries passengers for hire'. The hire contract, under general legal principles, is made at the place where notification of acceptance of the offer to hire occurs (and in the case of contracts by letter, where the letter of acceptance is posted). If the actual hire agreement is made outside the local licensing authority area, then even if the vessel is used within its area, no 'letting' arises within its jurisdiction.

1.10 TRAILERS AND TRAILING

1.10.1 ADVANTAGES AND PROBLEMS OF TRAILING

Small cruising boats, sail or power, can conveniently be moved from place to place on a road trailer. Apart from saving mooring fees, trailing allows the boat to be kept at home where it can readily be maintained, and of course it greatly extends the possible range of operation. It is, for example, perfectly feasible to trail a boat from Britain to the Mediterranean, whilst there are endless attractive options to explore our own home waters within the limits of holidays.

There are however practical difficulties if trailing a boat which is over about 6m (20ft) in length, notably the problem of getting a boat into the water and back on the trailer; much depends on the type of boat and her keel configuration. Fairly obviously, a heavy boat with a deep keel is much more difficult to handle than one with a centreboard or retracting keel – or a motor cruiser with a relatively flat bottom and outdrive engines which tilt out of the way.

But first consider your towing vehicle, be it an ordinary car or some kind of four-wheel drive off road vehicle. The latter has obvious advantages in terms of power, ruggedness and traction as you may discover on a wet ramp made slippery with seaweed! Most car manuals specify the maximum weight which the vehicle can tow and exceeding this can lead to prosecution. The law distinguishes between vehicles above and below an unladen weight of 1525kg. Below that figure there is no specific restriction on the weight of a braked trailer, but above 1525kg the vehicle, if used commercially, may be subject to a Gross Train Weight which is the combined gross weights of both vehicle and trailer.

1.10.2 SOURCES OF INFORMATION

From this brief foretaste it is apparent that the laws which govern road trailers are complex and forever changing. The situation is further complicated by a mass of European law and standards which apply both within the UK and abroad.

The best approach is to absorb as much advice as possible from well informed sources. Then shop around reputable trailer manufacturers some of whom provide much helpful advice and hard facts in their manuals and catalogues. For example Indespension produce a manual which contains much towing information and technical detail; it is obtainable for £3.00 from Indespension Ltd, Paragon Business Park, Chorley New Road, Horwich, Bolton BL6 6HG. Tel 01204 478500; Fax 01204 478583. www.indespension.co.uk

One of the best sources of information is the booklet "Towing and the Law" compiled by the Light Trailer and Trailer Equipment (LMTT) section of the Society of Motor Manufacturers and Traders Ltd (SMMT). This can be obtained from SMMT, Forbes House, Halkin Street, London SW1X 7DS. Tel 020 7235 7000; Fac 020 7235 7112. www.smmt.co.uk The Editor is indebted to SMMT for their kind permission to include extracts from their booklet.

The RYA also issues an Information Sheet, but check that the date is still current. The motoring organisations (AA and RAC) are valuable sources of information, particularly concerning trailing in Europe.

The principal UK and European legislation is contained in the following:
a. Construction & Use Regulations 1986 – SI 1078;
b. Road Vehicle Lighting Regulations, Schedule 18 – SI 1796;
c. Directive 94/20/EC: Mechanical coupling devices;
d. Directive 95/48/EC: Masses & Dimensions (Category M1).

Statutory Instruments (SI) are obtainable from TSO (The Stationery Office) Tel 020 7873 0011. British Standards are available from the BS Institution, Tel 020 8996 9000.

1.10.3 TRAILERS WITHOUT BRAKES

The law distinguishes between trailers with and without brakes. The two EC categories are:

O_1 Up to and including 750kg maximum gross weight;

O_2 From 750kg to 3500kg maximum gross weight. Above 3500kg, vehicle-operated air or power braking is required. Gross weight is the total weight of the trailer and load; the maximum value depends on its coupling, suspension, axles, wheels and tyres.

An O_1 trailer does not need to be fitted with brakes. It must be marked with its maximum gross weight. It is an offence to exceed the stated gross weight. It is illegal to tow an unbraked trailer unless the towing vehicle is at least twice the weight of the trailer and its load.

The various designs of towbars and primary couplings warrant careful attention as they are often subject to considerable loads and even abuse; see para (c) above.

A secondary coupling is a chain or cable required between vehicle and an O_1 trailer to maintain a safety link between the two if the primary coupling fails.

1.10.4   TRAILERS WITH BRAKES

Braking systems on new trailers must comply with EEC directive 71/320, which requires a coupling and correctly matched brakes and linkage, giving a minimum braking efficiency of 45%g, as tested on a special instrument. A parking brake must be fitted.

Braked trailers must have auto-reversing brakes, such that the trailer can be reversed without the driver having to leave the vehicle to operate an override. They should be fitted with a breakaway chain (or cable) which operates the trailer's brakes if the primary coupling becomes separated. It must be short enough to stop the front of the trailer meeting the ground.

1.10.5   UK REGULATIONS

1. Two red triangular reflectors must be fitted at the rear, and two white, non-triangular forward-facing reflectors at the front. Trailers over 5m long (excluding towbar) must be fitted with orange side-facing reflectors.
2. Two red rear lights and two red brake lights must be fitted   (operated by the brakes of the towing vehicle).
3. Trailers must have one or two rear fog lights.
4. Amber direction indicators, flashing in unison with those of the towing vehicle must be fitted.
5. The trailer's number plate must correspond with that of the towing vehicle, and must be lit at night; it must be yellow and reflective, with black letters/ numbers.
6. The speed limit for a vehicle towing a trailer on unrestricted roads is 50mph on single carriageways, and 60mph on dual carriageways and motorways. A vehicle towing a trailer must not use the right-hand (offside) lane of a three-lane carriageway unless passing another vehicle towing a load of such exceptional width that it can only be passed in that lane. Where the gross weight of towing vehicle and trailer exceeds 7500 kg, speed limits are 40mph on single carriageways, 50mph on dual carriageways, and 60mph on motorways.
7. There must be no dangerous projections. So, for example, outboards should be well padded and covered.
8. Tyres and tyre pressures must conform to legal requirements as with cars. Mudguards must be fitted.
9. The length of a trailer and its load (excluding towbar and coupling) must not exceed 7m, unless special conditions are fulfilled. The width of the trailer must not exceed 2·3m, and the width of the load must not project more than 305mm either side of the trailer. The maximum overhang of the load from the rear of the trailer is 3·05m.

1.10.6   INSURANCE AND MAINTENANCE

Most vehicle insurance policies provide third party cover whilst the trailer is attached to the towing vehicle. It is recommended that further cover for theft or damage to the trailer and its contents should be arranged. The boat loaded on it may be covered by marine insurance, but this should be pre-checked with the insurance company.

It is important to have a trailer which is suitable for the shape and weight of the boat concerned. It should support the weight of the boat, along the length of the keel, on rollers which also run the boat on and off the trailer. Side rollers support the boat athwarships, and should be adjusted to hold her steady with the minimum of transverse movement; the boat must be securely fastened. When loaded, the trailer weight at the coupling should be about 23kg (50lb).

Break-back trailers, which have a hinged backbone, can be used to facilitate loading and unloading. They may also eliminate the need to immerse the trailer's vulnerable wheel bearings in water. Where this is necessary, consider fitting Bearing Buddy seals or Bearing Savers. These replace the dust caps in the wheel hubs, and a spring-loaded piston maintains a slight pressure inside the hub, which is filled with grease, and keeps the water out. Otherwise it is necessary to clean and repack the bearings after every launching, or risk inconvenient and expensive failures. Against this possibility it is a wise precaution to carry a spare bearing kit in the car.

Even though it may not be used very often, a trailer needs regular maintenance. The tow hitch should be checked, cleaned and greased every three months, making sure that the jaws which grip the ball on the tow hitch are operating correctly. The ball itself should be cleaned and greased, and protected by the normal plastic cover, while the attachment of the bracket to the car needs checking occasionally.

Wheels and tyres require attention, as for a car. Check wheel nuts for security, and jack up the trailer once or twice a year to check the wheel bearings, which should be greased, but not too liberally. At the same time check the brakes and grease their linkages.

The jockey wheel needs examining from time to time, when the trailer is unloaded. Unwind the handle to remove the inner spindle, so as to clean and grease the assembly, together with the clamp. Check that it is securely bolted to the backbone.

Any rollers fitted need to be lubricated. If there is a winch, unwind the wire to make sure it is sound, and clean and grease the moving parts. An ungalvanised trailer is likely to need re-painting at intervals. Finally check the electric cable, connect it up to the car and make sure the lights function properly. If there is a problem, squirting WD 40 into the plug may be effective, but both plug and socket should be protected from the weather.

1.10.7   TRAILING IN EUROPE

In most European countries, particularly on inland water-ways, it is necessary to have an International Certificate of Competence (ICC), available from the RYA after a test, or as described in 1.1.7. Have available with you any other formal qualifications or licences.

Check that both boat and trailer are included in insurance documents, or on the Green Card required in most European countries. Some countries require separate cover for a trailer. Have an International Driving Licence if driving outside the EU.

In most cases it is wise to have Small Ships Register documentation (see 1.4.3) as evidence of your ownership of the craft. Evidence that VAT has been paid on the craft should be carried. This will normally permit tax-free importation, subject to the condition that the boat should not be sold or used for any commercial purpose while in the host country.

For any restrictions imposed by individual countries, consult their National Tourist Office in London before departing the UK. Such restrictions are unlikely to occur in EU countries, except at a very localised level.

1.11 BOOKS AND WEBSITES

Books

RYA Book of buying your first Sailing Cruiser by Malcolm McKeag (Adlard Coles).

RYA Book of buying your first Motor Cruiser by Robert Avis (Adlard Coles, 2001).
This is Sailing by Jim Saltonstall (Adlard Coles, 4th edn).
Sailing, a Beginner's Guide by David Seidman (Adlard Coles).
The Handbook of Sailing by Bob Bond.
Getting Afloat by Basil Mosenthal (Adlard Coles).
Learning to Sail by Basil Mosenthal (Adlard Coles).
Learning to Crew by Basil Mosenthal (Adlard Coles).
Yacht Crewing by Malcolm McKeag (Fernhurst).
The Complete Yachtmaster by Tom Cunliffe (Adlard Coles, 3rd edition).
Trailers and Towing (Indespension Ltd).
Trailing Sailing by JC Winters (Adlard Coles).
Where to launch by by Van der Klugt (Opus 5th edition).

RYA booklets relevant to this chapter:
G3   *Beginners' Dinghy Handbook (Levels 1 &2)*
G4   *National Sailing Logbook*
G8   *Marina Guide (UK and N France)*
G9   *The Yachtsman's Lawyer*
G10 *Buying a New Yacht*
G11 *Youth Sailing Logbook*
G12 *Advanced Dinghy Handbook (Levels 3 to 5)*
G14 *Dinghy Coaching Handbook*
G15 *Cruising Logbook*
G16 *Safety Boat Handbook*
G18 *Motor Cruising Logbook*
G19 *Powerboat Instructor Handbook*
G20 *Powerboating Logbook*
G21 *Buying a Second-hand Yacht*
G19 *Powerboat Instructor Handbook*
G27 *Cruising Instructor Handbook*

Websites
www.marina-info.com *directory to 13,000 marinas and 14,000 marine businesses world-wide.*
www.whamassoc.org.uk *West Highlands anchorage and moorings Association.*
www.yca.co.uk *Yacht Charter Association Ltd.*
www.asyc.co.uk *Association of Scottish Yacht Charterers.*

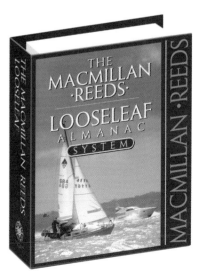

Chapter 2 Food and Clothing

CONTENTS

2.1 INTRODUCTION

Eating is a basic need and unsurprisingly it sits at the top of most lists, whether on a coastal cruise, passage making or racing. Careful planning makes the difference between enjoyment and survival.

We will assume that at least one member of the crew is a reasonably skilled cook. In a large crew or on an extended voyage a full-time cook takes care of provisioning and cooking and usually does not stand watches.

Recipes and cooking techniques are outside the scope of this chapter.

2.1.1 CHOICE OF FOOD
The choice of food at sea depends on several factors:

a. It needs to be sustaining, with sufficient calories, remembering that the physical effort in sailing a boat is often greater than might be imagined. Greasy meals should be avoided, because they make people more prone to seasickness.

b. Meals should not take too long to prepare, particularly when at sea, since the time involved must come out of the few hours that are available for sleep or relaxation between watches, unless the yacht boasts the services of a full-time cook.

c. Quite apart from the likely unavailability (and cost) of more exotic ingredients, recipes afloat should take account of the facilities available for the preparation and cooking of food on board. The average boat's stove is not likely to have more than two burners and a small oven, with only limited working space around it. So it is necessary to use as few saucepans as possible, and to limit the number of mixing bowls required. Incidentally this also reduces the subsequent washing up.

d. What food can be prepared under way will depend at least to some extent on the sea conditions and the point of sailing. It may sometimes be sensible to postpone a meal a short while, if the boat is just approaching shelter for example. But, in general, food at sea should be served punctually so that it fits in with the watchkeeping schedule and does not dictate it. Meals at sea must be easy to eat, preferably with only a spoon in bad weather so that the other hand can steady the bowl.

e. In deciding menus, consider the season of the year. In midsummer a sandwich with a cool drink should keep most people happy. But in spring or autumn, and always in bad weather, something hot is very welcome, even if it is only a warming mug of soup.

f. The fluid intake must be sufficient particularly in warm weather or to combat seasickness. Since water from a boat's tank is not always tasteless, other liquids may need to be provided according to individual taste. Alcohol should be controlled when at sea, whether cruising or racing.

g. On longer voyages a properly balanced diet is essential, as discussed in more detail below (2.2.6)

Certainly with the wide range of freeze-dried and instant foods now available, catering afloat has never been easier. Ocean racing has seen an increase in 'space-age' foods – to keep the weight down, remembering you need extra water or a watermaker to provide enough liquid to reconstitute the meals. Deep-frozen foods may only be applicable for larger yachts with the necessary refrigeration, but tinned foods come in all varieties, either as complete meals or as ingredients with which to embellish some basic dish. Long-life and vacuum-packed meals have been greatly improved. The ultimate in convenience are self-heating foods, but be warned that they are not only expensive but very heavy since each tin weighs about twice as much as the food it contains. A small microwave cooker is ideal for use aboard in a marina and can handle a wide variety of 'supermarket' foods.

2.1.2   COOKING METHODS

There are various basic ways of cooking food, both ashore and afloat, but some are more suitable than others in a small boat.

a. Boiling is a quick and efficient way of cooking. It brings out the natural flavour of vegetables and can help to retain their colour and maintain their nutrients. It softens meat by breaking down the protein collagen that forms its connective tissue. It is also used to cook pasta, shellfish, and eggs. Stews can be simmered more safely in the oven than on top of the stove. A pressure cooker provides a simple, safe and economical way of boiling food when afloat.

b. Frying means cooking in hot fat and most foods can be fried successfully providing that the right fat or oil is used, the process is quick and easy, although smelly in a boat. Use a splatter guard to stop the hot oil from splattering everywhere. Health

considerations demand that the amount of fried food eaten should be limited (see 2.2.6). For safety reasons deep fat frying should be avoided when afloat, and even normal frying is dangerous when under way.

c. Grilling is a useful way of cooking meats and fish, and most yachts have an adequate grill. For the food to be moist and tender you have to strike a delicate balance between rapid surface cooking and slower internal heat transfer. As a rule of thumb, always preheat the grill and put the food 4 to 6in from the grill element.

d. Roasting small joints of meat and poultry, for example, is entirely feasible in a reasonable oven. Most vegetables can be roasted, fibrous roots and tubers and vegetable fruits (aubergine, carrots, parsnips, potatoes etc.) But roasting takes time and therefore burns a lot of gas.

e. Baking fish, bread, cakes, biscuits in a hot, dry oven is, like roasting, heavy on fuel. But any sea cook worth his/her salt will bake bread on longer passages. This can be done in the oven, pressure cooker, frying pan or even under the grill. Dried yeast and, even better, easy-blend dried yeast are available in little packets, each enough for one loaf. Remember that yeast is a living organism and the temperature is very important – too hot and it will die; too cold and it never gets going at all.

2.1.3   THE RIGHT EQUIPMENT

Galleys, cookers, refrigerators and water systems are discussed in some detail in Chapter 19. The galley is the boat's kitchen. It should have a sink, cooker, stowage lockers and possibly a refrigerator. There is no such thing as the perfect galley – there are simply too many variables. But when buying a boat, it will soon become apparent where a builder or designer has put a lot of care and detailed design work into achieving an above average layout. The layout in Fig. 2(1) may set you thinking.

1.   Foot-operated water pump
2.   Fire blanket
3.   Fire extinguisher
4.   Handholds
5.   Twin sinks with fresh and salt water
6.   Mug stowage
7.   Plate rack, draining into sinks
8.   Refrigerator or ice box
9.   Plate stowages
10. Ready-use lockers and stowages

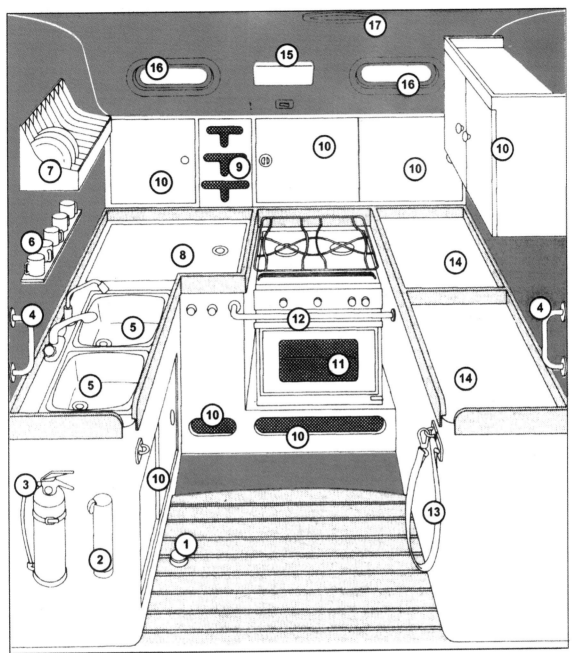

Fig. 2(1) Some features of a good galley.

11. Gimballed stove, with movable fiddles
12. Safetybar
13. Belt/harness
14. Working tops, with deep fiddles
15. Electric light over stove and sink
16. Natural light
17. Ventilation

Whatever type of cooker you use, have back-up means of cooking, eg a small Camping Gas stove, or in good weather a small charcoal barbecue could be suitable.

As with cooking ashore, you must have the right equipment and know how to use it safely and efficiently. The main difference between a house's kitchen and a boat's galley is the limited electrical power; most sailing cooks therefore have few equipment options. For every appliance a boat carries, the engine must run another hour or so a day just to keep the batteries charged. As a result the cook has to suffer the noise, vibration and heat of a diesel engine – invariably next to the galley.

Another difference is that stowage space is greatly restricted in a boat's galley.

Menu-planning will help decide what equipment you need in addition to the basics.

The Essential Gear

Besides a *good stove* with a least two burners and an oven, a good galley has *two deep sinks* side by side. Deep means sufficiently recessed to hold large dinner plates on edge while they wait to be washed, rinsed or dried. The second sink is then available for rinsing or, on rough days and nights, to hold food, flasks, bottles and cups etc. There may also be two water taps or a foot-operated pump for the water system, thus leaving the cook's hands free. One tap can supply fresh water (to be used sparingly) and the other seawater. As long as it is not polluted, seawater serves perfectly well for steaming vegetables, washing hands or dishes (with a final rinse in fresh water). When the crew go ashore, the seawater intake cock should be shut to avoid leakage.

A holder for paper towel
On a boat, sponges and tea-towels are not much help since, once used, they never dry out completely in the humid salty environment. Always take one roll for every one to two days of cruising.

Pressure cookers
These are highly recommended because they boil water, cook stews, soups and vegetables and even bake bread more quickly than regular pots. They also save on gas and with a tight-fitting lid are safer in rough seas. Some pressure cookers have internal dividers so that two or more items can be cooked simultaneously. But do allow it to cool before you release the top – a burn from the escaping steam is painful. Check that all your pots, pans and baking ware fit the cooker top and oven.

A minute timer
This would preferably the four hour kind with not too loud a tick, can be invaluable for cooking and for watch changes, weather forecasts etc. Fix it firmly to a dry bulkhead.

Stainless steel cutlery
This type of cutlery is vastly better than plastic knives and forks. Bring more cutlery than you need – it has a way of disappearing, particularly the teaspoons!

Plastic or china plates, bowls and mugs
Try to find mugs with large handles, so that you can put two or three fingers through for a real secure grip, preferably with non-skid rubber rings inset in their bases. Any boat venturing out into rough weather ought to have a spoon and a big, wide-mouthed, flat-bottomed plastic bowl for each crew member – you will end up eating most of your meals out of it. While some cooks use paper plates for sandwiches or other simple meals, paper goes soggy and takes up too much valuable rubbish space to be worth the saving in washing-up time.

Toaster
For those with no grill, there is a stove-top toaster which looks like a metal 'tent' and stands up over the flame with a piece of bread leaning against either side.

The detailed list of hardware below is a suggested minimum for the average yacht:

2 stainless steel saucepans with tight-fitting lids, side handles or a detachable handle, so they stow in a nest.
1 Pressure cooker; doubles up as large saucepan.
1 kettle, with whistle and flame trap around the base
2 non-stick frying pans
1 egg poacher. (A teflon-coated muffin tin doubles up as an egg poacher in the oven)
1 grill pan/toaster
2 heat-proof oven dishes
1 roasting/baking tin, with cover/roasting bags
1 flameproof, lidded casserole
2 asbestos mats with handles
1 slice
1 wooden spoon
1 slotted spoon
1 ladle (with hook so it does not slip into the pan)
1 spatula
1 pair of tongs (stainless steel)
1 pair of scissors
4 skewers of different lengths
3 sharp knives (large, medium, small)
1 knife sharpener
1 set of spoon measures/or cups
1 vegetable peeler
1 small egg whisk
1 measuring jug
1 grater
2 tin openers
2 corkscrews/bottle openers
1 chopping board
1 colander
1 strainer/sieve
1 sugar bowl/ lidded container
1 milk jug
1 salt cellar
1 pepper mill
1 butter dish (insulated)
1 bread bin
1 mug per crew member
1 bowl per crew member
1 large plate per crew member

1 small plate per crew member
1 egg cup per crew member
1 set of cutlery per crew member
2 kitchen plates
Stainless steel, pump-action vacuum flasks
1 gas lighter
1 pair oven gloves
6 drying-up cloths
1 plastic pan scourer
1 brush for washing dishes
6 plastic, screw-top containers for provisions

All these items need individual stowages, so that they are easily accessible and yet securely stowed at sea and can neither break loose nor rattle. A fitted drawer is ideal for cutlery, with a space for each knife, spoon and fork. Plates, bowls and mugs should be of the nesting variety, so that they stack neatly and securely on top of each other.

The lockers under the sink are convenient for the gash bucket; teacloths can be hung to the left of the stove beside the sink, and a kitchen-roll dispenser can be fitted under the lockers at top right.

2.2 PROVISIONING

2.2.1 PLANNING WHAT TO TAKE

Deciding how much food to take is neither simple nor straightforward. It is not an exact science, but rather a methodical and painstaking process. There are two general approaches: one is based on estimating food consumption per person and the other is derived from menu-planning. Neither is perfect, but combining the two will generally ensure that you have not left anything vital out. If you do use the menu-planning model, be sure to include snacking food and beverages.

Generally, developing a two week menu allows for sufficient variation to ensure that the galley crew are not keel-hauled! There should of course be a small reserve of food which can readily be carried in tins or packets, to allow for delays or emergencies. Surplus tinned food can always be left on board for future occasions, or taken home towards the end of the season. Stowage space in a small boat is always limited, and weight can be an important concern particularly in a racing yacht.

Provisioning for a lengthy cruise is a much more demanding business than collecting together the stores that are likely to be needed for a long weekend or for a cruise lasting a week or two. For a start, the sheer quantity of provisions that are needed will almost certainly pose a stowage problem. Single-handers are best off, with only one mouth to feed and lots of surplus space in and under unoccupied bunks. Small boats with large crews present the greatest challenge in selecting and stowing away everything that is likely to be required for more than about a week.

The worst scenario is a crew of four males, none of whom wish to take responsibility for buying, stowing and cooking food – still less washing up. Yet all expect to dine in gourmet splendour. The problem is exacerbated when individuals buy their own little goodies – at the end of the season the galley will sport six tins of peppercorns, four boxes of damp matches, two mildewed slices of salami, several opened bottles of flat soda water – but no whisky.

For a lengthy cruise it is worth finding out in advance the likes and dislikes of the intended crew, and also whether individuals are allergic to any particular food. Some people will only drink decaffeinated coffee, anybody suffering from gout should avoid offal, while others are allergic to shellfish in almost any form.

Fig. 2(2) is a suggested list, not necessarily comprehensive, but which can be amended or added to depending on circumstances. At the very least, if this stock of basic provisions is maintained the crew will not go hungry, or thirsty. There are few things more annoying than to find the first day on board that there is no marmalade for breakfast, or paper in the heads. Non-perishable items need to be supplemented by fresh foods, for which a separate list can be prepared.

Fig. 2(2) A checklist of stores to have on board during the season. Photocopy this list and use it when shopping or stowing foods.

Checklist – Non-perishable foods and Drinks

- ❏ Active dried yeast
- ❏ Baking soda
- ❏ Barley sugar
- ❏ Biscuits, chocolate
- ❏ Biscuits, plain
- ❏ Marmite
- ❏ Bread
- ❏ Bulgar Wheat/Couscous
- ❏ Butter, tinned
- ❏ Cake, tinned
- ❏ Cereals
- ❏ Cereal bars
- ❏ Cheese
- ❏ Chocolate, bars
- ❏ Chutney
- ❏ Cornflour
- ❏ Crackers
- ❏ Custard powder

- ❏ Dehydrated soups
- ❏ Dehydrated vegetables
- ❏ Detergent
- ❏ Dried fruits
- ❏ Eggs
- ❏ Fish, tins
- ❏ Flavouring essences
- ❏ Flour
- ❏ Foil
- ❏ Garlic
- ❏ Herbs, mixed
- ❏ Honey
- ❏ Jam
- ❏ Kitchen rolls
- ❏ Marmalade
- ❏ Mars bars
- ❏ Meat, tinned
- ❏ Mustard
- ❏ Noodles
- ❏ Nuts
- ❏ Oil, cooking
- ❏ Oil, salad
- ❏ Pasta
- ❏ Peanut butter
- ❏ Pepper
- ❏ Pickles
- ❏ Plastic bags
- ❏ Porridge oats
- ❏ Rice
- ❏ Ryvita
- ❏ Salt
- ❏ Sauces
- ❏ Scouring powder
- ❏ Snacks, assorted
- ❏ Soap
- ❏ Soups, tins
- ❏ Spaghetti
- ❏ Spices
- ❏ Sprouting beans
- ❏ Stock cubes
- ❏ Sugar
- ❏ Toilet paper
- ❏ Tomato Ketchup
- ❏ Tomato purée
- ❏ Vegetables, tins
- ❏ Vinegar
- ❏ Worcester sauce

Drinks
- ❏ Beer, cans
- ❏ Bovril
- ❏ Brandy
- ❏ Chocolate, drinking
- ❏ Coffee
- ❏ Gin
- ❏ Ginger ale, cans
- ❏ Juices, fruit, cans
- ❏ Lemon squash

- ❏ Lime juice
- ❏ Milk powder
- ❏ Milk, Long Life
- ❏ Orange squash
- ❏ Sherry
- ❏ Soda water, cans
- ❏ Tea bags
- ❏ Teas, herbal
- ❏ Tonic water, cans
- ❏ Vodka
- ❏ Whisky
- ❏ Wine, red
- ❏ Wine, white

2.2.2 NON-PERISHABLE STORES
Remember, everything deteriorates with time, especially humans on boats.

- ❏ Aluminum foil
- ❏ Apron
- ❏ Baking soda, Milton sterilising solution
- ❏ Band-aid plasters
- ❏ Burn cream/spray
- ❏ Cling film
- ❏ Cookery cards/recipes
- ❏ Indelible markers
- ❏ J cloths
- ❏ Matches in a watertight container
- ❏ Oven gloves
- ❏ Paper towel
- ❏ Rubbish bags, bin liners
- ❏ Scouring pads (non-rusting)
- ❏ Self-sealing polythene bags (Ziploc)
- ❏ Washing-up liquid
- ❏ Water purification tablets

2.2.3 STOWING FOOD
This is largely a matter of commonsense, but keep in mind two principles: (a) that the foodstuffs should be stowed safely and appropriately; and (b) that you should be able to find it quickly when needed. The latter is most important and is where the squirrel fails so dismally.

So, before you bring anything on board, be sure you know what spaces are available for food. The lockers around the galley will suffice for ready-use items, the day to day stuff which you will replenish from the longer term stowages.

Next, lay claim to a locker or two which are as near as possible to the galley, say under the two adjacent bunks. This is where your second-level of access items will stow. Handy, but not exactly on an immediate basis.

Finally the rest of the boat is your oyster. There is a considerable amount of space available if you are prepared to lift the boards of the cabin sole to get at bilges; or poke around at the bottom of lockers which are actually only half full of ship's stores – and could quite obviously be better utilised for your vital commodities.

At this point, having identified the spaces which you can call your own, pause and draw your plan of the boat as per Fig. 2(3). This is what squirrel failed to do. On the plan number the lockers, bilges and other stowages, so that anybody can go straight to Locker No 4 without constantly having to ask tedious questions.

Next come the Lists, or preferably one large Master List. Remember the list(s) are not solely for your benefit; they are a reference for any member of the crew and so should be readily accessible. It is the Cook's job, however, to write the lists in the first place and to keep them up to date thereafter. The latter is of course a form of basic stock-taking and if done carefully should ensure that you do not run out of marmalade when miles from nowhere. Some people list the contents of each locker in pencil on 5 x 7 index cards then keep the cards in a sealable plastic bag taped to the locker cover and revise as supplies are used. Before leaving harbour, check lockers and secure loose gear. Your stowage lists can of course be used in conjunction with, or be based on, the list at Fig. 2(2) which is partly a shopping list and partly a stock-taking list; it covers only non-perishables.

Obviously the list goes hand in glove with the Stowage Plan, so you might want to split the list up into the various numbered stowages. Whether you write in pencil, or encapsulate the list so that you can write in chinagraph (or simply cover it with clear Fablon) is up to you. Chinagraph is usually water-soluble, so be warned. If you are really with it, the whole thing can be done on the ship's computor or your own laptop. It is that Important!

Now at last you can get foodstuff aboard and start to stow it. Try if possible to assume the role of El Supremo with a number of slaves, or stevedores, running around at your command ... unlikely, I know, but stowing ship for even a month's cruise is a fairly major, physical task. Not for one poor soul!

Heavy, tinned foods must go in the bilges, as nearly amidships as possible. Remove labels from tins, and mark them with indelible ink; if they are likely to be in the bilges for long stow them in poly bags or varnish them to reduce rusting. Stow dry foods in poly bags in the upper lockers. Certain foods require special storage, as in 2.2.4. Glass bottles should be avoided because they may break, are heavy and clink together at sea. Most drinks are now obtainable in plastic bottles, or can at least be decanted into one. If essential, stow glass bottles in the bilges wrapped in bubble wrap, which is non-absorbent.

Many people organise stowage by meals, putting all the ingredients for an individual dinner together. Others group by type: for example, stowing all the canned vegetables in one place and all the canned fruits in another. If that method is used then the meal packs should be stored on opposite sides of the boat so that weight remains evenly distributed as the meals are consumed.

Plastic boxes, bags and bottles, aluminium foil and cling film all help to overcome the difficulties of sealing up perishable or semi-perishable foods.

Finally a word on stowing food and drinks in refrigerators. The arguments for and against top-openers versus front-openers are rehearsed in

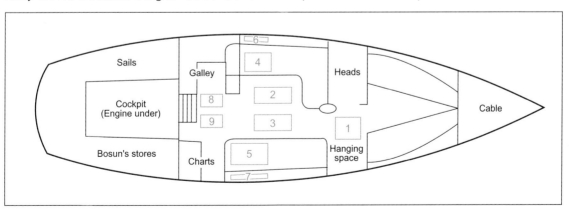

Fig. 2(3) Stowage plan for provisions. Lockers etc are numbered from forward to aft; evens to port, odds to starboard – by tradition.

1	*Bilge abreast the mast. Tinned goods.*	*2 & 3 Cabin bilges. Tinned goods.*
4 & 5	*Lockers under bunks.*	*6 & 7 Upper lockers, outboard.*
8 & 9	*Bilges between galley and chart table.*	

19.7.1, but it is too late now to change refrigerator as trolley loads of food arrive from the supermarket. Unquestionably front-openers are far easier for stowing and removing food, as we know from the home front. With a top-opener you are forced to stow in layers and the beer cans which in theory should be low down, in practice need to be visible near the top. The only solution is to build racks or more realistically to stow in plastic racks or baskets which can be removed in their entirety to get at the food below – not ideal, but ... Finally, do make a point of hucking out the fridge weekly so as to give it a thorough clean of all the debris and liquids which have accumulated – otherwise the smell will force you overboard.

2.2.4 KEEPING FOOD

1. *Biscuits* are a great stand-by at sea, because in airtight containers they will keep for several months. Once opened they soon go soft, so several small tins are better than one or two big ones.

2. *Bread* keeps best (up to ten days) in a dry but airy place, if such a spot exists in a small boat, rather than sealed in a plastic bag which breeds mildew. Sliced bread does not keep quite so well, nor does bread which has previously been frozen. There is a range of long-life bread (6 months) which is foil sealed, takes 5 minutes in the oven to warm: choose from rolls, baguettes or bloomers. Rye bread or pumpernickel keeps well and vacuum packed sliced rice bread will store for 6 months and is wheat and gluten free. On ocean passages various recipes are available for home-baked bread, using fast action dried yeast. You can also buy mixed grain bread mixes, which simply needs the addition of water.

3. *Butter* In temperate winters, well-salted butter will keep several months without refrigeration. But once in the tropics, butter, even in tins, tends to liquefy. If buying tinned butter, try shaking the tin gently, close to your ear. If you hear any liquid on the very first shake, then there is a good chance the butter inside is rancid. As a rule switch to tinned margarine when it gets hot.

4. *Cheese* Fresh, hard cheese keeps well in large portions, wrap in vinegar-soaked paper and put it in an airtight box with a couple of sugar lumps, while the vacuum-packed variety will stay fresh for months if unopened.

5. *Eggs* Eggs that are really newly laid will keep for at least three weeks, or longer if they are lightly smeared with Vaseline. Turn the boxes holding the eggs once a week, so that the yolks do not settle at one end. Do not buy eggs which have been stored in chilled counters, since they do not last. Keep old egg boxes for future use, since in most countries eggs are sold loose.

6. *Fruit* If bought when not quite ripe, citrus fruits (oranges, lemons, limes) will keep for several weeks. Hard apples keep well. Green bananas on the stem should be stowed in the dark and where they will not get bruised. Soft fruits quickly deteriorate. In hot climates any fruit (or vegetable) which may be eaten uncooked or unpeeled should be washed in dilute potassium permanganate. Foil pouches of semi-dried peaches, raisins, sultanas, pineapple, papaya, mango and prunes provide a good source of vitamin A, minerals, sugars and some roughage and last well.

7. *Meat* Vacuum-packed jars of meat keep better than tins. Good quality salami and smoked meats last months if hung up.

8. *Milk* Fresh milk will keep for several days in a refrigerator, but the longer-distance sailor must acquire a taste for good instant powdered milk or the condensed or evaporated variety. The former of course takes up less space, but tins of evaporated milk can be reconstituted to give normal milk by diluting with water. If you are coast-hoping and you have room to spare UHT (long-life) milk in cartons or plastic bottles with screw tops is good.

9. *Pasta* is quick and convenient to cook (risotto ready in 12 minutes) and the choice is wide: boil-in-the-bag rice, red, brown pre-cooked and wild rice, polenta, falafel (chick pea snack), gnocchi (Italian potato dumplings), instant noodles of various shapes and sizes, vacuum-packed fresh pasta, spinach, cheese, ham, and fish tortelloni, instant mash potatoes to name a few. For the real lazies, foil pouches of sauces from Indian, Chinese, South African and Mexican curries. They can work out to be expensive if you are cooking for quite a number. You might find that with a few spices taken along you could recreate some of the dishes easily and more cheaply.

10. *Poultry* Fresh chicken should be cooked and eaten within a couple of days, but can be kept a day or two longer in a refrigerator. Frozen chicken that is brought on board must be thoroughly thawed out before it is cooked. Hands, chopping board and knife must be thoroughly cleaned to stop a possible cross contamination of Salmonella.

11. *Vegetables* Depending on the season, potatoes will keep for several months if

they are stored in a dark, dry and airy place. Never eat green potatoes they are poisonous! Onions survive better in the light, which retards sprouting. Check that onions are really firm at both ends with no shoots showing. Tomatoes may be bought both red and green, firm to the touch. Store them stalk upwards. The green ones will last several weeks. Hard white cabbage will last at least a month. Quick-soak dried peas, sun-dried tomatoes and peppers, dehydrated onions, and mushrooms make welcome additions to meals.

12. *Tinned Meat and Fish* There is a good choice of meat meals: steak and ale, chicken and mushroom, minced beef and onion with puff pastry tops. All you do is open the tin lid and cook in the oven. Ideal as back up or for a small number of crew. There is tinned stewing steak and minced beef which form the basis of a variety of meals: stews, curries, pies, pasties, chilli, spaghetti bolognese and shepherds pie. Tinned hams, gammon and little meat puddings will last for three years!

    Tinned fish in oil or brine is more versatile then in tomato sauce. Choose from salmon, mackerel, tuna, pilchard, sardine and small tins of crab, squid and mussels offer an interesting addition to risotto.

13. *Sprouting Grains, Beans and Peas* are relatively simple. Using 6 a cup of seeds to 1 cup of water, soak overnight. Drain the liquid, place seeds in a wide mouth glass jar, cover with cheese cloth or a pair of tights. Place the jar on its side, tilted so it drains, and put in a dark, warm place. Rinse and drain the seeds once a day. Germination times vary but on average are 3-5 days except for mung and soybeans, which take 6-8 days. The following are some of the seeds that you might try: alfalfa, fenugreek, mustard, cress, radish, sesame, sunflower, grains, beans and peas.

    Do not eat the following seeds and beans: potato and tomato seeds which are toxic when sprouting; and fava and Lima beans are toxic if eaten raw.

14. *Vegetarian* instant long-life foods include: 'Beanfeast' a Soya mince range of ready meals – just add water. Tins of vegetarian pate, pulses, beans, Soya milk and marmite to name just a few.

15. *Instant Soups* can be found in tins, packets, foil sachets, cartons and plastic bottles the variety is enormous. Some of the thicker ones with the addition of pasta, noodles and pearl barley do make a fulfilling snack.

16. *Brownie, Cheesecake, Muffin and 'Bisquick'*

all-purpose baking mix are quick and easy to make, but ensure that you have bought cake, bread and muffin tins. Other instant puddings include: tinned custard with fruit, rice pudding, steamed puddings in minutes and jelly cubes to keep nails strong!

17. *Others*: Multi-grain morning bars made with wheat, wholegrain, oats and fruit are a good substitute for a quick breakfast snack in very rough weather. They are high in vitamins. Other long-life instant breakfast meals include potato rosti, with bacon and egg or sausage mix. Buy condiments in smaller pots as mustard, horseradish etc, tend to go stale and lose their flavour. Pickles, ketchup, etc last quite well.

2.2.5 FRESH WATER

"Water, water everywhere, Nor any drop to drink," lamented Samuel Coleridge's Ancient Mariner. It is ironic that at sea one is surrounded by oceans of salt water, but no matter how thirsty one becomes, it is always a big mistake to drink it.

People can survive more than a month without food, but only a few days without fresh water. Water must be carefully managed on a boat; it is essential to the health and well-being of the crew and having a sufficient supply makes life more enjoyable. Water requirements for one person for a two week period are seven gallons for drinking and seven gallons for washing, an average of one gallon per head per day. On ocean voyages carry a further 50% in reserve, if possible, in case of accidents to either water tank.

Always have two entirely separate supplies of water, so that if one tank leaks or is contaminated, there is another one to fall back on. It's also wise to have some portable containers either in the life-raft or at the ready to abandon ship.

There are notes about water systems and water storage in section 19.4 (Fresh water systems). The growth of marinas means more places around the coast where drinking water can be conveniently and safely topped up. To sterilize suspect drinking water, try purifying tablets, but test them first because some of them taste disgusting. If the water is clear, add 8 drops of household bleach to each gallon. If the water is cloudy, double the amount and allow the water to stand for 30 minutes; a taste of bleach should be noticeable. Two drops of 2% tincture of iodine to 500ml (1 pint) of water kills most bugs. This method is not recommended for persons with thyroid conditions. Or you can purify water by boiling it for 15 minutes, but that's a waste of fuel. Finally, potassium permanganate: Add just enough (the merest pinch) to turn the water slightly pink; let it stand for 15 minutes. The water is then ready for drinking.

2.2.6 DIET FOR LONGER VOYAGES

Food should be varied, appetising, attractive and nutritious within currently accepted nutritional guidelines. It must keep well and should pose few problems for stowage. Fresh provisions are ideal because they provide the most essential nutrients. But where preservation techniques must be used, it is essential that they have either preserved the original nutrients or that the food has been fortified with added nutrients – which can be determined from the label.

To perform well the body must have the correct amount of fuel or energy, which varies from person to person and with the activity performed. In port energy expenditure is low, and should be reflected in lighter meals. At sea more energy is expended with activity, and with the changed environment appetite increases disproportionately. Care must therefore be taken to satisfy the energy demand without eating too many calories to satisfy the increased appetite. In heavy weather much more energy is required due to the extra activity – not only when working on deck or to keep warm, but just to keep still, even when sleeping.

To determine how much food energy a typical person at sea requires for a voyage several things should be known:

- DAYS at sea, ie the distance divided by the estimated average day's run; and
- The individual's SEX, WEIGHT and physical ACTIVITY level.

ENERGY = Stored work measured in calories, joules or foot-pounds. Energy is used by the body to maintain body temperature, replace cells, and provide growth. It is acquired, of course, from the food we eat, as discussed below.

1. **Fat** is a rich source of energy (9 calories per gram) which readily contributes to obesity. Saturated fat in animal products increases the level of cholesterol in the blood and clogs up the cardiovascular system. Therefore choose leaner meats and remove excess fat, eat more poultry and fish in place of red meat, and avoid full fat milks. Semi-skimmed or skimmed milks are readily obtainable dried; they keep well and are fortified with vitamins. To reduce the amount of fat consumed avoid frying, which in any case can be dangerous in the confines of a yacht. Use margarines and cooking oils high in polyunsaturates (based on sunflower, safflower or corn oils). These oils have other advantages in that their keeping qualities are superior to the 'hard fats' (butter and lard).

2. **Sugar** provides no vitamins, minerals or other nutrients - just calories. It is the major source of tooth decay, often encouraged by infrequent cleaning. Dental problems at sea are almost invariably related to teeth that are decayed, so a reduction in sugar will result in less likelihood of toothache on passage. It is a fallacy that sugar is a major source of energy (3.75 calories per gram) - most foods supply energy. So avoid or reduce the addition of sugar in food preparation and in hot drinks. Select tinned products that are low in sugar, fruits that are tinned in fruit juice, and fizzy drinks that are diet or low calorie. Biscuits and cakes are not only high sugar foods but they contain much fat, therefore choose fruit in their place for snacks between meals.

3. **Salt** not only helps to raise blood pressure but also increases thirst. If that thirst is quenched with carbonated drinks it will contribute markedly to sugar intake (some fizzy drinks contain over eight teaspoonfuls of sugar). The imaginative use of spices and seasonings or the use of 'losalt' readily replaces the role of salt as a flavouring. There is no need to add salt to food even in the Tropics. All the salt we need (and a lot more) is to be found in the food we eat, most of it as a result of food processing. More than 75 per cent of the food eaten in Britain has been processed at least once, and food processors are renowned for adding liberal amounts of both salt and sugar to our food.

4. **Fibre** is the indigestible part of our diet and is found in cereal products, vegetables and fruit. It speeds the passage of food through the gut, helping to avoid constipation, piles, and (in longer term) gut disorders such as diverticulitis and cancer of the colon. Constipation at sea is indicative of a diet which is deficient in fibre and sitting down for long periods. Rather than easing the problem with proprietary laxatives, an increase in fibre element of the diet will prove much more beneficial. Potatoes in their skins, either baked, boiled or mashed, are not only a rich source of fibre but most of their vitamin C lies just under the skin. Pulses and pastas are not only easy to store and prepare, but are high in fibre and add variety. Tinned pulses are very convenient in

that they only need heating rather than soaking and long cooking. At least one piece of fresh fruit a day should be planned in all but the longest passages. Semi-dried prunes work wonders. Whole-wheat and multigrain breads are high in fibre and in nutrients, and are also more filling than their white counterparts, so that fewer are needed and less stowage space is required.

5. **Starch.** Complex carbohydrates should make up 55% of the diet. They add bulk and are digested very readily to give a steady source of energy. The main sources are bread, potatoes, pasta and rice.

Malnutrition and Dehydration

Most ocean passages last less than a month, so it is unlikely that you will stagger ashore with beriberi or pellagra at the end of your voyage, but I would still recommend taking a multi-vitamin/mineral pill once a day that contains thiamin (B12), A and C, plus magnesium. It takes up no space at all and has a shelf life of one year if kept perfectly dry.

Food at sea fulfills several roles. It is not only a source of nutrients to sustain normal body working, but it also satisfies the 'inner man' by creating a feeling of contentment and well-being, which sustains happiness and morale. By satisfying nutritional and social needs, correctly constituted food allows maximum body performance under all conditions. Whereas this may not be so important in day sailing, whilst undertaking longer passages a correct diet becomes vital as nutrient deficiencies may otherwise occur in the body.

Food		Amounts	Remarks
Meat and meat products		1.5kg	At least $\frac{1}{4}$ to be poultry
Fish		640g	May be increased at the expense of meat
Vegetables		4.25kg	1.6kg potatoes, 500g rice or pasta. Remainder fresh or tinned
Bread and flour		2.5kg	At least half to be wholemeal
Cereals		200g	High fibre, low sugar
Dairy produce:	Milk	2 litres	Skimmed or semi-skimmed
	Margarine	175g	Polyunsaturated
	Cheese	120g	
	Eggs	Three	Size 3
Fruit		1.25kg	Mainly fresh, but can also be dried or tinned
Biscuits		200g	
Sugar and preserves			350g
Oxo cubes		35g	

Fig. 2(4) Foods sufficient for one moderately active person for one week, providing 3100 calories daily. The amounts are for guidance only, but the proportions are balanced within current nutritional guidelines to provide adequate amounts of all nutrients. Any alcohol taken will increase the energy content and proportionately reduce the percentage energy contributed by other nutrients. Energy requirements may increase by up to 50% in adverse weather. See also Fig. 2(5).

Meat and meat products		Vegetables		Dairy produce	
Chicken, roast	500g	Potatoes	1600g	Milk, skimmed	1000ml
Beef, topside	250g	Rice/pasta	650g	– semi-skimmed	1000ml
		Peas, tinned	500g	Margarine, sunflower	175g
Lamb, chop	300g	Carrots, tinned	500g	Cheese	120g
Sausages, grilled	250g	Cabbage, fresh	400g	Eggs, fresh – size 3	165g
Bacon, grilled	200g	Beans in tomato sauce	300g		
Total	1500g	Tomatoes, tinned	300g	**Fruit**	
		Total	4250g	Oranges	375g
Fish				Apples	375g
Cod, fillet	180g	**Bread and flour**		Tinned fruit	500g
Plaice, fillet	180g	Flour, wholemeal	250g	Total	1250g
Mackerel, whole	180g	– white	250g		
Sardines/pilchards		Bread, wholemeal	1000g	**Sugar and preserves**	
(in tomato sauce)	100g	– white	1000g	Sugar	200g
Total	640g	Shredded wheat	200g	Preserves	150g
		Total	2700g	Total	350g

Fig. 2(5) List of individual foods contributing to the groups given in Fig. 2(4).

Depending on the efficiency of your refrigerator, you are most likely to run out of fresh produce and meats on long trips. While you will be unable to replace produce in large amounts, you can provide a good source of vitamins and proteins by sprouting beans and grains.

Dehydration is a serious concern especially in tropical climates. In the past people were advised to use salt tablets. The most current advice recommends the replacement of electrolytes by drinking beverages such as Gatorade ™ or Lucozade™ or any other isotonic drinks, or tea with lemon and sugar. Alcohol is not recommended as it causes further dehydration.

Fig. 2(4) shows under broad headings the foods needed by a moderately active person for one week, but note that more is required in bad weather.

2.2.7 NIGHT WATCH FOOD
Night watches consume a lot of energy and except in pilotage waters they can be very boring. A tempting and adequate Tupperware box with lid should be provided, containing a selection of sweet and savoury items:

- mini pre-wrapped cheese portions
- wholemeal crackers
- chocolate bars and boiled sweets
- muesli bars (granola bars)
- fruits, cakes, biscuits
- crisps and nuts
- dried fruit and trail mix

A snack box or rationing of snacks is important because it makes it clear to the crew what foods are off-limits. Otherwise you might find the lump of cheese for the next day's dinner has disappeared.

Fill insulated jugs with hot water for cup-a-soup, tea, instant chocolate and Bovril; the other jug with coffee, then stow them in the sink. Stainless steel is better than glass to avoid breakage – pump action is useful to avoid spillage and scalding.

2.3 THE COOK'S DOMAIN

2.3.1 GALLEY CHORES
Good cooking enhances a cruise or race, but it is still secondary to the sailing being done. The best sea cooks are not those valued for exotic dishes, but for their flexibility, creativity and persistence under dreadful conditions. It helps to have a cast-iron stomach and a sense of humour!

The cook's primary aim is to see that everybody gets enough tasty food to survive the cruise/race without suffering malnutrition, boredom or both.

The choice of food to be provided afloat depends on several factors: type of boat, length of passage, where sailing, racing or cruising etc.

It needs to be sustaining with sufficient calories, remembering that the physical effort in sailing a boat is often greater than might be imagined.

Meals should be quick to prepare; greasy foods should be avoided as they aggravate sea sickness.

Apart from the heads, nothing will get more use on your boat than the galley. Experience shows that much thought and planning will make life on board more enjoyable.

In most boats one individual is designated as cook or galley slave. From the start it is important to establish the exact role of such a person. Does he or she prepare, cook and serve each meal (and then clear it away and do the washing up) or do some other people help with one or more of these functions? Is this help allocated fairly among the rest of the crew, as it should be in a well-run yacht?

Another routine, more suitable for smaller boats, is for galley duties to be rotated, either for a day or perhaps a week at a time on a longer voyage. Whatever method is adopted, it must fit the routine for working the boat at sea. If only one of the crew is a competent navigator, then navigational duties must take priority over scrambling the eggs for breakfast, although in some circumstances it might be possible to combine these functions. A proper watchkeeping system depends very much on meals being punctual.

Even when galley duties are shared in some way, one individual should be in overall charge of the commissariat – generally planning menus, keeping an eye on the stocks of different items, and ensuring that the requisite standards of cleanliness and hygiene are maintained. In a small yacht this important duty will usually be delegated by the skipper.

2.3.2 MORALE BOOSTERS & SPECIAL OCCASIONS
When morale is low, the cook's additional duty is that of morale officer, probably because the galley is the primary source of diversion when weather or some other conditions have turned sour. Break up the routine and serve up some tins of stuffed olives, good quality tinned paté or some brownies – these will do wonders to lift the spirit.

Give some thought to any special occasions that

may occur during the time you are at sea. These range from the predictable Christmas, Birthdays and Valentine's Day to crossing the Equator or the International Dateline.

Additional supplies/gifts can add much pleasure to a long crossing, so be prepared with champagne, birthday candles, tins of good pate, stuffed olives etc – a great spirit lifter.

One final secret, when cooking for a crew save the best meals you can for the last four days of the voyage; crews like everyone else have short memories!

2.3.3   TOP TIPS
- Line shelves with non-slip matting to stop the contents sliding and rattling. It can be bought by the roll and cut to size to line lockers and galley counters or to make place-mats.
- A sugar cube in the cheese box will help stop the cheese from going mouldy. Or buy a cheese preserver with a unique micro-porous filter in the lid to regulate the humidity.
- Line both your stove (cut round gas rings) and grill pan with tin foil to save on washing up.
- Use square plastic storage jars which are 100% watertight and airtight. They save space and can be stacked more easily.
- Fleximats: unlike heavy chopping boards these are less than half a millimetre thick, but tough, lightweight and fully flexible for funneling into pans or the waste bin. Though semi-disposable, they will last for months. Ideal for weight-conscious racing yachts!
- Stay fresh Longer Bags keep fresh produce, eg fruits and vegetables, in peak condition. The bag's unique formula slows down the natural ageing process and helps prevent moisture and bacteria forming.
- A few grains of rice in the salt keeps it dry, or buy a small salt cellar with silica gel in the lid to absorb moisture. Make up a salt and pepper mix for cooking (5:1).
- Use herbs and spices to perk up tinned meats and fish.
- Ginger is helpful to sea-sickness sufferers: ginger herbal tea, ginger biscuits or fresh ginger added to a cup of warm milk.
- Milton sterilising solution or tablets added to the water when washing fruits, vegetables and salads helps guard against gastric problems and removes insects. Rinse in fresh water and dry.
- Label contents with an indelible marker pen. Use masking tape to label plastic containers

that have different contents at different times.
- To prevent dampness and the return of mildew and moulds, tie several pieces of chalk together in a net bag and suspend them in each locker. The chalk absorbs moisture.
- For off-shore racing, take a pair of washing-up gloves as hands constantly immersed in sea water can swell and get sore. Take a good barrier hand cream.

2.3.4   SAFETY IN THE GALLEY
The galley cooker can be the most temperamental piece of equipment on board – and one of the most dangerous. Do not even consider using the cooker until you are told exactly how to work it – the same goes for the heads. While showing you the cooker, the skipper should point out the fire blanket (for smothering flames), the use of the gas detector and fire extinguishers, the number and type depend on the size of the boat. Do not assume from looking at it that you know how to use it. Take it down from its mounting and read the instructions. Check the pressure gauge; if it reads low or empty, tell the skipper so that the extinguisher can be recharged before the cruise begins.

Most British yachts use liquefied petroleum gas (LPG) as fuel for the galley cooker. In Britain LPG is marketed by Calor Gas Ltd as butane (blue cylinders) or propane(red cylinders). Both are heavier than air, so any leak in the system is likely to result in an accumulation of gas in the bilges with the consequent serious risk of explosion. This danger can be minimised if the system and appliances are properly installed and are used carefully. Modern gas appliances are fitted with flame failure cut-offs and atmospheric sensors. It is also a wise precaution to fit an electronic gas detector called a sniffer, which sounds an alarm if the concentration of gas in the bilge approaches a dangerous level.

The best way to make sure that gas does not find its way into the bilge is to purge the line of unburned fuel. When you have finished cooking, before turning off the individual burner valve, shut off the valve at the cylinder. Allow the flame to die out, and then close the burner valve. This way, an accidental opening of a burner valve – say when a crew bumps against it in rough weather – will release air and not gas. When it is lit the stove should not be left unattended (except perhaps when heating water in a kettle in a calm sea.) Other fuels that may occasionally be used are paraffin and alcohol; see 13.3.5 and 19.2.2.

The cooker should be gimballed and fitted with

fiddles (retaining rails). Clamps or pot holders stop pots from flying across the cabin in rough weather.

Do not over fill pots. A strong safety bar across the front of the cooker stops the cook from falling onto the burners. Likewise a heavy belt or harness holds you in situ, and frees both hands for cooking. You should avoid serious cooking in rough weather and stick to quick instant foods until the weather eases.

The galley floor must be kept clean and dry, free from oil or grease. As a further safeguard the cook should wear oilskin trousers and sea boots in bad weather and use long-armed oven gloves and pot holders to protect against burns.

"Always clean your galley floors:
The portion dropped there could be yours!"

2.3.5 CLEANLINESS AND HYGIENE

Cleanliness is only an extension of good yacht husbandry. Surfaces on which dirt and dampness are allowed to accumulate soon deteriorate. Mildew can form on any material, and wooden structures are soon attacked by rot, given dampness and inadequate ventilation. Even small particles of food, left in some corner, can cause an unpleasant smell within the confines of a boat. A few days at sea will revive a sailor's olfactory nerves to pick up even the mildest odours, that ashore would be lost in the swirl of civilization – so it is important to keep the galley smelling nice.

The cooker, sink and working surfaces should be cleaned down after every meal, and the whole area given a special buff-up say every forenoon. The galley should be kept tidy, and utensils replaced in their proper stowages after use. These practices becomes increasingly necessary when the weather deteriorates. At the end of a cruise, and certainly at the end of the season, the entire galley, including the interiors of all lockers, needs to be thoroughly washed down with fresh water and mild detergent.

Gash, trash, garbage or plain rubbish

There must be a strict routine for dealing with gash. For a start it is illegal to jettison any rubbish within 3 miles of the coast. Plastic and other non-biodegradable substances must never be thrown overboard anywhere. The MCA recommends that no rubbish is dumped anywhere especially in the English Channel and North Sea. Certain items can go overboard when well offshore. All harbours and marinas will have a facility where skips and bins are provided. Most boaters would prefer to act in an environmentally responsible way. You can first reduce the sheer amount of rubbish to be ditched by simply doing the things listed below.

- ✓ Dispose of any unnecessary packaging before you stow purchases (ie cardboard boxes around cans, juice, toothpaste etc). Store vegetables in baskets instead of plastic bags.
- ✓ Separate gash – food scraps, vegetable peelings, coffee grinds etc can be thrown overboard (to leeward!) in deep water.
- ✓ Plastic, plastic bags and aluminum (rinsed in salt water to prevent smelling) are NEVER thrown overboard anywhere – plastic bags are a danger to sea life and likely to foul propellers and clog water intake valves.
- ✓ Tins and cans punctured in both ends a few times will sink rapidly and do no harm if well offshore. But if you are in enclosed waters or among islands or weekend sailing or racing, crush them and take them ashore.
- ✓ Bottles – take them ashore, most marinas have bottle banks. If cruising for long periods and in deep water, fill them with sea water and sink.
- ✓ Paper can be shredded and ditched over the side in deep water.

2.3.6 PEST CONTROL

Cockroaches

Do not bring on board any cardboard or paper bags, even cans or beer cases – roaches are known for laying their eggs on paper and cardboard. Check all fruit and vegetables. Various proprietary sprays and powders are available for the purpose, and a stock should be carried. They need to be used thoroughly and systematically, penetrating every corner and crevice. Remove the contents of each locker in turn and gain access behind fittings such as sink and cooker in order to treat the likely runs. If that does not succeed, consider fumigating the entire boat. This means sealing every opening, and the crew moving out for a day or more.

If mooring in cockroach areas, try sprinkling boric acid on shore lines, or if already onboard, icing sugar or sweetened condensed milk and powdered boric acid in a flat tin or match box away from children and pets.

Mice/Rats

Rats can climb mooring lines, but simply putting a metal cone half way up the mooring line will often keep them from making it on board – or on long distance cruising, take a cat!

Mosquitoes

Mooring in swampy areas or even off the west coast of Scotland are likely to increase the risk.

Mosquito coils work well, but take care to keep the coil in a well ventilated area and do not inhale smoke. Insect repellent is generally available in all locations or Oil of Lemon Grass, an aromatherapy oil, is said to work. In warmer waters put mosquito netting over sleeping areas.

Flies/Wasps
Can be killed with a fly swat. Flies are far more dangerous for spreading disease, so cover exposed food and, if desperate, use an aerosol spray.

Worms
Round worms are carried on fruit and vegetables, and tapeworm in undercooked meat. The eggs are not visible to the eye, but heat kills both types.

Wash salads and fresh fruit in a little potassium permanganate (a few crystals in water will suffice) just before eating them. Salt in washing water deals with slugs and caterpillars.

Weevils
Rarely encountered these days in well-packaged goods, but will be found in the West Indies and Eastern Mediterranean when buying semolina, pulses, cereals, couscous or rice from the sack or paper bags. Put the food stuffs in a freezer for 24 hours, in a plastic bag; this will kill any eggs, then transfer them to a beetle proof container. To de-weevil flour, use an extra fine sieve that holds back both weevil and their grub. Immersion in water: weevils float to the top, but sometimes with rice you will need to remove them manually by slowly and painstakingly panning through. Bay, Laurel and Eucalyptus leaves are supposed to act as weevil repellents.

2.4 WEIGHTS AND MEASURES

Recipes refer variously to metric or Imperial units and also to practical measures, eg tablespoons. For conversion factors and other details of units see Section 5.4 in Chapter 5, but here are some useful culinary equivalents for ready reference:

Weights
1oz	=	28g
4oz	=	113g (just over 0·1kg)
8oz	=	227g (just under 0·25kg)
16oz (1lb)	=	454g (just under 0·5kg)
100g	=	3·5oz
250g (0·25 kg)	=	9oz
500g (0·5 kg)	=	18oz (1lb 2oz)
1000g (1kg)	=	35oz (2lb 3oz)

Fluid measures
1fl oz	=	28ml
0·25 pint	=	142ml
0·5 pint	=	285ml
1 pint	=	568ml
0·1 litre (100ml)	=	3·5fl oz
0·25litre (250ml)	=	9fl oz
0·5 litre (500ml)	=	17.5fl oz

Practical units of measurement
2 teaspoons	=	1 dessert spoon (level)
4 teaspoons	=	1 table spoon (level)

12 tablespoons of 24ml (just under 1fl oz) fill a typical breakfast cup holding 285ml or 0·5 pint.

Since scales are unlikely to be on the average yacht, the following very approximate measures may be useful. They refer to level spoonfuls.

1·5 tablespoons	=	1oz (28g) rice, jam, syrup or honey
2 tablespoons	=	1oz (28g) cocoa, custard powder, cornflour, dried fruit, flour, grated cheese, lentils, sugar
4 tablespoons	=	1oz (28g) bread crumbs or porridge oats
8 tablespooons	=	1 cup
2 cups	=	1lb butter/ margarine or dried rice
4 cups	=	1lb non-fat dry milk solids or macaroni
5 cups	=	1lb spaghetti
6 cups	=	1lb noodles

2.5 SAILING CLOTHES

Having fed and watered the inner man/woman, all will be lost if the outer person is unable properly to combat the cold, wet and sometimes hot conditions which are part of the yachtsman's daily fare.

2.5.1 INTRODUCTION
In recent years sailing clothing has made great advances in design, materials and construction. Outwardly, it is more fashion conscious, often utilising bright colours in smart combinations, but the developments are more than skin-deep. Now materials are better than ever with breathable fabrics used from premium gear right down to budget level clothing, tailoring is much improved, and the detailed features built into modern foul-weather suits make them highly effective garments.

Sailors should be grateful for the fact that they do not have to endure bad weather clad in the traditional oilskin coat and sou'wester, made of fine canvas which was treated with an oil-based preparation (hence the name) to produce a material which was initially glossy and waterproof. But the garments were stiff and uncomfortable to wear, and exposure to sun and sea soon made them crack and become sticky, and far from waterproof.

Even the first breed of unlined PVC garments were not much better. The openings at the neck, wrists and ankles were so large that it was accepted that water would penetrate through them, even if the material or its seams did not leak. But now, with the modern materials available (discussed in more detail below), we can worry about such matters as reducing condensation inside suits, or eliminating it altogether with modern breathable fabrics, because they are so good at keeping from the outside getting in and getting the moisture from inside out.

The prices of modern sailing clothes may alarm some people, but there is a strong case for saying that they are very good value for money. Shore-going and more fashion orientated clothes attract high prices while offering little inherent value, but the same cannot be said of the best sailing gear. Look closely at the work that goes into a suit of foul-weather clothing, gauge the price of the accessories, feel the quality of the material, and they appear excellent value when compared with (say) tennis or ski clothing.

The real point about sailing clothes is that they must provide protection from wind, sun, salt, water and the cold. In temperate climates, such as prevail in Europe, cold is the biggest enemy and it can be a killer. Less dramatically, it can speed the onset of seasickness, and it can put newcomers off the sport simply because they feel cold and wet.

Cold is a killer in its own right. Deaths at sea were often attributed to drowning until hypothermia started to be widely understood in the 1960s. Stated simply, hypothermia is the body's inability to produce heat at a faster rate than it is being lost. Keeping the body core temperature at about 37·6°C (98·4°F) is vital for the correct working of the various organs. Conversely, being overheated (hyperthermia) can be just as dangerous. Hence you won't see a sportsman or woman nowadays very far from a bottle of water or specially formulated re-hydrating drink – something we could all learn from.

You do not have to fall overboard to become prone to hypothermia, since the air can draw out body heat just as effectively as the sea unless there is sufficient protection. Most sailors know the sensation of 'feeling the cold in their bones'

when on watch in miserable conditions. Along with low morale, an empty stomach and tiredness it is an early sign of the onset of hypothermia. The condition worsens through listlessness and weak, cumbersome movement – symptoms which most sailors will have experienced. In extreme cases, when life is endangered, sufferers can experience cramp, numbness, nausea, slurred speech, hazy vision and even unconsciousness. Urgent and correct treatment is required, as described in 13.9.17. So the correct clothing goes beyond questions of comfort and fashion. The right clothes are vital to safer sailing.

2.5.2 LAYERS FOR WARMTH

Many people still wear conventional shore-going clothes under their foul-weather gear. Frequently these are cotton based. Be warned. Whether you have breathable oilskins or not, cotton attracts moisture like a sponge – whether perspiration, rain or spray. If you've felt cold and clammy in cotton that is because it can absorb twice its own weight in water. When wet it can transfer heat away from the body at up to 30x the rate of dry air. Best save the cotton for sunny days or to change into when going ashore.

Far better synthetic fibre alternatives exist and virtually all sailing clothing makers offer them in a layering system of specially designed garments.

If you have breathable oilskins, then it is not so much desirable as essential to wear synthetic base layer clothing underneath in order to allow the outer shell to work effectively; see Fig. 2(6).

When the first Gore-Tex oilskins appeared in the early 1990s this phenomenon was not understood properly and many wondered why they still felt clammy inside supposedly breathable oilskins. Using synthetic materials next to the skin avoids this, even if means substituting swimming trunks or cycle shorts for cotton pants.

Natural materials such as cotton and wool are still regarded as very comfortable, but they have their disadvantages. Eiderdown, for example, may give the best heat insulation but it is very expensive and loses much of its efficiency when wet. Similarly, wool has long been a favourite for sweaters but these get smelly when wet and are slow to dry.

Artificial materials known as fibre pile (fur fabric) or the more expensive variations such as fleece (bunting in American terms) dry surprisingly quickly. If there is no circulation of air, or easy means of hanging them up, modern base and mid-layer garments will dry with body heat, when offwatch below deck. Artificial fibres such as polypropylene are more thermally efficient for underclothes, but their main advantage is their ability to transport, or wick, moisture away from the skin.

Whether artificial or natural fibres are preferred, keeping warm relies on the common principle that several thin layers are better than one thick one. A typical layer system has a specific job for each layer. The base should wick moisture away from the body. The mid layer should the prime means of insulating the body with warm air. And the outer layer should keep water out.

A typical base layer comprises thin T-shirt style vests and trousers, nowadays available in the full gamut of long and short sleeves/legs, and crew/polo/opening necks. The best items from the leading manufacturers will absorb as little as 0·5% of their own weight in moisture, so there will be no 'blotting-paper' effect.

The mid layer often comprises fleece type trousers or salopettes, topped with with a similar waistcoat or jacket. Experience will tell you if more is needed. So much depends on the individual's sense of cold, the amount of activity they are doing and the conditions in which they are sailing. Sailing downwind will seem much warmer in a given wind speed and air temperature than upwind.

Personal needs vary widely. Lean, thin people feel the cold quicker than thicker-set persons, who find that for once a layer of fat has a real benefit. Also the more you go boating either throughout the season or during an extended cruise, the lower the threshold of coldness becomes. Passage-makers will tell you that they feel less cold on the third day at sea than on the first.

For sailing outside the summer season more substantial clothing will be needed. Here the layer system will be more like: thermal T-shirt and long johns, a one-piece pile or quilted garment of long-john style (or thermal pile/quilted trousers with pile jacket), an additional bodywarmer waistcoat, and apart from oilskins special provision for hands, feet and head.

Thermal vests and trousers are now particularly soft and warm, often with a knitted inside surface to make them pleasant to wear next to the skin. Leading manufacturers such as Musto, Henri-Lloyd, Gill and Helly-Hansen offer a good choice both in styles and weight of garment to suit all types of sailing. Malden Mills' Polartec range of fabrics is one of the most widely used in premium quality brands.

Pile-type cloth has largely given way to polyester fleece with some excellent fabrics now being made. Generally quality follows price and one reasonably reliable way to assess the warmth properties of a fabric is to feel its weight and check its density against the light. If you are an active racing sailor, some of the heavy piles in mid-layers maybe too hot but ideal for long watchkeeping vigils by the cruising yachtsman and racing through the high latitudes.

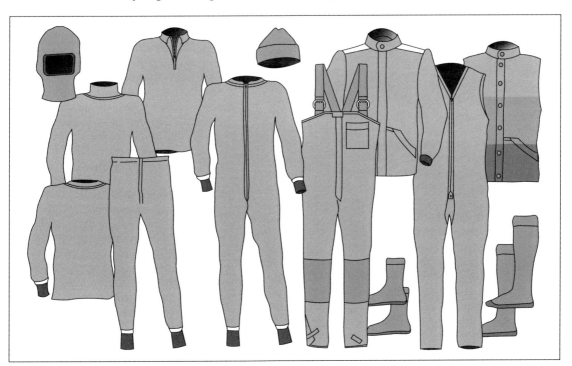

Fig. 2(6) On the layering principle, various bodywarmer garments can be worn beneath oilskins.

A key advantage of fleece over most other insulating fabrics is their lower water absorption and resistance to the fibres matting down when wet. When fabrics are dry and lofted they can trap air; and the better they retain this state, the warmer you will be.

2.6 FOUL-WEATHER GEAR

2.6.1 MATERIALS

More than anything, oilskins exemplify the adage that you get what you pay for. Top of the range, fully-featured breathable oilskins could cost ten times as much as a thin, budget set.

Be realistic in assessing your needs. Judge whether you'd rather spend the money on another item of gear for the yacht. A good chandler won't sell something more expensive than you'd rather buy. But do, whatever you chose, consider very carefully the choice between breathable and non-breathable oilskins. The former are invariably more expensive but ask anyone who has used them, and it would be rare to find one who would rather sail in anything else. More times than not, a convert is zealot-like in his enthusiasm.

Think of oilskins as part of your personal safety. Good foul-weather gear will protect the inner layers of clothing from sea, spray and rain and keep them dry which means you are warmer and more efficient.

Breathable fabrics

The American company, WL Gore, really made a breakthrough when they created Gore-Tex. Strange to imagine, but the clever part of this supple cloth laminate is actually expanded ePTFE, the same material as is used to coat non-stick pans. Stranger still, that something designed to keep the water out, comprises millions and millions of holes.

It is these micropores that let the fabric breathe. All sorts of analogies are used to explain the micro-pore. In terms of scale, Henri-Lloyd says think in terms of the pore as being 20,000 times smaller than a rain drop. Musto says if the pore is the same size as a kitchen, then a water droplet would be equivalent to a 200 mile meteorite whilst a water vapour molecule is the size of a coin. The idea is, therefore, to let the coins through but keep the meteorites out.

Gore-Tex is the top of the range material, but there are subtle differences between clothing makers. Some use a heavier, stiffer fabric scrim, the filling of the Gore-Tex laminate, because they have found that in extreme sailing, such as in the Southern Ocean, the more supple fabrics profile themselves to the body more, trapping less air

and heightening the sense of cold. This is not a problem for the vast majority of sailors.

For a time, WL Gore had strong patent protection in the breathable fabric market but there are now alternatives, many of them originating in the Far East with Japan's textile makers producing excellent cloths. Most however, are less efficient and not as durable as Gore-Tex, but they are cheaper and could be right solution for you.

The brand names of these fabrics are varied but the non-Gore-Tex breathables work on an entirely differently principle. Called hydrophilics, they transfer water by a chemical process.

Both Gore-Tex and the hydrophilics rely on osmotic pressure to an extent and this takes us back to the thermal under clothing. You want each layer to transmit water vapour better than the next one, hence base and middle layers ought to be more breathable than the outer layer. Cotton risks reversing the process and acts just like blotting paper.

This matters, because the body typically puts out 1/18 litre of water at idle. Moderate activity causes this to jump to 1/2 litre an hour and this can double with a series of heavy sail changes.

A top of the range suit of Gore-Tex oilskins are expensive but they are not cheap to make. The fabric is expensive because of its complex manufacturing process and very strict quality controls. Typically, it is double the price of the hydrophilics.

Making a top of the range ocean racing jacket for instance, could involve as many as 240 pieces of cloth. Study a hood and you'll appreciate why. And whereas in normal tailoring darts are used to give shape, oilskins use seams. Each seam uses a special Gore taping which is slow because it is a heat-set process. And the clothing manufacturer will carry out his own quality control, random pressure testing the seams. One jacket could take in excess of four hours to make. The price is high, but there is plenty of value too.

One thing you will notice in breathable oilskins is the lack of a lining; this is deliberate to allow the membrane to work properly. Breathable or not, use fabrics to which a waterproof finish has been applied; and do check the quality of construction and detailing.

Hoods, neck, wrist and ankle closures are now much more sophisticated. After all, there is little point using technically advanced cloths, if you can still get wet via a very unsophisticated hole.

PVC proofing

Polyvinyl chloride (PVC) is the traditional material for foul-weather gear but its day has past. Still prominent in the industrial and fishing markets, its presence in the yachting market is diminishing all the time. It has a distinctive glossy appearance and is rather heavy, but it is relatively cheap and its seams can be welded after they have been sewn to make them completely watertight. Although PVC garments have many proponents, fewer manufacturers offer them today.

One reason is colour, since there is little choice outside the standard range of yellow, blue, red or orange. In reality this is not such a disadvantage, because yellow or orange are sensible colours to wear at sea and to give good visibility in a man-overboard situation. More important, as foul-weather gear has become more sophisticated in design and detailing, so the limits of PVC have been reached.

PVC is still used however in light-weight budget oilskins as an alternative inside membrane to urethane. These are made of proofed nylon cloths, very different from old style material which often used a cotton base with a heavy PVC coating on the outside.

Neoprene proofing
Before breathable fabrics, neoprene was used as an interior coating on many top of the range garments. It is now rarely seen. Neoprene is much more expensive than PVC, and while it can be tailored in complicated ways, making the seams watertight is a much more involved process. Some companies dope the thread, but this is not enough since any load will open the stitching. The better suits have seams that are stitched not once but twice, and are then taped over on the inside.

Urethane proofing
Urethane proofing is the norm for lighter weight, bottom of the range oilskins and offer excellent value for money. Applied to the inside of nylon fabric it provides water and wind proof protection.

Additional waterproofing is often provided by spraying a treatment on the outside of the cloth to boost water repellency.

Clearly, the fewer seams that are included the better, and it is well worth looking at the styling of jackets and trousers to see where the seams are.

2.6.2 STYLE AND CONSTRUCTION
The knees and seats of trousers, and the elbows of jackets are all high-wear areas, where manufacturers try to avoid seams and sometimes fit reinforcing patches. Jacket seams across the top of the shoulder will also often be under load and manufacturers now take great care to move the seam away from the yoke of their jackets

Fig. 2(7) A good suit of foul-weather clothing has all the features listed below.

which is the part most exposed to the weather.

This gives rise to different cuts. Lower cost jackets use a simple inset seam to join an arm on to the body of the jacket. A tougher form of construction is the raglan style familiar from raincoats. Most complicated is the magyar seam, which takes the seam from the arm into the neck of the jacket at the top, and across the chest on the lower side.

There is a large choice of jackets. Smock styles have become popular again for specialized purposes, mostly for racing crews: lightweight spray tops for day racing, or blue water bowman's smocks with neoprene neck seals; see Fig. 2(7).

For most however, the conventional zip-fronted jacket is the best style, with a two-way, heavy duty zip, reinforced seat, reflective tape on hood and shoulders. The zip closure must be well protected with a single, or better still a double, storm flap. Linings are less common in breathables but where fitted, ought to be non-absorbent and with a draining facility. Hoods, shoulders, cuffs and jacket front can be fitted with retro-reflective patches which help identify a person overboard at night.

Pockets are useful for carrying knives, torches, personal man overboard beacons, handkerchiefs and so on. They should drain and be well protected by storm flaps. Fleece-lined hand-warmer pockets are a really useful feature. External pouches can be used to house mini-flares or radio beacons. Tabs for lifejacket and harness, crotch or thigh straps, pockets for whistle and light stick all enhance the safety aspects.

Careful attention to detail is essential at the openings for wrists and neck. No matter how good the material of the jacket is, water is always liable to find its way in at these points. Inner cuffs at the wrists together with external straps, both perhaps with Velcro adjusters, help to seam the arms. At the neck a good high zip helps, and careful shaping of the neck and hood ought to permit the collar to fit inside the hood to give protection up to the height of the cheeks. A peak on the hood boosts protection enormously, and some hoods fold back to allow the wearer to look up – to check sail trim for example. Sophisticated hoods have a storm flap which will fit around the chin, or unfolded, it can fit right up to ear height for really good protection. The best toggles can be worked easily with numb hands or when wearing gloves, and can be released quickly to permit conversation.

With trousers, very few waist-high styles are made nowadays. If a manufacturer does make them, they are often pitched at the motorboat market. Chest-high trousers are the best solution. They provide reasonable protection when no jacket is worn and a good overlap when sitting or crouching in a jacket.

When choosing chest-high trousers consider the problems of using the head, something that is difficult enough for men and certainly no easier for women. All manner of solutions have been tried, but one which works tolerably well for men is a long gusset down the chest which, with a bit a dexterity, does mean the trousers do not have be dropped every time.

It pays to consider the worst conditions that you have experienced or can envisage – changing sails on a pitching foredeck, clearing sheets down to leeward with water coursing past at ankle height, or sitting on the weather rail with waves landing in your lap. Even sitting huddled in the cockpit in driving rain and spray will expose any weakness in design or materials.

2.6.3 SAFETY HARNESSES AND PERSONAL BUOYANCY

For British Standards (BS) now read European standards (CEN) and in place of the old Kitemark, a CE number is now your guide; see also 13.3.6 & 13.3.7. Standards are evolving all the time. One terrible lesson learnt from the 1998 Sydney-Hobart Race was that even an approved safety harness can fail, especially if it has previously been exposed to sudden loading or not properly maintained and inspected.

Race and event organisers may make additional demands over and above the basic CEN standards, so be sure to check with the compliance requirements. Similarly, the vessel you are sailing might fall under other codes, such as those imposed by the MCA.

Safety harness

For instance, harnesses are subject to a drop test in order meet the CE 1095 standard, but Britain's Royal Ocean Racing Club and the Offshore Racing Council's Special Regulations committee are preparing an additional requirement to show if a harness or hook has been subjected to a shock load in subsequent use.

Notwithstanding increasing worries over liability and litigation, it is common sense for each individual to be responsible for his own personal safety gear. If you are using equipment supplied with the vessel or by another skipper, satisfy yourself that the gear meets the standard of any code which might be in operation and that you are willing to entrust your life to it; see Fig. 2(8).

The basic requirements for lifejackets and

harnesses have been discussed in 13.3.6 & 13.3.7. For a time harnesses were built into jackets; they were not considered as separate entities. But the compromises proved too great. Remember that being pulled through the water at even five knots exerts tremendous pressure, so an integral harness needs to be adjusted to the wearer's frame just as carefully as a harness worn externally. Improperly donned safety gear can only fulfil a small proportion of its potential capacity, and can endanger life in certain circumstances. A properly adjusted external harness, complying with CEN1095, is the most effective type.

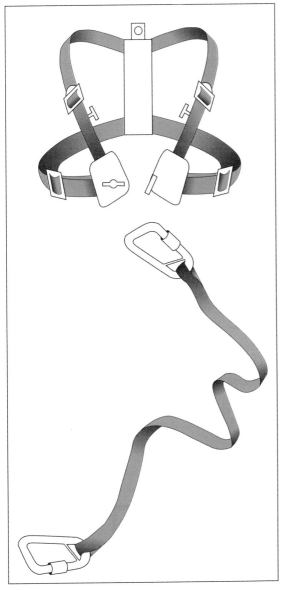

Fig. 2(8) Multifit safety harness with loop and toggle attachments.

Lifejackets

Personal buoyancy can be worn either inside or outside the jacket. Many leading makes, such as Musto, Henri-Lloyd, Helly-Hansen and Gill provide loops on the outside of jackets to permit a Multifit lifejacket to be worn. This fits like a collar round the neck and is held to the jacket by toggles mating with the loops, and with a substantial strap around the chest. It has no permanent buoyancy but uses gas bottle or oral inflation when needed. Careful shaping means that harness D-rings are unobstructed and that the lifejacket can be kept on the jacket if it is taken off when going below, ready for wear next time.

CEN 396 is the standard to look for here, provided 150 Newtons of buoyancy. There is a standard lower than this which provides only 100 Newtons, which to many is too little. By contrast the CE 399 standard demands 275 Newtons and full self-righting capability. It is the type used by lifeboatmen and rescue services, but many recreational users prefer to compromise some buoyancy for something less cumbersome.

2.6.4 SPECIALIST CLOTHING

Arguably the dry suit is the biggest single clothing innovation to have arrived in sailing in recent years. If made of breathable materials, it became tolerable to wear a suit with built-in socks and neoprene neck, wrist and waist seals; see Fig. 2(9).

Early versions, based on divers' drysuits, were not much fun thanks to high perspiration levels and difficult in regulating temperature. One-piece suits remain difficult to get into because they rely on one heavy, waterproof zip. Often this is situated at the back and across the shoulders as these tough brass zips are relatively inflexible. Some front fastening types are available.

These suits are very much the preserve of ocean racing crews in tough conditions or other specialised users such as operators of RIBs. Worn with base and mid-layer thermal clothing and an approved lifejacket they can conform to CEN standards for Abandonment. Tony Bullimore famously survived inside the upturned hull of his boat in the Southern Ocean for four days in such a suit. They are very expensive but worth every penny.

They are not survival suits in the strict sense, which tend to be insulated for floatation and heat retention and fitted with special features such as face visors. Nonetheless they work well in extreme conditions. Some manufacturers such as Musto fit a mouth piece so that the suit can be inflated.

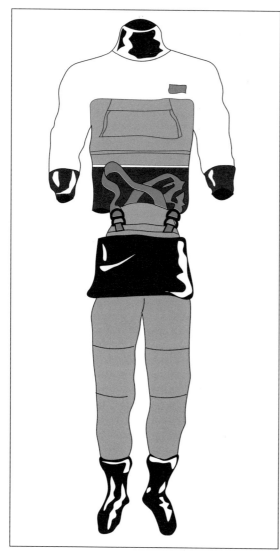

Fig. 2(9) Dry-suit top and trousers are joined at the waist by a special roll-up seal. The top has rubber seals at the neck and wrists. The trousers have waterproof socks attached.

Mock tops with sealable necks and wrist are also popular among ocean racing crews who have to stay on deck with only minimal time off watch.

2.6.5 FOOTWEAR

There is no real need to buy special sailing shoes provided you have a pair which grip well in the dry and wet, and which do not mark the deck. Trainers work well enough, although most people prefer to look the part in proper boating gear. Deck shoes can be nylon athletic-style or leather. Both are more durable than canvas; see Fig. 2(10).

Whatever the uppers are made of, the soles must grip the deck, but not pick up dirt which is then walked aboard. Many owners, quite

reasonably, expect visitors to take off shore-going shoes before coming on board.

The conflicting requirements of giving a good grip and not picking up dirt are best met by one of the varieties of razor-cut soles that are on the market though even the best grips can be rendered useless if the sole's material is inappropriate. Unbelievably, one of the best known deck shoe makers launched a short-lived model which used the wrong formulation. The grip was good in the dry; in the wet, it was lethal.

All eyelets and heel reinforcements should be non-rusting and non-magnetic. The leather, moccasin-style shoe can be worn comfortably without socks, but these are advisable for warmth in cooler weather and to absorb perspiration. The best varieties are hand-stitched with rot-proof thread. Shoes are made all over the world, as the legend under the tongue will reveal, with leather subject to all sorts of tanning processes. Some, it has to be said, can become smelly very quickly.

While deck shoes are fine for fair weather sailing or for use in harbour, when it comes to seagoing it is essential to wear a good pair of sea boots. Almost nothing is more demoralising than wet feet while on watch, and this should be preventable at least most of the time. Sea boots need just the same good grip on the soles as shoes. Fig. 2(11) shows the British and Continental sizes for footwear. For American sizes, add 5 to the British figure.

Provided there is a really good seal between the oilskin trouser and the boot, it should be possible to prevent water surging up inside and into the boot. Some boots have external gaiters to fit the bottom of the oilskins trousers. Best of all, is to wear Gore-Tex socks, if your sailing sees you knee deep in solid water. They are expensive but are a 'quality of life' purchase. Lined boots are the norm, though once wet they can take a very long time to dry out without a heat source.

Still relatively new to the market are Gore-tex boots. They tend to have a more shoe-like fit, so sizing needs to be done carefully.

Putting on and taking off boots with oilskin trousers can be awkward. A useful tip when taking them off is to roll the trousers down to the ankles and step out of the boots. Next time that they have to be worn it is a simple matter to step into the boots again and pull up the trousers.

2.6.6 HEAD, HANDS AND FEET

Keeping the extremities warm is fundamental to keeping the body trunk warm. The head for instance can lose as much heat as the body can

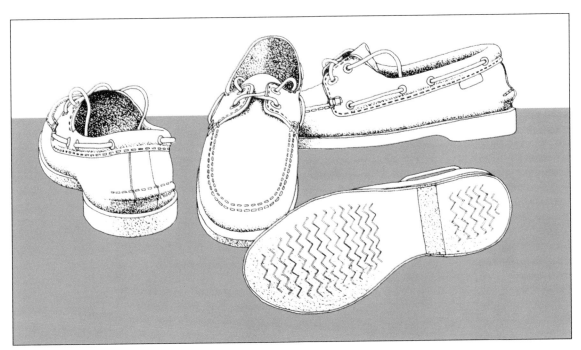

Fig. 2(10) Although leather deck shoes are more expensive, they last much longer than those with canvas/nylon uppers.

produce, so some form of headwear is essential in bad weather. A sou'wester or a hood incorporated in the jacket are the two alternatives for keeping water at bay and stopping it running down the neck, but both are inclined to restrict vision and communication.

Many people find that a woolly hat is adequate most of the time and can be worn under a hood. It is warm and gives some protection against knocks and bumps. Just as in thermal clothing, synthetic fleeces are much better than wool and for the same reasons: warmer when wet, low water

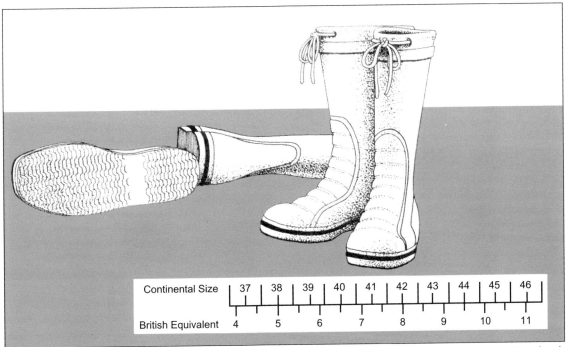

Continental Size	37	38	39	40	41	42	43	44	45	46
British Equivalent	4	5	6	7	8	9	10	11		

Fig. 2(11) A good pair of sea boots should have a hardwearing, non-slip sole; reinforcements at toe, heel and instep; arch support; quick-drying lining; broad fitting for warmth and comfort; and lightweight, flexible construction.

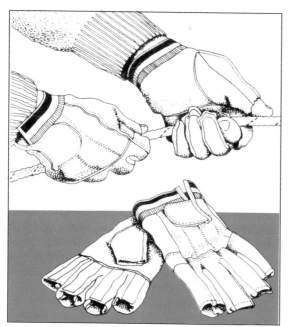

Fig. 2(12) A pair of sailing gloves can give useful protection.

absorption and quick drying. Some fabrics have a windproof layer for extra snugness.

In colder conditions a Balaclava-type hat can make a miserable watch more bearable – if necessary under a sou'wester or hood.

If hands are allowed to become cold, dexterity is lost. Leather sailing gloves protect hands in fine weather, but their fingerless style and cut-out backs mean that they are of little use during periods of inactivity in the cold. So two pairs of gloves makes sense – leather ones for warp and anchor handling, and fleecy mitts for cold conditions; see Fig. 2(12).

Cold feet are almost as bad as wet feet. Thick, fleecy, thermal socks can help, but they are not the whole answer. This is because the body cuts down the circulation of blood to the extremities when it is cold, in order to keep the vital organs in the core warm. You can warm up feet by movement to stimulate the flow of blood, and also by having boots which are not too tight.

2.7 CARE OF CLOTHES, AND WHAT TO TAKE

2.7.1   CARE OF CLOTHING

Washing codes now have to be shown on garments by law, and should be heeded with sailing clothing, which may need special treatment. Follow instructions to avoid damaging a garment and rendering it useless. Annoyingly, what might suit one style of fabric could ruin another.

For example, some polypropylene thermal wear clothes cannot be hot washed without risking shrinkage. Similarly, hot-air tumble drying may cause such garments to shrink to almost half their normal size. Others are inert to hot washing and tumbling, so read the labels.

Chandleries and outdoor activity shops sell specialised washing products for modern materials. They can wash clothing and restore water repellency.

For oilskins, regular washing is highly recommended. Even a fresh water rinse will help remove the salt. As a general rule avoid using detergents on proofed garments; use mild soap instead. Although oil, grease and petrol should not damage the proofing, such spillages can be removed with a gentle wash in warm soapy water. Some manufacturers allow machine washing, but hand washing is kinder. Do not spin dry proofed garments as the centrifugal action tries to force water out through the weave.

Breathables such as Gore-Tex react differently. Machine washing is good for them as it stops dirt becoming embedded in the micro-pores. Moreover, a tumble dry can re-set the molecules of the water-repellant treatments. WL Gore says ironing helps too; but do not try this on urethane or PVC treated fabric.

2.7.2   WHAT TO TAKE?

This is a Frequently Asked Question. Seagoing clothing has already been discussed mainly in the context of cold and wet weather. In warmer weather comfort and informality are the norm at sea.

In harbour, if invited aboard a strange boat for drinks, it is courteous to wear casually smart clothes – but the ambience and rapport with your hosts is the real key. When going ashore wear whatever you feel is appropriate for holiday circumstances and the type of restaurant, bar or nightclub you intend visiting. If invited to a formal evening function in a local yacht club, especially abroad, men would probably wear a jacket and tie (and ladies the equivalent). Some of the older-established yacht clubs in particular like to preserve a certain formality and, whilst they welcome visitors, they expect them to conform on matters of dress. You might for example be requested to move to the casual bar if so attired. It is usually obvious.

Of course you will probably know the relatives or friends with whom you sail well enough to be aware of how they dress on board and ashore – and any doubts about dress can be readily aired. But if you are amongst comparative strangers and a bit new to sailing customs, you might want to suss out whether informal gear is the norm or whether you will need something more formal.

The following is a slightly tongue-in-cheek check list of items which, apart from sailing gear, are mostly common sense:

Sailing gear

a. Most yachts have enough safety harnesses and lifejackets for all crew, but not foul weather gear or wellies. Borrowing onboard is rarely convenient, so bring your own; or for a one-off trip buy a cheap set at the local fisherman's cooperative.

b. Bring your own knife, waterproof torch, mini-flares, man overboard light, if you fear for your life – and a hand-held GPS if the navigator is known to be untrustworthy.

Personal Gear

c. Bring your own sleeping bag, towels, washing kit, suntan lotion, swimming gear and all the other paraphernalia of the optimistic sun-worshipper.

d. Enough shirts, trousers for at least one change if you get soaked. Go for synthetic fibres as they are quick drying. A neck towel to keep salt water at bay. Plenty of socks, including thick stockings for inside your wellies.

e. Warm clothing, including long johns and gloves, for those long night watches or just to cope with the British Summer.

f. At least one shower/wind proof jacket and whatever you like to wear on your head to cope with sun, rain, sea water and snow.

g. A shirt, tie and jacket/blazer for more formal occasions. Equivalent female rig, which no male would dare to specify.

h. Money, credit card, in-date passport, driving licence, mobile, alarm clock, personal medication.

Stowage space is often limited, so do not take too much gear and only ever in a soft holdall or bag; be prepared to live out of your bag if locker space is really short. Hard suitcases and framed rucksacks are definitely bad news on board.

Most boats are reasonably dry below, but smart clothes can be hung in poly bags from the cleaner, while other clothing is best wrapped in smaller poly bags. It only has to rain, or for there to be water in the bottom of the dinghy, for kit to get wet through even at the outset of a passage. A few black dustbin liners take up little space and could save your day. Some sailing holdalls have internal dividers to separate dry clothing from wet or damp.

2.8 BOOKS ABOUT COOKING AT SEA

Good Food Afloat: Every Sailor's Guide to Eating Right by John Betterley (Ashford Press).

The Gourmet Galley by Terence Janericco (Ashford Press).

Sell up and Sail by Bill and Laurel Cooper (3rd edition, Adlard Coles)

Living Afloat by Clare Allcard (Adlard Coles)

The Sailing Lifestyle by John Rousmaniere.

The Care and Feeding of the Sailing Crew by Lin and Larry Pardey (W.W. Norton & Co). Invaluable blue water catering.

The Great Cruising Cookbook by John C. Payne (Adlard Coles). International galley guide.

Boat Cuisine – the all-weather Cookbook by June Raper (Fernhurst).

Cruising Cuisine – Fresh Food from the Galley by Kay Pastorius.

A Boater's Guide to Provisioning by Dyan Farley.

Clothing

There are few books on Clothing, but all the major manufacturers publish informative publicity literature about their products. Taken in conjunction with this chapter, the reader should be able to gain a clear idea of what is likely to meet his needs at an affordable price.

Cruising Companions

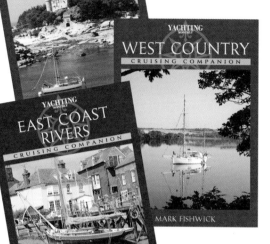

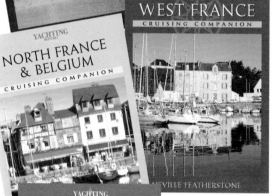

Produced in association with Yachting Monthly magazine, the Macmillan Reeds Cruising Companion range covers popular cruising grounds in NW Europe, with a fresh approach.

Superb quality port plans are used, alongside full-colour aerial photography, and the latest pilotage and approach information.

The Cruising Companion series adds 'what to do' information to the usual 'how to get there' pilotage, with thorough coverage of shore-side facilities and places of interest.

North Brittany & The Channel Islands	**£24.95**
West France	**£24.95**
East Coast Rivers	**£19.95**
West Country	**£19.95**
South West Spain & Portugal	**£24.95**
North France & Belgium	**£24.95**

Other planned editions in the Cruising Companion range include the following titles: Ireland Cruising Companion, Western Isles Cruising Companion, Northern Spain Cruising Companion, Netherlands Cruising Companion, South Coast Cruising Companion.

Chapter 3 Boat Handling

CONTENTS

3.1 INTRODUCTION

3.1.1 HANDLING UNDER SAIL

Many yachts habitually start their engines and lower their sails before the simplest manoeuvre – even just anchoring – and thereby miss the satisfaction of doing such things under sail. Their owners also forego the experience of handling their boats under sail, until the day when they must do so for real.

You may be unwise to enter a marina or a crowded anchorage under sail (with a serviceable engine), but a good skipper should be able to cope if need be. There are few problems that cannot be resolved under sail – albeit perhaps with the help of a warp or two, or even the anchor or the dinghy.

For manoeuvring under sail it is essential to have an understanding of hull and sail balance, as described in Chapters 15 and 17. Boat handling is something of an art, but an art which does need practice, especially in a strange craft. Every boat has different characteristics, which need to be learned. Find out how your boat handles under just the mainsail – how difficult is it to get her to bear away? Coming up head to wind, how much way does she carry, in different wind strengths? How well does she sail to windward under genoa alone? Try heaving-to, with the genoa backed, mainsheet well eased, and the helm down. At what angle to the wind will she lie a-hull, with no sail set?

When it comes to executing some special manoeuvre under sail, plan ahead for every eventuality. Navigational details and tidal problems should be sorted out well in advance. Explain to the crew exactly what has to be done, and have all gear likely to be needed ready at hand. If it is purely for training, by all means have the engine ticking over in neutral in case it should be needed.

Never be in a hurry, proceed as slowly as possible (while still retaining full control) so that there is time to make any manoeuvre within the limited space that may be available. It takes as much skill to sail a boat as slowly as possible as it does to achieve maximum speed on a spinnaker reach, maybe more, but there are plenty of opportunities to experiment with this in open water and to allow each member of the crew to share the experience. Find out how the boat handles under different combinations of sail, and in different wind strengths. Obviously more sail is needed in light airs, whilst at the other end of the scale it is necessary to know how the boat behaves under bare poles.

Apart from making the best use of tidal streams for coastal passages, they can be a great help when manoeuvring in confined waters. For example, with wind against tide, careful sail trimming should allow progress over the ground to be reduced to a fraction of a knot, greatly facilitating manoeuvres such as coming alongside or picking up a mooring. In other circumstances, when approaching a berth roughly against wind and tide, the latter may be used to ease the boat almost sideways into a small space. In these situations it is important to be able to lower whatever sail is set at a moment's notice, and also to note any local eddies in the tidal stream that can be used to advantage.

The successful boat handler must always be aware of the relative wind, the tidal stream and how each is (and will be) affecting the boat. Learn to assess the boat's movement by aligning static objects, such as piers, buildings, beacons etc. These can form transits to tell you whether the boat is moving sideways or tracking dead astern/ahead – and how quickly; or how fast the bow is swinging in a turn, and so on.

There are different factors to assess: the boat's progress throught the water under sail and/or engine; the effect of the wind also moving her through the water, and the influence of tidal stream or river current. The effect of sails or engine can be controlled by the skipper, the others cannot and they need to be continuously assessed because they are continually changing. The wind may funnel round the corner of a building, or disappear completely under its shadow. Tidal stream or river current vary in strength and direction from place to place, and from time to time. One moment the wind may be the dominant factor, the next the tide may take control.

While absorbed in this two-dimensional problem do not forget that there is a third dimension to consider – the depth of the water. Particularly in a strange harbour always have the echo sounder operating and, if available, set the alarm to warn of shoaling water. The nearest land to you is often that below your keel.

3.1.2 HANDLING UNDER POWER

The points in 3.1.1 also apply to handling under power when additional important factors should be understood. The factors at (a) and (b) lie at the root of all successful boat-handling under power. Their effects may eventually become second nature, but initially they will need careful thought, preferably whilst planning a manoeuvre. Ignore them at your peril.

a. **Propwalk**. As well as driving the boat ahead or astern, a rotating propeller generates sideways thrust, often referred to as paddlewheel effect or propwalk. Most single-engined boats have right-handed (RH) propellers, ie with ahead gear selected, they rotate clockwise as viewed from astern. When starting from rest, a RH propeller kicks the stern to starboard which makes it easier for the boat to turn to port (and harder to turn starboard). Conversely, when going astern, or going from ahead to astern, a RH prop kicks the stern to port, often very significantly. Hence a RH propeller boat will turn more tightly to port in both ahead and astern gears; a LH propeller does the opposite. These effects must always be at the forefront of your mind when manoeuvring, eg leaving/entering a finger berth, if the boat is to do what you want her to do. Remind yourself with a sketch as in Fig. 3(1).

Propwalk can be and usually is beneficial, if its action is known and anticipated. It can, for example, help greatly when turning round in a tight space, as in Fig. 3(2): (1) Go slowly ahead, with full starboard helm. (2) Neutral. (3) Full astern: propeller effect swings stern to port. (4) As boat gathers sternway, reverse helm; neutral. (5) Full ahead, starboard helm. (6) Throttle back, helm amidships.

If this 3-point turn were not needed, be sure to turn in your tightest direction, ie to

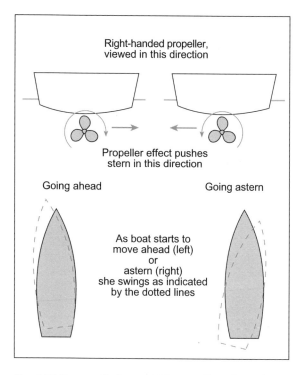

Fig. 3(1) Propwalk from a RH propeller, viewed from aft, pushes the stern of the boat sideways as arrowed. A LH propeller has the opposite effect. The lower sketches are an exaggerated reminder of the effects.

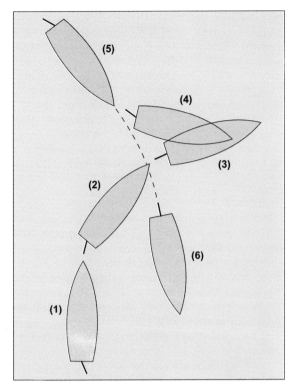

Fig. 3(2) Turning a boat with a single, RH propeller in a restricted space, nil wind.

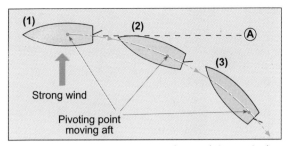

Fig. 3(3) The tendency to weathercock into wind.

port with a RH propeller, as if on a sixpence with some boats. When berthing port side-to with a RH propeller, the final burst astern to stop the boat will also tuck her in neatly parallel to the pontoon.

b. **Seeking the wind**. When motoring astern the boat will always want to 'weather cock' her stern into wind as the bow blows off downwind; this is aptly known as the stern 'seeking the wind', see Fig. 3(3): At (1) the boat is going astern, making for A. Due to the pivoting point moving aft, and the windage of the boat forward of that point, the stern tends to turn into wind (despite opposite rudder being applied), and the boat tracks through positions (2) and (3). It may be difficult to prevent this in a single-screw boat, depending on whether your propeller is left or right handed.

With a single-screw boat you must use this characteristic to your best advantage. Trying to fight it will often result in the boat being apparently unable to turn and lying almost broadside to the wind – a common sight in marinas. The helmsman has failed to appreciate the forces acting on his boat and on each other.

c. **Steering astern**. Coupled to this problem, many a helmsman is unhappy with steering

his boat astern. Admittedly some older boats have awkward propeller/rudder effects, but assuming your boat is 'normal': face aft, grasp the tiller firmly in both hands (so that it cannot take charge), go astern smartly, throttling well back as you gain steerage way. Only gentle helm movements are needed to maintain a straight course, provided you anticipate and correct any incipient yaw before it has become exaggerated. Point the rudder in the direction you wish the boat to go; the bow will follow along nicely like a dog on a lead. Find some open water and practice going astern through a figure-of-eight pattern; as you gain confidence do the same in more confined waters. It is time well spent.

Finally two basic points:

d. **Water flow**. A conventional rudder cannot steer unless water is flowing past it in one or other direction. Hence a burst of power is sometimes needed to gain steerage way as smartly as possible. Similarly, with an outboard or outdrive, there is no steering effect unless the propeller is driving ahead or astern.

e. **Pivoting point**. When a boat is turning under helm she swings around her pivoting point, whose position will vary. When stationary the pivoting point is amidships, but when going ahead it moves forward so that the stern swings out to describe a bigger circle than the bow; see Fig. 3(4): (1) Helm over. (2) Boat sliding sideways, hydrodynamic forces start to initiate the turn proper. (3) Established in the turn. Curves 'a' and 'b' show the lines taken respectively by the pivoting point (which has moved forward in the boat) and the stern (which has swung out). The turning circle of a single-screw boat is different to port and to starboard, depending on the direction of rotation of the propeller.

Conversely, when going astern the pivoting point moves well aft, so that as the boat turns under helm the bow describes a larger circle; make sure it does not strike another boat.

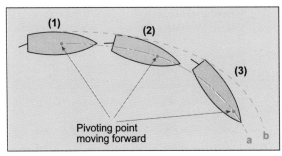

Fig. 3(4) Going ahead to starboard.

Before manoeuvring any boat at close quarters, it is wise to test her responses to helm and to throttle in open water. See how the wind affects her, how she steers at different speeds, how long she takes to stop from a given speed and how she handles astern. Keep as slow as will provide good steerage. Most boats will steer whilst the propeller is creating some slipstream over the rudder, so, when berthing throttle back well beforehand so that the engine can stay ticking over in ahead as long as possible, thus retaining steerage way.

Boats with outboard or outdrive propulsion have no rudders as such, but are steered by pointing the propeller in the required direction. This gives very positive handling whilst the propeller is rotating either ahead or astern – but none if in neutral. At close quarters therefore short bursts of low or moderate power are needed, making sure each time that the helm is first applied in the required direction before engaging ahead or astern; a helm indicator can be useful. Steering astern is very positive and the pivoting point of the boat is brought well aft which means that the bow can swing out widely.

Shallow water greatly modifies the normal flow pattern round the hull of a boat. Larger waves build up at bow and stern, increasing resistance. If excessive speed is maintained the boat becomes directionally unstable. It is also more difficult to turn a boat in shallow water.

In channels that are both shallow and narrow, such as a canal, steering can be made difficult by what is known as canal effect. Due to the restricted flow of water past the hull, waves build up ahead and astern of the boat. In between these two areas of higher pressure is a trough of low pressure amidships. A stream of water flows down each side of the boat, and in at each quarter: if this stream is disturbed, due to the boat getting close to the bank, the boat may take a sudden, violent sheer. The moral is to keep speed low.

A similar phenomenon (venturi effect) is the difficulty of avoiding collision between two craft which are proceeding too close to each other on parallel courses. While this more frequently occurs between power vessels it can also happen with sailing yachts, at crowded starts, for example, or when one boat luffs another during a race. It is caused by the speeding up of the water flow in the restricted gap between the two hulls, which results in a drop in pressure and consequently the two craft are drawn together. The effect increases with higher speeds so, before going alongside another craft under way, both should slow down.

3.1.3 TWIN-SCREW BOATS

With practice a twin-screw boat is easier to handle because with one shaft going ahead and the other astern she can be turned at rest in her own length. For best manoeuvrability a twin-screw boat should have outward rotating propellers, ie RH on the starboard side, and LH on the port side. Thus their propeller effect cancels out when both are running ahead or astern, and when turning at rest the joint effect of both propellers assists the swing.

Fast motor boats have very small rudders, in order to reduce drag at high speeds. But at low speeds such rudders are ineffective for manoeuvring, and it is best to put the helm amidships and steer by the engines.

3.1.4 FOULING A PROPELLER

A real danger, particularly to motor boats, is the possibility of fouling a propeller on moorings, or on lobster pots or other fishing marks. Even in daylight fishing marks are sometimes very difficult to see, particularly if the floats are almost submerged in a strong tidal stream.

If a rope cutter is fitted and does its job, you may only be aware of a temporary change in engine note. If it fails, several turns of rope may be bound tightly around the shaft before it is brought to rest and it may be necessary to cut them strand by strand. But if it is possible to get hold of the end of the rope, and if the shaft can be rotated by hand in the astern direction, the worst of the tangle may be unwrapped. Make certain, however, that the engine cannot possibly start while attempting this.

A face mask is better than nothing for underwater work, but some motor yachtsmen very sensibly carry sub-aqua gear for this purpose, and for other underwater work and examinations.

3.1.5 RUNNING AGROUND

Depending on the boat, the sea state and the type of bottom, running aground can be a serious matter or a trivial occurence. The deep keel of a sailing boat is the first thing to make contact, whereas with a motor boat the stern gear and rudder may be very vulnerable to damage. Therefore in a motor boat the first action should be to put the engine into neutral and assess the situation. On a rising tide, perhaps uncertain of the boat's true position, it is wise to anchor while the boat floats off and her position is checked. On a falling tide urgent action is needed, especially on a lee shore.

It is seldom wrong to turn the boat through 180°, if possible, and steer a reciprocal course until deeper water is regained. The draught of a keel boat can be reduced by heeling her over, by any available means, and the spinnaker pole can be used to swing her round or punt her. A shoal draught boat can be manhandled into deeper water, but it is important to be able to get people in the water back on board again and the engine must not be used if anybody is near the stern of the boat. A more seamanlike, but slower, operation is to lay out a kedge from the dinghy, using the longest warp that is available. Alternatively, it may be possible to tow the boat off, either with her own tender or with the help of some other craft with less draught, when the dinghy may be useful to pass a line across.

If a yacht is truly stranded on a falling tide, all that can be done is to safeguard her as far as possible. If she is on the edge of a bank it is most important to ensure that she heels over in an 'uphill' direction, not towards deep water. This can be done by transferring weights to the 'uphill' side, and by taking a masthead line ashore to pull her over in that direction.

If the hull is going to settle on rocks or stones, it must be padded with whatever is to hand – bunk cushions, sail bags etc.

3.1.6 PICKING UP A MOORING BUOY

Picking up a buoy is a good way to start boat handling, since it teaches the skipper to take charge of the boat, and if the buoy is small and in reasonably open water there is no risk of any damage – apart from the risk of getting the buoy rope round the propeller.

Under sail the aim must be to bring the boat to rest with the buoy nicely positioned close under one bow or the other. First check the directions and strengths of wind and tide, and in particular their relative effects on other moored boats nearby; how they are lying will determine the proper approach. If there is little or no tide it is usually best to lower the headsail early, and steer for a point to leeward of the buoy on a close reach; then luff up into wind when to leeward of the buoy, so that the boat stops at the buoy. This is a matter of judgement, depending on the

characteristics and displacement of the boat as well as the prevailing conditions. Do not lower the mainsail until the buoy is inboard, and if it becomes obvious that the manoeuvre has been misjudged do not hesitate to abandon that approach – bear away while still retaining steerage way, and go round again for another attempt.

The same tactics are employed if the tide is running strongly with the wind, except that of course the boat will not travel so far over the ground once she is brought head to wind.

When there is significant strength of tide, and it is against the wind, a different approach is needed – downwind, against the tide. Then it is best to come to the buoy under headsail only, trimmed so that the boat is just stemming the tide. Just before the boat reaches the buoy, let fly the headsail to spill the wind completely, and be ready to roll it as soon as the buoy rope has been secured.

When the wind is across the tide, which is often the case, the above tactics must be modified according to the conditions. It may be possible to approach under headsail, stemming the tide as for the downwind approach just described above. Or it may be best to come to rest head to wind just uptide of the buoy, and then drift down to it.

Care is needed when coming to a large mooring buoy, which could damage the boat if contacted. One of the patent boathooks which snaps a picking-up rope through the eye of a buoy can be most useful, particularly if short-handed.

Some of the considerations above apply equally when coming to a buoy under power. In a single-screw boat remember that if it is necessary to go astern at the last moment to check the boat's way, propeller effect (see 3.1.2) will throw the bow to starboard with a right-handed screw. In this case keep the buoy fine on the starboard bow during the final approach. On all occasions it is helpful if the person on the foredeck continually points in the direction of the buoy, because the helmsman inevitably loses sight of it at the critical moment. Other signs, such as 'come ahead' or 'go astern' can be mutually agreed.

When slipping a buoy under power it is best to drop astern initially, until the buoy is well clear ahead, so that there is no danger of fouling the mooring with the propeller. Tactics under sail depend on the relative directions of wind and tide. If the wind is against tide, and the boat is riding to the tide, it is preferable to slip from the buoy under headsail rounding up in open water to hoist the mainsail. If the boat is lying head to wind, hoist the mainsail and throw the boat off on the required tack by walking the buoy aft down whichever will be the windward side. The same effect is obtained by rigging a slip rope down whichever side of the boat is required (depending on which tack is decided on) to a position near the cockpit. Then let go the buoy rope and heave in on the slip rope to throw the bow off on the required tack.

In some harbours, to save space, boats moor fore-and-aft to buoys instead of swinging to a single buoy. The techniques for picking up and leaving head and stern buoys are similar to those employed for pile moorings, as in 3.4. The two buoys may be connected by a light line with a small buoy centred between them. This helps the picking up process, providing that the line does not foul the boat's propeller.

3.2 ANCHORING

3.2.1 ANCHORS AND CABLES

Anchoring is useful in so many ways and situations – perhaps for a yacht when the tide has turned foul, the wind has failed and so has the engine. But there are many other occasions when it is convenient to anchor: waiting for the tide before entering harbour, in fog when keeping clear of a shipping channel, or in a motor boat suffering engine failure. The anchor can also be used when manoeuvring in restricted space, or to regain deeper water when aground. And in a cruising boat anchoring is certainly the cheapest and often the most pleasant way to pass a night compared to the cost and sometimes dubious pleasure of a marina slot. But for anchoring to be enjoyable and safe, the right gear must first be aboard, as detailed in Chapter 18.

For a cruising yacht there is no substitute for chain cable: its weight helps to keep the pull on the anchor horizontal and the catenary which it forms absorbs the jerks on the cable as the yacht pitches; cable resists chafe, on the seabed and at the stemhead. The minimum amount of cable to be veered should be at least three times the depth of water at high water. But many amend this rule of thumb to 'four times', or add an extra 10 metres to the 'three times' whatever the depth. Much more chain will be needed in heavy weather and in really bad conditions an angel (anchor weight) can be lowered part way down the chain to maintain the catenary and reduce snubbing. In shallow water, less than about 5m, be aware that an anchor is more likely to drag because the chain will not be able to form a worthwhile catenary.

Boats up to about l0m (33ft) in length may be able to use a nylon warp in moderate conditions or when the boat will not be unattended for any length of time. Insert some 5m of chain between the warp and the anchor. This gives extra weight where it is most needed, and takes the chafe on the bottom. When warp is used, veer at least five times the depth at HW. Take great care to prevent chafe where the warp passes over the stemhead roller; a split polythene tube or canvas gaiter firmly seized to the warp should serve. The chain or anchor warp must be secured to a very strong point on the foredeck (anchor windlass, samson post, bitts, bollards or a stout cleat) which is itself well connected to the vessel's structure; on many modern boats the cleats are inadequate. A nylon warp secured inboard and to the chain with a chain hook outboard of the roller fairlead will reduce the shock loads of snubbing and also the noise of chain grinding in the bow roller; see 18.1. The inboard (bitter) end of the chain or warp should be secured in the chain locker by a line so that it can be cut on deck and slipped quickly if necessary, with a marker buoy attached. The cable or warp should be marked at intervals, so that it is easy to tell how much has been veered.

3.2.2 CHOOSING AN ANCHOR BERTH

Before reaching an anchorage study the chart carefully and decide where best to anchor, considering: depth (at high and low water), the holding ground, degree of shelter from the present and forecast wind direction, any obstructions in the area, and the position of any landing place. Always have an escape route should you have to clear out in a hurry, by day or night. Any boat which anchors must keep clear of craft already at anchor or on moorings nearby, so you must visualise how the boat will swing and where she will lie if the wind shifts or at the turn of the tide; equally how other nearby yachts will swing, and where their anchors are. A boat lying to chain will not range through such a large circle as one lying to a warp. Never anchor amid, or too close to, moorings because your anchor is very likely to become foul of the ground chains and you may swing too close to moored boats. You should also anchor clear of channels or fairways.

Work out the times and heights of HW and LW at the place that day – so that the present height of tide can be calculated. Then calculate the least depth in which the yacht can be safely anchored, whilst still remaining afloat at LW. The depth at HW will decide the amount of cable to be veered.

Before finally deciding on where to anchor, motor (or sail) around the immediate vicinity to check the actual depths from the echo sounder or lead line. Knowing the height of tide at the time, these soundings can be compared against the chart and serve as a useful check against anchoring where there will be insufficient depth at low water or where it is unnecessarily deep.

See which way any boats already at anchor are lying, because this will indicate the direction of your final approach to the chosen position for dropping the hook. Don't forget that after the anchor has been let go the yacht will drop back several lengths before she is riding to the cable – depending of course on the depth of water, how much cable is veered and how quickly the anchor gets a hold.

3.2.3   ANCHORING
Unless the sea is rough, it is wise to flake out on deck sufficient cable for three or four times the depth of water, ranged so that it will run out cleanly when the anchor is let go.

Normally you should come up head to wind (or head to tide, if this is stronger), let go the anchor as the boat comes to rest at the chosen spot, and then allow her to drop astern as the cable is veered. Initially don't let go much more cable than is needed to allow the anchor to reach the bottom, or the chain might pile up on top of the anchor and foul it. As the boat falls astern the cable (or warp) can be snubbed to help set the anchor; this effect can be increased by running the engine astern for a short burst.

In a sailing yacht it is easiest to come up head to wind, having already rolled any headsail and lowering the mainsail once the anchor has set. But there may be times, in a very strong tide for example, when it is necessary to anchor downwind. In such cases lower the mainsail first, to windward of the chosen position, and blow down to it under headsail alone. The speed of approach can be adjusted with the sheet, or by partly rolling the sail if necessary. The sail should be fully furled when the anchor is let go as the chosen position is reached.

If no engine is available, you must be able to set sail again quickly, should the anchor drag, or if there is any risk of fouling another vessel.

When the boat has 'got her cable', ie is riding to her anchor, take bearings of three conspicuous, charted objects and write them in the log, so that later you can tell if the anchor has dragged; or line up any prominent objects ashore. Also log the depth of water and the amount of cable veered.

If the bottom is foul it may be wise to buoy the anchor by securing a tripping line (longer than the depth at HW) to the crown of the anchor and the other end to a small buoy. If the anchor does become foul, hauling on the tripping line may help to clear it. Do not use floating line, and put a weight two metres below the buoy to keep the line clear of propellers etc.

It is sometimes useful to drop an anchor when coming alongside in a tideway under bad conditions – both to control the approach to the berth (in the case of a strong onshore wind, for example) and to help haul the boat off when leaving.

The anchor can also be used when turning the boat in a narrow channel with the tide under her, by dropping the anchor under the forefoot and allowing the boat to swing round on it.

3.2.4   MOORING WITH TWO ANCHORS
A boat lying to a single anchor swings through quite a big circle as wind or tide changes, and in restricted waters it may be helpful to moor with two anchors. In the event of bad weather, two anchors, if properly laid, also give greater security.

In a tideway the two anchors would normally be laid in line with the tidal stream, so that the boat lies to one on the flood and the other on the ebb, the heavier anchor being arranged to take the heavier load. This is best done by dropping the first anchor as normal, the upstream one on the ebb, or the downstream one on the flood. The boat is then allowed to drop back by veering twice as much cable as normal, when the second anchor is let go. Finally the boat is middled between the two as in Fig. 3(5). Or the kedge anchor can be laid by taking it away in the dinghy.

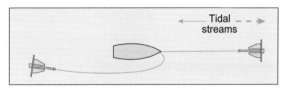

Fig. 3(5) Lying to two anchors in a tideway.

When lying to two anchors in a tideway, to avoid the likelihood of the chain and warp getting foul at the stemhead and damage to paintwork on the topsides, shackle the warp securely to the chain at deck level, and then veer them both to well below the waterline. The warp should be parcelled (wrapped) where it is in contact with the chain, to prevent chafe.

If bad weather exists or is forecast, it is always best to lie to two anchors if possible, both set ahead of the boat, one on either bow, with their cables or warps making an angle of not more that 40°, as in Fig. 3(6).

If the anchors are properly set, and their cables or warps adjusted correctly, they will share much of the load although there will be times when all the weight is on one. However two anchors do reduce the amount that the boat sheers about. If the boat has an engine, mooring with open hawse, as this is called, can be conveniently done when first anchoring. First let go one anchor in the normal way, preferably buoyed so that its position is known and so that the cable can be slipped if later it should prove difficult to recover both

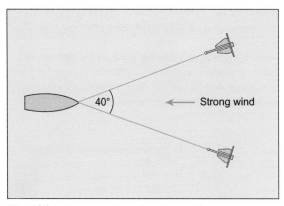

Fig. 3(6) Lying to two anchors, open hawse.

anchors. Once that anchor is set, veer a little more cable and motor forward at the required angle to drop the second anchor. Having set this, middle the vessel between the two, as in Fig. 3(6). Or in favourable weather the second anchor can be laid out later from the dinghy. When doing this it is important to decide on which bow to set the second anchor, and this, in the event of impending bad weather, will depend upon whether the wind is forecast to back or veer. See 3.2.5.

3.2.5 LAYING OUT A KEDGE, OR A SECOND ANCHOR

There are four distinct methods, involving different preparations, and as in many aspects of seamanship good preparation is the key to success.

1. The anchor together with the entire length of warp (plus chain where desirable) can be taken away in the dinghy. Make sure that what will be the inboard end of the warp is well secured to the stern of the dinghy, and then coil down the warp with the anchor on top. When at the chosen spot, lower the anchor to the bottom and row back to the yacht with the end of the warp. Take care transferring it inboard to the yacht. This method enables you fairly easily to select where to drop the anchor but be careful that this is not too far from the boat so that there is insufficient line for the return trip.
2. To avoid this, secure the end of the warp to the yacht, and then row away paying out the warp as you go. This means putting the anchor in the dinghy first, and then coiling down the warp on top of it.
3. Alternatively, put only the anchor in the dinghy and have somebody on deck to pay out the warp as the dinghy is rowed away. A prearranged signal tells the dinghy person when the end of the warp is reached.
4. But the simplest method is to lay the second

anchor from the yacht, using the engine. First flake the cable or warp to be used on deck, with a length equal to the scope to which the boat is lying. Go slow ahead, steering in the required direction, keeping the rode that is in the water fairly tight and clear of the boat's propeller. If necessary veer a little more cable so that the boat arrives at a position slightly ahead of the anchor already on the bottom. Let the second anchor go and allow the boat to lie back between the two.

3.2.6 WEIGHING ANCHOR
Before weighing anchor make all necessary preparations for getting under way and leaving harbour. If leaving under sail it is important to decide which tack to be on, once the anchor is aweigh. Normally only the mainsail should be set, to keep the foredeck clear. But with wind against tide it may be necessary to get under way with jib alone and set the mainsail later. Before setting sail much of the cable can be hauled in until the anchor is at short stay; it helps to go slow ahead on the engine while heaving in.

If lying head to wind and tide, and with no engine available, hoist the mainsail only and recover the anchor with a succession of short tacks to windward. On each occasion there will come a time when the cable leads astern, and the bight lying on the bottom can be brought in quite easily. Before it grows tight again, secure the cable and form another bight before tacking and repeating the process.

When unmooring with two anchors, first weigh the one which has less weight on it. This may be done from the dinghy, in which case it is useful to have rigged a tripping line.

If a tripping line has been used for the main anchor, recover the anchor buoy and bring it inboard. Once the cable is up and down (when the boat is directly over the anchor) it should be possible to break the anchor out, using the tripping line if necessary, and heave it in as quickly as possible. If the boat is reluctant to pay off on the required tack, back the headsail, and remember to reverse the helm if the boat gathers sternway. If necessary be prepared to re-anchor. Be ready to clean the anchor of mud etc as soon as it is brought inboard, and preferably beforehand.

3.2.7 FOUL ANCHOR
By misfortune the anchor may get foul on the bottom, usually on an old cable or a mooring chain. Or another boat may have dropped her anchor across your cable. This is where a tripping line may help. Otherwise try pulling on the cable from different directions, using the engine, to free it from the obstruction.

If the anchor is foul of a chain or cable it may be possible to bring it near enough to the surface to pass a warp under the obstruction, and the anchor then drops clear. Otherwise try lowering a loop of chain on a warp down the cable, in the hope that it can be manoeuvred near the crown of the anchor, and then pulled from the opposite direction to free it.

3.3 BERTHING ALONGSIDE

3.3.1 COMING ALONGSIDE

When arriving in a strange harbour first check the depth of water alongside any quay or jetty, the range of the tide, and the state of the tide at the time. Also check from the chart or pilot whether there are likely to be any underwater obstructions.

When coming alongside, always approach as slowly as possible consistent with maintaining steerage way, and head into wind or tide whichever is the stronger. Have fenders in position and warps rigged ready for taking ashore.

Under power in a boat with a right-handed screw, it is easier to berth port side to, because when going astern to check the boat's way the stern swings to port and helps to bring the boat parallel with the quay. If berthing on a quay where there are mooring bollards, it may be useful to put bowlines in the ends of the mooring warps in advance, especially if short handed.

If there are already one or more warps looped over a bollard, the eye of a fresh warp should be passed up through the eyes(s) of existing warp(s) before slipping it over the bollard. In this way any one warp can be let go without interfering with the others, as in Fig. 3(7).

Four ropes are normally needed to secure a boat alongside a jetty, quay or pontoon: a head rope led well forward and a stern rope led well aft; a fore spring led aft from the bow, and an after or back spring led forward from the stern; see Fig. 3(8).

In non-tidal waters, or when lying alongside another vessel, breast ropes can be added at right angles to the jetty. When lying on another vessel, whether alongside or at piles or buoys, always take your own lines forward and aft, and secure them to shore/piles/buoys as appropriate, and adjust them so that they are taking their share of the weight.

If you expect to dry out alongside, you should know the kind of bottom, and also what the wall is like to rest against. If there are piles along the face of the wall, a fender board should be placed across two or more fenders next to the hull so as to bear against convenient piles. A masthead line must be secured ashore to hold the boat against the wall.

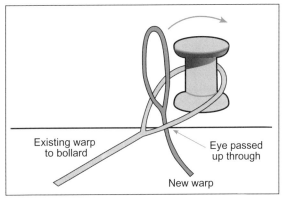

Fig. 3(7) Passing the eye of a warp up through the eye of a warp already on the bollard.

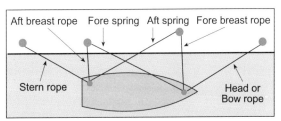

Fig. 3(8) Boat berthed alongside, with head and stern ropes, springs and breast ropes fore and aft. The latter should be dispensed with if there is any rise or fall of tide since they will need continual adjustment, but they are useful when mooring alongside another vessel.

When lying alongside a jetty or wall on a lee shore, a heavy anchor can be used to hold the boat away from the shore and prevent her bumping alongside. The anchor can either be let go from the yacht on arriving and before securing alongside, which is the simpler and preferred method, or subsequently taken away in the dinghy as described in 3.2.5. Such an anchor is also a great help when leaving the berth in these circumstances.

3.3.2 THE USE OF WARPS AND SPRINGS

Apart from securing a yacht alongside, warps can also be used to manoeuvre a boat, for example by the proper use of a spring when entering or leaving a difficult berth.

The effect of a warp secured to a boat depends upon its point of attachment and the direction of pull.

For a simple example, as in Fig. 3(9), if it is desired to haul a boat ahead along a quay, or a canal bank, a warp secured at the chainplates (at the deck edge, abreast the mast) will pull the boat ahead, clear of the wall, with little or no rudder needed. Should the warp be secured right forward, it continually pulls the bow towards the wall.

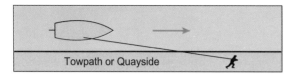

Fig. 3(9) Hauling a boat with warp attached to the chainplates.

By motoring ahead against a fore spring, with a suitably placed fender, the stern of the boat will swing out when the other lines are let go. Similarly, going astern against an aft spring will swing the bow out see Fig. 3(10) and Fig. 3(11).

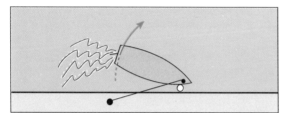

Fig. 3(10) Swinging the stern out by going ahead against a fore spring.

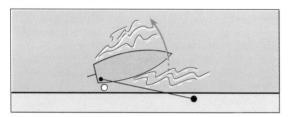

Fig. 3(11) Swinging the bow out by going astern against an aft spring.

A boat can be held temporarily alongside with just a spring, as illustrated in Fig. 3(12).

This can be very convenient because if the spring is led aft beforehand a single-handed person can do everything with little need to leave the cockpit, and without having to go on to the foredeck and leave the helm unattended. Similarly on departing, all that it needed is to let go the spring and recover the fender.

A spring can be most useful when a boat has to turn a significant corner, perhaps when leaving a difficult berth.

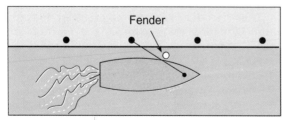

Fig. 3(12) Using a spring, whilst temporarily alongside. The engine is running slow ahead and the helm is adjusted to keep the boat parallel to the jetty.

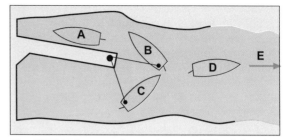

Fig. 3(13) Using a spring to leave a difficult berth.

For example in Fig. 3(13) the boat at A has to proceed in the direction E, involving a turn through 180° in a confined space. A spring is rove from her port quarter round a bollard at the end of the jetty, and brought back inboard. The boat then proceeds slow astern out of the berth. At B the spring is snubbed, and the boat starts to swing as shown, still going slow astern, until she reaches C; here the spring can be recovered, and the boat can go ahead with starboard helm as in D. During the manoeuvre the boat remains under complete control.

3.3.3   DRYING OUT ALONGSIDE

Apart from the occasional need to dry out alongside for a scrub, there are many attractive harbours which can only be visited by yachts able to take the ground.

The operation depends on several factors: the details of the wall or jetty, the nature of the bottom alongside it, the hull form of the boat, and the range of tide. If the boat is to take the ground soon after high water, make sure the next tide is big enough to re-float her.

Not all harbour walls are smooth or vertical; there may be protrusions below the water. The bottom may be uneven, perhaps rocky, or it may slope downwards from the foot of the wall at a dangerous angle; so seek advice. As a general rule never dry out alongside in a strange harbour until you have surveyed the site, unless in an emergency situation.

Some boats take the ground better than others. Catamarans or boats with twin bilge keels present no problem, unless the ground slopes significantly away from the quay. Cruising yachts with long, straight keels should dry out comfortably, but ensure that they lean towards the wall. Boats with shorter keels, and particularly the extreme fin and skeg type of hull, can give difficulty.

Much depends on which part of the keel touches first, and starts to take the weight. This in turn depends upon the shape of the keel and the slope of the bottom (not outwards from the wall, but along the length of the boat). If one end of the keel takes the ground first, the boat can pivot

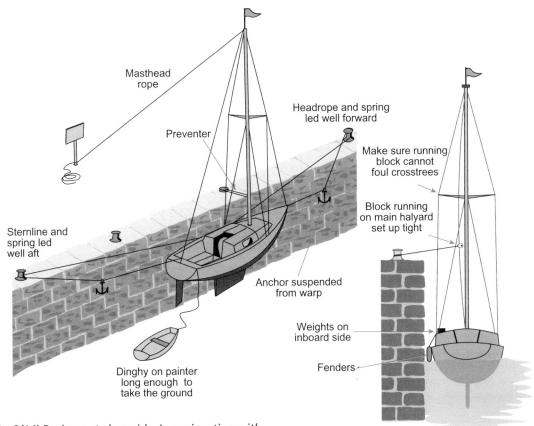

Fig. 3(14) Drying out alongside. In conjunction with Fig. 3(15), this diagram shows the basic precautions to be taken.

Fig. 3(15) As an alternative to a masthead rope, a running block can be attached to a halyard, set up tight against the mast.

laterally about this point as the water falls, so that either the bow or the stern may tend to swing towards the wall. The boat must therefore be firmly secured, with warps taken well out ahead and astern if there is any appreciable rise and fall: and she needs to be very well fendered at points about one-third and two-thirds along her length, where she will rest against the wall. To avoid continual adjustment of the headrope and sternline, heavy weights can be attached to the bight of each.

Weights, such as chain cable, should be transferred to the inboard side of the yacht so that she has a slight list towards the wall. If the boat is going to be alongside for just one tide a masthead rope can be rigged to some fixture ashore; a preventer round the mast to a convenient bollard on the quay as in Fig. 3(14) could act as a back-up. The masthead rope however needs constant adjustment, and for a longer stay it is more convenient to rig a mastline to a block running on a halyard close to the mast, as in Fig. 3(15).

Some of the above points apply to motor boats, but their main consideration is often the protection of sterngear and rudders. Many fast

motor cruisers are not suited to taking the ground without risk of damage to these items.

3.3.4 RAFTING

Rafting up of perhaps six or more boats alongside each other is quite common these days. Harbours often limit the number of boats that can raft up, but in any case always ask permission before berthing on another boat. The inner boats of a raft have to endure a lot of people and dirt across their decks and they should be shown every consideration.

As far as possible larger yachts should be inboard, and the smaller ones outboard. Masts of sailing boats should be staggered to prevent rigging and spreaders fouling. Plenty of springs and fenders are needed, and each boat should be secured to shore by her own head and stern lines.

When an inside boat wishes to leave, see Fig. 3(16), the procedure is relatively straightforward provided the crews of the outer boats assist. In order to control the outer boats the one leaving must depart in the direction of wind or tide, whichever is stronger. Then the semi-detached

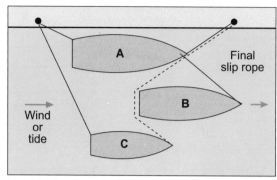

Fig. 3(16) B should depart with wind or tide, whichever is stronger; this helps to re-form the raft. Here B is about to let go her bow line, rigged as a slip rope, while the bow line of C has been passed under B's stern, ready to be hauled in once B has moved clear.

part of the raft is more easily reformed alongside; in some circumstances it helps if an outer yacht uses her engine for this purpose.

The departing boat lets go her shore lines, and then in succession the springs and other lines connecting her to the boats each side. Meanwhile the bow line(s) of the outer boat(s) has been brought round her stern, ready to be hauled in once the leaving boat is clear of the gap thus created.

If the outer boats are not manned, then one or two crewmen from the departing yacht must stay in the raft to re-secure them, being picked up from the outboard boat on completion.

3.3.5   LEAVING AN ALONGSIDE BERTH

First consider carefully the effects of wind and tide on the various options open to you; then decide in which order the various warps should be let go.

If the boat is heading into the stream, or a strong wind in still water, let go the lines in turn until the boat is held just on the after spring, which should have been arranged previously as a slip rope (taken round a convenient object ashore, and the end brought back inboard). Push the bow out, or go slow astern to spring the bow out; the tide or wind will then complete the process. Recover the spring and proceed ahead out of the berth. Watch your quarter against the quay or other craft and make sure the stern rope is kept clear of the screw; see Fig. 3(11). Once clear, unrig the fenders and make up all the warps.

When wind or tide is from astern, or if there is a wind blowing the boat on to the jetty, it is best to go astern out of the berth. The fore spring is rigged as a slip rope and is the last to be let go. One of the crew is stationed with a fender near the bow, and, having first checked that no other craft is approaching, the engine is put slow ahead

to swing the stern out from the jetty. When the boat has reached the required angle, let go the spring and go astern; see Fig. 3(10).

3.3.6   MOORING STERN/BOW-TO

In Mediterranean harbours boats often moor stern-to the quay or harbour wall, with an anchor out ahead; or bows-in to the wall, anchor astern. In a twin-screw motor boat this should present no problem, but it can be a different matter in a single-screw vessel that does not handle well astern, or in a strong cross wind. Before entering harbour have everything ready: warps aft, fenders each side and one over the stern, and the anchor cleared away on the foredeck; the boathook may also be useful.

Unless directed to a specific berth, spend a little time deciding where best to go. The obvious vacant berth may have underwater obstructions, the town sewer or other delights. It is usually best to lie among other yachts, who are more likely to take your lines than fishing boats or commercial craft.

The anchor must be let go opposite the chosen berth and about three boats' lengths from the quay, but not so far that you cannot reach the quay. If, as is likely, there are already other boats moored up, note how their cables are lying so as to avoid your anchor fouling theirs. If you cannot avoid crossing another boat's cable or anchor line with yours, let go your anchor well beyond. In a strong cross-wind you should let go the anchor slightly upwind of the berth, so that some tension in the cable will stop the bow being blown off as you go astern into the berth. Even in good conditions a little tension in the cable helps to keep the boat straight as the boat goes astern.

Good communication (perhaps by hand signals) is needed between the helmsman and the anchorman so that the required amount of cable is veered; and in a larger boat it is also needed with the stern as the boat gets nearer the quay. If single-handed it is slightly less difficult to go in astern, since helm, throttle and stern line are all within reach; the anchor warp can also be veered under control from the cockpit.

It is helpful to be able to lie temporarily alongside another boat, one side or other of the berth, while your stern lines are taken ashore. But if there is nobody to take your lines you have to get close enough to the quay for one of the crew to jump ashore.

Stern lines need to be led out in each direction so as to locate the boat sideways in the berth, as well as to hold her the required distance from the quay. In the Mediterranean they should not need adjusting thanks to the insignificant range of tide.

On the principle that it is easier to manoeuvre

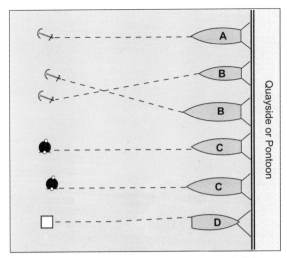

Fig. 3(17) Berthed stern-to: (a) is anchored; (b) have foul anchors; (c) are secured to buoys; and (d) is bows-to, secured to a permanent line/sinker.

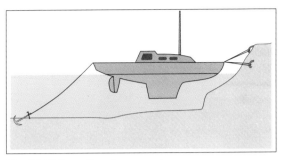

Fig. 3(18) Scandinavian mooring

out of a narrow space rather than into it, a different approach can be made in a boat that does not handle well astern or in bad conditions. Proceed ahead into the berth and pass a long line ashore. Then go astern to anchor in open water. The line to shore can then be passed aft so that the boat is hauled astern into the berth whilst the anchor cable is veered.

Leaving a stern-to berth is not difficult unless your anchor has fouled another boat's. This situation can sometimes be anticipated, and often remedied with the helpful co-operation of the other vessel (see 3.2.7). But it can be a tedious business and it is best to avoid the possibility in the first instance.

Other variations on the Mediterranean-moor include a berth where a stern line is permanently rigged from the marina pontoon out to a suitable sinker. Enter the berth bows-in and get bow lines ashore, whilst the stern line is picked up with a boathook; secure it to a quarter cleat and haul taut. Do not go astern into such a berth because of the risk of fouling the propeller.

3.3.7 SCANDINAVIAN MOORING

Norway and Sweden differ in two major respects from the UK, when it comes to mooring:

a. The tidal range is negligible; and
b. The steep-to rocky coast, sheltered by a myriad islets, lets you berth bows-in as if to a wharf, quay or pontoon. You are in effect securing to the scenery.

The bows-in technique is favoured by locals, taking bow warps to ring-bolts or cleats concreted into the rock, or around a convenient tree; a stern anchor or buoy holds the boat off the shoreline. A pair of posts (dolphins) serves the same purpose in

some harbours. Berthing stern-in is only feasible if you know your rudder will not strike the rocks or ledges. Handling techniques are similar to those described in 3.3.6.

Desirable equipment is a Scandinavian-style open pulpit with a clear gap through which one can step ashore with some elegance. In contrast the more usual pulpit presents fairly gymnastic problems, especially when climbing aboard over a high bow. The stern anchor should be as light as possible (for ease of handling); the Fortress range (18.1.1) combines light weight with good holding. An anchor plait warp, carefully flaked down into a bucket, will allow good control at the stern without impeding the bowman. Flat webbing warp stowed on a reel (Ankarolina) and attached to the pulpit is even better. Finally half a dozen mountaineering pitons and a lump hammer can be useful in wilder surroundings.

3.4 PILE MOORINGS

3.4.1 INTRODUCTION

Pile moorings are a means of fitting more boats into a harbour, often with two or more boats rafted between a pair of piles. In tidal waters the piles have sliding rings each side, to which warps can be secured. A line is secured to each ring so that it can be retrieved from below the water when necessary. Even when rafted against other boat(s) between piles, always take your own fore and aft lines to the piles.

On arrival first decide which way the boat should face; generally it is better to point into the stronger of tidal stream or river current (the ebb). In bad weather it may be preferable to face any strong wind that is forecast, while in other circumstances it may be easier to depart with the boat facing to seaward. However, all these considerations may be overridden by the sheer mechanics of getting into the berth in the first instance – particularly under sail with no auxiliary power. In all cases it is important to plan well ahead, to brief the crew on your intentions, and to have lines and fenders rigged. Possibly the dinghy may be needed to take out the stern line. The boathook should also be ready. It is often quicker and easier when initially securing to a ring on a pile to pass the line through the ring (or round the bar on which the ring travels) as a slip rope, bringing the end back inboard, and then make it fast properly later.

3.4.2 ARRIVAL UNDER POWER

If the berth is already occupied, it is easy enough to lie alongside and then take lines fore and aft to the piles, using the dinghy if necessary. But if the berth is empty the method will depend on the relative strengths and directions of wind and tide. Pile moorings are invariably laid in line with the stream, and if necessary the boat can always be turned through 180° later on.

With wind and tide together, approach into them, secure to the upstream pile, then ease the bow line to drift slowly back to allow the stern line to be secured.

An even neater manoeuvre, as in Fig. 3(19), is to take the stern line well forward along the deck, outboard of everything, and secure it to the downstream pile as the boat passes slowly by. Keep the stern line slack but clear of the propeller while continuing ahead to the upstream pile. Then middle the boat between the piles. This method is called a running moor.

With wind against tide, approach into whichever is the stronger. Under these conditions it is less easy to maintain directional control, and the running moor may be preferred. Alternatively, secure to the forward pile and take out the stern line by dinghy.

By the nature of things the wind is most likely to be blowing across the berth to make matters more difficult, and the method used will depend on its strength and direction relative to the tide. With twin screws there should be no difficulty, but in a low-powered sailing cruiser it may be useful to make a trial run to see how the boat behaves and how she drifts under wind and tide.

With the wind roughly at 90° to the line of

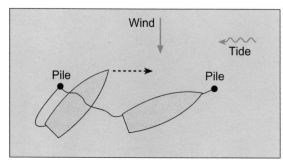

Fig. 3(20) With wind across the tide a variation of the running moor can still be used.

piles, approach close to leeward of the first (stern) pile and secure the stern line for a running moor. Then motor slowly ahead so that the combined action of wind and tide carries the boat slightly broadside to the further pile so as to secure the bow line, as in Fig. 3(20).

If however the boat is difficult to control, with the bow being blown off by the wind, it is safer to secure to the further pile and take out the stern line by dinghy, as in Fig. 3(21).

With a large crew have the dinghy already manned and in the water, perhaps with a line already made fast to the stern pile so that it can be passed quickly and easily.

3.4.3 ARRIVAL UNDER SAIL

As in the case of arrival under power, the line of approach will be decided by the relative strengths and directions of wind and tide. Except in a very strong wind it is usually best to head into the tide. The final approach must be very slow and well controlled, with the boat coming to rest in the required place.

With the wind forward of the beam, approach on a close reach under mainsail only, easing the mainsheet as necessary to reduce speed; then round up alongside the forward pile to secure the bow line. If the wind is blowing across the berth it will probably be necessary to take out the stern line by dinghy. See Fig. 3(22).

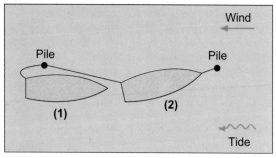

Fig. 3(19) With a running moor the stern line is secured to the aft pile as the boat passes, before securing the bow line. The boat is then middled between the piles.

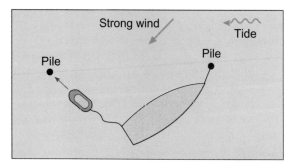

Fig. 3(21) With a strong wind across the berth it is likely that the stern line will need to be passed by dinghy.

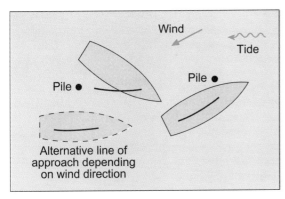

Fig. 3(22) With the wind ahead, approach under mainsail only, trimming it as necessary to control speed. Lower the mainsail as soon as the bow line is secured.

If the wind is aft of the beam, blow down into the berth under jib alone, adjusting speed by easing the jib sheet or by half rolling the sail if there is much wind. It should be possible to pass close to the downstream (aft) pile and execute a running moor as described in 3.4.2. See Fig. 3(23).

3.4.4 DEPARTURE UNDER POWER

If alongside another vessel between piles the procedure is similar to that used when leaving any alongside berth. Rig temporary slip lines to the other boat and let go the head and stern lines to the piles. If to leeward of the other vessel the wind will blow the boat off, but if to windward it may be more difficult to get away. In a strong tidal stream, depending on direction, it should be possible to go ahead or astern on a spring to swing out the stern or the bow.

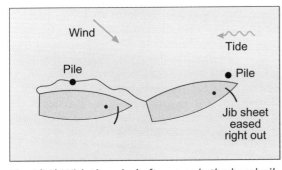

Fig. 3(23) With the wind aft, use only the headsail. Trim the sheet, and if necessary partly roll the sail, to control speed. Roll the sail as soon as the bow line is secured.

When she is the only one between piles, and lying head to wind and current, pull the boat ahead to rig the bow line as a slip rope, and then let her drop astern to release the stern line. If necessary the bow line can be led aft down one side of the boat or the other to give her a sheer in the required direction.

Lying stern to wind or tide, whichever is stronger, the above procedure is reversed. The stern line is rigged as a slip rope before the bow line is let go. Having given the boat a sheer by means of the helm, or by taking the stern line forward down the required side of the boat, proceed astern out of the berth. If the boat is underpowered, or does not handle well astern, turn her through 180° in the berth by warps – a procedure known as 'winding ship'.

With a beam wind, rig bow and stern lines as slip ropes, and allow the boat to be blown to leeward before letting go fore and aft and proceeding.

3.4.5 DEPARTURE UNDER SAIL

Since a sailing boat needs to leave the berth proceeding ahead (not astern), better control is given if this is done head to tide. If necessary, wind ship to achieve this. Rig head and/or stern line(s) as slip rope(s) on the same principle as in 3.4.4. If the wind is ahead, depart under mainsail but with the headsail ready for unrolling. If the wind is aft leave under headsail until it is convenient to round up and hoist the main.

When lying alongside another boat on piles the procedure is the same as for leaving any alongside berth; this is not too difficult when the wind is blowing the boat off, but more of a problem when it is in the opposite direction so that you may have to take a line to some object upwind to haul the boat off.

Unless the wind is aft, and in the same direction as the tidal stream, it is unwise to attempt to leave the middle of a raft under sail alone.

3.5 PRACTICALITIES AT SEA

3.5.1 PREPARATIONS FOR SEA

Before any trip to sea, particularly a lengthy passage, a thorough examination of the boat's material state must be made and a number of things checked. The details depend a good deal on the size and complexity of the boat, but the more common items which need attention are summarised below, for convenience under different headings.

On deck
- All deck gear, dinghy etc stowed and secured for sea
- All hatches and openings closed
- Anchor secured, but available for letting go
- Standing rigging checked. All bottlescrews and shackles moused
- Sails bent on, sheets led correctly, battens in
- Ensign and burgee hoisted
- Radar reflector in place

Engine
- Battery levels and state of charge
- Fuel tank (and spare cans) contents
- Engine and gearbox oil levels
- Fuel/oil for outboard
- Stern gland greased or water lubricated
- Cooling water: seacock open; water strainer clear; impeller condition; header tank contents
- Spares, tools, engine handbook on board
- Spare oil, grease and distilled water on board
- Inspect drive belts and hoses
- Bilges vented and dry
- No ropes over side, propeller clear
- Gearbox in neutral
- After starting check oil pressure, cooling water flow and charging rate
- Check gear operation in ahead/astern
- Read engine hour meter

Navigation
- Corrected charts and publications on board
- Tidal details extracted from almanac
- Functional checks of all electronic nav equipment
- Compare ship's head by steering compass and hand bearing compass
- Navigation and compass lights
- Paraffin for hurricane (anchor) light
- Foghorn functioning, spare cylinder
- Batteries for torches/lamps
- Log reading
- Barometer reading
- Clock checked and wound
- Obtain and record weather forecast
- Determine pilotage details, course to be steered on leaving harbour and passage plan complete

Safety equipment
- All crew should know where the following are stowed and how to use them:
- Gas detector, switch on and check
- Lifejackets, condition and gas cylinders in date
- Safety harnesses
- Flares in date and sufficient
- Fire extinguishers in date and charged
- Liferaft in date and secured
- Bilge pump, test operation
- Steering gear checked and tested
- Emergency steering arrangements
- First aid box in date and complete

Other items
- Gas cylinders for galley
- Provisions, water and fresh food embarked
- All moveable gear down below secured for sea.

3.5.2   NIGHT PASSAGES

Night passages greatly increase cruising range within a given period and may also allow full benefit to be derived from favourable winds or tide.

There is nothing difficult about sailing by night, and sometimes navigation is easier because lights can be readily identified by their characteristics. It is, for example, a good idea to make a landfall just before dawn, when lights are still available, and then make the final approach into a strange harbour in daylight.

Before it gets dark make a complete check of the boat. See that everything is secured on deck, and that any items which may be required during the night are to hand; check the navigation lights and compass light; pump the bilges; inspect the engine compartment; read the barometer; if bad weather threatens, consider the advisability of reefing or shortening sail before darkness falls. Prepare snacks or sandwiches which can be eaten as the watches change. Wear warm clothing and oilskins when on watch; even summer nights can be cold. Personal safety demands greater attention on deck in the dark. Safety harnesses should be worn and always clipped on when on deck and, when conditions warrant, in the cockpit.

Some skippers may leave clear instructions, preferably written, to the man on watch so that there is no doubt about navigation or other matters.

At night make every effort to preserve night vision: lights on compasses, navigational/engine instruments, should be dimmed to the minimum level. A red chart table light and subdued red lighting below deck allow you to see without being dazzled. In a sailing yacht the crew should be able to perform all normal sail drills in the dark, knowing the position of sheets and cleats by feel. Bright spreader lights may help on the foredeck but they leave the helmsman and navigator almost blind for the next few minutes. Do not point white torches at other people.

Show the correct navigation lights and be able to recognise the lights of other craft, as described in 4.1.

A good radar reflector, radar itself and navigation lights of the correct brilliance are the best safeguards against being run down. White flares to indicate your presence should be close at hand. Even a powerful torch is rarely adequate for this purpose, but an Aldis lamp or hand-held mini-searchlight with halogen bulb is very effective.

With nothing else to steer by (except perhaps a star) the compass is even more important by night than it is by day. Proper illumination, with a dimmer so that it can be adjusted to the minimum level depending on the conditions, is essential.

Preferably there should be stand-by compass lighting for emergency use.

3.5.3 FOG AND POOR VISIBILITY

Many of the remarks under 'Night passages' (3.5.2) apply equally to bad visibility, but essentially at sea in fog you should sound the required fog signal, slow down (or even stop if necessary), keep a careful eye on the radar, if fitted, and re-double the efforts of lookouts in detecting other shipping by eyes or ears.

The main danger is the risk of being run down by a larger ship, but this can often be avoided by keeping in relatively shallow water – just out of the main channel for example, rather than in it. A really efficient radar reflector is essential to safety. But there is still a risk of collision with small craft, or of grounding due to being unable to locate buoys or shore objects.

In fog radar on a small boat is a real bonus, both for collision avoidance and for navigation. But it will only be an advantage if the set is working efficiently and adjusted correctly, and if the operator has sufficient experience in interpreting what is on the screen.

It is usually possible to see that visibility is deteriorating, and the following action should be taken:

a. Slow down.
b. If possible plot a fix, noting time, log reading and speed. Review the course to steer in the changed circumstances.
c. Hoist radar reflector (if not permanently fitted).
d. Sound the prescribed fog signal. A sailing vessel sounds one long and two short blasts ('D') at intervals of not more than two minutes. A power-driven vessel making way through the water sounds one long blast (and if stopped two long blasts) at least every two minutes.
e. Switch on navigation lights.
f. If in relatively shallow water or where soundings may aid navigation, switch on the echo sounder and record depths at regular intervals.
g. Keep a very good look-out with, if possible, one person in the bow. If anything is seen or heard, he should point in the direction concerned.
h. Wear lifejackets, inflated if conditions and traffic warrant.
j. Check liferaft or dinghy is ready for launching.
k. In inshore waters prepare an anchor for letting go.
l. At night have flares or a powerful torch signalling lamp ready.
m. In a sailing yacht run the engine, or have it ready for instant starting.

In fog a small yacht without radar must keep an accurate plot of position, by GPS and DR, backed up by soundings and any other means. The helmsman must therefore maintain the course required, and any course changes must be properly recorded with times and log readings.

Tactics depend on the situation. If offshore the only danger is from other shipping. If a large ship is seen approaching at close quarters, only a radical alteration of course (preferably to starboard) plus the use of the engine may take the boat clear. In a fast motor boat the best initial action may be to turn sharply through 180° and increase speed, while deciding which way to avoid her without crossing her bows.

Always try to avoid shipping lanes. If possible get into shallow inshore water, where no large vessel can be, and anchor until the visibility improves.

If coasting it may be possible to progress slowly in comparative safety well inshore, by following a depth contour on the echo sounder, but this depends on the coastline and how the seabed shelves.

The best advice is to try to avoid fog. If the forecast even hints that visibility will be poor, stay in harbour, particularly if shipping lanes have to be crossed.

3.5.4 PREPARING FOR BAD WEATHER

With the number and frequency of forecasts available a yacht should always receive some prior warning of heavy weather. Even if her radio is out of action, or a vital forecast has been missed, the tell-tale signs of the sky and a falling barometer should give sufficient notice of bad weather in the offing (see Chapter 11).

The definition of bad weather varies from boat to boat and from crew to crew, but suffice it to say that it occurs when the conditions of wind and sea dictate the handling of the boat rather than the skipper's original passage plan. For a small sailing cruiser with a family crew this will probably be well before gale force 8 winds are experienced. Force 6, or the top end of force 5 in certain cases, is often quoted as the small craft's gale – with some justification. However most modern yachts, properly handled, are perfectly seaworthy; a crew's ability and physical endurance are often the limiting factors in rough weather.

Given enough warning of impending strong winds, certain actions should be taken before they arrive:

a. Decide on general strategy. If a suitable port or other shelter is within a manageable distance, then it is sensible to head for it –

always provided that it can be reached before conditions in the approaches are likely to become dangerous, and without hazarding the boat on a lee shore. If possible aim for a harbour to windward, ie within waters sheltered in the lee of the land. There are comparatively few harbours around the coasts of NW Europe which can safely be entered in bad weather and at any state of tide. Seas get shorter and steeper, and are more likely to break in shallow water. Wind against tide can greatly aggravate the sea state, and this may more be commonly experienced in the approaches to harbours and off headlands. So give careful consideration to the state of the tide at the likely time of arrival, and whether harbour marks or buoys will be visible.

Larger commercial ports, even if they lack normal yachting facilities, are usually safer to enter in bad weather. They are deeper and wider, with better marks and buoyage, and with lights which are more likely to be seen in poor visibility.

Motor cruisers with a limited fuel endurance should consider seeking shelter at an earlier stage than sailing boats, even though their higher speed permits them to get into harbour without undue delay.

b. If no suitable refuge is available within a safe distance the only option is to stay at sea. The primary consideration then becomes to ensure that the boat has or can gain plenty of sea room. Having once decided not to close the land, the main aim should be to keep as far offshore as possible, but also choosing a course which avoids tide races, shipping routes and shallow water.

If however the direction of the approaching storm is reasonably certain it may be possible to progress slowly towards a lee – provided by a stretch of coast for example – but only if an unexpected shift of wind is not going to put the boat on a lee shore.

c. Prepare the boat for the expected conditions. In a sailing boat it can never be too soon to reef, before conditions get too bad. Check that all gear on deck including the tails of halyards and the ends of sheets are well secured. Any rope which may be swept over the side could foul the propeller if the engine has to be started. All hatches, ventilators and other openings must be closed; if necessary blank off ventilators by stuffing in towels or tea cloths. Washboards should be fitted to the companionway leading below. Cockpit drains should be checked clear.

The bilge should be pumped dry and then examined at regular intervals. All moveable gear down below should be securely stowed. Shut all seacocks, and have buckets available in case pumps get clogged. Items such as storm canvas, foghorn, torches, flares, reefing gear, warps and sea anchor (if carried) must be readily accessible – not buried under other gear.

d. All the crew should be dressed in warm clothing, with lifejackets worn, even if uninflated. The skipper should insist that safety harnesses are put on at an early stage, and that they are always secured to a suitable strongpoint in the cockpit or on deck.

Since poor visibility may prevent visual fixing once the bad weather arrives, keep a close check on the boat's position and track made good by GPS. But maintain an accurate and independent plot of DR and EP. In strong winds expect that leeway will be more pronounced.

Get all available weather forecasts, so as to build up the best possible picture of the developing weather situation. The barometer should be read and recorded every half-hour. Record the estimated wind speed and direction, sea state, and type of cloud cover at similar intervals. In fact keeping abreast the weather situation is almost a full time job in bad weather, for which few small yachts have the human resources.

Meanwhile it is advisable to prepare sandwiches or similar food, and to put soup or coffee into a thermos flask for later consumption, when it may be impossible to use the cooker.

3.5.5   HANDLING IN BAD WEATHER
As wind and sea increase, and sail area is progressively reduced, further actions are likely to follow:

a. When it is imprudent or difficult to make any real progress in a particular direction, consider heaving-to. This can and should be practised under less demanding conditions. When cruising, and time is no object, it is often sensible to heave-to for an hour or so in order to eat in comfort.

Most yachts will heave-to satisfactorily under reefed main and storm jib but it all depends on balance, and boats with longer keels behave best in this respect, so it pays to experiment. The jib should be backed, that is the weather sheet should be hauled in, and the reefed main sheeted well in, with the helm lashed down to leeward. A boat may also be hove-to under trysail, or well reefed main, with no headsail – either being steered or with the helm lashed up – but this will depend upon the type of yacht and can best be determined by earlier trial and error.

b. In even more severe conditions it may be necessary to lie a-hull, ie with all sail lowered, allowing the boat to drift as she pleases. This is probably the best tactic for a multihull in really bad weather. It may help prevent the boat gathering way if the helm is lashed down, and this also reduces leeway. Seas will break on board (so the crew should stay below) and they may knock the boat onto her beam ends or even capsize her completely in extreme conditions. Then her survival will depend largely upon how well she was designed and built.

c. Most, but not all, authorities consider that a sea anchor is of doubtful benefit when streamed over the bow of a modern yacht, although it may be useful in a yawl or a ketch with the mizzen set to keep the boat head to wind – if indeed the sail remains intact when flogging in gale force winds. But very large strains are put upon the gear, and there is danger to the rudder when the yacht gathers sternway.

d. Under survival conditions the traditional alternative, but only if there is ample sea room to leeward, is to run before the wind and sea, streaming long warps over the stern to hold the boat steady and reduce her speed. Nowadays a specially designed drogue is better than warps. To be effective a drogue needs to be large, with a mouth diameter of at least 10% of the boat's waterline length. The shrouds need to have anti-tangle lines to prevent the drogue capsizing into its own shrouds. A weight should be fitted to keep the drogue well submerged at all times. A long line is required, of terylene (dacron) – not nylon, which is too elastic – adjusted in length depending on the length of the seas, and secured to the strongest point available, such as sheet winches. To minimise chafe you should 'freshen the nip' (veer, or haul in, some line) from time to time. Otherwise the stern of the boat should be vacated, with the helm lashed securely amidships, because seas will break aboard over the stern. All openings such as cockpit lockers must be well secured.

e. In recent years many yachts have successfully kept sailing (often racing) in extremely bad weather by steering downwind. This suggests that speed is needed to maintain control, and that the greatest danger is to reduce speed to the extent that steerage is lost in the troughs of the waves, just when good control is most needed to counter the next crest looming up astern. In these circumstances, when excessive speed is maintained the greatest risk is that the yacht surfs down a sea into an exceptional trough, and into the face of the wave ahead, and is consequently pitch-poled (somersaulted stern over bow).

3.5.6 FURTHER CONSIDERATIONS IN BAD WEATHER

Some general conclusions about the onset of surfing conditions and the risk of broaching include:

- Wave length about 1.25 times the waterline length of the hull is most likely to cause loss of steering and broaching.
- The maximum longitudinal force exerted by a wave occurs when its crest is just forward of the stern, and this peak force varies approximately with wave height.
- A reduction in boat speed, whether by lower rpm or particularly by towing a drogue, lessens the tendency to surf, with the consequent risk of broaching. A speed reduction is especially helpful when the boat is near the crest of a wave, in order to reduce the time spent in this potentially unstable position and with the rudder possibly half out of the water.
- When the boat is in a trough a boost of power can be given if necessary to assist steering and bring the boat back on course, rpm then being reduced as the next crest begins to overtake.

Motor boats can usually best cope with heavy seas by being kept almost bow on to them, speed being adjusted to give little more than steerage way. Under less severe conditions progress to windward may be possible by careful manipulation of the throttle(s) to help the boat over the waves, thus add power when the bow begins to fall and throttle back as the bow lifts to a wave. If it is necessary to run off before the sea, warps or a drogue towed astern will help to keep the boat running straight but care is obviously needed to prevent them fouling the propeller(s).

Bad weather can be very frightening for those who have not previously experienced it, but if the boat is well equipped and maintained, and if the correct preparations are made in advance, it can be faced with confidence provided the right decisions are taken in sufficient time. Everything will take much longer to do, and you can not afford to make mistakes. The severe motion and constant noise of wind and sea will be very wearing, but the human body can best tolerate such conditions when they are accepted as inevitable.

3.6 BOOKS ABOUT BOAT HANDLING AND HEAVY WEATHER

The following books give greater detail on:

Boat Handling

Boat handling under sail and power by Bill Anderson and Tom Cunliffe (Fernhurst)

The RYA book of boat handling under power by John Goode and Dick Everitt (Adlard Coles Nautical)

Powerboating, a guide to Sportsboat handling by Peter White (Fernhurst)

Helming and yacht handling by Stuart Quarrie (Crowood Press)

Heavy Weather Sailing

Heavy weather sailing by K. Adlard Coles, 5th edition revised by Peter Bruce (Adlard Coles)

The heavy weather guide by William Kotsch. US equivalent of Heavy weather sailing.

Fast boats and rough seas by Dag Pike (Adlard Coles)

Heavy weather cruising by Tom Cunliffe (Fernhurst)

Storm tactics Handbook by Lin and Larry Pardey (Waterline)

All weather yachtsman by Peter Haward (Adlard Coles)

How to cope with storms by D.V.Haeften (Adlard Coles)

A Manual of Heavy Weather cruising by Jeff Toghill (2nd edition, Adlard Coles)

Chapter 4 Rules of the Road

CONTENTS

4.1 INTRODUCTION

Every skipper and crewmember needs a sound working knowledge of the International Regulations for Preventing Collisions at Sea – often shortened to IRPCS, 'Rules of the Road', 'Collision Regulations' or 'ColRegs' – so that at sea or in a busy harbour they can be applied almost instinctively. Skippers and crews should also be able to recognize the lights, shapes and other signals prescribed for different types of vessels under various conditions.

The 1972 Regulations, which came into force on 15 July 1977, are printed in full overleaf (with a blue background). They are amended by IMO Resolutions, the most recent being effective 4 November 1995.

Explanatory diagrams and italicised notes are also included; these are not part of the official Regulations.

Notes

1. *The Rules, as set out above, are logically structured:*

   There are five Parts, A - E, containing 38 Rules. Parts A and B are at the very heart of the Regulations. Parts C and D cover Lights, Shapes and Sound signals – beloved of examiners. Part E contains the few Exemptions still in force. Finally there are four detailed annexes.

2. *It is far better to learn the Rules by understanding them and their implications – rather than parrot-fashion. Some helpful books are listed at the end of this chapter.*

The International Regulations for Preventing Collisions at Sea, 1972

Published by the International Maritime Organization (IMO) and reprinted with permission.

PART A – GENERAL

Rule 1   Application

(a) These Rules shall apply to all vessels upon the high seas and in all waters connected therewith navigable by seagoing vessels.

(b) Nothing in these Rules shall interfere with the operations of special rules made by an appropriate authority for roadsteads, harbours, rivers, lakes or inland waterways connected with the high seas and navigable by seagoing vessels. Such special rules shall conform as closely as possible to these Rules.

(c) Nothing in these Rules shall interfere with the operation of any special rules made by the Government of any State with respect to additional station or signal lights, shapes or whistle signals for ships of war and vessels proceeding under convoy, or with respect to additional station or signal lights or shapes for fishing vessels engaged in fishing as a fleet. These additional station or signal lights, shapes or whistle signals, shall, so far as possible, be such that they cannot be mistaken for any light, shape or signal authorized elsewhere under these Rules.

(d) Traffic separation schemes may be adopted by the Organisation for the purpose of these Rules.

(e) Whenever the Government concerned shall have determined that a vessel of special construction or purpose cannot comply fully with the provisions of any of these Rules with respect to the number, position, range or arc of visibility of lights or shapes, as well as to the disposition and characteristics of sound-signalling appliances, such vessel shall comply with such other provisions in regard to the number, position, range or arc of visibility of lights or shapes, as well as to the disposition and characteristics of sound-signalling appliances, as her Government shall have determined to be the closest possible compliance with these Rules in respect of that vessel.

Notes

1. *Rule 1(a): Harbour and similar authorities may make special rules for their own waters, but they should conform as closely as possible to these Rules.*

2. *Rule 1(c): Details of such lights and signals are in the Annual Summary of Admiralty Notices to Mariners.*

3. *Rule 1(d): See Rule 10. The organization is the International Maritime Organization (IMO).*

4. *Rule 1(e): To illustrate this one, lengthy sentence: Submarines, for example carry their steaming lights low down; aircraft carriers have their side and steaming lights offset to starboard. In other warships the disposition of the masts brings the steaming lights closer together than would otherwise be required, which can make it difficult to judge their aspect.*

Rule 2   Responsibility

(a) Nothing in these Rules shall exonerate any vessel, or the owner, master or crew thereof, from the consequences of any neglect to comply with these Rules or of the neglect of any precaution which may be required by the ordinary practice of seamen, or by the special circumstances of the case.

(b) In construing and complying with these Rules due regard shall be had to all dangers of navigation and collision and to any special circumstances, including the limitations of the vessels involved, which may make a departure from these Rules necessary to avoid immediate danger.

Notes

1. *Rule 2 implies that rules alone are not enough – it is the seamanlike actions (taking into consideration all the relevant factors) of*

those who have to interpret and apply them
that avoid collisions.
2. Rule 2(b) specifically states that a departure
from these Rules may be necessary in special
circumstances, and that to avoid immediate
danger a vessel is not merely justified in
doing this, but is expected to do so.
3. The Rules do not give any vessel a 'right of
way' over another completely regardless of
special circumstances which may apply.
Factors to consider might be the presence of
other vessels under way or at anchor, shallow
water, poor visibility, traffic separation
schemes, fishing fleets etc – or the handling
characteristics of the vessels concerned in the
prevailing conditions.

Rule 3   General definitions
For the purpose of these Rules, except where
the context otherwise requires:

(a) The word 'vessel' includes every
description of water craft, including non-
displacement craft and seaplanes, used or
capable of being used as a means of
transportation on water.
(b) The term 'power-driven vessel' means any
vessel propelled by machinery.
(c) The term 'sailing vessel' means any vessel
under sail provided that propelling
machinery, if fitted, is not being used.
(d) The term 'vessel engaged in fishing'
means any vessel fishing with nets, lines,
trawls, or other fishing apparatus which
restrict manoeuvrability, but does not
include a vessel fishing with trolling lines
or other fishing apparatus which do not
restrict manoeuvrability.
(e) The word 'seaplane' includes any aircraft
designed to manoeuvre on the water.
(f) The term 'vessel not under command'
means a vessel which through some
exceptional circumstances is unable to
manoeuvre as required by these Rules and
is therefore unable to keep out of the way
of another vessel.
(g) The term 'vessel restricted in her ability to
manoeuvre' means a vessel which from
the nature of her work is restricted in her
ability to manoeuvre as required by these
Rules and is therefore unable to keep out
of the way of another vessel. The term
'vessels restricted in their ability to
manoeuvre' shall include but not be
limited to:
  (i)   a vessel engaged in laying, servicing
        or picking up a navigation mark,
        submarine cable or pipeline;
  (ii) a vessel engaged in dredging,
        surveying or underwater operations;
  (iii) a vessel engaged in replenishment or
        transferring persons, provisions or
        cargo while underway;
  (iv) a vessel engaged in the launching or
        recovery of aircraft;
  (v)   a vessel engaged in mineclearance
        operations;
  (vi) a vessel engaged in a towing
        operation such as severely restricts the
        towing vessel and her tow in their
        ability to deviate from their course.
(h) The term 'vessel constrained by her
draught' means a power-driven vessel
which because of her draught in relation
to the available depth and width of
navigable water is severely restricted in
her ability to deviate from the course she
is following.
(i) The word 'underway' means that a vessel
is not at anchor, or made fast to the shore,
or aground.
(j) The words 'length' and 'breadth' of a
vessel mean her length overall and
greatest breadth.
(k) Vessels shall be deemed to be in sight of
one another only when one can be
observed visually from the other.
(l) The term 'restricted visibility' means any
condition in which visibility is restricted by
fog, mist, falling snow, heavy rainstorms,
sandstorms or any other similar causes.

Note
*Rule 3 (c): A sailing vessel under sail, with engine
running but not in gear, eg for battery charging,
is not a power-driven vessel.*

PART B – STEERING AND SAILING RULES
SECTION I - CONDUCT OF VESSELS IN ANY CONDITION OF VISIBILITY

Rule 4   Application
Rules in this Section apply in any condition of
visibility.

Note
*Rules 4 to 10 apply at all times, whether or not
ships are in sight of each other.*

Rule 5   Look-out
Every vessel shall at all times maintain a proper
look-out by sight and hearing as well as by all
available means appropriate in the prevailing
circumstances and conditions so as to make a
full appraisal of the situation and of the risk of
collision.

Notes

1. A vital rule for all seamen, including yachtsmen. Particular care is needed to cover arcs which may be obscured, eg in a sailing yacht by sails or by the heel of the boat; or in motor cruisers by the boat's structure.
2. During darkness take care to preserve night vision, by using only dim and well-screened red lights for the compass, over the chart-table and elsewhere below deck.
3. A look-out must use ears as well as eyes, especially in restricted visibility, when one crew member should if possible be stationed forward. Radar should also be used, if fitted, whatever the visibility.

Rule 6   Safe speed

Every vessel shall at all times proceed at a safe speed so that she can take proper and effective action to avoid collision and be stopped within a distance appropriate to the prevailing circumstances and conditions.

In determining a safe speed the following factors shall be among those taken into account:

(a) By all vessels:
   (i)   the state of visibility;
   (ii) the traffic density including concentrations of fishing vessels or any other vessels;
   (iii) the manoeuvrability of the vessel with special reference to stopping distance and turning ability in the prevailing conditions;
   (iv) at night the presence of background light such as from shore lights or from back scatter of her own lights;
   (v)   the state of wind, sea and current, and the proximity of navigational hazards;
   (vi) the draught in relation to the available depth of water.
(b) Additionally, by vessels with operational radar:
   (i)   the characteristics, efficiency and limitations of the radar equipment;
   (ii) any constraints imposed by the radar range scale in use;
   (iii) the effect on radar detection of the sea state, weather and other sources of interference;
   (iv) the possibility that small vessels, ice and other floating objects may not be detected by radar at an adequate range;
   (v)   the number, location and movement of vessels detected by radar;
   (vi) the more exact assessment of the visibility that may be possible when radar is used to determine the range of vessels or other objects in the vicinity.

Notes

1. Large ships going fast cannot stop quickly. The faster two vessels are approaching each other, the less time there is for either to appreciate the situation and take the necessary action to avoid a collision – and the greater the impact should such action fail.
2. For motor yachts the same considerations apply as for larger ships, particularly, of course, at night or in bad visibility. In sailing yachts sheer speed is not so much a problem as the way the boat is sailed. For example a boat under spinnaker and with her main boom guyed forward sacrifices considerable manoeuvrability in the quest for greater speed; even if she is only doing eight knots through the water, such action would contravene Rule 6 in poor visibility, or amongst a lot of other vessels.
3. Radar is not infallible. Experience is needed to adjust the set properly for the prevailing conditions, and to interpret correctly what is seen on the screen.

Rule 7   Risk of collision

(a) Every vessel shall use all available means appropriate to the prevailing circumstances and conditions to determine if risk of collision exists. If there is any doubt such risk shall be deemed to exist.
(b) Proper use shall be made of radar equipment, if fitted and operational, including long-range scanning to obtain early warning of risk of collision and radar plotting or equivalent systematic observation of detected objects.
(c) Assumptions shall not be made on the basis of scanty information, especially scanty radar information.
(d) In determining if risk of collision exists the following considerations shall be among those taken into account:
   (i)   such risk shall be deemed to exist if the compass bearing of an approaching vessel does not appreciably change;
   (ii) such risk may sometimes exist even when an appreciable bearing change is evident, particularly when approaching a very large vessel or a tow or when approaching a vessel at close range.

Fig 4(11) Navigation lights shown by power-driven and sailing vessels underway.

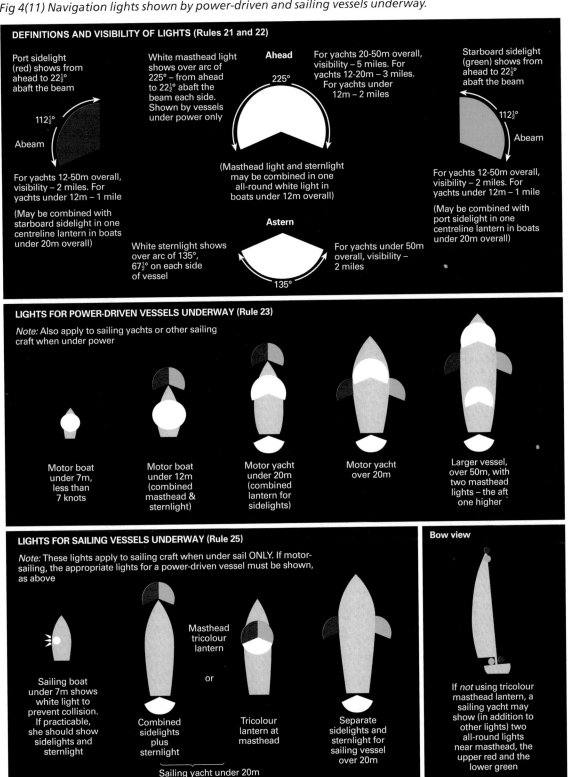

DEFINITIONS AND VISIBILITY OF LIGHTS (Rules 21 and 22)

Port sidelight (red) shows from ahead to $22\frac{1}{2}°$ abaft the beam

$112\frac{1}{2}°$

Abeam

For yachts 12-50m overall, visibility – 2 miles. For yachts under 12m – 1 mile

(May be combined with starboard sidelight in one centreline lantern in boats under 20m overall)

White masthead light shows over arc of 225° – from ahead to $22\frac{1}{2}°$ abaft the beam each side. Shown by vessels under power only

Ahead

225°

(Masthead light and sternlight may be combined in one all-round white light in boats under 12m overall)

Astern

White sternlight shows over arc of 135°, $67\frac{1}{2}°$ on each side of vessel

135°

For yachts 20-50m overall, visibility – 5 miles. For yachts 12-20m – 3 miles. For yachts under 12m – 2 miles

For yachts under 50m overall, visibility – 2 miles

Starboard sidelight (green) shows from ahead to $22\frac{1}{2}°$ abaft the beam

$112\frac{1}{2}°$

Abeam

For yachts 12-50m overall, visibility – 2 miles. For yachts under 12m – 1 mile

(May be combined with port sidelight in one centreline lantern in boats under 20m overall)

LIGHTS FOR POWER-DRIVEN VESSELS UNDERWAY (Rule 23)

Note: Also apply to sailing yachts or other sailing craft when under power

Motor boat under 7m, less than 7 knots

Motor boat under 12m (combined masthead & sternlight)

Motor yacht under 20m (combined lantern for sidelights)

Motor yacht over 20m

Larger vessel, over 50m, with two masthead lights – the aft one higher

LIGHTS FOR SAILING VESSELS UNDERWAY (Rule 25)

Note: These lights apply to sailing craft when under sail ONLY. If motor-sailing, the appropriate lights for a power-driven vessel must be shown, as above

Sailing boat under 7m shows white light to prevent collision. If practicable, she should show sidelights and sternlight

Masthead tricolour lantern

or

Combined sidelights plus sternlight

Tricolour lantern at masthead

Sailing yacht under 20m

Separate sidelights and sternlight for sailing vessel over 20m

Bow view

If *not* using tricolour masthead lantern, a sailing yacht may show (in addition to other lights) two all-round lights near masthead, the upper red and the lower green

Fig. 4(12)

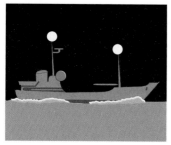

A power-driven vessel underway seen from abeam. **Rule 23(a)(ii)**

A power-driven vessel under 50m. **Rule 23(c)(i)**

A sailing boat under power with mainsail still set. **Rule 23 and Rule 25(e).**

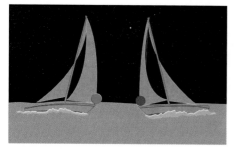

Sidelights of sailing yachts, when mounted low down as on the pulpit, may be obscured in a seaway.

The optional arrangement of a combined masthead light for sailing boats under 20m is more easily seen, and also conserves the battery. **Rule 25(b)**

A small boat under oars need only show a white light, in time to prevent collision. **Rule 25(d)(ii)**

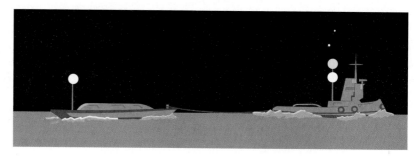

A tug and her tow seen from the starboard quarter. **Rule 21(d) and Rule 24**

The tug (left) and tow seen from ahead. From this aspect the two masthead lights of the tug might be confused with the masthead lights of a ship more than 50m in length. **Rule 24**

A vessel trawling, which should be given a wide berth. **Rule 26 (b)**

Fig. 4(13)

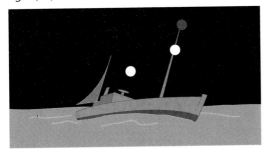

A vessel fishing (not trawling) and not making way (or she would show sidelights and sternlight). Gear extending more than 150m is shown by the white light. **Rule 26(c)(i) and (ii)**

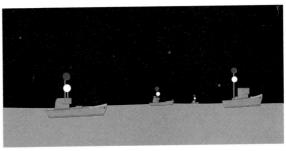

Fishing vessels often work together in a fleet, accordingly it is best to take substantial avoiding action.

Vessels engaged in pair trawling may exhibit a searchlight directed forward and in the direction of the other vessel of the pair. **Annex II. 2 (b) (i)**

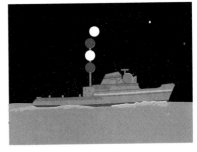

A vessel with restricted ability to manoeuvre. Masthead light and sidelights indicate she is making way through the water. **Rule 27 (b) (i)**

A tug (right) and tow, with restricted ability to manoeuvre. The three masthead lights of the tug indicate that the tow is more than 200m. **Rule 24 (a) (i) and Rule 27 (b) (i)**

A dredger dredging. The red over white over red lights show that her manoevrability is restricted; the two vertical red lights show her foul side, and the two vertical green her clear side. **Rule 27 (b) (i) and (d) (i) and (ii)**

A vessel constrained by her draught. **Rule 28**

Fig. 4(14)

A vessel engaged in pilotage duties, at anchor. **Rule 29 (a) (iii)**

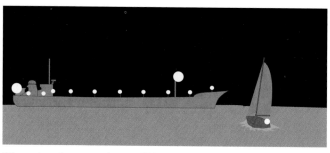

When at anchor, vessels over 100m in length are required to show their deck lights which may obscure other less bright lights. **Rule 30 (c)**

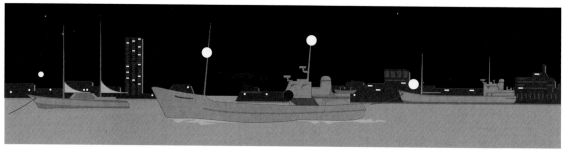

Great care is often needed to differentiate between navigation lights of nearby vessels and lights ashore. **Rule 6 (a) (iv)**

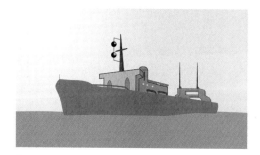

A vessel not under command. **Rule 27 (a) (ii)**

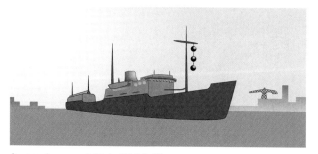

A vessel aground. **Rule 30 (d) (ii)**

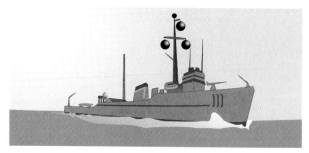

A minesweeper, with gear streamed. **Rule 27 (f)**

A divers' support boat exhibiting a rigid replica of International Code flag A; such craft should be given a wide berth. **Rule 27 (e) (ii)**

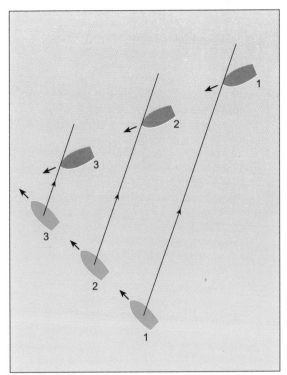

Fig. 4(1) Rule 7. The bearing of Black from Blue is steady. Long before position 2, Blue should have altered course to starboard by at least 45°, to pass under Black's stern.

Notes

1. *Always, and as early as possible, take and record a series of bearings of any approaching or crossing vessel to determine whether that vessel is on a collision course. If the actual (not the relative) bearing remains virtually steady, there is a risk of collision; see Fig. 4(1).*

2. *Rule 7(d)(ii) demands particular care. Taking bearings of the bow of a supertanker might show that a yacht would miss the bow, but possibly hit the stern.*

3. *If radar is fitted, it must be used, and used properly, ie by plotting a systematic series of ranges and bearings. Avoid jumping to conclusions about the collision risk, based on inadequate information.*

Rule 8   Action to avoid collision

(a) Any action taken to avoid collision shall, if the circumstances of the case admit, be positive, made in ample time and with due regard to the observance of good seamanship.

(b) Any alteration of course and/or speed to avoid collision shall, if the circumstances of the case admit, be large enough to be readily apparent to another vessel

observing visually or by radar; a succession of small alterations of course and/or speed should be avoided.

(c) If there is sufficient sea room, alteration of course alone may be the most effective action to avoid a close-quarters situation provided that it is made in good time, is substantial and does not result in another close-quarters situation.

(d) Action taken to avoid collision with another vessel shall be such as to result in passing at a safe distance. The effectiveness of the action shall be carefully checked until the other vessel is finally past and clear.

(e) If necessary to avoid collision or allow more time to assess the situation, a vessel shall slacken her speed or take all way off by stopping or reversing her means of propulsion.

(f) (i)   A vessel which, by any of these Rules, is required not to impede the passage or safe passage of another vessel shall, when required by the circumstances of the case, take early action to allow sufficient sea room for the safe passage of the other vessel.

(ii)   A vessel required not to impede the passage or safe passage of another vessel is not relieved of this obligation if approaching the other vessel so as to involve risk of collision and shall, when taking action, have full regard to the action which may be required by the Rules of this part.

(iii)   A vessel the passage of which is not to be impeded remains fully obliged to comply with the Rules of this part when the two vessels are approaching one another so as to involve risk of collision.

Notes

1. *This important Rule stresses the need to take **early and positive** action to avoid collision, and of monitoring the situation until the other vessel is well clear. Large and distinct alterations of course and/or speed are much more evident to another vessel than a succession of small ones. This is particularly so at night when, by altering course to show a different light, a vessel can make her intentions completely clear. But slowing down or even stopping is seldom obvious to others due to a yacht's limited speed range – even if the headsail is rolled, both to slow down and to advertise that you are doing so.*

2. While keeping clear of one vessel it is important to keep a good watch on others in the vicinity.
3. If necessary slow down, stop, or even go astern. Apart from minimising the effect of any collision, this gives more time to assess the situation. Such action can seldom be wrong when, in poor visibility, another vessel is detected forward of the beam (see Rule 19).
4. Rule 8(f) is in three parts which take account of three phases of a developing situation:
   Phase 1 (para (i)) tells a vessel that is required 'not to impede' the safe passage of another vessel to take early action to allow sufficient sea room for the other.
   Phase 2 (para (ii)) occurs when there is risk of collision, and states that the vessel required 'not to impede' retains this duty even though she may be a stand-on vessel under other Rules; and that any action taken must have regard for possible manoeuvres by the other vessel.
   Phase 3 (para (iii)) is reached when action or the lack of it under Phase 1 or 2 leads to a collision risk situation which requires the action of both vessels; here the Rules state that the vessel 'not to be impeded' must comply fully with the Rules of this part, ie Part B.
5. Small vessels and yachts navigating in traffic separation schemes (Rule 10) must be aware of their obligation not to impede vessels following traffic lanes, and of the attendant change to the traditional concept of steam giving way to sail.
6. Outside traffic separation schemes, in the open sea, many yachts deliberately initiate early avoiding action, to ensure that a risk of collision does not develop – knowing whose life is most at risk and the relative ease with which a yacht can take action as opposed to a large vessel; see also Note 1 to Rule 17.
7. The essence of Rules 7 and 8 may in practical terms be distilled into three basic questions which every skipper or crew should ask themselves – and answer, correctly – whenever a closing vessel is sighted:
   a. Is there a risk of collision?
   b. If there is, am I the give-way vessel?
   c. If I am, what action(s) must I take?

Rule 9   Narrow Channels

(a) A vessel proceeding along the course of a narrow channel or fairway shall keep as near to the outer limit of the channel or fairway which lies on her starboard side as is safe and practicable.

(b) A vessel of less than 20 metres in length or a sailing vessel shall not impede the passage of a vessel which can safely navigate only within a narrow channel or fairway.

(c) A vessel engaged in fishing shall not impede the passage of any other vessel navigating within a narrow channel or fairway.

(d) A vessel shall not cross a narrow channel or fairway if such crossing impedes the passage of a vessel which can safely navigate only within such channel or fairway. The latter vessel may use the sound signal prescribed in Rule 34(d) if in doubt as to the intention of the crossing vessel.

(e) (i)   In a narrow channel or fairway when overtaking can take place only if the vessel to be overtaken has to take action to permit safe passing, the vessel intending to overtake shall indicate her intention by sounding the appropriate signal prescribed in Rule 34(c)(i). The vessel to be overtaken shall, if in agreement, sound the appropriate signal prescribed in Rule 34(c)(ii) and take steps to permit safe passing. If in doubt she may sound the signals prescribed in Rule 34(d).
   (ii)   This Rule does not relieve the overtaking vessel of her obligation under Rule 13.

(f) A vessel nearing a bend or an area of a narrow channel or fairway where other vessels may be obscured by an intervening obstruction shall navigate with particular alertness and caution and shall sound the appropriate signal prescribed in Rule 34(e).

(g) Any vessel shall, if the circumstances of the case admit, avoid anchoring in a narrow channel.

Notes
1. A 'narrow channel' is not defined; it depends upon the relative sizes of the vessels and the waters concerned.
2. Sailing yachts are required to keep as near to the starboard side of a fairway as is practicable, just as much as power-driven vessels, and are equally bound by Rules 9(b) and 9(d).
3. Sailing yachts must not impede a vessel which can safely navigate only within a narrow channel or fairway, ie they must allow sufficient sea room to the other vessel so that risk of collision (or grounding) does not develop.

Rule 10   Traffic separation schemes

(a) This Rule applies to traffic separation schemes adopted by the Organisation and does not relieve any vessel of her obligation under any other Rule.

(b) A vessel using a traffic separation scheme shall:
  (i) proceed in the appropriate traffic lane in the general direction of traffic flow for that lane;
  (ii) so far as practicable keep clear of a traffic separation line or separation zone;
  (iii) normally join or leave a traffic lane at the termination of the lane, but when joining or leaving from either side shall do so at as small an angle to the general direction of traffic flow as practicable.

(c) A vessel shall so far as practicable avoid crossing traffic lanes, but if obliged to do so shall cross on a heading as nearly as practicable at right angles to the general direction of traffic flow.

(d) (i) A vessel shall not use an inshore traffic zone when she can safely use the appropriate traffic lane within the adjacent traffic separation scheme. However, vessels of less than 20 metres in length, sailing vessels and vessels engaged in fishing may use the inshore traffic zone.
  (ii) Notwithstanding sub-paragraph (d) (i) a vessel may use an inshore traffic zone when en route to or from a port, offshore installation or structure, pilot station or any other place situated within the traffic zone, or to avoid immediate danger.

(e) A vessel other than a crossing vessel or a vessel joining or leaving a lane shall not normally enter a separation zone or cross a separation line except:
  (i) in cases of emergency to avoid immediate danger;
  (ii) to engage in fishing within a separation zone.

(f) A vessel navigating in areas near the terminations of traffic separation schemes shall do so with particular caution.

(g) A vessel shall so far as practicable avoid anchoring in a traffic separation scheme or in areas near its terminations.

(h) A vessel not using a traffic separation scheme shall avoid it by as wide a margin as is practicable.

(i) A vessel engaged in fishing shall not impede the passage of any vessel following a traffic lane.

(j) A vessel of less than 20 metres in length or a sailing vessel shall not impede the safe passage of a power-driven vessel following a traffic lane.

(k) A vessel restricted in her ability to manoeuvre when engaged in an operation for the maintenance of safety of navigation in a traffic separation scheme is exempted from complying with this Rule to the extent necessary to carry out the operation.

(l) A vessel restricted in her ability to manoeuvre when engaged in an operation for the laying, servicing or picking up of a submarine cable, within a traffic separation scheme, is exempted from complying with this Rule to the extent necessary to carry out the operation.

Notes

1. Under Rule 10 the law requires that traffic separation schemes (TSS), which have been adopted by the International Maritime Organisation (IMO), must be observed. TSS are essential for the safety of larger ships, and while they may at times be inconvenient for yachtsmen they must be accepted as another element in passage planning, to be avoided if at all possible; see Fig. 4(2).

    TSS are marked on Admiralty charts which should be corrected in the usual way. TSS currently in force off the UK and NW Europe are summarised in the MRNA.

2. Yachtsmen should clearly understand that the whole of Rule 10 is applicable to yachts. Contrary to certain false impressions, TSS and Rule 10 do **not** modify the collision

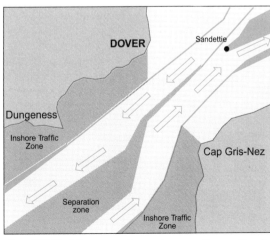

Fig. 4(2) Traffic separation scheme – Dover Strait.

regulations when two vessels meet or converge.

If for example a vessel is proceeding under power down a traffic lane, and another vessel which is crossing that lane appears on a collision course on her starboard bow, then the vessel in the lane must keep clear just as if she had been in mid-ocean.

However, if the crossing vessel is less than 20m (65ft) in length or a sailing vessel, then in this example she would have to comply with Rule 10(j), ie not impede.

3. The term 'shall not impede' is explained in Rule 8(f) as taking early action to give sufficient sea room for the safe passage of the other vessel (by navigating so as to avoid the risk of collision). If however a situation develops which does involve risk of collision, then the relevant Rules must be obeyed.

4. Yachts are usually well advised to navigate in the inshore traffic zone (keeping clear of the boundary of the adjacent lane) rather than along the lanes of a TSS – with the attendant risk of 'impeding' the safe passage of a power-driven vessel following the lane.

If using the lanes, a sailing yacht beating to windward must proceed 'in the general direction of traffic flow,' Rule 10 (b) (i), ie keep within the correct lane. She must certainly never beat to windward in the wrong lane – against the traffic flow.

If there is much shipping, it would be more prudent to motor to windward along the correct lane, rather than tacking to and fro with the risk of impeding some vessel.

5. If it is necessary to cross a traffic lane, the requirement to do so on a heading as near as possible at right angles minimises the crossing time and also presents an obvious 'beam-on' aspect to other lane users, who

again must not be impeded; see Fig. 4(3). In a sailing yacht, if the wind falls light and boat-speed drops below about three knots, the engine should be used if one is fitted.

Due to leeway and/or tidal stream, when crossing on a heading at right angles to the lane, a yacht's track (as seen for example by a shore radar) is unlikely to be at right angles to the traffic flow. This is accepted, and no official action will result in such cases if it is evident that the yacht was simply steering the required heading.

6. In order to comply with TSS, accurate navigation is important, so that a yacht knows exactly where she is in relation to the traffic lanes.

Note that 'YG' in the International Code means 'You appear not to be complying with the traffic separation scheme'. There are heavy fines for breaking the rules. A leading racing skipper was recently fined £12,000 with £3000 costs for navigating against the traffic flow.

PART B, SECTION II – CONDUCT OF VESSELS IN SIGHT OF ONE ANOTHER

Rule 11   Application
Rules in this Section apply to vessels in sight of one another.

Rule 12   Sailing vessels
(a) When two sailing vessels are approaching one another, so as to involve risk of collision, one of them shall keep out of the way of the other as follows:
  (i)   when each has the wind on a different side, the vessel which has the wind on the port side shall keep out of the way of the other;
  (ii) when both have the wind on the same side, the vessel which is to windward shall keep out of the way of the vessel which is to leeward;
  (iii) if a vessel with the wind on the port side sees a vessel to windward and cannot determine with certainty whether the other vessel has the wind on the port or on the starboard side, she shall keep out of the way of the other.
(b) For the purposes of this Rule the windward side shall be deemed to be the side opposite to that on which the mainsail is carried or, in the case of a square-rigged vessel, the side opposite to that on which the largest fore-and-aft sail is carried.

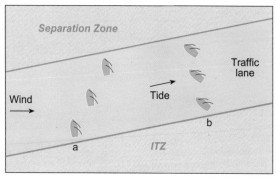

Fig. 4(3) When crossing a traffic lane, and considering the effects of wind and tide, (a) is correct – heading at right angles to the traffic lane, crossing as quickly as possible, and presenting an obvious beam aspect to other lane users. (b) is wrongly tracking at right angles.

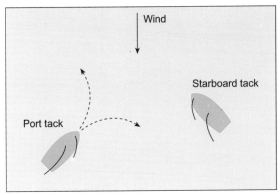

Fig. 4(4) Rule 12(a)(i). When two sailing boats are on opposite tacks the one on port tack (on the left above) must keep clear.

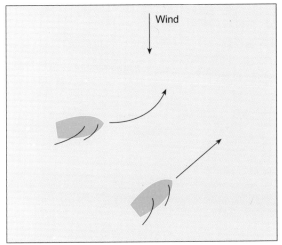

Fig. 4(5) Rule 12(a)(ii). When two sailing boats are on the same tack, the windward one (on the left above) must keep clear.

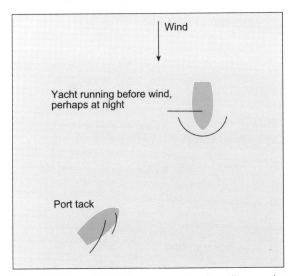

Fig. 4(6) Rule 12(a)(iii). If a port tack sailing yacht cannot decide whether an approaching vessel under sail to windward is on port or starboard tack, she shall keep clear.

Notes

1. The applications of this rule are shown in Figs. 4(4), 4(5) and 4(6) below. Rules 8, 13, 16 and 17(a), (b) and (d) also refer. Rule 12 does not apply if either of the two vessels under sail is also motoring.
2. Rule 12(a)(iii) is particularly applicable at night.

Rule 13   Overtaking

(a) Notwithstanding anything contained in the Rules of Part B, Sections I & II any vessel overtaking any other shall keep out of the way of the vessel being overtaken.

(b) A vessel shall be deemed to be overtaking when coming up with another vessel from a direction more than 225° abaft her beam, that is, in such a position with reference to the vessel she is overtaking, that at night she would be able to see only the sternlight of that vessel but neither of her sidelights.

(c) When a vessel is in any doubt as to whether she is overtaking another, she shall assume that this is the case and act accordingly.

(d) Any subsequent alteration of the bearing between the two vessels shall not make the overtaking vessel a crossing vessel within the meaning of these Rules or relieve her of the duty of keeping clear of the overtaken vessel until she is finally past and clear.

Notes

1. Rule 13 overrides all the other Rules in Part B, Sections I & II. A sailing vessel overtaking another, regardless of the tack each may be on, must keep clear.

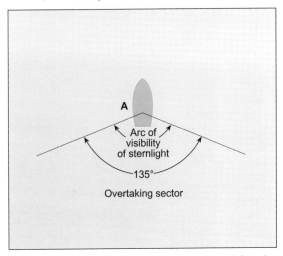

Fig. 4(7) Rule 13. Any vessel coming up with A in this sector (ie when her sternlight is visible but not her sidelights) must keep clear of A, whilst overtaking.

2. The vessel being overtaken also has a duty not to hamper the overtaker, Rule 17(a)(i). Therefore, before altering course always check that it is clear astern.
3. The overtaking vessel must continue to keep clear of the other, until finally past and clear. Prior to this, the overtaking vessel cannot become a crossing vessel – with any rights that this change of status might bestow on her.
4. The angle of $22\frac{1}{2}°$, eg in Rule 13(b) and elsewhere, stems from the use of 'points' in the magnetic compass. There being 32 points in 360°, two points equal $22\frac{1}{2}°$.

Rule 14   Head-on situation
(a) When two power-driven vessels are meeting on reciprocal or nearly reciprocal courses so as to involve risk of collision each shall alter her course to starboard so that each shall pass on the port side of the other.
(b) Such a situation shall be deemed to exist when a vessel sees the other ahead or nearly ahead and by night she could see the masthead lights of the other in a line or nearly in a line and/or both sidelights and by day she observes the corresponding aspect of the other vessel.
(c) When a vessel is in any doubt as to whether such a situation exists she shall assume that it does exist and act accordingly.

Notes
1. This Rule applies only to power-driven vessels, and makes both vessels meeting on nearly reciprocal courses responsible for altering course to starboard; see Fig. 4(8).
2. A substantial alteration may be required, accompanied by the appropriate sound signal, see Rule 34. Be wary of the potential collision risk where two head-on vessels look set to pass starboard to starboard; then one

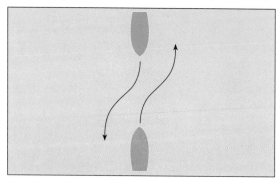

Fig. 4(8) Rule 14. When two power-driven vessels are approaching on reciprocal or nearly reciprocal courses, each shall alter to starboard so that they pass port to port.

turns port to increase the lateral separation, whilst the other turns starboard in accordance with this Rule ...

Rule 15   Crossing situation
When two power-driven vessels are crossing so as to involve risk of collision, the vessel which has the other on her own starboard side shall keep out of the way and shall, if the circumstances of the case admit, avoid crossing ahead of the other vessel.

Notes
1. 'If to starboard red appear, 'tis your duty to keep clear'. This applies even if the vessel which has the other on her starboard side is underway but stopped, unless she is not under command; see Fig. 4(9).

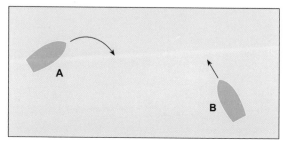

Fig. 4(9) Rule 15. Reminders: at night vessel A is 'warned' to give way on seeing B's red port light. B, seeing A's green stbd light, proceeds with caution.

2. Usually the give-way vessel turns starboard to pass astern of the other vessel, and/or reduces speed. Very exceptionally (if for example there is shallow water to starboard) an alteration to port may be justified – in which case a substantial alteration may be needed to avoid crossing ahead of the other vessel.
3. Rule 15 does not apply if one of the vessels is in the categories described in Rule 18(a)(i), (ii) or (iii).

Rule 16   Action by give-way vessel
Every vessel which is directed to keep out of the way of another vessel shall, so far as possible, take early and substantial action to keep well clear.

Note
"Early and substantial ... well clear" are the key words.

Rule 17   Action by stand-on vessel
(a) (i)   Where one of two vessels is to keep out of the way the other shall keep her course and speed.

(ii) The latter vessel may however take action to avoid collision by her manoeuvre alone, as soon as it becomes apparent to her that the vessel required to keep out of the way is not taking appropriate action in compliance with these Rules.

(b) When, from any cause, the vessel required to keep her course and speed finds herself so close that collision cannot be avoided by the action of the give-way vessel alone, she shall take such action as will best aid to avoid collision.

(c) A power-driven vessel which takes action in a crossing situation in accordance with sub-paragraph (a) (ii) of this Rule to avoid collision with another power-driven vessel shall, if the circumstances of the case admit, not alter course to port for a vessel on her own port side.

(d) This Rule does not relieve the give-way vessel of her obligation to keep out of the way.

Notes

1. *The stand-on vessel is only required to hold her course and speed under Rule 17(a)(i) in a two vessel situation, and not at long range before risk of collision develops – this is a sensible opportunity for a yacht to avoid confronting a larger vessel, especially since a yacht will usually see a large ship before that ship sees her.*

2. *The stand-on vessel is required to hold her course and speed, but may herself take avoiding action when it becomes apparent that the give-way vessel is not taking appropriate action. This must not conflict with possible belated action by the give-way vessel, and hence she should normally alter course substantially to starboard in accordance with Rule 17(c).*

3. *When collision can no longer be avoided, Rule 17(b) makes it compulsory for the stand-on vessel to take the best possible avoiding action in the circumstances. For a manoeuvrable yacht the best action may be a sharp 90° or 180° turn away from an oncoming ship. As a last resort turning onto the reciprocal of the give-way vessel's course may avoid or at least minimise the likely impact.*

Rule 18   Responsibilities between vessels

Except where Rules 9, 10 and 13 otherwise require:

(a) A power-driven vessel underway shall keep out of the way of:

(i)   a vessel not under command;
(ii) a vessel restricted in her ability to manoeuvre;
(iii) a vessel engaged in fishing;
(iv) a sailing vessel.

(b) A sailing vessel underway shall keep out of the way of:

(i)   a vessel not under command;
(ii) a vessel restricted in her ability to manoeuvre;
(iii) a vessel engaged in fishing.

(c) A vessel engaged in fishing when underway shall, so far as possible, keep out of the way of:

(i)   a vessel not under command;
(ii) a vessel restricted in her ability to manoeuvre.

(d) (i) Any vessel other than a vessel not under command or a vessel restricted in her ability to manoeuvre shall, if the circumstances of the case admit, avoid impeding the safe passage of a vessel constrained by her draught, exhibiting the signals in Rule 28.

(ii) A vessel constrained by her draught shall navigate with particular caution having full regard to her special condition.

(e) A seaplane on the water shall, in general, keep well clear of all vessels and avoid impeding their navigation. In circumstances, however, where risk of collision exists, she shall comply with the Rules of this Part.

Notes

1. *Rule 18 establishes a hierarchy of vessels which take precedence over others, noting the exceptions under Rules 9 (narrow channels), 10 (TSS) and 13 (overtaking).*

2. *A sailing yacht must keep clear of power-driven vessels under Rules 9(b), 10(j), 13 and 18(b). She must also avoid impeding a vessel constrained by her draught.*

3. *Although a power-driven vessel shall keep clear of sailing vessels Rule 18(a)(iv), it is much more seamanlike for a sailing yacht beating to windward to arrange her tacks so as to keep clear of larger ships; rather than having to invoke the provisions of Rule 17(a)(ii).*

PART B, SECTION III – CONDUCT OF VESSELS IN RESTRICTED VISIBILITY

Rule 19   Conduct of vessels in restricted visibility

(a) This Rule applies to vessels not in sight of one another when navigating in or near an area of restricted visibility.

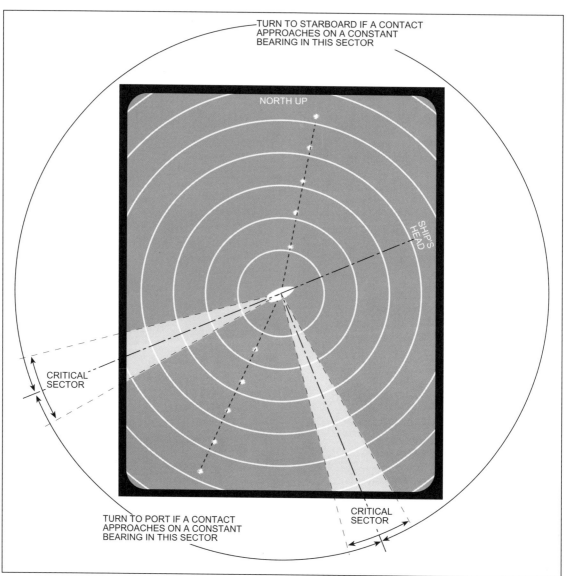

Fig 4(10). Rule 19 (d). Actions to avoid radar contacts closing on a constant bearing.

(b) Every vessel shall proceed at a safe speed adapted to the prevailing circumstances and conditions of restricted visibility. A power-driven vessel shall have her engines ready for immediate manoeuvre.

(c) Every vessel shall have due regard to the prevailing circumstances and conditions of restricted visibility when complying with the Rules of Section 1 of this Part.

(d) A vessel which detects by radar alone the presence of another vessel shall determine if a close-quarters situation is developing and/or risk of collision exists. If so, she shall take avoiding action in ample time, provided that when such action consists of an alteration of course, so far as possible the following shall be avoided:

(i) an alteration of course to port for a vessel forward of the beam, other than for a vessel being overtaken;

(ii) an alteration of course towards a vessel abeam or abaft the beam.

(e) Except where it has been determined that a risk of collision does not exist, every vessel which hears apparently forward of her beam the fog signal of another vessel, or which cannot avoid a close-quarters situation with another vessel forward of her beam, shall reduce her speed to the minimum at which she can be kept on her course. She shall if necessary take all her way off and in any event navigate with extreme caution until danger of collision is over.

Notes

1. *Section I of Part B (Conduct of vessels in any visibility) also applies. When vessels can see each other they are subject to the Rules in Section II. It is possible that of two vessels intent on not colliding with each other, one may be complying with the Rules in Section II and the other with those in Section III, ie Rule 19. This highlights the differences between these two Sections (which are not incompatible) and the fact that there is very much more to Rule 19 than meets the eye.*

2. *Rule 19 (d) – at the root of the matter – is negative in nature, in that it states two forms of avoiding action which if possible shall <u>not</u> be taken. By deduction, take, if possible, the **positive actions** illustrated in Fig. 4(10) to avoid radar contacts closing on a constant bearing, ie:*
   a. ***Alter to starboard** to avoid contacts on your port side or on your starboard bow;*
   b. ***Alter port** for contacts on your starboard quarter.*
   c. ***Slow down or stop.** Buys time and is not confusing.*
   Plot contact(s) in either critical sector with extreme care, so as to decide the best action to take. The critical sectors lie between the two major sectors in which avoiding action is more clear cut.

3. *Note that "close quarters situation" is introduced in addition to "risk of collision". A close quarters situation is not defined, but it implies the existence of an earlier hazardous situation, as well as a risk of collision.*

4. *Note also that give-way and stand-on vessels are not mentioned. **Every vessel is required to take avoiding action**, not knowing whether others are radar equipped.*

5. *Fog signals, 19 (e): If heard forward of the beam, slow down or stop. Navigate with extreme care until there is no risk of collision. A close quarters situation probably exists. For a vessel without radar these are basically the only actions available. The direction and proximity of sound (fog signals) at sea is notoriously hard to assess.*

6. *SAFETY. Safe speed, 19(b), is covered by Rule 6, and look-out by Rule 5. Other safety advice includes: Do not sail if fog/poor visibility is forecast; fit an efficient radar reflector, or preferably a good radar; be ready for immediate and drastic alterations of course; keep clear of TSS and narrow channels; seek shallow water to avoid shipping (beware of others doing the same thing).*

PART C – LIGHTS AND SHAPES

Rule 20   Application
(a) Rules in this Part shall be complied with in all weathers.
(b) The Rules concerning lights shall be complied with from sunset to sunrise, and during such times no other lights shall be exhibited, except such lights as cannot be mistaken for the lights specified in these Rules or do not impair their visibility or distinctive character, or interfere with the keeping of a proper look-out.
(c) The lights prescribed by these Rules shall, if carried, also be exhibited from sunrise to sunset in restricted visibility and may be exhibited in all other circumstances when it is deemed necessary.
(d) The rules concerning shapes shall be complied with by day.
(e) The lights and shapes specified in these Rules shall comply with the provisions of Annex I to these Regulations.

Rule 21   Definitions
(a) 'Masthead light' means a white light placed over the fore and aft centreline of the vessel showing an unbroken light over an arc of the horizon of 225° and so fixed as to show the light from right ahead to $22\frac{1}{2}$° abaft the beam on either side of the vessel.
(b) 'Sidelights' means a green light on the starboard side and a red light on the port side each showing an unbroken light over an arc of the horizon of $112\frac{1}{2}$° and so fixed as to show the light from right ahead to $22\frac{1}{2}$° abaft the beam on its respective side. In a vessel of less than 20 metres in length the sidelights may be combined in one lantern carried on the fore and aft centreline of the vessel.
(c) 'Sternlight' means a white light placed as nearly as practicable at the stern showing an unbroken light over an arc of the horizon of 135° and so fixed as to show the light $67\frac{1}{2}$° from right aft on each side of the vessel.
(d) 'Towing light' means a yellow light having the same characteristics as the 'sternlight' defined in paragraph (c) of this Rule.
(e) 'All-round light' means a light showing an unbroken light over an arc of the horizon of 360°.
(f) 'Flashing light' means a light flashing at regular intervals at a frequency of 120 flashes or more per minute.

1. Although in Rule 21(a) the term masthead light is used, the light does not necessarily have to be on a mast. It should however be above and clear of all other lights and obstructions.
2. With respect to Rule 21(c), a power-driven vessel of less than 12 metres may, under Rule 23(c) as revised, have her sternlight combined with the masthead light to form an all-round white light with improved visibility astern.

Rule 22   Visibility of lights

The lights prescribed in these Rules shall have an intensity as specified in Section 8 of Annex I to these Regulations so as to be visible at the following minimum ranges:

(a) In vessels of 50 metres or more in length:
   - a masthead light, 6 miles;
   - a sidelight, 3 miles;
   - a sternlight, 3 miles;
   - a towing light, 3 miles;
   - a white, red, green or yellow all-round light, 3 miles;

(b) In vessels of 12 metres or more in length but less than 50 metres in length:
   - a masthead light, 5 miles; except that where the length of the vessel is less than 20 metres, 3 miles;
   - a sidelight, 2 miles;
   - a sternlight, 2 miles;
   - a towing light, 2 miles;
   - a white, red, green or yellow all-round light, 2 miles;

(c) In vessels of less than 12 metres in length:
   - a masthead light, 2 miles;
   - a sidelight, 1 mile;
   - a sternlight, 2 miles;
   - a towing light, 2 miles;
   - a white, red, green or yellow all-round light, 2 miles.

(d) In inconspicuous, partly submerged vessels or objects being towed:
   - a white all-round light, 3 miles.

Rule 23   Power-driven vessels underway

(a) A power-driven vessel underway shall exhibit:
   (i) a masthead light forward;
   (ii) a second masthead light abaft of and higher than the forward one; except that a vessel of less than 50 metres in length shall not be obliged to exhibit such light but may do so;
   (iii) sidelights;
   (iv) a sternlight.

(b) An air-cushion vessel when operating in the non-displacement mode shall, in addition to the lights prescribed in paragraph (a) of this Rule, exhibit an all-round flashing yellow light.

(c) (i) A power-driven vessel of less than 12 metres in length may in lieu of the lights prescribed in paragraph (a) of this Rule exhibit an all-round white light and sidelights;

   (ii) a power-driven vessel of less than 7 metres in length whose maximum speed does not exceed 7 knots may in lieu of the lights prescribed in paragraph (a) of this Rule exhibit an all-round white light and shall, if practicable, also exhibit sidelights;

   (iii) the masthead light or all-round white light on a power-driven vessel of less than 12 metres in length may be displaced from the fore and aft centreline of the vessel if centreline fitting is not practicable, provided that the sidelights are combined in one lantern which shall be carried on the fore and aft centreline of the vessel or located as nearly as practicable in the same fore and aft line as the masthead light or the all-round white light.

Notes

1. The specifications for lights in Annex I are much more precise than used to be the case.
2. See pages 91-94 for the lights to be displayed by various classes of vessels.
3. Under Rule 23(c), as revised from 1 June 1983, a yacht of less than 12 metres in length under power may show sidelights (or a combined lantern) and a single all-round white light (combining the previously separate masthead light and sternlight).

Rule 24   Towing and pushing

(a) A power-driven vessel when towing shall exhibit:
   (i) instead of the light prescribed in Rule 23(a)(i) or (a)(ii), two masthead lights in a vertical line. When the length of the tow, measuring from the stern of the towing vessel to the after end of the tow exceeds 200 metres, three such lights in a vertical line;
   (ii) sidelights;
   (iii) a sternlight;
   (iv) a towing light in a vertical line above the sternlight;
   (v) when the length of the tow exceeds

200 metres, a diamond shape where it can best be seen.

(b) When a pushing vessel and a vessel being pushed ahead are rigidly connected in a composite unit they shall be regarded as a power-driven vessel and exhibit the lights prescribed in Rule 23.

(c) A power-driven vessel when pushing ahead or towing alongside, except in the case of a composite unit, shall exhibit:
   (i) instead of the light prescribed in Rule 23(a)(i) or (a)(ii), two masthead lights in a vertical line;
   (ii) sidelights;
   (iii) a sternlight.

(d) A power-driven vessel to which paragraphs (a) or (c) of this Rule apply shall also comply with Rule 23(a)(ii).

(e) A vessel or object being towed, other than those mentioned in paragraph (g) of this Rule, shall exhibit:
   (i) sidelights;
   (ii) a sternlight;
   (iii) when the length of the tow exceeds 200 metres, a diamond shape where it can best be seen.

(f) Provided that any number of vessels being towed alongside or pushed in a group shall be lighted as one vessel:
   (i) a vessel being pushed ahead, not being part of a composite unit, shall exhibit at the forward end, sidelights;
   (ii) a vessel being towed alongside shall exhibit a sternlight and at the forward end, sidelights.

(g) An inconspicuous, partly submerged vessel or object, or combination of such vessels or objects being towed, shall exhibit:
   (i) if it is less than 25 metres in breadth, one all-round white light at or near the forward end and one at or near the after end except that dracones need not exhibit a light at or near the forward end;
   (ii) if it is 25 metres or more in breadth, two additional all-round white lights at or near the extremities of its breadth;
   (iii) if it exceeds 100 metres in length, additional all-round white lights between the lights prescribed in sub-paragraphs (i) and (ii) so that the distance between the lights shall not exceed 100 metres;
   (iv) a diamond shape at or near the aftermost extremity of the last vessel

or object being towed   and if the length of the tow exceeds 200 metres an additional diamond shape where it can best be seen and located as far forward as is practicable.

(h) Where from any sufficient cause it is impracticable for a vessel or object being towed to exhibit the lights or shapes prescribed in paragraph (e) or (g) of this Rule, all possible measures shall be taken to light the vessel or object towed or at least to indicate the presence of such vessel or object.

(i) Where from any sufficient cause it is impracticable for a vessel not normally engaged in towing operations to display the lights prescribed in paragraph (a) or (c) of this Rule, such vessel shall not be required to exhibit those lights when engaged in towing another vessel in distress or otherwise in need of assistance. All possible measures shall be taken to indicate the nature of the relationship between the towing vessel and the vessel being towed as authorized by Rule 36, in particular by illuminating the towline.

Rule 25 Sailing vessels underway and vessels under oars

(a) A sailing vessel underway shall exhibit:
   (i) sidelights;
   (ii) a sternlight.

(b) In a sailing vessel of less than 20 metres in length the lights prescribed in paragraph (a) of this Rule may be combined in one lantern carried at or near the top of the mast where it can best be seen.

(c) A sailing vessel underway may, in addition to the lights prescribed in paragraph (a) of this Rule, exhibit at or near the top of the mast, where they can best be seen, two all-round lights in a vertical line, the upper being red and the lower green, but these lights shall not be exhibited in conjunction with the combined lantern permitted by paragraph (b) of this Rule.

(d) (i) A sailing vessel of less than 7 metres in length shall, if practicable, exhibit the lights prescribed in paragraph (a) or (b) of this Rule, but if she does not, she shall have ready at hand an electric torch or lighted lantern showing a white light which shall be exhibited in sufficient time to prevent collision.
   (ii) A vessel under oars may exhibit the lights prescribed in this Rule for sailing

vessels, but if she does not, she shall have ready at hand an electric torch or lighted lantern showing a white light which shall be exhibited in sufficient time to prevent collision.

(e) A vessel proceeding under sail when also being propelled by machinery shall exhibit forward where it can best be seen a conical shape, apex downwards.

Notes

1. *Rule 25(b), as revised, extends the length of sailing vessels which may show a tricolour light at or near the masthead from 12 metres to 20 metres.*

2. *A tricolour is highly visible for least battery drain. Yachts must however have additional side-lights (lower down) and a sternlight and masthead light for use when under power. See also Note 3 to Rule 23.*

Rule 26   Fishing vessels

(a) A vessel engaged in fishing, whether underway or at anchor, shall exhibit only the lights and shapes prescribed in this Rule.

(b) A vessel when engaged in trawling, by which is meant the dragging through the water of a dredge net or other apparatus used as a fishing appliance, shall exhibit:
  (i)   two all-round lights in a vertical line, the upper being green and the lower white, or a shape consisting of two cones with their apexes together in a vertical line one above the other;
  (ii)   a masthead light abaft of and higher than the all-round green light; a vessel of less than 50 metres in length shall not be obliged to exhibit such a light but may do so;
  (iii) when making way through the water, in addition to the lights prescribed in this paragraph, sidelights and a sternlight.

(c) A vessel engaged in fishing, other than trawling, shall exhibit:
  (i)   two all-round lights in a vertical line, the upper being red and the lower white, or a shape consisting of two cones with apexes together in a vertical line one above the other;
  (ii)   when there is outlying gear extending more than 150 metres horizontally from the vessel, an all-round white light or a cone apex upwards in the direction of the gear;
  (iii) when making way through the water,

in addition to the lights prescribed in this paragraph, sidelights and a sternlight.

(d) The additional signals described in Annex II to these Regulations apply to a vessel engaged in fishing in close proximity to other vessels engaged in fishing.

(e) A vessel when not engaged in fishing shall not exhibit the lights or shapes prescribed in this Rule, but only those prescribed for a vessel of her length.

Notes

1. *All vessels engaged in fishing show sidelights and sternlight when making way through the water, but not when stopped.*

2. *A fishing vessel may, in accordance with Rule 36, direct the beam of a searchlight in the direction of a danger.*

Rule 27   Vessels not under command or restricted in their ability to manoeuvre

(a) A vessel not under command shall exhibit:
  (i)   two all-round red lights in a vertical line where they can best be seen;
  (ii)   two balls or similar shapes in a vertical line where they can best be seen;
  (iii) when making way through the water, in addition to the lights prescribed in this paragraph, sidelights and a sternlight.

(b) A vessel restricted in her ability to manoeuvre, except a vessel engaged in mine clearance operations, shall exhibit:
  (i)   three all-round lights in a vertical line where they can best be seen. The highest and lowest of these lights shall be red and the middle light shall be white;
  (ii)   three shapes in a vertical line where they can best be seen. The highest and lowest of these shapes shall be balls and the middle one a diamond;
  (iii) when making way through the water, a mast head light or lights, sidelights and a sternlight, in addition to the lights prescribed in sub-paragraph (i);
  (iv)   when at anchor, in addition to the lights or shapes prescribed in sub-paragraphs (i) and (ii), the light, lights or shape prescribed in Rule 30.

(c) A power-driven vessel engaged in a towing operation such as severely restricts the towing vessel and her tow in their ability to deviate from their course shall, in addition to the lights or shapes prescribed in Rule 24(a), exhibit the lights or shapes prescribed in sub-paragraphs (b)(i) and (ii) of this Rule.

(d) A vessel engaged in dredging or underwater operations, when restricted in her ability to manoeuvre, shall exhibit the lights and shapes prescribed in sub-paragraphs (b)(i), (ii) and (iii) of this Rule and shall, in addition, when an obstruction exists, exhibit:
  (i) two all-round red lights or two balls in a vertical line to indicate the side on which the obstruction exists;
  (ii) two all-round green lights or two diamonds in a vertical line to indicate the side on which another vessel may pass;
  (iii) when at anchor, the lights or shapes prescribed in this paragraph instead of the lights or shape prescribed in Rule 30.

(e) Whenever the size of a vessel engaged in diving operations makes it impracticable to exhibit all lights and shapes prescribed in paragraph (d) of this Rule, the following shall be exhibited:
  (i) three all-round lights in a vertical line where they can best be seen. The highest and lowest of these lights shall be red and the middle light shall be white;
  (ii) a rigid replica of the International Code flag 'A' not less than 1 metre in height. Measures shall be taken to ensure its all-round visibility.

(f) A vessel engaged in mineclearance operations shall in addition to the lights prescribed for a power-driven vessel in Rule 23 or to the lights or shape prescribed for a vessel at anchor in Rule 30 as appropriate, exhibit three all-round green lights or three balls. One of these lights or shapes shall be exhibited near the foremast head and one at each end of the foreyard. These lights or shapes indicate that it is dangerous for another vessel to approach within 1000 metres of the mineclearance vessel.

(g) Vessels of less than 12 metres in length, except those engaged in diving operations, shall not be required to exhibit the lights and shapes prescribed in this Rule.

(h) The signals prescribed in this Rule are not signals of vessels in distress and requiring assistance. Such signals are contained in Annex IV to these Regulations.

Rule 28   Vessels constrained by their draught
A vessel constrained by her draught may, in addition to the lights prescribed for power-driven vessels in Rule 23, exhibit where they can best be seen three all-round red lights in a vertical line, or a cylinder.

Rule 29   Pilot vessels
(a) A vessel engaged on pilotage duty shall exhibit:
  (i) at or near the masthead, two all-round lights in a vertical line, the upper being white and the lower red;
  (ii) when underway, in addition, sidelights and a sternlight;
  (iii) when at anchor, in addition to the lights prescribed in sub-paragraph (i), the light, lights or shape prescribed in Rule 30 for vessels at anchor.

(b) A pilot vessel when not engaged on pilotage duty shall exhibit the lights or shapes prescribed for a similar vessel of her length.

Rule 30   Anchored vessels and vessels aground
(a) A vessel at anchor shall exhibit where it can best be seen:
  (i) in the fore part, an all-round white light or one ball;
  (ii) at or near the stern and at a lower level than the light prescribed in sub paragraph (i), an all-round white light.

(b) A vessel of less than 50 metres in length may exhibit an all-round white light where it can best be seen instead of the lights prescribed in paragraph (a) of this Rule.

(c) A vessel at anchor may, and a vessel of 100 metres and more in length shall, also use the available working or equivalent lights to illuminate her decks.

(d) A vessel aground shall exhibit the lights prescribed in paragraph (a) or (b) of this Rule and in addition, where they can best be seen:
  (i) two all-round red lights in a vertical line;
  (ii) three balls in a vertical line.

(e) A vessel of less than 7 metres in length, when at anchor not in or near a narrow channel, fairway or anchorage, or where other vessels normally navigate, shall not be required to exhibit the lights or shape prescribed in paragraphs (a) and (b) of this Rule.

(f) A vessel of less than 12 metres in length, when aground, shall not be required to exhibit the lights or shapes prescribed in sub-paragraphs (d)(i) and (ii) of this Rule.

Note

This Rule requires yachts to hoist anchor balls or show lights, the only exception (in certain circumstances) being for a boat of less than 7 metres in length (Rule 30(e)).

Rule 31   Seaplanes

Where it is impracticable for a seaplane to exhibit lights and shapes of the characteristics or in the positions prescribed in the Rules of this Part she shall exhibit lights and shapes as closely similar in characteristics and position as is possible.

PART D – SOUND AND LIGHT SIGNALS

Rule 32   Definitions

(a) The word 'whistle' means any sound signalling appliance capable of producing the prescribed blasts and which complies with the specifications in Annex III to these Regulations.

(b) The term 'short blast' means a blast of about one second's duration.

(c) The term 'prolonged blast' means a blast of from four to six second's duration.

Rule 33   Equipment for sound signals

(a) A vessel of 12 metres or more in length shall be provided with a whistle and a bell and a vessel of 100 metres or more in length shall, in addition, be provided with a gong, the tone and sound of which cannot be confused with that of the bell. The whistle, bell and gong shall comply with the specifications in Annex III to these Regulations. The bell or gong or both may be replaced by other equipment having the same respective sound characteristics, provided that manual sounding of the prescribed signals shall always be possible.

(b) A vessel of less than 12 metres in length shall not be obliged to carry the sound signalling appliances prescribed in paragraph (a) of this Rule but if she does not, she shall be provided with some other means of making an efficient sound signal.

Notes

1. *Rule 33(b) permits vessels less than 12 metres in length to carry alternative, efficient sound signals.*

2. *The effectiveness of a sound signal should be judged against its audibility from the bridge of a large ship, with conflicting noise from other sources. Some sound signals carried in yachts do not measure up to this standard.*

Rule 34   Manoeuvring and warning signals

(a) When vessels are in sight of one another, a power-driven vessel underway, when manoeuvring as authorized or required by these Rules, shall indicate that manoeuvre by the following signals on her whistle:
   - one short blast to mean 'I am altering my course to starboard';
   - two short blasts to mean 'I am altering my course to port';
   - three short blasts to mean 'I am operating astern propulsion'.

(b) Any vessel may supplement the whistle signals prescribed in paragraph (a) of this Rule by light signals, repeated as appropriate, whilst the manoeuvre is being carried out:
   (i)   these light signals shall have the following significance:
      - one flash to mean 'I am altering my course to starboard';
      - two flashes to mean 'I am altering my course to port';
      - three flashes to mean 'I am operating astern propulsion'.
   (ii) the duration of each flash shall be about one second, the interval between flashes shall be about one second, and the interval between successive signals shall be not less than ten seconds;
   (iii) the light used for this signal shall, if fitted, be an all-round white light, visible at a minimum range of 5 miles, and shall comply with the provision of Annex I to these Regulations.

(c) When in sight of one another in a narrow channel or fairway:
   (i)   a vessel intending to overtake another shall in compliance with Rule 9(e)(i) indicate her intention by the following signals on her whistle:
      - two prolonged blasts followed by one short blast to mean 'I intend to overtake you on your starboard side';
      - two prolonged blasts followed by

two short blasts to mean 'I intend to overtake you on your port side';

(ii) the vessel about to be overtaken when acting in accordance with Rule 9 (e)(i) shall indicate her agreement by the following signal on her whistle:
  - one prolonged, one short, one prolonged and one short blast, in that order.

(d) When vessels in sight of one another are approaching each other and from any cause either vessel fails to understand the intentions or actions of the other, or is in doubt whether sufficient action is being taken by the other to avoid collision, the vessel in doubt shall immediately indicate such doubt by giving at least five short and rapid blasts on the whistle. Such signal may be supplemented by a light signal of at least five short and rapid flashes.

(e) A vessel nearing a bend or an area of a channel or fairway where other vessels may be obscured by an intervening obstruction shall sound one prolonged blast. Such signal shall be answered with a prolonged blast by any approaching vessel that may be within hearing around the bend or behind the intervening obstruction.

(f) If whistles are fitted on a vessel at a distance apart of more than 100 metres, one whistle only shall be used for giving manoeuvring and warning signals.

Note
Rule 34(a), 3 short blasts means 'I am operating astern propulsion', but the vessel itself may not be going astern. A large ship takes some time to lose her way, even with the engines running astern.

Rule 35   Sound signals in restricted visibility
In or near an area of restricted visibility, whether by day or night, the signals prescribed in this Rule shall be used as follows:

(a) A power-driven vessel making way through the water shall sound at intervals of not more than 2 minutes one prolonged blast.

(b) A power-driven vessel underway but stopped and making no way through the water shall sound at intervals of not more than 2 minutes two prolonged blasts in succession with an interval of about 2 seconds between them.

(c) A vessel not under command, a vessel restricted in her ability to manoeuvre, a vessel constrained by her draught, a sailing vessel, a vessel engaged in fishing and a vessel engaged in towing or pushing another vessel shall, instead of the signals prescribed in paragraphs (a) or (b) of this Rule, sound at intervals of not more than 2 minutes three blasts in succession, namely one prolonged followed by two short blasts.

(d) A vessel engaged in fishing, when at anchor, and a vessel restricted in her ability to manoeuvre when carrying out her work at anchor, shall instead of the signals prescribed in paragraph (g) of this Rule sound the signal prescribed in paragraph (c) of this Rule.

(e) A vessel towed or if more than one vessel is towed the last vessel of the tow, if manned, shall at intervals of not more than 2 minutes sound four blasts in succession, namely one prolonged followed by three short blasts. When practicable, this signal shall be made immediately after the signal made by the towing vessel.

(f) When a pushing vessel and a vessel being pushed ahead are rigidly connected in a composite unit they shall be regarded as a power-driven vessel and shall give the signals prescribed in paragraphs (a) or (b) of this Rule.

(g) A vessel at anchor shall at intervals of not more than one minute ring the bell rapidly for about 5 seconds. In a vessel of 100 metres or more in length the bell shall be sounded in the forepart of the vessel and immediately after the ringing of the bell the gong shall be sounded rapidly for about 5 seconds in the after part of the vessel. A vessel at anchor may in addition sound three blasts in succession, namely one short, one prolonged and one short blast, to give warning of her position and of the possibility of collision to an approaching vessel.

(h) A vessel aground shall give the bell signal and if required the gong signal prescribed in paragraph (g) of this Rule and shall, in addition, give three separate and distinct strokes of the bell immediately before and after the rapid ringing of the bell. A vessel aground may in addition sound an appropriate whistle signal.

(i) A vessel of less than 12 metres in length shall not be obliged to give the above-mentioned signals but, if she does not, shall make some other efficient sound signal at intervals of not more than 2 minutes.

(ii) A pilot vessel when engaged on pilotage duty may in addition to the signals prescribed in paragraphs (a), (b) or (g) of this Rule sound an identity signal consisting of four short blasts.

Notes

1. A sailing vessel underway sounds one prolonged blast, followed by two short (−·· = 'D').
2. Sound signals are made when a vessel is near (not necessarily in) an area of restricted visibility.
3. The maximum interval between all whistle or foghorn signals is two minutes; they should be sounded more frequently if other craft are near.

Rule 36   Signals to attract attention

If necessary to attract the attention of another vessel any vessel may make light or sound signals that cannot be mistaken for any signal authorized elsewhere in these Rules, or may direct the beam of her searchlight in the direction of the danger, in such a way as not to embarrass any vessel. Any light to attract the attention of another vessel shall be such that it cannot be mistaken for any aid to navigation. For the purpose of this Rule the use of high intensity intermittent or revolving lights, such as strobe lights, shall be avoided.

Notes

1. A torch is rarely bright enough to attract attention. A small searchlight or high intensity Aldis-type lamp, shone in the general direction of an approaching vessel, or used to send five short and rapid flashes, Rule 34 (d), advertises a yacht's presence far more effectively. A white hand flare may be effective in the last resort.
2. Do not use any signal which may be mistaken for one elsewhere in the Rules, particularly distress signals. (See Rule 37 and Annex IV).
3. Strobe lights, which can be confused with a North cardinal buoy, must not be used.

Rule 37   Distress signals

When a vessel is in distress and requires assistance she shall use or exhibit the signals described in Annex IV to these Regulations.

Notes

1. Some of the authorised distress signals are more relevant to yachts than others. These are indicated in the notes to Annex IV and are also covered in more detail in Chapter 13.

2. A distress signal must only be used when a vessel is in grave and imminent danger, and requires immediate assistance.

PART E   EXEMPTIONS

Rule 38   Exemptions (a summary)

Any vessel (or class of vessels) provided that she complies with the requirements of the International Regulations for Preventing Collisions at Sea, 1960, the keel of which is laid or which is at a corresponding stage of construction before the entry into force of these Regulations may be exempted from compliance therewith as follows:

(c) The repositioning of lights as a result of conversion from Imperial to metric units and rounding off measurement figures, permanent exemption.

(d) (i) The repositioning of masthead lights on vessels of less than 150 metres in length, resulting from the prescriptions of Section 3(a) of Annex I to these Regulations, permanent exemption.

(h) The repositioning of all-round lights resulting from the prescription of Section 9(b) of Annex I to these Regulations, permanent exemption.

Notes

1. Only exemptions (c), (d)(i) and (h) above are still valid.
2. Most of the original exemptions granted for implementing changes to lights etc were for periods of four or nine years from 15 July 1977 when these Regulations came into force. They are omitted here, as time expired.

ANNEX I
POSITIONING AND TECHNICAL DETAILS OF LIGHTS AND SHAPES

1.   Definition

The term 'height above the hull' means height above the uppermost continuous deck. This height shall be measured from the position vertically beneath the location of the light.

2.   Vertical positioning and spacing of lights

(a) On a power-driven vessel of 20 metres or more in length the masthead lights shall be placed as follows:

(i) the forward masthead light, or if only one masthead light is carried, then that light, at a height above the hull of not less than 6 metres and, if the breadth of the vessel exceeds 6 metres, then at a height above the hull not less than such breadth, so however that the light need not be placed at a greater height above the hull than 12 metres;

(ii) when two masthead lights are carried the after one shall be at least 4.5 metres vertically higher than the forward one.

(b) The vertical separation of masthead lights of power-driven vessels shall be such that in all normal conditions of trim the after light will be seen over and separate from the forward light at a distance of 1000 metres from the stem when viewed from sea level.

(c) The masthead light of a power-driven vessel of 12 metres but less than 20 metres in length shall be placed at a height above the gunwale of not less than 2.5 metres.

(d) A power-driven vessel of less than 12 metres in length may carry the uppermost light at a height of less than 2.5 metres above the gunwhale. When however a masthead light is carried in addition to sidelights and a sternlight or the all-round light prescribed in Rule 23(c) (i) is carried in addition to sidelights, then such masthead light or all-round light shall be carried at least 1 metre higher than the sidelights.

(e) One of the two or three masthead lights prescribed for a power-driven vessel when engaged in towing or pushing another vessel shall be placed in the same position as either the forward masthead light or the after masthead light; provided that, if carried on the aftermast, the lowest after masthead light shall be at least 4.5 metres vertically higher than the forward masthead light.

(f) (i) The masthead light or lights prescribed in Rule 23(a) shall be so placed as to be above and clear of all other lights and obstructions except as described in sub-paragraph (ii).

(ii) When it is impracticable to carry the all-round lights prescribed by Rule 27(b)(i) or Rule 28 below the mast-head lights, they may be carried above the after masthead light(s) or vertically in between the forward masthead light(s) and after masthead light(s), provided that in the latter case the requirement of Section 3(c) of this Annex shall be complied with.

(g) The sidelights of a power-driven vessel shall be placed at a height above the hull not greater than three-quarters of that of the forward masthead light. They shall not be so low as to be interfered with by deck lights.

(h) The sidelights, if in a combined lantern and carried on a power-driven vessel of less than 20 metres in length, shall be placed not less than 1 metre below the masthead light.

(i) When the Rules prescribe two or three lights to be carried in a vertical line, they shall be spaced as follows:

(i) on a vessel of 20 metres in length or more such lights shall be spaced not less than 2 metres apart, and the lowest of these lights shall, except where a towing light is required, be placed at a height of not less than 4 metres above the hull;

(ii) on a vessel of less than 20 metres in length such lights shall be spaced not less than 1 metre apart and the lowest of these lights shall, except where a towing light is required, be placed at a height of not less than 2 metres above the gunwhale.

(iii) when three lights are carried they shall be equally spaced.

(j) The lower of the two all-round lights prescribed for a vessel when engaged in fishing shall be at a height above the sidelights not less than twice the distance between the two vertical lights.

(k) The forward anchor light prescribed in Rule 30(a)(i), when two are carried, shall not be less than 4.5 metres above the after one. On a vessel of 50 metres or more in length this forward anchor light shall be placed at a height of not less than 6 metres above the hull.

3. Horizontal positioning and spacing of lights

(a) When two masthead lights are prescribed for a power-driven vessel, the horizontal distance between them shall not be less than one half of the length of the vessel but need not be more than 100 metres. The forward light shall be placed not more than one quarter of the length of the vessel from the stem.

(b) On a power-driven vessel of 20 metres or more in length the sidelights shall not be placed in front of the forward masthead lights. They shall be placed at or near the side of the vessel.

(c) When the lights prescribed in Rule 27(b)(i) or Rule 28 are placed vertically between the forward masthead light(s) and the after masthead light(s) these all-round lights shall be placed at a horizontal distance of not less than 2 metres from the fore and aft centreline of the vessel in the athwartship direction.

(d) When only one masthead light is prescribed for a power-driven vessel, this light shall be exhibited forward of amidships; except that a vessel of less then 20 metres in length need not exhibit this light forward of amidships, but shall exhibit it as far forward as is practicable.

4. Details of location of direction indicating lights for fishing vessels, dredgers and vessels engaged in underwater operations

(a) The light indicating the direction of the outlying gear from a vessel engaged in fishing as prescribed in Rule 26(c)(ii) shall be placed at a horizontal distance of not less than 2 metres and not more than 6 metres away from the two all-round red and white lights. This light shall be placed not higher than the all-round white light prescribed in Rule 26(c)(i) and not lower than the sidelights.

(b) The lights and shapes on a vessel engaged in dredging or underwater operations to indicate the obstructed side and/or the side on which it is safe to pass, as prescribed in Rule 27(d)(i) and (ii), shall be placed at the maximum practical horizontal distance, but in no case less than 2 metres from the lights or shapes prescribed in Rule 27(b)(i) and (ii). In no case shall the upper of these lights or shapes be at a greater height than the lower of the three lights or shapes prescribed in Rule 27(b)(i) and (ii).

5. Screens for sidelights

The sidelights of vessels of 20 metres or more in length shall be fitted with inboard screens painted matt black, and meeting the requirements of Section 9 of this Annex. On vessels of less than 20 metres in length, the sidelights, if necessary to meet the requirements of Section 9 of this Annex, shall be fitted with inboard matt black screens. With a combined lantern, using a single vertical filament and a very narrow division between the green and red sections, external screens need not be fitted.

6. Shapes

(a) Shapes shall be black and of the following sizes:

   (i) a ball shall have a diameter of not less than 0.6 metre;

   (ii) a cone shall have a base diameter of not less than 0.6 metre and a height equal to its diameter;

   (iii) a cylinder shall have a diameter of at least 0.6 metre and a height of twice its diameter;

   (iv) a diamond shape shall consist of two cones as defined in (ii) above having a common base.

(b) The vertical distance between shapes shall be at least 1.5 metres.

(c) In a vessel of less than 20 metres in length shapes of lesser dimensions but commensurate with the size of the vessel may be used and the distance apart may be correspondingly reduced.

7. Colour specification of lights

The chromaticity of all navigation lights shall conform to the following standards, which lie within the boundaries of the area of the diagram specified for each colour by the International Commission on Illumination (CIE). The boundaries of the area for each colour are given by indicating the corner co-ordinates, which are as follows:

   (i) White
   x 0.525 0.525 0.452 0.310 0.310 0.443
   y 0.382 0.440 0.440 0.348 0.283 0.382

   (ii) Green
   x 0.028 0.009 0.300 0.203
   y 0.385 0.723 0.511 0.356

   (iii) Red
   x 0.680 0.660 0.735 0.721
   y 0.320 0.320 0.265 0.259

   (iv) Yellow
   x 0.612 0.618 0.575 0.575
   y 0.382 0.382 0.425 0.406

8. Intensity of lights

(a) The minimum luminous intensity of lights shall be calculated by using the formula:

$$I = 3.43 \times 10^6 \times T \times D^2 \times K^{-D}$$

where I is luminous intensity in candelas under service conditions,

   T is threshold factor 2×10^{-7} lux,
   D is range of visibility (luminous range) of the light in nautical miles,
   K is atmospheric transmissivity.

For prescribed lights the value of K shall be 0.8, corresponding to a meteorological visibility of approximately 13 nautical miles.

(b) A selection of figures derived from the formula is given in the following table:

Range of visibility (luminous range) of light in nautical miles D	Luminous intensity of light in candelas for K = 0.8 I
1	0.9
2	4.3
3	12
4	27
5	52
6	94

Note: The maximum luminous intensity of navigation lights should be limited to avoid undue glare. This shall not be achieved by a variable control of the luminous intensity.

9. Horizontal sectors

(a) (i) In the forward direction, sidelights as fitted on the vessel shall show the minimum required intensities. The intensities shall decrease to reach practical cut-off between 1° and 3° outside the prescribed sectors.

(ii) For sternlights and masthead lights and at 22½° abaft the beam for sidelights, the minimum required intensities shall be maintained over the arc of the horizon up to 5° within the limits of the sectors prescribed in Rule 21. From 5° within the prescribed sectors the intensity may decrease by 50 per cent up to the prescribed limits; it shall decrease steadily to reach practical cut-off at not more than 5° outside the prescribed sectors.

(b) (i) All-round lights shall be so located as not to be obscured by masts, topmasts or structures within angular sectors of more than 6°, except anchor lights prescribed in Rule 30, which need not be placed at an impracticable height above the hull.

(ii) If it is impracticable to comply with paragraph (b) (i) of this section by exhibiting only one all-round light, two all-round lights shall be used suitably positioned or screened so that they appear, as far as practicable, as one light at a distance of one mile.

10. Vertical sectors

(a) The vertical sectors of electric lights as fitted, with the exception of lights on sailing vessels underway, shall ensure that:
(i) at least the required minimum intensity is maintained at all angles from 5° above to 5° below the horizontal;

(ii) at least 60 per cent of the required minimum intensity is maintained from 75° above to 75° below the horizontal.

(b) In the case of sailing vessels underway the vertical sectors of electric lights as fitted shall ensure that:
(i) at least the required minimum intensity is maintained at all angles from 5° above to 5° below the horizontal;
(ii) at least 50 per cent of the required minimum intensity is maintained from 25° above to 25° below the horizontal.

(c) In the case of lights other than electric these specifications shall be met as closely as possible.

11. Intensity of non-electric lights

Non-electric lights shall so far as practicable comply with the minimum intensities, as specified in the Table given in Section 8 of this Annex.

12. Manoeuvring light

Notwithstanding the provisions of paragraph 2(f) of this Annex the manoeuvring light described in Rule 34(b) shall be placed in the same fore and aft vertical plane as the masthead light or lights and, where practicable, at a minimum height of 2 metres vertically above the forward masthead light, provided that it shall be carried not less than 2 metres vertically above or below the after masthead light. On a vessel where only one masthead light is carried the manoeuvring light, if fitted, shall be carried where it can best be seen, not less than 2 metres vertically apart from the masthead light.

13. High-speed craft

The masthead light of high-speed craft with a length to breadth ratio of less than 3·0 may be placed at a height related to the breadth of the craft lower than that prescribed in paragraph 2 (a) (i) of this Annex, provided that the base angle of the isosceles triangles formed by the sidelights and the masthead light, when seen in end elevation, is not less than 27°.

14. Approval

The construction of lights and shapes and the installation of lights on board the vessel shall be to the satisfaction of the appropriate authority of the State whose flag the vessel is entitled to fly.

ANNEX II
ADDITIONAL SIGNALS FOR FISHING VESSELS FISHING IN CLOSE PROXIMITY

1. General
The lights mentioned herein shall, if exhibited in pursuance of Rule 26(d), be placed where they can best be seen. They shall be at least 0.9 metre apart but at a lower level than lights prescribed in Rule 26(b)(i) and (c)(i). The lights shall be visible all round the horizon at a distance of at least 1 mile but at a lesser distance than the lights prescribed by these Rules for fishing vessels.

2. Signals for trawlers
(a) Vessels of 20 metres or more in length when engaged in trawling, whether using demersal or pelagic gear, shall exhibit:
  (i) when shooting their nets: two white lights in a vertical line;
  (ii) when hauling their nets: one white light over one red light in a vertical line;
  (iii) when the net has come fast upon an obstruction: two red lights in a vertical line.
(b) Each vessel of 20 metres or more in length engaged in pair trawling shall exhibit:
  (i) by night, a searchlight directed forward and in the direction of the other vessel of the pair;
  (ii) when shooting or hauling their nets or when their nets have come fast upon an obstruction, the lights prescribed in 2(a) above.
  (c) A vessel of less than 20 metres in length engaged in trawling, whether using demersal or pelagic gear or engaged in pair trawling, may exhibit the lights prescribed in paragraphs (a) or (b) of this section, as appropriate.

3. Signals for purse seiners
Vessels engaged in fishing with purse seine gear may exhibit two yellow lights in a vertical line. These lights shall flash alternately every second and with equal light and occultation duration. These lights may be exhibited only when the vessel is hampered by its fishing gear.

ANNEX III
TECHNICAL DETAILS OF SOUND SIGNAL APPLIANCES

1. Whistles
(a) Frequencies and range of audibility
The fundamental frequency of the signal shall lie within the range 70-700Hz.

The range of audibility of the signal from a whistle shall be determined by those frequencies, which may include the fundamental and/or one or more higher frequencies, which lie within the range 180 – 700Hz (± 1 per cent) and which provide the sound pressure levels specified in paragraph 1(c) below.

(b) Limits of fundamental frequencies
To ensure a wide variety of whistle characteristics, the fundamental frequency of a whistle shall be between the following limits:
  (i) 70-200Hz, for a vessel 200 metres or more in length;
  (ii) 130-350Hz, for a vessel 75 metres but less than 200 metres in length
  (iii) 250-700Hz, for a vessel less than 75 metres in length.

(c) Sound signal intensity and range of audibility
A whistle fitted in a vessel shall provide, in the direction of maximum intensity of the whistle and at a distance of 1 metre from it, a sound pressure level in at least one 1/3rd-octave band within the range of frequencies 180 – 700Hz (± 1 per cent) of not less than the appropriate figure given in the table below.

Length of vessel in metres	1/3rd-octave band level at 1 metre in dB referred to 2×10^{-5} N/m^2	Audibility range in nautical miles
200 or more	143	2
75 but less than 200	138	1.5
20 but less than 75	130	1
Less than 20	120	0.5

The range of audibility in the table above is for information and is approximately the range at which a whistle may be heard on its forward axis with 90 per cent probability in conditions of still air on board a vessel having average background noise level at the listening posts (taken to be 68dB in the octave band centred on 250Hz and 63dB in the octave band centred on 500Hz).

In practice the range at which a whistle may be heard is extremely variable and depends critically on weather conditions; the values given can be regarded as typical but under conditions of strong wind or high ambient noise level at the listening post the range may be much reduced.

(d) Directional properties
The sound pressure level of a directional whistle shall be not more than 4dB below the prescribed sound pressure level on the axis at any direction in the horizontal plane within ± 45° of the axis. The sound pressure level at any other direction in the horizontal plane shall be not more than 10dB below the prescribed sound pressure level on the axis, so that the range in any direction will be at least half the range on the forward axis. The sound pressure level shall be measured in that 1/3rd octave band which determines the audibility range.

(e) Positioning of whistles
When a directional whistle is to be used as the only whistle on a vessel, it shall be installed with its maximum intensity directed straight ahead.

A whistle shall be placed as high as practicable on a vessel, in order to reduce interception of the emitted sound by obstructions and also to minimise hearing damage risk to personnel. The sound pressure level of the vessel's own signal at listening posts shall not exceed 110dB (A) and so far as practicable should not exceed 100dB (A).

(f) Fitting of more than one whistle
If whistles are fitted at a distance apart of more than 100 metres, it shall be so arranged that they are not sounded simultaneously.

(g) Combined whistle systems
If due to the presence of obstructions the sound field of a single whistle or of one of the whistles referred to in paragraph 1(f) above is likely to have a zone of greatly reduced signal level, it is recommended that a combined whistle system be fitted so as to overcome this reduction. For the purposes of the Rules a combined whistle system is to be regarded as a single whistle. The whistles of a combined system shall be located at a distance apart of not more than 100 metres and arranged to be sounded simultaneously. The frequency of any one whistle shall differ from those of the others by at least 10Hz.

2. Bell or gong
(a) Intensity of signal
A bell or gong, or other device having similar sound characteristics shall produce a sound pressure level of not less than 110dB at a distance of 1 metre from it.

(b) Construction
Bells and gongs shall be made of corrosion-resistant material and designed to give a clear tone. The diameter of the mouth of the bell shall be not less than 300mm for vessels of 20 metres or more in length, and shall be not less than 200mm for vessels of 12 metres or more but of less than 20 metres in length. Where practicable, a power-driven bell striker is recommended to ensure constant force but manual operation shall be possible. The mass of the striker shall be not less than 3 per cent of the mass of the bell.

3. Approval
The construction of sound signal appliances, their performance and their installation on board the vessel shall be to the satisfaction of the appropriate authority of the State whose flag the vessel is entitled to fly.

ANNEX IV
DISTRESS SIGNALS

1. The following signals, used or exhibited either together or separately, indicate distress and need of assistance:
(a) a gun or other explosive signal fired at intervals of about a minute;
(b) a continuous sounding with any fog-signalling apparatus;
(c) rockets or shells, throwing red stars fired one at a time at short intervals;
(d) a signal made by radiotelegraphy or by any other signalling method consisting of the group ··· ––– ···(SOS) in the Morse code;
(e) a signal sent by radiotelephony consisting of the spoken word 'Mayday';
(f) the International Code Signal of distress indicated by N.C.;
(g) a signal consisting of a square flag having above or below it a ball or anything resembling a ball;
(h) flames on the vessel (as from a burning tar barrel, oil barrel, etc);
(i) a rocket parachute flare or a hand flare showing a red light;
(j) a smoke signal giving off orange-coloured smoke;
(k) slowly and repeatedly raising and lowering arms outstretched to each side;
(l) the radiotelegraph alarm signal;
(m) the radiotelephone alarm signal;
(n) signals transmitted by emergency position indicating radio beacons;
(o) approved signals transmitted by radiocommunication systems, including survival craft radar transponders;

2. The use or exhibition of any of the foregoing signals except for the purpose of

indicating distress and need of assistance and the use of other signals which may be confused with any of the above signals is prohibited.

3. Attention is drawn to the relevant sections of the International Code of Signals, the Merchant Ship Search and Rescue Manual and the following signals:
(a) a piece of orange-coloured canvas with either a black square and circle or other appropriate symbol (for identification from the air);
(b) a dye marker.

Notes

1. *A distress signal must only be made when a vessel is in grave and imminent danger, and immediate help is required.*
2. *Of the distress signals listed in paragraph 1, the following are most relevant to yachts and small craft: (b), (d), (e), (f), (g), (i), (j) and (k). Their use is more fully described in Chapter 13 'Safety'.*
3. *The radiotelegraph alarm signal (l) is twelve four-second dashes per minute sent at one second intervals.*
4. *The radiotelephone alarm signal (m) is alternate tones of 1300Hz and 2200Hz transmitted on 2182kHz for a period of 30 to 60 seconds.*

5. *The EPIRB signal (n) is either as in 4. above, or a series of single tones at a frequency of 1300Hz.*
6. *The DSC distress alerts are sent on VHF Ch 70, MF 2187·5kHz and on selected HF frequencies. They can also be sent via satellite with either absolute priority on general communications channels or on exclusive distress/safety channels.*

4.2 BOOKS ABOUT THE RULES OF THE ROAD

1972 ColRegs, obtainable from TSO.

Learning the Rule of the Road by Basil Mosenthal (Adlard Coles).

A Yachtsman's Guide to the Collision Rules by John Campbell (Waterline).

International Collision Regulations RYA/G2.

A Seaman's guide to the Rule of the Road (Morgan Technical Books).

A Small boat guide to the Rules of the Road by John Mellor (Fernhurst).

A Guide to the Collision avoidance Rules by Cockroft & Lameijer (Reed Books).

Seaway Code by James Stevens (RYA/TSO, 2001).

Boat Owner's Highway Code (Practical Boat Owner)

Collision Prevention Regulations (CD-ROM, PC Maritime).

Chapter 5 General Information

CONTENTS

5.1 LIMITS, VESSELS AND HAZARDS

Although we talk about the 'freedom of the sea', yachtsmen should be aware that various limits and restrictions are imposed by international agreements or by national decrees. These brief notes give limited legal treatment of such matters: international waters and fishing limits are complex subjects and liable to international dispute.

5.1.1 TERRITORIAL WATERS

The United Nations Convention on the Law of the Sea (UNCLOS) of 16 Nov 1994 gives detailed guidance on maritime zones, the jurisdiction which States may exercise and the right to freedom of navigation.

Countries may exercise sovereignty over the territorial sea along their coasts, but the breadth varies as does the method of measurement.

In general (as in the UK) the baseline is the low water line along the coasts of the mainland[1] and islands. Deep bays may be closed by a line up to 24 miles (38km) in length across the entrance, or at a point where the bay narrows to that distance. Coasts which are deeply indented or with a fringe of islands, such as Scotland's west coast, may have a system of straight baselines.

Waters on the landward side of baselines are internal waters (the territorial sea) over which

Country	Territorial waters	Fishing jurisdiction
Antigua/Barbuda, Argentina[1], Australia[1], Bahamas, Bangladesh, Barbados, Belgium, Belize[1], Bermuda, Brazil[1], Brunei, Bulgaria, Cambodia[1], Canada[1], Cape Verde Islands, Cayman Islands, Chile[1], Colombia[1], Comoros, Congo (Dem Rep, ex-Zaire), Cook Islands, Costa Rica, Cuba[1], Denmark[1], Djibouti[1], Dominica, Egypt[1], Equatorial Guinea, Estonia, Falkland Islands[1], Fiji, Gabon, Gambia, Georgia, Germany[1], Ghana, Grenada, Guatemala, Guinea, Guinea Bissau[1], Guyana, Haiti, Honduras, Iceland[1], India, Indonesia, Iran[1], Irish Republic[1], Ivory Coast, Jamaica, Japan[1], Kenya[1], Kiribati, Korea(North), Korea (South)[1], Latvia, Lithuania, Madagascar[1], Malaysia[1], Maldives, Marshall Is, Mauritania[1], Mauritius[1], Mexico[1], Micronesia, Morocco[1], Mozambique[1], Myanmar[1] (ex-Burma), Namibia, Nauru, Netherlands[1], Netherlands Antilles, New Zealand, Nigeria, Oman[1], Pakistan[1], Papua New Guinea, Philippines, Poland, Portugal[1], Romania[1], Russia[1], St Helena, St Kitts/Nevis, St Lucia, St Vincent & Grenadines, Sao Tome, Senegal[1], Seychelles, Solomon Islands, South Africa[1], Spain[1], Sri Lanka, Surinam, Sweden[1], Taiwan[1], Tanzania, Thailand[1], Tonga, Trinida & Tobago, Turks & Caicos[1], Tuvalu, Ukraine[1], UAE[1], United Kingdom[1], USA, Vanuatu, Venezuela[1], Vietnam[1], Western Samoa, Yemen.	12	200

Exceptions to the 12/200 miles limits

Country	Territorial waters	Fishing jurisdiction
Cyprus (Sovereign Base), Gibraltar, Jordan, Singapore.	3	3
Anguilla, British Virgin Islands, Faeroe Islands[1], Greenland[1], Montserrat, Palau (Belau), Pitcairn.	3	200
Norway[1]	4	200
Greece	6	6
Dominican Republic[1]	6	200
Bahrein, China PRC, Croatia[1], Eritrea[1], Iraq, Israel, Kuwait, Lebanon, Quatar, Saudi Arabia[1], Slovenia, Sudan.	12	–
Albania[1], Cyprus, Finland[1], France[1], Isle of Man, Italy[1], Monaco, Tunisia[1], Turkey[1], Yugoslavia[1].	12	12
Libya	12	20
Malta[1]	12	25
Algeria[1]	12	53
Angola	20	200
Togo	30	200
Syria	35	–
Cameroon	50	–
Benin, Congo (Rep), Ecuador[1], El Salvador, Liberia, Nicaragua, Panama, Peru, Sierra Leone, Somalia, Uruguay.	200	200

Note: [1]Uses straight baseline systems along all or part of the coast.

Fig. 5(1) The breadth of sea, in nautical miles, claimed for territorial waters and for fishing jurisdiction.

the country concerned has sovereignty. In the territorial sea foreign vessels have the right of innocent passage but must obey the laws and regulations of the state concerned. Innocent passage does not allow anchoring except where necessary for ordinary navigation or due to force majeure or distress.

Fig. 5(1) below shows the breadth of sea claimed by various countries as territorial waters and as fishing limits (see 5.1.2 below). The vast majority of States claim 12 miles territorial waters and 200 miles fishing limits; the UK does not recognise claims in excess of these limits. More detailed information is published annually in Notice to Mariners No 12.

5.1.2   FISHING LIMITS
Most States control fishing for 200 miles (322km) from the baselines referred to in 5.1.1. The UK (like other European countries) exercises fisheries jurisdiction to 200 miles from territorial sea baselines, or to a median line with other countries where that line is less than 200 miles. The UK claims exclusive fishing rights for six miles, with jurisdiction over a further six-mile zone in which other countries with established traditional rights may fish.

5.1.3   FISHING VESSELS
Yachtsmen should remember that, whether under sail or power, a yacht must keep clear of a vessel trawling or fishing. Such vessels should show the shapes or lights as in Rule 26 of the Collision Regulations (see Chapter 4). Fishing boats are often very insistent on their rights and it is best to give them a wide berth from an early stage.

Particular concentrations of fishing vessels around the coasts of Britain are likely to be met as outlined below. Keep a good look-out, and remember that drift nets may extend a mile or more, usually to windward of the fishing boat.

1. *England – South Coast.* Single and pair trawlers may be met from the Isles of Scilly to Start Point, generally within 12 miles (19km) of the coast, from September to March. Hand-line boats fish in this area throughout the year. Pots and nets are placed in areas all along the south coast, sometimes 15 miles (24km) offshore. Oyster dredgers operate in the Western Solent.
2. *England East Coast.* Fixed fishing gear is often met up to 12 miles (19km) offshore, from north Norfolk to the Scottish border.

3. *England North-east Coast*. Concentrations of vessels fishing for sprats may be met from October to March, up to 75 miles (120km) offshore between 53° 00' N (The Wash) and 55° 30' N (Craster). Small fishing boats with salmon drift nets may be concentrated from April to August up to 6 miles (10km) offshore between Whitby and Holy Island; the small floats are hard to see.

4. *England North-west Coast*. Concentrations of fishing boats, mostly single and pair trawlers, may be met during August and September within 12 miles (19km) of land between Chicken Rock (south tip of Isle of Man) and Douglas. Trawlers may be concentrated up to 25 miles (40km) west of Morecambe light-buoy in April/May and from mid-August to October.

5. *Scotland*. Concentrations of vessels fishing for mackerel and herring may be met June-December in the Minches and Firth of Clyde, and outside the Hebrides.

5.1.4 FISHING METHODS

Knowing how the professional fisherman goes about his business and the gear he uses is likely to help the yachtsman to keep clear of fishing boats and their equipment – to mutual benefit. Starting with the simplest of methods and moving on to large deep-sea fishing vessels with complex gear:

a. **Handlining and jigging**. A small, stationary, but not necessarily anchored, fishing boat is used, in inshore waters. Handlining is done with a weighted line and baited hook; jigging uses lure-like hooks attached to a line which is pulled or 'jigged' by hand or mechanically; see Fig. 5(2).

b. **Longlining**. A longline with baited hooks about 1m apart is anchored at both ends on the seabed and marked by buoys. A line may be up to 10 miles long with 50,000 hooks. The line is shot over the stern and recovered (hauled) over the bow of the fishing vessel. Longlining is used to catch ground-feeding fish in depths up to 180m; see Fig. 5(3).

c. **Pots** are used to catch shellfish, especially crab and lobster. They are made of wood, metal or plastic, covered with netting, in various sizes and shapes. They are set in lines of 10 to 60 pots, depending on the vessel's capacity, usually in rocky coastal areas, but also offshore. 100 pots on a line would be about 2M long. The lines are marked by floats. Pots are shot and hauled over the side; see Fig. 5(4).

d. **Gillnetting** is versatile in terms of the variety of fish caught. Nets may be anchored to the seabed or left to drift. A single net is about 100m long and may be joined to others to make lengths of several miles. If anchored they are marked by dan buoys and the net itself is held vertically above the seabed by underwater floats. They are shot over the stern and hauled over the bow.

Drift nets are about 35m long by 15m deep. They are suspended below the surface at the appropriate depth by lines supported by floats; up to 100 nets can be joined together. They are shot downwind and the drifter lies to the nets for 3 or 4 hours, before hauling them and shaking out the fish; see Fig. 5(5).

Fig. 5(2) Handlining and jigging

e. **Seine netting** is used to encircle fish on or just above the seabed. Depending on the depth of water the net used is between 250 and 900m long, with a towing warp attached at one end to an anchored dan-buoy and at the other to the vessel. The vessel circles the hoped-for shoal of fish and then hauls the net by recovering both ends, thus entrapping fish; see Fig. 5(6).

f. **Purse seining** uses a similar encircling process, but in addition a wire threaded through the bottom edge of the netting is pulled taut to close off the bottom of the net. The catch is hauled aboard and fish are pumped into tanks. The net may be 160m deep and enclose a circle with a diameter of 5 cables; see Fig. 5(7).

g. **Trawling** comes in various forms: One or two trawlers may be used, a pair being up to 3 cables apart towing a trawl extending up to 7 cables astern. The trawl may be towed along the seabed, in mid-water or very close to the surface. Otter trawling uses a cone-shaped net whose mouth is held open by water pressure on two otterboards each side. Trawling speed is 2-3kn for a seabed tow and 3-4kn for mid-water; see Fig. 5(8).

Stern trawling, the commonest form, uses a single net towed astern on the seabed or in mid-water, and held open by otterboards. It can be operated in most weather, but the stern trawler is less easy to manoeuvre; see Fig. 5(9).

Beam trawling uses nets held open by a steel beam 4 to 14m long and towed from derricks either side. When the derricks are horizontal, the beam is being towed on the seabed; when raised to 45°, the nets are alongside the trawler. Trawling speed is 2-6kn; see Fig. 5(10).

5.1.5 FISHING PORT REGISTRATION LETTERS

a. **United Kingdom**

A	Aberdeen
AB	Aberystwyth
AH	Arbroath
AR	Ayr
B	Belfast
BA	Ballantrae
BCK	Buckie
BD	Bideford
BF	Banff
BH	Blyth
BK	Berwick on Tweed
BM	Brixham
BN	Boston
BRD	Broadford
BS	Beaumaris
CA	Cardigan
CE	Coleraine

Fig. 5(3) Long lining

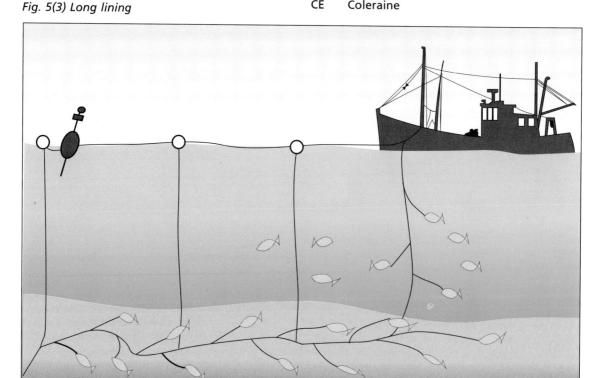

Fig. 5(4) Potting

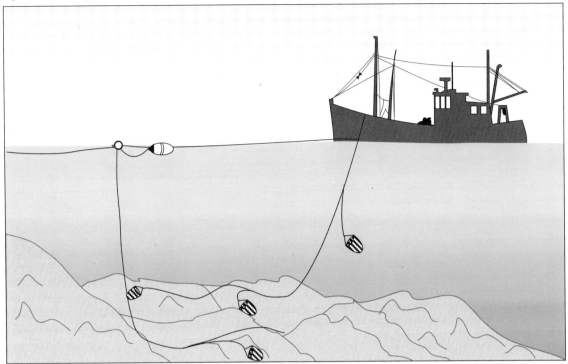

Fig. 5(5) Gillnetting

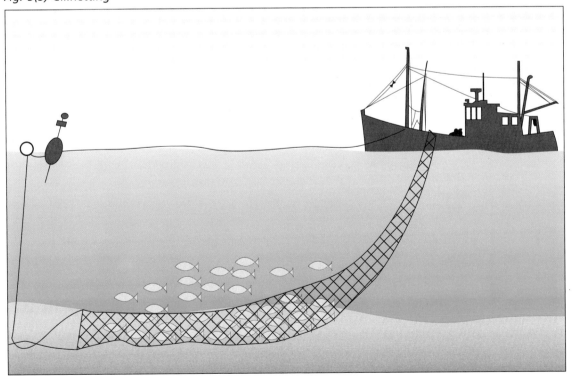

Fig. 5(6) Seine netting

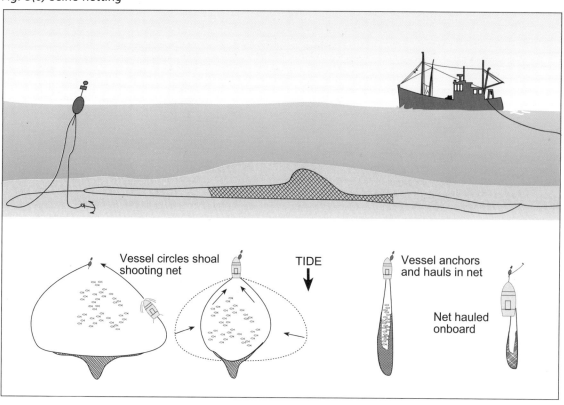

TIDE

Vessel circles shoal shooting net

Vessel anchors and hauls in net

Net hauled onboard

Fig. 5(7) Purse seining

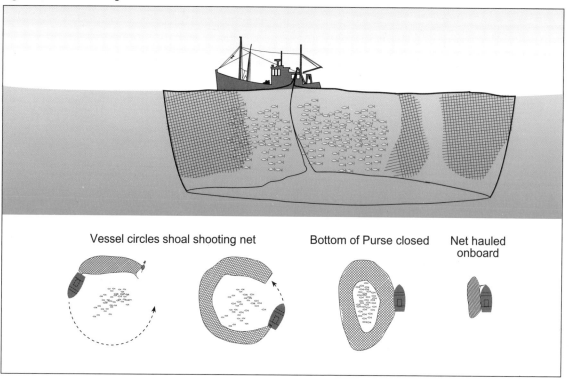

Vessel circles shoal shooting net

Bottom of Purse closed

Net hauled onboard

Fig. 5(8) Pair seabed trawling

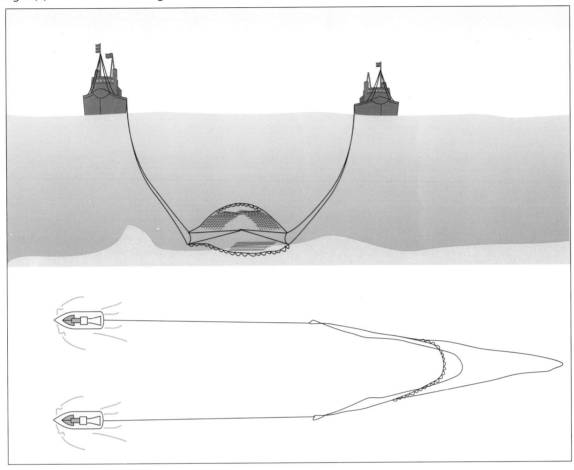

Fig. 5(9) Seabed otter trawling

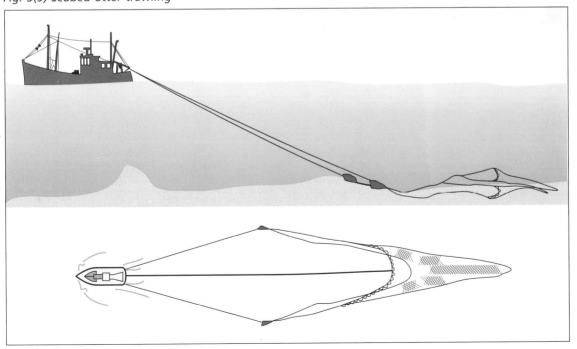

Fig. 5(10) Beam trawling

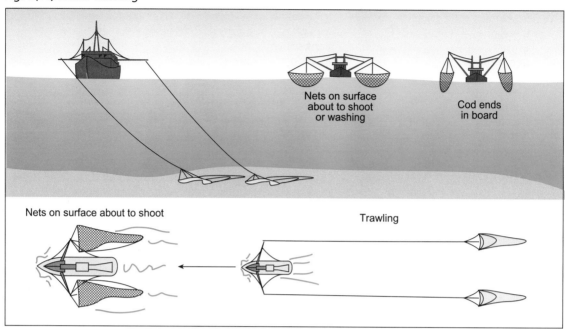

Nets on surface about to shoot or washing

Cod ends in board

Nets on surface about to shoot

Trawling

CK	Colchester	LT	Lowestoft	TN	Troon
CN	Campbeltown	M	Milford Haven	TO	Truro
CO	Caernarvon	ME	Montrose	TT	Tarbet
CS	Cowes	MN	Maldon	UL	Ullapool
CY	Castlebay	MR	Manchester	WA	Whitehaven
DH	Dartmouth	MT	Maryport	WH	Weymouth
DS	Dumfries	N	Newry	WK	Wick
E	Exeter	NN	Newhaven	WN	Wigtown
F	Faversham	OB	Oban	WY	Whitby
FD	Fleetwood	P	Portsmouth	YH	Great Yarmouth
FE	Folkestone	PD	Peterhead		
FH	Falmouth	PE	Poole	**b.**	**Eire**
FR	Fraserburgh	PH	Plymouth	B	Balina
FY	Fowey	PW	Padstow	C	Cork
GK	Greenock	PZ	Penzance	CE	Coleraine
GY	Grimsby	R	Ramsgate	D	Dublin
GU	Guernsey	RN	Runcorn	DA	Drogheda
H	Hull	RO	Rothesay	DK	Dundalk
HH	Harwich	RR	Rochester	G	Galway
HL	Hartlepool	RX	Rye	L	Limerick
IH	Ipswich	SA	Swansea	LY	Londonderry
INS	Inverness	SC	Scilly	NS	New Ross
J	Jersey	SD	Sunderland	S	Skibbereen
K	Kirkwall	SE	Salcombe	SO	Sligo
KY	Kirkcaldy	SH	Scarborough	T	Tralee
LA	Lanelli	SM	Shoreham	W	Waterford
LH	Leith	SN	North Shields	WD	Wexford
LI	Littlehampton	SR	Stranraer	WT	Westport
LK	Lerwick	SS	St Ives	Y	Youghal
LL	Liverpool	SSS	South Shields		
LN	Kings Lynn	SU	Southampton	**c.**	**France**
LN	London	SY	Stornoway	AC	Arcachon
LR	Lancaster	TH	Teignmouth	AD	Audierne

AY	Auray	AM	Amsterdam	**f.**	**Germany**		
BA	Bayonne	BH	Brouweshaven		(North Sea coast)		
BL	Boulogne	BI	Brielle	AA	Wester-Accumersiel		
BR	Brest	BL	Blankenham	AB	Bensersiel		
BX	Bordeaux	BOR	Borssele	AE	Emden		
CC	Concarneau	BR	Breskens	AG	Greetsiel		
CH	Cherbourg	BRU	Bruinisse	AJ	Juist		
CL	Calais	BZ	Bergen op Zoom	AL	Langeoog		
CM	Camaret	CP	Colijnsplaat	AN	Norderney		
CN	Caen	CZ	Cadzand	AS	Spiekeroog		
DK	Dunkirk	DD	Dordrecht	AU	Baltrum		
DP	Dieppe	DZ	Delfzijl	AW	Wilhelmshaven		
DA	Douarnenez	EG	Egmond aan Zee	AX	Borkum		
EL	Étel	EH	Enkhuizen	AY	Norddeich		
FC	Fécamp	EWD	Ellewoutsdijk	AZ	Neuharlingersiel		
GV	Guilvinec	GOE	Goes	BB	Bremen		
IO	Île d'Oléron	GRO	Groningen	BX	Bremerhaven		
LA	La Rochelle	HA	Harlingen	HC	Cuxhaven		
LH	Le Havre	HD	Den Helder	HH	Hamburg		
LO	Lorient	HI	Hinderloopen	OB	Brake		
LS	Les Sables d'Olonne	HN	Hoorn	OE	Elsfleth		
MA	Marseilles	HOE	Hoedekenskerke	ON	Nordenham		
MN	Marennes	HS	Hamsteede	OW	Wangerooge		
MT	Martigues	HV	Hellevoetsluis	SA	Amrum		
MX	Morlaix	HVH	Hoek van Holland	SB	Blankenese		
NA	Nantes	HVL	Hoogvliet	SC	Büsum		
NI	Nice	IJM	Ijmuiden	SG	Glückstadt		
NO	Noirmoutier	KP	Kampen	SH	Husum		
PL	Paimpol	KW	Katwijke	SP	Pellworm		
OV	Port Vendres	LW	Leeuwarden	SW	Wyk (Föhr)		
SB	St Brieuc	MA	Maasluis	SY	Teufelsbrück		
SM	St Malo	MD	Middelharnis				
SN	St Nazaire	ME	Medemblik	**g.**	**Denmark**		
ST	Sète	MK	Marken		(North Sea coast)		
TL	Toulon	ML	Maasland	E	Esbjerg		
VA	Vannes	MO	Monnikendam	F	Fanö		
YE	Île d'Yeu	MU	Muiden	HG	Hjöring		
		NI	Nieuwendam	L	Lemvig		
		NW	Nooordwijk	LN	Lökken		
d.	**Belgium**	NZ	Terneuzen	NF	Nykjöbing		
A	Antwerp	RO	Rotterdam	R	Ribe		
B	Blankenberge	SCH	Scheveningen	RL	Ringkjöbing		
BOW	Boechhowte	SL	Stellendam	S	Skagen		
C	Coxijde	ST	Stavoren	T	Thisted		
D	Doel	SV	Stavenisse	TR	Tönder		
H	Heyst	TR	Terschelling	V	Varde		
K	Kieldrecht	TX	Texel				
L	Lillo	VD	Volendam	**h.**	**Spain**		
M	Middelkerke	VE	Veere		(Atlantic coast)		
N	Nieuwpoort	VL	Vlaardingen	BI	Bilbao		
O	Oostende	VLI	Vlissengen	CA	Cadiz		
OD	Oost Duinkerke	VLI	Vlieland	CO	La Coruña		
P	La Panne	WK	Workum	FE	El Ferrol		
Z	Zeebrugge	WMD	Wemeldinge	GC	Las Palmas (de		
		YE	Yerseke		Gran Canaria)		
e.	**Netherlands**	ZK	Zoutkamp	GI	Gijon		
	(selected ports)	ZV	Zandvoort	HU	Huelva		
AK	Andijk	ZZ	Zieriksee	SS	San Sebastian		
AM	Ameland			ST	Santander		

125

j.	Portugal/Açores[A]
AH[A]	Angra do Heroísmo
AL	Albufeira
AN	Âncora
AV	Aveiro
BR	Barreiro
CM	Caminha
CS	Cascais
ER	Ericeira
ES	Esposende
FF	Figueira da Foz
FN	Funchal (Madeira)
FR	Faro
FZ	Fuzeta
HT[A]	Horta
LE	Leixões
LG	Lagos
LP[A]	Lajes (Pico)
LX	Lisboa
NZ	Nazaré
OL	Olhão
PD	Ponta Delgada
PE	Peniche
PM	Portimão
PS	Porto Santo (Madeira)
PT	Douro (Oporto)
PV	Póvoa de Varzim
QT	Quarteira
RE	Régua
RG	Ribeira Grande
SA	Sagres
SB	Sesimbra
SE	Setúbal
SF[A]	Santa Cruz (Flores)
SG[A]	Santa Cruz (Graciosa)
SM	S. Martinho do Porto
SN	Sines
SR[A]	São Roque (Pico)
TR	Trafaria
TV	Tavira
VC	Vila do Conde
VE[A]	Velas (S. Jorge)
VF	Vila Franca do Campo
VI	Viana do Castelo
VP	Vila do Porto
VR	Vila Real S. António
VV	Vila da Praia Vitória
VX	Vila Franca de Xira

5.1.6 SURVEYING SHIPS

While surveying, these display the signals prescribed in Rule 27(b) of the Collision Regulations, and may also show International Code group 'IR' ('I am engaged in underwater survey work. Keep clear of me and go slow'). During this work a survey ship may proceed across shipping lanes, and may tow gear up to 300m astern.

Vessels undertake seismic surveys to explore for oil or gas. They may tow detector cables between 3 cables and 3 miles long and initiate harmless explosions.

5.1.7 HOVERCRAFT

Hovercraft are mostly met in coastal waters. Since they can be blown sideways by the wind, their aspect may not indicate their true direction of travel. At night or in poor visibility they show a quick-flashing yellow light. Their noise may make sound signals inaudible.

5.1.8 HIGH SPEED CRAFT (HSC)

HSC continue to proliferate, creating an increased risk of collision due to their high speed and possibly unexpected direction of approach. Some HSC generate a significant shallow water effect in port approaches which can damage the shoreline, small craft and moorings.

HSC are defined by IMO as craft capable of a maximum speed equal to or exceeding 7.193 x Displacement to the power of 0.1667 (knots). Thus the criteria are a combination of both speed and displacement.

HSC show no special identifying signals and have no special privileges or obligations under the ColRegs.

In the UK the lead authority on HSC is the Maritime and Coastguard Agency which sponsors the annual Admiralty Notice to Mariners No 23, in which are listed all known HSC, their length, maximum speed and operating routes. They include various multi-hull configurations and hovercraft capable of speeds up to 50 knots.

5.1.9 DRACONES

Dracones are towed flexible oil barges, which float almost submerged in the water and are difficult to see. By day the towing vessel shows a black diamond shape, and the dracone (or last dracone, if more than one) tows a float with a similar shape. By night the towing vessel shows the lights prescribed by the Collision Regulations, and may illuminate the tow by searchlight. The dracone (or last dracone) tows a float with a white all-round light.

5.1.10 INCINERATOR VESSELS

Vessels burning chemical waste may be under way or at anchor in areas shown on charts and Sailing Directions. Such vessels have limited manoeuvrability, and show the signals prescribed in Rule 27(b) of the Collision Regulations. Avoid the noxious fumes by passing to windward.

5.1.11 WARSHIPS ON EXERCISES

Yachtsmen should appreciate the potential danger in approaching a formation of warships, or other vessels in convoy, too closely. Warships operating aircraft may have to steer as dictated by the wind, when they will show the lights or shapes as in Rule 27(b) of the Collision Regulations. Aircraft carriers may have masthead lights displaced to one side, normally to starboard, while their sidelights may be each side of the hull or of the island. They may also use red or white deck flood-lighting. Due to their configuration, other warships may not comply fully with the requirements for navigation lights.

Warships replenishing at sea are connected to auxiliary vessels by jackstays and hoses, and are severely restricted in their manoeuvrability and speed. They display the appropriate signals as in Rule 27(b), and other vessels must keep well clear (Rule 18).

5.1.12 PRACTICE AND EXERCISE AREAS (PEXA)

Around the UK, and in many other parts of the world, are areas designated for firing, bombing and other defence exercises. Those around the UK are shown on six small-scale Admiralty charts of the PEXA series. The extensive areas between the Isles of Scilly and to the SE of Selsey Bill and off the west coast of Scotland are shown in the MRNA.

Details of these areas are not currently (2001) shown on Admiralty navigational charts nor in their publications, but at the next **full** revision of UK navigational charts the limits of such areas will be included. Range beacons, lights and buoys which may help navigation will still be included, as now. Practice areas may be marked by yellow special buoys with the letters 'DZ' (Danger Zone) and name in black.

Annual Notice to Mariners No 5 describes the types of practices carried out. Warning signals, if any, are usually red flags by day, and fixed or flashing red lights by night. Range authorities are responsible for ensuring that the area is clear, and that there is no danger to vessels in the vicinity (see 6.1.2). Range Safety craft are clearly marked as such. If a yacht finds herself in an area where practices or exercises are in progress she should, if possible, maintain her course and speed; but if she is not able to do this for navigational reasons, she should clear the area as quickly as possible.

Information on when firing and exercise areas are active may be obtained from the following:

a. Routine MSI broadcasts on VHF by the Coastguard, including details of submarine (SUBFACTS) and gunnery exercises (GUNFACTS);

b. Navtex transmissions;

c. By VHF or telephone calls to Royal Navy operating authorities at Plymouth, Portsmouth and Faslane. Contact details are in the MRNA.

5.1.13 SUBMARINES

Submarines may be encountered anywhere at sea, not just in designated Submarine Exercise Areas.

a. Navigational lights: A submarine's masthead and side lights are placed well forward, and very low above the water; especially the stern light, which may be obscured by spray or wash. All submarines carry a quick-flashing yellow (amber) light, 1 to 2 metres above or below the after mast-head light, to assist identification in busy waters. The flashing rate is 90-105/minute, not to be confused with a hovercraft at 120/minute. A submarine at anchor or at a buoy shows an all-round white light amidships, as well as normal anchor lights. The aft anchor light may be located on the upper rudder which is some way aft of the hull's waterline; do not confuse such lights for those of two separate vessels of less than 50 metres length.

b. Warning signals: International Code group 'NE2' flown by a surface ship indicates that submarines are in the vicinity. The following pyrotechnics and smoke signals may be used by submerged submarines:

Smoke/flare	Signifies
White smoke candle (with/without flame or dye). Yellow smoke candles. Green flares launched about 60m (200ft) into the air, burning for about 5 secs.	Submarine's position in response to request from ship or aircraft.
Red flares (characteristics as for green flares above). If sighted and the submarine fails to surface within five minutes, assume she is in distress and sunk.	Clear the area immediately. Am carrying out emergency surfacing procedure. Do not stop propellers. Stand by to help.
Two white or yellow smoke candles released singly, about 3 minutes apart.	Clear the area immediately. Am preparing to surface. Do not stop propellers.

c. Sunken submarine: A submarine unable to surface will try to show her position by:

i Releasing an indicator buoy (with whip aerials) attached to the submarine by a 1000m long braid line, which must not be parted or hauled on; see below.
ii Firing candles with white flame and white smoke, or just yellow smoke. Some may have a yellow-green dye marker and a message carrier, which may be recovered.
iii Pumping out fuel or lubricating oil.
iv Blowing out air.

A submarine indicator buoy is semi-spherical in shape, 76cm in diameter and 90cm deep; see Fig. 5(11).

It has vertical strips of reflective tape, alternately red and white, or it may be plain orange. It bears the words 'SOS. FINDER INFORM NAVY, COASTGUARD OR POLICE. DO NOT SECURE TO OR TOUCH'; and a three-digit identification number under the words 'Forward' or 'Aft'. A white light flashes every two

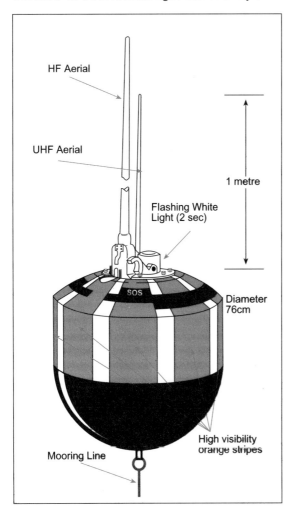

Fig. 5(11) Submarine Indicator Buoy.

HF Aerial

UHF Aerial

1 metre

Flashing White Light (2 sec)

SOS

Diameter 76cm

High visibility orange stripes

Mooring Line

seconds for about 72 hours. An automatic distress signal is transmitted on 8364kHz and 243MHz for at least 72 hours.

A submarine indicator buoy should not be confused with a sonobuoy, dropped by aircraft to detect submarines. A British sonobuoy is a thinner and longer cylinder, and although it has a whip aerial it does not have a light or the marking described above.

5.1.14 MINELAYING AND MINECOUNTERMEASURES

Minelaying and minecountermeasures (hunting and sweeping) exercises are normally confined to certain areas, published in annual Notice to Mariners No 10. A harmless practice mine which lies on the bottom and ejects green or white flares may be used.

The lights shown by mineclearance vessels are in Rule 27(f) of the Collision Regulations. Minehunters show the lights prescribed for a vessel restricted in her ability to manoeuvre, and usually work with small craft from which divers may be operating, or may be controlling a wire-guided submersible. Boats with divers exhibit Flag 'A' of the International Code. The minehunter shows Flag 'A' by day when divers are operating, or signals the letter 'A' by flashing light at night if approached by other vessels. Yachts should keep well clear of such operations, which may extend l000m from the minehunter.

Minesweeping and minehunting operations require the laying of small buoys, usually fitted with a radar reflector, which may have numeral or alphabetical flags attached. At night such buoys are lit by flashing green, white or red all-round lights, visible for about 1 mile.

5.1.15 MINEFIELDS

Many of the minefields laid during World War II have been swept or have had buoyed swept lanes cleared through them, but in a few unswept areas mines can still be a hazard – as may uncharted wrecks or shoals therein which have not been surveyed. Any drifting mine that is seen is likely to be a lost exercise mine, but it should be reported. Do not try to recover it or take it in tow. Annual Notice to Mariners No 6 gives more advice about mines especially those picked up in fishing trawls. The system of rewards for recovering mines has been discontinued.

5.1.16 THE EXAMINATION SERVICE

The Ministry of Defence may, in certain circumstances, control entry to special ports, and institute an Examination Service for vessels which approach them. If so, the following signals may be displayed ashore and also in the approaches by Examination or Traffic Control Vessels

By day	By night	Meaning
● red balls ● ●	Ⓡ flashing Ⓡ Ⓡ	Entry to port prohibited
Nil	Ⓖ Ⓖ Ⓖ	Entry to port permitted
A blue flag	Ⓡ Ⓖ Ⓡ	Movement of shipping within the port or anchorage prohibited.

Examination vessels wear a special flag, with a blue border and a square in the centre, the top half white and the bottom half red. They may be empowered to examine, identify and control vessels wishing to enter that port.

5.1.17 NAVIGATIONAL AIDS

Take care to pass navigational buoys, Lanbys, light-floats, etc at a prudent distance, especially in a tideway. Larger ships should be vigilant due to the damage they can cause to such aids, possibly with serious consequences for other vessels. However, yachts, rather than the buoy, are more likely to be damaged in any collision. Nevertheless, any contact should be reported at once via the Coastguard in case damage has been done to the navigational aid. It is an offence to make fast to any navigational aid.

5.1.18 MEASURED DISTANCES

Around the coast are measured distances, shown on charts and in Sailing Directions, where vessels run speed trials and calibrate logs, etc. Such vessels fly the International Code flags 'SM', and should be given a wide berth – including the turning area at each end of the run.

5.1.19 WRECKS

Under the Protection of Wrecks Act, 1973, wrecks may be protected due to their historic, artistic or archaeological importance. It is prohibited to anchor in these areas, or to dive, or to tamper with any part of the wreck. Under the same Act certain potentially dangerous wrecks are designated prohibited areas, eg the *'Richard Montgomery'* off Sheerness. These sites are shown on charts and in Sailing Directions, and in annual Notice to Mariners No 16.

5.1.20 OFFSHORE OIL AND GAS FIELDS

Where preliminary surveys show possible oil or gas in commercial quantities, a drilling rig is used to drill test wells. These rigs are large structures, marked by lights and fog signals, and with mooring wires extending a mile from the rig itself. Lighters and other support vessels may be moored nearby. These rigs are moved from place to place and hence their positions are not charted, although they may be promulgated in MSI broadcasts by the Coastguard or in Temporary Notices to Mariners.

Three main types of drilling rig are used:

1. Jack-up rigs, as used down to 120 metres, are towed into position, the steel legs are lowered to the sea bed, then the drilling platform is jacked-up above sea level.
2. Semi-submersible rigs are used down to about 1700m. They float on submerged caissons which may be self-propelled; and anchored or dynamically positioned.
3. Drillships are used in depths of 2000m or more, where mooring is impossible. They are kept precisely in position by electronic station-keeping gear which actuates a number of propellers around the vessels.

Several exploration wells may be drilled to establish the extent of a field. Those wells not needed are sealed, while others are capped with pipes etc projecting above the sea bed, and are marked on charts as 'Well' or 'Wellhead'.

When oil or gas is to be extracted from a field, a production platform is installed. These massive structures are shown on charts and in Sailing Directions, and are marked by lights and usually by fog signals. They may have mooring points for tankers, or mooring buoys and other dangers a mile or more away.

Permanent platforms show a main light(s), Fl 15s (U) (Morse ··—), while fog signals sound Morse 'U' every 30 seconds. Corners of the platform not marked by the main light are marked by lights Fl R 15 s (U).

Under international law, safety zones with radii of up to 500m are established around drilling rigs, production platforms and single point moorings (SPM). Yachts must not enter these zones except to save life, or on account of stress of weather or if in distress.

5.1.21 UNDERWATER CABLES

Cables, often carrying high voltage, are laid in coastal waters and are shown on charts. Damage to such cables can be very costly, and yachts should take every care to avoid anchoring near them. If a yacht fouls a cable, every effort should be made to clear it by normal means, taking great care not to damage the cable. If unsuccessful, the anchor warp or chain should be buoyed and slipped, but in no circumstances should the cable be cut or damaged.

5.1.22 OVERHEAD POWER CABLES

In various estuaries and rivers high-voltage overhead cables present a serious danger to craft passing underneath. Depending on the voltage concerned, a safety clearance of 2-5m should be allowed for the possible discharge of electric current to the mast of a yacht.

The elevation of cables (bridges and similar overhead obstructions) is shown on charts as the height above Mean High Water Springs (MHWS). Spurious radar echoes can be received when passing under power cables and can easily be misinterpreted.

5.1.23 TRAFFIC SEPARATION SCHEMES (TSS)

The International Maritime Organization (IMO) is responsible for establishing and recommending international measures for ships' routeing. For TSS which lie wholly within national waters, decisions about routeing lie with the national government, but schemes may be submitted to IMO for approval and adoption.

Rule 10 is quoted verbatim in Chapter 4, with explanatory Notes and diagrams. Diagrams of all IMO-adopted TSS are shown in the MRNA, on Admiralty charts and in Sailing Directions.

TSS in Europe which are not IMO-adopted include:

a. British Isles
   Approaches to Harwich; Dublin; and Holyhead harbour.
b. Netherlands Off Vlissingen.

5.2 HM CUSTOMS AND EXCISE

5.2.1 INTRODUCTION AND NOTICE 8

Since the European Union (EU) became a single market on 1 January 1993, EU yachtsmen have enjoyed unhindered movement for themselves and their boats within the EU, provided that all taxes due have been paid in a member country of the Community. As a result previous UK Customs procedures for yachts arriving directly from or going to other EU countries have been greatly relaxed.

Relaxations in other EU countries are similar, but vary in detail. There are also some changes to HM Customs procedures for yachts arriving from or departing to non-EC countries, although the general principles remain much as before.

The regulations for the temporary importation (TI) of boats into EU countries have also changed.

Member countries of the European Community (EC) or Union (EU) are: Austria, Belgium, Denmark, Finland, France, Germany, Greece, the Irish Republic, Italy, Luxembourg, the Netherlands, Portugal, Spain (but not the Canary Islands), Sweden, the UK (but not the Channel Islands).

Even if you are only cruising to or from EU countries, Customs officers may ask where you are from and where bound. They can still board your boat to check for drugs, firearms, animals that may carry rabies, and for prohibited and restricted goods (see 5.2.6).

Customs Notice 8 dated April 1996, which superseded Notice 8B of February 1993, gives details of Customs procedures. Notice 8 is entitled 'Sailing your pleasure craft to and from the United Kingdom'. It contains some minor, but time-wasting errors, for example the Dover Yacht Unit in paragraph 2 does not exist. For more up-to-date information visit the large and comprehensive Customs and Excise website at www.hmce.gov.uk

Copies of Notice 8 and further advice can be obtained from your local Customs Advice Centre of which there are nine in England, Wales and Scotland:

Centre	Tel	Fax
London (HQ)	020 7865 3100*	020 7865 3171
Southend	08450 199399	01702 367133
Newcastle	0191 201 1719	0191 201 1594
Glasgow	0345 442266	0141 308 3402
Cheadle	0161 261 7997	0161 261 7399
Nottingham	0115 971 2107	0115 971 2219
Cardiff	029 2038 6200	029 2038 6444
Plymouth	01752 777123	01752 765807
Reading	0118 964 4355	0118 964 4206

*If unable to contact your local Centre, call the National Helpline 020 7865 3100.

Notice 8 is based upon the following legislation:

1. The Customs and Excise Management Act 1979 (CEMA);
2. The Pleasure Craft (Arrival and Report) Regulations, made under sections 35(4) and 42(1) of the CEMA;
3. The Commissioners' Directions made under CEMA sections 35(1) and 64(2); and
4. Commission Regulation (EEC) 2454/93.

Notice 8 is not the law and does not change the law; it is the view of HM Customs & Excise of what the law says about pleasure craft and compliance with Customs & Excise requirements. Because of its obvious importance, the more relevant portions of Notice 8 are paraphrased below. Yachtsmen who intend to take their boats foreign are advised to study a copy. 'Foreign' means all countries outside the UK, including their territorial waters. The Irish Republic is foreign; the Channel Islands count as foreign; the Isle of Man does not.

5.2.2 LEAVING THE UNITED KINGDOM
If going directly to another EU state, you do not need to tell HM Customs that you are leaving, unless asked. But if going directly to a non-EU country you must pre-notify Customs as follows:

1. Complete sections (i) and (ii) on part 1 of Form C1331, available from Customs offices, most yacht clubs and marinas. A separate form is required for each voyage to or from a non-EU country. For telephone numbers of UK Customs offices see the MRNA or Notice 8.
2. Before leaving the UK deliver part 1 at the place of departure by putting it in a Customs post box, or taking it to a Customs office.
3. Retain part 2 onboard as evidence of your notification of departure.
4. If you have on board anybody who has no right of abode in the EU, you must inform an Immigration officer (usually the Customs officer) before you sail. This is not necessary if your first port of call overseas is expected to be in the EU, the Channel Islands or the Irish Republic. The form must be delivered as in (2) above before you expect to leave the UK.

If, after notifying your departure, your departure is delayed, notify the original Customs Office in writing of the delay; likewise if the voyage is abandoned.

You may be eligible to ship duty-free stores if you are going to a port south of Brest or north of the north bank of the River Eider in Germany. Application must be made in advance. Details of how to ship stores or to re-ship previously landed surplus duty-free stores can be obtained from Customs offices. You cannot take duty-free stores to the Irish Republic or to the Channel Islands.

If you are shipping stores under bond, or on which you are claiming repayment of customs charges, they must be placed on board under Customs seal, and must not be used in UK waters without paying duty.

If you carry any goods for industrial or commercial purposes, your boat is no longer a pleasure craft and becomes a commercial vessel.

5.2.3 ARRIVAL IN THE UK FROM AN EU COUNTRY
If arriving direct from another EU country (note that this does **not** include the Channel Islands),

there is no need to fly flag 'Q'. You need only report to HM Customs, if you have goods to declare in any of the following categories:

1. Prohibited or restricted goods (see 5.2.6).
2. Animals or birds on board (see 5.2.7).
3. Duty-free ship's stores.
4. The boat itself, if it is liable to VAT;

Any non-EC nationals on board will need to get immigration clearance; see 5.2.5.

Provided they are for your own personal use, there is no further tax to pay on goods which you have obtained in the EU. Personal use includes gifts, but if you receive any payment in return for buying alcohol and tobacco the transaction is dutiable and must be declared accordingly. EU law sets out the following guidelines for what constitutes 'personal use'. If you bring in more than these amounts, you must be able to satisfy the Customs officer that the goods are indeed for your own personal use:

800 cigarettes, 400 cigarillos, 200 cigars, 1kg smoking tobacco; 10 litres spirits; 20 litres fortified wine, eg port and sherry; 90 litres wine (of which only 60 litres may be sparkling); 110 litres beer.

HM Customs will continue to check for drugs, firearms, animals and other prohibited goods being brought into the country, and the penalties for infringement remain severe.

5.2.4 ARRIVAL IN THE UK FROM A NON-EU COUNTRY
The yellow 'Q' flag must be flown by a yacht arriving directly from outside the EU (this includes the Channel Islands), on entering UK territorial waters (the 12 mile limit). It must be clearly visible and suitably illuminated at night, and must not be lowered until all Customs formalities are complete. Failure to comply may result in a penalty.

On arrival telephone, or contact in person, a Customs officer; do what he tells you to do. Also fill in sections (i) and (iii) on part 2 of Form C1331, (using your outbound C1331 if applicable); or the Customs officer will provide if necessary. Retain the other part as your record. You must not land goods or persons, or transfer them to another vessel until a Customs officer says so.

You must declare the four categories of goods listed under 5.2.3, and in addition you must declare:

1. Any goods that are to be left in the UK.
2. Any tobacco goods, alcoholic drinks, perfumes and toilet waters in excess of the duty-free allowances (see Notice 1 'Customs guide for Travellers entering the UK').

3. If you are a returning resident of the UK or other EU State, any goods acquired on your trip whose total value exceeds £145. This includes equipment bought and fitted to the boat outside the EU.

The duty-free allowances for goods obtained **outside the EU**, as stated in Notice 1, are:

200 cigarettes; or 100 cigarillos; or 50 cigars; or 250gms of tobacco;

2 litres of still table wine;

1 litre of spirits or strong liqueurs over 22% volume; or 2 litres fortified wine, sparkling wine or other liqueurs;

60cc/ml of Perfume. 250cc/ml Toilet water.

£145 worth of all other goods including gifts and souvenirs.

People under 17 cannot have the tobacco or alcohol allowance.

Goods over the published (Notice 1) allowances may be:

a. Released, on payment of duty; or
b. Placed under seal in a compartment on board your vessel, until you leave the UK.

If goods are smuggled the boat may be seized and the person(s) concerned may have to pay a heavy fine or go to prison.

5.2.5 IMMIGRATION REQUIREMENTS

Anyone onboard who is not an EU national must get permission from the Immigration officer (normally the Customs officer) to enter the UK from a place other than the Isle of Man, the Irish Republic or the Channel Islands. The Customs officer can advise on this and the skipper is responsible for ensuring that this is done.

5.2.6 PROHIBITED OR RESTRICTED GOODS

Certain goods are either prohibited (banned) or restricted, to protect health and the environment. Restricted goods may only be imported into the UK under certain conditions, eg possession of an appropriate licence.

1. **Prohibited** goods include:

a. Unlicensed drugs, such as heroin, morphine, cocaine, cannabis, amphetamines, barbiturates and LSD.
b. Offensive weapons, such as flick knives, swordsticks, knuckledusters and some martial arts equipment.
c. Indecent and obscene material featuring children, such as books, magazines, films, videotapes, laser discs and software.
d. Adult obscene material (pornography).

e. Counterfeit and pirated goods and goods that infringe patents (such as watches, clocks and CDs and any goods with false marks of their origin) when brought into the UK from outside the UK.

2. **Restricted** goods include the following:

f. Firearms, explosives and ammunition, including electric shock devices (such as stun guns) and gas canisters.
g. Dogs, cats and other animals, including rabbits, mice, rats and gerbils, may not be imported unless you have a British import (rabies) licence.
h. Live birds, including family pets, unless they are covered by a British health import licence.
j. Endangered species, including birds and plants, whether alive or dead; also such things as fur, ivory or leather (or goods made from them) that have been taken from endangered species.
k. Meat and poultry, and most of their products including bacon, ham, sausages, pate, eggs, milk and cream. But you are allowed 1kg of meat per person as long as it is fully cooked and in airtight containers.
m. Certain plants and their produce. This includes trees, shrubs, potatoes, certain fruit, bulbs and seeds.
n. Radio transmitters such as CB radios that are not approved for use in the UK.

For further details of: g, h and k call 020 7904 6000 (MAFF); 'j' call 0117 987 8202 (DETR); 'm' call 01904 455195 (MAFF); and 'n' call 020 7211 0502 (RCA).

5.2.7 ANIMALS, BIRDS AND PETS

Animals and birds (including domestic pets) are subject to strict control. You must tell the Customs at the port of arrival, and have a 'British import (rabies) licence', issued in advance by the DEFRA or by the Scottish Office of Agriculture and Fisheries, to allow the import of any animal or bird at certain designated ports before they enter quarantine.

Animals and birds brought to the UK without a licence must always be kept in an enclosed part of the vessel below deck, and not allowed to come into contact with any other animals. Never let them ashore without the authority of the appropriate DEFRA officials. There are no restrictions on those animals, which are subject to rabies control, being imported from the Channel Islands and the Irish Republic which are at present free of rabies.

PETS (the Pet Travel Scheme) was introduced in

Feb 2000 to permit pet cats and dogs, including guide dogs for the blind and deaf, to enter the UK from certain countries without having to be quarantined in the UK. The 'veterinary' requirements (designed to prevent rabies reaching the UK) are rigorous, time-consuming and quite expensive. Some 28 European countries qualify as rabies-free. However pets may only travel to the UK on certain ferries, airlines and trains arriving at specific UK destinations. Thus pets are unable to return to the UK aboard their owner's yacht – *quel dommage!* For further details visit the excellent DEFRA website www.maff.gov.uk and click on the animal health and welfare section.

5.2.8   VAT AND BOATS

With the advent of the Single Market on 1 January 1993 there were important changes in the way in which VAT is charged on goods moving between member states of the EU. One useful source of information provided by HM Customs & Excise is Notice 725 "VAT and the Single Market" dated May 1998, amended October 1999. The subject is complex, but Notice 725 offers both an overview and some details of topics referred to below.

Liability for VAT

From 1 January 1993 an EU resident has been able to move a yacht on which VAT has been paid between EU countries without restriction. But because Customs authorities in different states are still establishing the VAT status of yachts moored therein, it is necessary to carry proof that VAT has been paid.

If the original VAT receipt for the boat is not held, such proof could be the boat's Part 1 registration documents, insurance policy, builder's certificate, records of surveys or repairs, berthing records, or correspondence with previous owners etc.

HM Customs have indicated that they will consider VAT to have been paid on any UK owned vessel for which it can be demonstrated that she was built before 31 December 1984 and was in EU waters at midnight on 31 December 1992.

All vessels 'designed or adapted for recreation or pleasure use' are liable to VAT. Vessels under 12m long are potentially liable to Customs duty.

If you are moving home from a non-EC country to an EU country, you may import a vessel free of customs duty and VAT subject to conditions listed in Notice 8.

Buying and keeping a new boat in the EU

From 1 January 1993, any EU national purchasing a new boat for use in EU waters is required to pay VAT on the purchase price. If keeping the boat in the UK, VAT due will be payable in the UK at the current rate of 175%. If you intend keeping the boat in another EU country, the rules are more complex. You should consult VAT Notice 728 'Motor vehicles, boats, aircraft: intra-EC movements by private persons'. This is a complex document dealing with 'New means of transport' (NMT), regardless of whether they have wheels, wings or hulls. VAT will always be due in the EU member state where the boat is to be kept. Notice 728 can be obtained from your nearest Customs Advice Centre or read on the Customs web site www.hmce.gov.uk

Buying a new boat in the EU, but keeping it outside

An EU national purchasing a boat in the EU, but intending to keep her permanently outside the EU, may be able to buy her VAT-free, as for example under the UK Sailaway Boat Scheme. This scheme is explained in VAT leaflet 703/3/93: You will need to complete Form VAT 436 and have it certified at your final point of departure from the EU. The vessel must be exported from the EU within 6 months of the date of delivery in the case of private non-EU residents (different periods apply to eligible EU residents and non-EU companies). HM Customs should be kept informed. Further details may be obtained from Mr Les Moorcroft, HM Customs & Excise, Floor 4 SW, Queen's Dock, Liverpool. Tel 0151 703 8654.

From the foregoing it is essential to carry onboard the following when visiting other EU states: preferably a VAT receipt; or failing that evidence of the boat's location on 31 December 1992; evidence of age if built before 31 December 1984, plus bill of sale where relevant, and registration certificate.

A boat will always be liable to VAT (and possibly to Customs duty) if she is purchased by an EU resident outside the EU and imported into the EU even if VAT has already been paid on the boat, or if she was first used before 1 January 1985, or if the tax due is 'insignificant'. This is a different situation to the re-importation by an EU resident of a boat which that person owned when she was last exported from the EC, when tax relief can be claimed if the facts can be proved.

5.2.9   TEMPORARY IMPORTATION (TI)

Under EU law pleasure craft from outside the EU may be temporarily imported into EU waters, free of duty and VAT, subject to conditions which depend on whether the boat is to be used for private or commercial purposes.

For private purposes these conditions are that:

a. The person responsible for the vessel normally resides outside the EU.
b. The boat will leave the EU before it has spent six months there (continuous or not) in the past 12 months.
c. The boat is used only by the owner or his immediate family who also live outside the EU.
d. The boat is not lent, hired, chartered or sold whilst in the EU.
e. If the person to whom TI has been granted wishes to leave the EU temporarily, keeping the boat in the EU until his return, he must first be authorised by HM Customs and comply with any conditions imposed.

The Channel Islands, being outside the EU, are subject to other conditions. Individual Channel Islands residents are allowed TI into the EU, including the UK, under the same rules as apply to other non-EU nationals.

5.2.10   LIAISON WITH HM CUSTOMS

Yachtsmen are encouraged to work with HM Customs in combatting the illegal importation of drugs, alcohol, cigarettes and tobacco. Owners and crews may be able to pass on information about drug smuggling and other serious Customs offences, but they should **never** act as law enforcement officers – dangerous criminals may be involved. All information received by HM Customs is treated in strict confidence. Be alert to suspicious activities and notify HM Customs as quickly as possible of:

a. Yachts, RIBs and other craft and/or their crews acting suspiciously. Ships signalling ashore or being met by smaller craft. Vessels operating at night without lights.
b. Packages being loaded or unloaded from small boats to large ships or fishing vessels in remote areas, beaches or at sea or at odd hours.
c. Vessels specifically adapted to conceal goods, or requests for such adaptations.
d. Light aircraft activity in unusual places, especially if goods are being handled or packages dropped from the air.
e. Vehicles transferring loads in suspicious circumstances or at unusual times.

Call (free, H24) the confidential Customs hotline on **0800 59 5000** and report in as much detail as possible what you have seen or heard. At sea it is best to log the details and report to Customs on arrival; it may be unwise to use radio communication because it is not secure. Your information will be treated confidentially and your identity protected. Even seemingly trivial information can be important. A cash reward may be payable for information leading to an arrest.

An owner should take all practical steps to make his vessel secure, particularly when unattended or abroad, so that items cannot be put aboard without his knowledge. HM Customs launches and staff on patrol duty will investigate suspicious activities or circumstances in and around moored vessels, and where practicable they will correct minor problems for the owner or report to the appropriate authority. This work can be minimised if owners act responsibly, and follow the required procedures for arrival and departure.

5.3 NATIONAL REGULATIONS IN EUROPE

5.3.1   INTRODUCTION

Before cruising to any foreign country be aware of the various formalities required, which are likely to include some or all of the items listed below. Brief notes on European countries are also given below in alphabetical order. More detailed information is given in the RYA booklets Cl and C2 *Planning a Foreign Cruise* (Vol 1, the Atlantic coast of Europe and the Baltic Sea; Vol 2, The Mediterranean and Black Seas); or from the London tourist office of the country concerned.

Generally all EU countries have relaxed their Customs procedures for yachts moving within the EU in a similar way to the changes in HM Customs requirements. But for non-EC countries, in the absence of specific information to the contrary it is necessary to report on arrival, and always if there are any exceptional goods or stores to be declared. Changes in procedures can be expected for countries joining the EC.

Further information on individual countries should be available from the authorities stated. Some countries require Customs to be cleared on final departure.

There are of course other matters, as listed in (a) to (g) below, to be considered when cruising abroad. Owners should as far as possible have done their homework before leaving the UK, so that they do not become a burden on others. However, if serious problems arise, the nearest British Consul can give limited help. For example he can issue an emergency passport, advise on the transfer of funds, help in the event of death or accident, advise on organisations which can trace missing persons, or assist with repatriation to the UK.

The following is a checklist of the essential items:

a. Comply with British Customs requirements, both on departure and return.

b. **Yacht** documents – carry the following:
- Certificate of Registry under Part I, or Part III (Small Ships Register) of the Merchant Shipping Act;
- Proof that VAT has been paid;
- Insurance policy and certificate of insurance, including at least £1 million third party cover. If necessary, arrange to extend the usual 'Home waters' cruising limits.
- Ship's Radio Licence;

c. **Personal** documents – carry the following:
- A crew list, including Passport numbers.
- Certificates of Competence (Yachtmaster Offshore, Coastal Skipper etc);
- International Certificate of Competence, validated if necessary for inland waterways by the inclusion of a CEVNI qualification.
- Radio Operator's Certificate of Competence and Authority to Operate.
- Passports for all the crew, plus any visas or special vaccination/medical certificates that may be needed.
- Form El11 (reciprocal National Health cover in EU countries). Health insurance, if thought necessary.

d. Comply with health, immigration and Customs requirements abroad. In most countries it is obligatory to fly Flag 'Q' on arrival, especially if carrying dutiable stores in excess of the normal 'tourist' allowance; if in doubt this is the safest procedure. Possibly the customs officer will visit the yacht, but more probably the skipper will need to go to the Customs office and produce the documents listed above. Always have the originals available, plus some photocopies for official records.

e. A British-owned yacht should wear a courtesy ensign and the Red Ensign in foreign waters. A special ensign, if eligible, may be worn although white and blue ensigns are liable to be misunderstood.

f. If taking part in any form of commercial activities, such as charter, be sure to comply with any national regulations.

g. Also comply with national regulations about disposing of waste over the side, or in special dumps ashore.

5.3.2 BELGIUM

Telephone code from UK 00 32; to UK 00 44. Craft from non-EU countries must fly flag 'Q' at port of entry. The yacht may be boarded by Customs officers and/or Immigration officers.

Seagoing craft must have basic safety equipment, and have their name and home port marked on the stern. There are special formalities for yachts staying more than two months. No restrictions on crew changes. On inland waters boats are required to fly the 'drapeau de navigation', a red flag with a white rectangular centre. The motor sailing cone is enforced. RYA Coastal Skipper Certificate required for navigating the Schelde estuary.

The Belgium (Flanders) Tourist Office, 31 Pepper St, London E14 9RW. Tel 0207 458 0044; Info 0207 867 0311; Fax 0207 458 0045. www.visitflanders.com ailsa@flanders-tourism.org Note: Belgium's coast is in Flanders. Wallonia and Brussels have a separate Tourist Office in London. Belgian Embassy, 103 Eaton Square, London SW1W 9AB. Tel 020 7470 3700.

5.3.3 DENMARK

Telephone code from UK 00 45; to UK 00 44. Yachts from an EU or Scandinavian country not carrying stores in excess of normal allowances need not report to Customs on arrival, but others must do so. Excess dutiable stores must be declared, and will be put under seal. No restrictions on crew changes. Danish authorities insist on one lifejacket per crew member.

Danish Tourist Board, 55 Sloane Street, London SW1X 9SR. Tel 020 7259 5959. Fax 020 7259 5955. Danish Embassy, same address; Tel 020 7333 0200.

5.3.4 FINLAND

Telephone code from UK 00 358; to UK 990 44. Marine emergency Tel 00230 1000. Access routes to harbours are strictly controlled; keep to the fairways. To clear Customs and passport control, call on VHF Ch 74 one hour before ETA, and go to any of the main commercial harbours. The major yacht harbours/marinas are at: Mariehamn, Kemi, Oulu, Vaasa, Naantali, Turku, Hanko, Helsinki and Hamina. Many areas are prohibited to foreign yachts. Government vessels may stop and search yachts (Flag 'L', ·—··), and actively enforce various regulations. Any excess alcohol or tobacco over the normal 'tourist' allowance must be declared on entry. Wines and spirits can only be bought from state liquor stores.

Finnish Tourist Board, 30/35 Pall Mall, London SW1 5LP. Tel 020 7839 4048. Finnish Embassy, 38 Chesham Place, London SW1X 8HW. Tel 020 72359 9531.

5.3.5 FRANCE

Telephone code from UK 00 33; to UK 00 44. British yachts must be registered, either under

Part I or Part III, Small Ships Register. No Certificate of Competence needed (unless required in the country of origin), but charterers of French motor boats under 15m must have an ICC and a copy of CEVNI. More stringent rules apply to vessels over 15m LOA.

Flag 'Q' is not required, nor Customs clearance, if the purpose of the visit is legitimate and no goods are carried which should be declared, and there is no notifiable illness onboard.

French Tourist Office, 178 Piccadilly, London W1V 0AL. Tel 020 7629 2869; Fax 020 7493 6594; Info 0891 244123.

French Consulate General, 6A Cromwell Place, London SW7 2EW. Tel 020 7838 2050.

5.3.6   GERMANY

Telephone code from UK: 00 49; to UK 00 44. Flag 'Q' is not needed if coming from an EU or Scandinavian country. Clear Customs (if necessary) at Borkum, Norderney, Norddeich, Wilhelmshaven, Bremerhaven, Cuxhaven (not Helgoland), Kiel or Travemunde (Baltic). Keep at least 1M clear of the outer limits of TSS. If only intending to transit Kiel Canal (for which special rules apply, obtainable at locks) it is not necessary to clear Customs, but fly Third Substitute. An International Certificate of Competence is required for inland waterways and the Rhine Police Regulations must be carried on the Rhine. The motor sailing cone is strongly enforced in German waters; instant fines are payable for non-compliance. No restrictions on crew changes.

German National Tourist Office, Nightingale House, 65 Curzon Street, London W1Y 7PE. Tel 020 7317 0908; Fax 020 7495 6129; Info 0891 600100.

German Embassy, 23 Belgrave Square, London SW1X 8PZ. Tel 020 7824 1300; Fax 020 7824 1435.

5.3.7   GREECE

Telephone code from UK 00 30; to UK 00 44. On arrival fly flag 'Q' and enter at one of the 50 or so recognised ports of entry where there are customs, immigration and health authorities. A 'Circulation' fee of 2000 drachmas/metre LOA is payable by visiting foreign yachts on first entry. On any subsequent entry within 30 days of the previous entry the fee is increased to 15,000 drachmas/metre LOA. Some reports suggest that this fee is not always levied. A Registration Certificate is required, plus proof of VAT payment; the skipper must have an ICC, or equivalent. If transiting the Corinth Canal it is advisable to have proof of net tonnage, as on Part I Registration. Yachts with Small Ship

Registration are charged on LOA, which may be more expensive. Wear a Greek courtesy ensign in good condition.

National Tourist Organisation of Greece, 4 Conduit Street, London, W1R 0DJ. Tel: 020 7734 5997.

Greek Embassy, 1A Holland Park, London W11 3JP. Tel 020 7221 6467.

5.3.8   IRISH REPUBLIC

Telephone code from UK 00 353; to UK 00 44. Yachts from non-EU countries (whether or not with dutiable stores) must fly flag 'Q' by day or show a red light over a white light by night, and report to local Customs or, if there is none, to a Garda (Police) station. Further details from the Revenue Commissioners, Dublin Castle, Dublin 2. UK citizens do not need passports.

Bord Failte Eireann (Irish Tourist Board), Ireland House, 150 New Bond Street, London W1Y 0AQ. Tel 020 7493 3201; Fax 020 7493 9065.

Embassy of the Republic of Ireland, 17 Grosvenor Place, London SW1. Tel 020 7235 2171; Fax 020 7245 6961.

5.3.9   ITALY

Telephone code from UK 00 39; to UK 00 44. In addition to the Certificate of Registration, a Certificate of Insurance is also required with an Italian translation, showing that your insurance company has reciprocal arrangements for third party liabilities with an Italian company. Other requirements are Proof of VAT status and a crew list with date and place of birth and passport numbers. An ICC is advisable.

Italian State Tourist Office (ENIT), 1 Princes Street, London W1R 8AY. Tel 020 7408 1254; Fax 020 7493 6695.

Italian Consulate General, 38 Eaton Place, London SW1. Tel 020 7235 9371.

5.3.10   NETHERLANDS

Telephone code from UK 00 31; to UK 00 44. Ports of entry are Vlissingen, Breskens, Terneuzen, Schiedam, Rotterdam, IJmuiden, West Terschelling, Den Helder, Lauwersoog, Harlingen and Delfzijl. In summer only: Roompotsluis, Oudeschild and Vlieland. On arrival from a non-EU country, report to Customs with documentation and passports. Fly flag 'Q' if dutiable goods are carried.

Yachts must carry and obey the Binnenvaart Politie Reglement (BPR: ColRegs/CEVNI etc in Dutch) which are included in Vol 1 of the Almanak voor Watertourisme. Special regulations apply to the Rivers Rhine, Lek and Waal. For boats over 15m LOA, or capable of more than 11 knots, an ICC is required on all inland waterways. For the Schelde, IJsselmeer or Waddensee the RYA Coastal Skipper Certificate or higher is required.

Yachts must keep watch on the various VHF frequencies applicable to VTS sectors, as listed in the MRNA.

Netherlands Board of Tourism, 18 Buckingham Gate, London SW1E 6LB. Tel 020 7931 0661.

Royal Netherlands Embassy, 12 Kensington Palace Gardens, London W8 4QU. Tel 020 7581 9615.

5.3.11 NORWAY
Telephone code from UK 00 47; to UK 095 44. Report to the Customs (Toll) at a Port of Entry such as Stromstad, Tonsberg, Oslo, Kristiansand, Mandal, Stavanger, Bergen or Alesund. Wear a courtesy ensign. Spirits in excess of 1 litre per head and tobacco are likely to be heavily taxed. Wines and spirits are only available from state liquor shops, and it is an offence to sell or give liquor to a local. It is important to clear Customs outwards on departure. There are no restrictions on crew changes.

Norwegian Tourist Board, Charles House, Lower Regent Street, London SW1Y 4LR. Tel 020 7839 6255; Fax 020 7839 6014.

Royal Norwegian Embassy, 25 Belgrave Square, London SW1X 8QD. Tel 020 7591 5500.

5.3.12 PORTUGAL
Telephone code from UK 00 351; to UK 00 44. Vessels must be registered and it is useful to have a crew list. No restrictions on crew changes. Skipper requires an ICC.

Portuguese National Tourist Office, 22 Sackville St, London W1X 2LY. Tel 020 7494 1441; Fax 020 7494 1868.

Portuguese Embassy, 11 Belgrave Square, London SW1X 8PP. Tel 020 7235 5331; Fax 020 7245 1287.

5.3.13 SPAIN
Telephone code from UK 00 34; to UK 07 44. Enter at a larger harbour and report to the Customs office where a Customs Permit (Permiso Aduanero) will be issued for the boat's stay in Spain. This permit is renewable and can be shown at other ports of call, and must be stamped on final departure. It is valid for six months in each calendar year for residents of EU countries. The yacht must be registered and the skipper must have an ICC or the equivalent. There are no restrictions on crew changes provided an individual's passport is suitably stamped.

Spanish National Tourist Office, 22 Manchester Square, London W1M 5AP. Tel 020 7486 8077; Fax 020 7486 8034.

Spanish Embassy, 39 Chesham Place, London SW1X 8SB. Tel 020 7235 5555; Fax 020 7259 5392.

5.3.14 SWEDEN
Telephone code from UK 00 46; to UK 009 44. Entry must be at a main harbour with Customs and passport control. The Swedish Tourism Council provides an informative leaflet *Customs Regulations for Leisure Craft*, which gives full details. On leaving you must go through passport control, but not Customs unless carrying stores or goods which must be declared. Alcohol and tobacco in excess of the normal tourist allowance may be sealed up on board, or even put ashore. There are strict import restrictions on various items, including live animals. There are some prohibited (military) areas.

Swedish Travel and Tourism Council, 11 Montagu Place, London W1H 2AL. Tel 020 7870 5600; Fax 020 7724 5872. Swedish Embassy, same address. Tel 020 7917 6400; Fax 020 7724 4174.

5.3.15 TURKEY
Telephone code from UK 00 90; to UK 00 44. Enter only at a designated port of entry. Fly flag 'Q' and a courtesy ensign. On arrival, if not visited, the skipper should take the ship's papers, crew list and crew passports to the harbour office where a Transit Log will be issued. The skipper should have an ICC. There are complex rules about crew changes and non-family crew members. For details see RYA Planning a Foreign Cruise, Vol 2.

Turkish Tourist Office, 170/73 Piccadilly, London W1V 9DD. Tel 020 7629 7771. Fax 020 7491 0773.

Turkish Embassy, 43 Belgrave Square, London SW1. Tel 020 7393 0202.

5.4 UNITS AND CONVERSIONS

5.4.1 BRITISH UNITS OF WEIGHTS AND MEASURES

Lengths
12 inches	=	1 foot
3 feet	=	1 yard
6 feet	=	1 fathom
1 shackle	=	15 fathoms
1 cable	=	1/10 nautical mile (approx 185 yards)
1 nautical mile	=	approx 6080 feet
1 statute mile	=	1760 yards (5280 ft)

Weights (avoirdupois)

16 drams	=	1 ounce
16 ounces	=	1 pound
14 pounds	=	1 stone
28 pounds	=	1 quarter
4 quarters	=	1 hundredweight
20 hundredweights	=	1 ton (2240 lb)

Volume

4 gills	=	1 pint
2 pints	=	1 quart
4 quarts	=	1 gallon
2 gallons	=	1 peck
4 pecks	=	1 bushel
8 bushels	=	1 quarter
5 quarters	=	1 load
36 bushels	=	1 caldron

Area

144 sq in	=	1 sqft
9 sq ft	=	1 sqyd
30 sq yd	=	1 sq pole
40 sq poles	=	1 rood
4 roods	=	1 acre (4840 sq yd)
640 acres	=	1 sq mile

Weight and volume of water

1 Imperial gallon	=	277.274 cu in, or 0.16 cu ft, or 10lb, or 4.546 litres
1 US gallon	=	231 cu in, or 0.133 cu ft, or 8.33lb, or 0.83 Imp gallons, or 3.8 litres
1 cu ft of water	=	6.232 Imp gallons, or 28.375 litres, or 0.284 cu metres, or 62.39lb
1 cu ft of salt water	=	64lb (or 1/35th ton)

Pressures

A column of water	=	Pressure of 0.434lb/sq in 1ft high
A column of water	=	Pressure of 1.43lb/1m high sq in
A column of water	=	Pressure of 1lb/sq in 2.3lft high

At 30in mercury (34ft water) atmospheric pressure is 1 atmosphere (14.71b/sq in)

Pressure in atmospheres = 0.068 x pressure in lb/sq in

5.4.2 SYSTÈME INTERNATIONAL (SI UNITS)

The SI version of the metric system is based on seven units denoting physical quantities. They are:

Quantity	Unit	Symbol
Length	metre	m
Mass	kilogram	kg
Time	second	s
Electric current	ampere	A
Thermodynamic temperature	kelvin	K
Luminous intensity	candela	cd
Amount of substance	mole	mol
(only used in physical chemistry)		

Note that the kilogram, unit of mass, is the only one with a multiple prefix. Prefixes denoting different sizes of this mass unit are attached to the 'gram', eg
1 kilogram = 1000 grams; 1 milligram = 1/1000 gram.

There are 15 derived units formed from base and/or supplementary units. They are:

Quantity	Name of SI derived unit	Symbol
Force	newton	N
Energy	joule	J
Frequency	hertz	Hz
Pressure and stress	pascal	Pa
Power	watt	W
Quantity of electricity	coulomb	C
Electric potential	volt	V
Electrical capacitance	farad	F
Electrical resistance	ohm	Ω
Electrical conductance	siemens	S
Magnetic flux	weber	Wb
Flux density	tesla	T
Inductance	henry	H
Luminous flux	lumen	lm
Illuminance	lux	lx

Prefixes

The following prefixes are used to designate multiples:

Prefix			Symbol	
giga	1 thousand million	1,000,000,000	10^9	G
mega	1 million	1,000,000	10^6	M
kilo	1 thousand	1000	10^3	k
hecto	1 hundred	100	10^2	h
deca	Ten	10	10^1	da
deci	1 tenth	0.1	10^{-1}	d
centi	1 hundredth	0.01	10^{-2}	c
milli	1 thousandth	0.001	10^{-3}	m
micro	1 millionth	0.000,001	10^{-6}	μ
nano	1 thousand millionth	0.000,000,001	10^{-9}	n
pico	1 million millionth	0.000,000,000,001	10^{-12}	p

5.4.3 CONVERSION FACTORS AND TABLES

To convert	Multiply by	To convert	Multiply by
Areas			
sq in to sq mm	645.16	sq mm to sq in	0.00155
sq in to sq cm	6.4516	sq cm to sq in	0.155
sq ft to sq m	0.0929	sq m to sq ft	10.76
sq yd to sq m	0.8361	sq m to sq yd	1.196
acres to sq m	4046.86	sq m to acres	0.000247
acres to sq yd	4840.0	sq yd to acres	0.0002
Consumption			
lb/hp/hr to gram/hp/hr	447.4	gram/hp/hr to lb/hp/hr	0.0022
Distances			
in to mm	25.40	mm to in	0.0394
in to cm	2.54	cm to in	0.394
ft to m	0.3048	m to ft	3.2808
yd to m	0.914	m to yd	1.094
fathoms to m	1.8288	m to fathoms	0.5468
statute miles to km	1.609	km to statute miles	0.6215
naut miles to statute	1.1515	statute miles to naut	0.8684
naut miles to m	1852	m to naut miles	0.00054
Force			
lbf to N	4.4482	N to lbf	0.2248
kgf to N	9.8066	N to kgf	0.101972
Mass			
oz to grams	28.35	grams to oz	0.0353
lb to kg	0.4536	kg to lb	2.205
ton to tonnes (1000kg)	1.016	tonnes to tons (2240lbs)	0.9842
tons to short (US) tons	1.12	short (US) tons to tons	0.893
Powers			
horsepower to kW	0.7457	kW to hp	1.341
hp to metric hp	1.014	metric hp to hp	0.9862
metric hp to kW	0.735	kW to metric hp	1.359
Pressures			
lb/sq in to kg/sq cm	0.0703	kg/sq cm to lb/sq in	14.22
lb/sq ft to kg/sq m	4.88	kg/sq m to lb/sq ft	0.205
lb/sq in to ft of water	2.31	ft of water to lb/sq in	0.433
lb/sq in to atmospheres	0.0680	atmospheres to lb/sq in	14.7
Speeds			
ft/sec to m/sec	0.3048	m/sec to ft/sec	3.281
ft/sec to knots	0.592	knots to ft/sec	1.689
ft/sec to miles/hr	0.682	miles/hr to ft/sec	1.467
ft/min to m/sec	0.0051	m/sec to ft/min	196.8
knots to miles/hr	1.1515	miles/hr to knots	0.868
miles/hr to km/hr	1.6093	km/hr to miles/hr	0.6214
knots to km/hr	1.852	km/hr to knots	0.5400
Torque			
lbf ft to Nm	1.3558	Nm to lbf ft	0.7376
kgf m to Nm	9.8066	Nm to kgf m	0.1020
lbf ft to kgf m	0.1383	kgf m to lbf ft	7.2330

To convert	Multiply by	To convert	Multiply by
Volumes			
cu in to cu cm	16.387	cu cm to cu in	0.061
cu ft to cu m	0.0283	cu m to cu ft	35.31
cu ft to galls	6.25	galls to cu ft	0.16
cu ft to litres	28.33	litres to cu ft	0.035
pints to litres	0.568	litres to pints	1.76
galls to litres	4.546	litres to galls	0.22
Imp galls to US galls	1.2	US galls to Imp galls	0.833
US barrels to cu m	0.16	cu m to US barrels	6.29

Feet to metres, metres to feet

How to use: The central columns of figures in bold type can be referred in either direction, ie to the left to convert metres into feet, or to the right to convert feet into metres. For example, five lines down: 5 feet = 1.52 metres, and 5 metres = 16.40 feet.

Feet		Metres	Feet		Metres	Feet		Metres	Feet		Metres
3.28	**1**	0.30	45.93	**14**	4.27	88.58	**27**	8.23	131.23	**40**	12.19
6.56	**2**	0.61	49.21	**15**	4.57	91.86	**28**	8.53	134.51	**41**	12.50
9.84	**3**	0.91	52.49	**16**	4.88	95.14	**29**	8.84	137.80	**42**	12.80
13.12	**4**	1.22	55.77	**17**	5.18	98.43	**30**	9.14	141.08	**43**	13.11
16.40	**5**	1.52	59.06	**18**	5.49	101.71	**31**	9.45	144.36	**44**	13.41
19.69	**6**	1.83	62.34	**19**	5.79	104.99	**32**	9.75	147.64	**45**	13.72
22.97	**7**	2.13	65.62	**20**	6.10	108.27	**33**	10.06	150.92	**46**	14.02
26.25	**8**	2.44	68.90	**21**	6.40	111.55	**34**	10.36	154.20	**47**	14.33
29.53	**9**	2.74	72.18	**22**	6.71	114.83	**35**	10.67	157.48	**48**	14.63
32.81	**10**	3.05	75.46	**23**	7.01	118.11	**36**	10.97	160.76	**49**	14.94
36.09	**11**	3.55	78.74	**24**	7.32	121.39	**37**	11.28	164.04	**50**	15.24
39.37	**12**	3.66	82.02	**25**	7.62	124.67	**38**	11.58	167.32	**51**	15.54
42.65	**13**	3.96	85.30	**26**	7.92	127.95	**39**	11.89	170.60	**52**	15.84

Inches to millimetres

inches	0	1/16	1/8	3/16	1/4	5/16	3/8	7/16	1/2	9/16	5/8	11/16	3/4	13/16	7/8	15/16
0		1.6	3.2	4.8	6.4	7.9	9.5	11.1	12.7	14.3	15.9	17.5	19.1	20.6	22.2	23.8
1	25.4	27.0	28.6	30.2	31.7	33.3	34.9	36.5	38.1	39.7	41.2	42.9	44.4	46.0	47.6	49.2
2	50.8	52.4	54.0	55.6	57.1	58.7	60.3	61.9	63.5	65.1	66.7	68.3	69.8	71.4	73.0	74.6
3	76.2	77.8	79.4	81.0	82.5	84.1	85.7	87.3	88.9	90.5	92.1	93.6	95.2	96.8	98.4	100.0
4	101.6	103.2	104.8	106.4	108.0	109.5	111.1	112.7	114.3	115.9	117.5	119.1	120.7	122.2	123.8	125.4
5	127.0	128.6	130.2	131.8	133.4	134.9	136.5	138.1	139.7	141.3	142.9	144.5	146.1	147.6	149.2	150.8
6	152.4	154.0	155.6	157.2	158.8	160.3	161.9	163.5	165.1	166.7	168.3	169.9	171.5	173.0	174.6	176.2
7	177.8	179.4	181.0	182.6	184.2	185.7	187.3	188.9	190.5	192.1	193.7	195.3	196.9	198.4	200.0	201.6
8	203.2	204.8	206.4	208.0	209.6	211.1	212.7	214.3	215.9	217.5	219.1	220.7	222.3	223.8	225.4	227.0
9	228.6	230.2	231.8	233.4	235.0	236.5	238.1	239.7	241.3	242.9	244.5	246.1	247.7	249.2	250.8	252.4
10	254.0	255.6	257.2	258.8	260.4	261.9	263.5	265.1	266.7	268.3	269.9	271.5	273.1	274.6	276.2	277.8
11	279.4	281.0	282.6	284.2	285.7	287.3	288.9	290.5	292.1	293.7	295.3	296.9	298.4	300.0	301.6	303.2
12	304.8	306.4	308.0	309.6	311.2	312.8	314.4	316.0	317.6	319.2	320.8	322.4	324.0	325.6	327.2	328.8

Feet and inches to millimetres

inches	0	1	2	3	4	5	6	7	8	9	10	11
feet												
1	305	330	356	381	406	432	457	483	508	533	559	584
2	610	635	660	686	711	737	762	787	813	838	864	889
3	914	940	965	991	1016	1041	1067	1092	1118	1143	1168	1194
4	1219	1245	1270	1295	1321	1346	1372	1397	1422	1448	1473	1499
5	1524	1549	1575	1600	1626	1651	1676	1702	1727	1753	1778	1803
6	1829	1854	1880	1905	1930	1956	1981	2007	2032	2057	2083	2108
7	2134	2159	2184	2210	2235	2261	2286	2311	2337	2362	2388	2413
8	2438	2464	2490	2515	2540	2565	2591	2616	2642	2667	2692	2718
9	2743	2769	2794	2819	2845	2870	2896	2921	2946	2972	2997	3023
10	3048	3073	3100	3124	3150	3175	3200	3226	3251	3277	3302	3327

Fathoms and feet to metres

The following table is useful for converting feet (or fathoms and feet) into metres, or vice versa:

Feet		6	12	18	24	30	36	42	48	54	60
Fathoms		1	2	3	4	5	6	7	8	9	10
Feet		1.8	3.6	5.5	7.3	9.1	10.9	12.8	14.6	16.4	18.3
1	0.3	2.1	3.9	5.8	7.6	9.4	11.3	13.1	14.9	16.7	18.6
2	0.6	2.4	4.2	6.1	7.9	9.7	11.6	13.4	15.2	17.0	18.9
3	0.9	2.7	4.5	6.4	8.2	10.0	11.9	13.7	15.5	17.3	19.2
4	1.2	3.0	4.9	6.7	8.5	10.3	12.2	14.0	15.8	17.7	19.5
5	1.5	3.3	5.2	7.0	8.8	10.6	12.5	14.3	16.1	18.0	19.8

Metres to nautical miles (m/M) (1m = 0.0005399 M)

m	0	100	200	300	400	500	600	700	800	900
0	0	0.054	0.108	0.162	0.216	0.270	0.324	0.378	0.432	0.486
1000	0.540	0.594	0.648	0.729	0.756	0.810	0.864	0.918	0.972	1.026
2000	1.080	1.134	1.188	1.242	1.296	1.350	1.404	1.458	1.512	1.566
3000	1.620	1.674	1.728	1.782	1.836	1.890	1.944	1.998	2.052	2.106
4000	2.160	2.214	2.268	2.322	2.376	2.430	2.484	2.538	2.592	2.646
5000	2.700	2.754	2.808	2.862	2.916	2.970	3.024	3.078	3.132	3.168
6000	3.240	3.294	3.348	3.402	3.456	3.510	3.564	3.618	3.672	3.726
7000	3.780	3.834	3.888	3.942	3.996	4.050	4.104	4.158	4.212	4.266
8000	4.320	4.374	4.428	4.482	4.536	4.590	4.644	4.698	4.752	4.805
9000	4.859	4.913	4.967	5.021	5.075	5.129	5.183	5.237	5.291	5.345

Nautical miles to metres (M/m) (1 M = 1852 m)

M	0.0	0.1	0.2	0.3	0.4	0.5	0.6	0.7	0.8	0.9
0	0	185.2	370.4	555.6	740.8	926.0	1111.2	1296.4	1481.6	1666.8
1	1852.0	2037.2	2222.4	2407.6	2592.8	2778.0	2963.2	3148.4	3333.6	3518.8
2	3704.0	3889.2	4074.4	4259.6	4444.8	4630.0	4815.2	5000.4	5185.6	5370.8
3	5556.0	5741.2	5926.4	6111.6	6296.8	6482.0	6667.2	6852.4	7037.6	7222.8
4	7408.0	7593.2	7778.4	7963.6	8148.8	8334.0	8519.2	8704.4	8889.6	9074.8
5	9260.0	9445.2	9630.4	9815.6	10008.0	10186.0	10371.0	10556.0	10742.0	10927.0
6	11112.0	11297.0	11482.0	11668.0	11853.0	12038.0	12223.0	12408.0	12594.0	12779.0
7	12964.0	13149.0	13334.0	13520.0	13705.0	13890.0	14075.0	14260.0	14446.0	14631.0
8	14816.0	15001.0	15186.0	15372.0	15557.0	15742.0	15927.0	16112.0	16298.0	16483.0
9	16668.0	16853.0	17038.0	17224.0	17409.0	17594.0	17779.0	17964.0	18150.0	18335.0

°F	°C	°F	°C	°F	°C
212	100	100	37.7	45	7.2
200	93.3	95	35.0	40	4.4
190	87.7	90	32.2	35	1.7
180	82.2	85	29.4	32	0.0
170	76.6	80	26.7	30	−1.1
160	71.1	75	23.9	25	−3.9
150	65.5	70	21.1	20	−6.7
140	60.0	65	18.3	15	−9.4
130	54.4	60	15.6	10	−12.2
120	48.8	55	12.8	5	−15.0
110	43.3	50	10.0	0	−17.7

Note: A more complete conversion scale is shown under Weather, Fig. 11 (22).

To convert °Centigrade to °Fahrenheit, multiply by 1.8 and add 32, eg 10°C x 1.8 = 18 + 32 = 50°F.

To convert °Fahrenheit to °Centigrade, subtract 32 and divide by 1.8.

5.5 GLOSSARIES

5.5.1 GLOSSARY OF NAUTICAL TERMS

Not surprisingly mariners have built up their own vocabulary of nautical terms, because many of the things which are expressed in nautical language have no equivalent ashore. In a boat precise instructions must often be given quickly, so clear communications can be very important. A sailor must therefore understand and use at least some of the more common terms. Here is a selection:

Aback	A sail is aback when trimmed so that the wind is on the forward side of it
Abaft	Behind; further aft than abeam
Abeam	On the beam; at right angles to the fore-and-aft line of the vessel
Aboard	In or on the vessel; on board
About, to go	To change tack
A-Bracket	Fitting shaped as an inverted 'A' supporting the end of the propeller shaft; cf P-bracket
Adrift	Loose; broken away; late
Afloat	Waterborne
Aft	At or towards the stern
Ahead	In front of; the direction of the bows
Ahoy	Hailing a vessel – plus her name
Amidships	Midway between bow and stern; position of the rudder or helm when fore-and-aft
Astern	Behind; the direction of the stern
Athwart	Across (the boat); athwartships

Avast	Stop (eg 'Avast heaving' – stop heaving)
Awash	Level with the surface of the water
A-weigh	When the anchor has broken out of sea bed
Back	Anti-clockwise change in wind direction. A sail is backed by hauling it to windward, so that the wind fills it on the other side
Backstay	A stay holding mast from astern
Bailer	A small receptacle for emptying water from a boat (bailing)
Ballast	Extra weight placed low down in a vessel to improve her stability
Bar	A shallow area (shoal) across the mouth of a harbour or river
Batten down	To secure hatches, openings etc before heavy weather or proceeding to sea
Battens	Flexible GRP or plastic strips inserted into pockets in the leech of a sail to keep its shape
Beacon	A fixed mark or structure to aid navigation
Beam	The width of a boat; a timber on which the decks are laid – hence 'on her beam ends'
Bearing	The direction of one object from another, usually expressed as a compass bearing
Bear away	To steer away from the wind direction
Bear off	To push away, eg from another boat or jetty
Beating	Sailing to windward, by alternately tacking across the wind
Beaufort scale	A numerical measure of wind speed
Becket	A loop or eye formed in a rope
Before	(the mast) Towards the bow
Belay	To secure or make fast a rope; (colloquially, to change or cancel an order, to cease)
Bend	A species of knot for joining ropes
Berth	Space for sleeping; or for a vessel to dock
Bight	The middle or loop of a rope (not the ends)
Bilge(s)	The curve of the underwater part of a boat, nearest the keel; space where water collects
Binnacle	The housing for a steering compass
Bitts	A pair of vertical posts for securing mooring lines or anchor warps
Bitter end	Inboard end of anchor cable

Block	A plastic, metal or wooden shell holding one or more sheaves through which ropes are led
Bluff	Steep-to, perpendicular
Boat hook	A stout pole with a hook at one end, used for picking up a buoy or in berthing a boat
Bollard	A vertical wooden or iron post on ship or shore, for securing mooring lines
Bolt rope	A rope sewn to the luff or foot of a sail
Boom	A spar used to extend the foot of a sail
Boom vang	A rope used to hold a boom forward and downward; see preventer
Boot-topping	Painted areas along the waterline
Bosun's chair	A seat which can be attached to a halyard for sending a man aloft
Bottlescrew	A rigging screw or turnbuckle used for tensioning standing rigging, esp shrouds
Bowline	A useful knot that forms a fixed loop
Bow	The forward end of a vessel
Bowse down	To tighten with a tackle (eg a rope or lashing)
Bowsprit	Spar projecting forward from the stem
Bring up	To come to an anchor or mooring
Broach	To swing over broadside on to the seas
Bulkheads	Vertical partitions within a vessel
Bulwarks	Solid wood or steel rails round the deck edge
Bunk	A bed
Buoy	A float used as a navigational mark; or for mooring to
Burgee	A triangular flag denoting membership of a club, flown at the masthead
By the head	A vessel trimmed bow down
By the lee	Running downwind, if the wind blows onto the lee side of the sail, risking a gybe
By the stern	A vessel trimmed stern down
Cable	Anchor chain or warp; or a distance of one tenth of a nautical mile, ie about 183 metres
Cardinal mark	Buoy or beacon indicating navigable water on the named side of the mark
Careen	To heel a vessel over to work on her bottom
Carry away	To break or part (spars, ropes) often violently
Carry way	To continue to move through the water
Carvel	Hull constructed to a smooth finish by laying planks edge to edge
Cast off	To let go (a warp or mooring line)
Catamaran	A twin-hulled, fast sailing vessel
Catenary	The curve of an anchor cable
Caulk	To make watertight the seams of a wooden deck or hull planking
Cavitation	Vibration and loss of power, caused by aeration of propeller working surfaces
Centre of buoyancy	Geometric centre of that part of a boat's hull which is below the waterline at any instant
Centreboard	A plate which can be lowered through a housing in the bottom of the hull, to increase lateral resistance, thus reducing leeway
Chainplates	Strong points on the hull each side of the mast, for attachment of shrouds
Chart Datum	The level to which charted depths and drying heights are referenced
Check	To ease out slowly (of a rope); slowly to stop a vessel's movement
Chine	The angle between the bottom and topsides in some designs of craft
Claw off	To get off a lee shore, usually close-hauled
Cleat	A fitting with projecting arms, around which a rope can be be layed or fastened
Clevis pin	A stout cylindrical pin (in standing rigging)
Clew	The lower, aft corner of a sail, where the foot meets the leech
Clinker	Method of wooden construction, where the edge of one plank overlaps the one below it
Close-hauled	Sailing as close to the wind as possible
Clutter	Unwanted returns (eg from waves or rain) on a radar display
Coachroof	Cabin top raised to increase headroom below
Companion	Ladder or stairs from on deck to below deck
Compass	Directional instrument, magnetic or fluxgate, pointing to magnetic north
Con	To give pilotage orders to the helmsman
Contour	A line on the chart joining points of equal elevation or equal depth

Counter	The overhanging portion of the stern	Fathom	A measure of depth, equals six feet
Course	The direction in which a boat is being steered	Fender	Protection against damage to a boat's side when alongside another vessel or a jetty
Cradle	Supporting frame for a boat out of the water	Fend off	To bear or push off a boat from a jetty
Cringle	A rope loop or metal eye attached to a sail, usually for reefing purposes	Fetch	To reach a desired destination; the distance which the wind has blown over open water
Crown	Where the arms of an anchor join the shank	Fiddle	A lip or batten around table tops to prevent objects falling or sliding off
Crutch	Metal jaw and pin which drops into gunwale of a boat to take an oar; see Rowlock	Fix	A position found from visual, astronomical or radio bearings, or by electronic means
Davits	Small cranes for hoisting boats, inflatables	Flare	Outward curve of the bow of a ship; pyrotechnic signal used to call attention
Dead reckoning	Position calculated from course steered, time and distance run	Flashing	Navigation light with period of light shorter than period of darkness
Deck	The floor(s) of a vessel, see also Sole	Flood	The tidal stream on a rising tide
Deckhead	Underside of the deck (cabin 'ceiling')	Fluxgate compass	Compass that electronically detects the earth's magnetic field by induced voltages
Deviation	Compass error due to the vessel's magnetism	Foot	The bottom edge of a sail
Dip	To lower, then re-hoist, the ensign as a salute	Fore-and-aft	The boat's major, or longitudinal axis
Displacement	The volume of water a vessel displaces, hence her actual weight in tons (35cu ft/ton)	Foreguy	Rope leading forward from boom end, to hold boom forward; also preventer
Dog watches	The two-hour watches from 1600-1800 and 1800-2000, known as the First and Last Dog	Forestay	Stay which runs from stem to mast(head)
Downhaul	A rope pulling downwards, usually on the tack of a sail; also on a spinnaker pole	Foretriangle	Triangle formed by forestay, mast and deck
Down helm	An order to the helmsman to put the tiller 'down', ie away from the wind	Forward	At or towards the bow
		Foul	Entangled, obstructed, eg 'foul anchor', 'foul bottom'; 'foul tide' ie adverse tidal stream
Dowse	To extinguish a light or lower a sail; also to spray with water, drench (also douse)	Fractional rig	A rig where the forestay attaches to the mast below the mast head (ie not a masthead rig)
Draught	The depth of a vessel from the waterline to the lowest part of the keel (also draft)	Frap	To bind together (rope, sails etc)
		Freeboard	The height of the deck above the waterline
Drogue	A form of stabiliser or sea anchor; used in yachts, boats, liferafts and lifebuoys	Freshen	A strengthening of the wind
		Furl	To lower or roll and secure a sail
Ebb	The tidal stream on a falling tide	Gaff	Spar at head of a fore-and-aft sail
Echo sounder	Electronic instrument to measure the depth of water	Gale	Wind of Beaufort force 8 (34-40 knots)
Ensign	A vessel's national maritime flag	Galley	The kitchen
Fairlead	Opening or fitting through which a (mooring) rope could be lead for working	Gimbals	Two pivoted concentric rings that hold items such as a compass or lamps level at sea
Fairway	A navigable, often buoyed, channel to a port	Go about	To tack, thus bringing the wind on the other side of the sails

Gooseneck	Fitting which holds the boom to the mast	Holiday	Area or gap left unpainted by mistake
Goose-winged	Running before the wind, with the foresail set on one side and the mainsail on the other	Hourglass	A spinnaker twisted in the middle, so that the wind fills the top and bottom parts
Ground tackle	Anchor, cable and associated gear	House flag	A rectangular, personal flag of owner
Gunwale	The upper edge along the sides of a boat	Hull	The structure of a boat, to deck level
Guy	A rope used to control a derrick or spar, eg in a yacht, the spinnaker guy; see also foreguy	Inboard	Towards the middle of, or within, a vessel
Gybe	Changing from one tack to the other by putting the boat's stern through the wind (as opposed to tacking)	Inshore	Towards, or close to, the shore
		Irons	A yacht is in irons when stationary, head to wind, unable to pay off on either tack
Halyard	Rope for hoisting a sail or flag	Isophase	A navigational light which shows equal periods of light and darkness
Handbearing compass	Portable magnetic compass for taking bearings; assumed to have no deviation	Jib	Triangular sail, set forward of the mast
Handsomely	Gently, or slowly	Jury	Makeshift (eg rudder, rig etc)
Hank	Fitting for attaching the luff of a sail to a stay	Kedge	A light-weight or secondary anchor
Hard	A place for beaching boats	Keel	The lower fore-and-aft structure of a vessel
Hard a-port	Helm order to use maximum helm in the stated direction (port or starboard)	Kicking strap	Tackle used to hold down boom, and reduce twist in sail; also vang, gas-kicker
Hatchway	A deck opening with a cover (hatch)	King spoke	The spoke of a steering-wheel which is vertical when the rudder is centred
Haul	To pull (a rope); or a wind shift		
Hawsepipe	Pipe from cable deck to outside of the bow, through which the anchor cable runs	Knot	One nautical mile per hour (speed)
Hawser	A heavy rope for mooring or towing	Landfall	First sight of land, seen from seaward
Head	The top corner of a sail	Lashing	Securing with a rope
Header	A wind shift bringing the wind further ahead	Lateral mark	Navigation buoy or beacon port or starboard side of a defined channel
Heading	The direction in which a boat is pointing	Latitude	Angular measurement of an object/position north or south of equator
Heads	Marine lavatory		
Headsail	A sail set forward of the mast		
Head sea	A sea from ahead	Launch	To slip into the water
Heave-to	To stop, or reduce speed, with vessel almost head to wind, helm a-lee and headsail aback	Lay	The twist in the strands of a rope; or to go in the direction indicated (eg lay aft)
Heaving line	A light line with a weighted end for throwing to another vessel or shore	Lazy	Extra or spare (eg sheet, the one not in use)
Heel	The angle of inclination (leaning) of a vessel	Lead line	Marked line with a lead weight, for measuring depth of water
Helm	The tiller or wheel	Leading marks/lights	Marks or lights which when aligned indicate the channel or best water
Hitch	Knots to secure a rope to a spar or object (eg rolling hitch), not for joining two ropes		
		Leech	The trailing (aft) edge of a sail
Holding	Quality of the bottom (ground) for anchoring	Lee helm	The tendency of a boat to fall off the wind, due to improper balance

Leeward	The side of a boat further from the wind (pronounced loo'ard; cf 'windward')	Nothing to port (or starboard)	Order to steer no further to port, or starboard
Leeshore	Shore on to which the wind is blowing	Null	The weakest signal from a D/F radio station, indicating its bearing
Leeway	The sideways movement of a boat, blown (to leeward) by the wind	Occulting	A navigational light, whose period of light is longer than the period of darkness
Lifeline	Line rigged to stop crew going overboard	Offing	Distance (safe) to seaward off the land
Lift	A wind shift allowing a boat to point higher (opposite to 'header'). Also a rope which supports a spar (eg main boom topping lift)	Off soundings	In deep waters; originally to seaward of the 100 fathoms line
		Off the wind	Sailing with the wind broad on, or abaft, the beam
List	Angle of heel	On the wind	Sailing as close to the wind as possible
Log	Instrument which measures distance run through the water	Overboard	Over the side of the vessel (into the water)
Log book	Record of vessel's movements, positions, etc	Overhaul	To ease the blocks of a tackle apart
Longitude	Angular measurement of an object/position east or west of the Greenwich meridian	Painter	The rope secured to the bows of a dinghy or tender, by which it is tied up or towed
Loom	The inboard end of an oar; reflection (of a light) on low cloud	Pay off	To allow the ship's head to swing away from the direction of the wind
Lubber line	Fixed mark on compass bowl, showing ship's head		
Luff	The leading edge of a sail.	Pay out	To ease out a chain or rope
To luff	To sail closer to the wind	P-bracket	Bracket supporting the aft end of the propeller shaft; cf A-bracket
Mainsail	Sail set on aft side of the main (principal) mast. Usually the largest working sail, and referred to as 'the main'	Pitch poled	When a boat is somersaulted, stern over bow, by a very large following sea
Mainsheet	Rope and tackle for trimming the mainsail	Pooped	When a vessel is overtaken by a sea which breaks over the stern (poop)
Make	To reach port; (of tides) when range is increasing	Port (side)	The left side of a vessel looking forward
Make fast	To secure a rope to a bollard or cleat	Port tack	Sailing with the wind over the port side of a vessel, whose main boom is to starboard
Make water	To leak		
Man	To provide the crew for certain tasks, eg to man the pumps	Preventer	A guy lead forward from the outer end of the boom; intended to prevent accidental gybing
Marline spike	Pointed steel tool, used for splicing		
Marry	To bring (the ends of) two ropes together	Quarter	Area from abeam to dead astern
Meridian	A north-south line through any point	Race	A localised area of tidally disturbed water
Messenger	A light line, used for example to haul over a large hawser, eg for towing	Racon	A beacon whose response to a radar set's transmission shows up on the display
Midships	Helm order to centre the rudder	Radar	Electronic instrument that displays the positions of ships, coastline, buoys etc
Miss stays	To fail to tack through the wind		
Mizzen	The aft mast in a yawl or ketch	Radio beacon	A radio transmitter of known frequency, position and signal, from which a navigator with a suitable receiver can obtain a bearing
Moor	To lie to two anchors, or secure to piles		
Neaps	A tide whose range is at a minimum		

Range	To flake down lengths of cable on deck, before anchoring; also	Snatch block	A single-sheave block which can be hinged open to take the bight of a rope
Range	The height difference between successive high and low waters	Snub	To check a line from running out round a winch or cleat; to pitch against anchor cable
Reach	A point of sailing with the wind roughly abeam	Sole	Deck of a cabin and fore-cabin
Reef	To reduce the area of a sail; a ridge of rocks	Sound	To ascertain (plumb) the depth (sounding)
Reeve	To pass the end of a rope through a block etc	Spinnaker	A triangular, full-bellied, light-weight sail set on a reach or running before the wind
Rhumb line	A course cuting all meridians at the same angle (a straight line on a Mercator's chart)	Spreaders	Struts (aka crosstrees) each side of the mast, to widen the angle of the capshrouds
Riding light	Anchor light	Spring	Mooring rope led forward from the stern, or aft from the bow, to a bollard or cleat ashore
Rigging	Wires which support the masts (standing), or ropes (running rigging) to control the sails	Spring tide	A tide whose range is maximum (cf 'neaps')
Rowlock	A gap in the gunwale, into which an oar fits; also, by common usage, a metal Crutch (qv), swivelling in the gunwale, for same purpose	Stanchion	Vertical support for guardrail wire running round the deck edge
		Standing part	The fixed (not running) part of a rope
Rubbing strake	A piece of wood (usually) secured along the hull, that takes the wear alongside a jetty	Starboard	The right side of a vessel looking forward
Rudder	Vertical plate, hinged on forward side, for steering	Starboard tack	Sailing with the wind over the starboard side of a vessel, whose main boom is to port
Run	To sail before the wind; or distance covered	Stay	Fore and aft support wires for mast
Samson post	Post for securing anchor or tow line	Steady	Helm order to maintain the present course
Scantlings	The dimensions of a vessel's timbers	Steerage way	When a vessel moves fast enough through the water to respond (answer) to her helm
Scuppers	Holes in bulwarks to allow water to drain from deck	Stem	The foremost part of the bow
Scuttles	Round openings in vessel's side	Stiff	Not easily heeled over
Seacock	A valve on a pipe connected to the sea	Stop	To secure a sail, especially a spinnaker, with cotton or elastic bands, so that it can be broken out (spread) after hoisting
Sheer	The upward curve of the deck, towards bow and stern; to move a vessel relative to her anchor (eg by applying helm in a tideway)	Surge	To ease out under control a rope around a winch or bollard
Sheet	Rope used to trim a sail's angle to the wind	Swage	A metal terminal pressed on to a wire rope
Ship	To take on board, especially of water	Swing	Procedure for finding compass deviation
Shoal	Shallow area of water		
Shrouds	Athwartships or lateral supports to mast	Tabernacle	Deck fitting in which the foot of a lowering mast pivots
Skeg	A fin aft of the keel, to protect the rudder	Tabling	Reinforcement sewn to edge of a sail
Slack water	When there is little or no tidal stream	Tack	The forward lower corner of a sail; to beat to windward, alternating port/starboard tacks
Slip(way)	Slope for launching boats; to let go (a warp)	Tackle	Ropes and blocks, to increase hauling power
Sloop	A sailing boat rigged with one mast		

Take a turn	To pass a rope around (typically) a cleat	Turn up	To make a rope fast
Tang	Mast fitting for attachment of shroud or stay	Under way	When a vessel is not anchored or secured to the land or shore in any way
Telltale	Wool, yarn or ribbon as wind indicator	Up & down	When the anchor cable is vertical
Thwart	Seat running across (athwart) an open boat	Veer	To pay out anchor cable; (of the wind) when it changes direction clockwise
Tidal stream	Horizontal movement of the sea, due to tide	Wake	Disturbed water astern of a vessel as she moves ahead
Tide	The rise and fall of the sea, caused by the attraction of the moon and sun	Warp	Rope used to moor or anchor, or move a vessel
Tiller	Bar connected to the rudder to move same	Wash	The waves caused by a vessel's progress through the water
Toggle	Metal fittings in rigging, to allow some free movement while retaining tension	Watches	Periods of duty for members of the crew
Topping lift	Lift (rope) to support the end of main boom or spinnaker pole	Weather	The side of a vessel nearer the wind ('wind-ward', as opposed to 'leeward')
Topsides	Sides of a yacht's hull above the waterline	Weather helm	When the tiller has to be held to windward to maintain a steady course
Track	A channel mounted to deck or spar, to take a traveller (eg sheet lead block, sail slide)	Weigh	To raise the anchor
Transom	The flat stern of some designs of vessel	Wetted surface	The area of the boat under water
Transducer	A sensor for passing data (eg depth or water speed) to a navigational instrument	Wind rode	When a vessel is lying to the wind (rather than to the tide)
Trick	A period or spell at the helm	Yard	A spar on a mast for spreading a sail
Trim	To alter the set of sails; the fore-and-aft attitude of a boat in the water	Yaw	Course deviation due to wind, sea or helm

5.5.2 FIVE-LANGUAGE VOCABULARY

Note: A five-language vocabulary of weather terms is given in Chapter 11 (Weather).

English	French	German	Dutch	Spanish
Types of boat				
Cruiser	Bateau de croisière	Kreuzeryacht	Toerjacht	Yate crucero
Cutter	Cotre	Kutter	Kotter	Cuter
Dinghy	Canot, dinghy	Dingi, Beiboot	Bijboot	Chinchorro
Ferry	Bac, ferry	Fähre	Veerboot	Pasaje
Fishing boat	Bateau de pêche	Fischereifahrzeug	Vissersboot	Pesquero
Ketch	Ketch	Ketsch	Kits	Queche
Launch	Vedette	Barkasse	Barkas	Lancha
Lifeboat	Bateau de sauvetage	Rettungsboot	Reddingboot	Bote salvavidas
Merchant vessel	Navire de commerce	Handelsschiff	Koopvaardijschip	Buque
Motor cruiser	Croiseur à moteur	Motorkreuzer	Motorkruiser	Motora
Motor sailer	Bateau mixte	Motorsegler	Motorzeiljacht	Moto-velero
Ocean racer	Bateau de course-croisière	Hochseerenyacht	Zeewedstrijdjacht	Yate de regatas oceánica
Pilot boat	Bateau pilote	Lotsenversetzboot	Loodskotter	Bote del práctico
Schooner	Goélette	Schoner	Schoener	Goleta
Sloop	Sloop	Slup	Sloep	Balandra

English	French	German	Dutch	Spanish
Tanker	Bateau citerne	Tanker, Tankschiff	Tanker, tankschip	Buque cisterna
Tug	Remorqueur	Schlepper	Sleepboot	Remolcador
Yacht	Yacht	Yacht	Jacht	Yate
Yawl	Yawl	Yawl	Yawl	Balandro de baticulo

Rigging Sails

English	French	German	Dutch	Spanish
Backstay	Pataras	Achterstag, Backstag	Achterstag	Popparrás
Batten pocket	Etui ou gaine de latte	Lattenasche	Zeillatzak	Bolsa del sable
Boom	Bôme	Baum	Giek	Botavara
Bowsprit	Beaupré	Bugspriet	Boegspriet	Baupré
Chain plate	Cadène	Rüsteisen, Puttings	Putting	Cadenote
Clew	Point d'écoute	Schothorn	Schoothoorn	Puño de escota
Crosstrees	Barres de flèche	Saling	Dwarszaling	Crucetas
Foot	Bordure	Unterliek	Voetlijk	Pujamen
Forestay	Etai avant	Vorstag, Fockstag	Voorstag, fokkestag	Estay de proa
Genoa	Génois	Genua	Genua	Génova
Halyard	Drisse	Fall	Val	Driza
Head	Point de drisse	Kopf	Top	Puño
Jib	Foc	Fock	Fok	Foque
Leech	Chute	Achterliek	Achterlijk	Baluma
Luff	Envergure	Vorliek	Voorlijk	Gratil
Mainsail	Grand'voile	Grossegel	Grootzeil	Vela mayor
Mast	Mât	Mast	Mast	Palo
Mizzen	Artimon	Besan	Bezaan	Mesana
Mizzen staysail	Voile d'étai d'artimon	Besanstagsegel	Bezaanstagzeil	Entrepalos
Reef point	Garcette	Reff'ose	Knuttel	Tomadores de rizo
Shackle	Manille	Schakel	Sluiting	Grillete
Sheet	Ecoute	Schot	Schoot	Escota
Shroud	Hauban	Want	Want	Obenque
Spinnaker	Spinnaker	Spinnaker	Spinnaker	Espinaquer
Staysail	Trinquette	Stagsegel	Fok	Vela de estay
Tack	Point d'amure	Hals	Hals	Puño de amura

Materials

English	French	German	Dutch	Spanish
Aluminium alloy	Aluminium	Aluminium	Aluminium	Aluminio
Bolt	Boulon	Bolzen	Bout	Perno
Bronze	Bronze	Bronze	Brons	Bronce
Glass fibre	Fibre de verre	Glasharz	Fiberglas	Fibra de vidrio
Gunmetal	Bronze de canon	Rotguss	Geshutsbrons	Brone de canon
Lead	Plomb	Blei	Lood	Plomo
Marine plywood	Bois contre plaque marin	Schiffsbausperrholz	Scheepstriplex	Contrachapado
Nut	Ecrou	Schraubenmutter	Moer	Tuerca
Nylon	Nylon	Nylon	Nylon	Nilón
Rivet	Rivet	Niet	Klinknagel	Remache
Screw	Vis	Schraube	Schroef	Tornillo
Stainless steel	Acier inoxydable	Rostfreier Stahl	Roestvrij staal	Acero inoxidable
Steel	Acier	Stahl	Staal	Acero
Terylene	Tergal	Polyester, Dacron	Dacron	Dacron
Washer	Rondelle	Unterlegscheibe	Ring	Arandela
Weld	Souder	Schweissen	Lassen	Soldar
Wood	Bois	Holz	Hout	Madera

Parts of a boat

English	French	German	Dutch	Spanish
Bilges	Cale	Bilge	Kim	Sentina
Bulkhead	Cloison	Schott	Schot	Mamparo

149

English	French	German	Dutch	Spanish
Cabin	Cabine	Kajute	Kajuit	Camarote
Cockpit	Cockpit	Plicht, Cockpit	Kuip	Bañera
Deck	Pont	Deck	Dek	Cubierta
Fo'c'sle	Poste avant	Vorschiff	Vooronder	Castillo de proa
Galley	Cuisine	Kombüse	Kombuis	Cocina
Gunwale	Plat-bord	Dollbord	Dolboord	Regala
Hatch	Ecoutille	Luk	Luik	Escotilla
Keel	Quille	Kiel	Kiel	Quilla
Lifeline	Filière	Rettungsleine Reling	Zeereling	Pasamano
Pulpit	Balcon avant	Bugkanzel	Preekstoel	Pülpito
Rudder	Gouvernail	Ruder	Roer	Timón
Stanchion	Chandelier	Stütze	Steun	Candelero
Steering wheel	Roue de gouvernail	Steuerrad	Stuurrad	Rueda de timón
Stem	Etrave	Vorsteven	Voorsteven	Roda
Stern	Poupe	Heck	Achtersteven	Popa
Tiller	Barre	Pinne	Helmstok	Cana
Wheelhouse	Timonerie	Ruderhaus	Stuurhuis	Timonera

Engine etc

English	French	German	Dutch	Spanish
Alternator	Alternateur	Wechselstromgenerator	Wisseistroomdynamo	Alternador
Atomiser, injector	Injecteur	Einspritzdüse	Inspuiter	Inyector
Battery	Batterie	Batterie	Accu	Bateria
Clutch	Embrayage	Kupplung	Koppeling	Embrague
Diesel fuel pump	Pompe d'injection	Einspritzpumpe	Brandstofinspuitpomp	Bomba de inyección
Distilled water	Eau distillée	Destilliertes Wasser	Gedistilleerd water	Agua destilada
Drive belt	Courroie de transmission	Treibriemen	Drijfriem	Correa
Fuel filter	Filtre à combustible	Treibstoffilter	Brandstoffilter	Filtro de combustible
Fresh water	Eau douce, potable	Trinkwasser	Drinkwater	Agua potable
Gearbox	Boitre de vitesse	Getreibe	Versneiiingsbak	Caja de cambios
Generator	Dynamo	Lichtmaschine	Dynamo	Generado
Grease	Graisse	Fett	Vet	Grasa
Hose	Tuyau	Schlauch	Slang	Tubo
Hydraulic fluid	Liquide hydraulique	Hydraulisches Öl	Hydraulischeolie	Aceite hidráulico
Ignition coil	Bobine d'allumage	Zündspule	Onsteking-bobine	Bobina
Oil	Huile	Schmierol	Olie	Aceite
Propeller	Hélice	Schraube	Schroef	Helice
Starter motor	Démarreur	Anlasser	Startmotor	Motor de arranque
Water pump	Pompe à eau	Wasserpumpe	Waterpomp	Bomba de agua

Navigation

English	French	German	Dutch	Spanish
Abeam	Par le travers	Querab	Dwars	Por el través
Ahead	En avant	Voraus	Voorwaarts	Avante
Anchorage	Mouillage	Ankerplatz	Ankerplaats	Fondeadero
Astern	En arrière	Rückwärts, achtern	Achteruit	Atrás
Bay	Baie	Bucht	Baai	Bahla
Beacon	Balise	Bake	Baken	Baliza
Binoculars	Jumelles	Fernglas	Kijker	Prismáticos

English	French	German	Dutch	Spanish
Buoy	Bouée	Tonne, Boje	Ton, boei	Boya
Channel	Chenal	Fahrwasser	Vaarwater	Canal
Chart	Carte marine	Seekarte	Zeekaart	Carta nautica
Compass	Compas	Kompass	Kompas	Compás
Course	Cap, route	Kurs	Koers	Rumbo
Degree	Degré	Grad	Graad	Grado
Depth	Profondeur	Tiefe	Diepte	Fondo
Deviation	Deviation	Deviation, Ablenkung	Deviatie	Desvío
Dividers	Pointes sèches	Kartenzirkel	Passer	Compas de puntas
East	Est	Ost	Oost	Este
Echo sounder	Echo sondeur	Echolot	Echolood	Sondar acustica
Estuary	Estuaire	Flussmundung	Mond	Estuario
Hand bearing compass	Compas de relèvement	Handpeilkompass	Handpeilkompas	Aguja de marcar
Headland	Promontoire	Vorgebirge	Voorgebergte	Punta
Island	Île	Insel	Eiland	Isla
Latitude	Latitude	Breite	Breedte	Latitud
Leading line	Alignement	Leitlinie	Geleidelijn	Enfilación
Longitude	Longitude	Lange	Lengte	Longitud
Mud	Vase	Schlick, Schlamm	Modder	Fango
North	Nord	Nord	Noord	Norte
Overfalls	Remous	Stromkabbeiung	Stroomrafeling	Escarceos
Parallel rulers	Regles parallèles	Parallellineal	Paralieliineaal	Paralelas
Patent log	Loch enregistreur	Patentlog	Patent log	Corredera de patente Babor
Port	Bâbord	Backbord	Bakboord	
Reef	Récif	Riff	Rif	Arrecife
Rocks	Rochers	Klippen, Felsen	Rotsen	Piedras
Shoal	Haut fond	Untiefe	Droogte	Bajo
South	Sud	Süd	Zuid	Sud
Starboard	Tribord	Steuerbord	Stuurbord	Estribor
Variation	Déclinaison	Missweisung	Variatie	Variación
West	Ouest	West	West	Oeste

Tides

English	French	German	Dutch	Spanish
Chart datum	Zero des cartes	Kartennull	Reductievlak: kaart-peil	Bajamar escorada
Depth	Profondeur	Tiefe	Diepte	Fondo
Ebb	Marée descendante	Ebbe	Eb	Vaciante
Flood	Marée montante	Flut	Vloed	Entrante
High water	Pleine mer	Hochwasser (HW)	Hoogwater (HW)	Pleamar
Low water	Basse mer	Niedrigwasser(NW)	Laagwater (LW)	Bajamar
Neap (tides)	Morte eau	Nipptide	Doodtij	Aguas muertas
Range	Amplitude	Tidenhub	Verval	Repunte
Rate	Vitesse	Geschwindigkeit	Sneiheid	Velocidad
Set	Porter	Setzen	Zetten	Dirección
Spring (tides)	Vive eau	Springtide	Springtij	Marea viva
Tidal stream	Courant	Gezeitenstrom	Getijstroom	Corriente

Numbers etc

English	French	German	Dutch	Spanish
One	un	eins	een	Uno
Two	deux	zwei	twee	Dos
Three	trois	drei	drie	Tres
Four	quatre	vier	vier	Cuatro
Five	cinq	fünf	vijf	Cinco
Six	six	sechs	zes	Seis
Seven	sept	sieben	zeven	Siete

English	French	German	Dutch	Spanish
Eight	huit	acht	acht	Ocho
Nine	neuf	neun	negen	Nueve
Ten	dix	zehn	tien	Diez
Six hours	Six heures	Sechs Stunden	Zes uren	Seis horas
Twelve hours	Douze heures	Zwolf Stunden	Twaalf uren	Doce horas
Eighteen hours	Dix-huit heures	Achtzehn Stunden	Achttien uren	Diez y ocho horas
Twenty-four hours	Vingt-quatre heures	Vier und zwanzig Stunden	Vier en twintig uren	Veinticuatro horas
Thirty-six hours	Trente-six heures	Sechs und dreissig	Zes en dertig uren	Treinta y seis horas
Forty-eight hours	Quarante-huit heures	Acht und vierzig Stunden	Acht en veertig uren	Cuarenta y ocho horas
Today	Aujourd'hui	Heute	Vandaag	Hoy
Tomorrow	Demain	Morgen	Morgen	Mañana
Radio				
Call sign	Indicatif	Rufzeichen	Roepsein	Señal de llamada
Frequency	Fréquence	Frequenz	Frequentie	Frecuencia
Operating time	Heures d'émission	Sendezeit	Seintijd	Hora de servicio
Radio beacon	Radiophare	Funkfeuer	Radiobaken	Radiofaro
Radio direction finder	Radiogoniomètre	Funkpeiler	Radio peiltoestel	Radio goniometro
Radio receiver	Poste récepteur	Rundfunkempfanger	Radio-ontvangtoestel	Receptor de radio
Radio station	Station d'émission	Rundfunksender	Radioomroepstation	Estación de radiodifusión
Radio telephone	Radio téléphone	Sprechfunk-Gerät	Radiotelefoon	Radio teléfono

5.6 USEFUL ADDRESSES

Amateur Yacht Research Society, BCM AYRS, London WC1N 3XX. ayrs@fishwick.demon.co.uk Tel/Fax: 01727 862268.

Association of Brokers and Yacht Agents (also YBDSA), Wheel House, Petersfield Road, Whitehill, Bordon, Hants GU35 7BU. Tel 01420 473862. Fax 01420 488328.

British Marine Industries Federation, Meadlake Place, Thorpe Lea Road, Egham, Surrey TW20 8HE. Tel 01784 473377; Fax 01784 439678. ashepard@bmif.co.uk www.bmif.com and www.bigblue.org.uk

British Sub-Aqua Club, Telford's Quay, Ellesmere Port, Cheshire CH65 4FL. Tel 0151 350 6200; Fax 0151 350 6215. postmaster@bsac.com www.bsac.com

British Waterways Board, Willow Grange, Church Road, Watford, Herts WD1 3QA. Tel 01923 226422; Fax 01923 226081.

British Waterways (Scotland), Regional Office, Canal House, Applecross Street, Glasgow G4 9SP. Tel 0141 332 6936; Fax 0141 331 1688.

Clyde Cruising Club, The Pentagon Centre, Suite 408, 36 Washington Street, Glasgow G3 8AZ. Tel 0141 221 2774; Fax 0141 221 2775. hazel@clydecruising.demon.co.uk www.clyde.org

Cowes Combined Clubs, (also Solent Cruising & Racing Association), 18 Bath Road, Cowes, Isle of Wight PO31 7QN. Tel:01983 295744. Fax: 01983 295329.

Cruising Association, CA House, 1 Northey St, Limehouse Basin, London E14 8BT. Tel 020 7537 2828; Fax 020 7537 2266. office@cruising.org.uk www.cruising.org.uk

HM Customs and Excise: Call the local Customs Advice Centre, as listed in 5.2.1, or visit www.hmce.gov.uk

Cutty Sark Trust, 2 Greenwich Church Street, London SE10 9BG. Tel 020 8858 2698; Fax 020 8858 6976. info@cuttysark.org.uk www.cuttysark.org.uk

Flag Institute, The, 44 Middleton Road, Acomb, York YO24 3AS. Tel 01904 339985. michael.faul@virgin.net

Hydrographic Office, Admiralty Way, Taunton, Somerset TA1 2DN. Tel 01823 337900; Fax 01823 284077.

Inland Waterways Association, PO Box 114, Rickmans-worth WD3 1ZY. Tel 01923 711114; Fax 01923 897000. iwa@waterways.org.uk www.waterways.org.uk

Inmarsat, 99 City Road, London EC1Y lAX. Tel: 020 7728 1000. Fax:020 7728 1044.

Institute of Marine Engineers, 80 Coleman St, London EC2R 5BJ. Tel 020 7382 2600; Fax 020 7382 2670.

International Institute of Marine Surveyors, Stone Lane, Gosport, Hants PO12 1SS. Tel 023 9258 8000; Fax 023 9258 8002.

International Maritime Organization (IMO), 4 Albert Embankment, London SE1 7SR. Tel 020 7735 7611; Fax 020 7587 3210.

Irish Lights, Commissioners of, 16 Lower Pembroke Street, Dublin 2. Tel 00 353 1 662 4525; Fax 00 353 1 661 8094. www.cil.ie

Irish Marine Emergency Services, Dept of the Marine, Leeson Lane, Dublin 2. Tel 00 353 1 662 0922; Fax 00 353 1 662 0795.

Irish Sailing Association, 3 Park Road, Dun Laoghaire, Co Dublin. Tel 00 353 1 280 0239; Fax 00 353 1 280 7558.

Junior Offshore Group, 28 Nodes Road, Cowes, Isle of Wight P031 8AB. Tel/Fax 01983 291192.

Little Ship Club, Bell Wharf Lane, London EC4R 3TB. Tel:020 7236 7729. Fax:020 7236 9100.

Lloyd's, One Lime Street, London EC3M 7HA. Tel 020 7327 5408; Fax 020 7327 6827. www.lloyds.com   lloyds-salvage@lloyds.com

Lloyd's Register (Passenger Ship and Special Service Craft Group), 71 Fenchurch St, London EC3M 4BS. Tel 020 7423 2325; Fax 020 7423 2016. psg-general@lr.org www.lr.org

Marine Accident Investigation Branch, 1st Floor, Carlton House, Carlton Place, Southampton SO15 2AN. Tel 023 8039 5500; Fax 023 8023 2459. maib@detr.gsi.gov.uk   www.open.gov.uk/maib

Marine and Coastguard Agency, Spring Place, 105 Commercial Road, Southampton, SO15 1EG. Tel: 023 8032 9100. Fax: 023 8032 9105.

Meteorological Office, London Road, Bracknell, Berks RG12 2SZ. Tel 01344 420242; Fax 01344 855921. (Moving to Exeter at a future date)

National Coastwatch Institution, 4a Trafalgar Sq, Fowey PL23 1AZ. Tel 0870 787 2147; Fax 0870 164 1893. info@nci.org.uk   www.nci.org.uk

National Federation of Sea Schools, Purlins, 159 Woodlands Rd, Woodlands, Southampton SO40 7GL. Tel/Fax 023 8029 3822. kay@nfss.co.uk www.nfss.co.uk

Nautical Institute, 202 Lambeth Road, London SE1 7LQ. Tel 020 7928 1351; Fax 020 7401 2817. sec@nautinst.org pubs@nautinst.org www.nautinst.org

Northern Lighthouse Board, 84 George Street, Edinburgh EH2 3DA. Tel 0131 226 7051; Fax 0131 220 2093. www.nlb.org.uk enquiries@nlb.org.uk

Port of London Authority, Baker's Hall, Hart Lane, London EC3R 6RB. Tel 020 7743 7900; Fax 020 7743 7999. www.portoflondon.co.uk

Radiocommunications Agency, Aeronautical & Maritime Services, Wyndham House, 189 Marsh Wall, London E14 9SX. Tel 020 7211 0211; Fax 020 7211 0507. ams@ra.gtnet.gov.uk www.radio.gov.uk

Radio Licence Centre, Ships Licences, PO Box 1495, Bristol BS99 3QS. www.radiolicencecentre. co.uk Tel 0870 243 4433.

Radio Licence Centre, Amateur Radio and CB Licences, PO Box 885, Bristol BS99 5LG. Tel 0117 925 8333.

Registry of Shipping and Seamen (RSS), PO Box 165, Cardiff CF4 5FU. Tel 029 2074 7333 extn 289; Fax 029 2074 7877; Helpline 0891 615353.

Royal Cruising Club, at the Royal Thames Yacht Club (see below).

Royal Institute of Naval Architects, 10 Upper Belgrade St., London SW1X 8BQ. Tel 020 7235 4622; Fax 020 7259 5912. hq@rina.org.uk www.rina.org.uk

Royal Institute of Navigation, 1 Kensington Gore, London SW7 2AT. Tel 020 7591 3130; Fax 020 7591 3131.

Royal National Lifeboat Institution, West Quay Road, Poole, Dorset BH15 1HZ. Tel 01202 663000; Fax 01202 663167. info@rnli.org www.lifeboats.org.uk

Royal Naval Sailing Association, 10 Haslar Marina, Haslar Road, Gosport, Hants PO12 1NU. Tel 023 9252 1100; Fax 023 9252 1122. e-mail rnsa@compuserve.com

Royal Ocean Racing Club, 20 St James's Place, London SW1A 1NN. Tel 020 7493 2248; Fax 020 7493 5252. rorc@stjames.demon.co.uk http// rorc.org

Royal Ocean Racing Club, Rating Office, Seahorse Building, Bath Road, Lymington, Hants SO41 9SE. Tel 01590 677030; Fax 01590 679478.

Royal Thames Yacht Club, 60 Knightsbridge, London SW1X 7LF. Tel 020 7235 2121; Fax 020 7245 9470. www.royalthames.com club@royalthames.com

Royal Yachting Association, RYA House, Romsey Road, Eastleigh, Hants SO50 9YA Tel: 023 8062 7400. Fax: 023 8062 9924. admin@rya.org.uk

Royal Yachting Association Scotland, Caledonia House, South Gyle, Edinburgh EH12 9DQ. Tel 0131 317 7388; Fax 0131 317 8566. helen@ryascotland.freeserve.co.uk

Society of Consulting Marine Engineers and Ships Surveyors, c/o 202 Lambeth Rd, London SE1 7LQ; Tel 020 7261 0869; Fax 020 7261 0871. scms@btinternet.com

Solent Cruising & Racing Association, see Cowes Combined Clubs.

Sport England (aka English Sports Council), 16 Upper Woburn, London WC1H 02P. Tel 020 7273 1500; Fax 020 7273 1868. info@english.sports.gov.uk www.sportengland.org

Stationery Office, The (TSO, former HMSO), St Crispin's House, Duke St, Norwich NR3 1PD. Tel 0870 600 5522; Fax 0870 600 5533. e-mail esupport@theso.co.uk www.the-stationery-office.co.uk Shop at: clicktso.com

Trinity House (Corporation of), Trinity House, Tower Hill, London EC3N 4DH. Tel: 020 7481 6900. Fax: 020 7480 7662. e-mail hcooper@admin.thls.org www.trinityhouse.co.uk

Yacht Charter Association Ltd, Deacon's Boatyard, Bursledon Bridge, Southampton, Hants SO31 8AZ. Tel: 023 8040 7075; Fax: 023 8040 7076; charter@yca.co.uk Website www.yca.co.uk

Yacht Designers and Surveyors Association (also Association of Brokers and Yacht Agents), Wheel House, Petersfield Road, Whitehill, Bordon, Hants GU35 7BU. Tel: 01420 473862. Fax: 01420 488328.

Yacht Harbour Association, Evegate Park Barn, Smeeth, Ashford, Kent TN25 6SX. Tel 01303 814434; Fax 01303 814364. sueheale@tyha.freeserve.co.uk

Chapter 6 Legal Advice

CONTENTS

Other legal references
Throughout this Handbook there are various references to legal matters in other chapters, where various problems of interest to boat owners are under discussion. These references are summarised below:

If legal advice is required, consult a solicitor who is well versed in maritime law. A list of such firms is available from the Royal Yachting Association.

6.1 PUBLIC RIGHT OF NAVIGATION

6.1.1 PUBLIC RIGHT OF NAVIGATION ON TIDAL WATERS

There is an inherent right of navigation on the sea. For the purposes of most cruising and racing yachtsmen, it is a safe generalisation that a public right of navigation exists over all tidal waters and that this can only be interrupted with the express consent of Parliament. However, the fact that tidal water may, on a spring high water, reach an otherwise dry ditch, does not necessarily meant that the right extends to that ditch. By the same token, while a large ship might under the most favourable circumstances negotiate a narrow crowded river, the automatic right that extends to smaller craft would not necessarily be enjoyed by that ship. It is a question of fact and degree in each case for each vessel as to whether the right exists.

The bed of all navigable tidal reaches of rivers up to high water mark is almost invariably the property of the Crown, but in most cases has been vested or leased to a harbour authority or conservancy, or to a local authority. The right of navigation is similar in many ways to the right of way on land. Just as on a public highway the right is enjoyed to pass and repass, and to stop for a reasonable length of time, so too on tidal waters a vessel may navigate and anchor, but may not permanently occupy an area of water by laying a fixed mooring without consent.

The right to navigate does not include the right to ground or rest on the seabed for repairing or cleaning the hull, although this is common and accepted practice.

There are a number of authorities who may purport to have a power to prevent navigation on tidal waters, but where such a power exists it may well be for limited purposes only.

6.1.2 MILITARY RANGES

Many coastal areas are used by the Ministry of Defence as gunnery or bombing ranges, or as proving ranges. During firing times these ranges, which are normally clearly marked by sea and/or land marks – and are depicted on more recent Admiralty charts, are patrolled by MOD Police who are entitled to request yachts to keep clear of certain limits. While it obviously makes sense to co-operate with reasonable requests where possible, all range Byelaws contain a specific exemption for vessels, in the ordinary course of navigation, crossing the sea area and taking no longer than is required for that purpose. The range Byelaws on all such ranges controlling the right to navigate are carefully worded so as not to exclude the bona fide right to transit the range at any time whether firing is scheduled or not. The effect of this exemption is to entitle cruising and racing yachts to cross the area or part of it, but not to enter only in order to round a mark and then leave it again, as in racing; nor to loiter, anchor nor start fishing.

6.1.3 PUBLIC RIGHT OF NAVIGATION ON NON-TIDAL WATERS

Public rights of navigation over non-tidal waters can be established by dedication (ie gift by the owner), by statute, by custom (in use since time immemorial) or by prescription (uninterrupted use as of right over a period in excess of 20 years). Both commercial and recreational vessels may keep this right alive; even canoeing may keep the right alive. A House of Lords ruling regarding the Yorkshire Derwent held that the general law governing the right of way over land does not apply to rivers or watercourses. Where there is no right to navigate, any attempt to do so will constitute a trespass and in the 1972 case of *Rawson v. Peters* an incursion by a canoeist into a valuable angling beat, even though it was not being fished on the day in question, was held to be an actionable trespass giving rise to damages and an injunction restraining further trespass.

A public right of navigation also exists on a number of lakes, reservoirs, major rivers and canals, where the right is generally subject to the payment of licence fees to the controlling authority.

6.1.4 NATURE CONSERVANCY AGENCIES
Statutory powers can be used to modify the public right of navigation so as to protect nature conservation interests in:

a. National and Local Nature Reserves
Such reserves can only extend to the low water mark, so it is only navigation in inter-tidal areas that can be affected. Conservation agencies (for national reserves) and local authorities (for local reserves) have powers to make byelaws, which can restrict or prohibit entry and movement of boats. As an alternative, voluntary arrangements may be possible. Examples are Lindisfarne National Nature Reserve and Pagham Harbour Local Nature Reserve. The relevant statute is the *National Parks and Access to the Countryside Act 1949*.

b. Marine Nature Reserves
Under the *Wildlife and Countryside Act 1981* (and equivalent legislation for Northern Ireland) the nature conservation agencies have the power to make byelaws excluding pleasure craft from certain parts of the reserve at certain times of the year. Marine nature reserves extend below the low water mark into the coastal marine area. At present there are only three such reserves designated: the island of Lundy, the island of Skomer and Strangford Lough. At Skomer, some small inshore areas are subject to restrictions on navigating and anchoring, otherwise no byelaws have been made. Advisory groups have been formed for these reserves, on which the RYA are represented.

c. European Marine Sites
An extensive network of marine sites, covering many areas of importance for yachting (eg the Solent, Plymouth, Essex Rivers, Falmouth, North Cardigan Bay, the Menai Strait, Strangford Lough and a number of others) are in the process of being designated as sites of European importance for nature conservation, under the European Habitats Directive. The relevant UK legislation is the *Conservation (Natural Habitats etc) Regulations 1994*. The conservation agencies have the same byelaw making powers as are given for marine nature reserves, but of more practical importance is likely to be the development of *schemes of management* which are the responsibility of a range of *relevant authorities*, such as local and harbour authorities, who are required to use their existing powers to manage the sites so as to achieve the conservation objectives established for them.

These sites have not yet been formally designated, and it may take some years before the full implications for recreational boating of the implementation of the Habitats Directive in marine areas becomes clear.

6.1.5 THE HARBOUR MASTER'S AUTHORITY
A Harbour Master may not exclude a craft for any reason except that it is carrying a dangerous cargo or may sink and create a danger to other vessels navigating within the harbour, nor may he prevent a craft from moving within the harbour except for the day-to-day control of traffic. As with all public authorities, harbour administrators are under a duty implied by law to exercise their powers reasonably and only for purposes associated with their undertaking.

In the leading case of *Pearn v Sargeant* (1973) the Harbour Master at Looe gave instructions that the harbour should be closed for a substantial part of the day so that a regatta could take place. The owner of a craft within the harbour was prosecuted for failing to comply with the Harbour Master's directions, even though the movement of his vessel could not conceivably have interfered with the craft competing in the regatta. The Lord Chief Justice said:

The function of the Harbour Master under the act is to regulate the traffic; after all it is a public harbour where the public have a right to be and it is not the Harbour Master's function, as such, to keep them out. His function is to control and regulate them rather like a traffic policeman regulating traffic. Of course there will be some cases where he has to go beyond these simple functions; of course there may be cases where necessity arises and he has to impose wider prohibitions for a particular time, but when that happens it is for consideration whether the directions he has given are reasonable for the emergency or circumstances which prompted them.

6.1.6 QUEEN'S HARBOUR MASTER (QHM)

The powers of QHMs in Naval Ports and Dockyards are very much wider than those applying to civil and commercial harbours. In Portsmouth Harbour for example the QHM has introduced regulations prohibiting the use of sailboards (which otherwise have all the rights and responsibilities attaching to other vessels through UK tidal waters) in clear conflict with the general principles governing the public right of navigation. The wide powers of the QHM make this a lawful exercise, as indeed would all regulations affecting the navigation of craft unless a complainant was able to show that the imposition of such regulations was entirely unreasonable. These powers derive from the Royal Prerogative without the need for any specific parliamentary authority.

6.2 HARBOUR LAW

6.2.1 DEFINITION OF HARBOUR

As we have seen most public harbours are under the jurisdiction of Harbour Authorities or Conservancies, or of the Harbour Committee of the relevant local authority.

By the terms of the Harbours Act 1964, 'harbour' is defined as *'any harbour whether natural or artificial, any port, haven, estuary, tidal or other river or inland waterway navigated by seagoing ships, and includes a dock, wharf and in Scotland a ferry or boatslip being used for marine work'.*

6.2.2 HARBOUR AUTHORITIES

The Harbours Act also defines a Harbour Authority for the purpose of the Act as *'any persons in whom are vested under this Act, by another Act or by any Order or instrument, powers or duties for improving, maintaining or managing a Harbour'.*

A Harbour Authority for a public harbour is generally established by statute, as the sea bed of a harbour, the fundus, is normally owned by the Crown. However, proprietors of a harbour entrusted with managing, maintaining or improving a harbour may also be recognised as non-statutory harbour authorities and generally exist in private harbours where the fundus is not owned by the Crown.

Nearly all harbours with a significant degree of commercial or recreational use are managed under statutory powers. One reason for this is that the taking of harbour dues and tolls is part of the Royal Prerogative and can only be assigned to a subject as a franchise by the Crown or by an Act of Parliament. Harbour Authorities which rely on grant or prescription from the Crown are now very rare and do not include any major Harbour authorities (with the exception of Naval Dockyards). Another reason why statutory powers are necessary to manage a harbour is that the construction and maintenance of harbour works below the high water mark may be open to challenge in the courts unless such construction and maintenance is authorised by statute, on the grounds that the works interfere with the public right of navigation. Moreover harbour authorities for large harbours need to have powers to regulate activities of persons using the harbour, and in particular the movement and berthing of vessels within the area. Adequate powers for these purposes can only be obtained by statute.

Local circumstances of the many harbour authorities in Britain are very varied. This is perhaps one reason why harbour authorities still operate to a large extent under local statutory powers. The nature and function of harbour authorities vary from one place to another as does the size of the area under jurisdiction.

6.2.3 CHARGES MADE BY HARBOUR AUTHORITIES

Charges made by harbour authorities are of two kinds:

a. Dues, a charge for a vessel entering, using or leaving the harbour, including charges in respect of marking or lighting the harbour. This is a payment for the enjoyment of the basic or essential harbour or port. Dues may be levied on all ships, passengers and goods using the port. The payment of dues is in the nature of a tax, as the amount payable is not directly related to the service received by the user. Under the *Harbours Act 1964*, a harbour authority may impose such claim for dues as they think fit, subject only to a right of appeal by users to the Secretary of State if harbour dues are thought to be unreasonable.

b. Other charges, a payment for the enjoyment, usually optional, of ancillary services, such as slipways, moorings and the use of other facilities.

Combined Charges are a payment combining both dues and charges. The practice of levying combined charges is expressly authorised under the *Transport Act 1981* and blurs the distinction between the two.

An objection to the charges can be made to the Secretary of State on the following grounds:

a) that the charge ought not to be imposed at all;

b) that the charge ought to be imposed at a lower rate than that at which it is imposed;

c) that, according to the circumstances of the case, the yacht ought to be excluded from the scope of the charge either generally or in circumstances specified;

d) that, according to the circumstances of the case, the charge ought to be imposed but at a lower rate than at which it is imposed on others.

The Secretary of State does not have the power to determine any legal issue.

6.2.4   MOORING RESPONSIBILITIES
The authority for consenting to the laying of moorings depends on the freehold ownership of the fundus. The authority to grant consent may be vested by statute in a harbour authority and no conflict of interest arises where the freehold ownership of the fundus has also been granted in the harbour authority by statute. Where the freehold interest of the fundus remains with the Crown or a party other than the Crown, such as a local council, then a conflict of interest is likely to arise. Where the laying of the mooring is within a harbour, then it may be necessary to gain consent from the both the harbour authority and the freehold owner of the fundus, such as the Crown Estate Commissioners. For the laying of moorings outside of a harbour authority area, consent of the freehold owner of the fundus should be sought.

Mooring is distinguished from the right of anchoring, the latter being an act incorporated in the right of navigation. Mooring is distinguished as it is the placing of a permanent fixture on the fundus.

The Crown Estate Commissioners will grant individual licences to boat owners wishing to lay moorings on their ground and leases to harbour authorities, local authorities, fairways committees and yacht clubs as appropriate. The Crown Estate Commissioners are under a statutory duty to obtain the 'best consideration' from their leases. The increasing demand for a fixed supply of mooring areas has enabled the Commissioners to increase rents considerably.

Individuals, clubs or even small harbour authorities negotiating Crown leases and rent reviews should seek advice from the RYA which maintains a current database of all new leases and rent reviews of mooring areas. Many harbour authorities of course provide mooring tackle in accordance with statutory powers to make facilities available for harbour users, and in such cases the cost of providing the tackle plus maintenance and replacement costs are properly charged to the mooring holder. Where the Crown Estate Commissioners lease the area of fundus to a marina operator for development, a very much higher rent is charged by the Crown in recognition of the profit element expected by the developer.

Where a club or harbour authority has taken a regulating lease, it is always subject to the condition that they should not 'uplift' the ground rent charged to individual boat owners by more than 25%, to cover administration and other charges.

Moorings which are used or intended to be used by yachts and are only equipped with a buoy attached to an anchor, weight or other device, which rest on or in the bed of the sea or any other water when used and which are designed to be raised from time to time for inspection are not subject to rates. (*Local Government Finance Act 1988*)

The principle of distinguishing moorings for the purpose of ratings was identified in the case of *Cory v. Bristow (1877)*, where it was held that moorings which were permanently embedded in the soil and could not easily be lifted gave rise to occupation and therefore rates were liable to be paid.

6.2.5   OTHER MOORING CONTROLS
So far as the laying of moorings is concerned, local authorities have a general planning jurisdiction down to the low water mark, or to the mid point of any narrow creek or river (which is defined by ancient case law as being a river not so wide that one cannot see what a man on the other side is doing). Under the terms of the Coast Protection Act 1949, consent for the construction of any works or deposit of any article (and this is interpreted to include mooring tackle) requires the consent of the Secretary of State for Transport. This consent will not be given where the proposal would cause an interference with, or danger to, navigation. The Department of Transport normally consults widely with all interested parties when proposals for development or new moorings are made, and conditions such as the size and type

of vessels using the moorings, together with a specification for ground tackle and mooring buoys, are often imposed.

6.2.6 ANCHORING AND THE USE OF MOORINGS

With the very much restricted space that is available for boats in most harbours and estuaries around our coasts, problems often arise with cruising yachts trying to find a place to anchor or moor even overnight. The right to navigate in tidal water implies a right to anchor at least for a reasonable time, or for purposes connected with navigation, as already mentioned in 6.1.1. But local byelaws often prohibit anchoring in certain areas, and sometimes throughout the entire harbour as applies in the Hamble River.

A vessel which anchors (where anchoring is permitted) must do so clear of other vessels already at anchor or on moorings. Consideration needs to be given to what will happen with the change of tide, or with a shift of wind to another quarter. Except in extreme conditions, dragging an anchor and causing damage to some other craft implies negligence, either due to not using the right ground tackle, failing to let go a second anchor when conditions so require, or leaving the boat unattended.

Moorings allocated to an individual by a harbour authority are private, for the use of that individual. In practice most yachtsmen do not object to some other craft using their mooring in their absence, always provided that the vessel is not too heavy for the mooring and that sufficient crew are left on board to shift berth should the absent owner of the mooring return.

A problem may arise however when an owner finds an unattended yacht on his mooring. As a last resort there may be a temptation to cast the stranger adrift, but this could amount to a criminal offence and would almost certainly entitle the owner to damages if the yacht was damaged. The only correct procedure is for the owner of the mooring himself to find an alternative mooring, or to move the stranger to some other safe berth in either case recovering the expense involved from the stranger, by legal action if necessary.

6.3 COLLISIONS

6.3.1 INTRODUCTION

Collisions include anything from the superficial scraping of a yacht to the total loss of a yacht. Common causes of collisions include adverse weather conditions, such as reduced visibility, and congestion in sailing areas, but the common factor in all collisions is human error. Human error has given rise to questions of poor seamanship, lack of foresight and an improper appraisal of other vessels' movements. These human elements are essentially issues of safety at sea.

Collisions typically happen where there has either been a failure to keep a proper look out, there has been a failure to slacken speed in a dangerous situation, there has been a failure to use up-to-date charts and Notices to Mariners, or there has been a failure to use recognised international and local navigational rules.

There is a presumption at law that all sailors have knowledge of the International Regulations for Preventing Collisions at Sea (IRPCS) which establish the rules of the road. Therefore, it is taken that a sailor knows these rules just as a motorist is taken to know the Highway Code. In a regatta, the infringement of the International Sailing Federation (ISAF) Racing Rules of Sailing, by prescription to Rule 68, does not in itself equate to a legal wrong and penalty taken for a breach of the Rules does not amount to an admission of a legal wrong. The prescription to Rule 68 specifically provides that the findings of fact of a protest committee can only be brought into evidence in a civil court with the written consent of both parties. In other words, such findings are irrelevant to the question of liability for damages. Courts are required by law to apportion liability for collisions in proportion to the degree in which each vessel was at fault, unless it is impossible to do so.

6.3.2 NEGLIGENCE

When dealing with a dispute concerning a collision, the courts will have regard to (but will not be limited to) the established facts, if relevant, the different skill levels of parties involved and the position of the parties under the Collision Regulations. Negligence is established where there has been a failure of necessary skill and care ordinarily expected of a competent, reasonable and prudent sailor. An owner of a yacht will become responsible for the negligence of those sailing his yacht for his benefit, including the helmsman and crew taken on board either for racing or cruising purposes. The yacht owner will not be responsible for any damage caused by the crew if not caused in the process of those people sailing the yacht for his benefit.

Negligence charged in a collision may include negligent navigation and negligent management of the vessel, such as the failure to properly care for equipment so that the steering gear fails or the mooring ropes part. However, liability is based on fault and not all instances of negligence amounts to such a degree of fault as to impose legal liability.

The burden of proving negligence rests on the party seeking to assert it, normally the claimant in the case. Having established negligence, the claimant must then prove that he has suffered some form of loss or damage as a result of that negligence. For instance, two yachts may have negligently come into contact with each other yet there was not even any scraped gel coat caused by that contact; therefore the claimant would have nothing to claim from the negligent sailor. Once these two issues have been established then the burden of proof shifts to the defendant, for him to prove any defence or contributory negligence. Each issue is decided on a balance of probabilities.

6.3.3   TYPICAL COLLISION SITUATIONS
A collision may or may not involve actual contact between two yachts. A collision may involve two or more yachts. The fault of each yacht involved in the collision will be assessed separately; fault will be attributable by consideration of blameworthiness. Instances where a yacht may be held liable for damage caused to another yacht although there has been no physical contact include:

i.   Excessive speed causing another vessel to sink;
ii. Chafing damage against the wharf caused by swell or wash of a passing boat;
iii. The negligent mooring or anchoring of a yacht, such as an unlit yacht lying in a navigation channel, causing an approaching yacht to take evasive action and running aground; and
iv. Proceeding along a designated shipping channel in the wrong direction, causing yachts, correctly using the shipping channel, to collide when taking evasive action. This has been likened to a motorist proceeding south on the north-bound carriageway of the M1.

The yacht need not be manned when damage is caused, such as a yacht breaking loose from its mooring and drifting into neighbouring yachts, for liability to be imposed on the yacht owner.

With all these scenarios, the yacht owner could avoid liability if he could prove in his defence that either there was a latent fault with the yacht and its equipment, such as a defect in a mooring chain, or that factors outside of the

yacht owner's control caused the damage. But the yacht owner must show that he took all reasonable care in order to escape liability.

6.3.4   THE COLLISION REGULATIONS
The IRPCS consist of rules relating to the steering and sailing of vessels, rules relating to the use of lights and shapes on those vessels and rules relating to sound and light signals. The Regulations are a matter of law as provided for by section 85 of the *Merchant Shipping Act 1995 (amended)* and SI 1996/75. Sailors in charge of all UK vessels anywhere and any other vessels in UK waters are presumed to have knowledge of the Regulations. The breach of these Regulations is of paramount importance in determining blame for a collision. Where the Regulations are breached, the yacht owner, the helmsman and any other person in a position of responsibility may be found guilty of the offence. Each rule is equally important although some salient points are identified here:

By Rule 5, the yacht shall use sight and hearing and all available means appropriate in the prevailing circumstances and conditions so as to make a full appraisal of the situation and of the risk of collision. The rule is intended to be all-embracing. By this rule, it is necessary to keep a satisfactory radar watch and to observe correctly lights on another vessel.

By Rule 6, the yacht must use a safe speed, therefore a speed adequate in the prevailing circumstances. The crew must always be in control of the yacht.

By Rule 7, every vessel shall use all available means appropriate to the prevailing circumstances and conditions to determine if a risk of collision exists. If there is any doubt as to whether a risk does exist, then it is deemed that a risk does exist.

An obligation is imposed on every yacht, by Rule 8, to avoid a collision by taking any necessary action, in ample time and with due regard to observation of good seamanship. Any such manoeuvre must be apparent to any observing yacht. A succession of small alternations of course or speed should be avoided, as should close-quarter situations.

6.3.5   LOSS OF LIFE AND PERSONAL INJURY CLAIMS
The skipper and owner of a yacht has liability to those on board, both crew and passengers, to take reasonable care in all circumstances and not to expose the crew and passengers to any unnecessary dangers. Not all insurance policies automatically cover this liability.

Where death or a personal injury results from a collision, a claim for these damages may be brought against any of the offending vessels, jointly or severally. Once the matter has been settled with one of the vessels, then the claim must be discontinued against the other offending vessels. The unsuccessful defendant has a right to claim a contribution or indemnity from the other vessels involved in the collision, but only where liability for the collision is established. A claim for death is governed by the *Fatal Accidents Act 1976*.

6.3.6 CONTRIBUTORY NEGLIGENCE
It is unlikely that full liability be will be imposed on only one of the yachts involved in the collision, as the actions of all parties to the collision will be taken into consideration to appreciate whether the collision could have at all been avoided. The level of liability will be graded. Those sailors who deliberately embarked on a negligent act will bear the greater degree of fault. Sailors who failed to cope adequately with a crisis thrust upon them will bear little to no degree of fault. The balance of liability is, of course, subject to the particular facts of the collision. The initial negligent act may have been so slight that a collision was easily avoidable, making the failure to take avoiding action so gross that the blame for the accident will fall largely on the yacht failing to avoid the consequences of the initial act of negligence. Such a scale of fault is imposed because although a human may choose not to deliberately break a rule, a human may not react perfectly to a crisis, thereby falling short of the requisite degree of reasonable care.

6.3.7 AGONY OF THE MOMENT DEFENCE
A defendant to a claim of collision may plead that he was forced, by circumstances out of his control, to take action with no time to think, form a plan nor carry out a deliberate and properly calculated plan or manoeuvre. The defendant is thereby seeking to override the general obligation to exercise due care and skill expected of a seaman. Therefore, although the act committed in the agony of the moment was the proximate cause of damage, it was not the probable cause to which blame can be attached. These circumstances often arise in the course of a yacht race where the helmsman is forced to make a snap decision as a reaction to the actions of another racing yacht in close quarters. A momentary inattention may have serious consequences.

6.3.8 ACT OF GOD
Act of God can be defined as an operation of natural forces which is so unexpected that any consequence arising from it must be regarded as too remote to be the foundation for legal liability. It need not be spectacular such as lightning or flooding; a rat gnawing through a wire can be held to be an Act of God. Such arguments can be used in defence.

6.3.9 INEVITABLE ACCIDENT
This is defined as an accident not avoidable by any such precaution as a reasonable man, doing such an act, there and then, could be expected to take. In the context of an action for negligence, it really amounts to a more specific means of denying a breach of the duty of care. In truth all accidents can be avoided, so long as adequate precautions are taken, but the law will never impose a higher standard of care than could be expected of a reasonable man under the circumstances.

6.3.10 VOLENTI NON FIT INJURIA
This is a defence by which it is pleaded that a person consented to an injury by consenting to the circumstances resulting in the injury and therefore cannot complain of it thereafter.

Thus an experienced yachtsman, who appreciates and accepts the intrinsic risks of yacht racing, can reasonably be expected to foresee that damage or loss may be occasioned as a result of starting a race or sailing a particular course in bad weather conditions, and may even be deemed negligent in so doing.

On the other hand, a competitor known to be inexperienced will not foresee the possible harm, nor could he reasonably be expected to, and would not necessarily be negligent in undertaking the risks. In such a case, the skipper of a boat and the organising club may owe a duty of care to a crew member, and the defence of *volenti* will fail.

Although consent is normally implied by the courts in all properly conducted sports, no one is deemed to consent to a deliberate fool. While one has to accept the risk of damage or injury arising from an honest mistake, carelessness, or error of judgment, a deliberate act outside the rules resulting in injury or damage will usually be actionable.

Where children are involved, the courts will take a practical view as to whether the child, in all the circumstances, and having regard to the nature of the risk, can sensibly be held to have consented to the risk. Below the age of 13 or 14 the onus of proof will be very much on the defendant to show that a child, particularly if inexperienced in the sport, knew the risks.

6.3.11 LIMITATION PERIOD AND COURT PROCEDURE

Legal proceedings in a collision suit should be commenced within two years from the moment of the collision. The court has the discretion to extend this period where the circumstances are considered to merit such extension. An extension of the claim period is unlikely where the delay was caused by the claimant. The claimant must have issued to the defendant a claim form within the two year period.

6.3.12 MEASURE OF DAMAGES

A claim for damages seeks to put the injured party in the position in which they were before the collision took place, as much as a financial quantification may so do. The successful claimant will be entitled to full compensation for all his losses arising from an incident. The claimant may claim for the repair of his yacht, towage, salvage, harbour dues, survey fees or delivery costs. Where there has been a total loss of a yacht, then the value claimed in court will be the market value of the yacht at the time the loss occurred. The court may take into consideration whether the yacht was being used in business such as for charter. Where two or more yachts are involved in a collision and liability is shared, then the cost of the damage to each yacht is added together and the aggregate is divided as apportioned by the court.

The repairs to a yacht, following a collision must be satisfactory and at a reasonable cost. The wrong doer has no right to choose the place of repairs.

6.4 TOWAGE AND SALVAGE

6.4.1 TOWAGE

Towage is in essence the service by one vessel to another for a fixed remuneration. Towage in its literal sense is distinct from salvage.

Towage is a negotiated contract to aid a vessel which lacks its own motive powers, such as a vessel emerging from a dockyard or a vessel manoeuvring in restricted water. "Towage" includes services such as escorting and guiding by the contractor's vessel. The terms and conditions of the contract are generally those of the UK Standard Conditions for Towage and Other Services (revised 1986), for which remuneration

may either be calculated daily or as a lump sum. The contract will also normally identify the Master and crew as the servants of the tow for the duration of the towage. This form places most liability for the towage on the tow, as the tug is generally held to be the servant of the tow. The Standard Conditions for Towage 1986 expressly preserve the tug-owner's right to limit his liability in addition to reserving his right to compensation for any other extra services rendered. A frequently used standard indemnity clause reads:

loss or damage of any kind whatsoever or howsoever or wheresoever arising in the course of and in connection with the towage.

6.4.2 SALVAGE

The right to salvage may or may not arise out of a contract, eg the Lloyd's Standard Form of Salvage Agreement (Fig. 6(1) overleaf), but salvage must be beyond the duty of any existing contract of employment between the parties, such as that of a pilot. The Standard Conditions for Towage 1986 expressly preserve all rights of the tug to claim salvage remuneration. Remuneration for salvage is by way of award and arises out of a legal liability created out of the fact that maritime property has been saved at sea. Salvage is supported by the courts' encouragement of seafarers to voluntarily protect lives and maritime property in danger at sea and the International Convention on Salvage 1989 is given the force of law in the *Merchant Shipping Act 1995*.

Lord Stowell, in a case concerning a vessel called *The Neptune* (1824), described a salvor as:

one who, without any particular relation to the ship in distress, proffers useful service and gives it as a volunteer adventurer without any pre-existing covenant that connected him with the duty of employing himself for the preservation of that ship.

A salvage award may only be claimed where:

i. the salvage has been rendered to a legally recognised subject of salvage, that being the vessel, its apparel, bunkers and so-called freight; and
ii. the service has been voluntary; and
iii. the service has been successful, if only partially.

It is for the salvor to prove beyond reasonable doubt that there existed a duty to render the service and that the duty was owed to the

LOF 2000

LLOYD'S STANDARD FORM OF
SALVAGE AGREEMENT

(APPROVED AND PUBLISHED BY THE COUNCIL OF LLOYD'S)

NO CURE - NO PAY

1. Name of the salvage Contractors: (referred to in this agreement as "the Contractors")	2. Property to be salved. The vessel: her cargo freight bunkers stores and any other property thereon but excluding the personal effects or baggage of passengers master or crew (referred to in this agreement as "the property")
3. Agreed place of safety:	4. Agreed currency of any arbitral award and security (if other than United States dollars)
6. Date of this agreement:	6. Place of agreement:
7. Is the Scopic Clause incorporated into this agreement ? State alternative : Yes/No	
8. Person signing for and on behalf of the Contractors Signature:	9. Captain or other person signing for and on behalf of the property Signature:

A. **Contractors' basic obligation:** The Contractors identified in Box 1 hereby agree to use their best endeavours to salve the property specified in Box 2 and to take the property to the place stated in Box 3 or to such other place as may hereafter be agreed. If no place is inserted in Box 3 and in the absence of any subsequent agreement as to the place where the property is to be taken the Contractors shall take the property to a place of safety.

B. **Environmental protection:** While performing the salvage services the Contractors shall also use their best endeavours to prevent or minimise damage to the environment.

(continued on the reverse side)

Fig. 6(1) Lloyd's Standard Form of Salvage Agreement

C. **Scopic Clause:** Unless the word "No" in Box 7 has been deleted this agreement shall be deemed to have been made on the basis that the Scopic Clause is not incorporated and forms no part of this agreement. If the word "No" is deleted in Box 7 this shall not of itself be construed as a notice invoking the Scopic Clause within the meaning of sub-clause 2 thereof.

D. **Effect of other remedies:** Subject to the provisions of the International Convention on Salvage 1989 as incorporated into English law ("the Convention") relating to special compensation and to the Scopic Clause if incorporated the Contractors' services shall be rendered and accepted as salvage services upon the principle of "no cure - no pay" and any salvage remuneration to which the Contractors become entitled shall not be diminished by reason of the exception to the principle of "no cure - no pay" in the form of special compensation or remuneration payable to the Contractors under a Scopic Clause.

E. **Prior services:** Any salvage services rendered by the Contractors to the property before and up to the date of this agreement shall be deemed to be covered by this agreement.

F. **Duties of property owners:** Each of the owners of the property shall cooperate fully with the Contractors. In particular:

(i)   the Contractors may make reasonable use of the vessel's machinery gear and equipment free of expense provided that the Contractors shall not unnecessarily damage abandon or sacrifice any property on board;

(ii)   the Contractors shall be entitled to all such information as they may reasonably require relating to the vessel or the remainder of the property provided such information is relevant to the performance of the services and is capable of being provided without undue difficulty or delay;

(iii)   the owners of the property shall co-operate fully with the Contractors in obtaining entry to the place of safety stated in Box 3 or agreed or determined in accordance with Clause A.

G. **Rights of termination:** When there is no longer any reasonable prospect of a useful result leading to a salvage reward in accordance with Convention Articles 12 and/or 13 either the owners of the vessel or the Contractors shall be entitled to terminate the services hereunder by giving reasonable prior written notice to the other.

H. **Deemed performance:** The Contractors' services shall be deemed to have been performed when the property is in a safe condition in the place of safety stated in Box 3 or agreed or determined in accordance with Clause A. For the purpose of this provision the property shall be regarded as being in safe condition notwithstanding that the property (or part thereof) is damaged or in need of maintenance if (i) the Contractors are not obliged to remain in attendance to satisfy the requirements of any port or harbour authority, governmental agency or similar authority and (ii) the continuation of skilled salvage services from the Contractors or other salvors is no longer necessary to avoid the property becoming lost or significantly further damaged or delayed.

I. **Arbitration and the LSSA Clauses:** The Contractors' remuneration and/or special compensation shall be determined by arbitration in London in the manner prescribed by Lloyd's Standard Salvage and Arbitration Clauses ("the LSSA Clauses") and Lloyd's Procedural Rules. The provisions of the LSSA Clauses and Lloyd's Procedural Rules are deemed to be incorporated in this agreement and form an integral part hereof. Any other difference arising out of this agreement or the operations hereunder shall be referred to arbitration in the same way.

J. **Governing law:** This agreement and any arbitration hereunder shall be governed by English law.

K. **Scope of authority:** The Master or other person signing this agreement on behalf of the property identified in Box 2 enters into this agreement as agent for the respective owners thereof and binds each (but not the one for the other or himself personally) to the due performance thereof.

L. **Inducements prohibited:** No person signing this agreement or any party on whose behalf it is signed shall at any time or in any manner whatsoever offer provide make give or promise to provide or demand or take any form of inducement for entering into this agreement.

IMPORTANT NOTICES:

1. **Salvage security.** As soon as possible the owners of the vessel should notify the owners of other property on board that this agreement has been made. If the Contractors are successful the owners of such property should note that it will become necessary to provide the Contractors with salvage security promptly in accordance with Clause 4 of the LSSA Clauses referred to in Clause I. The provision of General Average security does not relieve the salved interests of their separate obligation to provide salvage security to the Contractors.

2. **Incorporated provisons.** Copies of the Scopic Clause; the LSSA Clauses and Lloyd's Procedural Rules may be obtained from (i) the Contractors or (ii) the Salvage Arbitration Branch at Lloyd's, One Lime Street, London EC3M 7HA.

Tel.No. + 44(0)20 7327 5408

Fax No. +44(0)20 7327 6827

E-mail: lloyds-salvage@lloyds.com.

www.lloyds.com

LLOYD'S

15.1.08
3.12.24
13.10.26
12.4.50
10.6.53
20.12.67
23.2.72
21.5.80
5.9.90
1.1.95
1.9.2000

owners of the maritime property; time charterers can stand in the shoes of the owner of the yacht.

A receiver will detain the salvaged property unless security is given by its owner. Once the salvage award claimed is verified, then the receiver may sell the property and apportion the monies between the salvor and the owner. The value of the award for a saved vessel is assessed according to the circumstances in which it was saved. The vessel will be valued either as a going concern or as her value to the owners in the damaged condition. *The Merchant Shipping Act 1995* provides that a claim has to be made to the Admiralty Court within two years of the salvage.

Towage becomes salvage when the duty performed is beyond that required by the towage contract and fulfils the criteria for salvage; the duty performed was beyond the reasonable contemplation of the parties when the original towage contract was negotiated. The burden of proof lies on the party claiming the salvage.

6.4.3 LIFE SALVAGE

Life salvage is established where there has been actual, or a substantial apprehension of, danger to persons whose lives have been saved. Where only lives have been saved, then there will be no legal obligation to pay any remuneration. Masters have a duty to save lives at sea providing that his own vessel and persons thereon are not endangered.

Only where both maritime property and lives are saved together is it customary practice to award greater remuneration than if property alone had been saved.

6.4.4 SALVAGE CLAIMS

The normal yacht insurance policy covers salvage, but be warned that it might not cover the full sum if the boat is under-insured. It does not cover a convenient tow if the boat is becalmed or the engine has broken down. In such cases it is always important to agree beforehand a price for a pluck into harbour. Although yachtsmen can be expected to give such a service free to their fellows, the same cannot be said of commercial craft to whom time is money.

If the situation is such that a claim for salvage may arise, there are two suggested courses of action:

1. It may be possible to agree a reasonable sum in advance either verbally or better still (if feasible in the circumstances) by Lloyd's Standard Form of Salvage Agreement, as shown in Fig. 6(1). In emergency this could be torn out of the Handbook and used for

the purpose. If a verbal agreement is made, be sure that your crew witness what is discussed and the price quoted, and write down the conversation promptly. Do not disclose the value of your boat to the claimant.

In practice it may be impossible to agree a figure, or even to establish proper communication, in which case resort to the second course of action:

2. To turn the whole business over to your insurers either by mobile phone or as soon as possible on reaching harbour, so that they can negotiate a settlement. They will need to know the full facts, including the degree of risk to your own vessel and also to the salvor. It is therefore important to be able to produce the boat's log, the chart with previous course and position correctly plotted, and relevant information on the present and forecast weather.

If and when a salvage claim comes to court for adjudication the court will examine all the circumstances of the case, not only the value of the vessels concerned and the time and danger involved, but also the degree of skill shown in the salvage and whether the salvor's vessel was specifically engaged as a salvage vessel or whether the salvage was simply opportune.

A claim for salvage may succeed if the claimant can show that, while he was not performing any legal or official duty, he voluntarily saved, or helped to save, a vessel and perhaps her crew, which was in danger on tidal waters; danger must have existed. Another basic principle of salvage is 'no cure, no pay'.

Some acts of salvage are self-evident – for example where a boat is towed off a lee shore or off rocks in a rising wind – but other cases may not be so obvious. A claim might be upheld because a vessel answered a distress signal, even if that had been made hastily and prematurely (and hence also illegally). The moral here is that if you require assistance, but are not actually in distress, you should use the appropriate signal such as 'V' (Victor) in the International Code of Signals, meaning 'I require assistance'.

A vessel might claim salvage just because she stood by and gave advice; or if she assisted in pilotage to avoid a local danger; or if she provided equipment such as pumps, fire extinguishers, or even a towing warp to a boat in danger. For the last reason it is better (when possible) for a boat to use her own warp when being taken in tow in emergency, or at least to show that she has a suitable rope for the purpose.

Other factors which might support a salvage claim could be the physical condition, ignorance or lack of skill of the crew of a boat in danger. Even their unguarded remarks might be construed as evidence that the boat was in real trouble.

Unless the boat is really in danger, do not accept help from a stranger without politely making it quite clear that you have the situation well in hand, and that you are only availing yourself of his kind offer of assistance as a matter of convenience.

In salvage cases, in the unusual event of the claim not being settled out of court, awards tend to be very much lower than feared by the owner. In the highest cases an award of more than 50% of the salved value is unusual, and that would presuppose a skilful operation in circumstances of great danger, where the loss of the salved vessel was virtually certain and where the operation took a great deal of time and effort involving an expensive salvage vessel. In other cases the award will be proportionally less, and an award of a few per cent may be all that is merited.

Once the salvage has been effected, the salvor has a maritime lien on the property salved. This is a right to arrest the vessel at any time, even if she has subsequently been sold to a third party, and to sell her to meet the claim. Since this lien gives good legal protection to the salvor, he is not permitted to detain the vessel after she has been brought to port unless he found her abandoned and derelict, or can prove that there is a substantial risk that his claim may not be met (eg if the owner lives abroad and has no resources or property in the jurisdiction of the British courts). Apart from having a claim against the vessel herself, the salvor also has a claim against the other personal assets of the owner if he is unable to satisfy his claim from the sale proceeds.

The RNLI never claims salvage or charges for rescuing persons or property. Yachtsmen who benefit from the RNLI should at least make a significant donation to RNLI funds, whilst personal gratitude to the crew is always appreciated. Occasionally a lifeboat crew may claim salvage, but if they do they have to bear the cost of the rescue and of any damage to the lifeboat, regardless of the outcome of the claim.

6.5 POLLUTION

6.5.1 GENERAL

Pollution is governed by various International Conventions, such as MARPOL (The International Convention for the Prevention of Pollution from Ships 1973), which are recognised by the *Merchant Shipping Act 1995*, but mainly relate to oil pollution. It is an offence to throw anything over board within 12 miles of land – even food waste, paper packets or wrappers, plastic, glass or tins. A heavy fine will be imposed on offenders and the owner and Master of a yacht will be held responsible.

6.5.2 SEWAGE

So far as sewage pollution is concerned, only craft 'certified' to carry more than 10 people are affected. In practice this is interpreted to cover craft with 11 or more permanent berths, which are prohibited from discharging sewage less than 12 miles from the nearest land. The effect of this is to require all such vessels to be fitted with holding tanks. The regulations also provide that holding tanks should not be discharged instantaneously, but at a moderate rate with the vessel proceeding at a speed of 4 knots or more. As an alternative, vessels may be fitted with approved sewage treatment plants. Vessels subject to the regulations also require a standard shore connection for sewage discharge. A certificate of compliance must be obtained from the Department of Transport when the vessel is first commissioned, and be renewed at five-year intervals thereafter.

6.5.3 GARBAGE

Annex V of the International Convention for the Prevention of Pollution from Ships (1973) is given legal effect by the *Merchant Shipping (Prevention of Pollution by Garbage) Regulations 1998* SI 1998/1372. The Regulations apply to all UK vessels, although documentation of the matter is only required of vessel of 400 gross tons and above.

"Garbage" means all kinds of victuals, domestic and operational waste excluding fresh fish and parts thereof, generated during the normal operation of the ship and liable to be disposed of continuously or periodically except sewage originating from ships.

The controls established by Annex V of the Convention are strict and vary according to the type of garbage and area in which the vessel is operating, as follows:

(1) The disposal into the sea of all plastics including synthetic ropes, synthetic fishing nets and plastic garbage bags is absolutely prohibited.

(2) Floating dunnage, lining or packing materials may not be disposed of into the sea less than 25 miles from land.

(3) Food waste, and all other garbage including paper products, rags, glass, metals, bottles,

crockery and similar refuse may not be disposed of less than 12 miles from land unless ground or fragmented as required to less than 25mm across, in which case not less than 3 miles from land.

Special rules apply to the Mediterranean Sea, Black Sea, Baltic Sea, Red Sea and Persian Gulf, prohibiting all disposals, except for food wastes which may be disposed of at least 12 miles from land.

6.5.4 THE ENVIRONMENT

The following notes are adapted from an RYA leaflet *Tidelines*, by kind permission of the RYA. They offer practical guidance, mainly directed at newcomers to sailing, on waste disposal and the protection of the natural environment. Please observe the following:

a. In principle never ditch rubbish at sea.
b. Keep it onboard and dispose of it ashore in proper receptacles. These are available in all marinas and elsewhere in properly managed harbours and rivers of which Looe and the Helford River are particularly good examples.
c. Readily degradable foodstuffs may be ditched at sea when more than 3 miles offshore, 12 miles in the English Channel and North Sea.
d. Foodstuffs which are not readily degradable, eg skins and peelings, should not be ditched at sea.
e. Other rubbish, eg packaging of plastic, glass, metal, paper and cardboard; fabrics; ropelines and netting, should never be ditched at sea.
f. Do not discharge anything except 'washing-up' water into a marina, anchorage or moorings.
g. Oils and oily waste are particularly harmful to the water, fish and wildlife. Take used engine oil ashore in a well-sealed container or bottle for proper disposal. Do not pump oily bilge water overboard.
h. Avoid fuel spillage when topping up outboards.
j. Rowing ashore provides better exercise, less noise and no pollution compared with a 2-stroke outboard!
k. Sewage. If possible use shoreside toilets; and only use the onboard heads in tidal waters.
l. Consider fitting and using a holding tank. These are already compulsory in some countries. Pump-out facilities are shown in the MRNA. If there are none, only pump out more than 3 miles offshore.

m. Toxic waste, eg some antifoulings, cleaning chemicals, old batteries, should be disposed of ashore at a proper facility.
n. Wild birds, plants, fish and marine animals are usually abundant along coastlines. Respect protected sites; keep away from nesting sites and breeding colonies. Minimise noise, wash and disturbance.
o. Go ashore at recognised landing places. Do not anchor or dry out where important and vulnerable seabed species exist, eg soft corals, eel grass.

6.6 LAW FOR YACHTS, BOATS AND CLUB LAUNCHES

6.6.1 PASSENGERS AND CREW

The purpose of the Merchant Shipping Act 1995 and related Regulations are primarily to promote the safety of persons on board a vessel.

"Passenger" means a person carried on a vessel, except:

i. a person employed or engaged in any capacity on board the vessel on the business of that vessel;
ii. a person on board the vessel either in pursuance of the obligation laid upon the skipper to carry shipwrecked, distressed or other persons, or by reason of any other circumstances that neither the skipper nor the owner nor the charterer (if any) could have prevented; and
iii. a child under one year of age.
   "Crew" means a person employed or engaged in any capacity on board the vessel on the business of that vessel. "Engaged" has been taken by the courts to mean a binding contractual agreement. Thus, a person engaged may be unpaid, or may even have paid the shipowner for the voyage, or have come aboard a sail training yacht as a trainee, he will be deemed to be a member of the crew if he has signed some contractual document relating to the voyage.

6.6.2 COMPULSORY REQUIREMENTS FOR PLEASURE YACHTS USED ENTIRELY FOR PRIVATE PURPOSES

A "pleasure vessel" is defined in the *Merchant Shipping (Vessels in Commercial Use for Sport or Pleasure) Regulations 1993* SI 1993/1072 as:

1. any vessel which at the time it is being used is:
(a) (i) in the case of a vessel wholly owned by an individual or individuals is used only for the sport or pleasure of the owner or the immediate family or friends of the owner; or

(ii) in the case of a vessel owned by a body corporate, the persons on the vessel are employees or officers of the body corporate, or their immediate family or friends; and

(b) on a voyage or excursion which is one for which the owner does not receive money for or in connection with operating the vessel or carrying any person, other than as a contribution to the direct expenses of the operation of the vessel incurred during the voyage or excursion; or

2. any vessel wholly owned by or on behalf of a members' club formed for the purpose of sport or pleasure of members of that club or their immediate family; and for the use of which any charges levied are paid into club funds and applied for the general use of the club; and

3. in the case of any vessel referred to in paragraphs (1) and (2) above no other payments are made by or on behalf of the users of the vessel, other than by the owner.

Pleasure yachts used entirely for private purposes tend to be exempt from many of the shipping regulations. The following is a summary of the legal requirements for privately used pleasure craft:

a. United Nations Convention on the Law of the Sea, to which the United Kingdom is signatory, requires all craft going into foreign territorial waters to fly the flag of their state and to carry documents as evidence of the right to fly that flag. Thus, registration in effect remains compulsory under international law for foreign venturing vessels.

b. Customs formalities between EU member states are at a lower level than as between an EU member state and a non-EU member state. Form C1331 must be completed on departure from and arrival in the UK for all trips outside UK territorial waters. The 'Q' flag need only be flown on arriving in the UK from a non-EU member state. Customs Notice 8 is a guide to procedures and is governed by sections 35(4) and 42(1) of the *Customs and Excise Management Act 1979 (amended)* and the *Pleasure Craft (Arrival and Report) Regulations (1990)*.

c. The employment of a master and crew is governed by Part III sections 24-84 of the *Merchant Shipping Act 1995*, by which the Secretary of State has issued a number of Statutory Instruments. Generally, these Regulations do not apply to pleasure

vessels, used for non-commercial purposes and not manned by a professional crew.

d. Pleasure yachts in Class XII, over 45ft (13.7m) in length, are subject to lifesaving and fire appliances rules.

6.6.3 COMPULSORY REQUIREMENTS FOR PLEASURE YACHTS ENGAGED IN A COMMERCIAL CAPACITY

The Blue Code (*A Code of Practice for the Safety of Small Commercial Sailing Vessels*) and the Yellow Code (*A Code of Practice for the Safety of Small Commercial Motor Vessels*) set a standard of safety and protection for all on board, although the Codes recognise that total safety at sea can never be guaranteed. These Codes satisfy the requirements under the *Merchant Shipping (Vessels in Commercial Use for Sport or Pleasure) Regulations 1993* (SI 1993/1072) recognised in law by Schedule 14 of the *Merchant Shipping Act 1995*. The Regulations apply to vessels owned by proprietor's clubs and associations, including sail training vessels. These vessels are still required to comply with any local authority licensing.

The Codes apply to all vessels of up to 24 metres load line, which are engaged at sea in activities on a commercial basis, which do not carry cargo nor carry more than 12 passengers. The Codes relate to the construction of the vessel, its machinery, equipment, stability and the correct operation of the vessel to maintain safety standards. The vessel must be examined as complying with the Codes and certificate issued to that effect.

These Codes establish safe manning conditions by providing a structure for necessary qualifications to be held by crew. Vessels other than those on bare-boat charter are subject to these safe manning conditions. Persons included within the scope of the Codes are trainees and passengers.

Pleasure yachts in commercial usage must be surveyed and the Load Line Regulations applied.

6.6.4 CLUB LAUNCHES

Launches owned and used solely by members' clubs are classified as pleasure craft and therefore subject to little regulation. However, club launches may be used for a more commercial purpose such as ferrying non-members, for a fee, around the moorings and therefore become subject to greater regulation.

Vessels which are no more than 24 metres at load line, carry no more than 12 passengers, do not carry cargo, operate only in favourable weather and daylight from a nominated departure point and are in commercial use for sport or pleasure are subject to the "Red Code"

(Code of Practice for the Safety of Small Vessels in Commercial Use for Sport or Pleasure Operating from a Nominated Departure Point). The Code is the accepted Code in accordance with the *Merchant Shipping (Vessels in Commercial Use for Sport and Pleasure) (Amendment) Regulations 2000* SI 2000/482. The Code governs the standard and certification of such vessels. The RYA and RYA-recognised establishments have gained exemption for its support boats attending training and racing events.

Vessels operating in categorised waters (areas of varying distances from a safe haven), as identified by the Merchant Shipping (Categorisation of Waters) Regulations 1992, are not governed by the "Red Code" but instead are governed by local byelaws. Club launches carrying more than 12 passengers will require a survey and a licence from the Department of Transport. Launches carrying 12 or fewer passengers will not need a licence from the Department of Trade but may be required to hold a local licence if they are 'let on hire to the public' or are 'used for carrying passengers for hire'. A licence will not necessary relieve the boat owner from complying with any legal requirements of the local harbour authority.

6.6.5 INLAND NAVIGATION AUTHORITIES – INCLUDING THE BRITISH WATERWAYS BOARD, THE ENVIRONMENT AGENCY AND THE BROADS AUTHORITY

There are over 30* inland navigation authorities in the UK, although in mileage terms, the majority of inland waters fall within the jurisdiction of either the British Waterways Board, the Environment Agency or the Broads Authority.

The use of inland waterways in Great Britain is regulated by local bye-laws and national legislation. Most inland navigation authorities have statutory jurisdiction to license all craft using their navigations and to attach conditions and requirements to such licenses. In general, most boats licensed to use the rivers and canals administered by British Waterways Board and the Environment Agency must conform to the requirements of the Boat Safety Scheme** (BSS). The Broads Authority are currently considering the extension of the BSS to the waters under their control.

Further information from the Association* of Inland Navigation Authorities, or the Boat Safety Scheme**, both of which are located at Willow Grange, Church Road, Watford, Hertforshire WD1 3QA.

6.6.6 MERCHANT SHIPPING LOAD LINES

Merchant shipping load lines are governed by section 89 and schedule 3 of the *Merchant Shipping Act 1995* and apply to all ships except warships, fishing vessels and pleasure yachts, except pleasure vessels in commercial usage. Clearly therefore, if a vessel can be described as a pleasure yacht, she does not fall within the rules. There is some doubt whether the owners of pleasure vessels which are used for commercial or semi-commercial purposes, such as sail training or charter, should be liable if they fail to comply with these rules. It was held by the High Court, in *The Chalice* (1991), that it was wrong to apply the Merchant shipping load lines to pleasure yachts simply because the yacht was being used for a commercial purpose. The court held that a pleasure yacht was entitled to any exemptions given to it by Act or Regulation whatever use it was being put to at the time. This case was decided before the Merchant Shipping Act 1995 came into force.

6.6.7 THE OFFICIAL LOG BOOK

Section 77 of the *Merchant Shipping Act 1995* gives powers to create Regulations of shipping documents, notably an official log book. Log books are governed by SI 1983/1801 (amended), but this does not apply to any vessel less than 25 GT nor to pleasure yachts; the Statutory Instrument otherwise specifically provides that official log books shall be kept in every ship registered in the United Kingdom.

6.7 CLUBS AND SAILING SCHOOLS

6.7.1 POTENTIAL LIABILITIES OF YACHT CLUB OFFICERS AND SAILING SCHOOL INSTRUCTORS

Every Yacht Club and Sailing School will organise or engage in activities in the normal course of its business which, by their very nature will involve some element of risk.

A person will owe a duty of care that they will not injure another through their carelessness or negligence; this is particularly so of persons in positions of responsibility, such as yacht club officers and sailing instructors. When confronted with a claim from a competitor or a trainee injured in the course of sailing activities, the court examining the problem will look at the following criteria:

1. What was the relationship of the injured person to the club or school?
2. What would a reasonable yacht club or sailing school have done in similar circumstances?

3. What may be the normally accepted activities of a club or school in that context and in particularly what responsibilities should be assumed in the course of the organisation of a regatta or sailing course?
4. What standards do the club or school, or other comparable clubs or schools, maintain?

The Courts are more willing to find a duty of care to exist in particular circumstances. However, if the injured party can establish a case that there was a breach of duty to take care or negligence, the defendant may still be able to show a defence.

Where a club is an unincorporated association, no action can be taken directly against the club because the club has no separate legal capacity. Instead, an action will stand against an officer of that club who was directly involved in the matter at issue. The normal rules of tort apply where a member wishes to bring an action against another member of the club. No member may be made the subject of a legal action simply because he is a member of that club. An increasing number of clubs and most sailing schools are incorporated as limited companies, thereby creating a separate legal capacity for the organisation. Where this is the case, actions may be taken directly against the club or school and a member will be able to sue the organisation.

6.7.2 CLUBS' AND SCHOOLS' PREMISES

Most yacht clubs and sailing schools own or lease premises and are subject to the legal requirement to exercise care to avoid injury to visitors, including trespassers, who come onto those premises. If a visitor is harmed in some way and can prove negligence on the part of the organisation, he will be entitled to receive damages.

Premises may include the club house, bar, any other buildings, jetties, slipways, piers and even the adjacent seabed if it is relevant. The organisation has a duty to warn sailors using the facilities of any particular and unusual hazards in the are, such as rocky outcrops on an otherwise smooth and sandy sea bed.

A club or school with paid employees or who provide equipment for members are subject to the Health and Safety at Work Act 1974 and a series of related Regulations.

6.7.3 CLUB ORGANISING REGATTAS

Persons likely to be affected by a club's activities will be the competing owners and skippers of vessels, the crew members and third parties. These parties owe a duty in tort to each other. By the signing of a Race Entry Form, which is accepted by the organisers of the regatta, a contractual relationship also arises between the each and every competitor and the organisers; the acceptance of the signed Entry Form forms a tripartite contract.

With regard to competitors and crew, the club must adopt a reasonable standard of care, having regard to the age and experience of the competitors in such matters as the laying of the course, determining the classes of entrants, starting and finishing the race, the weather conditions, making arrangements for support boat cover and scrutineering of any equipment provided. Although it is a fundamental principle of yacht racing that competitors enter the race at their own risk, this rule cannot be enforced against competitors below the age of eighteen years, nor against competitors who are too inexperienced to understand the risks that they race.

So far as the position of safety regulations is concerned, it is for each club to decide whether a code of safety regulations should be imposed, in the light of the experience and competence of its race officers and available man power. What ever the policy the club follows, it is important that it be followed consistently and a reasonable attempt be made to ensure compliance with any safety rules that are imposed.

When faced with a claim for damages, a club or school may form a defence, which includes that of *volenti non fit injuria*, in that competitors and crew cannot be heard to complain of injury or damage if they voluntarily accepted the risk of damage. Thus a competitor in a race may reasonably be assumed to accept the following risks:

1. Racing without proper lifesaving equipment.
2. The perils of the sea including adverse weather conditions.
3. That other competitors will not be as competent as he himself is.
4. Racing in an unseaworthy yacht owned by another.
5. Using an inexperienced crew.
6. Sailing in an area which he knows may be unsafe.

6.7.4 OTHER SOURCES OF LIABILITY

The launching of vessels and their subsequent recovery are activities in which a club or school will from time to time engage. Such activities, if not carried out in a proper manner, could cause damage for which a club or school could be liable. For example, a club or school could either manage the launching in a negligent manner or they could have allowed the slipway to have deteriorated into an unsafe physical condition, a condition which is not of a reasonable standard.

6.7.5 ORGANISING ESCORTS, RESCUE BOATS ETC.

Any escorts or rescue vessels must be managed in a proper manner, although in cases of emergency the standard required at law will not necessarily be as high. Where the operator owns the vessel, he stands in the same position as any other boat owner. If some other person's boat is being borrowed, then the club or school will be responsible for the safe navigation of the boat. Where an officer or employee is in charge, even though the vessel remains under the control of her owner, the club or school may very well find itself liable under the law of vicarious liability for the negligence of the owner. It is emphasised therefore that the vessels and personnel appointed for escort and/or rescue operations should be suitable and capable, and insurance arrangements confirmed.

Where the owner of the vessel 'volunteers' himself and his vessel rather than being requested, the club or school is not likely to be liable for the vessel owner's negligence unless it can be said that he acts as an agent on behalf of the club.

6.7.6 EXCLUSION AND EXEMPTION CLAUSES

Contracts for the purpose of either:

  i. things done in the course of business; or
 ii. arising from the occupation of premises used for the business purposes of the occupier;

are subject to the Unfair Contract Terms Act 1977. In the case of a school or large yacht club habitually used and visited by non-members, the activities will invariably be classified as 'business' and therefore will fall within the scope of the Act. Such activities include contracts formed by the acceptance of entry of a competitor to a regatta and a pupil attending a sailing course, where both persons are paying money.

The competitor or pupil should be referred to any exclusion clauses in the document which he signs, especially if the clauses are not contained in that same document but, such as at regattas, may be held in the Notice of Race or the rules governing the race. Essentially, liability for death and personal injury may not be excluded by a term of the contract. Other liabilities may not be excluded or limited unreasonably. In assessing the reasonableness of an exclusion clause, the equality of the bargaining powers of parties to the contract will be taken into consideration. Occupiers' liability, where the occupation is for the purpose of business, will be assessed in the same manner.

Rules such as ISAF Rules of Racing do not appear to offend the Act. The parts of these rules about laying marks, provision of information about tides and weather, choosing courses etc, could give rise to liability where such tasks are performed negligently, but it is not really desirable to seek to exclude such liability since the club or school can always protect itself by insurance. On the other hand, exclusion of liability is usually desirable to protect a club from liability arising from matters beyond its control – such as seaworthiness of vessels and the provision of lifesaving equipment. The ISAF Rules of Racing, as they stand, adequately serve this purpose.

Chapter 7 Navigation and Passage Making

CONTENTS

7.1.1 STANDARD NAVIGATIONAL TERMS

Some navigational terms are used rather loosely and may mean different things to different people depending on context. In any boat where more than one individual is involved in navigation, the precise meanings of such terms must be established in order to avoid confusion. Certain standard terms, as listed below, are now used in shorebased courses and these should be used at all times.

*The word 'angle', as asterisked below, is normally omitted unless there is a possibility of confusion.

Course (Co) – the intended heading.

COG (Course over the Ground) – at a given moment; a GPS output.

Course to steer – the compass course to be steered by the helmsman, as directed by the navigator.

Dead reckoning (DR) – the process of maintaining or predicting an approximate record of progress by projecting course and distance from a known position.

DR position – (1) the general term for a position obtained by DR, plotted on the chart as a +; and (2) specifically a position obtained using course and distance run, the latter derived from the log impeller or engine revolutions as considered more appropriate.

Drift – the distance covered in a given time due solely to the speed (rate) of a tidal stream and/or a current.

*Drift angle** – the angular difference between the ground track and the water track.

Estimated position (EP) – a DR position refined by the addition of set and drift and estimated leeway, plotted on the chart as a ⌂. EP is the best possible approximation of a present or future position. It may also take account of extrapolation from earlier fixes.

Heading – the horizontal direction of the ship's head at a given moment. (This term does not necessarily require movement of the vessel.)

Leeway – the movement of a vessel to leeward caused by wind effect.

*Leeway angle** – the angular difference between the water track and the ship's heading.

Rate – the speed of a tidal stream and/or a current.

Set – the direction towards which a tidal stream and/or a current flows.

SMG (Speed made good) – over the ground, over a given period; a GPS output.

SOG (Speed over the Ground) – at a given moment; a GPS output.

Track – the path followed or to be followed between one position and another. It may be track over the ground (*Ground track*) or through the water (*Water track*).

*Track angle** – the direction of a track.

Track made good – the mean track actually achieved over the ground during a given period.

VMG – Velocity, ie direction and speed, made good towards a waypoint or destination, irrespective of the track/speed currently being made good; a GPS output.

7.1.2 LATITUDE AND LONGITUDE

The positions of vessels or objects on a chart are referred to by their latitude and longitude. The latitude of a point is its angular distance north or south of the equator, measured from 0° – 90° N or S. The longitude is its angular distance east or west of the prime (Greenwich) meridian, measured from 0° – 180° E or W.

In angular measurement there are 360 degrees in a circle, and 60 minutes of arc to a degree. For greater accuracy there are 60 seconds to a minute, but latitude and longitude are more often shown in degrees, minutes and tenths of a minute, eg latitude 51°07'·60N. The scale of latitude is given vertically along each side of the chart, and longitude horizontally along the top and bottom.

Fig. 7(1) illustrates how the latitude and longitude of point A are referred to the equator

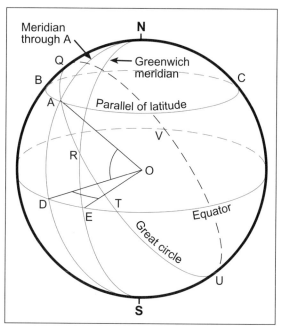

Fig. 7(1) Parallels of latitude, meridians and great circles.

and the Greenwich meridian respectively. Angle AOD is the latitude (north of the equator) and angle DOE is the longitude (west of Greenwich). BAC is the parallel of latitude through A, and NADS is the meridian through A.

7.1.3 GREAT CIRCLES

A great circle is the intersection on the surface of a sphere of a plane passing through its centre. The earth may be treated as a sphere, and in Fig. 7(1) it is clear that all meridians are great circles passing through the poles. The equator is the only parallel of latitude which is a great circle. The circle depicted by QARTUV is also a great circle.

The shortest distance between any two points on the surface of the earth lies along the great circle through them. Over long distances, eg across an ocean, great circle sailing is sometimes adopted, either by means of special (gnomonic) charts, or by computing the courses and distances by formula, tables or calculator.

7.1.4 COURSES AND BEARINGS

In order to get from place to place the navigator needs an indication of direction. Also if he knows the directions (bearings) of certain fixed objects marked on the chart he can fix his position. Courses and bearings are most easily measured in relation to true north, as given by the meridian passing through the place concerned, ie a line pointing straight up towards the top of a Mercator chart.

Courses and bearings are measured clockwise from north, and are always expressed in three

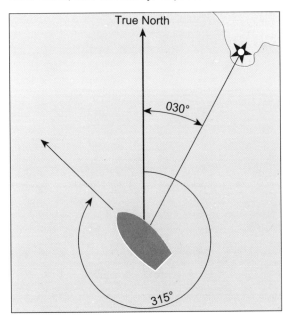

Fig. 7(2) A true bearing and a true course, related to true north.

figures. A true bearing of 090° is due east for example, and 180° is due south. In Fig. 7(2) the lighthouse bears 030° from the yacht, which is steering 315° (north west).

Rhumb line course

The true course of a boat is the angle between true north and the direction in which she is heading, measured clockwise. Thus her steady course cuts all the meridians at the same angle; this is called a rhumb line course. If drawn on a globe it will normally appear as a spiral towards one of the poles, but on a Mercator's chart (7.3.1) it is conveniently represented by a straight line.

So a yacht, steering a steady course from one place to another, proceeds along a rhumb line. This is not quite the same as the line she would follow for the *shortest* distance between the two places, which is the great circle joining them, but for practical navigation over comparatively short distances the difference is insignificant.

7.1.5 VARIATION

In yachts and boats, courses and bearings are actually measured by a magnetic compass, which points to the magnetic north, not true north. The angular difference between magnetic and true north is called Variation. If magnetic north is to the west of true north, variation is labelled west; if it is to the east, variation is labelled east.

Variation alters from place to place on the earth's surface and, to a lesser extent, with the passage of time. In 2001 around the British Isles it ranges from about 2°W in the Dover Strait to about 8°W off the Western Isles and NW Ireland. Variation is clearly shown in Fig. 7(3) and on small scale charts (eg AC 2 of the British Isles) by isogonals, lines joining points of equal variation, with the value and annual rate of change, say 6°W (5'E).

Variation on medium/large scale charts is printed inside the compass rose as, for example, 6°41'W 2001 (5'E) meaning that it is decreasing about 5' annually. Older charts print the information in full, for example:

Variation 8°46'W (1985) decreasing about 5' annually.

To convert a magnetic bearing or course to a true one, subtract westerly variation or add easterly. When converting from true to magnetic the opposite applies, ie add westerly variation or subtract easterly. In the examples below only westerly variation is used as this applies in UK waters. If in doubt, it helps to draw a small sketch like the ones shown.

In Fig. 7(4) a magnetic bearing of 081°(M) with a variation of 8°W results in a true bearing of 073°(T).

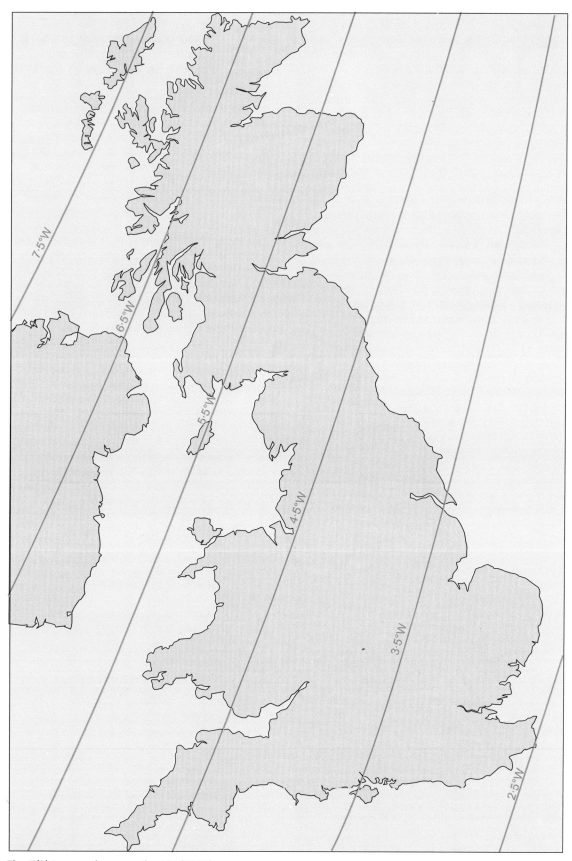

Fig. 7(3) Isogonals across the UK (2001)

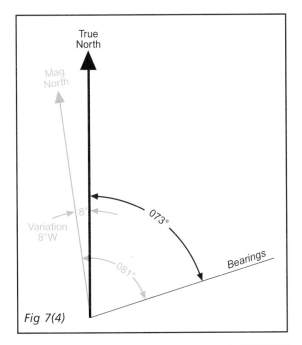

Fig 7(4)

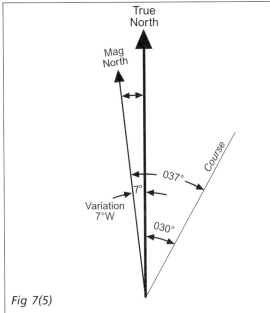

Fig 7(5)

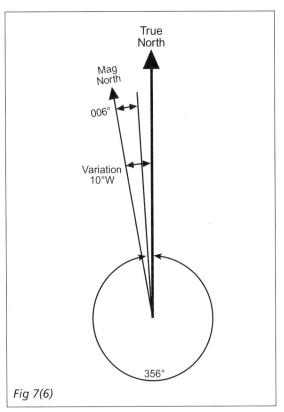

Fig 7(6)

Figs 7(4) – 7(6) The relationship between true and magnetic courses and bearings.

legend "Local Magnetic Anomaly (see Note)" is shown at the position; the Note is below the chart title.

7.1.6 DEVIATION

Deviation is caused by the influence of the boat's own magnetic field on the compass; it deflects the compass needle away from magnetic north to which it would otherwise point. So this must be allowed for, in addition to variation. If the compass is deflected to the west of magnetic north, deviation is west: if it is deflected to the east of magnetic north, deviation is east.

Unlike variation, deviation alters with the direction in which the boat is heading. It may be westerly when the boat is pointing one way, and easterly when it is pointing another.

Deviation can be very significant in steel boats, or where the compass is placed too close to a magnetic mass such as the engine or iron ballast keel. Temporary deviation can be caused by inadvertently placing any magnetic object, eg a knife, too close to the compass. Permanent deviation can be caused by lightning.

In most boats deviation can largely be eliminated by a skilful compass adjuster, who places small corrector magnets near the compass so that they cancel out the local magnetic field.

In Fig. 7(5) a true course of 030°(T) and a variation of 7°W gives a magnetic course of 037°(M).

In Fig. 7(6) a true course of 356°(T) with a variation of 10°W gives 356°(T) + 10° = 366°(M), ie 006°(M).

Areas of Local Magnetic Anomaly are found in certain isolated places. These are indicated on Admiralty charts by a wavy line encircling figures such as ± 15° in the centre, indicating that within the enclosed area the magnetic variation may deviate from the normal by the value shown. If the area affected cannot easily be defined, a

When the adjustment is complete, and as much of the deviation as possible has been removed, the boat is finally 'swung' on various headings (usually every 15°) to find out what deviation still remains, and a deviation card is drawn up as shown in Fig. 7(7). The procedures for checking, adjusting and swinging a compass are described in sections 7.2.2 to 7.2.6.

DEVIATION CARD: Main steering compass		
Yacht		
Date		
Magnetic course°	Deviation°	Compass course°
000	2W	002
015	2W	017
030	3W	033
045	3W	048
060	4W	064
075	3W	078
090	3W	093
105	3W	108
120	2W	122
135	1W	136
150	1W	151
165	1W	166
180	0	180
195	0	195
210	0	210
225	0	225
240	1E	239
255	2E	253
270	2E	268
285	3E	282
300	2E	298
315	1E	314
330	0	330
345	1W	346
360	2W	002

Fig. 7(7) Typical deviation card.

Deviation is applied in just the same way as variation. A useful mnemonic is the word CADET, standing for 'Compass to True, Add East'. The two end letters show the conversion from 'Compass to True', and the three centre ones mean 'ADd East', ie when converting from compass to true add easterly variation or deviation (and subtract westerly). Conversely when converting from True to Compass, ie add westerly and subtract easterly.

Variation and deviation are summed to give the total compass error to be applied on that occasion. For example, if variation is 7°W and the deviation on the course being steered is 3°E, the total compass error is 4°W. In this case a course of 168°(C) would be 164°(T).

7.1.7 RELATIVE BEARINGS

Relative bearings are sometimes used at sea to indicate the direction of an object or another vessel in relation to the fore and aft line of one's own boat. Relative bearings to port are designated 'Red', and those to starboard 'Green', each being numbered from 000° (dead ahead) to 180° (dead astern). So a relative bearing of 'Green 080' indicates a direction 10° ahead of the starboard beam. 'Red 135' indicates a bearing on the port quarter.

The clock code is another way of indicating relative bearing. 12 o'clock is dead ahead, 3 o'clock is on the starboard beam, 6 o'clock dead astern and so on. Thus a vessel or feature at 11 o'clock is 30° off the port bow.

7.1.8 DISTANCES

Distances at sea are as important as directions. They are measured in nautical miles, often abbreviated to n mile or M, which are longer than statute or land miles. The nautical mile is the length of a minute of latitude at the place concerned, and because the earth is not a perfect sphere it varies slightly in length from 1843m (6046ft) at the equator to 1862m (6108ft) at the poles. However this is not a problem because the Mercator chart has a built-in scale of distances in the form of the latitude scale, which is marked down the margin either side.

Fig. 7(8) shows how a distance between two points on the chart is transferred with dividers to the latitude scale, to determine how far they are apart in nautical miles.

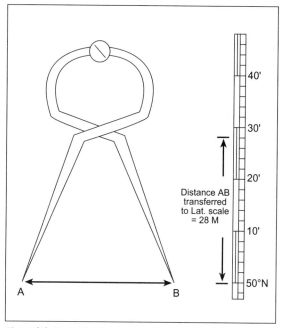

Fig. 7(8) Use dividers to measure AB on the chart and read off the distance from the latitude scale.

Instruments such as logs and radar sets which measure distances are calibrated on a mean figure of 1852m (6076ft), now universally adopted as the International Nautical Mile.

A cable is one-tenth of a nautical mile, or for practical purposes 185m (200yd). Cables, abbreviated to ca, are often quoted in Pilot books for distances less than a mile.

7.1.9 SPEED

Speed at sea is measured in knots (abbreviated to kn). A knot is one nautical mile per hour, equivalent to 1.15 statute miles per hour.

A log is the instrument used to measure distance at sea, as nautical miles run through the water. Most logs also measure speed through the water in knots. GPS invariably provides SOG (Speed over the Ground), SMG (Speed made Good) and VMG (Velocity made Good); see 7.1.1.

A Dutchman's Log measures the boat's approximate speed if all else has failed. A person in the bows drops a chip of wood, or similar, in the water ahead of the boat and signals as it passes the bow. A second person right aft times it passing the stern. Use the formula: Speed (kn) = $(0.592 \times LOA(ft)) \div T(secs)$. Or enter the following table with LOA, go down to time in seconds and read across to speed in the lefthand column:

	LOA (ft)				
Knots	20'	25'	30'	32'	36'
1	11·8	14·8	17·8	18·9	21·3
2	5·9	7·4	8·9	9·5	10·6
3	3·9	4·9	5·9	6·3	7·1
4	3·0	3·7	4·4	4·7	5·3
5	2·4	3·0	3·6	3·8	4·3

7.1.10 DISTANCE, SPEED AND TIME

The distance, speed and time equation is D = S x T, where D is nautical miles, S is knots and T is hours. It lies at the root of most forms of navigation, ie planning, DR, pilotage, passage-making, oceanic crossings. The mnemonic 'DST: 60, 30, 2' is an arithmetical reminder of the equation, especially useful for quick mental calculations.

In the MRNA a table, partly shown in Fig. 7(9), gives distance run for a known time and speed; or any permutation of these three variables. The speed band is from 2.5 to 20 knots, and times are up to one hour at one minute intervals. For passages measured in days and weeks a navigational slide-rule is a more convenient tool.

Example How far does a boat sail in 8 minutes at 6·5 kn? From the 8 minute line at the side of the table go across to the 6·5 kn column. Answer = 0·9M.

Alternatively use the table to find out how long it takes to cover a known distance at a certain speed; or what speed is required to go a certain distance in a given time.

A useful rule of thumb helps with short distance mental DR, for example buoy-hopping in fog. Based on a convenient period of 6 minutes (one tenth of an hour), at X knots you will cover X cables. Thus in 6 minutes at 5kn you will cover a distance of 5 cables; at 3kn, 3 cables and so on. GPS and radar may not always be working.

7.1.11 DEPTHS

Depth of water is always of concern to yachts-men. The nearest land to you is often that below your keel. Modern echo sounders are reliable,

Distance for a given speed and time

Time		Speed in knots																Time	
Decimal of hr.	Mins	2.5	3	3.5	4	4.5	5	5.5	6	6.5	7	7.5	8	8.5	9	9.5	10	Mins	Decimal of hr.
.0167	1				0.1	0.1	0.1	0.1	0.1	0.1	0.1	0.1	0.1	0.1	0.2	0.2	0.2	1	.0167
.0333	2	0.1	0.1	0.1	0.1	0.1	0.2	0.2	0.2	0.2	0.2	0.2	0.3	0.3	0.3	0.3	0.3	2	.0333
.0500	3	0.1	0.1	0.2	0.2	0.2	0.2	0.3	0.3	0.3	0.3	0.4	0.4	0.4	0.4	0.5	0.5	3	.0500
.0667	4	0.1	0.2	0.2	0.3	0.3	0.3	0.4	0.4	0.4	0.5	0.5	0.5	0.6	0.6	0.6	0.7	4	.0667
.0833	5	0.2	0.2	0.3	0.3	0.4	0.4	0.5	0.5	0.5	0.6	0.6	0.7	0.7	0.7	0.8	0.8	5	.0833
.1000	6	0.2	0.3	0.3	0.4	0.4	0.5	0.5	0.6	0.6	0.7	0.7	0.8	0.8	0.9	0.9	1.0	6	.1000
.1167	7	0.3	0.4	0.4	0.5	0.5	0.6	0.6	0.7	0.8	0.8	0.9	0.9	1.0	1.1	1.1	1.2	7	.1167
.1333	8	0.3	0.4	0.5	0.5	0.6	0.7	0.7	0.8	0.9	0.9	1.0	1.1	1.1	1.2	1.3	1.3	8	
.1500	9	0.4	0.4	0.5	0.6	0.7	0.7	0.8	0.9	1.0	1.0	1.1	1.2	1.3	1.3	1.4	1.5		
.1667	10	0.4	0.5	0.6	0.7	0.8	0.8	0.9	1.0	1.1	1.2	1.3	1.3	1.4	1.5	1.6	1.7		
		0.5	0.5	0.6	0.7	0.8	0.9	1.0	1.1	1.2	1.3	1.4	1.5	1.6	1.6				
					0.8	0.9	1.0	1.1	1.2	1.3	1.4	1.5	1.6	1.7	1.8				
						1.0	1.1	1.2	1.3	1.4	1.5	1.6	1.7	1.8					
								1.3	1.4	1.5	1.6	1.7	1.9						
									1.5	1.6	1.8	1.9							

Fig. 7(9) Portion of time, speed and distance table.

cheap and a most useful aid to navigation. But to gain full benefit from them it is necessary to appreciate exactly what they measure.

First, a yachtsman must understand the charted depths marked on a chart and how the height of tide is expressed above chart datum. For tidal information and definitions see Chapter 12. The echo sounder (or lead line) then tells him rather more than that he is about to run aground.

Second, decide how to set up your echo-sounder so that you get the information you want without excessive mental arithmetic. There are two options:

a. Make it read the true distance of the sea bed below sea level; cross-check this with a lead line. This simplifies tidal/depth calculations. Subtracting the height of the tide at any moment (see tide tables) from the echo-sounder's reading gives the charted depth, for comparison with the depths shown on the chart. This may help to establish your position and is highly relevant when anchoring. But mentally you will always have to subtract your draught to be aware of depth below the keel.

b. Make it read the actual distance of the seabed below the base of your keel. The merit of this is that you know with rock-hard certainty that when the echo-sounder reads zero your keel is touching the bottom.

Note: Most echo-sounders can be set to display depth below the waterline, or below the keel, ie taking account of the position of the transducer relative to waterline/keel.

The echo sounder can also be used, perhaps in poor visibility or to avoid a foul tide, for 'contour navigation' following a certain depth contour, maybe just clear of the main shipping channel or close inshore.

When anchoring, the height of the tide at that time must be known so that, in conjunction with the depth of water shown by the echo sounder (or lead line), you can calculate what will be the greatest and least depths of water at that place. The greatest depth will dictate how much scope should be given to the anchor cable, while the least depth will of course govern whether or not the boat will remain safely afloat at low water.

7.2 EQUIPMENT

7.2.1 COMPASSES
The compass is arguably the most important navigational instrument on board. Buy the best you can afford, preferably two on a tiller steered

yacht, to avoid the difficulty of sighting across a beamy cockpit to read the one and only compass. Two or even three compasses also permit cross-checking, so that at least errors are obvious, even if you do fail to have them removed by a compass adjuster.

There is a wide range of magnetic compasses on sale. Get one which has a reputation for reliability, is easy to read by day and especially at night when integral lighting is often too dim or too bright and requires a dimmer to be fitted. Corrector magnets should be incorporated. Bulkhead or binnacle mounting will be largely dictated by tiller or wheel steering and cockpit layout. The bulkhead compass can often usefully be read from inside the cabin.

The conventional magnetic compass is being challenged by electronic fluxgate instruments with no moving parts to wear. As well as serving as a steering compass these can also serve as a heading sensor for various electronic devices, eg autopilot, Loran, GPS or plotter. A fluxgate compass is even available which can continuously measure the deviation of the and compensate accordingly to an accuracy of ± 0.5 degrees. Perhaps the days of the professional compass adjuster are numbered.

7.2.2 COMPASS CHECKS
Take every opportunity to check the accuracy of the steering compass. A quick comparison can always be made with a hand bearing compass, held on the fore and aft line well away from any metal object. This should show up any serious deviation on a particular course.

A more accurate method is to take a bearing of a known transit (two objects in line) and compare it with the bearing from the chart, remembering to allow for variation. It is good practice to check the compass against all available transits, for example leading marks when entering or leaving harbour.

The sun, or any other celestial body, can also be used; its azimuth angle (Z) at the time and place concerned is given in sight reduction tables (Chapter 9). The azimuth angle is the true bearing of a celestial body, measured (in the northern hemisphere) eastward or westward from true north. The azimuth (Zn), which is the true bearing of the celestial body in 360° notation, measured from true north, is easily derived from the azimuth angle.

The relationship between Z and Zn depends upon the Local Hour Angle (LHA) of the celestial body, which is the angle measured westwards at the pole between the observer's meridian and the celestial body's meridian. In northern latitudes if LHA is greater than 180°, Zn = Z. If LHA is less than 180°, Zn = 360° − Z.

TABLE 2(5) True bearing of sun at sunrise and sunset.

LAT	0°	1°	2°	3°	4°	5°	6°	7°	8°	9°	10°	11°	LAT
	°	°	°	°	°	°	°	°	°	°	°	°	
30°	90	88.8	87.7	86.5	85.4	84.2	83.1	81.9	80.7	79.6	78.4	77.3	30°
31°	90	88.8	87.7	86.5	85.3	84.2	83.0	81.9	80.6	79.5	78.3	77.1	31°
32°	90	88.8	87.6	86.5	85.3	84.1	82.9	81.7	80.5	79.4	78.2	77.0	32°
33°	90	88.8	87.6	86.4	85.2	84.0	82.8	81.6	80.4	79.2	78.0	76.8	33°
34°	90	88.8	87.6	86.4	85.2	84.0	82.7	81.5	80.3	79.1	77.9	76.7	34°

Under the column heading a vertical arrow points to the DECLINATION 9° column; an arrow at the left points to the 33° row, which is boxed at the value 79.2.

Fig. 7(10) Extract from Table in the MRNA.

In order to achieve sufficient accuracy for checking a compass an azimuth mirror is needed, and the altitude of the celestial body should not be more than about 35°.

7.2.3 COMPASS CHECK BY SUN'S BEARING

At sea the compass may readily be checked against the sun's azimuth as it rises or sets, without needing a sextant or sight reduction tables. Given the approximate latitude of the boat, obtain the declination of the sun from a Table in the MRNA so as to enter Table 2(5), partly shown above as Fig. 7(10), and extract the tabulated bearing.

For example, in latitude 33° and with declination 9°, the tabulated bearing is 79·2 (say 79°). This is the true bearing of the sun, measured from north if the declination is north, or from south if the declination is south; towards the east if rising, or towards the west if setting.

The following examples show how to derive the true bearing in different circumstances:

DR Lat	Declin-ation	Sun rise/set	Tabulated bearing	True bearing
33°	9°N	Rising	79°	N79°E = 079°
33°	9°N	Setting	79°	N79°W = 281°
33°	9°S	Rising	79°	S79°E = 101°
33°	9°S	Setting	79°	S79°W = 259°

Having obtained the true bearing, apply the local magnetic variation and compare the resulting figure with the compass reading in order to determine the deviation on the course being steered.

Due to refraction, which is about 34' when observing bodies on the horizon, the bearing of the sun should be taken when its lower limb is a little over half a diameter above the horizon.

It is impossible to take bearings with most yachts' steering compasses which are not designed for the task. To overcome this difficulty steer the boat directly toward, or away from, the rising or setting sun, aligning it with the mast, forestay etc. In all cases it is important to remember that the deviation obtained applies only to the course being steered at the time of the observation.

7.2.4 COMPASS ADJUSTING

The steering (or master) compass is the key navigational instrument in any yacht, and its accuracy is most important. No compass should be relied on unless it has at least been checked by 'swinging', to determine the deviation on various headings. The procedure is outlined below.

If a compass swing shows that the deviation is not more than a degree or two on any heading, no further action is required. But very often larger deviations will be disclosed on certain courses, and when these are plotted against their respective headings a sine curve, such as is shown in Fig. 7(11), will be found.

This deviation curve is the sum of five different coefficients, called A, B, C, D and E. Coefficients A

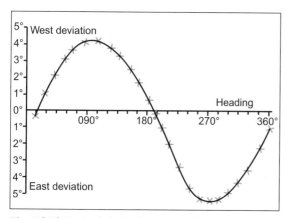

Fig. 7(11) Typical deviation curve, from a compass swing prior to making any corrections.

and E can normally be ignored in small vessels, and no means are provided to correct for them. Coefficient D is caused by items such as steel decks, not usually present in yachts, so that normally the yachtsman is only concerned with coefficients B and C.

Coefficient B causes deviations on east-west headings, and coefficient C causes deviations on north-south headings. Fortunately the effects of both B and C can be greatly reduced or eliminated by placing small correcting magnets near the compass, so as to counteract the local distortion of the earth's magnetic field.

Unlike poles of magnets attract each other, while like poles repel each other. In compass adjusting a north-seeking pole (eg the north end of a compass needle) is marked as a red pole, and a south-seeking pole is marked as a blue pole. Hence the north magnetic pole is a blue pole, and the south magnetic pole is a red pole.

Coefficient B, which causes the trouble on east-west headings, can be corrected by using fore and aft magnets which fairly obviously have no effect on the direction of the compass needle when the boat is heading north or south (because they only strengthen or weaken the earth's magnetic field). If the magnet is placed red (north) end forward, it corrects easterly deviation on easterly courses and westerly deviation on westerly courses. Conversely, if the magnet is placed blue (south) end forward, it corrects westerly deviation on easterly courses and easterly deviation on westerly courses.

Similarly, coefficient C, which gives rise to deviation on north-south courses, can be corrected by adding athwartships magnets – which have no effect on the compass when the boat is heading east or west. A magnet with its red (north) end to starboard corrects easterly deviation on northerly headings, and corrects westerly deviation on southerly headings. A

magnet with its blue (south) end to starboard corrects westerly deviation on northerly headings, and corrects easterly deviation on southerly headings.

The effect of either fore and aft or athwartships magnets can be increased or reduced by varying the strength of the magnet or its distance from the compass card. Older compasses had wooden corrector boxes, drilled with holes into which small magnets could be inserted. Modern compasses have built-in correctors, which can be adjusted by a screw.

7.2.5 HEELING ERROR

There is, however, another source of compass error which should be attended to first, and that is heeling error – especially in sailing boats which may spend long periods on one tack or the other. Vertical magnetic forces do not affect the compass when the boat is upright, but can cause heeling error when she is inclined. This is more important in sailing boats, but even in a motor boat heeling error can make the compass unstable when the vessel rolls. Heeling error can only be removed if vertical magnets can be placed below the compass. The adjustment is made with an instrument called a dip needle, which is a horizontal magnet balanced on a knife edge. This is set up ashore, away from any magnetic influence, so that it is levelled with the north end pointing north (south in the southern hemisphere) by adjusting a balance weight. The dip needle is then put exactly in the position occupied by the compass, with the boat on an east/west heading and the needle pointing north. If it does not lie horizontally it can be adjusted by vertical correctors – red end up if the north end is dipped down, blue end up if the north end is raised.

Correction for heeling error must be done before any other corrections are made. By the same token, if any alteration is made to the vertical magnets used for heeling error correction, it is important to carry out a compass swing to check the deviation on all courses.

7.2.6 COMPASS SWINGING

The compass should be swung on specific occasions, or whenever its accuracy is in doubt. Many yachts are not swung often enough, since with the passage of time the compensating magnets lose their magnetism. It should be done when the boat is new (or when a new compass is fitted); at the start of each season; if additional equipment (including electrical items) is fitted anywhere near the compass; and on any major change in latitude say more than 10°.

A compass can be swung by taking bearings, from a known position, of an object at least 5M

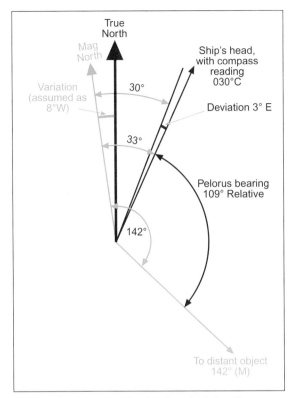

Fig. 7(12) Compass swinging in principle. The relative bearing of a distant object, related to its known bearing from a certain position, gives the deviation on a particular heading, in this case 030°.

away, using a pelorus or bearing plate. This is an azimuth ring graduated from 0°-360°, with a sighting arm for viewing the distant object; it is usually only found in larger boats. The pelorus may be set up on a tripod with its zero mark on the fore and aft line of the boat, so that the relative bearing of the object can be read for various headings, and compared with the bearing from the chart. The principle is shown in Fig. 7(12) and in the table below.

Ship's head (°C)	Pelorus relative bearing	Compass bearing °C of object	Known bearing (°M)	Deviation
000°	140°	140°	142°	2°E
030°	109°	139°	142°	3°E
060°	081°	141°	142°	1°E
090°	052°	142°	142°	0°
120°	023°	143°	142°	1°W

... and so on

If a pelorus is not available, a sextant, held horizontally, can be used to take the bearings. First it is necessary to place two reference marks, accurately located on the centreline of the boat

say with one on the aft side of the mast and the other at the aft end of the coachroof, and the observer near the stern.

Professional compass adjusters may use the sun rather than a distant terrestrial object, working from prepared azimuth tables. Unless conditions are very smooth, the yacht must be moored between three or four points, so that she can be warped round and held steady while the bearings are taken. Alternatively she can be kept under way, in the immediate vicinity of a buoy or beacon whose position is known. It is important however that the boat should not be close to large magnetic objects, and also to ensure that there are no tools or spare corrector magnets anywhere near the compass.

The procedure is then briefly as follows: With the boat heading due east, fore and aft magnets are placed so as to remove the deviation. The procedure is then repeated with the boat heading due north, using athwartships magnets. The effect of these magnets is then checked with the boat heading due west and due south. If there is no appreciable deviation (say, less than 2°) no further correction is necessary, but if there is, then remove half of it by placing the appropriate magnets. Then check again on east and north headings.

Having completed the adjustment so that the deviation on the four cardinal points is minimal, and hopefully only 1° or so in each case, the boat is then swung through 360° to measure the residual deviation at steps of, say, 30° and these readings form the deviation card; see Fig. 7(7).

Do impress upon all crew members the importance of keeping magnetic objects well away from the compass at all times. Camera light meters, metal spectacle cases and tools may have a misleading influence on even the best adjusted compass – and on some autopilots.

7.2.7   HAND BEARING COMPASS

A good hand bearing compass is essential for coastal navigation, and at sea for taking bearings of an approaching vessel to see whether there is a risk of collision. It can also be used for a quick check of the yacht's steering compass, and in emergency it can be taken aboard the liferaft or tender.

Such a compass needs to be accurate, with a scale that is easy to read, and sufficiently damped for the card to settle quickly. Illumination must be provided for use at night, and this is now almost universally achieved with Betalights.

The traditional type of Sestrel (arm's length) compass is an excellent instrument, with which very accurate bearings can be taken, but it is relatively bulky and the prism somewhat vulnerable to damage. In emergency this type of hand bearer can be used as a steering compass. Other designs, such as the well-known Mini compass, are more compact, and by using modern optical systems the compass can be held close to the eye, to eliminate parallax, with both the object and the figures on the card readily visible. Other makes include Silva, Plastimo, Ritchie and Suunto, and such compasses can be hung on a lanyard round the neck, and stuffed inside one's oilskin jacket, so that they are readily available when required.

Working on a different principle is the Autohelm fluxgate personal compass which can take and store up to nine bearings at the touch of a button. Pressing another button brings the bearing up on a LCD display. There is also a stopwatch facility to time the interval between bearings, or the period of a flashing light.

7.2.8 OTHER NAVIGATIONAL ITEMS

To perform the basic navigational tasks a fair sized chart table and suitable instruments are needed. A flat, smooth surface large enough to take an A0 chart (840 x 1186mm) folded to about 530 x 710mm is essential. If space is very limited some form of portable board will suffice, but without a fixed surface chartwork at sea is much harder. Charts normally stow in a shallow drawer below the chart table. Good lighting is important, interchangeable red/white and screened to avoid dazzling people on deck. A magnifier, with integral light, is useful.

Above the chart table this Handbook, the MRNA and Cruising Companions etc can be stowed on a small shelf or bookcase. A ship's log-book is essential, for keeping navigational records; see 7.4.5. Most navigators use a notebook for calculating tidal heights, compass courses etc and for reference later. This book may also be used for passage planning, and for recording snippets of information from various sources.

A reliable clock or watch is needed, with an alarm for reading the hourly log, copying the shipping forecast etc. A stop watch is essential for precise timing of lights.

A radio receiver able to receive LW, MW and FM is needed for the shipping forecasts. A built-in tape recorder which can be pre-set is valuable. Navtex is however more versatile than an ordinary radio receiver and requires no attention. The two should be regarded as complementary. An aneroid or digital barometer, or barograph, completes the weather requirements.

A good pair of dividers, preferably of the crossover type which can be operated with one hand, are essential for chartwork, and a pair of compasses for drawing arcs and circles can be useful for some problems.

A protractor, or similar, for measuring and plotting courses and bearings on the chart is needed and the various types are discussed below. Many yachtsmen use one of the purpose-built plotters which are available, eg a Douglas protractor or the Breton and Hurst plotters.

Protractors, plotters and parallel rulers

A **Douglas protractor** is a perspex square, graduated round the edge from 0° to 360° in both directions, and with a small hole in the centre. The square is engraved with a grid, parallel to the sides. To measure the course from A to B the centre hole is placed over the line AB, the square is lined up with the nearest meridian or parallel of latitude with the north point at the top, and the course is then read off the edge of the square on the outer (clockwise) set of figures. A similar procedure is followed to determine the direction or bearing of an object.

The **Breton or Portland plotter** has a perspex base, approx 14" x 5", in the centre of which is a rotatable compass rose with an engraved grid inside. It is simple, strong and easy to use. To measure a track or line on the chart, place either long edge of the plotter against the track line; turn the engraved grid to align with a convenient parallel of latitude or meridian, or

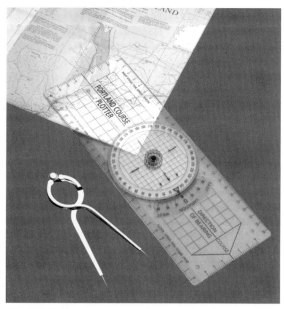

Fig. 7(13) A protractor such as the Portland Plotter is purpose-built for use on a yacht.

better still both. Then read off the bearing of the track against the correct value on the variation scale. Converting between true and magnetic, either mentally or on the chart, is not required.

Conversely to plot the bearing of a feature, say 082°M, as taken with a hand-bearing compass, set that value against the local variation, say 4°W. Place the plotter on the chart so that one long edge touches the feature; then jockey the plotter around so as to align its squared grid with a convenient parallel or meridian. Draw the line. The long edges have useful graduations at scales of 1:25,000, 1:50,000, 1:75,000 and 1:150,000. Incomparable.

The **Hurst plotter** is similar in principle, but, in addition to its compass rose and squared grid, has a long rather vulnerable perspex arm which can be aligned with the required course or bearing against the plotter's own compass rose. It is relatively simple to use, and does away with true to magnetic conversions and vice versa, but appears to be a forerunner of the Breton plotter.

Some navigators use **navigational set squares**, which are right-angled, isosceles triangles in perspex, graduated in degrees from the centre of the hypotenuse from 0° to 180° on the outer scale, and from 180° to 360° on the inner. Each to his own.

Parallel rulers are of two kinds: the hefty roller type which could be lethal on a yacht; and the traditional type with two parallel strips of perspex connected by metal arms each end; this has to be 'walked' across the chart, calling for dexterity and patience in a rough sea.

A handy stowage is needed for soft pencils (2B), a quality soft rubber, dividers, and plotter or protractor.

At least one pair of efficient **binoculars** is needed, but better still have one pair for the skipper/navigator, and a spare pair for general ship's use. The correct choice is important. Prismatic binoculars are described by two sets of figures, thus 7x50. The first figure or figures refer to the magnification, 7 for example meaning that an object viewed will appear seven times larger and seven times nearer than if viewed with the naked eye. The second set of figures is the diameter of the objective lens (furthest from the eye) in mm, and this determines the amount of light admitted.

Another important dimension which is not immediately apparent but which can be quickly derived is the diameter of the exit pupil, the lens nearest the eye. This is determined by dividing the diameter of the objective pupil by the magnification. Hence for a 7x35 binocular the diameter of the exit pupil is 5mm. A large exit pupil passes more light to the eye and gives a brighter image. About 7mm is a desirable figure. This is particularly important in poor light, and is assisted by special coatings on the lenses and prisms of good quality binoculars.

At sea binoculars with a magnification of more than 7 or 8 are impossible to hold sufficiently steady to get a good image. Exceptionally 9 x or 10 x can be used in large yachts which provide a steady platform, but for good all-round use 7x50 is recommended. In a yacht binoculars need to be sturdy and waterproof. Those which have individual focusing for each eyepiece are more resistant to water than those with central focusing. Some kind of rubber coating helps to protect binoculars from the knocks which they may receive onboard a yacht. Treat them with care, put them down gently since it does not take much of a jolt to knock them out of collimation.

For general daytime use it is difficult to fault the Tasco Offshore 54-1 binoculars which include a compass (plus a rangefinder reticle if required). They are light and compact with excellent optical qualities and the compass is extremely deadbeat. At £150 they are good value. Other well-known makes include Steiner and Canon.

7.2.9 LOGS AND SPEEDOMETERS

Distance run, together with course steered, forms the basis of dead reckoning (see 7.4.3). The speed of a vessel through the water is almost as important. So some form of log is essential for any seagoing boat which is going to make coastal cruises.

The traditional Walker log is simple, accurate and reliable. It consists of a rotor at the end of a long line connected to the instrument on the stern of the boat. The mechanical simplicity is obvious, although seaweed can stop the rotor working and the line may be bitten off by large fish. The accuracy stems from the rotor operating well astern of the hull, and reliability is ensured because, apart from routine cleaning and lubrication, maintenance is minimal. The whole log and line can be stowed away in its box when not needed. It is, however, wise to carry a spare line and rotor.

When streaming a log, first hook it onto the indicator and then (retaining the rotor inboard) stream the bight of the line before letting the rotator go; otherwise the rotor will twist the line into knots while it is being streamed. Conversely, when recovering it, unhook the end of the line from the indicator and pay it out astern as the rotor is pulled in – allowing the line to untwist as it is eventually hauled aboard from the rotor end.

Modern types of log are more convenient to use, but not necessarily any more accurate. Some have a small impeller or paddlewheel mounted almost flush with the underside of the hull. The rotating part incorporates a small magnet so that the magnetic impulse is passed to a unit inside the boat, which counts the number of pulses and hence records speed and distance run.

Some logs work without any moving parts, so avoiding the problems of fouling by weed etc. An electro-magnetic log works on the principle that if a conductor moves in a magnetic field an electric current is induced in it, and the faster the movement the greater the current. The magnetic field is produced by an electromagnet inside the hull fitting, and the potential difference is sensed by two electrodes mounted flush with the outside of the hull.

Doppler logs measure the apparent shift in frequency between a transmitted signal and the signal reflected back from the water or (in shallower depths) from the bottom. When picking up the bottom signal the log measures distance and speed over the ground, rather than through the water. Others work on the speed of sound.

If it is to be relied on, any log should be calibrated by timing the boat over a measured distance.

Most electronic logs incorporate some form of adjustment for calibration, and few have theoretical operating errors of less than ± 15 per cent. In practice the error is likely to be greater than this and may vary with speed. So log readings must be used with caution when (for example) approaching dangers in poor visibility.

7.2.10   ECHO SOUNDERS

An echo sounder is the most useful item of electronic equipment for a boat of any type, and there is a large range of models available. Properly used as described above, an echo sounder is a navigational aid, not just a means of preventing involuntary grounding.

All echo sounders work on a similar principle, but with different ways of presenting the information. An electronic pulse, usually at 150 or 200 kHz, is transmitted downwards from the transducer, fitted in the bottom of the boat. The signal received back from the sea bottom is amplified and then made into a readable display. For small boats the most common is the flashing display with a rotating arm, at the end of which there is a light source. The light flashes at zero when the pulse is emitted, and it flashes again when the amplified signal is received back. For practical purposes the speed of sound in water is

constant at about 1490m/sec (4900ft/sec), although it is slightly affected by differences in temperature and salinity. Since the arm rotates at a constant speed, the time taken for the pulse to go to the bottom and back is represented by the angular displacement between the two flashes.

The receiver will also record echoes that are returned from intermediate objects (fish, weed etc), between the transducer and the sea bed. Also, with experience, the echo from a hard bottom, such as rock, can be distinguished from soft mud.

Other types of display incorporate either a needle on a dial (ie an analogue display) or a digital readout. Either may include a special microprocessor which tries to sort out the extraneous signals from fish etc which otherwise may cause the display to fluctuate wildly.

Most modern echo sounders are sufficiently powerful to allow the transducer to be installed inside a glassfibre hull. Apart from eliminating the need for a hole through the bottom, this also solves any problem of fouling on the face of the transducer. It does however reduce the sensitivity at maximum depths.

Some echo sounders have shallow-water alarms which can be useful, particularly if cruising short handed. In addition, some models have a deepwater alarm, or anchor watch features.

The most versatile type of echo sounder has a visual record display whereby the flash (similar to that of a rotating flashing display) marks a moving sheet of paper and thus provides a recorded picture of the echoes from the sea bed and from the water above it. Some such echo sounders combine this graphical display with a flashing light display which can be used in isolation (to save paper).

Yet another method of presentation is by cathode ray tube and in colour so that different types of echoes (fish shoals, surface contamination, plankton layers and type of bottom) can readily be distinguished. Forward and sideways-looking beams can forewarn of an imminent grounding. Such sophisticated equipment is expensive and is normally only used for fish finding.

7.2.11   LEAD LINE

Even though most yachts are fitted with an echo sounder it is a good idea to carry a hand lead and line. Apart from being required if the electronic instrument fails, it may also be useful at anchor, to tell whether the anchor is dragging. The nature of the seabed can also be determined by 'arming the lead', ie pressing tallow or heavy grease into a hole at the base of the lead. Shingle, gravel, mud, sand and shells will stick to the tallow.

Since most charts are now metric a lead line should be calibrated in metres, and the following traditional markings could be appropriate:

2 metres	Two strips of leather
3 metres	Three strips of leather
5 metres	A piece of white duck
7 metres	A piece of red bunting
10 metres	A piece of leather with a hole in it
13 metres	A piece of blue serge
15 metres	A piece of white duck
17 metres	A piece of red bunting
20 metres	Two knots

These marks were based on the fathom (6 feet), ie about two metres, and at night could be identified by feel. Lines could of course be marked with paint; whatever marks are used should be easy to remember and are best entered in a 'Ship's booklet' for ready reference.

A 20 metre lead line is more than adequate for most yachting purposes, particularly when mainly used as a stand-by for the echo sounder. Depending on the boat's normal cruising waters, a line of 10 metres should suffice. The lead should be heavy enough, say 7lbs (3kg), to cope with a strong tidal stream or current and penetrate a layer of mud to find the underlying bottom.

7.3 CHARTS

7.3.1   MERCATOR'S PROJECTION

An adequate chart of an area is the first requirement for any form of navigation. Without it the sailor has no idea of the relative positions or distances of one feature from another, or of what goes on beneath the surface of the sea.

A chart, like a map, must be a compromise because it has to represent the curved shape of the globe on a flat piece of paper. Details of the coastline, for example, are slightly distorted to get them onto a flat surface.

Most charts are drawn on Mercator's projection with the meridians shown as equally spaced parallel lines running up and down the chart whereas in reality they converge towards the poles. The parallels of latitude, which in reality are equally spaced, are drawn on the chart further and further apart towards the poles.

Thus on a Mercator's chart land masses are greatly distorted in high latitudes, but this is not important around the British Isles.

A Mercator's chart has the following characteristics:

a. A rhumb line, which cuts all the meridians at the same angle, appears as a straight line on the chart.

b. The scale of distance is given by the latitude scale – at the latitude concerned.

c. Angles on the earth's surface equal the corresponding angles on the chart.

d. Meridians are parallel straight lines, equally spaced, and the scale of longitude is constant for all latitudes.

e. A great circle, which is the shortest distance between two points, appears as a curve. Unless long distances are involved, this is not a serious disadvantage.

7.3.2   GNOMONIC CHARTS

Some charts are based on a gnomonic (pronounced know-món-ic) projection. Apart from large scale harbour plans this projection is also used for polar charts and for great circle sailing. A gnomonic chart is a projection of the earth's surface from the centre on to a tangential plane, so that all great circles appear as straight lines. Large scale gnomonic charts, as used for harbour plans, are used in just the same way as a Mercator's chart.

7.3.3   SCALE

The amount of detail shown on a chart depends upon its scale. Large scale charts (typically 1:7,500) are used for harbour plans; medium scale (1:50,000) is used for port approaches and coastal detail, while smaller scale charts (eg 1:200,000) may be used for longer coastlines. A smaller scale still (1:1,000,000) covers whole sea areas, eg Admiralty chart 1104, The Bay of Biscay. Scale is the relationship between a distance shown on the chart and the actual distance on land or sea, eg 1:50,000 means that 1cm on the chart represents 50,000cm on land/sea. So large scale charts have small numbers in their scale and cover small areas, while small scales charts have big numbers and cover big areas.

The scale is shown near the chart's title. It is always important to use the largest scale chart available, particularly for inshore pilotage, because a lot of inshore details are necessarily omitted from small scale charts.

A good idea of the scale of a chart can be obtained by looking at the latitude scale, remembering that one minute is one nautical mile. On Admiralty charts the design of the latitude scale varies with the scale of the chart. Care is needed in reading latitude and longitude scales. Read off the correct number of degrees first (taking the lower of the two figures on either side of the position), and then the number of minutes. If cruising near the Greenwich meridian, ensure that you are reading in the correct (West or East) hemisphere.

7.3.4 CHART CORRECTIONS

It is false economy and possibly dangerous to carry too few or out-dated charts. Admiralty charts show at the bottom their date of publication, the date of the latest edition and the number of the last correction inserted.

Corrections to charts and other navigational publications published by the Hydrographic Office (such as the ALL and the ALRS) are issued in the weekly Admiralty Notices to Mariners, which can be obtained from chart agents or are available for study at Mercantile Marine Offices and Customs Offices. They are also available free on the Internet at www.nms.ukho.gov.uk at 1200 noon the day before the official publication date of Thursday.

A Small Craft Edition of Admiralty Notices to Mariners (NP 246) is published in February, May, July and September. It lists the corrections which are of direct interest to yachtsmen navigating the waters around the British Isles and from the Gironde to the Elbe.

NP 294 'How to correct your charts the Admiralty way' sets out simply and clearly the essentials of good chart correcting – sadly a much neglected practice; cost £7.95.

7.3.5 SMALL CRAFT CHARTS

Commercially produced charts are available specifically intended for use in small craft. They either have relatively small sheets or can be folded like a map, making them handy to use in a small space.

Stanfords charts cover Dublin to The Wash, Ushant to Den Helder and, in booklet form, major yachting areas. They give pilotage notes and tidal data, and are available from chandlers and Stanfords Charts, PO Box 2747, West Mersea CO5 8FT. sales@allweathercharts.co.uk Tel/Fax 01206 381580. www.allweathercharts.co.uk (Nothing to do with Stanfords' book/map store Long Acre, London).

Imray, Laurie, Norie & Wilson (Imrays) publish three types of chart: 'C' charts of the UK and Europe from Denmark to Gibraltar; 'Y' charts cover the UK's S and SE coasts and harbours; the 2000 series are handy size charts of the SE UK and Clyde. Available at chandlers or from Imray, Wych House, The Broadway, St Ives, Huntingdon, Cambs PE27 5BT; Tel 01480 462114; Fax 496109. ilnw@imray.com   www.imray.com

Admiralty Small Craft charts are standard Admiralty charts modified to meet the needs of yachtsmen. They fold down to 215mm x 355mm (slightly bigger than A4), for convenient stowage. On the reverse useful information includes Coastguard, radio, weather, safety, navigation warnings and tidal streams. 122 Small

Craft charts cover sailing areas in the UK and northern France and retail at £12.50 each (2001).

Small Craft Folios cover eight popular yachting areas. Each folio contains 10-12 charts at A2 size (594mm x 420mm) to fit yacht chart tables. Stowed in clear plastic wallets and costing £37 each, the folios are as follows:

SC 5600   The Solent and Approaches
SC 5601   E Devon & Dorset, Exmouth to Christchurch
SC 5602   The West Country, Falmouth to Teignmouth
SC 5603   Falmouth to Padstow, inc Isles of Scilly
SC 5604   The Channel Islands
SC 5605   Chichester to Ramsgate, inc Dover Strait
SC 5606   Thames Estuary, Ramsgate to Tower Bridge
SC 5607   Thames Estuary, Essex and Suffolk coast.

ALRS Small Craft (NP 289 UK to the Med, including Azores and Canaries) is a new publication containing marina and port communications, MSI, GMDSS and Navtex information at £17.95; see also section 8.7.

All charts and publications are available from bookshops, chandlers and Admiralty Chart Agents. For further information contact the Hydrographic Office, Taunton, Somerset TA1 2DN. Tel 01823 337900; Fax 284077. www.ukho.gov.uk

7.3.6 ADMIRALTY CHARTS

The full Admiralty Chart Catalogue (NP 131, at £19) lists some 6000 charts and publications covering most of the world. When ordering charts, give both their number and title; they cost £16.30 each. NP 131 also lists Admiralty chart agents, as repeated in Admiralty Notice to Mariners No. 2 each year. In Chapter 9 of the MRNA, Admiralty chart agents are shown by 'ACA' under a port entry, but without the address.

A mini-catalogue (NP 109) listing charts of the British Isles and north-west Europe is published every January; as is a similar mini-catalogue (NP 106) of Mediterranean charts including the Bay of Biscay, Spain, Portugal, the Canaries and the Black Sea. Both catalogues are free.

The Hydrographic Office also issues a variety of other charts, diagrams and publications, of which the following may be of interest to yachtsmen:

a. Chart 5011, a booklet giving the symbols and abbreviations used on Admiralty charts; £8.00.
b. Astronomical charts, azimuth diagrams and star charts. NP 400, sight reduction forms; £5.25.
c. Routeing charts for ocean passages. The data includes routes and distances between

ports, ocean currents, wind roses, ice limits, air and sea temperature, barometric pressure, and the incidence of fog and gales.

d. The Fisherman's Pilot:
NP 150 Western North Sea
NP 151 North & West Scotland
NP 152 Ireland & Irish Sea.

e. Instructional charts in the 5000 series. These are uncorrected charts for navigational classes; £3.50.

f. Plotting charts.

g. PEXA (Practice & Exercise Areas) charts of the UK (Q series); £8.00.

h. Co-tidal and Co-range charts (5057-5059); £8.00.

j. Admiralty Sailing Directions (Pilots) covering the world (£37.00); see 7.10.3.

k. Admiralty List of Lights and Fog Signals (Vols A to L); see 7.10.4.

l. Admiralty List of Radio Signals (Vols 1-6 & 8); see section 8.7.

m. Tide Tables (£19.00) & Tidal stream atlases (£7.00), as listed in Chapter 12.

n. The Mariner's Handbook (NP 100); £37.00.

o. Ocean Passages for the World (NP 136); £45.00.

7.3.7 ADMIRALTY CHART SYMBOLS AND ABBREVIATIONS

There is a huge amount of information on a chart, and to make the most of it you should know at least the more common symbols and abbreviations, which optimise the use of limited space. Rocks, wrecks and most of the commoner symbols and abbreviations are shown in Figs. 7(14) to 7(17). But for complete details and a constant reference you need Admiralty Chart 5011 (edition 2, Dec 1998; £8.00), which is actually an A4 size booklet.

The information below and in Figs. 7(14) to 7(17) refers to metric charts, unless otherwise stated. There are still a few fathoms charts in use, probably not corrected. Their rather cluttered black-and-white appearance is distinctive; their symbols and abbreviations are obsolete, but comparable to those on metric charts.

One obvious function of a chart is to show the outlines of the coast and of off-lying islands. On Admiralty metric charts these features are distinguished by the land being tinted buff, and drying areas (between high water and low water) being tinted green. Features such as lights, radio aids, traffic separation schemes, prohibited anchorages, submarine cables, explosive dumping areas, submarine exercise areas, pipelines etc are shown in magenta.

Depths on metric charts are shown in metres (and tenths of metres in shallower waters). Depths of less than 5 metres are tinted blue, and the 10 metre depth contour has a ribbon of blue tint. Shades of blue vary and may be shown to different depth limits according to the scale and purpose of the chart.

Drying heights (above chart datum) are also in metres and tenths of metres, and are underlined. Clearances below bridges etc are given in metres above MHWS. Heights of lights, hills etc are in metres above MHWS.

7.3.8 ELECTRONIC CHARTS

The advent of digitised charts, supplied on CD, is revolutionising navigation – and many other tasks on board; see 8.4.5. A large number of charts can be stored on a single CD for display on a Personal Computer (PC) screen. Increasingly sophisticated software allows the navigator to zoom in to a particular area of the chart or to zoom out for an overview of the navigational situation. Waypoints and routes can be plotted and stored and a section of the chart printed out for use in the cockpit. As the laptop and CDs are easily portable they can be taken home, allowing passage planning to be done in advance. On board, with the yacht's GPS connected to the computer, the current position is superimposed on the chart. Some software will control an autopilot to keep the yacht on the planned track and with the more complex programmes – and a suitable interface – radar contacts can also be displayed on the chart.

Electronic charts are technically of two different kinds:

a. Raster charts. These are electronically scanned from a paper chart (or its original film) and thus retain with remarkable accuracy and fidelity the familiar appearance and almost the feel of paper charts. It is this familiarity which plays a major part in inspiring confidence among users of these charts. The image is similar to that of a newspaper photograph, ie it is made up of a grid of different sized coloured dots (or pixels) which form a computer file; these files can be very large. If you zoom in on raster charts the dots will soon be visible, whilst zooming out will cause the image quality to be degraded.

b. Vector charts. Any feature, coastline or object on a chart may be described, in terms of shape and size, by mathematical vectors, ie lines of a known direction and length. Thus if you start from a known point and 'trace round' the outline of say an islet you will end up with a large number of vectors which precisely define the islet. The chart is built up of a number of layers each of which usually carries similar types of information. Vector chart files are smaller than raster which means they open up on the screen more quickly and can give greater sharpness and clarity at different levels of zooming.

Both raster and vector charts have their strengths and weaknesses; neither is better than the other. Vector charts certainly carry more intelligence than raster, but this may only be significant in certain specialised applications. It is of course possible to have an electronic chart system which can handle both types of chart. Other factors which will affect your choice include cost and the extent of chart coverage for the area(s) in which you will cruise.

Chart manufacturers are rightly jealous of their copyright because producing charts is an expensive business. To guard against copying of electronic charts a security key (otherwise known as a 'dongle') is required without which the PC cannot run the charting software. A dongle contains both physical hardware and some electronic circuitry; it is very reliable and hence unlikely to deprive the yachtsmen of his electronic charts at sea.

Most British Admiralty (BA) and American government charts are now available in electronic format as well as those from many other hydrographic offices. BA charts are available from chart agents and chandlers in Maptech (producers of American government charts) and ARCS (Admiralty Raster Chart Service) formats, both of which store raster facsimiles of the familiar paper charts.

With Maptech charts the basic software to read them is included free on the chart CD, although more sophisticated Maptech software is available at additional cost. As these programmes are designed specifically for the leisure user, as well as to display Maptech charts, the software is simple to learn and use and the speed of the display impressive. The Maptech chart folios of around 25 charts per CD are much cheaper than the ARCS series and like ARCS are facsimiles of official charts. Covering all popular cruising and racing areas, Maptech charts can be corrected and often include additional features such as aerial and approach photography, 3D bathymetric data, port plans and data, lights and tides. Privately produced charts (such as the Imray series) are also available.

To view ARCS charts a suitable navigation programme is needed – these vary in price and sophistication and chart agents can supply a list of compatible software. ARCS charts in the 'Navigator' range are designed primarily for large

ships and the user buys a licence for a number of charts, thereafter a new licence must be purchased annually. The ARCS 'Skipper' range allows the leisure user to buy a permanent licence for one or more folios of 10 charts per CD. Standard folios cover most popular cruising areas; alternatively a folio of 10 specific charts can be selected. For a further fee quarterly or annual correction discs can be purchased.

Using electronic charts can significantly reduce the number of paper charts carried, but there must still be some on board. Should the PC fail there must be a means of navigating the yacht safely into harbour. This requires a general chart of the area together with approach and entry charts for several all weather harbours of refuge. Should the computer breakdown then one of these harbours can be entered instead of the planned destination. The normal navigation instruments such as hand bearing compass, log, dividers and protractor or plotter, must be available so that conventional navigation can be carried out. A written log must be maintained even when the PC is the primary means of navigation.

7.3.9   CHART PLOTTERS AND PCS
Electronic position fixing systems, primarily GPS and to a far lesser extent Loran-C (see Chapter 8) are now the norm amongst yachtsmen. But a latitude and longitude, displayed on whatever Navaid is in use, must still be transferred to the chart so that the position can be related to other features such as navigational dangers. So for some time to come many yachtsmen will continue to use the conventional paper chart which provides all the detail needed, to a good standard of accuracy, and is simple to correct when required.

The Yeoman plotter is/was a first generation electronic device which provides the essential link between the Navaid in use and the paper chart on the chart table. It dispenses with dividers, parallel rulers or mechanical plotting aids. It consists of a digitised mat or electronic grid on top of which the paper chart to be used is clipped and located. It can be used with any Mercator chart or harbour plan, and will accept an Admiralty chart folded in half. The electronic grid under the chart allows the Yeoman plotter (or puck) on the chart surface to convert any chosen position into latitude and longitude. Conversely, given latitude and longitude by (say) GPS, the Yeoman will guide you to that position on the chart by means of four illuminated red arrows pointing 90° apart. When the red lights go out, the puck is in the designated position.

Fig. 7(14)   Abbreviations used on Admiralty charts. †Obsolescent

Coastal Features		
Anch.	Anchorage	
Appr.	Approaches	
B.	Bay	
C.	Cape	
Chan.	Channel	
Cr.	Creek	
Ent.	Entrance	
Est.	Estuary	
G.	Gulf	
Hn.	Haven	
Hr.	Harbour	
I.	Island, Islet	
L.	Lake, Loch, Lough	
Lndg.	Landing place	
Mt.	Mountain, Mount	
Mth.	Mouth	
P.	Port	
Pass.	Passage	
Prom.	Promontory	
Pt.	Point	
R.	River	
Rds.	Roads, Roadstead	
Rk.	Rock	
Sd.	Sound	
Str.	Strait	

Units	
cm	Centimetre(s)
dm	Decimetre(s)
fm	Fathom
ft	Foot, Feet
Ht†	Height
km	Kilometres
kn	Knots
Lat	Latitude
Long	Longitude
m	Metre(s)
M	Sea Mile(s)
mm	Millimetres
No	Number

Adjectives etc	
abt	About
Aero	Aeronautical
Anct†	Ancient
approx	Approximate
conspic†	Conspicuous
dest	Destroyed
discont	Discontinued
dist	Distant
exper	Experimental
explos	Explosive
Gt, Grt†	Great
Hr†	Higher
(illum)	Illuminated
Lit†	Little
LL	List of Lights
Lr†	Lower
Mid†	Middle

NM	Notice(s) to Mariners
Obscd	Obscured
(P)	Preliminary (NM)
(priv)	Private
prohib	Prohibited
proj	Projected
prom	Prominent
S.	Saint
SD	Sailing Directions
SD	Sounding doubtful
subm	Submerged
(T)	Temporary (NM)
(vert)	Vertically disposed

Buildings etc	
Ave	Avenue
Baty	Battery
Bldg	Building
Cas	Castle
Cath†	Cathedral
Cemy†	Cemetery
CG	Coastguard station
Ch	Church, Chapel
Chy	Chimney
Const	Construction
Cup	Cupola
Dk	Dock
FS	Flagstaff
Ho	House
Hosp	Hospital
LB†	Lifeboat
Mon	Monument
NB	Notice Board
Obstn	Obstruction
PO	Post Office
Ru (ru)	Ruin
Sch	School
Sig	Signal
Sp	Spire
SS	Signal Station
St	Street
Sta	Station
Tel	Telephone
Tr	Tower

Dangers	
Bk.	Bank
cov	Covers
dr	Dries
ED	Existence doubtful
Le.	Ledge
Obstn	Obstruction
pos	Position
PA	Position approximate
PD	Position doubtful
Rep	Reported
Rf.	Reef
Sh.	Shoal
uncov.	Uncovers
unexam	Unexamined

Nature of the Seabed	
Ba†	Basalt
bk	Broken
Bo†	Boulders
c	Coarse (sand)
Ck†	Chalk
Cy	Clay
f	Fine (sand)
G	Gravel
ga†	Glacial
h	Hard
l†	Large
m	Medium (sand)
M	Mud
Ml†	Marl
Ms†	Mussels
Oy†	Oysters
Oz†	Ooze
P	Pebbles
Qz†	Quartz
R	Rock
S	Sand
Sh	Shells
sf	Stiff
Si	Silt
S/M	Sand over mud (layers)
sm†	Small
Sn†	Shingle
so	Soft
St	Stones
sy	Sticky
Wd	Weed (inc Kelp)

Tides and Currents	
CD	Chart Datum
DW	Deep Water
HAT	Highest Astronomical Tide
HW/LW	High Water/Low Water
LAT	Lowest Astronomical Tide
MHW	Mean High Water
MHWN	Mean High Water Neaps
MHWS	Mean High Water Springs
MLW	Mean Low Water
MLWN	Mean Low Water Neaps
MLWS	Mean Low Water Springs
MSL	Mean Sea Level
MTL	Mean Tide Level
OD	Ordnance Datum
Sp/Np	Spring Tides/Neap Tides
Vel	Velocity

Compass	
annly	Annually
decrg	Decreasing
incrg	Increasing
Mag	Magnetic
Var	Variation

Fig. 7(15)   Admiralty chart symbols.

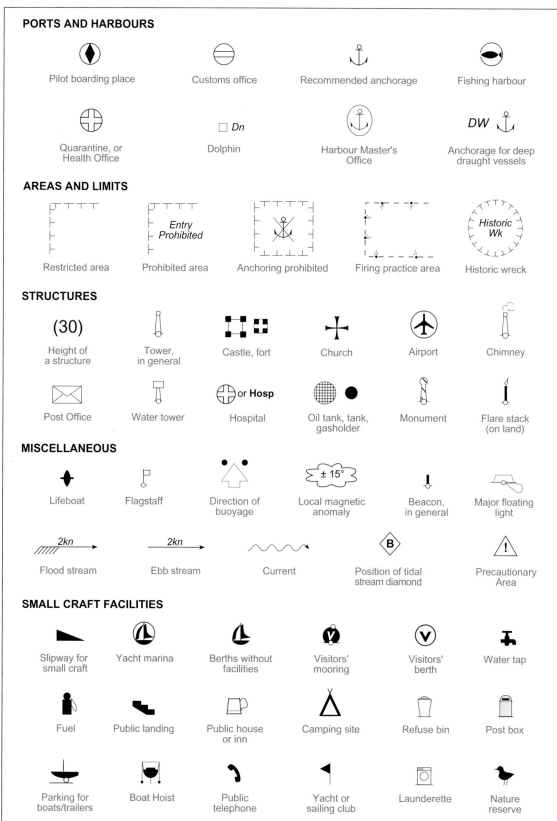

Fig. 7(16)

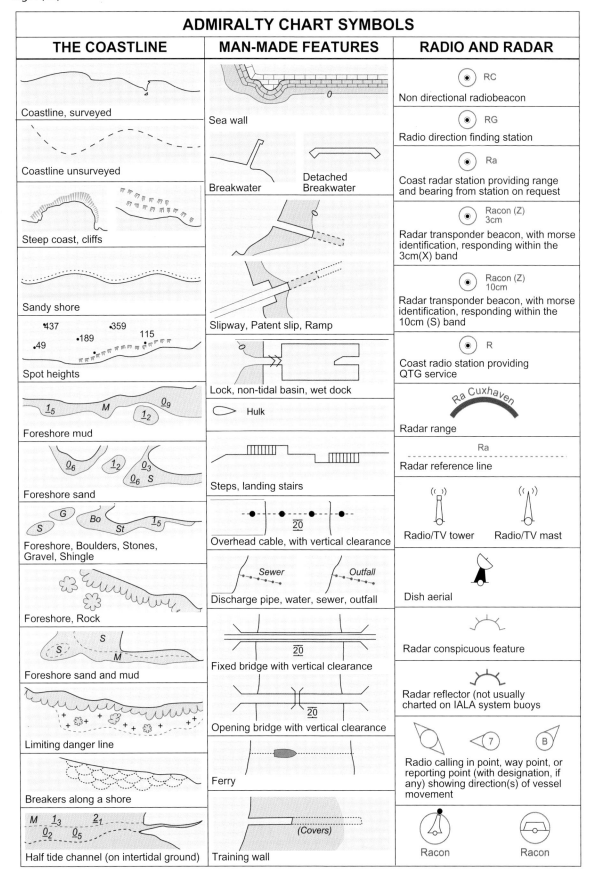

ADMIRALTY CHART SYMBOLS

THE COASTLINE	MAN-MADE FEATURES	RADIO AND RADAR

THE COASTLINE

Coastline, surveyed

Coastline unsurveyed

Steep coast, cliffs

Sandy shore

Spot heights

Foreshore mud

Foreshore sand

Foreshore, Boulders, Stones, Gravel, Shingle

Foreshore, Rock

Foreshore sand and mud

Limiting danger line

Breakers along a shore

Half tide channel (on intertidal ground)

MAN-MADE FEATURES

Sea wall

Breakwater   Detached Breakwater

Slipway, Patent slip, Ramp

Lock, non-tidal basin, wet dock

Hulk

Steps, landing stairs

Overhead cable, with vertical clearance

Discharge pipe, water, sewer, outfall

Fixed bridge with vertical clearance

Opening bridge with vertical clearance

Ferry

Training wall   (Covers)

RADIO AND RADAR

RC — Non directional radiobeacon

RG — Radio direction finding station

Ra — Coast radar station providing range and bearing from station on request

Racon (Z) 3cm — Radar transponder beacon, with morse identification, responding within the 3cm(X) band

Racon (Z) 10cm — Radar transponder beacon, with morse identification, responding within the 10cm (S) band

R — Coast radio station providing QTG service

Ra Cuxhaven — Radar range

Ra — Radar reference line

Radio/TV tower   Radio/TV mast

Dish aerial

Radar conspicuous feature

Radar reflector (not usually charted on IALA system buoys

Radio calling in point, way point, or reporting point (with designation, if any) showing direction(s) of vessel movement

Racon   Racon

193

Fig. 7(17)

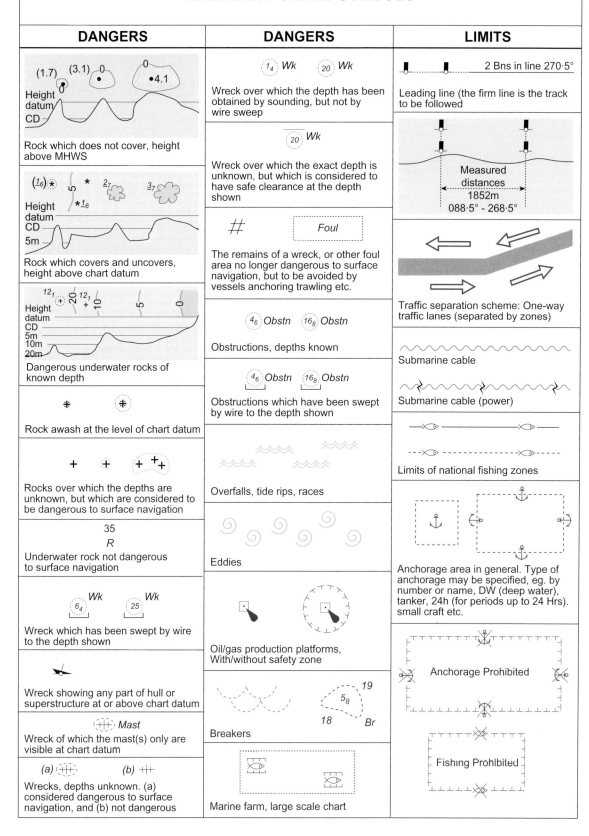

ADMIRALTY CHART SYMBOLS

DANGERS	DANGERS	LIMITS

DANGERS

(1.7) (3.1) 0 0 •4.1
Height datum CD
Rock which does not cover, height above MHWS

(1₆)* * 2₇ 3₇
*1₆
Height datum CD 5m
Rock which covers and uncovers, height above chart datum

12₁ 20 12₁ 10 5 0
Height datum CD 5m 10m 20m
Dangerous underwater rocks of known depth

Rock awash at the level of chart datum

Rocks over which the depths are unknown, but which are considered to be dangerous to surface navigation

35
R
Underwater rock not dangerous to surface navigation

6₄ Wk   25 Wk
Wreck which has been swept by wire to the depth shown

Wreck showing any part of hull or superstructure at or above chart datum

Mast
Wreck of which the mast(s) only are visible at chart datum

(a)   (b)
Wrecks, depths unknown. (a) considered dangerous to surface navigation, and (b) not dangerous

DANGERS

1₄ Wk   20 Wk
Wreck over which the depth has been obtained by sounding, but not by wire sweep

20 Wk
Wreck over which the exact depth is unknown, but which is considered to have safe clearance at the depth shown

Foul
The remains of a wreck, or other foul area no longer dangerous to surface navigation, but to be avoided by vessels anchoring trawling etc.

4₆ Obstn   16₈ Obstn
Obstructions, depths known

4₆ Obstn   16₈ Obstn
Obstructions which have been swept by wire to the depth shown

Overfalls, tide rips, races

Eddies

Oil/gas production platforms, With/without safety zone

19
5₈
18   Br
Breakers

Marine farm, large scale chart

LIMITS

2 Bns in line 270·5°
Leading line (the firm line is the track to be followed

Measured distances 1852m 088·5° - 268·5°

Traffic separation scheme: One-way traffic lanes (separated by zones)

Submarine cable

Submarine cable (power)

Limits of national fishing zones

Anchorage area in general. Type of anchorage may be specified, eg. by number or name, DW (deep water), tanker, 24h (for periods up to 24 Hrs). small craft etc.

Anchorage Prohibited

Fishing Prohibited

Fig. 7(33)

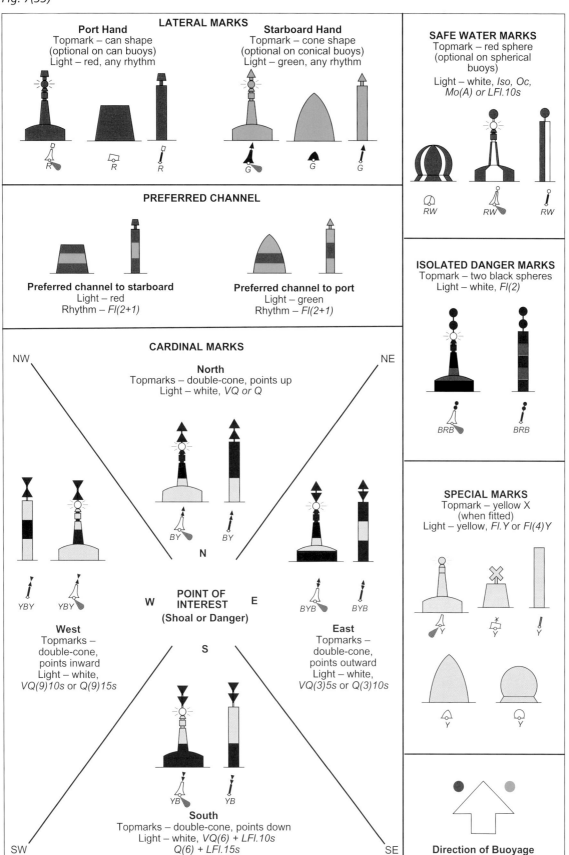

LATERAL MARKS

Port Hand
Topmark – can shape
(optional on can buoys)
Light – red, any rhythm

R   *R*   *R*

Starboard Hand
Topmark – cone shape
(optional on conical buoys)
Light – green, any rhythm

G   *G*   *G*

PREFERRED CHANNEL

Preferred channel to starboard
Light – red
Rhythm – *Fl(2+1)*

Preferred channel to port
Light – green
Rhythm – *Fl(2+1)*

CARDINAL MARKS

NW   NE

North
Topmarks – double-cone, points up
Light – white, *VQ or Q*

BY   *BY*

N

YBY   *YBY*

West
Topmarks –
double-cone,
points inward
Light – white,
VQ(9)10s or Q(9)15s

W   **POINT OF INTEREST** (Shoal or Danger)   E

East
Topmarks –
double-cone,
points outward
Light – white,
VQ(3)5s or Q(3)10s

BYB   *BYB*

S

YB   *YB*

South
Topmarks – double-cone, points down
Light – white, *VQ(6) + LFl.10s*
Q(6) + LFl.15s

SW   SE

SAFE WATER MARKS
Topmark – red sphere
(optional on spherical buoys)

Light – white, *Iso, Oc, Mo(A)* or *LFl.10s*

RW   *RW*   *RW*

ISOLATED DANGER MARKS
Topmark – two black spheres
Light – white, *Fl(2)*

BRB   *BRB*

SPECIAL MARKS
Topmark – yellow X
(when fitted)
Light – yellow, *Fl.Y* or *Fl(4)Y*

Y   *Y*   *Y*

Y   *Y*

Direction of Buoyage

195

Fig. 7(39) International Port Traffic Signals (IPTS)

No.	Lights		Main Message
1	 ●●●	Flashing	Serious emergency — all vessels to stop or divert according to instructions
2	●●●	Fixed or Slow Occulting	Vessels shall not proceed (Note: Some ports may use an exemption signal, as in 2a below)
3	 ●●●		Vessels may proceed. One way traffic
4	 ●●○		Vessels may proceed. Two way traffic
5	 ●○●		A vessel may proceed only when she has received specific orders to do so (Note: Some ports may use an exemption signal, as in 5a below)
	Exemption signals and message		
2a	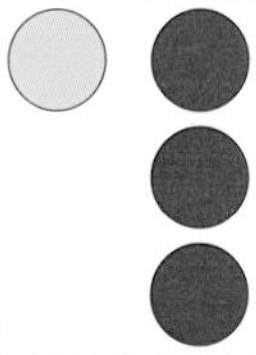 ○ ●●●	Fixed or Slow Occulting	Vessels shall not proceed, except that vessels which navigate outside the main channel need not comply with the main message
5a	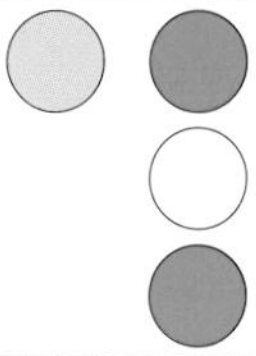 ○ ●○●		A vessel may proceed only when she has received specific orders to do so, except that vessels which navigate outside the main channel need not comply with the main message
	Auxiliary signals and message		
	White and/or yellow lights, displayed to the right of the main lights		Local meanings, as promulgated in local port orders

The rules for the IPTS (7.7.9) are:

a. The main movement message always comprises three vertical lights. No additional light is added to the column carrying the main message. Thus three vertical lights are recognisable as a traffic signal, not navigational lights.

b. Red lights mean 'Do not proceed'.

c. Green lights mean 'Proceed, subject to the conditions stipulated (if any)'. To avoid confusion, red and green lights are never displayed together.

d. Some signals may be visible in all directions to all vessels. Others may be directional, ie visible only to vessels entering, or to others leaving, harbour.

e. The 'Serious Emergency' signal must be flashing, at least 60 flashes per minute. All other signals must be fixed or slow occulting (the latter more discernible if background glare is a problem). A mix of fixed and occulting lights must not be used.

f. Signal No 5 requires some other means of communication, eg VHF radio, signal lamp, loud hailer, or auxiliary signal, as a specific order that a vessel may proceed.

g. A yellow light, to the left of main signals Nos 2 or 5, and level with the top light (see signals 2a and 5a), may be used to mean 'Vessels which can safely navigate outside the main channel need not comply with the main message'. This signal is clearly significant to yachtsmen.

h. Signals which are auxiliary to the main message may be devised by local authorities. These auxiliary signals should be only white and/or yellow lights, displayed to the right of the main signal lights.

From the above it is evident that the IPTS are simple, and easy to memorise. Ports with complex entrances and much traffic may need many auxiliary signals, which will have to be documented. Smaller harbours with less traffic often use only main signals Nos 2 or 4.

When a chart is to be used for the first time it must be referenced. Three convenient positions, at the intersections of meridians and parallels of latitude, are entered as latitude and longitude into the Yeoman memory, which can accommodate references for 100 charts. Each chart is numbered by the user from 00 to 99. With these positions entered into the memory the plotting hole in the puck lens is placed over each reference point in turn, and the 'enter' key pressed. Thereafter, whenever that chart is clipped to the mat, it is only necessary to enter the chart number for the plotter to be ready for use.

Chart plotters are the next step forward to displaying a chart electronically. They process a vast amount of data received from navaids and instrument sensors which can then be displayed on a small high-resolution screen, usually about 200mm (8in) in size, in full colour. The pictorial electronic plot shows current position, tracking, course to new waypoints, or whatever other data your GPS is able to produce. Additional types of information such as bottom contours, buoys, lights, traffic routes, or wrecks can be superimposed on the basic chart according to the degree of information and sophistication required. Most chart plotters will store at least 20 waypoints, and a number of event markers, and also display any tabulated data in a separate window on the screen.

Chart plotters are now available in different forms:

a. Stand-alone plotters which provide all the essential functions and are not linked to other tasks.
b. Plotters which are combined with an echo-sounder giving a pictorial display both in plan and cross section.
c. Plotters which provide the features in (b) with a radar screen display as well.

The merit of such a triple combination is space-saving; one unit is providing three quite separate facilities which if properly interpreted give the navigator one coherent picture of where the boat is geographically, both relative to land and other vessels, and in what depth. The de-merit is potential confusion unless the user is well versed in selecting and interpreting a variety of inputs. Each display is also bound to be somewhat miniaturised.

Even allowing for the versatility which a combined chartplotter/echosounder/radar display apparently gives, a prospective purchaser must decide whether the use of a PC gives him/her even more power to the elbow. The pros and cons of a PC are discussed in Chapter 8 in more detail, but

may be briefly summarised here as follows:

Pros – A PC is more adaptable than a chart plotter in terms of taking advantage of the constant advances in technology. Software can be readily upgraded and extra memory added. The PC display is usually of higher quality than that of a chart plotter, and – importantly – is larger. A PC is not limited to one or even three functions. Astro (Chapter 9), Communications (Chapter 10), Weather data (Chapter 11) and Tidal calculations (Chap 12) can all be done more easily or quickly on a PC, along with a variety of domestic tasks.

Cons – the average chart plotter is designed to cope with the marine environment. Most of them are waterproof and can safely be mounted in the cockpit. Electrical supply is invariably 12v/24v from the boat's DC supplies. The PC however will need a good quality stable sinewave invertor to provide the necessary AC supply for regular usage. Most PCs are relatively fragile, ie not built to withstand physical shocks and rough handling and very few can tolerate rain or spray, still less solid water. There are some good quality stowage boxes available which are well padded and waterproof when closed, but inevitably they inhibit full use of a PC which has to be removed for normal use. It must then be securely fixed to a chart table.

7.4 CHARTWORK

7.4.1 PROCEDURES
Three basic procedures form part of routine chartwork:

1. To establish the (compass) course to steer to get the boat from A to B, allowing for tidal streams and other factors, whilst avoiding any dangers along the route.
   For various reasons (eg wind direction) it may not be possible to steer the required course in practice, so:
2. To keep a Dead Reckoning plot of the boat's position in order to monitor progress; see 7.4.3.
3. To fix and plot the boat's position regularly, adjusting the course so as to reach the destination; see 7.5.

7.4.2 COURSE TO STEER
Courses, (and headings and bearings) may be expressed as True, Magnetic or Compass, annotated respectively as (T), (M) or (C). But the symbol (T) is usually omitted, as for example in Admiralty Sailing Directions and in most yachtsman's pilot guides which state in the explanatory notes that all courses and bearings are true.

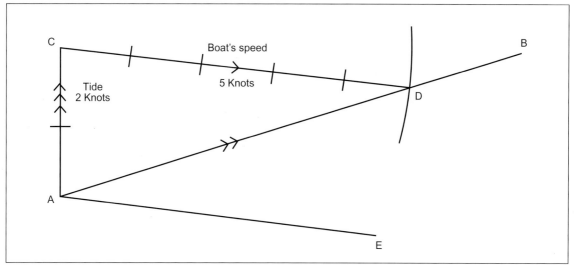

Fig. 7(18) How to determine the course to steer to allow for tidal stream.

Assuming that you plan to sail from point A to point B, first study the route on the chart to ensure that it does not pass over or near to shallow water, obstructions, prohibited areas, tide rips or other hazards.

Place the plotter along the line AB and read off the true course; suppose this is 073°. If variation is (say) 8°W, the magnetic course is 081°(M). From the specimen deviation card in Fig. 7(7) note that the deviation is 3°W on this heading. The compass course from A to B is therefore 084°(C).

However the course to steer differs from the ground track between two points, whenever allowance has to be made for set and drift due to a current and/or tidal stream.

Fig. 7(18) assumes that the tidal stream is setting north at 2 knots, and that the boat's speed through the water is 5 knots. From A construct AC pointing in the direction in which the tide is running (north), and two convenient units in length. From C, using a pair of compasses or dividers measure a length equal to five units (boat's speed) so that it meets AB at D. Draw AE parallel to CD. This is the course to steer. The boat starts from A, steering a course in the direction AE, but the tide carries it steadily north so that the ground track of the boat is along the line ADB.

The above assumes that the rate of the tidal stream remains constant at two knots, and that the speed of the boat is steady at five knots. On an actual passage either or both of these figures may change and the tidal stream may change or even reverse direction. In this case the passage must be divided up into a suitable number of parts, and the necessary course to steer

calculated for each part, if it is desired to follow the track AB.

7.4.3 DEAD RECKONING (DR)

Referring to Fig. 7(19) if on sailing from point A the log reading is zero, after two hours on a course of (say) 080° it is possible to plot a rough position on the chart. If the log reading is ten miles, then assuming that the course of 080° has been maintained and neglecting any effects of wind or tide, the boat will have moved to B. B is called the Dead Reckoning position, or DR, and is marked on the chart with a cross and the time alongside it.

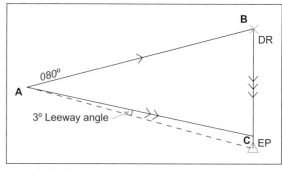

Fig. 7(19) Plotting: By convention the DR position is shown by a cross, and EP by a triangle. Course has a single arrow, tidal stream three arrows, and the resultant track two arrows.

Estimated Position (EP)

Still referring to Fig. 7(19), if while the boat is sailing from A to B the tidal stream is setting due south at a steady two knots, it will carry the boat four miles south during the two hours. The effect of the tidal stream is shown by the tidal vector BC in the diagram, and the boat will end up at C and not at B.

Leeway is another ingredient which must be

NAVIGATION AND PASSAGE MAKING

estimated and applied in order to arrive at an Estimated Position (or EP). It is the angle between a boat's heading and the actual direction she is moving through the water (water track); the difference being caused by the 'sideways' component of the wind. The amount of leeway a boat will make depends upon the strength and direction of the wind relative to the boat, her speed through the water and wave action. The windage of her rig and hull, her draught and hull design also contribute. About 5° may be a typical figure for the average cruising yacht when beating to windward. Leeway is less on a reach, and of course zero when the boat is running dead before the wind.

For example in Fig. 7(19) if the wind is from the north and leeway is estimated at 3°, then re-plot line AC 3° further south. Where the tidal vector cuts this new line at C_1 is called the Estimated Position (or EP) which by convention is marked by a small triangle with a dot in the middle, and the time alongside.

You may also need to take into account surface drift which (as distinct from tidal stream or ocean current) is caused by the wind blowing in a certain direction for a considerable time, and which may persist for a while after the wind has changed direction.

Finally the navigator must apply the mean heading which the helmsman has *actually* achieved over a certain period (perhaps every half-hour or hour). This may not be the same as the course to steer, because the helmsman will not always be able to achieve this for a variety of reasons. It makes quite a difference to the DR/EP.

7.4.4 VMG

The definition of VMG in 7.1.1 bears repetition. It is the Velocity, ie direction and speed, Made Good towards a waypoint or destination, irrespective of the course/speed currently being made good (COG/SOG). In effect it is a measure of the progress you are making towards your goal. VMG is displayed by virtually all GPS receivers. It is very important to racing yachtsmen, but oddly many cruising yachtsmen pay it little more than lip service.

If you can lay your course direct to a waypoint or mark then VMG, COG and SOG are virtually all one and the same thing. If however you are beating to windward then VMG becomes a key factor in tactical decision making. It tells you at the very least which is the favourable tack.

When running downwind VMG is equally important as Fig. 7(20) demonstrates. In this example, either the yacht can run dead downwind towards the mark with a SOG, and VMG, of say 5 knots. Or she can 'tack downwind'

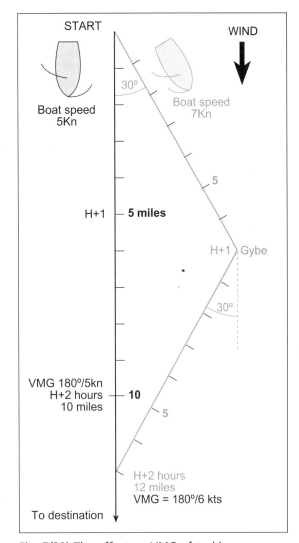

Fig. 7(20) The effect on VMG of tacking downwind.

in a series of long boards. Thus, if she comes up to windward by no more than 30°, her speed will increase to say 7 knots, but naturally she will have further to go to the mark. Her progress, or VMG, towards the mark can be calculated by the simple formula:

VMG = Boatspeed(kn) x Cosine of the off-course angle.

In this case VMG = 7 x Cos 30° = 6·06 kn, say 6 knots.

If the boat makes two boards each of one hour, she will cover 14M through the water, but 12M towards her goal. In the same two hours, if running downwind at 5 knots, she would have covered only 10M towards her goal. With GPS continuously displaying VMG, this worthwhile gain is there for the taking.

199

7.4.5 THE LOGBOOK

It is in the logbook that navigational events of all kinds will be recorded, although this is not a legal requirement. But most entries support basic navigational DR, your trusty fallback, should other electronic navaids fail you. Note that by tradition small craft always record in the log that they are sailing *towards* a destination, since it could be tempting fate to assume that you will reach the planned destination.

The following should therefore be recorded regularly in a proper logbook or ruled notebook:

a. Course to steer; and course actually steered.
c. Log reading and distance run.
e. Wind speed and direction.
f. Barometer reading.

Each entry should be made against Time in the lefthand column. The same applies to details of fixes, course alterations, weather changes. A wide Remarks column is for narrative or expanded details, although a separate notebook is better for rough jottings which are of only passing value.

Much of this data can be invaluable when something goes wrong. If for example the visibility starts to deteriorate it may be vital to recall the log reading when passing a buoy an hour earlier, and what course has been maintained since then. One test by which a well-kept logbook might be judged is whether or not the passage can be re-constructed from the various log entries. In this respect it is akin to an electronic Flight data recorder on an airliner.

Engine readings, whether on a sailing yacht or a motor cruiser, should be recorded regularly, so as to detect any changes in oil pressure, cooling water temperature and other vital parameters. These readings can show whether the rate of change is significant or purely transitory (for known reasons). A trend may be discerned, allowing any problem to be checked before it becomes really serious.

Other details will depend on the installation, but engine rpm, ammeter, fuel gauge, and turbocharger boost pressure (where applicable) are all useful indicators. They too could be recorded in the log, perhaps on the opposite page to navigational entries.

Engine(s) starting/stopping times will contribute to a record of engine running hours, if this is not automatically done. Engine hours will of course trigger maintenance at the appropriate intervals, and a separate maintenance schedule can call up work due on an hours basis. This might include cleaning fuel filters and injectors, renewing oil filter elements and changing lubricating oil, checking drive belts

and flexible hoses, and other similar routines. Fuel, oil and fresh water consumption, batteries' charge state, and even marina charges may all be noted in the log.

7.5 POSITION FIXING

7.5.1 BEARINGS AND TRANSITS

Fixing is part of routine navigation; how often depends on circumstances, but consider the following guidelines:

a. Hourly on a coastal passage, perhaps two hourly on an offshore passage;
b. Every half hour, or more often, in narrow waters;
c. Immediately, if there is any doubt about position;
d. Immediately, in emergency, man overboard etc.

This section concentrates on fixing by more traditional means in order of decreasing accuracy. Thus a good three bearing visual fix is always going to be more reliable than a running fix (7.5.8). Fixing by GPS needs little explanation, but the methods described here are those which will be needed if GPS fails for any reason.

A visual fix requires two or more position lines (P/L); where they cross gives the position of the boat at the time of the observations. Even a single reliable P/L can be very useful; example a P/L astern or ahead can establish whether the boat is on her required track.

The most positive form of P/L is a transit, ie when two known objects are in line with each other. Simply join the two objects on the chart,

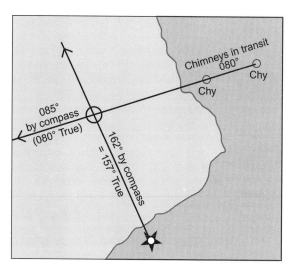

Fig. 7(21) The transit of two known objects, cut at nearly 90° by a bearing of a third object, should give a reliable fix.

extend the line seaward, and the boat is somewhere along it. If you also take a compass bearing of the transit and check it against the bearing shown on the chart, you will have confirmed, or otherwise, that the objects have been correctly identified. Bearings of transits or leading marks, as shown on the chart or in sailing directions, are true bearings taken from seaward so it is necessary to apply variation. Taking the bearing is also a useful check on the compass.

A transit of two objects and a bearing of another object roughly at right angles gives a useful fix, particularly if as suggested above the bearing of the transit is taken so as to check the total compass error, and this is then applied to the second bearing. The procedure is shown in Fig. 7(21).

If the transit is 080° on the chart, but 085° by compass then the total compass error is 5°W. Hence if the bearing of the single object is 162° by compass its true bearing is actually 157° and should be plotted accordingly.

Visual compass bearings of two objects, if carefully taken, can give a reasonable fix but it is desirable to take at least three. This is what is involved in plotting on the chart one of these bearings – that of the church in Fig. 7(22). Assume that the reading from the hand bearing compass is 073°(M). As indicated, this is a magnetic bearing, so variation, say 7°W from the chart, must be taken into account.

On a Breton plotter set 073° against 7°W variation. Place the long edge of the plotter against the church and move the plotter so as to align its grid with any convenient meridian or parallel; draw a P/L to seaward. Mark it at the

end with a single arrowhead and with the time of observation (1521).

Note. With this type of plotter there is no need to convert arithmetically from magnetic to true, or vice versa, nor to use the compass rose on the chart. ii. 066° is the true bearing, against the zero mark on the variation scale.

Repeat the process with the other two objects. If all three bearings are completely accurate the three P/Ls will cross at a point. This rarely happens; in practice the P/Ls form a small triangle called a cocked hat. The size of the cocked hat is a good indication of the accuracy of the fix.

If a cocked hat of a reasonably small size has been obtained, the fix is taken as its centre and is marked with a small circle and the time alongside, as in Fig. 7(22). If however there are dangers nearby then the fix is taken as the corner of the cocked hat nearest the danger, so that the worst situation is assumed.

If a large cocked hat is obtained, one or more of the bearings must be wrong or incorrectly plotted. This is why it is important to take at least three bearings; if only two objects are observed there is no check on reliability.

Objects must be selected so that their P/Ls give a good cut at a sufficient angle. When three bearings are taken the P/Ls should ideally meet at angles of about 60°. Be wary of fixes from P/Ls which cross at less than 30°.

7.5.2 BEARING AND DISTANCE

A bearing and distance of a known object, as marked on the chart, will give a fix. Radar will give the range of any good radar target, noting that ranges are more accurate than radar bearings. So take a radar range and a visual bearing with the hand bearing compass, ensuring in each case that you observe the same object. The use and limitations of radar in yachts is discussed in Chapter 8.

With accurate radar ranges of two or more objects, a fix can be obtained by drawing the appropriate arcs on the chart and seeing where they intersect. If the ranges of only two objects are taken it is of course possible for the arcs to intersect in two feasible positions, and therefore approximate bearings should be taken of each.

Alternatively a rangefinder may be used, but these are not very accurate at ranges of over a mile. The range reticle and compass fitted to some binoculars are ideal.

Range can also be calculated or extracted from tables, having taken a vertical sextant angle of an object of known height, eg a lighthouse; see 7.5.3. Coupled with a bearing of the object, this will give a good fix.

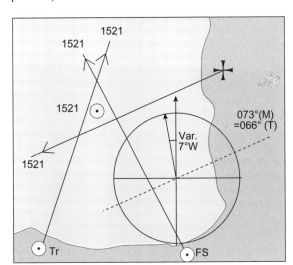

Fig. 7(22) If possible always take bearings of at least three objects. The size of the resulting cocked hat indicates the reliability of the fix.

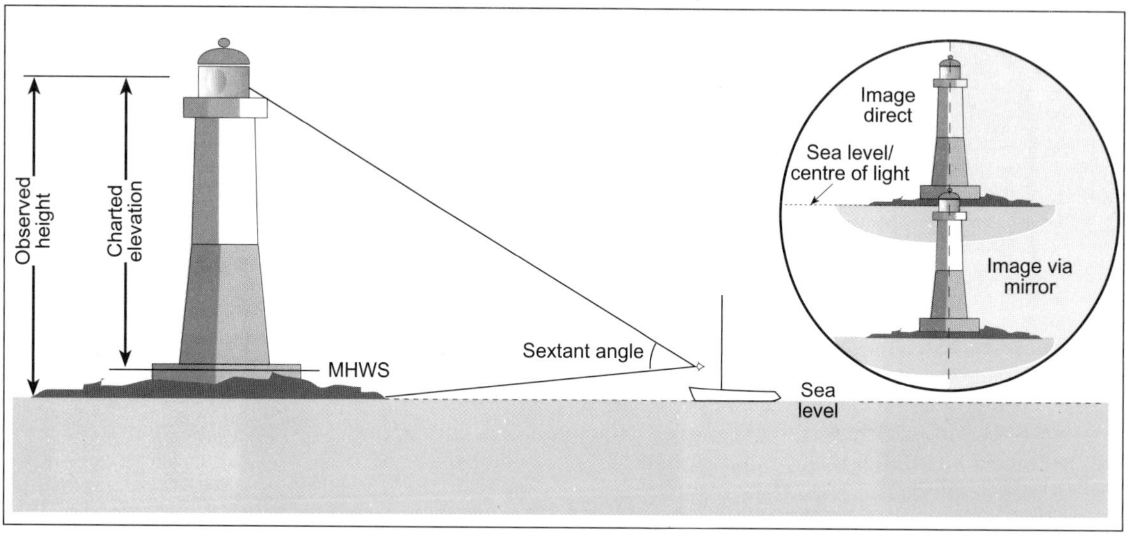

Fig. 7(23) A vertical sextant angle, and bearing, of an object of known elevation gives a reliable fix.

7.5.3 VERTICAL SEXTANT ANGLES

If the elevation of an object, eg as a lighthouse, is known, and if its vertical angle is measured with a sextant, then its distance away can be calculated or extracted from the tables in the MRNA. A bearing of the object taken at the same time will accurately fix the boat's position.

Elevations of prominent objects above MHWS are shown on the chart or are given in Sailing Directions in metres (m). For lights the elevation is to the centre (focal plane) of the lantern. Do not confuse (m) with the range of lights, shown in miles (M).

In practice the height of tide and height of eye are usually ignored, since by so doing the object is made to appear a little closer than it actually is. This gives a safety margin if any danger is assumed to be inshore of the yacht (but not if it is to seaward). The sextant angle must always be corrected for index error (IE).

The sextant angle to be measured is from the top of the object (or the centre of the lantern, for a lighthouse) to the sea at its base – not to the horizon, see Fig. 7(23).

From a height of eye of 3m, about the maximum feasible in a small yacht, the visible horizon is only 3·6M away. Therefore at any greater distance the base of a lighthouse, for example, is below the horizon and not visible to an observer. Consequently a measured sextant angle will be less than it should be, making the object seem further away than it actually is; in which case be wary of the distance off by vertical sextant angle.

Distance off by Vertical Sextant Angle

Height of object ft	m	Distances of object (nautical miles) 0.1	0.2	0.3	0.4	0.5	0.6	0.7	0.8	0.9	1.0	1.1	1.2	1.3	1.4	1.5	Height of object m	ft
		° ′	° ′	° ′	° ′	° ′	° ′	° ′	° ′	° ′	° ′	° ′	° ′	° ′	° ′	° ′		
33	**10**	3 05	1 33	1 02	0 46	0 37	0 31	0 27	0 23	0 21	0 19	0 17	0 15	0 14	0 13	0 12	**10**	33
39	**12**	3 42	1 51	1 14	0 56	0 45	0 37	0 32	0 28	0 25	0 22	0 20	0 19	0 17	0 16	0 15	**12**	39
46	**14**	4 19	2 10	1 27	1 05	0 52	0 43	0 37	0 32	0 29	0 26	0 24	0 22	0 20	0 19	0 17	**14**	46
53	**16**	4 56	2 28	1 39	1 14	0 59	0 49	0 42	0 37	0 33	0 30	0 27	0 25	0 23	0 21	0 20	**16**	53
59	**18**	5 33	2 47	1 51	1 24	1 07	0 56	0 48	0 42	0 37	0 33	0 30	0 28	0 26	0 24	0 22	**18**	59
66	**20**	6 10	3 05	2 04	1 33	1 14	1 02	0 53	0 46	0 41	0 37	0 34	0 31	0 29	0 27	0 25	**20**	66
72	**22**	6 46	3 24	2 16	1 42	1 22	1 08	0 58	0 51	0 45	0 41	0 37	0 34	0 31	0 29	0 27	**22**	72
→ 79	**24**	7 23	3 42	2 28	1 51	1 29	1 14	1 04	0 56	0 49	0 45	0 40	0 37	0 34	0 32	0 30	**24**	79
85	**26**	7 59	4 01	2 41	2 01	1 36	1 20	1 09	1 00	0 54	0 48	0 44	0 40	0 37	0 34	0 32	**26**	85
92	**28**	8 36	4 19	2 53	2 10	1 44	1 27	1 14	1 05	0 58	0 52	0 47	0 43	0 40	0 37	0 35	**28**	92
				3 05	2 19	1 51	1 33	1 20	1 10	1 02	0 56	0 51	0 46	0 43	0 40	0 37		
					2 28	1 58	1 39	1 25	1 14	1 06	0 59	0 54	0 49	0 46	0 42	0 40		
							1 45	1 30	1 19	1 10	1 03	0 57	0 53	0 49				
								1 35	1 24	1 14	1 07	1 01	0 56					

Fig. 7(24) Portion of table of distance off by vertical sextant angle.

Distance of horizon for various heights of eye

Height of eye		Horizon distance	Height of eye		Horizon distance	Height of eye		Horizon distance
metres	feet	n. miles	metres	feet	n. miles	metres	feet	n. miles
1	3.3	2.1	21	68.9	9.5	41	134.5	13.3
2	6.6	2.9	22	72.2	9.8	42	137.8	13.5
3	9.8	3.6	23	75.5	10.0	43	141.1	13.7
4	13.1	4.1	24	78.7	10.2	44	144.4	13.8
5	16.4	4.7	25	82.0	10.4	45	147.6	14.0
6	19.7	5.1	26	85.3	10.6	46	150.9	14.1
7	23.0	5.5	27	88.6	10.8	47	154.2	
	26.2	5.9	28	91.9	11.0			
			29	95.1				

Fig. 7(25) Portion of table of distance of horizon for various heights of eye.

For a more precise range, the distance that sea level is below MHWS should be added to the elevation of the object (above MHWS) before entering the tables.

Enter the table, see Fig. 7(24), in the MRNA with the elevation (m) of the object; read horizontally to the observed sextant angle (corrected for IE). Go vertically to read the distance (M) of the object, interpolating if need be. For example, the vertical sextant angle of an object with a height of 24m is 1°04' (after correction for index error). By inspection, the distance off is 0·7M.

If in this case the sea level was known to be 2m below the level of MHWS, the table would be entered with a height of 26m. By interpolation, it can be seen that an angle of 1°04' would then give a distance of approximately 0·75M.

To keep a certain distance away from an object of known elevation, extract the relevant 'danger angle' from the table, and then ensure that it is not exceeded.

7.5.4   DISTANCE OF THE HORIZON
The distance of the sea horizon for a certain height of eye can be obtained from a table in the MRNA, Fig. 7(25). Actual distance may be affected by abnormal refraction.

Note that for a typical height of eye of 3m the sea horizon is only 3·6M away which is why even quite a large pillar buoy may not be seen until 3M or so. This underlines the advantage of climbing up onto the boom say for a higher viewpoint; even an extra 2m of eye height will increase the horizon distance by about 1M.

7.5.5   RANGE OF LIGHTS WHEN RISING/ DIPPING
The range of a light, when it first rises above or finally dips below the horizon, can be calculated or extracted from tables, for various heights of eye; see Fig. 7(26). This often gives a useful fix when making a landfall. It is the light source, not the loom, which rises or dips.

Enter the table in MRNA, Fig. 7(27), with the elevation of the light and height of eye, to give the range at which a light may be seen to dip below or rise above the horizon.

7.5.6   HORIZONTAL SEXTANT ANGLES
Horizontal sextant angles (HSA) are an accurate but little used means of fixing a boat's position. Even the cheapest plastic sextant is perfectly suitable, as an accuracy of half a degree is quite sufficient. The method entails measuring the

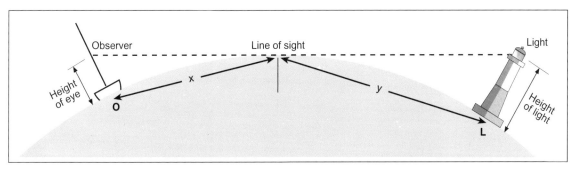

Fig. 7(26) The distance at which an observer can just see a light on the horizon is the sum of x and y, ie the distance from the observer's eye to the horizon plus the distance from the light to the horizon.

Lights — distance off when rising or dipping (n. miles)											
Height of light		**Height of eye**									
	metres	1	2	3	4	5	6	7	8	9	10
metres	feet	feet	3	7	10	13	16	20	23	26	30	33

metres	feet	1	2	3	4	5	6	7	8	9	10
10	33	8.7	9.5	10.2	10.8	11.3	11.7	12.1	12.5	12.8	13.2
12	39	9.3	10.1	10.8	11.4	11.9	12.3	12.7	13.1	13.4	13.8
14	46	9.9	10.7	11.4	12.0	12.5	12.9	13.3	13.7	14.0	14.4
16	53	10.4	11.2	11.9	12.5	13.0	13.4	13.8	14.2	14.5	14.9
18	59	10.9	11.7	12.4	13.0	13.5	13.9	14.3	14.7	15.0	15.4
20	66	11.4	12.2	12.9	13.5	14.0	14.4	14.8	15.2	15.5	15.9
		11.9	12.7	13.4	14.0	14.5	14.9	15.3	15.7	16.0	16.4
			13.1	13.8	14.4	14.9	15.3	15.7	16.1		
				14.2	14.8	15.3	15.7				

Fig. 7(27) Portion of table showing the distance off lights when rising or dipping.

angles, as seen from seaward, between three shore marks, holding the sextant horizontally (not vertically, as when taking a sight of a celestial body).

The angle between only two marks gives an infinite number of possible positions on the circumference of a 'position circle' radius AO/BO; see Fig. 7(28). A third mark must be used to obtain a second position circle. Where the two circles intersect is the fix.

The geometry relies on the fact that, at the centre of a circle, the angle $\angle$AOB subtended by a chord (AB) is double the angle subtended at the circumference (AY$_2$B). Knowing the HSA between two marks enables a position circle to be drawn. For example, if the HSA between known objects

A and B is 50°, then $\angle$AOB at the centre of the position circle will be 100°. Hence $\angle$OAB and $\angle$OBA are both 40°; construct lines at A and B which are each 40° to AB. Where they meet at O is the centre of the position circle. Using radius OA/OB draw the position circle. (Yacht positions Y$_1$ and Y$_3$ are included to show how any HSA taken from a yacht on the position circle will also be 50°; hence the need for a second position circle).

If the HSA is greater than 90°, subtract 90° from it and construct AO and AB on the opposite (landward) side of the line AB, as shown in Fig. 7(29). Here for example $\angle$ASB is 110°, so $\angle$OAB and $\angle$OBA are both 20°.

A station pointer, if you happen to have one, provides an easy, mechanical way of plotting HSAs. It has three arms which can be set at the

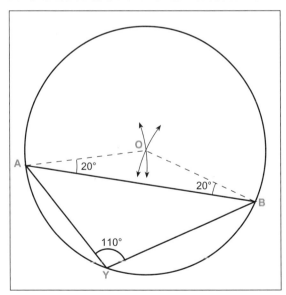

Fig. 7(29) If the HSA is more than 90°, as shown here, subtract 90° from it and construct the two radii OA and OB on the opposite side of the line AB.

Fig. 7(28) The geometry of a position circle.

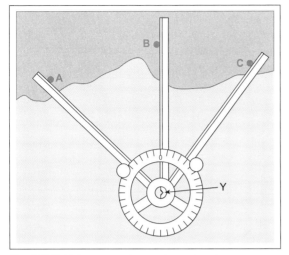

Fig. 7(30) Using a station pointer to plot a position by horizontal sextant angles.

two HSAs. Jockey the station pointer around until the bevelled sides of each of its arms lie against the three marks (A, B, and C). The fix will be at the hole 'Y' in the centre of the pivot, through which a pencil mark can be made, as in Fig. 7(30).

Without a station pointer, it is equally easy to draw the two HSAs on a piece of tracing paper, and then move it about on the chart until the three lines lie over the marks. A Douglas protractor could also be used. The fix can also be obtained by geometric plotting; or by extracting from tables the radii of the two position circles, having entered with the HSAs and distance apart of the marks.

The advantages of HSAs are that accuracy is not affected by compass errors, log readings or tidal streams; and deviation or variation are not involved. The angles can, with practice, be measured very accurately.

Even without a sextant, the same method can be used with compass bearings, if the differences between the bearings are solely considered rather than the actual values of the bearings; this too eliminates any errors due to deviation or variation.

The geometric layout of the three marks and the yacht can be important. The following limitations apply when choosing marks for fixing by HSAs:

a. They should be at least 30° apart;
b. All three should be on or near a straight line; **or**
c. The centre mark must be nearer the yacht than the line joining the two outer marks (if the centre mark is beyond this line, a reliable fix will be impossible); **or**
d. The boat must be inside the triangle formed by the three marks, as might occur within a bay or bight.

e. If the three marks and the boat all lie on or near a circle, no fix can be obtained.

7.5.7 LINE OF SOUNDINGS
Echo sounder readings, along with bearings of shore marks, can help provide a fix. Such readings should in any case always be near the front of the navigator's mind, as the land below is often that nearest to the boat.

Soundings must first be corrected by deducting the height of the tide at the time and place concerned, so that they can be compared with the depths on the chart. A line of soundings taken at regular intervals is best, although even a single sounding can be helpful. Mark the corrected soundings at the proper distance intervals (allowing for tidal streams) on the edge of a piece of tracing paper and then move it about the chart with its edge parallel to the track of the boat, until it matches the depths on the chart.

Such a position line should obviously be used with caution, but in poor visibility for example it can be very helpful, especially if the sea bed has distinctive contours. The Hurd Deep, north of the Channel Islands, is a good example of a distinctive trench.

7.5.8 RUNNING FIX
If only a single object or light can be positively identified on a stretch of coast, a running fix on it, as in Fig. 7(31), will still give the boat's approximate position.

At 1600 a yacht steering east at 8kn takes a bearing of 040° on light L. The log is read at 1600, as usual. When the bearing of L has changed by at least 45°, and preferably more, a second bearing (320°) is taken, again noting the time (1630) and log reading.

Next work out how far the boat has travelled over the ground between the two bearings. From the log readings and course steered plot the distance (AB) through the water. Add the

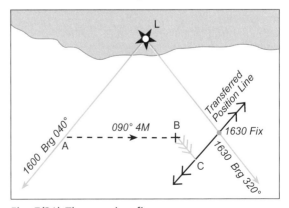

Fig. 7(31) The running fix.

tidal stream (135°/1kn) during this period (BC). Thus AC represents the movement of the boat between the two bearings. Now transfer the first P/L by this amount to lie through C. (Mark this transferred P/L by double arrows at each end). Where it crosses with the second P/L is therefore the yacht's position at 1630, when the second bearing was taken.

The quality, ie accuracy, of a running fix is only as good as your DR, including tidal stream and leeway. It is a little better than an ordinary Estimated Position.

7.5.9 DOUBLING THE ANGLE ON THE BOW

This is a special and easily calculated form of running fix. Although quick, it is not very accurate and should not be trusted where there is any appreciable tidal stream. Assume in Fig. 7(32) that the boat is sailing along the line AC. At A a relative bearing is taken of object L when it is (say) 40° off the bow; time and log readings are noted. When this bearing has doubled to 80° off the bow, the time and log reading are again noted and the second bearing is plotted. Geometrically ABL is an isosceles triangle and so AB (the distance by log between the two bearings) equals BL (the distance of the boat from L). Mark it off to show the fix at B.

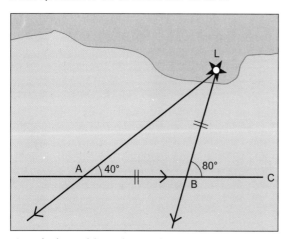

Fig. 7(32) Doubling the angle on the bow is a special type of running fix.

7.5.10 FOUR POINT BEARING, AND OTHER SPECIAL ANGLES

If, when doubling the angle off the bow as described above, the first relative bearing is 45° and the second is therefore 90°, then the distance run between the two bearings equals the distance by which the object is abeam (when the second bearing is taken). This is called a four point bearing fix because under the old method of compass notation a point is $11\frac{1}{4}°$ and four points are 45°.

There are other special pairs of angles of an object off the bow which, if accurately taken and used when there is *no tidal stream* to consider, result in the distance run over the ground between the bearings being equal to the distance by which the boat will pass abeam of the object. These pairs of angles off the bow are 22° and 34°; 25° and 41°; 32° and 59°; 35° and 67°; and 37° and 72°.

All running fixes must be used with caution. You must be sure of the distance the boat has made over the ground between the bearings, and that a steady and accurate course has been maintained.

7.6 HIGH SPEED NAVIGATION

7.6.1 INTRODUCTION

The basics of navigating at high speed are no different from those used at lower speeds. It is just that the time factor is compressed and things happen far more quickly. Instead of having the luxury of time to sort out the navigation, the compressed time frame means that the available time for making navigation decisions may have to be measured in seconds rather than minutes.

There are therefore two key elements in successful high speed navigation:
    a.   Concentration, to keep ahead of the navigation; and
    b.   Preparation, to have all the navigation information you need readily at hand.

Whether you are navigating by electronics or by visual means, time spent in preparation is never wasted and this is the time to look at all the possible options. It is much easier to weigh these up in harbour than when being tossed about at sea.

7.6.2 PLANNING AND ELECTRONICS

Electronic navaids, charts and plotters have made a huge difference to high speed navigation because they can present the information needed for navigation in a readily useable form. Before electronics, much of a navigator's time was spent in working out the position. Now GPS provides a constant update of the position, but the latitude and longitude produced by the GPS are just meaningless figures until they are plotted on the chart. As we have seen, plotting on a paper chart is difficult at high speed, but the electronic chart does it all automatically. It will constantly update the position on the chart display to show the track you are maintaining, but at higher speeds that alone is not enough. You are not so much interested in where you are, as in where you are going.

The electronic chart will not give you this information without some help, and to get the best out of an electronic chart system you need to tell it the route you want to take. One of the basic rules of high speed navigation is that, because the often rough ride makes it difficult to do navigation tasks at sea, you have to do most of the preparation before leaving harbour. In the comfort of calm water it is much easier to plot your proposed route on the electronic chart, to check it against the paper chart and to ensure that all is well before leaving. When navigating an aeroplane (at much higher speeds), it used to be said that two hours preparation are needed for every hour in the air – not a bad rule of thumb at sea.

7.6.3   PLANNING AND PAPER CHARTS
Always keep in mind the possibility of electronic failure – which is why you plot your course on the paper chart as well. Write down the courses and distances between each waypoint (alter course point) on the paper chart and then you will have a reference to work from if the electronics do let you down.

The paper chart is also useful to carry out a double check on the proposed route. In planning the route on the electronic chart, you will select points through which you want to pass. These waypoints will be selected to pass clear of all dangers, and you need to check carefully along the line that appears on the screen, that there are no dangers such as rocks or shoals close by the planned route. The scale of an electronic chart, as often used for route planning, may be small and may not show all the dangers near the route, which is why a double check on the paper chart is advisable.

When you are plotting the course on the paper chart, check along the route, not only for dangers but also for navigation marks and other easily identifiable features. Put a pencil ring around these marks so that they stand out on the chart. This highlighting will also serve to remind you about the marks coming up which can serve as a reassuring visual check on the navigation progress.

At high speed, navigation is a combination of checking by visual observation the information provided on the electronic chart; such checking helps to instil confidence in what the electronic chart shows. It may also be a good idea, when selecting a route, to inject deviations off the direct track so that the boat passes close enough to be able to see and verify navigational marks such as buoys.

If navigating without the benefit of electronics, then the shorter the distance between waypoints, the better. The compass and steering accuracy on a fast boat may not always be as accurate as you might like, so the shorter the distance between waypoints, the better the chance of seeing the mark at the waypoint.

7.6.4   NAVIGATING AT SEA
Once you have done the preparation, it is simply a case of switching into the plot to the first waypoint and continuing from waypoint to waypoint until you reach your destination. With a fast boat you can make an allowance for the tide and for leeway but any such allowance will be relatively small and a better solution may be to wait and see if the plot of the vessel is drifting away from the track line and then alter course to bring it back on to the track.

It is always best to operate a fast boat on the autopilot. This can be set on the 'follow track' mode so that the autopilot will automatically make the necessary corrections to keep the boat on the programmed track line. But use this way of navigating cautiously because you do not want a fast boat to make any sudden alterations of course. It is probably better to make course alterations manually, but still use the autopilot because it will give much more precise course control than any manual steering could hope to achieve. As well as being more efficient, it will make the radar much easier to use because the display will be that much more stable.

And finally remember that you can always slow down if you are not happy with the navigation situation. This will buy valuable time which can often be lacking in fast boat navigation.

7.6.5   RADAR
A stable radar picture can help enormously when you are navigating at night or in poor visibility. Radar is used both for navigating and for collision avoidance and it can be very difficult to use when the boat is yawing through 10 ° or 20 ° as it could under manual steering. Most small boat radars operate in a relative mode and any yawing in direction means that the targets seen on the radar display are also swinging about which can make them difficult to identify. Radar can be particularly valuable for fast boat navigation as the heading marker can be set to a safe distance off a headland or danger. Because the fast boat is only minimally affected by the wind and tide, you can be confident that the boat will pass very close to the required distance off.

Steering by autopilot also has considerable benefits on a fast boat at night. The steady course maintained by the autopilot will make it much easier to identify flashing lights at night because they will be in or near the same place on the horizon each time they flash. At night it is best to navigate from an open steering position if possible because the visibility will be much better and there will be fewer blind spots. When you are travelling at one mile every 2 minutes (30 knots) you need to be acutely aware of your surroundings and in this situation the radar outline of adjacent land can be very reassuring.

Navigating in fog demands that your speed is reduced considerably to match the prevailing conditions. As a guide to reducing speed slow down to a speed which allows you to stop well within the visibility range, plus allowing time to detect and assess other vessels' course and speed. This will probably take you out of the realm of fast boat operations, but at least you and others will be much safer. Radar is a wonderful tool in poor visibility, but it does have limitations in detecting small vessels particularly in waves, so must be used with caution.

Maintaining the highest level of concentration should enable you to navigate safely at speeds in excess of 30 knots. When speeds rise to 40 or 50 knots, the margins of safety are correspondingly reduced, and whilst concentration can compensate to a degree, this has to be combined with a high level of preparation. This preparation should not only cover the main route to be followed, but should also encompass alternative routes to follow if conditions change en-route.

7.6.6   SEA CONDITIONS
Fast boats can be very sensitive to wave conditions and so you will need to assess the expected en route conditions as part of your planning.

Tides and currents may have only a relatively small effect on your speed and direction, but they can have a significant effect on the waves. With wind against tide, the wave length is shortened, the wave becomes steeper and may be liable to break – all of which creates adverse conditions for the progress of a fast boat. This can be disconcerting or even dangerous if the tide changes direction during the course of the passage, and the changing conditions could affect the speed of comfortable progress. Tide-generated sea states can be exaggerated around headlands and in shallow water, so as part of your prior preparations be on the look out for such conditions.

With a fast boat there are possible alternative courses to follow in order to reduce the effects of bad sea states. Seas from directly ahead or astern are probably the worst conditions for a fast boat and even a 10° or 20° course alteration

can make a significant difference to progress. It may mean a slightly longer route, but if it allows a higher speed to be maintained or the comfort of the ride to be improved, then the extra distance can be justified.

Crossing a wide bay with a head sea can be a slow and punishing experience. Altering course to follow the coast around the bay may be a viable option, with the initial alteration putting the wind just off the bow; eventually the route takes the boat into the lee of the land where the conditions are better. This is one possibility amongst many options which may be available to a fast boat.

7.7 PILOTAGE, MARKS AND LIGHTS

7.7.1   PILOTAGE TECHNIQUE
Pilotage is the navigation of a vessel in narrow and/or shallow waters, using geographical features, buoys and other marks (or their lights) in conjunction with the chart, compass, echo sounder and radar, if fitted.

Pre-planning is the keyword, whether it be a first time approach at night into the busy waters of Plymouth Sound or a relatively simple entry to Scrabster near the Pentland Firth. First study the charts and Pilots with meticulous care so as to visualise the overall geography and be aware of hazards. As far as possible memorise the route and salient features. Back up your memory with a sketch plan in a notebook of the tracks and distances between turning points or waypoints. Note the marks and lights you expect to use in order to maintain track. The navigator must be continuously aware of objects appearing ahead, abeam and astern so that he can relate them to his present position and thus maintain the pre-planned track.

Pilotage is often most difficult when there are many confusing objects available, like the lights of a large sea port when first seen from seaward. But if the position of the boat is known or can be verified at any time, it is simple enough to take a bearing of an object or a light which appears in order to identify it from the chart. Or possibly the object will come in transit with one that has already been identified.

You should work ahead by plotting what the bearings of important marks will be when the boat reaches some future position. Then a quick check with a hand-bearing compass will identify these marks. Do not be distracted by the welter of lights and buoys all around, many of which will not affect you. Pre-plan those you wish to use and concentrate on identifying them alone. Keep one jump ahead of the game. Talk the helmsman's eyes onto the next mark, then helmsman's eyes onto the next mark, then yourself find the subsequent marks. If things do not materialise where and when expected, stop the boat and sort things out in slow time rather than pressing on when things are clearly not right.

Pilotage is obviously much easier (and safer) if one person steers the boat and follows the courses ordered, and the navigator is completely free to concentrate on his job. The helmsman should never jump to his own conclusions or ignore the navigator's guidance. Things at sea are rarely exactly as you first see them. In a difficult situation it pays to use two people for pilotage – one up top taking the bearings, and passing them to the other who is at the chart table. This is particularly helpful at night, because it preserves the night vision of the person on deck. A third person can keep the lookout and time/identify lights.

7.7.2 LEADING MARKS AND CLEARING LINES

Most charts contain examples of leading marks – objects placed at a harbour entrance or in a narrow channel, so that by keeping them in line the best water is followed. The true bearing of the transit from seaward is shown on the chart by a caption, eg 047°, against the solid line of the transit. It is also sometimes shown as 'Ldg Lts 047°' or as ' Oc & OcR ≠ 047°'. The symbol ≠ means 'in transit'. Note that a solid line shows the track to be followed; where it changes to a pecked line, the transit ceases to be valid. This might occur, for example, in a well marked fairway, where one transit ends as you alter course to align on the next. If lit, pairs of leading marks sometimes have the same light characteristics, to help identify them. The 'Pilot' describes what the leading marks look like by day. When using any form of transit always take a bearing of it, and check this against the chart or sailing directions, to see if the correct objects are being observed. It is absolutely vital that every helmsman knows which way to adjust his course to stay on a transit or regain it; especially when tracking on a transit which is astern of the boat.

Clearing lines are usually pre-plotted bearings between which a boat will keep clear of hidden dangers. In most cases the bearing of a conspicuous object will be used. A clearing line may sometimes be a transit.

7.7.3 IALA BUOYAGE SYSTEM (REGION A)

International buoyage conforms to a single IALA Maritime Buoyage System (IALA = International Association of Lighthouse Authorities). This system applies world wide, except that in Region

A (which includes Europe and the Mediterranean) lateral marks are red to port and green to starboard, whilst in Region B (the Americas and parts of the W Pacific) these colours are reversed; the shapes of lateral marks are the same in both regions.

Region A uses the following five types of marks, in any combination, see Fig. 7(33) (see page 195):

1. Lateral marks, used in conjunction with a conventional direction of buoyage, indicate the port and starboard sides of a channel to be followed.
2. Cardinal marks, used in conjunction with a compass, show where dangers exist or where the mariner may find navigable water.
3. Isolated danger marks show isolated dangers of limited size and with navigable water all around them.
4. Safe water (also landfall or mid-channel) marks show that there is navigable water all round that position.

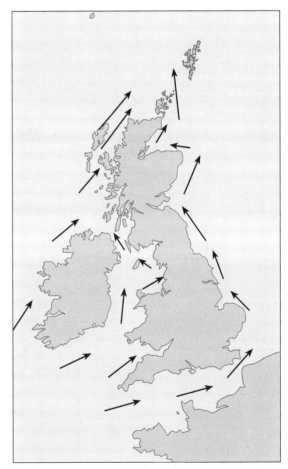

Fig. 7(34) General Direction of Buoyage around the UK.

Fig. 7(35) Local and General directions of buoyage.

5. Special marks are not primarily for navigation, but indicate an area or feature used for special purposes, eg spoil grounds, recreational zones, TSS, firing ranges and outfall pipes.

Any mark can be identified by its unique features: by day colour, shape, topmark; and at night the colour or rhythm of its light, if any.

Lateral marks (Region A)

Lateral marks are laid in conformity with a Conventional Direction of Buoyage which is either:

a. A Local direction, ie inwards from the sea towards a harbour, estuary or river; or
b. A General direction, which is broadly from SW to NE off the open coasts of the British Isles; see Fig. 7(34).

Where these two directions conflict, a changeover occurs: For example, off the Suffolk coast a boat coasting south from Lowestoft sees red PHM buoys on her starboard side (laid in conformity with the General direction). But south of Orfordness green SHM buoys lie to starboard (in conformity with the Local direction, ie inwards to the Thames Estuary). If doubt exists the direction (local or general) is shown by a special arrow on the chart; see Fig. 7(15). Off Orfordness there are two such opposing arrows; see Fig. 7(35).

Port hand marks:

Colour	Red
Shape	Can, pillar or spar
Topmark (if any)	Single red can
Light (when fitted)	Red, any rhythm, except (2+1)

Starboard hand marks:

Colour	Green (see note)
Shape	Conical, pillar or spar
Topmark (if any)	Single green cone point up
Light (when fitted)	Green, any rhythm, except (2+1)

Where port or starboard lateral marks do not rely on can or conical buoy shapes for identification they carry the appropriate topmark, where practicable. Any numbering or lettering follows the direction of buoyage, normally even numbers on PHM marks, odds on SHM marks.

Preferred channel marks (PCM)

At the point where a channel divides, when proceeding in the direction of buoyage, the preferred or main channel is indicated by a modified port or starboard lateral mark as appropriate. The modification is a green band around a red PHM mark and a red band around a SHM mark; the light, if fitted, will always be Fl (2+1) R or G. To help remember, the PCM mark as a whole applies to the main channel, whilst the R or G band relates to the secondary channel. The light uniquely identifies it as a PCM.

Preferred channel marks

	To starboard	To port
Colour	Red, with one broad green band	Green with one broad red band
Shape	Can, pillar or spar	Conical, pillar or spar
Topmark (if any)	Red can	Green cone, ▲
Light Rhythm	Red Fl (2+1) R	Green Fl (2+1) G

Cardinal marks

A cardinal mark may indicate that the deepest water is on the named side of a mark; or show the safe side on which to pass a danger; or indicate a feature in a channel such as a bend, junction, fork, or the end of a shoal.

Cardinal marks are laid in one of the four quadrants (North, East, South and West) as bounded by the true bearings NW –NE, NE – SE, SE – SW and SW – NW, taken from the point marked. They indicate where the best navigable water lies, relative to the danger or point marked. The name of a cardinal mark indicates the side on which it should be passed. For example, pass north of a North cardinal mark (situated in the quadrant between NW and NE from the point marked). Similarly keep east of an East cardinal mark, and so on.

Because of their colour scheme, topmarks and light characteristics, Cardinal marks are rarely difficult to identify by day or night and in poor visibility. They are pillar or spar shaped, distinctively painted black and yellow, and carry two unique black cone topmarks, one cone above the other. Two mnemonics: the double cones of north and south cardinal topmarks point north (up) and south (down) respectively. Cones for west cardinals are point to point, or waisted. East cones have their points apart or extended. Secondly, regard the points of a cone as 'black' in terms of the overall colour scheme; thus the points of an ECM topmark equate to black bands at top and bottom of the buoy/mark itself (yellow in between).

Their lights are always white, either quick flashing (Q), 50 or 60 flashes per minute; or very quick flashing (VQ), 100 or 120 flashes per minute; or Group Q or VQ. The number of flashes corresponds to the hour positions on a clock face: 12 or more at 12 o'clock (north), 3 at 3 o'clock (east), 6 at 6 o'clock (south) and 9 at 9 o'clock (west). A South cardinal also shows one long flash of not less than 2 seconds duration (in addition to six short), to distinguish it easily from 3 or 9 flashes.

North cardinal mark

Topmark	–	Two black cones, points up
Colour	–	Black above yellow
Shape	–	Pillar or spar
Light (when fitted)	–	White, Q or VQ.

East cardinal mark

Topmark	–	Two black cones, base to base
Colour	–	Black, with yellow band
Shape	–	Pillar or spar
Light (when fitted)	–	White, Q (3) 10s or VQ (3) 5s.

South cardinal mark

Topmark	–	Two black cones, points down
Colour	–	Yellow above black
Shape	–	Pillar or spar
Light (when fitted)	–	White, Q (6) + L Fl 15s or VQ (6) + L Fl 10s

West cardinal mark

Topmark	–	Two black cones, points together
Colour	–	Yellow, with black band
Shape	–	Pillar or spar
Light (when fitted)	–	White, Q (9) 15s or VQ (9) 10s.

Isolated danger marks

Isolated danger marks are moored on or above, or erected on, an isolated danger of limited extent, such as a rock or a wreck, which has navigable water all around it.

Topmark	–	Two black balls (vert)
Colour	–	Black, with one or more red bands
Shape (buoys)	–	Pillar or spar
Light (when fitted)	–	White, Fl (2).
Mnemonic	–	Two balls, two flashes

Safe water marks

Safe water marks indicate that there is navigable water all round the mark, and are used for mid-channel, landfall or fairway marks.

Topmark (if any)	–	A red ball (not on spherical buoy)
Colour	–	Red and white vertical stripes
Shape	–	Spherical, pillar or spar
Light (when fitted)	–	White, isophase, or occulting, or L Fl 10 s, or Morse 'A'.

Special marks

Special marks are not primarily for navigation, but indicate a special area or feature such as leisure areas, spoil grounds, military exercise areas, cable, pipe line outfalls, Ocean Data Acquisition Systems (ODAS) buoys, or traffic separation schemes where conventional channel marking might cause confusion.

Topmark (if any)	–	A yellow 'X' shaped cross
Colour	–	Yellow
Shape	–	Optional; not in conflict with lateral or safe water marks*.
Light (when fitted)	–	Yellow, but different rhythm from cardinal, isolated danger, or safe water marks.

*For example, a special mark outfall buoy on the port side of the channel could be can-shaped but not conical.

New dangers are marked in accordance with the IALA sytem. They may include naturally-

CLASS OF LIGHT	International abbreviations	Illustration Period shown ⊢————————⊣
FIXED	F	
OCCULTING (total duration of light longer than dark) Single-occulting	Oc	
Group-occulting	eg	Oc(2)	
Composite group-occulting	eg	Oc(2+3)	
ISOPHASE (light and dark equal)	Iso	
FLASHING (total duration of light shorter than dark) Single-flashing	Fl	
Long-flashing (flash 2s or longer)	L Fl	
Group-flashing eg	Fl(3)	
Composite group-flashing	eg	Fl(2+1)	
QUICK (50 to 79, usually either 50 or 60, flashes per minute) Continuous quick	Q	
Group quick	eg	Q(3)	
Interrupted quick	IQ	
VERY QUICK (80 to 159, usually either 100 or 120, flashes per minute) Continuous very quick	VQ	
Group very quick	eg	VQ(3)	
Interrupted very quick	IVQ	
ULTRA QUICK (160 or more, usually 240 to 300, flashes per minute) Continuous ultra quick	UQ	
Interrupted ultra quick	IUQ	
MORSE CODE	eg	Mo(K)	
FIXED AND FLASHING	F Fl	
ALTERNATING	eg	Al. WR	

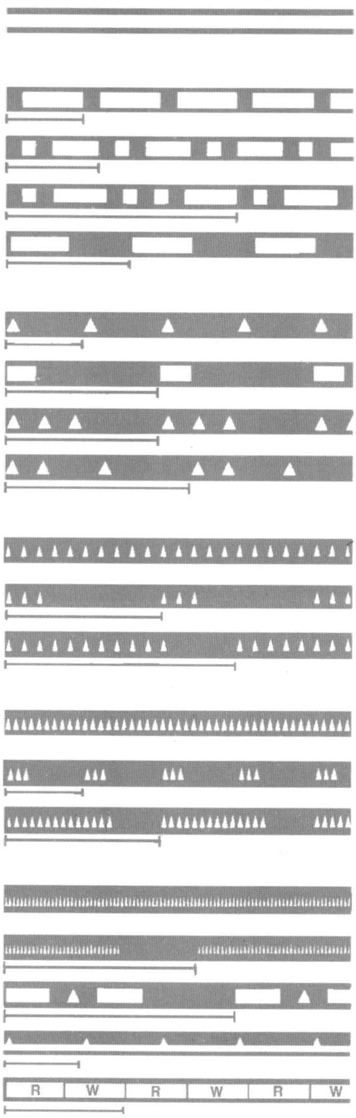

COLOUR	International abbreviations	NOMINAL RANGE in miles	International abbreviations
White	W (may be omitted)	Light with single range eg	15M
Red	R	Light with two different ranges eg	15/10M
Green	G	Light with three or more ranges eg	15-7M
Blue	Bu		
Violet	Vi	PERIOD is given in seconds eg	30s
Yellow	Y	DISPOSITION horizontally disposed	(hor)
Orange	Y	vertically disposed	(vert)
Amber	Y	ELEVATION is given in metres (m) above MHWS	

Fig. 7(36) Light characteristics.

recurring obstructions such as a sandbank or rock, or man-made dangers such as wrecks. At an especially grave danger one of the marks may be duplicated. Lights will be appropriate to a cardinal (Q or VQ white), or lateral mark (Q or VQ, R or G).

7.7.4 LIGHTS

Lights from lighthouses, light vessels and light buoys are shown on a chart by a magenta coloured flare, with the light's characteristics alongside. The international abbreviations shown in the second column of Fig. 7(36) apply to both metric and fathoms charts.

Lighthouses sometimes show different coloured light sector(s) to warn of offlying dangers or indicate the safe channel. Their arcs of visibility and colour of light (if other than white) are given on the chart. The bearings T° are **as seen from seaward**, measured clockwise from 000° to 359°, and define the limits of the various arcs.

The way in which these sectors are quoted in the Admiralty List of Lights, or in a Navtex message if the sectors have recently been changed, can be misinterpreted – with a potentially dangerous result. For example a light, quoted as having the following sectors R343°–153° (170°), G153°–333° (180°), is correctly depicted in Fig. 7(37).

But it has been known for it to be wrongly drawn as a mirror image, ie with the Red sector to the east, the Green sector to the west and the unlit 10° sector to the north. The correct procedure (applicable to all lights) is:

a. Make a sketch with the ☆ (the light) in the centre.
b. Draw the first bearing (343° in this example) as a line pointing NNE to end at the ☆, ie as seen from seaward.
c. Do the same for the 153° bearing.
d. The (170°) sector drawn clockwise from 343° to 153° is obviously the Red sector.

e. The (180°) Green sector continues clockwise from 153° to the final bearing of 333°, which is of course the reciprocal of 153°.
f. The unlit 10° sector lies to the SSE of the light, between the Green and Red sectors.

A directional light shines over a narrow arc, indicating a direction to be followed. The arc may be flanked by arcs of different colour, characteristic or lesser range. Try the following example of a more complex light, checking your result against Fig. 7(38):

Q WRG 9m 10M, G015°–058° (43°), W058°–065° (7°), R065°–103° (38°), G103°–143·5° (40·5°), W143·5°–146·5° (3°), R146·5°–015° (228·5°).

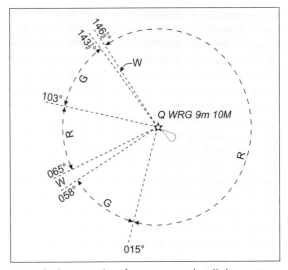

Fig. 7(38) Example of more complex light sectors.

The elevation of a light is the height of its focal plane (centre of the lamp) in metres above MHWS, or above MSL if there is no tide. In describing a light structure's visual appearance, horizontal divisions of colour are called 'bands', vertical divisions are 'stripes' and spiral divisions are 'diagonal stripes'.

Leading lights are two or more lights aligned so as to form a leading line which should be followed, usually between dangers; see 7.7.2. The rear leading light is at a higher elevation than the front. Lights described as 'Lts in line' mark the sides of a channel, and are not leading lights; in that sense the term is obsolescent.

Fog detector lights may be fitted on or near some light structures. They automatically detect fog, switch on fog signals and/or transmit the range of visibility to a data centre for broadcasting. Some types are visible over a narrow arc, some show a powerful bluish white flash, and others sweep back and forth and may be mistaken for signals. Fog detector lights operate by day and night.

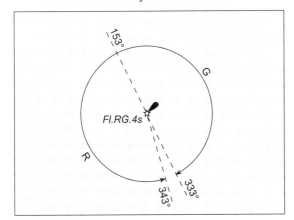

Fig. 7(37) Example of light sectors.

7.7.5 RANGES OF LIGHTS

Two basic criteria determine the maximum range at which it is possible to see a light:

a. it must be above the observer's horizon; and

b. it must be powerful enough to be seen at range (a).

The range of a light can be stated in three ways:

1. Geographical range is the maximum distance at which a light can reach an observer, as determined only by the observer's height of eye, the light's elevation and the curvature of the earth. A Table in the A.L.L gives such ranges for light elevations up to 400m and heights of eye up to 45m. Or it can be found from a Table of 'Distances at which a light dips (or rises)', as given in the MRNA.

2. Luminous range is the maximum distance at which a light can be seen, as determined only by the intensity of the light and the prevailing visibility. It takes no account of the light's elevation, the observer's height of eye, or the curvature of the earth. In lay terms Luminous range expresses the brilliance of a light in the current visibility.

3. Nominal range is the luminous range when the meteorological visibility is 10M. This notional range is printed on charts, in the A.L.L and in the MRNA.

Distance from a light cannot be estimated from its apparent brightness. A Table in the A.L.L enables the yachtsman to find the maximum range at which a light may be sighted at night in the prevailing visibility. Due to their intensity, many lights will be sighted at distances greater than the estimated visibility; for example in a prevailing visibility of 5M, a light with a nominal range of 16M will be seen at 10M. A light may be seen further due to abnormal refraction, and the loom (diffused glow) of a powerful light can often be detected well beyond its geographical range.

Conversely in thick weather a weak light can easily be obscured at distances well below its nominal range. For example in a prevailing Met visibility of 1M, a light with a nominal range of 5M will be seen at under 1M. Lights placed at a high elevation may be obscured by cloud. Glare from background light (eg a major city) can halve the range at which a light will be visible.

7.7.6 LIGHT-VESSELS

Light-vessels, major light-floats and LANBYs are all shown on the chart by one generic symbol; see Fig. 7(15). Trinity House light-vessels and floats around the UK are unmanned and are being converted to solar power. They show a white riding (anchor) light forward at night, in addition to their main light. In fog or low visibility a fog detector light activates a foghorn, sounding as shown in the MRNA. Most are equipped with a Racon.

If a light-vessel is out of position or is hit by a ship, an alarm is automatically triggered at the Operations Control Centre, Harwich. The OCC can switch off the main light and Racon and take other appropriate actions.

7.7.7 OIL AND GAS PLATFORMS

Offshore oil and gas platforms are shown on the chart by a small square with a dot in the centre. They show a main light Mo (U) 15s 15M, and red lights, Mo (U) R 15s 3M, may mark any projections. They sound a fog signal, Horn Mo (U) 30s.

7.7.8 FOG SIGNALS

Various fog signals are sounded by lighthouses, light-vessels and some navigational buoys. Sound is very unpredictable in fog, and signals may be heard at varying distances. Under sail it may help to heave-to when trying to pick up a fog signal; under power, the engine should be stopped for the same purpose.

The following are the main types of fog signals, with abbreviations in brackets:

1. Diaphone (Dia). Operated by compressed air, producing a powerful, low-pitched sound often ending with a grunt. Now rarely encountered.

2. Horn (Horn). Compressed air or electricity vibrates a diaphragm. Some produce sounds of differing pitch.

3. Siren (Siren). Operated by compressed air. Various types produce sounds of different intensities.

4. Reed. Uses compressed air to emit a weak high-pitched sound.

5. Explosive (Explos). Produces reports like the sound of a gun. Now very rarely encountered.

6. Bell, Gong and Whistle (Bell, Gong, Whis). May be operated by hand, by machinery, or by wave motion.

Fog signals in Morse code are shown by 'Mo' and the letter(s) of the signal, eg Horn Mo (AR).

7.7.9 INTERNATIONAL PORT TRAFFIC SIGNALS (IPTS)

An international system of port signals is in fairly wide use in NW Europe (see page 196), but elsewhere they may not be adopted for many years. A few countries retain existing national signals; see 7.7.10. Whatever the system, the purpose is to regulate the entry and exit of all kinds of vessels to/from harbours for reasons of safety. IPTS help to reduce VHF calls and language problems, although IPTS and VHF may at times be used together. It behoves the yachtsman to be as well aware of the meanings of IPTS as the Master of the QE II.

7.7.10 NATIONAL PORT TRAFFIC SIGNALS
France
The IPTS are in general use in France. However in some small French ports, where there is not much traffic, a simplified code may be used as follows:

By day	By night	Meaning
A red flag	Ⓡ	Entry prohibited
A green flag	Ⓖ	Exit prohibited
A red over a	Ⓡ	Port closed in both
green flag	Ⓖ	directions

Netherlands
IPTS are in general use. If the government takes control of entry to Dutch harbours, the following signals indicate that entry is prohibited, and that a yacht should proceed towards the Examination vessel flying the same signal.

By day	By night
3 red balls (vert),	3 Ⓡ (vert)
or:	or:
Two cones, points	Ⓖ
together,	Ⓡ
over a ball	Ⓦ

Germany
IPTS are in general use. There is a complicated series of visual, lights and sound signals for bridges and locks, some of which are shown in the MRNA.

7.8 PASSAGE PLANNING

7.8.1 A LOGICAL PROCESS
Apart from using the correct navigational techniques, essential preparation and planning must be completed before any passage – even for short coastal trips. A passage of whatever length has three phases: a Beginning, Middle and End. The three phases are:

a. Departure from the present harbour or anchorage;
b. The Passage itself which is likely to be by far the longest phase; and
c. The Landfall or arrival at a destination.

Planning is, or should be, a logical and well thought out process which addresses each phase. The demands of one phase may conflict with another. Having identified these, the skipper and navigator (who may be the same person) might have to modify the developing plan so as to resolve any such conflicts.

It is often best to study the middle phase first, because the most time and effort will be spent on passage, taking advantage of tidal streams and minimising the adverse effects of headwinds and/ or poor weather. If planning, for example, a coastal leg of some 30 – 40M you might reasonably plan (hope) to carry a fair tide the whole way. You should therefore identify when the fair stream starts to make and time your departure accordingly. But a longer passage of say 100M is likely to take three tides, of which two must be fair and one foul, if at all possible. On longer passages still, say 200M, the tidal streams have to be taken more or less as they come and other factors are likely to predominate.

Having devised an outline plan for the Passage proper, consider next how best to dovetail in your departure. Much depends on whether the departure port is available at all hours. If it is, your plan may only have to include pilotage details and the need to be at the fairway buoy, or other departure point, at the right time. If, however the departure port is tidally limited, by a bridge, a lock or sheer lack of water, you may have to settle for the earliest time at which you can leave and modify the passage plan accordingly. Alternatively you may be able to leave one tide earlier and anchor outside to await the original departure time. It is often worth plugging the last of a foul tide so as to take full advantage of the next six hours of favourable stream.

Similar constraints might apply at your arrival port, or delays on passage may cause you to anchor off and wait. There is usually a solution, one of which may be diverting to a more accessible port either short of, beyond or abeam your planned destination. Such a possibility ought to have been considered in the planning stage, when the need to think laterally is important – you are after all only making a plan which cynics would say is something from which to deviate. Once at sea the need to stay flexible is equally important. Do not be hellbent on the delights of port X, when it is obvious that other options have become more feasible or even perhaps safer. Indeed never be too proud to abandon the leg and return whence you came.

7.8.2 PLANNING CONSIDERATIONS
The amount of planning required depends upon the scope of the passage, and to some extent upon the experience of the skipper and crew.

(Assume, for the purposes of this section, that the sea-worthiness of the boat and the crew strength, in relation to the waters concerned and the likely weather conditions, are not in doubt – although in reality they may all limit your passage).

Planning tasks will include:

a. Obtaining the necessary charts and other publications for the area concerned and adjacent areas, in case of a weather diversion.

b. Studying charts to select the best route in the light of principal dangers, tidal streams, tidal gates and/or races, navigational marks, distances and the likely time needed.

    Certain headlands are notoriously hard to round due to strong tides and wind bends. Information on such points is in the various Pilots and should be carefully heeded.

c. Choosing alternate harbours or ports of refuge which will give adequate shelter in bad weather, plus any restrictions on entry due to tidal or weather conditions.

d. For motor cruisers consider the distance to be covered relative to the cruising range of the boat. Check fuel availability at destination and along the way.

Quite a lot of reading and thinking is required when planning a passage or cruise to a strange place or coast, but the work will be amply repaid, particularly if events do not go entirely as planned.

The area in which you are sailing will influence your planning. For example the mudbanks and narrow swash-ways of the Thames Estuary are very different from the deep water and rocky coastlines of western Scotland. In the former depth of water and tidal streams are always a concern, as are obstructions and identifying navigational marks. Choose channels which are wide enough to permit some margin of error should the visibility be bad, even if they add to the distance. Alternative routes may not be readily available and short cuts can lead you into trouble with lack of marks and water as well.

In western Scotland careful pilotage amongst rocks is the norm. There are often no navigational marks in the more remote places, so learn to identify islets against a matching background, read the mountain contours and orientate yourself in twisting, featureless channels.

More detailed tasks include cleaning up the charts and stowing them in the order in which they will be used. Mark up the tidal stream atlas with hourly times for ease of reference; sometimes this can be done for a week in advance. Record the times and heights of HW and LW for departure, arrival and alternative ports along the route. All this data can be written in a pocketbook for quick reference in the cockpit; or on a planning proforma, eg Figs. 7(41) and (42), at the chart table. Principal lights, port radio channels and the times/frequencies of weather forecasts can also be included.

The more pre-planning that can be done, the less there will be to worry about when the boat is at sea. Everything should be at your fingertips. Preliminary chart work is especially important in fast, planing motor cruisers in which writing or plotting when under way is often impossible – so all courses and distances should be worked out and listed in advance; see 7.6. Record the fuel state accurately, knowing the likely boat speed and fuel consumption at various engine rpm. Make allowance for factors such as a strong head wind, dirty bottom, or an exceptional load on board.

Non-navigational matters, eg fuel, food, water, gas, documents, passports, money and customs formalities, are dealt with separately.

7.8.3   PLANNING WITH ELECTRONIC AIDS

Modern position fixing systems such as GPS and Loran-C are highly accurate and reliable, and will probably be used as the primary navigational method. However traditional methods are by no means obsolete and should be routinely practised in parallel with electronic navigation as a mutual check that all is well.

Electronic systems give quick and accurate solutions to navigational problems, but only if correct data is inserted. Waypoints must be entered carefully and methodically into the GPS, since human errors are all too easily made if you are tired, distracted or in a rush.

The first step, therefore, is to study the chart, select your route and draw it on the chart; see also 8.4.3. Ensure that it clears all dangers, eg rocks, shoals and headlands. When satisfied, enter the lat/long of all waypoints, and the tracks and distances between them measured off the chart, on a tabular Form, as in Fig. 7(40). Cross-check these for accuracy against those computed in the GPS route plan.

Armed with this mini-plan, punch the waypoints into the GPS and then build the electronic route. Compare the electronic tracks/distances between waypoints with those measured off the paper chart. If there are errors of more than, say, 2° or 0·2M, then either you

WPT 1.	Track & Distance ➞			WPT 2.	Track & Distance ➞		
Name	By chart	°/	M	Name	By chart	°/	M
Lat .... N/S	By GPS	°/	M	Lat .... N/S	By GPS	°/	M
Long .... W/E				Long .... W/E			
WPT 3.	Track & Distance ➞			WPT 4.	Track & Distance ➞		
Name	By chart	°/	M	Name	By chart	°/	M
Lat .... N/S	By GPS	°/	M	Lat .... N/S	By GPS	°/	M
Long .... W/E				Long .... W/E			
WPT 5.	Track & Distance ➞			WPT 6.	Track & Distance ➞		
Name	By chart	°/	M	Name	By chart	°/	M
Lat .... N/S	By GPS	°/	M	Lat .... N/S	By GPS	°/	M
Long .... W/E				Long .... W/E			
WPT 7.	Track & Distance ➞			WPT 8.	Track & Distance ➞		
Name	By chart	°/	M	Name	By chart	°/	M
Lat .... N/S	By GPS	°/	M	Lat .... N/S	By GPS	°/	M
Long .... W/E				Long .... W/E			

Fig. 7(40) Form for checking that Waypoints and the Tracks & Distances between them are correct.

plotted wrongly on the paper chart, or you inserted inaccurate waypoints. Go back and find out where you went wrong; correct the error(s) and check again.

Never ignore the paper chart work just described. It is the only sure way of identifying and bowling out errors or discrepancies, which 90% of the time are caused by 'finger' trouble. Total reliance on electronic planning is as absurd as it is dangerous. No GPS can reveal a rock, a tiderace or even a headland on the track between two waypoints. A chart plotter may be a step in the right direction, and is undoubtely convenient, but it still lacks the essential autonomy and independence upon which cross-checking utterly depends.

7.8.4 PASSAGE PLANNING CHECK LISTS

The two check lists in Figs. 7(41) and (42) aim simply to ensure that all relevant navigational information is obtained and can be readily referred to at sea. This enables the skipper/navigator to make informed decisions and to be better prepared for any unforeseen eventuality. No doubt skippers/navigators will devise their own check lists and this is sensible since everybody works in a slightly different way towards achieving the same end.

Figs. 7(41) and (42) are short term, ie concerned with the minutiae of the immediate passage being planned. Fig. 7(41) contains details of the departure and destination ports; the times and heights of tide which will affect them; and the tidal streams which will influence the passage itself. The lower half is a simple navigational plan

showing tracks and distances between the various waypoints and an estimate of the time required for each leg. The way in which this plan is actually achieved, or deviated from, is of course recorded in the ship's log.

Fig. 7(42) is a bank of information which you will have culled together from various sources. It gives you on one sheet of paper all the background data needed for a particular passage. Much of the information can be worked out and written down in advance.

By the time you have finished this planning you will have in your brain or at your finger tips:

a. The weather situation.
b. The navigational plan itself.
c. Potential dangers en route: clearing lines, distance-off dangers, TSS, shipping lanes, etc.
d. Visual marks and electronic waypoints to be used.
e. Tidal streams, noting when they turn and any tidal gates, typically off headlands and in narrow channels.
f. Critical times and heights of tides which affect the departure and destination harbours, eg crossing bars, sills.
g. A detailed pilotage plan for entry to any unfamiliar harbour, final destination or port of refuge.

Fig. 7(43) is really a **cruise** planning check list. It takes a longer view, in this case a week at a time, and helps you to judge whether you are likely to achieve your goals on schedule, assuming that time is a factor (as it usually is). It also records details, such as Standard Port tide times and times of sunrise/set, which will serve throughout the

DATE .... ETD .... FROM .... TOWARDS .... DISTANCE ....M ETA ....

❑ CHARTS REQUIRED (IN ORDER)   ❑ CUSTOMS   ❑ MARINA BILL   ❑ COASTGUARD (TR)

DEPARTURE PORT - INFORMATION	DESTINATION PORT - INFORMATION

TIDAL DATA   SPRINGS/BETWEEN/NEAPS   SUNSET .... SUNRISE ....   MOONRISE .... MOONSET ....

STANDARD PORT ....

HW TIMES/HEIGHTS LW TIMES/HEIGHTS	OTHER PORTS	HW TIMES/HEIGHTS	LW TIMES/HEIGHTS

TIDAL STREAMS

FAIR, FROM .... TO.............

FOUL, FROM .... TO.............

TIDAL GATES ....

NOTES

❑ TRAFFIC SEPARATION SCHEMES   ❑ PROHIBITED AREAS   ❑ WAYPOINTS ENTERED

PASSAGE PLAN

FROM	TOWARDS	TRACK°/DIST (M)	LEG TIME AT .... KTS	REMARKS

Fig. 7(41) Passage planning check list (1)

Alternate Harbours & Ports of refuge

Port				
Pilot book				
Access				
Tides				
Dangers				
Shelter				
Local regs				
VHF				

Dangers on route

Danger	Marked by	Clearing brgs

Visual aids on route (DAYMARKS, BUOYS AND LIGHTS)

Forecasts	On sailing	Forecast	Outlook period
Wind			
Weather			
Visibility			
Barometer			
Sea state			

Watch System

System Checks
❑ Engine ❑ Fuel ❑ Water ❑ Electrics

Notes

Fig. 7(42) Passage planning check list (2)

DAY/DATE	MON	TUE	WED	THU	FRI	SAT	SUN
SUN RISE/SET							
HW DOVER Sp/Nps/Coeff							
STANDARD PORT HW/LW							
DEPARTURE PORT HW/LW							
Exit Window Bar/lock/sill							
ARRIVAL PORT HW/LW							
Arrival window Bar/lock/sill							
TIME 0000 PLAN 0400 0800 1200 1600 2000 2359							

Fig. 7(43) Weekly Planning Proforma

week. A 24 hour time plan focuses on daily events, such as watch-keeping, or the sea/shore ratio. In essence it gives The Big Picture and the benefits of an overall plan.

These check lists are largely self-explanatory in that they contain boxes to be completed or items to be ticked off. Navigational planning is not a chore; it is interesting and thought provoking. For many it is one of the main reasons for going to sea and visiting strange harbours.

7.9 NAVIGATIONAL WARNINGS

7.9.1 INTRODUCTION

Navigational Warnings, a part of MSI, are essentially Hazard warnings. They are described in ALRS Vol 3 and in Annual Notices to Mariners No 13.

For the purposes of the Navigational Warning Service, the world is divided into 16 vast sea areas (NAVAREAS), numbered I – XVI . Fig. 7(44) shows the NAVAREAS, the Area Coordinators (a nation) and the transmitting stations. Area Coordinators for Areas I, II and III (the Mediterranean) are respectively the UK, France and Spain. Within NAVAREA I, which extends from 48°27′N to 71°N and out to 35°W, Sweden coordinates a Baltic Sea Sub-Area. NAVAREAS and METAREAS (Chap 11) are geographically the same.

There are three types: Long range, Coastal and Local.

Long range radio NavWarnings are collated and issued by each Area Coordinator for the whole of his area. They are numbered consecutively throughout the year and are specific to the area concerned. They are transmitted at least twice daily at scheduled times by radiotelephony, radiotelex, facsimile and Navtex, in English and one or more other languages. They promulgate data which ocean navigators need or which may affect routeing, eg failures or changes to navigational aids, wrecks and navigational dangers of all kinds, SAR operations, cable laying operations, naval exercises, pollution etc.

Coastal and Local NavWarnings are also issued, within each area. Coastal warnings, promulgated by a national co-ordinator, cover waters up to 100 – 200M offshore; they are broadcast in English and in the national language by coast radio stations or Coastguards.

Local warnings are issued by harbour or port authorities for their domains, only in the national language.

7.9.2 NAVWARNINGS – UK

Radio NavWarnings, issued by the Hydrographic Office, provide immediate information on dangers to navigation. Less essential matters, or dangers within harbour limits, may not be broadcast but appear in Notices to Mariners.

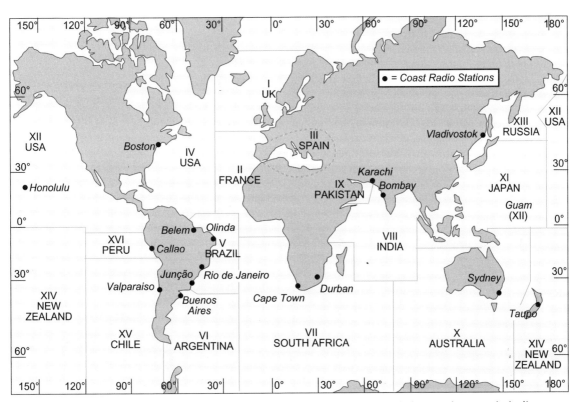

Fig. 7(44) NAVAREAS I – XVI. Area Coordinators are in CAPITALS. Transmitting stations are in italics.

NavWarnings are broadcast by the following means:

a. Long range warnings for NAVAREA I are broadcast via the international SafetyNET service, ie by Inmarsat satellites. Messages are numbered in sequence, and the text is published in weekly Notices to Mariners, together with a list of those warnings still in force.

b. NAVTEX warnings for the British Isles are broadcast by Cullercoats, Portpatrick, Niton, Valentia and Malin Head. For a description of NAVTEX see 11.2.7; the areas concerned are shown in Fig. 11(26).

c. Coastal warnings, also known as WZ warnings, are broadcast by MRCC/MRSCs at scheduled times (see the MRNA) for Sea Regions A – N around the UK, as shown in Fig. 7(45). These broadcasts are on any or all of VHF working channels 10, 23, 73, 84 or 86 (and exceptionally on Ch 67) – so you must listen to the prior announcement on Ch 16. Important warnings may be broadcast at any time on the distress frequencies of 2182kHz and VHF Ch 16, prefixed by Securité.

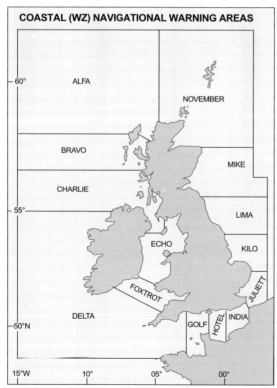

Fig. 7(45) Sea Regions A – N, for which UK Coastal (WZ) NavWarnings are issued.

d. Local warnings may be broadcast by harbour authorities. The Coastguard broadcasts local warnings of dangers in inshore waters which are outside the limits of harbour authorities. These broadcasts are on the same working channels as in para (c), but there is no schedule or numerical sequence; however there may be repeats.

e. Ship reports: Vessels encountering dangers to navigation or severe weather conditions should notify other craft in the vicinity and the nearest MRCC/MRSC.

7.9.3 NAVWARNINGS – EUROPE
The following notes describe the NavWarnings broadcast by certain European countries. For details of frequencies, schedules and the area of coverage, see the MRNA.

Norway
NavWarnings for Norwegian waters are issued in English by the Norwegian Coast Directorate (KystDirektoratet). They are broadcast by Navtex and by Coast radio stations on the appropriate RT frequencies. Urgent and important warnings will be announced at any time on VHF Ch 16, 2182kHz and by DSC on 2187·5kHz and VHF Ch 70. Rogaland (L) is the nearest Norwegian Navtex station to the UK; see 11.2.7, Annex.

Denmark
NavWarnings for Danish waters are broadcast by Lyngby Coast radio station (near Copenhagen) in Danish and English on MF. They are also broadcast on VHF by Coast radio relay stations.

Germany
NavWarnings are issued by VTS centres for their areas of responsibility and by the Sea Warning Service Centre at Cuxhaven for the whole German warning Area. North Sea VTS centres are Ems, Jade, Bremerhaven Weser, Cuxhaven Elbe, Brunsbüttel Elbe and German Bight; all use the callsign 'Traffic' after the name. Warnings are broadcast in German and English on receipt and after the next silence period, and may be repeated as necessary. VHF warnings are broadcast by Bremen MRCC. Navtex warnings for the North Sea coast are broadcast by the Netherlands Coastguard IJmuiden (P) and for the Baltic coast by Stockholm Radio (Gislövshammar) (J).

Yachts encountering dangers to navigation should inform Seewarndienstzentrale Cuxhaven through the nearest coast radio station. Oil pollution should also be reported to Cuxhaven Central HQ, prefaced by the word Oelunfall (oil accident).

Netherlands

NavWarnings for the North Sea are announced by Netherlands Coastguard (IJmuiden) on DSC 2187·5kHz and VHF Ch 70, before being broadcast on MF and by relay stations on VHF. IJmuiden Navtex (P) also broadcasts warnings in English.

Belgium

Oostende coast radio station announces NavWarnings on VHF Ch 16, 2182kHz and DSC on 2187·5kHz and VHF Ch 70 and broadcasts them in Dutch and English on MF and VHF. Antwerpen broadcasts them on VHF for the Schelde. Navtex broadcasts by Oostende (M) cover the Belgian/French coasts from 3°E to Calais and from 3°E to the UK coast between Lowestoft and North Foreland. Oostende (T) covers the Belgian coast.

France

Long range warnings for NAVAREA II are issued by SHOM and broadcast via SafetyNET in English and French. (North France is in NAVAREA I).

Coastal and Local warnings are known as AVURNAVs (AVis URgents aux NAVigateurs); they are coordinated by the following regional maritime authorities:

a. Cherbourg, for the North Sea and the eastern Channel (Belgian frontier to Mont St Michel, including the Channel Islands).
b. Brest, for the western Channel and Atlantic coast (Mont St Michel to the Spanish frontier).
c. Toulon, for the south coast of France and Corsica.

Avurnavs are broadcast by Navtex, Niton (K) and Corsen (A), and by the appropriate CROSS station; urgent warnings are transmitted on receipt and at the end of the next silence period, as well as at scheduled times. RT warnings are prefixed 'Sécurité Avurnav' with the name of the station. Latitude and longitude are normally given in three groups: the first is four figures for latitude in degrees and minutes; the second is four or five figures for longitude in degrees and minutes; and the third is two letters to show the hemisphere, eg 4622 0233 NW.

Vessels encountering dangers to navigation should inform ships in the vicinity and the nearest CROSS station, using the Sécurité prefix.

Spain

Long-range warnings for NAVAREAs II and III are broadcast on SafetyNET in English.

Coastal warnings are broadcast by coast radio stations on MF and VHF in Spanish and English. 'Vital' or 'Important' warnings (AVURNAVES) are announced on 2182kHz and are prefaced by the safety signal (Sécurité); they are broadcast on receipt, after the next silence period, and at scheduled times. 'Routine' warnings (AVISO) are announced on 2182kHz and are also prefaced by the safety signal; they are broadcast after the next silence period and at scheduled times.

Local warnings are broadcast by coast radio stations on VHF in Spanish, and are classified 'Avurnave' or 'Aviso'. Avurnaves are announced on Ch 16 and are prefaced by the safety signal; they are broadcast on receipt and at scheduled times. Avisos are broadcast on the station's working channel at scheduled times.

Portugal

The Portuguese Hydrographic Institute issues Coastal Warnings for up to 200M offshore, including Madeira and the Azores. They are broadcast by Coast radio stations in Portuguese and English on MF. Local warnings are broadcast only in Portuguese on VHF.

Italy

Warnings are broadcast in Italian and English by Coast Radio stations on receipt and at scheduled times; the most recent warnings are broadcast first. Urgent warnings are also broadcast in Italian and English, on receipt and at scheduled times.

Greece

Hellenic NavWarns (sic) are issued by the Hydrographic Office and broadcast in Greek and English at scheduled times by coast radio stations.

7.9.4   SUBFACTS AND GUNFACTS

Subfacts are warnings that submarines are or will be operating on the surface, at periscope depth and fully submerged, in certain sea areas around the UK. They are of obvious interest to yachts and fishing vessels.

The areas most used by RN submarines are (a) in the English Channel from the Isles of Scilly eastwards to a position 50°15'N 01°15'W, 37M SSE of Selsey Bill; and (b) off the west coast of Scotland from the Isle of Man to Cape Wrath.

Warnings are broadcast on VHF at scheduled times by Falmouth and Brixham MRCC/SCs for the South coast, and by Clyde, Belfast, Oban and Stornoway MRCC/SCs for Scotland. The sea areas are divided into much smaller sub-areas which are referred to by name and/or number in the broadcasts. Information is also available on

Navtex, from Naval authorities and via a Fisherman's Hotline Tel. Details are in the MRNA and in ALRS volume 3.

Submarines on the surface will comply strictly with the IRPCS. Submarines at periscope depth will not close to within 1500 yards of a fishing vessel without that vessel's express permission. For their own safety yachts are advised to listen to Subfacts and to avoid active areas. If in or near active areas keep a doubly sharp lookout – a vessel flying the Code flags NE2 indicates that submarines are in the vicinity; monitor VHF Ch 16; keep the engine (or a generator) and the echo-sounder running, so that the submarine's sonar will hear them; and at night show deck-level, rather than masthead, navigation lights.

Gunfacts are warnings of naval gun firing practices which mainly take place in the English Channel and West Scottish sea areas described above. They are broadcast at the same times and by the same MRCC/SCs as Subfacts. Where gun firing is due to take place outside these areas broadcasts will be made by the ship(s) concerned, normally on VHF Ch 06 or 67 at 0800 and 1400LT, after a prior announcement on Ch 16. Gun firing in this context is a generic term; it includes missiles, underwater explosions and pyrotechnics/illuminants.

7.10 BOOKS

All books shown below are those in the 2001 catalogues of leading publishers and distributors of nautical books. Not listed are other books which may be out of print, but still have an enduring value, for example the French Pilot, four volumes by Malcolm Robson, which depend largely on the traditional technique of the transit line. Books on electronic navaids and Astro-navigation are listed in Chapters 8 and 9 respectively.

7.10.1 BOOKS ABOUT NAVIGATION
The RYA Book of Navigation by Tim Bartlett (Adlard Coles).

The RYA Book of Navigation Exercises by Alison Noice and James Stevens (Adlard Coles).

Learn to Navigate by Basil Mosenthal (Adlard Coles).

Basic Coastal Navigation by Conrad Dixon (2nd edition, Adlard Coles).

Coastal Navigation by Gerry Smith (3rd edition, Adlard Coles).

Inshore Navigation by Tom Cunliffe (Fernhurst).

Coastal and Offshore Navigation by Tom Cunliffe (Fernhurst).

Understanding Navigation by Tim Bartlett (Fernhurst).

7.10.2 ALMANACS, PILOTS AND CRUISING COMPANIONS
When navigating in narrow waters, you should have on board Pilot books which complement the data shown on even the largest scale chart. Such information is almost indispensable for pilotage into many attractive places and secure anchorages.

The new series of Cruising Companions, published by Nautical Data Ltd in association with Yachting Monthly magazine, offer much additional information about facilities and attractions ashore, as well as full pilotage data.

Inclusion of a publication in the following list is not necessarily a recommendation. Pilot books for yachtsmen vary considerably in their scope, accuracy and usefulness.

Almanacs
Macmillan Reeds Nautical Almanac (Nautical Data Ltd) in bound and looseleaf editions NW Europe: Skagen to Gibraltar.

Macmillan Reeds Channel Almanac wire-bound edition (Nautical Data Ltd).

Macmillan Reeds Western Almanac wire-bound edition (Nautical Data Ltd).

Macmillan Reeds Eastern Almanac wire-bound edition (Nautical Data Ltd).

PBO Small craft Almanac (Nautical Data Ltd).

Votre Livre de Bord (Bloc Marine) in two volumes: NW Europe and Mediterranean.

The Nautical Almanac (TSO). The only source of daily ephemerides for Sun, Moon, Aries and the planets.

England – South Coast
West Country Cruising Companion by Mark Fishwick (Nautical Data Ltd, 5th edition 2001).

The Shell Channel Pilot by Tom Cunliffe (Imray, 3rd ed'n 2000). Ramsgate to Scilly/Dunkerque to L'Aberwrac'h.

Solent Hazards by Peter Bruce (Boldre Marine, 4th edition 1994).

Wight Hazards by Peter Bruce (Boldre Marine, 1989)

Inshore along the Dorset coast by Peter Bruce (Boldre Marine, 1996)

Yachtsman's Guide to the Scillies by Norm (Armorel Studio, St. Mary's).

Isles of Scilly revised by John and Fay Garey (RCC/Imray, 2nd edition 1999).

The Waypoint Directory (English Channel) by Peter Cumberlidge (Adlard Coles, 2nd edition 2001)

England – East Coast

East Coast Rivers Cruising Companion by Janet Harber (Nautical Data Ltd, 2001).

North Sea Passage Pilot (Cromer to Den Helder/Dover to Calais by Brian Navin (Imray, 3rd edition 1998).

Tidal Havens of the Wash and Humber by Henry Irving (Imray, 4th edition 1995).

Sailing Directions, Humber Estuary to Rattray Head (Royal Northumberland Yacht Club, 4th edition 1989).

The East Coast: The Wash to Ramsgate by Derek Bowskill (Imray, 4th edition 1998).

North Sea Waypoint Directory by Peter Cumberlidge (Adlard Coles, 1999)

Scotland

Western Isles Cruising Companion by Mike Balmforth and Patrick Roach (Nautical Data Ltd, 2002)

Clyde Cruising Club Sailing Directions *(4 parts)*:
1. *Firth of Clyde, inc Solway Firth and Isle of Man* ('98).
2. *Kintyre to Ardnamurchan* (1998).
3. *Ardnamurchan to Cape Wrath* (1997).
4. *Outer Hebrides* ('95). Note: Shetland, Orkney and N & NE Coasts of Scotland are to be revised by about *2003*.

Yachtsman's Pilot (5 vols) by Martin Lawrence (Imray):
1. *Clyde to Colonsay* (3rd edition, 2001).
2. *Isle of Mull and adjacent coasts* (1999).
3. *Skye and NW Scotland* (1997).
4. *The Western Isles* (1996).
5. *North and East Scotland, C Wrath to Farne Is* (2001).

West Highland Shores by Maldwin Drummond (Adlard Coles).

Scottish Islands by Hamish Haswell-Smith (Canongate 1996); not a Pilot, but a work of art by a yachtsman.

East Coast of Scotland Pilot Handbook, Berwick-upon-Tweed to Fraserburgh (FYCA, 3rd edition 2000).

Irish Sea

Lundy and Irish Sea Pilot (Land's End to Portpatrick) by David Taylor (Imray, 2nd edition 2000).

Cruising Anglesey and adjoining waters (Liverpool to Pwllheli) by Ralph Morris (NW Venturers YC, 6th edition 2000).

Isle of Man SDs (Hunter Publications, 1998).

Solway SDs, Loch Ryan to Ravenglass inc Solway Firth (SW Scotland Sailing Association, 1996).

Ireland

East and North Coasts of Ireland (ICC, 9th edition 1999). *South and West Coasts of Ireland* (ICC, 9th edition 1999).

Inland Waterways – British Isles

Port of London Authority Pleasure Users Guide PLA Yachtsman's Guide (PLA).

The River Thames Book by Chris Cove-Smith (Imray, 2nd edition 1998).

Visiting Yachtsman's Guide to the tidal Thames (CA).

Inland Waterways of Great Britain by Jane Cumberlidge (Imray, 7th edition 1998).

Inland Waterways of Ireland by Jane Cumberlidge (Imray, 2001).

Map of the Inland Waterways of Great Britain (Imray).

The Broads and Fens – A waterway Guide by Derek Bowskill (Imray, 1999)

North West Europe – General

Cruising Association Handbook (CA, 8th edition) British Isles and Europe: Baltic approaches to Gibraltar.

Planning a Foreign Cruise, Vol. 1 Atlantic Europe and the Baltic (RYA/CA, 2000).

The RYA book of Euro-Regs for Inland Waterways by Marian Martin (RYA 1998).

France and Channel Islands

North Brittany and Channel Islands Cruising Companion by Peter Cumberlidge (Nautical Data Ltd, 2001).

North Brittany and the Channel Islands by John Lawson (RCC/Imray, 2001).

The Channel Islands by Nick Heath (RCC/Imray, 2000).

Normandy and Channel Islands Pilot Mark Brackenbury (Adlard Coles, 9th edition 1995).

France – North and West Coasts

North Brittany and Channel Islands Cruising Companion by Peter Cumberlidge (Nautical Data Ltd, 2001).

North France and Belgium Cruising Companion (Cap de la Hague to Antwerpen) by Neville Featherstone (Nautical Data Ltd, 2001).

West France Cruising Companion (L'Aberwrac'h to Hendaye) by Neville Featherstone (Nautical Data, 2001).

The Shell Channel Pilot by Tom Cunliffe (Imray, 3rd ed'n 2000). Ramsgate to Scilly/Dunkerque to L'Aberwrac'h.

North Biscay (Ouessant to Gironde) revised by Gavin McLaren (RCC/Imray, 6th edition 1999).

South Biscay (Gironde to La Coruña) revised by John Lawson (RCC/Imray, 5th edition 2000).

Inland Waterways – France

North France and Belgium Cruising Companion (inc R. Seine to Paris) by Neville Featherstone (Nautical Data Ltd, 2001).

Through the French Canals by Philip Bristow, revised by David Jefferson (Adlard Coles, 9th edition 1999).

Inland Waterways of France by David Edwards-May (Imray, 7th edition 2001).

Map of the Inland Waterways of France (Imray, 1999).

Paris by boat by David Jefferson (Adlard Coles, 1998)

Notes on French Inland Waterways (CA).

Cruising French Waterways by Hugh McKnight (Adlard Coles, 3rd edition).

River Seine Cruising Guide by Derek Bowskill (Imray 1996).

The Channel to the Med by Derek Bowskill (Imray 1995).

Netherlands

Cruising Guide to the Netherlands by Brian Navin (Imray, 3rd edition 2000).

Vetus Marina Guides: the Netherlands (Adlard Coles)

Almanak Voor Watertoerisme (ANWB Vols. I and II, in Dutch); Royal Netherlands Touring Club.

Germany

Cruising Guide to Germany and Denmark (North Sea & Baltic coasts) by Brian Navin (Imray, 2nd edition, 2001).

Through the German Waterways by Philip Bristow (Adlard Coles).

The Inland Waterways of Germany by Barry Sheffield (Imray, 1996)

Scandinavia

Norwegian Cruising Guide by John Armitage and Mark Brackenbury (Adlard Coles, 2nd edition 1996).

The Baltic Sea compiled by Barry Sheffield (RCC/Imray, 1992).

Atlantic Spain and Portugal

Northern Spain Cruising Companion (French border to La Coruña) by Detlef Jens (Nautical Data Ltd, 2002).

Spain and Portugal Cruising Companion (La Coruña to Gibraltar) by Detlef Jens (Nautical Data Ltd, 2001).

Atlantic Spain and Portugal Oz Robinson revised by Anne Hammick (RCC/Imray, 4th edition 2000).

Yachtsman's Guide (Guia Navegante) to Spain and Portugal by Richard Edmund (Ashton, 11th ed'n 2000).

Mediterranean – West

Mediterranean Almanac 2001-2 by Rod Heikell (Imray).

Mediterranean Cruising Handbook by Rod Heikell. (Imray, 4th edition 1998). Companion to the Almanac.

Planning a Foreign Cruise, Vol. 2 The Mediterranean and Black Seas (RYA/CA, 2001).

Votre Livre de Bord, Méditerranée (Bloc Marine, 2001).

Straits Sailing Handbook by Colin Thomas (RCC/Imray, 2001). Handy guide to Gib and adjacent coasts.

Mediterranean Spain, in two volumes by Robin Brandon, revised by Oz Robinson:

Costas del Sol and Blanca (RCC/Imray, 3rd ed'n 1999); and

Costas del Azahar, Dorada and Brava (RCC/Imray, 3rd edition 1999)

Islas Balearas revised by Anne Hammick (RCC/Imray, 6th edition 2000).

South France Pilot, Golfe du Lion by Robin Brandon (RCC/Imray, 1993).

La Corse and adjacent Sardegna by Robin Brandon, revised by John Marchment (RCC/Imray, 2nd edition 2001).

Mediterranean France and Corsica Pilot by Rod Heikell (Imray, 2nd edition 1997).

North Africa: Morocco, Algeria and Tunisia by Hans van Rijn, revised by G. Hutt (Imray, 3rd edition 2000).

Italian Waters Pilot by Rod Heikell (Imray, 5th edn 1998).

Adriatic Pilot by Trevor and Dinah Thompson (Imray, 3rd edition 2000).

Navigational Guide to the Croatian coast Locally published in Zagreb, available through Imray (2nd edn 2000).

Mediterranean – East

Greek Waters Pilot by Rod Heikell (Imray, 7th edn 1998).

Ionian by Rod Heikell (Imray, 4th edition 2000).

Saronic by Rod Heikell (Imray, 2nd edition 2001).

Turkish Waters & Cyprus Pilot by Rod Heikell (Imray, 6th edition 2001).

Turkey's Mediterranean coast by Rod Heikell (Imray, 2001). A handy softback covering Bodrum to Kerkova.

Turkey and Dodecanese Cruising Pilot by Robin Petherbridge (Adlard Coles).

Black Sea Cruising guide by Rick and Sheila Nelson (Imray 1995). Turkey, Bulgaria, Romania, Ukraine and Russia.

Red Sea Pilot by Elaine Morgan and Stephen Davies (Imray 1995).

Caribbean

A Cruising Guide to the Caribbean by Michael Marshall (Adlard Coles).

Cuba: A Cruising Guide by Nigel Calder (Imray, 2nd edn 1999).

The Yachtsman's Guide to Jamaica by John Lethbridge (Imray 1996).

Street's Cruising Guide to the Eastern Caribbean, five volumes by Don Street (to be re-published in 2001).

Cruising Guide Publications, five volumes:

Virgin Anchorages by Nancy & Simon Scott; aerial photos.

The Virgin Islands by Nancy & Simon Scott; 9th edn 2000.

The Windward Islands by Chris Doyle; 10th edn 2000.

The Leeward Islands by Chris Doyle; 6th edn 2001.

Trinidad and Tobago by Chris Doyle; 1997.

Venezuela and Bonaire by Chris Doyle & Jeff Fisher; 1997.

Central & Southern Bahamas by Stephen Pavlides, 1997.

The Turks and Caicos Guide by Stephen Pavlides, 1997.

The Atlantic Coast, Maine to Florida (Embassy Marine 1998).

Oceanic

Atlantic Crossing Guide by Anne Hammick (RCC/Imray, 4th edition 1998).

Ocean Passages for the World (NP 136), (UK HO, 1987).

Atlantic Pilot Atlas by James Clarke (Adlard Coles, 3rd edition, 2000).

Atlantic Islands by Anne Hammick (RCC/Imray, 3rd edition 1999)

Canary Islands Cruising Guide by Doina Cornell (World Cruising Publications).

World Cruising Handbook by Jimmy and Doina Cornell (Adlard Coles, 3rd edition 2001).

World Cruising Routes by Jimmy Cornell (Adlard Coles, 3rd edition 1998).

Indian Ocean Cruising Guide by Rod Heikell (Imray 1999).

Pacific Crossing Guide by Michael Pocock (RCC/Imray 1997)

7.10.3 ADMIRALTY SAILING DIRECTIONS

Admiralty Sailing Directions cover the World in 74 volumes, referred to as Pilots and costing £37·00 in 2001. Those covering Europe from Denmark to Gibraltar, including the British Isles, are listed below. More recent editions (ie all those below) are revised and re-published in full every three years by a continuous revision process. Older titles are updated by Supplements every three years. All volumes are updated by NtM for matters of immediate importance.

NP	Ed'n	Date	Title and Area of coverage
22	8th	9/2001	*Bay of Biscay Pilot.* Pointe de Penmarc'h to Cabo Ortegal.
27	4th	1999	*Channel Pilot.* Scilly to Selsey Bill, including the Channel Islands, and Ouessant to Cap d'Antifer.
28	5th	1999	*Dover Strait Pilot.* Selsey Bill to Orford Ness, and Cap d'Antifer to Scheveningen.
37	14th	1999	*West Coast of England and Wales Pilot.* Land's End to Mull of Galloway, including Isle of Man.

NP	Ed'n	Date	Title and Area of coverage
40	15th	2000	*Irish Coast Pilot*. All of Ireland.
52	4th	2000	*North Coast of Scotland Pilot,* including Orkney, Shetland and Faeroes.
54	5th	2000	*North Sea (West) Pilot.* Southwold to Rattray Head.
55	3rd	1999	*North Sea (East) Pilot.* Scheveningen to Skagen.
66	14th	9/2001	*West Coast of Scotland Pilot.* Mull of Galloway to Cape Wrath, including the Hebrides.
67	7th	1999	*West Coasts of Spain and Portugal Pilot.* Cabo Ortegal to Gibraltar.

The Mediterranean is covered in five volumes:

45	10th	1978	Vol I, E Spain, N Africa to Malta, Sicily, toe and heel of Italy.
46	10th	1978	Vol II, S of France, W Italy down to 39°N, Corsica and Sardinia.
47	10th	1988	Vol III, Ionian and Adriatic Seas.
48	11th	2000	Vol IV, Aegean Sea.
49	7th	1999	Vol V, Libya to Syria, Cyprus and Crete.

Vols IV & V are re-published in full every three years.

7.10.4 ADMIRALTY LIST OF LIGHTS AND FOG SIGNALS

The Admiralty List of Lights (ALL) is published annually in 11 volumes (A – L; not I) and is the definitive guide to lights and fog signals world-wide; cost £21.00. It is corrected by weekly NMs and includes lights on buoys which have an elevation of 8m or more.

Europe and the Mediterranean are covered by volumes:

A   British Isles and North France (inc Chenal du Four); Vol A is available as a Windows based CD-ROM (DP 561), updated free by weekly e-mail or CD-ROM.

B   South and East sides of the North Sea, including Belgium, Netherlands, Germany, West Denmark and South Norway.

C   The Baltic Sea.

D   West France, Spain, Portugal (and all of Africa).

E   The Mediterranean.

Chapter 8 Electronic navigation and Radar

CONTENTS

8.1 ELECTRONIC NAVIGATION SYSTEMS

8.1.1 DEVELOPMENTS

Some 50 years ago the first radio direction finding (RDF) receivers became available for use in small boats. Since then the silicon chip and ubiquitous microprocessors have revolutionised both electronic equipment and navigation techniques. The marine world initially was less willing than the space and aviation communities to accept new high technology equipment and to adopt the new navigational techniques needed to exploit fully the capability and advantages that accrued.

Since the 1980's when Decca (withdrawn in 2000) first became widely available to yachtsmen, existing radio navaids have been substantially developed, whilst others, including

Consol and Omega, have gone out of service. Marine RDF is obsolescent, although still used in some European countries. Aeronautical RDF beacons remain in service, probably for some years yet, and are of use to mariners. The 'Transit' satellite navigation system has been superseded by the more accurate and reliable Global Positioning System (GPS) which is complemented by the still more accurate Differential GPS (DGPS). The hyperbolic Loran-A has given way to the much more advanced Loran-C and wide coverage is available in NW Europe, although it has yet to be widely adopted by yachtsmen.

At the same time there has been a steady shift away from the traditional belief that electronic navaids are only an aid to navigation. By virtue of their proven reliability and exceptional accuracy they are now widely accepted as the primary means of navigating, whilst more time-honoured and independent methods are regarded as little more than desirable back-ups.

The dangers in this philosophy are twofold:

a. that the electronic navigator may through disuse forget the basic skills, if indeed they were ever learned; and

b. he/she may be unable to detect when a complex electronic navaid is malfunctioning – usually insidiously.

If an electronic navaid goes off the air or is degraded, or the yacht loses all electrical power, this will occur at the most awkward and potentially dangerous time. Hence whatever sophisticated equipment is fitted, the navigator must practise and retain the basic skills which have been outlined in the previous chapter. To this end conventional and electronic navigational techniques need to be employed in parallel; the former should not be neglected.

8.1.2 SYSTEMS AVAILABLE

The individual yachtsman can select from a huge range of equipment depending on how he uses his boat, what his requirements and interests are, where he sails, and how much he can afford. Whether you own a world-girdling yacht or a small coastal or offshore cruising boat sailed occasionally across the North Sea or the English Channel, a GPS receiver which can provide continuous fixing anywhere on the world's waters, to an accuracy of 10-15 metres, must be the minimum equipment. By virtue of its obvious navigational advantages, GPS frees yachtsmen to enjoy their sport in greater safety, to manage the boat more efficiently in adverse conditions and to cope more effectively with emergencies.

The following summarises the position fixing systems and radio navigational aids available or being developed in 2001:

1. GPS (GLONASS)
2. Differential GPS
3. Loran-C and Eurofix
4. Radar, including radar beacons (Racons)
5. Marine Radio Direction-finding (RDF) stations
6. Aeronautical RDF beacons
7. HM Coastguard MF/VHF DF (Emergency only)
8. VHF Direction-finding

Each of the above has advantages and disadvantages in terms of cost, accuracy, space occupied (including that for the aerial), power supply, ease of operation, reliability, and the presentation of information. In some cases, one set on board a yacht can cover two (or more) of

the above. For example, 1 and 2 are closely allied; 1 and 3 can also be inter-linked; a suitable MF receiver will cover 5 and 6 (the latter is gradually been withdrawn from service, depending on national needs).

Finally a VHF R/T set will cope with 7 and 8. Because both these are used in emergency, they are dealt with in Chapter 13, Safety and Distress.

8.1.3 ACCURACY

The navigator should appreciate the accuracy that can be expected from any navigational system in the prevailing conditions. Although technical specifications may include terms such as Root Mean Square (RMS) error and dRMS (distance RMS), the commonsense definition of accuracy (absolute accuracy) is the distance between the boat's actual position and the position obtained from the system in use. Two other terms amplify the meaning of accuracy:

1. Absolute accuracy is a measure of the receiver's ability to determine geographic position (latitude and longitude), the accuracy of which varies depending on where the vessel is within the coverage area. Use absolute accuracy to keep track of true position.
2. Repeatable accuracy. This is the accuracy with which a user can return time and again to a position whose coordinates have been measured at a previous time, using the same navigational aid. Good repeatable accuracy helps to find a particular buoy having previously determined its coordinates, or to return safely to harbour when the visibility is poor.

Do not be misled by the fact that a digital readout may give figures to two or more decimal places. High resolution of a display does not necessarily mean high accuracy.

8.2 SATELLITE FIXING SYSTEMS

8.2.1 GLOBAL POSITIONING SYSTEM (GPS)

GPS, sometimes called 'Navstar', is a second generation satellite navigation system developed in the USA for military purposes; it became fully operational in 1995. It provides highly accurate worldwide, three-dimensional position-fixing coverage (latitude, longitude and altitude), together with velocity and time information in all weather conditions. GPS satellites have a design life of 7.5 years. The constellation consists of 24 operational satellites (+ 3 in-orbit spares) which are available for navigation, and provide the two levels of service shown below. Fig. 8(1) shows how these

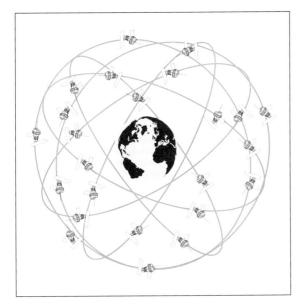

Fig. 8(1) 24 GPS satellites, plus 3 spares, are arranged in 6 orbital planes inclined to the equator at 55°. This configuration ensures that at least 4 suitably elevated satellites are in view anywhere on earth.

are deployed in six orbital planes, evenly distributed, circling the earth every 12 hours at heights of about 10,900n miles.

GPS offers two levels of service: Standard Positioning Service (SPS) and a Precise Positioning Service (PPS).

a. SPS was available to all users at no cost and provided horizontal positioning to an accuracy of about 100 metres by imposing a deliberate degradation called Selective Availability (SA) – for reasons of national security.

b. PPS provides maximum accuracy, about 10-15m, and was intended solely for military purposes.

However on 1 May 2000 the USA cancelled the imposition of Selective Availability (SA) on non-military users, who can now enjoy the full PPS accuracy of GPS.

It is possible that the USA could re-impose SA, either locally or globally, if its national security is threatened at some future date; in which case civil users would revert to SPS.

GPS information, including any planned disruption in peacetime, is provided by the US Coast Guard Navigation Center, 7323 Telegraph Rd, Alexandria, Va 22315; Tel +1 703 313 5907; Fax +1 703 313 5920; e-mail nisws@smtp.navcen.uscg.mil Web www.navcen.uscg.mil   Information is also available on NAVTEX.

8.2.2 PRINCIPLES

The principle on which GPS works is the accurate measurement of distance from a receiver to a number of satellites whose precise positions in space are known. In over-simplified terms, each satellite transmits the PPS and/or SPS code saying 'this is my position and this is the time'. From the exact times of transmission and receipt of the signal, the signal transit time is established. When this is multiplied by the speed of light (161,829 n miles per second), the distance to the satellite is obtained. If similar measurements are made on three satellites, three intersecting circles each centred on the satellite's position at the time of its transmission are obtained. If no errors are present, the intersection of the circles represents the yacht's position.

Since accurate time is so important, each satellite is fitted with two caesium and two rubidium atomic clocks which gain or lose less than one second every 300,000 years. Timing accuracy is vital because a timing error of only 1/1000th of a second can produce a distance error of around 161 n miles.

Satellites are positioned so that at least four are always visible at elevations greater than 5°, and five will usually be above the horizon anywhere on earth. In conjunction with control and monitor stations, a marine receiver whose altitude above the surface of the earth is already known, requires only three satellites to produce a fix. GPS provides continuous global two-dimensional (latitude and longitude), or three-dimensional (latitude, longitude and height) fixing in all weathers.

Each satellite transmits navigation and time data on two downlink frequencies of 1575.42 and 1227.6 MHz. The former frequency transmits both the SPS and the PPS codes; the latter frequency transmits the PPS code only.

8.2.3 ACCURACY

Inherent system errors associated with GPS are small, ie of the order of 7-8m using PPS, and 19-20m using SPS. The major causes of such errors are: ionospheric and atmospheric (signal delays); multipath errors (ghosting); clock errors (very small); satellite position errors (minute); geometric dilution of position (GDOP) or poor satellite geometry; and unusual solar activity (forecast to be much increased between 1999 and 2003).

Overall accuracy of PPS is about 10-15m, whilst SPS is limited to 100m horizontally and 156m vertically for 95% of the time, and 300 metres for 4.99% of the time.

The accuracy of a GPS fix also depends on the sophistication of the user's receiver, ie the accuracy of its mathematical models and the number of channels it can receive on. A wide range of GPS receivers is available, including handheld instruments. Typically these display: latitude/ longitude, course and speed made good, track error, ETA, an estimate of fixing accuracy, satellite status, and the best satellites to use for fixes (see 8.4).

A greater source of inaccuracy arises from the different geodetic framework, or horizontal datum, used by GPS (WGS 84) and the chart on your chart table.

8.2.4 HORIZONTAL DATUM

Note: The term Horizontal Datum avoids any confusion with the vertical Chart Datum used in tidal calculations.

GPS fixes are based on a world-wide datum called the World Geodetic System (WGS 84) reference spheroid. WGS 84 often differs from the horizontal (or geodetic) datum found on the majority of marine charts in use at present. Admiralty charts always state on which datum a chart is based, with a note "SATELLITE - DERIVED POSITIONS" showing how to apply the lat/long adjustments manually before plotting a GPS fix on that chart, for instance:

Positions obtained from satellite navigation systems, such as GPS, are normally referred to the WGS 84 Datum. Such positions must be adjusted by 0·06 minutes NORTHWARD and 0·09 minutes EASTWARD before plotting on this chart. For example:

Position by WGS 84 datum 48°21'·50N 04°28'·50W
Lat/Long adjustments   +0'·06N   −0'·09E
Adjusted position   48°21'·56N 04°28'·41W

Admiralty charts of the UK use the Ordnance Survey of Great Britain Datum (1936), abbreviated to OSGB 36; the Irish Datum (OSI 1965) is virtually identical. In European waters, including the Channel Islands, the datum used is usually European Datum 1950 (ED 50); but the Lisboa Datum applies in Portuguese waters.

However most modern, good quality GPS receivers automatically compensate for the differences between WGS 84 and the horizontal Datum applicable to the local chart, by offering a choice of horizontal Datums. The user has only to ensure that his receiver is selected to the same Datum as the chart in use. But be warned: this automatic correction relies wholly on the excellence, or otherwise, of the software in your particular receiver. Because of the random nature (see below) of the differences, a single software correction may not be adequate; for example the difference between WGS 84 and ED 50 as applied in Norway is very different to that

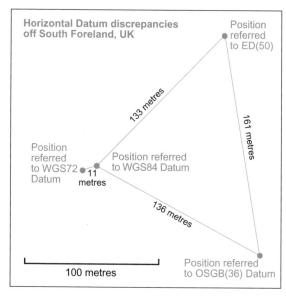

Fig. 8(2) Effect of using different Horizontal Datums in the Dover Strait.

applicable in Egypt, although both countries use the same Datum.

In practical terms, failure to use the correct horizontal Datum could result in significant errors which would nullify the accuracy of PPS and could even put you on the rocks if navigating in very narrow waters. For example, in the Dover Strait the difference between ED 50 and WGS 84 would amount to 133m, and to 136m between OSGB 36 and WGS 84; see Fig. 8(2).

The differences are not constant and vary irregularly for every location, the largest so far found being 7M in the Pacific. The importance of setting a GPS receiver to the local chart datum is obvious in the light of GPS PPS accuracy of around 10-15m.

In June 2000, therefore, the UKHO began changing Admiralty charts of the UK from OSGB 36 to ETRS 89 Datum (European Terrestrial Reference Datum) which is the equivalent of WGS 84 for Europe – now referred to as "a WGS 84 compatible datum". The first 310 UK charts will take 3 years to be changed, the remainder including N Ireland, Eire and the Channel Islands will follow in due course. Charts will be re-published as far as possible in geographic groups, for example the approach and entry to a major port, to minimise disruption. The legend "WGS 84 POSITIONS can be plotted directly on this chart" is now printed in magenta at top and bottom of the new charts, plus other notes.

Positions quoted in Notices to Mariners will be referenced to the Datum of the latest edition of the chart concerned, ie not necessarily WGS 84 compatible.

Small craft charts and Folios will be converted to a WGS 84 compatible datum at some unspecified period after their standard chart equivalents. In the interim the yacht navigator can either rely on his GPS receiver to convert positions from WGS 84 to OSGB 36 or ED 50, as appropriate, or he can manually apply the conversions as shown under "Satellite-derived positions".

Realistically there will be a longer period during which such arrangements continue, simply because individuals may not find it affordable or economic to replace all their charts in one fell swoop.

8.2.5   DIFFERENTIAL GPS (DGPS)

DGPS represents a means of enhancing the accuracy of GPS, either SPS with SA super-imposed, or PPS. Even the highly accurate PPS service may not be accurate enough to meet the stringent demands of navigating large vessels within certain harbours and approaches. DGPS may not appeal to all yachtsmen, especially now that SA has been removed and the PPS is freely available to all users. But since the DGPS service is free and suitable receivers are already available for around £600, they may become more popular in due course.

Suitably located DGPS reference stations detect any errors by comparing actual GPS signals with the signals predicted for the specified reference point, and then provide corrections. These corrections are transmitted to specially equipped users navigating in the local area over MF frequencies formerly used by marine RDF beacons. See Fig. 8(3).

On board the user ship a radio receiver able to receive the MF frequencies and equipped with a demodulator appropriate to the DGPS corrections, is linked to the GPS receiver and automatically applies the transmitted corrections to the navigation data. DGPS can provide navigational accuracy of better than 10 metres.

Integrity monitoring stations in a number of countries indicate whether the DGPS reference stations are healthy, unhealthy or simply unmonitored.

8.2.6   GLONASS

GLONASS (*Global'naya Navigatsionnaya Sputnikova Sistema* or GLObal NAvigation Satellite System in short) is the Russian equivalent of GPS. The first satellites were launched in 1982 by the Soviet Union and the system was declared fully operational in 1996; but the satellites have proved unreliable – only 11 out of 24 are currently operational. More satellites were due for launch in 2001.

The principles are the same as for GPS, but some of the parameters differ: For example 24 (same number) satellites are at an altitude of 10,300M in 3 orbital planes inclined to the equator at an angle of 64·8°. This inclination and the 3 planes significantly favour coverage at high (polar) latitudes whilst GPS favours mid-latitudes. The accuracy of both systems is about the same (15 – 20m), provided SA is not activated. A few more detailed technicalities are given in ALRS Vol 8, or contact:
CSIC of Russian Space Forces, PO Box 14, Moscow 117279. Tel/Fax +7 095 333 8133.
E-mail   sfcsic@mx.iki.rssi.ru
Web   www.rssi.ru/SFCSIC/SFCSIC_main.html

8.2.7   GNSS

A receiver able to operate with GPS and GLONASS would therefore obtain the best of both worlds, whilst the extra available satellites would improve geometry, acquisition times and coverage. The combined system, known as Global Navigation Satellite System (GNSS) exists in a basic form. Several commercial companies now make receivers capable of receiving and processing signals from 14 (or more) navigational satellites, ie GPS or GLONASS, individually or in combination. Coordinates could be expressed in US or Russian Horizontal Datums.

Problems encountered relate to Time differences and the use of different Horizontal Datums. GPS time is based on UTC, as defined by the USN Observatory, while GLONASS uses UTC (Soviet Union). UTC (SU) differs from UTC by about 7 seconds; UTC (USNO) differs from UTC by a mere 20ns (nanoseconds). The Russian authorities may start to bring GLONASS time closer to UTC.

GPS uses an ellipsoid based on the WGS 84 coordinate frame. GLONASS uses a PZ 90 frame, also referred to as Soviet Geocentric Co-ordinate System 1990 (SGS90). The difference between coordinates of positions referenced to WGS 84 or SGS90 is less than 15m with a mean of 5m. This relationship must be very precisely defined if dual operation is to be effective.

Future developments, in the quest for dual operation, involve the overlaying of Satellite Based Augmentation Systems (SBAS) onto basic GNSS. SBAS will use a suite of geostationary satellites giving greater accuracy, availability, integrity and continuity. Its development is driven by aeronautical requirements. It will have three major components: EGNOS (European Geostationary Navigation Overlay System); WAAS (the American Wide Area Augmentation System); and MSAS (the Japanese Multi-functional Transport Satellite). Successful overlaying of SBAS

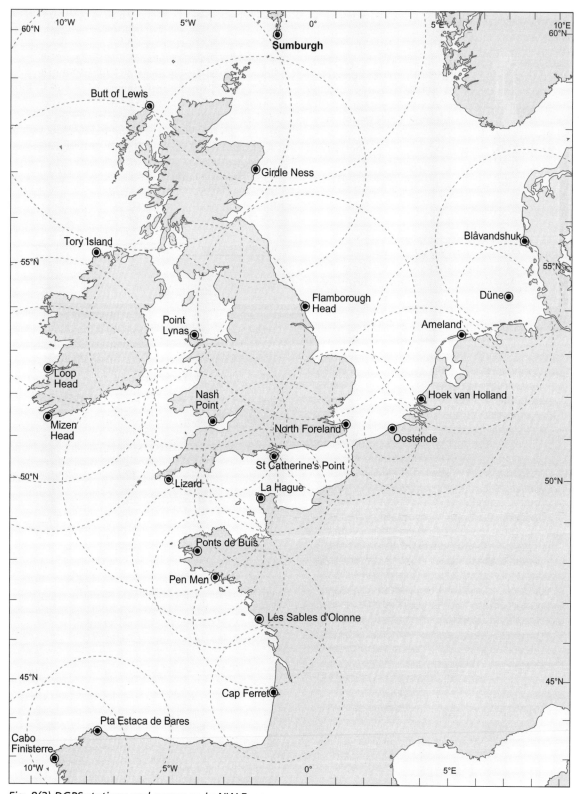

Fig. 8(3) DGPS stations and coverage in NW Europe.

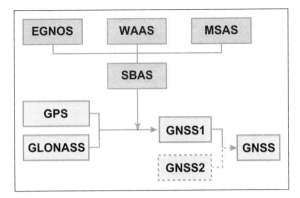

Fig. 8(4) The development of GNSS.

will lead to GNSS 1. If combined with GNSS 2, which is still at the discussion stage, the final result will be simply GNSS in its ultimate form. Fig. 8(4) illustrates the building blocks outlined above.

8.2.8 GALILEO

Galileo is a civilian project, within Europe, to launch a satellite fixing system which is wholly independent of the American, military sponsored and funded GPS. In effect Galileo would be a third generation GPS for the early 21st century.

As mentioned in 8.2.7, GPS needs to be augmented so as to overcome its shortcomings. These include the fact that it has no 'safety of life' or performance guarantees; it does not carry out self-checking to the level which non-military equipment might. The building blocks above are part of the augmentation process; EGNOS is the European contribution. The ultimate goal is GNSS 2 which is where Galileo would play a part.

Galileo is directed by the EU in conjunction with the European Space Agency. 30 satellites are planned in medium earth orbit at about 12,400M above earth. Trial satellites are due for launch in 2004 and operational status is supposedly 2008. In December 2000, at the end of project definition, a decision to give Galileo a clear go-ahead was postponed. Definition comprised four main projects:

a. GALA, the overall system led by a French company;
b. GalileoSat (space and earth segments) led by Italy;
c. Geminus (services) led by Racal UK; and
d. Integration of EGNOS into Galileo, led by Italy.

Keep watching this space ..... There are all the signs of over-complex management structures, funding difficulties, a lack of political conviction and compatibility problems with GPS.

8.3 HYPERBOLIC FIXING

8.3.1 HYPERBOLIC THEORY

The theory of hyperbolic position lines is briefly as follows. A hyperbola is a curved line joining a series of points whose distances from two fixed points always differ by a constant amount. Loran's operating principle depends on measuring the difference in time taken by radio waves travelling from two fixed stations on shore to reach a vessel at sea. (Decca, now obsolete, measured the phase difference between continuous-wave signals from two fixed stations). Because the speed of radio waves is constant, the actual difference in range from the two fixed stations can be derived from the time difference; hence the appropriate hyperbola which forms a position line – see Fig. 8(5). A similar measurement from another pair of fixed stations gives a second position line, and hence a fix. Since a hyperbola consists of two parts which are symmetrical about the axis of the fixed stations, the system is designed to be able to determine which half forms the position line.

In practice, two to four fixed slave stations are set up around a master station to form a 'chain'. The two pairs giving the best cut can be selected for a fix.

Most hyperbolic receivers give a convenient

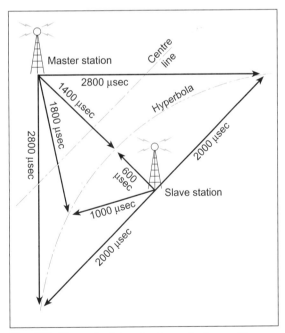

Fig. 8(5) The principle of a hyperbolic position line. At any point on the curved line (hyperbola) the time difference between receiving synchronised signals from the master station and slave station is 800 µsec.

direct read-out of latitude and longitude. Earlier systems displayed figures which corresponded to lines on a latticed chart, from which the position was derived; this gives the most accurate results.

8.3.2 LORAN-C

Loran-C is a LOng RANge hyperbolic fixing system. It is suitable for coastal, landfall and offshore navigation within coverage. The original Standard Loran system, later known as Loran-A, was invented in the USA during the early 1940s. By the end of World War II, some 70 transmitting stations were in operation, but only a few chains off China now remain. The improved version, Loran C, first became operational in 1957.

There are 24 Loran-C chains in operation (2001), all in the northern hemisphere. Coverage is of the US eastern seaboard, the northern rim of the Pacific from Mexico to Singapore, NE and NW India, Persian Gulf and Red Sea.

A typical Loran chain consists of three to five transmitting stations spaced several hundred miles apart. One of the stations is designated as the master station (M). The other slave stations are identified as W, X, Y and Z, as appropriate. These identification letters are used on lattice charts and in publications. The stations are geometrically located so that signals from the master and at least two slaves can be received throughout the required area of coverage. Loran-C uses pulsed transmissions at low frequency (100kHz).

The stations transmit as sequenced pairs: master and slave W; master and X; and so on, depending on the number of slaves in the chain. Precise time is the very essence of Loran, so each transmitter is accurately controlled by caesium clocks. Each station transmits groups of pulses at a specified interval, called the group repetition interval (GRI). Slaves transmit in a predetermined sequence after a fixed time delay. This delay between a master and slave is known as the coding delay and is different for each station. Coding delays are so arranged that no matter where a vessel is within the coverage area, she will always receive the signals in the same order.

The Loran receiver accurately measures the time difference (TD) in arrival of the pulse signals sent out from the master and slave stations. These measurements are made first by matching the pulse envelopes (coarse difference) and then by matching the phase of the 100 kHz carrier within the envelope (fine difference). TDs are measured in micro-seconds (millionths of a second) and these readings, as shown on older receiver displays, can then be transferred to a Loran lattice chart overprinted with hyperbolic curves for the stations concerned. Selecting the correct hyperbola, or interpolating as required, gives a position line. The procedure is repeated with a different slave station to get a fix.

Modern Loran-C receivers automatically convert the TDs and display position as latitude and longitude. If the highest accuracy is required always use corrected time differences and plot on a lattice chart. Loran-C sets also display position continuously, accept waypoints and compute bearings and distances, cross-track information, course and speed made good, course to steer, ETAs etc.

Dependent on the power of transmitters and other factors, ground wave reception at ranges of 800 – 1200M is possible, but a more practical figure for normal operational use would be up to 600M from transmitters. Loran-C pulses also propagate as skywaves, the incidence of which varies from day to night and from place to place. Skywaves may be received at ranges up to 2300M, but with much less accuracy.

Accuracy, using groundwaves, varies from about 100m at a range of 200M to about 250m or more at 500M from transmitters.

8.3.3 NELS

The Northwest European Loran-C System (NELS), established by Eire, France, The Netherlands, Germany, Denmark and Norway, became operational in 1995. Nine stations form four chains, as shown below:

1. LESSAY Chain, Rate 6731. Master: Lessay. Slaves: Sylt (Z), Soustons (X) and Loop Head (Y, at a later date).
2. SYLT Chain, Rate 7499. Master: Sylt. Slaves: Lessay (X) and Vaerlandet(Y).
3. EJDE Chain, Rate 9007. Master: Ejde. Slaves: Jan Mayen (W), Bø (X), Vaerlandet (Y) and Loop Head (Z, at a later date).
4. BØ Chain, Rate 7001. Master: Bø. Slaves: Jan Mayen (X) and Berlevåg (Y).

Fig. 8(6) shows the predicted coverage of NELS. The provisional Control Centre is at Bø, Norway until the permanent Centre at Brest is completed. Further information can be obtained from: Norwegian Defence Communications and Data Services, Oslo mil/Akershus, N-0015 Oslo. Tel: +47 23 09 24 76; Fax +47 23 09 23 91.

Data on the accuracy and coverage of Loran-C is given in publications issued by the US Hydrographic office, including Publication No. 221, but only for certain North American chains.

Chayka is the Russian equivalent of Loran-C.

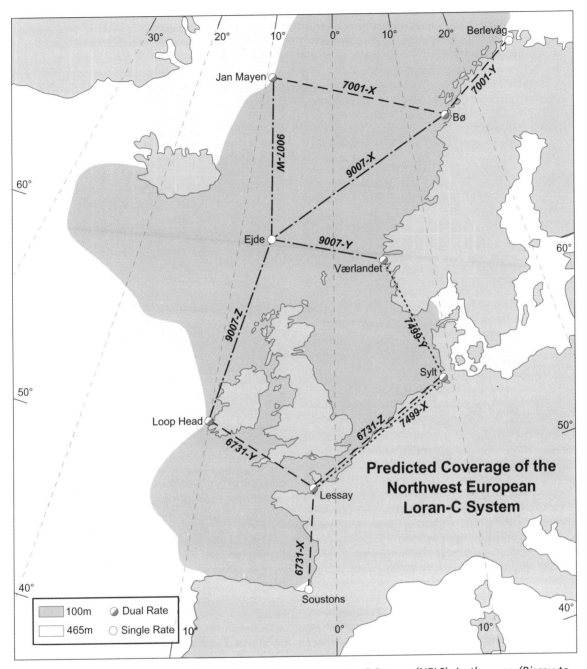

Fig. 8(6) Predicted coverage of the Northwest European Loran-C System (NELS). In the area (Biscay to Iceland to Spitsbergen and North Cape) accuracy is predicted to be about 100m. Outside this area, as shown, accuracy is about 465m.

8.3.4 EUROFIX

Eurofix is a navigational system which combines Loran-C and DGPS. To do this it sends differential satellite corrections to users as time modulated signal information on the Loran-C signal, without interfering with Loran-C's normal navigational functions. It allows both DGPS and Loran-C to be used in parallel, or in isolation if one fails, and to be compared for best results.

Following successful Eurofix test transmissions from the Loran-C station at Sylt, Eurofix is being implemented at Lessay, Vaerlandet and Bø. Eurofix coverage is estimated to be 1000km from each Loran-C transmitter with an absolute accuracy of 5 metres and 99·99% availability per month. There is potential for further expansion in Europe and into the Mediterranean, using Chayka (8.3.3).

For further information contact NELS Co-ordinating Office at the Norwegian address/tel/fax given in 8.3.3.

8.4 ELECTRONIC NAVIGATION TECHNIQUES

The most important principle in any form of navigation is always to cross-check any piece of information by another means before relying on it. Sensibly used, modern electronic fixing aids can greatly assist navigators, whilst cross-checking them against traditional techniques or other instrumentation. A suspicious mind and a refusal to make assumptions are other great assets.

8.4.1 PREREQUISITES

An adequate power supply, battery voltage and capacity is vital to satisfactory performance. Arrange a fused 12V (or 24V) supply to prevent damage to the receiver caused by voltage surges. Ensure that the boat's electrical supply is 'clean' and that no undue electrical noise is present.

Logs and compasses play an important role with any receiver or DR computer requiring an input of speed or heading. Before such data is used for navigation, either via an automatic interface or manually for dead reckoning, the log and compass should be accurately calibrated. The best results are always obtained if electronic equipment is automatically interfaced with log and compass. Such a combination provides a more accurate DR plot and takes account of steering errors.

8.4.2 WAYPOINTS

A waypoint is a specified position, for example a place of departure, a selected point along the planned route (perhaps where a course alteration is intended), or your destination. Before starting a passage, waypoints are entered as latitude and longitude, or perhaps as bearing and distance from a position or from another waypoint. Most receivers have enough memory for a library of several hundred waypoints, with waypoint names added – this makes the entry of waypoints more reliable. From this library waypoints are selected to form a Route, ie the legs (tracks and distances) which you plan to follow. You can then select a wide range of navigational information, such as position, course and speed made good, bearing and

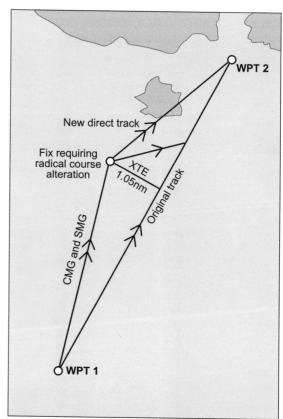

Fig. 8(7) Waypoint navigation does not eliminate the need for conventional plotting techniques. Maximum cross-track error should be related to dangers on the chart, eg an island. Here a substantial alteration of course is needed to regain the original track.

distance to the next waypoint (either by great circle or rhumb line), cross-track error, time to go, estimated time of arrival (ETA) and Man Overboard position.

Waypoints lie at the heart of electronic navigation. An error in the entry of waypoint coordinates will cause a navigational error if undetected. You should develop a procedure (a-e below) to eliminate human error, as far as possible, when inserting waypoints into receivers. Work without interruption and be highly self-critical, always ready to believe that you are capable of making an error.

As formats vary between receivers, you should learn the format used to key in data and where to position any decimal points. Wrongly placed decimal points can cause sizeable errors in bearing and distance. Check whether E or W longitude is the default setting of your receiver. If necessary, key in the appropriate hemisphere.

The simple precautions below can help to avoid errors being made when inserting waypoints:

a. Lay off tracks and distances on the chart, check they are safe and record waypoints on a route plan, 8.4.3.
b. Check that the coordinates of waypoints as taken off the chart are correct. If using published waypoints, plot them on the chart to confirm that they are accurate.
c. Verify that waypoints have been correctly entered.
d. Get someone else to check your work if possible.
e. Build the waypoints into a route. Compare the tracks and distances computed by the receiver with those in (a); investigate any discrepancies.

8.4.3   THE ELECTRONIC ROUTE

A simple table of the intended route serves two purposes: (a) it is a record of the data which you will key in; and (b) it allows a cross-check of any errors. Such a table is given in Chapter 7, Fig. 7(40) along with other navigational check lists. It should include:

1. Waypoint Number and name, in sequence.
2. Charted position in latitude/longitude.
3. Track & distance to next waypoint, from the chart. This should be compared with the Track & Distance as calculated by your GPS receiver within the Route Plan.
   Additional data might include:
4. Maximum XTE (maximum distance allowable to left or right of intended track, to keep clear of dangers).
5. DR time for that leg, at estimated speed. With any receiver it is advisable to catalogue and record frequently-used waypoint data. Most receivers will automatically list their waypoint library in alphabetical order. An indexed address book can be used to record in geographical sequence the coordinates for anchorages, buoys, harbours or turning points. Subsequently, as these places are visited, record their actual coordinates so as to take advantage of the high repeatability, which enables a vessel to return again and again to the same position on the basis of previous readings.

8.4.4   DISPLAYS

A major advantage of waypoint navigation is that (as well as current position) the computer continuously displays ever-changing navigational data such as distance to go, cross-track error, course and speed made good.

Once the required waypoints have been entered, it is a simple matter to call up a display of continuously updated range and bearing as the vessel approaches the selected waypoint, as illustrated in Fig. 8(7).

The range and bearing between WPT 1 and WPT 2 defines the track required. If the vessel remains on track, the bearing does not change; if she goes off-track, then the bearing will increase or decrease.

The most useful parameter to indicate deviation from a required track is cross-track error (XTE). XTE is the distance that the vessel is to left or right of the intended track. This is valuable information in its own right, but even more so if, whilst planning, the navigator defines the maximum off-track distance that can be accepted, based on the proximity of potential navigational dangers; see 8.4.3 (4). If XTE is indicated, but no navigational danger lies between the present position and the destination waypoint, the boat can sail direct to the destination. But if some danger is present, as shown in Fig. 8(7), it may be necessary to regain the original track as soon as possible. The golden rule is that, if off-track, always check the track from the present position to destination for proximity to dangers.

On a longer passage, when allowing for the effect of tidal stream, the vessel will invariably be to one or other side of track and, if no dangers exist, it is pointless trying to keep rigidly to the required track.

You should check regularly that read-outs of Course Made Good (CMG), Speed Made Good (SMG) and Velocity Made Good (VMG) tie in with the track required to reach the next waypoint.

Finally, check whether bearings are true or magnetic. Most sets prompt you to insert magnetic variation. Be aware that a bearing and distance to a waypoint is not a course to steer. Some sets can accept a tidal stream input and give a course to steer, but most do not, so the effects of set, drift and leeway will have to be applied manually in the normal way.

8.4.5   USING A COMPUTER ON BOARD

Although many people go sailing to 'get away' from them, personal computers (PCs) are increasingly useful afloat. In addition to its everyday shore-based uses, an onboard PC can help the yachtsman with navigation, provide communication facilities, give access to weather information and calculate tidal data. The range of software available for marine use is growing and, with the increasing power of computers, programmes are becoming easier to use and offer a wider range of features. Advice about using a PC for specific tasks is contained in Chapters 7 (Navigation), 9 (Astro), 10 (Communications), 11 (Weather) and 12 (Tides). General advice on using a computer afloat is given here.

Only the largest yachts will carry a built-in, full size desktop machine. Most will make do with the laptop or notebook PC that is used mainly for non-yachting applications ashore. Whatever computer is used the more powerful it is the better. At a minimum it should have CD and floppy disc drives, at least 250MB of free hard disc space and 32MB of RAM, although 64MB or more will enable programmes to run more efficiently. The faster the processor the better, but the performance of a slow machine can be greatly enhanced by increasing the RAM. Windows 95, or a more recent version of Windows, will be required. If it is to be connected to a GPS or radio receiver the PC must have a serial port – many modern notebook computers have only USB ports and at present most programmes do not support these, although an adapter can be obtained.

Some method of recharging the computer battery is needed. If only short passages are to be made, then this could be done at home or when connected to shore power. In these circumstances a spare battery will be more than a luxury. A small inverter to convert the yacht's 12 volt supply to mains voltage is cheap and much more convenient and will permit unlimited use of the PC at sea. For most notebook computers an inverter of 150-watt capacity should be adequate.

PCs and water do not mix and it is vital that an onboard computer is protected from the elements. Soft computer cases are available from many office equipment suppliers and will protect the PC and its peripherals when in transit to and from the yacht, but most are barely even splashproof. Truly waterproof bags, which should provide protection even if the computer is dropped in the water, are available from chandlers. They are similar to those produced for handheld radios but they do not fit all laptop PCs. An alternative DIY cover can be made from a single piece of PVC backed material folded over the computer and stitched at the sides – rather like a large envelope. The seams should be coated with neoprene rubber solution to seal the stitch holes. If a generous flap is provided, folded over and secured with Velcro, such a case will protect the computer from most accidents. A secure, dry

stowage must be found for the PC, which should be kept in its cover or bag when not in use.

When in use on board the computer must be situated so that there is no chance of it either coming adrift or of being exposed to splashing or spray. If used for 'real time' navigation or communications then care must be taken that drips from wet foul weather gear or hands do not get onto the machine. A simple way of doing this is to protect the keyboard with a sheet of cling film wrapped loosely around the body of the open PC, leaving only the screen exposed. Keys can be operated easily through the film. A conventional mouse (plugged into the back of the computer) should be used rather than a touchpad or other built in tracking device. The mouse can also be protected from wet hands with a sheet of cling film laid loosely over it.

Finally, if space can be found for one, a small colour printer will be useful. These are now very cheap and compact. It is often easier to read weather fax pictures or complex forecasts on paper than it is from the screen. If electronic charts are used, sections covering intricate pilotage can be printed for use in the cockpit.

8.5 RADAR

8.5.1 INTRODUCTION
The size, price, and power consumption of small-boat radars have fallen dramatically over recent years, so radar is now a practical proposition for almost any boat more than about 8m in length, so long as it has a 12v power supply.

Despite the fact that it depends on electrical power, radar has a lot in common with traditional navigation aids. In particular, you need some background knowledge if you are to get the best performance out of the equipment, and it takes some skill and experience to make best use of the information it can provide.

There are good reasons why the International Regulations for the Prevention of Collisions, Rule 7 (b) and (c), insist that *"Proper use shall be made of radar equipment if fitted and operational"* but go on to say that *"Assumptions shall not be made on the basis of scanty information, especially scanty radar information."*

8.5.2 HOW RADAR MEASURES RANGE
The principle of radar is like that of an echo sounder; it transmits a short pulse of energy, which is reflected by solid objects so that some of the energy is returned as an echo. Knowing the speed at which the pulse has travelled and the

time it has taken, it is possible to work out the distance it has covered.

In practice, radar uses super high frequency radio waves, often called microwaves. Most marine radars are known as "X-band" or "three centimetre" radars because they operate at a frequency of about 9400MHz and a wavelength of about 3·2cm. Some commercial vessels also use S-band or "ten centimetre" radar operating at about 3000MHz.

Microwaves travel at 161,860M per second. This means that radar pulses have to be very short, and the timing very precise. For example, the echo from an object 8M away will return only 100 microseconds (0.0001 second) after the pulse was transmitted.

8.5.3   HOW RADAR MEASURES BEARING

A radar aerial is highly directional; it focuses the microwaves into a fairly well-defined beam, and rotates to sweep the beam around the horizon.

In principle, radar pulses should only be reflected from targets that are within the radar beam. This means that if an echo is received, the target that produced it must lie in the direction the antenna is pointing.

In practice, this isn't quite true, no radar aerial is perfectly directional, and radar pulses can sometimes ricochet off large structures such as cliffs, harbour walls, and large ships to produce misleading echoes. Most of these false echoes, however, are short-lived or intermittent.

8.5.4   THE MAIN PARTS OF A RADAR

The **transmitter** consists of a special type of radio valve called a magnetron. It produces a stream of very short but powerful pulses of microwave energy; see Fig. 8(8).

The **antenna** (also known as an aerial, scanner, or radiator) is designed to radiate microwaves in a narrow beam. Some radars use a parabolic reflector, rather like the reflector of a car headlamp; some use a "slotted waveguide" system, in which the microwaves are transmitted from accurately-machined slots in a rectangular metal pipe called a waveguide. Increasingly, small boat radars use a "patch array", in which the antenna is a made up of lots of little copper pads, each acting rather like one of the slots in a slotted waveguide.

Whichever type is used, the width of the beam depends on the size of the antenna. The larger the antenna, the narrower the beam.

The antenna also captures the returning echoes, and passes them to the receiver.

The **receiver** amplifies the returning echoes. It is difficult to process microwave frequencies, so in

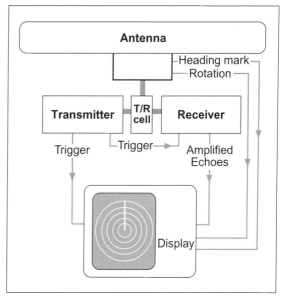

Fig. 8(8) Block diagram showing information flow.

practice the first stage of the receiver reduces the frequency of the returning echoes to a more manageable intermediate frequency.

To stop the powerful transmissions of the magnetron from wrecking the sensitive receiver, the two are isolated from each other by the **Transmit/Receive cell** (T/R cell).

The bearing and time/distance information from the scanner unit is passed to the **display**, where it is used to build up a map-like picture known as a Plan Position Indicator (PPI).

Until the 1980's, most radars had **radial scan displays**, using relatively simple technology to produce a picture that was generally of good quality, but was so dim that it could not be seen in daylight. All modern radars, however use a combination of computer and TV technology to produce a "**raster scan**" picture that is visible in daylight.

More recently still, raster scan techniques are used in radars with liquid crystal displays, which are cheaper, slimmer, and use less power than conventional "TV-type" screens.

8.5.5   BEAMWIDTH AND DISCRIMINATION

No radar can produce a sharply-defined parallel-sided beam. In real life, the sides of the beam flare outwards, and some energy spills out from the sides and back of the antenna to form sidelobes.

The angle through which the intensity of the beam is at least half of its maximum is known as its **beamwidth**. The beamwidth depends primarily on the size of the antenna, roughly following the rule that:

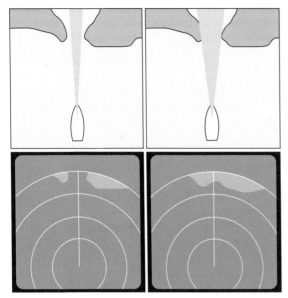

Fig. 8(9) Radar discrimination: on the left a 3° beam; on the right a 7° beamwidth is unable to distinguish the entrance, until much closer.

Beamwidth = 70 x wavelength ÷ antenna width.

For a typical small boat radar with a 60cm antenna, this works out to about 4°.

Beamwidth is important, primarily because it affects the radar's ability to discriminate between two objects that are close together.

Suppose, for example, you are approaching a harbour, whose entrance appears to be 5° wide; see Fig. 8(9).

A radar with a beamwidth of 3° would detect the land on the left hand side of the entrance. Then, as the antenna rotated, the beam would pass straight through the entrance without producing an echo, so the display would show a gap. Then, as the beam moves on further, it would detect the land to the right of the entrance.

A 7° beam would be too wide to pass through the entrance without being reflected from one side or the other, so a radar with a 7° beamwidth would not pick up the entrance until it is considerably closer.

The **vertical beamwidth** of most radars is in the order of 25–30°, considerably bigger than their horizontal beamwidth. This is to ensure that at least some of the main beam is directed horizontally even when the vessel rolls.

8.5.6 PULSE LENGTH AND PRF

The radar has to finish transmitting a pulse before it can receive any echoes. That means the pulses have to be very short, usually less than 1 microsecond (1 millionth of a second). In practice, for short range operation, radars often use pulses that are very much shorter still.

"Long" pulses (about 1 microsecond) are good for long range or small targets because each pulse contains more energy.

"Short" pulses (about 0.1 microsecond) are good for short ranges because they allow the radar to start listening for echoes sooner and because they give good range discrimination.

Range discrimination refers to the radar's ability to distinguish between objects that are at slightly different ranges.

If the radar is using a long pulse, its discrimination suffers because the leading edge of the echo from the second object may return before the radar has finished receiving the echo from the first object. The two echoes merge together, producing a single contact on the screen instead of two.

The designers of a radar have to be absolutely certain that all the echoes from one pulse will have been received before the radar transmits the next pulse. To do this, the pulses are widely separated.

"Short" pulses are typically about 500 microseconds apart. There are about 2000 of them per second, so they are described as having a pulse repetition frequency (PRF) of 2000Hz.

"Long" pulses are typically about 2000 microseconds apart: their PRF is about 500Hz.

8.5.7 SWITCHING ON AND SETTING UP

Radar controls vary widely between different makes and models, as advancing technology allows some controls to be automated, and market forces have driven manufacturers to add extra features whilst reducing the number of visible controls.

Nevertheless, most radars have only six or seven main controls:

On/Off: turns the power on, and warms up the magnetron, but does not transmit.

Transmit/Standby: switches the transmitter and receiver on, or into a "standby" mode, in which it is ready for immediate use.

Brilliance: controls the brightness of the screen image, but does not affect its content – like the brightness control on a TV. Adjust it to produce a clear but not dazzling picture.

Contrast: found only on LCD radars, contrast regulates the appearance of the picture. It may need to be adjusted to suit changing lighting or viewing angles.

Gain: regulates the sensitivity of the receiver. It should be turned up until the picture is full of speckles, then down until most of the speckles have just disappeared. Setting the gain too low will reduce the chance of detecting small targets or poor reflectors.

Range: adjusts the scale of the picture. A 12-mile range, for instance, means that the outer edge of the picture is 12 miles from its centre. The range control also affects the pulse length and PRF.

Tuning: adjusts the receiver to allow for slight changes in the transmitted frequency, usually caused by temperature changes. Adjust it by looking for a weak contact near the edge of the screen. Concentrate on that contact while adjusting the tuning so as to make the contact as strong, bright, and consistent as possible. Allow 3 seconds between each adjustment, to allow the radar to update its picture!

The controls should usually be adjusted in this order. It's easy to remember because once the set has been switched on and is transmitting, the other controls follow in alphabetical order.

8.5.8   OTHER CONTROLS
Numerous other controls may be used to improve the picture or to operate special functions.

Echo Stretch (ES) or expansion: artificially enlarges contacts in range to make them more conspicuous.

HM delete: a bright line called the Heading Mark extends from the centre of the display to indicate your own vessel's heading. It can be temporarily deleted by pressing the HM delete button.

Interference Rejection (IR): removes the mass of speckles, mainly caused by transmissions from other radars, that can sometimes clutter the radar picture. It is often said that use of the IR facility will hide racons, but this was only true of certain types of racons that are now obsolete.

Rain clutter (anti clutter rain, or FTC): used to remove clutter caused by echoes from rain and clouds. It should be used with caution, because it can weaken other contacts, especially those from low-lying coastlines.

Rings: a pattern of concentric range rings is usually provided to help estimate ranges: they can be deleted or restored by using the rings control.

Sea clutter (anti clutter sea, or STC): used to remove the dense clutter around the centre of the picture, caused by echoes from the sea surface. It should be used with extreme caution, as it can wipe out any contact within its radius of operation.

8.5.9   MEASURING RANGE AND BEARING
The **Variable Range Marker** (VRM) is a range ring whose radius can be varied to measure the range of a target. Expand the VRM until it just touches the closest part of the contact; the range to the target is then shown in a data box on the screen.

The **Electronic Bearing Line** (EBL) is a line which can be swept around the screen. Its bearing is shown in a data box on the radar screen. The EBL can be used as an electronic substitute for a hand-bearing compass, but it is important to be aware of the fact that radar bearings are generally much less accurate than radar ranges.

Unless the radar is connected to a compass, any bearing shown will be relative to your boat's heading. To convert relative bearings to compass bearings, add the heading, for example:

134° (R)	Relative Bearing
080° (C)	Heading by compass
214° (C)	Compass Bearing

Note that if the result is greater than 360°, you will have to subtract 360° to reduce it to a meaningful number; and that you may still need to allow for variation and deviation.

8.5.10   HEADING MODES
On most small-boat radars, the standard picture represents your own vessel at the centre of the screen, heading straight upwards.

This **head-up mode** is good because targets on the port side of your vessel produce contacts on the left side of the screen, and so on. Unfortunately, if you are trying to relate the radar picture to a chart it can be difficult. A more fundamental problem is that as the boat yaws, the whole picture rotates around the centre.

North-up mode requires heading data from a compass. In North-up mode, the radar picture is rotated to put North at the top. This stabilises the picture, and makes it easy to relate the radar picture to a chart.

Course-up mode also requires heading data from a compass. In course-up mode, the radar picture is turned round to put the boat's course at the top. The result looks very similar to head-up mode, except that it is stabilised; as the boat yaws only the heading marker swings from side to side.

Course-up is good for collision avoidance, but it is important to remember to re-set the radar when you make a deliberate alteration of course.

8.5.11 WHAT RADAR CAN "SEE"
Five factors decide whether an object will show up well, or not.

Material: Some materials absorb microwaves; others are transparent to them. Others absorb microwaves but immediately re-radiate them; these are "good reflectors". In general, materials such as steel, or salt water, which conduct electricity, are good reflectors. Non-conductors such as wood and plastic are poor reflectors.

Size: By the time the radar pulse has travelled a mile or so from the radar, it occupies quite a large volume; at one mile for instance, it may be 300m x 100m x 500m – and still growing! A small object will only be struck by part of the pulse, so it can only reflect a small proportion of the energy. A large object can reflect considerably more.

Orientation: A flat, surface at right angles to the radar beam reflects radar waves straight back. If the surface is not at right angles, the echo won't bounce back the way it came, so it won't reach the antenna and won't be detected.

Shape: Flat surfaces are usually good reflectors, but only if they are at precisely the right orientation. Other shapes behave differently: a sphere, for instance, always presents a tiny part of its surface at right angles to any approaching radar beam, so it is a weak but reliable reflector.

Texture: In general terms, a "rough" surface is a more reliable reflector than a "smooth" one because it is less prone to the effects of orientation. "Rough", in this context, means having surface imperfections measurable in centimetres.

8.5.12 WHAT RADAR CANNOT SEE
A target can only produce an echo if it is struck by at least part of the radar pulse. An obstruction such as a headland can hide targets from the radar just as effectively as it can hide them from the naked eye.

Radar cannot see round corners!
In general, a radar antenna should be mounted clear of all obstructions. Obstructions that are considerably smaller than the scanner (such as a yacht's mast) will weaken the radar's transmissions in the affected area, but the effect is usually slight. Large obstructions (such as funnels or superstructures) may produce significant blind arcs.

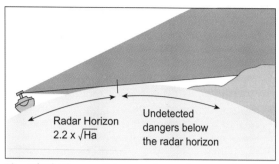

Fig. 8(10) The earth's curvature obscures the low-lying coast, whilst inland hills can be 'seen'.

The biggest obstruction of all is the earth itself. Radar's "view" is limited by a horizon, just as our own eyesight is; see Fig. 8(10) which includes the formula for calculating the distance of the radar horizon.

The radar horizon is slightly further away than our visual horizon, so the distance at which a radar will "see" a good reflector can be found by adding about 5% to the figure extracted from the dipping distance tables in the MRNA.

Alternatively, use the formula:

$$Range = 2{\cdot}2 \left(\sqrt{H_a} + \sqrt{H_t} \right)$$

where Range is in nautical miles; H_a is the antenna's height and H_t is the target's height, both in metres. This gives the distance at which the target will be 'seen' above the radar horizon. For example, with an antenna height of 9m and a 50m high cliff as target: R = 2·2(3 + 7) = 22M.

8.5.13 RADAR REFLECTORS
Wood and plastic are poor reflectors, so most small craft do not show up well on ships' radars, particularly when they are surrounded by waves of highly reflective salt water!

To overcome this problem, there have been many attempts to produce radar reflectors which combine the reflective efficiency of a flat metal plate with the all-round reliability of a sphere.

Unfortunately, such devices can never be big enough to capture and reflect more than a minute proportion of the energy contained in a radar pulse.

Official advice is that radar reflectors should be used by small craft. Some research, however, shows that their effect is limited and that in some cases they are even counter-productive. If you choose to use a radar reflector, make sure it is fitted correctly and the right way up, and remember that it offers no guarantee that you will be seen.

8.5.14 RADAR TRANSPONDERS
Unlike passive reflectors, transponders transmit their own signals on radar frequencies whenever

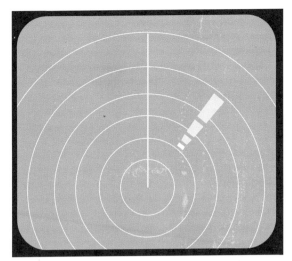

Fig. 8(11) A Racon 'flash', in this case broken up to indicate 'U' (··—), as often shown by an oil/gas rig.

they receive pulses from a radar. There are three main types:

Radar target enhancer (RTE): instantaneously transmits an exact copy of any radar pulse it receives, to produce a strong and consistent contact on the radar screen.

Search and Rescue Transponder (SART): intended solely to mark the position of a vessel in distress. Its signal is a string of twelve pulses, which appear as a row of blobs on the radar screen.

Racons: used only on major buoys or navigation marks. When triggered by a radar pulse, a Racon responds with a much longer

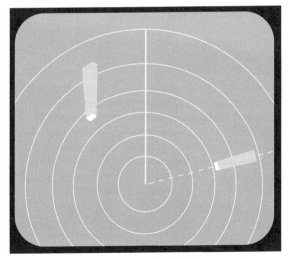

Fig. 8(12) The contact on the left is not a threat, as shown by its wake. The one on the right is a collision risk.

pulse which shows up as a distinctive streak about 2-3 miles long on the radar screen. The signal may appear in sections, to represent a morse identification; see Fig. 8(11).

A Racon signal is always intermittent, typically visible for about ten seconds every 1-2 minutes.

8.5.15 ASSESSING THE RISK OF COLLISION
The standard test for whether a risk of collision exists is in Rule 7d(i) of the Collision Regulations: *"risk shall be deemed to exist if the compass bearing of an approaching vessel does not appreciably change"*.

On radar, the same test applies: simply swing the EBL to cut through the centre of an approaching contact. If the contact appears to be sliding along the EBL, then it is on a steady bearing so a collision risk exists; see Fig. 8(12).

It is easy to see why this is true. Our own vessel is at the centre of the screen, at the root of the EBL, so if a contact is making steady progress along the EBL, then eventually – unless one of us does something to change the situation – it will end up joining us at the centre of the screen.

8.5.16 CLOSEST POINT OF APPROACH (CPA)
If the approaching contact is not sliding along the EBL, the risk of collision is less, but the situation could still develop into a near miss. Radar enables us to estimate how near it is likely to be; see Fig. 8(13).

If you plot the position of the contact over a period of time – either by drawing on the radar screen with a grease pencil or a dry-wipe marker, or by transferring the information to a paper plotting sheet – you should see that it moves in a straight line.

By drawing a straight line through the plots representing the contact's past movement, we can predict its future movement, and see how closely it approaches the centre of the screen.

8.5.17 WORKING OUT ANOTHER VESSEL'S COURSE AND SPEED
A contact sliding along the EBL suggests that a vessel is approaching us on a collision course. That does not mean that it is heading straight towards us! Common experience suggests that collision risks usually occur when you are looking at the side of another vessel, rather than its bows.

In other words, **the movement of the contact across the screen does not show the move-ment of the other vessel through the water.**

To work out the other vessel's course and speed, we need to compare it with some

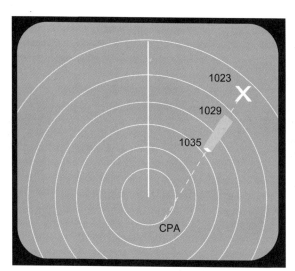

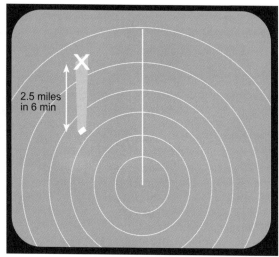

Fig. 8(13) Plotting shows that this contact is not on a collision bearing, but its projected track indicates a CPA of just under 1M (inside the 1st range ring).

Fig. 8(14) A fictitious stationary target appears to move down the screen at our own speed up the screen; in this example at 25kn we have moved 2·5M in 6 minutes.

stationary object. Of course, we can't rely on a suitable stationary object being available when we want it, but we can predict how the contact representing a stationary object would behave; see Fig. 8(14). It would either:

a. move parallel to the heading mark; or
b. move in the opposite direction to the heading mark; and
c. move at the same speed as our own boat speed.

Now, imagine that the approaching vessel dropped a marker at the moment we started observing it. The marker isn't visible on radar, but we can plot its movement on the screen or on a plotting sheet, using these three rules.

After six minutes, the marker and the vessel will be in different positions on the screen. We know that the marker is stationary, because we made it obey the rules applicable to a stationary object; see Fig. 8(15).

The separation between them must, therefore, be due to the movement of the ship.

The direction between the position of the imaginary marker and the vessel is the vessel's course. The distance it has travelled in six minutes is one tenth of the distance it would travel in an hour, so we can find its speed by multiplying the distance it has travelled in six minutes by ten. Thus the other vessel is converging on us at an angle of about 40° and a speed of 18kn (1·8M in 6 minutes).

The 'fiction' of a hypothetical stationary marker has been found to be the easiest way of understanding what is a straightforward Relative Velocity problem. Another approach is to forget

W (the fictitious marker), and draw the pecked velocity vector AX of our own ship up the screen and parallel to the heading marker. Measure OX which represents the course and speed of the other vessel.

The Editor acknowledges with thanks the technical assistance and advice given by Tim Bartlett who revised sections 8.5.1 to 8.5.17.

8.5.18 RADAR BEACONS

The two types of Radar navigational beacon are Racons and Ramarks:

A Racon is a form of transponder which, when triggered by another vessel's radar, paints a distinctive return on the radar display. This

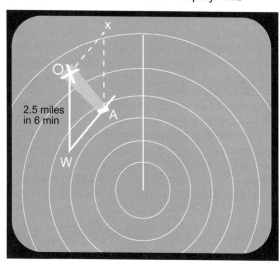

Fig. 8(15) After 6 minutes, the 'marker' is at W and the ship at A. Join W to A, to find the other vessel's course & speed by measurement.

positively identifies the feature concerned and is of real value when navigating on radar. Racons are fitted to many major light-vessels, buoys and lighthouses, and are marked on the chart by a magenta circle and the word Racon.

Most Racons respond to 3cm (X-band, 9300 – 9500 MHz) radar emissions only, but newer Racons also respond to 10cm (S-band, 2900 – 3100 MHz) emissions. Some Racons are called frequency-agile; their response is always within the bandwidth of a yacht's radar, and they may cease to respond for a few seconds every minute to allow echoes otherwise obscured by the Racon signal to be discerned. The response is a Morse identifying signal, typically T (−), M (−−) or O (−−−), the length of the response depending on the number of Morse characters. Racons coded D (−··) are used to mark new dangers, eg wrecks. The response paints on the display as a line extending radially outwards from a point slightly beyond the actual position of the Racon, as shown in Fig. 8(12), due to the slight delay in the response of the transponder. Thus the vessel's actual distance from the Racon is a little less than the distance to the Racon return.

The maximum range of a Racon is typically 10-15M, but varies from 3-35M. In practice, picking up a Racon at greater distances depends also on the power of the boat's radar and the elevation of both the Racon and the radar scanner. A yacht with an X-band radar transmitting 3kW from a scanner at 5m above sea level would expect to pick up the response from a 5m high Racon at 6M. The same Racon would be picked up at 15M by a large ship's radar transmitting at 25kW with a scanner height of 35m. With abnormal radio propagation, a spurious Racon return may be seen at much greater distances than the beacon's nominal range, appearing at random along the correct bearing on the display. Only rely on a Racon return if its appearance is consistent, and the boat is believed to be within its range. At short ranges a Racon may cause unwanted interference on the display; this can be reduced by adjusting the rain clutter control.

The characteristics of Racons around the UK and Europe, are given in the MRNA, including: The name, latitude and longitude, nominal range (M), identifying signal; and the sector, if less than the usual 360°, within which the Racon responds.

A Ramark is a radar beacon which transmits independently, ie without having to be triggered by a ship's radar. It is otherwise similar to a Racon, except that a Ramark's response gives no indication of how far away it is, since it extends from the ship's position in the centre out to the circumference of the display.

8.6 RADIO DIRECTION FINDING (RDF)

RDF is mentioned here briefly because in some countries Marine beacons remain in service. Aeronautical RDF MF beacons are likely to stay in service for some years to come. There are also two forms of shore-based VHF DF which can help to locate a vessel in distress, and are therefore mentioned in 13.6.7.

8.6.1 MARINE RDF BEACONS
For many years this was the only form of radio navigational aid aboard yachts. It enables bearings to be taken of RDF beacons ashore which when plotted will produce a cocked hat of manageable proportions. The RDF MF receiver onboard is battery operated and therefore independent of the yacht's electrical system. RDF requires skilful handling to achieve accuracy, but it is much better than nothing and can usefully up-date the DR plot.

The UK, Ireland, France, Belgium, Netherlands, Germany, Denmark and Portugal withdrew their Marine RDF beacons from service between 1999 and 2001. Some of these beacons now transmit DGPS signals.

In the Mediterranean and Black Seas, Italy, Turkey, Tunisia, Algeria, Egypt, Morocco, some Balkan nations and former USSR Republics retain RDF beacons.

Spain retains marine RDF beacons, but it is not known for how much longer they will continue. Listed below and in ALRS Volume 2 are her Atlantic coast beacons.

North and North-west Spain

Name	Lat/Long	Ident	kHz	M
C. Machichaco	43°27'·45N 2°45'·08W	MA	284·5	100
C. Mayor	43°29'·48N 3°47'·37W	MY	304·5	100
Llanes	43°25'·20N 4°44'·90W	IA	303·5	50
C. Peñas	43°39'·42N 5°50'·80W	PS	297·5	50
Pta Est. de Bares	43°47'·17N 7°41'·07W	BA	309·5	100
Torre de Hércules	43°23'·23N 8°24'·30W	L	301·5	50
C. Villano	43°09'·68N 9°12'·60W	VI	290·5	100
C. Finisterre	42°53'·00N 9°16'·23W	FI	288·5	100
C. Estay (Vigo)	42°11'·19N 8°48'·73W	VS	312·5	50
C. Silleiro	42°06'·33N 8°53'·70W	RO	293·5	100

South-west Spain

Name	Lat/Long	Ident	kHz	M
Rota	36°37'·69N 6°22'·77W	D	303·0	80
C. Trafalgar	36°11'·06N 6°02'·06W	B	297·0	50
Tarifa	36°00'·13N 5°36'·47W	O	299·0	50

8.6.2 AERONAUTICAL RDF BEACONS
Aeronautical beacons range from powerful, long range coastal beacons (usually as a back-up for

VOR beacons) to short range locator beacons associated with an airport's Instrument Landing System (ILS). The long range coastal beacons are of obvious value to mariners; the short range beacons, if located near a coastal airport, may provide some guidance. Aero beacons transmit continuously, using a NON A2A emission mode which requires the BFO to be selected On.

Frequencies etc are no longer listed in ALRS, so users will require access to aeronautical publications such as the UK (or other national) Air Pilot.

8.6.3 EMERGENCY RDF

This service is available on either VHF or MF and is only for use in emergency. Each VHF DF station is remotely controlled by a nearby MRCC/MRSC and is marked on the chart as RG. A ship transmits for a bearing on Ch 16 if in distress; otherwise on Ch 67. The ship's bearing **from** the station is passed on the same channels.

8.7 BOOKS ABOUT MARINE ELECTRONICS

Admiralty List of Radio Signals (UKHO) in 7 Volumes:
1. Coast Radio Stations (Pts 1 & 2);
2. Radio Navigational Aids;
3. Maritime Safety Information Services (Pts 1 & 2);
4. Meteorological Observation Stations;
5. GMDSS;
6. Port Operations, Pilots, VTS (Pts 1 to 5);
7. (Not used, 2001);
8. Satellite Navigation Systems;

NP 289: Admiralty Maritime Communications for Yachtsmen. Extracts from Vols 1-8. UK and Med;

NP 290: Admiralty Maritime Communications for Yachtsmen. Extracts from Vols 1-8. Caribbean.

Simple GPS Navigation by Mik Chinery (Fernhurst).

A Small Boat Guide to Electronics afloat by Tim Bartlett (Fernhurst).

GPS afloat by Tim Bartlett (Fernhurst).

Radar afloat by Tim Bartlett (Fernhurst, 2000).

The RYA book of electronic navigation by Tim Bartlett (Adlard Coles, 2001)

Using Radar by Robert Avis (Adlard Coles).

How to use Radar by H.G. Strepp (Adlard Coles).

Using GPS by Conrad Dixon (Adlard Coles, 2nd edition).

Using PCs on board by Rob Buttress and Tim Thornton (Adlard Coles, 2000)

Chapter 9 Astro-navigation

CONTENTS

9.1 INTRODUCTION TO ASTRO-NAVIGATION

9.1.1 OUTLINE

Astronomical navigation, astro-navigation (or just astro, as it is widely called) remains the most basic method of fixing a vessel's position out of sight of land. To some extent modern electronic navigational aids, GPS in particular, have diminished the need for astro, but it still remains the one system that is universally available, self-contained and free; furthermore, it is not controlled by political or commercial bodies. Thus astro continues to fascinate many navigators, perhaps due to its place in history, celestial nature and freedom from outside influences.

The astro-navigator's tools are:
- a sextant to measure the angle (altitude) above the horizon of a celestial body (sun, moon, star or planet);
- a clock or watch to give the precise time of this sight;
- an almanac (ephemeris) to give the body's coordinates at that time; and
- sight reduction tables (SRT) or other methods to convert ('work up') the data into a form which can be plotted on a chart to give an astronomical fix.

The 'other methods' can range from physical models of the Earth through numerous 'short' techniques (many associated with the names of famous astronomers and navigators) employing tables, calculators and most recently computers to 'reduce' the effort involved. A navigation computer contains the ephemeris and therefore does the work of both almanac and sight reduction tables. The recent trend has been to move away from dedicated computers to the more flexible PC, which can be used to tackle many other tasks such as plotting.

If however the computer fails, you must be able to revert to pencil, paper, almanac and SRT. The almanac and SRT recommended for used on yachts are *The Nautical Almanac* and *Sight Reduction Tables for Air Navigation* produced jointly by the UK and US Nautical Almanac Offices. Ideally a preparation in coastal navigation should precede an ocean passage, to acquire the skills of taking a running fix and using the sextant in horizontal angles and distance off, before taking a departure and "shooting" the Sun.

9.1.2 THE BIG PICTURE

The work sequence which you the navigator will follow is shown diagrammatically in Fig. 9(1).

Study it now to gain an idea of what you have to do, even if at this stage it does not make total sense. Later it may prove a useful reference if you lose the thread. So:

1. Take the sight(s) with a sextant, getting someone else, if possible, to time the sight(s) very precisely.
2. Go below and start to fill in a sight reduction form (a work-sheet designed to cue you through the various tasks).
3. Enter the almanac with the Observed Altitude of the body and the time of the sight. Extract True Alt(itude), Dec(lination) and GHA (Greenwich Hour Angle).
4. From GHA jot down an Assumed (convenient) Longitude and work out LHA (Local Hour Angle).
5. Next enter the Sight reduction Tables at your nearest Assumed Latitude with Dec and LHA to emerge with Tab(ulated) Alt(itude) and Azimuth.

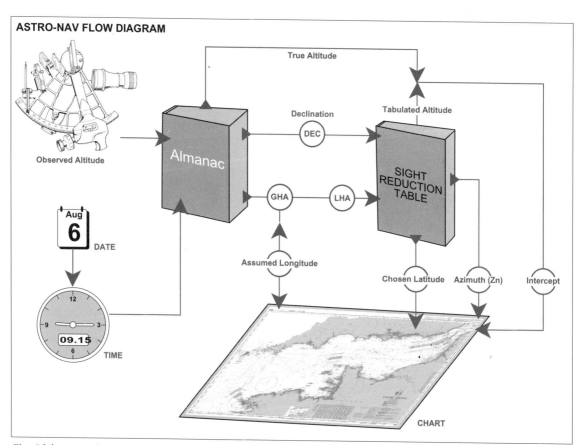

Fig. 9(1) Astro Flow diagram.

6. Compare True Alt with Tab Alt to give an Intercept (or distance) for plotting purposes.
7. On your chart or plotting sheet you can now plot the Lat/Long of your Assumed or Chosen position (a little bit of convenient fiction, courtesy of Marcq St. Hilaire).
8. From this slightly fictitious position lay off the Azimuth (bearing) of the body which you shot with your sextant and measure off the intercept.
9. At 90° to the azimuth draw a single position line (P/L) and your actual position is somewhere on it.
10. If possible take shots of at least 3 bodies to get 3 P/Ls. Where they intersect is your position. Alternatively:
11. If, as is likely, you have only shot the Sun, you will have only one P/L, not a fix. Take a second Sun sight later in the day and plot its P/L. Then run on the first P/L along the track and distance made good (by conventional DR). Your fix is where the two P/Ls cut.

The navigator needs to acquire two basic skills:

a. The art of wielding a sextant efficiently; and
b. Meticulous accuracy in working up the sight.

9.1.3 SCOPE OF THIS CHAPTER
In the rest of this chapter a Glossary first defines the principal terms used in astro navigation. The principles of astro are then summarised, to simplify the transition from theory into practice. An explanation of the astronomical triangle follows.

Next the sextant is described, with its errors and adjustments, and the altitude corrections which must be applied, followed by notes on practical sight-taking.

Sight reduction is next discussed: *The Sight Reduction Tables for Air Navigation* (issued in the UK as AP 3270 and in the USA as Pub No 249) are here recommended. These tables, in three volumes, are sufficiently precise for all practical purposes at sea. Their use is fully explained and examples are given under Sight Reduction (9.7).

The Nautical Almanac, compiled by the Nautical Almanac Office and published by TSO, will be needed. In addition to tabulations for the Sun, Moon, planets and stars, it contains concise reduction tables.

A dedicated navigation computer is a convenient way of reducing sights although Personal Computers have recently taken over the role. With computers there is no need to look up an almanac or a sight reduction table, all that

is done by appropriate software within the machine, and at the end of the calculation it will display the fix in terms of latitude and longitude. However, this must be referred to a chart (particularly when close to hazards); also computers are vulnerable to damage of one kind or another at sea and it is not wise to rely solely on them.

Whether stars are to be identified for sights by using AP 3270 or by planisphere, or other method, it is a good idea for navigators, and indeed other crew members, to be sufficiently familiar with the sky at night as to be able to pick out the principal constellations, the main navigational stars and the planets. The star chart in Fig. 9(11) and the accompanying text are intended mainly for this purpose.

Finally position lines are discussed with ways of analysing the plot to establish the most probable position.

9.1.4 GLOSSARY OF TERMS
Altitude Angular distance, along a vertical circle, from the horizon.

Altitude difference a. Intercept; b. Difference in consecutive tabular entries of altitude.

Amplitude Angular distance, measured along the horizon, clockwise or anticlockwise from the prime vertical.

Apogee The point at which a body in orbit around the Earth reaches its furthest distance from the Earth.

Apparent motion Motion, especially of astronomical bodies, relative to a reference point which may itself be in motion.

Apparent time Time based upon the rotation of the Earth relative to the apparent, or true, Sun.

Astronomical fix A position determined from astronomical data.

Astronomical triangle The navigational triangle solved in sight reduction.

Astronomical twilight Ends (or begins) when the centre of the Sun is 18° below the horizon. At the end (or beginning) of astronomical twilight, twilight is less than the contribution from starlight, and it is dark for most practical purposes.

Atmospheric pressure correction The value applied to a sextant altitude to correct for non-standard atmospheric pressure.

Autumnal equinox That equinox at which the Sun crosses the celestial equator from north to south.

Azimuth Angular distance, measured along the horizon, eastward from the principal vertical circle.

Azimuth angle Angular distance, measured along the horizon, clockwise or anticlockwise from the direction of the elevated pole, or occasionally from either this or the reciprocal direction, whichever is nearer.

Calculated (or computed) altitude (Hc) Altitude of an astronomical body as determined by calculation or equivalent means.

Celestial equator The intersection of the plane of the Earth's equator and the celestial sphere.

Celestial horizon The great circle on the celestial sphere midway between the zenith and nadir.

Celestial meridian A great circle through the celestial poles and the observer's zenith.

Celestial pole Either of the two points of intersection of the celestial sphere and the extension of the Earth's rotational axis.

Celestial sphere An imaginary sphere of arbitrary radius on which astronomical bodies are considered to be located. According to the situation the celestial sphere is normally centred at the observer or at the centre of the Earth.

Civil twilight Ends (or begins) when the centre of the Sun is 6° below the horizon. Before morning and after evening civil twilight the brightest stars and planets are visible.

Computed altitude (Hc) Calculated altitude.

Co-ordinated Universal Time (UTC) A timescale available from broadcast signals. It is maintained within +0.9 seconds of Universal Time (UT) by the introduction of one second steps (leap seconds).

Corrected sextant altitude Observed altitude.

Declination Angular distance north or south of the celestial equator.

Dip The apparent angle between the sensible horizon and the visible horizon.

Diurnal circle The apparent daily path of an astronomical body.

Ecliptic The apparent annual path of the Sun round the celestial sphere.

Elevated pole The celestial pole above the horizon.

Equation of time The difference between mean and apparent solar times.

Equinox Either of two times when the Sun is at zero declination. In the northern hemisphere the vernal equinox occurs around March 21 when the declination changes from south to north, and the autumnal equinox occurs around September 23 when the declination changes from north to south.

Ex-meridian observation An observation of the altitude of an astronomical body taken near the celestial meridian, for conversion to a meridian altitude.

First point of Aries Vernal equinox.

Geographical pole Either intersection of the surface of the Earth and the Earth's axis of rotation.

Geographical position (GP) a. Sub-point. b. A position defined by geographical co-ordinates, usually latitude and longitude.

Geometrical horizon The intersection of the celestial sphere and an infinite number of straight lines from the eye of the observer tangent to the surface of the Earth.

Great circle The intersection of the surface of a sphere with a plane through its centre.

Greenwich apparent time Apparent time on the Greenwich meridian.

Greenwich hour angle (GHA) Angular distance, measured along the equator, west of the Greenwich celestial meridian.

Greenwich mean time (GMT) Mean time on the Greenwich meridian. Superseded by Universal Time.

Greenwich sidereal time Sidereal time at the Greenwich meridian.

Horizon That great circle of the celestial sphere midway between the zenith and nadir, or a line approximating this circle.

Horizontal parallax The geocentric parallax when the body is on the horizon.

Hour circle Great semi-circle of the celestial sphere connecting the celestial poles and another fixed point of the celestial sphere.

Intercept The difference between calculated and observed altitudes.

International nautical mile (M) The linear unit internationally accepted as the nautical mile = 1852m or 6076ft.

Local apparent noon The instant of upper transit of the apparent Sun.

Local apparent time Apparent time at a specified meridian.

Local hour angle (LHA) Angular distance, measured along the equator, west of a specified celestial meridian.

Local mean time (LMT) Mean time at a specified meridian.

Local sidereal time Sidereal time at a specified meridian.

Lower branch That half of a celestial meridian that passes through the nadir.

Mean Sun A fictitious Sun conceived as moving eastward along the celestial equator at the average rate of the apparent Sun along the ecliptic.

Mean time Time based upon rotation of the Earth relative to the mean Sun.

Meridian altitude (Mer Alt) Altitude of an astronomical body on the celestial meridian.

Meridian transit The passage of an astronomical body across a celestial meridian.

Nadir That point on the celestial sphere vertically below the observer.

Nautical mile (M) Generally, the length of 1' of a great circle of the Earth. Specifically, the international nautical mile of 1852m or 6076ft.

Nautical Twilight Ends (or begins) when the centre of the Sun is 12° below the horizon. At the end (or beginning) of nautical twilight the horizon is not visible in general, and it is not possible to make altitude observations with a marine sextant.

Navigational triangle The spherical triangle solved in sight reduction or great-circle sailing.

Nutation Small irregularities in the precession of the equinoxes.

Observed altitude (Ho) Actual altitude of an astronomical body above the celestial horizon.

Parallactic angle The navigational triangle angle at the astronomical body or destination.

Parallax Difference in apparent position of an object as viewed from different positions.

Parallax in altitude Geocentric parallax of an astronomical body at any specified altitude.

Parallel of altitude A circle of the celestial sphere parallel to the plane of the celestial horizon.

Parallel of declination A circle of the celestial sphere parallel to the plane of the celestial equator.

Parallel of latitude A circle on the surface of the Earth parallel to the equator.

Perigee The point at which a body in orbit around the Earth reaches its nearest distance from the Earth.

Polar circle The parallel (N or S) equal to the maximum co-declination of the Sun.

Polar distance Angular distance from a celestial pole.

Polar motion Wobbling motion of the geographical poles of the Earth, affecting measurement of universal time.

Precession of the equinoxes Conical motion of the Earth's rotational axis about the vertical to the plane of the ecliptic, caused by the attractive force of other bodies of the solar system on the equatorial bulge of the Earth, and resulting in a slow drift of the equinoxes and solstices.

Prime meridian The Greenwich meridian from which longitude is reckoned.

Prime vertical circle The vertical circle through the east or west point of the horizon.

Principal vertical circle The vertical circle through the true north point of the horizon.

Proper motion The component of motion of an astronomical body perpendicular to the line of sight.

Refraction The change in direction of travel (bending) of a light ray as it passes obliquely through the atmosphere. Refraction is always added to the geometric altitude to produce the observed altitude.

Retired (transferred) position line A position line moved back to allow for motion of the observer between the earlier time to which the line is retired and the time of observation.

Right ascension (RA) Angular distance, along the equator, measured in time east of the hour circle of the vernal equinox.

Running fix Position determined by a. plotting two or more P/L's at any selected DR position on the vessel's run or b. advancing previous P/L's by course and distance run between the times of observation and the fix, as in coastal navigation.

Sea-air temperature difference correction The correction applied to a sextant altitude to correct for error in tabulated dip because of difference in the temperature of the water and air at their interface.

Semidiameter The angle at the observer produced by the radius of the disc of the Sun or Moon.

Sensible horizon A small circle of the celestial sphere marking the intersection of a plane parallel to the plane of the celestial horizon, through the eye of the observer.

Sextant altitude (Hs) Altitude of an astronomical body as measured by a sextant.

Sidereal Of or pertaining to stars.

Sidereal hour angle (SHA) Angular distance, along the equator, measured west of the hour circle of the vernal equinox.

Sidereal time Time based upon rotation of the Earth relative to the vernal equinox.

Solstice Either of two times when the declination of the Sun reaches a maximum or minimum. The maximum occurs around June 21 and the minimum around December 21.

Tabulated altitude (Ht) Calculated altitude for an assumed position

Time sight Observation of an astronomical body for determination of longitude by calculation of meridian angle and its comparison with Greenwich hour angle.

Transferred position line See Retired position line.

True altitude Corrected observed altitude.

Twilight Twilight is caused by the scattering of sunlight in the upper layers of the Earth's atmosphere, when the Sun is below the visible horizon.

Universal Time (UT) The equivalent of GMT, for all practical purposes.

Upper branch That half of a celestial meridian that passes through the zenith.

Upper transit The passage of an astronomical body across the upper branch of a celestial meridian.

Vernal equinox That equinox at which the Sun crosses the celestial equator from south to north.

Vertical circle A great semi-circle joining the zenith and nadir.

Visible horizon The projection of the line where Earth and sky appear to meet on the celestial sphere. In the absence of atmospheric refraction, visible and geometrical horizons coincide.

Zenith (Z) That point on the celestial sphere vertically overhead.

Zenith distance (ZD) Angular distance from the zenith.

Zone description The number, with its sign, applied to zone time to convert it to the corresponding GMT or UT.

Zone time Mean time at a standard reference meridian whose time is kept throughout a designated area.

9.2 PRINCIPLES OF NAUTICAL ASTRONOMY

9.2.1 CONCEPTS AND RELATIONSHIPS

To grasp the basic principles of astro-navigation you need to understand certain concepts and relationships. In this chapter the Earth is assumed to be spherical; in practice the navigator will not need to correct for its oblateness since this is accounted for in charts, tables etc.

The distances of the celestial bodies are irrelevant for the purposes of navigation. You can envisage all of them as lying on the inner surface of a sphere concentric with the Earth and known as the celestial sphere. This purely notional device makes it easier to understand position and apparent movement of the celestial bodies in relation to the Earth's surface.

The plane of any great circle on a sphere passes through the centre of the sphere, dividing it into two equal parts or hemispheres.

The celestial horizon is the great circle, which cuts the celestial sphere midway between the zenith and nadir; its plane is horizontal to the observer.

The True altitude of a celestial body is the angle at the centre of the Earth between that body and the celestial horizon.

A nautical mile is the average length of a great circle of the Earth, which subtends an angle of one minute of arc at its centre. Since the radius of the Earth is known, so is the length on its surface of 1 minute of arc. Note that minor differences have arisen through accepting different values for the size and shape of the Earth. The International Nautical Mile is standardised at 1852m (6076ft); this fact, as such, has no direct navigational significance.

The counterparts on the celestial sphere of terrestrial latitude and longitude are respectively declination, measured north or south (N or S) of the celestial equator; and hour angle, by convention measured west from a chosen meridian (not east and west as is longitude). Greenwich hour angle (GHA) is measured along

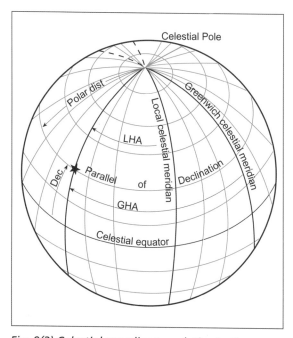

Fig. 9(2) Celestial coordinates relative to the Earth.

the equator west from the Greenwich celestial meridian, see Fig. 9(2).

The geographical position (GP) or sub-point of a celestial body is where an imaginary line from the centre of the Earth to the body would cut the Earth's surface. To an observer at that point the body would be at the zenith, right overhead. The celestial coordinates (lat/long) of that GP would be the body's declination, north or south of the celestial equator; and its GHA measured west from the Greenwich meridian.

9.2.2 ANGULAR MEASURE AND GEOGRAPHICAL DISTANCE

Fig. 9(3) shows how measuring a body's altitude gives the observer's distance in nautical miles from that body's GP.

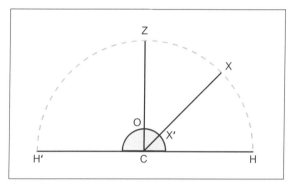

Fig. 9(3) Arc and distance on the Earth's surface.

Thus an observer at O on the Earth's surface measures, after correction, the altitude of the body X above the celestial horizon H'CH. Subtracting this angle from 90° gives the angle XCZ, between X and the zenith (Z). The arc XZ on the celestial sphere is clearly the same as the arc X'O on the Earth's surface; hence, knowing the Earth's radius, this angular measure OCX' in degrees and minutes gives the linear distance in nautical miles. This relationship lies at the heart of all nautical astronomy.

9.2.3 TIME AND HOUR ANGLE

If the celestial bodies were all stationary on the celestial sphere, **time** would not feature in astro-navigation. But, the Earth's rotation about its polar axis gives the stars (which we regard as fixed, because of their immense distances away from Earth) an apparent motion from east to west across the celestial sphere; one complete cycle takes approximately 23 hours, 56 minutes, 4 seconds, the length of a sidereal (or star) day. The Earth, of course, not only rotates about its axis but also orbits around the Sun completing

one circuit every year. This makes the solar day slightly longer than the sidereal day, by about one part in 365.

The movement of the apparent Sun in its orbit is not, for various reasons, entirely regular and for timekeeping the concept of a fictitious mean Sun whose passage over successive meridians takes exactly 24 hours has been introduced. The difference between apparent time and mean time is the equation of time given on the daily pages of *The Nautical Almanac*.

Both time and longitude are by convention measured from the Greenwich or prime meridian. Since the Earth rotates 360° relative to the Sun in 24 hours, 15° of longitude is equivalent to 1 hour of time. For every 15° of longitude west of Greenwich the local mean time will be 1 hour earlier than Universal Time, almost the same as Greenwich Mean Time. (To preserve the Greenwich date an international date line runs along the meridian of 180° E and W, with detours around certain islands). The entries on the daily pages of the ephemeris are tabulated for Universal Time but the navigator will in general be more directly concerned with local time.

For various reasons the longitude of a celestial body is specified by its hour angle, that is the angle measured along the equator west of a celestial meridian. When the Greenwich or prime meridian is the celestial meridian chosen, the angle will be the Greenwich hour angle (GHA); if it is the observer's meridian it will be the local hour

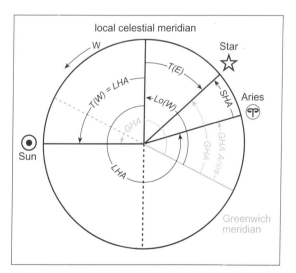

Fig. 9(4) Time diagram (seen from above the South Pole) showing the relationship between time (T) and hour angle. Lo (W) means Longitude West; subtract it from the Sun's GHA to give the sun's LHA.

angle (LHA). The ephemeris tabulates GHA of the Sun, Moon and planets. This is converted to LHA by subtracting westerly or adding easterly, thus:

LHA = GHA + observer's longitude east
or – observer's longitude west

(where necessary adding or subtracting 360°). Fig. 9 (4) illustrates these relationships.

Because the stars may be regarded as fixed (whereas the planets of the solar system move rapidly around the celestial sphere) the GHA of each navigational star is not usually included in the ephemeris.

Instead the ephemeris gives the GHA of the First Point of Aries, a fixed point in the sky, and sidereal hour angle (SHA) is tabulated for each navigational star. SHA is the angular difference between GHA Aries and the GHA of the star. Thus GHA Aries + SHA = GHA of the star.

9.3 THEORY INTO PRACTICE

9.3.1 THE ASTRONOMICAL TRIANGLE

Since, as we have seen (9.2.2), zenith distance measured in arc can be equated with distance on the Earth's surface in nautical miles, it follows that a sight of a celestial body, whose GP (9.2.1) can be established, will locate the observer on a circle of position whose centre is the GP and radius the zenith distance. In Fig. 9(5) the outer sphere represents the celestial sphere, the inner one the Earth; X is the body observed, and X′ is its GP; O is the observer and Z his zenith; P is the pole and RQ

is a part of the celestial equator. The altitude ZCX subtracted from 90° gives the zenith distance ZX and the arc OX′ is the distance on the Earth's surface stated in nautical miles.

For the time of the sight the navigator extracts from the ephemeris the body's coordinates (declination and hour angle) which in principle enables the GP to be plotted and a circle of position to be drawn, somewhere on which the observer must be. In practice, however the vast distances involved make plotting to the required scale totally impossible – except when very high altitudes put the body within a degree or two of the zenith.

This is where the astronomical or 'PZX' triangle, tinted 'blue' in Fig. 9(5), comes into play. It contains:

at Z the azimuth angle PZX;
at P the local hour angle ZPX of X from Z;

and

at X the parallactic angle, which is not normally required. The Greenwich celestial meridian is PGS, therefore the Greenwich hour angle of X is GPX and the longitude of Z is GPZ.

Two sides of the triangle are known:

ZX (zenith distance or ZD for short) = 90° – Hs, the altitude of X, as measured by sextant; and

PX is established by the chronometer and ephemeris.

To solve the triangle a third part is required, which can be found by various different mathematical methods of sight reduction.

In the Intercept (or Marcq St Hilaire) method, which is almost universal today, in various forms, a convenient position (usually the DR or a position near it suited to the method in use) is assumed for Z. The ZD of the assumed position is then calculated and compared with the observed ZD. The difference between the two ZD's is the *Intercept* which is plotted from the assumed position towards or away from the body, according to whether the assumed position is nearer or further away from that body. Unless the radius of the position circle is very small (as with very high altitudes), the part of it in the vicinity of the observer can, with no discernible error, be regarded as a straight line at right angles to the body's bearing. This is the P/L.

There are many solutions to the problem of deriving the intercept and azimuth of a celestial body from a timed observation of its altitude – whether trigonometric, tabular, graphical or by computer or electronic calculator. Only two are considered in any detail here:

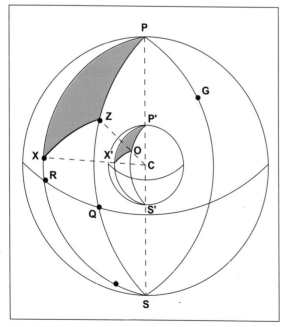

Fig. 9(5) The astronomical triangle.

a. Tabular (direct entry or inspection tables; see 9.7.3 and 9.7.4) which, for an assumed position, give pre-calculated values of altitude and azimuth for whole degrees of declination and hour angle; and

b. PC's with navigational software and dedicated navigation computers (9.7.2) programmed to give the intercept and azimuth from the DR position, without reference to almanac or reduction tables; and to display the latitude and longitude of the fix with an assessment of its precision.

9.4 THE SEXTANT

9.4.1 DESCRIPTION

Fig. 9(6) shows the marine sextant in a simplified form.

The telescope and horizon glass are attached to the frame although minor adjustments can be made with adjusting screws. The index mirror is similarly fixed to the index arm which rotates about the centre of curvature of the arc. The latter has at its lower end an index, or pointer, against which the graduated arc is read. The index mirror and horizon glass should be parallel when the index reads zero.

Fig. 9(7) shows diagrammatically how the sextant measures angles. The arc of the sextant subtends an angle of 60° but, due to the principle of double reflection, the scale is graduated to 120°. Older sextants carry a vernier scale on the index arm opposite the arc to facilitate reading fractional parts of the smallest graduations on the scale. Modern sextants have micrometer tangent screws, or drums, which serve the same purpose and are far easier to read.

9.4.2 HANDLING

Handle and treat your sextant with tender, loving care; it is a delicate precision instrument. Only lift it by the frame or handle, never by the arc, and

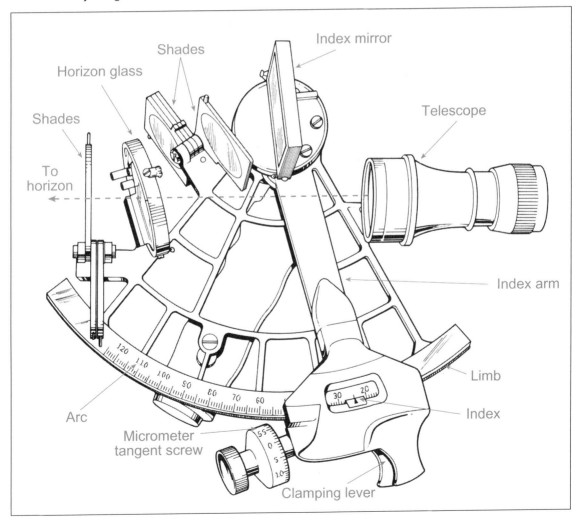

Fig. 9(6) The sextant.

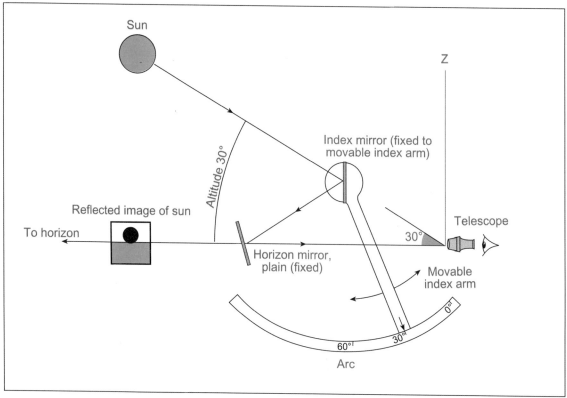

Fig. 9(7) Measuring angles by sextant.

always replace it in its box after use. A lanyard secured to the handle and around your neck is a safety measure before going on deck. The glasses and mirrors should be wiped dry with a clean soft chamois leather or linen cloth to stop moisture damaging the silvering. Wipe the glasses with great care to avoid altering their adjustment. A bag of silica gel in the sextant box will help combat moisture. A little light oil applied occasionally to the worm gear at the back of the arc is the only lubrication necessary.

Many modern sextants are made of aluminium alloys and are lighter and therefore easier to handle. Plastic sextants are light and cheap but require careful treatment to prevent warping or distortion. The choice of telescopes is largely an individual matter, but a single telescope suitable for all bodies may be preferred to a range of telescopes for different purposes (star, inverting etc). Your first Sun sights will be easier and safer for your eyes without the telescope – medical examinations have revealed burns on the retina of many professional navigators.

9.4.3 ERRORS AND ADJUSTMENTS

Sextants are subject to certain errors. Instrument error cannot be corrected by the navigator, but in a good sextant it is usually small enough to be

ignored. If it exists, it is tabulated by the manufacturer and applied as corrections to different altitudes. The three principal causes of instrument error are centring error from a faulty location of the pivot of the index arm, graduation error on the scale, and prismatic error where the two sides of the mirrors or shades are not parallel.

Errors adjustable by the navigator are perpendicularity, side error, index error and collimation error. Because they interact, correct them in the order given below:

Perpendicularity error arises when the index mirror is not perpendicular to the frame. To check, hold the sextant horizontally and sight the arc simultaneously through the mirror and directly. Perpendicularity error exists if the reflected and direct views of the arc do not appear as a single unbroken line. Remove the error by a screw at the back of the mirror.

Side error exists if the horizon glass is not perpendicular to the frame. It is another form of perpendicularity error, strictly speaking. To check, set the index to zero and sight the horizon which should appear as a continuous straight line in both the direct and double reflected views. If either moves up or down with respect to the other when the sextant is rocked about the line of sight, side error exists. It is corrected by a screw at the base of the glass. Another way of checking side error is to sight a low altitude star (low in the sky). With the index set to zero, two images of the star side-by-side indicate side error.

Index error exists when, with the index set at zero, the index mirror and horizon glass are not parallel, such that the direct and reflected images of the horizon appear as a broken line. Check it as for side error, observing the horizon with the sextant vertical. When corrected, the direct and reflected images of the horizon will appear as a continuous straight line. Several readings should be taken, the sextant being offset in different directions each time.

Another way of checking for index error is to observe the Sun on and off the arc, the limbs of the two Suns visible just touching in either case. The index error will be half the sum of the two readings; a useful check on the accuracy of these observations is that the sum should be four times the semi-diameter of the Sun as given in *The Nautical Almanac*.

Perhaps the best way of all is to use a low altitude star and one that is not too bright, which will allow greater accuracy and be less tiring than using the Sun.

Index error is corrected by a screw or screws at the base of the horizon glass. Since it will directly affect the angles measured, index error should be checked every time the sextant is used. However, adjusting the sextant each time index error is found would tend to wear the thread of the adjusting screws; it is usual to allow errors up to 2' or 3' as a correction to the observations.

If the index correction is on the arc of the sextant the reading will be too high by that amount and must be subtracted to get the observed altitude, and conversely added if it is off the arc. An aide memoire for the sign of the correction is: "If it's on it's off, and if it's off it's on".

Collimation error is caused by the telescope not being parallel to the frame and will result in greater angles being measured than the correct values. To check, place the sextant horizontally on a flat surface and make a mark on the wall or bulkhead opposite in line with the line of sight along the upper surface of the frame. Another mark is made above it corresponding to the distance between the frame and the telescope. The two will be parallel when the second mark is in the centre of the field of view of the telescope. If correction is possible, adjustment is by a pair of screws on the collar of the telescope.

Regular checks
Normally the only errors which need to be checked with any regularity are index error and side error; unless it exceeds about 2' the former is generally included as a correction to the altitude, while the latter will so far as possible be eliminated by adjustment.

9.5 ALTITUDE CORRECTIONS

9.5.1 GENERAL
After correcting the altitude read off a sextant as in 9.4.3, an allowance should be made, if relevant, for personal error (i.e. the amount an observer habitually over- or under-reads the sextant). The result is known as Sextant altitude (Hs for Height sextant), to which several altitude corrections must then be applied; the outcome will be Observed altitude (Ho for Height observed).

Corrections for dip, refraction, semi-diameter and parallax are applied to Hs as appropriate; semi-diameter applying only to Sun and Moon, and horizontal parallax only to the Moon. Formulae for calculating and applying the corrections are given in the section on Sight Reduction Procedures in *The Nautical Almanac*. Using the correction tables in *The Nautical Almanac*, the Hs is first corrected for index error and dip to give an apparent altitude with which the table of correction for refraction and semi-diameter is entered. The altitude corrections are considered in turn below. Fig. 9(8) illustrates the various horizon systems referred to in the text.

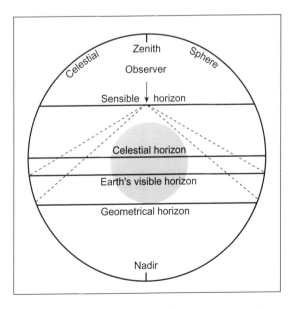

Fig. 9(8) Horizon systems used in astro-navigation.

9.5.2 DIP
Dip of the sea horizon arises because the observer's eye level is above the surface of the sea which causes the horizon to be depressed (dip) below the horizontal plane at the observer's eye. The correction, which is always subtracted, increases numerically with height. Anomalous conditions, e.g. a large difference between sea and air temperature, can cause errors in the calculated dip values. Taking sights on opposite horizons or equally spaced around the horizon are ways of overcoming this difficulty. The dip correction includes an allowance for the fact that light from the horizon will be affected by terrestrial refraction.

9.5.3 REFRACTION
Astronomical refraction is the angular difference between the true and apparent altitude of a celestial body. Light from a celestial body entering the Earth's atmosphere is progressively bent towards the vertical by variations in the density of the medium which makes the body appear higher in the sky than it actually is; see Fig. 9(9).

The density of the air is affected by temperature and atmospheric pressure and the refraction corrections given in *The Nautical Almanac* are for a mean temperature of 10°C and pressure of 1010mb. Refraction decreases with altitude, from about 34' at the horizon to zero at the zenith. The correction is always subtractive. Anomalous conditions such as those affecting the dip also affect astronomical refraction; however, since refraction decreases rapidly with altitude, the effect will be minimised by avoiding low altitude sights, say below 10°. An additional table for non-standard atmospheric

conditions is provided and may be used with low altitude sights.

9.5.4 SEMI-DIAMETER
Semi-diameter corrections apply only to the Sun and Moon, because the coordinates given in the almanac for celestial bodies are for the centre of the body; whereas either the upper or lower limb of the Sun and Moon will have been observed. Stars and planets appear in the sextant telescope as points of light, although Venus at its nearest approach has in fact a semi-diameter of over 0'·5. Semi-diameter varies with the body's altitude and its distance from the Earth, but only in the case of the Moon is this augmentation navigationally significant, due to its nearness to Earth. In *The Nautical Almanac* (TSO) the position of Venus is given for the centre of its light.

9.5.5 PARALLAX
Parallax is the difference in apparent position of an object as viewed from different positions. In the context of an altitude correction, it refers to the angle between a point on the Earth's surface from which the body is viewed and the place it would occupy if it were to be viewed from the centre of the Earth.

Parallax is zero at the zenith, increasing, as the altitude decreases, to a maximum on the observer's sensible horizon, Fig. 9(10). This value is known as the horizontal parallax (HP).

In *The Nautical Almanac* corrections for parallax are already taken into account in the altitude correction tables for the Sun, Moon, Venus and Mars. Any correction for stars would be negligible and is ignored. Only in the case of the Moon, because of its close proximity to the Earth, is horizontal parallax used as an argument to enter the tables.

9.6 PRACTICAL SIGHT TAKING

9.6.1 NOTES ON OBSERVATIONS
In a small boat there is little choice about the height from which sights will be taken. For dip corrections, the height of eye will be above the waterline. The higher the height of eye, the less rapidly the correction for dip of the horizon changes and thus the more reliable the observation. Further, in a rough sea the horizon is often hidden from view by wave tops. On the other hand in poor visibility it is often possible to take satisfactory sights by getting closer to the sea surface such that the horizon shrinks to within the prevailing visibility. Thus at 0·61m/2ft above the water, which might be obtained by taking

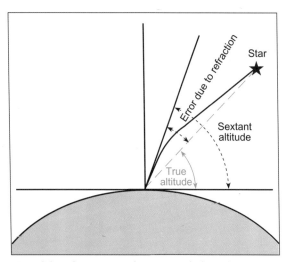

Fig. 9(9) Refraction and measured altitude.

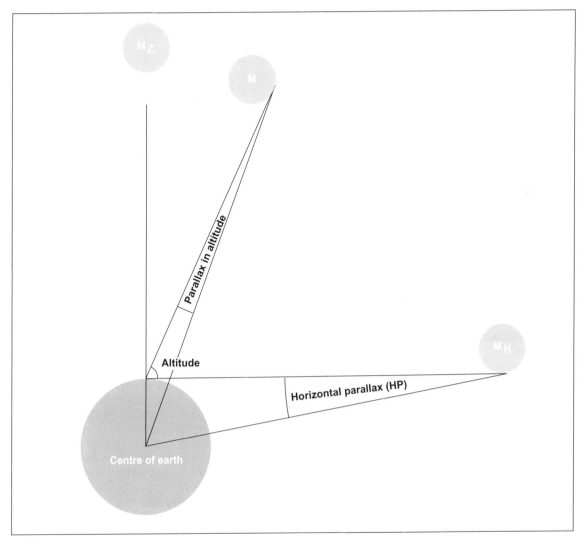

Fig. 9(10) Parallax is only relevant to the Moon.

sights from a companionway, or in calm weather from a dinghy, the horizon will only be about 1·25M. Physically the best posture for taking sights is to sit, wedged from the waist down and with both hands free.

A sight is taken by bringing the celestial body down to the point on the horizon immediately below it. The Sun's lower limb will usually be used and whichever limb of the Moon is fully visible. The point of tangency with the horizon is defined by rocking the sextant laterally through about 20° either side of the line of sight, until the body is seen to be exactly 'kissing' the horizon. The higher the altitude the more important this becomes.

Considerable practice is needed to use a sextant accurately from such an unsteady platform as a small boat. The advice of an experienced observer may initially be helpful.

There are several ways of bringing the body down to the horizon, including initially holding the sextant upside down to allow the horizon to be brought up to the body. With the Sun, and occasionally the Moon, quite a good tip is to half close the eye and be guided by the ambient light as to when the body is in the field of view. Take extreme care not to be blinded; the proper use of shades requires cautious removal from the line of sight.

Statistically the random error of the mean of a number of sights is reduced as the square root of the number. Averaging a series of sights will not necessarily reduce the error by this amount because the errors will not all be random. However, because of the difficulties of taking sights in small vessels, with rapid accelerations and a low height of eye, it is customary to take a series of sights and mean the times and altitudes. Take care, however, not to include rogues which are usually obvious. If the sights are more or less evenly timed, a series of three or five (or even seven) sights allows the middle one to be treated as a yardstick as to how good the series is; its time and altitude should be close to the mean. A quick plot on graph paper of time versus Hs serves a similar purpose.

Nowadays digital wrist watches have almost totally replaced clockwork chronometers or deck watches. They are reliable, highly accurate, usually water-resistant and virtually shockproof. The type most convenient for timing sights has a stopwatch with a lap function which allows the times of each sight in a series to be recorded. With a digital display there is little chance of a gross misreading error. Keep an electronic clock at the chart table for use as the master for stopwatch work. If it is automatically regulated by long-wave time signals from a transmitter (Rugby, Frankfurt etc), it will always be accurate to within one second.

It is very helpful to have another crewmember who will record the time and altitude of each sight. The time must be recorded to the nearest second, which represents 0.25 minute of arc. You can of course take accurate times on your own (as single-handers have to) by attaching to the sextant a stopwatch or your wristwatch, synchronised with a master clock down below, as described above. Any notion of counting out loud the interval between taking a sight and looking at a clock is unlikely to be accurate.

9.6.2 THE ACCURACY OF SIGHTS

There is a tendency for some navigators to exaggerate the accuracy of sights at sea, perhaps due to some confusion between the accuracy attainable, which is quite high, and the average accuracy which might be expected. First therefore what is meant by accuracy?

In theory any sextant sight can be accurate to within the limits to which altitude and time can be read; the resultant position line will pass near enough through the observer's position. The question is how often is this, or any other predicted result, likely to occur? The confidence level in such predictions is usually expressed as a percentage. The level with which practising navigators are normally most concerned is the 95% level which defines the number of occasions out of every 100 on which the error is unlikely to exceed a stated value. To say, for example, that the 95% level accuracy of sextant observations at sea is 4 miles is to say that out of every 100 observations only five may be expected to have an error exceeding 4 miles.

Some years ago the Royal Institute of Navigation, the Royal Navy, the Royal

Netherlands Navy and several British shipping companies, investigated the accuracy of astronomical observations at sea. The following results were obtained from an analysis by HM Nautical Almanac Office of some 4000 observations:

Percentage Error	Average observer	Best observer	Error exceeded in
50	0'.7	0'.5	10 out of 20
90	2'.4	1'.4	2 out of 20
95	3'.1	2'.0	1 out of 20

The errors in question are of course position-line errors, not errors in position.

Most of the observers were professional seamen taking sights from a comparatively steady platform and at an elevated height of eye. Besides being a useful guide for the navigator, these results shed light on how precise almanacs and tables need to be. Almanacs and tables for marine navigation are normally tabulated to a precision of 0'.1 of altitude and 0°.1 of azimuth, mainly because the next convenient unit is 1' or 1°. But where there is scope for unavoidable error, in this case that of observation, it can be shown that there is little to be gained by reducing other sources of error beyond a certain point. That is why the standard method of sight reduction proposed in this Handbook is the combined British and American *Sight Reduction Tables for Air Navigation* (known respectively as AP 3270 and Pub No 249) tabulated to 1' of altitude and 1° of azimuth, a precision sufficient for all practical purposes at sea.

9.6.3 SUN SIGHTS

The Sun is the body most frequently observed at sea, generally in successive sights with an allowance for the dead reckoning run between sights. Partial cloud cover especially when the gaps are small can be riskiest for the eyes.

Except when hidden by cloud, the lower limb of the Sun is normally observed. If the upper limb is brought to the horizon the altitude correction for semi-diameter will, clearly, be subtractive. Occasionally the outline of the Sun is so indistinct that it will be easier to estimate when the centre of its disc is on the horizon than to use either limb. In which case the altitude correction obtained from the combined altitude correction table is the mean of the corrections for the upper and lower limbs.

A clear horizon makes accurate sights much easier, but a clear horizon can also occur in conditions conducive to abnormal dip. Tell-tale signs of abnormal atmospheric conditions generally include the distortion of the outlines of ships on the horizon.

9.6.4 MOON SIGHTS
The upper or lower limb of the Moon can be observed, whichever is the more complete. The altitude correction tables for the Moon with horizontal parallax as argument give separate corrections for each limb.

Generally Moon sights are only taken in daylight when the resulting position line can often usefully be crossed with a position line from the Sun in order to give a fix. The Moon takes rather longer than other bodies to cross the same meridian and in that respect is marginally easier to observe.

9.6.5 STAR SIGHTS
Star sights are normally taken in the morning and evening when the Sun is about 8° or 10° below the horizon, in the interval between civil and nautical twilights. The interval lasts about 24 minutes on the equator, longer as latitude increases. In this twilight period the brighter stars will be visible in the sextant telescope while the horizon will be clear enough for sight taking. Generally stars to the east will appear first in the evening and disappear first in the morning. The brightest star should normally be taken first in the evening and last in the morning.

Star sights are usually pre-planned by working out the time of twilight at the DR position (from data given in *The Nautical Almanac*) and then by means of a planisphere or the Selected Star Tables of AP 3270 calculating the altitudes and azimuths for the approximate time. The stars may then most easily be observed by setting the approximate altitude on the sextant rather than attempting the more difficult task of bringing them down to the horizon.

Although single observations should be the exception rather than the rule, the time for taking stars is limited by the light. It is therefore generally better to take single sights of a larger number of stars well distributed in azimuth, than to take several shots of a smaller number.

Star sights are sometimes possible by moonlight, but the results should be treated with some caution because the horizon can be deceptive. The planet Venus is occasionally visible in daylight through the sextant telescope and can be crossed with a position line from the Sun or Moon. Because of the difficulty of picking it up it is usual to observe Venus at its meridian altitude.

The planet Jupiter too is often visible long after sunrise or before sunset.

Because several stars can generally be observed more or less simultaneously, star sights tend to yield the most accurate astro-fix at sea. In principle two well observed stars at a reasonable angle of cut suffice for a fix, but a third will add reliability by enabling any errors in the observation or reduction of either sight to be detected. Four stars or more, if the plot is intelligently analysed (see 9.9.2), give the best chance of an accurate and reliable fix.

Star identification
Stars can be identified by their constellation, catalogue designation (within that constellation) and in some cases by name. The constellations, of which there are nearly 90, are groups of stars which appeared to different cultures to resemble mythical figures or objects; their names are expressed in Latin. A star's designation is the Latin name (genitive case) of its Constellation name (nominative case) prefixed by a lower-case Greek letter usually in descending order of brightness; thus α Leonis is the brightest star in the constellation Leo, β Leonis the second brightest, and so on. But the principal navigational stars have proper names, so navigators seldom need the constellation and catalogue designations. Thus α Leonis is Regulus, a star of first magnitude 1·3.

A star's apparent brightness is measured in terms of magnitude: the lower the magnitude number, the brighter the star. The 20 brightest stars are rated first magnitude (ranging from a negative value to 1·5), and the faintest stars just visible to the unaided eye under perfect conditions are rated sixth magnitude. A navigator will rarely use more than about 20 of the 57 stars 'selected' for navigational use, but at times it helps to be able to identify and observe some of the lesser used bodies.

Of the planets Venus, Jupiter, and sometimes Mars, obtain negative magnitudes, making them extremely bright. Venus, Mars, Jupiter and Saturn, the navigational planets, are easy to pick out in the sky since they are relatively much brighter and shine with a steady light, as opposed to the twinkling light of a star. Mars can often be recognised by its reddish tint. All planets stay fairly close to the ecliptic. On rare occasions, Mercury could be confused with one of the navigational planets when it is close to maximum elongation from the Sun.

Fig. 9(11) shows the relative positions of the northern stars as seen from Earth. The coordinates are declination and sidereal hour

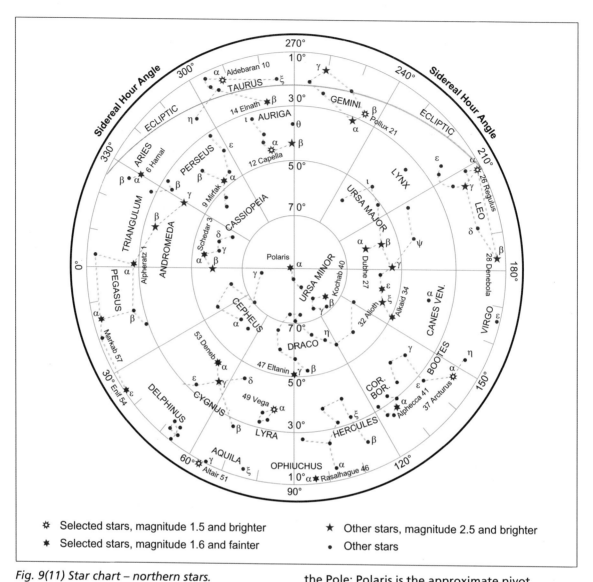

Key:
☼ Selected stars, magnitude 1.5 and brighter   ★ Other stars, magnitude 2.5 and brighter
✸ Selected stars, magnitude 1.6 and fainter   • Other stars

Fig. 9(11) Star chart – northern stars.

angle. Equatorial stars can be displayed separately as their locations are obviously distorted by the projection. The shapes of the constellations, as devised by the ancients, are traced by lines joining component stars. The key shows how different magnitudes are depicted.

A beginner can best start to locate stars in the northern hemisphere by first identifying Ursa Major, the Great Bear or Plough. Follow the transit of the two Pointers at the 'front end' of the Plough (Merak the lower one and the brighter Dubhe, a selected navigational star), which leads almost to Polaris. Polaris, the Pole Star, is roughly the pole of the heavens around which the sky appears to rotate. Polaris is itself part of Ursa Minor, a constellation very similar to Ursa Major, which rotates anticlockwise around

the Pole; Polaris is the approximate pivot. Extending the curve of the Plough handle leads to Arcturus, a first-magnitude reddish star. Continue the arc to another first magnitude star, the bluish-white Spica, equatorial and therefore not shown here.

On a summer evening, to an observer in the northern hemisphere the Plough will lie west of Polaris with the Pointers nearly horizontal. The brilliant blue-white Vega, brightest star in the northern hemisphere, will be visible to the east, with Altair, an equatorial star, almost midway between the two Guardians which point towards it.

The 'summer triangle' of Altair, Vega and Deneb is conspicuous. Antares, a noticeably red, first-magnitude star, is found in the constellation of Scorpius at about this time, fairly low in the southern sky. In the sky, though not on the star chart, the likeness to a scorpion is obvious.

In the autumn, the Plough is low in the northern sky in the evenings, and CASSIOPEIA'S CHAIR, (which looks like the letter W) can be picked out on the other side of the Pole at about the same distance. On winter nights the Plough lies to the right of Polaris, and Cassiopeia to its left. At this season Orion's Belt can be seen to the south, with Betelgeuse, a bright yellowish-red star, to the north-east, and Bellatrix, a fainter, white star to the north-west. Rigel, a bright bluish star, lies south-west of the Belt. Continuing the line of the Belt south-eastward leads to Sirius, a brilliant blue-white star, the brightest in the heavens (magnitude −1·6).

The quickest way to become familiar with the night sky is to identify one or two of the constellations and the brightest stars within them, and to follow their progress across the sky, first hour by hour and then night by night. More bodies can be added from the star chart as time goes on, until recognition becomes virtually automatic once a pattern in the sky is discernible. The pleasure is enhanced by scanning the heavens through binoculars from well offshore, clear of the glare and haze of land.

9.7 SIGHT REDUCTION

9.7.1 HISTORICAL INTRODUCTION

The term sight reduction embraces the whole process of calculating the observer's position from an astronomical observation (or series of observations). It particularly refers to the use of tables (and other means) to derive an astro position line, usually by comparing a calculated altitude with the observed one. The notion of the position line was first conceived by the American shipmaster Thomas H. Sumner in 1837 and it is sometimes known as the Sumner line. The device of comparing the observed and calculated altitudes to obtain the intercept was introduced by the French naval officer Marcq St. Hilaire in 1875, after whom the method is named; it is now the standard method of sight reduction, whatever means are used to calculate the intercept.

Tabular methods of solving the astronomical triangle by spherical trigonometry have often made use of the haversine formula. The azimuth is usually derived from a separate table or diagram as for instance the ABC tables or Weir's azimuth diagram. Books of nautical tables such as Norie's, Inman and Burton cater for sight reduction by such methods, as well as other,

sometimes obsolescent, methods such as Longitude by Chronometer. The major disadvantage of all such methods is the large amount of calculation involved.

'Short' methods, as they became known, were devised precisely to shorten the amount of calculation and simplify the sight reduction process generally. They usually entail dividing the astronomical triangle into two right angled triangles by dropping a perpendicular from a vertex to the side opposite, a method originally suggested by Napier. Such tables have usually appeared in quite slim volumes devoted solely to sight reduction. Typical of the 'short' methods were those devised by the following people: Ageton, Aquino, more recently Sadler, Pfab, Davies, Janiczek, Kotleric, Pepperday and Bennett (a complete list would run into nearly one hundred names). The recent publication *The Complete On-Board Celestial Navigator* by George G. Bennett (1999), McGraw Hill, has finally exhausted all the remaining possibilities upon which such tables can be based, and is strongly recommended.

Unfortunately certain 'short' methods do not always work with the same accuracy over all regions of the sky. When the problem areas are known about, complex rules may have to be applied to maintain the accuracy of the tables. For this reason they have been superseded by tables of the modern direct entry or inspection type in which great simplicity is achieved, although often at the expense of bulk, so that more than one volume is required to cover the sky. The effect of precession on the star places also means that a new edition has to be published every five years or so.

9.7.2 RECOMMENDED METHODS

The direct entry tables recommended in this Handbook are the *Sight Reduction Tables for Air Navigation* produced jointly in the United Kingdom as AP 3270 and in the United States as Pub No 249. In three volumes they tabulate altitude to 1' and azimuth angle to 1°, precise enough for all normal astro requirements at sea. This gives at least a marginal advantage over *Sight Reduction Tables for Marine Navigation,* also produced jointly in the United Kingdom as NP 401 and in the United States as Pub No 229, which, in six volumes, tabulate altitude to 0'·1 and azimuth angle to 0°·1, a precision not normally necessary at sea.

The Nautical Almanac also contains a set of concise reduction tables. Like most 'short' methods these concise tables divide the astronomical triangle by dropping a perpendicular from the observer's zenith. Full instructions and an example are provided. The entries are at intervals of 1° for all latitudes and hour angles and the table has to be entered twice, the second time with arguments extracted in the first entry. As with inspection tables a whole degree of latitude is chosen and a longitude such that the LHA is a whole degree.

The entries, in seven steps, are straightforward but take care to observe the rule of signs. Altitude is given to the nearest 1' of arc, although rounding off errors could increase the error to 2'. This stated accuracy of the tables has been checked over all regions of the sky, and there are no special cases to be considered.

As noted in 9.1.3, personal computers are now capable of storing ephemerides and

LAT 49°N

LHA ♈	Hc	Zn	Hc	Zn	Hc	Zn	Hc	Zn	Hc	Zn	Hc	Zn	Hc	Zn
	♦ Dubhe		REGULUS		PROCYON		♦ SIRIUS		RIGEL		ALDEBARAN		♦ Mirfak	
90	47 45	043	27 11	104	41 26	146	23 31	168	31 56	193	53 17	215	64 58	287
91	48 12	043	27 49	104	41 47	147	23 39	169	31 47	194	52 54	217	64 20	287
92	48 39	044	28 27	105	42 08	149	23 46	170	31 36	196	52 30	218	63 42	288
93	49 07	044	29 05	106	42 28	150	23 52	171	31 25	197	52 06	219	63 05	288
94	49 34	044	29 43	107	42 48	151	23 58	172	31 14	198	51 40	221	62 28	288
95	50 01	044	30 21	108	43 06	152	24 03	173	31 01	199	51 14	222	61 50	289
96	50 29	044	30 58	109	43 24	154	24 07	174	30 48	200	50 47	224	61 13	289
97	50 56	044	31 35	110	43 41	155	24 10	175	30 34	201	50 20	225	60 36	289
98	51 24	045	32 12	111	43 57	156	24 13	177	30 20	202	49 52	226	59 59	290
99	51 52	045	32 49	111	44 13	158	24 15	178	30 04	203	49 23	227	59 22	290
100	52 19	045	33 25	112	44 27	159	24 16	179	29 48	205	48 54	229	58 45	291
101	52 47	045	34 02	113	44 41	160	24 17	180	29 32	206	48 24	230	58 08	291
102	53 15	045	34 38	114	44 53	162	24 17	181	29 14	207	47 54	231	57 31	291
103	53 43	045	35 13	115	45 05	163	24 16	182	28 56	208	47 23	232	56 55	292
104	54 11	046	35 49	116	45 16	165	24 14	183	28 38	209	46 51	234	56 18	292
	♦ Dubhe		Denebola		REGULUS		♦ SIRIUS		RIGEL		ALDEBARAN		♦ Mirfak	
105	54 39	046	22 32	094	36 24	117	24 12	184	28 18	210	46 19	235	55 42	292
106	55 07	046	23 12	094	36 59	118	24 09	185	27 58	211	45 47	236	55 05	293
107			23 51	095	37 34	119	24 05	186	27 38	212	45 14	237	54 29	293
				096	38 08					213	44 41	238		
117	60 19	046						196						
118	60 48	046	30 57	104		131	22 38	197	23 14				47 58	298
119	61 16	046	31 36	105	43 58	132	22 26	198	22 46	224	38 13	249	47 23	298
	♦ Kochab		Denebola		♦ REGULUS		SIRIUS		RIGEL		♦ ALDEBARAN		CAPELLA	
120	43 22	021	32 13	106	44 27	133	22 13	199	22 19	225	37 36	250	62 35	279
121	43 37	022	32 51	107	44 55	134	21 59	200	21 51	226	36 59	251	61 57	280
122	43 51	022	33 29	108	45 23	136	21 45	201	21 22	227	36 22	252	61 18	280
123	44 06	022	34 06	108	45 50	137	21 31	202	20 53	228	35 44	253	60 39	281
124	44 21	022	34 44	109	46 17	138	21 15	203	20 24	229	35 06	254	60 01	282
125	44 36	022	35 21	110	46 42	139	20 59	204	19 54	230	34 28	255	59 22	282
126	44 51	022	35 57	111	47 08	141	20 43	205	19 24	231	33 50	256	58 44	283
127	45 06	023	36 34	112	47 32	142	20 26	206	18 53	231	33 12	256	58 05	283
128	45 21	023	37 10	113	47 56	143	20 08	207	18 22	232	32 34	257	57 27	284
129	45 36	023	37 47	114	48 19	145	19 50	208	17 51	233	31 55	258	56 49	284
130	45 52	023	38 22	115	48 41	146	19 31	209	17 19	234	31 17	259	56 11	285
131	46 07	023	38 58	116	49 03	148	19 11	210	16 47	235	30 38	260	55 33	285
132	46 23	023	39 33	117	49 24	149	18 51	211	16 15	236	29 59	261	54 55	286
133	46 38	023	40 08	118	49 44	150	18 31	212	15 42	237	29 20	261	54 17	286
134	46 54	024	40 43	119	50 03	152	18 09	213	15 09	238	28 42	262	53 39	287

Fig. 9(12) Portion of page from AP 3270, Epoch 2000, Vol 1, page 62 for latitude 49°N and LHA Aries 123°.

running programmes to work up and plot sights. NavPac and Compact Data for 2001 to 2005 is such a package produced by HM Nautical Almanac Office and used by the RN and other navies throughout the world. The astronomical data and the software package are provided on a CD ROM, which is easy to protect from a harsh environment. The non-uniformity and the unpredictable nature of the Universal Time scale means that the astronomical data needs to be updated every five years or so. Moreover as PCs become smaller and more popular, there will never be a problem with the software package becoming unusable. For these reasons PC-based navigation packages have become more popular than dedicated packages. The dedicated package CN-2000, which uses the methods devised by G. Bennett can be strongly recommended. It is hard wired, and even if the batteries are removed for any length of time the package will work again once new batteries have been installed. Unfortunately it has a limited shelf life, because the calculator upon which it is based has now gone out of production.

The ease with which sights can be reduced using a package like NavPac places astro on a stronger footing with GPS. With both methods available, the prudent mariner requires to understand the concepts involved and relate them to the presence of hazards, and have traditional techniques polished and available in case of failure.

9.7.3 SIGHT REDUCTION TABLES FOR AIR NAVIGATION, AP 3270

These tables are in three volumes and tabulate altitude to the nearest l' of arc and azimuth to the nearest 1°. As their name implies, they were originally intended for use in the air but they are commonly used at sea, and some of the correction tables have been modified for marine purposes. The tables were designed for use with *The Air Almanac*, which tabulates GHA and declination for every l0 minutes of UT, but they are just as easily used with *The Nautical Almanac*. The tables include an auxiliary table, which in emergencies, enables the GHA and declination of the Sun to be calculated for some years ahead without the use of an almanac. Although for various reasons (see 9.6.2) a tabulated precision of 0'·l of altitude and 0°·l of azimuth is normally adopted in marine tables and almanacs, the accuracy that can be obtained with the Air tables suffices for all practical purposes at sea.

Volume 1 is for star sights only (see Fig. 9(12)). It gives, for whole degrees of latitude and argument LHA Aries, the calculated altitude (Hc) and azimuth (Zn) of sets of 7 stars selected for their brightness and angle of cut. No interpolation is needed. The brightest stars are shown in capitals and the best combination for a fix from three stars is marked by ♦ diamond-shaped

---

Example 9(1): A four star fix using AP3270 Volume 1, Epoch 2000.

Date 4 April 2001. DR 48° 55'N 39° 55'W. Sights are taken 10 minutes after end of civil twilight at 22h 00m UT. From Table 4 of AP 3270, Volume 1, Epoch 2000, GHA Aries = 163°. Subtract longitude west from GHA Aries to give LHA Aries. LHA Aries = 123° (163° – 40°W).
The seven selected stars on page 62 for assumed latitude 49°N and LHA Aries 123° are:
♦ Kochab (44 06 022); Denebola (34 06 108); ♦ REGULUS (45 50 137); SIRIUS (21 31 202); RIGEL (20 53 228); ♦ ALDEBARAN (35 44 253); and CAPELLA (60 39 281).

The following stars were observed and reduced using AP 3270:

	♦ Kochab	Denebola	♦ REGULUS	♦ ALDEBARAN
UT	22h 03m 14s	22h 06m 12s	22h 09m 05s	22h 11m 15s
GHA, Table 4(a)+4(b)	163° 17'	163° 17'	163° 17'	163° 17'
Increment, Table 4(c)	48'	1° 33'	2° 16'	2° 49'
GHA Aries	164° 05'	164° 50'	165° 33'	166° 06'
Assumed longitude	40° 05'	39° 50'	39° 33'	40° 06'
LHA Aries	124°	125°	126°	126°
Hc	44° 21'	35° 21'	47° 08'	33° 50'
Zn	022°	110°	141°	256°
Ho	44° 17'	35° 19'	47° 02'	33° 42'
Intercept	4' away	2' away	6' away	8' away

Astronomical Fix   48°55'N, 39° 54'W

Fig. 9(13) Plot of the four-star fix as in Example 9(1). Note that AP1 and AP4 are very close together. This is coincidental and not unusual; it is not a cause for concern.

symbols. Since both north and south hemispheres are catered for, the azimuth (Zn), rather than the azimuth angle, is extracted direct. Because of precession of the equinoxes the star tables become inaccurate with the passage of time and so are calculated for a particular epoch and republished every five years. Corrections for later years are tabulated as a displacement to apply either to a position line or to the fix; in the case of the correction table for marine use to the nearest degree and 0.1M.

Plot each position line from the assumed latitude and longitude to determine the fix. The entry in Table 5, Precession and Nutation page 322, for 2001, LHA Aries 120°, and latitude N50°, requires the fix to be transferred by 1M on bearing 100°, which places the OP 2M East of the DR position.

The time to take stars is between civil and nautical twilight (see glossary) when the horizon is still firm and the stars visible. In the evenings this will be from the beginning of civil twilight and in the mornings from the end of nautical twilight. The values for twilight are given in the daily pages of *The Nautical Almanac*.

The tables are most effectively used by preplanning the observations, estimating according to the DR position and GHA Aries at the time of twilight, the LHA Aries and from the tables seeing the selection of stars available. The approximate altitude of the stars the navigator intends to take can then be set on the sextant,

identifying each in turn by its bearing (remembering to apply magnetic variation). This will enable the navigator to see the stars on the horizon well before they can be picked out in the sky, and so avoid the time-consuming and sometimes difficult business of bringing each down to the horizon.

To use the star tables a position near the DR position is assumed with a whole degree of latitude and a longitude such that it will combine (adding easterly and subtracting westerly longitudes) with the GHA to give a whole degree of LHA; see Example 9(1). The tables are entered at the appropriate latitude page, north or south, with argument LHA Aries, and the tabulated altitude (Hc) and azimuth (Zn) of the stars observed are extracted and the intercept derived in the usual way.

Volumes 2 and **3** are permanent tables, which provide for navigation by the Sun, Moon and planets and for navigational stars with declinations less than 30°. They are similar in principle to Volume 1 but tabulate, for integral degrees of latitude, declination and LHA, the calculated altitude (Hc), a quantity d used to adjust the altitude for increments of declination, and azimuth angle (Z). Selection of the page to enter is made according to the chosen latitude, the declination range (0°–14° or 15°–29°) and whether the declination and latitude have the same or contrary names. Volume 2 covers latitudes 0° to 39°, Volume 3 latitudes 39° to 89°.

Date 22 July 2001. Position to nearest degree 39°N 7°E.
The Sun is observed at 10h 23m 06s (GHA = 334° 10', Dec = N 20° 13') and at 12h 50m 42s (GHA = 11° 04' and Dec = N 20° 12'). Add longitude east to GHA Sun to give LHA Sun.

UT	10h 23m 06s	12h 50m 42s
GHA (Sun)	334°10'	11°04'
Assumed Longitude	+6°50'	+6°56'
LHA°	341°	18°
LAT°	39°N	39°N
Dec (Sun)	20°13' N	20°12'N
Degrees of Dec (Dec°)	20°	20°
Minutes of Dec (Dec')	13'	12'
Observed Altitude Ho	64°56'	65°27'
Tabular Altitude Ht	64°55'	65°29'
Tabular Difference d	+48'	+48'
Correction	+10'	+10'
Calculated Altitude Hc	65°05'	65°39'
where Hc = Ht + Correction		
Intercept p = Ho – Hc	9' away	12' away
Azimuth angle Z	135°	136°
True Azimuth	135°	224°

Example 9(2): A Sun-run-Sun fix using The Nautical Almanac for GHA and Dec and AP3270 Volume 3 for sight reduction.

The tables can also be used to check the compass from a bearing of the Sun, taking the time to the nearest minute.

Each volume carries clear instructions for use and an example of reducing a sun sight is shown below. As before an assumed position is chosen such that the latitude is a whole degree and the longitude combined with GHA gives an integral degree of LHA. The GHA and declination of the body are extracted from *The Nautical Almanac* in the usual way and the tables entered at the appropriate page with argument LHA. The altitude is corrected (Table 5) for the increments of declination and the tabulated altitude (Hc) compared with the (corrected) observed altitude

(Ho) to give the intercept, towards or away according to whether Ho is greater (to) or less (away) than Hc. Where necessary the azimuth angle (Z) is subtracted from 180° to give the azimuth according to the rule printed on each page of the tables.

Determining the astronomical fix
Assuming the ground Track is 300° (T) and the ground distance made good between the observations is 25M, determine the fix at the time of the afternoon observation. First plot the two P/Ls from their assumed latitude and longitude. Next transfer the first P/L parallel to itself on bearing 300°, distance 25M. Then the

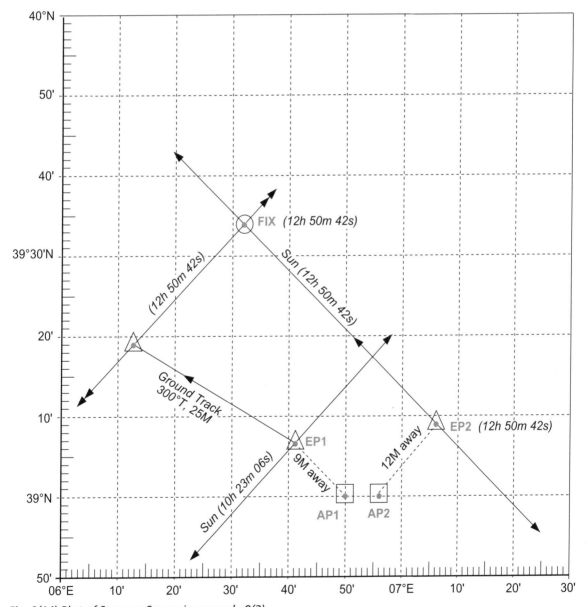

Fig. 9(14) Plot of Sun-run-Sun as in example 9(2).

astronomical fix at the intersection of the transferred P/L and the second P/L is 39° 34'N 006° 32'E; see Fig. 9(14).

For the morning observation, enter the table on page 5 of AP3270, Volume 3, Lat 39°, Declination (15° – 29°), <u>same</u> name as latitude, Dec = 20°, LHA = 341°, and extract Ht = 64 55, d = 48, Z = 135. Minutes of declination = 13, Table on page 344 gives correction to Ht for minutes of declination = 10. Use the rule at top left hand corner of page, N Lat, LHA greater than 180, Zn = Z = 135.

For the afternoon observation, enter the table on page 5 of AP3270, Volume 3, Lat 39°, Declination (15° – 29°), <u>same</u> name as latitude, Dec = 20°, LHA = 18°, and extract Ht = 65 29, d = 48, Z = 136. Minutes of declination = 12, Table on page 266 give correction to Ht for minutes of declination = 10. Use the rule at top left hand corner of page, N Lat, LHA less than 180, Zn = 360 – Z = 224.

9.7.4 SIGHT REDUCTION TABLES FOR MARINE NAVIGATION (NP 401)

These tables are in six volumes, each covering 16 degrees of latitude from 0° to 90° with an overlap of one degree between each volume. They are intended for use with *The Nautical Almanac* and tabulate calculated altitude (Hc) to the nearest 0'·1 of arc and azimuth angle (Z) to the nearest 0°·1. The principle is identical to that of AP 3270, but an integral degree of LHA rather than latitude decides which page to use. A sight reduction form (NP400 single sheet, NP400a 24 sheet pad) is available from the UK Hydrographic Office and serves both publications, although many navigators design their own for the former. An interpolation table for increments of declination printed on the inside covers is necessarily more elaborate than its equivalent in AP 3270, to match the greater precision of the main tables.

Although intended primarily for astro-navigation at sea, the tables constitute a fundamental solution to the spherical triangle in which two sides and the included angle are given; they can be used for a wide variety of purposes (eg great-circle sailing) other than sight reduction. More elaborate interpolation techniques are available for some of these.

Their increased accuracy is normally of little practical consequence, but they have the marginal advantage over AP 3270 of covering all declinations, ie not just 0° – 29°. However they lack the convenience of the separate and very much simplified star tables.

9.7.5 LATITUDE BY MERIDIAN ALTITUDE

By far the simplest form of sight is the determination of latitude by observation of the meridian altitude, usually of the Sun. It is also an easy sight to take because during the period of meridian passage the altitude changes very slowly. At the time of transit the Sun appears to hang in the sky for a period of a minute or so.

The approximate time of meridian passage, generally to the nearest minute, is calculated by applying to the UT (GMT) of meridian passage given in the ephemeris the DR longitude at noon converted into hours and minutes. In west longitudes meridian passage will be later than on the Greenwich meridian, in east longitudes, earlier.

In some circumstances a timed altitude, generally to the nearest minute, is preferable to judging the maximum altitude but it is common practice at sea to observe the meridian altitude by taking a series of, say five, sights over two or three minutes when the Sun appears to be at its highest, before it dips. In that case the sight is not timed and no plotting is involved.

The altitude corrections are applied in the usual way and the zenith distance (90° minus true altitude) added to the declination when it is the same name as the latitude and subtracted when it is not. This gives the observer's latitude.

9.7.6 LATITUDE BY THE POLE STAR

Polaris, the Pole Star, is easily picked out in the night sky by following the line of the pointers at the leading end of the Plough. It is not quite in line with the axis of the Earth's rotation and a correction to its altitude has to be made to obtain the latitude, which otherwise would correspond precisely with the true altitude. The star revolves very slowly around the pole of the heavens at an angular distance of about 1°. Its apparent movement is only about 1' in 3 min so that an observation for latitude need only be timed to the nearest minute.

For the time of the sight GHA Aries is extracted from *The Nautical Almanac* and the longitude applied to give LHA Aries. With LHA Aries as argument the Pole Star Tables in *The Nautical Almanac* give a correction to the altitude from which the latitude is deduced. Alternatively, when a lesser precision is acceptable, the Q correction (Table 6 in AP 3270, Volume 1, page 324) may be used. In each case a separate table gives the azimuth of Polaris.

When the star is above or below the pole of the heavens, near the meridian, its altitude will change least and time will be less important. Half an hour either side of meridian altitude, the change in altitude will only be about 1' and this is the best time to observe so that a series of shots can be averaged to eliminate random error.

9.7.7 PLOTTING THE SUN'S GEOGRAPHICAL POSITION

In the tropics when the Sun's declination is not more than about 2° from the latitude, it is possible to obtain an extremely accurate fix by plotting the Sun's geographical position as it passes the meridian and from it describing two (or more) arcs with radius the zenith distance. About 5 to 10 minutes before meridian passage, and at about the same time after it, timed altitudes are taken in the normal fashion. The geographical position of the Sun at these times is then plotted with declination as latitude and GHA as longitude (360° minus GHA for easterly longitudes). With the three positions (the meridian altitude can conveniently form the third) as centre, arcs are described with zenith distance as radius; where they intersect constitutes the fix. Fig. 9(15), in tropical latitudes and easterly longitudes, illustrates an example. If it is necessary to transfer the first position circle for the course and distance sailed, as it might be at high speeds, this is most conveniently done by shifting the first geographical position the course and distance made good.

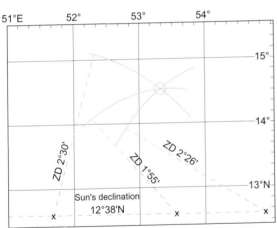

Fig. 9(15) Plotting the Sun's geographical position in the tropics from arcs of small circles; this can only be done when declination is within 2° of latitude. In this method, declination is used as latitude and GHA is used as longitude.

9.7.8 EQUAL ALTITUDES

In certain circumstances, when the difference between the observer's latitude and the Sun's declination does not exceed about 10°, longitude may be determined by taking equal altitudes of the Sun on either side of the meridian. At the same time the latitude can conveniently be found by meridian altitude, thus giving a fix. A correction must be made for the change in declination between the successive observations and for any change in latitude between the sights. In this case

the assumption that meridian passage takes place at maximum altitude will not lead to significant error. Serious errors will occur if the method is used outside the rather confined limits in which it is valid. These are that the Sun should be not less than 20° in bearing from the meridian, not more than 10° in hour angle and at an altitude of not less than 70°.

The time of meridian passage is first worked out in the normal way and the first altitude taken, typically, about 15 minutes before it, and the time noted. Altitude corrections need not be applied, provided the afternoon sight is taken from the same height of eye. The meridian altitude is then observed as usual and (unless a second sextant has been available) the altitude of the first sight is set on the sextant again. At about the same interval after meridian passage the time is noted when the Sun is at the altitude set on the sextant. The mid-time of the observations is obtained by adding the two times together and dividing by 2; the GHA of the Sun for that time is the longitude west (or 360° minus GHA, the longitude east).

If the observer's latitude has changed and/or the Sun's declination has changed between the sights a correction is made to the first altitude to obtain the second. The quantity d given on the daily pages of *The Nautical Almanac* is the change of declination, north or south, in an hour; change of latitude will be obtained by working out a DR for the time of the second observation, or from the traverse table. The corrections can be combined and will be added to the first altitude if the Sun is getting nearer to the observer and subtracted if it is getting further away.

9.8 THE POSITION LINE

9.8.1 THE USE OF A SINGLE POSITION LINE

A single astronomical position line can be used together with other information such as a line of soundings or a bearing (whether obtained visually by compass or by any radio method) to produce a fix. The accuracy of the fix will depend upon both the accuracy of the information and the angle of cut. The accuracy of a visual bearing will depend on the distance of the object; the accuracy of radio bearings on that of the system which is being used.

A useful fix can often be obtained by observing a planet or bright star shortly before sunrise, and crossing it later with an altitude of the Sun when it has reached at least 10°; the angle of cut should be at least 30°. In this way any uncertainty as to the course and distance used to transfer the first position line will be minimised.

Angle	Error
°	′
90	1.0
85	1.0
80	1.0
75	1.0
70	1.1
65	1.1
60	1.2
55	1.2
50	1.3
45	1.4
40	1.5
35	1.7
30	2.0
25	2.4
20	2.9
15	3.9
10	5.8
5	11.5

Fig. 9(16) The effect of angle of cut on fix accuracy.

A single position line can also be used to clear a point or danger in the same way that a visual bearing can, making due allowance for the accuracy of the sight. Where appropriate the position line can be shifted to clear the danger by the required distance; the direction and distance the line has been shifted will then be the course and distance to make good.

9.8.2 ANGLE OF CUT
For a two-body fix, whether Sun, Moon, star or planet (and whether obtained from simultaneous or successive altitudes) the optimum angle of cut is 90°, so as to minimise the effect of errors in either position line. However, the error introduced by smaller angles of cut decreases so slowly that for all practical purposes any angle between about 60° and 120° will be as good as the right angle. See Fig. 9(16) and the accompanying table. With three position lines the optimum angle of cut is 60° and with four position lines, as with two, it is 90°.

9.8.3 RATE OF CHANGE OF BEARING AND ALTITUDE
In terrestrial navigation it is obvious from the technique of doubling the angle on the bow that rate of change in bearing increases until the object is abeam. The maximum rate of change will be on the beam.

The same principle applies to a celestial body as it approaches the meridian. The altitude on the other hand changes most rapidly when the body is rising or setting, and very slowly around the time of culmination. Further, the higher the altitude (in other words the closer the declination is to the latitude) the faster the change in bearing. In low latitudes it is thus possible on occasions to obtain a right-angled cut by successive observations of the Sun on either side of the meridian within the space of a comparatively few minutes.

For historical reasons that go back to before 'the problem of longitude' was solved, the noon position is always logged as the principal position for the day. However, noon is, navigationally, far from the best time to take a fix and whenever possible successive sights should be taken either side of the meridian. The most important criterion is the shortest possible run between sights, consistent with an adequate change in bearing.

9.9 PLOTTING AND EVALUATING THE SIGHT

9.9.1 PLOTTING
For oceanic purposes the chart in daily use is unlikely to be on a scale convenient for plotting sights. Mercator plotting sheets for different latitude bands are available from the Hydrographic Office but they are not essential, take up room and cost money. Any navigational chart in the right latitude band can of course be used to plot sights by simply altering the longitude labels.

If the sight is worked from the DR position (rather than from the assumed position used with inspection tables) the simplest form of plot is to erect, for example in the work-book, a perpendicular to represent the meridian and use the lines of the work-book on any convenient scale for latitude. (Squared paper serves the same purpose). The sights are then plotted, using a protractor, from the DR position and the resultant fix transferred to the chart either as a bearing and distance from the DR position or in terms of latitude and longitude, departure being converted into difference of longitude by the traverse or any other suitable table. If the DR position for successive sights is worked up from that used in the first sight, the run between the sights need not be considered.

The most convenient form of plotting sheet to use with an assumed position, where each sight will be plotted from a separate longitude, is the 'Universal' plotting sheet (Fig. 9(17)) issued by the US Defense Mapping Agency, and also published by private firms in Europe and USA.

The vertical line (meridian) is graduated in

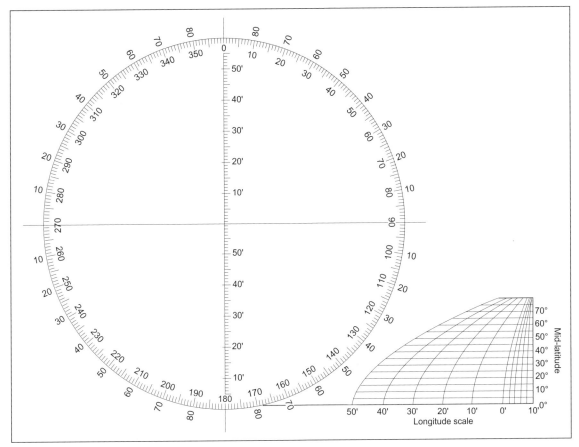

Fig. 9(17) The 'Universal' plotting sheet.

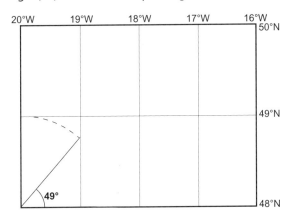

Fig. 9(18) Construction of a plotting sheet for a limited area.

nautical miles and the compass rose is marked on the inside from 0° to 360° and on the outside from 0° to 90° north and south of the horizontal line (parallel). This parallel is labelled as the assumed latitude. The plotting sheet is converted to a Mercator chart by joining the graduations north and south corresponding to the assumed latitude. This defines meridians either side of the central one.

For example, in DR latitude 50° (north or south), join the two fifties on the outer graduation east of the central meridian (one north and one south of the central parallel). This establishes the line of longitude 1° east of the central meridian. Minutes of longitude are measured from the longitude scale at the bottom of the sheet using the mid-latitude.

A plotting sheet effective over a limited area can be constructed by drawing equally spaced vertical lines to represent the meridians with horizontal lines correctly spaced in relation to the meridians as parallels of latitude (a relationship defined mathematically by the cosine of the latitude or its complement the secant).

An example construction is shown in Fig. 9(18): the meridians are drawn to a convenient scale and the spacing of the parallels is determined by drawing a line from one parallel towards the next at an angle equal in degrees to the mid-latitude between them. The length of the inclined line between the meridians represents the correct spacing between parallels; the inclined line can then be graduated to measure nautical miles.

9.9.2 EVALUATING POSITION LINES

The software package NavPac can be used to apply probability and statistical techniques to three or more position line observations up to a maximum of fifteen. Either by plotting or inspecting the intercepts it is possible to delete mistakes or remove poor observations, and additional observations can be included to determine the fix as the passage proceeds. In principle this should increase the accuracy of the position and the taking of sights.

Manual techniques for evaluating position lines to establish the most probable position is an important part of the art of astro-navigation at sea. A plot of six star sights, for example, may show position lines intersecting at nine separate points within a reasonable distance of the DR, and some method will be required to analyse the plot and see which of the lines is likely to be the more reliable and to detect the presence of gross errors or blunders. Observational errors are of course an integral part of navigation and the first thing to realise is that a position line more accurately represents a band of position the width of which corresponds to the probable error of the observation. Thus if the error from all causes in an observation is estimated, to a given confidence level, to be, say, half a mile, the observer's position should lie within a band of position a mile wide (ie half a mile either side of the position line). The confidence level most generally used in navigation is the 95% level at which the stated error will be exceeded only once in twenty occasions.

When two position lines cut at an angle of 90°, and each position line is assumed to be equally reliable, the error configuration will be a box which is usually shown as a circle of error with radius slightly larger than the position-line error. When the cut angle is other than 90°, the bands will form a diamond of error, which may

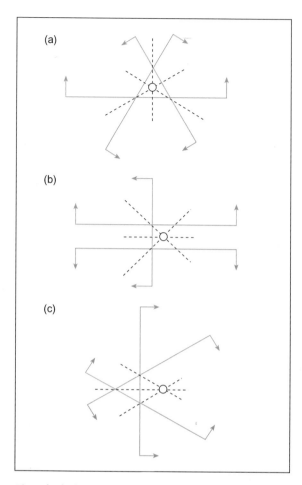

Fig. 9(20) The bisector method of establishing the most probable position. The arrows point toward the body observed.

conveniently be drawn as an ellipse. Fig. 9(19) shows examples. In practice these configurations will seldom be drawn on the chart but the experienced navigator will always think of position lines as bands with a certain width and of the resultant fix as a small area within which his ship lies rather than as a point.

When three position lines intersect at an angle of about 120°, the in-centre of the cocked hat is generally assumed to be the position. This will be so if the errors in each sight are equal and in the same direction, as they usually are; however, if there is a blunder in one of the position lines, the position may well lie outside the triangle.

There are several ways of analysing the astro plot, all of which involve marking on each position line, generally by a small arrow, the bearing of the body observed. The bearing will of course be at right angles to the position line.

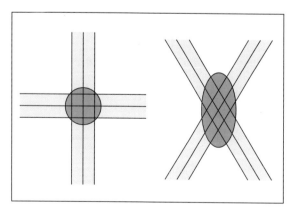

Fig. 9(19) Error configuration and angle of cut.

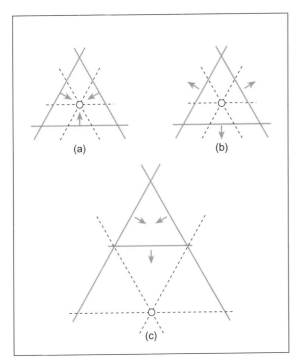

Fig. 9(21) Shifting astro-position lines an equal amount towards or away from the bodies observed to establish the most probable position from a cocked hat.

Unless there is an abnormal cause of error the arrows should all point towards or away from the centre of the figure described by the position lines. In the bisector method the (external) angle between two position lines whose azimuth arrows both point either towards or away from each other is bisected (by eye); the intersection of the bisectors is taken as the fix. The use of bisectors, which are in fact position lines obtained from equal differences of altitude, eliminates systematic error and averages random errors in the observations. However, there are constraints on the method. The best bisector will be derived from sights separated in azimuth by 180° but, because of the slow variation of the sine curve, this figure can be extended to 150°. The method should not be used where the difference in azimuth is less than 60°.

An alternative to the bisector method is to shift all the position lines the same amount and in the same direction, either towards or away from the body observed, thus closing or opening out the pattern, until they meet at a point. This will both eliminate systematic error and reveal gross errors or a blunder. The two methods are illustrated in Figs. 9(20) and 9(21).

Two position lines constitute a fix. A third line,

however, will increase the reliability of the fix; but it will not enable the navigator to distinguish between any systematic errors and blunders. A 'cartwheel' fix of four stars whose bearings differ by 45° will give a more reliable fix, but four stars 90° apart will often indicate, by the spacing of the two sets of reciprocal position lines, the size of the systematic error and the probable size of the random error. On the other hand, since the bisector method eliminates systematic error, the soundest procedure is to take four stars 90° apart and analyse the plot by that method which will indicate whether the set has been influenced by random error. A fifth sight as a stand-by, which need not be worked up, can indicate a blunder if that is suspected.

9.10 BOOKS ABOUT ASTRO-NAVIGATION

The Nautical Almanac – NP 314 (TSO, Annual)

AP 3270 Sight Reduction Tables for Air Navigation, Vol 1, Epoch 2000, (TSO, 1997),

Admiralty Manual of Navigation, Vol 2, – not currently available to the general public, but retail sales in bookshops are being investigated; (TSO, 2000)

NP 401 Sight Reduction Tables for Marine Navigation (six volumes), TSO

American Practical Navigator, by Nathaniel Bowditch US DMA Pub. No 9, (US Government Printing Office, 1995).

NavPac and Compact Data 2001 – 2005, by B D Yallop & C Y Hohenkerk, (TSO, 2000)

AstroNavPC and Compact Data 2001 – 2005, Astro-navigation Methods and Software for the PC, HM Nautical Almanac Office (Willmann-Bell, 2000)

The Complete On-Board Celestial Navigator, by G.G.Bennett (McGraw Hill, 1999)

Celestial Navigation by Tom Cunliffe (Fernhurst, 2001)

Celestial Navigation for Yachtsmen, by Mary Blewitt, (Adlard Coles, 11th edition, 1997)

Celestial navigation (programmed learning) by Gerry Smith, (Adlard Coles, 2nd edition 2001)

Elements of Navigation and Nautical Astronomy, by C H. Cotter, (Hollis and Carter, 1995)

Lecky's Wrinkles in Practical Navigation, (Out of print), 23rd edition by G. Cobb, (George Philip)

Ocean Navigator by Kenneth Wilkes, rev'd by P. Langley -Price & P. Ouvry, (Adlard Coles, 7th edition 2000)

The Yacht Navigator's Handbook, by Normal Dahl, (Ward Lock, 1983)

Ocean Sailing by Tom Cunliffe, (Fernhurst, 2000)

Reed's Heavenly Bodies (Annual) by Lt Cdr H. Baker, Reeds

Ocean Yachtmaster by P. Langley-Price & P. Ouvry, (Adlard Coles, 1996)

Ocean Yachtmaster Exercises by P. Langley-Price & P. Ouvry, (Adlard Coles, 1986)

Philip's Stargazer Pack, inc Night Sky notes, star chart and planisphere

Collins Guide to Stars and Planets by Ian Ridpath

From Sails to Satellites by J E D Williams, (OUP, 1994)

Using PCs on Board by R. Buttress and T. Thornton, (Adlard Coles, 2000)

Chapter 10 Communications

CONTENTS

10.1 MEANS OF COMMUNICATING

Communications are a means to an end, not an end in themselves. Usually the content of a message is more important than the means. This principle is reflected in the Handbook: the subject of a message is best covered in the chapter which deals with that subject, as in real life. For example, in emergency situations all the means of communications used, including GMDSS, are described in Chapter 13, "Safety and Distress". Or again, the means used to disseminate Navigational warnings are described in Chapter 7, "Navigation and Passage Making". Thus the yachtsman should instinctively find in one comprehensive chapter all the information relating to a particular topic.

Yachtsmen should be able to communicate at sea with other vessels, port authorities, marinas, the Coastguard, foreign coast radio stations, race officers and personal or business contacts. They

may also wish to receive Marine Safety Information (MSI), ie weather forecasts and gale warnings, navigational warnings and safety or distress messages.

Various means of communication are mentioned or described in detail below. Some are slow and obsolescent, but simple and reliable, best used over short distances. Others are much quicker, longer range, more sophisticated and invariably more expensive.

By far the commonest way by which yachts communicate is Radiotelephony (speaking on the radio, or R/T for short) which therefore forms the bulk of this chapter.

10.2 INTERNATIONAL CODE OF SIGNALS

10.2.1 FORMAT
The International Code of Signals (ISBN 011 551015X, available from The Stationery Office),

was revised in 1964 and came into force in 1969; it was consolidated in 1991. It is the time-honoured, procedural basis for most forms of communication afloat. It adopts the principle that each signal has a complete meaning, and omits the vocabulary method used in earlier versions, so as to avoid language difficulties. For that reason, if for no other, yachtsmen should have an outline knowledge of its content and a few simple messages. But for comprehensive use of the Code, the complete code book must be held on board.

The Code plays a part in today's plain language voice communication (radiotelephony), even though users may be unaware that they are following its procedures. Coded messages in nine languages alleviate the problems of translating international communications.

Methods of transmission
Messages can be sent by the Code in the following ways:

1. Radiotelephone: by voice in plain language or Code.
2. Flashing light, using the Morse code; see 10.2.2. By day and night, in plain language (preferably) or code, singly or in groups.
3. Voice, over a loud hailer in plain language.
4. Sound signalling in Morse, eg with a foghorn. Slow, and possibly confusing in poor visibility.
5. Radiotelegraphy in Morse. Not for yachtsmen.
6. Signal flags (see page 292) displayed singly for the most important messages (or in groups for more complex meanings). Flags are slow, need good visibility and do not lend themselves to use on a small yacht.
7. Hand flags (or arms) in Morse; little known method.

Method 1 is of course the norm, but if your VHF fails or you are dismasted, consider method 2 to make contact. Method 3 is very short range and requires a megaphone. The remainder are either impracticable on a yacht or so dated as to elicit no response. Not listed is semaphore which can be very efficient over short distances when sent and read by competent people – train your crew.

Types of signals
The present International Code (in English, French, German, Greek, Italian, Japanese, Norwegian, Russian and Spanish) consists of:

a. Single-letter signals whose meanings are very urgent, important, or much used.
b. Two-letter signals in the General Section.
c. Three-letter signals beginning with the letter 'M' in the Medical Section.

Complements are used to amplify the available groups, vary the meaning, or ask a question. These are beyond the scope of the yachtsman.

The Code is arranged under the following subjects:
Distress, Emergency, Casualties, Damage; Aids to Navigation, Navigation; Manoeuvres; Miscellaneous; Meteorology; Communications; Pratique; Medical.

10.2.2 USE BY YACHTSMEN
Yachtsmen are most likely to use the Code in R/T or Morse. If there are language problems, plain language messages can be spelled phonetically, eg "Am at Brehat – I spell: Bravo, Romeo, Echo, Hotel, Alfa, Tango".

Although not an RYA requirement, it is worth knowing the Code flags, the meanings of single-letter signals, the Morse code and the phonetic alphabet; all in colour on page 292. There are 26 alphabetical flags, 11 pendants (numerals 0-9 plus the Answer Pendant or Code Flag), and three triangular flags the First, Second and Third Substitutes.

Sending Morse code by light is best on an Aldis lamp with a proper flashing trigger and a reasonably accurate way of aiming it at the recipient. An ordinary torch may be better than nothing – but not much. Assuming you have learned Morse (and it is well worthwhile), it should be possible to read and send messages at about five to ten words per minute.

10.3 THE RADIO SPECTRUM

It is the task of the Radiocommunications Agency (RA) to manage the non-military part of the Radio Spectrum so as to ensure that it runs efficiently and effectively. There are three main aspects:

a. Frequency planning and allocating;
b. Assigning and licensing users; and
c. Keeping the Spectrum free of harmful interference.

One has only to compare the result with the piecemeal way in which the Internet has evolved to appreciate that the RA has been largely successful.

The RA regulates the use of radio equipment installed or used on board, so that all who use the radio spectrum can do so without transmissions being subjected to interference, particularly in emergencies. In general the regulations are contained in the International Radio Regulations and the Wireless Telegraphy Act 1949, as amended, which provides that a licence issued by the Secretary of State is required to install or use any radio apparatus on board a UK registered vessel or one whose moorings are predominantly in the UK; see 10.4.2.

Radiocommunications Agency, Wyndham House, 189 Marsh Wall, London E14 9SX. Tel 020 7211 0211; Fax 020 7211 0507. amcb@ra.gtnet.gov.uk www.radio.gov.uk

10.3.1 FREQUENCIES

Radio transmissions are normally referred to by their frequency rather than wavelength. The two are of course closely inter-related, as shown by the formula:

Wavelength (metres) x Frequency (kHz) = 3×10^5
Thus 1500 metres wavelength equals 200kHz, and 200 metres equals 1500kHz, and so on.

Frequencies are expressed in kiloHertz (kHz), once called kilocycles per second. For frequencies of 3000kHz and above, the MegaHertz (MHz) is used, one MHz being 1000kHz.

The frequency bands in use in marine radio are:

Band	Frequency	Wavelength (m)
Low (LF)	3 – 300kHz	10,000 – 1000
Medium (MF)	30 – 3000kHz	1000 – 100
High (HF)	3 – 30MHz	100 – 10
Very High(VHF)	30 – 300MHz	10 – 1

Typical frequencies (in kHz) covered by a yacht's radio equipment are:

150 – 400	RDF beacons, LW shipping forecasts;
550 – 1600	Receiving MW broadcasts;
1600 – 4000	MF/HF communications; and
90 – 105MHz	Receiving FM/AM broadcasts.

10.3.2 MODES OF EMISSION

Intelligence is impressed upon a radio emission by modulation, which entails different modes of emission. A continuous emission of constant amplitude (or strength) and of constant frequency carries no information. The simplest way of impressing intelligence upon it is to switch it on and off (or key it), eg make Morse Code characters. This type of modulation is designated as AlA and is used for the identification signal of radiobeacons and in radiotelegraphy.

The amplitude of the radio emission, however, can be fluctuated at a rate and to a degree corresponding with a sound wave to produce speech, music or a plain musical tone. The latter may be keyed as necessary. These emissions are referred to as 'amplitude modulation' (AM). There are various types depending on whether the original (carrier) radio wave is transmitted with the

so-called 'sidebands' generated in the process of modulation, or whether the sideband is wholly or partially suppressed. One of the sidebands may also be suppressed so as to make better use of the transmitter's power and of the radio-frequency spectrum. The resulting 'single-sideband' (SSB) emission is the standard for maritime medium frequency (MF) radio, enabling the number of MF channels to be doubled.

The designation A2A refers to AM, the type of emission being telegraphy by the keying of an amplitude-modulating audio frequency (or frequencies), or by keying the modulated emission. It is commonly used for the identification signals of aeronautical radiobeacons.

A second way of impressing intelligence on a radio wave is to fluctuate the frequency, with the amplitude staying constant. This is called 'frequency modulation' or FM, and is used in VHF radiotelephones. It suffers less than AM from outside interference, and is simple and relatively cheap; but it occupies more spectrum width per channel and therefore is unsuitable for the HF and MF bands.

The modes of emission most commonly used in marine radio are:

Al A	Continuous wave telegraphy, Morse code.
A2A	Telegraphy by the on-off keying of a tone modulated carrier, Morse code: double sideband.
H2A	Telegraphy by the on-off keying of a tone modulated carrier, Morse code: single sideband, full carrier.
A3E	R/T using amplitude modulation: double sideband.
R3E	R/T using amplitude modulation: single sideband, reduced carrier.
J3E	R/T using amplitude modulation: single sideband, suppressed carrier.
H3E	R/T using amplitude modulation: single sideband, full carrier.
F1B	Telegraphy using frequency modulation: Narrow-band direct-printing (Telex/Navtex).
F3E	Telephony using frequency modulation (Sound broadcasting).
FXX	Cases not covered by FIB, F3E nor frequency modulation facsimile, in which the main carrier is frequency modulated.

10.3.3 VHF RADIO

The general subject of VHF radiotelephones for yachtsmen is well covered in RYA booklet G22, which gives the various procedures in detail. Virtually all ships, sea-going yachts, commercial ports, marinas, MRCC/MRSCs and other elements of the rescue services are fitted with VHF.

VHF range is slightly more than line of sight distance between the aerials, so the aerial needs to be as efficient and as high as possible. 35M is a typical range between a yacht's masthead aerial 9m above sea level and a shore station aerial. The formula for range (M) to the horizon is $2.25 \times \sqrt{\text{aerial height in metres}}$. Thus two boats, each with 9m high aerials can expect 13 – 15M range. If dismasted, an emergency aerial is well worth having on board.

The maximum permitted output of a VHF set is 25W. A low power output, usually 1W, is used for short range communication. Hand-held VHF sets operate on 5W and 1W and are ideal in the cockpit, or if short-handed.

Most VHF sets are 'Simplex', ie they transmit and receive on the same frequency, so that only one person can talk at a time. 'Semi-duplex' sets transmit and receive on different frequencies, while fully 'Duplex' sets can do this simultaneously, so that conversation is normal.

Most sets have 'dual watch', whereby Ch 16 and one other channel can be monitored at the same time. All international channels can usually be scanned.

Frequencies and Channels

The frequencies allocated by international agreement for marine VHF are in the range 156.00 –174.00 MHz, as shown below.

Ch 16 (156.80MHz) is used for distress and safety, and for calling and answering. Once in

TRANSMITTING FREQUENCIES IN THE VHF MARITIME MOBILE BAND

Channel	Ship station	Coast station	Inter ship	Single frequency	Two frequency	Public correspondence
60	156.025	160.625			•	•
01	156.050	160.650			•	•
61	156.075	160.675			•	•
02	156.100	160.700			•	•
62	156.125	160.725			•	•
03	156.150	160.750			•	•
63	156.175	160.775			•	•
04	156.200	160.800			•	•
64	156.225	160.825			•	•
05	156.250	160.850			•	•
65	156.275	160.875			•	•
06	156.300		•			
66	156.325	160.925			•	•
07	156.350	160.950			•	•
67	156.375	156.375	•	•		
08	156.400		•			
68	156.425	156.425		•		
09	156.450	156.450	•	•		
69	156.475	156.475	•	•		
10	156.500	156.500	•	•		
70	156.525	156.525	DSC (GMDSS)			
11	156.550	156.550		•		
71	156.575	156.575		•		
12	156.600	156.600		•		
72	156.625		•			
13	156.650	156.650	•	•		
73	156.675	156.675	•	•		
14	156.700	156.700		•		
74	156.725	156.725		•		
15	156.750	156.750	•	•		
75	156.775		Guard band			
16	156.800	156.800	Distress, Safety, Calling			
76	156.825		Guard band			
17	156.850	156.850	•	•		
77	156.875		•			
18	156.900	161.500			•	•
78	156.925	161.525			•	•
19	156.950	161.550			•	•
79	156.975	161.575			•	•
20	157.000	161.600			•	•
80	157.025	161.625			•	•
21	157.050	161.650			•	•
81	157.075	161.675			•	•
22	157.100	161.700			•	•
82	157.125	161.725		•	•	•
23	157.150	161.750			•	•
83	157.175	161.775		•	•	•
24	157.200	161.800			•	•
84	157.225	161.825		•	•	•
25	157.250	161.850			•	•
85	157.275	161.875		•	•	•
26	157.300	161.900			•	•
86	157.325	161.925		•	•	•
27	157.350	161.950			•	•
87	157.375	161.975		•	•	•
28	157.400	162.000			•	•
88	157.425	162.025		•		

NOTES

1. For intership communication, those channels (ie 06, 08, 72 and 77) assigned solely for this purpose should be used in preference to other frequencies. Ch 06 may also be used by ships and aircraft on SAR operations, when interference must be avoided.
2. Ch 10, 67 and 73 may be used by ships, aircraft and land stations for SAR co-ordination and for anti-pollution operations.
3. Ch 13 is an international inter-ship navigational safety channel, sometimes called "Bridge-to-bridge".
4. In 1972 the original 50kHz channel spacings were reduced to 25kHz, and extra channels were interleaved between the existing ones. Hence the oddly sequenced channel designations, since channels 29 to 59 inclusive are allocated to other services.
5. Ch 10, 23, 73, 84, 86 and 67 (exceptionally) are used by the UK Coastguard for broadcasting MSI.

contact, stations must switch to a working channel, except for safety matters; or in the UK they may be switched to Ch 67. Ch 16 will be monitored at least until 2005 by ships, CG stations and any remaining Coast radio stations. Vessels are encouraged to monitor Ch 16, in the following words:

Every ship should make its contribution to safety by guarding one or other of the radio distress frequencies for as long as practicable, whether or not required to do so by regulation.

VHF channels are grouped for three main purposes, as shown below, and in their preferred order of usage. Some channels are used for more than one purpose.

- a. **Public correspondence** (via coast radio stations) channels are: Ch 26, 27, 25, 24, 23, 28, 04, 01, 03, 02, 07, 05, 84, 87, 86, 83, 85, 88, 61, 64, 65, 62, 66, 63, 60, 82, 78, 81. All these can be used for duplex working if the set is so equipped.
- b. **Inter-ship**. These are all simplex channels: Ch **06**, **08**, 13, 09, 10, **72**, 73, 69, **77**, 15, 17.
- c. **Port operations** (pilotage, tugs etc). The simplex channels are: Ch 12, 14, 11, 13, 09, 68, 71, 74, 69, 73, 17, 15. Duplex channels are: Ch 20, 22, 18, 19, 21, 05, 07, 02, 03, 01, 04, 78, 82, 79, 81, 80, 60, 63, 66, 62, 65, 64, 61, 84.

The following channels have specific uses:

Ch 0 (156·00MHz) is for use by HM Coastguard, lifeboats and SAR helicopters. It may only be fitted in a yacht if specially authorised by the RA.

Ch 67 (156·375MHz) is used in the UK (only) for yacht and small craft safety, accessed via Ch 16.

Ch 70 (156·525MHz) is reserved for Digital Selective Calling for distress and safety purposes; see Chapter 13.

Ch 80 (Tx 161·625MHz; Rx 157·025MHz) is the UK's primary working channel between yachts and marinas.

Ch M (157·85MHz) is the secondary channel.

Ch M2 (161·425MHz) is used by yacht clubs for race control, with Ch M as a stand-by. Ch M and Ch M2 are 'private' channels that pleasure craft are authorised to use when granted a Ship Radio Licence. Marinas or yacht clubs wishing to use Ch M, Ch M2, or Ch 80 must apply for a Maritime Coastal Licence.

10.3.4 MF AND HF RADIO

Medium Frequency (MF) and High Frequency (HF) can conveniently be considered together, because there are basic similarities and sets are available which span the MF (1605 – 4200kHz) and HF (4 – 25MHz) marine bands. MF radiotelephones provide communication at ranges of up to 300M (555km), considerably greater than can be achieved by VHF. An HF set can give worldwide coverage. But MF/HF sets are a little larger and heavier than VHF, consume more power, and are more expensive.

MF/HF sets are single sideband (SSB, 10.3.5) and must be type-approved for a licence to be obtained. Many channels are available at different frequencies. The MF international RT distress frequency, 2182kHz, is used for distress and calling, EPIRB signals, urgency and safety messages. Some UK and foreign Coastguard Centres, and those foreign Coast Radio Stations still in being, keep watch on 2182kHz. There is a silence period on this frequency for three minutes after every hour and half-hour, ie at H to H+03 and H +30 to H+33. During these silence periods all transmissions except distress, urgency and safety communications must cease on 2182kHz.

HF means High Frequency, Short wave, Long distance. It also means quite a high degree of technical skill and perseverance to communicate successfully when radio propagation conditions are anything other than ideal. In that respect it is far inferior to the clarity of SatCom, but is of course free, apart from capital outlay which applies equally to SatCom. It is better compared with Amateur (ham) Radio (10.3.7).

HF propagation is by skywave which is hugely influenced by the reflective, and attenuating, properties of the ionosphere. The ionosphere is a broad region in the earth's atmosphere which extends from about 60km to 10,000km above the earth's surface, depending on time of day/ night and season. Within it are free electrons and ions produced by the ionizing action of solar radiation. These disturb the propagation of radio waves by refracting, reflecting and attenuating them. At night the reflective effect is usually strongest and the radio waves will be bounced between earth and ionosphere over vast distances. But sunspot activity and solar flares will reduce range and increase interference.

A good quality SSB MF/HF radio will cost from £2000 to £2500, whilst the ham equivalent can cost from £700 to £2000. Hams are more versatile and work through an amazing network of amateur operators ashore who are often prepared to go to great lengths to assist a fellow ham in say mid-Pacific. SSB traffic (10.3.5) has declined with the advent of SatCom, so that it is now easier to find a clear working frequency. Many long-distance yachtsmen will opt to have aboard both SSB and ham. Much depends on your need to communicate and the effort, and money, you are prepared to put into it.

10.3.5 SINGLE SIDEBAND (SSB)

In single sideband (SSB), the carrier and one sideband (usually the lower) are suppressed, thus reducing the width to the upper sideband only. This therefore reduces the band width, and greatly reduces interference with adjacent channels. Also, where otherwise the output power of a transmitter would have been divided between the carrier and both sidebands, it is now concentrated on one sideband, thus increasing power output.

H3E full carrier SSB working should be used for calling and listening on 2182kHz, and for all Safety working between ship and shore. R3E reduced carrier SSB working is seldom used in practice. All other broadcasts (ie MSI) on working channels are made in the J3E mode (fully suppressed carrier, SSB), as are link calls and other transmissions on working channels.

If using French documentation, the term for SSB is BLU (Bandes Latérale Unique); and for Dutch it is EZB (Enkel Zyband).

SSB frequencies (kHz) used for Distress, Calling and Intership working are as follows:

Band MHz	Calling/ Distress	Intership	Remarks
2	2182	2065, 2079	MF, up to 200M
4	4146, 4149	4125	
6	6215	6224, 6227, 6230	Most popular
8	8291	8294, 8297	
12	12290	12353, 12356	Long range
16	16420	16528, 16531	

10.3.6 CITIZEN'S BAND RADIO (CB)

CB radio is a short range radio service that can be used for business or pleasure. You do not need technical qualifications to operate the multitude of CB equipment that is available. CB is specially designed not to cause interference to other radio users, hence only radios meeting the required specifications can be used. There are 31,000 licensed CB operators in the UK.

Afloat, CB is not a substitute for proper marine band VHF, if only because the CB emergency channel (Ch 09) is not monitored in the same way as VHF Ch 16. But CB radio is a relatively cheap method of communicating between a yacht and a shore station, eg the yacht club or marina – or even with the owner's house if within range. In particular CB radio can be used for some of the social talk for which marine VHF is not intended.

Send the licence application form and the fee

(£15 in 2001) to: Radio Licensing Centre, PO Box 885, Bristol BS99 5LG. Tel 0117 925 8333. Unless you are using CB radio under the supervision of another CB licence holder, you must have a licence in your own name; the minimum age is 14. Information on CB Radio (Licensing, Equipment, Interference and Abuse) is available from the RA.

The CB Code of Practice includes the following:

a. Read the licence carefully.
b. Listen before transmitting, with the Squelch control turned down (and Tone Squelch turned off if you have Selective Call facilities), to ensure the channel is clear.
c. The calling channel is Ch 14. Once contact is established move to another channel.
d. Pause before replying, so that other stations may join the conversation.
e. Use plain language.
f. At all times and on all channels give priority to calls for assistance. Leave Ch 09 clear for emergencies. If you hear a call for help, wait. If no regular volunteer monitor answers, then offer help if you can.
g. In emergency, if there is no answer on Ch 09, try Ch 14 or 19.
h. Keep transmissions and chat as brief as possible.

10.3.7 AMATEUR RADIO

Amateur, or 'ham', Radio is a hobby for everyone interested in communicating. It is not a substitute for official maritime facilities, available on VHF, MF and HF. But it can be a useful additional way of communicating, particularly for yachts which cruise extensively. There are two million licensed amateur radio enthusiasts in the world, and at least some of them are seagoing. Several 'nets', operating on agreed frequencies, function for specific sea areas such as the UK, the Atlantic, the Caribbean, and the coastal waters of the United States.

Amateur Radio, like other radio services, is controlled by the International Telecommunications Union in Geneva, which allocates strictly defined frequencies. All countries require that amateur radio enthusiasts pass an examination to ensure that they can operate without causing interference to other radio services.

Although most amateur operators communicate by voice, other forms of transmission are by Morse, by slow-scan television, or by teletype. A good set is relatively expensive, and it is essential to have very efficient aerial and earthing arrangements.

For details of Amateur licences, cost £15, contact the Radio Licensing Centre; see 10.3.6. There are five licence categories:

1. Amateur Radio Licence (A). Permits the use of all frequencies allocated, including HF for global communications. The Radio Amateurs' Examination and a Morse test at 12 words per minute (wpm) must be passed.
2. Amateur Radio Licence (A/B). A new licence introduced in 1999, it permits use of all frequencies in the UK, but abroad only frequencies above 30MHz can be used. The qualifications are the same as for the (A) licence, except Morse is at 5wpm.
3. Amateur Radio Licence (B). Permits the use only of frequencies above 30MHz, which does not usually allow communication over more than a few hundred miles (unless the Amateur Satellite Service is used). The Radio Amateurs' Examination must be passed, but no Morse.
4. Amateur Radio (Novice) Licence (A). Permits use of all novice frequencies. The Novice Radio Amateurs' Examination and a Morse test at 5 wpm must be passed.
5. Amateur Radio (Novice) Licence (B). Permits the use of novice frequencies above 30MHz. The same exam as (4), but no Morse, is required.

Full details of the above licences, training courses, Morse tests, and technical details are contained in the booklet 'How to Become a Radio Amateur' (RA190), obtainable from the RA; see 10.3.

The Radio Society of Great Britain (RSGB) has a HQ building which houses the National Amateur Radio Museum and Library, The GB3RS Radio Shack and a book shop. RSGB, Lambda House, Cranbourne Road, Potters Bar, Herts EN6 3JE. Tel 0870 904 7373; Fax 0870 904 7374. postmaster@rsgb.org.uk   www.rsgb.org

10.3.8   PERSONAL MOBILE RADIO (PMR)
Another name, another acronym! This has been around a long time, a sophisticated version of the old Walkie-Talkie. Operating in the UHF band on eight channels at around 446 MHz, these little sets are cheap, need no licence and mostly have a range of some 2-3M. Pocket-sized, they work on either AA or AAA batteries and of course in pairs. Prices in the High Street range from £35 to £100 for each unit. Uses on a boat could include helm to foredeck comms, request to be picked up by tender from ashore, rendezvous arrangements, race control, cruising in company, working at the masthead and much more.

10.4 DOCUMENTATION

10.4.1   THE SHIP RADIO LICENCE
A single Ship Radio Licence, introduced on 1 April 1995, covers all types or combinations of radio equipment including VHF (fixed and portable), UHF Portable, MF, HF, SatCom equipment (Standard A, C, B, M), radar, VHF DSC, MF/HF DSC, SART and EPIRBs operating on 121·5/ 243 MHz, 406 MHz and 1·6 GHz. It does not cover television for which a separate licence is required. A licence is not needed for a radio receiver.

If transportable equipment, eg a hand-held VHF set, is used on several different vessels, or on a vessel which is not covered by a Ship Radio Licence, each item of transportable equipment must be separately licensed. No callsign attaches to a transportable Licence.

Ships Radio Licences are issued on behalf of the RA by the Radio Licensing Centre, PO Box 1495, Bristol BS99 3QS. Tel 0870 243 4433; Fax 0117 975 8911.   www.radiolicencecentre.co.uk You will be sent the Licence Disc and holder, plus Validation Document, and a Terms Booklet (RA 336) which should be read as an integral part of the Licence. Owners of 406 MHz EPIRBs should fill in the relevant part of the Licence Amendment form within the Booklet, to help the MCA to maintain their database for SAR purposes.

The Radio Licensing Centre (formerly operated by Wray Castle Ltd, Cumbria) is part of the Post Office's specialist customer management unit. It has for some years issued licences for Amateur Radio and Citizen's Band Radio. Ship Radio licence fees (in 2001) for vessels used solely for pleasure have been reduced by £2 to £20.

A licence is required regardless of whether the vessel is actually in use, since it is granted for establishing a station. If radio equipment is removed and stored a licence is not required, but one must be obtained if and when the equipment is refitted. If you sell your boat write to the Radio Licensing Centre with details of the new owner, and return the old licence. It is a condition of the licence that the equipment meets certain minimum standards in terms of spurious emissions, power output, frequency deviation etc. Before buying a set make sure that it has passed the RA's Type Approval testing.

When the Ship Radio licence is first issued, an internationally recognised call sign, eg MSUN4, is allocated and remains with the vessel despite change of ownership or change of name. It is registered with the ITU in Geneva, along with details of your vessel which may be supplied to other authorities for SAR purposes. Callsigns are not transferable; a new licence (and therefore a new callsign) must be obtained when buying another vessel.

The flag letters/numerals of the callsign itself may be flown from the starboard yardarm, normally when entering and leaving harbour; they are the vessel's Visual signal letters (VSL).

An MMSI (Maritime Mobile Service Identity) may also be issued on request and free of charge by the Radio Licensing Centre. An MMSI is a 9 digit number which identifies a station and under GMDSS forms part of DSC; see Chapter 13.

Other licences, which may be relevant to yachts, are:

a. Citizens' Band (CB) Radio Licence; see 10.3.6.
b. Amateur Radio Licence; see 10.3.7.

10.4.2 REGULATIONS

Apart from the licensing arrangements described above, other regulations govern R/T afloat (other than CB and amateur radio). These are contained in the *Handbook for Marine Radio Communication* (Lloyd's of London Press Ltd). Here is a brief summary:

1. Operators must preserve the secrecy of correspondence, and not divulge the contents of any transmissions which they may receive or intercept.
2. Stations must identify themselves when transmitting. Vessels are identified by name and callsign, amplified if necessary by nationality or type. Yacht names may be prefaced by the word 'Yacht', eg Yacht JUNO, MSUN3. MRCC/MRSCs are normally identified by their name followed by Coastguard, eg Stornoway Coastguard.
3. A yacht with R/T must carry her Ship Radio Licence, a copy of Section 11 of the Post Office (Protection) Act, 1884; the Certificate(s) of Competence of the operator(s); and a Radiotelephone Log.
4. For a vessel in distress, the nearest MRCC/MRSC becomes the co-ordinating station for the incident.
5. While at sea a yacht may call other vessels, shore stations (or aircraft). In harbour she may not communicate with other vessels, except on safety matters; but only with shore stations eg a local Port authority, Coastguard centre, or station (marina) by authorised private channel (Ch M or M2). Messages must not be transmitted to an address ashore except through a coast radio station (if one is within range) or by other means.
6. Operators must not interfere with the working of other stations. Before transmitting, an operator must always listen on the appropriate frequency or channel in order to check that it is not already in use.
7. Unnecessary or superfluous transmissions are forbidden. Test transmissions must not interfere with other stations, and

must include the vessel's callsign.
8. Absolute priority must be given to distress calls and messages. The transmission of false distress, safety or identification signals is strictly prohibited.
9. The transmission of profane, indecent or obscene language is strictly forbidden.
10. Under the regulations any vessel fitted with a radiotelephone should keep a radiotelephone log. The following entries should be made:

The operator's name; the time of arrival at and departure from ports, with names; a summary of communications relating to distress, urgency and safety traffic; a record of communications exchanged with coast stations and other ship stations; a reference to any important service incidents (breakdowns of the apparatus); and the boat's position, at least once each day.

10.4.3 CERTIFICATES OF COMPETENCE

Approved marine radio installations must be controlled by a person aged 16 or over and holding a Marine Radio Operator's Certificate of Competence and Authority to Operate (one sheet of A4 plus passport photograph), valid "until further notice". The minimum standard was the Restricted (VHF-Only) Radio Telephony Certificate of Competence, which is no longer being issued, although existing Certificates remain valid for VHF-only radios. The (VHF-Only) Certificate has been superseded by the Short Range Certificate (SRC) of Competence, valid for both DSC and VHF-only radios; see Chapter 13, 13.7.5.

10.4.4 EQUIPMENT ONBOARD

A seagoing yacht should have on board at least a radio receiver able to receive the BBC Radio 4 shipping forecasts. The vast majority of cruising yachts will also have a marine band VHF transceiver radio. A Navtex receiver (see chapter 11) for MSI, in particular weather forecasts, is a great boon. For long range communications MF and/or HF radio will be required, together with HF Radio Facsimile receiver for long range weather. If you can afford it, some form of satellite communications will provide genuine global calling. GMDSS (see chapter 13) for safety and distress will by 2005 be virtually essential for offshore yachtsmen and even now (2001) it offers huge advantages over the earlier generation of safety and distress calling. Much of this more sophisticated equipment will link up with your onboard computer which will provide access to the Internet and e-mail messaging.

The ubiquitous mobile 'phone is not a

requirement, but, as many have found, its versatility places it at the forefront of communications at least in harbour and inshore waters. When your life is at stake, it is hard to disregard what it can do. A recent incident (Feb 2001) highlighted its unique capability: a damsel aboard a yacht in the Lombok Strait sent a distress message, via SMS, to her boyfriend in the UK who alerted the UK Coastguard. They in turn contacted the Australian and Indonesian Coastguards and the rescue services responded.

10.4.5 INSTALLATION

Radiotelephones need careful, professional installation to ensure they work efficiently. The set should be mounted where it is accessible, but protected from spray and damp. A waterproof extension speaker, or a hand-held VHF set, is useful in the cockpit.

The radio will usually run off the ship's battery which should be mounted as high as possible, remote from bilge water or from possible fire in the engine compartment.
MF and HF radiotelephones need to be properly earthed, usually to a metal plate on the underside of the boat.

All electrical equipment must be effectively suppressed in accordance with the requirements of BS1597, which defines the permitted interference levels over a frequency range of 15kHz to 100MHz.

A good aerial is vital. Since the power of a VHF transmitter is limited to 25W, an antenna should be used which will transmit the maximum beam in a horizontal direction, and not up into the sky. This, however, can be overdone, so that there is a loss in signal strength when the boat heels appreciably. The antenna must be matched to the transmitter, with the right impedance, expressed in terms of the 'voltage/standing wave ratio' which should be as near unity as possible over the range of frequencies employed. Connecting cables must be kept as short as possible (consistent with placing the antenna as high as possible), and be of good quality co-axial cable; this should normally be 6·5mm, although 13mm may be required for some masthead installations. If dismasted, an emergency aerial should be available for rigging on deck.

10.5 R/T PROCEDURES

10.5.1 WORKING PROCEDURES
The following procedures apply to all non-DSC R/T transmissions (other than CB). Except for Distress, Urgency or Safety messages, communications between a ship and coast station are controlled by the coast station; ship

stations must comply accordingly. Between two ship stations, the station called controls the working (under DSC the reverse is true; see Chapter 13). If a coast station intervenes both ships must comply with its instructions.

Voice communication
Before making an R/T call decide exactly what you are going to say. Write the message down if you are hesitant or inexperienced. Speak directly into the microphone, held a few inches from the face, about as loudly as for normal conversation. Speak clearly, distinctly and at a steady rate; or at dictation speed if you know the message is being written down by the recipient. Pitch your voice a little higher than normal; do not drop the pitch at the end of words or phrases.

Complicated or important words or figures should be given more slowly than other parts of the message; they may need to be spelled phonetically. It is normally not necessary to use the full phonetic spelling for figures, but the following pronunciations are helpful:

Numeral	Pronunciation	Numeral	Pronunciation
0	ZE-RO	5	FIFE
1	WUN	6	SIX
2	TOO	7	SEV-en
3	TREE	8	AIT
4	FOW-er	9	NINE-er

Procedure words (Prowords)
In RT communication brevity and clarity are enhanced by using prowords. These are listed in 'The Standard Marine Navigational Vocabulary' (M. 1252). Some of the commoner words and their meanings are shown below:

ACKNOWLEDGE	*Have you received and understood?*
CONFIRM	*My version is ... Is that correct?*
CORRECTION	*An error has been made in this transmission; the correct version is ..... (Spoken during a message)*
I SAY AGAIN	*I repeat (normally important words or numerals in the message).*
I SPELL	*I will spell out a word or part of the message phonetically*
OUT	*End of working*
OVER	*I have completed this part of my message and am inviting you to reply. Never say OVER AND OUT; it is a contradiction in terms.*
RADIO CHECK	*Request the strength and clarity of my transmission*

RECEIVED	*Receipt acknowledged*
SAY AGAIN	*Repeat your message* (or part indicated by ALL BEFORE or ALL AFTER)
STATION CALLING	*Used when a station is unsure of the identity of a station which is calling*

Calling procedure

Before transmitting, a station must first listen to ensure it will not interfere with communications already in progress, and if necessary await an appropriate break. Apart from distress, urgency or safety communications, calling and signals preparatory to the exchange of traffic should not exceed one minute when using 2182kHz (MF) or Ch 16 (VHF).

To make a call, the calling station must use a frequency on which the other station keeps watch. Normally a ship calls a coast station on the frequencies or channels given in the MRNA and in ALRS Volume 1.

However a coast station may call a ship station for which it has traffic if it knows the ship is within its area.

An initial call consists of:

The callsign or name of the station being called, x 3;

This is .... callsign or name of the calling station, x 3; OVER.

For VHF communication the name of the station called need only be given once, and that of the calling station twice. When contact is made the name need only be transmitted once.

If a station does not reply, the call may be repeated at three-minute intervals, providing this does not interfere with any communication in progress. Where reliable VHF communication is practicable, the calling ship station may repeat the call as soon as it is known that other traffic has terminated.

Replying to calls

Reply on the frequency monitored by the calling station, unless it has specified another frequency. The reply is made in a similar form to the initial call. If the station is unable to accept traffic immediately it instructs the other station:

'WAIT .... MINUTES'; or if other ships are waiting: 'YOUR TURN IS NUMBER ....'

'All Ships' broadcasts

Messages from Coastguard Centres and other authorities about gale warnings & navigational warnings for general consumption are normally prefaced by 'All Ships' or 'All Stations'. No reply or acknowledgement is needed.

10.5.2 PORT OPERATIONS

Most commercial ports, harbours and marinas have VHF R/T facilities. A few also use MF, mainly for pilotage services, which rarely concern yachtsmen.

VHF channels for Port Operations are listed in the MRNA and in ALRS Volume 6; those most commonly used are Ch 12 and Ch 14. Communications on these channels must be restricted to operational handling, the movements and safety of ships and, in emergency, to the safety of persons. For example it is quite in order at a strange harbour for a yacht to call the Harbour Office and request berthing instructions. In some busy commercial ports permission to enter or leave must be requested, so as to deconflict from other vessels, especially if the fairway is narrow or visibility is obstructed by buildings. These channels must not be used for public correspondence messages (link calls).

Call on a nominated working channel, stating which it is, since the Port Radio may be monitoring more than one channel; for example: 'Lerwick Harbour – This is Aida, Aida on Channel One Two – Over'.

Useful information can often be obtained simply by monitoring the appropriate channel in a commercial port or its approaches. In some ports scheduled broadcasts of information on local traffic, weather and tidal conditions are made. Do not use those working channels which are reserved for VTS, tug operations, pilot services etc.

10.5.3 TRAFFIC REPORTS (TR)

A Traffic Report is a safety measure by which a yacht can inform the Coastguard (or a Coast Radio Station, if any exist) of her intended passage from A to B, together with her ETA and number of people on board. In remote areas where routine radio contact is difficult or impossible, this is particularly important. Sometimes the Coastguard may actually request your passage details. This could be vital information if the boat becomes overdue or is involved in a distress situation. It is important to report the boat's safe arrival at her destination, or any change of plan en route, so that safety services are not alerted for no good reason.

After the initial contact, a TR call might be as follows:

'SHETLAND COASTGUARD, this is Yacht FULMAR, MIKE ZULU ZULU 3, – TANGO ROMEO: DEPARTED FAIR ISLE, ESTIMATING EYEMOUTH 26.1200UT JULY, FOUR PERSONS ONBOARD – OVER.'

On arrival at Eyemouth yacht Fulmar reports to the nearest Coastguard MRCC/MRSC:

'FORTH COASTGUARD, this is yacht FULMAR, ARRIVED EYEMOUTH 26.1430UT, REQUEST YOU ADVISE SHETLAND COASTGUARD – OVER'

10.5.4 COAST RADIO STATIONS

In the last few years, the convenience and popularity of mobile 'phones have caused a dramatic decline in the number of calls made through Coast Radio Stations (CRS). As a result the UK, France and Netherlands have closed down their CRS. In Germany a limited number of commercially operated CRS provide a public correspondence (link calls) service.

However CRS are still operational in Ireland, Belgium, Denmark, Spain and Portugal. But some or all of these will possibly cease to operate in the next few years.

Details of all coast radio stations, worldwide, are contained in the Admiralty List of Radio Signals, Vol 1. Those in North-West Europe are given in the MRNA.

Where CRS still exist their main purpose is to serve as a link between ships and the shore telephone network. They also transmit routine Traffic lists (telling ships of message traffic for them), navigational warnings (of wrecks, lights not functioning etc) and weather bulletins. Gale warnings are broadcast at the end of the next silence period and at other scheduled times.

CRS also have an important role to play in handling Distress, Urgency, Safety and Medical messages, but this role is handled by the Coastguard in the UK, France and Netherlands; see Chapter 13.

10.5.5 LINK CALLS FROM SHIP TO SHORE

CRS can link ships to shore stations via R/T and then into the international telephone network. Personal calls can be made to certain countries and transferred charge (collect) calls to a UK subscriber. It is not possible to make a call through a foreign CRS on a Ship Radio (Transportable) Licence, ie on a hand-held set.

Charges for link calls made via foreign CRS (including Jersey and Guernsey) can be billed to you via one of the following Accounting Authorities recognised by the ITU, provided you have pre-arranged a company and quote the relevant 'Accounting Authority Indicator Code' (AAIC). CRS hold copies of the ITU List of Ship Stations, giving the Accounting Authority for each vessel.

AAIC   Accounting Authority

GB 01   A-N-D Group plc, Tanner's Bank,
North 05 &15 Shields, Tyne & Wear
NE30 1HJ. Tel 0191 258 1635;
Fax 0191 296 4484.

GB 02   Cable & Wireless, East Saxon House,
27 Duke St, Chelmsford, CM1 1HT.
Tel 01245 702000; Fax 01245 348972.

GB 03   International Marine Radio Co Ltd,
Morley House, Badminton Court,
Church St, Amersham HP7 0DA.
Tel 01494 434000; Fax 01494 431993.

GB 06   Peninsular Electronics Ltd,
Broadquay House, Orpen Park,
Ash Ridge Road, Almondsbury,
Bristol BS12 4QD. Tel 01454 201777;
Fax 01454 205201.

GB 08   GEC-Marconi, Marine Division,
Marconi House, New St,
Chelmsford CM1 1PL.
Tel 01245 353221; Fax 01245 358776.

GB 11   ABB Nera Ltd, 20 Imperial Way,
Croydon CR0 4RR.
Tel 020 8686 5701; Fax 020 8680 8206.

GB 12   Bachmann Marine Services Ltd,
Frances House, St William Place,
St Peter Port, Guernsey GY1 4HQ.
Tel 01481 723573; Fax 01481 711353.

GB 13   Helexco Co Ltd, 31 High St,
Colliers Wood, London SW19 2JE.
Tel 020 8542 4916; Fax 020 8540 8047.

GB 19   CI Maritime Services, PO Box 601,
St Peter Port, Guernsey.
Tel/Fax 01481 54506.

GB 20   Yacht Electronic Services (UK)
Ltd, 2 Mill Row, Bexley DA5 1LA.
Tel 01322 556633; Fax 01322 556634.

GB 21   BPI Communications Ltd,
Equinox House, Oriel Court, Alton
GU34 2YT. Tel 01420 544533;
Fax 10420 544766.

Remember, if you are cruising world-wide, that the above companies operate globally and that not all countries are served by mobile 'phone networks.

To make a VHF Link Call

Do not call on a designated broadcast channel, particularly around the times of scheduled broadcasts. Monitor each working channel in turn until a free one is located, with no transmissions. A channel in use is indicated by either speech or by an engaged signal, a series of pips. Your initial call should last at least three seconds in order to activate equipment at the CRS. If you do not succeed in 'switching on' a CRS's transmitter, you may be out of range. Try another channel or another station, or call again when closer.

Example: A VHF link call from yacht Seabird to a Tel number in the UK. The yacht calls the nearest CRS, say Coruña Radio, on Ch 26 the relevant working channel:

'CORUÑA RADIO, CORUÑA RADIO, THIS IS SEABIRD, SEABIRD – MSAS3, MSAS3 – ONE LINK CALL – OVER.'

You may then hear pips automatically acknowledging your initial call (in which case you await an operator) or Coruña Radio may respond at once:

'SEABIRD, THIS IS CORUÑA RADIO – WHAT NUMBER – OVER.'

Seabird states the number to be called and her AAIC:

'CORUÑA RADIO THIS IS SEABIRD – LINK CALL:

ZERO ZERO-FOUR FOUR-ONE NINE THREE FIVE-SIX TWO SEVEN EIGHT THREE ZERO – ALFA ALFA INDIA CHARLIE: GOLF BRAVO ONE ONE – OVER.'

If communications are good, it should not be necessary to repeat the numbers, but do so if in doubt or if requested.

The CRS would then call the telephone number and connect it to the yacht. If radio channels are busy, calls may be limited to six minutes. The timing of a call ceases when the shore telephone is put down, not when the yacht signs off. The CRS normally so informs the ship station at the end of the conversation.

The procedure for an MF Link call is similar:

a. Call the relevant CRS on 2182 kHz;
b. An operator will then designate a working frequency; switch when instructed.
c. The operator will request the following information: vessel's callsign, name, accounting code (AAIC), category of traffic (eg telephone call, telex), and the telephone number required.

Autolink RT

Autolink RT enables you to dial directly into national and international telephone networks without going through a Coast radio station operator. It works through an onboard unit which is easily connected to the radio, and does not interfere with normal manual operation. This service on VHF, MF and HF gives quicker access, call scrambling on some units where privacy is required, and simplified accounting. Last number redial and a ten number memory store are available.

To make an Autolink call switch on the radio and the Autolink unit. Select a working channel and enter your PIN number (see below) as prompted. Key in or recall from memory the required telephone number in response to the prompt. If the channel is free, press the Send key on the Autolink unit, and connection is automatic. If the radio channel is already in use, either wait until it is free or select another channel if available. Then press the Send key again.

With full duplex radios press the PTT key throughout the conversation. With semi-duplex sets press the PTT key only when speaking. The connection is ended and charging stops when the receiver is replaced on the telephone ashore, but press the Send button if the 'call-off' indicator is not displayed.

If you own an Autolink unit, on registering with BT you may pay for calls by one of three methods: (1) a nominated UK telephone number, (2) a BT Chargecard, or (3) a ship's Accounting Authority. There is no registration or subscription charge, and you may change your method of payment on request. For charging you are identified by the PIN number allocated. Up to 99 different PIN numbers can be issued with the serial number of each Autolink unit, so the unit is available for 99 different people, each charged individually.

10.5.6   CALLS TO SHIPS AT SEA

Link calls can be made by a telephone subscriber to a vessel at sea, provided the caller knows roughly where the vessel is and there is a CRS within range. The subscriber calls the relevant CRS (remember that these no longer exist in the UK, France and Netherlands). Give your name and telephone number, the name of the person you wish to speak to, the yacht's name, callsign and position (if known). The yacht is then called. When she responds you will be called back and connected via VHF or MF. All calls are controlled by a radio operator. A booking can be made, valid for 24 hours, after which it is cancelled. The charge starts only when you speak to the nominated person on board.

If no reply is received, the vessel's name will be placed on a Traffic List which is broadcast at scheduled times every day. Traffic Lists are first announced on Ch 16 and then broadcast on the stated working channel(s) at the times listed in the MRNA. Shift to that channel and listen; if there is traffic for you, call the CRS on the working channel.

If the yacht has a satellite terminal, you can make a phone, fax or data call via BT's Inmarsat service. Either call the yacht's satellite terminal direct, if your phone is digital, by dialling 00 then the appropriate Oceanic code, followed by the yacht's identification number. The Oceanic codes are: Eastern Atlantic 871; Western Atlantic 874; Pacific 872; and Indian Ocean 873. The yacht's identification number can be obtained from international directory enquiries on 153.

Alternatively, if you have difficulty or do not have a digital phone, call 155 and ask the international operator for an Inmarsat call. Again give the ship's identification number and Oceanic region (if known).

10.6 SATELLITE COMMUNICATIONS

Satellite Communications (or Satcom) have developed to the point where they are the norm rather than the exception in the field of marine communications. The principle of using satellites in space to reflect signals from one point on earth to another is readily understood. The technicalities however are literally the stuff of "rocket scientists" and need not greatly concern the average yachtsman. Jargon abounds.

The following paragraphs outline Who provides What; What it can do for you, the Customer; within What limitations; and at What approximate expense? In a highly competitive industry some of the major protagonists are listed below. For the aspiring buyer of Satcom equipment the best advice is to study the rapidly developing market in as much depth as possible; and then to seek further advice from intermediary companies. One such company, to whom the Editor is indebted for their help in writing this section, is Macrocosm Ltd, 33 Halifax Road, Bowerhill, Melksham SN12 6TU. Tel/Fax 01225 353505. mark@macrocosm-uk.com www.macrocosm-uk.com

There are three elements in any satellite communications system:

a. The satellite network, provided for example by Inmarsat.
b. The Land Earth Stations (LES) which are owned by the telecommunications organisations in the countries in which they are located; eg Goonhilly LES and BT.
c. Telephonic terminals onboard ships and boats worldwide; also known as Ship Earth Stations (SES).

10.6.1 INMARSAT

Inmarsat (INternational MARitime SATellite organisation) was established in 1979 to serve the maritime industry. This 80 nation private conglomerate of finance companies is the biggest and longest established player in the Satcom market.

The Inmarsat satellite network consists of 9 satellites in geo-stationary (GEO) orbit 22,223M (36,000km) above the earth. Four of these satellites provide overlapping operational coverage of the globe (apart from the extreme polar regions beyond 70°N and 70°S). The other five are in-orbit spares or offer leased capacity. Each satellite covers about a third of the earth's surface, including the three oceans as follows: The Atlantic is covered by AOR-W and AOR-E, the Pacific by POR and the Indian Ocean by IOR. See Fig. 10(1).

Each satellite operates up to seven spot beams, which are focused around the globe to provide continuous voice and data coverage. Around the world there are 34 LES and over 150,000 User terminals operating via Inmarsat services.

The type of onboard terminal fitted to the boat determines which Inmarsat channel is used. The following terminals are available:

Sat B

An advanced communications system capable of digital voice and data messaging at 64 kbps – slightly faster than a normal PC with a modem.

This system has a very large fixed radome and is used predominantly on commercial ships. Equipment prices are about £18000, airtime about £7 per minute.

Sat C

A cheaper version of Sat B with a small omni-directional antenna, but will only handle text messages and fax data. The baud rate (transmission speed) is very low, 640 kbps, and it is expensive to run at approximately £5/page.

Mini M

This is the most recent addition to the Inmarsat inventory; it is considerably smaller and cheaper than the Sat B and has put satellite communications into an affordable price bracket at around £3000.

This system uses 3 satellites radiating narrow spot beams to a small dome antenna onboard. The dome is fixed to the boat and a number of servos inside keep the antenna pointed at the satellite, thus compensating for the boat's movement.

The most positive feature of this compact equipment is that it can be used like a normal phone-fax machine, with a mobile phone type handset and plugs on the unit to connect a PC or fax machine. The down side is that the baud rate (transmission speed) is still only 2400 kbps.

M4

The M4 service is relatively new and currently only land based, but a marine based unit is not out of the question. It offers voice and data speeds of up to 64kbps (the same as Sat B) but at a fraction of the equipment cost and at cheaper airtime rates.

Inmarsat is at the moment the world leader, but several emerging technologies, as shown below, already offer, or soon will, stiff competition.

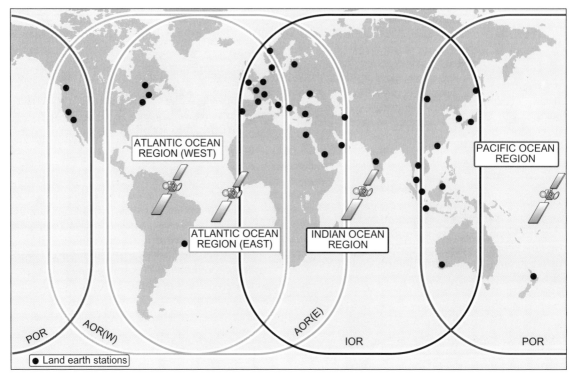

Land earth stations

Fig. 10(1) Inmarsat coverage and Earth Stations.

10.6.2 GLOBALSTAR

Globalstar is a consortium of leading international telecommunication companies, established in 1991, to provide mobile and fixed satellite-based telephony services. The promoter of Globalstar is the American company Loral who manage the programme in association with Qualcomm. Numerous local partners, equipment manufacturers and telecommunications operators involved in the operation include Vodafone, Hyundai, Daimler Benz Aerospace and Ericsson. Globalstar's service providers are long established companies such as TESAM, Vodafone, DACON, Elsacomm and China Telecom thus lending some stability to a fairly new company.

Globalstar has a constellation of 48 low earth orbit (LEO) satellites orbiting at 1414 km (763M) above the earth. These are regularly spaced over 8 orbital planes inclined at 52° to the equator. Each orbital plane is occupied by 6 satellites that provide continuous coverage within a defined area. The LEO avoids long distance echo and time transmission delays experienced with conventional geo-stationary (fixed) satellite networks.

Within the coverage callers have simultaneous access to 2 or 3 satellites. This innovative "path diversity" ensures reliability because even if a signal is blocked, the call is not interrupted.

Globalstar handsets are small and portable, often dual mode units which means that where GSM coverage is available the handset can be used as a normal mobile telephone, thus avoiding costly satellite telephone calls. When the handset is outside GSM coverage it switches to satellite mode to make and receive calls. A Marine kit designed for yachts has a satellite antenna small enough to be mounted on a pushpit. Together with the dual-mode handset this kit retails at around £2000.

The drawback of the Globalstar service is the lack of coverage in vast areas of the Pacific and Asia; it is not known when, or indeed if, these areas will be covered.

Globalstar has service agreements in over 100 countries, and these roaming agreements provide access to high quality transmission. Coverage at sea extends to 200 nautical miles from the coastlines of the respective countries where globalstar coverage has been established.

10.6.3 OTHER SATCOM OPERATORS

a. ACeS

(Asia Cellular Satellite system) is the first regional GEO designed exclusively for the Asia Pacific region, where in many parts fixed communications are largely non-existent. It came online at the end of 2000.

b. Emsat

Provided by the Paris-based Eutelsat company who until now have been primarily concerned with broadcasting satellite television. This is a pan-European satellite-based mobile telephony system. It can be used for voice communication and the transmission of faxes, data and short

Flag Etiquette – *see also Chapter 10.8*

White Ensign

Blue Ensign

Red Ensign

Defaced Blue Ensign

Defaced Red Ensign

Club Burgee

Commodore's Flag

Vice-Commodore

Rear-Commodore

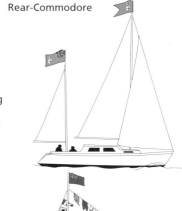

Left: yacht flying club burgee and wearing the Red Ensign.

Right: ketch-rigged yacht flying a Flag Officer's flag, and wearing a special ensign at the mizzen masthead.

Left: yacht in a foreign port flying a house flag at the fore, with a courtesy ensign at the starboard yardarm.

Right: yacht dressed overall for a British national festival.

International Code of Signals – Code Flags, Single Letter Signals, Phonetic Alphabet and Morse Signals

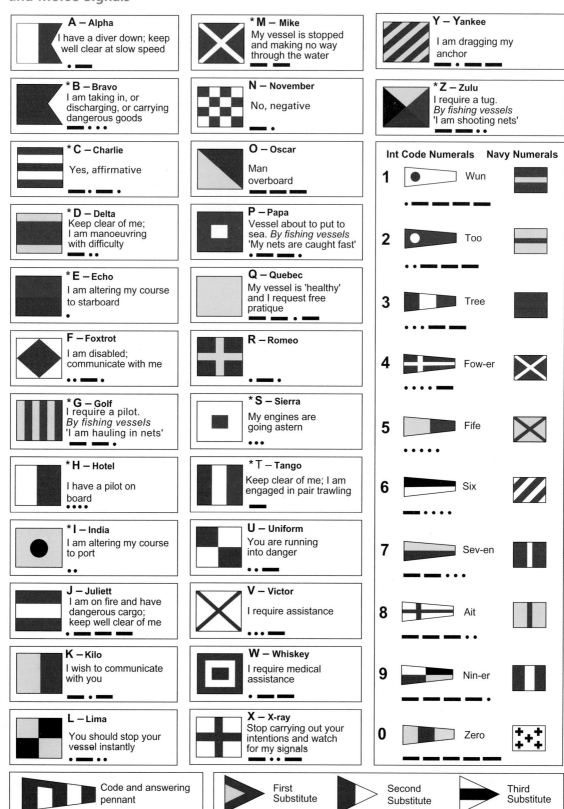

A – Alpha
I have a diver down; keep well clear at slow speed

* B – Bravo
I am taking in, or discharging, or carrying dangerous goods

* C – Charlie
Yes, affirmative

* D – Delta
Keep clear of me; I am manoeuvring with difficulty

* E – Echo
I am altering my course to starboard

F – Foxtrot
I am disabled; communicate with me

* G – Golf
I require a pilot.
By fishing vessels
'I am hauling in nets'

* H – Hotel
I have a pilot on board

* I – India
I am altering my course to port

J – Juliett
I am on fire and have dangerous cargo; keep well clear of me

K – Kilo
I wish to communicate with you

L – Lima
You should stop your vessel instantly

* M – Mike
My vessel is stopped and making no way through the water

N – November
No, negative

O – Oscar
Man overboard

P – Papa
Vessel about to put to sea. *By fishing vessels* 'My nets are caught fast'

Q – Quebec
My vessel is 'healthy' and I request free pratique

R – Romeo

* S – Sierra
My engines are going astern

* T – Tango
Keep clear of me; I am engaged in pair trawling

U – Uniform
You are running into danger

V – Victor
I require assistance

W – Whiskey
I require medical assistance

X – X-ray
Stop carrying out your intentions and watch for my signals

Y – Yankee
I am dragging my anchor

* Z – Zulu
I require a tug.
By fishing vessels
'I am shooting nets'

Int Code Numerals   Navy Numerals

1   Wun
2   Too
3   Tree
4   Fow-er
5   Fife
6   Six
7   Sev-en
8   Ait
9   Nin-er
0   Zero

Code and answering pennant

First Substitute

Second Substitute

Third Substitute

* Asterisked signals, when made by sound, must comply with IRPCS Rules 34 & 35

National Maritime Flags

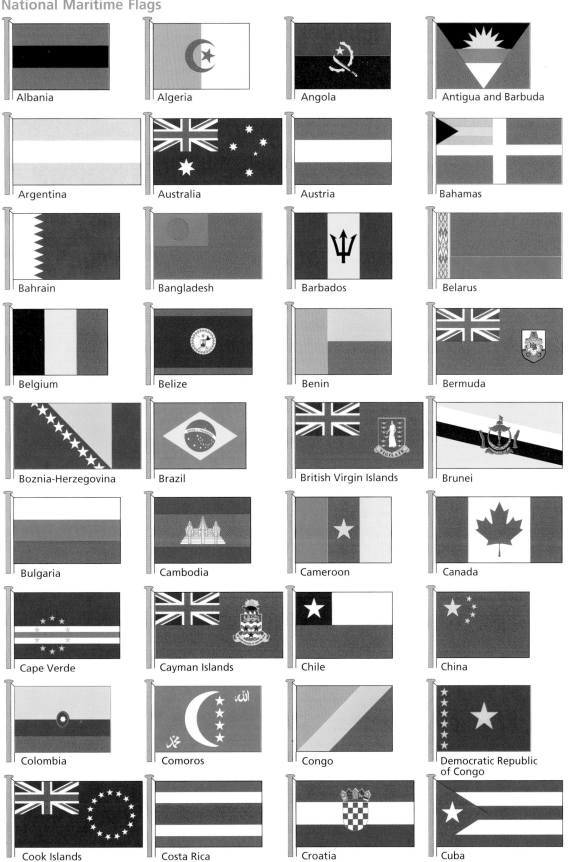

Albania

Algeria

Angola

Antigua and Barbuda

Argentina

Australia

Austria

Bahamas

Bahrain

Bangladesh

Barbados

Belarus

Belgium

Belize

Benin

Bermuda

Boznia-Herzegovina

Brazil

British Virgin Islands

Brunei

Bulgaria

Cambodia

Cameroon

Canada

Cape Verde

Cayman Islands

Chile

China

Colombia

Comoros

Congo

Democratic Republic of Congo

Cook Islands

Costa Rica

Croatia

Cuba

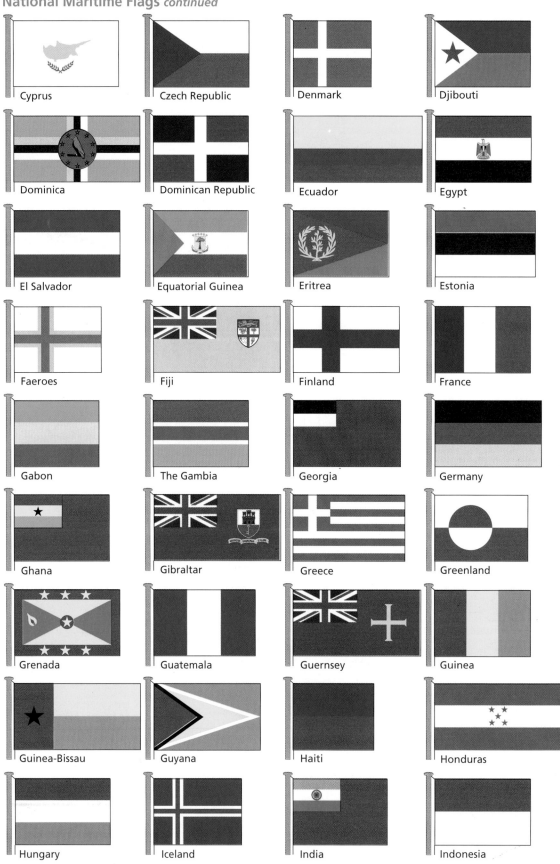

Cyprus

Czech Republic

Denmark

Djibouti

Dominica

Dominican Republic

Ecuador

Egypt

El Salvador

Equatorial Guinea

Eritrea

Estonia

Faeroes

Fiji

Finland

France

Gabon

The Gambia

Georgia

Germany

Ghana

Gibraltar

Greece

Greenland

Grenada

Guatemala

Guernsey

Guinea

Guinea-Bissau

Guyana

Haiti

Honduras

Hungary

Iceland

India

Indonesia

National Maritime Flags *continued*

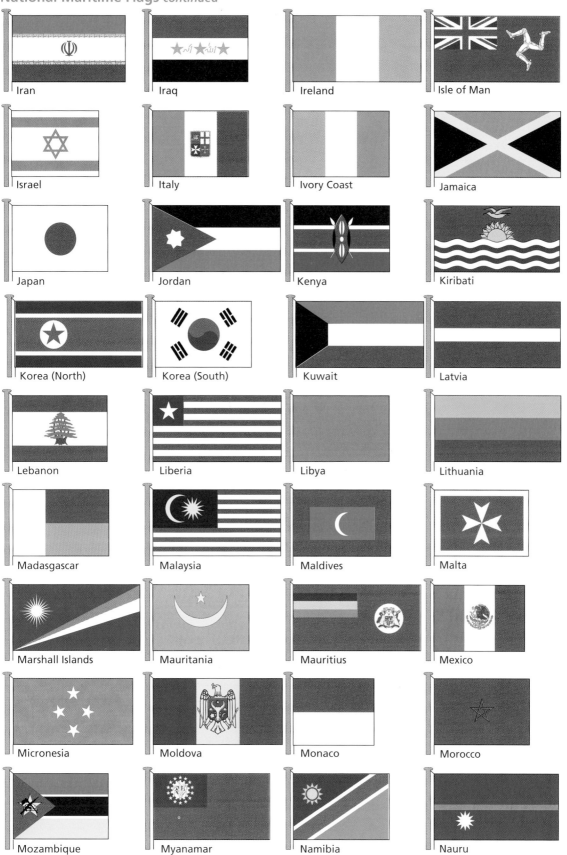

Iran

Iraq

Ireland

Isle of Man

Israel

Italy

Ivory Coast

Jamaica

Japan

Jordan

Kenya

Kiribati

Korea (North)

Korea (South)

Kuwait

Latvia

Lebanon

Liberia

Libya

Lithuania

Madasgascar

Malaysia

Maldives

Malta

Marshall Islands

Mauritania

Mauritius

Mexico

Micronesia

Moldova

Monaco

Morocco

Mozambique

Myanamar

Namibia

Nauru

National Maritime Flags *continued*

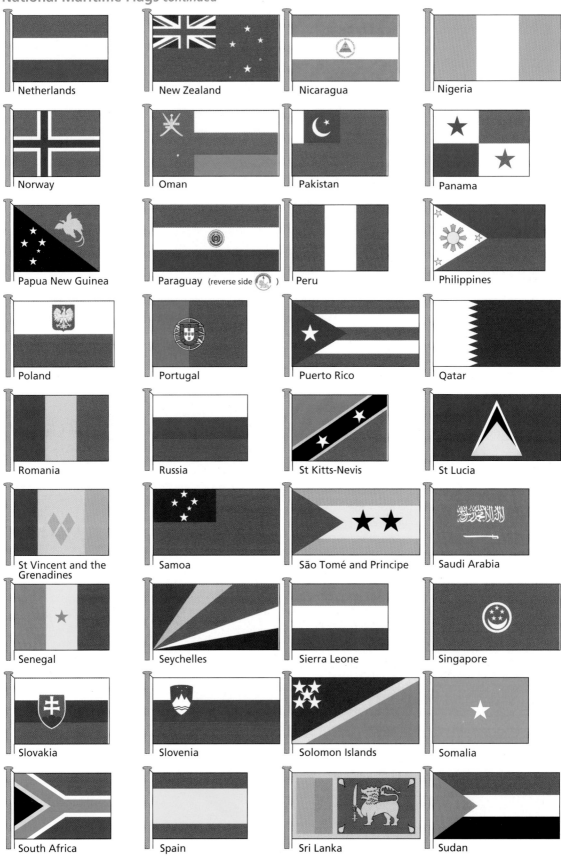

Netherlands

New Zealand

Nicaragua

Nigeria

Norway

Oman

Pakistan

Panama

Papua New Guinea

Paraguay (reverse side)

Peru

Philippines

Poland

Portugal

Puerto Rico

Qatar

Romania

Russia

St Kitts-Nevis

St Lucia

St Vincent and the Grenadines

Samoa

São Tomé and Principe

Saudi Arabia

Senegal

Seychelles

Sierra Leone

Singapore

Slovakia

Slovenia

Solomon Islands

Somalia

South Africa

Spain

Sri Lanka

Sudan

Norfolk Broads Yacht Club

North Devon Yacht Club

Orwell Yacht Club

Parkstone Yacht Club

Penarth Yacht Club

Penton Hook Yacht Club

Perth Sailing Club

Poole Harbour Yacht Club

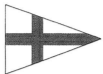

Poole Yacht Club

Portmadoc & Trawsfynydd Sailing Club

Portrush Yacht Club

Ribble Cruising Club

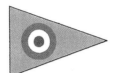

Royal Air Force Yacht Club

Royal Anglesey Yacht Club

Royal Artillery Yacht Club

Royal Burnham Yacht Club

Royal Channel Islands Yacht Club

Royal Cinque Ports Yacht Club

Royal Corinthian Yacht Club

Royal Cork Yacht Club (incorporating Royal Munster Yacht Club)

Royal Cornwall Yacht Club

Royal Cruising Club

Royal Dart Yacht Club

Royal Dorset Yacht Club

Royal Eastern Yacht Club

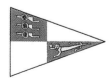

Royal Engineer Yacht Club

Royal Findhorn Yacht Club

Royal Forth Yacht Club

Royal Fowey Yacht Club

Royal Gourock Yacht Club

Royal Harwich Yacht Club

Royal Highland Yacht Club

Royal Irish Yacht Club

Royal London Yacht Club

Royal Lymington Yacht Club

Royal Mersey Yacht Club

Royal Motor Yacht Club

Royal Naval Club & Royal Albert Yacht Club

Royal Naval Sailing Association

Royal Norfolk & Suffolk Yacht Club

Royal Northern & Clyde Yacht Club

Royal North of Ireland Yacht Club

Royal Northumberland Yacht Club

RNVR Yacht Club

Royal Ocean Racing Club

Royal Plymouth Corinthian Yacht Club

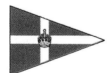
Royal St. George Yacht Club

Royal Scottish Motor Yacht Club

Royal Solent Yacht Club

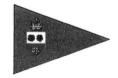
Royal Southampton Yacht Club

Royal Southern Yacht Club

Royal Tay Yacht Club

Royal Temple Yacht Club

Royal Thames Yacht Club

Royal Torbay Yacht Club

Royal Ulster Yacht Club

Royal Victoria Yacht Club

Royal Welsh Yacht Club

Royal Western Yacht Club

Royal Western Yacht Club of England

Royal Yachting Association

Royal Yacht Squadron

Royal Yorkshire Yacht Club

Salcombe Yacht Club

Scarborough Yacht Club

Seaview Yacht Club

Severn Motor Yacht Club

Solway Yacht Club

South Caernarvonshire Yacht Club

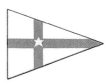
Starcross Yacht Club

St. Helier Yacht Club

Strangford Lough Yacht Club

Sunderland Yacht Club

Sussex Motor Yacht Club

Sussex Yacht Club

Teign Corinthian Yacht Club

Thames Estuary Yacht Club

Thames Motor Yacht Club

Thorpe Bay Yacht Club

Thurrock Yacht Club

Walton & Frinton Yacht Club

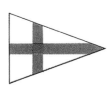
Waveney & Oulton Broad Yacht Club

Welland Yacht Club

West Lancashire Yacht Club

West Mersea Yacht Club

West Stockwith Yacht Club

Whitby Yacht Club

Whitstable Yacht Club

Yealm Yacht Club

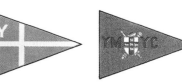
York Motor Yacht Club

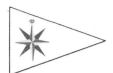

Clube de Vela
Atlântico
(Portugal)

Deauville Yacht Club
(France)

Kongelig Dansk
Yachtklub
(Denmark)

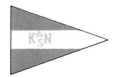

Kongelig Norsk
Seilforening
(Norway)

Koninklijke Jacht Club
Oostende en Motor
Jacht Club van Belgie
(Belgium)

Koninklijke
Nederlandsche
Motorboot Club
(Netherlands)

Koninklijke
Nederlandsche Zeil-en
Roeivereeniging
(Netherlands)

Koninklijke Roei-en
Zeilvereeniging 'De
Maas'
(Netherlands)

Kungl. Svenska Segel
Sällskapet
(Sweden)

New York Yacht Club
(USA)

Point Yacht Club
(South Africa)

Royal Belgian Sailing
Club
(Belgium)

Royal Bermuda Yacht
Club
(Bermuda)

Royal Hong Kong
Yacht Club
(Hong Kong)

Royal New Zealand
Yacht Squadron
(New Zealand)

Royal Nova Scotia
Yacht Squadron
(Canada)

Royal Perth Yacht
Club of Western
Australia
(Australia)

Royal Suva Yacht
Club
(Fiji)

Royal Sydney Yacht
Squadron
(Australia)

Royal Yacht Club de
Belgique
(Belgium)

Segelkamaradschaft
'Das Wappen von
Bremen'
(Germany)

Société des Régates
du Havre
(France)

Société Nautique de
la Baie de St. Malo
(France)

Société Nautique de
Quiberon
(France)

Union National Pour
La Course Au Large
(France)

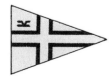

Vlaamse Vereniging
Voor Watersport
(Netherlands)

Watersportvereniging
'Haringvliet'
(Netherlands)

Watersportvereniging
'Texel'
(Netherlands)

Yacht Club
Argentino
(Argentine)

Yacht Club
d'Arcachon
(France)

Foreign Yacht Club Burgees *continued*

Yacht Club de
Cherbourg
(France)

Yacht Club de France
(France)

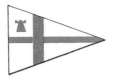

Yacht Club de Morlaix
(France)

Yacht Club de
Nieuwpoort
(Netherlands)

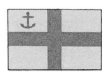

Yacht Club du Nord
de la France
(France)

Yacht Club du Trieux
(France)

Yacht Klub Polski w Gdyni
(Poland)

Other flags

Flag of Europe   or

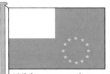

With appropriate national
flag in the canton

Many places have local flags (see 10.8.6), including
Scotland, Northern Ireland, Wales, Isle of Man,
Jersey, Sark, Alderney, Herm and Normandy – which
should *not* be used as courtesy flags.

Scotland

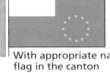

Northern Ireland

Wales

Isle of Man

Jersey

Guernsey's official
maritime flag is on
page 294

Sark

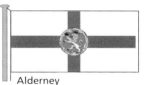

Alderney

Normandy

Brittany (Independent)

Cornwall

Some unofficial flags are
not fully recognised in the
places or countries concerned.

Fig. 11(7) and Fig. 11(8) The Beaufort scale and sea states.

Wave heights given below are probable mean heights in the open sea, remote from land, when the wind has been blowing for some time. In enclosed waters, or near land, with an offshore wind, wave heights will be less and the waves steeper. Wave height for a given wind strength depends upon the fetch and the length of time for which the wind has been blowing.

Photography
© Crown – Force 0, 11
© G.J.Simpson – Force 1, 2, 7
© I.G. MacNeil – Force 3, 4, 5, 6
© W.A.E. Smith – Force 8
© J.P. Laycock   Force 9
© G. Allen – Force 10
© J.F.Thomson – Force 12

Force 0   0-1 Kts
Calm   Wave Ht 0m

Force 1   1-3 Kts
Light Air   Wave Ht 0.1m

Force 2   4-6 Kts
Light Breeze   Wave Ht 0.2m

Force 3   7-10 Kts
Gentle Breeze   Wave Ht 0.6m

Force 4   11-16 Kts
Moderate Breeze   Wave Ht 1m

Force 5   17-21 Kts
Fresh Breeze   Wave Ht 2m

Force 6   22-27 Kts
Strong Breeze   Wave Ht 3m

Force 7   28-33 Kts
Near Gale   Wave Ht 4m

Force 8   34-40 Kts
Gale   Wave Ht 5.5m

Force 9   41-47 Kts
Severe Gale   Wave Ht 7m

Force 10   48-55 Kts
Storm   Wave Ht 9m

Force 11   56-63 Kts
Violent Storm   Wave Ht 11.5m

Force 12   64 plus Kts
Hurricane   Wave Ht 14m

messages (SMS) at low cost. Designed for specialist fleet operators, the service can extend into areas not yet covered by the terrestrial cellular networks. The coverage footprint is fairly small and excludes America, Asia and Australasia.

c. ICO

ICO intends to launch commercial satellite services in 2003 after a period of testing in 2002. The service will provide global Internet protocol services, including Internet connectivity, data, voice and fax services. The system will operate in both circuit-switched mode – based on the GSM standard – and in packet-switched and Internet protocol (IP) modes.

The ICO Space segment will consist of 12 satellites operating in medium Earth orbit (MEO) at an altitude of 10,390km (6,400 miles). Divided equally between two planes, each inclined at 45° to the equator and at right angles to the other, the satellites will provide complete, continuous overlapping coverage of the Earth's surface. Each satellite will circle the Earth approximately once every six hours. Of the 12 satellites, 10 will form the active constellation and the remainder will be in-orbit spares. An additional two spare satellites will be built and kept on the ground ready for launch if needed.

ICO's satellites will use a "bent-pipe" architecture, a configuration where the satellites act like mirrors to reflect signals between the user equipment and the ground station. In a bent-pipe system the satellite is used to relay communication between the end-user equipment and a ground station that is part of the terrestrial infrastructure. The terrestrial infrastructure, rather than satellite-to-satellite communications links, provides the connection to the destination network or end-user.

The satellites will communicate with terrestrial networks through a ground segment known as ICONET, which will be a high-bandwidth global IP network. This will consist of 12 Earth stations, or satellite access nodes (SANs), located around the globe, connected via high-speed links. Six SANs have been equipped as telemetry, tracking and control stations. They are expected to provide nearly continuous monitoring of the satellites in orbit, which will be controlled from the company's Satellite Control Centre in the UK.

10.7   MISCELLANEOUS SIGNALS

10.7.1   RADIO TIME SIGNALS
Radio Time signals are transmitted at hourly intervals from 0600 – 1900UTC on BBC Radio 4 and much less frequently on BBC Radio 1, 2 and

3. BBC time signals consist of six pulses representing successive seconds: the first five pulses are each of 0·1s, followed by a final 0·5s pulse. The start of the final, longer pulse marks the exact start of the next minute. BBC World Service transmits time signals on a number of MF and HF frequencies.

The BBC Time Standard equipment is at Broadcasting House in London. It receives UTC information from the GPS satellites and from Rugby [MSF] to generate the 'pips'. These can be received in the UK with an accuracy better than 0·05 secs (50ms). Signals from relay stations abroad which receive their signals through a satellite link will be delayed by about 0·25 secs (250ms).

10.7.2   PRATIQUE MESSAGES
All yachts arriving in the UK from abroad (including the Channel Islands) are subject to Customs, Public Health and Home Office (Immigration Department) requirements, whether carrying dutiable stores or not. Details are given in Customs Notice No. 8 (April 1996). This is summarised in 5.2 and is available from any Customs and Excise office (but not VAT offices). Customs Officers normally act for the Immigration and Health authorities.

UK regulations require flag 'Q' to be flown on entering territorial waters, but it need not be illuminated at night. It means: *My vessel is healthy and I request free pratique.* Pratique is in effect a licence to have dealings with a port, granted after showing a clean bill of health.

10.8 FLAGS AND THEIR USAGE

10.8.1   SEA AND LAND FLAGS
The flags which may be displayed by a yacht include the national maritime ensign, a yacht club's burgee, the flag of a yacht club's Flag Officer, a house flag, a courtesy flag when abroad, and flags connected with signalling or racing; see page 291 for where they should be hoisted.

The Union Flag is not an ensign; it is flown at the bows of warships at anchor or berthed alongside, and this is the only time when it is correct to call it the Union Jack. The broad white diagonal band near the hoist must always be uppermost. The Merchant Jack (formerly Pilot Jack) does not apply to yachts, but may be seen on certain civil ships; it is a Union Flag within a broad white border.

Land flags, as distinct from sea flags, include the Union Flag (the national flag of the UK), the crosses of St George (as flown by an Admiral in the Royal Navy), St Andrew (the national flag of Scotland), St Patrick (Ireland) and the Welsh

Dragon. The EU flag, blue with 12 gold stars, is not a sea flag.

10.8.2 ENSIGN

The ensign is the national maritime flag, often the same as the national flag, eg France, but not so in the UK. For British yachts and commercial vessels the Red Ensign is the national maritime flag. The Geneva Convention 1956 requires vessels to wear their national ensign. The ensign is also referred to as the Colours, ie a symbol of national identity. As such it is a matter of pride to wear a smart, clean ensign – and the same goes for other flags.

In addition to the Red Ensign, and often to the confusion of foreign nations, some 80 clubs (see the Navy List) are privileged to wear a special Ensign, under strict conditions and with penalties for contravention. The special Ensign for a yacht may be the White Ensign (Royal Yacht Squadron only); the Blue Ensign; a defaced Blue Ensign, ie with a badge; or the defaced Red Ensign. A special Ensign may only be worn under a warrant issued by the Ministry of Defence prior to 1 April 1985, or under a permit subsequently issued to the owner by his club and in accordance with the following rules:

The yacht must be registered under either Part I of the Merchant Shipping Act 1894, or the Merchant Shipping Act 1983. She must be not less than 2 tons gross if registered by tonnage, or 7m LOA if registered by length. The owner(s) must be British and be member(s) of the club concerned. The yacht must be a cruising boat (not a houseboat) and must not be used for any commercial purpose. Her name must not incorporate a name, product or trademark used for business purposes. The permit must be carried on board, and a special Ensign may only be worn if the owner is on board or ashore nearby, and if the club's burgee (or Flag Officer's flag) is flown.

If an owner belongs to more than one club eligible to wear a special Ensign, he must obtain a separate permit for each Ensign. The loss or theft of a permit must be reported immediately, and if the owner ceases to be a member of the club, or if the yacht is sold, the permit must be returned at once to the secretary of the club.

When chartering a permit may be issued to a club member for short periods. Further details of the issue and conditions for permits for special Ensigns are available from secretaries of clubs concerned.

The Ensign, being the yacht's national colours, should be worn in the most prominent position normally at a staff on the stern. In sailing yachts however this may be impossible: in gaff-rigged yachts it is usually worn at the peak of the sail on the aftermast (if more than one); in bermudan yawls and ketches on a staff at the mizzen masthead; and in others at a position twothirds of the way up the leech of the aft sail. In power-driven yachts with a gaff on an aft mast, the Ensign may be worn at the peak of this gaff at sea.

The Ensign should be worn when entering or leaving harbour, and must be worn when a yacht arrives at or departs from a foreign port. At sea it need not be worn except when meeting other craft or when coming near to land especially when passing coastguard or signal stations etc. Yachts which are racing do not wear Ensigns.

In harbour the Ensign should be hoisted at 0800 in summer and at 0900 from 1 November to 14 February. It should be lowered at sunset or 2100, whichever is earlier, or when the crew go ashore if before that time (all local times). It is incorrect to leave the Ensign flying overnight in harbour, but this is more often done than not, and when abroad serves to identify the yacht's nationality. In the Royal Navy the ceremony of hoisting/lowering the ensign is known as Colours.

In a yacht with a permit for a special Ensign, the Red Ensign should be hoisted in the morning if the owner is not present being replaced by the special Ensign when he arrives. Conversely if the owner departs from the yacht and the port, the special Ensign must be lowered, and replaced by the Red Ensign if the yacht is still manned.

Ashore, ensigns should only be used at yacht clubs where they should be hoisted/lowered at the times above.

See pages 293 – 297 for illustrations of ensigns and some examples of flag positions on page 291.

10.8.3 BURGEE

Each club has its own burgee, a triangular flag which can be flown on members' yachts. The design is optional provided it does not conflict with official signals or other established flags. The burgee signifies that the owner, or person in charge of the yacht, is a member of that club, and a club burgee must never be flown under any other circumstances. A yacht should not fly more than one club burgee at a time. A selection of British and foreign YC burgees are shown on pages 298 to 305.

The burgee should if possible be flown from a staff at the masthead. Despite the lights, aerials and anemometers which may sprout from the masthead, it is not difficult to secure the burgee staff (swivelled) to a long stout bamboo cane and hoist it so that the burgee flies in pride of place above all else. Alternatively the burgee should be flown from the starboard spreader. But when abroad the burgee will have to be shifted to the port spreader to allow the courtesy flag to fly from the starboard spreader – with no other flag above it on the same halyard.

In harbour a burgee should be flown at the same times as the Ensign; where a special Ensign is worn the related club burgee must be flown. In recent years, however, it has become the norm to leave the burgee flying at night in harbour, when the owner is on board or ashore in the vicinity. At sea a burgee is normally flown in sight of land or other ships.

An owner who belongs to a club in the harbour where his boat is lying should fly the burgee (and special ensign, if any) of that club. If he belongs to more than one local club he should use the burgee (and special ensign, if any) of the senior one, unless one of the other clubs is holding a regatta or similar function. Anybody lent or chartered a yacht flies a burgee of a club of which he is a member – not a burgee of the absent owner or charter company.

10.8.4   FLAG OFFICERS' FLAGS

Most clubs authorise their flag officers to fly broad pennants, special swallow-tailed flags similar in design to the club burgee. The Vice- and Rear-Commodore's flags are distinguished from the Commodore's by one and two balls respectively in the cantons next to the hoist. Some clubs provide for their past Commodores to fly a special flag at the masthead. This flag incorporates the design of the club burgee but is either a different shape (eg rectangular) or has some other distinguishing feature.

A flag officer's flag is flown day *and night* while the owner is on board or in effective control. Normally a flag officer of a club always flies his flag officer's flag (with appropriate special ensign, if any) in preference to the burgee of some other club of which he is a member. But there are exceptions to every rule – for example when he attends a rally or regatta which another club is staging.

10.8.5   COURTESY FLAG

It is customary in a foreign port to fly at the starboard spreader a miniature version of the maritime Ensign of the country being visited; some countries insist on this. Yachts do not normally wear more than one courtesy flag.

Do not fly a courtesy flag inferior to (ie below) any other flag on the same halyard – that would be an obvious discourtesy.

The courtesy flag for foreign yachts visiting Britain is the Red Ensign (not the Union Flag). In

the illustrations, the flags of Italy, Poland and Romania have crests in the centre, which are omitted when these flags are used as courtesy flags.

Local flags

Brittany and Normandy, for example, have local flags (see page 305) which indicate support for an independent Brittany or Normandy. They should not be used in lieu of the French Tricolour at the starboard spreader, but can be flown from the port spreader. Note: If cruising through the Spanish Basque country, it may be wise to take advice on whether to fly the Spanish courtesy flag or the Basque regional flag or neither – especially in times of tension.

There is no need for a British yacht to wear a courtesy flag anywhere within the British Isles, but it may be polite to acknowledge any local flag, by flying it from the starboard spreader. There are local flags for Scotland, Northern Ireland, Wales, Isle of Man, Jersey, Guernsey, Alderney, Sark and Herm (see page 305).

Of these, Guernsey is unique in having an official maritime flag (see page 294), which can be used in lieu of the Red Ensign by any boat registered in the Bailiwick of Guernsey (which includes Alderney, Sark and Herm). Conversely, it can officially be used as the courtesy flag, in lieu of the Red Ensign, by any foreign yacht visiting the Bailiwick.

10.8.6   HOUSE FLAG

Some owners and organisations have a private, distinguishing flag, square in shape, which is normally flown at the port spreader, but only in harbour. It should be hoisted and lowered at the same times as the burgee and Ensign. The design of a house flag must not conflict with that of any other official or existing flag. Generally a house flag is only flown when the owner is on board.

10.8.7   YACHT RACING

The various flags and signals used in yacht racing are detailed in the Racing rules of sailing; see Chapter 14 and RYA booklet YR1. Yachts which are racing do not wear an ensign, burgee or a flag officer's flag.

10.8.8   SALUTES

It is customary for yachts to salute all warships and Royal Yachts of any nation, and flag officers of the club whose burgee the yacht is flying (but normally only once a day). Salutes are made by dipping the Ensign only, ie lowering it about two thirds of the way, but to a position where it will still fly. The salute is acknowledged by the other vessel dipping and re-hoisting her Ensign, whereupon the saluting yacht rehoists hers.

10.8.9 DRESSING SHIP

Ships can be dressed in two ways: overall – the more usual, only in harbour; or with masthead flags – normally only when under way in or near a harbour, but may be used as an alternative to dressing overall in vessels not fitted with dressing lines. Dressing lines are the dedicated lines on which the flags are hoisted; normally a yacht will use her halyards in harbour.

Dressing overall is done by flying the flags of the International Code (only) from stem to masthead, from masthead to masthead if there is more than one mast, and down to the stern. The triangular flags and pendants should be spaced out between the rectangular flags. The recommended order of flags, from forward, is:

E, Q, p3, G, p8, Z, p4, W, p6, P, p1, I, Code, T, Y, B, X, 1st Sub, H, 3rd Sub, D, F, 2nd Sub, U, A, O, M, R, p2, J, p0, N, p9, K, p7, V, p5, L, C, S.

Note: p0 to p9 are the numeral pendants. The size of flags should be appropriate to the size of the yacht.

The Ensign should be worn at its normal position, and there should be a flag (normally another similar Ensign) at each masthead.

For British national festivals (see below) a British Ensign is worn at each masthead, and at the main masthead the Ensign and club burgee fly side by side. But if the owner is a flag officer he flies his flag at the masthead without an Ensign.

The principal occasions for dressing ship in this country are currently: Accession Day (6 Feb), Commonwealth Day (March), HM The Queen's Birthday (21 April), Coronation Day (2 June), HM The Queen's Official Birthday (June), HRH The Duke of Edinburgh's Birthday (10 June) and HM The Queen Mother's Birthday (4 August).

For foreign national festivals (at home or abroad), the Ensign of the country concerned is flown at the masthead alongside the burgee in single-masted yachts, at the mizzen masthead (in place of a British Ensign) in ketches and yawls, and at the fore masthead (in place of a British Ensign) in a schooner-rigged yacht. In the case of a flag officer, flying his flag (alone) at the masthead of a single-masthead yacht, the foreign Ensign should be flown at the starboard spreader.

When dressing ship for a local occasion (eg a regatta) the club burgee should be flown at the main masthead, and no Ensign. An Ensign should be worn at any other masthead. On all occasions of dressing ship it is important that the same design of Ensign is worn in different parts of the vessel.

Dressing with masthead flags is carried out by wearing Ensign(s) at the masthead(s), as described above, without dressing lines.

10.8.10 MOURNING

On occasions of national or private mourning colours are half-masted. This is done by first hoisting them close up, and then lowering them to the dipped position; similarly before hauling them down they are first raised to the masthead. For national mourning only the Ensign is half-masted; for private mourning both the Ensign and burgee.

National mourning is observed on such occasions as the death of a member of the Royal Family. The Ensign (only) is half masted when news is received, and kept at half mast until sunset; or if news is received at night, then the Ensign is flown at half mast throughout the next day. Colours are again half masted while the funeral is in progress.

HM Ships half mast Ensigns and Jacks when the funeral of an officer or rating takes place in a port where they are lying. Yachts present should conform.

Private mourning may be observed when the owner of a yacht dies, or when for example a flag officer or a past flag officer of a club dies. On such occasions both the Ensign and burgee are half masted, the procedure otherwise being similar to national mourning described above.

10.8.11 FLAG TERMINOLOGY AND SIZES

Vexillology is the study of flags. The Flag Institute is the main UK authority; contact the Editorial Office, 44 Middleton Road, Acomb, York YO24 3AS. Tel 01904 339985 or institute@flags.net

Flags of the World at www.fotw.net is probably the most extensive flag website in the world. The latest flag news is available on www.flagwire.com Flags of all kinds and friendly advice can be obtained from The Flagmakers, United Flag Traders Ltd, 20 Clarion Court, Llansamlet, Swansea SA6 8RF. Tel 01792 700795; Fax 01792 700802 and www.flagcentral.com

A flag, like a sail, may be described as follows: The Hoist is the 'leading edge' nearest the staff or halyard. The Fly is at the opposite end. A flag is divided into four Cantons or quarters: Upper and Lower Inner, ditto Outer.

Ensigns are rectangular in the ratio 2:1 and are traditionally sized by the yard; thus a $1\frac{1}{2}$ yard ensign measures 54in x 27in.

As a rough guide the following table, by courtesy of Captain R. Yeoward of the Cruising Association, shows for different LOA the appropriate flag sizes:

LOA ft	Ensign	Burgee	Courtesy	House	Jacks	Signals
21-26	$\frac{3}{4}$ yard	15"	7"	6" x 9"	14" x 21"	6" x 8"
27-34	1 yard	15"	8"	8" x 12"	18" x 27"	9" x 12"
35-42	$1\frac{1}{4}$ yds	18"	10"	10" x 15"	20" x 30"	12" x 15"
43-50	$1\frac{1}{2}$ yds	24"	12"	12" x 18"	27" x 40"	18" x 21"
51-60	$1\frac{3}{4}$ yds	30"	15"	15" x 22"	32" x 48"	20" x 30"

10.9 BOOKS ABOUT COMMUNICATIONS AND FLAG ETIQUETTE

Admiralty List Of Radio Signals (UKHO):
- Vol 1 Coast Radio Stations;
- Vol 3 Maritime Safety Information (MSI);
- Vol 5 GMDSS; and
- Vol 6 Port Operations, Pilot Services and VTS (Pts 1-5).

Two books intended for yachtsmen are NP 289 and NP 290, as shown below under their grandiloquent and rather misleading titles of:

Admiralty Maritime Communications (NP 289) UK/Med;

Admiralty Maritime Communications (NP 290) Caribbean.

RYA booklets
C4 Flags and Visual signals
G22 VHF radio including GMDSS
Using PCs on board by R. Buttress and T. Thornton (Adlard Coles, 2000)
Using VHF Radio by B. Faulkner (Adlard Coles)
Marine SSB Operation by M. Gale (Fernhurst)
The VHF GMDSS Handbook by M. Gale (Fernhurst)
VHF afloat by Sara Hopkinson (Fernhurst)
The VHF Companion by Sara Hopkinson (Fernhurst)
The Complete book of World Flags (Dorling Kindersley)

MACMILLAN REEDS NAUTICAL ALMANACS

Where would you be without them?

These almanacs include:
- Extensive coverage of smaller ports with additional chartlets
- Full colour plans and illustrations throughout
- A directory of marine services and supplies
- Wire binding allows the almanacs to be opened flat
- Large type size makes information easy to read even in adverse conditions
- These handy volumes are a very practical addition to the navigation station

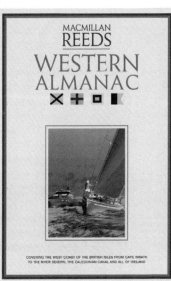
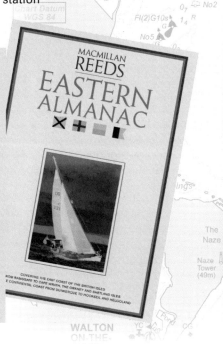

Channel Almanac

The Macmillan Reeds Channel Almanac offers the cruising and racing yachtsman ready access to essential information by virtue of its clear layout and user friendly format.
The Channel Almanac covers the south coast of England from the Scillies to Dover, the Channel Islands and northern France from Calais to L'Aberildut. Topics include pilotage, tides, safety, navigation, radio, lights, waypoints, weather and forecasts around UK and European waters, communications, MAYDAY and distress procedures - in fact everything the cruising yachtsman needs to know.

Wire binding allows the almanac to be opened flat on the chart table and the large type size makes information easy to read even in adverse conditions. At 272 pages, this handy volume is a very practical addition to the navigation station.

Western Almanac

The Macmillan Reeds Western Almanac follows the same format as the Channel Almanac and covers the west coast of the UK from Cape Wrath to Padstow and the whole of Ireland. It contains all the information needed for crossing the Irish and Celtic seas and visiting the delightful harbours, lochs and estuaries found in these waters.

Eastern Almanac

The Macmillan Reeds Eastern Almanac follows the same format again but covers the east coast of the UK from Ramsgate to Cape Wrath (including the Orkney and Shetland Islands) and the European coast from Dunkerque to Hooksiel in Germany, plus Helgoland. All the vital information is here for crossing the North Sea to Belgium, Holland and Germany, and many other passages such as the cross-Thames Estuary.

Chapter 11 Weather

CONTENTS

11.1 WHAT MAKES THE WEATHER

11.1.1 INTRODUCTION

Of all leisure activities sailing is one of the most weather sensitive. Anyone going to sea should therefore know how the weather works and be able to interpret weather forecasts. Some of the RYA certificates of competence also require a certain amount of meteorological knowledge to be demonstrated before they are granted.

Modern aids such as weather satellites and powerful computers have done much to improve the accuracy of forecasts in recent years but weather forecasting is not, and probably will never be, an exact science. In any case, no forecast covering an area could be sufficiently detailed to include all the variations within the period and across the area covered by the forecast. The mariner must therefore be able to interpret forecasts to obtain maximum benefit from them. Part of the interpretation process is to be able to monitor the weather so that any departure from the forecast can be quickly detected, so as to anticipate what is likely to happen in the future and take the appropriate action.

A general understanding of the weather is not difficult and a great deal can be learned from studying current weather charts and by listening to the more detailed forecasts on radio, eg those on BBC Radio 4. Much can also be learned by observing the weather, especially cloud formations and wind changes, and attempting to find the reasons for the various weather phenomena seen. However, some knowledge is needed of how the atmosphere produces the weather around us.

11.1.2   THE AIR AROUND US

Air is a mixture of gases. By volume, dry air contains about 79% nitrogen, 20% oxygen and the rest is small quantities of other gases. However, completely dry air does not exist in the free atmosphere. Water, up to about 3% at the surface, is the most important constituent from the aspect of producing 'weather'.

The visible symptoms of the earth's weather and most of the significant changes occur in a relatively thin layer of air near the ground called the troposphere. This extends to about 16km (10 miles) above ground at the equator and to about 9km ($5\frac{1}{2}$ miles) at the poles.

The temperature of the air in the troposphere generally decreases with increasing height, allowing air to move vertically and, as we shall see at 11.1.6, vertical movement is essential for the formation of cloud. The troposphere ends at the tropopause (approximately 36,000 ft or six miles high) above which is the stratosphere. Here the temperature gradually increases with height which means that cloud formation is generally inhibited.

11.1.3   HOW THE ATMOSPHERE WORKS

The atmosphere can be regarded as a big heat engine, driven by the sun. But, how does the engine work and why do we get continual movement and change?

First, the sun heats the earth more at the equator than near the poles. In addition, the heating varies with time of day, the time of year, and the nature of the earth's surface. Oceans heat up and cool slowly. Deserts, other dry areas and conurbations, heat up quickly by day and cool quickly by night, while farm land heats and cools more slowly. Slopes facing the sun will heat up quicker than those facing away from the sun.

In turn, the earth both heats and cools the air above it. The resulting temperature differences of the air lead to pressure differences. Pressure differences lead to air movement, ie winds (see 11.1.9), which causes a redistribution of the air; hence the pressure patterns change leading to changes in the winds – and so on.

Air cools as it rises, either by flowing up over hills, by convection or by air converging. Cooling also can occur when the air is in contact with cold ground. As the air cools it is able to hold less and less water until eventually water vapour starts to condense into droplets. This releases latent heat. If the air continues to cool then the drops may freeze to become ice or snow, again releasing latent heat. If the ice melts then latent heat is needed. This comes from the air, so cooling takes place. Again, if water drops evaporate, then latent heat is required from the air and again cooling takes place. These latent heat effects change the air temperatures and therefore the pressure patterns and hence the winds.

Air warms as it descends, after crossing hills or, see 11.1.8, in a high pressure area. Again, the pressure pattern changes.

The formation of drops of water in the air causes cloud to form. Cloud cuts off the radiation from the sun and reflects it back out to space – that is why cloud appears so bright when you fly above it. But, cloud also absorbs radiation from the ground and re-radiates it back to earth.

11.1.4   GLOBAL WEATHER

Heating at the equator creates a low pressure area into which air from north and south flows, leading to the air, initially, being carried upward. Because pressure decreases with increasing height, the rising air expands leading to cooling. The tropopause acts as a lid and the air can rise no further. It then spreads out to the north and south until after further cooling it sinks back towards the ground where some air returns to the equator at low level and some flows towards the poles.

Cooling over the poles makes the adjacent air colder and denser. This air sinks and flows to lower latitudes where it meets low level air from the subtropics. The resulting upward movement reaches the troposphere where again there is a northward and southward flow completing the vertical circulation.

This is shown schematically in Fig. 11(1). As can be seen areas of rising air are associated with lower air pressure at the surface and descending air with higher surface pressure. This much simplified model is greatly modified because of the many heating and cooling effects described earlier.

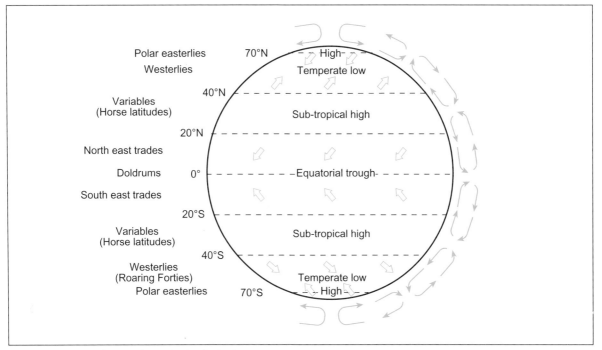

Fig. 11(1) From left to right: principal winds, surface pressure systems and air circulation over the globe.

Local weather patterns must be studied in the context of broader considerations, ie the global distribution of pressure around the world and the weather patterns they produce. The general flow and the pressure systems shift northwards with the sun during the northern hemisphere summer. The reverse happens during the northern winter; see also Fig. 11(2).

Air flowing from high to low pressure at the surface sets up circulations of air (more detail of this at 11.1.7). The land masses distort the circulations around the highs and lows, breaking them into separate cells so that movement between equator and poles occurs in bursts. These circulations are greatly affected by the distribution of land and sea. (See 11.1.6 and 11.1.9 for more detail on the relationship between pressure systems and wind).

The subtropical high pressure belts, around 30°N and 30°S are split into separate regions of high pressure commonly situated over the eastern part of each ocean, eg the Azores high. Similarly the belt of low pressure round the world at about 50 - 60°N is divided into two regions of low pressure near Iceland and the Aleutians. In the southern hemisphere the belt of low pressure does extend more or less round the world because there are no major land masses in these latitudes.

Over large land masses pressure tends to build in the winter and fall in the summer; such

seasonal changes can greatly modify the wind system over nearby oceans, eg the monsoon winds which blow over the Indian Ocean. The belts of high and low pressure drift somewhat north and south during the year, following the sun. To a lesser extent, ocean currents (see 12.1.15) affect the pressure over the world's surface, as they are able to transfer heat from one place to another.

11.1.5 ATLANTIC WEATHER

Fig. 11(2) shows the principal regions of high and low pressure and the major wind systems throughout the world in January and July, but the following discussion is confined to the Atlantic Ocean. The Equatorial Trough (Doldrums) represented by the heavy dotted line, is a low pressure area between the NE trade winds north of the equator and the SE trades to the south of it. Although renowned for their light winds, the Doldrums have very changeable weather; their width varies greatly, but is typically 200 – 300 miles (322 – 483km).

The NE and SE trade winds blow persistently, mostly about Force 4 and sometimes stronger, but seldom at gale force. The weather is usually fair, with small detached cumulus clouds, described in 11.1.11, rather wetter on the western side of the Atlantic. The amount of cloud and rain experienced increases towards the Equatorial Trough. Normally the barometer is steady, apart from the diurnal variation noted in 11.1.14, but if this diurnal rise and fall ceases, or if the barometer rises or falls markedly, it may foretell a tropical disturbance (see 11.1.20).

JANUARY

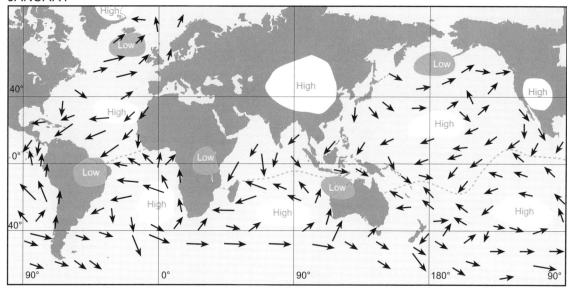

JULY

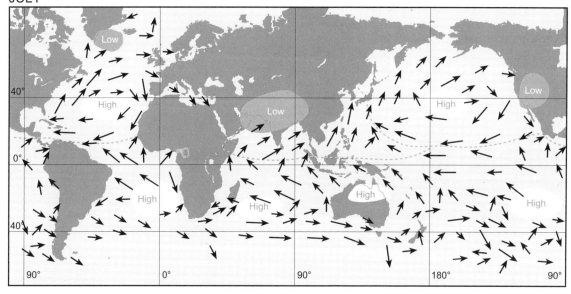

Fig. 11(2) Pressure distribution and wind systems in January and July. The dotted line indicates the Equatorial Trough. The relative strength of wind is shown by the length of the arrows.

On the polar side of the trade wind belts lie areas of anticyclones called The Variables (or the Horse Latitudes), with calms, or light to moderate winds variable in direction. Here the weather is usually fine, with only small amounts of cloud and rain.

North of 35°N, and south of 35°S, the winds become more predominantly westerly as latitude increases – more especially in the southern hemisphere where the significance of the Roaring Forties needs little explanation. In

the northern hemisphere the westerlies of the North Atlantic are in general lighter and less constant in direction, due to the large land masses and the effects of the depressions which form along the Polar Front (11.1.13). Fog is common in summer on the western side of the North Atlantic.

The polar regions are largely unnavigable due to ice. The wind is generally easterly, and the weather often cloudy with frequent fog in summer.

11.1.6   STABILITY AND INSTABILITY
Weather systems are of course 3-dimensional and their weather characteristics depend largely upon how air temperature changes with height.

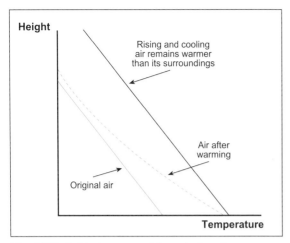

Fig. 11(3) Cold air warmed from below becomes unstable.

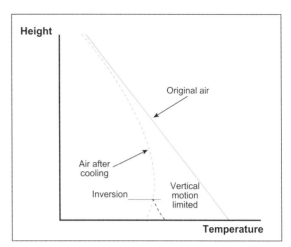

Fig. 11(4) Warm air cooled from below, making it stable.

The temperature profile of the air at any place depends upon where the air originated, and how it has been changed during its journey.

Air originating from a polar region is naturally cold, and its simplified temperature/height graph might look like the solid blue line in Fig. 11(3). If that air is then carried to lower latitudes (for example in the wake of a cold front) the temperature of the lower layers will be increasingly raised by the warmer underlying surface, thus changing the shape of the graph as indicated by the dotted line. If further heating is applied to the air at the surface – perhaps by sunshine – the air will rise by convection. The rising air cools, but provided that it stays warmer than its environment it will continue its upward motion. This condition is known as 'unstable' air, and is associated with good visibility, cumuliform cloud and gusty wind.

The reverse process occurs when a large mass of air is taken to higher latitudes, as indicated in Fig. 11(4). A situation is reached when any parcel of rising air will soon cool to the temperature of its surroundings, and can rise no further (unless mechanically lifted – as it may be by turbulence or by being forced up over a mountain range). This condition is known as 'stable' air, which often brings layered cloud, fairly steady winds, and sometimes poor visibility. As shown in Fig. 11(4) the surface cooling can lead to a layer of warmer air above the cooler layer beneath; this is called a temperature inversion.

11.1.7 AIR MASSES

Air masses are homogeneous in that they have almost uniform temperature and humidity throughout. They originate from either polar or tropical regions; and on their way towards the

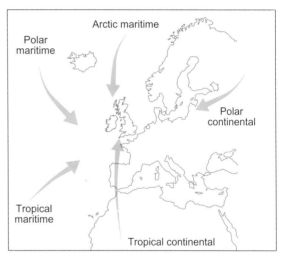

Fig. 11(5) The various air masses which influence our weather have widely different characteristics, depending upon their origins and tracks.

UK they track over either sea or land (maritime or continental); see Fig. 11(5).

After passing over a sea surface the air becomes humid, whilst its movement over a continental land surface renders the air drier. Thus four main air masses affect Britain and NW Europe, very briefly categorised by source and track, as follows:

   a. Tropical maritime (warm, stable, humid SW winds);
   b. Polar maritime (cold, unstable, humid NW winds);
   c. Polar continental (cold, dry, slightly unstable NE winds); and
   d. Tropical continental (warm, dry, slightly unstable Southerly).

Note: The (in)stability of continental air masses varies with summer or winter.

Tropical maritime air

While it may have started as unstable air, it has been cooled at the surface during its journey over the water towards northwest Europe and become stable and more humid. The weather is typically fairly warm with layered cloud (see cloud photographs 7 and 8) from which rain or drizzle may fall. The visibility at sea is rarely good and advection (sea) fog is a problem over the SW Approaches (see 11.1.17). With the air being constrained beneath a temperature inversion near the surface, the wind is usually quite steady from the SW quadrant.

Polar maritime air

This air originated over the polar region and has typically moved south towards Greenland before turning southeast towards Britain. It is naturally cold, and initially stable, air but has been modified near the surface as it moved over the relatively warmer waters of the north Atlantic. Therefore the air is unstable by the time it reaches Britain. The weather is typically fairly cold with passing showers. The clouds have a good deal of vertical development (see cloud photograph 10). The visibility is usually very good, except in any showers. The wind tends to be variable in speed with a large range between gusts and lulls and sometimes very blustery conditions occur, especially in the vicinity of heavy showers, with possible squalls. The wind blows from the NW quadrant, but will vary in direction with the gusts and lulls.

A variation of polar maritime air is *Arctic maritime air*. This air mass is unstable for similar reasons, but the difference is that the air is carried more directly from the polar region and thus it is colder. This air mass often reaches Britain when there is a low pressure area over Scandinavia which adds to the upward movement of unstable air. This leads to a greater frequency of blustery showers, especially over the North Sea and the waters around northern Scotland. Gustiness is a feature of the winds, particularly to the north and east of Britain. While visibility is generally good it will obviously decrease during showers, and in the winter snow showers can bring a sudden and dramatic decrease in visibility.

Polar continental air

There is usually a marked seasonal difference in the general weather brought by this air mass to Britain. In summer the skies are often cloudless, especially over waters in the south and west. Although the air tends to become unstable as a result of day-time heating over mainland Europe,

it is normally too dry to produce much in the way of cloud and showers.

In winter the air has started its journey being cold and remains so as it passes over the cold ground of continental Europe. The sky tends to be either clear due to the dryness of the air or covered with layers of low cloud trapped under an inversion. A generally dry pattern can be expected, although convection caused by the relatively warm waters of the North Sea can cause occasional light rain or snow. An introduction of moisture can bring heavier falls of rain or snow to southern Britain. At all times of the year, visibility can be moderate or good well out at sea. However advection fog can be a problem on the east coast of the UK (see 11.1.17).

Tropical continental air

Like polar continental air the weather produced by this air mass varies seasonally. It occurs infrequently in the winter and when it does it is similar to a warmer form of polar continental air. A low-level inversion tends to develop as the air passes over the cold land and thus any cloud will be layered similar to cloud photograph 8. The wind tends to be steady and rarely strong. While the visibility is not usually very good, fog is fairly infrequent with western areas being more likely to be affected.

In summer the precise track of the air is critical with regard to its effect upon the weather. If the air has come from due south or a little east of south the air will be dry with little cloud. Daytime heating results in some instability so there is a degree of gustiness to the wind. The visibility is usually quite good but often hazy.

The situation is changed considerably if the flow veers bringing air from over the waters off northwest Africa and Iberia. The increased humidity coupled with instability from strong day heating will cause deep clouds to form (cloud photographs 9 and 10) with thunderstorms over Spain and southwest France. These storms often migrate northwards to Britain with their attendant risks of extreme gustiness and wind shifts and sudden deterioration of visibility. The brunt of these storms is usually taken by the southwestern part of Britain. Thundery weather of this type often occurs at the end of a settled spell when the air flow gradually veers and the air mass changes from polar continental to tropical continental and eventually to a maritime type.

Although the above describes the most common air mass types that affect Britain and northwest Europe, every weather situation is unique and there are many variations.

11.1.8 ATMOSPHERIC PRESSURE

The air pressure at any point is the total weight of the air above that point. At the surface, this is about 10,000 kg (10 tonnes) per metre^2, or 14 lb/in^2. Perhaps surprisingly, one cubic metre of air weighs about one kg. For many years pressure was expressed as the height, in inches or millimetres, of a column of mercury needed to balance the weight of the air in a mercury barometer. In more recent times, one bar has been defined as a near average total atmospheric pressure, divided for convenience into 1000 millibars (mb).

Following the adoption of the pascal as the SI unit of pressure, meteorologists chose the hectopascal as the international unit for measuring atmospheric pressure; 1 hPa = 100 pascals = 1 mb. The millibar is still often used in weather reports and forecasts for the public, but the term hectopascal is increasingly being used, especially on the Continent. A conversion scale from mb/hPa to inches and millimetres of mercury is shown in Fig. 11 (28).

The distribution of pressure at any given time is vital information for the meteorologist who needs pressure readings taken at the same time in many different places. For consistency, readings are adjusted to a datum of mean sea level to take account of the reduced pressure at places above sea level (1hPa at or near sea level equals approximately 7·5m or 25 feet in height). From these readings a pressure chart can be produced by drawing on it isobars (lines that connect places with equal atmospheric pressure). Isobars are usually drawn either side of 1000hPa at equal intervals, typically 2, 4 or 8hPa, depending upon the chart scale. Areas of high (anticyclones) and low (depressions) pressure can thus be readily identified.

Pressure readings give the yachtsman invaluable information and assist in monitoring weather changes and forecasts. Changes in pressure, particularly if rapid, are often of most importance, but it is useful to compare the change of pressure at one's own location with thast expected from any forecast charts received.

11.1.9 WIND AND THE BEAUFORT SCALE

Isobars are like contours on a map. When contours are close together the gradient is steep: similarly for isobars. Gravity makes a ball roll down a slope. So too, gravity makes air try to flow directly from high pressure to low pressure, but it only does this near the equator. Elsewhere, due to the rotation of the earth (the Coriolis effect), it is deflected to the right in the northern hemisphere and to the left in the southern.

The Dutchman Buys Ballot recognised the relationship between isobars and wind. His law can most easily be remembered as: 'If in the northern hemisphere you stand with your Back to the Blast (wind), the Low pressure will be on your Left'. Or, more prosaically, in the northern hemisphere winds blow anti-clockwise around a low and clockwise round a high, while in the southern hemisphere the reverse is true.

Since wind is caused by the effect of gravity and the pressure gradient, it follows that stronger winds will be experienced where the isobars are closely spaced. Isobars spaced further apart indicate lighter winds. Thus in Fig. 11(6) the winds at A could be expected to be stronger than at B.

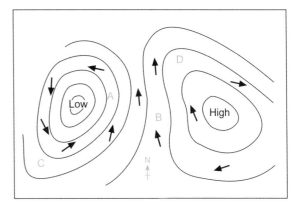

Fig. 11(6) How isobars depict an area of low pressure, (depression) on the left, and an area of high pressure (anticyclone) on the right. The arrows show typical wind circulations in the northern hemisphere.

The curvature of the isobars also affects wind speed. When the isobars are curved cyclonically, ie round a low, the wind speed is less than around high pressure, for the same isobar spacing. Although the isobars at C and D are equally spaced, the wind at D will be much stronger. The extension of a low as shown at C is called a trough, while the extension of a high as at D is a ridge.

The Coriolis effect varies with latitude and becomes increasingly significant with increasing latitude; it is showing its hand by about 10°. One result of importance to the sailor is that the wind resulting from a given pressure gradient will be stronger in lower latitudes. Those used to sailing in home waters can be surprised at the wind strength in relation to the isobar spacing when in the subtropics. A second consequence is that, very near the equator, the wind really does blow across the isobars. Any low pressure area will quickly fill and any high area will collapse.

Wind strengths are commonly expressed in forecasts and in other applications in terms of the Beaufort scale; see Fig. 11(7). This originally related the strength of the wind (when there were no instruments to measure its speed) to the amount of sail a ship could carry, and later to the effect of the wind on the sea state (Chapter 12). Terms such as 'Force 5' or 'Force 7' are not a direct measure of the physical force of the wind, on a sail for example. The actual force exerted on a sail is proportional to the square of the wind speed. Thus a wind of Force 7 (say 30 knots) has more than twice the weight of a wind of Force 5 (say 20 knots) – which is why even a fairly small increase in wind speed has a significant effect on a sailing yacht; see Fig. 11(8) for sea states.

Use of the Beaufort scale may seem slightly arcane. However, winds are never constant and the use of one number to represent a range of wind speeds is convenient. It gives a realistic average and a range of speed. A skipper will soon get to know what effect a given force has on his boat and its handling characteristics. The good Admiral's scale is a sensible pragmatic tool, as valid as ever.

Winds at about 600m (2000ft) are free of the earth's frictional effect, so blow roughly parallel to the isobars, ie in the direction that low cloud is moving (see 11.1.11). At the surface, friction causes the wind to be backed from the free flow wind in the northern hemisphere and veered in the southern hemisphere. The wind backs/veers about 30° over land and 10° – 15° over the open sea. The lighter the wind, the greater is the effect.

The wind speed over the open sea can be twice what it is over the land, which is worth remembering when you are in harbour, trying to decide whether or not to sail. It applies particularly in sheltered harbours with off-shore winds. Remember too that the wind is less at sea level than it is even 9m (30ft) above. As we have seen at 11.1.7 the character of the wind, that is, its short-term variability in speed and direction, will depend upon the air mass.

Some weather maps have a geostrophic wind scale against which the spacing of isobars, often at 4mb intervals, can be stepped off with dividers to give the approximate wind speed in knots or Beaufort force. Other such scales, as shown in Fig. 11(9), can be placed at right angles to the isobars at the place required, with the higher end of the scale on one isobar; the reading is taken where the next isobar (higher or lower) cuts the scale. Scales used by meteorologists give the wind speed at 600m (2000ft). Over the sea, due to the small surface friction, this 2000ft wind is likely to be about the same as that at sea level. The RYA weather map scale uses 2mb, the corresponding Beaufort force and gives the wind at sea level.

11.1.10 HUMIDITY

The importance of water in the air was mentioned in 11.1.2 and 11.1.3. In rather more detail, water exists naturally in three forms: liquid (water or water droplets), solid (ice) and as an invisible vapour. The amount of vapour air can hold depends upon the temperature. The lower the temperature the less moisture the air can hold in vapour form. For example, air at 0°C (32F) can hold only half as much water vapour as air at 10°C (50°F). If air is progressively cooled it eventually reaches a condition when it can no longer hold the vapour without condensing into a liquid or solid state – water droplets or ice crystals. The temperature to which air needs to be cooled so that vapour condenses to form water, is called the 'dew point'. Apart from cooling due to contact with a cold surface, the usual way for air to be cooled is by upward motion. Becauses pressure decreases with increasing height, rising air expands and cools.

Moisture in the air is most commonly manifested by the presence of clouds whose various forms are described in the following section.

11.1.11 CLOUDS

It is a great help when studying the local weather or making your own forecast, to be able to recognise the different types of cloud, and know how they form, move, change and decay.

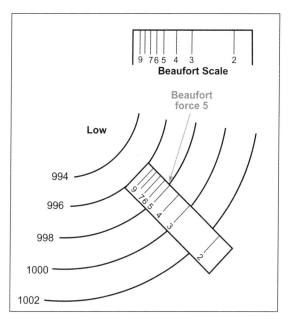

Fig. 11(9) Scale for measuring the Beaufort force from isobar spacing on an RYA weather map.

When observing clouds, try to record the extent of cover (usually expressed in octas, a way of dividing the whole sky into eighths, such that four octas is half cover and eight octas is total cover), the heights and types of cloud, and their directions of movement. If this is too daunting a task, try to distinguish the main types of high, medium and low altitude cloud.

Cloud can be categorised into four different types, each depending on how the air is made to rise and is thereby cooled to its dewpoint.

1. Convection cloud
In unstable conditions rising air is cooled to its dew point and forms heaped up cumulus cloud described later.

2. Clouds due to turbulence
Over the sea turbulence may extend up to about 600m (2000ft) when the wind is strong. If the air is sufficiently damp to be cooled to its dew point at this height, a sheet of stratus cloud may be formed.

3. Orographic cloud
This is the type of cloud formed when moist air is forced to rise over hills or mountains. By its nature it is not of much direct consequence to yachtsmen.

4. Frontal cloud
This forms when a relatively warm air mass meets a cooler air mass, so that the warm air, being lighter, rises above the cold air (or is forced upwards by the cold air driving underneath).

Clouds may also be grouped into three altitude bands – high, medium and low – measured from their base. Sometimes it may be hard to judge the actual heights of clouds, but it is usually simple to decide their other main feature, ie whether they have vertical development and individual form (cumulus type) or are a shapeless kind of spreading layer cloud (stratus type). Certain Latin words are used to describe cloud types or characteristics:

Cirrus	–	feathery
Stratus	–	layers or sheets
Cumulus	–	heaped
Alto	–	medium altitude
Nimbus	–	rain bearing
Fracto	–	broken

The various types and height bands are:

Name	Abbrev'n	Type	Height band
Cirrus	Ci	High	Usually above
Cirrocumulus	Cc	clouds	22,000ft
Cirrostratus	Cs		(6700m)
Altocumulus	Ac	Medium	7000-20,000ft
Altostratus	As	clouds	(2135–6100m)
Nimbostratus	Ns	Low	Usually below
Stratus	St	clouds	7000ft(2135m)
Stratocumulus	Sc		
Cumulus	Cu	Ditto	but they often
Cumulonimbus	Cb		build upward into High cloud

The ten more common types of cloud, as listed above, are described below and illustrated on pages 404-405. These pictures show:

1 – 6	A typical cloud sequence on a warm front (cirrus, cirrocumulus, cirrostratus, altocumulus, altostratus and nimbostratus)
7 – 8	Warm sector clouds (stratus, stratocumulus)
9 – 10	Cold front clouds (cumulus, cumulonimbus). The growth of cumulus cloud.

High cloud

1. Cirrus (Ci)
White, feathery, isolated clouds of ice crystals which cast no shadow; often called 'mares' tails' when thin and tufted. Usually indicate strong wind at altitude. Thin, high level cirrus means good weather; but thickening Ci which consolidates into cirrostratus and altostratus heralds an advancing low or frontal system.

2. Cirrocumulus (Cc)
Banks or rows of small white flakes, sometimes rippled or patterned (mackerel sky). Thicker than cirrostratus and usually contrasted against the blue sky. May indicate changeable weather. A transient cloud often developing from cirrus or cirrostratus, and then changing back to these or other forms.

3. Cirrostratus (Cs)
A thin white veil of transparent cloud, frequently giving haloes around the sun and moon. Often follows cirrus and precedes altostratus, heralding a depression and deteriorating weather.

Medium cloud

4. Altocumulus (Ac)
Longish layers or patches of white or pale grey cloud, usually in groups or lines. Rather similar to cirrocumulus, but larger and thicker, with a darker pattern. If much vertical development is evident it means instability which may give rise to thunderstorms.

5. Altostratus (As)
A sheet of cloud which may follow cirrostratus (although it is lower and thicker), in which case rain almost invariably follows with an approaching

front. Altostratus often varies in density – dark in some parts but the sun can be seen through others. It may cover the whole sky.

Low cloud

6. Nimbostratus (Ns)
A dense grey layer of low cloud which forms below altostratus, covering the whole sky and giving steady precipitation; often with scud detached from the main cloud layer.

7. Stratus (St)
Low sheet of uniform grey cloud, like fog not resting on the ground. The sun can sometimes be seen through it. It may cover the whole sky, or only be patches trailing over the sea. Often associated with drizzle and poor visibility.

8. Stratocumulus (Sc)
Irregular masses or rolls of large puffy clouds, with varying degrees of darkness, and often a thick wavy appearance. Common in winter, bringing drizzle rather than rain.

9. Cumulus (Cu)
Clouds with clear outlines, separated from each other. They have flat, grey bottoms; white, puffy sides; and billowing tops, with considerable vertical development. Cumulus comes in all sizes. Small puffy cumulus indicates fair weather.

10. Cumulonimbus (Cb)
Towering and forbidding storm clouds; when well developed, marked by anvil tops indicating powerful rising air currents – often producing squally winds with rain, heavy showers of hail or snow, and frequently thunder. Frequently embedded in intense cold fronts and vigorous troughs.

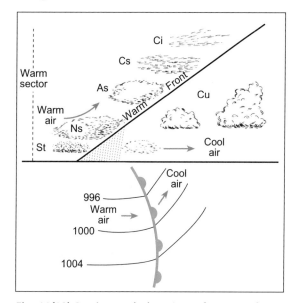

Fig. 11(10) Section and plan view of a warm front.

11.1.12 FRONTS AND OCCLUSIONS
Where different air masses, 11.1.7, are brought together the boundary between them is called a 'front'. Although some mixing occurs between the air masses they retain their individual identity for several days and the passage of a front is the most common, sometimes dramatic, way for a change of air mass over Britain.

Warm front
Around a frontal low (11.1.13) the advancing warm air, being lighter than the cold air it is replacing, tends to rise up over the cold before any significant mixing takes place. This is called a warm front, see Fig. 11(10). As the warm air is forced upwards it is cooled and is likely to produce cloud and rain.

Cold front
Behind the warm front is a warm sector, followed by a colder air mass overtaking the warm, along a broad line called a cold front – with the cold air driving in under the warm in a wedge action – pushing the warm air upwards even more vigorously, see Fig. 11(11).

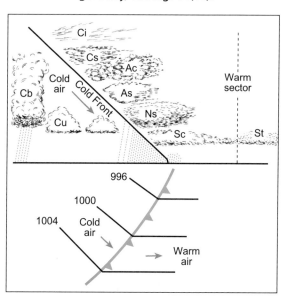

Fig. 11(11) Section and plan view of a cold front.

Occlusions
Sometimes the cold air lifts all the warm air off the surface of the land or sea, in which case the front is said to be occluded. There are two types of occlusion, cold and warm – depending on whether the air ahead of or behind the occluded front is the colder; both types of occlusion behave like fronts of the same name.

With the more usual cold occlusion, Fig. 11(12), cold air has overtaken a warm air mass,

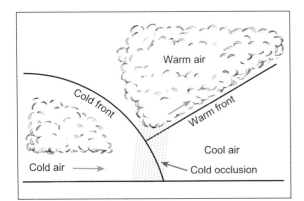

Fig. 11(12) Cross section of a cold occlusion.

lifting it off the surface; and then has caught up with air which is cool, but not as cold as itself. This usually results in rain from the warm front, continuing for a while after the front has passed, followed by a typical wind veer and cooler weather after the cold front has gone through.

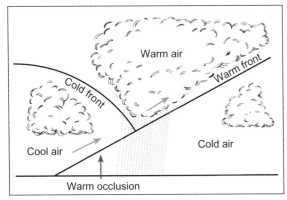

Fig. 11(13) Cross section of a warm occlusion.

A warm occlusion, Fig. 11(13), occurs when the overtaking air is cool but not as cold as the air ahead of the front. The warm occlusion is less active than a cold occlusion and is followed by somewhat warmer air.

11.1.13 FRONTAL DEPRESSIONS

Depressions affecting the British Isles mostly originate from a distortion of the Polar Front, the global feature which marks the broad boundary between polar air to the north and tropical air to the south. In a North Atlantic context the Polar Front extends from the American coast at roughly 30°N to the east at about 50°N. It moves a few degrees south to give us our winter, and a few degrees north in the summer, in theory to put the UK under the more benign influence of the Azores High. It is however the breeding ground for the

succession of depressions which afflict the UK and NW Europe.

All frontal depressions have a finite life: some persist longer than others, some become deeper and more vigorous, while others quickly disappear. But during their varying lives the Atlantic depressions are all continually changing as they meet up with or absorb other air masses in their general movement, which is often in an ENE direction crossing north of the UK.

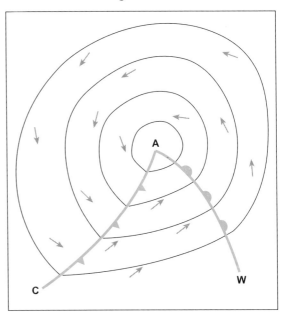

Fig. 11(14) A model depression. The arrows indicate wind directions.

Fig. 11(14) shows a classic or 'model' depression with its associated warm and cold fronts. AW is the warm front and AC is the cold front. Between the two fronts is the warm sector.

The frontal symbols are placed on the forward side of a front to show the direction of movement as well as type of front. On coloured charts a warm front is marked red, a cold front is blue, and an occlusion is purple. An occlusion is symbolised by alternate round and triangular marks. Arrows indicate the probable wind directions.

The movements (speed and direction) of depressions and their associated fronts are complex, and it is best to rely on forecast information. However RYA and other weather charts have scales, Fig. 11(15), for measuring the likely speeds of warm and cold fronts, in a similar way to wind speeds, Fig. 11(9). Cold fronts and occlusions usually move faster than warm fronts.

Depressions vary considerably in size and their speed of movement. They can be a thousand miles or more in diameter, or barely cover a shipping forecast area. They can travel at over 50 knots or linger interminably; those which cover a large area are usually the slower moving ones. With the model depression the isobars are roughly circular but those in the warm sector are usually straight. Often a depression can be elongated in shape, with the worst of the weather in troughs of low pressure extending from the centre. All fronts lie in a trough, but not all troughs are 'frontal'.

11.1.14   THE PASSAGE OF A DEPRESSION

Around the British Isles depressions and their associated fronts usually approach from the west and pass through to the east, with the centre of the depression often tracking north of the mainland.

The typical weather sequence thus causes is illustrated in Fig. 11(16). But keep in mind the approximate scale of this model: (A) could well be 200 miles or more ahead of (D), the surface position of the warm front. The horizontal and vertical scales are grossly mismatched; for example the cirrus cloud is probably about five miles above sea level.

Initially at (A), with a warm front still well to the west, the weather is fine with a moderate south-westerly wind; there may be some cumulus cloud around, and probably cirrus spreading from the west. The speed and amount of the cirrus is a good sign of the depth of the likely depth of the depression and of resulting strong winds. The barometer shows a tendency to fall.

At (B), as the warm front approaches, the wind starts to back southerly, the barometer falls, and cloud cover increases – initially thin cirrus with streaky white tufts or mares' tails, but steadily thickening into cirrostratus, possibly with a halo.

At (C), nearer the warm front, the cloud lowers and thickens, first into altostratus and then nimbostratus; the glass drops faster, and the wind increases and perhaps backs south east. It starts to rain and visibility shortens.

At the warm front (D), the rain eases or stops, the barometer steadies, and the wind veers to the south west. In the stable air of the warm sector visibility is poor, with low cloud and mist. If the centre of the depression passes some distance away to the north the cloud may break.

The cold front approaches from the west with a thick bank of cloud, but often this is not visible due to overcast conditions in the warm sector, so its sudden arrival may not be expected.

With the passing of the cold front (E), the wind veers sharply to the west or north west, perhaps with a squall. The clouds start to break as the rain ceases, visibility improves and the barometer starts to rise.

As the cold front clears away to the east (F), the glass rises further and the weather brightens with cumulus clouds developing in the unstable air; these may extend vertically into cumulo-

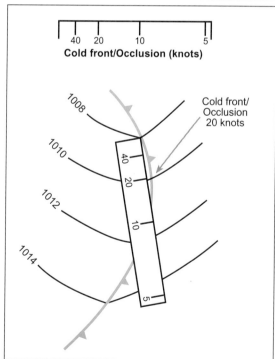

Fig. 11(15) Scales for measuring frontal speed: above, for warm front; below, for cold front or occlusion.

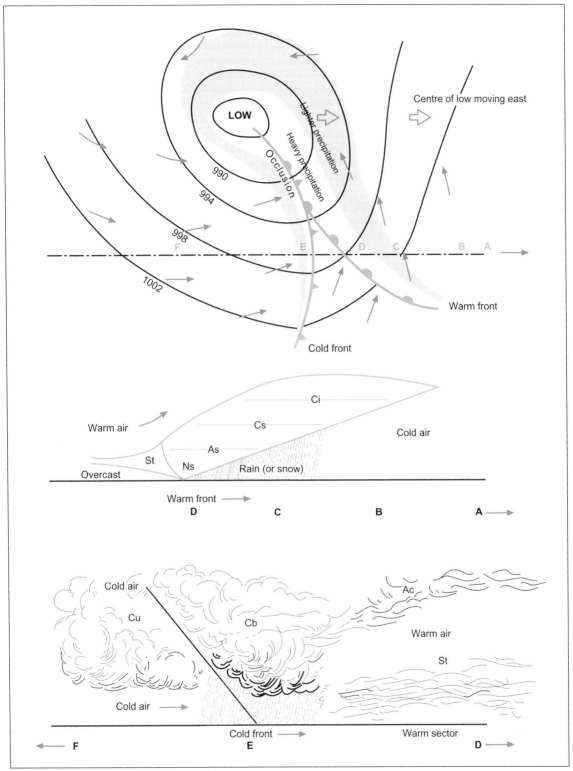

Fig. 11(16) The passage of a depression.

nimbus, causing showers, perhaps with anvil tops and thunderstorms.

Depending on the yacht's position relative to the centre of the depression, very different weather conditions and wind strengths will be experienced. Depressions do not always move as predicted: they can speed up, slow down, deepen, fill or change direction.

If the centre of the depression passes to the south of the yachtsman there is an altogether smoother sequence of weather, without the sudden changes and veers of wind which occur when negotiating the fronts south of a low. Instead the wind continually backs, initially with increasing cloud, as the glass falls. By the time the centre of the low is almost south of the observer the glass is steadier, the wind roughly from the east, and it is raining. When the centre has passed to the south the wind backs to north east, the barometer rises, and the rain may slacken. As the depression clears to the east the wind backs through north to north-west, and convective cumulus or cumulonimbus clouds become established – as behind the cold front further south.

The foregoing describes a 'typical' frontal depression, crossing the British Isles from the west, but each one is unique with its own variations.

11.1.15 SECONDARY DEPRESSIONS AND NON-FRONTAL LOWS

Secondary depressions will sometimes form in a trough, more frequently in a frontal trough some distance from the parent depression. They may be very vigorous and completely absorb the primary. Such secondaries can develop quickly (within 12 to 24 hours) and move very rapidly, causing a sudden and occasionally unforeseen wind increase. The strongest winds are likely to be on the side of the secondary furthest from the parent low, where the circulation of the former intensifies that of the latter.

The formation of a secondary used to be hard enough for a professional meteorologist to detect, still more so for a yachtsman at sea with limited knowledge of the exact position, movement and characteristics of the parent primary. Current numerical weather prediction methods have significantly improved matters, but it is still prudent to be alert for secondaries forming in the area of large occluded lows, particularly when there is a long trailing cold front. Look, also, for the point of occlusion pushing well ahead of the main low to form a very sharp trough – often a breeding ground for a secondary low (in this case known as a triple-point low, ie where the warm, cold and occluded portion of the fronts meet).

Non-frontal lows may develop due to surface heating, instability and orographic effects. Polar lows most commonly form in northerly air streams between Greenland and Iceland. Without satellites they were hard to detect and could give embarrassingly large amounts of snow. In summer, with light southerlies, heat lows are likely to form over France and drift northwards towards southern England to give severe thunderstorms and locally torrential rain.

11.1.16   ANTICYCLONES

Large highs are usually slow moving, but smaller ones can move or collapse quite quickly. A ridge has similar characteristics. Britain's summer climate often benefits from the north or northeast extension or movement of the semi-permanent Azores High, Fig. 11(2), which forces lows onto a more northern track.

As we saw at 11.1.4, high pressure is associated with descending air (subsidence) which warms the air, thus creating stability and inhibiting upward motion – hence the generally fair weather. As this process continues an inversion often develops near the surface under which the visibility is rarely good and a cloud layer can be trapped, especially in the winter. In winter poor visibility, stagnant air and overcast skies produce the dull, leaden light often referred to as 'anticyclonic gloom'.

Anticyclones are usually associated with light winds blowing clockwise around the centre (11.1.7), but an established high often deflects lows around its periphery bringing occasional poor weather and strong winds of Force 6 or more. Also, in 11.1.9 we saw that anticyclonic curvature could create stronger winds than straight or cyclonically curved isobars. This, coupled with strengthening around headlands and other coastal effects (see 11.1.18) can make winds around highs surprisingly strong. This is especially so off the south coast of England when a high to the north gives easterlies along the English Channel.

The inversion from a well-established high can also affect some radio signals and radar.

11.1.17   FOG

Fog develops in a similar way to cloud by air being cooled to its dew point. It follows that fog is more likely to form when the air is more humid, ie when the dew point is relatively high and the air requires less cooling before the dew point is reached. When coastal sailing one should be wary of any fog banks that are seen offshore; a tidal change can cause the fog to change position with the speed of the tidal flow.

Fog and mist are visible water droplets in the atmosphere. Haze is the presence of dust or smoke particles in the air. The distinction is made because further cooling can cause mist to get worse. With haze, this is not so.

Fog can be classified according to the way in which it forms. The two types of interest to the sailor are:

1.   Advection fog

This is the commonest type encountered over the seas of NW Europe and can occur whenever air moves towards colder waters. The RYA weather maps have average sea temperatures for September and February (annual maxima and minima). With any known or expected fetch of wind, these help the yachtsman to see when sea fog is likely or not. Most likely conditions are when the wind is Force 4 or less; the sea temperature is relatively low (spring/early summer); and the air has had a long enough sea track to acquire moisture and salt particles which encourage the water droplets to form. Such conditions are routinely met in warm sectors over the SW approaches to the English Channel in spring/early summer.

In the North Sea at any time of the year the waters over the Dogger Bank can be somewhat warmer than near the east coast of Britain. That is why, with an easterly wind, sea fog, or haar, can persist for many days near the coast and some way out to sea. Even with a northerly wind, sea fog can occur around the north coast of East Anglia.

Advection (or sea) fog is not readily 'blown away' and can persist in quite strong winds (eg gales off the Grand Banks of Newfoundland). A clearance is usually brought about simply by a change in wind direction, a post-cold front change of air mass, or occasionally when the fog-laden air moves over warmer water. A temporary clearance may result when close to a weather shore, off the north Brittany coast for example, due to the higher overland temperature; but after dusk fog may quickly reform. The fog layer is often quite shallow, so a masthead lookout may be able to con you clear of big ships! See also 11.1.7 for notes about fog in tropical maritime air and haar in continental air.

2. Radiation fog

As the earth radiates heat into space, especially on still clear nights, the lowest layer of air becomes cooler and when the air temperature falls to, or below, its dew point, fog develops and is trapped below a low-level inversion; 2 or 3 knots of wind act as a good mixing agent. By the nature of its development it is most frequent later in the night and during the few hours after dawn, and is most persistent during the winter months. The fog is cleared by an air mass change, a rise in temperature ('the sun will burn it off by 1030'), an increase in the wind (when the fog often lifts into low cloud) or a combination of these changes. Radiation fog, also known as land fog, is mainly a problem in harbour or close inshore when it drifts off the land. The sea temperature is usually sufficiently high to disperse the fog, although occasionally it can be a problem off the coasts of eastern Scotland and northeast England in the spring.

Other kinds of fog

Frontal fog is caused by the mixing of warm and cold air at a front. It may develop because the air is saturated in continuous rain ahead of a warm front or occlusion, and is usually confined to a relatively narrow belt near the frontal boundary; but sea fog may form in the warm moist air behind the front.

Air that has not been cooled enough to give advection fog may be cooled a little more by being forced to rise up a fairly small hill or coastal cliff. In itself, it has no consequence for the sailor. Nevertheless, it does indicate that the air is very near to saturation and that sea fog might occur at any time.

When thundery lows develop over France and drift north across the Channel, they create slow moving areas of very moist air. These give localised, very dense and therefore dangerous fog banks.

11.1.18 COASTAL WINDS

Many yachtsmen cruise largely in inshore waters (up to 12 miles off the shore) where the coastline itself often causes significant changes to the general wind. Such coastal effects rarely occur in isolation but in combination with each other and with the gradient (geostrophic) wind. The main effects in the northern hemisphere are discussed below.

Sea breezes

The theory of the sea breeze is simple: The land warms up by day and cools down at night much more quickly than the sea, which tends to change its temperature only over a long period (a function of their different thermal properties). Thus on a sunny morning as the land warms, the air above it is quickly heated and expands. This creates pressure gradients, initially at 100 or so metres above ground level giving a flow of air from land to sea at that height. The compensating reverse flow at sea level is the sea breeze, Fig. 11(17).

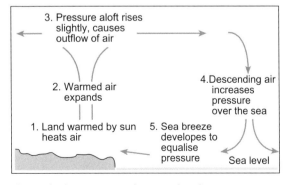

Fig. 11(17) How a sea breeze develops.

The effect depends upon there being little or no cloud over the land; the more cloud cover the less likely is a sea breeze.

The timing and strength of the sea breeze, and its subsequent behaviour, depend however on other factors. The most important is the wind already blowing in the morning. Around the UK an on-shore wind of force 3 or more can inhibit the vertical circulation described and a sea breeze is unlikely to develop. Conversely, a light off-shore wind will help the initial flow above ground level and so allow sea breeze development although its timing will be later than if the early morning were calm. In the western Solent an ENE 3-4 off the land can be reversed to a WNW 3-4 by the Southampton sea breeze.

Sea breezes are encouraged by low coastal areas with hills behind and are more pronounced when the atmosphere is unstable rather than stable. The sea breeze sets in earlier on east-facing coasts, rather than west, since the former warm up more quickly; and when there is no cloud over the land nor an existing off-shore wind.

A sea breeze cannot flow directly onto a cliff, but will flow around it. For example the Southampton sea breeze pulls the air around both sides of the Isle of Wight to give a WSW in the western Solent and a ESE to the east. Similarly, at Tor Bay air is dragged in from around Berry Head to the south and around Hope's Nose to the north; see Fig. 11(18). The classic sight in both areas is that of two yachts running towards each other under spinnaker.

The sea breeze begins along the shoreline, and slowly spreads seaward. Its onset may be seen by the build-up along the coast of a line of cumulus cloud which gradually moves inland. This is due to convergence as the sea breeze meets air over the land – the 'sea breeze front'. The sky will be clear over the sea, where the air is descending to feed the developing on-shore wind.

Under favourable conditions a sea breeze may be felt 10 miles or so offshore probably by early afternoon (but later if it has had to overcome an off-shore wind); in some areas its effect may extend further offshore. As the sea breeze strengthens during the day, the wind over inshore waters tends to veer (due to the Coriolis effect).

By early evening, as the sun's power wanes, the sea breeze starts to ease and will have gone by sunset, perhaps earlier if the off-shore gradient wind increases or cloud spreads across the land.

Off the UK sea breezes are most common in late spring, but they are also experienced in early spring and summer.

Land breezes

Land breezes blow at night, in the opposite sense from sea breezes by day, but not usually so strongly. They are caused by the land cooling more quickly than the sea – by radiation on a clear night, as typifies anticyclonic conditions. These off-shore breezes may start a couple of hours after sunset and blow until dawn, or a bit later. Since they depend on the temperature difference between land and sea they are more likely to occur in autumn (when the sea is warmest) than in spring or early summer.

The land breeze may be strengthened in some areas by a katabatic wind – caused by air being cooled on the slopes of coastal hills and mountains in settled weather with clear skies, and draining down the valleys to the sea. The effect is local and is usually not very strong in UK waters, except in steep-sided estuaries such as Scottish lochs. Nevertheless the effect can be quite marked where there are valleys such as around some river estuaries in SW England and Wales. The land breeze effect does not extend so

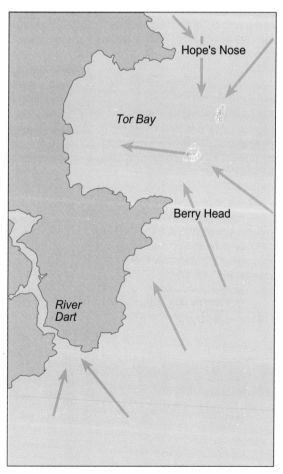

Fig. 11(18) Sea breeze effect in Tor Bay.

far from the coast as the sea breeze by day, usually not more than about five miles offshore.

The air which rises over the sea may form some cloud of a cumulus type, while the upper air moving back inland and sinking over coastal areas helps to keep them clear of cloud.

Le vent solaire

During the summer when the Azores high extends a ridge towards NW Europe, a particularly well marked land/sea breeze cycle (known locally as the *vent solaire*) occurs off the French Atlantic coast, particularly around Baie de Quiberon area. Because of the strong heating, even a NE 4-5 early morning wind can be reversed by the sea breeze effect. The sea breeze then veers, classically, to the NW. As the land cools at night, the wind reverts to its gradient direction of NE. Land breezes then enhance the offshore wind and anyone anchored on the east sides of Belle Île, Houat or Höedic can have an uncomfortable night.

Off-shore wind

With an off-shore wind, as the land is approached the wind can be expected to back. As we have seen in 11.1.7, due to friction the wind over the land is backed from the wind caused purely by the pressure force (the geostrophic wind), and it is backed by a greater amount than over the sea. There is a lag before the smaller amount of backing over the water takes full effect. When the wind is blowing over cliffs there is also the possibility of an eddy developing so that close inshore the wind can become flukey with an on-shore component.

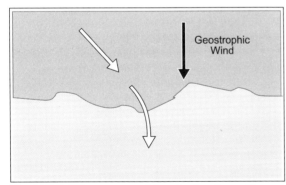

Fig. 11(19) When approaching the land an off-shore wind can be expected to back.

Wind along the coastline

The difference in the land and sea friction also has an effect upon the wind when it is blowing more or less parallel to the coastline. There are two cases to consider:

i. Back to the wind, land on your right.
   Here the greater backing of the wind over

the land causes it to converge just offshore with the wind over the sea, leading to an increase in the overall wind speed. This convergence can help the sea breeze to develop.

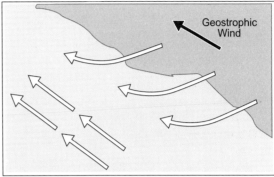

Fig. 11(20) With your back to the wind and the land on your right, an increase in wind speed can be expected immediately offshore.

ii. Back to the wind, land on your left.
   Here, conversely, the difference in the frictional effect causes the airflow over the water to diverge from that over the land. Therefore a lighter wind could be expected as the shoreline is approached. The divergence makes sea breezes less likely.

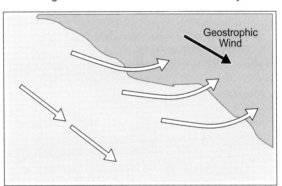

Fig. 11(21) With your back to the wind and the land on your left, less wind can be expected just offshore.

Headlands

The air tends to go around obstacles in its path rather than over them. This is more marked when the air is stable, especially when there is a low-level inversion. Near to and on the windward side of a headland the flow will be 'squeezed' causing the wind to be stronger while, as might be expected, there will be a decrease on the leeward side but possibly with an eddy.

Funnelling

The reluctance of air to go over obstacles will also tend to increase the wind when it blows up or down an estuary or fjord, especially when there is rising ground on both sides (Carlingford Lough in Ireland is a good example when a NW wind blows down the lough). In addition there is the effect of the wind blowing along a coastline, as described above. As a general rule with the back to the wind, the strongest wind will be towards the right-hand shore. With winds from a NE or SW direction, such funnelling explains the stronger winds through the Dover Strait.

Diurnal weather variations

Changes to the weather that tend to recur over a 24-hour period are called 'diurnal' changes. Most such changes are a result of the normal heating and cooling cycle. Thus the onset of sea breezes and to a lesser extent the formation of radiation fog have a diurnal pattern.

Such changes are most marked over the land, which responds to daytime heating and night-time cooling, and therefore these effects will be most noticeable in coastal waters. The open sea's surface temperature varies little from day to night so the diurnal effect is negligible, particularly in windy conditions, but some diurnal change can be experienced under light wind or calm conditions with clear skies.

11.1.19 THUNDERSTORMS

A thunderstorm is a particularly vigorous type of storm accompanied by strong winds, heavy precipitation and a bravura display of *Son et Lumière* (Thunder & Lightning) from towering cumulonimbus; it demands respect.

For a thunderstorm to form, the following are needed:

a. Marked instability over a substantial height band of the atmosphere; this implies a very pronounced decrease in air temperature with height and/or strong heating at the surface.

b. Adequate moisture from below (eg rain forest); and

c. Air which has reached saturation in ascent triggered by some form of lifting (advective heating, frontal lifting, convergence and, over or near land, by orographic lift and solar heating).

There are two basic types of thunderstorms, classified by their means of formation:

i. Heat or air mass; and

ii. Frontal.

The air mass storm is more likely to occur over a large land mass subject to intense heating, eg mid-west USA. But a polar maritime air mass moving south over an increasingly warm sea surface may develop sufficient instability to trigger off a thunderstorm. The air mass thunderstorm is usually isolated or well scattered. But very strong heating can create a heat low and a large area of thunderstorms – a typical example being the thundery outbreaks that drift northwards from France to cover much of southern England.

A frontal storm usually occurs where a cold air mass undercuts a warm mass, eg at a cold front or occlusion, although warm front and occluded front thunderstorms can also occur. A line of such thunderstorms may therefore be as much as 100 miles long. Thunderstorms are much less frequent over sea than over land.

The distinctive cumulonimbus cloud associated with a thunderstorm is a tall towering cloud often with a dark base at say 2000 ft, rising perhaps 30,000 feet or more to a spreading anvil-shaped head of cirrus cloud. It is a complex structure composed of several cells each having its own updraughts and downdraughts which affect the surface wind in its vicinity. Individual thunderstorm clouds may be 10 miles in diameter, but when embedded in a frontal trough they may extend many more miles in a narrow belt.

Lightning is caused by an electrical discharge between positively and negatively charged areas, whether from cloud base to top, cloud base to ground or cloud top to space. Lightning is frequently 'forked' due to the ionisation of the air along its path. So-called 'sheet' lightning is simply forked lightning obscured by cloud or rain.

Thunder is the noise caused by the sudden expansion of the air heated by the lightning flash. Although flash and noise occured simultaneously, the latter is heard after the flash is seen due to the slower speed of sound. Thus a thunderstorm's distance away can be estimated by timing the interval between lightning and the associated thunder; each 5 seconds represents approximately one mile.

The wind changes around a vigorous cumulonimbus can be sudden and dramatic. In the development phase, the large up-currents create strong inflows to the cloud. When heavy rain starts to fall it drags down air causing strong downdraughts and outflows. The result is windshifts up to 180° with extreme gusts. This gives rise to the oft-quoted but misleading comment that a thunderstorm 'comes up against the wind'. A thunder cloud, like all other clouds, is moved by the general wind but the thunderstorm has its own surface wind pattern. This should be borne in mind when deciding how best to take avoiding action.

A thunderstorm is capable of producing sudden very heavy rain and often hail with a rapid deterioration in visibility to less than 100m; so in addition to monitoring the progress of the storm keep a good lookout for other mariners who may also be avoiding it.

A lightning strike can be a real and frightening hazard, especially with stainless steel rigging and masthead fittings, but a metal mast acts as a lightning conductor by providing a low resistance path for the current to pass to earth (the sea). Some experts say that damage to the yacht can be minimised by connecting an earthing strap from the base of the mast to the keel bolts or a plate on the vessel's bottom (13.3.5). However, others claim that a lightning strike can blow the plate or keel bolts off the boat with disastrous effects. An alternative being marketed looks like a wire brush at the masthead. The makers claim that this diffuses the static charge at the masthead and prevents development of the strong electrical gradient needed for damaging lightning strikes.

When lightning is about, stay below deck if possible and avoid handling metal fittings at all costs. Night vision will be temporarily destroyed and switching on deck floods before the event may restore orientation.

Compasses, radios, GPS and other electronic equipment are likely to be adversely affected or even burned out; it may help to disconnect aerials and power leads if time allows. It is a wise precaution to put the spare hand-held GPS in the oven which will act as a Faraday cage; or, just keep it in encased in metal foil.

Occasionally the conditions needed to create thunderstorms can lead to the development of a tornado. In NW Europe these are usually a few metres, exceptionally up to 100m, across unlike their larger and far more devastating US cousins. Nevertheless, any violent vortex with intense vertical motion that is capable of uprooting trees, can do damage to or knockdown a yacht. A good sign that tornados are about is when a funnel-shaped extension to the cloudbase is seen with disturbed water and a cloud of spray beneath. A more vigorous tornado with very low core pressure will appear to lift the water into a waterspout. Fortunately these are fairly rare over British waters and occur mainly in a very humid late summer southerly. A favoured location seems to be off the south coast of the Isle of Wight. Watch the cloud base of a Cb and avoid tornados or waterspouts just as you would another vessel.

11.1.20 TROPICAL REVOLVING STORMS (TRS)

This is the generic name given to typhoons of the China Sea, cyclones of the Indian Ocean, Arabian Sea and Bay of Bengal and hurricanes in the Caribbean and around Australasia. They are intense depressions forming in low latitudes. Fig. 11(22) gives details of areas and months of activity so providing invaluable planning information for long distance cruising.

The trigger is usually a trough in the easterly winds either side of the equator, see Fig. 11(2). These troughs create areas of very vigorous convection with very strong upward currents giving similarly strong inflows. At about latitude 10° N or S the Coriolis effect starts to be felt (11.1.9) causing the inflows to form cyclonically circulating winds spiralling into the centre. Heat from the sea, plus the latent heat released by the condensation of vast amounts of moist air, are critical factors. Large areas (over 8.5×10^6 km^2, or about the size of the USA) of sea warmer than 26°C may be required, which is why hurricanes have never been observed in the South Atlantic.

In the North Atlantic, the process starts off the coast of west Africa. The storms continue to move towards the Caribbean. In lower latitudes the tracks are usually fairly straight, with speed of movement 10-15 knots WNWly. Around 15° latitude, the whole storm is affected by Coriolis causing deflection to the right sometimes to an ENE direction to join the mid-latitude lows.

Winds are often very violent and the sea state dangerously high and confused. Gale force 8 winds are likely within 200-100 miles of the centre, rising to hurricane force 12 inside 100 miles. Mean winds of well over 100 knots are on record and gusts to 175 knots have been reported. At the centre, or eye, of the storm (which may be 10 miles across or 30-40 miles in a large TRS) there is a temporary lull. Outside the eye the wind blows at hurricane force, torrential rain and driven spray reduce visibility to almost nil, and massive, dense clouds extend to the tropopause.

Weather satellites now identify and track hurricanes so that position, intensity and likely movement can be regularly broadcast – but such predictions are not infallible. Ships and especially a slow-moving yacht should therefore take early avoiding action.

Fig. 11(23) shows the typical path of a hurricane, and identifies the dangerous and navigable semicircles. The former lies to poleward (north in the N Atlantic) of the storm's path, where the wind is strongest and a yacht tends to be blown into the eye of the storm. If the wind steadily veers, the yacht must be in the dangerous semicircle. The most dangerous quadrant is ahead and to the poleward side of the storm. If the hurricane recurves, the eye of the storm may pass over the yacht.

Area & Local name	Jan	Feb	Mar	Apr	May	Jun	Jul	Aug	Sep	Oct	Nov	Dec	A	B
North Atlantic, West Indies region (hurricane)													10	5
North-East Pacific (hurricane)													15	7
North-West Pacific (typhoon)													25-30	15-20
North Indian Ocean Bay of Bengal (cyclone)													2-5	1-2
North Indian Ocean Arabian Sea (cyclone)													1-2	1
South Indian Ocean W of 80°E (cyclone)													5-7	2
Australia W, NW and N coasts & Queensland coast (hurricane)													2-3	1
Fiji, Samoa, New Zealand (North Island) (hurricane)													7	2

Start/Finish of season

Period of greatest activity

Period affected when season early/late

Column A: Approximate average frequency of tropical storms each year
Column B: Approximate average frequency of tropical storms each year which develop Force 12 winds or stronger

Fig. 11(22) Table of TRS activity v Location

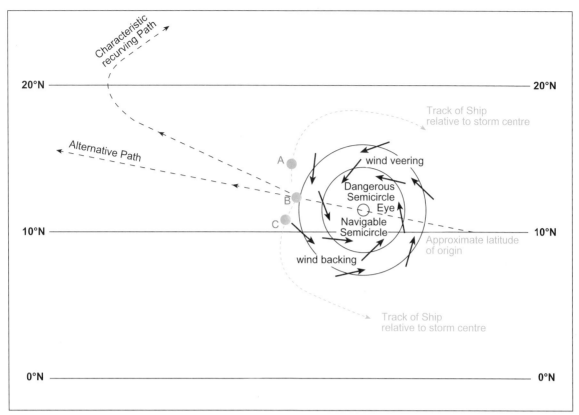

Fig. 11(23) Typical path of a hurricane, showing the dangerous and navigable semicircles.

Avoiding actions in the northern hemisphere include:

  a. If the wind is veering, you are north of the storm's possible track and at risk from the approaching dangerous semicircle. So turn to keep it 10°- 45° off the starboard bow, tracking as shown by the pecked line. Note: If however the TRS is close and recurves sharply, it could pass near to a vessel following this action. Another course of action would therefore be to turn south, ahead of the storm's path and into the navigable semicircle.

  b. If the wind is steady, turn to keep it on your starboard quarter, making best speed into the navigable semicircle.

  c. If the wind backs, turn to keep it on your starboard quarter, tracking well clear as shown by the dotted line.

11.2 SOURCES OF WEATHER INFORMATION

Yachtsmen around NW Europe and the W Mediterranean are well served with weather information, most of which originates from National Weather Services, such as the UK Met. Office and is disseminated in many different ways. Information from other countries is often in the national language but there are some services, mainly under the GMDSS umbrella, that are in English. Marine forecasts in other languages are not usually difficult to understand and it is worthwhile learning a few of the words used; see 11.5.2.

11.2.1 SHIPPING FORECASTS – BBC RADIO 4

Shipping forecasts, primarily designed for commercial vessels on passage, necessarily cover very large sea areas. It is therefore impossible, in 3 minutes and 300 words, to include much detail, especially about the many variations that are of interest to yachtsmen. Their main strength is that they are revised every 6 hours – after each run of the Met Office weather prediction model, based on the six hourly international exchange of weather observations. This means that changes to the weather situation and expected evolution can readily be identified.

Definitions of terms used are in 11.3. Recording and using the forecast are discussed in 11.4. Check the latest times of forecasts in the MRNA and ALRS Vol 3. See also Figs. 11(31) and (32).

Contents

The forecasts include:

  a. Areas with gale warnings† in force;
  b. A general synopsis of weather systems and their expected development over the next 24 hours;

c. Sea area forecasts (in a fixed order) for the next 24 hours, giving wind direction and force, weather and visibility.

† Gale warnings are broadcast on Radio 4 at the first programme juncture and news bulletin after receipt.

Times
The Shipping forecasts are broadcast daily by BBC Radio 4 on 198kHz LW at the following local times:

0048*, 0535*, 1201 and 1754.

* These broadcasts are also on FM and MW. Sea area Trafalgar is included only in the 0048 Shipping forecast.

On Sundays at 0542 a seven day forecast for all sea areas is broadcast on LW, FM and MW frequencies.

Radio 4 FM and MW frequencies
FM broadcasts are on the following frequencies (MHz):
England 92·4-94·6; Scotland, Wales and Northern Ireland 92·4-96·1 or 103·5-104·9; Channel Islands 94·8.
MW broadcasts are on the following frequencies (kHz):
Tyneside 603; London and Northern Ireland 720; Redruth 756; Plymouth and Enniskillen 774; Aberdeen 1449; and Carlisle 1485.

11.2.2 WEATHER REPORTS FROM COASTAL STATIONS
These are **only** broadcast after the 0048 and 0535 Shipping forecasts on Radio 4 LW, MW and FM. They give the actual wind direction and force, weather, visibility, pressure and tendency at 2300 and 0400 respectively for the following stations:
Tiree, Stornoway, Lerwick, Fife Ness, Bridlington, Sandettie Lt V*, Greenwich Lt V*, Jersey, Channel Lt V*, Scilly*, Valentia, Ronaldsway and Malin Head.
* *Automatic weather station; does not yet report weather.*

11.2.3 INSHORE WATERS FORECASTS – BBC RADIO 4
These cover UK waters up to 12 miles offshore. They are broadcast by BBC Radio 4 after the 0048 and 0535 Shipping Forecasts and on the same LW, FM and MW frequencies. These forecasts are intended to take some account of local phenomena such as land and sea breezes and the effects of topography on inshore weather. They cover the coast clockwise in 9 sections, divided by salient features such as Cape Wrath, Duncansby Head, Orkney, Shetland, Berwick-

upon-Tweed, Whitby, North Foreland, St Catherine's Point, Land's End, Colwyn Bay and Mull of Kintyre.

After the 0048 forecast only, reports are broadcast of the actual weather at the following coastal stations:
Boulmer, Bridlington†, Sheerness, St Catherine's Point, Scilly†, Milford Haven, Aberporth, Valley, Liverpool (Crosby), Ronaldsway†, Larne, Macrihanish, Greenock, Stornoway†, Lerwick†, Wick, Aberdeen and Leuchars.
With five exceptions†, these are not the same as the stations featured at the end of the Shipping forecast.

11.2.4 GENERAL FORECASTS – BBC RADIO 4
Land forecasts can be useful to yachtsmen as they often include an outlook period up to 48 hours beyond the detailed forecast and the shipping forecast, and some reference to weather along the coasts. They may also give more recent information which was not available in the previous shipping forecast. The more detailed land area forecasts are broadcast on Radio 4 on 198kHz and FM. They are also available by fax from 09065 300 138, or by telephone from 09068 500 438.

On Saturdays at 0556 a topical leisure forecast for the UK and parts of Europe is broadcast on LW, FM and MW.

11.2.5 LOCAL RADIO STATION FORECASTS
The scope, details and therefore value of forecasts broadcast by local radio stations vary considerably. Some give no more than an indication of the present weather conditions; others are comprehensive and detailed. Many local radio stations in coastal areas broadcast 'Small Craft Warnings' when winds of Force 6 or more are expected within the next 12 hours on the coast or up to five miles offshore. These warnings are handled in a similar way to gale warnings on Radio 4, being broadcast at the first programme juncture after receipt and then repeated on the next hour or after the next news bulletin.

Local radio stations' weather forecasts which are of particular interest to yachtsmen are given in the MRNA and in ALRS, with times and frequencies; times may vary to fit in with other programmes.

11.2.6 MRCC/MRSC BROADCASTS
HM Coastguard is one of the most important and easily accessible sources of weather information for ships and yachts at sea. They broadcast the following:
a. Gale and strong wind (> F6) warnings on receipt.

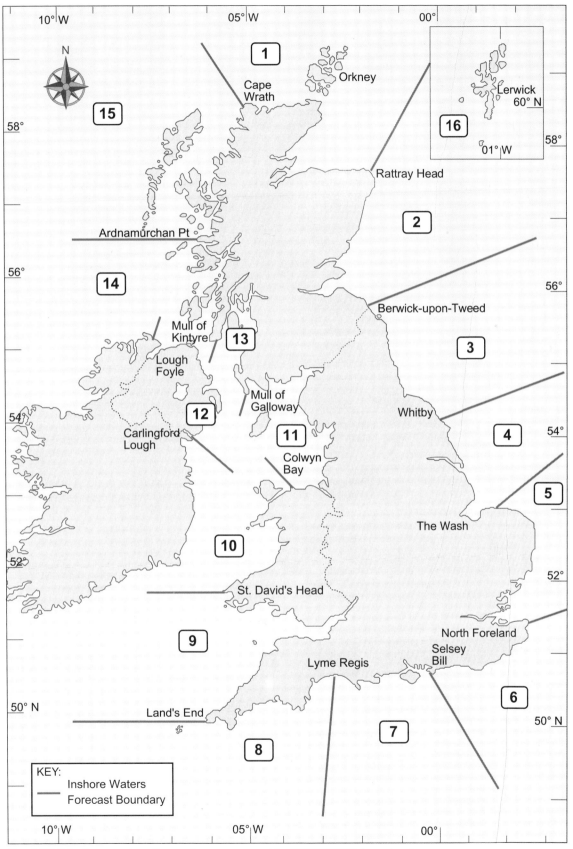

Fig. 11(24) Inshore waters forecast areas as used in MRCC/MRSC broadcasts.

b. Shipping forecasts for adjacent Sea areas, twice daily.

c. Forecasts for local inshore waters, (16 areas around the UK; see Fig. 11(24)), every 4 hours including gale and strong wind (> F6) warnings. The forecasts are updated twice a day and cover the first 12 hours from 0700 or 1900 UT and an outlook for the next 24 hours.

The 16 Areas referred to by the Coastguard in their Inshore waters broadcasts are defined as:

Area Boundaries

1 Cape Wrath to Rattray Head, including Orkney
2 Rattray Head to Berwick-upon-Tweed
3 Berwick-upon-Tweed to Whitby
4 Whitby to The Wash
5 The Wash to North Foreland
6 North Foreland to Selsey Bill
7 Selsey Bill to Lyme Regis
8 Lyme Regis to Land's End, including Scilly Isles
9 Land's End to St David's Head, inc Bristol Channel
10 St David's Head to Colwyn Bay, inc St George's Channel
11 Colwyn Bay to Mull of Galloway, inc Isle of Man
12 Carlingford Lough to Lough Foyle
13 Mull of Galloway to Mull of Kintyre, including the Firth of Clyde and North Channel
14 Mull of Kintyre to Ardnamurchan Point
15 Ardnamurchan Pt to Cape Wrath, inc Western Isles
16 Shetland Isles (60M radius from Lerwick)

Note: The numbers 1-16 have no significance; they are merely a reference and are not included in the broadcasts.

The Table below gives for each Centre the times UTC of the Shipping forecasts in **bold** type and Inshore forecasts in plain type every 4 hours. Broadcasts are on any or all of VHF working channels 10, 23, 73, 84 or 86 (and exceptionally on Ch 67) – so it is important to listen to the prior announcement on Ch 16. Shipping forecasts are also broadcast by Centres* on the MF frequencies as pre-announced on 2182kHz.

MRCC/MRSC Inshore and Shipping forecasts

South coast

Falmouth*	0140	0540	**0940**	1340	1740	**2140**
Brixham	0050	0450	**0850**	1250	1650	**2050**
Portland	0220	0620	**1020**	1420	1820	**2220**
Solent*	0040	0440	**0840**	1240	1640	**2040**
Dover	0105	0505	**0905**	1305	1705	**2105**

East coast

Thames	0010	0410	**0810**	1210	1610	**2010**
Yarmouth*	0040	0440	**0840**	1240	1640	**2040**
Humber*	0340	**0740**	1140	1540	**1940**	2340
Forth	0205	0605	**1005**	1405	1805	**2205**
Aberdeen*	0320	**0720**	1120	1520	**1920**	2320
Shetland*	0105	0505	**0905**	1305	1705	**2105**

West coast

Stornoway*	0110	0510	**0910**	1310	1710	**2110**
Clyde*	0020	0420	**0820**	1220	1620	**2020**
Belfast	0305	**0705**	1105	1505	**1905**	2305
Liverpool	0210	0610	**1010**	1410	1810	**2210**
Holyhead*	0235	**0635**	1035	1435	**1835**	2235
Milford Hvn*	0335	**0735**	1135	1535	**1935**	2335
Swansea	0005	0405	**0805**	1205	1605	**2005**

Check in the MRNA for any changes to these schedules. Note that the Shipping forecast will be that of the previous Radio 4 broadcast unless there has been some significant change, eg gale warning issued/cancelled.

As a courtesy yachtsmen should make every effort to listen at the scheduled times. It can be time consuming for a busy Coastguard to have to repeat a forecast that has just been broadcast, often twice on different aerials.

The Coastguard also reports actual weather on request, but based solely on 'looking out of the window' or on reports from nearby vessels.

Other European countries have similar services, sometimes in English as well. MRNA and ALRS Vol 3 contain details of schedules and VHF channels and/or MF frequencies. Nearer to home Jersey Met Office has a particularly good service on VHF and MF covering the area bounded by 50°N, the French coast and 3°W (about Ile de Bréhat). The Irish Met service also has a good service covering areas around its coasts.

11.2.7 NAVTEX

The MCA encourages all seafarers to use NAVTEX, an integral part of the GMDSS in disseminating Marine Safety Information (MSI), ie weather, navigational and safety data, to vessels within range of shore stations. An unobtrusive black-box, using little power, automatically receives such information transmitted in text form, mostly on 518 kHz. Skippers of small vessels probably use NAVTEX mainly to get weather data – hence it features here, but is also mentioned under Safety (Chapter 13) and Navigation (Chapter 7). See also 11.2.17.

The basic installation consists of an aerial and receiver. Messages may be either read from a 'soft copy' LCD display or printed onto paper rolls 80 mm (3 in) wide. The paper is expensive but allows information to be reviewed in slow time, filed and/or passed on to any non-Navtex yachts nearby. It is vital to have the aerial

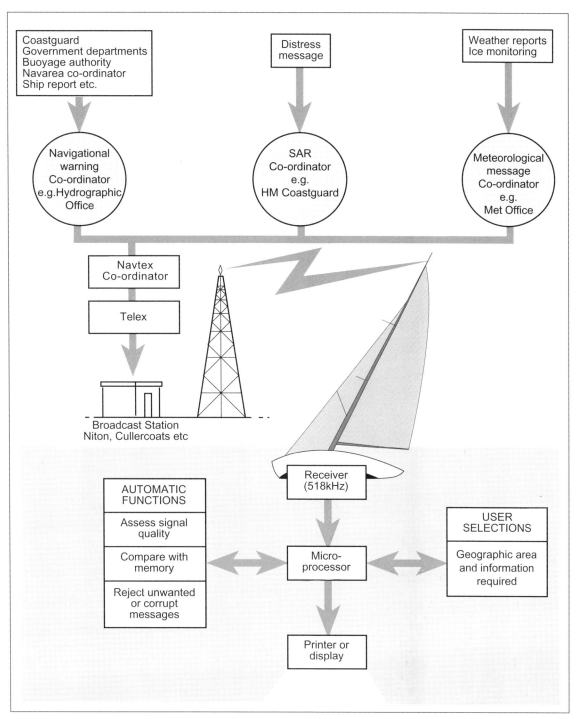

Fig. 11(25) Navtex inputs and components.

properly earthed for optimum reception, especially near a station's maximum range.

Fig. 11(25) shows the Maritime Safety Information (MSI: Safety, Met and Nav warnings) and their sources as provided by Navtex.

Each message is prefixed by a four character alpha-numeric group. The first letter is the identity code of the transmitter, eg G for Cullercoats; the second letter indicates the message category as in the code below. The third and fourth characters are message serial numbers, from 01 to 99 in order of receipt. At 99 the numbering starts again at 01 using the numbers of any expired messages. The serial number AA 00 denotes a message of extreme urgency which will always be printed, regardless of how the receiver has been programmed.

Message categories

A Navigational warnings
B Gale warnings
C Ice reports
D SAR information and Piracy warnings
E Weather forecasts
F Pilot Services
H Loran-C
I Not allocated
J Satnav
K Other electronic Navaids
L Subfacts and Gunfacts in the UK
M to U Not allocated
V Amplifying Nav warnings initially sent under A; plus Oil and Gas Rig weekly list
W to Y Special services
Z No messages on hand

Receivers are easily programmed to select station(s) and categories of messages. After switch-on, first select the required stations, noting that one, more, or all in-range stations can be chosen. Then select the required message categories. With some (eg ICS) sets, messages in categories A, B and D can not be deselected; they are always printed/displayed. Messages which are corrupt will be rejected and receivers with paper printout will also reject messages received within the last three days. Other receivers (eg NASA) allow all messages except D to be deselected.

All information is available in English, although some stations also broadcast in the local language. The MF frequency of 518 kHz gives excellent coverage of the waters for which the system is intended, ie to about 300M offshore. Interference between stations is minimised both by time sharing and by limiting the transmitters' power.

Five stations cover the Sea Areas clockwise around the British Isles:

Niton (S) Thames to Fastnet; plus Biscay, Fitzroy, Sole and Lundy
Portpatrick (O) Lundy to Fair Isle and SE Iceland
Valentia (W)* Sole, Fastnet and Shannon
Malin Head (Q)* Shannon, Rockall, Malin, Bailey
Cullercoats (G) Fair Isle to Thames, but not N & S Utsire, Fisher and German Bight

*Malin Head also broadcasts the High Seas forecasts for the East Northern and East Central sections of MetArea I, *Valentia the East Central section only; see Fig. 11(27).

The weather information broadcast by these British and Irish stations originates from the Met. Office and is identical to that broadcast in the Shipping Forecasts, except as indicated in 11.2.6.

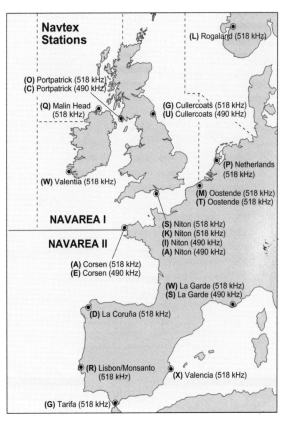

Fig. 11(26) Navtex stations.

There are no reports of actual weather on Navtex. The contents of a Navtex broadcast apply only to the area for which that station is responsible.

Navtex forecasts also contain a brief outlook for the following 24 hours, concentrating on hazards. In addition an extended three day outlook, valid from when the 24 hour outlook ends, is transmitted by Portpatrick at 2220, Niton at 2300 and by Cullercoats at 0100 (all UTC).

A second frequency 490kHz (used abroad for broadcasts in the national language) now broadcasts twice daily a 12 hours forecast, plus a 24 hours outlook, for Inshore waters. The contents are the same as the CG broadcasts in 11.2.6. This is followed by a three day National outlook. Strong wind warnings are also issued by the 490kHz UK stations, as listed below. Note that their identification letters differ from those of the 518kHz stations. Their broadcast times (UTC) and features which demarcate the coastal stretches are as follows:

Niton (I) – 0520, 1720. The Wash, N Foreland, Selsey Bill, Lyme Regis, Land's End, Scilly, St David's Head, St George's Channel and Colwyn Bay.

Portpatrick (C) – 0820, 2020. St David's Head, Colwyn Bay, St George's Channel, Mull of Galloway including Isle of Man, Carlingford Lough, Lough Foyle, Mull of Kintyre, Firth of Clyde, North Channel, Ardnamurchan Pt, Cape Wrath, Outer Hebrides and the Shetland Isles.

Cullercoats (U) – 0720, 1920. Cape Wrath, Orkney Isles, Rattray Head, Berwick upon Tweed, Whitby, The Wash and North Foreland.

Note: **Niton (A)** on 490kHz is the equivalent of Niton (K), ie it covers the north coast of France, but in French.

To receive 490kHz broadcasts on existing 518kHz sets, NASA have produced a second aerial. The existing aerial on ICS sets must be replaced with a dual frequency aerial. In both cases users switch manually between frequencies. ICS also market a new set that receives both frequencies simultaneously and stores the information to be read on screen or paper.

Full details of NAVTEX broadcasts are given in ALRS Vol 3 (NP 283) and in the Small Craft ALRS (NP 289).

ANNEX   NAVTEX STATIONS IN METAREAS I, II AND III

Times UTC of weather messages are in **bold**; if no bold type, that station broadcasts Navigational warnings only.

METAREA I. Co-ordinator: UK

R	Reykjavik, Iceland						
	0318	**0718**	**1118**	**1518**	**1918**	2318	
L	Rogaland, Norway						
	0148	0548	0948	**1348**	1748	2148	
B	Bodø, Norway						
	0018	0418	0900	**1218**	1618	2100	
V	Vardø, Norway						
	0300	0700	**1100**	1500	1900	**2300**	
C	Murmansk, Russia						
	0120	0520	0920	1320	1720	2120	
F	Arkhangel'sk, Russia						
	0200	**0600**	1000	1400	**1800**	2200	
J	Gislövshammar, Sweden						
	0330	**0730**	1130	1530	**1930**	2330	
H	Bjuroklubb, Sweden						
	0000	0400	**0800**	1200	1600	**2000**	
U	Tallinn, Estonia						
	0030	0430	**0830**	1230	1630	**2030**	
P	Netherlands Coast Guard, IJmuiden						
	0348	0748	1148	1548	1948	2348	
T	Oostende, Belgium (Sea areas Dover and Thames)						
	0310	**0710**	1110	1510	**1910**	2310	
M	Oostende, Belgium						
	0200	0600	1000	1400	1800	2200	
G	Cullercoats, UK						
	0100	0500	**0900**	1300	1700	**2100**	

O	Portpatrick, UK						
	0220	**0620**	1020	1420	**1820**	**2220**	
S	Niton, UK						
	0300	**0700**	1100	1500	**1900**	**2300**	
K	Niton, UK (Channel median line to N France)						
	0140	0540	0940	1340	1740	2140	
W	Valentia, Eire						
	0340	0740	1140	1540	1940	2340	
Q	Malin Head, Eire						
	0240	0640	**1040**	1440	1840	**2240**	

METAREA II. Co-ordinator: France

A	Le Stiff, Ushant (CROSS Corsen), France						
	0000	0400	0800	**1200**	1600	2000	
D	La Coruña, Spain						
	0030	0430	0830	**1230**	1630	2030	
R	Lisboa (Monsanto), Portugal						
	0250	**0650**	**1050**	**1450**	**1850**	**2250**	
G	Tarifa, Spain						
	0100	0500	**0900**	1300	1700	**2100**	
F	Horta, Azores, Portugal						
	0050	**0450**	**0850**	**1250**	**1650**	2050	
I	Las Palmas, Islas Canarias, Spain						
	0120	0520	**0920**	**1320**	**1720**	2120	

METAREA III. Co-ordinator: Spain

X	Valencia, Cabo de la Nao, Spain						
	0350	**0750**	1150	1550	**1950**	2350	
W	Toulon (CROSS La Garde), France						
	0340	0740	**1140**	1540	1940	**2340**	
T	Cagliari, Sardinia, Italy						
	0310	**0710**	1110	1510	**1910**	2310	
O	Malta						
	0220	**0620**	1020	1420	**1820**	2220	
V	Augusta, Sicily						
	0330	**0730**	1130	1530	**1930**	2330	
R	Roma, Italy						
	0250	**0650**	1050	1450	**1850**	2250	
U	Trieste, Italy						
	0320	**0720**	1120	1520	**1920**	2320	
Q	Split, Croatia						
	0240	**0640**	1040	1440	**1840**	**2240**	
K	Kerkyra, Greece						
	0140	**0540**	**0940**	**1340**	**1740**	**2140**	
H	Iraklion, Crete, (Greece)						
	0110	**0510**	**0910**	**1310**	**1710**	**2110**	
L	Limnos, Greece						
	0150	**0550**	**0950**	**1350**	**1750**	**2150**	
I	Izmir, Turkey						
	0120	0520	0920	1320	1720	2120	
F	Antalya, Turkey						
	0050	0450	0850	1250	1650	2050	
M	Troodos, Cyprus						
	0200	**0600**	1000	1400	1800	2200	
P	Haifa, Israel						
	0020	**0420**	0820	1220	1620	2020	
N	Alexandria, Egypt						
	0210	0610	1010	**1410**	1810	2210	
D	Istanbul, Turkey						
	0030	0430	0830	1230	1630	2030	

E	Samsun, Turkey					
	0040	0440	0840	1240	1640	2040
J	Varna, Bulgaria					
	0130	**0530**	0930	1330	**1730**	2130
C	Odessa, Ukraine					
	0230	0630	**1030**	1430	**1830**	2230
B	Mariupol', Ukraine					
	0100	**0500**	0900	1300	**1700**	2100
A	Novorossiysk, Russia					
	0300	0700	**1100**	1500	**1900**	2300

11.2.8 SHORT MESSAGE SERVICE (SMS)

Introduction

The Met Office provides two different text services for mobile 'phone users, depending on the Service Provider:

1. via Vodafone (and perhaps some other networks);
2. via any other Service Provider.

First, over Vodafone, the following weather messages can be obtained either as a 'one-off' or by regular automatic updates. Payment is through the call charge.

    a. Shipping forecasts for all UK Sea areas;

    b. Reports of actual weather at 48 UK coastal stations.

    c. Forecasts for Inshore waters from North Foreland clockwise to Hartland Point.

How to use SMS

Dial 08700 767 838 and follow the recorded main menu. It will prompt you to press:

1   for service information
2   to receive index of products on fax
3   to order a product
4   to cancel a regular update
9   to connect to customer helpline
0   to return to main menu

After pressing 3, press 1 for a one-off order or 2 for a regular order. A regular order ensures that a product, eg shipping forecast for sea area Tyne, is automatically sent to your mobile as it is updated four times during the day.

Then order the product by keying in the appropriate four digit code from the three lists below. The information will duly appear on the screen of your mobile. It can then be read, stored in memory or deleted.

Shipping forecast Sea Areas

Updated at 0001, 0500, 1100 and 1700LT; valid for the same period as the BBC Radio 4 broadcasts.

4411	Viking	4412	North Utsire
4413	South Utsire	4414	Forties
4415	Cromarty	4416	Forth
4417	Tyne	4418	Dogger
4419	Fisher	4420	German Bight
4421	Humber	4422	Thames

4423	Dover	4424	Wight
4425	Portland	4426	Plymouth
4427	Biscay	4428	Finisterre
4429	Sole	4430	Lundy
4431	Fastnet	4432	Irish Sea
4433	Shannon	4434	Rockall
4435	Malin	4436	Hebrides
4437	Bailey	4438	Fair Isle
4439	Faeroes	4440	SE Iceland

Coastal station reports

Updated hourly, except places* which are updated every 3 hours, ie 0000, 0300, 0600, etc ... All local times.

4301	Ballycastle, Bangor Hbr (Belfast Lough)*
4302	Oban*, Greenock
4303	South Uist, Tiree
4304	Aultbea (Loch Ewe), Stornoway
4305	Macrihanish, Prestwick
4306	Walney Island, St Bees Head
4307	Rhyl (N Wales), Crosby (Liverpool)
4308	Aberdaron, Valley (Anglesey)
4309	Aberporth, Milford Haven
4310	Cardiff, Mumbles
4311	Falmouth*, St Mary's (Scilly)
4312	Brixham, Plymouth
4313	Channel lt vessel, Guernsey
4314	Jersey, Île de Bréhat*
4315	Thorney Island, Lee-on-Solent
4316	St Catherine's Pt (IoW), Greenwich lt vessel
4317	Dover, Newhaven*
4318	Walton-on-the-Naze, Sheerness*
4319	Weybourne (The Wash), Holbeach
4320	Bridlington, Donna Nook (R Humber)
4321	Boulmer, Tynemouth*
4322	Aberdeen, Fife Ness
4323	Peterhead*, Lossiemouth
4324	Sule Skerry, Wick

Forecasts for the Inshore waters of the UK South coast

Valid for 6 hours. Updated 0530 for period 0600-1200; at 1130 for period 1200-1800; and at 1630 for period 1700-2300, all LT. Other inshore areas are to be added.

4561	North Foreland to Beachy Head
4562	Beachy Head to Selsey Bill
4571	Selsey Bill to Durlston Head
4572	Durlston Head to Lyme Regis
4581	Lyme Regis to Looe
4582	Looe to Padstow
4583	Padstow to Hartland Point

Charging information and Notes

Shipping forecasts are charged at 10p and Coastal reports (two stations) at 30p/message. Inshore waters forecasts are charged at 50p/ message. Charges are only made for those messages received.

Other Service Providers, using SMS or WAP
The second service, via any mobile provider, gives:
  a. "Time and Place" forecasts;
  b. National Inshore waters forecasts (for 9 areas around the UK); and
  c. Gale warnings.
Note: Route forecasts and buoy reports are planned.

Register at no charge. Payment is in advance, a minimum of £10, by credit card: 20p per message for regular order, 50p for one-offs. Users can check via the mobile when to top up the kitty. To set up and use the services go to www.metoffice.gov.uk and click on Mobile services. Messages can be directed to your digital mobile phone screen, to a palm top device or laptop PC.

'Time and Place' are very localised forecasts covering 2 sq miles. Fine scale topographic data allows prediction of effects of headlands, river estuaries, sea breezes etc. Specify the places where you need weather information, using brief names of your own choice. The places can be up to 6M offshore around the whole of the UK and up to 16M near 100 popular coastal resorts; they can be added to or changed at any time. Forecasts are for a specific time up to 6 hours ahead, and can be ordered on a regular or one-off basis.

WAP (Wireless Application Protocol)
Mobiles using WAP will be generally cheaper to use because they access an Internet Service Provider. The Shipping forecasts and gale warnings will be free. The address for a WAP mobile handset is mymetoffice.com/main.wml

For further information and detail of the above SMS and WAP services, call Tel 0845 300 0300, Fax 0845 300 1300 or visit www.metoffice.gov.uk/leisuremarine/

11.2.9 WEATHER INFORMATION BY RECORDED TELEPHONE MESSAGE (MARINECALL)

Marinecall provides three types of recorded message:
  a. **Inshore waters Forecast** (Wind, weather, vis, sea state, temp) for 16 areas (to 12M offshore), valid for five days; updated 0700 and 1900LT. All calls cost 60p/min. Dial 09068 500 and the 3-digit code for the areas below:

National (3-5 days forecast)	450
Cape Wrath to Rattray Head, inc Orkney	451
Rattray Head to Berwick-upon-Tweed	452
Berwick-upon-Tweed to Whitby	453
Whitby to The Wash	454
The Wash to North Foreland	455
North Foreland to Selsey Bill	456
Selsey Bill to Lyme Regis	457
Lyme Regis to Hartland Point	458
Hartland Point to St David's Head	459
St David's Head to Colwyn Bay	460
Colwyn Bay to Mull of Galloway, inc IoM	461
Mull of Galloway to Mull of Kintyre	462
Mull of Kintyre to Ardnamurchan Pt	463
Ardnamurchan to C. Wrath and Western Isles	464
Lough Foyle to Carlingford Lough	465
Channel Islands (issued by Jersey Met. Office)	432

  b. **Offshore forecasts**, for planning days 2 to 5, cover:

English Channel	992
NW Scotland	985
North Sea (south)	991
Irish Sea	954
North Sea (north)	955
Biscay	953

Dial 09068 500 + codes above. Updated at 0800LT daily.

  c. **Reports of Actual weather** at coastal stations, using information from the Met. Office, updated hourly. Dial 09068 226 plus the 3-digit code below. All calls cost 60p/min. There are no reports from the Channel Islands.

Cape Wrath, Wick, Lossiemouth	451
Peterhead, Aberdeen, Fife Ness	452
Boulmer, Tynemouth	453
Bridlington, Holbeach	454
Weybourne, Walton-on-the-Naze, Sheerness	455
Dover, Greenwich Lt V, Newhaven	456
Thorney Is, Lee-on-Solent, St Catherine's Pt	457
Brixham, Plymouth, Falmouth, St Mary's (Scilly)	458
Cardiff, Mumbles, Milford Haven	459
Aberporth, Aberdaron, Valley	460
Rhyll, Crosby, Walney Island	461
Prestwick, Greenock, Macrihanish	462
Oban, Tiree	463
Benbecula, Aultbea (L. Ewe), Butt of Lewis	464
Bangor, Ballycastle, Malin Head	465

11.2.10 WEATHER INFORMATION BY FAX (METFAX)

MetFAX provides two types of forecasts by fax:
  a. **Inshore waters** forecasts, plus weather charts, about 4 mins @ £1/min. Dial 09060 100 + the same 3-digit code as used in Marinecall (11.2.9), except that the Channel Islands code is 466 (not 432).
  b. **2-5 day planning forecasts** (time 3 mins), plus charts for 2, 3, 4 and 5 days ahead, cover the same areas as 11.2.9. Dial 09060 100 + different 3-digit codes, ie:

English Channel	471	NW Scotland	468
North Sea (south)	472	Irish Sea	473
North Sea (north)	469	Biscay	470

Additional services + their 3-digit numbers include:

401	Marine index	17 mins
426	2, 3, 4, & 5 day forecast charts	2 mins
441	24 hrs Shipping forecast	15 mins
444	Surface analysis chart	16 mins
445	Surface forecast chart	16 mins
447	UK actual weather plot	15 mins
474	Europe/Med actual weather plot	17 mins
499	Satellite Images	36 mins

Cost is £1/minute, premium rate, (Index free); the length of calls varies from 16 to 35 minutes. MetFax Helpline Tel is 08700 750075; Fax 08700 750076.

11.2.11   MEDITERRANEAN WEATHER (METFAX MED)

From the UK dial 09060 100 + a 3-digit code below and follow the menu options for fax forecasts and charts:

Gibraltar to Malaga	435
Valencia to Barcelona	438
Malaga to Cartagena	436
Balearic Islands	439
Cartagena to Valencia	437

Payment is by most major credit cards.

11.2.12   TELEPHONE DIRECT TO FORECASTER

This is a 24 hours consultancy service with a specialist marine forecaster, available from any 'phone, anywhere. The consultancy usually includes a briefing on the synoptic situation, outlook and weather windows, followed by questions/answers. Call 08700 767 888 or from abroad +44 8700 767 888. A flat rate charge of £17 is payable by most major credit cards. Or call the same number for a fax forecast at £3.

A similar consultancy with a marine forecaster in Gibraltar covers the Mediterranean and Canary Isles. Call 08700 767 818 or +44 8700 767 818 from abroad for a flat rate of £15 by credit card. Or call the same number for a 5 day forecast for Spain and the Balearics, delivered to a fax machine in Spain for £3 per forecast.

11.2.13   ROUTE FORECASTS

Forecasts for an individual yachtsman or organisation for a specific route can be specially prepared by private weather forecasting companies, for example:
Noble Denton Weather Services Ltd, 131 Aldersgate St, London EC1A 4EB. Tel +44 (0)20 7606 4961; Fax +44 (0)20 7606 0773. e-mail: fcst@ndws.demon.co.uk

The Met Office has discontinued its MetROutE service. But see the Weather Wizard 11.2.14.

11.2.14   FORECASTS ON THE INTERNET
Finding useful Internet sites

www.franksingleton.clara.net is an excellent Weather Site produced by a former Met Office Senior Forecaster who is also an active yachtsman. There are leads to sites useful to sailors as well as informative articles on the weather.

The following are a few of the more worth-while sites:

UK Met Office

On the main website at www.met-office.gov.uk there is much information including 36-hour inshore forecasts with 3 day outlooks, shipping forecasts, gale warnings, satellite pictures.

For premium rated services register on 0845 300 0300 and buy £10 of "virtual" tickets using credit card. This gives access to MetWEB (at no charge) where there are reports of actual weather at coastal stations (free), surface pressure charts, 2 to 5 day planning forecasts, and 5 day forecasts for five areas in the western Mediterranean.

A Marinecall 2-day text costs £1 and two synoptic charts another £1 which is less than half the cost over the telephone line. Download times are quite fast which is useful for a mobile phone link.

Weather Wizard

This service is provided by Transas Marine Ltd using data direct from the UK Met Office computers. Visit www.transasdataco.com or Tel +44 (0)2380 332730; Fax +44 (0)23 802 3439. £50 buys the software but you can then receive £50 worth of information. Simply e-mail Transas with a request and they supply it via a telephone circuit to your PC. When the £50 runs out, buy more by prepayment, minimum of £30. Cost of products depends upon the volume of data provided. Forecasts of isobars, winds, sea state (wave and swell) are available world-wide out to 5 days ahead. A chart of forecast wind vectors for the western Mediterranean would cost about £1.

The various services offered include weather routeing advice although this is probably more useful to ships than yachts. Graphical displays are on good-looking marine chart format.

Météo France

Go to www.meteo.fr/naviweb/ sous_panneaux_salon.html for a very comprehensive set of marine products. Follow your nose, with minimal French, to locate: coastal forecasts (in French); various NAVTEX and INMARSAT texts (in English); forecast charts of isobars, wind arrows, wind waves and swell – all at 12 hour intervals out to 3 days. These are all free.

Try www.meteo.fr/naviweb/sous_panneaux_ guide.html for much information on Météo France services to mariners, schedules of VHF, LW, MF and HF broadcasts and various premium rated services.

Spanish Met Service

www.inm.es/wwc/html/dtemint/metmar/ altmar.html has links to coastal forecasts for the whole of Spain and for the offshore Atlantic and the Mediterranean. All are in understandable Spanish.

Warning

Many links used by yachtsmen are provided by Universities which have no operational requirement to ensure that the information is up-to-date. Also, the information provided by the National Meteorological Services via the Internet is not part of an operational service. Internet Service Providers have no operational requirement to stay working at all times. It follows that the Internet should be used to complement and not replace GMDSS services.

11.2.15   FORECASTS BY TELEPHONE FOR SHIPS AT SEA

Since the closure of many Coast Radio Stations, it has become virtually impossible to call the Met Office by ship to shore links. Those with a mobile phone may always use the Direct service (11.2.12) via terrestrial or Satellite links. Anyone wishing to do so at sea or wishing to use email via INMARSAT should first check with the Met Office (or private Met company) on the most appropriate number or address to use.

11.2.16   HF BROADCASTS

The three means of transmission are shown below:

By voice

Radio France Internationale broadcasts in clear, slow French a daily forecast at 1140 UTC for the N Atlantic (15°N to 55°N and out to 35°W, thence to the Antilles). It can be heard from the equator to the North Sea.

Monaco Radio [3AC] broadcasts on HF/SSB at about 0930 UTC daily to cover METAREA II. This includes the eastern Atlantic from 48°N to 6°S and out to 37°W. Monaco broadcasts also cover the western Mediterranean; they are spoken first in slow, clear French and then in English. Schedules and frequencies are in ALRS, Le guide marine de Météo France and on the Météo France web site, see 11.2.14.

Radio Fax

This is simply a method of receiving weather maps by HF/SSB radio using a dedicated receiver/ printer or, often more conveniently, a link from the radio to a laptop using specialist software. Charts can be viewed on screen or printed out. Products available include actual and forecast isobaric charts, wind direction and force, sea state.

In western Europe the sources are Northwood (UK Navy) and Offenbach (Germany). Frequencies and times of broadcasts are listed in the MRNA and ALRS, Vol 3. Bracknell (GFA) ceased broadcasting 3 April 2001. Among the many charts issued, the most useful are the surface actual and forecast synoptic charts from one to five days ahead.

On the Internet the following links give schedules:

Northwood   www.hffax.de/HF_Fax/Gya_98.txt
Offenbach   www.dwd.de/services/gfsf e_faxpln.html

A very comprehensive site describing global radio fax is http://www.nws.noaa.gov/om/ marine/radiofax.htm This site contains a link to world-wide schedules, and there are many, although this does require an Acrobat reader.

Radio teleprinter

Offenbach (Deutscher Wetterdienst/German Met Office) has a very useful radio teleprinter broadcast also on HF/SSB. The commercial radio fax software packages will usually receive these data also. Many of the broadcasts are coded weather observations from land stations and ships, but there are also forecasts in text, some in English. Some of these are point forecasts direct from the German weather computer and are valid to as much as five days ahead. These are particularly valuable for getting indications of Mistral winds in the Mediterranean. Schedules are in ALRS Vol 3 and at www.dwd.de/services/ gfsf/e_telexpln.html

11.2.17   WEATHER BY SATELLITE INMARSAT

The INMARSAT satellite system is described in detail in Chapter 10. Under the SOLAS convention vessels over 300 grt normally carry equipment enabling reception of MSI on the EGC SafetyNET via an INMARSAT satellite; this is the blue waters equivalent of NAVTEX. The net effect is that the many HF services, such as those described in 11.2.16, are being gradually phased out.

Weather information is supplied by the UK Met Office for METAREA I, see Fig. 11(27); and by Météo France for METAREAs II and III. Note: Geographically METAREAs and NAVAREAs (see 7.9.1) are the same.

Yachts are most likely to use the INMARSAT-C

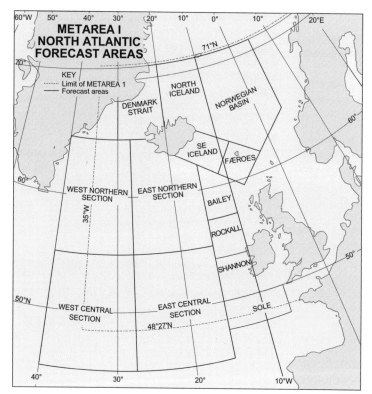

Fig. 11(27) METAREA I. North Atlantic forecast areas.

and 13264 kHz (Sunrise to sunset). Airports covered include: Shannon, Keflavik, Helsinki, Stockholm, Oslo, Bergen, Copenhagen, Prestwick, Dublin, Amsterdam, Lisbon, Santa Maria (Azores), Barcelona, Rome and Athens. Details are in the UK Air Pilot, published by the Civil Aviation Authority.

RAF SSB Volmet broadcasts on 5450 kHz and 11253 kHz. The broadcasts include actual weather reports for: Keflavik, Prestwick, Bardufoss, Bodo, Oslo, Kinloss, Lossiemouth, Leuchars, St Mawgan, Porto, Gibraltar, Brindisi and Akrotiri (Cyprus). Details from No 1 AIDU, RAF Northolt, West End Rd, Ruislip, Middx HA4 6NG.

11.2.19 TELEVISION

Programmes

Several TV forecasts include a synoptic chart. Together with satellite weather pictures, this gives a useful guide to the general weather situation before starting a passage. A BBC programme on Sunday, around noon, has a weekly outlook. This is updated during the midweek, day-time broadcasts. In more remote areas, especially abroad or with poor radio/phone links, a TV forecast in a restaurant, bar or even a shop window can be valuable.

Teletext

BBC Ceefax page 400 is an index containing five-day outlooks and forecasts for inshore waters. ITV's Teletext weather index is at page 151. It gives a Shipping forecast and an inshore waters forecast. But, note that these are not produced by the Met Office so there may be differences between these and other broadcasts.

11.2.20 PRESS FORECASTS

The delay between the forecast being issued and the paper being on sale reduces the value of press forecasts to yachtsmen. However forecasts in the broadsheets may include a pictorial weather map and a synoptic chart for noon with expected changes. If no other data is available, this can help to interpret the shipping forecast on first putting to sea. Some regional newspapers print useful forecasts and charts for up to a week ahead. Newspapers can also be useful where radio reception is difficult, eg in the deep Rias of northern Spain.

and Mini-M systems for reasons of cost, physical size and power consumption. INMARSAT-C allows transmission and reception of telex-type messages, including MSI broadcasts. As well as receiving MSI information, Mini-M can also be used for voice messages and e-mail. However, it is far too slow to download graphics.

Satellite telephones

The technology is advancing rapidly and, in time, affordable equipment will probably become available, allowing economic reception of weather charts from the Internet. In the meantime the service available using the Weather Wizard (11.2.14) is worth consideration by blue water sailors, since much good information can be received in a fairly small message size.

11.2.18 VOLMET

Volmet broadcasts of airfield weather are of limited value because they require an HF radio and some knowledge of aviation terminology. Two stations which broadcast H24 on HF SSB (H3E) are Shannon and the RAF.

Shannon Volmet broadcasts on 3413 kHz (Sunset to sunrise); 5505 kHz and 8957 kHz (H24);

11.2.21 VISUAL STORM SIGNALS

The International System of Visual Storm Warning signals (prescribed by SOLAS) uses cones, balls and flags with the following meanings:

Quadrant from which gale expected	Day	Night
NW	▲	Ⓡ
		Ⓡ
SW	▼	Ⓦ
		Ⓦ
NE	▲	Ⓡ
	▲	Ⓦ
SE	▼	Ⓦ
	▼	Ⓡ
Near gale expected (any direction)	●	Ⓦ
		Ⓖ

A ● and, say, a ▼ mean a near gale is expected from the SW. One flag with any of these signals means that the wind is expected to veer; two flags, it is expected to back.

Storm signals are obsolescent and are no longer shown in the UK, Eire, Netherlands, Germany and Denmark. They are shown in France at Fécamp, Dieppe, Ault, Boulogne and Dunkerque, and may be shown in Spain and Portugal.

Strong wind warnings may also be shown. In France, at Ouistreham and Port Navalo only, light signals (by day only to avoid ambiguity) warn yachts and small craft that winds of Force 6-7 are expected within a certain time:

Q (quick flashing) IQ 8s	Within 3 hours
(interrupted quick flashing)	Within 6 hours

In Belgium at Nieuwpoort, Oostende and Zeebrugge craft under 6m LOA are prohibited from going to sea, while the following warnings are shown:

By day	Two black cones points together;
By night	A flashing violet light.

These indicate onshore winds of Force 4 or more.

11.3 TERMS USED IN WEATHER BULLETINS

Specific terms regularly used in marine and land forecasts are defined below (see also the glossary at 11.5.1).

11.3.1 VISIBILITY

Good	> 5M	Moderate	2 – 5M
Poor	1000m – 2M	Fog	< 1000m

11.3.2 TIMING AND SPEEDS OF WEATHER SYSTEMS

Timing (usually of a gale) from issue to arrival:

Imminent	Within 6 hours
Soon	6 – 12 hours
Later	12 – 24 hours

Speed of movement (eg lows and highs):

Slowly	0 – 15 knots
Steadily	15 – 25 knots
Rather quickly	25 – 35 knots
Rapidly	35 – 45 knots
Very rapidly	Over 45 knots

11.3.3 BAROMETRIC PRESSURE TENDENCIES

Terminology	*Rate of change*
Steady	Less than 0·1mb in 3 hours
Rising or Falling	1·6 – 3·5mb in 3 hours, unless qualified by:
Slowly	0·1 – 1·5mb in 3 hours
Quickly	3·6 – 6mb in 3 hours
Very rapidly	More than 6mb in 3 hours

11.3.4 GALE WARNINGS

A warning MUST be issued if the forecaster <u>thinks</u> that winds of gale force 8 <u>may</u> occur, up to 12 hours ahead, somewhere in a sea area. Beyond 12 hours he can use the words 'perhaps .... later', if he thinks that there is a risk in the 'later' period but is not sure enough to issue a warning. But to a small vessel, it is tantamount to a full warning.

'Gale now ceased' is only issued if the forecaster is as sure as he can be that there is no longer a wind of Force 8 <u>anywhere</u> in the sea area. Gale warnings are self cancelling after 24 hours, unless renewed. A gale warning is a forecast, while a cancellation should be a fact.

Gales, see Fig. 11(7), are defined as follows:

Gale	– at least force 8 or gusts to 43 knots.
Severe gale	– at least force 9 or gusts to 52 knots.
Storm	– at least force 10 or gusts to 61 knots.
Violent storm	– at least force 11 or gusts to 69 knots.

Hurricane force – force 12 (64 knots or more). The term 'hurricane' on its own is only used for a true tropical revolving storm.

11.3.5 LAND FORECASTS, WIND AND VISIBILITY

Wind strength in land forecasts is described by the terms below which equate to the Beaufort forces shown:

Calm	0	Fresh	5
Light	1 – 3	Strong	6 – 7
Moderate	4	Gale	8

Visibility terms in land forecasts are defined as follows:

Mist	200 – 1000m
Fog	< 200m
Dense fog	< 50m

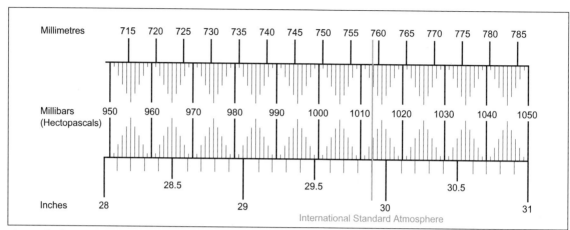

Fig. 11(28) Atmospheric pressure: equivalent values of millibars (or hectopascals), inches of mercury, and millimetres of mercury.

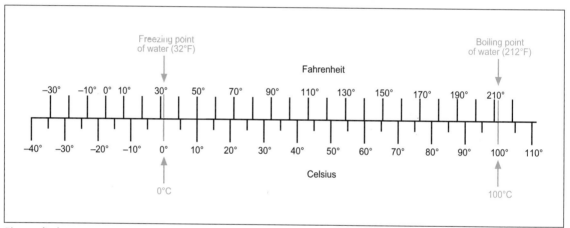

Fig. 11(29) Temperature: °Fahrenheit and °Celsius equivalents. See also 5.4.3.

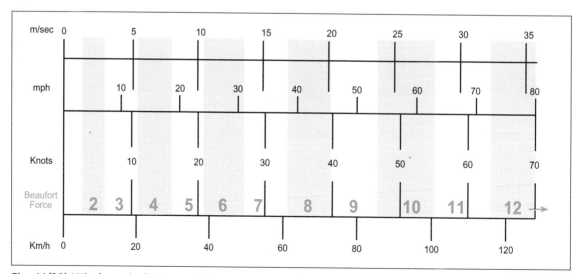

Fig. 11(30) Wind: equivalent speeds in metres/second, miles/hour, knots, kilometres/hour and Beaufort force.

11.4   APPLYING THE FORECAST

11.4.1   RECORDING THE SHIPPING FORECAST

There are many forecasts available to the yachtsman. Although the shipping forecast is very broad brush it does provide an invaluable framework within which other, more localised forecasts and your own observations can be used. Beyond 25 miles or so offshore it is, in any case, the only type of broadcast forecast in text form available. Details are in 11.2.1.

It rarely suffices just to listen to a forecast, especially the shipping forecast which is packed with potentially useful information. A copy is essential, whether by pencil and paper, tape recorder or Navtex. But tape recorders can be fiddly. Navtex broadcasts are only twice daily and never include reports of actual weather from 'coastal stations'. So it is sensible to write down the forecast as it is read out, using your own brand shorthand, see below.

First, be ready well before the broadcast starts; recap on the previous forecast to be aware of weather systems which may recur in the general synopsis. When the broadcast begins, concentrate solely on writing down all the essentials: gale warnings in force, general synopsis, the forecasts for all sea areas (not just the nearest ones); and, at 0048 and 0535 the actual weather reported from the various coastal stations. Record the times when the forecast was issued and the time of the actual weather at coast stations. These are easy to omit and are needed to get the correct timing on your finished synoptic chart.

To achieve all this, use some kind of shorthand and a proforma. The RYA and the Royal Meteorological Society jointly publish a Metmap in pads of 40. The Metmap, Figs. 11(31) and (32), is on two pages: one contains a map of the Sea areas with scales for geostrophic wind and frontal movement, a compass rose annotated in points and a distance scale. The other is a form for writing or ticking off the broadcast details.

In the synopsis, for example, 'Low 998 moving NE rather quickly' can be abbreviated as 'L98 ↗ rq'. 'High 1020 300 miles southwest of Ireland stationary' as 'H 20 300 SW Ire st'; and so on. Wind directions are easy: W, NW etc. Calm is simply a ⊙, cyclonic a C, Variable a V. Veering, backing or becoming can be V, B or →. Imminent, soon, later are I, S, L. For weather and visibility, use the Beaufort letters or symbols shown in 11.4.3. In station reports, the first 9 or 10 can be left off the pressure without ambiguity, eg 97 = 997mb. Visibility can be just

the number: obviously 1500 is metres and 15 is miles.

11.4.2   DRAFTING A SYNOPTIC CHART

If ashore, or with a recent synoptic chart – perhaps by MetFAX or radio fax, then the shipping forecast can be studied in relation to what was expected earlier. Compare the winds in the forecast with what you see on the chart, particularly the wind directions. Does the forecast weather and visibility match up to what is on the chart?

The RYA Metmap is a useful way to 'see' the forecast. It is particularly valuable if you have been at sea for some while and do not have a recent chart. It can be used to draft your own mini-synoptic chart using all the information in the broadcast. Although the RYA syllabus no longer requires the ability to draw such charts, it is a useful skill which can only enhance your understanding of what you hear or see in the forecast.

Begin by plotting the actual weather reports onto the Metmap. Since these are now broadcast only twice a day (0048 and 0535), your chart is probably best built around the 0048 forecast because there are also reports at this time from the inshore waters forecast. However, ashore or at anchor, 0535 might be more sociable, using actual weather reports timed at 0400 LT. See Fig. 11(33) for a complete plotting model produced by a National Met Service as might appear in some marinas. You, of course, can plot only the pressure, wind, weather and visibility.

Then plot the information contained in the general synopsis. At the 0535 broadcast the details in the synopsis will be for the midnight just past; this is the last full chart that the forecaster has available to him. Therefore, to conform with the time of the observations, advance the positions of highs, lows, fronts etc by using the forecast speeds ('rather quickly' etc), so that your synoptic chart is valid for 0400LT.

Finally add the wind, weather and visibility forecasts for the Sea areas (Forth, Tyne ....), concentrating on the 'at first' forecasts if there are other predictions for 'later'. By now a coherent weather picture is emerging.

To get a better view and to aid your understanding, start sketching in the isobars, lightly because the eraser is as important as the pencil. Interpolate or extrapolate from the data for the coastal station pressures, heeding the general pattern indicated by lows or highs given in the general synopsis. The isobars can then be extended over the sea using the forecast wind directions and spaced according to the geostrophic scale for the forecast wind speeds

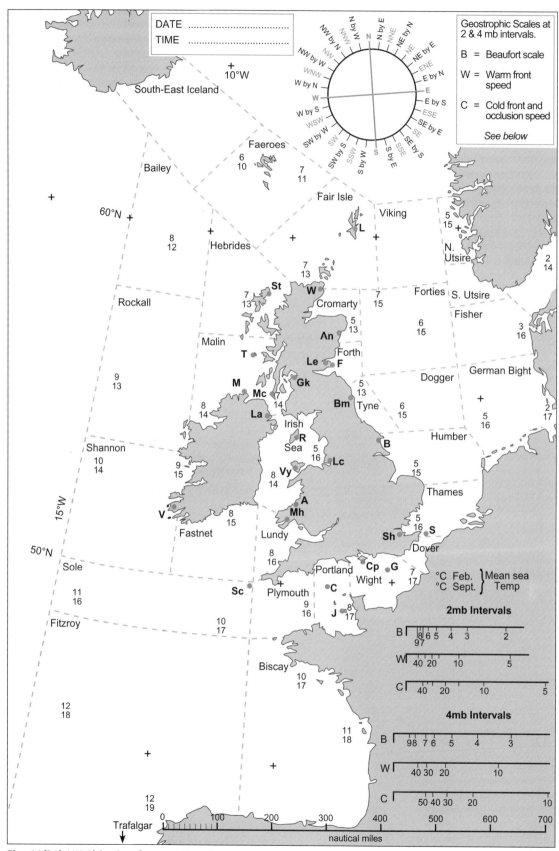

Fig. 11(31) UK Shipping forecast Sea Areas.

GENERAL SYNOPSIS   at .... BST/UT .... Day/Date ....

Gales	SEA AREA	Wind	Weather	Visibility
	Viking			
	N.Utsire			
	S.Utsire			
	Forties			
	Cromarty			
	Forth			
	Tyne			
	Dogger			
	Fisher			
	German Bight			
	Humber			
	Thames			
	Dover			
	Wight			
	Portland			
	Plymouth			
	Biscay			
	Trafalgar			
	Fitzroy			
	Sole			
	Lundy			
	Fastnet			
	Irish Sea			
	Shannon			
	Rockall			
	Malin			
	Hebrides			
	Bailey			
	Fair Isle			
	Faeroes			
	SE Iceland			

COASTAL REPORTS (Shipping Forecast) at .... BST/UT

		Wind Direction	Force	Weather	Visibility	Pressure	Trend
Tiree	T						
Stornoway	St						
Lerwick	L						
Fife Ness	F						
Bridlington	B						
Sandettie Auto	S						
Greenwich LV Auto	G						
Jersey	J						
Channel LV Auto	C						
Scilly Auto	Sc						
Valentia	V						
Ronaldsway	R						
Malin Head	M						

COASTAL REPORTS (Inshore Waters) at...............BST/UT

Boulmer	Bm					
Bridlington	B					
Sheerness	Sh					
St Catherine's Pt	Cp					
Scilly Auto	Sc					
Milford Haven	Mh					
Aberporth	A					
Valley	Vy					
Liverpool Crosby	Lc					
Ronaldsway	R					
Larne	La					
Machrihanish Auto	Mc					
Greenock	Gk					
Stornoway	St					
Lerwick	L					
Wick Auto	W					
Aberdeen	An					
Leuchars	Le					

Fig. 11(32) Form for recording the Shipping forecast .

and the observations of wind at the light vessels. At other stations, the wind may be affected by local topography.

Remember that at troughs or fronts the isobars should change direction, sometimes markedly, at other times imperceptibly. It is initially a matter of trial and error, but practice helps to speed up the process so that a very useful weather map can be produced in a few minutes. Armed with this it is much easier to understand what is, or should be, happening to the weather in your area, to identify trends and to keep an eye on dubious areas.

11.4.3 SYMBOLS AND THE STATION CIRCLE

Synoptic charts are often on display in harbours, marinas and yacht clubs. Observations are shown by symbols and numbers, a "pictorial" shorthand. Fig. 11(33) is a chart of actual weather reported at various stations, as provided by MetFax. The station circles are in abbreviated format and that for Manchester is itemised below the main chart. Note that the various observations always appear in the same (clock) position around the circle, with the obvious exception of the wind arrow and total cloud amount in octas (eighths) inside the circle. The bottom part of this Figure shows extra data which might have been included in a full report from Manchester. This kind of plotting can be used on the Metmap for information from the shipping forecast. The commoner symbols are shown below.

Wind symbols

Wind direction is symbolised by arrows, flying downwind. Thus the examples below show westerly winds. By international convention each long feather indicates 10 knots, and each half feather indicates 5 knots. A solid triangular feather indicates 50 knots, at which point the long and half feather notation recommences. Convert Beaufort Forces to knots and vice versa, if necessary.

The Station Circle

The actual Met conditions observed at a reporting station are depicted on some synoptic charts by a Station Circle. The amateur who can 'decipher' this Circle will understand the weather situation more fully.

Fig. 11(33) (a) shows a number of station circles plotted over the UK and Ireland. In (b) the report for Manchester is analysed: Wind is southerly at 10kn; cloud cover is six octas; temperature is +3°C; pressure is 999mb; present weather is rain showers, and the past weather is also showers (that's Manchester for you).

Symbols	Knots	Symbols	Knots
	1 — 2		28 — 32
	3 — 7		33 — 37
	8 — 12		38 — 42
	13 — 17		43 — 47
	18 — 22		48 — 52
	23 — 27		53 — 57

Other useful wind symbols include:

Calm	⊙
Variable force 3	V3
Cyclonic variable force 4	④

Weather Symbols

	Beaufort notation	Plotting symbols
Rain	r	•
Drizzle	d	،
Shower	p	▽
Snow	s	✳
Hail	h	△
Thunderstorm	t	☒
Fog	f	≡
Mist	m	=
Haze	z	∞

Symbols may be combined or elaborated as in the example below for rain

	Beaufort notation	Plotting symbols
Intermittent slight rain	r_o	•
Continuous slight rain	$r_o r_o$	• •
Intermittent moderate rain	r	• •
Continuous moderate rain	r r	• • •
Intermittent heavy rain	R	• • •
Continuous heavy rain	R R	• • • •

In (c) the items which might appear in a full weather report have been added: low cloud is at 6 o'clock, both amount and type, in this case five octas Cumulo-nimbus at 1500 ft; medium cloud is at 12 o'clock (four octas cirrus at an unspecified

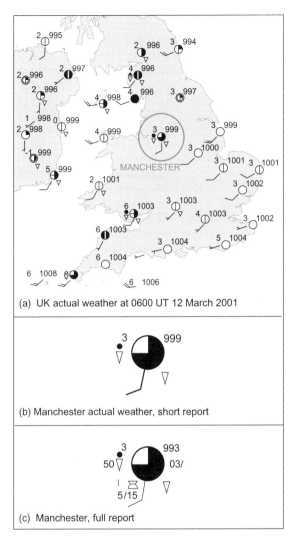

(a) UK actual weather at 0600 UT 12 March 2001

(b) Manchester actual weather, short report

(c) Manchester, full report

Fig. 11(33) Actual weather and the Station circle.

height); the pressure is 999·3mb (at 1 o'clock), which has risen 0·3mb in the last 3 hours (pressure tendency is at 3 o'clock); the dewpoint is +1°C (at 8 o'clock); and visibility is 5km (at 9 o'clock).

Visibility in kilometres is coded as follows:

Code No		Visibility in km
0 – 10	=	Fog, less than 1 km.
11 – 50	=	each number is 100m; thus 38 = 3·8 km.
51 – 80	=	deduct 50; eg 55 = 5 km; 80 = 30 km.
> 81	=	deduct 80, each digit is 5 km over 30 km; eg 82 = 40 km.

11.4.4   WEATHER AND PASSAGE PLANNING

A weather forecast is just that. How to use this imperfect tool depends to some extent upon the nature of the sailing being undertaken. Consider the following scenarios:

a.   **Day sailing** – off the berth and back.

Check the weather at least 24 hours ahead. Record the shipping forecasts. Look for trends, changes in emphasis and/or timing of events. Variations in content may indicate an uncertain situation.

For local conditions, use weather info from HMCG, MetFAX, Marinecall, local radio or SMS, as convenient. But, most importantly use your own local knowledge of local wind variations, sea breezes and their effects near headlands, cliffs, straits and channels.

b.   **Offshore/coastal passages** – up to 100 miles or so.

Start studying synoptic charts about 5 days in advance. Check the consistency of the forecasts from one day to the next. Inconsistency might well imply greater than usual uncertainty. Consider the further outlook: if northerly gales are in the offing, a wine run to Cherbourg will be stymied if you have to return by ferry.

If you decide to go, use the forecast winds to determine your strategy. Your destination may not be feasible unless for example you work up to windward to avoid being headed. Keep other options and ports of refuge up your sleeve. Think laterally; above all, Think.

If lightly crewed consider wind strengths. A forecast Force 5 can become a 6. The forecast direction 'west' means anywhere from SW to NW. Try to judge from the weather data which is more likely. Plan accordingly.

On passage keep listening to the radio, especially if the wind is already fairly brisk. Review the strategy and short term tactics. Is it time to tack or sensible to reef?

c.   **Longer passages**

Much the same advice applies. Think carefully about any passage likely to exceed 2 days, if for example the longer range 3 to 5 day forecasts are suggesting too much wind, or from the wrong direction. Having got an apparent weather window, never assume that the 5 day forecast will work out to be exact, especially beyond day 3. Keep monitoring all radio, Navtex and radio fax information. Look for any indication that the weather is not panning out as expected. If in doubt, be prepared to divert or even heave to and wait a while.

d.   **Ocean passages**

Any blue water sailor has to be able to cope with the worst weather. Obviously, take avoiding action if at all possible, but this may not be easy as it will be based on 4 or 5 day predictions. It is useful to have radio fax, or a service such as Weather Wizard (11.2.14) or being able to download charts from the Internet via a Satphone. In practice, the forecasts will probably help decide when to hoist storm sails and ride out the gale.

For all kinds of sailing, ultimately the broad questions to be answered will be: What weather is likely to hit me in the next 12 to 48 hours, 3, 4 or 5 days? What should I do to take advantage of the good and avoid the bad?

11.4.5   WATCHING THE WEATHER

As well as studying the forecast, it is good seamanship to keep a "weather eye" open. Coupled with the forecasts, watching the sky, the barometer and the wind can help you to be just that half step ahead.

Cloud

General cloud types and the reasons for their shapes were described in 11.1.11. Layered cloud suggests stable air and a fairly steady wind. An increasing depth of instability cloud indicates that winds are likely to become more gusty and variable in direction. With cumulonimbus clouds, it is wise to watch for squalls in their vicinity (see 11.1.19).

A line of small cumulus developing a little inland is a good indicator that a sea breeze has started to develop.

When sailing offshore shallow cumulus-type clouds are often noticed forming in lines or 'streets' aligned with the wind direction. This tends to happen most frequently when the wind is between Force 4 and 6. Bands of lighter and stronger winds blow parallel to the cloud streets with the stronger winds in between the lines of cloud.

Pressure

A steady fall in pressure can confirm the approach of a forecast depression or frontal system with the associated deterioration in conditions. Conversely a steady rise in pressure occurs while such systems are moving away.

Frequently the rate of pressure change indicates the intensity of a system – the greater the fall (or rise) the stronger are the accompanying winds likely to be. As a general rule if the pressure changes more than 3 mb in three hours, increasing winds can be expected. A change of around 6 mb in three hours indicates a gale, and one of 10 mb a severe gale.

Note too that a steady barometer does not rule out a significant increase in wind. The boat could be between an anticyclone and an advancing depression, so that, although the barometric pressure at the place is steady, the pressure gradient is starting to increase.

An aneroid barometer should be on board, either of the analogue variety whose glass is tapped in time-honoured fashion; or, better still, one with a digital read-out. A barograph which continuously records the pressure on a paper-covered drum is not really practical due to the yacht's movement. Readings from a barometer will suffice, so long as they are regularly logged and plotted on a graph as a record similar to that from a barograph.

Some modern barometers contain a solid-state pressure transducer with a digital readout showing present pressure and rate of change of pressure over the past 3 hours. They store past pressures every 15 minutes over a 24 hour period. One such is the battery powered Weathertrend made by Prosser Scientific Instruments Ltd.

To make a valid comparison between forecast and actual pressures, the ship's barometer should have been calibrated. This is best done when the pressure is steady and winds are light. Read the pressure at, say, 1200 UT. Then, either get the pressure from the nearest reporting station using the SMS service (see 11.2.8) or by reference to a synoptic chart for that time. If winds are light, the pressure gradient will be slack (11.1.9) and any errors in estimating pressure at your location will be small.

Wind

Always log wind force and direction so that changes can be readily detected and considered in the context of the weather chart. Measuring the wind is easily done using masthead equipment, but remember that the apparent wind is being measured – so allow for the boat's course and speed. A simple hand-held ventimeter and a hand-bearing compass can be used to measure the wind, taking care to do this on the windward side. Better seamanship, and more practicable, is to get into the habit of relating sea state and boat handling to the Beaufort force.

11.5 METEOROLOGICAL TERMS

11.5.1   GLOSSARY

Anabatic wind A wind that blows up a slope as a result of heating; as opposed to the more common katabatic wind.

Anaprop Anomalous radio propagation: interference to radio transmissions (especially radar and VHF radio) as a result of meteorological conditions.

Anemometer Instrument for measuring wind speed.

Anticyclone An area with a centre of high barometric pressure.

Aurora Borealis Bright streaks of light in the northern sky, caused by electrical discharges; the 'northern lights'.

Backing An anti-clockwise change in wind direction.

Bora A cold blustery NE wind blowing down mountain sides on the eastern coast of the Adriatic.

Clouds Aggregate of minute water droplets or ice crystals suspended with its base above ground level; see 11.1.11.

Cold front The boundary of a cold air mass.

Coriolis An effect on the wind direction caused by the earth's rotation; after an Italian mathematician.

Corona A series of tinted rings around the edge of the sun or moon due to diffraction of light by water droplets.

Cyclone Generic name for an area with a central low pressure, usually called a depression in mid-latitudes. A tropical cyclone in the Indian Ocean, Arabian Sea or Bay of Bengal is also called a cyclone.

Cyclonic Anti-clockwise circulation around a depression.

Depression see Cyclone.

Dew Water droplets formed by water vapour in the air condensing on surfaces cooled by radiation at night.

Dew point The temperature at which cooling air becomes saturated, before condensation (eg dew) is formed.

Doldrums An area of calm or light and variable winds over equatorial waters.

Drizzle Small (<0·5mm) water drops of near uniform size usually falling steadily from low stratus cloud.

Equinoctial gales Gales believed (wrongly) to blow with greater severity and frequency at the equinoxes than at other times of the year.

Eye of the storm An area of light winds and often broken cloud at the centre of a tropical revolving storm.

Eye of wind The direction from which the wind blows (now rarely used).

Föhn wind A warm dry wind in the lee of a mountain range; of Alpine origin.

Front A sloping zone separating two different air masses.

Further outlook A brief summary of the future weather conditions for a period after that covered by a more immediate forecast.

Geostrophic wind The wind that would blow parallel to the isobars, due to the balance of Pressure Gradient Force and Geostrophic Force, if friction, curvature of the isobars, latitude, and other local effects were ignored.

Gust A rapid but brief increase in windspeed relative to its general strength.

Haar A type of sea fog in some north-eastern parts of Scotland and England.

Hail Hard pellets of ice from cumulonimbus clouds, often associated with thunderstorms.

Halo A circle of light around the sun or moon caused by refraction of the light by ice crystals.

Hectopascal The international unit of atmospheric pressure, equivalent to a millibar.

Hurricane A tropical revolving storm in the West Indies, off the American seaboard and Australasia. A wind of hurricane force, ie 12 on the Beaufort scale.

Hygrometer An instrument for measuring air humidity (also psychrometer).

Inversion An increase in air temperature with altitude.

Isobars Lines on a synoptic chart or weather map joining points of equal barometric pressure.

Isotherms Lines on a weather map joining points with the same temperature.

Jetstream A narrow band of very high speed wind near the tropopause.

Katabatic wind A wind that blows down mountain slopes, due to cooling by radiation.

Land and sea breezes Off-shore and on-shore winds caused under clear skies by the land respectively cooling and heating up more quickly than the sea.

Levanter A humid easterly wind in the Strait of Gibraltar.

Lightning An electrical discharge between positively and negatively charged areas within thunderclouds or to earth.

Line squall A sudden, violent squall often associated with a cold front or a line of thunderstorms.

Lull A drop in windspeed relative to its general strength.

Mackerel sky Appearance of the sky when cirrocumulus or altocumulus cloud form a pattern like mackerel scales.

Mirage The appearance in the sky of images which are in reality over the horizon, due to abnormal refraction.

Mistral A dry, cold wind blowing down the Rhône valley and over the northwest Mediterranean. Similar winds in parts of Spain are known as the Maestral.

Occlusion The merging of cold and warm fronts which lifts the warm sector above the land or sea surface.

Polar front The global boundary between polar and tropical air masses, where depressions often originate.

Precipitation A generic name for rain, drizzle, snow, sleet and hail.

Rain Drops of water (>0·5mm) usually falling, often with variable intensity, from frontal cloud

Recurvature A curving change in direction, or near reversal, of the initial track of a tropical revolving storm.

Ridge Extended portion of an area of high pressure.

Roaring Forties Popular name for the strong prevailing westerlies in middle latitudes of the southern hemisphere.

Scirocco A warm southerly wind in the Mediterranean.

Scud Seaman's term for fractostratus cloud, low shreds of racing cloud, often beneath rain clouds.

Sea breeze See land breezes.

Sea fret Sea fog (also haar) in parts of NE England.

Sea smoke Evaporation fog formed when cold air moves over warm water; aka 'Arctic sea smoke', 'steam fog' or 'water smoke'.

Secondary depression A low formed in the circulation of a primary depression, often on a trailing cold front.

Showers Short spells of precipitation from convective cloud.

Sleet In the UK, a mixture of rain and snow or snow that melts as it falls; has a slightly different meaning in some other countries.

Snow Ice crystals which coalesce and fall as snowflakes.

Squall A sudden blast of wind lasting several minutes, usually associated with a cold front or thunderstorm.

Synoptic chart A weather map, showing at a certain time pressure distribution, principal features, visibility, wind, temperature and cloud over a large area (a 'snapshot').

Thunder The noise made by lightning causing the air to heat and expand rapidly.

Tornado A violent vortex usually cyclonic and associated with thunderstorm clouds.

Trade winds Winds of near constant speed and direction blowing from the sub-tropical highs toward the equator.

Tramontana A northerly wind blowing across Italy to the Tyrrhenian Sea. NW winds in Spain are known as Tramontane.

Trough A V-shaped 'valley' extending from a depression, shown on a weather chart by a sharp bend in the isobars.

Typhoon A tropical revolving storm in the West Pacific.

Veer A clockwise change in the wind direction.

Ventimeter A small hand held instrument for measuring wind speed or force.

Warm sector The area of warm air between warm and cold fronts in the circulation around a frontal depression.

Waterspout A vertical vortex of low pressure extending down from the cloudbase to the sea.

11.5.2   FIVE LANGUAGE WEATHER VOCABULARY

Navtex information is always in English and may also be in the originator's national language. Some French radio stations, particularly along the Channel coast, broadcast weather information in English. But CROSS stations broadcast Inshore waters forecasts in French only. In the Netherlands English is the second language. Several Spanish CGs broadcast in English as well as in Spanish. Details of foreign stations including frequencies, times of forecasts and coverage are in the MRNA. A vocabulary of some of the commoner terms in English, French, German, Dutch and Spanish is given below.

English	French	German	Dutch	Spanish
Anticyclone (High)	Haut pression	Hoch	Hoge drukgebied	Anticiclón
Area	Region	Gebiet	Gebied	Zona
Backing	Retournant	Krimpen	Krimpend	Rolada a la izquierda
Calm	Calme	Stille, Kalme	Stil	Calma
Centre	Centre	Zentrum	Centrum	Centro
Clouds	Nuages	Wolken	Wolken	Nubes
Cold	Froid	Kalt	Koud	Frio
Cold front	Front froid	Kalt front	Koud front	Frente frio

English	French	German	Dutch	Spanish
Cyclonic	Cyclonique	Zyklonisch	Cyclonisch	Ciclónico
Decrease	Affaiblissement	Abnahme	Afnemen	Disminución
Deep	Profond	Tief	Diep	Profundo
Deepening	Se creusant	Vertiefend	Verdiepend	Ahondamiento
Depression (Low)	Depression (bas)	Depression (Tief)	Depressie	Depresión
Direction	Direction	Richtung	Richting	Dirección
Dispersing	Se dispersant	Zerstreuend	Verstrooiend	Disipación
Drizzle	Crachin	Spruhregen	Motregen	Llovizna
East	Est	Ost	Oosten	Este
Extending	S'étendant	Erstreckend	Uitstrekkend	Extension
Extensive	Etendu	Verbreitet	Uitgebreid	General
Falling	En baisse	Fallend	Vallend	Bajando
Filling	Se comblant	Auffüllend	Vullend	Relleno
Fine	Beau	Schönwetter	Mooi	Buen tiempo, sereno
Fog	Brouillard	Nebel	Mist	Niebla
Frequent	Frequent	Haufig	Veelvuldig	Frecuente
Front	Front	Front	Front	Frente
Frost	Gelée	Frost	Vorst	Escarcha
Gale	Coup de vent	Sturm	Stormachtig	Viente duro, vendaval
Gale warning	Avis de coup de vent	Sturmwarnung	Stormwaarschuwing	Aviso de viente duro/temporal
Good	Bon(ne)	Gut	Goed	Bueno
Gusty	Rafale	Boig	Buiig	Granizo
Hail	Grêle	Hagel	Hagel	En rachas
Heavy	Abondant	Stark	Zwaar	Aumentando
Increasing	Augmentant	Zunehmend	Toenemend	Fuerte, violento
Isolated	Isolé, éparse	Einzelne	Verspreid	Aislado
Light (slight)	Faible	Schwach	Licht, zwak	Ligero, débil
Lightning	Éclair	Blitz	Bliksem	Relámpago
Local	Locale	Ortlich	Plaatselijk	Local
Mist	Brume legère	Dunst	Nevel	Neblina, bruma
Moderate	Modéré	Massig	Matig	Moderado
Moderating	Se modérant, se calmant	Abschwächend, abnehmend	Matigend, afnemend	Disminuyendo
Moving	Se déplacant	Bewegend	Bewegend	Moviendo
North	Nord	Nord	Noorden	Norte
Occasional (showers)	Eparse(s)	Gelegentlich	Nu en dan	Ocasional
Overcast	Couvert	Bedeckt	Geheel bewolkt	Cubierto, encapotado
Poor	Mauvais	Schlecht	Slecht	Malo
Precipitation	Precipitation	Niederschlag	Neerslag	Precipitación
Pressure	Pression	Druck	Druk	Presión
Quickly	Rapidement	Schnell	Zeer snel	Rapidamente, pronto
Rain	Pluie	Regen	Regen	Liuvia
Rising	En hausse, montant	Steigend	Ryzend, stygend	Ascendente
Rough	Agité	Sturmisch	Guur	Duro, bravo
Scattered	Sporadiques	Verstreut, vereinzelt	Verspreide	Difuso
Shower	Averse	Schauer	Stort bui	Chubasco
Slowly	Lentement	Langsam	Langzaam	Lentamente
Snow	Neige	Schnee	Sneeuw	Nieve
South	Sud	Süd	Zuiden	Sur
Squall	Grain	Bo	Bui	Turbonada
Stationary	Stationnaire	Stationär, ortsfest	Stationair, stilstand	Estacionario
Steadily	Regulièrement	Stetig, standig	Regelmatig	Sin parar
Storm	Tempéte	Sturm	Storm	Temporal
Strong	Fort	Stark	Sterk	Fuerte
Swell	Houle	Dunung	Deining	Mar de fondo/leva
Thunder	Tonnerre	Donner	Donder	Trueno

English	French	German	Dutch	Spanish
Thunderstorm	Orage	Gewitter	Onweer	Tormenta, tronada
Variable	Variable	Veränderlich	Veranderlijk	Variable
Veering	Virant	Rechtsdrehend	Ruimend	Girando
Warm	Chaud	Warm	Warm	Cálido
West	Ouest	West	Western	Oeste
Wind force	Force du vent	Windstärke	Windkracht	Fuerza del viento

11.6 WEATHER BOOKS AND WEBSITES

The following books and websites provide further reading and reference about weather as it affects yachting:

Books

Weather Forecasts (RYA booklet G5) by David Houghton Basic guidance on forecasts. Useful pocket reference.

Yachtmaster shore-based course notes (RYA). This includes a brief but well-illustrated weather section.

Marine Weather Services Excellent free booklet; annual update from the Met. Office.

Le Guide Marine de Météo France. Annual booklet with up-to-date French weather sources.

Instant Weather Forecasting by Alan Watts (Adlard Coles 2nd edition). Good cloud photographs.

Instant Wind Forecasting by Alan Watts (Adlard Coles Nautical). A companion volume to the previous title.

This is practical weather forecasting by Dieter Karnetzki (Adlard Coles Nautical). Basics for cruising yachtsmen.

Weather at Sea by David Houghton (Fernhurst). A good basic description of how the elements behave.

Wind Strategy by David Houghton (Fernhurst). A companion title, for racing yachtsmen and race officers.

Ocean Passages for the World (NP 136), UKHO. Classic advice on long distance routeing and global weather.

The Weather Handbook by Alan Watts (Waterline, 2nd edition). Interpreting what you see.

A sailor's guide to wind, waves and tides by Capt Alex Simpson (Waterline). Weather systems and their effects.

The weather companion by Tim Bartlett (Fernhurst). Revision for RYA courses on flip-cards.

Weather to sail by Mike Brettle and Bridget Smith (Crowood Press ,1999).

The world weather guide by Pearce and Smith. Mostly weather statistics for 200 countries.

Understanding weatherfax by Mike Harris (Adlard Coles). How to receive and interpret weatherfax.

Meteorology for Mariners by the Met. Office (TSO). New edition due. Detailed textbook for professional mariners.

Cloud Types for Observers by the Met. Office (TSO). A good reference for cloud recognition.

Meteorological Glossary (TSO). The definitive glossary from the Met. Office; good if storm-bound in harbour.

Admiralty List of Radio Signals, Vol 4: Meteorological Observation Stations (UKHO).

Websites

www.bbc.co.uk/weather   *The BBC is putting increasing amounts of weather on this site*

www.dmi.dk *Danish Met Institute*

www.franksingleton.clara.net   *Brilliant site by current yachtsman/ex-forecaster. Topical and practical articles.*

www.infomet.fcr.es   *Links to charts from several centres*

www.inm.es *Spanish Met Office; texts in Spanish of coastal and offshore forecasts*

www.nws.fsu.edu/buoy   *MOAA weatherbuoys*

www.meteo.fr/marine/   *French Met Office. Some forecasts in English; good for free charts*

www.meto.gov.uk/leisuremarine *UK Met Office's definitive site.*

www.nottingham.ac.uk/meteosat   *Specialists in satellite imagery*

www.onlineweather.com   *Weather bulletins by e-mail or WAP phone, includes sailing*

www.sunba2.ba.infn.it/images/faxes   *Quick downloads of charts from various centres including Bracknell.*

www.wmo.ch   *Comprehensive listing from the WMO. Leads to Met services worldwide*

Chapter 12 Sea and Tide

CONTENTS

12.1 THE SEA

12.1.1 HOW WAVES ARE FORMED

Any sensible yachtsman prefers to sail in smooth water, but once at sea waves will inevitably be encountered. A little knowledge of the subject helps to understand their behaviour and their potential dangers. For colour photographs of waves and sea states associated with different wind speeds, see Fig. 11(8), page 306.

Waves are created by wind. Friction between the water and the air moving over it causes energy to be transferred from the wind to the surface of the sea. This energy manifests itself by forming waves, and is why wind speed at sea level is less than at the top of a mast. When wind first starts to blow over a calm sea, small ripples are formed. These cause pressure fluctuations and turbulence above the surface of the water, both of which help to increase the size of the ripples into wavelets and eventually into proper waves. The windward side of each wave is more affected by the wind than the leeward side, and hence each wave collects extra energy from the wind, causing it to grow bigger.

The wave-making process does not however continue indefinitely. As a wave grows larger, it begins to move faster, thus reducing its speed relative to the wind; hence energy is lost within the wave itself due to the motion of the water, particularly if the wave breaks. So eventually a state of equilibrium is reached, and unless the wind speed changes or the wave reaches shallow water or some other obstruction the wave will maintain a steady state.

12.1.2 WAVE FORMS AND DEFINITIONS

Although waves at sea vary endlessly in both size and type, a train (succession) of theoretical waves should first be considered in order to study their form and behaviour; initially the waves should also be in deep water, unaffected by the seabed.

Fig. 12(1) shows a wave diagrammatically, with some of the key terms and dimensions which are used to describe it.

In the diagram, C is the celerity (velocity) in ft/sec of the wave, as it moves from left to right. The period of a wave (T) is the time in seconds between two successive crests passing a given point. If the wave length in feet is L, then

$$C = \frac{L}{T}$$

In deep water it can be shown that:

$$C = \sqrt{\frac{gL}{2\pi}}$$

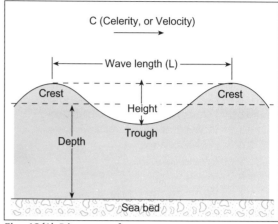

Fig. 12(1) Diagram of a wave.

(where g = 32.2ft/sec/sec, and π = 3.14) and hence

$$C = 2.26 \times \sqrt{L}$$

From the equations above it follows that:

$$L = 5.12 \times T^2 \text{ and}$$
$$C = 5.12 \times T$$

Thus it is shown that whereas the celerity (velocity) of a wave varies directly with its period, its length varies as the square of the period.

If celerity is expressed in knots

$$C = 3.03 \times T$$

Fig. 12(2) shows the relationships between celerity (knots), wavelength (feet) and wave period (seconds).

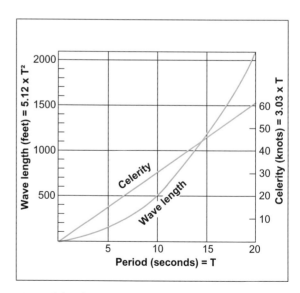

Fig. 12(2) Relationships between celerity and period, and wave length and period of waves.

When a wave passes, any particle of water on or near the surface moves in nearly a circular orbit. Although the wave moves forward, the surface of the sea does not – or only very slightly. If the movement of an object, such as a floating can, is observed it will be seen to move in an almost closed orbit, in a vertical plane; not quite a closed orbit because, as suggested above, there is a small movement of the surface water in the direction of wind and wave.

Particles below the surface also describe orbits, the end of each orbit being approximately the same as its starting point. The size of these orbits decreases very quickly with depth below the surface, and becomes negligible at a depth equal to 7 x the wave length.

12.1.3   WAVE SIZE

In the open sea, the size of waves depends on the strength of the wind, the length of time for which it has blown, and the fetch (distance upwind of the observer) over which it is blowing. Thanks to data collected and published by the Marine Information and Advisory Service of the Institute of Oceanographic Sciences – and with their kind permission to publish Figs. 12(3), (4) and (5) – it is possible to predict wave heights and periods with reasonable accuracy. These predictions must, however, be for some approximate mean value because larger waves can be expected to appear from time to time, as explained below.

Sometimes strong winds blowing for only a short time produce higher waves than lesser winds blowing for a long time; on other occasions moderate winds blowing for a considerable time produce larger waves.

To predict wave height, enter Fig. 12(3) on the left with the surface wind speed in knots. Go

Fig. 12(3) Wave height prediction graph for coastal waters (depth typically 20 – 200m).

horizontally to the right to intersect either the pecked curve for the appropriate duration (in hours) or the vertical line corresponding to the fetch (in nautical miles) as shown on the bottom scale, whichever is reached first. The predicted height in metres is read from the solid curve intersected at that point. Consider, for example, a 30 knot wind blowing for 12 hours over a fetch of 60 nautical miles. Entering the diagram on the left at 30 knots, and moving horizontally to the right, the 60 mile fetch line is reached before the duration of 12 hours, and the resulting height is 3m.

Fig. 12(4) is used similarly to determine the period. Both graphs give predictions for coastal waters, with depths typically 20 – 200m. Except in very strong winds the predicted wave heights are only slightly too small for deeper waters, but in deep water the wave periods will be about 10 – 20% longer than suggested by Fig. 12(4).

The predicted height (H_s) obtained from Fig. 12(3) is the 'Significant Wave Height', defined as the average value of the heights of the one-third highest waves. If, for example, 60 waves are observed, H_s is the average height of the 20 biggest. The 'Significant Wave Period' is the average value of the periods of those same (one-third highest) waves. Theory, together with actual measurements at sea, shows that on average the highest single wave in any ten-minute period is likely to be about 1.6 times the significant wave height, as expressed in the formula:

$$H_{max(10\ min)} = 1.6 \times H_s$$

Hence, if the significant wave height (H_s) is 3m, as determined in the example above, $H_{max(10\ min)}$ will be 4.8m. Having calculated this figure, it is then possible to refer to Fig. 12(5).

This is a graph of 'Wave Height Factor' for coastal waves plotted against the duration of gale conditions in hours. If, as in the example used

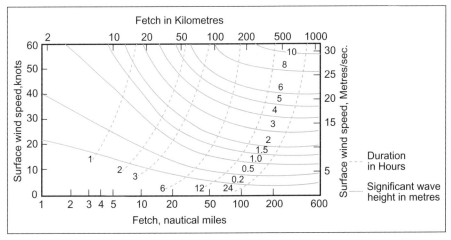

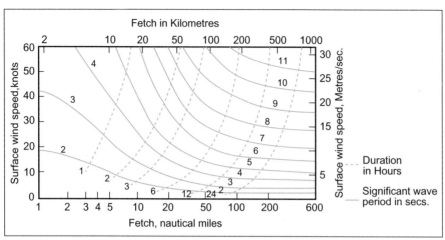

Fig. 12(4) Wave period prediction graph for coastal waters (depth typically 20 – 200m).

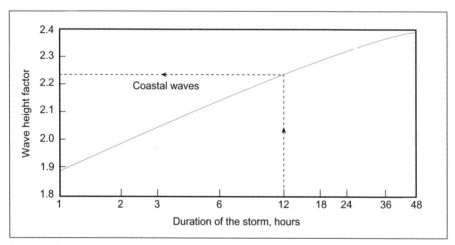

Fig. 12(5) Curve relating wave height factor to duration of storm (coastal waves).

above, the wind has blown for 12 hours, the factor from the curve is 2.23 and this figure is used to multiply $H_{max(10\,min)}$ to give the most probable height of the highest wave in the storm, thus:

$$4.8 \times 2.23 = 10.7m.$$

12.1.4 FREAK WAVES

From observation at sea it is clear that waves vary considerably in height. This is because any individual wave in practice consists of a large number of wave components, each with its own height and period. In any wave system the faster components (with longer periods) continually overtake the slower components. When crests get into step with each other, exceptionally large waves occur. When crests of some components coincide with troughs of others, there is a brief spell of relative calm.

In a small yacht it is very difficult to judge the heights of waves with any accuracy, but wave recording stations are established at many points around the UK. It has been shown that about one wave in 23 is twice the average height, and one in 1175 is three times the average height. Only about one wave in 300,000 (the equivalent of about a month at sea) exceeds four times the average height, and such a wave is very seldom encountered by yachtsmen or recorded on any instrument. In the foregoing the average height corresponds to about 0.6 times the significant wave height, as defined previously.

12.1.5 BREAKING WAVES

As the wind speed increases, some waves become too steep, and tend to break. In a theoretical train of waves this happens when the wave height is one-seventh of the wave length, although in reality (due to the fact that waves are not uniform in character) a figure of one-twelfth is more typical. In the open sea, once the wind reaches force 7 or more, breaking seas are likely to be encountered. When a wave breaks, its kinetic energy is partly absorbed by the following wave, causing it to grow.

12.1.6   SWELL
Swell consists of waves that are generated by meteorological disturbances, and which persist after that disturbance has ceased. Swell can travel a long way from where it originated, and in deep water it will maintain a constant direction. With distance travelled its height decreases, but its length and speed stay the same. The following terms describe the length and height of swell:

Length:	Short	0 – 100 m
	Average	100 – 200 m
	Long	over 200 m
Height:	Low	0 – 2 m
	Moderate	2 – 4 m
	Heavy	over 4 m

Quite commonly swell from one direction converges with swell from another. When this happens there will be occasions, even in deep water, when two crests (or two troughs) are superimposed, resulting in abnormal waves. When such conditions already exist, and a strong wind starts to blow from yet another direction, a very confused and dangerous sea is likely to result.

12.1.7   WIND AGAINST TIDE
When a wave system encounters an adverse tidal stream (or current) the wave length becomes shorter. Hence the waves become steeper and more likely to break; they also tend to become higher, thus aggravating the situation. These conditions can produce a very dangerous sea, particularly when the tidal stream is strong and running over a shallow and uneven bottom.

Conversely, when the wind is blowing with the tidal stream (or current), the length of the waves increases and their height reduces.

12.1.8   WAVES IN SHALLOW WATER
When waves move into shallow water they start to feel the effect of the sea bottom once the depth equals three-quarters of the wave length. Due to friction against the bottom, the orbiting movement of the water beneath the wave is upset and the celerity of the wave is reduced.

Because $C = L/T$ (see 12.1.2 above), the wave length is reduced and the waves become steeper to the point where they break, a process which is assisted by the decreasing depth of water.

When a wave breaks upon a beach its total energy content is destroyed, as anybody who has experienced heavy surf can testify. The force generated by breaking waves can be very considerable, and has been known to shift structures weighing hundreds of tons. As a wave starts to break some of the surface water moves forward with the wave form itself. In the open sea this energy, from a breaking wave, is transferred to other overtaking waves, but when approaching a beach the whole accumulated force is spent upon the shore. This moving mass of water is called a 'wave of translation'.

A special situation arises when waves of translation are approaching an estuary. As they meet the outflowing river current the breaking wave can continue for a great distance upstream as a special form of bore; see 12.1.14.

12.1.9   BARS
Where, because of the local configuration of the shelving bottom, waves tend to break repeatedly at a certain distance from the shore, a bar may be formed. Smaller waves may pass over the bar without breaking, but they are affected by the shallow water, which shortens their wave lengths. Larger waves break on the bar, throwing large quantities of water over it so that there is a tendency for the sea level inshore of the bar to rise. This water has to return seawards, often through one or more channels scoured through a narrow part of the bar an extremely dangerous area for boats and swimmers.

Many popular yachting harbours are fronted by a bar. In moderate weather most such bars do not present any great hazard, but it is normally advisable to cross them before (and not after) local high water. Some bars are potentially very dangerous however, and a stretch of harmless-looking water can soon be transformed into a death trap once the ebb starts to run, particularly if there is any strength of wind blowing onshore.

12.1.10   OVERFALLS AND TIDE RACES
Some of the worst sea conditions that can be experienced occur quite close to land off headlands where the tidal stream runs strongly. Any promontory (or a narrow channel, say between two islands) constricts the natural flow of the tidal stream, and hence speeds it up. If at the same time the sea bottom is irregular in depth, considerable turbulence can be created in the area concerned.

These factors, combined with a wind blowing against the tidal stream, can create tide races where very dangerous overfalls are formed – conditions naturally being worst at spring tides and in gale force winds.

The more significant tide races can be unpleasant for a small yacht even in good conditions and are best avoided at all times.

Others are passable in safety in good weather and at the right state of the tide, usually at slack water. Any tide race, or area where there are heavy overfalls, should be given a wide berth in bad weather, or when wind of any strength is against the tide.

12.1.11 REFRACTION OF WAVES
When waves pass from one depth of water to another – as happens when they meet a coastline at an angle, or when they pass the end of a headland, or down either side of an island – they are refracted (or bent) in much the same way as a ray of light is bent when passing from one medium to another.

The most common example of this is where a train of waves approaches a beach at an angle, as illustrated in Fig. 12(6). As soon as the inshore end of a wave gets into shallow water, it slows down so that the whole wave train eventually alters course somewhat, and the waves start to approach the shore roughly parallel to it.

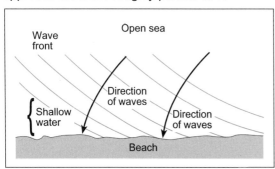

Fig. 12(6) Refraction of waves approaching a beach.

Refraction can be very pronounced around the sides of an island. Where the two refracted wave trains meet on the leeward side of the island there can be an uncomfortable stretch of confused water, just where a peaceful lee might have been anticipated, see Fig. 12(7).

Waves become diffracted (broken up) as they spread out after passing an obstruction, eg a pronounced headland or a breakwater, tending in general to reduce wave height.

12.1.12 REFLECTED WAVES
Where waves which are in relatively deep water meet a vertical object such as a cliff or harbour wall, they are reflected back to seaward, much as light is reflected by a mirror. This can set up an area of standing waves, in which both peaks and troughs are very pronounced. An unpleasant and confused sea can result, particularly if two separate wave trains happen to be reflected at the same time. Care is needed in the approaches to certain harbours where these conditions are relatively common.

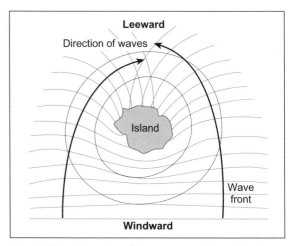

Fig. 12(7) Refraction of waves round an island.

12.1.13 TSUNAMIS
This Japanese name meaning 'harbour wave' is given to waves caused by submarine earthquakes, volcanic eruptions or coastal landslips; also known as 'seismic waves' and, incorrectly, as 'tidal waves'. They occur (mostly in the Pacific) on a scale far surpassing any waves generated by the wind, and can be over 100 miles in length, less than a metre high, and travelling at speeds of 300 - 500 knots.

In the open sea they present no danger, but once they enter shallow water the series of waves become shorter and very much higher (up to 20m), and their effect can be disastrous. The first crest is often preceded by a trough, so any abnormal lowering of sea level could give warning of a tsunami arriving within a few minutes. If possible, get out to sea fast. Due to their great wave length the waves arrive at intervals of 10 to 40 minutes. The tsunami international warning centre is in Hawaii.

12.1.14 BORES
A bore is a form of wave which rolls up certain estuaries and rivers, induced by resonant tidal oscillations. A bore in simple terms is caused either by the meeting of two tides or, more commonly, by the general constriction of the advancing tide into a narrowing and shelving channel. The effect is increased by spring tides, previous heavy rainfall, following winds and low barometric pressure.

The most impressive bores occur on the Rivers Hooghli, Amazon, Petticodiac (Bay of Fundy), and Chien Tang Kiang in China. In Europe the Mascaret on the R. Seine used to be significant, but is now much reduced due to improvements in the channel, except at springs between Villequiers and Rouen when yachts should stay in mid-channel. The R. Severn bore starts above Sharpness, but is not fully developed until it reaches Longney, 9 miles below Gloucester, where it rushes upstream at a height of some 1 to 1.5m and is dangerous to boats where it breaks along the banks. It usually occurs when the Avonmouth range exceeds 13·5 metres. The bore on the River Trent is only slightly less impressive.

Eagre also means a bore but is archaic Old English.

12.1.15 OCEAN CURRENTS

Currents are the semi-permanent movements of water not caused by the tide. Navigationally horizontal movements are of prime interest, although vertical components may exist in sub-surface currents. Currents are caused mainly by either seasonal or more permanent wind systems blowing over the sea, or to a far lesser extent by changes in the density of sea water induced by differences in temperature (just as air temperature affects the wind). The set of a current is the direction in which it flows, so a westerly current flows *to* the west whereas a westerly wind blows *from* the west.

The established atmospheric circulations over the oceans, such as the NE and SE trade winds which blow towards the equator, are the principal causes of currents – in this instance the

North and South Equatorial currents which flow in the Atlantic, Pacific and Indian Oceans in close alignment with the Trades and which in turn result in the flow of compensating countercurrents.

A simplified diagram, Fig. 12(8), of the main world currents shows how, in the Atlantic, the North Equatorial current is augmented by a split in the South Equatorial current off the coast of Brazil, and flows into the Caribbean and the Gulf of Mexico before swinging north up the east coast of North America to form the Gulf Stream. Off Newfoundland the Gulf Stream is deflected by the cold Labrador current, and sets towards Europe. In the North Atlantic part of it divides to form the Canaries current and then to rejoin the North Equatorial drift. The rest flows past the British Isles towards Norway.

In southern latitudes no land masses disrupt the westerly drift caused by the Roaring Forties, resulting in a general easterly current flowing around the bottom of the world.

Currents are important considerations for long distance passage making, and more detailed information is available in *Ocean Passages for the World* and in *Meteorology for Mariners*. Notes for particular areas are contained in Admiralty Sailing Directions.

Fig. 12(8) Principal ocean currents of the world (black arrowheads indicate cold currents).

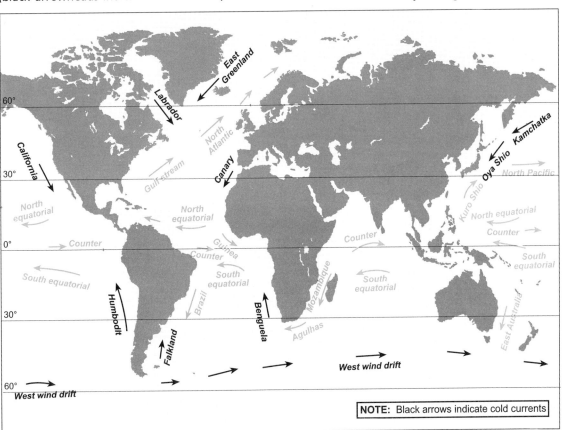

12.1.16 CORIOLIS EFFECT

The earth's rotation, called the Coriolis force, has the effect of deflecting any moving thing to the right in the northern hemisphere and to the left in the southern, but not on the equator. This effect applies to the water both in ocean currents and tidal streams. The effect is greater in higher latitudes, and in practice results in a typical deflection of 20°. It is why north-flowing currents such as the Gulf Stream and the Kuro Shio current off Japan, or the south-flowing ones like the Brazil and Agulhas currents, drift away from their respective coasts.

The Coriolis force also influences the bigger range of tide on the French side of the English Channel, since the Channel flood is deflected to the right towards the French coast. Conversely, the ebb is diverted towards the English coast.

12.1.17 DENSITY OF SEA WATER

The density of sea water depends on temperature, pressure and salinity. Density decreases as temperature rises; and increases both as pressure rises (with depth below the surface), and as salinity rises.

For normal calculations the density of fresh water at surface level is taken as 1000kg/m³. Sea water at surface level varies from about 1021kg/m³ in equatorial regions to about 1027kg/m³ at the poles. Generally the density of sea water is less in coastal regions than in the open sea. In the ocean depths it can reach 1070kg/m³.

For convenience, density is often expressed in the form *sigma-t*, where:

$$sigma\text{-}t = (\text{Density in kg/m}^3 - 1000)$$

Hence a density of 1025.6kg/m³ has a value of 25.6 in *sigma-t* terms.

12.1.18 SALINITY OF SEA WATER

For our purposes, the salinity of water may be defined as the amount of dissolved solids present, expressed in parts per thousand. In fresh water the figure is zero, and in the open sea it is typically 35 parts per thousand and generally within the 33 – 37.5 range. The salinity is less in higher latitudes, in regions of high rainfall, or where there is dilution by rivers or melting ice. Where there is considerable evaporation the figure may reach more than 40 parts per thousand.

The North Atlantic has a higher salinity than the South Atlantic, and the Atlantic as a whole is more saline than the Pacific Ocean.

In estuaries, where rivers and streams flow into the sea, changes in salinity have a great influence on plant and animal life. Salinity fluctuates with the tides, and with the prevailing weather conditions. The well-defined zones in which different species live and breed depend largely on the tolerance of the species concerned to varying degrees of salinity. Nature finds ways to meet these natural changes, but not to resist man's pollution of rivers and estuaries with sewage, pesticides, industrial chemicals, oil and other destructive matter.

12.1.19 THE COLOUR OF THE SEA

In the open ocean the natural colour of the sea is a very intense blue, but this is modified in higher latitudes and in coastal regions to a green or blue/green colour due to the presence of plankton (very small animal and vegetable life) floating in the sea. In a few areas, eg the Red Sea, the density of the plankton may produce a brown or red/brown colour.

Temporary discolorations may be caused by a number of factors: plankton dying (due, for example, to changes in temperature); sand or dust particles carried offshore by the wind; or sand or mud produced by submarine earthquakes.

Cloud shadows can often cause what appears to be a change in colour of the sea, and may be mistaken for shoal water.

Around coral reefs the colour of the sea is a good indication of the depth of water if the sun is high. Depths over 18m (60ft) show as a deep blue-black colour, which becomes a deep blue over sand or more dark green over rock. In 9m (30ft) rock shows as a mottled brown, and sand as light green. In shallower water, sand shows up as very pale green, and rock as light yellow-brown, probably distinguishable by eye.

12.2 TIDES – INTRODUCTION

12.2.1 GENERAL THEORY

The tide is the periodic rise and fall of sea level caused by the gravitational attraction of the Moon and, to a lesser extent, of the Sun. The gravitational effect of the Moon is not uniform over the earth's surface. At a point nearest to the Moon it is greater than at the centre of the earth, where it is in turn greater than at a point on the far side of the earth. This causes the sea level to be raised at the points nearest to and furthest from the Moon – at A and B in Fig. 12(9).

When the Sun and Moon lie in a straight line with the earth they are said to be 'in conjunction' or 'syzygy' (a useful Scrabble word). Their combined gravitational effect is greatest, and this produces the largest rise and fall of tide. These are called spring tides, and occur just after new moon and full moon; see Fig. 12(10).

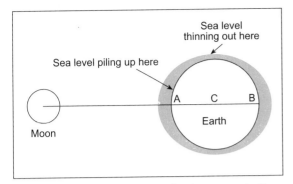

Fig. 12(9) Diagram showing the (exaggerated) effect of the Moon's gravitational pull on the sea.

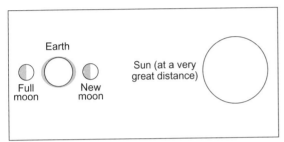

Fig. 12(10) When the Sun and Moon lie in a straight line with Earth, their gravitational forces act in conjunction, causing a large rise and fall in sea level (spring tides).

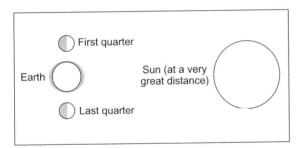

Fig. 12(11) When the Sun and Moon form a right angle with Earth, their combined effect is minimised, resulting in a smaller rise and fall in sea level (neap tides).

When the Moon and the Sun form a right angle with the earth they are said to be in quadrature; Fig. 12(11). Their respective gravitational effects are acting at places which are one-quarter of the earth's circumference apart, and hence their combined effect is minimised. The result is a smaller rise and fall in sea level, ie neap tides, which occur just after the first and last quarters of the Moon.

Since the earth rotates on its axis every 24 hours, the actual areas nearest to and furthest from the Moon are continually changing. Hence the level of the sea at any point is also continually changing.

A lunar day (the time between two successive passes of the Moon across a given meridian) is about 24 hours 50 minutes. In the Atlantic Ocean, and along the coasts of NW Europe, two complete tidal cycles (each of one high and one low water) occur every lunar day. These are called semi-diurnal tides, with a period of about 12 hours 25 minutes between successive high waters.

Some parts of the world have diurnal tides, with only one high water and one low water every 25 hours or so. Diurnal tides usually have very little rise and fall.

Other parts of the world experience mixed tides, which are partly semi-diurnal and partly diurnal in character. Mixed tides, like semi-diurnal tides, have two complete tidal oscillations per day but often one of the cycles is much more pronounced than the other.

Tides are influenced by the physical layout of ocean basins and the surrounding land. For example in the Mediterranean and the Baltic there is virtually no tide, because the entrances to these seas are too narrow to allow the flow of water necessary to create any significant rise and fall in the time available. On open coasts, the tide usually rises and falls at about the same rate on any given day, but in estuaries it normally rises more quickly than it falls; see 12.9.6.

The height of the tide is measured against a reference level called chart datum, as defined in 12.3.1. Predictions for the times and heights of high water and low water at places all over the world are published annually in tide tables, which include differences for calculating times and heights at Secondary ports.

Tide refers to the vertical movement of water, the rise or fall in sea level. This in turn causes horizontal movements of water, called tidal streams. Information on the strength and direction of tidal streams is available from various sources, as described in 12.9.

12.2.2 LOCAL TIDE CONDITIONS

The physical shape of the coast and the sea bed can cause local tidal conditions which differ substantially from the semi-diurnal (or diurnal) pattern. A good example is the complex tidal regime between Swanage and Selsey Bill on the south coast of England, where double high waters and a sharply defined low water also occur. There is often no simple explanation for such phenomena.

The Coriolis force (induced by the earth's rotation on any object which moves on the surface of the earth, except at the equator) can also affect local tidal conditions, and helps to explain (see 12.1.16) why the French side of the

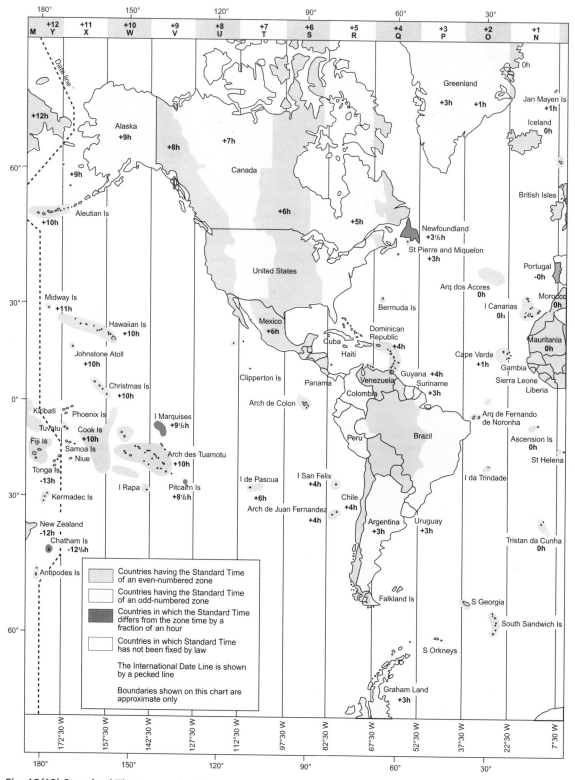

Fig. 12(12) Standard Time zone chart.

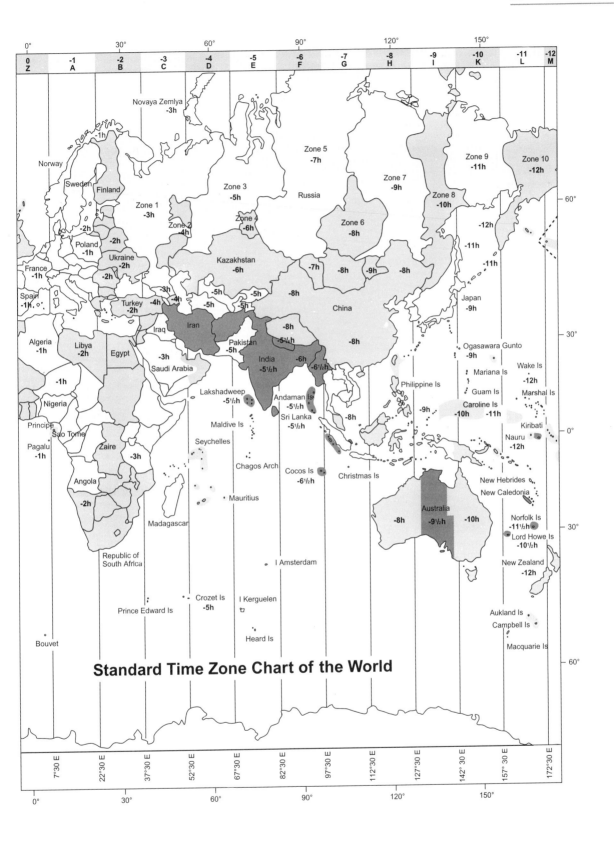

Standard Time Zone Chart of the World

English Channel has bigger tides than the English coast opposite.

Other tidal phenomena, such as bores, together with non-tidal changes in sea level caused by abnormal meteorological conditions, are mentioned in 12.1.14 and 12.8.

12.2.3   EQUINOXES AND SOLSTICES

Twice a year, at about the times when the Sun crosses over the equator at the vernal equinox on 21 March and the autumnal equinox on 23 September, spring tides are larger than normal. These are called Equinoctial Spring Tides, and they occur when all the factors which contribute to big tides – such as the phase of the Moon, the Moon's declination and the Sun's declination – are working in concert. Around the solstices (21 June and 22 December) the tides are smaller than normal.

12.2.4   TIDE TABLES

Admiralty Tide Tables (ATT) are published annually in four volumes (each £18.00) covering:

Vol 1 – UK and Eire, plus European Channel ports.
Vol 2 – Europe (excluding the UK and Eire), the Mediterranean Sea and the Atlantic Ocean.
Vol 3 – Indian Ocean and South China Sea.
Vol 4 – Pacific Ocean.

Vols 3 and 4 also include tidal stream tables (12.9.5).

Vol 1, and similarly Vol 2, are divided into three parts:

Part I gives the predicted daily times and heights of HW and LW at Standard Ports, computed by the UK HO for all UK and Irish ports, and by their national authorities for foreign ports. Vol 1, Part Ia gives hourly height predictions for certain UK ports.

Part II gives time and height differences for Secondary Ports, as referenced to a Standard Port in Part I.

Part III gives the harmonic constants for use with the Simplified Harmonic method of tidal prediction (12.7.10).

The UK and European information in Parts I and II of Vols 1 and 2 is reproduced in the MRNA.

Tidal predictions and related products can also be provided by the Proudman Oceanographic Laboratory, Bidston Observatory, Prenton, Wirral CH43 7RA. Tel 0151 653 8833; Fax 0151 653 8345. www.pol.ac.uk

12.2.5   TIME ZONES AND TIME
DIFFERENCES

There are 24 Time zones around the world, each with a width of 15° of longitude. In each zone, the same time (Zone Time) is kept. The Greenwich meridian is the reference centre of the system, and lies in the middle of Zone 0, which extends from 7°30'E to 7°30'W. It is the zone in which the Standard Time is Universal Time (UT) or GMT; the two are virtually the same and UT is gradually replacing GMT in common parlance.

Zones to the east of Zone 0 are numbered –1, –2, –3 etc; and those to the west +1, +2, +3 etc. The twelfth zone is divided into two by the International Date Line, the part to the west being –12, and the part to the east +12. Ashore, zones are adapted to suit geographical areas or administrative convenience. For example, all France is physically in Zone 0, but keeps Zone –1 (or –0100) as Standard Time. Portugal which lies just within Zone +1, used to keep Zone –0, then went to Zone –1, but about 5 years ago changed back to Zone 0, by popular demand.

A Zone's number represents the hours by which Zone Time must be decreased (if east of Greenwich) or increased (west of Greenwich) to obtain UT. For example in Zone –1 (–0100) the time kept is one hour in advance of UT, and so 2000 local time is 1900 UT.

Zone Time may also be referred to by the letters A – Z. Thus Zone 0 is Z, or UT; zones to the east are lettered A to M (omitting J), and those to the west N to Y.

The International Date Line is a modification of the 180° meridian, drawn so as to include islands of particular groups on the same side of the line; but a few anomalies remain. When crossing the Date Line heading east, change to yesterday's date; when heading west, change to tomorrow's date.

The Standard times kept in different countries, together with those countries which observe Daylight Saving Time (DST), are shown in the MRNA and ALRS Vol 2, as are the details of radio time signals broadcast by the BBC; see 10.7.1. Larger countries, eg the USA, may adopt several Standard Times.

Co-ordinated Universal Time (known internationally as UTC, a language-independent abbreviation) was introduced in 1972 to provide a globally accessible and precisely defined timescale for Earth-rotation time (UT) and International Atomic Time (TAI). TAI is based on the atomic second of fixed duration, established through the quantum resonance of isolated caesium 133 atoms. The master atomic clocks run undisturbed, generating time markers at intervals of exactly one second to give the minutes, hours and days of the TAI scale. TAI was initially set to agree with UT in 1958, but the scales have since slowly drifted apart due to small changes in the Earth's rate of rotation. UTC is formed by occasionally breaking the normal counting sequence to insert or delete a second (known as a 'leap second') to keep UTC within one second of UT. This is done as the final second of a UTC month – December or June as first choice, and March or September as second choice. It happens on average about once a year. UTC is for all practical purposes the same as UT.

Daylight Saving Time

To extend daylight in the evening, many countries change to Daylight Saving Time (DST or Summer Time) as their legal time for part of the year. In most European countries DST operates from the last Sunday in March until the Saturday before the last Sunday in October.

During the winter months in the UK, Eire and Portugal clock time is UT. During summer months, clock time is BST which is Zone A, –0100, ie one hour ahead of UT.

During winter months in France, Belgium, the Netherlands, Germany, Denmark and Spain local (clock) time is Zone –0100. During the summer, local (clock) time is –0200, or two hours ahead of UT.

Time differences

Tidal predictions for Standard Ports are in the Standard Time normally kept at the place; they take no account of BST or other Daylight Saving Times. The zone time used is shown on each page of tidal predictions in the MRNA. Yellow tinting on these pages shows when Standard Time is in force. The pages are untinted for DST months, when one hour must be added to convert to clock or local time.

Time differences for Secondary Ports, when applied to the predicted times of HW and LW at Standard Ports, will give times of HW and LW in the zone time listed for the Secondary Port. Be aware that the same is true when the Standard and Secondary Port(s) are in different zones. For example some Spanish harbours (Zone –0100) to the north and south of Portugal are referred to Lisboa (UT) as the Standard Port. But this is already accounted for in the Secondary Port time differences.

Any change in zone time at the Standard Port, or any difference between zone times at Standard and Secondary Ports has no significance. Only changes in zone time at the Secondary Port, where different from those tabulated, may be corrected for. In some parts of the world it should be verified that the zone time tabulated for a Secondary Port is in fact valid, since changes are not always notified in time for inclusion in tide tables.

12.3 DEFINITIONS

12.3.1 CHART DATUM (CD)

Chart datum is a level so low that the tide will rarely fall below it. In the UK this level is approximately that of the Lowest Astronomical Tide (LAT). Tidal predictions for British ports are based on LAT (see 12.3.2). Charted depths and drying heights on a chart are referenced to CD, as are all calculations of height of tide. Admiralty metric charts of the British Isles use LAT as CD.

12.3.2 LOWEST ASTRONOMICAL TIDE (LAT)

LAT is the lowest sea level (HAT is the highest) predicted to occur under average meteorological conditions and under any combination of astronomical conditions. Although it is only reached very occasionally, it is not the extreme level. Still lower sea levels may be caused by abnormal meteorological conditions; see 12.8.

LAT is used as CD for Admiralty metric charts of the British Isles. LAT is also the reference level for Admiralty Tide Table predictions for ports in Great Britain.

12.3.3 CHARTED DEPTH

A charted depth, as printed on the chart, is the vertical distance of the sea bed below chart datum at that place. Depths are shown in metres and tenths of metres on modern metric charts where, for example, 5_2 indicates 5·2 metres. Depths will still be found expressed in fathoms and/or feet on some older charts, where 5_2 would indicate five fathoms and two feet. It is obviously important to know which units are in use. Admiralty metric charts have the legend DEPTHS IN METRES clearly printed in magenta on the top and bottom margins. Fathoms and feet charts are usually obvious by their lack of colour.

12.3.4 DEPTH (ACTUAL)

The actual depth of water at any place is the sum of the charted depth and the height of the tide at that time and place. If there are no errors in the chart, or in the tidal calculation, the depth so calculated should be the same as a sounding by lead line or by an accurate echo sounder.

12.3.5 SOUNDING

The term 'sounding' means the depth of water from sea level to the sea bed, as measured by echo sounder or lead line. It should not be confused with the figures on a chart showing the depth of water below chart datum, which are correctly known as 'Charted depths' (see 12.3.3).

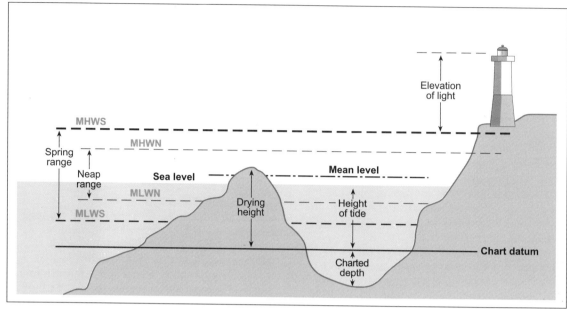

Fig. 12(13) Diagram depicting the main terms used in tidal predictions and calculations.

12.3.6 DRYING HEIGHT

The drying height is the vertical distance above chart datum of the top of any feature which from time to time is covered by water. Figures for drying heights are underlined on the chart in metres and tenths of a metre on metric charts, and in feet on older charts. For example, on a metric chart, 5₂ indicates that the place concerned dries 5·2m above CD. The actual depth of water above such a place is the height of the tide at the time less the drying height indicated. If the result is minus, then that place is uncovered at the time selected.

12.3.7 CHARTED HEIGHT

The elevation above MHWS of a feature such as an islet or large rock which is never covered by the sea.

12.3.8 CHARTED ELEVATION (LIGHTS, BUILDINGS ETC)

The elevation of lights or structures shown on a chart in metres above the level of MHWS; see Fig. 12(13).

12.3.9 CHARTED VERTICAL CLEARANCE

The vertical distance in metres from the level of MHWS to the underside of a bridge span/arch or to overhead power cables; see 12.6.2. Not to be confused with the vertical clearance between a mast head and bridge.

12.3.10 HEIGHT OF TIDE

The height of the tide is the vertical distance between CD and sea level at any given time.

12.3.11 RISE/FALL OF TIDE

Rise of tide is the amount in metres by which the tide has risen above the last LW. Fall of tide is the amount in metres by which the tide has fallen below the last HW. Not to be confused with height of tide which relates to CD.

12.3.12 MEAN LEVEL (ML)

ML is loosely used in three different senses:

a. As 'Mean Sea Level' (MSL) which is the mean level of the sea over a period of about 18·6 years, or the average level which would exist if there were no tides. In this context monthly variations in ML are shown in Part II of ATT. Where the variation is less than 0.lm it is entered as 'negligible'. For short periods the ML may vary by as much as 0.3m, above or below the predicted figures. In non-tidal waters, eg the Baltic, MSL is used as CD.

b. ML also refers to 'Mean Tide Level' (MTL), which is calculated by meaning the heights of Mean High Water Springs (MHWS), Mean High Water Neaps (MHWN), Mean Low Water Neaps (MLWN) and Mean Low Water Springs (MLWS).

c. ML finally describes the average of a large number of hourly heights, which can produce a different figure.

12.3.13 RANGE

The range of the tide is the difference in height between successive high and low waters. Mean Spring range is the difference between MHWS and MLWS. Mean Neap range is the difference between MHWN and MLWN. The range is therefore an indication of the 'size' of a tide.

12.3.14 CO-TIDAL AND CO-RANGE LINES

Co-Tidal lines join points of equal Mean High Water Interval. Co-Range lines join points of equal Mean Spring Range. See 12.7.9 for the use of these lines.

12.3.15 INTERVAL

The interval is the period between the time of HW and any given time, expressed as hours and minutes before or after high water, ie HW – or +.

12.3.16 DURATION

The duration of a tide is the interval between the times of HW and the previous LW; it is normally slightly more than six hours where semi-diurnal tides apply, as around the coasts of NW Europe. Duration can be used to calculate the time of LW where only the time of HW is known.

12.3.17 FLOOD

The flood is the movement of tide as it rises from LW. It runs for about six hours and is described in three parts: the first two hours being the 'young flood', the middle two hours the 'main flood' and the final two hours the 'last of the flood'.

12.3.18 EBB

The ebb is the movement of tide as it recedes from HW. With semi-diurnal tides it runs for about six hours and is sometimes referred to in three parts: the 'first of the ebb', the 'strength of the ebb' and the 'last of the ebb'.

12.3.19 SLACK WATER

Slack water is the period at HW between the end of the flood and the start of the ebb, or similarly at LW between the end of the ebb and the start of the flood. At HW an extended period of slack water is known as a 'stand'.

12.3.20 SPRING TIDES (SPRINGS)

Spring tides rise highest and fall lowest above/below the Mean Level, ie their range is maximum. Springs occur when the Moon and Sun are acting in conjunction; see 12.2.1. At springs the tidal streams run more strongly.

12.3.21 EQUINOCTIAL SPRING TIDES

Unusually large tides which can be expected with spring tides at about the equinoxes, which occur on 21 March and 23 September; see 12.2.3.

12.3.22 NEAP TIDES (NEAPS)

Neap tides have the smallest range and the slowest tidal streams. They occur between springs, ie at the first and last quarters of the moon when the influences of the Sun and Moon are in quadrature; see 12.2.1.

12.3.23 MAKING

An expression describing that stage in the two-weekly tidal cycle when the range starts to increase from a minimum (neaps) to a maximum (springs).

12.3.24 TAKING OFF

An expression describing that stage in the two-weekly tidal cycle when the range starts to decrease from a maximum (springs) to a minimum (neaps).

12.3.25 STANDARD PORTS

Standard Ports are those with tidal characteristics suited to being a reference for other ports, usually along the same stretch of coast. They are often chosen as being large commercial or naval ports, or for historical reasons. Their predicted daily times & heights of HW and LW are given in Admiralty Tide Tables.

12.3.26 SECONDARY PORTS

A Secondary Port has tidal characteristics which are similar to those of its Standard Port, even though the latter may not necessarily be the nearest. 'Secondary Port' does not imply lesser importance. Tidal predictions for Secondary Ports are made by applying time and height differences to the times and heights predicted for the relevant Standard Port (see 12.5).

12.4 STANDARD PORT CALCULATIONS

12.4.1 LIST OF STANDARD PORTS

Daily time and height predictions of HW and LW at all Standard Ports are given in Admiralty Tide Tables. These predictions are based on observations over a period of at least a year, and usually much longer.

Daily predictions for the following Standard Ports are given in the MRNA:

UK: Falmouth, Plymouth, Dartmouth, Portland, Poole (not HW times), Southampton, Portsmouth, Shoreham, Dover, Sheerness, London Bridge, Burnham-on-Crouch*, Walton-on-the-Naze, Lowestoft, Immingham, River Tyne (North Shields), Leith, Aberdeen, Lerwick, Stornoway, Ullapool, Oban, Greenock, Liverpool, Holyhead, Milford Haven, Avonmouth, Belfast.   * Not a Standard Port.

Channel Islands: St Peter Port, St Helier.
Eire: Cobh (Cork, Ringaskiddy), Dublin, Galway.
Gibraltar. *Portugal:* Lisboa.
France: Pointe de Grave, Brest, St Malo, Cherbourg, Le Havre, Dieppe, Dunkerque.

Netherlands: Vlissingen, Hook of Holland.
Germany: Wilhelmshaven, Cuxhaven and
    Helgoland.
Denmark: Esbjerg.

12.4.2   TIMES OF HW AND LW
For Standard Ports the times (and heights) of HW
and LW are read direct from the tide tables. The
MRNA uses the same format as the Admiralty
Tide Tables (ATT).

  The Zone Time of the predictions is shown at
the top of each page. In the British Isles, UT
(GMT) is used throughout so one hour must be
added when BST is in force (non-shaded areas).
The same is true for other daylight saving times
elsewhere; see 12.2.5. For convenience the dates
of Neaps and Springs are coloured blue and red
respectively. The relationship between CD and
Ordnance Datum (Newlyn), or other national
equivalents, is shown at the foot of each page.

12.4.3   HEIGHTS OF HW AND LW
Daily heights in metres of HW and LW at
Standard Ports are shown in ATT and the MRNA,
referenced to CD.

12.4.4   HEIGHTS OF TIDE AT
SPECIFIED TIMES
The height of tide at any desired time between
HW and LW is predicted by using the tidal curves,
which lie next to the tide tables for each
Standard Port.

  Fig. 12(14) shows the Galway curves: The
Mean Spring curve is a solid line and the Mean
Neap curve, where it differs from the spring

*Fig. 12(14) Galway Spring and Neap curves and
calculation of height of tide at a specific time.*

curve, is pecked. Note the reference heights of
MHWS/ MHWN and MLWS/MLWN at top and
bottom; and the Mean range values at springs
and neaps in a box to the right of the diagram.
Do not extrapolate beyond the spring or neap
curves, ie if ranges are greater than spring values
use the spring curve, and if less than neaps use
the neap curve.

Example problem
*Find the height of tide at Galway at 1100 on a
day when the predictions are:*

	21	0107	0·3
		0731	5·4
Su		1331	0·3
		1955	5·0

1. On Fig. 12(14) plot the heights of the
    relevant HW (5·4m) and LW (0·3m) at the
    top and bottom respectively of the left-
    hand part of the diagram; join the two with
    a diagonal line.
2. In the boxes below the curves, enter the
    time of HW (0731) and other times needed
    to span the relevant period, ie 0831, 0931,
    1031 and 1131.
3. From the required time of 1100 (3½h after
    HW) go vertically to the spring curve (in this
    case).
4. From the curve go horizontally to the
    diagonal line, thence vertically to the scale
    for height. Read off the height of 2·1m.

12.4.5   TIMES OF SPECIFIC HEIGHTS OF TIDE
The time when a specific height of tide between
HW and LW is reached can be predicted by using
the tidal curves in a reverse sense to that
discussed in 12.4.4.

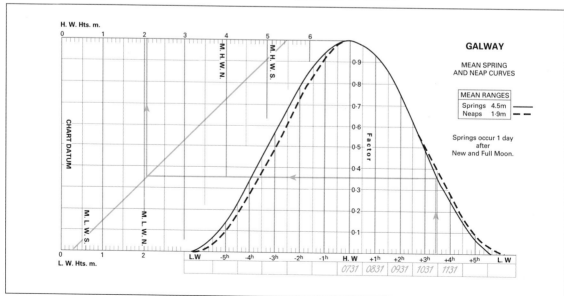

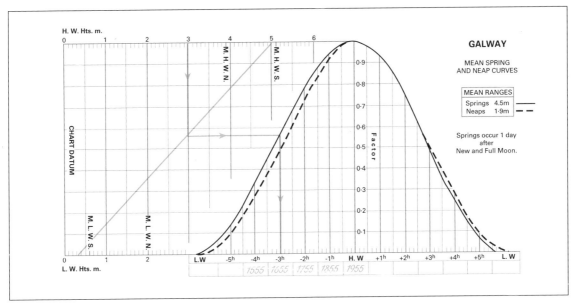

Fig. 12(15) Finding the time when the tide reaches a certain height.

Example problem
Find the time in the afternoon when the tide reaches a height of 3m at Galway, the predictions being as in the previous example.

1. On Fig. 12(15) plot the heights of LW and HW which bracket the required time (ie at 1331 and 1955) at the bottom and top respectively of the left-hand part of the diagram; join the two with a diagonal line.
2. In the boxes below the curves, enter the time of HW (1955) and other times spanning the relevant period.
3. From the required height (3m) drop vertically to the diagonal line, and thence go horizontally to the spring curve (in this case).
4. From the curve drop vertically down to the time scale. Read off the required time: HW – 3h = 1655.

12.5 SECONDARY PORT CALCULATIONS

12.5.1 TIMES OF HW AND LW
The approximate times of HW and LW are calculated by adding/subtracting the published time difference to/from the time of HW or LW at the relevant Standard Port. The time differences given are approximate, as will occur in normal weather. Although usually given to the nearest minute, do not assume that they are so accurate. Note too that the times thus obtained are in the Zone Time of the Secondary Port, as was explained more fully in 12.2.5.

Predictions for times falling between those given in each column for the Standard Port must be interpolated.

Example problem
Consider the tidal information for Maseline Pier on the east coast of Sark:

Standard Port ST HELIER

Times				Height (metres)			
High Water		Low Water		MHWS	MHWN	MLWN	MLWS
0300	0900	0200	0900	11·0	8·1	4·0	1·4
1500	2100	1400	2100				
Differences SARK (MASELINE PIER)							
+0005	+0015	+0005	+0010	–2·1	–1·5	–0·6	–0·3

If HW St Helier is at about 0300 or 1500, the difference to be added/subtracted to get the time of HW Sark is +0005 (ie, add 5 minutes). If HW St Helier is at about 0900 or 2100, the time difference to be applied to obtain HW Sark is +0015 (add 15 minutes).

Similarly for the LW times: If LW St Helier is at about 0200 or 1400, LW Sark is 5 minutes later. If LW St Helier is at about 0900 or 2100, LW Sark is 10 minutes later.

Such data can conveniently be recorded in boxes 9 and 10 of the tidal prediction form at Fig. 12(16). The procedure is included in the example given in 12.5.3.

Interpolation by eye
To find the appropriate time difference for the Secondary Port at times which fall between the given Standard Port times (0300/1500, 0900/2100, 0200/1400 and 0900/2100) one must interpolate between the columns, either by eye, by arithmetic or by graph.

For example when HW St Helier is at 0300, the time difference for Sark is +0005 and when HW St Helier is at 0900 the time difference is +0015. Hence for HW St Helier at 0600, the time difference for Sark will, by eye, be +0010. The figures used in this example were convenient ones, because for HW St Helier at 0600 (midway between 0300 and 0900), the Sark time difference was clearly midway between +0005 and +0015, ie +0010.

Interpolation by graph

If interpolation by eye or by arithmetic seems difficult, the graphical method, as depicted in Fig. 12(17), is a simple way of solving more complex problems. Use any suitable squared paper to construct a graph with Standard Port times on the vertical axis, and the Secondary Port time differences on the horizontal axis.

Example

Using the St Helier data above, find the time difference for HW Sark when HW St Helier is at 0700.

Fig. 12(16) Tidal prediction form for calculations when using Admiralty Tide Tables or the MRNA.

1. Establish the Standard Port time bracket in which 0700 occurs, ie between 0300 and 0900.
2. Plot 0300 against the relevant time difference, +0005, and 0900 against +0015. Draw a line between these two points, and mark it HW.

   (Note: The LW line for times between 0200 and 0900 is also shown on the graph as a dashed line).
3. Enter the graph at 0700 and go horizontally to meet the HW diagonal. Thence go up to the top scale and read off the time difference of +0012. Ergo the required time of HW Sark is 0712.

A graph is particularly suitable where calculations are to be repeated over several tides. For example yachtsmen whose home port is tidally constrained may find it helpful to construct a suitable graph.

Height differences can be similarly interpolated; see 12.5.2 and Fig. 12(18). Or

Time or Height required ....

		TIME		HEIGHT	
		HW	LW	HW	LW
Standard Port		1	2	3	4
Differences		5	6	7	8
Secondary Port		9	10	11	12
Duration (or time from HW to LW)		13	9 – 10 or 10 – 9		14

Range Stand. Port   3 – 4

Range Secdy. Port   15   11 – 12

* **Springs/Neaps/Interpolate**

Start: height for given time ↓

	Time reqd.	16	17 + 18
9	Time of HW	17	9
17 – 16	Interval	18	

Date ....

	Factor	19

Time zone ....

	Rise above LW	20	22 – 21
19 x 15			
12	Height of LW	21	12 ↑ **Start: time for given height**
20 + 21	Height required	22	

* **Delete as necessary**

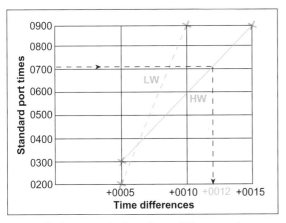

Fig. 12(17) Interpolating time differences by graph.

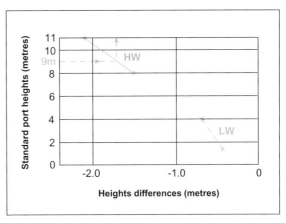

Fig. 12(18) Interpolating height differences by graph.

Interpolation of both time and height differences can conveniently be done on one piece of graph paper as shown in Fig. 12(19).

12.5.2 HEIGHTS OF HW AND LW

To find the heights of HW or LW at a Secondary Port apply the height differences for that harbour to the height of HW or LW at its Standard Port. Note that these height differences are averages for Mean Spring and Mean Neap levels and predicted heights so obtained are approximate. The variation in height differences is assumed to be linear. Heights for dates between Springs and Neaps must be found by interpolation.

Example A: using the Sark tidal data in 12.5.1, by simple arithmetic the height of MHWS at Sark is 8·9m (11·0 – 2·1); and the height of MHWN is 6·6m (8·1 – 1·5); and so on for MLWN and MLWS.

Example B: find the height of LW at Sark midway between springs and neaps: At Sark MLWN is 3·4m and MLWS is 1·1m; midway between these two values is 2·25m, QED.

Height differences for HW or LW on any day between springs and neaps can be interpolated graphically, like time differences; see 12.5.1 and Fig. 12(18).

Example C: find the HW height difference for Sark when the predicted height of HW at St Helier is 9·0m.
1. Using suitable scales, insert Standard Port heights on the vertical axis and height differences on the horizontal.
2. Plot the Standard Port heights of 11·0m (MHWS) and 8·lm (MHWN) against the height differences of –2·1m and –1·5m respectively, and join these two points by a diagonal.

3. Enter the graph at the Standard Port HW height of 9·0m; go horizontally to the diagonal, thence up to the top axis to find the required height difference of –1·7m.

12.5.3 HEIGHTS OF TIDE AT SPECIFIED TIMES

Heights of tide at Secondary Ports for times other than HW and LW are predicted from the Mean Spring and Mean Neap curves for the relevant Standard Port in a similar way to 12.4.3.

This assumes that along the coast in question there is little change in the shape of tidal curves between adjacent Standard Ports, and that the duration of rise or fall at the Secondary Port is similar to that of its Standard Port.

Enter the curves with the times and heights of HW and LW at the Secondary Port, calculated as in 12.5.1 and 12.5.2 above.

Interpolate (where necessary) by eye between the curves. Do not extrapolate – use the spring curve for spring ranges or greater, and the neap curve for neap ranges or less.

Example problem

Find the height of tide at Fanad Head at 1300 UT, when the predictions for the Standard Port (Galway) are:

5	0326	4·2
	0919	1·6
Sa	1536	4·4
	2143	1·5

The tidal differences for Fanad Head are:

Standard Port GALWAY

Times				Height (metres)			
High Water		Low Water		MHWS	MHWN	MLWN	MLWS
0200	0900	0200	0800	5·1	3·9	2·0	0·6
1400	2100	1400	2000				
Differences FANAD HEAD							
+0115	+0040	+0125	+0120	–1·1	–0·9	–0·5	–0·1

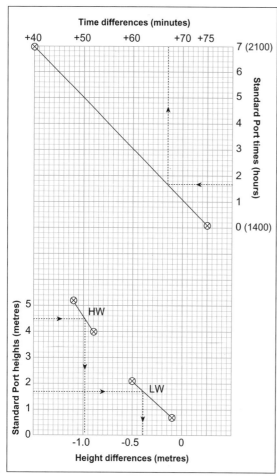

Time differences (minutes)

+40 +50 +60 +70 +75

Standard Port times (hours)

7 (2100)

6

5

4

3

2

1

0 (1400)

Standard Port heights (metres)

5   HW

4

3

2   LW

1

0

-1.0   -0.5   0

Height differences (metres)

Fig. 12(19) Interpolating time and height differences by graph (Fanad Head on Galway).

1. Find the time and height differences for Fanad Head by interpolation as described in 12.5.1/2 and shown in Fig. 12(19). The HW time difference is +0107 and the HW/LW height differences are –1.0 and –0.4m respectively.

2. Record these differences in boxes 5, 7 and 8 of the form shown in Fig. 12(20).

3. The resultant figures for Fanad Head are HW at 1643, height 3.4m, and LW height 1.2m.

4. On the Galway curves diagram at Fig. 12(21) enter the Fanad Head heights for HW (3.4m) and for LW (1.2m) top and bottom on the left of the diagram, and connect the two points by a diagonal line.

5. Enter the time of HW Fanad Head (1643) in the HW box, and insert 1543, 1443, 1343 and 1243 in the boxes to the left, ie before HW.

6. From the time required (1300), which is 3h 43m before HW, go upward to a point between the spring and neap curves. (This point reflects the fact, by inspection, that the range is rather nearer neaps than springs).

7. Then go horizontally to the diagonal, and down to the height scale to find the required figure of 2·0m.

12.5.4 TIMES OF SPECIFIC HEIGHTS OF TIDE

Example problem
Find the time when the afternoon tide reaches a height of 2·5m, using the tidal data in 12.5.3 and the previous example already drawn on Fig. 12(21).

1. Enter the diagram at 2·5 metres on the bottom axis and go up to the diagonal, thence horizontally to a point nearer to the neap than the spring curve.

2. Go down to the time scale at the bottom, to read off HW –2h 40m, = 1403.

12.6 PRACTICALITIES

Many yachtsmen find tidal calculations difficult to work out and even more difficult to apply in the real world. The first problem becomes easier with experience, or you may decide to buy some sort of tidal calculator or get your PC to do the calculations for you. The second problem is largely a case of being able to see the wood for the trees. Having scribbled seemingly endless calculations on a pad, what is the net result?

12.6.1 ANCHORING

Anchoring is probably the commonest scenario for such difficulties. There are really only two tidal questions to answer, before you decide where to let go the hook:

   a. What is the least depth to anchor in so as to remain afloat at LW? and

   b. How much chain should you veer?

Clear your mind by drawing a sketch to show the relevant parameters. These include the boat's draught, underkeel safety clearance, heights of tide (as calculated) now and at LW, and echo sounder reading.

Example: It is 1600; the height of tide is calculated to be 4·2m. Draught is 1·5m and you choose 1·0m as underkeel clearance. LW is calculated to be at 1800, height 1·8m.

1. Sketch the situation at LW: Draught + keel clearance = 2·5m; deducting 1·8m (height of LW) gives 0·7m. This is the charted depth required to keep you afloat at LW.

2. Now relate the 0·7m to the present time and state of tide. Height of tide 4·2m + charted depth 0·7m = 4·9m. That is the least depth by echo-sounder (calibrated to read below sea level) in which you can now anchor.

3. Find that sounding (4·9m) and (if clear of other boats, near enough to the jetty etc) let go the anchor.

Time or Height required .... *1300 and 2.5m*

	TIME		HEIGHT	
	HW	LW	HW	LW
Standard Port *Galway*	1 *1536*	2 *0919*	3 *4.4*	4 *1.6*
Differences	5 *+0107*	6	7 *-1.0*	8 *-0.4*
Secondary Port *Fanad Head*	9 *1643*	10	11 *3.4*	12 *1.2*
Duration (or time from HW to LW)	13	9 – 10 or 10 – 9	Range Stand. Port	14 *2.8* 3 – 4
			Range Secdy. Port	15 *2.2* 11 – 12

* ~~Springs/Neaps/~~Interpolate

Start: height for given time ↓	Time reqd.	16 *1300*	17 + 18
9	Time of HW	17 *1643*	9
17 – 16	Interval	18 *-0343*	Date .... *5th May*

	Factor	19 *0.37*	Time zone .... *UT*
19 x 15	Rise above LW	20 *0.8*	22 – 21
12	Height of LW	21 *1.2*	12 ↑ **Start: time for given height**
20 + 21	Height reqd.	22 *2.0*	

* **Delete as necessary**

Fig. 12(20) Using the tidal prediction form to find the height of tide at a given time.

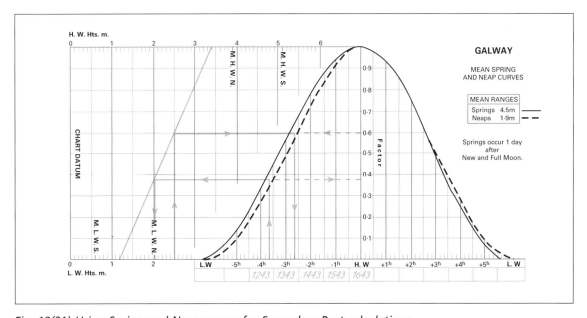

Fig. 12(21) Using Spring and Neap curves for Secondary Port calculations.

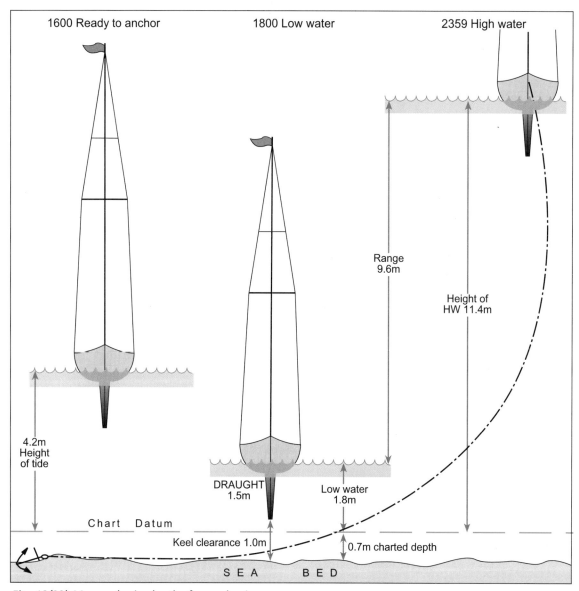

Fig. 12(22) Max and min depths for anchoring.

Question (b) hinges partly on how you decide the amount of chain to veer relative to depth at HW. (You should certainly veer a minimum of 3 x depth at HW, **PLUS** a constant 10m; there are other rules of thumb). But in the purely tidal context you need to check there is enough chain aboard to satisfy two other anchoring parameters:

4. Deep water, eg off West Scotland; and
5. Large range of tide, eg off the Channel Islands.

In the example given, you can deduce (rule of 12ths) that the range of tide is about 9·6m, so depth at HW will be about 9·6 + 1·8 + 0·7 = 12·1m. Using the chain rule of thumb above, (12·1 x 3) + 10 = 46m. Do you carry that length of chain? Many boats have only about 30m.

The principle is similar when working out the time at which there is enough water to get over a sill; or the time band when the height of tide permits your masthead to clear the underside of a bridge, with a safety margin.

12.6.2 OVERHEAD CLEARANCES
Yachtsmen must sometimes calculate whether a boat can pass safely below objects like bridges or power lines. Their heights are shown on the chart above MHWS, so the clearance will nearly always be greater than the figure shown. Below bridges the height clearance (metres) is in black with a $\overline{20}$. Below power lines a safe overhead clearance (metres) is in magenta $\overline{28}$.

A diagram, as in Fig. 12(23), often helps to show how the measurements relate to CD. The following 'formula' also applies, but heed the

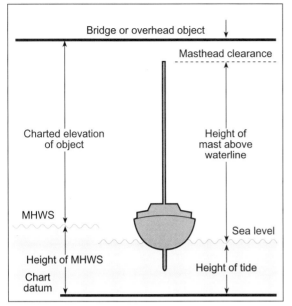

Fig. 12(23) Calculating overhead clearance.

brackets carefully or else the result will be totally incorrect:

Masthead clearance = (Elevation of object + height of MHWS) – (height of tide + height of mast above water).

12.7 PREDICTION METHODS

The calculations already described for times and heights of tide are based on the methods recommended when using Admiralty Tide Tables (ATT), as reproduced in the MRNA. These may seem long-winded and even difficult, but they help to understand what is actually being done; with experience they become routinely easy. Other means of calculating tides, eg by computer and by short-hand or rule of thumb, are discussed below. In some countries, slightly different methods may be used, but the principles are essentially the same.

12.7.1 TIDES BY COMPUTER

As the prediction of tides is a mathematical process PCs are an ideal way of carrying it out. With a suitable programme, times of HW and LW can be predicted for any standard or secondary port quickly and easily as well as heights at intermediate times. A tidal graph can be displayed on the screen or printed out. Several software packages are available.

The most comprehensive is TotalTide produced by the UK Hydrographic Office; see below. This is an expensive programme aimed at commercial shipping and in addition to the basic software cost, data for a particular geographic area must be purchased separately. TotalTide provides HW

and LW data for all ports and includes tidal stream information for many coastal and offshore positions.

Other commercially produced programmes are probably more suitable for most yachtsmen. These vary in price from a few pounds upwards, with the more expensive ones having more features. All will predict the times of HW and LW at a range of ports as well as heights at intermediate times – some have worldwide cover whilst others are limited to a local geographic area. Most programmes allow the yachts draught to be entered and many will print out a section of 'tide tables' for any port covered. It is worth looking at several programmes before choosing one and most suppliers will provide a demonstration disc or have a web site where demonstration software can be downloaded.

Whatever programme is chosen, for yachts sailing in areas where tides are significant such as the English Channel, there must be other means on board to work out approximate tidal data should the PC fail. At the very least this should be a table of times of HW and LW at Dover with the corrections to be applied for other ports, together with a small scale tidal stream atlas of the area.

Simplified harmonic method of tidal prediction (NP 159)

NP 159 is basically a graphical system requiring the use of a pencil, protractor, proforma, and a set of ATT. The method can be very time consuming if many predictions are required, but computers will normally be used to save time; see TotalTide and SHMW programmes below. Data can be produced for Standard or Secondary ports world-wide using one standardised prediction method. A variant of NP 159 is given in the introduction to ATT for those who prefer to use a pocket calculator.

Predictions are displayed graphically as hourly plots of height versus time together with tabulated predictions for each hour. To obtain a prediction, it is only necessary to key in the day, month and year, and the relevant port harmonic constants obtained from ATT or from NP 160 'Tidal harmonic constants, European Waters'. Since harmonic constants change from time to time, for best results use those listed in the latest tide tables.

Several commercial programmes, based on the NP 159 method, are now available and can be obtained from Positron Navigation, Dolphin Software, or PC Maritime. Pilotage Software also market good programmes for use on Psion hand-held calculators.

TotalTide 2001

TotalTide 2001 replaced Tidecalc (NP 158) which was withdrawn from service by the UK HO in March 2001. Tidecalc area disks (NP 158A, 1 - 13) will be supported until November 2001 when they too will be withdrawn.

TotalTide 2001 (DP 550-01) is a new Windows-based tidal prediction programme (DP = Digital Publication). It consists of one CD-ROM containing the calculation programme, and seven area data sets which are accessed through a permit key system. These provide world-wide coverage. Area 1 covers the UK, Europe, Mediterranean and far Northern waters.

TotalTide provides instant tidal heights and tidal stream predictions, using the same algorithms and Harmonic Constants as ATT. Tidal heights for all Standard and Secondary Ports can be displayed graphically or in a table. They can be calculated for up to seven consecutive days, including under keel and overhead clearances. Tidal streams for more than 3000 positions are presented on a chart-based diagram.

TotalTide runs on a PC with a 200MHz processor or better, at least 64Mb RAM and using Windows 95, 98, NT or 2000. Because it is designed for the commercial market (SOLAS vessels) it is priced accordingly, ie £130 for the calculation programme and £70 for each Area data set. However a less expensive version, modified for leisure use, is expected to be marketed in early 2002.

Simplified Harmonic Method for Windows (SHMW).

Another new HO product, also released in March 2001, is the Simplified Harmonic Method of Tidal Prediction for Windows (SHMW – ref: DP 560).

SHMW replaces the old DOS-based NP 159A which will be withdrawn at the same time. SHMW, supplied on CD-ROM is safe, accurate, speedy and user friendly. The user is required to input Harmonic Constants from Part III of ATT or from NP160 if in European waters. Predictions are then displayed as a graph of height v time for a period of up to 24 hours and over 7 consecutive days. Data for up to 20 ports can be stored. SHMW is everlasting and is expected to retail at £30. It is better suited to the leisure market than TotalTide, if only on grounds of cost.

12.7.2 FACTORS

A factor scale (0 to 1) appears vertically in the centre of the tidal curves for Standard Ports. The factor may be regarded as that percentage of the total range which has been reached at the time in question. By definition a factor of 0 implies LW, and a factor of 1 implies HW. A factor of 0.5 means that half of the mean range has been reached at the time shown on the curve, either before or after HW.

Using factors the height of tide at times between HW and LW can be calculated by simple arithmetic. Multiplying the range by the factor gives the rise (height) of the tide above LW in metres at the time concerned:

Range x Factor = Rise (above LW)

In tidal calculations with factors, use the lower part (boxes 16 – 22) of the tidal prediction form illustrated in Fig. 12(20), as well as boxes 1 – 15.

Problem (a) What is the height of tide at 1300? Using the Fanad Head data in 12.5.3 and the Galway curves at Fig. 12(21), proceed as follows:

1. Fill in boxes 1 – 15 of Fig. 12(20), as required.

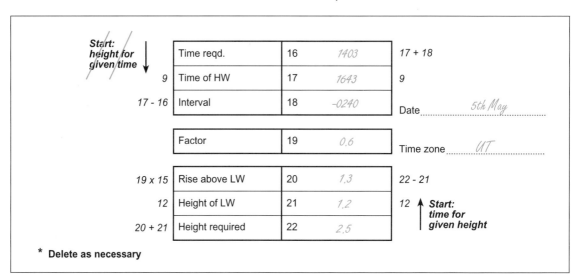

Fig. 12(24) Using the tidal prediction form to find when the tide reaches a certain height.

2. Enter in box 16 the time required (1300).
3. Enter in box 17 the time (1643) of HW Fanad Head.
4. Enter in box 18 the interval from HW (–0343), by subtracting box 16 from box 17.
5. Enter the Galway curves at the bottom with the interval (0343 before HW) and go up to the curves.
6. Interpolate as before between springs and neaps, but go right, as shown by the dashed line, to the factor scale to extract the factor (0·37). Enter this in box 19.
7. Enter Rise in box 20, having ascertained it from the formula:
Rise = Range (2·2m) x Factor (0·37) = 0·8m
8. Enter the height of LW (1·2m) in box 21. Add boxes 20 and 21 to give the height required, ie 2·0m. QED.

Problem (b) When after lunch does the tide reach 2·5m?

Complete the lower part of the tidal prediction form, but in reverse, ie box 22 to 16, as illustrated in Fig. 12(24).

1. Boxes 22 and 21 are respectively 2·5m and 1·2m.
2. Box 20 is box 22 minus box 21 = 1·3m.
3. Transpose and complete the formula, thus:
Factor = Rise (1·3m) ÷ Range (2·2m) = 0·6
4. Re-enter the Galway curves at 0·6 on the factor scale.
5. Go the left to the curves, as indicated by the dashed line, to a point, as before, nearer the neap curve.
6. Thence go down to the time scale and read off the interval required, viz –0240 (2h 40m before HW). Thus the tide reaches 2·5m at 1403. QED.

This method is far quicker in practice than in the telling!

12.7.3   SOLENT TIDES
Special curves are given in ATT and in the MRNA for some 20 Secondary Ports on the south coast of England, between Bournemouth and Selsey Bill. Here the tides are particularly complex and the tidal regime is much distorted. The most obvious feature is that double HWs occur, and these are ill-defined and the exact times of either HW are indeterminate. However LW is sharply defined and therefore the time of LW is used as a basis instead of HW. The curves appear to be the inverse of the normal shape, but in other respects they are used in the normal way, remembering to substitute LW for HW. They are referenced to Portsmouth (Standard Port).

12.7.4   HOURLY TIDAL HEIGHTS
The predicted heights of tide at each hour are given in ATT Vol 1 for Plymouth, Poole, Southampton, Portsmouth, Rosyth, Liverpool, Avonmouth and St Helier. Most of these are deepwater ports, naval and/or commercial, easily accessible by leisure craft. The obvious exceptions are St Helier where both marinas are only accessible above half-tide, and Poole which is shallow and has a small tidal range.

The hourly heights are predicted by a method different from the usual Standard Port HW and LW predictions. Hourly heights do not give precise times of HW and LW, as can be verified by inspection. They are also incompatible with Secondary Ports' time and height differences which cannot be used with hourly heights to predict tidal data at Secondary Ports.

12.7.5   TWELFTHS RULE
The 'Twelfths Rule' can provide approximate heights of tide between HW and LW. However, unless the tide at the place concerned rises/falls in a regular sine wave pattern (as in Fig. 12(14), where the rate of rise and fall is proportional to the interval) the method can seriously mislead. It can not for example be used where double HWs or LWs occur or where there is a marked stand.

The Rule assumes that the tide rises and falls by:

1/12 of the range during the first hour
2/12 of the range during the second hour
3/12 of the range during the third hour
3/12 of the range during the fourth hour
2/12 of the range during the fifth hour
1/12 of the range during the sixth hour

Thus, for example, where the range is (conveniently) 3·6m, each 1/12 represents 0·3m. If it is HW +5, the tide will have fallen in the preceding 4 hours by 9/12, ie 2·7m. Subtract this from the height of HW to get a rough height of tide. A simple mnemonic '1, 2, 3, 3, 2, 1' shows by how many 1/12s the tide rises/falls during each hour.

12.7.6   TIDES BY POCKET CALCULATOR
Assuming a sinusoidal variation in tide height, a calculator can be used to determine the height correction to be applied relative to the nearest HW or LW, using the formula:

$$\text{Height correction} = \frac{R}{2}\left(1 - \cos\frac{180 \times t}{T}\right)$$

where R = range of tide concerned
t = interval from nearest HW or LW
T = duration of rise or fall

More advanced scientific calculators are programmable to provide heights of tide for a limited number of places at any time required.

A calculator can also be used to apply the Admiralty method of tidal prediction, as mentioned in 12.7.1.

12.7.7 FRENCH TIDAL COEFFICIENTS

In France a non-dimensional coefficient is quoted to quantify the size, ie range, of every tide in the year. These figures are based on a scale for which the key reference coefficients are as follows:

120	=	Extreme equinoctial spring tide
95	=	Mean spring tide
70	=	An average tide
45	=	Mean neap tide
20	=	The smallest neap tide

Unlike range, which requires knowledge and memory of the spring and neap values of the Standard Port in use (Brest, Wilhelmshaven, Margate, Stornoway etc ...), it is always easy to recall the coefficients above and to know instantly the state of the tide. The coefficients for Brest are included in the MRNA and apply to the whole of NW Europe.

Coefficients are often used at ports which dry or are tidally constrained to indicate the likely access hours at neaps, springs and between times. For example at Perros-Guirec in north Brittany, hours of access are quoted as:

Coeff >70,   approx HW ±1½;
Coeff 60-70,   HW ±1;
Coeff 50-60,   HW −1 to +½;
Coeff 40-50,   HW −½ to HW.

This simple presentation can save a lot of mental gymnastics and may even prevent you from being neaped.

Tidal coefficients could also be used to determine rates of tidal streams on any given day, on a similar principle to that described in 12.9.2 and illustrated in Fig. 12(27). They should simply be substituted on the vertical axis for the values of range, based on coefficient 45 against the neap rate, and coefficient 95 against the spring rate.

French tide tables provide similar information to that in ATT. Standard Ports (below), which as such are not in ATT, may save time and make for greater accuracy: Fécamp, Paimpol, Roscoff, Concarneau, Port-Tudy, Port-Navalo, St Nazaire, Les Sables d'Olonne, La Rochelle, Bordeaux, Bayonne (Boucau) and St Jean-de-Luz.

Secondary ports' time and height differences will need to be interpolated in the same way as in the ATT if proper accuracy is required. However for less precision it could suffice to use spring differences when the coefficient is 70 or more; and neap differences for less than 70.

SHOM produce a useful graph (9004 HQG) for plotting heights/times of HW and LW, enabling heights and times of tide at 5 minute intervals to be quickly extracted.

The terms below describe some of the more common tidal data displayed in French ports:

Chart datum	Zéro des cartes
High water	Pleine mer (PM)
Low water	Basse mer (BM)
Spring tide	Vive-eau (VE)
Neap tide	Morte-eau (ME)
MHWS	Pleine mer moyenne de VE
MHWN	Pleine mer moyenne de ME
MLWN	Basse mer moyenne de ME
MLWS	Basse mer moyenne de VE
GMT/UT	Temps universel (TU)
Below keel allowance	Pied de pilote
Stand (of tide)	Étale
Flood tide	Flot or Flux
Ebb tide	Jusant or Reflux
Standard Port	Port principal
Secondary Port	Port rattaché
Tidal curve	Courbe type de marée
Draught	Tirant d'eau

12.7.8 FRENCH TIDE SIGNALS

At French ports two types of tide signals may be displayed from signal masts, indicating:

a. The height of the tide above CD. The day time signals are a combination of cone, cylinder and ball (or lights by night) as follows:

By day	By night	Meaning
▼	Ⓖ	0.2m (about 8in)
■ (cylinder)	Ⓡ	1.0m (3.3ft)
●	Ⓦ	5.0m (16.4ft)

The three day shapes (or equivalent lights) are hoisted at a yardarm, so that, viewed from seaward, the cones are to the left, and balls to the right of the cylinders in the middle; as shown below. Thus three cones, three cylinders, and one ball means 8.6m height of tide.

b. The state of the tide, as follows:

By day	By night	Meaning
A blue	Ⓖ	Low water
pendant	ⒼⒼ	stand
▲	Ⓖ Ⓦ	Tide rising
White flag with a black St Andrew's cross	ⓌⓌ	High water stand
▼	Ⓦ Ⓖ	Tide falling

12.7.9 CO-TIDAL AND CO-RANGE CHARTS

These charts are used to obtain a tidal prediction (time and height) for some place offshore, as opposed to port or coastal locations which are covered by tide tables. The charts depict Co-Tidal and Co-Range lines, as defined below and in 12.3.14, for the following areas off NW Europe:

5057   Dungeness to Hoek van Holland;
5058   British Isles and adjacent waters; and
5059   Southern North Sea.

Detailed instructions for use are given on the charts.

A Co-Tidal line joins points of equal 'Mean HW (or LW) Time Interval' which in turn is defined as 'the mean time interval between the passage of the Moon over the Prime (Greenwich) Meridian and the time of the next HW (or LW) at the place concerned'.

A Co-Range line joins points of equal 'Mean Spring (or Neap) Range' which in turn is defined quite simply as 'the difference in level between MHWS and MLWS (or MHWN and MLWN)'.

In some tidal regions there are amphidromic points, where the range is very small (less than 1m), but increases away from the centre, sometimes by as much as 1m in 15M. Amphidromic points are depicted by the Co-Range lines. Around the centre the times of HW and LW progress clockwise or anti-clockwise, as portrayed by Co-Tidal lines.

Around the British Isles amphidromic points are found in the southern North Sea, off Poole Bay, off Arklow (SE Eire) and NW of the Mull of Kintyre.

Perhaps a more practical requirement to find time and height of tide at an offshore location occurs in the Thames Estuary, where some pre-planning may pay dividends if intending to navigate through a shallow gat. To this end the 'Tidal Stream Atlas for the Thames Estuary' (NP 249) also contains Co-Tidal and Co-Range charts. These are more clearly arranged and described than charts 5057 – 5059, but prior study would still be worthwhile. The calculations require predictions for Sheerness, Walton-on-the-Naze or Margate, depending on where you are.

12.7.10 HARMONIC CONSTANTS

The study of tides is considerably facilitated by the fact that tidal movements are to all intents and purposes linear with respect to the tide-generating forces. This means that the resultant tide is the direct sum of all the constituents: for example, if the lunar tide is calculated and then the solar tide is calculated, the resultant tide will be the direct sum of the two, there being no inter-action between them.

The harmonic method of tidal analysis and prediction is based on the principle that a complex tidal curve can be broken down into a number of sine curves and that these can be calculated for future dates, reassembled in their correct relationships and so give predictions of hourly heights of the tide. From these values it is possible to determine the times and heights of the turning points of the curve, which are, of course, high water and low water.

Admiralty Tidal Handbook No 1 (NP 122) offers the layman some thought-provoking information about the Admiralty method of harmonic analysis of long term tidal observations (long term meaning about 30 days). The objects of the analysis are to make full and flexible use of the observations; to minimise the amount of arithmetic required; and to get the maximum number of tidal constituents out of the observations.

The following brief summary is for interest or for the purist: Tide-raising forces (Sun and Moon) were discussed in 12.2.1. Their net effect is an oscillatory force which rises to a maximum in one direction, falls to zero, then rises again to a maximum in the opposite direction. A complete cycle lasts about 12 hours (half a lunar day), so the tide is said to be semi-diurnal. The force however is far from regular, for a variety of reasons; but it can be resolved into a number of constituents, each of which is a regular and simple oscillation. For each constituent the Amplitude is the constant maximum to which the constituent rises in either direction; and its Phase is an angle which increases at a constant rate (speed) with time.

Each constituent can be shown to have 'lag', ie behind the tide-raising constituent which produced it. When related to GMT, 'lag' is known as 'g°', a speed in degrees per hour. Its amplitude is known as 'H' in metres. These two quantities for every constituent collectively form the Harmonic 'Tidal Constants' for the place in question; and these appear in Part III of ATT.

The four most important constituents, as shown in Part III of ATT, are:

M_2 The Lunar semi-diurnal constituent
S_2 The Solar semi-diurnal constituent
K_1 The Luni-Solar diurnal constituent
O_1 The Lunar diurnal constituent

Many others can be discovered and normally up to 60 are used in calculating tidal predictions for a Standard Port; in some complex cases up to 120 are used. Distortions of the tidal curve are catered for by using higher harmonics of the basic constituents usually consisting of the Quarter and Sixth diurnals. These are represented in the Admiralty method by F4, f4, F6 and f6. Shallow

Place	Lat	Long	Heights in metres above datum				Datum and Remarks
	N	W	MHWS	MHWN	MLWN	MLWS	
Port of Bristol (Avonmouth)	51°30'	2°44'	13.2	9.8	3.8	1.0	6.50m below Ordnance Datum (Newlyn)
Shirehampton	51°29'	2°41'	12.5	9.1	3.0	1.0	5.80m below Ordnance Datum (Newlyn)
Sea Mills	51°29'	2°39'	11.8	8.3	2.1	0.9	5.00m below Ordnance Datum (Newlyn)
Cumberland Basin Entrance	51°27'	2°37'	10.3	6.8	-	-	3.35m below Ordnance Datum (Newlyn)
Portishead	51°30'	2°45'	13.1	9.7	-	-	6.50m below Ordnance Datum (Newlyn)

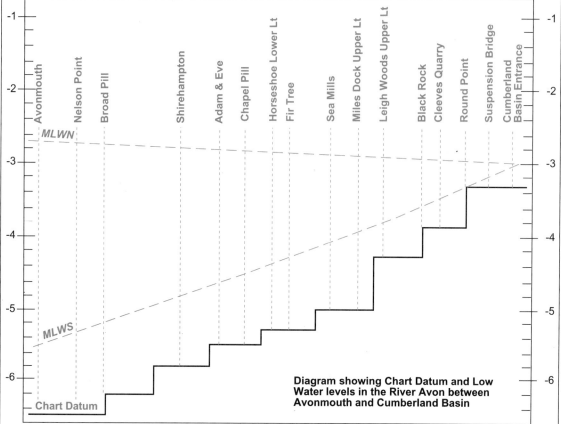

Diagram showing Chart Datum and Low
Water levels in the River Avon between
Avonmouth and Cumberland Basin

Fig. 12(25) Chart Datums and LW levels in the River Avon (Bristol); see chart 1859.

water corrections may also be applied where the effect is noticeable. Seasonal changes in mean sea level are much less significant.

Harmonic constants, as given in Part III of ATT for both Standard and Secondary Ports, are intended for use with the Simplified Harmonic Method of Tidal Prediction (NP 159). These figures enable the most accurate prediction possible to be made, both of the times of HW and LW and of the hourly heights between. The degree of accuracy produced by this method is not normally needed by yachtsmen, since meteorological conditions probably produce a greater difference to the published predictions, than the increased accuracy provided by this method. The results will always differ slightly from the predictions given in Part I which use

many more harmonic constituents, sometimes more than 100 and thus can be expected to be more accurate.

12.7.11 TIDAL DATA ON ADMIRALTY CHARTS

Most large scale charts of the British Isles contain a panel entitled "Tidal levels referred to Datum of Soundings" which shows the heights of MHWS, MHWN, MLWS and MLWN above CD at certain places on the chart. These heights of tide are approximate values at springs and neaps under average conditions, but at extreme springs the range may increase by 20-30%; see Fig. 12(25).

It also shows in the remarks column the height (m) of CD at these places relative to Ordnance Datum (Newlyn); usually below, occasionally above, OD (Newlyn). This is a horizontal plane, or Land Survey Datum, based on mean sea levels recorded at Newlyn from

1915 – 21. The sea level has risen since then, so that OD (Newlyn) is now about 0·2m below the mean sea level at Newlyn.

Any changes in the relative levels of land and sea may be determined by reference to permanent benchmarks ashore. Table III in ATT Vol 1 tabulates the difference in metres between CD and OD (Newlyn) at all UK Standard and Secondary Ports. Table IV does the same for certain foreign ports relative to their national Land Datum. Most of these differences are shown in the MRNA at the foot of each page of the Standard Port Tide tables.

12.8 METEOROLOGICAL INFLUENCES

Meteorological conditions can significantly affect tidal levels and streams. Sea level tends to rise in the direction towards which the wind is blowing, and to be lowered in the other direction. The stronger the wind and the longer it blows, the greater the effect. If the wind shifts direction substantially, say from south to north, it can cause the sea level to oscillate thereby much affecting predicted heights.

Strong winds blowing along a coast can set up long waves which raise sea level at their crest and lower it at their trough. Under exceptional conditions this can raise the height of the tide by two or three metres in what is known as a storm surge; conversely a negative surge can lower the height of low water by one or two metres, which may be more serious for yachtsmen. The southern North Sea is particularly affected by storm surges and by negative surges, especially in the winter.

Tidal heights are predicted for average barometric pressure. When the barometer is high, tidal heights are likely to be lower than predicted, and vice versa. A change of 34 mb/hPa can cause a change of 0.3m in the height of sea level, although this may not occur at once. Severe conditions giving rise to a storm surge, as described above, are likely to be caused by a deep depression, and the low barometric pressure tends to raise sea level still more. The result of these abnormal conditions is naturally more serious at springs than at neaps.

An intense depression or the passage of a line squall can have local effects on the height of water by causing an oscillation (known as a seiche) which can raise or lower sea level a metre or more in the space of a few minutes. Seiches quite often occur around the British Isles, particularly in the winter.

In some parts of the world seasonal changes in the weather, such as the monsoon, can affect sea level. This is taken into account in tidal predictions where sufficient data is available.

12.9 TIDAL STREAMS

12.9.1 INTRODUCTION
Tidal streams are the horizontal movement of water caused by the vertical rise and fall of the tide. With semi-diurnal tides, as occur around the British Isles, the tidal streams reverse their direction every six hours or so, and can be predicted by reference to a suitable Standard Port.

They are quite distinct from ocean currents, which run for long periods in the same direction and are described in 12.1.15. 'Flow' describes tidal stream plus current. Tidal streams (and currents) are described by the direction to which they set, ie a tidal stream setting 180° is flowing from north to south; they may also be referred to as ingoing and outgoing, especially in a river or estuary. Streams are further categorised as rectilinear and rotary; the former implies a set in only two directions, for example east- or west-going as in the English Channel. Rotary streams change direction through 360° in a complete cycle; a good example of this occurs around the Channel Islands.

Fig. 12(26) shows the direction of the main flood stream around the British Isles. It sets mainly to the NE, but also enters the Irish Sea through the North Channel and then sets SE towards the Isle of Man. From Shetland and the Pentland Firth it sets southwards down the east coast as far as the Thames Estuary.

Tidal streams greatly affect yachtsmen in many parts of NW Europe, because they often run at about two knots, and much more strongly in some areas and at springs. In a few places they can reach six to eight knots or more.

Along open coasts the tidal stream does not necessarily turn at HW or LW, but more often near half-tide. The stream usually turns earlier inshore than offshore, sometimes resulting in significant eddies. In open waters round the British Isles, non-tidal currents are not included in tidal stream predictions. But in rivers and estuaries there is often a permanent current caused by river water; such currents are included in tidal stream predictions.

12.9.2 TIDAL STREAM ATLASES
For NW Europe the rate (speed) and set (direction) of tidal streams is shown in the following 17 booklets of Admiralty Tidal Stream Atlases, £7.00 in 2001.

NP	Ed'n	Date	Title
209	4	1986	Orkney and Shetland Islands
218	5	1995	North coast of Ireland, West coast of Scotland
219	2	1991	Portsmouth Hbr and apprs
220	2	1991	Rosyth Harbour and apprs
221	2	1991	Plymouth Harbour and apprs
222	1	1992	Firth of Clyde and apprs

Note: No official tidal stream data is available for the W coast of Ireland, but unofficial tidal arrows are included in the MRNA by courtesy of the Irish Cruising Club.

Each atlas contains 13 charts of the same area (or pairs of charts for wider areas), showing the hourly rate and set of the tidal streams from 6 hours before to six hours after HW at a Standard Port, usually Dover, and often with times at a local Standard Port in brackets. Tidal atlases, due to their small scale, cannot show details of inshore eddies or the tidal inset towards the coast in bays.

The set of the stream is shown by arrows which are graded in weight and length to indicate the rate. Thus → indicates a weak stream, and ➔ indicates a strong stream. The figures against the arrows give the mean neap and spring rates in tenths of a knot, eg 19,34 indicates a mean neap rate of 1·9 knots, and a mean spring rate of 3·4 knots. The position of the comma is approximately where the observations were taken.

The rate at dates between neaps and springs can be interpolated on the graph at Fig. 12(27), which is on the inside front cover of all Atlases with full instructions. The graph has a vertical axis showing values of mean range at Dover or some other Standard Port; note that the mean values for Spring and Neap ranges are shown by two horizontal dotted lines across the graph. The horizontal axis is calibrated in tenths of a knot.

Fig. 12(26) The main flood stream around the UK

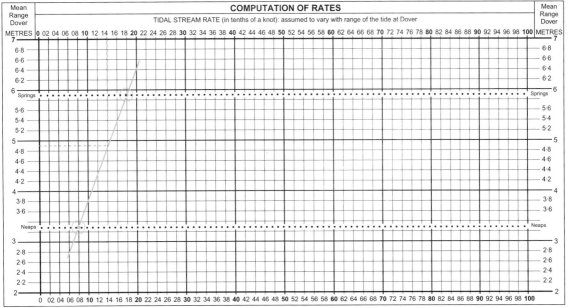

Fig. 12(27) Graph for interpolating tidal stream rates at times between neaps and springs, using Dover predictions and range.

Example problem:

Find the tidal stream rate off the northern tip of Skye at 0420 UT on a day when the predictions for Dover are:

0328	1·4
0819	6·3
1602	1·1
2054	6·4

1. From the tide tables extract the range of tide at Dover for the morning only, in this example 4·9m = (6·3 – 1·4).

	A	51°41'·1N 5°08'·8W		B
Hours	Dir	Rate Sp	(kn) Np	Dir
6		0.0	0.0	
5	013	0.3	0.1	
4	023	0.8	0.4	
3	027	1.1	0.5	
2	023	1.0	0.5	
1	017	0.7	0.	
HW	354	0.3		
1	214	0.5		
2	207	0.9		
3	207			

(left margin labels: "Before HW" brace for hours 6–1; "After HW" brace for hours 1–3)

Fig. 12(28) Tidal stream diamonds on Admiralty charts give hourly set and rate at Springs and Neaps.

2. Note from the tidal stream atlas the mean spring and neap rates for the time and position required. The appropriate chart in Tidal Stream Atlas NP 218, or in 9.8.3 of the MRNA, is that for '4 hours before HW Dover' which shows mean rates of 08,18 (0·8 knots at neaps and 1·8 knots at springs).

3. In the graph (Computation of Rates) plot these rates on the mean Neap and Mean Spring dotted lines and join them with a diagonal line.

4. From where this diagonal cuts the horizontal line for Dover range that day (4·9m), go vertically to the top or bottom scale and read off the rate, 14 or 1·4 knots. QED.

A perspex sheet or tracing paper can be laid on top of the graph to preserve it for future use.

12.9.3   TIDAL STREAM DIAMONDS

On some Admiralty charts hourly tidal streams (rate and set) can be read from a Table. Diamond-shaped symbols, identified by letters, are marked in positions for which the Table gives the latitude and longitude, followed by the set and spring/neap rates for each hour before and after HW at the local Standard Port. Where relevant, any river current is normally included.

The example shown in Fig. 12(28) is for position Ⓐ on chart 3274, where tidal streams are referenced to HW Milford Haven. The set is given in °T far more precisely than the vectors shown in a Tidal stream atlas. In the approaches to a large or complex port area there may be a generous distribution of diamonds, principally for the benefit of large ships.

Also on some charts the flood and ebb streams

are depicted by an arrow, respectively with ⟶ _3kn_ ⟶ and without feathers ⟶ _3kn_ ⟶ . The mean spring rate is given alongside as, say, 3kn.

12.9.4 TIDAL STREAMS IN SAILING DIRECTIONS

Admiralty Sailing Directions describe tidal streams along each section of the coast in some detail. This will usually include times of slack water and when the tide turns; the rate at springs and neaps; and tidal hazards, such as races, overfalls, eddies and whirls. Times are referenced to HW at the nearest Standard Port using a four-figure group, in which the first two figures are hours and the last two are minutes, usually to the nearest five minutes, eg –0615 means 6¼ hours before HW. This data, in as much detail as space allows, is included in the MRNA under Passage Information.

12.9.5 TIDAL STREAM PREDICTIONS IN TIDE TABLES

In some parts of the world, tidal streams are not related to the predicted times of HW at any Standard Port, or are completely unrelated to the tidal pattern. For such places, eg the entrance to San Francisco Bay, Vols 3 and 4 of the ATT give: the direction of the rectilinear set, and daily predictions of the times of slack water and of the maximum rates and their values. The tables also show curves for three types of tidal stream (dominant semi-diurnal, mixture of semi-diurnal and diurnal, and dominant diurnal); and how currents may be taken into account.

12.9.6 TIDAL STREAMS IN RIVERS

Generally the flood stream is slightly stronger than the ebb, and it runs harder during the first half of the rise of tide, but its duration is less.

In rivers tidal streams are influenced by local weather conditions as well as by the phases of the Moon. Strong and prolonged winds blowing up an estuary will increase both the rate and duration of the flood stream, and correspondingly reduce the ebb. This may increase the height of tide within the river, at least temporarily. When the wind decreases the ebb stream runs more strongly until the normal level is restored.

At or near springs, in a river which is obstructed for example by sandbanks at the entrance, the time of HW gets later going up river. The time of LW also gets later, but more rapidly. So the duration of the rise of tide becomes shorter, and the duration of the fall of tide becomes longer. At

the entrance the flood stream starts at an interval after LW which increases with the degree of obstruction to the channel, and this interval between LW and the start of the flood increases with the distance up river. However, the ebb begins soon after local HW along the length of the river. Thus the duration of the flood is less than that of the ebb, and the difference increases with the distance up river.

At neaps the flood and ebb both start soon after local LW and HW respectively, and their durations and rates are roughly equal.

Both at springs and neaps recent precipitation can affect the stream, such that the ebb's duration and rate are increased, whilst the flood's are reduced.

12.10 BOOKS ABOUT THE SEA AND TIDES

The Mariner's Handbook, Chapter 4 (NP 100).

Ocean Passages for the World (NP 136).

Admiralty Manual of Tides (NP 120).

Admiralty Tide Tables, (NP 201, 202, 203 & 204):
Vol 1 – UK and Eire, plus European Channel ports.
Vol 2 – Europe (excluding the UK and Eire), the Mediterranean Sea and the Atlantic Ocean.
Vol 3 – Indian Ocean and South China Sea.
Vol 4 – Pacific Ocean.
Vols 3 and 4 also include tidal stream tables.

Admiralty Method of Tidal Prediction (NP 159).

Admiralty Tidal Handbooks (NP 122, 1–3):
No 1   Admiralty Method of Harmonic Tidal analysis for long period observations (1985)
No 2   Datums for Hydrographic Surveys (1975)
No 3   Admiralty Method of Harmonic Tidal analysis for short period observations (1986)

Tidal Harmonic Constants, European waters (NP 160).

Dynamic Oceanography by J. Proudman.

Seastate and Tides by Ken Duxbury (Stanford Maritime).

The Tide by H. A. Marmer (Appleton & Co).

The Tides and Kindred Phenomena by G. H. Darwin (Murray).

Waves and Beaches by W. Bascorn (Doubleday & Co).

Tides and Currents by David Arnold (Fernhurst)

Chapter 13 Safety, Distress and First Aid

CONTENTS

Assuming that a boat is handled sensibly and prudently, implying that good seamanship is used, safety afloat is ultimately a matter of preparation: making sure that the boat is well found and properly fitted out, and that the skipper and his crew are ready to cope with any emergency by knowing how to use the right equipment.

Prevention is always better than cure, and at sea it is easier to forestall an accident than to retrieve the situation. For example, fire prevention is infinitely preferable to fire fighting; careful pilotage is more satisfactory than having to kedge off the shore; listening to the weather forecast (and interpreting it correctly) is a lot more comfortable than getting caught out unexpectedly in gale force winds; and proper engine maintenance is safer and cheaper than a tow into harbour.

However accidents can sometimes happen even on board the best organised boat, and on such occasions it is vital that all on board know how best to deal with the particular emergency, and the correct procedures for seeking help should it be required.

The owner or skipper has a direct and inescapable responsibility for the safety of the crew and the boat. He must be knowledgeable, prepared to make quick decisions on all matters, and able to anticipate what the next problem might be.

The Crew

As regards the crew he has an important responsibility for their proper management and training.

Young people should themselves grasp every opportunity to learn the basic skills of seamanship and navigation by getting afloat in boats belonging to relatives or friends – you can never start too young. In addition, newcomers to the sport are encouraged to participate in the various proficiency and training schemes which are administered by the Royal Yachting Association. These cover every aspect of the sport: dinghy sailing, wind-surfing, ski-boats and runabouts, coastal and offshore cruising under either sail or power. All these training courses lead to recognised RYA/DTp Certificates for those who qualify at the various levels of expertise.

Individual crew members are responsible for taking with them personal items of equipment, some of which are discussed in more detail below. For comfort and for the safety of the individual, and ultimately of the entire crew, it is essential to be properly clothed at sea. Non-slip shoes or sea boots should be worn by everybody on board, and even in mid-summer all should have foul weather clothing with close fastenings at neck, wrists and ankles, and with a hood or suitable hat. Take at least two changes of sailing clothing, including warm sweaters and towelling neck scarves. Other personal items include a sailor's knife and spike, on a lanyard; a waterproof electric torch, and a personal supply of anti-seasickness pills if you are a sufferer.

Lifejackets and safety harnesses (which are discussed in 13.3.6 and 13.3.7) are usually supplied on board, but if an individual prefers to take his own, the owner or skipper should check that they are to the required standard.

The Boat

The skipper must ensure that the boat meets various safety criteria and that she has a number of safety factors built-in to her, in particular that:

i. Her basic design and construction are suitable for her intended purpose.
ii. She is properly maintained.
iii. She has a competent crew, with some reserve of strength for unforeseen events.
iv. She is fitted with suitable gear which will withstand all conditions likely to be met.
v. In the event of an accident, emergency equipment must be on board enabling the crisis to be overcome – and the crew must know how to use it.

Safety check list

Before going to sea, check the following items:

❑ Boat in seaworthy condition
❑ Engine in running order
❑ Lubricating oil checked
❑ Engine coolant checked
❑ Handbook, tools, spares onboard
❑ Sufficient fuel onboard
❑ Bilge clear and pump working
❑ Anchor gear correct
❑ Fire extinguishers
❑ Flares in date
❑ Lifejackets for all onboard
❑ Seagoing clothing
❑ VHF radio working
❑ Safety harnesses
❑ Compass and charts
❑ Torches and batteries
❑ Radar reflector
❑ Man overboard gear
❑ First Aid box
❑ Liferaft
❑ Local weather forecast
❑ Tidal state
❑ Somebody ashore knows where you are bound, and estimated time of arrival/return

13.2 SAFETY AND THE LAW

13.2.1 LEGAL REQUIREMENTS

Certain safety equipment is required by law to be carried in yachts. Owners of larger yachts, more than 13·7m (45ft) LOA, must comply with the requirements of the Merchant Shipping (Life Saving Appliances) Rules 1980 and the Merchant Shipping (Fire Appliances) Rules 1965, obtainable from TSO.

All yachts must be equipped with the necessary navigation lights and means of giving sound signals as required by the IRPCS.

Yachts when racing are usually required to carry at least a certain minimum of safety equipment, as prescribed by the class, club or organisation involved. For example yachts competing under the International Offshore Rule (IOR) or in other offshore events must normally comply with special safety regulations prescribed for different categories of races by the Offshore Racing Council (ORC), available from the Royal Ocean Racing Club Rating Office, Seahorse Building, Bath Road, Lymington, Hants SO41 9SE. Tel 01590 677030; Fax 01590 679478.

Commercially operated UK yachts up to 24m LOA are subject to the Merchant Shipping (Vessels in Commercial use for Sport and Pleasure) Regulations 1993. The Sail Training Ship Code of Practice has been amended to cover all such vessels, with a parallel code for motor yachts used commercially.

13.2.2 RYA RECOMMENDATIONS FOR BOATS UP TO 13.7M (45FT) LOA

The RYA (see booklet C8/98) puts yachts in categories A-D depending on LOA, where they sail and the risk of being caught out in rough weather, as follows:

A	Ocean	Ocean passages of any length. LOA likely to be longer than 10m.
B	Offshore	Yachts which make offshore passages of 50 - 500M around the UK & NW Europe. LOA likely to be 8-13·7m.
C	Inshore	Coastal cruises by day/night, within 10M of land and 4 hours of a port of refuge. LOA likely to be less than 8m.
D	Sheltered	In estuaries, inshore or inland waters, day only. Within 1 hour of a port of refuge. LOA of yachts likely to be less than 6m.

TABLE 1. Based on these risk levels, the following is a precis of the main items of safety equipment recommended to be carried. Note: A bullet • recommends that the item be carried, but the number, method or contents is left to the skipper.	CATEGORY			
	A	B	C	D
1. **Means of propulsion (**Sailing yachts only)				
1.2 A trysail, or deep reef to reduce the mainsail luff to 60% of full hoist, and a storm jib	•	•	•	
1.3 For engine starting, a battery isolated from all other electrical systems, or hand cranking	•	•	•	
2. **Number of anchors,** with appropriate lengths/diameter of warp & chain or chain only	2+	2	2	1
3. **Bailing and bilge pumping** (see 13.3.2)				
3.2 Buckets of 9-14 ltrs capacity with lanyard and strongly secured handle	2	2	2	
3.3 Manual bilge pumps, operable with all hatches closed	2	2	1	
3.4 Softwood bungs attached adjacent to all through-hull fittings, able to be closed	•	•	•	•
4. **Detection equipment**				
4.1 Radar reflector properly mounted and as big as is reasonable (see 13.3.1)	•	•	•	
4.2 Fixed nav lights, iaw IRPCS; 4.3 Foghorn; 4.4 Powerful torch	•	•	•	
Motoring cone (sail only); anchor ball and light	•	•	•	•
5. **Pyrotechnics (in date)**				
5.1 Hand-held red flares	6	4	4	2
5.2 Buoyant orange smoke signals	2	2		
5.3 Red parachute rockets	1	2	4	2
5.4 Hand-held orange smoke signals			2	2
5.5 Hand-held white flares	4	4	4	
6. **Fire fighting equipment** (see 13.3.5 and 13.8.3)				
6.1 Fire blanket (BS EN 1869) for all yachts with cooking equipment	•	•	•	•
6.2 For yachts with a galley or carrying engine fuel: multi-purpose extinguishers of minimum fire rating 5A/34B to BS EN 3	3	2	1	1
6.3 Additionally, for yachts with both a galley and carrying engine fuel: multi-purpose extinguishers of minimum fire rating 5A/34B to BS EN 3	1	1	1	1
6.4 Additionally, for yachts with engines over 25hp, a fixed automatic or semi-automatic fire fighting system to discharge into the engine space	•	•	•	•
7. **Personal safety equipment for each crew member** (see 13.3.6, .7 and .8)				
7.1 Warm clothing, oilskins, seaboots and hat	•	•	•	•
7.3 Lifejacket (BS EN 396) 150 Newtons	1	1	1	
7.4 Lifejacket light	1	1		

TABLE 1. *continued*

		A	B	C	D
7.5	Spray face cover; 7.7 Immersion suit, per crew member	1			
7.6	Safety harness, per crew member (for yachts with enclosed wheelhouse, one harness for 50% of the crew)	1	1	1	
7.8	Jackstays and cockpit clip-on strong points	•	•	•	•
8.	**Liferaft** (see 13.3.10)				
8.1	Inflatable dinghy, designed or adapted for saving life, sufficient for all on board		1	1	
8.2	Liferaft, designed solely for saving life, sufficient for all on board	1			
8.3	Emergency grab-bag (see text for contents)	1	1	1	
9.	**Man overboard recovery equipment** (see 13.3.9)				
9.1	Horseshoe life-belts fitted with drogue and self-igniting light	2	2	1	
9.2	Buoyant sling on floating line – may replace 1 horseshoe lifebelt if 2 are carried	1	1		
9.3	Buoyant heaving line, at least 30m long, with quoit	1	1	1	
9.4	Boarding ladder capable of rapid and secure attachment	1	1	1	
9.5	Dan buoy with a large flag	1	1		
10.	**Radio**				
10.1	Radio receiver able to receive forecasts on 198kHz and local radio station forecasts	1	1	1	1
10.2	VHF Marine band radio telephone	1	1	1	1
10.3	Digital Selective Calling controller to class D (MPT 1279)	1	1		
10.4	Marine band HF/SSB radio; 10.5 406 MHz EPIRB registered in the vessel's name	1			
10.6	Navtex; 10.8 Emergency VHF radio aerial; 10.9 Waterproof hand-held VHF radio	1	1		
10.7	Radar transponder (SART)	1			
11.	**Navigational equipment**				
11.2	Charts, tide tables and navigational publications of the cruising area and adjacent areas	•	•	•	
11.3	Steering compass, able to be illuminated	1	1	1	1
11.5	Drawing instruments; 11.6 Barometer; 11.7 Echosounder & lead-line; 11.9 Watch or clock	1	1	1	
11.8	Radio nav system, Loran C and/or GPS	1	1		
11.10	Distance measuring log; 11.11 Binoculars	1	1	1	
11.12	Sextant, the Nautical Almanac (TSO) and sight reduction tables	1			
12.	**First aid kit and manual** (see 13.8.28/30)	1	1	1	
13.	**General equipment**				
13.1	Emergency tiller (all wheel-steered vessels)	1	1	1	1
13.2	Towing warp; 13.10 Bosun's chair (sit harness BS EN 813 1997)	1	1	1	
13.3	Warps and fenders; 13.6 Repair tools; 13.7 Spares, engine, electrics, shackles and twine	•	•	•	•
13.4	Waterproof torch	3	2	2	1
13.5	Rigid or inflatable tender	•	•	•	
13.8	Emergency fresh water, separate from main tanks; 13.9 Emergency repair materials	•	•		

13.2.3 MARINE ACCIDENT INVESTIGATION BRANCH (MAIB)

The MAIB is the government organisation that investigates accidents involving UK vessels anywhere in the world, and any vessels inside the UK 12-mile limit. Most of their work involves merchant ships and registered fishing vessels, but serious yachting accidents may be investigated, particularly if the yacht is being operated commercially.

The MAIB is entirely independent of the MCA. They do not prosecute nor attribute blame – their investigations seek to find out how and why an accident happened and what lessons might be learned to prevent it happening again. All their reports are published and Safety Digests, containing brief reports of investigations and their findings, are distributed free of charge, three times a year, to whoever requests them. A good deal of information is available via MAIB's website www.maib.detr.gov.uk

The MAIB can be contacted at: Marine Accident Investigation Branch, First Floor, Carlton House, Carlton Place, Southampton SO15 2DZ. Tel 023 8039 5500; Fax 023 8023 2459. maib@detr.gov.uk

13.3 SAFETY EQUIPMENT

13.3.1 RADAR REFLECTORS

Steel or aluminium objects (the most likely metals used in yacht construction) will reflect a radar beam if they are hit at the correct angle, but timber and glassfibre return no worthwhile echo at all; even a metal mast is a poor reflector, due to its shape. So the average yacht can be considered almost invisible to radar.

To avoid collision a ship should be able to detect and plot an echo from a boat at a range of at least 5 n miles, and to achieve and sustain this detection it is essential that the boat has an efficient radar reflector.

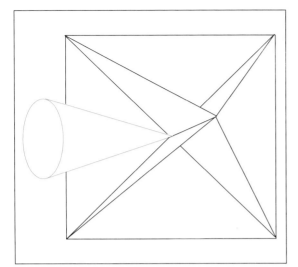

Fig. 13(1) A standard octahedral reflector showing an imaginary cone in which the best reflections are returned.

Many yachts rely on a simple octahedral reflector, consisting of three metal surfaces (usually aluminium sheet) mounted at right angles to each other. This type of reflector has six points around it, and eight internal corners each of which forms a 're-entrant trihedral'. When a radar beam encounters one of these re-entrant trihedrals, it is reflected off the sides (usually all three) and returned in a direction parallel to that whence it came.

Maximum reflection is obtained when the radar beam is directed into a corner within a cone, as in Fig. 13(1). In an octahedral reflector there are eight such corners, and hence eight such cones for maximum reflection. Within these eight cones reflection is good, elsewhere less so.

For the best 360° reflection, an octahedral reflector should be mounted in the aptly called 'catch rain' position (the attitude it adopts when standing on a level surface). But in this position one of the optimum cones is pointing straight upwards and one is pointing straight downwards. The other six point sideways, three of them angled 20° above the horizontal and three of them 20° below. So that, when the boat is upright, none of the six reflecting corners are working at maximum efficiency.

If the polar diagram is plotted to show the strength of reflection for the complete 360° around the boat, this will typically indicate six equally spaced sectors of about 35° each where reflection is good, with gaps in between where reflection is considerably reduced. A different pattern will emerge when the boat is heeled.

For adequate responses an octahedral reflector needs to be quite large, with a diagonal length of at least 460mm (18in), so that each

reflecting corner has sides of 230mm (9in). It must be stoutly made so that the plates remain flat and perpendicular to each other. The reflector must be hoisted in the 'catch rain' attitude already described, and at a height of at least 4m (13ft) above the waterline.

Some octahedral reflectors have circular (rather than pointed) corners, formed by the intersection of three circular plates at right angles to each other, instead of three square plates. These have some advantage because the reflecting ability is increased relative to overall size.

More sophisticated types of reflector overcome some of the shortcomings of the octahedral. One is the Firdell Blipper 210-7, an array of reflecting corners stacked vertically and enclosed in a cylindrical plastic case for protection and to reduce windage. This is permanently mounted on the mast as high as is feasible. It measures 595mm long by 240mm diameter and weighs 1.8kg.

A French reflector contains reflective metal discs in a tube approx 50mm diameter by 500mm long. It can be hoisted on a halyard or secured to the wire shrouds.

The most uniform reflection through 360° in azimuth (right round the horizon) is provided by the Lensref reflectors, which work on the principle of the Luneberg dielectric lens. This consists of a spherical lens, so constructed that the density of the material is graded as a function of the radius, being greatest in the centre. This has the effect of focusing an incoming radar beam on to a reflecting band, which is fitted round the 'equator' of the sphere and returns the beam along a path parallel to that on which it arrived. The width of the reflecting band dictates the angle of heel which the device can accommodate, but the width cannot be too much or it blanks off an undue proportion of the incoming beam. Performance is good up to 15° of heel, but then falls off sharply.

Yet another reflector is the Visiball Mk II designed for mounting on the top of the mast, with a navigation light fixed above it. The Visiball is said to be unaffected by heel and to provide uniform, consistent 360° coverage.

13.3.2 BILGE PUMPS

Modern GRP hulls should not normally take water into the bilge, but in any boat adequate pumping arrangements must be provided, and periodically tested, in case they are ever needed for emergency use.

Any seagoing boat should have at least two suitable pumps, which can be operated off the engine, electrically driven or worked manually. If an engine driven or electrical pump is fitted it must be augmented by a powerful manual pump in case no power is available. An electrical pump can be float controlled, and therefore cope with any water accumulated while the boat is lying idle.

A manual bilge pump must be sited where it is easy to use, remembering that considerable and prolonged effort may be called for in an emergency, and also so that it can be conveniently dismantled for cleaning and inspection. The diaphragms, seals and valves of manual pumps should be examined at least once a season, and it is sensible to carry spares for these parts. Any bilge pump should be fitted with a good strainer in the bilge, which must be easily accessible for cleaning.

Limber holes in the bilges must be kept clear so that water can drain to the pump section. Any dirt which is allowed to accumulate in the bilges will soon cause a blockage, and for this reason alone it is important that bilges be kept clear of all forms of dirt and debris.

Any opening below the waterline is a threat to the watertight integrity of the boat, and must be fitted with a seacock which can be shut in the event of any failure of pipes or fittings. It is important that these are kept free, and are easy to access. A few soft wood plugs of different sizes are useful for stopping leaks.

13.3.3   UNDERWATER HULL DAMAGE

Although thankfully it is not common, it is not unknown for a yacht to suffer underwater damage – perhaps due to collision with submerged wreckage, or even a whale. Large baulks of timber and semi-submerged containers are particularly dangerous. If such impact damage results in cracks or splits in the hull, most of the inflow of water may be stemmmed by driving in small, soft wood wedges wrapped with pieces of rag, always provided that the damaged area is accessible.

If the hull is actually holed, rather than just cracked or split, a very large quantity of water will start to pour into the boat, far above the capacity of any pumps installed. For example, a hole 6 inches square at 2 feet below the waterline will admit about 2275 litres (500 gallons) of water a minute, which is sufficient to sink a small yacht within a couple of minutes. Certain smaller yachts (such as the Etap range, built in Belgium, and the Sadler 29 in this country) have two skins with foam buoyancy in between them, to make the boat unsinkable – a commendable safety feature. The survival of an ordinary yacht, however, will depend on finding the damage very quickly, and immediately

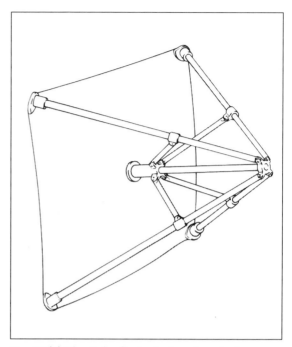

Fig. 13(2) The Subrella leak-stopping device can be pushed through a hole in the hull and then opened on the outside, to make a seal.

reducing the rate of flooding to something that can be controlled by the pumps.

Collision mats were invented more than a century ago. and have proved their efficiency on many occasions. Traditionally made of heavy canvas with ropes at each corner, a collision mat can be drawn over the outside of the hull so that it covers the damaged area, whereupon the pressure of the seawater presses it tightly against the hull, to stem at least most of the leak. It is obvious, however, that this would need to be done very quickly indeed to cope with a hole of any significant size.

More practical for easy stowage and rapid deployment is the Subrella, an umbrella-like device made in three sizes, which is pushed through the hole from the inside and then opens on the outside; see Fig. 13(2). Water pressure spreads the patch over the hole and forms an effective seal. If it is impossible to get at the hole from inboard, due to parts of the boat's structure, the Subrella can also be inserted from outboard. To be effective (and it is) the Subrella must be instantly available, ie stowed in a handy spot – not at the bottom of a cockpit locker. It is available from DCG Banbury, 1 Longfellow Rd, Banbury, Oxon OX16 9LB. Tel/Fax 01295 257707. e-mail subrella97@aol.com Website http:// members.aol.com/subrella97 or via www.ybw.com

Typically hull damage may not allow repairs to be made from inside the hull. GRP often

fractures or splits over a relatively small area –
which is still able to let in a huge amount of
water. For example a 2in diameter hole, 1ft
below the waterline, will admit about 2,200 galls
in the first hour. The Kollision Kit is purpose built
to deal with such damage, and other minor
repairs to pipes and structures. It contains a fast
curing, two-part Epoxy specially formulated for
use underwater and tolerant of inexact mixing
ratios (when you are in a hurry). Apply to a
suitably sized patch and press into place on the
outside of the hull; water pressure will hold it
there and the epoxy will harden in about 5
minutes to a strong watertight seal. Available
from IES, Unit 6, Braxton Court, Lymore Lane,
Milford on Sea SO41 0TX. Tel 01590 641444; Fax
01590 641222. info@epoxysolutions.co.uk
www.epoxysolutions.co.uk

13.3.4 GUARDRAILS
A seagoing boat should have double guardrails,
the top one not less than 0.6m (2ft) above the
deck, well supported by stanchions at intervals of
not more than about 2.15m (7ft). The heel
fittings of the stanchions must be through
bolted, so that they are securely fitted.
Guardrails should be kept taut by bottlescrews or
lanyards.

A sturdy pulpit forward gives much needed
security for sail changing or anchor work. It, too,
needs to be firmly bolted through the deck.
Cruising boats usually have a pushpit (or similar
arrangement) aft. This can be used for stowing
lifebuoys, some liferafts, man overboard devices,
antennae, outboard mounting bracket and
dodgers with the boat's name clearly shown to
port and starboard.

13.3.5 FIRE PREVENTION
Any boat contains a lot of flammable equipment
even discounting such obvious hazards as fuel
and bottled gas. Hence fire prevention is the first
priority. See also 13.8.3 for fire fighting.

Even if smokers are careful with matches,
lighters, ash etc; and the fuel and gas systems
are properly installed, well maintained and
sensibly used, the risks should never be under-
estimated. There are more than 350 fires every
year on leisure craft, many of which are
apprently well maintained and sensibly manned.
Carelessness, fatigue and inexperience all
contribute to a potential hazard of frightening
proportions and consequences.

Smoking in a small boat should be
discouraged. Even if it is acceptable to all
aboard, great care is needed when disposing of
matches, ashes and cigarette ends; smoking in
bunks is too risky to be allowed. Precautions are

also necessary on deck to make sure that lighted
material does not go down an open hatch or
locker lid. Cigarette ends have been known to
enter open port holes and cause fires.

Most galley fires are caused by the ignition of
hot fat or oil, and deep fat frying should be
avoided afloat. If liquid fuels such as paraffin or
alcohol are used there is an obvious danger from
spillage.

Electrical faults are a major cause of fires. Do
not assume that a 12 volt system is innocuous;
Chapter 21 makes clear that excessive current, as
caused by a typical short circuit, is a very real
hazard. So too is poor insulation due to chafing
or old age.

Gas systems
Bottled gas (normally butane) is the commonest
cooker fuel in British boats. Propane is similar, but
can be used in lower temperatures than butane.
Both are heavier than air, so if they leak they sink
to the bottom of a space or into the bilge, where
they can collect until an explosive mixture (about
2% to 11% by volume) is built up.

It is a sensible precaution to fit a gas detector
which will warn of any leak before a dangerous
concentration is reached. The sensor should be
fitted in the lowest part of the bilge, but above
the normal level which any bilge water might
reach. Gas detectors should be wired up so that
they can be switched on before any other
electrical equipment in the boat is used. The
simplest detectors have a single head, whilst
dual-alarms allow detectors to be fitted in the
bilge and near the cooker. Some of these have a
solenoid-operated shut off valve in the pipeline.

The smallest leak in a gas system will be
indicated by a 'bubbler' gas leak detector, such
as the Alde 4071-905, available from Calor Gas
dealers. It should be connected in the pipeline
close downstream of the regulator. It gives an
instant visual check that the system is gas-tight
from the regulator outlet side to each installed
appliance, a leaking system being positively
indicated by bubbles appearing in the glass
sighting chamber.

If gas is smelt extinguish all naked lights and
smoking materials, do not run any electrical
equipment or engines, and ventilate the boat
thoroughly. Pump the gas from the bilges with a
manual diaphragm-type bilge pump. Check the
entire gas system for leaks by carefully testing all
pipe unions with soapy water; do not use gas
until the defect has been found and repaired.

All work on gas installations and fittings must
be done by a 'competent person', somebody
with suitable work experience and trained in
accordance with the Health and Safety
Commission's 'Approved Code of Practice'. The

British Standard BS 5482 for LPG installations in boats has been replaced by European Standard EN ISA10239.

Gas bottles should be stowed in a dedicated locker on deck with an overside drain at the bottom. Failing this, the locker must be gas tight to the hull, but again with an overboard drain which emerges above the waterline. The bottle(s) must be securely fixed with a metal bracket or a strong lashing; shock cord is inadequate. If the bottle is thrown on its side or inverted, liquid gas may enter and pass through the regulator, causing a seventy-fold rise in pressure in the low pressure section of the installation. Bottles may be linked together by a manual or automatic change-over valve, so that when one is empty the other can be turned on to operate through the same regulator and supply pipe. If this means too big a locker it is not much trouble to bring in a spare and link up after taking away the empty. Gas should always be turned off at the cylinder after every cooking or heating session – not just at the end of the day.

Gas piping must be stainless steel or seamless copper, routed high in the boat, well clipped and kept as short as possible. Flexible connections should only be used at the cylinder end or at a gimballed stove, and must conform to BS 3212 Flexible Tubing or Hose for Use in Butane/Propane Gas Installations.

Gas appliances (cookers and water or cabin heaters) must be designed for butane/propane gas and conform to the European Standard. New appliances must carry the CE mark in accordance with the European Gas appliance Directive. Appliances with pilot lights, such as water heaters, should incorporate a flame failure device to shut off the gas supply if the pilot light goes out. Adequate ventilation must be provided to prevent a build up of carbon monoxide or carbon dioxide. When a cooker or similar appliance is not in use, or in bad weather, and always before leaving the boat, the gas should be turned off at the bottle. Remote control valves are available.

To maintain safety and efficiency the system should be serviced annually by a competent person. More information on gas systems is given in 19.2.3.

Fuel systems

A boat's fuel system is the other major fire risk, particularly if the fuel is petrol. Even the smallest leak must be eliminated, and care must be taken with spills when refuelling. The fuel filler must be on deck so that any overflow does not go into the bilges, and so that fumes displaced from the tank are vented into the fresh air. The air vent

from the tank should go to a protected place on deck and be covered with a gauze.

There must be a shut off valve (easily accessible) on the fuel line where it leaves the top of the tank, and the entire fuel system should be professionally fitted using materials of approved standards.

Particular care must be taken when refuelling or when working on any part of the fuel system – cleaning filters for example. At such times it is essential to stop smoking and have no naked lights in the vicinity. On completion of the work make quite certain that all joints are tight. In the event of a spill mop up as much fuel as possible and thoroughly ventilate the area.

Before starting an engine, always first run the engine compartment exhaust fan (where fitted) for five minutes, and inspect the engine space for any smell of fuel.

13.3.6 LIFEJACKETS

Good lifejackets are quite expensive but they are essential items of equipment for any sea-going boat. They should be worn in bad conditions, or by non-swimmers whenever they are on deck or in the cockpit of a boat at sea. Lifejackets may also save lives when going ashore in a smaller tender in a tideway – or returning, particularly at night or in adverse weather.

For each person on board a sea-going boat there should be a lifejacket which conforms to the EC Standards (see below) which in July 1995 superseded the former BS 3595. Both Standards stipulated minimum buoyancy levels for adults and children; and the ability to support the head of an unconscious person so that the mouth is clear of the water; and turn an unconscious or exhausted person from being face down onto his back in five seconds. Another requirement is a becket (loop) to enable the wearer to be lifted from the water.

Lifejackets and Personal Buoyancy Aids (PBA) are two separate items: the former is inflatable and has a higher degree of buoyancy than the latter which is of closed cell foam; there are hybrid versions. All lifejackets can be inflated orally and the better ones by a small CO_2 gas cylinder either manually or automatically activated.

Gas inflation must not be used if the lifejacket has already been inflated orally; nor must the lifejacket be inflated orally before entering the water. Automatic inflation is achieved by a hydrostatic valve which operates by water pressure when 150mm (6in) below the water; this has the significant advantage that the lifejacket will inflate itself even if the wearer is unconscious on entering the water.

The European specifications for buoyancy aids and lifejackets carry the CE Mark of Approval. The new EN standard is measured in Newtons (N), where 10N = 1kg or 2·2lbs. There are four levels of minimum performance; the higher the Newton number, the greater the buoyancy. The ratings quoted below are for adults:

(1) A 50N Buoyancy Aid gives 5·5kg (11 lbs) of buoyancy; only suitable for competent swimmers in sheltered waters with help close at hand, (EN 393).

(2) A 100N Buoyancy Aid gives 11kg (22lb) of buoyancy; suitable for swimmers and non-swimmers in calm coastal waters. Self-righting is not guaranteed, (EN 395).

(3) A 150N Lifejacket with 16kg (33lb) of buoyancy is the standard that should suffice for the average yachtsman who cruises off NW Europe in the summer, but it may not immediately self-right an unconscious person, (EN 396).

(4) A 275N Lifejacket is a high performance device providing 28kg (63lb) of buoyancy for offshore use and severe conditions. It is most suitable in commercial use when, for example, oilrig workers are using tools and heavy waterproof clothing in hazardous conditions. In most conditions it can turn an unconscious person from face-down to on his back in the minimum time, (EN 399).

For inland waters, where help is readily at hand for a person who goes overboard, a PBA is

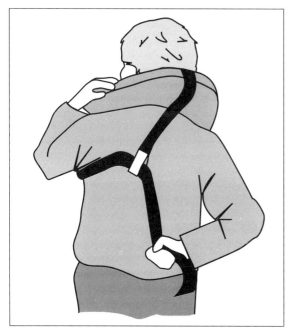

Fig. 13(3) To put on a lifejacket, read the instructions, then put your head through the hole, and secure the waistband at side or front.

acceptable. It is more comfortable to wear than the average lifejacket, but provides less flotation and is only intended to be sufficiently buoyant to help a conscious person reach safety.

When buying a lifejacket try it on inflated. It should provide firm support to the neck, and should not allow the head to fall forward. The straps must be properly adjusted to suit individual wearers; this is particularly important in the case of youngsters. Special sizes are available for children.

Most lifejackets are bright orange or red in colour, which makes them more visible in the water. Some have strips of retro-reflective tape around the collar and an anti-spray hood. They should also be fitted with a whistle attached to a lanyard, and preferably have an automatic light which switches on when immersed in water. It is recommended that a lifejacket or a combined lifejacket-and-harness should be fitted with a crutch or thigh strap to stop it riding up.

Lifejackets must be checked periodically and stowed in a dry, accessible locker, of which the crew is aware.

One of the main UK manufacturers of life-jackets and associated gear is Crewsaver, Mumby Rd, Gosport, Hants PO12 1AQ. Tel 023 9252 8621; Fax 023 9251 0905. sales@crewsaver.co.uk www.crewsaver.co.uk

13.3.7 SAFETY HARNESSES

In bad weather or at night it becomes doubly important to prevent any crew member falling over the side; so the skipper must ensure that those on deck are wearing safety harnesses, and that these are clipped to suitable strong points – not to the guardrails or parts of the standing or running rigging.

Safety harnesses must conform to EN 1095, the European Standard, which is based on the three main reasons for wearing a safety harness:

a. To secure the wearer on deck;
b. Prevent a wearer from falling in the water; and
c. To assist their recovery back on deck.

NB: They are not intended to prevent falls from a height.

EN 1095 requires minimum sizes and strengths for all the component parts – the webbing straps, the securing line, and the snap hook at the end. Apart from being strong enough, metal fittings must also be non-magnetic. A harness must be properly adjusted for the wearer, so that the point of attachment for the safety line is high on the chest. It is desirable that a safety harness should be fitted with a crotch strap, and RORC Special Regulations insist on this.

It is useful if the harness has two clips, one

on short stay and one on a longer line for working on deck. In bad weather a crew member should be hooked to a fixed part of the boat's structure before emerging from the cabin into the cockpit. Jackstays (13.3.8) rigged along the deck allow people to move forward and aft without continually having to alter their attachment to the boat.

Some sailing jackets have a built-in harness (and some have an inflatable lifejacket too). These garments help overcome the problem of ensuring that people on deck are wearing harnesses when the weather deteriorates.

Harnesses need to be checked regularly to ensure that there is no wear or damage to the webbing or the safety line. In particular the adjusting buckles and the snap hook need to be kept free and in good condition, and the hinges lightly oiled.

There is not the same requirement for safety harnesses in motor boats, but one or two should be carried in case it is necessary to work on deck in bad weather. Remember however that anybody wearing a safety harness and going overboard at more than about 8 knots is liable to injury.

An experienced crew knows when it is sensible to be hooked on, but often the skipper or whoever is in charge on deck must insist that everybody hooks on.

13.3.8   LIFELINES (JACKSTAYS)

Whatever the deck layout of a cruising yacht, lifelines are a wise precaution. A crewman can attach the lanyard of his safety harness to them when going forward to the mast or foredeck in rough weather or at night. They are often plastic-covered stainless steel wire on each side of the boat, running forward at deck level, or along the coachroof, from the aft end of the cockpit to the foredeck and well secured at both ends. They should lie inboard of the shrouds if possible. Their securing plates fore and aft must obviously be through-bolted, not just screwed down, with substantial ply or stainless steel backing pads. The round cross section of the wire can in itself be a safety hazard even in calm weather, as it tends to roll from under the foot; flat webbing lifelines avoid this. Webbing is more elastic and therefore better able to absorb shock loads. On bigger boats, or those with a centre cockpit, four lines may be necessary.

13.3.9   MAN OVERBOARD (MOB) GEAR

The gear which can help to save a MoB (see 13.8.4) must satisfy three urgent requirements, in sequence:

i. Keep the MoB afloat;

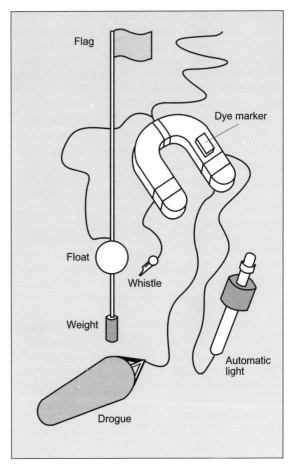

Fig. 13(4) Lifebuoy with dan buoy and safety equipment.

ii. Find him; and

iii. Get him back on board; all as quickly as possible.

The first need is to throw a lifebuoy as quickly and as close as possible to the MoB. This may be a simple round lifebelt or a U-shaped lifebuoy with a floating strobe light. More elaborate types of sling are mounted on the pushpit and attached to the boat by about 45 metres of line. The Jon-Buoy recovery raft is similarly deployed and allows a MoB to get aboard the raft which then can be winched back aboard. Whatever the type, speed is of the essence.

Secondly a dan buoy, Fig. 13(4), is thrown overboard to mark the MoB's position; two dan buoys thrown in succession will help the helmsman's orientation. Dan buoys have a 2-3m high pole with a light and flag Oscar atop, to make them easy to see. In addition to the MoB function on a yacht's GPS, the MoB may be carrying a mini-flare pack or small personal locator beacon attached to lifejacket or clothing. The Sea Marshall PLB8, for example, is a well-proven Class-B mini EPIRB, about the size of a cigarette packet, which transmits for about 30 hours on 121·5MHz. It can be activated manually or automatically to trigger an alarm onboard. Its aerial contains a high visibility light and can be hung around the neck. On the yacht a receiving aerial, if linked to a simple compass, gives the bearing of the MoB. Contact: Sea Marshall Rescue Systems Ltd, 1st & 2nd Floors, 36 Market Place, Beverley HU17 9AG. Tel 01482 679779; Fax 679780. www.seamarshall.co.uk

Finally, the MoB can be brought alongside by various patent line-throwing devices. But the problems of getting a semi- or unconscious body back aboard are well known, particularly if he is not wearing a safety harness. The Jon-Buoy recovery raft (above) has a lifting point on the end of four inflatable arms to which a halyard can be secured; raft and MoB are then winched aboard with relative ease.   Alternatively the Tri-Buckle is a simple aid resembling a small headsail, made of polyester mesh. The 'tack' and 'clew' are secured to the yacht's toe rail amidships and the head to a halyard. The MoB is floated horizontally into the bight and winched up no higher than the toe rail where he is rolled inboard onto the deck – without having to be lifted over the guardrail. The Tri-Buckle, which stows in a bag attached to the pushpit, is available from: Blue Sea Safety, Old Hele Post Office, Bickington Road, Barnstaple EX31 2BX. Tel/Fax 01271 374911. e-mail: bss@orchardcare.co.uk Website: www.safetyatsea.co.uk

13.3.10 LIFERAFTS

If, for whatever reason, a crew has to abandon ship (and, for good reasons, never do so prematurely), a liferaft which will accommodate

Fig. 13(5) Inflated liferaft showing features and safety equipment.

all on board should ensure their safety for a considerable period; large yachts may need more than one raft. Because of the shelter it provides, its relative stability and the survival equipment which it should contain, a liferaft is far better than a rigid or inflatable dinghy, and is therefore recommended even for coastal waters; see Fig 13(5).

Desirable features include an automatically erecting canopy to protect the occupants and prevent total inversion; two independent buoyancy compartments either of which will support the raft and occupants; and (particularly for ocean passages or in cold waters) an inflatable double floor. To provide stability there should be water-ballast pockets underneath. To help prevent capsizing and to reduce drift the raft should have a large and effective drogue made of slightly porous material and attached to anti-tangle shroud lines.

Liferafts are stowed in either a soft valise or a hard canister, secured by quick release straps, and stowed where it can be easily got over the side. The inboard end of the painter must be securely fastened to the boat. Once the valise or canister is in the water (preferably on the lee side of the boat) the painter is given a really strong jerk or series of jerks, whereupon the liferaft will automatically inflate itself and break out of its container. Don't worry about the subsequent wailing sound, which is only surplus gas venting to avoid over-inflation. If the raft inflates upside down, it is easily righted although somebody may have to enter the water. It is far better if the crew can get into the liferaft directly from the yacht, rather than via the water, and therefore keep dry. In any case it is not easy to get into a liferaft when wearing an inflated lifejacket.

When first inflated a liferaft is unstable because it is unloaded, the water ballast pockets have not had time to fill, and the drogue has not been streamed. In bad weather the liferaft should be boarded as soon as possible after inflation, and the weight of the crew should be evenly distributed.

Even a loaded liferaft can become unstable in bad weather. Factors which influence instability include the shape of the canopy in very strong winds, the design and strength of water ballast pockets, the position of the access hatch in the canopy, and in particular the design of the drogue. These and other factors were the subject of detailed investigation after the unsatisfactory performance of liferafts in the 1979 Fastnet Race.

Liferafts are available with a choice of survival equipment, and the scale carried depends upon what sort of cruising is intended. Obviously more items are desirable for an ocean voyage than for a passage across the North Sea or the English Channel. A minimum contents, which equates to the ORC scale, would be: Sea anchor(drogue), safety knife, quoit and 30m line, bailer, pump, paddles, water, 3 hand-held red flares, 3 leak stoppers, 2 sponges, instructions card, signals card, anti-seasickness pills (6 per head), waterproof torch, repair kit, first aid kit and sick bags. The contents of a supplementary 'panic bag' are listed in 13.3.11.

Hand-operated watermakers, working on the reverse osmosis principle, are available – at considerable cost. Also on the market is a solar watermaker which works by condensation, and is said to give 1 pint of water a day in UK waters, and 3 or 4 times more in warmer climes.

Information about abandoning ship and the use of a liferaft is given in 13.8.1.

Since liferafts have been found at sea, apparently lost from the parent craft in error, it is a good idea that the raft should have the yacht's name clearly painted on it in order to assist identification (which otherwise can only be done through the serial number, which takes some time).

Liferafts and the survival equipment within require annual servicing to ensure that they will function correctly in an emergency. This servicing is quite expensive, and coupled with an outlay of at least £1000 for buying a middle of the range 4 man liferaft, hiring a liferaft for the season becomes a reasonable proposition: a fully serviced 4 man liferaft can be hired for about £300 for 6 months.

13.3.11 SURVIVAL EQUIPMENT
As well as the survival equipment provided in a liferaft, it is a good idea to keep a readily available 'panic' or 'grab' bag close to the companionway. The contents will supplement that in the liferaft and should include:

Fresh water, at least 1 gall (4·5 ltrs) per head in 1 ltr screw-top containers for ease of handling and rationing; hand-held VHF; hand-held GPS; EPIRB or 121·5MHz locator beacon; SART; mobile phone; compass; torch and spare batteries; 2 red paraflares; 3 red hand-held flares; heliograph (signalling mirror); whistle; First aid kit; anti-seasickness pills; bin liners; money, passports; paper & pencils; RYA Sea Survival Practical Notes; fishing gear; spare clothing; thermal protective suits; food (eg Mars Bars, barley sugar, fresh fruit etc).

Finally, the four survival priorities are:

1 Protection; 2 Location; 3 Water; and 4 Food – in that order. But, underpinning all the equipment in the world, is the **Will to Survive** – an absolute determination that you will come through, possibly against all the odds.

13.4 SEARCH AND RESCUE (SAR) ORGANISATION – UK

Around the coasts of Britain we have excellent rescue services, manned by skilled and dedicated personnel. All seafarers should understand how these various resources are organised and co-ordinated, and the procedures to be followed, should they find themselves in difficulty.

The Global Maritime Distress and Safety System (GMDSS; see 13.7) is already mandatory for larger ships and SAR authorities are fully equipped to take advantage of the undoubted benefits which it bestows. Pleasure craft will also benefit enormously from GMDSS and yachtsmen are steadily becoming indoctrinated into the several elements of the system. They need only to acquire a DSC compatible radio and get themselves trained in its use.

The roles of the MCA, HM Coastguard, NCI, RNLI, Royal Navy and the Royal Air Force are outlined and discussed in subsequent sections.

13.4.1 THE MARITIME AND COASTGUARD AGENCY
The Maritime and Coastguard Agency (MCA) is responsible for:

a. developing, promoting and enforcing high standards of safety at sea;
b. minimising loss of life among seafarers, both in offshore and coastal waters;
c. responding to maritime emergencies 24 hours a day;
d. reducing the risk of ships polluting the marine environment; and
e. where pollution does occur, minimising its impact on UK interests and the environment.

MCA Headquarters are at Spring Place, Commercial Road, Southampton. Branches and responsibilities within the MCA include: HM Coastguard, Counter Pollution and Salvage, Survey, Inspection and Enforcement. The MCA produces a range of safety information as leaflets or brochures. A particularly good one is the *Voluntary Safety Code for Leisure Craft*, a set of cards covering all types of craft from kayaks to yachts.

13.4.2 HM COASTGUARD
Organisation
HM Coastguard is an on-call emergency organisation responsible for the initiation and co-ordination of civil maritime Search and Rescue (SAR) within the UK Search and Rescue Region (SRR). It responds to requests for assistance from or for persons in distress and/or danger at sea or on the coastline.

HM Coastguard co-ordinates search and rescue via 6 Maritime Rescue Co-ordination Centres (MRCC), 12 Maritime Rescue Sub Centres (MRSC) and a network of Sector Bases. A corps of 3150 volunteer Auxiliary Coastguards undertake coastal rescue, searches and surveillance.

The UK SRR covers the waters around the UK from latitude 45°N to 61°N and from the median line in the North Sea and English Channel out to 30°W. Within these limits the Irish Coast Guard is responsible for the waters around the Irish Republic.

The UK SRR is divided into four Regions (see Fig. 13(6)) managed by:

a. Southern – Falmouth and Dover MRCCs;
b. Eastern – Yarmouth MRCC;
c. Scotland and Northern Ireland – Aberdeen and Clyde MRCCs; and
d. Wales and Western England – Swansea MRCC.

Each Region is sub-divided into three Districts, each run by an MRSC). The telephone numbers of the MRCC/SCs are given in the MRNA.

Within each District there is an organisation of Auxiliary Coastguard watch and rescue stations, grouped into Sectors and managed by regular Coastguard Officers.

Communications

The Coastguard is the authority responsible for maintaining a continuous listening watch on the International Distress, Safety and Calling frequencies of VHF Channel 16 and MF 2182kHz. VHF coverage is provided out to at least 30M from the coast, and MF ground wave coverage extends out to 150M. An electronic watch is also maintained on VHF DSC channel 70 and MF DSC 2187.5kHz.

All leisure craft owners/skippers should be aware of the importance of both VHF radio and VHF DSC, particularly when considering the purchase of new radio equipment. Some foreign SAR Authorities, in accordance with GMDSS, only maintain an electronic distress watch on DSC, reverting to Ch 16 for subsequent voice distress communications. HM Coastguard will maintain a dedicated 'headset' watch on Ch 16 until 31 January 2005. There are currently (2001) no plans for HM Coastguard to cease monitoring Ch 16.

All VHF users should undertake training to obtain a suitable VHF Operator's Licence. A VHF Distress call (MAYDAY) will be heard by the Coastguard and by vessels within range of the signal, each of whom will respond and maintain communications on Ch 16 with the vessel in distress. MRCCs and MRSCs do not monitor CB frequencies and yachtsmen should be aware of

the limitations of Mobile telephones. Aerial coverage, battery life and the person-to-person nature of the mobile phone are all limiting factors and therefore mobiles should not be relied upon for distress alerting and other safety calls.

Maritime Safety Information (MSI)

HM Coastguard has taken over responsibility for broadcasting MSI, following the closure of BT Coast Radio Stations. MSI includes information about SAR operations and in some areas GUNFACTS/SUBFACTS. Weather broadcasts are covered in Chapter 11; Navigational Warnings are dealt with in Chapter 7. Times and frequencies/channels for MSI broadcasts are listed in the MRNA. MSI is also contained in the regular Navtex broadcasts.

Safety Identification Scheme

This voluntary and highly recommended Scheme, formerly known as the Yacht and Boat Safety Scheme (or simply as the CG66), provides specific details of your boat and its equipment to the Coastguard for inclusion on their database. This information will help to mount a successful SAR operation, and also promotes closer links with small boat users.

An application form (CG66) can be obtained from the local MRCC/SC, harbour master or marina, on which to fill in details of your boat and her equipment. This includes name of boat and where displayed, usual base or mooring, where normally operated, type of boat, colours of hull and sails, rig, sail number, speed and endurance under power, liferaft and serial number, dinghy type and colour, details of safety equipment, radio type and call sign, owner's name, address and telephone number, shore contact's name, address and telephone number, and yacht club or association. A photograph of the boat is useful.

This information about your boat is available to all MRCC/SCs, if she becomes overdue or in distress. The CG66 is valid for two years; if not renewed it will be considered invalid and deleted from the database. A different card can be given to a relative or reliable friend, so that they will know the MRCC/SC to contact if they are concerned for the boat's safety.

Traffic Reports (TR)

It is obviously not easy for the Coastguard to maintain continuous watch for all small boats on coastal passages, but they will record any TRs received by phone, or via VHF Channel 67 while on passage. A TR contains your destination's name, other ports of call, number onboard and

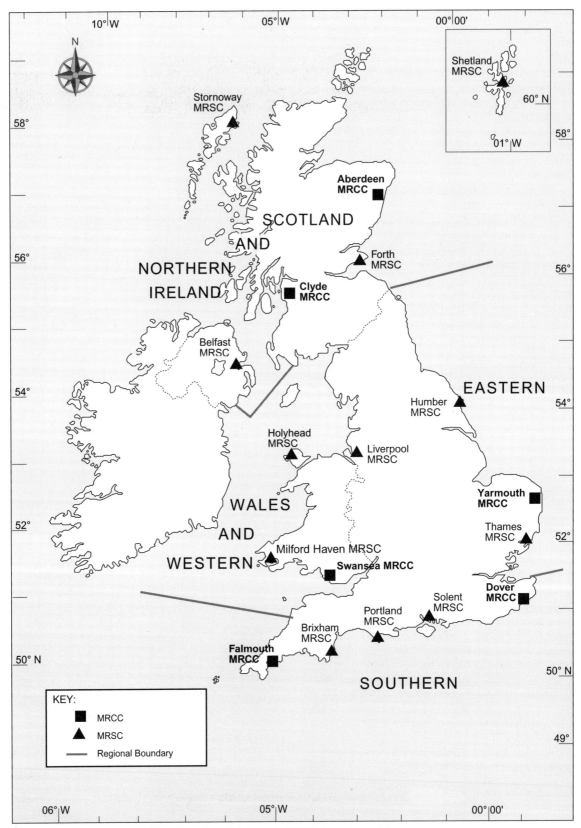

Fig. 13(6) The Coastguard Regions for which each MRCC is responsible.

Fig. 13(7) Distress signals as listed in Annex IV of the Collision Regulations.

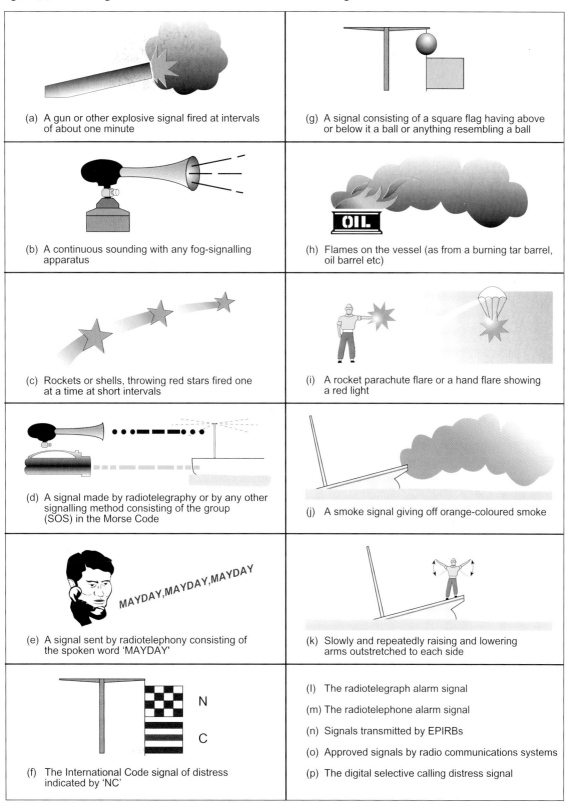

(a) A gun or other explosive signal fired at intervals of about one minute

(g) A signal consisting of a square flag having above or below it a ball or anything resembling a ball

(b) A continuous sounding with any fog-signalling apparatus

(h) Flames on the vessel (as from a burning tar barrel, oil barrel etc)

(c) Rockets or shells, throwing red stars fired one at a time at short intervals

(i) A rocket parachute flare or a hand flare showing a red light

(d) A signal made by radiotelegraphy or by any other signalling method consisting of the group (SOS) in the Morse Code

(j) A smoke signal giving off orange-coloured smoke

(e) A signal sent by radiotelephony consisting of the spoken word 'MAYDAY'

(k) Slowly and repeatedly raising and lowering arms outstretched to each side

(f) The International Code signal of distress indicated by 'NC'

(l) The radiotelegraph alarm signal

(m) The radiotelephone alarm signal

(n) Signals transmitted by EPIRBs

(o) Approved signals by radio communications systems

(p) The digital selective calling distress signal

1. Cirrus (Ci) Very high white feathery clouds (mares' tails) consisting of ice-particles, usually indicate wind aloft. If it thickens it indicates weather deterioration with the approach of a low.
© *RK Pilsbury*

2. Cirrocumulus (Cc) Mackerel sky. Rows of small white puffs very high up sometimes forming banks. Thicker than Cirrus. Harmless, but these clouds can foretell changeable weather.
© *RK Pilsbury*

3. Cirrostratus (Cs) A thin high milky film, through which the sun can be seen, sometimes with a halo. Harmless until the cloud thickens, when it again can indicate an approaching depression.
© *CS Broomfield*

4. Altocumulus (Ac) A larger version of Cirrocumulus in areas of high pressure or edges of warm zones. Clouds developing vertically by mid-morning may foretell thunderstorms by after-noon.
© *CS Broomfield*

5. Altostratus (As) Sheet-like grey cloud like a layer of medium level fog. The sun may be seen through it, without halo. Following Cirrostratus, rain and front can be expected within 1-3 hours.
© *S Cornford*

6. Nimbostratus (Ns) A mass of low, grey, rain-bearing cloud. Normally following Altostratus with the passing of a front. Steady rain will set in.
© RK Pilsbury

7. Stratus (St) Soft, grey, fog-like layer of cloud as low as 1000 or even 500 feet. If dense, Stratus can produce drizzle and poor visibility, and will be found between warm and cold fronts.
© Crown

8. Stratocumulus (Sc) Dense, lumpy grey cloud at 2300 – 5000 feet. As it intensifies to form a solid grey layer across the sky, it will rain within one or two hours.
© GA Watts

9. Cumulus (Cu) Typical fair weather cloud formed by rising warm air. Builds in the morning but leaves large areas of blue sky. Disappears by evening. Thickening foretells a change on the way.
© RK Pilsbury

10. Cumulonimbus (Cb) Larger and more dramatic cloud than cumulus rising to great heights with huge tops. Expect heavy rain and thundery squalls. The higher the cloud the stronger the squalls.
© Crown

Fig. 13(8) Lifesaving Signals.

LIFE SAVING SIGNALS (Shore-to-Ship) – see 13.6.5

Signals (1) to (4) may be indicated by a white flare, a rocket showing white stars on bursting, or an explosive sound signal.

(1) Landing signals for the guidance of small boats with crews or persons in distress

		Other signals	*Meaning*
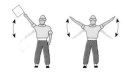	**Vertical** motion of a white flag (or white light or flare by night) or of the arms	International Code letter 'K' by light or sound ▬ • ▬	**'This is the best place to land'** (An indication of direction may be given by a steady white light or flare at a lower level)
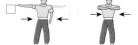	**Horizontal** motion of a white flag (or white light or flare by night) or of the arms extended horizontally	International Code letter 'S' by light or sound • • •	**'Landing here is highly dangerous.**
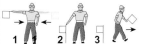	**Horizontal** motion of a white flag followed by 2. placing the white flag in the ground and 3. by carrying another white flag in the direction to be indicated. By night white lights or flares are used instead of white flags	1. Signalling the code letter 'S' (•••), followed by the code letter 'R' if the better landing place is more to the right in the direction of approach, or 2, by the code letter 'L' (• — ••) if the better landing place is more to the left in the direction of approach	**'Landing here is highly dangerous. A more favourable location for landing is in the direction indicated'**

(2) Signals to be made in connection with the use of shore apparatus for life-saving

Vertical motion of a white flag (or white light or flare by night) or of the arms 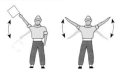	**In general:** affirmative. Specifically: rocket line is held - tail block is made fast - hawser is made fast - man is in the breeches buoy - haul away	**Horizontal** motion of a white flag (or white light or flare by night) or of the arms 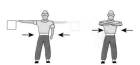	**In general:** negative. Specifically: slack away-stop hauling

(3) Replies from life-saving stations etc. to distress signals made by ships or persons

Pyrotechnic signals Orange smoke signal 	White star rocket - three single signals fired at intervals of about one minute	Combined light and sound signal - three single signals fired at intervals of about one minute	**'You are seen - assistance will be given as soon as possible'**

(4) Signals to be used to warn a ship which is standing into danger

International Code signals **'U'** [flag] or **'NF'** [flags] } **'You are running into danger'**

International Code signals **'U'** by light or sound • • ▬

(5) Signals used by Sub-Aqua divers

Left: 'I am OK' Right: 'I need assistance'

where your CG66 has been registered. The nearest Coastguard **must** be advised by radio or telephone on reaching your destination, or of any change of plan.

13.4.3 NATIONAL COASTWATCH INSTITUTION (NCI)

The NCI is a charity dedicated to the safety of all who use the UK coastal waters. Formed in 1994, it functions by re-introducing Visual Watch Stations around the coast, usually by re-opening former Coastguard lookouts, now abandoned. Huge stretches of coastline are solely reliant on the volunteer NCI watchkeepers to provide the vitally important visual watch link with HM Coastguard, the RNLI and the other SAR services. In any one year hundreds of life-threatening incidents occur and many lives have been saved as a direct result of the vigilance of an NCI watchkeeper.

In addition, VHF channel 16 is monitored to detect weak distress transmissions, all passing small boat traffic is logged to assist in the search for craft reported missing and a watch is kept on the adjacent Coastal Footpaths. The NCI further serves the mariner by informing local tourist offices and radio stations of actual weather conditions. In daylight hours the same service is provided to any yachtsman who telephones for information of conditions outside the shelter of a harbour. It is hoped that some stations will shortly be authorised to transmit on VHF channels M and M2.

For further information contact your local NCI station or NCI Head Office, 4a Trafalgar Square, Fowey, Cornwall PL23 1AZ. Tel 0870 787 2147; Fax 0870 164 1893. info@nci.org.uk www.nci.org.uk

The following 18 NCI stations were operational in 2001:

St Ives	01736 799398
Cape Cornwall (Land's End)	01736 787890
Gwennap Head (Land's End)	01736 871351
Bass Point (Lizard)	01326 290212
Polruan-by-Fowey	01726 870291
Rame Head (Plymouth)	01752 823706
Prawle Point	01548 511259
Exmouth	01395 222492
Portland	01305 860178
St Alban's Head	01929 439220
Peveril Point (Swanage)	01929 422596
Folkestone	01303 227132
Holehaven (Canvey Island)	01268 696971
Felixstowe	01394 670808
Gorleston (Great Yarmouth)	01493 440384
Mundesley (Norfolk)	01263 722399
Hartlepool	01429 274931
Wylfa Head (Anglesey)	01407 711152

If the flag is flying, NCI are watching over your safety at sea. Stations under development for 2001 include Stepper Point (Padstow), Barry (S Wales) and Herne Bay (Kent).

13.4.4 THE CHANNEL ISLANDS

There is no Coastguard in the Channel Islands. SAR tasks are directed by the harbour masters of St Peter Port and St Helier for the North and South areas respectively. The liaison with CROSS Jobourg is close, such that a French yacht in distress in Channel Island waters might well be handled by Jobourg; whilst a British yacht in adjacent French waters could be directed by St Peter Port or Jersey Radios. These two stations provide all communications needed for SAR. They are DSC VHF (not MF) equipped, both monitor Ch 16 and Jersey guards 2182kHz at present. There are offshore lifeboats at Braye (Alderney), St Peter Port, St Helier and St Catherine (Jersey). The Channel Islands Air Search operates a dedicated SAR Islander aircraft from Guernsey airport.

13.4.5 ROYAL NATIONAL LIFEBOAT INSTITUTION (RNLI)

The RNLI (founded in 1824) is a charitable organisation, supported entirely by voluntary contributions. There are over 220 RNLI stations around the coasts of the UK, the Republic of Ireland, the Isle of Man, and the Channel Islands. From them are deployed more than 300 all-weather and inshore lifeboats. Lifeboats are manned by volunteer crews. Each station with an all-weather lifeboat normally has one full-time RNLI employee who may be the motor mechanic or a coxswain-mechanic.

When launched on service all-weather lifeboats keep watch on Ch 16 and 2182kHz. They can also use other frequencies for contacting other vessels, SAR aircraft, Coastguard and other authorities, and are fitted with VHF direction-finding equipment. Inshore lifeboats are fitted with VHF. All-weather lifeboats and the larger inshore lifeboats show a quick-flashing blue light.

It is a sobering thought that in 1999 27% of the 5621 launches were to assist sailing yachts whilst 20% were to help powered pleasure craft. In these two categories 313 and 268 lives were saved respectively.

Yachtsmen can help support the activities of the RNLI by joining *Offshore*, full details of which can be obtained from the RNLI, West Quay Road, Poole, Dorset BH5 1HZ. Tel 01202 663000; Fax 01202 663167. info@rnli.org www.lifeboats.org.uk

13.4.6 ROYAL NAVY

The Royal Navy assists casualties by means of ships and aircraft, including helicopters (see also 13.8.2). RN Sea King Mk V helicopters, based at Culdrose and Prestwick, have a radius of action of about 200M depending on equipment fit, and are at 15 minutes readiness to fly by day and 45 minutes at night.

13.4.7 ROYAL AIR FORCE

The Aeronautical Rescue Co-ordination Centre (ARCC) at RAF Kinloss (Moray Firth) controls rescues for civilian and military aircraft in the UK SRR. The COSPAS/SARSAT UK Mission Control Centre is co-located. The ARCC directs helicopter and Nimrod aircraft to assist ships in distress. RAF SAR helos are based at Wattisham, Leconfield, Lossiemouth and Valley. Air Traffic Control Centres sometimes request aircraft to keep visual or radio watch for vessels in distress.

13.5 SAR IN WESTERN EUROPE

In Western Europe SAR arrangements are comparable to those for the UK, as described in 13.4. There are also notes on each country in the Safety chapter of the MRNA.

ALRS, Vol 5, Section 10 has more detailed information at national and international levels. The 'Bible' on SAR is the *International Aeronautical and Maritime Search and Rescue Manual* (IAMSAR Manual), published jointly by IMO and ICAO in 3 volumes; only Volume 3 is likely to be of interest to yachtsmen.

13.5.1 REPUBLIC OF IRELAND

The Irish Coastguard (formerly Irish Marine Emergency Service) has its HQ in Dublin at the Dept of the Marine, Leeson Lane, Dublin 2. Tel: 01 662 0922; Fax 01 662 0795. The Irish CG is responsible for co-ordinating SAR operations, Pollution control, safety awareness and a commercial radio communications service.

There are approximately 65 full-time staff at Dublin MRCC, Malin Head MRSC, Valentia MRSC and Cork where there is an Engineering Unit. Each Centre is responsible for a designated sub-region of the Irish SRR. They keep continuous listening watch for distress calls on VHF Ch 16, DSC Ch 70 and MF DSC 2187·5 kHz.

Coast Radio Stations are co-located at these MRCC/SCs and are operated by the same staff; 14 remote relay stations form a national CG communications network.

Each Centre can call on the RNLI, Coast Life Saving Service, military helicopters, civilian aircraft, the Irish lighthouse service, and the civil police (Garda). Centres liaise with the UK and

France, and act as a clearing house for all messages received during SAR operations within 100 miles of the Irish coast.

The CG has two Sikorsky S61N helicopters based at Shannon and Dublin airports. 50 volunteer CG units are equipped with breeches buoys, cliff rescue gear and support boats. Team leaders' home tel nos are quoted in the MRNA, plus details of MRCC/SCs. The RNLI has 26 all-weather and community-run inshore lifeboats on call around the coast.

13.5.2 FRANCE

France has four Regional Surveillance and Rescue Operations Centres (*Centres Régionaux Opérationnels de Surveillance et de Sauvetage* – or CROSS,) on the Atlantic coast at Gris-Nez, Jobourg, Corsen and Étel. They provide a permanent operational presence along the coast and liaise with foreign equivalents as required. CROSS Étel specialises in providing medical advice and responds to alerts from the COSPAS/SARSAT satellites.

CROSS coordinates the following tasks:

1. Maritime Search and Rescue.
2. Traffic surveillance, especially within the 12M limit.
3. Fishery surveillance out to 200 n miles.
4. Monitoring pollution.
5. Collection of data for future use.

Traffic surveillance includes policing the TSS and ITZ in the English Channel and off Ushant. MSI broadcasts, including reports of vessels which appear to be violating Rule 10 (TSS), are relayed from VHF stations along the coast. Some broadcasts are in French and English.

CROSS can be called on VHF Ch 16, 'phone, fax or telex; and via French Navy signal (semaphore) stations, the Gendarmerie Nationale and Affaires Maritimes. More details of the CROSS organisation, including broadcast channels and times, are given in the MRNA.

The French lifeboat service is administered by the Société Nationale de Sauvetage en Mer (SNSM), 9 Rue de Chaillot, 75116 Paris. Tel 01.56.89.30.00; Fax 01.47. 20.72.33.

13.5.3 BELGIUM

The Sea Rescue Co-ordination Centre is at Sir Winston Churchillkaai 2, 8400 Oostende. Tel: 059 55 29 11; Fax 059 70 36 05. The Belgian Coastguard Service, callsign "Coastguard Oostende", is situated at MRCC Oostende and is responsible for co-ordinating SAR services. There are MRSCs at Nieuwpoort and Zeebrugge. Oostende Radio (OST) and Antwerpen are the coast radio stations. All these stations keep listening watch on Ch 16 and DSC Ch 70, 2182kHz and DSC 2187·5kHz. Belgian lifeboats are administered by the Ministerie van Verkeerswezen, Aarlenstraat 104, 1040 Brussels. Offshore and inshore lifeboats are based at Nieuwpoort, Oostende and Zeebrugge. SAR Sea King helicopters are at Koksijde Belgian Air Force base, which is a Rescue sub-centre.

13.5.4 NETHERLANDS

Netherlands Coastguard is responsible for co-ordinating SAR operations through the MRCC at IJmuiden (at the entrance to the North Sea Canal). The MRCC keeps watch (H24) on VHF Ch 70 (and Ch 16 until 1 Feb 2005) and 2187·5kHz and uses callsign "IJmuiden" (pronounced eyemowden) during SAR operations. Tel no is +31 (0)900 0111 for alerts H24; Fax (0)255 546599. A network of relay stations, some with antennae pointing inshore only, broadcasts MSI on Ch 23 or 83; times are in the MRNA.

24 coastal and 10 inshore lifeboat stations are operated by the Koninklijke Nederlandsche Redding Maatschappij (KNRM). SAR helicopters are based near Den Helder and Leeuwarden.

13.5.5 GERMANY (NORTH SEA)

The Deutsche Gesellschaft zur Rettung Schiffbruchiger, Werderstrasse 2, D-28199 Bremen; Tel 0421 53.68.70, co-ordinates SAR operations off the North Sea coast. The co-located MRCC keeps listening watch H24 on VHF Ch 16 and DSC Ch 70. Interestingly a dedicated emergency number **124 124** is available for use by mobile phones within the network coverage.

Offshore and inshore lifeboats are stationed along the whole coast. Naval warships and military helicopters are made availble for SAR.

13.5.6 SPAIN (ATLANTIC)

The HQ of the SAR organisation (Sociedad Estatal de Salvamento y Seguridad Maritima) is in Madrid; it is also an MRCC. On Spain's north coast there are MRCCs at Bilbao, Gijon and Finisterre and MRSCs at Santander, La Coruña and Vigo. In SW Spain are MRCC Tarifa and MRSC Cadiz. All monitor the distress frequencies H24 and communicate via the Coast Radio Stations.

13.5.7 PORTUGAL

The Portuguese Navy co-ordinates SAR operations off mainland Portugal, Madeira and the Azores. There are MRCCs at Lisboa and Ponta Delgada and a MRSC at Funchal. Communications are via Coast Radio Stations.

13.6.1 R/T PRE- AND POST-GMDSS

VHF Channel 16 and 2182kHz MF are the internationally recognised frequencies for sending and receiving emergency messages (Distress, Urgency and Safety). But the turn of the century is a period of transition, at least for yachts, from the long established equipment and procedures which have been in place for the last 50 years – to the more complex and sophisticated technology of GMDSS. This is fully covered in 13.7, the next section.

Channel 16 and 2182kHz continue as the international emergency frequencies, but with the important difference that fewer and fewer merchant ships and shore stations keep watch on these frequencies, both now and more so after 2005. Although not obligatory for yachts, GMDSS will by default become the norm and Channel 16 will only be used after initial contact has been made on the DSC frequencies, Channel 70 and 2187·5kHz. The HF DSC frequencies are '4207·5, 6312·0, 8414·5, 12577·0 and 16804·5 kHz.

In progressing from the familiar to the unfamiliar, yachtsmen should fully appreciate that they are reaping the benefit of a system which automatically alerts other ships and safety services to a vessel in distress. Lives will be that much less at risk.

13.6.2 EMERGENCY MESSAGES AND PROCEDURES

Few emergency situations fall into watertight categories and if in doubt (and under stress) remember the principle that it is far better to put the Coastguard (or other authority) in the picture early, rather than too late. For example a Pan-Pan, or even a Securité call could alert the safety services to a problem which is currently under control, but which might later escalate into a more serious situation requiring outside assistance. The vastly experienced Coastguard are well able to judge how best to deploy SAR resources to cope with such a situation.

The three levels of emergency messages (Distress, Urgency and Safety) are discussed below.

1. Distress

The R/T distress signal 'MAYDAY' means that a **ship, aircraft, vehicle or person is in grave and imminent danger, and requires immediate assistance**.

The procedure for a Mayday call is as follows:

Check that the yacht's main battery switch is 'ON'. Switch on the radio, and in the case of VHF ensure that it is on 'high power'. Switch the transmitter to Ch 16 (or 2182kHz, as appropriate). Press and hold the transmit button, then say slowly and distinctly:

> MAYDAY, MAYDAY, MAYDAY
>
> THIS IS TINA, TINA, TINA (boat's name x 3)
>
> MAYDAY, TINA (boat's name once)
>
> MY POSITION IS ...... (Latitude and longitude, or true bearing and distance from a known point)
>
> NATURE OF DISTRESS ....
>
> ASSISTANCE REQUIRED ....
>
> NUMBER OF PERSONS ONBOARD ....
>
> OVER.

Release the 'transmit' button at the end of the message. The yacht's position is vital and should be repeated if time allows. An immediate acknowledgement should be expected in coastal waters, either from another vessel or from a shore station. If not, check the set and repeat the distress call and message.

If it is difficult to send an MF distress message, try during one of the three minutes' silence periods starting at H and H + 30, which are intended for this purpose. During these silence periods all transmissions on 2182kHz, except for Distress or Urgency traffic, must cease. There is no equivalent on Ch 16.

The distress signal (MAYDAY) imposes general radio silence, which is maintained until the vessel concerned or some other authority cancels the distress. A distress signal should be cancelled as soon as (but not before) the emergency is over.

A distress message is acknowledged as follows:

> MAYDAY
>
> TINA, TINA, TINA (name of boat in distress x 3)
>
> THIS IS ADA, ADA, ADA (name of boat acknowledging x 3)
>
> RECEIVED MAYDAY ...... (eg, coming to help)

A yacht which hears a distress message from a vessel in her immediate vicinity and is able to give assistance should acknowledge accordingly, but only after giving an opportunity for the nearest shore station or some larger vessel to acknowledge.

If a yacht hears a distress message from some more distant vessel, and if it apparently has not been acknowledged, then the yacht should do everything possible to pass on the distress message. The intercepted distress message is preceded by the words:

> MAYDAY RELAY, MAYDAY RELAY, MAYDAY RELAY
>
> THIS IS .... (name of relay vessel x 3)
>
> Then read out the intercepted distress message.

Controlling distress traffic

If necessary, the station controlling distress traffic may impose radio silence by transmitting on the frequency in use for distress purposes:

> SEELONCE MAYDAY, then its own name/ident.

If any other station nearby believes it essential to impose radio silence, it may transmit:

> SEELONCE DISTRESS, then its own name/ident.

When complete silence is no longer necessary on a distress frequency, the station controlling traffic may relax the silence by a signal indicating that restricted working may be resumed, as follows:

> MAYDAY
>
> ALL STATIONS (x 3)
>
> THIS IS .... (name/ident of controlling station)
>
> TIME .... (eg 1615 UT)
>
> NAME .... (of station in distress)
>
> PRU-DONCE.

When distress traffic has ceased, the controlling station indicates that normal working may be resumed, thus:

> MAYDAY
>
> ALL STATIONS (x 3)
>
> THIS IS .... (name/ident of controlling station)
>
> TIME .... (eg 1745 UT)
>
> NAME .... (of station which was in distress)
>
> SEELONCE FEENEE.

2. Urgency

The Urgency Signal consists of the words 'PAN PAN', spoken three times, and indicates that the station has a **very urgent message to transmit about the safety of a vessel or person**. Messages prefixed by the Urgency Signal, which in other respects are similar in format to a distress message, take priority over all messages except distress, and are sent on Ch 16 or 2182kHz, or on any other frequency which may be used in case of distress.

The Urgency Signal is appropriate when someone has been lost overboard or when urgent medical advice is required. In the latter case, when communication has been established, it may be better to transfer to a working frequency. The Urgency Signal should be cancelled by the station concerned when the need ceases.

3. Safety

The Safety Signal consists of the word SECURITE (pronounced SAY-CURE-E-TAY) spoken three times. It indicates that the station is about to transmit a message concerning safety matters, often an important navigational or meteorological warning, eg a buoy adrift, a light extinguished, a wreck, or a gale warning. Such messages usually originate from a shore station, and are sent on a working frequency after an announcement on the distress frequency.

Portable RT equipment
Hand-held VHF radios, operating on Ch 16 and other channels, are useful because as well as being operable from the yacht they can be taken into the liferaft in the event of abandoning ship.

Mobile telephones
Note that while mobile 'phones may be useful for various purposes in coastal waters, they should not be used for distress or safety communications, if proper marine VHF or MF equipment is available.

13.6.3 DISTRESS SIGNALS
Recognised visual and sound distress signals are listed in Annex IV to the International Regulations for Preventing Collisions at Sea. See Chapter 4 and the colour plate in Fig.13(7). Those signals best suited for use on yachts and small craft are shown below, with amplifying notes. (The letters of the sub-paragraphs are those in Annex IV).

b. Continuous sounding with any fog signalling apparatus. *To avoid any ambiguity, the letters SOS (in Morse ··· ——— ···) should be continuously sounded.*

d. A signal made by radiotelegraphy or by any other signalling method consisting of the group ··· ——— ··· (SOS) in the Morse Code. *On a yacht this means a sound signal as in (b) by day, or a signalling lamp at night.*

e. A signal sent by radiotelephony consisting of the spoken word MAYDAY. *The procedure is given in 13.6.2.*

f. The International Code signal of distress 'NC'. *Hoist flag N above flag C at any convenient halyard.*

g. A signal consisting of a square flag having above or below it a ball or anything resembling a ball. *Hoist a square flag above an anchor ball; more obvious than (f).*

i. A rocket parachute flare or a hand flare showing a red light. *A red flare is undoubtedly the most effective visual distress signal at night. See below for further details.*

j. A smoke signal giving off orange-coloured smoke.
    By day orange smoke signals (hand-held

for short ranges, or the larger buoyant type for longer range) are more obvious than flares, although the smoke disperses quickly in a strong wind. The table at 13.2.2 recommends the number of flares and smoke signals for different sized boats and levels of risk.

k. Slowly and repeatedly raising and lowering arms outstretched to each side. *Raise and lower the arms above and below the horizontal, in unison; a very obvious and easy short-range signal.*

Except in genuine Distress or Urgency, as defined, the use of any of the above signals is strictly forbidden. They always require the skipper's approval, either in respect of one's own boat or on behalf of another vessel in distress which for some reason is unable to make a distress signal.

If subsequently the danger is overcome, the distress call must be cancelled by whatever means are available.

Other Distress signals
These include: 'V' ('Victor') in the International Code, which means 'I require assistance'. This can be sent by light or sound in Morse code 000 1; or by flag, but flag signalling from a yacht is barely worth trying; the flags are too small and few people understand their meaning.

Flares
Flares serve to raise the alarm and to pinpoint the boat's position. A hand flare, which lasts about a minute, will do both tasks if no more than three miles offshore. Hold hand flares firmly, downwind of yourself.

Further offshore a red parachute rocket, which projects a suspended flare to more than l000ft and burns for more than 40 seconds, raises the alarm, but hand flares will still be needed to pinpoint the boat's position. Parachute rockets turn into the wind; fire them vertically in normal conditions, or aimed about 15° downwind in strong winds. Do not aim them into the wind, or they will not gain altitude. If there is low cloud, fire rockets at 45° downwind so that the flare burns under the cloud.

When parachute rockets are used two should be fired initially, about one minute apart, to give safety services an approximate line of bearing. Then wait several minutes before firing another pair. Do not fire parachute rockets when a helicopter is nearby. Verey pistols require a firearms certificate from the police.

See 13.2.2 for the scale of flares or pyrotechnic signals which the RYA recommend should be carried on board yachts of different

LOA and categorised as sailing across Oceans, Offshore, Inshore or in sheltered waters.

Flares should conform to SOLAS 83 (Safety of Life at Sea convention), as amended. Mini-flares are satisfactory for personal use by dinghy sailors for example, but are not a substitute for proper SOLAS flares offshore.

Flares must be stowed where they are easily accessible, but protected from damp. All the crew must know where they are and how to use them. In good storage conditions they should have a life of three years; examine them regularly for any signs of deterioration and replace them by the expiry date.

Outdated flares are not dangerous, but they become increasingly unreliable. They must never be discharged for practice reasons or thrown overboard. Liferaft service stations can arrange disposal, but in the event of any difficulty contact the Police or the Coastguard. Pains Wessex will accept outdated flares through their agents.

White flares are not distress signals, but are used for collision warning, ie to highlight the presence of your boat to another vessel sighted on a collision course. An outfit of four is suggested. To retain your night vision, shield your eyes when using them.

13.6.4 RESPONSE TO A DISTRESS CALL

Raising the alarm

If you are in distress at sea, ie in grave and imminent danger and in need of immediate assistance, do not delay in sending a Distress Alert on DSC and on Channel 16. The CG will respond and may request further information not already provided. Other vessels will be alerted by a MAYDAY RELAY and the appropriate SAR units will be tasked to assist (see below).

If at sea you pick up a distress signal, or information about any vessel or aircraft in distress, you are obliged to proceed with all speed to give assistance (assuming you are in a position to do so), unless or until you are specifically relieved by the coordinating MRCC/SC. Write down the most important details such as the casualty's name and position. If no other vessel acknowledges, you must make a MAYDAY RELAY call as in 13.6.2. Cease all other transmissions that might interfere with distress traffic and continue listening on the frequency concerned. Similarly, if you see a red flare or other distress signal or situation, you must render all assistance possible and immediately contact the Coastguard.

If you are ashore and see an accident afloat, dial 999 on the nearest telephone and ask for the 'Coastguard'. You will be asked for details of the incident, and possibly to stay near the telephone for further communications.

Response to a Distress call

When alerted, the Coastguard will summon the most appropriate assistance available. This might be a Coastguard Emergency Towing Vessel (ETV) of which there are four based at Fair Isle*, Minches*, the Dover Strait and the Western Approaches* (*winter only). An RNLI all-weather or inshore lifeboat might be requested to launch; an SAR helicopter belonging to the Coastguard, Royal Navy or RAF could be scrambled (13.4); other Coastguard stations might be contacted; or shipping in the vicinity might be directed to the scene. Normally the first vessel to arrive assumes the role of 'on-scene Commander', but a larger or better equipped vessel may take over the job.

13.6.5 VISUAL SIGNALS FROM UK SHORE STATIONS TO SHIPS IN DISTRESS

The 'Annual Summary of Admiralty Notices to Mariners' (NP 247, a red-covered book) lists NMs 1 to 24 which are re-issued every year with amendments if necessary.

NM No 4 'General Arrangements for SAR' covers a variety of Distress situations and procedures. Amongst these are the signals which should be used by shore stations to a vessel in distress, or stranded, off the coast of the UK. They may seem somewhat archaic in this age of GMDSS and electronic communications, but are reproduced here in case they are ever encountered. They are listed below and illustrated in Fig. 13(8):

1. **Acknowledgement of distress signal**

By day. Orange smoke signal or combined light and sound signal (thunderlight) consisting of three single signals fired at about one minute intervals,	'You are seen – assistance will be given as soon as possible'.
By night. White star rocket consisting of three single signals fired at about one minute intervals.	(Repetition of such signals has the same meaning)

If necessary the day signals may be given at night, or the night signals by day.

2. **Landing signals for the guidance of small boats with persons in distress**

By day. Vertical motion of a white flag or the arms, or signalling the code letter 'K' (−·−) by light or sound.	'This is the best place to land'
By night. Vertical motion of a white light or flare, or signalling the code letter 'K'(−·−) by light or sound. An indication of direction may be given by placing a steady white light or flare at a lower level and in line with the observer.	'This is the best place to land'

By day. Horizontal motion of a white flag or arms extended horizontally, or signalling the code letter 'S' (···) by light or sound.

'Landing here is highly dangerous'

By night. Horizontal motion of a white light or flare, or signalling the code letter 'S' (···) by light or sound.

'Landing here is highly dangerous'

By day. Horizontal motion of a white flag, followed by the placing of it in the ground and the carrying of another white flag in the direction indicated, and/or a white star-signal in the direction of a better landing place. Or signalling the code letter 'S' (···) followed by the code letter 'R' (·—·) if a better landing place is more to the right in the direction of approach; or by code letter 'L' (·—··) if a better landing place is more to the left in the direction of approach.

'Landing here is highly dangerous. A more favourable location for landing is in the direction indicated'

By night. Horizontal motion of a white flare or light, followed by the placing of the white light or flare on the ground and the carrying of another white light or flare in the direction to be indicated, and/or a white star-signal in the direction towards the better landing place. Or signalling the code letter 'S' (···)followed by the code letter 'R' (·—·) if a better landing place is more to the right in the direction of approach, or by code letter 'L' (·—··) if a better landing place is more to the left in the direction of approach.

'Landing here is highly dangerous. A more favourable location for landing is in the direction indicated'

3. Signals used in connection with shore life saving apparatus

By day. Vertical motion of a white flag or the arms
By night. Vertical motion of a white light or flare.

In general 'Affirmative'. Specifically: 'Rocket line is held'; 'Tail block is made fast'; 'Man is in breeches buoy'; 'Haul away'

By day. Horizontal motion of a white flag or arms extended horizontally.
By night. Horizontal motion of a white light or flare.

In general 'Negative'. Specifically: 'Slack away' 'Stop hauling'

4. Signals to be used to warn a vessel standing into danger

The International Code signals 'U' or 'NF', or the letter 'U' (··—) flashed by lamp or made by foghorn, whistle etc.

'You are running into danger'

If necessary, a white flare, a rocket showing white stars on bursting, or an explosive signal may draw the vessel's attention to these signals.

13.6.6 SIGNALS USED BY AIRCRAFT ON SAR OPERATIONS

As aircraft are routinely used in SAR, yachtsmen should be able to understand the signals which may be made. A survivor in a liferaft may well not have a radio. The search aircraft's tasks are to:

i Find the casualty and give her exact position;
ii Guide ships to the scene;
iii Keep the casualty under observation;
iv Mark her position by smoke or flare floats; and
v Drop survival equipment.

The survival equipment dropped by aircraft such as the RAF Nimrod consists of a 10-man liferaft and 2 canisters of supplies.

Search procedures

The pattern of search and the spacing between tracks flown by an aircraft depends upon the visibility, cloud base, the kind of object being searched for (eg yacht or liferaft) and the type, if any, of electronic search aid used. The most likely patterns are 'creeping line ahead' and an 'expanding square search'. The search may prove futile, unless the casualty can indicate its position to the aircraft, ie by radio, flashing lamp, flares, smoke, heliograph etc.

An aircraft normally flies through the search area at 3000 – 5000ft, or below cloud, firing a green Very at roughly every 5 to 10 minutes and at each turning point. When a green flare is sighted, do the following:

a. Wait for the glare of the green flare to die out.
b. Fire one red flare.
c. About 20 seconds later fire another red flare (this enables the aircraft to line up on the bearing).
d. Fire a third red flare when the aircraft is overhead, or if it appears to be going badly off course.

Obviously (but it bears repeating), a boat or liferaft must carry at least 3 red flares to comply with the above. If the aircraft has been diverted to the search from another task it may fire flares of any colour (except red). Do not fire pyrotechnics aimed directly at aircraft, particularly helicopters overhead.

RAF aircraft diverted to SAR are equipped with some or all of UHF, VHF, HF and MF RT. Royal Navy SAR helicopters and other RN aircraft carry HF/VHF/UHF RT equipment. RAF aircraft on SAR operations usually maintain a continuous watch on 121·5 and 243MHz, and 2182 kHz. The aircraft can home onto transmissions on these frequencies and Marine Band FM frequencies.

Dedicated SAR helicopters in the UK can communicate with RNLI lifeboats and HM Coastguard on the VHF/FM marine distress calling and safety frequency Channel 16, and on working frequencies. UK and most European SAR aircraft use voice callsigns comprising the word 'Rescue' followed by two or three numerals.

Directing signals

The following signals may be used by SAR aircraft to direct searching ships towards a vessel, aircraft or person in distress:

1. In sequence, the aircraft circles the search ship at least once. It then crosses low, ahead of that ship, opening and closing the throttle or changing the propeller pitch. Finally It heads in the direction in which that ship is to steer. The sequence may be repeated.	The aircraft is directing a ship towards the vessel or aircraft in distress.
2. The aircraft passes close astern of the search ship, at low altitude, rocking the wings or opening and closing the throttle or changing the propeller pitch. The aircraft may repeat the signal as necessary.	The aircraft is indicating that the assistance of the ship is no longer required.

13.6.7   EMERGENCY VHF DF AND MF QTG

There are two ways in which a vessel in distress can obtain RDF bearings from shore station(s) (and thus fix her position):

a. On VHF from the Coastguard or foreign equivalent. The vessel herself does not require any DF equipment on-board; only a VHF radio. She transmits for a bearing on Ch 16 if in distress; otherwise on Ch 67, or 82 off Jersey or 11 off France. Her bearing **from** the DF station is given on the same channels. This is not a routine navigational procedure; it is intended only for use in emergency.

Each VHF DF station is controlled by a nearby MRCC/MRSC and is shown on charts as ⊙ RG; see Fig. 7(16) and Fig. 13(9) for a map of DF sites in the UK and France. The Lat/Long of the stations are:

Falmouth MRCC

Trevose Head	50°32'·91N	05°01'·89W
St Mary's (Scilly)	49°55'·70N	06°18'·17W
Land's End	50°08'·13N	05°38'·19W

Brixham MRSC

Rame Head	50°18'·99N	04°13'·10W
Prawle Point	50°13'·14N	03°42'·55W
Berry Head	50°23'·97N	03°29'·05W

Portland MRSC

Grove Point	50°32'·93N	02°29'·20W
Hengistbury Head	50°42'·95N	01°45'·64W

Solent MRSC

Boniface Down	50°36'·21N	01°12'·03W
Selsey Bill	50°43'·82N	00°48'·20W
Newhaven	50°46'·90N	00°03'·13E

Channel Islands

Guernsey	49°26'·27N	02°35'·77W
Jersey	49°10'·85N	02°14'·30W

Dover MRCC

Fairlight	50°52'·19N	00°38'·83E
Langdon Battery	51°07'·93N	01°20'·69E
North Foreland	51°22'·50N	01°26'·82E

Thames MRSC

Shoeburyness	51°31'·34N	00°46'·69E
Bawdsey	51°51'·60N	01°25'·00E

Yarmouth MRSC

Caister	52°39'·63N	01°42'·90E
Trimingham	52°54'·57N	01°20'·60E
Hunstanton	52°56'·95N	00°29'·59E

Humber MRSC

Easington	53°39'·13N	00°05'·95E
Flamborough Head	54°07'·08N	00°05'·12W
Whitby	54°29'·40N	00°36'·25W
Hartlepool	54°41'·79N	01°10'·47W
Tynemouth	55°01'·08N	01°24'·90W
Cullercoats	55°04'·00N	01°28'·00W
Newton	55°31'·01N	01°37'·10W

Forth MRSC

Crosslaw	55°54'·50N	02°12'·20W
Fife Ness	56°16'·78N	02°35'·25W

Aberdeen MRCC

Inverbevie	56°51'·10N	02°15'·65W
Windyhead	57°38'·90N	02°14'·50W
Thrumster	58°23'·55N	03°07'·25W
Dunnet Head	58°40'·31N	03°22'·52W

Shetland MRSC

Compass Head	59°52'·05N	01°16'·30W
Wideford Hill	58°59'·29N	03°01'·40W

Stornoway MRSC

Sandwick	58°12'·65N	06°21'·27W
Rodel	57°44'·90N	06°57'·41W
Barra	57°00'·81N	07°30'·42W

Clyde MRCC

Tiree	56°30'·62N	06°57'·68W
Kilchiaran	55°45'·90N	06°27'·19W
Law Hill	55°41'·76N	04°50'·46W

Belfast MRSC

West Torr	55°11'·91N	06°05'·60W
Orlock Head	54°40'·41N	05°34'·97W

Liverpool MRSC

Snaefell (IoM)	54°15'·84N	04°27'·66W
Walney Island	54°06'·61N	03°16'·00W

Holyhead MRSC

Great Ormes Head	53°19'·98N	03°51'·11W
Rhiw	52°49'·98N	04°36'·69W

Milford Haven MRSC

St Ann's Head	51°40'·97N	05°10'·52W

Swansea MRCC

Hartland Point	51°01'·20N	04°31'·32W

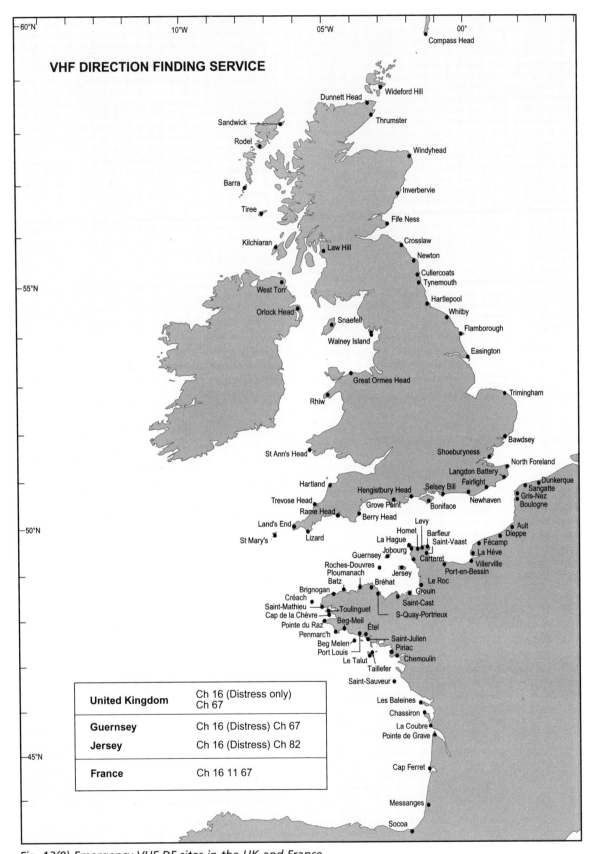

VHF DIRECTION FINDING SERVICE

Compass Head

Wideford Hill
Dunnett Head
Thrumster
Sandwick
Rodel
Windyhead
Barra
Inverbervie
Tiree
Fife Ness
Kilchiaran
Crosslaw
Law Hill
Newton
Cullercoats
Tynemouth
West Torr
Hartlepool
Orlock Head
Whitby
Snaefell
Flamborough
Walney Island
Easington
Great Ormes Head
Trimingham
Rhiw
Bawdsey
St Ann's Head
Shoeburyness
North Foreland
Langdon Battery
Hartland
Fairlight
Dunkerque
Hengistbury Head
Selsey Bill
Sangatte
Trevose Head
Grove Point
Newhaven
Gris-Nez
Rame Head
Berry Head
Boniface
Boulogne
Land's End
Levy
Ault
St Mary's
Lizard
Homet
Barfleur
Dieppe
La Hague
Saint-Vaast
Fécamp
Jobourg
La Héve
Guernsey
Carteret
Villerville
Roches-Douvres
Jersey
Port-en-Bessin
Ploumanach
Le Roc
Batz
Bréhat
Grouin
Brignogan
Saint-Cast
Créach
Saint-Mathieu
Toulinguet
S-Quay-Portrieux
Cap de la Chèvre
Beg-Meil
Pointe du Raz
Étel
Penmarc'h
Saint-Julien
Beg Melen
Piriac
Port Louis
Chemoulin
Le Talut
Taillefer
Saint-Sauveur
Les Baleines
Chassiron
La Coubre
Pointe de Grave
Cap Ferret
Messanges
Socoa

United Kingdom	Ch 16 (Distress only) Ch 67
Guernsey	Ch 16 (Distress) Ch 67
Jersey	Ch 16 (Distress) Ch 82
France	Ch 16 11 67

Fig. 13(9) Emergency VHF DF sites in the UK and France.

415

DF stations are controlled by a CROSS monitoring Ch 16; or by a Signal Station (Semaphore) or a Naval Lookout. The latter two types of station monitor Ch 16 and also scan Channels 1-29, 36, 39, 48, 50, 52, 55, 56, and 60-88.

Dunkerque	51°03'·40N 02°20'·40E
Sangatte	50°57'·10N 01°46'·39E
Gris Nez (CROSS)	50°52'·20N 01°35'·01E
Boulogne	50°44'·00N 01°36'·00E
Ault	50°06'·50N 01°27'·50E
Dieppe	49°56'·00N 01°05'·20E
Fécamp	49°46'·10N 00°22'·20E
La Hève	49°30'·60N 00°04'·20E
Villerville	49°23'·20N 00°06'·50E
Port-en-Bessin	49°21'·10N 00°46'·30W
Saint Vaast	49°34'·50N 01°16'·50W
Barfleur	49°41'·90N 01°15'·90W
Levy	49°41'·70N 01°28'·20W
Homet (Cherbourg)	49°39'·50N 01°37'·90W
Cap de la Hague	49°43'·60N 01°56'·30W
Jobourg (CROSS)	49°41'·50N 01°54'·50W
Carteret	49°22'·40N 01°48'·30W
Le Roc	48°50'·10N 01°36'·90W
Grouin	48°42'·60N 01°50'·60W
Saint-Cast	48°38'·60N 02°14'·70W
St Quay-Portrieux	48°39'·30N 02°49'·50W
Île de Bréhat	48°51'·30N 03°00'·10W
Roches-Douvres	49°06'·39N 02°48'·80W
Ploumanac'h	48°49'·50N 03°28'·20W
Ile de Batz	48°44'·80N 04°00'·60W
Brignogan	48°40'·60N 04°19'·70W
Créach	48°27'·60N 05°07'·70W
Créach (CROSS)	48°27'·60N 05°07'·80W
Saint-Mathieu	48°19'·80N 04°46'·20W
Toulinguet	48°16'·80N 04°37'·50W
Cap de la Chèvre	48°10'·20N 04°33'·00W
Pointe du Raz	48°02'·30N 04°43'·80W
Penmarc'h	47°47'·90N 04°22'·40W
Beg-Meil	47°51'·30N 03°58'·40W
Beg Melen (Groix)	47°39'·20N 03°30'·10W
Port Louis (Lorient)	47°42'·60N 03°21'·80W
Étel (CROSS)	47°39'·80N 03°12'·00W
Saint-Julien	47°29'·70N 03°07'·50W
Taillefer (Belle Île)	47°21'·80N 03°09'·00W
Le Talut (Belle Île)	47°17'·70N 03°13'·00W
Piriac	47°22'·50N 02°33'·40W
Chemoulin	47°14'·10N 02°17'·80W
Saint-Sauveur (Yeu)	46°41'·70N 02°18'·80W
Les Baleines (Ré)	46°14'·60N 01°33'·70W
Chassiron (Oléron)	46°02'·80N 01°24'·50W
Pointe de la Coubre	45°41'·90N 01°13'·40W
Pointe de Grave	45°34'·30N 01°03'·90W
Cap Ferret	44°37'·50N 01°15'·00W
Messanges	43°48'·80N 01°23'·90W
Socoa (Hendaye)	43°23'·30N 01°41'·10W

b.   By the QTG service (QTG is part of the Q code). When sent on MF from a ship to a shore station it means 'Request you send two dashes of 10 seconds each, plus your callsign, on the specified working frequency'. The shore station complies with that request and

the ship is able, with her onboard DF equipment, to obtain a bearing of the shore station from the yacht. A QTG station is shown on the chart by D R, see Fig. 7(16), but few such stations now operate in Europe.

13.7 GLOBAL MARITIME DISTRESS AND SAFETY SYSTEM (GMDSS)

13.7.1   INTRODUCTION

The abbreviation GMDSS does not roll off the tongue; it is even a little intimidating. However it is only a Global Maritime System which deals with Distress and Safety – at once things look much simpler. Perhaps Safety should precede Distress (as in the title of this chapter), because, importantly, it is by careful attention to Safety measures that we strive to avoid Distress. As always Prevention is better than Cure. It is also worth stressing that GMDSS is a 'System' with various sub-systems and components. See 13.10.3 for other abbreviations.

GMDSS can be regarded as nothing more than a vast communications umbrella which allows ships and shore stations to be in touch with each other over huge distances – in fact almost anywhere on the waters of this planet – a far cry from the *Titanic* in 1912 and even from the communications which have served us over the last 50 years.

Safety is the raison d'etre for GMDSS. Ships and yachts at sea can now receive a steady stream of Safety information about weather, navigational matters and emergency situations; forewarned is forearmed. Such information, which is nothing new, is called Maritime Safety Information – or MSI, if you must.

Finally we should understand, and be thankful for, the knowledge that when everything has gone wrong and we are, almost literally, on our beam ends ie in Distress, then the press of a button will alert others to our predicament. Our position and yacht identification are electronically transmitted within 5 seconds. Amplifying details could be transmitted if 15 more seconds were to be available.

This is not to say that we can duck our responsibilities; it is simply to acknowledge that technical advances can save lives which might otherwise have been lost. Against this background it is plain commonsense that yacht owners should embrace GMDSS, even though it is not, and probably never will be, compulsory for leisure craft below a certain size. It is however compulsory for vessels of over 300 tons which are regulated by the Safety of Life at Sea (SOLAS) convention, ie almost all merchant ships.

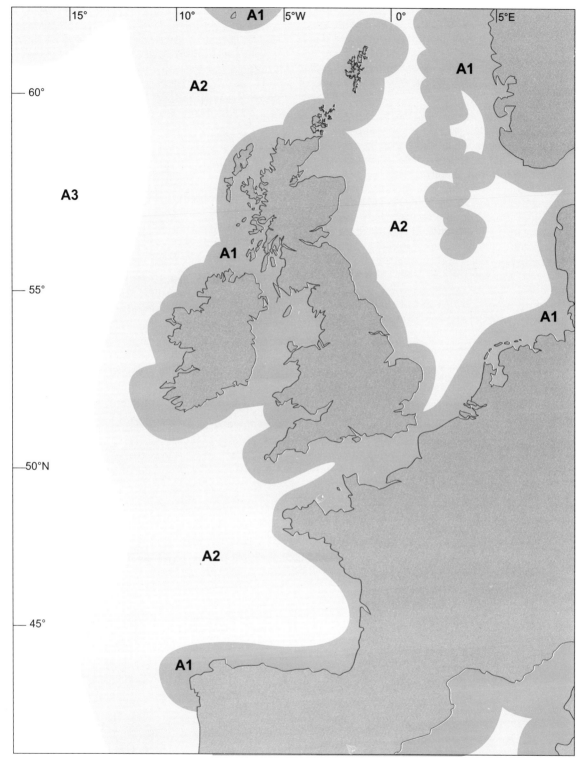

Fig. 13(10) Sea Areas around NW Europe.

13.7.2   COMMUNICATIONS

Communications lie at the heart of the system and divide into short, medium and long range, which in turn apply to four designated Sea Areas; see Fig.13(10) for European waters. Short range (30-55M offshore) is provided by VHF radio; Medium range (100-300M) by MF radio; and Long range between Lat 70°S and 70°N by Satellite communications. HF radio covers the polar regions.

These four Sea Areas are designated A1 to A4 depending on the type of communications required:

A1 is an area within VHF range of coast stations.
A2 is an area within MF range of coast stations.
A3 is an area within coverage of Inmarsat satellites.
A4 are the remaining Sea areas beyond the reach of the equipments which cover Al, A2 and A3 areas.

It is therefore obvious that the type of radio equipment which a ship must carry depends on the Sea Area(s) in which she normally operates.

VHF and MF radio need little introduction beyond saying that as part of GMDSS two dedicated initial contact channels or frequencies are used: Channel 70 for VHF and 2187·5kHz for MF. These loosely equate to VHF Ch 16 and 2182kHz in the pre-GMDSS era. Both these latter remain the primary voice communication Distress channel/frequency – and continue to be used as such after DSC has alerted other ships and shore stations.

Unsurprisingly Ch 70 and 2187·5kHz are associated with yet another abbreviation, DSC or

Digital Selective Calling. Digital means it is quick, efficient, machine-generated and more powerful than non-digital transmission. Selective because it allows individual ships or shore stations and specific groups of ships to be called.

For picking up Distress alerts both COSPAS/ SARSAT and INMARSAT satellites may be used (see 13.7.8). There are three types:

a. COSPAS/SARSAT satellites in Low Earth Orbit (LEO) from pole to pole, operating on 406 MHz;
b. Three COSPAS/SARSAT geo-stationary (GEO) satellites, which enhance the coverage of (a); and
c. Four Inmarsat GEO satellites which cover the three oceans, but not the polar regions, and operate in the 1·5 and 1·6 GHz bands.

Under GMDSS radio watchkeeping at sea is compulsory and automatic, the latter meaning any receipt of Distress and Urgency alerts rings an alarm to tell the crew. This is an important feature,

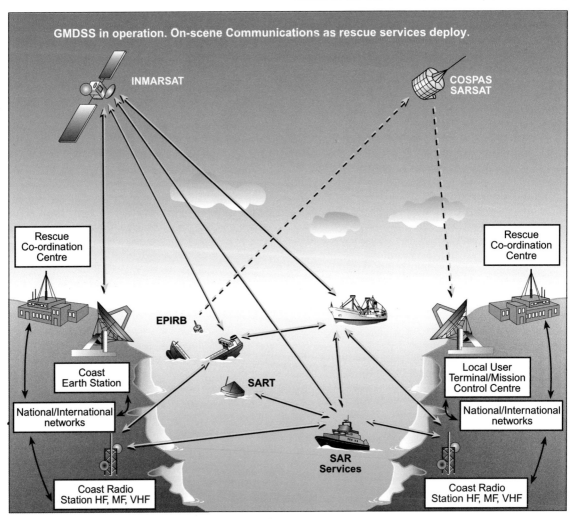

Fig. 13(11) GMDSS on-scene rescue communications.

as much on yachts as on commercial vessels.

The distinction between terrestrial and satellite communications should perhaps be emphasised. Consider a typical (if there is such a thing) Distress situation:

- The Distress alert is likely to be detected by the COSPAS/SARSAT system, which has no communications role as such; see Fig. 13 (11).
- The COSPAS/SARSAT satellite passes its findings to a Mission Control Centre (MCC) ashore. The MCC uses landlines to forward the information to Coastguard MRCC/MRSCs and Coast Radio Stations (if in existence)
- The Coastguard links by landline via Coast Earth Stations (eg Goonhilly) into the Inmarsat satellite system (if the long range so requires); see Chapter 10.
- Satcom, via Inmarsat, now enables the ship in distress to communicate with other ships, rescue services and the Coastguard. The ship may of course already be communicating by terrestrial means.

In terms of broadcasting MSI, Navtex (see Chapter 12) on 518 kHz MF takes care of A2 waters, out to about 300M from the transmitter. Further offshore, at scheduled times, Inmarsat satellites broadcast MSI over the three Oceans which they serve. This service is called SafetyNET and may simply be regarded as the long-range equivalent of Navtex.

Enhanced Group Calling (EGC) is another abbreviation to add to your list, but may never be encountered in practice by yachtsmen, because it features only in the Inmarsat-C system. Small to medium-sized yachts are unlikely to be fitted with Sat-C terminals as Mini-M equipment may be more suitable. EGC is a means of sending messages to selected groups of vessels; in that sense it bears some resemblance to DSC.

13.7.3 MARITIME MOBILE SERVICE IDENTITY (MMSI)

An MMSI is a nine-digit number used in DSC to identify a ship or shore station, either individually or in groups. It is similar to a telephone number or an ordinary non-DSC callsign. An MMSI is automatically granted, free of charge, by the RA to any holder of a Ship Radio Licence. It is unique to that ship (or shore station) and is usually inserted by the dealer from whom you buy the equipment. Unless this has been done, you cannot operate DSC. As a side issue, because the MMSI cannot be changed, a DSC set is a very much less attractive target for thieves.

The nine digits indicate the station's type (ship or shore), nationality, specific identity and whether individual or group. The following examples of MMSI show how the nine digits are utilised:

a. 232123456 = a single UK ship. UK identifiers are 232, 233 and 234; the ship is identified by the last six digits.
b. 023412345 = a group (as shown by the prefix 0) of UK ships. The group is identified by the last five digits.
c. 003661234 = an American (366) shore (prefix 00 means shore) station, identified by the last four digits.

Thus a single ship never has any prefixed zeros. A group MMSI always starts with a single zero. A shore station MMSI always starts with two zeros. The next three digits are nationality identifiers which always feature in MMSIs of all kinds; they are also known as Maritime Identification Digits (MID). Finally, the last four, five or six digits are the station's own unique identifying digits – making up the total to nine digits.

There is no published book (directory) of MMSIs, but they can be found at the ITU's web site www.itu.int Your DSC Controller or DSC/VHF set usually has a small built-in Directory able to accept 10 to 20 MMSI's which you commonly use.

13.7.4 DSC CONTROLLERS AND DSC RADIOS

First, whatever you buy must be type-approved by the RA to ensure its technical compliance with certain agreed standards. The European Standard EN 301.025 was first published in 1998 and specifies the minimum standards for small craft VHF DSC. However national standards (eg the UK's MPT 1279 specification) have since been introduced. Most recently, April 2001, a R & TTE Directive has usurped National standards and must now be complied with. This Directive is less demanding than the National standards and it is expected that in due course it will be brought into line with EN 301.025.

DSC Controllers can be "added-on" to a VHF radio which must itself be DSC compatible. Thus two boxes sit next to each other in a rather space-wasting manner. The Controller is outwardly distinguished by its large display window, an alpha-numeric keyboard and a guarded red Distress button. More recent sets, such as the Simrad RD 68 in Fig. 13 (12), are completely integrated into one box, not much bigger than a typical non-DSC VHF radio, but the display window has shrunk correspondingly.

DSC Controllers have been catgorised by IMO into seven classes of which only Class D and possibly Class F are of interest to yachtsmen:

Class D is the minimum DSC capability for small craft and other non-SOLAS vessels for whom DSC is not compulsory; often referred to as 'voluntary fit' vessels.

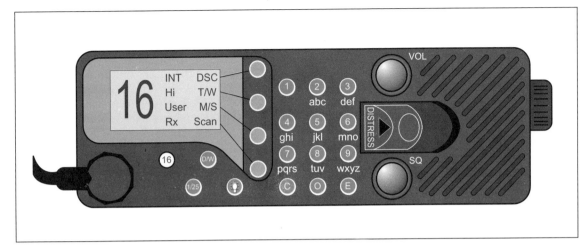

Fig. 13(12) Integrated DSC controller and VHF radio.

Class F relates to a hand-held VHF radio with very limited DSC facilities. It has since been withdrawn, but may be re-instated at a later date as hand-held sets far outnumber fixed installations.

13.7.5 CERTIFICATES OF COMPETENCE

Since February 1999 GMDSS has been a compulsory fit for all vessels over 300 tons, commercial vessels under 300 tons and some categories of passenger vessesl – but not leisure craft. A new Short Range Certificate (SRC) of Competence has been introduced so that yachtsmen can benefit from the greatly enhanced safety standards of GMDSS. It is called SRC because VHF is the short range element of GMDSS communications and is valid for both VHF-only and DSC radios. Specifically the SRC requires a candidate to demonstrate, by continuous assessment and passing a written examination, his ability to operate a DSC controller (or that part of a VHF/DSC radio). Training may take the form of a one day course (and examination) for those who have never had a 'VHF-only Certificate of Competence'; or for those with that Certificate, a half day conversion course is available. The examination can of course be taken at established Centres without any prior training other than self-study.

All RYA trainers/assessors use an RYA-approved, hands-on DSC Simulator. Fig. 13(13) shows a diagram of this simulator which is an excellent training aid, both for groups and individuals. It cost £20 from LightMaster, 18 Stanley Gardens, South Croydon CR2 9AH. Tel 020 8405 8200; Fax 020 8405 8300. admin@lightmaster.co.uk

RYA booklet G22/99 "VHF Radio (inc GMDSS)" gives sound advice on how to use the equipment, both pre- and post-GMDSS. Booklet G26/20 "VHF Radio SRC assessments" contains details of the SRC syllabus and examination. In essence G22 trains you and G26 tells you how to pass the assessment/examination. Most people will find it worthwhile to do a little prior revision on Distress definitions and the precise format of various messages.

A Long Range Certificate (LRC) is desirable for the many yachtsmen who routinely cruise offshore beyond VHF range, ie outside A1 areas. This deals with MF, HF and Satellite communications, as well as Navtex, EPIRBs and SARTs. The syllabus can be covered in modules, ie 'DSC module', 'Satellite module', each taking a day including the examination.

13.7.6 DSC PROCEDURES

The four main DSC procedures permit you to send, or receive:

a. A Distress Alert and its associated Distress message;

b. An Urgency Alert and associated Urgency message;

c. A Safety Alert and its associated Safety message; and

d. A Routine Alert, followed by a ship-to-ship or ship-to-shore message.

The first three Alerts correspond respectively to the Mayday, Pan Pan and Securite calls on non-DSC radio, which you will make once your Alert has gone out. The Routine alert is a DSC way of contacting another vessel or shore station without having to clutter up Ch 16 with the usual initial contact call – which is a useful benefit on a busy channel.

Before you start using DSC the display window will be showing your Lat/Long (assuming the GPS is linked to the DSC), the time UT, your MMSI,

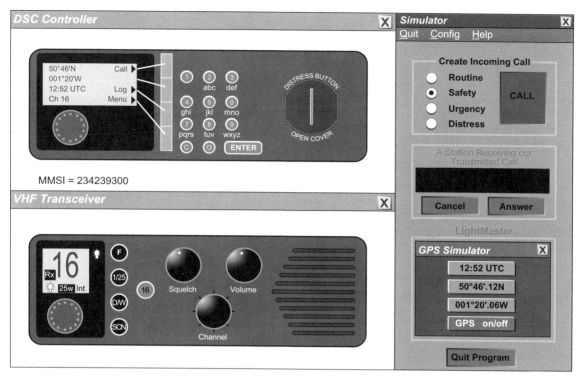

Fig. 13(13) DSC training Simulator

Fig. 13(14) The DSC display after the first press.

the VHF Ch selected and power output 1W or 25W, as shown in Fig. 13(13). Note that, although selected to Ch 16 on 25W in this example, the DSC Controller is listening on Ch 70 at 25W, ready for any incoming Alert.

To send a Distress Alert:

i Lift the spring-loaded cover and press the Red button for a moment. The window will display 'Distress UNDESIGNATED'; see Fig. 13(14).

ii If you are in extremis, ie abandoning ship without delay, press and hold the red button for 5 seconds. The window will change to 'Mayday sent' with a prompt to send a Mayday call on Ch 16 – which the non-DSC part of the radio has already selected on 25W.

iii If however time permits, after the first press scroll through the various types of distress to select the situation which you are in (Fire, sinking, collision, piracy etc). Then press the red button for 5 seconds and you will have sent a full Distress Alert, ie with a brief description of the problem; Fig. 13(15).

You would now hope to receive an acknowledgement on Ch 70 from the Coastguard; Fig. 13(16).

You would then send a conventional Distress call and message on Ch 16, for the benefit of any non-DSC vessels in the vicinity, eg:

MAYDAY, MAYDAY, MAYDAY
This is JUNO, JUNO, JUNO
MMSI 233 654321
MAYDAY, JUNO
Position ....
Holed and sinking
Request immediate assistance
Four persons on board
Abandoning to liferaft
OVER

Note: The first 3 lines are the Distress Call with your MMSI added so as to tie in with your DSC Distress Alert.

The remainder is a standard Distress message.

This should be acknowledged on Ch 16 with some indication of what help is being activated. If your Distress Alert was not acknowledged it will automatically be repeated every four minutes on Ch 70 until it is acknowledged.

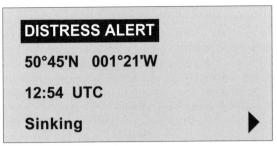

DISTRESS ALERT

50°45'N   001°21'W

12:54 UTC

Sinking   ▶

Fig. 13(15) The DSC display after the second press.

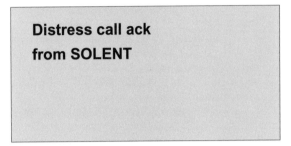

Distress call ack

from SOLENT

Fig. 13(16) Distress ackowledged.

Receiving a Distress Alert
If a Distress Alert is received an aural alarm will sound to notify you. You cannot respond on DSC with a Class D Controller, so switch to Ch 16, listen and copy the Mayday message. If no other

Fig. 13(17) The menus in a DSC Controller.

authority acknowledges, you are obliged to. Be realistic in assessing whether you are able to render practical assistance. It may in any event be sensible to send a MAYDAY RELAY in the hope of alerting a shore authority to the situation.

The DSC Controller Menu
Study the built-in menu, as in Fig. 13(17); it shows how you were cued through the Distress Alert. It also shows the various options available to you for dealing with other situations including setting up routines and 'house-keeping' procedures. Options and terminology may vary in detail depending on individual manufacturers, but the broad principles hold good.

To send Urgency or Safety Alerts, select the 'All Ships' Call and proceed accordingly. In Fig. 13(18) a Safety message is about to be broadcast on Ch 16 to all ships by a UK shore station.

As with a Distress Alert, you will continue with a conventional Pan-Pan or Securité message on Ch 16.

The Routine Alert is a way of 'paging' another vessel to say that you wish to converse.

If you do know her MMSI, then go ahead with the Alert, noting that unlike non-DSC VHF, the station calling nominates the intended working channel – Channel 77 in this case; see Fig. 13 (19).

If you do not know the other ship's MMSI, you cannot call her on DSC. You will have to make a

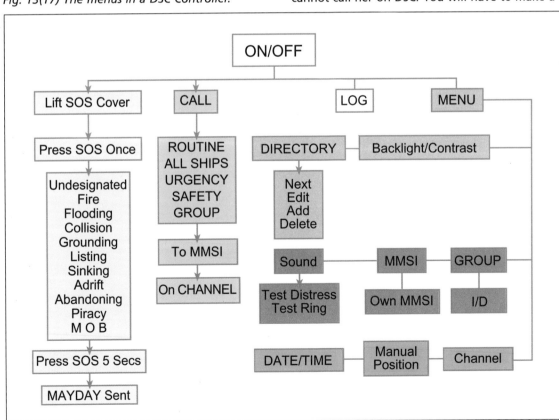

Fig. 13(18) A Safety message is about to be broadcast on Ch 16 to all ships by a UK shore station.

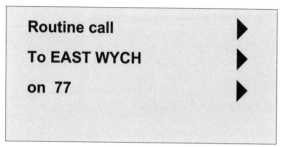

Fig. 13(19) A Routine call to another yacht on Ch 77.

voice call on Ch 16 and she will nominate the working channel. You may be more likely to get a response if you call on Ch 13 rather than 16; the former is designated as a bridge-to-bridge channel. Many yachtsmen now find it worthwhile to monitor Ch 13/16 on Dual Watch.

13.7.7 OTHER COMPONENTS OF GMDSS

It is a requirement of GMDSS that ships, including voluntary-fit yachts, should be able to send Distress Alerts by two out of three possible means. These are:

a. DSC calling on VHF Ch 70, MF 2187·5 kHz or the HF distress and alerting frequencies in the 4, 6, 8,12 and 16 MHz bands;

b. EPIRBs; and

c. Satellite communications through Inmarsat.

DSC is probably the primary means for participating yachts, which are also likely to fit a 406 MHz EPIRB not only on the grounds of its obvious ability to pinpoint your position in a Distress situation, but also because it is far cheaper than SatCom. The latter however is steadily becoming more affordable and offers good quality global communications at all times and in all areas except the Polar regions.

EPIRBs are discussed in the next section, SatCom is covered in Chapter 10 and Navtex in Chapter 11.

13.7.8 EMERGENCY POSITION INDICATING RADIO BEACONS (EPIRB)

EPIRBs are self-contained battery-operated, watertight and buoyant radio transmitters. They

are designed to be used by mariners during a distress situation to transmit an alert via satellite to maritime authorities.

Larger vessels, such as those operating under SOLAS conventions, over 300 gross tonnes or fishing vessels over 12m LOA must carry EPIRBs as part of their GMDSS fit. But many smaller vessels, pleasure craft in particular, are advised to carry a beacon, especially if cruising far from a safe haven. These beacons provide a secondary back-up means of alerting when alternative radio contact fails. They should be regarded as a supplementary rather than a solitary means of alerting.

Types of beacon

The two types of COSPAS/SARSAT approved EPIRBs suitable for small craft usage operate on: either 121·5/243 MHz (the civil/military aeronautical distress frequencies); or 406 MHz, for the more sophisticated beacons. The main difference between the two types is the way they transmit an alert.

Other types of beacon include:

a. Search and Rescue Transponders (SARTs) intended for use aboard a liferaft (see 13.7.9);

b. Personal Locator Beacons (PLBs) for use by individuals; and

c. Emergency Locator Transmitters (ELT) for use in aircraft.

The 121·5/243 MHz beacons transmit an analogue signal at around 75 – 100mW. More modern types can transmit the vessel's callsign and position or MMSI in Morse. All 121·5MHz beacons are manually activated and work with low-earth orbit satellites, but they cannot be detected by the geostationary satellites that provide instantaneous alerting over 85% of the globe. The position of a 121·5/243 MHz beacon is normally accurate to within 10·8M. Note that 121·5/243 MHz beacons will be phased out between 2006 and 2009.

Users are therefore recommended to consider buying a 406 MHz model. These transmit a uniquely coded digital signal to the satellites as well as having a built-in 121·5 MHz homing device.

406 MHz beacons come in two categories, depending on how they are activated: Type I float free EPIRBs are activated either automatically or manually. They are either stowed in canisters or in special mounting brackets fitted with a hydrostatic unit which releases the beacon when 2-4 metres below the water. The beacon then floats to the surface and begins to transmit, for its battery life of 48 hours. The beacon must be properly mounted where it can float free without snagging the vessel.

Fig. 13(20) A 406MHz EPIRB with built-in GPS.

Type II beacons can only be manually released and have a 24 or 48 hour battery life.

Both categories transmit a signal at 5 watt every 50 seconds and have a 98% detection probability on the first satellite pass. They can be picked up by geostationary satellites as well as by those in polar orbit. The positional accuracy of 406 MHz beacons is normally within 2·7M, depending on the number of satellite passes.

The most recent 406 MHz GPS beacons transmit alerts which also include their position to within 100 metres, using their own in-built GPS. They also transmit on 121·5MHz for homing purposes; see Fig. 13(20).

SAR Satellites

As far back as the 1960s satellites were used to track emergency beacon transmissions on 121·5/243 MHz. These are the international frequencies for VHF civil aeronautical distress and its military UHF equivalent.

By the mid 1970s the USA, Canada and France had developed the SARSAT (Search and Rescue Satellite- Aided Tracking) system. It uses 406 MHz, a frequency specific to EPIRBs, as well as being able to detect 121·5/243 Mhz. The beacons are digitally coded with a unique identifying signal and importantly their details are registered with the relevant authorities.

A similar system, known as COSPAS (*Cosmicheskaya Systema Poiska Aariynyich Sudov* – roughly translated as "Space system for the detection of vessels in distress") was developed by the USSR at the same time. In 1979 the two merged into today's COSPAS/SARSAT system.

SARSAT instrumentation is on board the US NESDIS- operated satellites which are in Low Earth Orbit (LEO) from pole to pole. At an altitude of 528M, inclined at 99° to the equator, these satellites take 100 minutes per orbit and have a footprint (radius of view) of 2500 km. They carry a Search and Rescue Processor (SARP)

which receives and stores 406 MHz beacon data. The satellite measures the frequency of the EPIRB and also date/time stamps it. Its position is calculated from the transmission data, thus the more hits the greater the accuracy of the position. The SARP transmits the data to the nearest ground station tracking the satellite, which are known as LUTs (Local User Terminals). If the footprint encompasses a LUT as well as the beacon position simultaneously, the information is transferred immediately (Real-time mode). Otherwise the signal is stored and passed to the next available LUT (Global mode), thus providing global coverage on 406 MHz. These satellites also carry a SAR repeater which receives and re-transmits 121·5 and 243 MHz signals. However this data is only transmitted if a LUT is within the footprint at the same time as the beacon, otherwise the data is lost.

COSPAS instrumentation is carried onboard the NAZEZHDA navigational satellites in LEO polar orbit at an altitude of 620M with an 83° inclination. Each orbit takes 105 minutes and has a footprint of 3000 km. The main difference between the COSPAS and SARSAT is that the Russian satellites do not receive 243 MHz distress signals. The LUT processes the downloaded data and passes it to the Mission Control Centre (MCC). The UK MCC is at Kinloss, Morayshire.

Additionally COSPAS/SARSAT now have three 406 MHz receivers on geostationary earth orbiting (GEO) satellites. These satellites continuously view large areas of the Earth and provide immediate alerting and identification of 406 MHz distress signals. However as there is no relative motion between themselves and the beacon, they cannot locate the EPIRB by Doppler. Positional data has therefore to be verified on the next available pass by a COSPAS/SARSAT LEO satellite. The registration details of the beacon can however be checked at this point and passive Search and Rescue can begin.

Inmarsat, a leading provider of global mobile maritime communications, also has a network of four geostationary satellites covering the Atlantic, Indian and Pacific Oceans. These pick up alerts from their own brand, Inmarsat-E EPIRB. These beacons are currently less well known than the Cospas/Sarsat types, but as prices reduce this will change. They are registered with Inmarsat in London; for further details visit their website: www.inmarsat.org

False alerts

Around the UK in 2000AD there were 451 distress alerts from 406 MHz beacons, of which 425 were false – a false alert rate of approximately 94%. Careful handing of beacons can reduce such statistics. EPIRBs are made to be extremely sensitive and are designed for use in a emergency;

false alerts are therefore easily generated in a number of ways. These include: mishandling, incorrect testing, washing down decks or just bad weather. Ensure that the beacon is handled as per the manufacturer's instructions and that manually activated types are easily retrievable. Batteries and hydrostatic releases must also be checked and replaced regularly, again referring to manufacturers' advice.

Beacon registration

If you own a UK encoded EPIRB, it is now **compulsory** by law to provide the Registry at Falmouth MRCC with information about your vessel: ie number of people on board and, most importantly, how to contact you in an alert, or a shore-based contact who is aware of your planned trip; also loss or theft of the EPIRB. Registration is free of charge and forms are available from the Registry and in various publications, including a section in the Ship Radio Licence application form.

Once registered you will be provided with a database entry printout and two 'proof of registration' labels. If the EPIRB is properly registered, a false alarm can be resolved by just a quick telephone call without using vital SAR resources which could be deployed more usefully elsewhere.

The role of each Registry is to provide 24 hour access to database information on EPIRBs, so as to assist in maritime SAR operations. When a beacon alert is received by an MCC, part of the data refers to the Country Mid code, eg: 232 – Great Britain, which immediately identifies the country or administration where the beacon's registration details are held. This information is passed by the MCC to the appropriate Rescue Centre(s).

406 MHz EPIRBs can be identified in one of three main ways (although different countries apply different rules), ie by using a MMSI, Callsign or Unique Serial No (serialised protocol). The only beacons which can be registered are those that have been UK Type approved and have been programmed using, preferably, UK Serialised Protocol or a UK MMSI number. Refer to MSN 1732 (M&F) and MGN 150 (M&F), Merchant Shipping Notices or Guidance Notes available from the MCA.

Further details from: The EPIRB Register, Falmouth MRCC, Castle Drive, Pendennis Point, Falmouth, Cornwall TR11 4WZ. Tel 01326 211569; Fax 01326 319264.

Useful Web sites include:

www.mcga.gov.uk	MCA
www.cospas-sarsat.org	Cospas/Sarsat
www.sarsat.noaa.gov	USA satellites & registration

13.7.9 SEARCH AND RESCUE TRANSPONDER (SART)

A SART is the main means of actually pinpointing a ship in distress or, more probably, her crew in a liferaft. A SART is akin to a Racon, ie when swept by the radar of a searching aircraft or ship it responds with a series of signals which are clearly seen on radar. It will only respond to a 3cm (X band) radar.

The SART should be mounted vertically on the liferafts, at least 1m above sea level. It can then be detected at up to 40M by a helicopter at 3000ft; and at up to 5M by a ship. Tests have shown a severe reduction in range if the SART is not properly mounted, ie if floating in the water or lying flat on the floor of a liferaft the detection range will be as little as 1·8 – 2·0M. If upright on the liferaft floor, range improves to 2·5M. Battery capacity should allow 96 hrs in standby mode and at least 8 hours whilst actively responding.

When first detected the SART signal is seen as 12 dots orientated towards the transponder. At about 1M range from the SART, the dots broaden out into arcs which grow progressively wider until they form concentric circles as the SART is closed. This form of signal is far easier to detect than a single radar contact.

13.8 EMERGENCY SITUATIONS

13.8.1 ABANDON SHIP

Although preparations should be made, it is unwise to leave a yacht until it is certain that she is doomed. A boat is a much better target for rescue craft than a liferaft and while it is possible to remain on board it may be feasible to use her various resources (such as the radiotelephone for distress calls) to good effect and to select equipment which can be taken into the liferaft, or perhaps be securely lashed into the dinghy – which should be taken too if circumstances permit.

Action needed, if time permits, before entering the raft and cutting it adrift from the yacht:

1. If the radio is available, send a Distress alert and/or a Mayday call, stating that the crew are abandoning ship into the liferaft, and giving the position. If a hand-held VHF is carried it should of course be taken in the liferaft.
2. Dress warmly with sweaters etc under oilskins and lifejackets on top. Take extra clothes in bin liners.
3. Fill any available containers with screw tops about $\frac{3}{4}$ full of fresh water, so that they will float.

4. Take the emergency/panic/grab bag; see 13.3.11.
5. Collect additional food, including tins and tin opener.
6. Collect any equipment which will help to navigate and manage the liferaft - such as charts, hand bearing compass, pencils and paper, torch, extra flares, bucket, length of line, first aid kit, knife, fishing gear.
7. If possible, salvage such items as passports, money and ship's papers. *Sea Survival – A Manual* by Dougal Robertson (Paul Elek) is recommended reading.

In the liferaft

Around the British Isles it is unlikely that survivors would be adrift in a liferaft for any length of time, but it is best to plan for the worst from the outset. If there has not been time to collect useful items from the yacht, there may be a chance to salvage all sorts of flotsam when she sinks. Almost anything may prove useful, but beware of sharp objects or wreckage which might pierce the raft.

8. Keep the inside of the raft as dry as possible. Cold is likely to be a problem even in summer – huddle together for warmth. Close the opening to the raft as necessary, but always keep a lookout for shipping. Activate EPIRB.
9. Stream the drogue if it is desired to stay near to the scene of abandoning ship, or if the weather is bad.
10. Ration fresh water to $\frac{1}{2}$ litre ($\frac{3}{4}$ pint) per person per day. Do not drink sea water or urine. Collect rain water; a gutter and drain is usually provided on the raft's canopy.
11. Use flares sparingly, and only on the skipper's orders. See 13.3.10 and 13.6.6.
12. Take anti-seasickness pills as soon as possible.

13.8.2 HELICOPTER RESCUE

When a helicopter comes to the aid of a yacht in distress, it helps if the yacht crew has some working knowledge of the procedures and limitations. Helicopters cannot hover close above a yacht with a mast, for safety reasons. While hovering the pilot has limited vision of a boat or a survivor below him and relies on conning instructions from his aircrewman. Hover height depends on keeping clear of the yacht's mast, on the size of the target and the type of transfer being effected.

The helicopter has first to find the yacht. An accurate position (latitude and longitude, or bearing and distance from some charted feature) in the yacht's MAYDAY call is essential. Identifying the yacht from the air, particularly if other craft are in the vicinity, is easier if the boat's name is clearly painted on the hull, deck or on dodgers; the sail number also helps if sails are hoisted.

The yacht in distress, on sighting the helicopter, will assist recognition by showing an orange smoke signal by day or a red flare at night; even an Aldis lamp trained on the helicopter and flashing SOS will help. Do not fire parachute rockets when a helicopter is in the vicinity. The yacht can call the helicopter on VHF Channel 16. SAR helicopters use the callsign 'Rescue' plus two or three numerals, eg 'Rescue 193'. A message might also be relayed by the Coastguard or by a lifeboat in the vicinity.

The helicopter will normally use the Hi-line method of transferring survivors, because a yacht's mast and rig inhibit the more usual direct winching procedure; Fig. 13 (21). A yacht is also a very small and erratic target and offers poor visual references to the pilot. The Hi-line itself is like a heaving line and provides an umbilical from yacht to the helicopter's winch wire during the transfer. It is a terylene rope (90, 150, 200 or 250 feet long) with a soft eye at each end and a weak link (150lb breaking strain) where it attaches to a hook at the end of the helicopter's winch wire. It is dipped (earthed) in the sea before handling to dispel any static charge. Its weighted lower end will be lowered to or trailed across the yacht for the crew to retain and tend, but it must **never** be secured to the yacht. To the hook are also attached the lifting strop or stretcher for lifting survivors. With the Hi-line aboard the yacht, the helicopter is free to manoeuvre into the optimum winching position, initially conned by the Aircrewman until the pilot has the necessary references.

On the yacht meanwhile, all sail should be lowered and the boom lashed on deck away from the transfer area. It helps if the yacht's drift can be reduced by a sea anchor, or by streaming the anchor and cable over the bows. If able to motor, maintain steerage way with the wind 30° to 40° off the port bow. The helicopter can then hover almost dead into wind, so that the pilot on its starboard side can see the yacht. The crew should be prepared for the helicopter's deafening noise (use sign language), and for the severe rotor downwash which will whip up spray and blow unsecured items overboard. As the helicopter pays out the winch wire, the crew should take down the slack on the Hi-Line; coil it carefully, free of snags. The Hi-Line is used to guide the winch wire to the yacht, until the winch hook and strop are onboard. Keep it just taut, but do not pull it in faster than the winch wire is lowered, or the weak link will part, with consequent delay.

The lift. The strop is put over the head and shoulders, and fitted under the arm pits with the

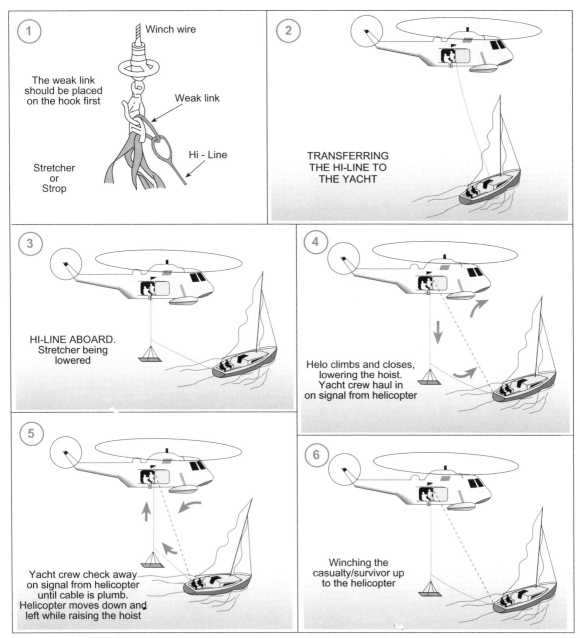

Fig. 13(21) Hi-line lift technique.

padded part in the small of the back; Fig. 13(22). The sliding toggle at the front is then pulled down towards the body to tighten the strop. The survivor gives a thumbs up when ready to be hoisted. The arms should then be kept extended downwards, close to the sides of the body. When the survivor is secured in the strop, and the thumbs up signal is given, the helicopter ascends and takes in the wire. The crew on deck pay out the Hi-Line, keeping it just taut; hold on to it until the aircrewman indicates that he is ready to recover it. But if a further lift is to be made, the end of the line should be retained on board anyway (but not made fast), so as to recover the

strop for the next lift. The diver may or may not be lowered with the strop. To raise two survivors in one lift, two strops may be offered together.

At the door of the helicopter, obey the instructions of the diver and/or the Aircrewman. Once the survivor is inside the aircraft the strop will be removed, and the survivor should strap himself in to a seat, as directed. On leaving the helicopter follow the Aircrewman's directions, to avoid the risk of walking into the tail rotor.

The normal way, depending on sea state and deck movement, of lifting a survivor from a boat with no mast is with a direct winch transfer, ie without the Hi-line.

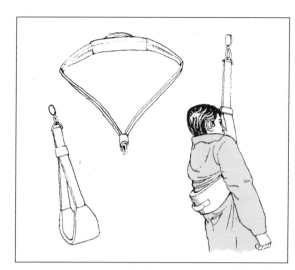

Fig. 13(22) The strop used in helicopter rescue lifts.

If the diver descends to the yacht, or to rescue somebody from a liferaft or from the water, obey his instructions exactly and as quickly as possible, since time may be precious. A diver will accompany a survivor in a double lift, as illustrated in Fig. 13(23). The survivor in his strop faces the diver, who puts his legs round the survivor's waist. An injured person is strapped into a special helicopter stretcher and winched up, accompanied by the diver. Small children are carried by the diver when being lifted.

It is NOT always necessary for survivors to be picked up from a dinghy or liferaft streamed astern of the yacht. The decision to abandon or

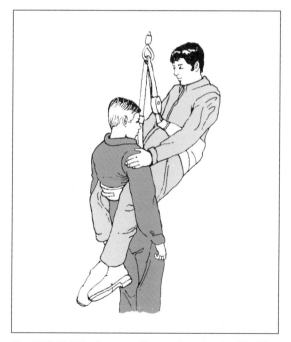

Fig. 13(23) Winchman with survivor in double lift.

stay with the yacht rests with the skipper, ideally having taken advice from the helicopter. In a small sailing boat which has no dinghy or liferaft, survivors (who should of course be wearing lifejackets) may have to jump into the water on the end of a long warp so that they can be picked up. This problem does not arise in the case of a motor cruiser with no mast, or a small sailing dinghy. The latter, if still upright, should lower any sails.

The Sea King (Mk 5 as used by the RN, and other Mks by other navies, the RAF and the Coastguard) is the SAR workhorse. It may be crewed by 2 pilots, 1 observer (navigator), 1 Aircrewman, 1 SAR diver, and medics as required. It has an unrefuelled radius of action of about 200M, a maximum speed of 120kn and time on task of at least 30 minutes (depending on range). It can carry 10 survivors or an underslung payload of 6000lbs. It has radar and a full radio fit, including marine band VHF with which to contact a yacht. Like most modern SAR helicopters it operates by day and night in all weathers. RN SAR helicopters are at 15 minutes notice to fly by day, 45 minutes at night.

The above notes were revised with the kind assistance of 771 Naval Air Squadron at RNAS Culdrose, Cornwall.

13.8.3   FIREFIGHTING

To start and sustain a fire three things are needed: Fuel, oxygen and heat, the last named being needed to start the fire which then becomes self-sustaining by virtue of its own heat. Remove any one of the three ingedients and the fire will go out – but be on your guard against re-ignition. Fire extinguishers therefore aim to cool the fire down, smother it, or react with it chemically; or sometimes a combination of these methods. So much for heat and air (oxygen).

Cutting off the fuel supply is the one way that an owner has of preventing a fire in the first place or starving it if it should start. He must devise ways of storing and cutting off such flammable fuels as gas, petrol, diesel, paraffin, paint and solvents. He may have to accept the fire risk of more mundane combustibles such as wood and paper. But he should at least instal fire-retardant upholstery and deckhead linings. He should insist on commonsense in the galley, ie good gas discipline and rigorous care with oils and fats. Finally he must remain on his guard against the great risk of ignition sparked by faulty electrics.

Fires are categorised by fuel type, as follows:

Type   Fuel
A   Solid materials: wood, paper, upholstery.
B   Liquids: Petrol, paraffin, oil, solvents etc.

C   Gases: Propane, butane, LPG.
E   Electrical: the principal cause of fire aboard.

Extinguishants are discussed in some detail below and are summarised in Fig. 13(23). Most extinguishers are of the stored pressure type (dry nitrogen) with a pressure gauge. Powder or foam are held in suspension and therefore do not consolidate over a period of time. The best types have a controlled discharge, allowing some of the contents to be retained for use in the event of re-ignition.

a. **Water** is excellent for cooling down a fire, and on a boat there is always a plentiful supply, readily hauled aboard in a couple of buckets with lanyards. Water is less damaging to the interior of a boat than chemicals, and does not give off harmful fumes. Water can prevent re-ignition of a fire which has been temporarily extinguished by other means. But water must not be applied to burning liquids such as fuel or cooking fat since a violent reaction will occur, spreading the fire in every direction. Also, since water is heavier than fuels or cooking fat, the latter will float on the water and continue burning. Nor must water be used on electrical fires where high voltage is present, due to the danger involved.

b. **Dry powder** is the best choice for use below decks as it does not give off dangerous fumes, nor conduct electricity, is non-corrosive and is suitable for most types of fire. It does make rather a mess, but not as much as foam. Powder stops combustion chemically, and absorbs some heat as it melts, thereby giving a slight cooling effect. When triggered, the powder emerges as a fine jet which should travel at least 2m; when this hits the flames it causes dense white non-toxic smoke, which can be alarming in the confines of a boat. The average powder extinguisher discharges fully in less than 10 seconds, so it is important to get as close as possible and aim carefully at the base of the fire, to ensure that the first burst from the extinguisher is really effective.

c. **Foam** extinguishers are best for AB type fires. The foam is known as AFFF (Aqueous Film Forming Foam) which is water-based and forms a clinging blanket over the surface. Thus it cuts off the supply of oxygen and also effectively cools the surface, preventing re-ignition. It should not be used on CE fires. It is little used in boats largely because Dry powder does rather more.

d. **Carbon dioxide** (CO_2) acts by blanketing a fire and has no cooling effect. It is good on liquid or electrical fires, but much less so on 'A' type fires where re-ignition is likely. It is stored under high pressure, and the weight of the cylinders (5kg minimum) makes it unsuitable for small boats. In larger craft it may be used (like BCF) for fixed installations in engine rooms. It works by depleting the oxygen level to a point (less than 15%) where combustion cannot be supported – and humans may suffocate.

e. **BCF** (Halon 1211) is only legal in automatic extinguishers in the engine room until Dec 2003. Otherwise it is banned due to its alleged ozone-depleting properties (a pity because it is very effective on all types of fire). Heat from the fire activates the sensing head to release the extinguishant, which fills the compartment with gas. This eliminates any need to open up the engine room, which can only make matters worse. It is important that the extinguisher is large enough in relation to the volume of the space: 1·0kg of BCF is sufficient for up to 1·8m³ of engine room, and 1·5kg for 3·6m³ (no deduction being made for space occupied by engines etc). Vaporising liquids such as Halon 1211, ie BCF (bromo-chloro-difluoro-methane), and Halon 1301, ie BTM (bromo-trifluoro-methane) are excellent all-round extinguishants, but fumes given off by them can be dangerous in the confined spaces of a boat.

The following table, Fig. 13(24), briefly summarises which extinguishants are effective on which types of fire. Clearly dry powder emerges as the best all-rounder, despite the mess it leaves behind. All extinguishers are now red (water cylinders being totally red), but a smallish label on the bottle is colour-coded (as shown below) to identify the type of extinguishant.

Type of fire	Water (Red)	Foam (Cream)	Powder (Blue)	CO_2 (Black)
A	Yes	Yes	Yes	V. limited
B	No	Yes	Yes	Yes
C	No	No	Yes	No
E	No	No	Yes	Yes

Fig. 13(24) Summary of uses for extinguishants.

Minimum fire rating

Table 1 in 13.2.2 gives the number of extinguishers which the RYA recommends should be carried aboard yachts in categories A-D. One or two extra extinguishers are strongly

429

recommended. Table 1 also specifies a minimum fire rating for extinguishers, for example 5A/34B to BS EN 3. This rating states the type and size of fire which that extinguisher can tackle. In this example 5A means that under test conditions the extinguisher was able in 1 minute to put out a 0·5m length of test material in a type A fire. Similarly 34B refers to a liquid fire where in 1 minute the extinguisher could put out a 50:50 test mixture of 34 litres of petrol and water. A 5A/34B rating would typically apply to a 1kg dry powder extinguisher. BS EN 3 shows compliance with British and European standards.

A fire blanket, stowed near (but not above or behind) the cooker, is ideal for smothering galley flare ups, ie fat fires. Do not use water, which only scatters the burning liquid. If a fire blanket is not available, a towel or blanket soaked in water will serve. Make as good a seal as possible with the blanket round the edge of the pan, and try to prevent the blanket falling into the actual liquid. Leave the blanket in place until the pan and its contents are thoroughly cooled.

Speed is essential in firefighting, so it is important that there should be an extinguisher ready to hand in each compartment of a boat, and that all the crew should know how to use them. An extinguisher just inside the companionway and another in the forecabin should ensure that the fire can be fought whilst preserving an escape route.

If a serious fire develops, steer the boat so that the wind will not spread the flames further along the boat. Batten down all hatches to avoid fanning the flames.

Fire extinguishers do not remain efficient, or even operable, if left indefinitely in a marine environment. Some (more expensive ones) are fitted with pressure gauges, which should be checked regularly. BCF or BTM extinguishers can be checked by weight. But dry powder extinguishers should be discharged & refilled or replaced about every five years. Weighing them is ineffective, because a leak only causes loss of the propellant, which has negligible weight compared to the powder.

The above notes were revised with the kind assistance of Mr John Scott, Chief Executive of Firemaster Extinguisher Ltd, Firex House, 174-176 Hither Green Lane, London SE13 6QB.

Tel 020 8852 8585; Fax 020 8297 8020.
info@firemaster.co.uk
www.firemaster.co.uk

13.8.4 MAN OVERBOARD PROCEDURES

If somebody goes overboard, despite all normal precautions, you need not only the gear to locate and recover him, but also a clear understanding of the drill to be used – which should be practicable for nearly all situations.

There are four phases:

1. Alarm and alert.
2. Locate the MoB.
3. Recover him/her onboard; and
4. Rescuscitate and revive.

Phase 1: Shout 'Man overboard, port/starboard' x 3. Press the MoB key on the GPS. Tell a crewman, ideally whoever saw him go over the side, to lock his eyeballs onto the MoB regardless and keep pointing at him. Throw a life buoy over; the sooner this is done, the nearer it will be to the MoB. 20 seconds later throw a second life buoy over, to give a line of bearing. All crew should be on deck.

Phase 2: Manoeuvre the boat back to the MoB. This is easier said than done and circumstances vary widely. The following principles and methods emerge on which a skipper must base his particular plan on the day:

a. It is often best to use the engine, simply because as a generalisation it is easier than under sail. Much of the MoB training is done under sail to guard against the day when the engine will not start. This should not obscure the fact that the engine is often the best bet. Take all the usual precautions against getting lines around the prop.

b. RYA teaching is not dogmatic about any

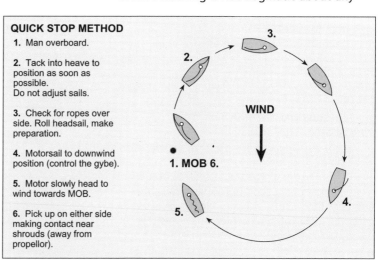

Fig. 13(25) The quick stop method.

one method. The key is to learn the simplest possible method which will work on most boats, in most conditions when reasonably short-handed, ie helmsman plus one or two crew.

c. Stay as close to the MoB as possible, so as to keep him in sight. To stop the boat quickly, tack into the hove-to position. Then bear slowly away, rolling the genoa before you turn downwind. Start the engine, ensure you have enough turning room, and after passing abeam the MoB, gybe round carefully and motor slowly head to wind toward the MoB. Aim to stop with the MoB abeam the shrouds and preferably on your lee side. Take great care in using the engine when manoeuvring close to the MoB, to avoid injury by the propeller; see Fig. 13(25).

d. Another method, with or without engine assistance, is to reach away from the MoB, taking careful note of the course steered and time A-B, which equals B-A. This gives the crew a chance to prepare. When ready tack round onto or just beyond the reciprocal, and then make the final approach hard on the wind. Roll the genoa

and ease the main, to control speed, aiming to luff up alongside the MoB; see Fig. 13(26).

e. With more crew available, an established method when beating to windward or reaching is to bear away, gybe, and then luff back onto a course which will take the boat back to the required spot. Approach the MoB almost close-hauled, in order that speed may more easily be adjusted to round up alongside him; see Fig. 13(27).

f. If a yacht is running under spinnaker (or a preventer is rigged on the main boom, or a mizzen staysail is set), even with a competent crew, it may be 5 minutes before the boat is ready to come on the wind and beat back to the MoB – perhaps half-a-mile away. Here some accurate navigation is needed to ensure that your tacks will bring the boat as near as possible to the scene.

g. When running or broad reaching, especially in a lot of wind, it is probably best to luff gradually until the wind is about on the beam (lowering the spinnaker beforehand, if it is set), and then come about so as to return on a roughly close-hauled course (if originally running) or on more of a reach (if originally on a broad reach).

h. Plenty of practice is needed in different wind speeds and on different points of sailing. It is vital that the sails are trimmed and handled as the skipper or helmsman requires. Success is more likely to be achieved by keeping control of the boat, than by hasty action which may leave her helpless. A Mayday call is in order if help is needed to locate the MoB.

Phase 3: First secure the MoB to the yacht, either by a heaving line if he can grab it; or by a crewman going into the water to secure a line to his lifejacket or around his chest. It is usually best to stop close to windward of the MoB so as to recover him on the lee side, where there is some shelter and freeboard is reduced. The risk of the yacht being thrown on to him by a sea is not too great. On the other hand if the boat is brought to rest immediately to leeward of the MoB, there is a real likelihood that he will not be secured before the boat drifts away to leeward.

Some of the special gear

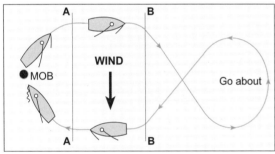

Fig. 13(26) The reach–tack–reach method.

THE GYBING METHOD

1. Man overboard

2. Stand on for 5 seconds

3. Bear away onto a reach, making preparations.

4. Controlled gybe.

5. When MOB just abaft the beam, harden up

6. Roll headsail. Control speed on mainsail

7. Recover MOB on lee side below boom

Fig. 13(27) The gybing method.

available to help get the MoB back on board was discussed in 13.3.9. The weight of a waterlogged, unconscious man is considerable and to get him inboard over the guardrail may demand more than a halyard, a powerful winch and a gorilla. Both the Jon-buoy recovery raft and the Tri-buckle have the merit of lifting the MoB horizontally and the latter rolls him on deck below the guardrail.

Some boats have a bathing ladder aft, which usually hinges down into the water. This may be useful, but it is close to the propeller(s) and there is likely to be considerable pitching motion at the aft end. A boarding ladder amidships can be used, but since this may not even reach to the waterline the MoB will need a bight of rope about 0.6m (2ft) below water, into which he can put one or both of his feet so as to get on to the bottom rung of the ladder. A rope ladder is usually much harder to climb.

By this time however the MoB is likely to be cold and exhausted and in need of assistance. A strong crewman may be able to haul him aboard on a halyard as already mentioned. Or most mainsheets have considerable power: unshackle the lower block and secure it to his harness or lifejacket, set up the topping lift and then haul him in; or the falls of davits may be used in the same way. The main halyard is probably a better bet as it has the power of a winch directly behind it.

Another suggested method is to lower the headsail partly into the water so that the MoB can be manoeuvred into the bight of the sail and then bowsed inboard by the sheet winch, together with an auxiliary halyard transferred to the clew of the sail. This method is similar to, but less effective than using the Tri-buckle.

Perhaps a more practicable method is to secure an inflatable dinghy or even a liferaft alongside the yacht, so that the MoB can at least be got out of the water and into it as a first phase of his rescue. It may help to remove the guardrails round that part of the boat in order to transfer him inboard.

Phase 4: The battle is not yet won. You have a half-drowned unconscious person on deck. Carry out the ABC of rescuscitation (13.9.16) with all speed on deck. Then manhandle him down below (an exhausting business) to treat him for hypothermia (13.9.17). If you encounter problems at any stage, do not hesitate to make a PAN-PAN MEDICO call (13.9.31) and get medical advice.

An MoB situation demands thought and pre-planning in every phase. To avoid delay all crew must understand the procedure to be used, and know where the necessary gear is stowed.

Man overboard from a motor cruiser

In a motor boat it is normally easy enough to turn round and return to somebody who has gone over the side. If the helmsman sees the incident, or has early enough warning from somebody else, he should apply helm so as to swing the stern away from the MoB, thus reducing the risk of injury from the propeller(s).

As in a sailing boat, a lifebuoy should be released as quickly as possible and somebody should be told to watch the person in the water continuously.

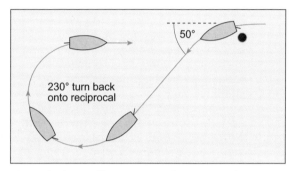

Fig. 13(28) A Williamson turn (50° away, then a 230° reversal) returns a motor cruiser with reasonable certainty to a MoB.

Depending on the type and speed of boat the quickest and simplest way of getting back to the MoB is using the Williamson turn, Fig. 13(28). After any initial helm has been applied to swing the stern away from the MoB, keep turning in that direction until about 50° off the original course. Then apply full opposite rudder to turn the boat through 230° back onto the reciprocal of her original course. The MoB should then be right ahead; aim about 10 ft to windward of him. With practice in one's own boat this manoeuvre can be made quite precisely.

The principles of Phases 3 and 4 apply equally to the motor cruiser procedures. The best lifting gear is likely to be the davits, whether manual or powered, but usually the vertical lift onto the stern platform is not great.

13.8.5 TOWING PROCEDURES

Every seagoing yacht should have at least one 50m long warp of three-strand 16mm nylon or 18mm polyester. This can also be used for kedging, or as an extra long mooring warp, or for towing at sea. In smooth water a boat can be towed on a short warp, whilst in a congested harbour the towing boat may secure herself alongside the boat to be towed.

Good co-operation between the crews of both boats is needed, even in good weather. In calm water the tow can be passed by the towing craft manoeuvring with her stern close to the other's bows. Both boats must be almost stationary, or moving at the same speed through the water, while the tow is being passed. In any wind or sea throw a heaving line and haul the tow rope across. In severe conditions a line can be floated down to the other craft. It is usually more sensible for the towing craft to supply the tow line, since she will probably be to windward of the other; but see 6.4.4 about the implications of salvage.

The towing boat ...

Only tugs are designed to tow. The average yacht is poorly equipped to tow, because it is impossible to get the point of tow far enough forward. In a tug the tow hook is almost amidships and well forward of the propeller, but in a yacht this is usually prevented by the pushpit, backstay and guardrails. Hence the tow rope has to be made fast to a cleat near the stern, which stops the towing boat from manoeuvering freely. Towing from one quarter will make steering even more difficult, but the problem should be solved by rigging a bridle between cleats on each quarter.

It should be possible to slip or release a towrope which is under load, especially in an emergency. In large boats an axe comes in handy; a pair of bolt cutters or sharp knife may also be effective. When towing a runabout or a dinghy, the line should be turned up on a cleat and tended by hand, so that it can be slipped immediately.

Quite a strong initial pull on the towline is needed to get a boat dead in the water moving, so the tow must be taken up very gently to avoid parting. The towing craft must not go ahead until the other signals that she is ready. If a tow parts, anybody standing near could be injured. The casualty is initially likely to be lying beam-on to any swell or sea, so the towing vessel should start towing across the swell before gradually altering course into it, if this is necessary.

When towing, avoid sudden alterations of course, particularly if the tow is unable to steer; and try to give advance warning of your intentions. When reducing speed, do so gradually, especially when towing a heavy vessel which carries her way. Do not tow too fast, a common fault when yachts are being towed by larger ships. When towing a small boat which has been swamped proceed very slowly, otherwise the boat

will be damaged or the tow will part.

In calm water it is easier to tow from alongside if any manoeuvring is involved. The towed boat should be positioned well aft, on the other's quarter. The choice of side may be dictated by the job in hand – for example where the other boat is to be berthed. When going ahead the weight is taken by a spring led aft from the bow of the towing boat; similarly when going astern the pull is by a spring led forward to the boat being towed. A properly positioned towing craft with warps correctly adjusted has surprising freedom of manoeuvre, but good fendering is essential.

If towing more than one boat the biggest should be next astern, and the lightest at the end of the tow. If towing a large number of dinghies two lines, one from each quarter, are better.

... and the towed

Securing the tow rope is difficult in bad weather; success depends largely on how well prepared the crew are. Think in advance about how and where to connect the tow. The average boat has very few points strong enough to take the strains involved in a seaway. A towing bridle should if possible be rigged before the 'rescue' vessel arrives.

Towing at sea puts a tremendous strain not only on the tow rope but on the samson post, bollard, bits or cleat to which it is secured. In many modern yachts there is no foredeck fitting strong enough to take a tow in a seaway. A keel-stepped mast, at deck level, may be the strongest point of attachment; the towline at the stemhead may have to be lashed down to avoid damaging the forestay and will have to be protected against chafe at this point. Or a bridle of strong warps may be rigged around the superstructure and cockpit at deck level, attached to strong points such as sheet winches, backed up onto other winches. This is never easy, and will certainly take time if done properly – any hasty lash-up will soon come adrift once the tow is taken up.

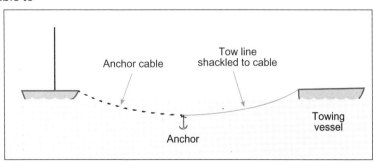

Fig. 13(29) Towing at sea, using the anchor chain.

It may help to attach the towing vessel's warp to the casualty's anchor; chain can then be veered as in Fig. 13(29). The weight of the anchor and cable gives some spring to the tow. Chain is of course much stronger than the average warp and chafe-free, but it will still need to be secured very firmly on deck.

The boat under tow should if possible be steered so that she does not yaw from side to side. She should be trimmed somewhat by the stern, and not by the bow.

In any sea or swell, the tow length should be adjusted so that the two craft are 'in step' relative to the waves. The towing boat, for example, should not be going down a wave when the boat in tow is climbing the face of a wave astern.

Most tows are taken or given informally, as a matter of convenience between the parties concerned, especially between yachts. If commercial bargaining is necessary, as for example with a fishing vessel, agree on a reasonable sum before accepting a tow, even if it is just a short pluck into harbour. What may start as a simple towing operation can develop into a salvage claim (6.4.4), if for example the tow gets into danger through no fault of the towing boat or the weather deteriorates.

If under tow by an RNLI lifeboat, obey the coxswain's orders implicitly – they are the experts. They may pass you a small canvas drogue to stream astern and give a steadier tow, especially if you have lost your rudder. This will reduce the tendency to broach in following seas.

13.8.6   TOWING AND IRPCS

The International Regulations for Preventing Collision at Sea require vessels towing or under tow to show certain signals, which are given in Chapter 4, Rule 24. A vessel being towed should show sidelights and sternlight, but not a masthead light.

Yachts or other craft not normally used for towing do not have to show the special towing signals required by Rule 24(a) and (c), but must indicate the relationship between the towing vessel and the vessel being towed, in particular by illuminating the towline by searchlight; see Rule 24 (i) and Rule 36.

In poor visibility a vessel towing sounds one long blast followed by two short blasts ('D'), at intervals of not more than two minutes. The vessel being towed sounds one long blast followed by three short blasts ('B'), when practicable immediately after the signal sounded by the towing vessel; see Rule 35 (c) and (e).

13.8.7   COMMUNICATION WHILST TOWING

Communication between the two vessels is essential and will usually be on VHF. Without VHF or if there are language problems, and especially in bad weather, the following signals are almost universally understood:

Thumbs up/down = Good/no good.

Arms extended at waist height with the palms of the hands paddling downwards = Slow down.

Arms extended slightly higher with palms upwards = Increase speed.

Arms waved criss-cross in front of and above the head = No good or Stop what you are doing.

The same meaning is conveyed by a 'throat-cutting' action with the edge of one hand.

The International Code of Signals contains the following two-letter groups which, in the absence of any other form of communication, may be made by loud hailer (voice), light or flags – but of course it pre-supposes that both yachts understand the Code:

KK	Towing is impossible under present weather conditions
KL	I am obliged to stop towing temporarily
KM	I can take you in tow
KN	I cannot take you in tow
KP	You should tow me to nearest port or anchorage
KQ	Prepare to be taken in tow
KR	All is ready for towing
KS	You should send a line over
KT	You should send me a towing hawser
KU	I cannot send towing hawser
KV	I intend to use my towing hawser/cable
KW	You should have towing hawser/cable ready
KX	You should be ready to receive the towing hawser
KY	Length of tow is . . . (numbered) fathoms
KZ	You should shorten in the towing hawser
LA	Towing hawser/cable has parted
LB	You should make towing hawser fast to your chain cable
LD	You should veer your hawser/cable
LE	I am about to veer my hawser/cable
LF	You should stop veering your hawser/cable
LG	You should prepare to cast off towing hawser
LI	I am increasing speed
LJ	I am reducing speed
QD	I am going ahead
QE	I have headway
QF	I cannot go ahead
QG	You should go ahead
QH	You should not go ahead any more
QI	I am going astern
QJ	I have sternway

QK I cannot go astern
QL You should go astern
QM You should not go astern any more

RL You should stop your engines immediately
RM My engines are stopped
Z   I require a tug

13.9 FIRST AID AFLOAT

The objectives of First Aid at sea are:

a. to preserve life;
b. to prevent further damage;
c. to relieve pain and distress; and
d. to deliver a live casualty ashore.

13.9.1 EMERGENCY RESUSCITATION – ABC
The immediate procedure to follow for any collapsed or unconscious person is:

A Airway.
Clear mouth of teeth or debris with fingers. Listen at mouth for breathing. Tilt head backwards, using head tilt and chin lift to maintain clear airway – Fig. 13(30).

Fig. 13(30) Ensuring clear airway: head tilt and chin lift.

Place in recovery position if breathing – Fig. 13(31).

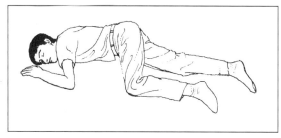

Fig. 13(31) Recovery position.

B Breathing.
If not breathing and airway clear, start mouth to mouth ventilation, Fig. 13(32).

Kneel beside patient, maintain head tilt and chin lift, pinch nostrils. Take a deep breath and blow two full breaths into patient's mouth. Watch for rise and fall of chest. Feel carotid pulse, Fig. 13(32). If pulse present, continue one inflation every five seconds until breathing recommences.

Fig. 13(32) Mouth to mouth ventilation. Maintain head tilt and chin lift. Pinch nose. Blow into victim's mouth; watch chest rise.

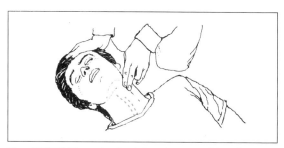

Fig. 13(33) Place to feel for the carotid pulse.

C Circulation.
If carotid pulse absent after checking for 10 seconds, start external chest compression. Lay patient on hard, flat surface. Kneel beside patient, place heel of one hand just below middle of breastbone, Fig. 13(34).

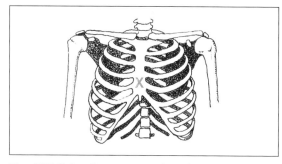

Fig. 13(34) Cardiac massage: hand position on breastbone.

Place other hand on top of this hand. Depress breastbone 40 - 50mm (15 - 2in) then release, Fig. 13(35).

One operator: 100 chest compressions per minute. Two breaths after every 15 compressions; see Fig. 13(36).

Two operators: 100 chest compressions per minute. One breath after every five compressions; see Fig. 13(37).

Children
Blow into both mouth and nose if necessary: use a faster breathing rate (one inflation every three

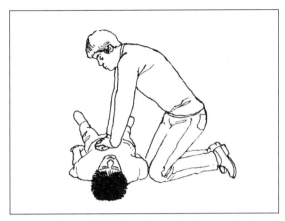

Fig. 13(35) Chest compression: body and hand position. Press firmly, then release.

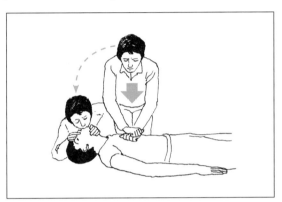

Fig. 13(36) One operator: chest compression rate 100/min, two breaths after every 15 compressions.

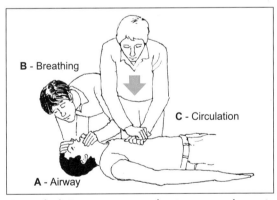

B - Breathing

C - Circulation

A - Airway

Fig. 13(37) Two operators: chest compression rate 100/min, one breath every 5 compressions.

seconds), and smaller breaths. For external chest compression use gentle compression with one hand only, or just fingers for a baby; use a compression rate, of up to 100 per minute, one breath every 5 compressions.

Do not stop
Feel carotid pulse every three minutes. Stop chest compression as soon as pulse returns but continue mouth to mouth ventilation if breathing still absent. Continue until both pulse and breathing return or patient is obviously dead after one hour (skin cold and pale, pupils widely enlarged, no breathing, no pulse, no heartbeat).

Exception: hypothermia victim (see 13.9.17).

Problems during resuscitation
Vomiting
This occurs commonly during resuscitation (especially after immersion). To prevent vomit entering the lungs, turn the patient rapidly on to his side. Clear the airway before recommencing resuscitation.

Fractured ribs
External chest compression moves blood around the body by directly compressing the heart, and by increasing the pressure in the chest cavity. Use your body weight to compress the breastbone, do not lift your hands between compressions and do not press anywhere but directly on the breastbone. Avoid erratic or violent compressions.

Drowning and hypothermia
These casualties may exhibit all the signs of apparent death, yet may still recover totally. Abandon resuscitation reluctantly and only after thorough and repeated attempts have been made to warm the victim.

13.9.2   BLOCKAGE OF AIRWAY AND CHOKING
If blockage by some object (e.g. a peanut) is suspected, turn the casualty on his side and give up to five sharp back slaps with the flat of the hand between the shoulder blades. Check mouth and remove any obstruction.

If unsuccessful, wrap both your arms around the victim's waist from behind, and give five sharp upwards thrusts with both fists into the abdomen above the navel but below the ribs so as to imitate coughing. Clear object from mouth.

In unconscious adult administer abdominal thrusts with the victim lying on his back. Attempt mouth to mouth breathing. Do not give up; repeat the abdominal thrusts.   Infants and small children should first be given five forceful blows on the back before proceeding to abdominal thrusts.

13.9.3   SHOCK
Shock can result from almost any accident or medical emergency and, depending upon the cause, may range in severity from a simple faint to near death. Shock occurs when the delivery of oxygen to the tissues is impaired because of inadequate or inefficient circulation of the blood. Possible causes include:

a. Loss of blood – internal or external bleeding.
b. Loss of fluid – diarrhoea, peritonitis, burns.
c. Heart failure – heart attack.
d. Lung failure – drowning.
e. Brain failure – stroke, head injury.
f. Illness – diabetes.

Signs and symptoms

Thirst, apathy, nausea, restlessness. Pale, cold, clammy skin, sweating. Rapid, weak pulse. Rapid, shallow breathing. Dull, sunken eyes, bluish lips, leads to collapse.

Management

a. ABC – airway, breathing, circulation (see 13.9.1).
b. Control bleeding, if present.
c. Lie flat; elevate legs to 20°. Exceptions:
  i   Bleeding from mouth – recovery position.
  ii Unconscious – recovery position.
  iii Chest injury – sitting may be preferred.
d. Splint any fractures; avoid movement.
e. Avoid chilling, keep warm.
f. Relieve pain – give pain killers. Exceptions:
  i Head injury with impaired consciousness.
  ii Cases with severe breathing difficulty.
g. Reassure the patient.
h. Fluids may be life saving in cases of dehydration (e.g. diarrhoea, vomiting, severe burns). Give half a cup of water at 15 minute intervals. Add a pinch of salt and a little sugar. Never give alcohol. Avoid in severe abdominal pain or internal injury.

Never attempt to give fluids by mouth to an unconscious person.

Collapse and signs of shock after an accident when external blood loss is absent or slight must suggest internal bleeding. Clues may be few. The patient may cough or vomit blood, or pass blood in urine or from bowel. He may complain of worsening pain in abdomen or chest. **Urgent help needed**.

Medical illnesses, such as diabetes, severe infections or heart disease, may produce shock without giving many clues as to the cause. **Urgent help needed**.

Acquaint yourself with any medical problems of crew before a long passage. There should be a record on board of any medication being taken by any member of the crew, including the skipper (see 13.9.21).

13.9.4   BLEEDING – OPEN WOUND

Bleeding is often very dramatic, but is virtually always controllable.

Management

a. Apply firm continuous direct pressure; bandage on a large pad. If bleeding continues, bandage more pads on top of initial pads; then press directly over wound for at least 10 minutes (blood takes this time to clot).
b. Elevation if wound is on a limb.
c. Do NOT apply a tourniquet. The whole limb may be lost if the tourniquet is left on for too long.

13.9.5   BLEEDING – INTERNAL (CLOSED INJURY)

Follows fractured bones, crush injuries, or rupture of organs such as the liver or spleen. Shock may appear rapidly. **Urgent help needed**.

13.9.6   NOSE BLEED

Lean forwards and pinch the soft part of the nose firmly for at least 10 minutes to allow the blood to clot. Do not blow nose or try to remove clot.

If bleeding continues repeat the pressure for longer than 10 minutes. If still bleeding after 30 minutes insert as much 50mm (2in) gauze bandage (moistened with water) as you can, using forceps to feed the bandage into the nose. **Urgent help needed**.

13.9.7   CUTS AND WOUNDS

Often dramatic but only potentially serious if nerves, tendons or blood vessels are severed.

a. Clean thoroughly with antiseptic. Remove dirt or other foreign bodies in the wound.
b. Small clean cuts can be closed using Steristrips Skin must be dry. Use as many Steristrips as necessary to keep the skin edges together. Leave for five days at least. See Fig. 13(38).
c. Larger deep cuts may require special suture techniques; apply a dressing and seek help. Do not try amateur surgery at sea.
d. Ragged lacerations or very dirty wounds. Do not attempt to close these; dead tissues may have to be trimmed away to prevent

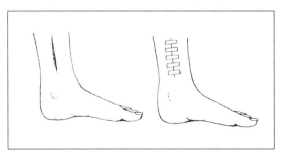

Fig. 13(38) Use of Steristrips to close a superficial wound.

infection. Clean as well as possible, sprinkle antibiotic powder in wound and apply a dressing. *Seek help.*

If in doubt a wound is best left open and lightly covered to keep it clean and dry. If contemplating an extended passage, seek tuition from your doctor.

Fingers and toes
Blood may collect under the nail following an injury. Release the blood by piercing the nail with a red hot needle or paper clip. It will not hurt!

13.9.8 FRACTURES AND DISLOCATIONS – GENERAL
Fracture = a broken bone. Dislocation = a displaced joint. Both result from major trauma and will produce pain (which is worse on attempted movement), localised swelling, abnormal shape, and a grating feeling on movement (when a fracture is present). Blood vessels or nerves around the fracture or dislocation may also be damaged resulting in a cold, pale, or numb limb below the site of the injury. Fractures of large bones such as the femur (upper leg) will result in major internal bleeding and may cause shock. When complications occur **urgent help is needed**.

Early application of a splint and elevation of the injured limb where possible will reduce pain and minimise complications. Treat for shock and pain.

13.9.9 SPECIFIC FRACTURES AND DISLOCATIONS
Skull. See head injury (13.9.12).

Nose. Control bleeding by pinching. Straighten the nose immediately after the accident if possible.

Cheek. Caused by a direct blow. Rarely serious but requires specialist care.

Jaw. Beware of associated brain or spine injury. Remove blood and teeth fragments; leave loose teeth in place; protect broken teeth (see 13.8.22). Ensure airway is clear. Commence regular antiseptic mouth washes and antibiotics. Support jaw with bandage over top of head. Give only fluids by mouth.

Neck. May result from a direct blow, a fall or a whiplash type injury. If conscious, patient may complain of pain, tingling, numbness or weakness in limbs below the injury. *Mishandling may damage the spinal cord, resulting in paralysis or death.* Avoid movement and support head. Immobilise by wrapping a folded towel around the neck. If movement is necessary then lift the victim as one rigid piece, never allowing the neck to bend. **Urgent help needed.**

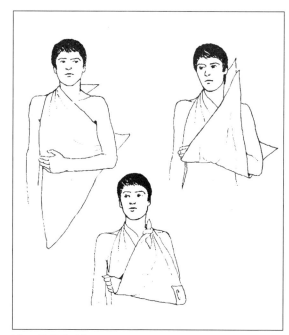

Fig. 13(39) Sling.

Spine. Fracture of the spine may occur below the neck but the results may be similar and mishandling of the victim may greatly worsen the damage. Avoid movement if possible. Lift the patient without allowing the spine to sag. **Urgent help needed**.

Ribs. See chest injury (13.9.13). Often very painful. Strapping is not much use.

Upper Limb
  a. Collar bone (clavicle). Support arm in sling, Fig. 13(38).
  b. Dislocated shoulder. If this has happened before, the patient may reduce the dislocation himself; otherwise do not attempt reduction in case a fracture exists.
  c. Upper arm (humerus). Support the arm with a collar and cuff inside the shirt. Tie a

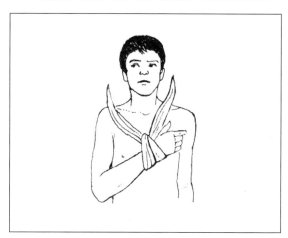

Fig. 13(40) Collar and cuff.

438

clove hitch around the wrist, loop the ends behind the neck, Fig. 13(40).

d. Forearm and wrist. Splint (e.g. with battens or pieces of wood). Do not bandage tightly. Elevate or support in a sling.

e. Fingers. Elevate hand and, unless badly crushed, leave unbandaged; keep moving. If very wobbly, bandage to adjacent finger.

Lower Limb

a. Thigh. Shock may be considerable. Splint by strapping to other leg with padding between the legs. Do not bandage too tightly.

b. Knee. Twisting injuries or falls damage the ligaments and cartilages of the knee. Very painful and swollen. Treat as for fracture.

c. Lower leg. Pad very well. Splint using oar, broom handle or similar pieces of wood.

d. Ankle. Fracture or severe sprain may be indistinguishable. Immobilise in neutral position with foot at right angles. Elevate the limb.

To be really effective a splint must be rigid and extend to the joints above and below the fracture. This is not always possible. The splint must be very well padded. Inflatable splints may seem useful but can interfere with the circulation; see under tourniquet, 13.9.4c.

If the limb beyond the bandage or splint becomes swollen or discoloured, the bandage must be loosened to improve circulation. If you improvise a splint (e.g. fibre glass) it is essential not to enclose the whole limb and risk cutting off the circulation.

13.9.10   COMPOUND FRACTURES
If a deep wound overlies the fracture or the bone ends are visible do not try to close the wound or replace the bone ends. Clean thoroughly with antiseptic and cover with sterile dressing. *Seek help.* Commence antibiotics if help delayed.

13.9.11   STRAINS AND SPRAINS
Torn ligaments, pulled muscles and other injuries. Rest the injured part; elevate if possible; apply ice packs (wrapped in a towel) if possible at sea; administer pain-killers. If in doubt, treat as a fracture and immobilise.

13.9.12   HEAD INJURY
A blow to the head, with or without fracture, may result in immediate unconsciousness or more delayed effects.

Management
a. Immediate unconsciousness, but quick recovery with slight drowsiness or headache. Prescribe rest and watch carefully.

b. Immediate unconsciousness, no sign of recovery. Put in recovery position (beware of associated spine injury). Check airway. Observe the following and record every 10 minutes: pulse rate, breathing rate, pupil size (both sides), responses to verbal command, response to firm pinching. **Urgent help needed**.

c. Delayed deterioration (either not unconscious immediately, or apparently recovering then worsening). Increasing drowsiness, change in mental state and eventually unconsciousness. Treat as (b) above. **Urgent help needed**.

Scalp wounds may bleed profusely. Control with very firm pressure; cut away hair, and close using Steristrips if no fracture beneath. *If in doubt seek help.* Avoid giving drugs after head injury.

13.9.13   CHEST INJURY
May result in fractured ribs. These are very painful, and breathing may be uncomfortable and shallow. The fractured ribs may puncture the lung, or if a number of ribs are each broken in two places (e.g. after crush injury) then this flail segment of the chest may seriously impair breathing.

Management
a. Airway, breathing, circulation (see 13.9.1).
b. Patient may be more comfortable sitting up.
c. Plug any hole with a pad if air is sucking in and out.
d. Support any unstable chest segment with your hand.
e. For fractured ribs prescribe rest and strong pain-killers if necessary. Very painful.

Avoid tight strapping lest it restricts breathing even further. **Urgent help needed** for any case with impaired breathing.

13.9.14   EYE PROBLEMS
All eye injuries or illnesses are potentially serious. Never put old or previously opened ointment or drops into an eye; serious infection could result.

a. Foreign object. Flush the eye with clean water, pull the bottom lid out to inspect, remove object with a clean tissue. To inspect beneath upper lid, pull the lid out and then roll it upwards over a matchstick. After removal of object, instil sterile antibiotic ointment inside pulled out lower lid. Cover with pad.

b. Corrosive fluid. Continuous flushing with water for 15 minutes. Give pain-killers and chloramphenicol ointment; cover with pad. *Seek help as soon as possible.*

c. Infection (conjunctivitis). A sticky, weeping eye with yellow discharge. Chloramphenicol ointment four times per day.

13.9.15   BURNS AND SCALDS

a. Move the victim to fresh air to avoid inhaling smoke.
b. ABC – Airway, Breathing, Circulation.
c. Stop further injury: dip the whole of the burnt part into cold water for 10 - 15 minutes. Seawater is excellent but may be very painful.
d. Remove only loose clothing. Do not pull off clothing stuck to the skin.
e. Cover with sterile dressing. If skin broken or blistered, use sterile paraffin gauze beneath the dressing. Separate burnt fingers with paraffin gauze. Never use adhesive dressings.
f. Do not prick blisters or apply ointments.
g. Elevate burnt limb and immobilise.
h. Give strong pain-killers.
i. Treat for shock: give frequent and copious drinks of water.
j. Commence antibiotics for major burns.
k. If burns extensive or deep, **urgent help needed**.

Sunburn may be very severe. Treat as for any other burn. If skin unbroken apply calamine lotion; give pain-killers. For prevention use only filter preparations with high protection factor.

13.9.16   DROWNING

The resuscitation of an apparently drowned person may be complicated by two factors: i, a sudden illness (eg a stroke) or an accident (eg a blow to the head) may have precipitated the fall into the water; ii, the time spent in the water may have produced marked hypothermia. The water around the UK is rarely warmer than 15°C (60°F).

Management
a. **A Airway**. Clear the airway: seaweed, false teeth etc.
b. **B Breathing**. If not breathing start mouth to mouth ventilation as soon as possible and in the water if practicable. See 13.9.1(2).
c. **C Circulation**. If pulse absent, start chest compression as soon as aboard. See 13.9.1(3).
d. If stomach bulging, turn on to side to empty water, or he may vomit large quantities of water which could be inhaled.
e. Prevent cooling. Remove wet clothes; wrap in blankets to warm.

f. Continue resuscitation until victim revives or death is certain. Hypothermia may mimic death. Do not abandon resuscitation until person has been warmed or signs of death persist despite attempts at warming:
g. Once revived, put in recovery position, Fig. 13(30).
h. Any person rescued from drowning may collapse in the next 24 hours as the lungs react to inhaled water. **Urgent help needed**.

13.9.17   HYPOTHERMIA

Lowered body temperature will follow immersion in sea – Fig. 13(41) – or prolonged exposure on deck.

Fig. 13(41) Estimated survival time after which only 50% of immersion victims would still be alive. Adult males in conventional dress. (By kind permission Surg. Cdr. Frank St. C. Golden RN.)

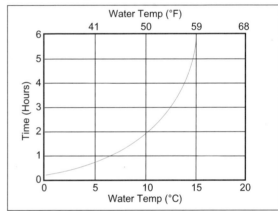

Symptoms include: unreasonable behaviour followed by apathy and confusion; unsteady gait, stumbling, slurring of speech; pale, cold skin; slow, weak pulse; slow breathing; shivering. Leads to collapse, unconsciousness and ultimately death.

Management
a. *A Airway* control; put in recovery position.
b. *B Breathing*. If not breathing, start mouth to mouth ventilation.
c. *C Circulation*. A slow feeble pulse may be present: unwise to use chest compression.
d. Remove wet clothing. Avoid wind chill. Dry and wrap in blankets or sleeping bag, another person in the sleeping bag will generate heat.
e. Give hot sweet drinks if conscious.
f. Do not give alcohol, or rub the skin, or place very hot objects against skin.

13.9.18   FROSTBITE

Usually affects toes, fingers, ears or nose. The affected part may be very painful, numb, stiff and discoloured. Warm gently (e.g. on someone else's back). Immersion in water less than 43°C (110°F) is satisfactory; higher temperatures will cause more damage. Do not rub the affected part with anything.

13.9.19   POISONING
Poison may reach the body when swallowed, inhaled or injected through the skin (e.g. bites and stings).

General management
    a.   ABC: Airway, Breathing, Circulation.
    b.   Recovery position if unconscious.
    c.   *Seek help.*

Swallowed poison
For swallowed poison the container may have instructions or suggest antidote(s). For corrosive or petroleum products (e.g. acids, alkalis, bleach, detergent, petrol) *do not induce* vomiting. Administer copious fluids (eg milk).

For other substances (e.g. pills, medicines) do not induce vomiting – it is often ineffective and may cause further harm to the casualty. If collapsed or unconscious, **urgent help needed**.

Inhaled poison
Poison may be inhaled from sources such as carbon monoxide or other exhaust fumes, bottled gas which has leaked into bilge, or fire extinguisher gas. Carbon monoxide inhalation produces cherry red lips and skin. Move into fresh air immediately. If breathing absent, commence resuscitation. **Urgent help needed**.

Bites and stings
Injected poison from bites and stings usually only causes local swelling and discomfort, but some individuals may react severely. For insect stings, resuscitate if collapse occurs; otherwise give rest, pain-killers, antihistamines (e.g. chlorpheniramine). In warmer water, sea snakes and various sea stingers can inject extremely deadly poison: prevent drowning, resuscitate if necessary; if sting caused by jelly fish or Portuguese Man O'War etc, pour vinegar onto sting to reduce further poison release.

If the victim becomes weak and breathless, lightly compress the limb above the wound with a roller bandage to delay spread of poison; do not apply a tourniquet. Commence resuscitation. **Urgent help needed**.

Many large cities maintain a 24-hour poison information centre. Use the radio for advice.

13.9.20   SEASICKNESS
Basically an inner ear disturbance caused by motion. Fear, anxiety, fatigue and boredom aggravate the condition. May manifest itself as lethargy, dizziness or headache as well as nausea and vomiting.

Avoid strong food tastes, and too much alcohol. Take small amounts of fluid and food (e.g. biscuits) frequently if you feel ill. Avoid fatigue; adequate sleep will often relieve the sick feeling. Keep warm. Stay on deck, and concentrate on some task if possible. Ensure that sick crew on deck are secured by lifeline. Turn in if all else fails. Intractable vomiting may cause serious loss of fluid.

No one remedy is suitable for every person. Try the various preparations until you find one that is effective with minimal side effects; most tend to cause a dry mouth and some tiredness. Available tablets include: Dramamine (dimenhydrinate), Avomine (promethazine) and Stugeron (cinnarizine). Take the first tablet some hours before sailing, and then regularly for as long as necessary. Take a tablet just before going to sleep if possible. Various preparations can be applied behind the ear or worn as a wrist band.

13.9.21   SUDDEN ILLNESS
Acquaint yourself with any medical problems of the crew (and skipper!) before a long passage. Ask medical advice on likely symptoms and treatment; unless forewarned, diagnosis may otherwise be very difficult once at sea.
    a.   Abdominal pain (minor).
        i   Upper abdomen, intermittent, burning, no tenderness, otherwise well. May follow large alcohol intake. Eased by milk or antacid. Bland meals. No alcohol.
        ii More generalised, cramping or colicky pain, no tenderness, may have diarrhoea or vomiting. May be gastroenteritis or food poisoning. Take oral fluid with a pinch of salt added. Avoid dehydration.
    b.   Abdominal pain (major). Severe abdominal pain, usually constant and generalised. Abdomen may be rigid or very tender to touch, fever may be present, rapid pulse rate, generally unwell, nausea and vomiting. Make the patient comfortable, give pain relief (injection if possible). Give nothing to eat or drink. **Urgent help needed**.
    c.   Allergies. Mild cases may just have a rash which responds to calamine lotion and antihistamine tablets. Severe cases may collapse with breathing difficulty and require emergency ABC resuscitation.
    d.   Constipation. Common at sea. Prevent by eating fruit, vegetables, bran and if necessasry, anti-constipation medication (e.g. senna preparations).

e. Convulsions. Patient may be a known epileptic. Insert twisted cloth between teeth to protect tongue. Prevent injury. Recovery position; protect airway (he may still look very blue). After fit, allow him to sleep. **Urgent help needed**.

f. Diabetes. A diabetic may become unconscious if his blood sugar is too high or too low. For hyperglycaemia (too much sugar) insulin is needed. Hypoglycaemia (too little sugar) may be caused by too much insulin, unusual stress or exercise, or too little food. In either case first give sweets, sugar, soft drinks. If recovery not rapid, **urgent help needed**.

g. Diarrhoea. Can become serious, especially in young children if much fluid is lost. Stop food, give plenty of fluid. Kaolin may be useful. Lomotil or Imodium tablets very effective in adults.

h. Fever. May be associated with anything from common cold, appendicitis, heat stroke to an infected toe. Except for major abdominal problems, prescribe copious fluids, paracetamol or aspirin (not in children) and antibiotics if infection is present.

j. Heart attack. Severe central chest pain; may spread to shoulders, neck or arms. Sweating, then bluish lips, then collapse. Breathing and heart may stop (no carotid pulse in neck).
   i Early symptoms; rest, reassure. **Urgent help needed.**
   ii If unconscious: recovery position; observe breathing and pulse.
   iii If breathing stops or pulse absent, commence mouth to mouth ventilation and chest compression immediately and do not stop. See 13.9.1.

k. Heat stroke. Cool patient by sponging with cold water; encourage drinking (one teaspoon of salt per pint of water). If patient stops sweating, has a rapid pounding pulse and is becoming unconscious, **seek help urgently**.

l. Stroke. Sudden unconsciousness, paralysis or weakness on one side of body, slurring of speech. Recovery position, air way control. **Urgent help needed**.

13.9.22   TOOTHACHE

Dental pain seems worse at sea, and prevention is better than cure. For a long voyage consider carrying a dental mirror, tongue spatula, pen torch, cotton wool rolls, tweezers, zinc oxide powder and oil of cloves (or a ready-mixed temporary filling, e.g. Coltisol). Dentanurse is an emergency treatment pack which enables an amateur to make basic temporary repairs, eg replacing crowns, lost fillings. It contains zinc oxide and Eugenol.

Management

a. Throbbing toothache, made worse by hot or cold or when bitten on. If an obvious cavity is present, clean out and apply zinc oxide paste (made by incorporating as much zinc oxide powder as possible into three drops of oil of cloves, to form a thick putty). Take paracetamol.

b. Dull toothache, tender to bite on; gum swollen or red with possible discharge. Treat as above but also take an antibiotic.

c. Broken tooth or filling. Cover exposed surfaces with zinc oxide paste.

d. Bleeding gums. Clean teeth more thoroughly. If accompanied by foul odour and metallic taste, use regular hot salt water rinses and antibiotics.

e. Pain round wisdom tooth. Toothbrush to clean area; use hot salt water rinses; take antibiotics and painkillers.

f. Mouth ulcers. Hot salt water rinses.

13.9.23   CHILDREN

Children may become ill with alarming rapidity. Ear and throat infections are especially common. Children are also more susceptible to effects of dehydration, so if ill encourage to drink copious fluids. Reduce drug dosage to a proportion of adult dose based on weight. Average adult 70kg (155lb).

13.9.24   DRUGS

Paracetamol 500mg tablets	painkiller	1–2 tablets 4 hourly
Dihydrocodeine 30mg tablets	strong painkiller	1–2 tablets 4 hourly
Chlorpheniramine 4mg tablets	antihistamine	1 tablet 8 hourly
Aludrox	indigestion	1–2 before meals
Loperamide 2mg capsules	diarrhoea	2 capsules initially followed by 1 after each loose stool, up to a maximum of 8 per day
Senokot tablets	constipation	2–4 tablets daily
Tetracycline 250mg	antibiotic	1 capsule 4 times daily
Amoxicillin 250mg	antibiotic	250–500mg every 8 hours (beware penicillin allergy)
Erythromycin 250mg	antibiotic	For penicillin-allergic adult 4 tablets daily
Cinnarizine 15mg tablets	seasickness	2 before voyage then 1 every 8 hours

13.9.25   INJECTIONS

A doctor's prescription is required for injections. Stringent regulations apply to injectable painkiller drugs, which are probably only warranted for long passages. It is safest to inject into the muscle on the outer part of the mid-thigh. Clean the area, then plunge the needle swiftly an inch or so through the skin, pull back on the plunger to ensure that a blood vessel has not been entered, then slowly complete the injection.

13.9.26   NORMAL PHYSIOLOGICAL MEASUREMENTS

a.   Pulse rate.   Adults 60–80/minute.
                          Children up to 100/minute.
b.   Breathing.   12–15/minute.
c.   Temperature.   36·7°C (98·4°F)

13.9.27   MEDICAL ADVICE BY R/T

Medical advice can be obtained almost anywhere in European waters (and elsewhere) by making an all-stations 'PAN-PAN MEDICO' call or a DSC Urgency Alert to the Coastguard, or to a Coast Radio Station (CRS) in those countries where CRS are still in being. You will be connected to a suitable medical authority – usually a doctor or the nearest hospital.

The Urgency signal 'PAN PAN MEDICO' is alway advised, especially abroad because it is internationally understood and cuts through most language problems. **Urgent help needed** is shown in bold type against the more serious medical problems in the preceding pages and this implies a Pan-Pan Medico call. You should also recognise that as a layman you are not qualified to judge how serious the casualty's condition is – so get the best possible advice and/or help as quickly as possible.

Be prepared to give a detailed summary of the patient's symptoms, eg pulse rate, breathing rate, temperature, skin colour, conscious state (with reference to pupil size, responses to verbal command and to firm pinching; see 13.9.12), site and description of any pain, site and type of injury, amount of blood lost.

If medical help is needed by way of a doctor coming aboard, or if a serious casualty has to be off-lifted, the arrangements will be made by the Coastguard. For what it's worth, the message is passed free of charge.

If the situation is truly not urgent, then either it can wait until you get into harbour or at least you can forewarn the port authority so that a doctor or para-medics can meet you on arrival. Such a call could be made in adequate time on the harbour's working channel.

13.9.28   SUGGESTIONS FOR A FIRST AID KIT

A made-up Offshore First Aid Kit can be bought for about £55.95. Your doctor or chemist may suggest alternatives. Prescriptions are needed for most of the drugs; see 13.9.24. Out of date drugs are potentially dangerous – destroy them. Special preparations are available for children. Stow the following suggested items in a readily accessible, clearly marked waterproof container:

Triangular bandage x 2 (doubles as bandage or sling) Crepe bandage 75mm x 2
Gauze bandage 50mm x 2
Elastoplast 75mm x 1
Band Aids (or similar) various shapes and sizes
Wound dressing bpc, 1 large, 1 medium
Sterile non-adhesive dressing (Melolin) x 5
Paraffin gauze sterile dressings x 5 packs
Steristrips x 5 packs
Cotton wool
Scissors and forceps, good stainless steel
Safety pins
Thermometer
Disposable gloves
Antiseptic solution (e.g. Savlon)
Sunscreen with high protection factor
Antibiotic powder or spray
Tinaderm powder (athlete's foot)
Calamine lotion (bites, stings and sunburn)
Insect repellent (DEET, diethyltoluamide)
Individual choice of anti-seasick tablets
Chloramphenicol eye ointment

Additional items for extended cruising

Do not forget vaccinations – a course may need to start as much as 6 months before departure.

Syringes 2ml x 2 (if carrying injections)
Dental kit – see 13.9.22
Moisture cream (for cracked hand and lips)

13.9.29   FORM E111

For cruising in European waters it is sensible to carry Form E111, *Certificate of entitlement to benefits in kind during a stay in a member state*. Form E111 is actually contained within a very informative 52 page booklet *Health advice for travellers*, aka T6; this is obtainable from a Post Office where the E111 must be completed and stamped. It is useful to have several photocopies of the Form E111 as the foreign doctor or pharmacist may need to retain a copy.

E111 allows yachtsmen to obtain medical treatment on a reciprocal basis, although it will not cover the full charge. Details of how to claim in the 18 member countries of the EEA (the 15 EC members plus Iceland, Liechtenstein and Norway) are given in the T6 booklet. A further 40+ countries world-wide have reciprocal health care agreements with the UK. But many others, including USA, Latin America, Canada, India, the Far East and Africa, do not; if cruising these areas private health insurance may be advisable.

Yachtsmen cruising abroad may naturally be concerned about the possibility of being given infected blood. Under normal circumstances it is not possible to carry blood or plasma in a yacht. If a blood transfusion is essential, try to ensure that the blood used has been screened against HIV and Hepatitis B.

If you are cruising to distant destinations you may wish to take additional sterile needles and syringes, for example if you or a crewman are diabetic, and you should seek advice from your doctor or local hospital before leaving. Syringes and needles are attractive to intravenous drug abusers so should be locked up in a very secure place.

13.9.30   FIRST AID TRAINING
Most of us would benefit from and probably welcome regular attendance at a refresher training course, perhaps every other year. This enables us to keep abreast of the latest methods, treatments and medical opinion – and to remind ourselves of techniques which happily we are not often called upon to utilise. Such courses are run by the First Aid specialists at the St John Ambulance; at bodies like the RYA, Cruising Association and by yacht clubs as part of their winter training schedules.

13.10 BOOKS ABOUT SAFETY AND FIRST AID

13.10.1   SAFETY, INCLUDING GMDSS
RYA booklets
C8 Cruising Yacht Safety
Sea Survival: Practical Notes
Survive the Savage Sea by D Robertson (Adlard Coles)
G22 VHF Radio including GMDSS
G26 VHF Radio SRC assessments
VHF DSC Handbook by Sue Fletcher (Thomas Reed)
GMDSS for Small Craft by A Clemmetsen (Fernhurst)
GMDSS, ALRS Vol 5 (UKHO)
GMDSS – a User's Handbook by Denise Bréhaut (Adlard Coles)
The VHF GMDSS Handbook by M Gale (Fernhurst)

13.10.2   FIRST AID
The following books give detailed advice and at least one should be on board:
First Aid Manual of St John Ambulance, St Andrew's Ambulance Association and the British Red Cross (Dorling Kindersley, 7th edition 1997, £10.99). Clear and authoritative text, profusely illustrated in colour. A quick reference guide is included on Emergency First Aid.
The Ship's Captain Medical Guide (TSO, 22nd edition, £33.00). Official handbook for merchant ships.
First Aid at Sea by D Justins & C Berry (Adlard Coles, 3rd edition 1993, £9.99). Easy reference guide.
The First Aid Companion by Dr R Haworth (Fernhurst)
First Aid Afloat by Dr R Haworth (Fernhurst)
Advanced First Aid afloat by Dr Peter Eastman
Your Offshore Doctor by Dr Michael Beilan (Adlard Coles).

13.10.3   GMDSS ABBREVIATIONS
AOR-E	Atlantic Ocean Region (East); Inmarsat
AOR-W	Atlantic Ocean Region (West); Inmarsat
CES	Coast Earth Station
COSPAS/ SARSAT	Russian/US satellite-aided SAR System
DSC	Digital Selective Calling
EGC	Enhanced Group Calling; Sat-C
EPIRB	Emergency Position Indicating Radio Beacon
GEOSAR	Geostationary SAR satellite system
GMDSS	Global Maritime Distress & Safety System
IMO	International Maritime Organisation
Inmarsat	International Mobile Satellite Organisation
IOR	Indian Ocean Region; Inmarsat
ITU	International Telecommunication Union
LES	Land Earth Station
LEOSAR	Low Earth orbiting SAR satellite system
LUT	Local User Terminal; COSPAS/SARSAT
MSI	Maritime Safety Information
MCC	Mission Control Centre; COSPAS/ SARSAT
MID	Maritime Identification Digits (eg 233: UK)
MMSI	Maritime Mobile Service Identity code
MSI	Maritime Safety Information
NBDP	Narrow-Band Direct-Printing (Navtex)
NCS	Network Co-ordination Station; Inmarsat
POR	Pacific Ocean Region; Inmarsat
SafetyNET	MSI broadcasting service; Inmarsat
SART	Search and Rescue Transponder
SRR	Search and Rescue Region
SES	Ship Earth Station; a vessel at sea
SOLAS	Safety Of Life At Sea, Convention.

Chapter 14 Starting to race

CONTENTS

14.1 INTRODUCTION

14.1.1 THE ATTRACTIONS

Most yachtsmen like to make their boat sail faster on occasions – maybe on passage in order to catch the tide at some critical spot, or to get into harbour in time for a meal or before the pubs shut. Eventually this quest for speed can be translated into the idea of competing in races. Sadly many people find this difficult to achieve because the sport of yacht racing is surrounded by countless rules and regulations which are rife with terms that are incomprehensible to the ordinary sailor.

But take heart. This chapter aims to explain some of these mysteries, at least to a level sufficient for the average sailor to compete in club events without causing disruption or damage. If you wish to race more seriously – as may well happen once you have tried it – you will need to make a detailed study of the rules so that you are able to take advantage of various tactical situations which present themselves. There are many good books available for this purpose, and a selection is given in the bibliography at the end of the chapter.

Races are mainly organised by individual clubs, whose standards and methods can vary considerably. Some are large, well-run concerns which cater primarily for the more expert sailors and which hold regattas that attract large fleets of yachts in different classes, possibly including competitors from abroad. Other clubs are smaller and less formal, perhaps giving races for a few local boats, and without the cut and thrust of national or international competition.

The local geography largely dictates the type of racing that will be found in any one place. Small stretches of inland waters such as lakes and reservoirs are necessarily only suitable for dinghy racing or perhaps the smallest sizes of keelboats. These small craft may also flourish in estuaries and other sheltered waters around the coast, but here too will be larger yachts which are suitable and equipped for racing from port to port and even offshore. Yet these different categories of racing all have certain things in common.

For a start they all compete under the same basic rules, as will be discussed below. With no spectators to cheer them on their way they will all take part for the satisfaction of defeating the elements as well as their rivals, whether they are near the front of the fleet or bringing up the rear. With no umpires afloat to oversee proceedings, they all share a sense of trust in adhering to the rules. And within each class there is likely to be a wide spread of ages, with the experience of older men and women compensating for the physical agility of their more youthful opponents.

14.1.2 THE ORGANISATION OF YACHT RACING

As described below, bona fide competitive events will usually be organized by a sailing club or yacht club that is recognised by the national authority, which in the case of the United Kingdom is the Royal Yachting Association (RYA). In return the RYA is represented, like the national authorities of all principal countries which control yacht racing, on the International Sailing Federation (ISAF). ISAF frames and administers the racing rules, which are revised every four years following the Olympic Games, while various sub-committees deal with technical, measurement and other related matters.

So every individual who races, even in a modest handicap event at a local club, is racing under the same rules as people all round the world. Disputes between boats are settled by protest hearings, and a boat which claims the race committee (and, sometimes, another competitor) has done something that seriously affects the boat's finishing position may seek redress. If a competitor disagrees with a protest or redress decision, he or she can appeal against the decision to the RYA.

ISAF recognises and administers a limited number of 'International' classes. These include those classes of boats that compete in the Olympic Games every four years, but also some other classes which have either been used in past Olympics or which have special international appeal.

In a similar way the RYA recognises various 'National' classes, which are mostly dinghies but include for example the National Swallow, a 22ft keelboat used in the 1948 Olympic and the National Squib, a 5.8m (19ft) one-design keelboat of which more than 750 have been built.

14.2 THE RACING YACHTS

There are a bewildering number of different types of boat that race, even just around the shores and inland waters of Britain. They vary in size from tiny dinghies like the Optimist, intended for children, to large (and very expensive) seagoing craft which are quite capable of racing across the oceans as well as participating in coastal regattas. Between these two extremes lie a variety of 'classes' which in general belong to one of the following headings.

14.2.1 ONE-DESIGN CLASSES

As the name implies, boats of a one-design class are as near as possible identical in all important respects. With modern GRP construction it is likely that all hulls have been produced from one mould, thus ensuring the same external shape even if the distribution of the building materials (resin and glass) within the hull may not be very precise. However, most one-design classes are governed by a minimum weight.

The dimensions and weights of spars and sails are also closely controlled within fairly small tolerances. Some classes require spars and sails to come only from nominated firms. There will certainly be regulations about the equipment that may or may not be carried, together with a minimum outfit of safety gear. Some classes have limitations on the maximum and minimum number of crew to be carried.

Before competing in races a one-design boat must have whatever certification is required by the club or class association concerned. This is likely to mean inspection and measurement by an approved measurer, and quite possibly a requirement to weigh the boat. Naturally the owner is not at liberty to alter any item without a repeat measurement.

Most one-design classes are of commercial origin, where a designer or builder has set out to provide a specific boat for racing purposes as well as for cruising or day sailing. In such cases it is in the builder's interests to try to ensure that all boats are as similar as possible, and to avoid any changes in building procedures that may deviate from the original standards. The success of such a class depends greatly on how carefully the class rules are drafted initially, and on how closely they are controlled by the class association which administers them.

One-design classes provide the purest and closest racing, boat against boat and with no handicapping. Success depends on how well a boat is tuned and sailed. A one-design boat should hold her value well, because she is not outdated by subsequent developments in hull or rig.

Most dinghy racing is in one-design classes with most cruiser racing undertaken on handicap. There are however several very successful one-design cruiser classes which race boat for boat.

Classes such as the International Melges 24 and the National Sonata at the smaller end of the scale and the Mumm 30 and Sydney 40 at the larger end are among the more popular. These and similar classes can usually muster sufficient yachts to enable separate fleets to compete within some major events or series. They will usually run their own area, national, and sometimes international championships. A yacht belonging to a one-design class is not precluded from participating in handicap events.

14.2.2 RESTRICTED CLASSES
Restricted classes have rules similar to those for one-designs, but the tolerances stipulated are a good deal wider, and there is much more choice in materials, spars, sails and general equipment. By definition anything not specifically prohibited by an *open class* rule is permitted. Hence there is greater scope for development, which may appeal to the racing enthusiast or amateur boat builder. Against this the older boats become less competitive and do not hold their value. In general costs are higher.

14.2.3 FORMULA (OR RATING) CLASSES
A quite different approach is where, instead of certain measurements being stipulated with defined tolerances, actual measurements of the completed boats are fed into a formula which must not result in more than a certain figure (of length). If that figure is exceeded the boat is not 'in class'.

The formulae that have been used over the years are varied and often very complicated, embracing certain prime measurements such as length, beam, draught and sail area plus various allowances (or penalties) for factors considered desirable (or undesirable) as the case might be. Even the measured length may only be arrived at after a calculation to establish exactly where and how it is measured. In essence, those factors such as length, sail area and low freeboard which improve speed are pluses or multipliers in the formula, while those which decrease speed like abnormal beam or draught are minuses or dividers.

These attempts to relate mathematical formulae to actual speed on the water have inevitably caused designers to search for combinations of measurements that will produce a shape of hull to give a little more speed. This has often introduced unwelcome characteristics such as poor stability or difficult steering – as well as some very unattractive looking yachts.

A rating formula can be used in two different ways: One is to produce a number of yachts that

have the same rating, and hence the same potential speed. This gives yachts of 'level rating', which race against each other boat for boat with no time allowances. They have the same theoretical speeds, but they are not identical. For example, one boat might have slightly more length at the expense of a little sail area.

Although formula class yachts designs will differ one from another, class racing will be undertaken boat for boat without the application of any handicap. The first boat to cross the finishing line is the winner.

Metre yachts are one group of formula yachts, although better known due to the Twelve Metres formerly raced in the America's Cup.

The Metre formula is:

$$\frac{L + 2d - F + \sqrt{S}}{2 \cdot 37}$$

where:

L = length (m),
d = girth difference* (m),
F = freeboard (m),
S = sail area (m²)

* skin girth (following contours of hull) less chain girth (bridging concavities) at approx mid-section.

Alternatively a measurement formula may be used to produce numerical ratings of boats of different sizes and with different characteristics. Each individual rating can be then transferred into a time allowance, based on elapsed time or on course distance, to provide a handicapping system.

14.3 HANDICAPPING METHODS

14.3.1 HISTORICAL
The history of how successive handicapping formulae have evolved over the last 150 years, and how each in turn has been abandoned, makes interesting reading – albeit of a rather mathematical nature. But here we are more concerned with what is in force today, or with rules of the recent past that have influenced the shape of countless yachts which are still afloat in the 21st century.

Rating rules, normally applied to cruiser and offshore yachts, are applied similarly to formula class rules except that the formula is used to produce numerical ratings of boats of different sizes and with different characteristics. Instead of the yacht being designed and built with dimensions that, when fed into the formula, give a common result or *rating*, the actual dimensions of the yacht will be used to determine that yacht's rating. Most modern ratings are, in theory, directly proportional to the yacht's speed and so, by simple multiplication provide a system from which race results can be calculated.

The various handicapping systems most likely to be encountered today are described below.

14.3.2   INTERNATIONAL OFFSHORE RULE (IOR)

From the early 1930s until the 1970s, yachts that took part in offshore races or raced in the coastal waters of Western Europe, the Mediterranean and Australasia were measured and rated under the then Royal Ocean Racing Club (RORC) rule. It should be emphasised that the RORC rule originally came into being as a means of handicapping, as fairly as possible, yachts of diverse types and sizes, few of which had been specifically designed for racing.

Any measurement rules become 'type forming' as designers learn how best to exploit the formulae involved, but in general the RORC rule produced good seaworthy yachts many of which are still actively sailed and raced. Across the Atlantic the Cruising Club of America (CCA) rule produced seaworthy boats from different formulae.

From a yacht's linear rating must be calculated a factor for handicapping purposes. In Britain a 'time correction factor' (TCF) – the equivalent of the modern 'time multiplying factor' (TMF) – was calculated from a formula based on the square root of the rating. TCF multiplied by elapsed time gave corrected time, and this 'time on time' method is still used today. Yachts racing under the CCA rule traditionally used 'time on distance', expressed in so many seconds per mile and calculated from special tables. Both systems have their disadvantages with boats of disparate size that may be sailing under very different conditions of wind and tide during a long race.

There were obvious disadvantages, particularly in respect of international competition, in having two different measurement rules each side of the Atlantic, and in 1970 there came into being the new International Offshore Rule (IOR). This incorporates some features from both the previous RORC and CCA rules. The calculations are complex and are intended to be done by computer. Hull measurements are taken at fixed points or stations much as before. An innovation was an inclining experiment in which the yacht is heeled a small amount by known weights in order to determine a 'centre of gravity factor' (CGF) which is a multiplier in the basic formula.

In its early years many boats around the world had IOR certificates, up to 10,000 in 1977, but numbers have now dropped dramatically. In 1994 only 200 boats in the UK and Ireland held current certificates, and by 1996 there were none.

14.3.3   INTERNATIONAL MEASUREMENT SYSTEM (IMS)

In 1975 in the USA, the Massachusetts Institute of Technology developed Velocity Performance Predictions (VPPs) for a range of wind speeds and directions, and this subsequently became the Measurement Handicap System (MHS). In 1985, as IOR declined, the MHS was adopted as the International Measurement System (IMS) for international use. The IMS' main advantage is the ability to apply VPPs to assess handicaps. Thus the previous state of affairs where certain boats would perform well on corrected time in heavy weather while others might prevail in light conditions, is taken into account. In theory a boat does not win 'in her own weather'.

An advantage is that by machine-measuring the computer programme draws a full lines plan of the hull - eliminating problems caused in the IOR by taking measurements only at selected points and thus allowing designers to exploit the rule with artificial bumps in what would otherwise be a fair surface. Wetted surface is also measured and, like IOR, there are measurements afloat, for freeboard and inclining.

From the available data the IMS programmme produces a boat's certificate, giving a table of some 35 time allowances for different wind conditions and courses, from which a race officer can work a computer programme. A refinement is to have each boat's data stored in the race computer. The race officer then inputs the course type and length, starting times and finishing times. The computer works out the average speeds to assess the wind, and then produces the required handicaps.

Soon after its introduction in 1985, IMS became established in the United States, Italy, Australia, Holland, Germany, Sweden and Finland, but made poor progress in the UK and Ireland where only 330 yachts ever held certificates. This was probably due to the rule's sophistication, complexity and cost. Today few countries have any real IMS fleets, with no racing whatsoever under this rule in the UK.

14.3.4   INTERNATIONAL LEVEL CLASS (ILC)

More recently introduced are International Level Class yachts designed to the relevant ILC Rule. In 1994 only two sizes existed, the ILC 40 (LOA 11.5m to 12.5m) and the ILC 46 (LOA 13.4m to 14.5m). It is however planned to introduce ILC 30s and ILC 70s, and possibly others in the future. As the name implies, these various classes will each race level (without handicapping) and are seen primarily as a replacement for the old Ton cup classes.

14.3.5 CHANNEL HANDICAP SYSTEM (CHS)

For the average cruising yachtsman who intends to enter the occasional race, the Channel Handicap System (CHS) is the likely starting point. It is a time on time rating system for all types of monohull cruising yachts to be handicapped for coastal or offshore racing at club level. CHS was originated jointly by the Royal Ocean Racing Club (RORC) in this country and the *Union National pour la Course au Large* (UNCL) in France.

Each yacht is given a time correction factor (TCF) depending on her key hull measurements, hull and keel type, principal sail measurements and materials, etc. An owner should be able to take all the required dimensions, and many of them can be extracted from a valid IOR or IMS certificate if held, but if preferred a measurer can be arranged. In some races and regions measurement is compulsory. The RORC rating office, which administers the scheme in the UK has a vast amount of data on boats of all types and sizes, and will check measurements submitted. Increasingly race organisers require official weights of hulls, obtained with an authorised load cell. For some events an endorsed certificate, CHS(E), is required, which may need official check measurements.

To discourage design optimisation, TCF formulae are not published. They are revised annually to refine handicapping and to allow for new design trends. So a certificate has to be revalidated annually.

CHS was always intended for cruising yachts with proper accommodation, and while yachts designed for racing are not excluded they are at some disadvantage compared to genuine cruiser/racers. Light displacement boats and day boats may be rated CHS, but should be classified as such so that they race in special divisions.

Handicaps are influenced by the boat's sail wardrobe, with sail cloth classified into three grades. Low-tech sails must be woven, soft-finish polyester (or nylon or cotton). By accepting a rating penalty a boat may use mid-tech cloth which includes a wide range of materials from highly resinated woven dacron to dacron/mylar laminates. For an increased penalty hi-tech cloths may be used, for example, Kevlar and Spectra laminates. Only sails declared for rating purposes can be carried on board.

TCFs for CHS are calculated to three decimal places, whilst IOR TMFs are shown to four places and are normally slightly lower in value. No attempt should be made to compare the two systems with each other, nor with IMS time on distance allowances.

14.3.6 THE RORC / UNCL IR 2000 RATING (IRC AND IRM)

The RORC's IR 2000 rating rule, launched in Jan 2000, comprises two separate rating systems: IRC and IRM, embraced in one overall structure.

14.3.7 IRC

IRC, that is IR Club (the initials IR have no meaning), is in effect a re-naming of the highly successful and popular Channel Handicap System (CHS). The IRC System enables all types of monohull cruising yachts to be handicapped for racing in coastal or offshore waters at club level on an international basis. Self-measurement, together with the difficulties of optimising designs to the rule, makes IRC a very cheap, simple and attractive system.

IRC was originally conceived for domestic use but, due to its popularity and the developmental input of the RORC, IRC is today used in over 25 countries. More than 5000 IRC certificates were issued worldwide in 2000AD, just under half of these outside the UK. Thus the IRC is one of, if not the, most popular rating rule both in the UK and worldwide.

IRC is a rating system which derives a *handicap* from the physical dimensions of a yacht's hull and keel type, principal sail measurements, sail materials, and so on.

At its simplest, an owner should be able to take all the required dimensions and declare his yacht's measurements, obviating the need for costly independent measurement. At the more serious end of the racing scale an IRC endorsed Certificate may be issued following measurement by an RORC measurer. The RORC rating office, which administers the scheme in the UK has a vast amount of data on boats of all types and sizes, and will check measurements submitted. Increasingly, race organisers are requiring official weights of hulls, obtained with an authorised load cell (electronic weighing device). For some events an endorsed certificate is required.

The IRC formulæ produce a Time Corrector (TCC) which, when applied to a yacht's elapsed time for a race, gives a Corrected Time on an equal scale to other competitors. The formulæ used to calculate the TCC are deliberately secret and under constant review. This makes it difficult to design to the rule and discourages any means of artificially reducing a TCC or increasing performance. However, IRC does not exclude yachts designed specifically for racing. It can be used to rate Ultra Light Displacement Boats (ULDBs) and Dayboats, although race organisers are encouraged to provide separate classes for these craft whenever possible.

To assist in the operation and development of the rule, the RORC welcomes the input of ideas or comment from clubs, race organisers and owners. An IRC Council with regional representation has been formed to facilitate this.

14.3.8 IRM

IRM was introduced with effect from 1 January 2000. This is the measured part of the IR 2000 Rule (hence the M) with published formulæ. Every boat, except those of a recognised one-design, must be independently measured, weighed and inclined in order to obtain a certificate.

IRM produces a Time Corrector, in this case a TCM, which is used to calculate race results. The IRM and the IRC Time Correctors are calculated from different formulæ and are not compatible. A boat with an IRC certificate cannot use its TCC to equate a race result against another boat's TCM. However, every boat measured and weighed under IRM and issued with a TCM is also issued with an IRC certificate giving a TCC. This is how the two parts of IR 2000 come together.

With IRM, owners and designers are able to calculate ratings by using the published formulæ. This will tend to make IRM "type-forming", designs will be optimised and inevitably converge on the "best shape". The RORC therefore reserve the right to make adjustments or amendments at any time in order to prevent undesirable or unforeseen lines of development.

In its first season, 57 boats held a valid IRM certificate. The fleet consists of 30 designs, from 15 design offices, and includes recognised one-designs. The average length of yachts was 11.59 metres (38 feet). The majority of the fleet were British but there were also boats from Greece, Ireland, New Zealand, Holland, Germany, France and the USA.

The emphasis of IRM is on simplicity and concise rules and it is hoped that it will soon become the premier system used throughout the world. The RYA gives its wholehearted support to this RORC initiative.

14.3.9 THE SPORTSBOAT RULE (SBR)

Sportsboats, by their very nature, are designed as out-and-out racing boats; so a TCC issued to a sportsboat rated under IRC is inclined to be harsh. To overcome this and to enable sportsboats to race on equal terms the RYA and RORC have jointly developed the Sportsboat Rule (SBR).

The SBR is designed to meet the rating needs of small to medium sized light displacement, large sail area racing keelboats. Like IRC, the SBR uses self-measurement and secret formulæ to calculate a boat's Time Correction Factor (TCF) from the physical dimensions of a boat.

Recognised one-design sportsboats which meet set criteria are issued their TCF's by the RYA. One-offs or limited numbers of similar boats are issued individual certificates by the RORC.

14.3.10 RYA PORTSMOUTH YARDSTICK SCHEME

The RYA Portsmouth Yardstick Scheme (PYS), originally conceived for dinghy racing and later extended to keelboats, cruising yachts and multihulls, is operated jointly by the RYA and the Clubs and has gained international recognition. It quantifies the speed of class yachts on the basis of past race results and is thus a performance scheme requiring no measurement or central certification. Full details are contained in the RYA booklet YR2, published annually, and in the RYA website. The booklet also gives full recommendations on the use of the PYS and is a must for any club running yardstick races.

Some definitions help to understand how the scheme works:

1. The **Portsmouth Number** (PN), expressed as whole numbers from 600 to 1700, is the measure of performance. The ratio between PNs reflects the ratio difference in the performance of yachts. Assuming yacht Alpha has a PN of 700 and yacht Beta one of 1400, if Alpha completes a race in 70 minutes then, for Beta to beat Alpha on Corrected Time, she has to finish the same race in under 140 minutes. On another day in different conditions and over a different course, Alpha may take 35 minutes to complete the race in which case, the ratio between the PNs being the same, Beta would need to finish in under 70 minutes to beat Alpha.

   To establish a PN for a new yacht or one without a PN she must race against yachts with known, well-established PNs (classified as a Primary or Secondary Yardstick) against which the new class can be assessed.

   If, in the first example above a new yacht Delta had raced and finished in 100 minutes then her PN assessed against Alpha (assuming Alpha to be a Yardstick class) would be 1000. (700/70 x 100 = 1000). At club level this assessment would be carried out over a number of races and the PN for Delta continually adjusted until such time as it became stable.

2. **Primary Yardsticks** (PY). These are Portsmouth Numbers which are published by the RYA and which have become well established by the experience of many clubs over several years. For example, for cruisers (in 2001) they include:

Yacht	Primary Yardstick Nos
Sigma 33	923
J/24	936
Impala	943
MG C27	959
Contessa 32	994
Westerly GK 24	1014
Sonata	1038
E Boat	1050
Ruffian 23	1060
Sadler 25	1060
Achill 24	1076
Westerly Centaur	1206

3. **Secondary Yardsticks** (SY). These are less well established PNs also published by the RYA.
4. **Recorded Numbers** (RN). These are PNs published by the RYA on the basis of limited information.
5. **Club Numbers** (CN). These are PNs which are allocated by a club. They may be derived from Trial Numbers (see below) or adjusted by a club from RYA lists.
6. **Trial Numbers**. These are numbers that are allocated by a club on a trial basis until a CN can be determined.

Within any (except one-design) class of cruising yacht there may be significant variations in, for example, rig. Some boats may have only small headsails, or carry no spinnaker. These variations from what is defined as 'Base Trim' are allowed for by small additions to the PN for example, plus 40 for a yacht with no spinnaker. A similar scale of allowances is laid down for different engine/propeller configurations and for different keel configurations.

A Portsmouth Certificate may be issued to a yacht when she is allowed a Club Number, and should specify what allowances have been made for variations from Base Trim.

Every July clubs which use the scheme are asked to render a 'Yardstick Return' to the RYA, to assess how the system has worked and to make recommendations for any changes in PNs.

The main advantage of the PYS is that no yacht measurement or certification is required, thus saving the owner money. One disadvantage is that the Scheme is not designed to cope with one-off or non-standard class yachts where the performance of the helmsman and crew cannot be averaged out from the yacht's performance.

14.3.11   OTHER HANDICAPPING SYSTEMS
Many regional or local handicapping systems exist. These include for example ECHO in Ireland, NECRA in the North Sea, Clyde Handicap Nationale (HN) in France, Scandicap Mk II and Danish Handicap (DH). There are about a dozen systems in the United States. For their annual 'Round the Island' race the Island Sailing Club uses the West Solent Handicap Formula, adjusted in some cases by comparison with the Portsmouth Yardstick.

Many clubs run their own handicapping systems for local club events. In some ways these are the most satisfactory of all with a fixed fleet of boats – until some stranger appears and sweeps the board.

14.4   RACING YACHT SAFETY

Water is potentially dangerous. Sailing therefore always contains an element of danger. Some dangers inevitably increase when racing.

Decisions on safety ultimately lie with skippers, who should get all the facts needed to make a well informed decision. However rules, regulations and schemes exist which make a racing yacht a safer vehicle and a skipper more aware of its limitations.

14.4.1   ORC SPECIAL REGULATIONS
For many years the RORC issued its own Special Regulations governing minimum equipment and accommodation standards for yachts racing offshore. These were replaced by the similar regulations of the Offshore Racing Council (ORC), the international body which now governs the sport.

Apart from specifying that a boat must be strongly built, properly rigged and fully seaworthy, the regulations cover many details which include: engine installations, security of hatches, sizes and watertight integrity of cockpits, seacocks on hull openings, lifelines, stanchions, pulpits, fire extinguishers, bilge pumps, anchors and cable, first aid kit, foghorn, radar reflectors, compasses and navigational equipment, navigation lights, storm sails, emergency tiller, tools and spares, radio receiver, lifejackets, whistles, safety harnesses, liferaft and flares, and specific minimum standards for safety harnesses and liferafts.

Various degrees of compliance with the regulations are arranged by categorising races as follows:

Race Categories

Category 0 trans-oceanic races, including races which pass through areas in which air or sea temperatures are likely to be less than 5° Celsius other than temporarily, where yachts must be completely self-sufficient for very extended periods of time, capable of withstanding heavy storms and prepared to meet serious emergencies without the expectation of outside assistance.

Category 1 races of long distance and well offshore, where yachts must be completely self-sufficient for extended periods of time, capable of withstanding heavy storms and prepared to meet serious emergencies without the expectation of outside assistance.

Category 2 races of extended duration along or not far removed from shorelines or in large unprotected bays or lakes, where a high degree of self-sufficiency is required of the yachts.

Category 3 races across open water, most of which is relatively protected or close to shorelines, including races for small yachts.

Category 4 short races, close to shore in relatively warm or protected waters normally held in daylight.

For example, most RORC races are now Category 3 (plus liferaft), with yachts recommended to equip to Category 2 which applies to the Fastnet Race. Most clubs which run races for handicap classes, even inshore, specify the standard of equipment by reference to ORC Special Regulations. For example, yachts racing in the Solent might be required to comply with Category 4.

ORC Special Regulations are published in RORC's annual programmes and website, and may also be obtained from ISAF and ORC.

As an extension of the ORC Special regulations in the UK, the RYA publishes recommendations for equipment to be carried in category 5 & 6 for use in small boats and where the race conditions are likely to be less severe than in the ORC Categories. This information is published in the RYA booklet YR9 – Racing Yacht Safety.

14.4.2 RORC STABILITY AND SAFETY SCREENING (SSS)

The SSS or 'Triple S' numeral scheme was developed by the RORC for race organisers to assess the suitability of yachts for offshore races; it can also be applied to inshore and dayboat racing. The SSS numeral comes partly from the yacht's dimensions and partly from her compliance with ORC Special Regulations.

The organisers' general rule of thumb

assumed that the longer a yacht, the more capable it is of withstanding bad conditions. This has served very well over the years but gave only a very rough guide to safety and stability. Other physical characteristics will add to or subtract from an assumed level of safety and stability based solely on length. The RYA and RORC believe that the correct consideration of these other factors, in addition to length, will produce a far better guide to seaworthiness.

Under the SSS Scheme each yacht, whether or not it possesses any safety equipment or features, will have a Base Value. The yacht's dimensions and the application of the formulæ are the sole ingredients.

Base Value is the yacht's Base Size Factor adjusted up or down by applying eight calculated modifying factors. Base Values range from 10 to 70; the higher values suggest a more seaworthy yacht.

Base Size Factor is the primary factor related to the physical size of the yacht and sets a suitable scale. Each modifying factor results in a value close to unity and is used to adjust the Base Size Factor to take account of variations from the norm.

The modifying factors are:

i **Length Displacement Factor** which notes that light displacement for size may cause control and stability problems in extreme conditions. Within limits, heavy displacement for length may be considered desirable for seaworthiness.

ii **Beam Displacement Factor** recognising that high beam, particularly when related to low displacement and large topside flare, has been shown to increase the risk of both wave induced capsize and inverted stability.

iii **Sail Area Displacement Beam Length Ratio** relates the normal sail area to the size of a yacht in terms of its displacement, length and beam. Power to carry sail effectively is directly related to displacement.

iv **Rig Factor** recognises the ease of sail handling and sail reduction associated with certain rig configurations. It also notes the greater structural integrity of rigs not requiring sophisticated control.

v **Keel Factor** recognises the potential reduction in the basic ballast stability of yachts with drop keels or centreboards.

vi **Engine & Propeller Factor** notes the advantages of having effective auxiliary propulsion.

vii **Dayboat Factor** recognises the limitations of dayboats.

viii **Self Righting Factor** gives credit for a yacht's proven self righting ability from a knockdown. This can give credit to a yacht which has been inclined for IR2000, IMS, or other rating purposes (and is still in the same trim). If a yacht has not been inclined, the factor defaults to 1.0.

An **Adjustment Value** takes account of non-dimensional safety features such as compliance with ORC Special Regulations. This value will normally default to 0, unless specific features have been declared and incorporated. The maximum Adjustment Value allowed depends on the Base Value already calculated (Table 1) with the features which may be included in Adjustment Value, and their values (Table 2).

Table 1: Limits on Adjustment

Base Value Range Adjustment	Max. Value
< 8	0
8 - 14	3
15 - 23	5
24 - 32	6
33 - 41	7
> 41	8

Table 2: Adjustment allowances
For yachts which fully comply with ORC Special Regulations:

Compliance with ORC Race Category:	Max adjustment allowed
4	+ 3
3	+ 5
2	+ 6
1	+ 7
0	+ 8

or, for cruising yachts which do not fully comply with the ORC Special Regulations requirements, Adjustment Values up to +3 may be awarded.

Thus the **SSS Numeral** (SSSN) is the sum of Base Value and Adjustment Value and is the qualifying number to be used for races with minimum SSS requirements. A yacht's IR2000 certificate will show, in the top right hand corner, three figures: **SSS Base Value, Adjustment Value and the SSS Numeral.**

An advantage of the SSS scheme is that it gives a measure of each yacht's stability and safety which can be applied to a particular race. Race organisers can specify a minimum SSS numeral for each race having regard to the type and duration of the race and the likelihood of sailing at night or encountering adverse conditions. As a guide, the RORC suggests that the following minimum SSS numerals are related to ORC race categories:

Table 3: Suggested minimum SSSN

ORC Race Category	Minimum SSSN
4	10
3	20
2	30
1	40
0	50

An owner can use a SSS numeral as a standard against which to judge the likely capability of his vessel. It can also give some comparative guidance as to how the safety of any yacht may be enhanced from the aspect of seagoing. For example, Table 4 shows the Base Value calculated for certain well known designs.

Table 4: Typical SSS Base Values

Yacht	Base Value
E Boat	10
J/24	11
Sonata	15
Formula 28	16
X 99	20
HB 31	22
X 3/4 Ton	24
DB1	26
Hustler SJ30	26
Sigma 33	29
Oyster 41	37
Sigma 38	38
Contessa 32	39
Nicholson 43	50
Nicholson 55	60

For most of their races the RORC requires a minimum SSS figure of 20, but more for certain races – for example, 30 for the Fastnet Race.

Most yachts over 12m LOA can achieve a figure of 30 fairly easily, but this may not apply with smaller boats, particularly those of very light displacement or with flimsy rigs. In such cases the SSS figure will alert a race committee to an entry which may be disallowed, while at the same time encouraging an owner to make all possible improvements.

14.4.3   ISO STABILITY INDEX (STIX)
The ISO's (International Standards Organisation) standard on the stability and buoyancy for recreational craft (ISO 12217) has developed into a stability index (STIX) as a result of previous work undertaken by the RORC and RYA on the SSSN. The principle of calculating a Base Size Factor and adjusting this up or down by modifying factors is the same with STIX as with SSSN.

The difference is however, in the meaningfulness and calculation of some of the modifying factors. STIX has seven modifying factors three of which include features of the yacht's righting moment. The RORC and the RYA are jointly working to incorporate the STIX index into the existing SSSN scheme. This work is expected to be complete for the 2002 racing season.

14.5 CONDUCT OF YACHT RACES

14.5.1   RACE ORGANISATION

Before taking part in a race it is necessary to understand the general procedure. Races are run mainly by individual clubs, who are bound to follow in all important respects the rules prescribed by the International Sailing Federation (ISAF).

A club gives the outline arrangements for a forthcoming event in 'a Notice of Race', which among other details such as time and date should prescribe the method of entry. For a major regatta the Notice of Race is a lengthy document. The entry form will usually require an owner to declare that the boat has the necessary measurement certificate and that he or she will conform to the rules.

The owner then obtains the 'Sailing Instructions' – an important document which deserves very careful study because it includes such details as the starting signals and arrangements, the course to be sailed, and finishing line, the time limit, the method of shortening the course and many other matters as appropriate. Do not forget to take it afloat with you, and for major events it is best to take a photocopy.

14.5.2   OWNERS' OBLIGATIONS

Racing imposes obligations as well as offering enjoyment and competition. When entering a race an owner undertakes to be bound by the racing rules, to conform to the written sailing instructions which spell out such details as the course to be sailed, and where appropriate to obey whatever regulations may be imposed by the class to which the boat belongs. These may specify various details such as safety equipment to be carried and the number of persons on board.

When a yacht has been measured for handicapping purposes, or if she belongs to a one-design class, the owner must not make any changes that will invalidate the boat's rating (measurement). A boat can be entered in an open event by a member of any recognised club, or by a personal member of any National Authority.

However, many clubs rather naturally require an owner to be a member in order to compete in the regular club races, probably run on a weekly basis during the season, even if they stage less frequent open meetings to which outsiders are very welcome. So you must join a suitable club, which so far as the racing rules are concerned may or may not be the club providing the racing.

For identification purposes a yacht must carry numbers, of a specified size, on her mainsail and spinnaker. Larger boats may also be required to have numbers on their headsails. These numbers may be allocated by the national authority (the RA in the United Kingdom), or by an organisation such as the Royal Ocean Racing Club or the boat's class association.

There are regulations about advertising that may be displayed on racing yachts. For some club events and for racing some classes that have chosen to limit advertising this is restricted to the small marks such as sailmakers placed near the tack of a sail, or other manufacturers on spars. Full details are given in ISAF Regulation 20, Appendix 1 of the Racing Rules of Sailing.

As has already been mentioned, sailing races are self-policing. There is no umpire afloat (apart from special match races) to call foul. It depends on each individual skipper to make sure that the rules are obeyed from start to finish – a situation which prevails in few other competitive sports.

If you touch a mark (an infringement) you may be the only person to know. But it is up to you to retire from the race or take whatever alternative penalty is available. For example making two 360° turns with two tacks and two gybes for not keeping clear of, or not giving room to, another boat when required to do so by a rule, and making a single turn for touching a mark. The responsibility lies with the offender to do the right thing without prompting from any other competitor.

Of course there are occasions between two boats when both helmsmen in an incident feel that they are in the right, and if a collision occurs this must be dealt with fairly under the protest procedure described below, not by verbal abuse across the water. If you make a mistake and baulk another boat, regardless of what penalty you may accept, it is polite to apologise as soon as possible, either during the race, at the finish, or on getting ashore.

Finally, if you are not satisfied with the course or with some other arrangements regarding a race do not complain too much to the Race Officer. He is almost certainly a volunteer, who is taking his turn at a thankless task. Where you have constructive ideas about running the race they are best passed to the Sailing Secretary for consideration at the next meeting of the Sailing Committee.

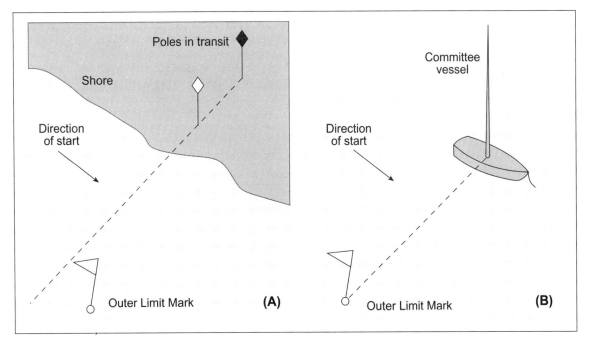

Fig. 14(1) Two types of starting line: (a) the transit of two poles or flagstaffs ashore, plus an outer limit mark (OLM); and (b) in open waters the line may be between the mainmast of the Committee Vessel (CV) and a buoy.

14.5.3 RACE COMMITTEE

To organise even a single race properly takes some effort, and for a major regatta where there are several classes and many entries a large number of helpers are needed. In some clubs competitors are expected, or even required, to assist on the race committee on a regular basis and this can be interesting and instructive. A newcomer to racing could do worse than help on the race committee before actually competing, because this will soon give an insight to the general procedure and from quite a different viewpoint.

14.5.4 COURSE TO BE SAILED

One of the first duties of the race committee is to decide and signal the course to be sailed. The method of doing this will be described in the sailing instructions, but it is helpful to know the location of the possible marks in advance, rather than have to locate them on the chart in the hectic minutes before the start.

The marks will be stated in order, and in each case it will be indicated whether the mark is to be rounded or passed, and whether it is to be left to port or to starboard. Note that there is a distinction between rounding and passing. If a string represents the wake of the yacht from start to finish, it must when drawn taut lie on the

required side of each mark. If the mark is a rounding mark, the taut string must touch it, which it will do automatically in most cases, but also occasionally when it is explicitly required that the mark be 'looped' so that a boat will cross her own wake. Otherwise, the mark is what is called a 'passing' mark, and the tautened string will not touch it. Rounding marks are the 'corners' of the course and boats will usually come very near them. Passing marks usually keep boats away from hazards, and boats may never need to be in their vicinity.

It is an infringement to touch a mark while rounding or passing. However, a yacht may exonerate herself from this offence by making one complete 360° turn, which must include one tack and one gybe. This must be taken as soon as the yacht can sail clear of other competitors.

When possible the course should be set in order to give a good test of sailing to windward, and of reaching and running. When circumstances permit the opening leg will normally be a beat.

14.5.5 STARTING

Two types of starting line are in use, Fig. 14(1):

For races conducted from a shoreside club (a) the starting line is usually the transit of two poles or flagstaffs ashore, with probably a buoy to mark the outer limit of the line. This buoy, called the 'outer limit mark', will not necessarily be exactly on the starting line, but probably a boat's length or so on the course side of the line. This has lulled many beginners (and experienced sailors) into making a premature start.

If in open water (b) it will be an imaginary line between two objects – usually a buoy and the mast of the committee vessel which is running the race. This type of starting line can be orientated at 90° to the wind direction to give a windward start.

The standard starting sequence for most races is:

Five minutes before the start the 'Warning Signal' (class flag) is broken out, with a sound signal (gun or hooter).

Four minutes before the start the 'Preparatory Signal' (Flag P of the International Code, or a flag indicating a penalty if a boat is on the course side of the starting line at any time in the last minute before her starting signal) is broken out, with another sound signal. From this moment the yachts must take a penalty or retire for breaking a racing rule, or risk disqualification.

A yacht must be away from her mooring (though she may be anchored), and she must not be propelled other than by sail (no engine, no paddling). Also note that a yacht should not wear an ensign while racing, so if an ensign has been worn (quite correctly) while sailing out to the starting area, it ought to be removed at or before the Preparatory Signal.

Three minutes later, the preparatory signal is removed with a long sound signal. There is now one minute to the starting signal, during which a penalty may apply if any part of the boat is on the course side of the line (including at the moment of the starting signal). If flag I (India) was used as or with the preparatory signal, the penalty is to return to the pre-start side round one end and start (again) – which will usually result in a late start – while flag Z means a 20% place penalty in the race results and a black flag means disqualification from that race.

The start is signalled by removing the warning signal, with a sound signal.

Note that on each occasion it is the flag which is the actual signal from which the time is taken. The sound signal is only to call attention. However, in a well run race the two should be synchronised.

If any part of a boat is across the starting line at the starting signal, or had crossed it when flag I applied and not yet returned round an end, a further sound signal is made and Flag X is hoisted. The offender must then return – keeping clear of the other boats which have started correctly – and start properly (when Flag X will be lowered). This 'individual recall' signal is not made when a boat is to be disqualified under the 'black flag' procedure.

If a large number of boats are over the line, and if they cannot be identified, the race committee will signal a 'General Recall'. This is done by hoisting the First Substitute and making two sound signals. Then the whole fleet (including any boats which started correctly) must return for a fresh start, with the Warning Signal hoisted one minute after the First Substitute is lowered.

Other flags are used in connection with starting races. The most common are the Answering Pendant which is the postponement signal, and Flag N which indicates that the race cannot be started, usually because of too little or too much wind, and is abandoned, either for the day or until after the fleet has returned to harbour.

One end of the start line will often be favoured by the line not being precisely square to the wind direction if the first leg is a beat, or to the direction of the first mark if the opening leg is either a reach or a run.

It is therefore important to decide the best place to start, and in open water this can best be done with the boat's compass, by comparing the bearing of the starting line with the wind direction or the direction of the first mark. Remember that both of these can change in the minutes before the Preparatory Signal. The effect of any tidal stream across the course also needs to be considered.

It is also important to decide whether it is likely to be better to work one side of the course or the other, due to predictable wind shifts or tidal stream, or maybe to tack up the middle of the course on wind shifts which are sometimes quite pronounced in coastal waters.

Having decided where to start, the next problem is to be there when the starting gun fires, and with plenty of boat speed. Here experience and a good knowledge of the rules count, because other boats will aim to be at the same point at the same time.

14.5.6 SOME GENERAL RACING RULES

It is a fundamental principle of sportsmanship that when competitors break a rule they will promptly take a penalty (when available) or retire.

Certain fundamental rules must always be obeyed:

A. A boat or competitor shall give all possible help to any person or vessel in danger (Rule 1.1).
B. A boat and her owner shall compete in compliance with recognised principles of sportsmanship and fair play. A boat may be penalised under this rule only if it is clearly established that these principles have been violated (Rule 2).

C. A boat is solely responsible for deciding whether or not to start or to continue racing (Rule 4).

The right-of-way rules between two boats when racing are summarised in section 14.6 below, where different circumstances are dealt with. Here some general rules applicable throughout a race are stated. The relevant ISAF rule number is given in brackets. In the Racing Rules of Sailing, all types of vessels that are racing are described as 'boats'.

A boat shall avoid contact with another boat if reasonably possible. However a right-of-way boat or one entitled to room

a. need not act to avoid contact until it is clear that the other boat is not keeping clear or giving room, and
b. shall not be penalised unless there is contact that causes damage (Rule 14.)

When a boat acquires right of way, she shall initially give the other boat 'room' to keep clear, unless she acquires right of way because of the other boat's actions (Rule 15).

When a right-of-way boat changes course, she shall give the other boat 'room' to keep clear (Rule 16).

Subject to these rules, a right-of-way boat is free to alter course as she wishes, even if done with the specific objective of impeding the other boat, but special rules apply when one boat is overtaking another to leeward (Rule 17), and at marks and obstructions (Rules 18 and 19).

If possible, a boat shall avoid a boat that is at anchor, aground or capsized, or is trying to help a person or vessel in danger (Rule 21).

A boat may anchor during a race, but must not secure to a buoy or alongside a jetty etc (Rule 45).

A boat intending to protest shall hail 'Protest' and conspicuously display a red flag as soon as possible. She must also notify the other boat of her intention to protest, and may be required to inform the race committee at or before the finish if the sailing instructions say so. A written protest must be submitted within a prescribed time, but may later be withdrawn on request. Protests and requests for redress are heard after racing by a protest committee of disinterested individuals, usually three or four in number (Rules 61 and 62).

14.5.7 FINISHING

The finishing line will be described in the sailing instructions in a similar way to the starting line, and may be the same. Note that the finishing line must be crossed from the direction of the last mark. A boat remains subject to the racing rules until she has cleared the finishing line. In some races a competitor may be required to record her own finishing time, and this is often a wise precaution in case of subsequent dispute.

14.6 RACING RIGHT-OF-WAY

14.6.1 DEFINITIONS

These notes on the racing right-of-way rules (Part 2 of the ISAF Racing Rules of Sailing) are not intended to be comprehensive or to cater for the expert sailor. They should however be sufficient to keep a beginner out of trouble, and to allow him or her to race without causing disruption or damage. If at any moment you are unsure of your rights, play it safe and keep well clear of other boats.

Certain terms appear repeatedly in the ISAF rules, and will need to be used in what follows, so it is important that they are understood. Two are not defined but are in general sailing use:

Tacking. A yacht is tacking from the moment she starts to luff until she has borne away to close-hauled.

Close-hauled. A yacht is close-hauled when sailing as close to the wind as she can with advantage when going to windward.

Many other terms used regularly in the rules have the following specific definitions:

Clear Astern and *Clear Ahead; Overlap* One boat is *clear astern* of another when her hull and equipment in normal position are behind a line abeam from the aftermost point of the other boat's hull and equipment in normal position. The other boat is *clear ahead*. They *overlap* when neither is *clear astern* or when a boat between them *overlaps* both. These terms do not apply to boats on opposite *tacks* unless rule 18 applies. See Fig. 14(2).

Keep Clear One boat *keeps clear* of another if the other can sail her course with no need to take avoiding action and, when the boats are overlapped on the same tack if the leeward boat can change course in both directions without immediately making contact with the *windward* boat.

Leeward and Windward A boat's *leeward* side is the side that is or, when she is head to wind, was away from the wind. However, when sailing by the lee or directly downwind, her *leeward* side is the side on which her mainsail lies. The other side is her *windward* side. When two boats on the same *tack overlap*, the one on the *leeward* side of

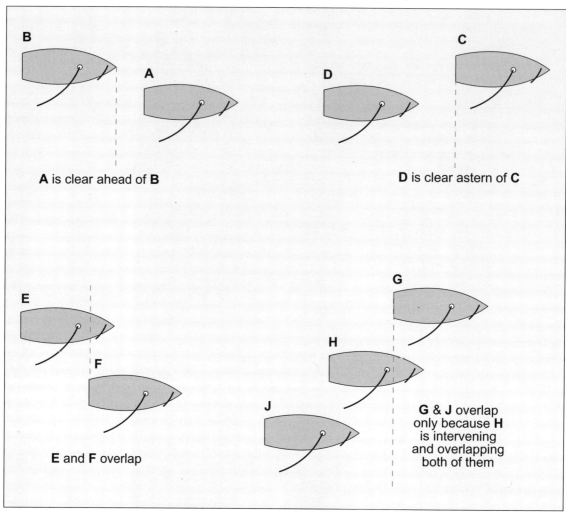

Fig. 14(2) Illustrations of Clear ahead, Clear astern and Overlapping, as defined above.

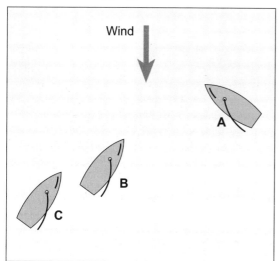

Fig. 14(3) Boat A on the starboard tack has right of way and is an obstruction to B. B may require C to tack so that B may then do likewise to keep clear of A.

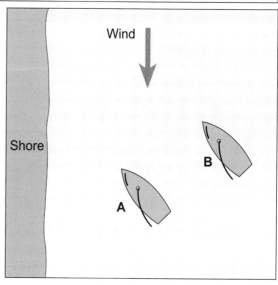

Fig. 14(4) The shore is an obstruction, and A may call upon B for room so that she may tack to avoid it. B must either tack when hailed or reply 'You tack', and give B room to tack and keep clear of her. (Rule 19).

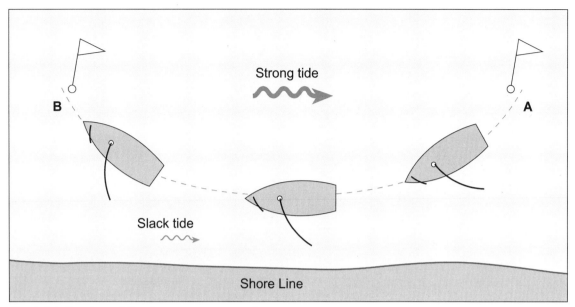

Fig. 14(5) The dotted line is a proper course for the yacht sailing from A to B. if for example there is less tidal stream or more wind inshore.

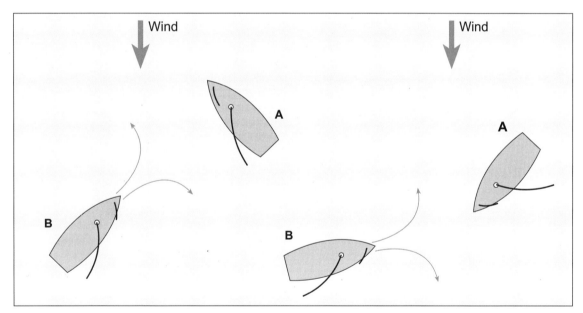

Fig. 14(6) Basic rule - opposite tacks. In each case B on port tack must keep clear of A on starboard tack. (Rule 10).

the other is the *leeward* boat. The other is the *windward* boat.

Obstruction An object that a boat could not pass without changing course substantially, if she were sailing directly towards it and one of her hull lengths from it. An object that can be safely passed on only one side and an area so designated by the sailing instructions are also *obstructions*. However, a boat *racing* is not an

obstruction to other boats unless they are required to *keep clear* of her, give her *room* or, if rule 21 applies, avoid her. See Figs. 14(3) and (4).

Proper Course A course a boat would sail to *finish* as soon as possible in of the other boats referred to in the rule using the term. A boat has no *proper course* before her starting signal. See Fig 14(5).

Protest An allegation made under rule 61.2 by a boat, a race committee or a protest committee that a boat has broken a *rule*.

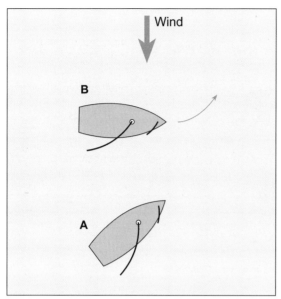

Fig. 14(7) Basic rule - same tack, overlapped. B, the windward yacht, must keep clear of A to leeward. (Rule 11).

Room The space a boat needs in the existing conditions while manoeuvring promptly in a seamanlike way.

14.6.2   RIGHT-OF-WAY IN OPEN WATER

In open water the basic rules which govern the right-of-way between two or more boats are similar to the 'Collision Regulations' for ordinary vessels:

On opposite tacks – port tack keeps clear of starboard tack (Rule 10). See Fig 14(6).

On the same tack, overlapped – windward boat keeps clear of leeward boat (Rule 11). Fig 14(7).

On the same tack, not overlapped – boat clear astern keeps clear of boat clear ahead (Rule 12).

When a boat which has been clear astern establishes an overlap to leeward of a boat on the same tack, she must initially allow her room to keep clear. This requires and deserves some explanation: Initially the boat clear astern must keep clear, but the moment she establishes an overlap the responsibility passes to the windward boat; Rule 11. In the extreme case it would be unfair if the leeward yacht could establish her overlap just a few inches from the windward boat's stern, since the latter would then be physically incapable of luffing to keep clear. Given the initial opportunity, which is not a continuing one, the windward boat must respond and keep clear (Rule 15).

In these circumstances the leeward boat may not sail above her proper course while the overlap exists and she is within two boat-lengths of the other boat (Rule 17.1).

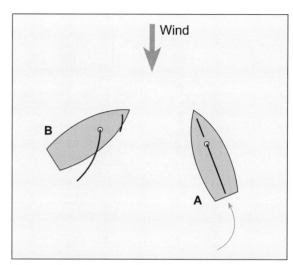

Fig. 14(8) Basic rule – changing tacks, tacking and gybing. Here A has tacked too close to B. A must tack far enough from B to allow the latter to keep clear without having to alter course before A completes her tack (or gybe). (Rule 15).

14.6.3   TACKING

A boat which is tacking must, having passed head to wind until she reaches a close-hauled course, keep clear of a boat that is not so doing, under rule 13. A boat must not tack or gybe into a position giving her right-of-way unless she does so far enough from a boat on a tack to allow the latter to keep clear without starting to alter course before the tack or gybe is completed (Rule 15). This is illustrated in Fig. 14(8) where A has tacked too close to B to allow the latter to keep clear. It is a situation which is difficult to judge, so when in doubt do not tack.

14.6.4   BEARING AWAY

When two boats are on the same tack on a free leg of the course (not beating to windward), a boat must not sail below her proper course when she is within two of her hull lengths of a leeward boat or of a boat clear astern which is steering a course to leeward of her own (Rule 17.2). Note that this only applies on a free leg of the course. A boat ahead or overlapped to windward may bear away if she can justify this as her proper course, (provided that, if windward boat, she continues to keep clear) or she may bear away and gybe provided that if she gains right of way in so doing (by changing from a windward boat on port tack to starboard-tack boat) she gives the other boat room to keep clear (Rule 15).

14.6.5   RULES AT THE START

This is an exciting and hectic phase of any race, but only one special rule applies before a boat

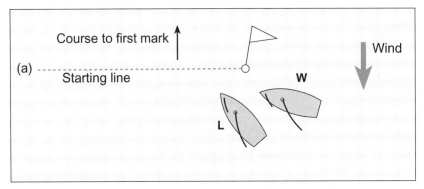

Fig. 14(9) The anti-barging rule. Approaching the starting line to start, a leeward boat need not give a windward boat room to pass to leeward of a starting mark (either end of the line) that is surrounded by navigable water. L does not have to give room to W and may sail above a close-hauled course to deprive her of room, provided that any course change gives the other boat room to keep clear (Rules 18.1(a) and 16).

within two lengths of the mark, the outside boat must give the inside boat room to round inside her; see Rule 18.2(a). Room is defined as the space a boat needs in the existing conditions while manoeuvring promptly in a seamanlike way; see Fig 14(10).

Otherwise, if the boats are not overlapped when the first of them enters the two-length zone, the one astern must keep clear until they have passed the mark, regardless of which tack they are on, unless the boat ahead tacks; see Rule 18.2(c).

The written rule is complicated, because it has to cater for different situations, but for our purposes simply remember that if you have established an overlap on an outside boat on the same tack in ample time, you may call for water and expect to get it. Remember, however, that there may be a boat or boats ahead who are already almost at the mark, and on whom you may not have established an overlap in sufficient time. Also, having rounded the mark the situation may change. Having been the leeward and inside boat with right-of-way actually rounding the mark, you may both then gybe while rounding so you become the windward boat and responsible for keeping clear of the boat to leeward of you (which however must give you room to finish your rounding).

Never try to establish an overlap at the very last moment. If you fail you will probably be forced the wrong side of the mark, because it will be too late to go under the stern(s) of the boat(s) ahead – which is where you should have gone in the first place.

Rule 18 does not apply to boats on opposite tacks when approaching a windward mark or an obsruction to windward. Nor, as has already been seen, does it apply at a starting mark surrounded by navigable water when approaching the line to start. It applies at marks between boats that are required to leave the mark on the same side and are doing so. At an obstruction, it applies when boats are passing the obstruction on their same sides (to port or starboard), so it does not apply when, for instance, they are reaching along the shore approaching each other on opposite tacks – one is leaving the obstruction to port and the other to starboard.

has cleared the starting line. Also there is no 'proper course' before the starting signal.

In the period after the Preparatory Signal boats will be sailing in all different directions, and a very sharp lookout is needed to prevent collision. In the final minute or so they will be jockeying for the best position at the start, and until a helmsman is really familiar with the rules it is best not to get too involved.

When a boat is returning after a premature start, she must keep clear of all other boats which have started correctly (Rule 20).

14.6.6 APPROACHING THE SHORE, OR OTHER OBSTRUCTIONS

With two boats on the same tack approaching the shore, or some other obstruction, it would obviously be dangerous if the boat to leeward or close ahead was unable, if already close-hauled, to escape sailing up the beach. In these circumstances she may hail 'Water' for room to tack. The other boat must then tack (followed by the hailing boat), or she may reply 'You tack', in which case the hailing boat must tack immediately and be given room by the other. Rule 19.) See Fig. 14(4).

14.6.7 ROUNDING MARKS

Much of Section C of the rules is devoted to special rules that apply when boats are 'about to round or pass' a mark or an obstruction. The rules are complicated and deserve careful study. Here we will only discuss the basic principles.

There is no definition of 'about to round'. It certainly applies when a boat is within two lengths of a mark, but it could be a greater distance when yachts are sailing fast and perhaps down tide.

In essence the rule says that if an inside boat establishes an overlap before the outside one is

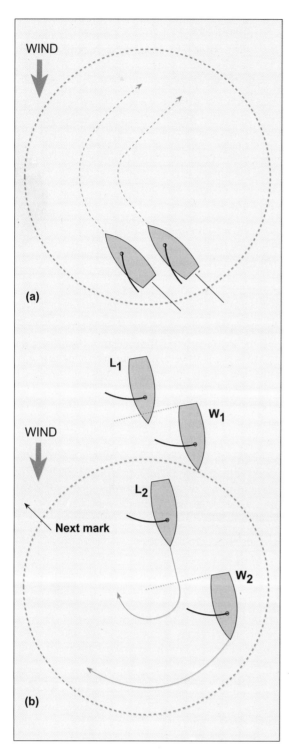

Fig. 14(10) An inside, overlapping boat must be given room to round or pass a mark or obstruction, as in (a). She must establish her overlap at least before the outside boat is within two lengths of the mark or obstruction. In (b) above L1 has established an overlap on W1 before the latter is within two lengths of the mark. Even if the overlap is subsequently broken, W2 must still give room to L2; see Rule 18.2(b).

14.7 RACE PREPARATION

14.7.1 PREPARING THE BOAT

If a yacht has not previously been used for racing, several items will need to be examined and possibly improved. The underwater hull must be as clean and smooth as you can reasonably get it, not forgetting the keel and especially the rudder where good preparation can really help the boat's performance. Clean off the propeller and if, as is common, it has two blades, mark the shaft inboard so that they can be arranged vertically behind the keel with the engine in gear. Remove all superfluous cruising gear from the boat, except any safety equipment which commonsense or class rules require to be retained on board. Concentrate all heavier items amidships, and as low down as possible.

Do not assume that the way a mast is rigged in a cruising yacht is necessarily ideal for racing. It may not be possible to move the heel of the mast without major surgery, but mast rake and shroud tensions should be easily adjustable. The basic procedure for setting up the rigging is described in Chapter 17 (17.2.5).

In a fractionally rigged (ie not masthead) boat the degree and distribution of the mast bend can be altered, depending on the flexibility of the spar. Mast bend affects the amount and position of draught (fullness) in the mainsail, as well as forestay tension and the tightness of the mainsail leech. The most obvious method of controlling fore and aft mast bend is with backstay tension, provided there is a simple way of adjusting it. A small amount of pre-bend can be exerted on a keel-stepped mast by moving the heel and adjusting the chocks at deck level.

When racing, speed in setting and changing sails is vital, so all the gear must function correctly and smoothly, with the minimum effort for the crew. Check over all the items such as snap shackles and halyard stoppers or clutches. To minimise the risk of somebody pulling the wrong rope, all sheets, halyards and other control lines should be colour coded. All halyards should be marked, say at the exit point from the mast or at their cleat, at the point where the sail is fully hoisted.

The various sail controls already described in 15.6 need to be provided, and it is important that they can be operated easily and positively. Wherever possible there should be some form of graduated scale so that optimum settings can be determined, recorded, and repeated as necessary. This is particularly important for items such as the positions of genoa sheet cars.

14.7.2 SAIL NUMBERS

One of the RYA prescriptions to the ISAF Racing Rules of Sailing requires that any British owned yacht racing shall display on its sails a unique Sail Number conforming to a specific series. In addition, where the boat belongs to an International class or might race (or sail) outside of UK waters, its Sails Number should be prefixed by the letters GBR. (GBR is no more nor less than the GB used to identify a British car). Other national letters for countries near to the UK are FRA – France, NED – Holland, IRL – Ireland, BEL – Belgium.

The series of numbers recognised by the RYA for offshore racing yachts are suffixed with the single letter Y, T, L, N, M, C or R. The first four (Y, T, L and N) are general series issued by the RYA to monohull yachts. M is a general series for multi-hull boats. The Clyde Yacht Clubs Association issues C numbers, whereas R numbers come from the RORC. The letter suffix is used simply to give unique Sail Numbers without resorting to five numerical digits, which can be hard to read.

Dinghies and small boats, not subject to search and rescue involving safety agencies, will normally display a Sail Number qualified by a class insignia. For example the Dragon uses D as its class insignia whereas a Laser will use a stylised laser symbol.

14.7.3   PREPARING THE CREW
Even quite large yachts can be handled by two or three people when cruising. But for racing the number must be increased significantly. Speed in tacking and in sail handling demands several pairs of hands, and it is a sad fact that most modern yachts when going to windward require human ballast on the weather rail for best performance in any breeze.

Certain key positions need to be filled by people who are familiar with the boat and who are sufficiently competent and experienced to fulfil their particular role without too much supervision. The key personnel are:

a. Helmsman, who steers the boat and who is probably, but not necessarily, in overall charge.
b. Tactician, who thinks the boat around the course – deciding the best route and tactics vis-à-vis other competitors, tidal conditions, predicted weather and actual wind shifts, and navigational features in the area. In a small yacht he may also be in charge of the deck – planning and supervising sail changes, gybing, reefing and so on – but in a larger boat this needs to be a separate person.
c. Bowman, who works the foredeck when shifting headsails, gybing the spinnaker etc.
d. Headsail and spinnaker trimmers (two), who operate and trim the sheets and guys to obtain optimum boat speed.

e. Mainsail trimmer, who handles the mainsheet and traveller. He may also help with other jobs around the cockpit, such as tailing genoa sheets.

The six people nominated above can be augmented or assisted by other hands depending on the size of the boat. Obtaining (and retaining) the necessary number of persons of the required calibre can be a daunting task, particularly for a boat with a very heavy racing schedule where a 'crew secretary' may well take over the job from the owner.

Good crewing depends not just on skill but also on teamwork, and this can only be achieved by practice. Early in the season spend a whole day going through all the standard drills: changing headsails, hoisting, gybing and lowering the spinnaker, and reefing the mainsail. It is often possible to practise some of these by getting out early to the start of a race.

14.7.4   PRE-RACE PREPARATIONS
Before any race several essential preparations must be made. The more basic requirements are listed below, but these will be multiplied when entering an important regatta, perhaps away from the boat's home port.

1. Make the necessary entry for the race, obtain and study the sailing instructions. Ensure that the boat conforms to requirements for insurance, measurement certificates etc.
2. Check such details as time of start, how far to sail from mooring to race area.
3. Arrange crew and tell them when and where to join the boat.
4. See that all outstanding repairs (eg to sails) are completed, and all items returned on board.
5. Study tidal conditions for the day of race, and work out predictions for tidal streams. When racing in shoal waters it is also useful to work out hourly tide heights over the period of the race, so that instant decisions can be taken about crossing sand banks etc.
6. Complete all material preparations on the boat: bottom clean, surplus gear removed, fuel and water tanks in race condition, all necessary safety equipment on board, chart(s) and tide tables etc. available, navigational instruments all functioning.
7. As the day of the race approaches, study the weather pattern and outlook period.
8. On day of race, final check that all necessary items such as sailing instructions are on board. Ensure no amendments to sailing instructions. Obtain weather forecast as late as possible. Embark food and drink. Check bilges dry. Have correct sails on board. Check watch/stopwatch and compass.

14.7.5 AFTER THE RACE

A race does not end for skipper or crew when the finishing line is crossed. There needs to be a wash-up to discuss what went right and what went wrong, and this is best conducted while events are fresh in the memory, perhaps while sailing into harbour. No race is ever sailed without a few mistakes being made, and the boat with the fewest errors is usually the winner. In order to make sure that everything is covered it is helpful to make a list of the different points which may be relevant.

1. Material preparation. Were there any gear or equipment failures, and what can be done to avoid any repetition? Can the performance of any items be improved, and how? Sails are very important to a racing boat – were any shortcomings exposed? Were the correct sails on board?
2. Rig and sail adjustments. Are fundamental items like mast position, mast rake and rig tension correct? Was proper use made of the various sail controls: sheeting positions, Cunningham, kicking strap, mainsheet traveller, main clew outhaul etc?
3. Crew. Was the crew strong enough for the conditions? Were there errors in sail handling, and were these due to the wrong drill or poor execution? Were fundamental drills such as tacking and gybing performed as well as possible?
4. Conditions and tactics. Was sufficient information available to helmsman and tactician about wind and weather forecasts, tidal stream predictions over the course area? Was such information acted on correctly, or were opportunities missed – detecting major wind shifts, for example?
5. The start. Did the boat start at the right end of the line, on the gun, and in clear wind? Was the boat on the right tack after the start, to choose the right side of the beat?
6. The racing rules. Were the crew in doubt about how any of the rules were interpreted?

This is also a useful occasion to brief crew about the next race or future programme.

Any defect, however small, needs to be carefully recorded for action to be taken. Experience shows that it is much better to note such items in a proper defect book rather than on odd scraps of paper. Before leaving the boat make sure that everything is stowed away, clean the boat up and take any rubbish ashore.

Do not forget that in some events a declaration that the rules have been obeyed must be signed, on getting ashore.

14.8 BOOKS ABOUT RACING

Racing - A Beginner's Manual by John Caig and Tim Davison (Fernhurst).
Racing Crew by Malcolm McKeag and Bill Edgerton (Fernhurst, 2nd edition).
Tactics by Rodney Pattison (Fernhurst, 2nd edn).
RYA Book of Race Training by Jim Saltonstall (Adlard Coles, 3rd edition).
The Secrets of Sailboat Racing by Mark Chisnell (Fernhurst).
Yacht Rating by Peter Johnson (Fernhurst).
Racing Skipper by Mike Goulding (Fernhurst, 2000).
Navigation Strategy and Tactics by Stuart Quarrie (Fernhurst).
The Offshore Race Crew's Manual by Stuart Quarrie.
The Racing Rules for Sailors: 2001-2004 by Mary Pera.
Paul Elvstrom Explains the Racing Rules of Sailing (2001-2004) by Paul Elvstrom, Editor Søren Krause (Adlard Coles, 14th edition, 2001).
The Rules Book: 2001-2004 Eric Twiname, revised by Bryan Willis (Adlard Coles, 7th edn, 2001).
Winning Races by J. Heyes (Adlard Coles).
The Rules in Practice: 2001-2004 by Bryan Willis (Fernhurst, 2001).
The Racing Rules Companion by Bryan Willis (Fernhurst, 2001).
Protests and Appeals by Bryan Willis (Fernhurst).

RYA Booklets
YR1   Racing Rules of Sailing, 2001-2004
YR2   Portsmouth Yardstick Scheme, 2001
YR6   Yacht and Sail Measurement, 2001
YR7   Handy Guide to the Racing Rules, 2001
YR9   Racing Yacht Safety, 2001

Websites
www.sailing.org   *ISAF official site*
www.sailing source.com   *ISAF magazine*
www.rorc.org   *RORC*
www.seahorse.co.uk   *RORC magazine*
www.rya.org.uk   *RYA*
www.btchallenge.com   *Round the world the wrong way*
www.americascup200.org.nz   *Official Cup site with links to the challengers*
www.offshorechallenges.com   *Figaro and Vendée Globe*
www.orma-60.org   *60ft mutihulls*
www.sailingweek.com   *Official site for Antigua Race week and other Caribbean regattas*
www.volvo-ocean-race.com   *Used to be the Whitbread rtw*
www.the race.org   *Non-stop, no limits round the world*
www.yachtracingclub.com
www.regattas.com

Chapter 15 Hulls

CONTENTS

15.1 THE DESIGN PROCESS

Any new design will start life as a set of hopes and requirements. These may include an idea for the layout of the accommodation, a desire for performance, a yearning for aesthetics and (usually) a need for economy. It is seldom if ever the case that all requirements are complementary, in many cases some will be in direct conflict and all design requires a certain amount of compromise. This situation ensures that no one solution will suit all purposes, it accounts for the tremendous variety of boats on the water and fuels the lively debate on their various merits and shortfalls.

The job of the designer or design team is to translate the requirements and preferences of the client into a set of information from which the boat can be built. The output of the design process may be in several forms, but in all cases it is an exercise in communication – a description of a finished product and guidance on how this result is to be achieved.

Traditionally, the majority of design work would be presented as a set of hand drawings accompanied by a written specification. The advent of computer systems has changed the way in which these drawings are produced, but in most cases the output of the design process is still the same. Computers have revolutionised the way designers work, but they have not taken the decision- making away from the designer.

In its simplest form, Computer Aided Design (CAD) entails the use of a two dimensional drawing programme as an electronic drawing board. The operator places lines or groups of lines as he would by hand – the CAD file is merely a very accurate and easily adjustable drawing. Other software enables the creation of a "model", constructed from solids or surfaces, which may be manipulated and formed to the desired shape. Hull modelling software will calculate various facts and figures relating to this form, all of which help the designer to achieve the shape which is felt to be most suited to the task. These 3D models can be detailed and rendered to produce very impressive images.

The use of computers also allows the modern designer to increase the scope of his or her work into areas which were previously impractical due to the laborious nature of the calculations. The tireless electronic brain will churn though countless numeric operations in seconds, where previously the relatively unreliable human equivalent would take days. This has accelerated the process of evolution of design and doubtless will continue to do so.

15.2 HULL DESIGN

15.2.1 INTRODUCTION
A hull is a three dimensional form which can be described using various measurements, ratios and coefficients. The numbers alone are not enough to define the exact hull form, it is possible to generate many shapes which have identical measurements and it is down to the designer to produce a fair hull which will have the desired attributes. In developing the hull shape, the designer will have a set of figures in mind, but will also be aiming for a certain appearance and may well be considering additional requirements such as the need for a large aft cabin or the influence of a rating rule.

Hull form coefficients in particular help to quantify what will be observable characteristics. For example the ends may look pinched or "fine", and the Prismatic Coefficient will indicate just how fine they are. All these factors help the designer to achieve the desired shape and characteristics and enable small and methodical changes to be made.

The aim of this chapter is to explain the various measurements, ratios and coefficients that may be used to describe a hull. It is seldom the case that one factor can be changed in isolation, and deviation from the ideal or optimum in one area is frequently required to satisfy another. Evaluation of a hull requires that all things are considered, with differing requirements leading to various blends of factors.

15.2.2 LINES PLAN
The lines plan is the final output of the hull design process. It is the drawing that describes the shape of the hull to the builder or any other interested person.

The lines plan is presented with three views of the boat, and although there may be some variety in the way these views are arranged each view will usually contain the outline of the vessel and other contour lines. These contour lines are shown on Fig. 15(1).

- Buttock lines – These are defined by vertical planes passing through the boat parallel to her centreline. They appear as straight lines (eg B1 and B2) when viewed from above (in the plan view) and ahead or astern (in the body view), but in the profile view they will appear as curves where the vertical planes intersect the hull surface.

- Waterlines – These are horizontal planes parallel to the waterline. They appear as straight lines (WL –1, DWL & WL1) in profile and body plans and as curves in plan view.

- Sections – These are athwartships slices (S1–11) through the boat, and appear as curves in the body plan.

The contours of a lines plan can be read in a similar manner to the contours on a map, only in the lines plan there are three views to give a more comprehensive description of the form.

Fig. 15(1) A typical Lines plan.

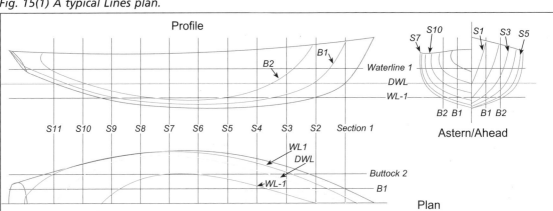

Great importance is traditionally attached to the fairness of a lines plan, ie the smoothness and blending of the curves. The lines of a hull will hint at the hull form coefficients (15.2.4), and those well practised in reading and drawing lines plans will only refer to the coefficients in passing to confirm an already comprehensive appreciation of the shape. The development of a fair hull form is where the artistry of the designer qualifies the numerical rigour of the mathematician or engineer.

In a traditional drawing office, the lines plan would be produced by hand, using curves, battens and spline weights to position and adjust each of the lines. The three views would be built up gradually, with constant cross checking to ensure the accurate agreement of the views. Various methods have been developed to help the draughtsman arrive at a hull form with the correct displacement and form. However the process of adjustment in three views and constant checking is very time consuming; it takes several days' work to produce a fully faired lines plan.

In the modern design office, hulls are modelled using computers. Most hull fairing software operates in a similar manner, using a grid of "control points" to distort a flexible surface into a three dimensional form. This form is viewed on the screen in the usual three views with the surface contours (buttocks, waterlines and sections) being generated by the computer. The software can calculate all the dimensions and coefficients associated with the hull form in a matter of seconds, so the designer can make adjustments and see their effects very quickly. The final form is arrived at by a methodical process of trial and error, with refinements being made until the numbers and appearance of the hull contours are as desired. Like the curves and splines of the traditional draughtsman, the hull fairing software is a tool requiring skilled use if the eventual result is to be satisfactory. The computer itself knows nothing about good or bad design, it will happily model and calculate as instructed and the ability of the modern designer to manipulate the surface is as fundamental as his traditional counterpart's dexterity at his drawing table.

Once the designer is satisfied with the hull model, the lines generated by the software can be transferred to a 2D draughting package for presentation as a traditional lines plan and further design drawings. Alternatively, the hull shape can be exported as a 3D surface to form the basis of a full computer model of the boat. Design offices may use other software to perform stability calculations or make predictions of the boat's performance or powering requirements. Most of these programmes will use the model from the hull fairing programme as the basis for their calculations.

15.2.3 DISPLACEMENT AND WEIGHT
The chosen displacement of a new boat is critical for it to satisfy the various requirements. It can be expressed as a volume of displaced water (given the symbol ∇), or the weight associated with this (symbol Δ). Displacement affects performance and handling characteristics as well as being one of the best indicators of the general size of the boat.

When comparing boats, it is important to consider more than just the displacement in tons, kg or other units – this must be related to the length of the hull to be able to evaluate the boat as being relatively heavy or relatively light. There are various displacement/length (D/L) ratios in common use. For sailing boats at least, one of the most common is calculated as follows:

$$D/L = \frac{\Delta}{(0.01 \times L_{WL})^3}$$

This is an imperial ratio, where displacement (Δ) is in long tons (2240 lbs; 1016 kg) and waterline length (L_{WL}) in feet. Those interested in the mathematics will notice that the length is cubed, to make it dimensionally similar to displacement which is a function of volume. This is an important feature of useful ratios, most of which are non-dimensional and can therefore be used to compare boats of differing sizes without scaling effects distorting the values.

Use of this formula on a normal boat's vital statistics will yield a number between 100 and 400. 400 indicates a boat which is very heavy by modern standards and more akin to a traditional design. Ultra Light Displacement Boats (ULDBs) are sometimes loosely defined as having D/L ratios of under 100. Most modern cruising yachts will fall in the 175 to 300 range, with racing boats from under 100 to around 200.

When launched, the boat will float such that the weight of water she displaces is equal to her total weight. Having chosen the preferred design displacement, the designer has the task of ensuring that the finished boat will actually turn out to be the correct weight and will float on her marks. During design and building, careful calculations are made to estimate the weight of all the various items of structure, machinery and gear that go into the boat. Knowing this, the designer can adjust the hull shape to provide this displacement, or in the case of sailing boats, specify the appropriate ballast to ensure the grand total weight is correct. As well as the weight, the position of the items must also be considered to ensure that the boat will float level.

The Ballast Ratio of a sailing boat will provide an indication of her stability and power to carry sail and is usually given by expressing the weight of ballast as a percentage of the total displacement. A high ballast ratio could suggest several things, of which two possibilities are as follows:

   a. The hull has a relatively large designed displacement, so considerable ballast is needed to make up the correct weight; and

   b. The boat has a very light hull structure and fit out, allowing a greater proportion of her total weight to be carried as ballast.

The above reasons suggest different approaches to the design of the boat, and hint of rather differing requirements. This shows that it is important to consider the overall D/L ratio at the same time as the ballast ratio and in general this is necessary when considering all ratios or characteristics. No one figure will provide the whole picture.

15.2.4   CURVE OF AREAS

As well as aiming for a particular displacement, the designer will have an idea of how this volume should be distributed down the length of the boat. The fullness of the ends of the boat and where the total centre of the displaced volume should lie, all need to be considered. This volume distribution is described by the "Curve of areas of displacement", which is effectively a graph where the immersed area of each section is plotted down the length of the boat; see Fig. 15(2).

Fig. 15(2) Typical curve of areas of displacement.

From the general particulars of the hull and the curve of areas, various descriptive figures and coefficients can be calculated and envisaged:

   a. The Longitudinal Centre of Buoyancy (LCB) is the point through which the total buoyancy could be considered to act. This is usually expressed as a percentage of waterline length (measured from forward or occasionally amidships), and is represented as the centre of the area under the curve of areas of displacement. Typically, the LCB will lie between 50% and 55% aft of the forward end of the waterline. When launched, the hull will take up a position such that the LCB is vertically in line with the Longitudinal Centre of Gravity (LCG) – as mentioned above, either may have been adjusted by the designer to ensure that the boat will float level.

   b. Block Coefficient (C_B), is a crude description of the fullness of a hull. It is calculated as follows:

$$C_B = \frac{\nabla}{L_{WL} \times B_{WL} \times T_C}$$

where ∇ is the displacement of the hull in m³; L_{WL} and B_{WL} are the waterline length and beam; T_C is the draught of the hull

The block coefficient represents the proportion of the volume of a box with the same length, width and depth as the hull, that the hull shape actually occupies. C_B for a box shaped hull would be 1, and barges

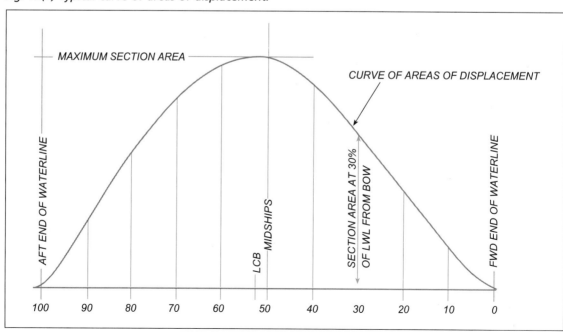

can come pretty close to this figure. Normal sailing yachts will have a CB of around 0·38.

c. Prismatic Coefficient (C_p) is a rather better indicator of the fullness of the ends of the hull, as it relates the actual displaced volume of the hull to that of the prism formed by extruding the greatest section area over the length of the waterline.

$$C_P = \frac{\nabla}{A_M \times L_{WL}}$$

Where A_M is the maximum section area, usually just aft of midships.

A hull with very fine ends could have a Prismatic coefficient as low as 0·50. Most sailing boat hulls have C_p values between 0·54 and 0.56, power boats can have figures up to around 0.65. As can be seen from the small range of these figures this is a very sensitive indicator of hull form.

The shape of the curve of areas will give an indication of prismatic coefficient. A fine ended hull with a low C_p will have a bell-shaped curve of areas, with very flat ends rising quickly to the maximum area around amidships. A full ended power boat hull, perhaps with an immersed transom, will have more area under the ends of the curve. The immersed transom would be indicated by the curve not returning to zero at the aft end, ie there is some immersed area at the aft end of the waterline.

15.2.5   WATERPLANE

The waterplane is one term for the waterline on which the boat floats, ie in plan view this is the outline of the 'hole' that the boat makes in the water. Various characteristics of the shape of the waterplane will have an effect on performance and the designer will need to consider them when developing the hull form.

a. The **Longitudinal Centre of Flotation** (LCF) is the fore and aft position of the centre of area of the waterplane. Like the LCB, this can be expressed as a percentage of the waterline length. This is the point about which the hull will pitch, and it is usually placed a few percent aft of the LCB.

b. **Half Angle of Entry** is the angle that the waterplane makes with the centreline at the bow. Another indicator of the fineness of the bow.

c. The **Transverse Inertia** of the waterplane (I_{xx}) has a large effect on the initial stability of the hull. It is easiest to consider inertia as a resistance to acceleration, and in this case a resistance to the rotational acceleration of the waterplane in roll. If you consider a piece of card cut into the shape of the waterplane, with a stick threaded down the centreline, the transverse inertia is the resistance you would feel when trying to twist the stick to start the card spinning. In calculating I_{xx}, the beam dimension is cubed and thus is very powerful, and it is easy to envisage this when trying to twist the stick. Thus waterline beam has a dominating effect on I_{xx}, and is one of the most influential factors governing the stability of the boat.

d. The area of the waterplane will determine the hull's **Sinkage**. This figure indicates how far the boat will settle into the water when weight (Crew, stores, fuel, water etc) is added. If a hull sinks by 1cm, a slab of water 1cm thick, with the same area as the waterplane will have been displaced. The weight of this displaced water will be the same as the weight of the load added. Sinkage is sometimes expressed as Tonnes per Centimetre of Immersion (TPC), ie how many tonnes it takes to sink the boat by one centimetre.

15.2.6   MIDSECTION

The Midsection is (unsurprisingly) the section through the boat amidships, ie the middle point of the waterline length of the hull. When drawing a lines plan by hand this is one of the the first curves to be added and its shape will be given much considerqtion by the designer. As the hull of a boat is a three dimensional form, the centre of buoyancy can be described not only in the longitudinal sense (LCB), but also the transverse and vertical dimensions. As the hull is symmetrical, the transverse centre of buoyancy will be on the centreline. The Vertical Centre of Buoyancy (VCB) however will be determined by the section shape of the hull. A slab sided barge will have her VCB at half the draught, whereas a light and beamy yacht with a deep fin keel will have her VCB rather nearer the waterline. VCB is another factor which has a significant effect on stability.

The Deadrise angle is the angle that the bottom of the boat makes with the waterline. This is an important consideration for fast power craft, a "Deep V" hull form being synonymous with high deadrise.

15.3 APPENDAGES AND FOILS

15.3.1   DESIGN CONSIDERATIONS

Anything that is stuck on the outside of the hull below the waterline is termed an appendage. For modern sailing boats, the main appendages are the keel and rudder; however P-brackets and struts also come under this broad heading. In terms of the boat's performance, P-brackets and the like produce only drag and the main consideration when designing them is to reduce this to the absolute minimum whilst still providing the necessary support.

Keels and rudders however are also foils. They exist to develop forces to balance those from the rig, and to control the heading of the boat. The keel also provides a conveniently low location for ballast, and its role in lowering the total centre of gravity is fundamental to the performance of the boat. That said, keels and rudders also produce drag, so clearly it is possible to have too much of a good thing.

Before examining the factors affecting performance of a foil, it is necessary to understand how this performance and the various characteristics of the foil are described. These terms apply to any foil, be it the wing of a Boeing 747 or the keel of a yacht.

- Chord – This is the dimension of the foil in the direction of the fluid flow. For yacht keels and rudders the chord is the length of the keel.
- Span – The foil dimension perpendicular to the flow. This is the depth dimension of a keel.
- Thickness – The measurement through the thickness of the section.
- The Root and Tip – For keels the Root is the hull end of the foil and the Tip is the bottom end.
- Planform – For a keel, the planform is the general shape of the keel when viewed in profile. For an aircraft wing, the planform is the appearance from above (which is rather more logical!).
- Taper Ratio – This is the ratio of tip chord to root chord, ie how the foil narrows towards its tip.
- Sweepback – This describes the degree to which the tip of the foil is aft of the root. Sweepback is usually expressed as the angle of the "quarter chord line" that is the line joining the points one quarter of the chord length back from the leading edge at the root and tip.
- Aspect Ratio (AR) Best calculated as:

$$AR = Span^2 \div Area,$$

which gets around problems with determining a suitable value of chord for irregularly shaped foils.

- Lift (L) – This is the force developed by the foil perpendicular to its centreline.

- Coefficient of Lift (C_L) – Defined as:

$$C_L = \frac{L}{\tfrac{1}{2}\rho S v^2}$$

where L is the lift developed in units of force (Newtons); ρ is the density of the fluid, seawater for keels most of the time; S is the planform area of the foil; and v is the speed of the fluid passing over the foil.

Like all coefficients, the coefficient of lift is a way of expressing the lift generated without having to consider the size of the foil. Coefficients are non-dimensional and allow valid comparisons of performance between foils of differing sizes.

- Section Drag – The category of drag associated with the frontal area of the foil. Best envisaged as the drag associated with pushing the fluid out of the way as the foil advances.
- Viscous Drag – The frictional drag resulting from the passage of fluid over the surface area of the foil.
- Induced Drag (D_I) – Another type of drag that a foil is subjected to. Induced drag is a by product of the generation of lift.

- Coefficient of Induced Drag (C_{DI}) – Defined as:

$$C_{D_I} = \frac{D}{\tfrac{1}{2}\rho S v^2}$$

D_I is the Induced drag in units of force (N)
- Angle of attack (a) – The angle the flow of fluid ahead of the foil makes with the foil centreline.

- Lift Curve Slope

$$\left(\frac{\delta C_L}{\delta \alpha}\right)$$

The coefficient of lift increases as the angle of attack, α, is increased, the process being represented by the lift curve for the foil. Those familiar with mathematics will recognise the symbol δ as representing a change; the lift curve slope is a measure of how quickly C_L increases with increasing α.

15.3.2   FACTORS AFFECTING PERFORMANCE

A description of how a foil develops lift is beyond the scope of this chapter. However various characteristics of the foil will have an effect on how much lift it is capable of developing, how much drag is associated with this lift and how quickly the lift is generated as the angle of attack increases.

In discussing causes and effects, it is usually best to consider one cause at a time. For example, in assessing the effects of increased aspect ratio, other variables such as planform area and taper ratio should be constant. Unfortunately in reality one is seldom able to adjust one factor without affecting another; however it is possible to add up the various effects to give a total outcome for a series of modifications.

Most of the options for foil optimisation will be the different ingredients in the overall planform. These could be expected to have the following effects:

Foil area

One of the keel's main jobs is to produce sideforce to balance that developed by the rig. The quantity of sideforce is determined by (amongst other things) the area of the foil. If the keel is too small, too much leeway will result, since the keel's angle of attack will have to be quite high before enough sideforce is produced. However, the bigger the keel, the greater the wetted surface and so a compromise must be found which provides enough area and yet tolerable frictional resistance.

Alterations to aspect ratio

This is one of the most fundamental contributors to foil performance.

The coefficient of induced drag C_{DI} is almost entirely dependent upon aspect ratio, the higher the aspect ratio the lower will be C_{DI}. Similarly, lift curve slope is also affected by aspect ratio above all other parameters, and will be increased with increasing AR. The expected result in terms of sailing performance is a boat which will sail faster (due to the reduced drag) and point higher, as less leeway (angle of attack α) will be needed for the foil to develop enough sideforce to oppose the rig.

Aspect ratio is not all good news however, and there are a few practical and handling considerations which will be compromised by extremes. The stall angle of the foil will be reduced by increasing the aspect ratio, ie it will be easier to cause the foil to stall by applying too much rudder angle, or by overloading the keel at low speeds. Also, given that a certain area of keel is required, the high aspect ratio foil will be deeper and this may not be practical for inshore sailing.

Sweepback and Taper ratio

In general, sweepback and taper ratio affect the lift distribution along the span of the foil. They are generally considered together and the theoretical aim is for an elliptical lift distribution, ie a graph showing the lift distribution along the span would resemble a quarter ellipse with the greatest value at the root, tapering to zero at the tip.

Sweepback encourages spanwise flow, that is a slant in the flow over the foil towards the tip. It is easy to imagine this shifting some of the foil's lift generation towards the tip.

Taper ratio obviously effects the area distribution of the foil, and thus it has a logical effect on the lift distribution.

The theoretical aim of elliptic lift distribution suggests an elliptical planform, and this is seen in some cases. In practice, this planform is not usually the best as the very tip of the ellipse generates a disproportionate amount of frictional drag and if this is considered it is better to cut off the tip. One of the better illustrations of this is the wing of the Spitfire, which started off with an elliptic planform but was subsequently modified to have a square tip, the reasoning being that the very tip of the elliptic wing was producing more drag in one department than it was saving in another.

When considering sweepback and taper ratio it is not really possible to ignore the hull above the keel. Particularly for a heavy and deep bodied yacht, the hull will contribute to the generation of side force, and there will be considerable flow across the bottom of the canoe body. This cross flow effectively increases the angle of attack at the root of the foil, and thus the loading at the root is rather greater than would otherwise be the case. It is therefore normal to see more sweepback on these keels in an attempt to spread this high load towards the tip and maintain as near an elliptic lift distribution as possible.

In general it is the planform which has the greatest effect on foil performance as its various facets dominate lift production, induced drag and frictional drag. The section shape of the foil is more closely connected with what might be termed the handling characteristics as well as the section drag of the foil. Section shape and foil thickness will also be fundamental to the weight of the foil, ie how much ballast it may contain and where this will be situated.

There are a great many variations in section shape and all have characteristic influences on stall angle and section drag. In general, a straightforward tear drop shape provides a good starting point which will not encourage early stalls and will offer reasonably low drag. The NACA 00 series of sections are not dissimilar to this and are frequently used for rudders where stall tolerance is important.

Other more specialist sections have their

maximum thickness further back from the leading edge. This can lead to earlier stalling, however the aim is to keep the flow laminar over as much of the foil as possible which can reduce drag dramatically. There is also a danger of flow separation at low speed aft of the maximum thickness on these sections which can result in a huge drag penalty. Generally they are at their best at relatively low angles of attack.

Like all other aspects of design, selecting the right foil section will involve a certain amount of compromise. For keel and rudder design in general, it is possible to expend a great deal of time, effort and consequentially money in determining the best compromise.

15.3.3 LONG KEELED HULLS

With a hull where it is not easy to separate the keel and/or rudder from the main hull, it becomes harder and less valid to apply the theories discussed above. There comes a point where the general approach must shift to "low aspect ratio" theory, where lift generation is considered in a different way. With this theory, lift is primarily dependent on the leading edge, and the span of the foil becomes the most powerful feature.

Similarly to the approach for high aspect ratio foils, this is a general theory which can be applied to yacht underbodies, aircraft wings or any other foil of the appropriate proportions. The "delta" planform used on Concorde for example could be treated in the same way as the keel of some older racing yachts. As suggested by its pedigree, this is a very respectable solution in terms of lift and induced drag, although there is a price to pay in terms of wetted surface and thus viscous drag.

15.4 RESISTANCE AND PERFORMANCE

15.4.1 RESISTANCE COMPONENTS

The total resistance of a hull can be split into various categories. Of these, two are responsible for the majority of the resistance:

Frictional resistance

Frictional resistance is the obvious consequence of forcing a body through a fluid. The frictional resistance (R_F) may be calculated as follows:

$$R_F = \tfrac{1}{2}\rho S v^2 C_F$$

where ρ is the density of the fluid; S is the total surface area of the hull or other body; v is the speed of the hull or body through the fluid; and C_F is the coefficient of friction, described below.

The coefficient of friction is calculated for each

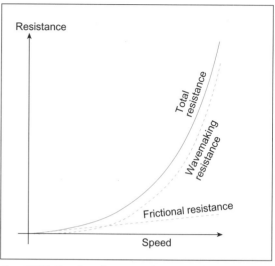

Fig. 15(3) Total resistance, the sum of Frictional and Wavemaking resistance, increases with speed.

circumstance, and depends on the length and speed of the body and the viscosity of the fluid. C_F is greater for short bodies and for this reason the keel and rudder of a yacht will contribute a greater proportion of the total frictional resistance than their area would suggest. Careful fairing and smoothing of the foils is particularly worthwhile when preparing for a race.

Wavemaking resistance

A body passing through the interface of two fluids will generate waves. Generation of waves involves the transfer of energy from the moving body to the fluid and thus creates resistance. Unlike frictional resistance, wavemaking resistance can not be calculated directly as it will depend on too many factors of hull form, speed and length.

Fig. 15(3) shows how wavemaking resistance and frictional resistance contribute to the total hull resistance as speed increases. It should be noted that this illustration is valid for displacement hulls only, high speed hulls are discussed further below.

At low speeds, frictional resistance is the larger of the two contributors, but as speed increases wavemaking becomes the dominating factor and presents the greatest barrier to increased speed. The total resistance of the boat underway will also be contributed to by factors such as the induced drag of the foils, and added resistance due to seastate.

15.4.2 SPEED/LENGTH RATIO

Particularly when considering wavemaking resistance, the length of the boat has a large bearing. A wave has a speed of forward travel which is directly related to its length (the distance from crest to crest). Waves generated by the passage of an object will travel at the speed of that object and so their length is thus dictated by the speed of the boat.

Two sorts of wave systems are set up by a yacht's hull:

a. Divergent waves are created at the bow and stern; these move away from the hull in a diagonal pattern; and
b. Transverse waves are also generated at the bow and stern. These have their crests and troughs across the boat and effectively travel along with her. As the length of these waves is dictated by the speed of the hull, the position of the second crest of the transverse bow wave will move aft as the speed increases. At a certain speed, this crest will coincide with the first crest of the stern wave, and the positive interference will increase the size of the resultant stern wave. This dramatically increases the energy in the wave and thus the wavemaking resistance of the hull. For a displacement hull the maximum speed of the boat is effectively limited by this occurrence.

Obviously, a longer hull can travel faster before the second crest of the bow wave reaches the stern, and thus any consideration of wave making resistance must be linked to the Speed/Length ratio of the boat.

There are various methods for calculating the Speed/Length ratio, the usual value quoted for yachts is an imperial ratio calculated as follows:

$$S/L = \frac{v}{\sqrt{L_{WL}}}$$

where v is the speed of the boat in knots; and L_{WL} is the waterline length in feet.

This is easily calculated and the highest practicable speed for a displacement hull coincides with a value of around 1.3. Very light or narrow hulls are able to increase this value somewhat before the wavemaking resistance becomes crippling.

The modern Naval Architect uses a more dimensionally correct ratio known as Froude Number:

$$F_N = \frac{v}{\sqrt{gL_{WL}}}$$

where v is the speed in metres per second (m/s); g is the acceleration due to gravity (m/s²); L_{WL} is the waterline length in metres (m).

The ratio is named after William Froude, who conducted much of the early work on ship hull resistance.

15.4.3 HULL FORM AND SPEED/LENGTH RATIO

Given that wavemaking resistance is caused by a hull's displacement disturbing the surface of the water, if a vessel is to travel faster than her attendant wave speed she must climb out of the water and thus reduce her displacement. This is achieved by the development of hydrodynamic lift on the aft sections of the hull, the support from which replaces that provided by buoyancy when the vessel is at rest. As she climbs out of the water, the wetted surface of the hull also decreases which helps the boat to travel faster.

The amount of planing surface required and thus the shape of the aft body of the boat will be dictated by the speed length ratio which is desired. No one hull form will provide the attributes for lowest resistance at all speed length ratios. The flat afterbody and immersed transom of a planing craft will produce significant turbulence and thus high resistance at low speeds. For each point on the scale of speed length ratio, an optimum hull form can be identified which will provide the lowest resistance. If high top speed is required, efficient low speed operation must be sacrificed – this is easily deduced by observing the waves set up by a planing powerboat moving at slow speed. Fig. 15(4) shows the resistance curves of three generalised categories of hull form.

It can be seen that each of the three basic hull forms has a band of speed/length ratio where it is most efficient. However if one wants to travel fast, there is a penalty to be paid in the form of inefficiency at lower speeds. As an aid to consideration of the curves, the speed of a 40ft (12.2m) waterline boat is shown alongside the speed/length ratio.

15.4.4 TANK TESTING

When attempting to decide upon the engine size for a power boat, or trying to predict how fast a sailing boat will go, it is necessary to estimate the resistance of the hull at various speeds. The frictional resistance can be calculated however this can not be done for wavemaking resistance.

To get around the problem, a scale model of the hull can be made and towed in a tank at varying speeds. If the resistance of the model is known, it is possible to scale this up and predict the resistance of the full sized craft. If this looks unsatisfactory, adjustments can be made to the model to attempt to reduce the resistance or alternatively a series of models with systematic variations of hull form can be tested to identify those factors which have the greatest effect.

When tank testing, it is the total resistance of

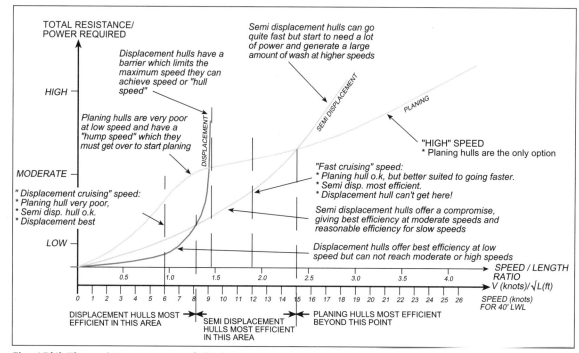

Labels within the figure:

TOTAL RESISTANCE/
POWER REQUIRED

Displacement hulls have a barrier which limits the maximum speed they can achieve speed or "hull speed"

Semi displacement hulls can go quite fast but start to need a lot of power and generate a large amount of wash at higher speeds

HIGH

Planing hulls are very poor at low speed and have a "hump speed" which they must get over to start planing

SEMI DISPLACEMENT

PLANING

DISPLACEMENT

"HIGH" SPEED
* Planing hulls are the only option

MODERATE

"Fast cruising" speed:
* Planing hull o.k, but better suited to going faster.
* Semi disp. most efficient.
* Displacement hull can't get here!

" Displacement cruising" speed:
* Planing hull very poor,
* Semi disp. hull o.k.
* Displacement best

Semi displacement hulls offer a compromise, giving best efficiency at moderate speeds and reasonable efficiency for slow speeds

LOW

Displacement hulls offer best efficiency at low speed but can not reach moderate or high speeds

SPEED / LENGTH RATIO
V (knots)/√L(ft)

0.5   1.0   1.5   2.0   2.5   3.0   3.5   4.0

0 1 2 3 4 5 6 7 8 9 10 11 12 13 14 15 16 17 18 19 20 21 22 23 24 25 26   SPEED (knots) FOR 40' LWL

DISPLACEMENT HULLS MOST EFFICIENT IN THIS AREA

SEMI DISPLACEMENT HULLS MOST EFFICIENT IN THIS AREA

PLANING HULLS MOST EFFICIENT BEYOND THIS POINT

Fig. 15(4) The resistance curves of displacement, semi-displacement and planing hulls.

the hull that is measured. Owing to the nature of the components of resistance, the total resistance can not be directly scaled up to full size, but must be separated into its frictional and wavemaking constituents. Skin friction for the full sized hull can be calculated, so the primary purpose of the tank testing is to determine the wavemaking resistance and this must be separated from the tank data by subtracting the skin friction component as calculated for the model.

The procedure then goes something like this:

Step 1.   Tank test model and measure the total resistance.

Step 2.   Calculate the frictional resistance of the model and subtract this from the total to leave the wavemaking resistance.

Step 3.   Scale up the wavemaking resistance of the model to the full size boat.

Step 4.   Calculate the frictional resistance of the full size boat and add it to wavemaking to determine the total resistance.

As the wavemaking resistance of the hull is closely associated with speed length ratio, it is necessary to test the model at the same speed length ratio as the full sized boat. This will ensure that the wavemaking resistance scales accurately.

Tank testing can provide far more than just wavemaking resistance data. As mentioned in the section on foils, the interaction of hull and keel is often hard to appraise. In the test tank, various foil options can be tested and the sideforce and drag they develop can be measured, and this can be very useful in selecting the best keel option.

Some test tanks have wave generators and these can be used to generate sea states in the tank. The model can be tested in waves to observe the effects on resistance and also to make an appraisal of the handling characteristics of the boat in a seaway.

The main drawback with tank testing is the time and expense that is needed for a productive testing program. Hiring tank facilities is very expensive and usually this is not practical in the context of a small boat design.

15.4.5   PERFORMANCE PREDICTION

Although tank testing is expensive, the data from a series of tests can be applied to more than one vessel. As mentioned above, a series of tests on models with small and incremental differences in hull form can be used to identify factors that are influential in wavemaking resistance. Using large amounts of this data as a basis, various "systematic series" have been developed which allow designers to predict the resistance of their own designs, based on the resistance of similar models.

This data, in addition to similar data regarding the lift and drag produced by sails and rigs, has enabled the development of "Velocity

Prediction Programmes" (VPP's). VPP procedures involve repetitive "trial and error" calculations which are best done by computer. Powerful software has been developed which will effectively develop a polar diagram for a boat by considering its various features of hull form and rig. It should be stressed that any of these processes can only be applied to boats which fall within the range of the basis data. It is extremely risky to extrapolate this data and attempt to use it for dissimilar vessels. To use an obvious example, it would be foolish to base yacht performance predictions on data sourced from container ships.

Despite the best efforts of tank testing and computer analysis, performance prediction is not a precise science. Neither can the tank or computer modify the hull form or rig to enhance the performance. It is up to the designer to test various options and compare the results in the hope that one particular avenue of development will be suggested as being profitable.

15.5 STABILITY, SAFETY AND SEAKINDLINESS

15.5.1 INTRODUCTION
The seakeeping abilities of a boat will result from various contributory factors. A yacht's stability concerns her will to stay upright and is obviously fundamental to safety, comfort and performance. Her seaworthiness in general will be contributed to by her stability, her structural integrity, the suitability of her gear and the preparedness of her crew. Her seakindliness is more of a comfort consideration and is defined by her reactions to waves or other conditions at sea.

As with any other area of design, the desire for performance and other requirements may conflict with seakeeping considerations. Compromise will be reached bearing in mind the intended use of the boat and the likelihood that the seakeeping abilities of the boat will be put to the test.

15.5.2 MECHANICS OF STABILITY AND KEY FACTORS
There are several key factors which will effect the stability of the yacht. These result mostly from the hull shape and the position of the centre of gravity. Examination of what has a bearing on these critical factors reveals the contributions of the commonly discussed features such as beam, ballast and depth of keel.

When discussing stability, the term Righting Moment refers to the moment which is attempting to return the boat to an even keel. If the vessel is at a steady angle of heel, this is because the righting moment is equal and opposite to the heeling moment, ie there is equilibrium. The righting moment which is developed as the hull heels occurs because the centre of buoyancy moves off to one side as hull volume is immersed to leeward and emerges to windward. The transverse separation of the forces of weight and buoyancy creates a restoring moment to balance the heeling moment imposed by, for example, the rig.

The mechanics of stability and the generation of righting moment are considered using a series of points which are described below. The relative position of these points will define many of the stability characteristics of the boat. For the purposes of this section the size of the rig is not considered (although its presence does have an effect on one of the critical points (G) as will be seen). This is because stability is a response mechanism and the precise nature of the disturbing force, be it an offset load or heeling moment from a rig, need not be considered. Fig. 15(5) illustrates the likely position of three critical points:

B is the **centre of buoyancy**. This is the point through which the upward force of buoyancy acts. The height of B (the VCB) is defined by the shape of the hull section.

G is the **centre of gravity**. The total weight of the boat acts down through this point. The vertical position of G (the VCG) is determined by the weight and position of all the items on board, and providing none of these moves G will remain in the same place.

M is the **metacentre**. When the boat heels, say to 15° as in Fig. 15(6), the metacentre is seen to be the point on the centreline which is vertically above the centre of buoyancy.

The vertical position of B results directly from the shape of the hull, that of G is determined by the weight distribution. The position of the metacentre (M) is calculated to be a certain distance above B as follows:

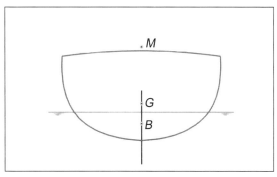

Fig. 15(5) Centres of Buoyancy, and Gravity and the Metacentre with the boat upright.

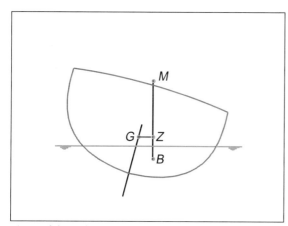

Fig. 15(6) With 15° heel, the relative positions of M, G and B have changed.

$$BM = \frac{I_{XX}}{\nabla}$$

Where BM is the height of M above B. I_{XX} is the transverse inertia of the waterplane. ∇ is the volume of displacement of the hull.

It can be seen that BM is determined by the shape of the hull. G is the only point which is affected by weight distribution.

As mentioned above, the righting moment is developed as the centres of buoyancy (B) and gravity (G) move out of line. The horizontal distance between them is referred to as GZ, Z being the point vertically above B that is level with G; see Fig. 15(6). So we arrive at a formula for righting moment:

$$Righting\,Moment = Displacement \times GZ$$

Obviously a greater value of GZ will increase the righting moment. Looking at Fig. 15(6), it is easy to see that if M were higher above G, if the boat is heeled to the same angle, GZ would be greater. The distance GM is known as the Metacentric Height and is one of the fundamental measurements connected with stability, linking the factors (B and M) determined by hull form, with the material factor G.

Up until now, stability has been treated as one subject in order to define the various contributory factors. In reality, it should be considered in two parts.

15.5.3   SMALL ANGLE STABILITY
Small angle stability is primarily concerned with the sailing performance and comfort of the boat which are the primary issues when sailing in normal circumstances. It is usually the case that for small angle stability the boat wants to be as stiff (stable) as possible so maximum sail can be carried for best performance.

To understand how the various factors affect the small angle stability of the boat, it is best to consider a few examples. Most of these effects can be intuitively predicted, however they are treated from a theoretical standpoint using the basic points and formulae described above. It is hoped that this approach will enable the reader to consider more complex situations where intuition does not provide a clear answer. It is best to consider only one variable at a time, even though changes in one characteristic are often accompanied by changes in another.

a.   Increased beam
Increasing beam increases I_{XX}, which in turn increases BM, ie M moves up. Providing G stays in the same place, GM is increased and thus righting moment for a given angle of heel is greater.

b.   General increase in displacement.
Righting moment is dependant on Displacement and GZ. So an increase in Displacement leads to a direct increase in Righting moment. However, the formula for BM has the volume of displacement on the bottom line, so as displacement rises, BM reduces (M moves down), GM is decreased and some of the gain in stability is lost.

c.   Increase in weight of ballast.
Firstly, the effect is the same as a general increase in displacement. However, as the ballast is presumably added to the keel, the centre of gravity of the whole boat (G) will move down. GM is therefore increased, and the righting moment increases with it.

d.   Increase in draught.
The likely effect is that the ballast will be lower and as above, G moves down leading to increased stability.

e.   Modification to section shape.
Even without changing beam and displacement, it is possible to alter the shape of the section. If the section area is concentrated high up, with a "hard" turn to the bilge, B will move upwards. BM remains the same as neither I_{XX} nor ∇ has changed, so M moves up, thus GM is increased. A "slack" bilge section will have its area lower so B moves down. M goes with it and GM is decreased. This explains the common understanding that boats with "hard" bilges are stiffer than their "soft" bilged counterparts.

f.   Multihulls
Here all sorts of things are changing, but the mechanics of stability are still the same. Considering the two separate hull waterplanes as

one (albeit with a rather large gap in the middle), the most important factor is the huge increase in beam. This leads to a vast increase in I_{xx} and consequentially large BM. Displacement will be small as there is no ballast to consider, and G may be rather high also, but BM is so big that GM is also large and the resultant righting moment is considerable.

g. Addition of water ballast or crew on the rail

With the previous illustrations, G has always been on the centreline. Adding a weight to one side of the boat or moving a weight already on board will cause the total centre of gravity (G) to move off to one side. G moves directly away from Z, and thus righting moment increases.

15.5.4   LARGE ANGLE STABILITY

Beyond an angle of heel of say 45°, the emphasis on aspects of stability is changed somewhat. At this angle and beyond, the boat is hardly sailing at her most efficient and life on board is not particularly comfortable. The situation is likely to be temporary, and concern is focussed on ensuring that this is indeed the case.

To discuss large angle stability it is first necessary to look at what happens to the theory as the angle of heel increases. For very small angles of heel (up to about 5°), M remains in more or less the same position. Once the angle gets beyond around 30° however, M moves down towards G as can be seen in Fig. 15(7). All this contributes to the value of GZ, which will increase as the boat heels, and then start to decrease again. The GZ curve of the boat is drawn by calculating the value of GZ for a range of angles of heel and plotting these on a graph. This shows very clearly how GZ changes as the boat heels.

At around 110° in the example of Fig. 15(7), M will coincide with G and then pass it, resulting in a negative value of GM. This is the Angle of Vanishing Stability (AVS). At this point the boat has passed the point of no return and now all the mechanisms of stability are working in reverse, attempting to capsize her. This is indicated by the negative values on the GZ curve, in this area, the vessel's initial stability is working the wrong way round and she will be stable upside down unless something happens to roll her back to the point where GM and thus righting moment are positive again.

When considering small angle stability any of the several mechanisms used for increasing stiffness is good news. More stability gives more power to carry sail leading to better performance etc. With large angles, the issues are a little more complex as not all methods of increasing GM will pass the large angle test.

What is obviously critical is the point on the GZ curve where M passes G, and the values of GZ become negative.

As is clear in the previous section, if increased stability is desired without increased displacement, some means must be found of increasing the metacentric height. For small angles, the overall position of G and M does not matter, we are interested only in their separation (GM). The difference when considering large angle stability is best visualised by examining two vessels with equal displacement and metacentric height.

Vessel A is the example used in Fig. 15(7). She is a beamy and shallow bodied yacht, with a high waterplane inertia (I_{xx}) and large BM. This gives her a generous metacentric height despite the fact that her centre of gravity (G) is rather high.

Vessel B is shown in Fig. 15(8). She has a deep and narrow hull and achieves her metacentric height (equal to that of vessel A) not because of great beam and large BM, but as a result of her centre of gravity (G) being very low due to her low slung ballast.

The first thing to notice is the relative positions of B and G in the two examples at zero angle of heel. Despite the fact that the boats have identical GM, the points G and M are both very much lower on vessel B, in fact G is actually below B. Note that for simplicity keels are not shown on the diagrams, however particularly for vessel B, significant draught and a high ballast ratio would be needed to achieve the VCG shown. In terms of small angle stability, due to their equal values of GM the boats behave in a very similar fashion (their GZ curves are more or less coincident), once they heel beyond 30° however, differences become apparent; see Fig. 15(9).

As her angle of heel gets large, Vessel A starts to lose stability as her GZ values fall rapidly. Her high centre of gravity is in danger of toppling over her centre of buoyancy, and indeed she reaches her AVS relatively quickly. She is then very stable upside down.

Vessel B on the other hand, thanks to her low centre of gravity, still has plenty of positive stability at the point where vessel A reaches the point of no return. She has to heel over a lot further before M passes G and her GZ becomes negative.

The next step is to consider how the safety of the boat in extreme conditions is affected by the points raised so far. This is begun by establishing a set of events or circumstances which may conspire to put the large angle stability of the boat to the test.

It is fairly obvious that more than wind action

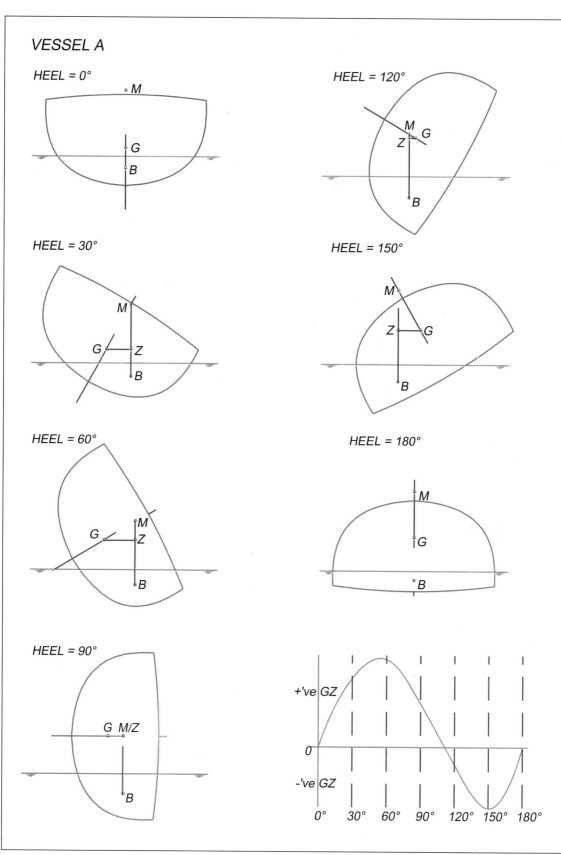

Fig. 15(7) Vessel A, the relationship between G, B and M with increasing angles of heel.

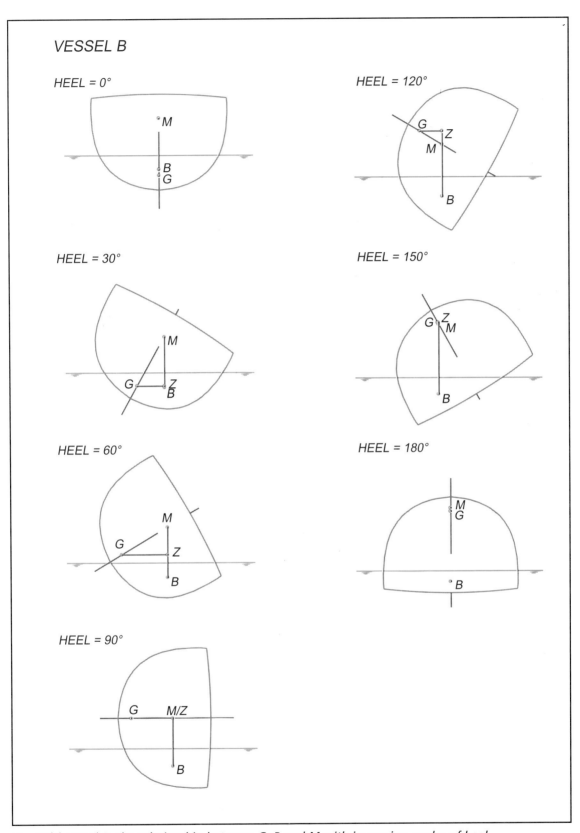

Fig. 15(8) Vessel B, the relationship between G, B and M with increasing angles of heel.

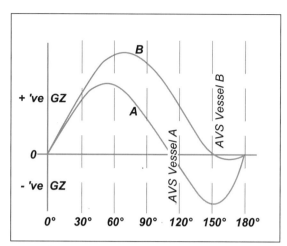

Fig. 15(9) Comparison of the GZ curves and AVS of Vessels A and B.

alone is needed to capsize a yacht of normal proportions. Clearly there must be some other external force which pushes the boat beyond the angle of heel where the sails are effectively flat in the water. By far the most likely candidate is a breaking wave.

With normal wave action, water does not travel with the wave but moves up and down as the wave energy passes. There is a small amount of movement backwards and forwards, but this is small compared with the speed of the wave itself which is linked to wave length and can be up to 30 knots. When a wave becomes unstable and breaks, the crest tumbles over and a large mass of water cascades down the face of the wave at high speed.

A yacht lying along the wave will receive a tremendous blow on her topsides and bilge as the wave crest hits her. Some of the massive energy of this moving water is translated into rolling the yacht, and she will continue to roll until the force stops or the energy is absorbed by her righting moment. The GZ curve and the large angle stability characteristics it describes contribute to the outcome of this situation, however there are other considerations.

As noted above, righting moment is the product of GZ and displacement, so multiplying the individual values of GZ by displacement will produce a righting moment curve. As displacement is constant for any one boat, the curve will have exactly the same shape as the GZ curve, but the area underneath the curve up to a certain angle of heel will represent the energy which is needed to roll the boat to that angle. What this has done is incorporate the vital factor of vessel size into the stability curve.

Using and extending the examples above, the following are illustrations of some common

attributes and their consequences for the large angle stability of the boat:

a. Size: The first thing to note is that sheer size is the single biggest factor in considering the safety of the boat. The larger boat will require more energy to roll to her AVS, and thus a bigger and more violent breaking wave will be needed. It follows therefore, that any consideration of a "safe" or "suitable" AVS must be put in context by the size of the boat, ie a larger boat will not require so high an AVS to be as resistant to capsize as her smaller counterpart. Work done in America following various disturbing events, including the Fastnet disaster of 1979, produced a formula for "Capsize Length", which can be used to calculate the "size" of a yacht as it relates to capsize resistance. The formula includes the various influential factors, and produces a number which when subtracted from 160° suggests a suitable minimum range of positive stability.

b. Low centre of gravity: As with small angle stability, a low centre of gravity is always a valuable asset in terms of large angle characteristics. This is clearly illustrated by Vessel B's behaviour. A low centre of gravity is generally achieved with large amounts of low slung ballast, and by avoiding an excessively heavy rig.

c. Large beam: Beam is useful to stability in boosting BM and hence GM, however a hull which is too dependent upon beam alone for stiffness runs the risk of sacrificing large angle stability in the search for sail carrying power.

d. High freeboard: Increasing freeboard generally helps range of stability as it delays deck edge immersion. When this happens the stability curve starts to fall off because of the rapid decrease in (heeled) waterline beam (effecting BM). A more intuitive explanation is the lack of any more reserve buoyancy on the leeward side. The effect of increased freeboard is slightly offset by the potential rise in the centre of gravity.

e. Deck structures: In much the same way as increasing freeboard, deck structures provide increased waterline beam at high angles of heel. Put another way, they provide buoyancy to leeward as they become immersed. All this helps increase the angle of vanishing stability although the danger of raising the centre of gravity with heavy deck structures should not be ignored.

f. Roll inertia: When the wave crest hits the side of the boat, its energy is in the form of momentum, ie there is a certain mass of water travelling at a certain speed. This momentum is transferred into rolling the boat. The resulting speed of roll will be determined partly by the roll inertia of the complete boat. As previously described, inertia is best thought of as a resistance to acceleration, and this is a particularly useful approach in this case. It is easy to imagine that one of the largest contributions to the roll inertia of the boat is the rig. Its centre of mass is a long way from the centre of gravity of the whole boat, and thus its contribution to the total inertia can be up to 65%. If the rig greatly increases the roll inertia, and thus limits the acceleration of the rolling motion, it is clear that keeping the rig upright is hugely important in avoiding capsize.

g. Appropriate handling and control: The actions of the crew will always be a relevant factor when considering safety. Much has been written on storm survival and the measures that the beset yachtsman may take. From the design point of view, it is important to ensure that the crew will have control over the boat in extreme conditions and will therefore be in a position to influence the outcome. The reliability of the steering gear is obviously fundamental to the control of the boat and steering gear failure is at the root of many capsize incidents.

h. Structural integrity: The forces of impact involved with breaking waves are very large. Ensuring that the basic structure of the hull and deck can withstand the blows is fundamental to the survival of the boat in extreme conditions.

15.5.5 MOTIONS AND SEAKINDLINESS

A floating object has six "degrees of freedom" or ways in which it may move (motions). These are as follows:

a. Heave: The movement of the hull up and down.

b. Sway: The movement of the hull from side to side.

c. Surge: The movement of the hull forwards and backwards.

d. Pitch: Rotation of the hull about a transverse axis. The bow and stern move up and down.

e. Yaw: Rotation of the hull about a vertical axis. Bow and stern move side to side.

f. Roll: Rotation of the hull about a longitudinal axis.

All of these motions are responses to external forces or movements of weight on board. These could result from the influences of waves, wind, impacts or any other form of disturbance. The motions of heave, pitch and roll are most often under scrutiny as they have the greatest effect on the performance of the boat and the comfort of those on board.

The way the boat responds to the disturbance will result from a combination of three factors.

1. Excitation: Any motion results from some sort of excitation, be it a wave or other disturbance. The excitation destroys the equilibrium of the forces of buoyancy and gravity. In the case of a wave, as the wave passes the boat it will momentarily change the waterline, and thus the volume of displacement and the way this volume is distributed.

2. Response: If the excitation destroys the equilibrium of the floating boat, the response is the result of this as the various forces act on the boat. Response can not be separated from stability as it is the mechanisms of stability that will generate the response, ie the stability of the hull in each of the degrees of freedom attempts to restore it to a state of equilibrium.

3. Damping: Having had its equilibrium disturbed, the hull will react and move back towards a state of equilibrium. As the moving hull has a certain amount of momentum, it will pass through the point of equilibrium and beyond, at which point the forces reverse and start the boat moving back again. The result of this is an oscillation, with the hull perhaps rolling or pitching in a rhythmic manner. The boat has been given energy by the excitation and if there were no damping influence, the motion would continue as none of this energy would be used up.

From a designers point of view, only the response and damping can be altered. The excitation is an external influence and other than placing limitations on the use of the boat there is little that can be done about it.

As mentioned above, the response of the boat to disturbances results from her stability. It is perhaps ironic that the mechanism commonly associated with comfort is at the root of the motions that will destroy it! The boat with little or no stability will respond only very slightly to the excitation, whereas the extremely stable boat will be vigorous in her attempts to conform to every ruffle of the surface of the sea.

Stability may cause forces and moments to be developed, however these are acting on a body with considerable mass and inertia, and these factors will mollify the effects somewhat. Mass and inertia introduce a time element to the response, ie there is some delay in the boat responding to the excitation. Rather as a pendulum of a certain length will always want to swing at a certain rate, the combination of stability, mass and inertia determine the "natural frequency" for the motions of a boat. It is easy to envisage a stiff and light boat having a quick roll and an overall roll period (the time for one complete oscillation) which is relatively short.

A rolling motion caused by a single wave or other disturbance will die down once the damping has absorbed the energy. However, boats travel through a sea state which has its own frequency and if this is the same or close to the boat's natural frequency in roll, pitch or heave the resulting resonance can be extremely uncomfortable. There is a certain amount of luck to this, sometimes the frequency of encounter is just "right" and starts the boat rolling or pitching in a particularly vigorous manner. Changing the boat's course slightly so the waves are encountered at shorter or longer intervals may be enough to stop the resonance.

The motions of a boat in a seaway can have a marked effect on performance, and by changing the weight distribution on board it is possible to adjust the inertia and thus the response characteristics of the boat. This is most commonly put into practice by avoiding excessive weight in the ends of the hull. Weight in the ends can increase the inertia of the boat in pitch, and thus slow the pitch motion to a point where it becomes ponderous and the boat does not respond well to a head sea. For best performance, minimum weight in the ends results in a quick pitch motion allowing the boat to "contour" relatively small waves and not be stopped by them. This can be taken too far however, and in a cruising yacht this sharp pitching motion may not be deemed particularly comfortable.

Damping is the remaining weapon in the hands of the designer to limit motions. This will not change the natural frequency of a motion, however it can lessen the effect of resonance and cause motions to die down relatively quickly. Damping can come from various sources:

i   Appendages: Keels and rudders provide large amounts of roll damping. It is easy to picture the water having to swirl around them as the boat rolls and this absorbs the roll energy. Ships are occasionally fitted with long and shallow bilge keels to provide additional roll damping.

ii Hull section: A hull section with a pronounced "V" form or hard chine shape will produce damping in roll.

iii Rigs: Even when there is no wind, a sail sheeted flat will provide effective roll damping. The rig can also provide considerable pitch damping as causing the luffs of the sails to move back and forth will require energy. This is very noticeable on some traditional boats with long bowsprits, where the relatively horizontal luff of the jib has a significant pitch damping effect.

15.6 CONSTRUCTION

15.6.1   MATERIAL CHOICE

The hull structure has several jobs to do and depending on the emphasis on cost, light weight, robustness and personal preference various materials can be suggested as being appropriate. Whatever material is chosen, the structure will be designed and engineered to provide the required strength and stiffness. Comparison of materials on the basis of "strength" can be misleading as it goes without saying that whatever material is used should be applied in sufficient quantity. Overall, the following factors may be considered:

a. Cost: An obvious and fundamental consideration. Cost will not only be affected by the material choice – the complexity of the structure will also have a bearing.

b. Weight: Varying materials will need to be applied in varying amounts to provide the required strength and stiffness. Those with impressive material properties in relation to their weight will yield a lighter structure. Cost and weight are almost directly at odds. Engineering a structure with the required mechanical properties and yet reduced weight nearly always results in a more expensive hull as more exotic materials and processes may need to be applied.

c. Robustness: This is the property of a material or structure that is frequently confused with strength. Robustness is not readily quantifiable and involves consideration of the nature of a possible failure. Metal structures are commonly viewed as being very robust, partly because a failure due to impact may result in significant distortion but not always a catastrophic loss of integrity or watertightness.

d. Longevity: Linked to maintenance and the ease with which the structure can be repaired, this requirement will be given very differing importance depending on the use and required life span of the boat.

e. Aesthetics and atmosphere: Again these are considerations that will vary hugely between boats and owners, with differing preferences dictating a range of approaches.

f. Building practicalities: For various reasons, some materials may suggest themselves or be ruled out due to the nature of the project. Any form of moulded construction lends itself strongly to a production building, whereas for a one off build this may not be the most practical approach.

15.7 COMPOSITES

15.7.1   REINFORCING MATERIALS

The term GRP stands for "glass reinforced plastics" and defines the great majority of small craft being built today. However materials other than glass fibre can be used for reinforcing, and the standard polyester resin can be replaced on high performance craft by stronger resins which are also more water and weather-proof. The more general term "fibre reinforced plastics" (FRP) applies to these structures, and the whole approach comes under the broad heading of Composites.

Glass reinforcing is made up from filaments extruded to a diameter of something like 0·01mm (0·0004in) and then bundled together to make strands. From there on the reinforcing can take on various guises. The strands may be randomly deposited and bound together with a high solubility binder to form a sheet, known as chopped strand mat. This is the cheapest and easiest to work of the reinforcings that are normally used, but offers the least impressive structural properties. There is nothing wrong with an all-chopped strand mat laminate, it will simply be heavier for equal strength than most of the alternatives.

Glass strands may also be woven together using various patterns. There is a huge variety of cloths available, each offering a different weave pattern or perhaps more material laid in one direction than another. When weaving the strands together, they are bent slightly which can lead to a certain amount of elasticity in the cloth. The best stiffness properties can be obtained from fabrics where the strands are laid across each other and stitched together.

If a load is anticipated in one place and its orientation can be predicted, the area can be reinforced using unidirectional tape. This is a band of fibres lying in one direction (UD), perhaps loosely stitched together. UD's are usually applied to the inside faces of frames or perhaps to reinforce the hull in way of the chain plates.

All the descriptions so far have been of normal glass reinforcement whose strands have a tensile strength of about 37,000kg/cm² (500,000lb/sq in). This is known as E-glass, probably because it was first developed for electrical applications. Alternative reinforcing materials are also available offering superior material properties but at increased cost. With these reinforcements hull and superstructure weight may be reduced by 12-15% over conventional GRP building, and by even more if sandwich construction is employed (see below). It is difficult to be dogmatic about weight saving since its potential varies with how far the builder is prepared to go in exploiting new materials and with the size of the vessel. It is easier to save weight on a big boat than a small one. Though weight saving on the hull is only part of the story – there being great scope on the fitting-out side as well – dedicated racing men are prepared to pay handsomely for even quite small reductions.

There are various alternative reinforcing materials available as follows:

a. S-glass has 30 - 40% higher tensile, impact and flexural strengths than the usual E-glass.

b. Kevlar is an organic fibre closely linked to nylon chemically, but called an Aramid. Its specific gravity is about half that of E-glass, and it is stronger in tension and stiffer. It is less good in compression, however. Kevlar has very good impact resistance and is the material used for bullet proof vests. It can be applied in areas of the hull structure where impacts are more likely to occur to increase the robustness of the laminate.

c. Carbon Fibre is another organic fibre material. Carbon comes in various degrees of strength and stiffness, however in the high strength and stiffness varieties there is a penalty to be paid in terms of brittleness. Carbon has now become the material of choice for high performance boats which demand the lightest and stiffest structures possible. Carbon uni-direction tapes can also be used to reinforce certain areas of the structure where high loads can be anticipated. Carbon is an extremely useful material for spars and offers very significant weight savings over the alternative Aluminium or Timber material options.

It is possible to obtain "Hybrid" cloths woven with two different types of reinforcing, such as Kevlar and S-glass or Kevlar and Carbon Fibre. Such reinforcements are often used in uni-directional rovings designed to exploit the different advantages of different materials. Thus Kevlar with high impact resistance and tensile strength can be combined with the compressive strength and stiffness of carbon fibre.

15.7.2   RESINS
The standard laminating resin is what is called an unsaturated polyester resin. Unsaturated meaning that it is capable of being converted from a liquid to a solid state in the right conditions. The resin on its own is not particularly strong (typical tensile strength being $6.3kg/mm^2$ (9000lb/sq in), and is only used to bind the reinforcing materials together. It follows that the lightest most efficient structure will have the minimum required amount of resin. Resin-to-glass ratio (by weight) will depend to a large extent on the type of reinforcing used. Chopped strand mat needs a large amount of resin to consolidate it properly, woven cloths need less. On a hull having chopped strand mat only, the ratio by weight will be something like 2:1; a high quality cloth laminate should have around equal weights of resin and reinforcement.

Normal boat building resins burn spectacularly as any witness to a boat fire can testify. There are self-extinguishing resins on the market which will not support combustion and will cease to burn once the source of ignition has been removed, but they are less weather resistant and less waterproof than conventional resins. It may be worthwhile employing them on the innermost laminations in the engine space but they are not really used much in yacht building. One application is for the hulls of tankers' lifeboats.

The unsaturated polyesters are good, moderately priced all-rounders. Greater strength, adhesion and waterproofing qualities can be had by using epoxy resins, though the cost increase is significant. Epoxy resins will flex more than polyesters before failing, which leads to a more durable laminate. Where exotic reinforcing materials are used epoxy resins will enable the most efficient laminate to be produced.

Vinylester resins are a sort of halfway house between polyesters and epoxies both in regard to cost and performance. Like epoxies, vinylester resins will flex more before failing and are consequently less brittle than a polyester resin.

15.7.3   CORED STRUCTURES
Any structural member relies to a certain extent upon thickness to develop its strength and stiffness. Sandwich panels offer the stiffness and strength benefits of great thickness, without the obvious weight penalty as the heavy reinforcing materials are confined to the skins of the sandwich. The core can consist of foam, low density timber (balsa) or a honeycomb of "Nomex" (a form of Aramid paper) or Aluminium.

In a sandwich panel, the skins either side of the core deal with the tension and compression that results from flexural loading, and the core carries the shear loading. The core must also support the thin skins which have little stability in compression and prevent them from buckling.

15.7.4   PRODUCTION BUILDING
Most production building involves laying the laminate inside a female mould. By this means the tooled surface of the finished hull is on the outside and no further fairing and finishing is required. The smoothness of the inside face depends entirely on the skill of the laminators, but is likely to be concealed with an interior lining and joinery in any case.

When a new female mould is required a wooden plug is built which is the same size and shape as the desired finished moulding. The plug is sanded and smoothed to as good a finish as can be achieved since every imperfection is likely to be faithfully reproduced on the production craft. The plug is then coated with a release agent, and layers of glassfibre and resin are laid over it in the normal moulding process until a sufficient thickness has been achieved. The mould is then lifted off the plug and with supports bonded to it is stood on the floor for work to commence.

Small boat moulds are normally made in one piece but for bigger craft they may be split longitudinally down the middle and bolted together so that after the hull has been laid up inside, it can be supported from above while the two halves of the mould are unbolted and moved apart. Such a split mould is also necessary if there is appreciable tumblehome in the sections. If a one-piece mould were used the hull could not be lifted out since it is wider at some distance below the deck line than it is at the deck line itself. Moulds are sometimes arranged so they can be tipped. This allows the men laying up the layers of glass and resin inside to work downhand from a staging projecting into the mould. Failing such a set-up they have either to scramble about in the bottom or work from stages lowered from above.

A mould has a limited life since it is sometimes

damaged when a hull sticks while it is being lifted out due, maybe, to the laminating resin penetrating the release agent. The damage can be repaired but it may be difficult to get the repair to match exactly the contours of the mould. Further, the mould is frequently polished to achieve a good finish on the hull taken from it and this polishing can wear flats into surfaces that were originally curved.

A male mould is virtually the same thing as the plug used when creating a female mould, though it is built to give the hull shape to the inside of the skin and not the outside. It may be an accurate representation of the hull completely planked up, or it may consist of frame patterns covered in closely-spaced, though not necessarily touching, battens. Though it must be faired and cleaned off it is not usually necessary to bring it to the high degree of finish of a plug, since it acts more as a former against which veneers or sheets of foam may be laid and attached than as a genuine mould. Hence it is cheap by comparison. The finished hull is lifted off the mould which can then be used again if required.

The process of lamination of the final hull shell is usually achieved by hand layup, where the specified layers of chopped strand mat or cloth are laid into the mould and saturated with resin. If an all chopped strand structure is specified, the laminate can be built up using a chopper gun, which chops strands and sprays them into the mould at the same time as spraying resin. This is a more economical process but it is hard to regulate the finished thickness of the shell and it is generally not associated with high quality building.

15.7.5   CUSTOM BUILDING
Custom building of composite structures is more likely to involve a male mould which removes one procedure (the layup of a female mould over a plug) from the process. In the case of cored structures, the male mould need only consist of frequently spaced battens over sections. In general, custom built composite structures will involve a higher specification of materials and more exotic fabrics may be used. These require more elaborate consolidation techniques to achieve the best results.

Production building usually involves hand consolidation of the laminate, ie the materials and resins are worked by hand and rollers are used to ensure that the cloth is fully saturated with no air gaps. Where a more even resin distribution and more reliable consolidation with minimal resin weight is desired, vacuum bagging may be used. When using this

technique, the assembled laminate is covered with a plastic film which is sealed to the mould tool at the edges. The air is then removed from under the sheet with a vacuum pump, and atmospheric pressure consolidates the laminate whilst it cures.

Where absolute minimal use of resin is desired to achieve the best possible laminate properties, pre-impregnated cloths may be used. These materials are impregnated with the appropriate amount of epoxy at the factory, and then chilled to arrest the curing of the resin. When required for assembling the laminate, the material is removed from a freezer, cut to shape and laid up as specified. The complete laminate is then vacuum bagged and rolled into an oven where the structure is baked to cure the resin. Depending on the sophistication of the system used, cure temperatures may be as high as 120°C (250°F).

15.8 METALS

15.8.1   STEEL
For many cruising yachts, especially those which will be voyaging into ice or other remote and potentially impact-ridden locations, steel construction is an option which will be worthy of serious consideration. Modern coatings (epoxies or chlorinated rubber) applied after thorough shot blasting mean that maintenance requirements are low and rusting is no longer the problem it once was. Steel is extremely robust and will merely distort under an impact that would shatter a GRP or timber hull, and which might tear a hole in Aluminium alloy. The material itself is comparatively inexpensive and is quickly converted to boat form with proper thought in the design and planning stages.

The thickness of steel plating required for adequate strength is frequently below that which may be welded easily without undue distortion. This leads to plating which requires little in the way of internal stiffening members. The hull will weigh maybe twice as much as one of GRP or alloy, though the completed boat will not weigh twice as much, since fitting out weights will be similar on boats of every form of construction.

In the days of riveting (which avoids the problems of heat distortion) very light plates could be and were used (the Thornycroft-built launch *Arie* of 1863 vintage had iron hull plates 0·6mm thick), but today a riveted hull would be expensive as compared with welding, not least because rivets for very thin plating would probably have to be specially made.

Steel used in boat building is usually to

BS4360 43A which is a fairly conventional mild steel. Special steels such as Corten, which has a low carbon content and additions of copper and manganese, have been tried but have not been found to offer sufficient advantages to outweigh their higher initial cost.

Framing on small craft is normally flat bar, and on bigger boats angle bar with the toe welded to the shell. The same types of section are used for the longitudinal stiffeners. Because large, flat areas of steel are unattractive to look at, may even be wavy and anyway are heavy, bulkheads are usually of marine ply. The exceptions may be the forward collision bulkhead and possibly another just forward of the engine room. These will frequently be steel and watertight. Decks and upperworks are often of steel, too, though an all-steel boat can have compass problems, especially if the compass cannot be mounted on the centreline. Though a compass adjuster can usually cope, if cost is not of primary importance there is a case for making the surrounding structure (such as the wheelhouse or indeed the whole superstructure) of timber or Aluminium alloy. Failing that, the compass can always be mounted at some distance from magnetic materials, and it is normally happy enough set in a pedestal on deck.

Integral tanks are simple to arrange on steel boats but it is important to ensure that there are adequate manholes in them to allow inspection and repair as required. Too many steel boats are built without real thought, using traditional wood building as a basis for construction. This leads to a proliferation of unwanted objects such as chine, keel and stem bars. It is easier, cheaper and just as satisfactory simply to butt plates together in these areas and weld. Welding may be of the simple electric arc type, or the more sophisticated and slightly more expensive shielded arc process where the arc is shrouded in an inert gas such as CO. This last type of welding makes for less distortion.

15.8.2   ALUMINIUM
Aluminium alloy cannot rust or rot. It needs painting, apart from antifouling, only for cosmetic purposes and it is light and tough. Its principal disadvantage is that it is incompatible with many other of the traditional non-ferrous materials used in boat building, such as the brasses and bronzes. In their presence under water it is quickly eaten away through electrolytic or galvanic action. However it is generally possible to substitute some other material. Thus, seacocks may be bought made in Aluminium alloy, and stainless steel (which produces no fierce

reaction) can often be used. As a last resort just about anything can be hard chrome plated for complete protection.

Similarly to a steel vessel, one of alloy may be of any shape desired but if she is of single or double chine form labour costs will be reduced. Alloy is normally welded (with an inert gas type of welder), although it is often riveted on small boats to eliminate distortion and to allow thin plates to be used. A typical hull structure will weigh about half as much as steel and about the same as GRP. An alloy plate with equal resistance to bending as steel will be about 1·5 times as thick, but about half as thick as ply or a GRP laminate. An alloy boat is built in very much the same way as a steel boat, with frames and longitudinals reducing unsupported panel size. Since it is non-magnetic, alloy presents no compass problems. The Aluminium alloy used is normally a British Standard alloy 5083 and although a hull might cost two or three times as much as the steel equivalent, the hull alone represents only a small percentage of complete boat cost and so this figure is not as damning as it first appears.

15.9 TIMBER

15.9.1   TRADITIONAL METHODS
Before the development of modern adhesives and composite construction methods, traditional timber construction was the norm for yachts. This method has been developed and refined over many years of experience to make the most of the material properties of timber and yet accommodate its various shortcomings. The differing uses and circumstances of boats built using this method have resulted in many variations to the theme. Most of these use a system of longitudinal planking over transverse frames, although the nature of these elements can and does vary greatly.

Carvel planking is butted edge to edge, with either a watertight fit or some sort of caulking to seal the seam. In clinker planking, the edges of the planks overlap and are fastened together to form a watertight seam. Framing may be sawn to shape from logs with appropriately curved grain, or can be steamed into position, the application of steam for an appropriate length of time rendering the timber flexible.

The quality of the materials and the skill and consideration with which the hull is built will have a large bearing on its longevity and a traditional timber boat requires a certain amount of maintenance to ensure that the various materials used do not degrade. That said, the structure consists of a number of discrete members, and any one of these can be removed and replaced. The construction is in effect infinitely replaceable and this capacity for repair and renewal means that traditionally- built boats can have a very long lifespan.

15.9.2   MODERN METHODS

The development of modern adhesives has allowed timber construction to be developed into a range of more efficient techniques. The use of these adhesives and particularly the sealing properties of epoxy resins allow two fundamental departures from traditional construction:

a. The timber is effectively sealed and its moisture content is prevented from changing dramatically. This stabilises the timber and limits the dimensional changes that traditional timber construction has developed to accommodate. If the moisture content can be kept below around 12%, degradation due to rot is eliminated and timber choice can be made without undue emphasis on durability.

b. The ability to join small pieces of timber effectively without using fastenings allows the timber to be applied in many more different combinations and orientations than was previously practical. With large baulks of timber less readily available to builders, the ability to use several smaller pieces with fewer flaws makes timber construction a practical proposition. Several strips of timber can be bent easily and laminated together to form frames which previously would have required careful selection of timber and significant wastage.

The general approach is more akin to composite construction, and in a similar manner timber is used as a reinforcing material and can be applied in whatever thickness and orientation is appropriate.

The majority of modern wood-epoxy boats are built using strip planking techniques. Strip planking can be laid over reasonably widely spaced moulds or frames, and the result is that a basically fair hull can be achieved relatively quickly and without an expensive mould. The strip planking can have diagonal veneers applied to the outside to give strength across the grain of the strips, or alternatively a glass sheathing can be laid in epoxy resin to do much the same job. Glass can also be applied to the inside of the hull, resulting in a sandwich type structure although it should be recognised that the timber planking will behave differently to a normal core material as used in composite construction and

this will have an effect on the way the structure is engineered.

The shell can be supported by laminated frames or plywood bulkheads or some combination of the two. The entire structure is encapsulated in epoxy resin to limit the changes in moisture content of the timber. Where diagonal veneers are used it is often the case that a thin layer of glass cloth will still be applied to provide abrasion resistance and act as a very serious paint job to ensure the structure remains sealed.

The Editor acknowledges with thanks the contributions in Sections 15.1 to 15.9 from Ed Burnett of Burnett Yacht Design, Staverton Bridge Mill, Totnes, Devon TQ9 6AH. Tel/Fax 01803 762113. ed.burnett@btinternet.com www.byd.btinternet.co.uk

15.10   PRACTICAL CONSIDERATIONS

15.10.1   HULLS IN PRACTICE

The previous sections have dealt with basic design considerations and briefly described building methods. This is interesting information on how your current boat came to be as she is. It is also valuable background if you are about to buy, or have built, a new boat.

However, most owners are stuck with what they have. They cannot radically alter its inherent characteristics, although, with some knowledge of hull balance, stability, resistance, trim, or any of the other subjects already covered, they may be able to improve their craft in certain ways. For example even quite minor changes may create, perhaps, a safer, drier or more manageable boat.

15.10.2   DECKS

With GRP construction it is extremely difficult to mould-in a really satisfactory non-slip deck surface. It is often tried but, though the result may be quite good on the first few craft of the production run, gradually the non-skid pattern becomes less prominent in the mould and less effective in practice. Moulding-in a pattern is cheap, but a better result is normally achieved by bonding one of the excellent non-skid materials available on to a smooth deck. The material should be placed wherever people are likely to walk or be working the boat, ie around the mast and the forestay, with sections elsewhere on deck providing a safe walkway.

Or use a non-skid deck paint, which is basically a low gloss paint with silver sand mixed in. It is tough, effective, easy on the eye and value for money. Sachets of anti-skid granules can also be mixed in to a suitable undercoat or gloss marine paint.

15.10.3 WINDOWS, PORTS AND HATCHES

Windows tend to leak, especially if they follow the curve of a cabin side and are bolted to the irregular thickness of a typical GRP moulding. This tendency is exaggerated where alloy frames have been distorted. No amount of sealant is likely to succeed. Usually a leaking window has to be removed, cleaned out and re-bedded.

Ports, being generally smaller are less prone to distortion. They are also held tight shut by side and bottom clamps, and a perished seal is therefore the likeliest source of a leak. On steel, alloy and wood the tendency to leak is minimized by the fact that the cabin sides are uniformly thick.

Fig. 15(10) A modern heavy duty hatch in Lewmar's Ocean range, designed for offshore yachting.

Modern, well designed and engineered hatches are less likely to leak, except perhaps where the frame is bedded in around the deck opening.

15.10.4 COCKPIT DRAINS

Too many cockpit drains are based on standard household waste systems for reasons of economy, and are consequently hopelessly inadequate in area. According to the Norwegian authorities, all craft with cockpit soles 35cm (l4in) or more above the waterline should have drains of an area calculated by the formula:

Total drain area (sq cm) = 40 + (15 x area of cockpit sole in sq m).

Alternatively, in imperial units, that is:

Area of drains (sq in) = 0.155 x (40 + 1.4A),

where A is the cockpit sole area in sq ft.
If, for example, the cockpit sole was 6ft x 3ft

(l8sq ft) the cross-sectional area of the drains should total:

Area = 0.155 x [40 + (1.4 x 18)] = 0.155 x 65 = l0 sq in.

That requires two drains each of 2½in diameter. They can be crossed if desired, such that the port side drain exhausts on the starboard side and vice versa. Thus the leeward drain outlet, which may well be under water, will not flood the cockpit. On the other hand it will not drain it very well either. On a cockpit with its sole well above the waterline it is probably better to have straight-through drains with as short a pipe length as possible, exiting above the waterline. The two last suggestions are to help speed the flow of water through the pipe.

A rough guide to the length of time taken to empty a cockpit is given by the formula:

$$T = \frac{A \times \sqrt{D}}{2B}$$

where T is the emptying time in seconds; A is the cockpit sole area in sq ft; D is the depth in feet of water in the cockpit; and B is the drain area in sq ft.

For example a 6ft x 3ft cockpit with two 3in diameter drains, if flooded to a depth of 2ft, would empty in about 2 minutes. With twin 1½in drains it would take about 10½ minutes; and with 1in drains about 21 minutes. The last two are clearly not very comforting figures.

Cockpit drains should have seacocks at their outlets.

15.10.5 STANCHIONS AND TOERAILS

These are safety items and need to be substantial and very well fastened. Stanchions shorter than about 0.6m (2ft) are of little use in preventing a body catapulted from one side of the deck to the other from going overboard. If they are 0.75m (2ft 6in) they will be better and anything more is better still. The strains that a flailing body puts on the stanchion base fastenings are enormous, and they must be through-bolted, not screwed. On a GRP hull there must be thick and wide backing plates (usually of marine ply) under the bolts, which might otherwise be pulled clean through the deck. Toe rails around the deck edge are a safety feature, and also stop small items rolling over the side. They should be approximately 75mm (2½ to 3in) high and again be through-bolted.

15.10.6 MAINTENANCE AND REPAIR

If a hull and deck are to be kept in tip-top condition, they should be closely examined at regular intervals. Small blemishes in paint or varnish work can turn into large blemishes unless attended to early on; the same applies to cracks in the GRP gel coat. Stress cracks, which may be seen in areas of high stress, for example around the chain plates, should be looked at by an expert and some repair work done. They indicate that something is at fault, so that the chain plates might need to be lengthened or have arms welded to them to distribute their load over a wider area. Check small items too: The loss of a cheap shackle can lead to the loss of a boat.

When the boat is out of the water examine the sacrificial anodes (see also 15.10.7) for excessive wasting; check on the state of the propeller shaft and its bearing (seize the prop and shake it violently – if there is much movement the shaft or bearing or both need renewing); and check on rudder bearing wear. If these bearings are bolted to the hull the bolts themselves ought to be examined. Take a couple out and see if they are wasted, which may be the case if they are brass or stainless steel. If the bearing cannot be removed hit the bolt heads hard with a hammer to see if they fall off – they might! Metal items below the waterline can suffer other problems, from rusting and stress corrosion to dezincification (15.10.7.)

Blisters on the bottom of a GRP vessel may be the result of osmosis which is not quite the disaster that it was originally thought to be – with early professional treatment it can be completely eliminated. Pitting on the bottom of a steel hull probably means that the mill scale that is present on the surface of all steel plate after rolling was not properly removed during shot blasting, and a more thorough examination is indicated. On a wooden boat check for softness or rot with a sharp bradawl, especially along the waterline and at the ends where the planking is rebated into the stem, keel and transom. Seacock fastenings should be checked and, if possible, a keel bolt drawn for examination. If this cannot be done hit the heads with a hammer, as with the rudder bearings, to check on the state of the metal.

Leaks where wooden superstructures join the deck affect both wooden and GRP craft. Fresh water leaks can lead to rot and not just discomfort below. If the joint or connection is at all suspect clear away all the previous water-stopping treatment, which might be an ineffectual quarter-round beading lightly bedded onto a compound; then bond the joint with glassfibre tape and epoxy resin. Epoxy putties are good for filling holes and dents in all materials, but take a great deal of sanding off afterwards.

Probably car body repair kits are best for work on GRP construction.

Major damage to GRP must be ground back to sound laminate and carefully cleaned out; then dry and degrease the area. If the damage has not penetrated right through the hull the repair consists of filling the hole with resin and glassfibre mat, as in normal laminating, until the repair is slightly proud of the surface. Then a plastic sheet like cellophane is smoothed on and taped over the repair and everything is left to dry. Finally the surface can be ground smooth and painted with two-pot polyurethane.

If the damage has penetrated the hull, it is best tackled from inside, as shown in Fig. 15(11).

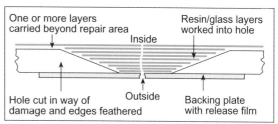

Fig. 15(11) Repairing a damaged GRP hull from the inside.

The damaged area is ground out and feather-edged. A backing piece of ply is held or wedged against the outside of the hull and coated with a release agent and then, if possible, gel coated. The hole is made good with layers of glassfibre and resin with a few layers taken beyond the damaged area. This is covered with a cellophane film and allowed to dry. The backing piece and film are removed and the repair ground smooth on the inside and, if gel coat was not available, painted outside.

All GRP work should be done in reasonably calm, dry conditions. Warmth speeds up the resin curing time, and an electric hot air blower or infra red heater will help. GRP hulls respond well to regular washing and polishing with one of the many proprietary polishes on the market, but avoid the silicone variety which is difficult to remove if the boat ever needs painting.

Repairing other forms of construction entails seeing how the job was done in the first place and then copying the method as far as possible. Modern gap-filling epoxy resins will make good many defects in workmanship, easily filling gaps up to 6mm (6in) wide, and even more if extended with a suitable filler. Epoxy paints can be used on all forms of construction and are very waterproof and hard. After a while even wet and dry paper does not seem to touch them, but they do tend to 'chalk' quite quickly. For this reason a final coat of two-pot polyurethane is often applied over an epoxy for a good finish.

15.10.7 ELECTROLYTIC ACTION

Sea water is an all too excellent electrolyte, so two dissimilar metals in close proximity underwater tend to form a cell with the current flowing from one to another. This has the effect of wasting away the anodic or more 'base' of the metals.

Some typical boatbuilding metals are listed below in an approximate electro-chemical sequence with the noble, or cathodic, materials at the top.

Galvanic series in sea water
Noble or cathodic end
Stainless steel type 316 (2% molybdenum)
Stainless steel type 304
Stainless steel type 321 (0·4% titanium)
Monel
Gunmetal
Phosphor bronze
Admiralty brass
Red brass
Copper
Naval brass
Manganese bronze
Muntz metal
Lead
Stainless steels with oxide destroyed
Cast iron
Mild steel
Aluminium alloys
Cadmium plating
Galvanised steel
Zinc
Magnesium
Base or anodic end

Stainless steel appears, confusingly, in two positions in the table. As delivered, and in normal use with the oxide film that forms naturally to protect the metal intact, stainless steel is among the most noble and corrosion-resistant of materials. However the maintenance of that oxide film requires the presence of oxygen which in certain places (such as under a barnacle) may be absent. In other areas, for example, where a shaft passes through a rubber bearing, the oxide film may be worn away and the oxygen prevented from reaching the surface. Here 'crevice corrosion' may occur, and where this happens stainless steel drops down the galvanic series towards the base end and is liable to corrosion. The metal does not change; it is simply that its protective skin (which is formed in other alloys, such as aluminium alloy, in much the same way) is destroyed locally. Adding molybdenum, as in the 316 alloys, minimises crevice corrosion. The presence of titanium, on the other hand, though it makes for easier welding, reduces resistance to corrosion. If the oxide film is restored the material will again move to the noble end of the scale.

Zinc anodes are used because they will be attacked before any of the usual metals and therefore will protect them. Magnesium anodes are generally preferred in fresh water, incidentally. The size, positioning and installation of all such sacrificial anodes is best left to the professionals. These anodes should never be painted, because paint protects against galvanic corrosion (and so is very important) but anodes are meant to be attacked and corroded. Even where cathodic protection is fitted, leakage from insulation faults in electrical circuits can cause rapid corrosion under water, see Chapter 21 (21.6.4).

When deciding which metals to use underwater the distance they are apart on the galvanic series is one important factor (the greater the distance the more serious the action); the other is their relative bulk. For example, if iron fastenings were used on a copper-sheathed yacht, the iron would be attacked which would be dangerous. On the other hand if for some reason gunmetal bolts were put through an iron keel, though the iron would still be wasted that would not be too serious. Taking an even more extreme example, stainless steel shafts are sometimes used in conjunction with aluminium alloy hulls, and though the aluminium will be attacked, because its area is so vast compared with that of the shafts the effect is generally not serious. But aluminium alloy shafts in a stainless hull (if that is conceivable) would be asking for trouble.

Mill scale on steel plating is another example of dissimilar metals in action. Mill scale, which occurs as the plates are being rolled, comprises various ferric oxides, among them magnetite. This is about as cathodic to iron as copper, and where paint has been removed and sea water can get at the scale, the plating will be attacked and eaten away. Thus the removal of mill scale by shot blasting or other means is most important on steel craft, just as is the maintenance of a protective film of paint.

Brass is an alloy of copper and zinc. In the presence of sea water the zinc will be wasted away. This is called de-zincification and leaves the metal copper-coloured, crumbly and quite lacking in strength.

15.10.8 PAINTING

Painting is still extensively used on yachts, both to protect surfaces above and below the water and for cosmetic reasons. Even a GRP hull needs antifouling unless the boat is normally kept out of the water, and epoxy paints are commonly used on GRP hulls to combat osmosis, or to restore and protect the surface after osmosis has been treated (see 15.10.6).

Terms like two-pot polyurethane, wet edge time and pot life may sound rather forbidding – and modern paint systems are chemically very complex – so it is vital to follow in detail the instructions which are issued by paint makers. Nevertheless, there are some general rules which apply, no matter what paint or varnish is being used.

First, it is essential to choose a paint suitable for each particular application. Some paints are incompatible with others, and cannot be satisfactorily applied on top of them, so it is important to keep a record of what products are used on various parts of the hull, boot-topping, topsides, upperworks, deck, spars, varnished surfaces, deck fittings, interior surfaces, chain locker, bilges etc. It is also necessary to use the right type of paint for the material being covered, whether GRP, timber, alloy, steel or ferro-cement. All paint manufacturers provide helpful literature on their products, and if carefully read and heeded there should be no problems, but do not hesitate to seek their advice if in doubt.

Take great care when handling most of the substances used in painting a boat and in the prior preparation of the surfaces. Paints, strippers and the like should come with safety notes indicating the risks that they present and how they should be used. Good ventilation is important, but special precautions are needed with antifoulings even when these are removed or applied in the open air. Take advice on choosing a proper industrial respirator or face mask. Eye protection is also important and goggles must be worn when applying poisonous liquids, or using a power tool for sanding etc. Many substances can irritate the skin or cause dermatitis, so wear a pair of disposable gloves. Paints, thinners etc all present a fire risk, so due care needs to be taken in this respect.

Good surface preparation is absolutely essential for all paintwork, and will account for 75% of the work needed, probably more when applying a single-coat, epoxy resin-based paint. The surface must be smooth, clean and free of grease and, usually, of all traces of the previous paint. Dust must be removed by washing with water or white spirit, and finally wiping off with a tack cloth. Keep the atmosphere dust-free: damp down the floor, and do not wear woollen garments which may shed small hairs.

With most paint systems a primer or undercoat must be overcoated within a certain period (say 6 to 24 hours) which means that careful planning is needed. Consider also the weather and temperature: never paint in damp conditions.

Paints and varnishes either contain, or need added to them, thinners which allow the covering to spread evenly in a thin film and which then evaporate. Consequently the final film may only be half as thick as the wet film that is applied – one reason why dust particles mysteriously appear when the paint dries. Make sure that the correct thinners are used, and in the right proportions. If a can of paint is to be used which has been previously opened, it is important to strain it carefully to remove any portions of skin which have formed. Mix the components of the paint and/or thinners as directed, and allow the pot to stand for a few minutes to get rid of air bubbles.

Most paints can be applied by brush, roller or spray. Professional painters may use spray systems, for which proper equipment and precautions are essential. Paint spraying can be dangerous unless proper safety measures are taken. The amateur is therefore likely to use brush or roller; the latter is quicker but does not give such a good finish as a brush. A brush is better for priming coats, which must be brushed well into the surface. Some paints can be applied adequately with a pad.

Brushes must be best quality and, of course, scrupulously clean. Because speed is important in applying paint (a polyurethane, for example, sets quite quickly) it is necessary to use as large a brush as can be easily handled for the area concerned. If a roller is used, have one of the shaved mohair type.

It is essential to plan the work, dividing the area to be covered into manageable sizes, and working from one to another while the paint is still wet and the boundaries can merge together. Immerse the bristles of the brush not more than half-way into the paint, and do not wipe off the brush against the sides of the tin which causes loss of thinners from the paint running back into the tin. Transfer the paint to the surface as evenly as possible, using fast horizontal strokes, but finally laying off in one direction with the brush angled at about 45°. Do not reverse the brush while it is in contact with the paint film, or air bubbles will be trapped.

After about half-an-hour, paint may start to gel in the top of the brush, so either wash the brush with thinners or change brushes to prevent bits of dried paint getting to the paint film.

Brushes must be thoroughly washed out with thinners after use, and then with warm water and detergent. After rinsing and drying they should be wrapped in greaseproof paper and stowed carefully away, not left stuck in a tin.

15.11 BOOKS ABOUT BOATS

Stability and Buoyancy RYA booklet G23.

ISO 12217 – Small craft, Stability and Buoyancy assessment and Categorisation (ISO).

Teach yourself Naval Architecture by B. Baxter (Warsash Nautical Bookshop).

Boat Data Book by Ian Nicolson (Adlard Coles, 4th edn).

The Boatbuilding Book by Geoffrey O'Connell (Ashford).

The Boatbuilding Manual by Robert M. Stewart (International Marine).

Boatbuilding with Steel by Gilbert Klingel (International Marine).

Fibreglass Boats by Hugo du Plessis (Adlard Coles).

Elements of Boat Strength by David Gerr (Adlard Coles).

Build Your Own Boat by Ian Nicolson (Hyman).

Cold-Moulded & Strip-Planked Wood Boatbuilding by Ian Nicolson (Adlard Coles).

Metal Boats by Ken Scott.

Yacht Design explained by Steve Killing & Douglas Hunter.

Complete Amateur Boatbuilding by Michael Verney (Adlard Coles, 4th edition).

Practical Small Boat Designs by John Atkin. (International Marine).

Principles of Yacht Design by Lars Larsson and Rolf Eliasson (Adlard Coles, 2nd edition).

Osmosis and Glassfibre Yacht construction by Tony Staton-Bevan (Adlard Coles, 2nd edition).

Desirable and undesirable characteristics of offshore yachts by the Technical Committee of the Cruising Club of America, edited by John Rousmaniere. (Nautical Quarterly Books; WW Norton & Co).

Aero-hydrodynamics of Sailing by CA Marchaj (Adlard Coles, 3rd edition).

Seaworthiness, the forgotten factor by CA Marchaj (Adlard Coles).

Yacht and small craft construction – Design Decisions by Gordon Trower.

Chapter 16 Multihulls

CONTENTS

16.1 INTRODUCTION

16.1.1 EARLY HISTORY AND ADVANTAGES

Multihulls go back a long way in history. Captain Cook noticed their presence in Polynesia long before any interest was shown in them in Europe or America. He was evidently impressed by their speed, but only much later did it emerge that the Polynesians and Melanesians had emigrated huge distances, populating most of the Pacific sometimes with whole villages carried on huge catamarans. They transported not only people but livestock, plants, food and water, navigating by systems that were only more recently rediscovered by such eminent multihull sailors as Dr David Lewis and Sir Robin Knox-Johnston.

The generic term multihull includes catamarans, trimarans and proas. A catamaran is a vessel with two hulls of equal size, joined by cross-beams or a bridgedeck. These are by far the most popular type of cruising multihull. The proa, is one with two unequal-sized hulls which are symmetrical fore-and-aft, and rigged so that it can be sailed in either direction. Experimentation went on with these craft in the 1960s and 70s, but they are all but extinct in the West today. A trimaran refers to a vessel with three hulls, where the central hull is usually larger than the two outriggers (or amas). While catamarans and proas have their origins in the Pacific, the trimaran is a more modern Western creation. Today trimarans are popular for racing

and make more performance orientated cruising boats, but are not nearly as popular as catamarans.

The advantages that the multihull employed so successfully in the Pacific are still apparent, although much developed, in their modern day equivalents. The inherent wide beam gives a stability which allows racing multihulls to have a formidable power/weight ratio, and a living area which is so attractive in cruising multihulls. They are easily the fastest sailing boats afloat, the largest examples capable of sailing more than 600 miles in a day. Multihulls, like monohulls, come in all forms and for all manner of functions, which they achieve in a more extreme way.

Multihulls have some unique benefits when compared to monohulls. They are inherently stable and heel little. Put a cup of tea on the saloon table and it will probably stay there. Because of their stability they also do not require a ballasted keel to keep them upright. This not only makes them much lighter, improving their performance, but means that they have shallow draught. This potentially opens up new cruising grounds, such as the exploration of the upper reaches of rivers and creeks. It also allows multihulls to be anchored or put on a drying mooring which would be unsuitable for most monohulls. Their inherent stability means they can take the bottom in tidal areas with relative ease and thus can be beached over a low tide for repairs or simply to enjoy a day or night on the beach without any of the hassles of anchoring.

They also have several less obvious attributes. Many larger multihulls have a diesel engine in each hull and this makes them highly manoeuvrable. Put one engine astern and the other forward and they will spin on a sixpence. The large flat deck area – and in particular the trampoline – is ideal for relaxing.

Multihulls may typically be fast, spacious or cheap. By and large you can have two of these things, but not three. It is for example possible to have a fast, spacious cruising catamaran, but its hulls and rig must usually be made of lightweight, costly materials such as carbon fibre and so will not be cheap. A simplified version of this is that with multihulls you can either have accommodation equivalent to the finest cruising yacht or speed greater than the largest maxi, but not both.

16.1.2 LATER PROGRESS

In the 1660s the English eccentric, Sir William Petty, caused a catamaran to be built which resembled nothing so much as a conventional boat sawn in half lengthways and planked up the middle both sides, with a bridgedeck joining the two halves. A more serious attempt was by the inspired American yacht designer Nathaniel Herreshoff. In 1875 he designed, built and raced the surprisingly modern *Amaryllis* which was 7.6m (25ft) long and an unbelievable 5.5m (18ft) wide. Originally fitted with a lateen rig, she was fast but not very stable. In trying to avoid the use of daggerboards he had omitted a basic fact, that fine slim bows do not offer much buoyancy and can easily trip over a lee bow. Herreshoff found out the hard way.

In Britain the multihull story began with such pioneers as Bill O'Brien, James Wharram and the Prout brothers; in America the likes of Piver, Cross and Brown produced cruisers, whilst Dick Newick became known for his more performance orientated craft and race winners.

16.2 ACCOMMODATION

16.2.1 CATAMARAN LAYOUTS

One of the most popular reasons for buying a cruising multihull, along with their shoal draught, is their great internal volume. The layout of a cruising catamaran is very different from that of an equivalent monohull. In particular the saloon on the bridgedeck allows a good all round view outside, but gives a feeling of being 'on the water' and not 'down below'. In addition, the layout makes for greater privacy in the cabins.

Many catamarans have at least three bunks situated in the ends of the hulls. In the smaller sizes, on boats like the 24ft Striders and 26ft Tikis,

these bunks are singles but as length increases they become progressively wider so that at 13.7m (45ft) plus they can be 'Queen sized' doubles. In this configuration the fourth corner is often taken up by the heads/shower compartment as in the Prout range. On most catamarans the saloon is rarely used for sleeping, although often the table can be dropped down to form a large double bunk.

With this accommodation layout a catamaran gives great privacy, even in the smallest sizes. However some catamarans have their bunks on the bridgedeck, forward of the saloon, for example the 34ft Gemini, see fig 16(1). A disadvantage is that access can be a problem.

Typically, midships in one hull will be the navigation area where there is room for a full-sized chart table and repeater instruments. Midships in the other hull will be a galley which would not shame a small apartment, with plenty of room for food, stowage, refrigerator, work tops and sinks. The main drawback is that often the cook is blocking the way to one bunk and the navigator is obstructing access to the heads.

Modern catamarans have a wider beam than their predecessors and so some boats larger than 35ft, such as those in the French Fountaine Pajot range, can have the chart table and galley on the bridgedeck. This makes the chart table more accessible to the cockpit, and the galley to the saloon area, even if it leaves the cook under the scrutiny of the crew. With this configuration a narrow heads compartment is usually shoehorned in midships in each hull and there are cabins in all four corners of the boat.

Finally, there are a small number of open bridgedeck cruiser/racer catamarans being produced to order, for example Newton's 15 metre cruiser racer.

16.2.2 TRIMARAN LAYOUTS

Cruising trimarans are typified by the speedy Dragonflys from Quorning Yachts in Denmark and the Corsair Marine range of Ian Farrier designs, built in California. On these the accommodation is similar to a monohull - except narrower - with the usual fo'c'sle berth, heads compartment, saloon with dinette/ double berth, galley opposite the chart table, companionway up to cockpit, and possibly an aft cabin.

The trimaran was not always a performance machine. The American designers mentioned earlier and some British designers such as Derek Kelsall, developed the trimaran as a cruising yacht. Those of 30+ft would have bunks in the wings connecting the main hull to the amas or outriggers. This is a little like sleeping on a windowsill with little overhead space. The amas

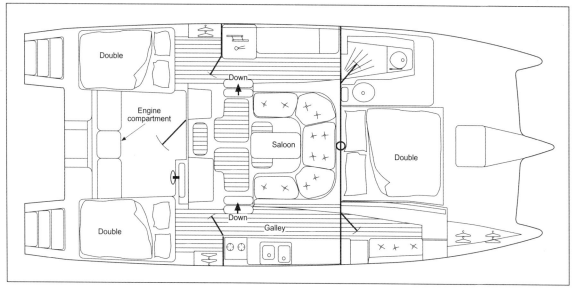

Fig.16(1) The Gemini 105 is a 34' live-aboard boat for a couple or small family. A single 27 hp diesel or outboard motor is mounted centrally.

themselves were only used for light stowage, such as fenders, warps, sails, deflated inflatables, etc.

On their larger trimarans of 12m (40ft) or more LOA, the amas were also used for accommodation with a narrow corridor running along them to reach a wing-bunk and with a heads in the bow. Effectively each ama was a private ensuite double cabin as in Fig. 16(2).

At this size there was usually a grand luxe cabin aft in the main hull with another large double forward, leaving the centre part of the main hull for the saloon, galley and chart table, and occasionally an inside steering position.

Large trimarans make ideal charter boats, with the bigger ones providing guest accommodation for eight as well as a private suite for the crew. The main problem is that there is almost too much room, and where there is space something will be found to fill it and weight, as we shall see, kills a multihull's performance.

16.3 PERFORMANCE AND RACING

16.3.1 THE PROFESSIONAL RACERS

For sheer speed around the buoys or around the world no one can beat the big multihulls. The French dominate this area, as these monsters appeal to the French craving for style, speed and macho image, and this has attracted huge television, radio and newspaper coverage which in turn has produced extensive sponsorship money.

For the last decade the top Grand Prix class has been the ORMA circuit for 60ft trimarans. They race in a series of dramatic televised round-the-

buoys events, usually at French ports such as La Trinité-sur-Mer or Fécamp. They also take part in long distance transatlantic events such as the four yearly singlehanded Route du Rhum and Europe 1 New Man STAR (formerly the OSTAR) and the bi-annual two handed Transat Jacques Vabre.

The 60ft trimarans are now highly developed and substantially faster than the giant 85ft catamarans that were the class 1 fleet in the mid-1980s and the class is currently (2001) experiencing a rebirth. Most are almost as wide as they are long with floats as long and with almost as much under water volume as their centre hulls. They all have rotating wingmasts and on most this can be canted to weather for added performance by giant hydraulic rams on the shrouds. Other European countries are joining this fleet, which is an awesome spectacle at full speed.

Large catamarans also made a comeback during the 1990s with the advent of the Jules Verne Trophy, originally for sailing around the world in less than 80 days, now for the fastest non-stop circumnavigation starting and finishing from a line between Ushant and the Lizard. The first winner of the Trophy was Bruno Peyron in 1993 and his time was subsequently bettered by Peter Blake and Robin Knox-Johnston on board *ENZA New Zealand* and then by Frenchman Olivier de Kersauson on board the trimaran *Sport Elec*.

Due to Bruno Peyron's effort, large multihull sailing took a quantum leap at the end of the millenium with the creation of 'The Race' – the ultimate round the world yacht race, with no design and size constraints. The ultimate expression of Peyron's concept was Pete Goss' ill-fated *Team Philips*, a radical catamaran, 120ft long with slender wave-piercing bows and unstayed rotating wingmasts mounted in each hull. However it was the more conservative designs of

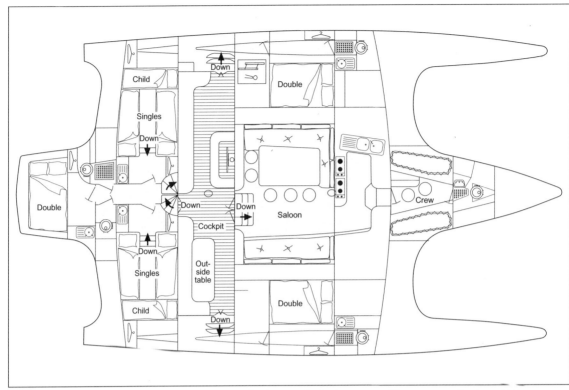

Fig. 16(2) In larger trimarans it is common to find double bunks in the wings, reached from the amas, and double bunks forward and aft in the main hull.

Gilles Ollier which proved most successful. Three such yachts were built for 'The Race', at 107-110ft LOA, skippered by some of the world's top names – Whitbread winner Grant Dalton, top trimaran sailor Loick Peyron and American multihull sailor Cam Lewis.

These giants represent the limits of current technology and have dramatically increased the maximum speed that can be achieved under sail over a sustained period. For many years the record for the most number of miles sailed in 24 hours hovered around 520-540 held by 60ft trimarans, but the first of this new generation, Steve Fossett's *PlayStation*, covered 687 miles in 24 hours whilst reducing the west to east transatlantic record to 4 days 17 hours 28 minutes. The skippers of these boats feel that in the right conditions a 700 mile day is achievable.

16.3.2 THE MID-SIZE
In France there is an active class called Formula 28, but there is almost no serious racing for multihulls between this size and the 60 footers.

By contrast in the UK there has been highly competitive offshore racing for a handful of boats in the 30-45ft size range. Part of the reason for this is because of the number of classic events in

which they can still compete: the Royal Western Yacht Club's Round Britain and Ireland, the Royal Torbay Yacht Club's Triangle Race and the Royal Cornwall's Azores and Back. They have also been very popular in sailing and hill climbing events such as the Three Peaks Race and the Scottish Three Peaks, although multihulls are now prohibited from the former.

16.3.3 MICRO-MULTIHULLS
At the modest end of the scale are the micro-multihulls. This class was started in England by Richard Woods and his Strider range and then picked up by the Multihull Offshore Cruising and Racing Association. MOCRA organises a series of races for those who do not have to spend too much on their sport. A Strider can be raced competitively for an outlay no greater than £15,000. The beauty of these boats is that by definition they must be transportable by trailer, which in itself limits size, weight and thus expense. Over the last decade the class has matured and become highly competitive with the elegant Firebirds, Dragonflies and Farriers dominating.

For trailerable multihulls see also 16.5.4.

16.3.4 CRUISER/RACERS
Club racing is available to cruising boats and by far the most popular event in the UK is the annual Round the Island Race where the multihull classes are sent off first to get them out of the way. The event is a clear demonstration that

racing multihulls with a crew of perhaps two or three are often more than a match for racing monohulls twice their size with a huge crew lining the windward rails.

Many clubs have classes for cruiser or cruiser/racer multihulls in their series. In particular the Royal Ocean Racing Club allows multihulls to participate in their prestigious events. In the Solent the Royal Southampton Yacht Club also has a very active programme for multihulls as well as several short-handed events.

16.4 SAILING CHARACTERISTICS

16.4.1 DISPELLING THE MYTHS

There are many myths surrounding the performance of multihulls. 'They don't sail to windward' was a popular criticism and certainly true of some older cruising multihulls. Most modern cruising catamarans have solved this problem through the use of stiffer rigs and hulls, better sails and underwater appendages and although they may not point as high as a monohull will sail much faster when freed up slightly so their overall pace upwind will be similar, and, of course, very much faster when reaching.

A majority of the most popular cruising catamarans will sail no faster than an equivalent cruising monohull and this is down to one simple factor: weight. By this we mean not just the weight of the boat itself but of all the gear with which it is so tempting to fill the large interior volume of a multihull. For a comparable weight and sail area, a heavy multihull will always be much slower than a light one.

All designers are familiar with the upward spiral of 'more weight means more sail area', necessitating a taller mast, and in turn heavier rigging, scantlings and a bigger engine. This upward spiral inevitably leads to a much bigger, heavier, slower and more expensive boat than was envisaged. On the other hand, if at a stroke you can halve the weight of the boat by removing ballast, the spiral goes the other way. Sail area can be smaller, masts shorter, rigging perhaps a little lighter, hull scantlings reduced, and the engine smaller in terms of size, weight, price and fuel consumption. This is exactly the case with multihulls.

For example, a typical 9m (30ft) catamaran, fully rigged and engined, weighing a mere 2.5 tons, is powered by a 9.9 hp four-stroke outboard and has a working sail area of under 50sq m (500sq ft) providing excellent speed. Another 11.3m (37ft) cruising catamaran may well fit a 17hp diesel, with the 27hp option being the largest recommended, to give a very respectable 8 knots.

16.4.2 THE CAPSIZE BOGEY

The primary reason people are put off buying multihulls are the alarming stories about them capsizing. This is perhaps fuelled by images of dinghy cats and the giant racing machines blasting around with their windward hulls (and in the case of the 60ft trimarans their centre hulls) clear of the water. Cruising cats simply are not designed to sail like that. If they are over-pressed the lee hull will start digging in causing a lot of lee helm. Reducing sail will not only bring the helm back in balance but will also cause an increase in boat speed.

The fact is multihulls *can* capsize and there are two instances when this happens. If they are sailing off the wind, being pushed hard or raced and have too much sail up for the conditions, the excitement will come to a quick, wet end as the boat dives into the back of a wave, buries its lee bow and trips over it, a capsize called a 'pitchpole'. (The type of capsize where the windward hull lifts until the boat is over on its side practically never happens.)

This type of capsize was very real in the early days of multihulls, when the sportier catamarans were being raced to the limit and were crewed by men who were still learning. There is a simple rule to avoid this: reef early. The time to reef is when you first wonder "is the boat over-pressed?" Today, improvements in design make this very rare among cruising multihulls, which now have more buoyancy in the ends of their hulls and more stability through having much more beam than their predecessors.

The second occasion is in the ultimate conditions, when there are storm or hurricane force winds and, in particular, giant breaking seas. Multihulls are lighter than their monohull counterparts, and they dislike confused or beam-on seas even more, so they must be sailed with great caution under less sail. However, one of the multihull's final advantages is that they do not sink, because there is no ballasted keel to drag them down, and they are usually inherently buoyant. Escape hatches are commonly fitted enabling the crew to make their way onto the upturned hull and wait for rescue.

16.4.3 SURVIVING STORMS

In the worst weather conditions multihulls have many attributes to prevent them from the ultimate capsize disaster. While monohulls will be knocked down and/or rolled, the high initial stability of multihulls means when all the sails are dropped they behave like a giant raft. This is aided by their lack of a deep keel. Without this they can be washed down waves with nothing to trip them up.

In survival conditions there are several courses of action. You can run with it. Often it will help the stability of the boat if as much gear as possible is moved aft. Racing multihulls even have aft water ballast tanks which can be filled when racing downwind in heavy conditions. To slow the boat down many trail heavy warps or even anchor chain tied in a large loop, or some of the excellent parachute drogues now available, although it is important to have a very strong attachment point for them.

Quite often the easiest thing to do is to heave to if not racing, although it is amazing how rarely this old fashioned remedy is used. Most multihulls are well enough balanced to lie quite comfortably under a backed storm jib and triple reefed main. If things get worse most of these boats will lie a-hull. The noise is the most frightening thing, with breakers coming normally from just forward of the beam and, as the windward hull lifts, crashing on to the windward side of the lee hull. This is very trying for the nerves of the crew, but the boats themselves should be designed to withstand it – as described in 16.5.3.

16.4.4   SAILING WITH SAFETY

Certain basic rules should be remembered. Reef early, and never let the windward hull lift. In gusts, if capsizing seems a possibility, when close hauled or reaching, luff up to spill wind from the sails; when broad reaching, bear away to flatten the boat down. Do not sail with sheets cleated in strong winds. Check that quick-release jammers really do work when under maximum load.

At over a certain wind speed the boat may be reduced to storm jib only. This will not give much progress to windward in a seaway, but it may be helpful to run the leeward engine at modest rpm.

A theoretical assessment of the safe wind speed for different sail areas can be made from formulae for static and dynamic stability, as explained below.

Fig. 16(3) shows the forces acting on a catamaran under sail, around a point (P) of rotation taken as the foot of the leeward hull. If 'a' is half the distance between the centrelines of the hulls, and 'b' is the height of the centre of effort of the sail plan above P, the boat will capsize if:

Wind pressure x 'b' > Displacement x 'a'

'a' can be measured, or found from the boat's drawings, while 'b' can be calculated geometrically or may be given by the builder – remembering that it varies with the amount of sail actually set. Wind pressure (F) on the sails in lb/sq ft can be taken as:

$0.0051 \times \text{Wind Speed}^2$

where wind speed is in knots.

From the above, at the moment when the boat is about to capsize:

$0.0051 \times \text{Wind Speed}^2 \times \text{Sail Area} \times \text{'b'}$
$= \text{Displacement} \times \text{'a'}$

From this the formula can be expressed as:

$$\text{Wind Speed (knots)} = 14 \times \frac{\text{Displacement} \times \text{'a'}}{\sqrt{\text{Sail Area} \times \text{'b'}}}$$

where displacement is in lbs, sail area in sq ft and dimensions 'a' and 'b' in feet.

The formula above refers to what is termed 'static stability'. It has become customary to adopt a safety factor of 60% in calculating 'dynamic stability' of practical sailing, because for any wind force there are gusts which often greatly exceed the average wind speed. Thus:

Dynamic stability = 0.6 x Static stability;

$$\text{or} = 8.4 \times \frac{\sqrt{\text{Displacement} \times \text{'a'}}}{\text{Sail Area} \times \text{'b'}}$$

This can be used for working out in advance, for a known displacement, in what wind speeds different combinations of sail can be carried.

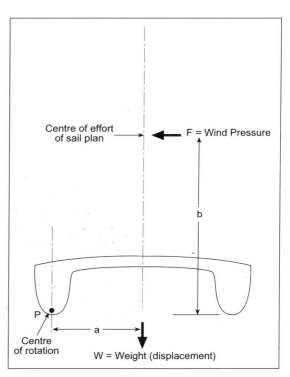

Fig. 16(3) The forces acting on a catamaran under sail. Taking moments about the bottom of the leeward hull (P), for the boat to capsize F x b must be greater than W x a.

16.4.5 HANDLING

A multihull is a lightweight yacht, floating on top of the water rather than in it. In practice this means that unless she is fitted with deep daggerboards she will not point as high as a monohull and should not be asked to do so. On most multihulls it is best to bear away a little. By doing this the weight will be more evenly distributed between the hulls, and the speed will rise. Usually, by sailing freer but faster, the overall performance to weather should be similar to a monohull.

Off the wind it is often preferable to tack downwind when the genoa is blanketed by the main and it is either not possible to run goose-winged or for some reason to hoist a cruising chute. The beam of a multihull makes it possible to tack down the spinnaker or cruising chute to the bows without a pole. Set flying in this way the sail can more easily be handled, without all the attendant problems and dangers of a pole and its rigging. Most modern performance multihulls tend to use flatter cut gennikers instead of spinnakers and sail bigger angles downwind. An advantage of gennikers is that they can be hoisted on a furler and then unrolled, making for easy handling.

Safety lies in keeping the boat moving fast and easily. The boat will tell you by her speed and general ease of motion whether she is giving her best possible performance for the prevailing conditions, but the sensation of heel which shows a monohull is overpressed, is not there on a multihull. You should therefore have a clear idea of the maximum wind speeds at which you should reef and err on the conservative side if there is an awkward sea. Always reduce sail early so that the boat is not too hard pressed: the speed will not be reduced, it may even increase.

Going about or picking up a mooring needs careful judgement because multihulls are light, have little momentum, high windage and consequently lose way very quickly and then gather sternway. When stuck in irons, reversing the helm will bring the bow round but the technique is undoubtedly to shoot round, backwinding the headsail for a second or two to give the bow a final push. So when picking up a mooring under sail, you should get much closer to it before rounding up. This will certainly cause panic and consternation on the foredeck if your crew is used to sailing monohulls. However, having secured the mooring they will realise that the catamaran, being light, is not so difficult to hold.

Light weight and high windage mean that at anchor or on a mooring a multihull is more likely to be affected by the wind direction than by the tidal stream. This can be embarrassing in a tight anchorage, with the multihulls lying to the wind and the monohulls to the tide. However, as the multihull can often find some shallow corner unavailable to the deep keelers it is not too often a problem. When a catamaran is fitted with centreboards these can be partly lowered where it is desirable that the boat lies to the tide.

The excessive beam of a multihull can present difficulties. For yachtsmen who want to use the French canal system where the maximum beam is 5m or sometimes less, this restricts buyers of a modern catamaran to about 9.75m (32ft) LOA. Marina berthing can be expensive when beam is a function of price and you find yourself moored between much longer monohulls, although some marinas can usually find a berth at the end of a pontoon.

In gale force conditions, it is normally possible to continue under reduced rig – reefing down to storm jib or rolled up genoa, balanced by a suitably reefed main. Roller reefing headsails have made this job much easier, particularly on the Prouts where the headsail area is about twice as big as the main. However, most modern catamarans have a roller-furling headsail and a large slab-reefing mainsail with a reasonable amount of roach that drops down neatly into lazy jacks.

Multihull rigs tend to be quite different from those of monohulls. Firstly their beam allows for twin backstays. On cruising boats this makes it possible to have a very stable rig and a mainsail with generous roach without the need for running backstays. Often the mast is stayed with diamonds rather than shrouds and this makes for a potentially tight sheeting angle when sailing upwind. Performance multihulls often have rotating wingmasts, similar to those used on beach cats. These allow the mast and mainsail to form a more efficient aerodynamic shape and ultimately a more powerful sail plan. Carbon fibre spars, rotating or fixed, are becoming increasing popular on cruising multihulls.

Performance multihulls tend to carry about half as many sails as the equivalent monohull. This is partly due to reasons of weight, but also due to the multihull's characteristics. With multihulls a greater increase of windspeed is needed to force a sail change and they usually have a more dominant mainsail which, of course, is reefed rather than changed.

16.5 DEVELOPMENTS

16.5.1 HULL SHAPE

The evolution of hull shapes, for cruising multihulls has been quite different from their monohull counterparts. Wharrams are mostly built out of sheathed marine ply, and are V-sectioned to give useful resistance to leeway, but this results in narrow footroom and wide deckspace.

The Prouts opted for a canoe stern giving them a very quiet wake but also made them prone to hobby-horsing in critical wave lengths until they introduced bow bulbs, which dampen down the motion. Many manufacturers have long shallow keels, often fitted with a sacrificial shoe. These keels are small enough to maintain shoal draught but deep enough to grip the water without the use of centreboards. During the 1980s almost no cruising catamarans were fitted with centreboards, but there has been an about turn in recent years as designers have appreciated their value in improving windward performance.

Most modern cruising catamarans have a symmetrical hull section, semi-circular beneath the waterline, the size of which depends upon the necessary load carrying capacity of the yacht. An exception is the French-built Catana range where the hulls are angled outwards at the base to maximise overall beam.

16.5.2   STRUCTURE

Compared to a monohull, a multihull represents a far more complicated structure to engineer and build. In bad weather crucial parts of a multihull get thoroughly tested and these are typically the joints where the crossbeams meet the hulls, where the impact strains are enormous. Equally crucial is the middle beam structure as this carries the mast step. Many builders, even for production boats, use hi-tech, expensive materials such as Kevlar and carbon fibre to ensure this structure does not fail.

The other area where stress is evident is at the points where the bulkheads are attached to the hulls and deckhead. These are always worth checking on older boats, as the joints can be too soft, making for a sloppy fit all round and in storm conditions the bulkheads may pop out of their joints. If the hull is too flexible the bulkhead can cause vertical hairline cracks in the hull at that point, where impact from waves cause the hull sides to flex either side of the bulkhead.

While Prouts traditionally used to mount their masts on the cockpit bulkhead, on others the mast is supported by a massive composite or steel A-frame which stretches across the bridgedeck to spread the load to the hulls. Between the A-frame and the deck is a mast support and on top of this sits the mast tabernacle. Most modern catamarans have found another solution – moving the mast step forward of the saloon where it sits on a substantial double bulkhead arrangement.

The forward trampoline found on the old

MacAlpine-Downie cats has also undergone a renaissance and is to be found on many modern catamarans. This prevents bridgedeck pounding forward – as well as being excellent for sunbathing and a fun area for children to play on.

As multihulls often dry out it is essential that they have a rudder and keel system strong enough to allow this. The rudders in particular can be a problem. There have been many solutions to this. On the older Prouts the rudder was integral with a skeg beneath the canoe-shaped sterns. Others had transom-hung rudders with swinging or retractable blades, but these may suffer from a lack of grip when running before the wind in sizeable waves. Most popular these days are normal spade rudders where fixed keels give the rudders sufficient clearance to be well short of the ground when dried out.

16.5.3   CONSTRUCTION

All the early multihulls in the USA and Europe were constructed in marine plywood, either forced into the conventional shape or, more often, if they were designed to be amateur built, V-shaped like the Wharrams or hard chined like the Pivers or early O'Briens. Originally paint was all that protected the ply from water, and the integrity of the hull depended very much on the quality of the ply. Top quality Bruynzeel, though heavy, lasts for a very long time but some of the other cheaper imports will have a considerably shorter lifespan.

It soon became general practice to sheathe the ply with GRP in the form of chopped strand mat or woven cloth, or Cascover. The most popular form of wood construction today is the WEST System, where the wood is saturated in waterproof epoxy. This is an ideal, cost effective system for one-off construction.

Foam sandwich construction, although not invented by Derek Kelsall, has been imaginatively developed by him. Over the years Kelsall has refined this type of construction where glassfibre is laminated to a core of foam. His most successful building system using this material is his 'flat panel technique'. Huge flat panels of foam sandwich are laminated on a table 9m (30ft) long and 1.5m (5ft) wide. These panels are then used exactly like plywood sheets. He has refined this system by laminating the sheets so that they can be bent to form the underwater panels. The advantage of this system is that it saves many hours of construction time, and keeps the work of sanding and filling to a minimum.

Today nearly all production cruising multihulls are built in GRP. However GRP is a term that covers a huge range of materials. Today's manufacturers use glass in a variety of mats and cloths and in areas of high load, uni- or bi-directional fibres are usually specified. Some even use carbon fibre. Most significant has been their use of more modern resins which seem to offer better protection from osmosis, to the extent that some manufacturers are now offering guarantees against it.

Many top French builders have developed fast resin infusion systems and are vacuum bagging (15.7.5) laminates for an efficient wetting out.

In the racing world it is a very different story. Techniques for building multihulls have merged with those of building monohulls, carbon fibre with a Nomex core being the current state of the art specification. In France most yards prefer to build one-off racing boats in a female mould, but in the rest of the world, it seems one-offs are built over male moulds. Those with particularly big budgets are using specialist high modulus and high strength types of carbon fibre, particularly in the spars.

16.5.4 TRAILERABLE MULTIHULLS
As marina charges become more and more excessive in line with the increasing value of property, the attraction of a boat that you can tow home each weekend becomes apparent. The Telstar 26, a small trimaran with fairly basic accommodation for a conventional family of four was an early example and there are many still afloat.

The most significant aspect of the Telstar design was the system that enabled her amas to hinge down under the main hull on immensely strong hinges, so that the boat can easily be trailed behind a two-litre car.

More recent marques applying the same trailerable trimaran philosophy have been the successful Ian Farrier-designed trimarans built by Corsair Marine in California and the Dragonfly range built by Quorning Yachts in Denmark. Both started out with models of 25-27ft LOA and have since increased their ranges, keeping the accent on performance.

The Corsair trimarans use a clever cantilever system of raising and lowering the folding amas, which can easily be done singlehanded. Release two pins, wind on a winch and the crossbeams start to rise as the ama slides in beneath the flair in the mainhull. For their size the accommodation on these trimarans is a little cramped, but owners of these craft buy them for the thrill of fast sailing and are prepared to sacrifice some creature comforts.

The beauty of all these 'trailer sailers' is not only the added security and cost saving of having your boat parked in the garden, but also the facility of being able to avoid long and tedious

passages, and to be able to arrive at a distant cruising ground without wasting precious holiday time.

16.5.5 ENGINES
Trimarans are almost always powered by a single engine. They either have an outboard, operating on a sliding bracket as on the Telstar, or else a more conventional petrol or diesel engine under the cockpit driving through normal shafting.

On sailing catamarans up to 9m (30ft) outboards are still favoured, the most popular being the remarkably quiet Yamaha 9.9hp four-stroke. It gives good torque at quite low rpm and can push even a 30-footer along at an acceptable six knots without causing drag when not required. The bigger sizes of boat (where weight is less critical) have twin-engined installations, in small engine rooms separated from the accommodation by a watertight bulkhead and driving a conventional shaft. If the buoyancy aft is sufficient, the engines are mounted quite well aft, under the double berths and drive through outdrives.

16.5.6 OTHER APPLICATIONS
Quite distinct from the role of multihulls as boats for cruising or racing under sail, the catamaran in particular has lent itself to many other applications. Multihulls make very stable platforms on which new rigs have been developed including foils, wing sails, air propellers driving water screws and modern dipping lugsails. Jacques Cousteau even used a 32m catamaran for experiments with a Flettner rotor.

Catamarans have found a particular niche for themselves in powerboat racing. These craft consist of a wing between two hulls, forming a 'tunnel'. The wing provides lift in proportion to its size and the speed of the boat, thereby reducing the amount that the hulls are immersed – to the extent that the drive units are virtually all that is in the water at speed.

While catamarans initially made their impact on the inland circuit racing scene, it took some while for the same thing to happen in offshore racing. However in 1977 *Yellowdrama III*, designed by James Beard and built by Cougar Marine, won the Cowes/Torquay/Cowes race at an average speed of 65 knots and became the world's first class I catamaran to get the better of the long, sleek monohulls that had previously prevailed. By the time of the 1991 Cowes/Torquay race 30 of the 35 entries were catamarans.

A relatively recent development has been that of motor cruisers as catamarans where the slim, easily driven hulls give good speed and economy; the increased internal space, the lateral stability, especially in a following sea or at anchor in a swell is also a great improvement over single hull equivalents.

If powered catamarans have yet to make a real impact as pleasure craft, this is far from true so far as commercial applications are concerned. Their large and stable deck area makes them suitable for many roles, such as diving, fishing and survey work, and of course for carrying passengers.

Catamaran ferries are becoming increasingly common. Large and fast catamarans have been introduced on many short sea routes all around the world. Warships as well are turning to multihulls to give more stable gunnery platforms or higher chase and evasion speeds.

16.5.7   THE PRESENT MULTIHULL SCENE

As we have seen, the present multihull scene is very different from that of 10 or 20 years ago. In the UK, although the economic climate was partly responsible for the demise of many multihull manufacturers, by contrast solid throughout this has been Prout, who have survived through manufacturing to a consistent high quality.

There is, however, no lack of specialist designers in the UK whose excellent designs are being built on a one-off basis, such as John Shuttleworth, Darren Newton or Richard Woods.

One does not have to study the cruising multihull market too long to see that it has in fact polarised. There are the small performance trimarans and the larger more sedate cruising catamarans. It is telling for example that the smallest catamaran available from the large French manufacturers is 38ft long and a majority of their models fall into the 40-60ft category. Part of the reason for this is the availability of features that make boats of this size manageable by a crew of two, such as bow thrusters, furling headsails – both on and offwind – and electric winches and windlasses.

16.5.8   THE FRENCH CONNECTION

With the tremendous interest stirred up by the media about high performance multihulls in France, designers and builders there turned to cruising boats. Several small independent manufacturers sprang up and in the 1980s even Beneteau, the world's most prolific builder of yachts, introduced a model. The life of the radical looking Blue II was short though and Beneteau pulled out of the race when this series was discovered to have osmosis problems.

Today the largest multihull production builders are to be found in France.

16.5.9   MOCRA

The leading multihull organisation in the UK is the Multihull Offshore Cruising and Racing Association (MOCRA). MOCRA was formed in 1969 to encourage and foster the sailing of multihull cruisers and to help improve their seaworthiness; to protect the interests of owners and to offer help when required; to encourage cruising and racing in UK waters, and to disseminate information on multihulls. MOCRA is affiliated to the RYA and is recognised as the National Authority for British cruising and racing multihull sailors.

Membership Secretary: Mike Butterfield, Old Thatched House, Fairmile Avenue, Cobham, Surrey KT11 2JB. Tel 01932 862190. 101517.337@compuserve.com

16.6 BOOKS ABOUT MULTIHULLS

The Sailor's Multihull Guide by Kevin Jeffrey and Charles E. Kanter (Avalon House).

The Cruising Multihull by Chris White (Waterline).

Multihull Cruising Fundamentals by Chris White (Press media Publishing).

Multihull Seamanship by Dr Gavin LeSueur (Fernhurst).

Multihull Seamanship Illustrated by Gavin LeSueur (Press media Publishing).

Multihull Voyaging by Thomas Firth Jones (Adlard Coles)

The Catamaran Book by Brian Phipps (Fernhurst)

Catamaran Sailing by Derek Kelsall (Press media Publishing).

Cruising Catamarans (Amateur Yacht Society).

Design for Fast Sailing by Edmund Bruce and Henry Morss (Amateur Yacht Research Society).

Catamaran Racing by Kim Furniss and Sarah Powell (Fernhurst)

Chapter 17 Spars, Rigging, Ropes and Sails

CONTENTS

17.1 SPARS

17.1.1 MASTS – GENERAL

The mast of a sailing yacht supports the sails which drive her through the water. Most yacht masts depend on standing rigging to hold them in position, but a few are unstayed. In a typical cruising yacht the mast is relatively sturdy, and is kept as straight as possible by the standing rigging. A modern racing yacht mast is made as light and narrow as possible, and can be bent by varying amounts in order to optimise the set of the mainsail. This type of rig is more complicated, and must be carefully controlled, since any error may cause dismasting.

17.1.2 MASTS – MATERIALS AND CONSTRUCTION

Originally masts were made of solid timber – usually pine, or spruce for small racing yachts. It was not always easy to find suitable timber of uniformly good quality; so as better glues were developed it became feasible to build up a mast in sections. Short lengths of timber which might have been a source of weakness could then be rejected, and by reversing the natural grain of the wood in adjacent sections it was possible to minimise the risk of distortion as the timber matured. Hollow wooden masts were developed. The development of epoxy resins for structural joints and surface coating has allowed

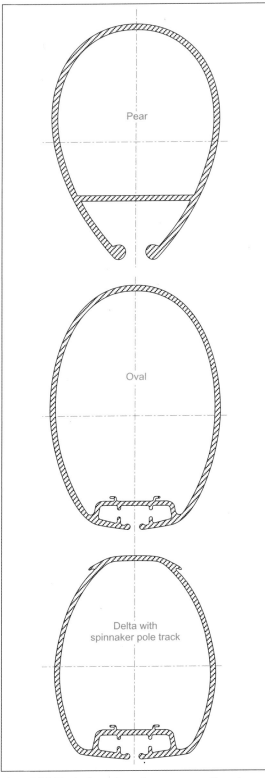

Fig. 17(1) Typical sections for a conventional mast. The chain dotted lines indicate the neutral axes of each section about which the areas of material on either side balance.

wood to be used in more adventurous ways.

Masts for large vessels such as sailing ships and the bigger yachts, were built up from steel plates, originally rivetted together but later of welded construction.

Aluminium alloy began to be generally adopted for yacht masts in the 1950s, and is now in almost universal use. The material has a tensile strength of about 20 tons per square inch, and an alloy spar can be about two-thirds the weight of a hollow one laboriously fashioned in silver spruce. Although aluminium masts are strong and relatively cheap, aluminium is not an ideal material in one important respect. An extrusion cannot have any variation in the wall thickness of a mast from heel to truck. Some racing mast sections are light weight, but have additional localised reinforcement.

Carbon fibre spars are considerably lighter than aluminium. But construction is very labour intensive and materials are relatively expensive, so overall production costs are increased by a large factor. At present, the technique is confined to very special applications.

Masts are manufactured from extruded tubes of the required section, Fig. 17(1), and incorporate a track or groove for the mainsail as required. After being extruded, the tubes are heat treated. This confers additional strength. At this stage, most mast sections are cleaned, chemically etched and then anodised. The anodised surface is very durable, and prevents surface corrosion.

Masts usually have a larger fore-and-aft dimension (and hence more resistance to bending), partly to resist the pull of the luff of the mainsail, but mainly because they have better support athwartships. The top of a mast may be tapered, reducing windage and weight. The benefits of tapering are more pronounced on a fractional rig. Spars for smaller yachts are made in one extruded length, but bigger masts can be constructed from two or more sections joined together.

Welding aluminium alloy requires specialist skills and equipment. Even minor repairs to masts (or other aluminium alloy spars) are usually beyond the capabilities of the average boatyard. During the welding process, localised changes are made to the material characteristics. If welding is done without due care, it can cause a localised weakening of a previously heat treated tube.

The mast is usually fitted out with various discrete components. These must be selected and secured with due regard for strength and resistance to corrosion and fatigue. Cast alloy components are usually compatible with

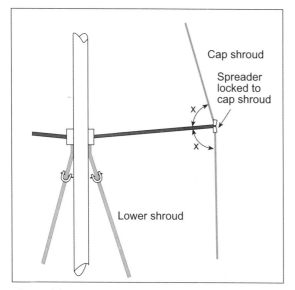

Fig. 17(2) It is important that the spreader bisects the angle of the cap shroud, and that it is locked to same.

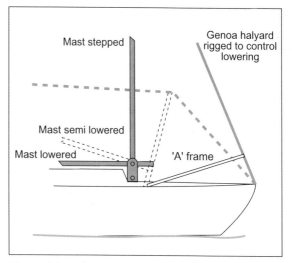

Fig. 17(3) 'A' frame rigged to control lowering of mast stepped on deck in tabernacle, using genoa halyard.

aluminium alloy, but brass or other copper-based alloys must be used with great caution. Stainless steel fittings such as shroud attachments and spreader brackets should be well insulated from the mast. The insulation may be nylon sheet, elastic sealing compound or zinc chromate paste. Many winches have bronze bases, which must be isolated from their mounting pad by some suitably inert material such as nylon or Tufnol. Rivets should be monel metal or stainless steel. Stainless steel machine screws are often used for high load applications, but must be well insulated. Self-tapping screws may be used for lightly loaded fittings, but must have their sharp points blunted to avoid damage to internal halyards.

17.1.3 BOOMS AND POLES
The construction of a boom is similar to that of an alloy mast, but the loads are completely different. A mast must resist high compression, but a boom must resist bending. Almost all modern booms are tall and narrow in section, having greater strength in the vertical plane; see Fig. 17(1). The section used depends on the yacht's power, boom length and mainsheet position. Round booms for roller reefing are rarely produced these days.

Spinnaker poles are circular in cross-section, and designed to resist compression. The diameter is selected by reference to pole length and the yacht's power. On medium and larger yachts, poles can be relatively heavy and difficult to handle. This is one instance where the benefits of carbon fibre outweigh the extra cost for some crews.

Whisker poles are subject to much lower loads than spinnaker poles, so are usually smaller in diameter. However, to be fully effective with a large overlap genoa, they may require to be longer than the spinnaker pole.

17.1.4 SPREADERS
The length of spreaders is usually determined by the naval architect, and relates to the chainplate position. Spreaders must be carefully designed, and their attachment to the mast must be well engineered. Modern spreaders are firmly fixed to the mast, which improves mast stability. Older types were usually allowed to swing fore-and-aft. It is most important that the outer end of the spreader is securely fixed to the cap shroud, and that it bisects the angle of the shroud. Normally therefore the spreader is cocked up about 5° or 6° above horizontal, see Fig. 17(2).

Some spreaders have clamps at the outer end for this purpose, otherwise bulldog grips can be used, well taped over to prevent any damage to sails.

Spreaders and their attachments are among the major components of a rig structure; any failure commonly causes dismasting.

17.1.5 MAST STEP
Masts on small and medium sized yachts are usually stepped on deck. This allows a more simple deck moulding, more flexibility in accommodation layout and avoids leaks at deck level. Larger yachts usually have their mast stepped on the keelson, and obtain support at the partners where they pass through the deck. This additional support usually allows a slightly lighter mast section to be used.

Some yachts have their mast stepped in a tabernacle or hinged heel fitting on deck, which allows the mast to be lowered for passing under bridges etc. As the mast is lowered, the effective angle between the forestay and the mast reduces, so some kind of frame must be rigged forward of the mast to serve as a strut, as shown in Fig. 17(3). Also, as the mast is lowered the tension on the shrouds is removed, and so it must be steadied laterally to avoid damage to the tabernacle or heel fitting.

17.1.6 MAINTENANCE

During the sailing season there is little actual maintenance to be done on aluminium alloy spars, but there is a continual need for inspection aloft to ensure that all is in order and to prevent trouble developing. Maintenance of standing rigging is discussed in 17.2.6, and should be done at the same time.

For going aloft a good bosun's chair is needed, preferably one with a safety belt to prevent the occupant slipping out. Modern bosun's chairs have handy pockets for tools and spares, but otherwise these can be hoisted separately in a bucket. Normally the main halyard is used – make sure that the shackle is properly screwed up. It is advisable to have a second halyard attached for safety, or the person going aloft may take a safety line which can be secured aloft. When anybody is aloft, a crewman should be in attendance below; somebody else might let go the halyard by mistake – it has been known!

Starting at the masthead check that halyard sheaves are free and in good condition. Take the weight of the halyard off each sheave in turn, to check the clearances in the bearings. Worn bushes or sheaves should be renewed before they cause halyards to wear or jam. A good wash down with fresh water to remove salt deposits from bearing surfaces will not come amiss, followed by lubrication. Use modern teflon-based fluid, gel or greases.

Examine all the fittings at the masthead, to make sure that pins are in good order and that the holes through which they pass are not elongated. Check all split pins for security. Look for any signs of cracks in the mast itself or in the attached cast fittings, and for any movement in screws or rivets. Unless these details are inspected methodically it is easy for something to be overlooked.

Coming down the mast check the security of the mast track, if externally fitted, and wash out the track so that the slides can run freely. Inspect each shroud fitting, check the security of any through-mast bolts, and look for any sign of distortion to the mast wall itself. Localised

bulging of the section can de detected by a slight change in colour.

At the spreaders, check that they bisect the shroud angle correctly, that the tips are secured to the shrouds where appropriate, and that anti-chafe arrangements are in place. See that the spreaders are secure in their sockets, and that the latter are properly attached to the mast with all securing arrangements tight and correct.

At deck level check round the main boom gooseneck, winch pads, cleats, sheave boxes etc, for any visual sign of deterioration. Carefully inspect cables where they pass though the mast wall. If the insulation is damaged, very rapid corrosion can develop. Only close inspection may detect a tiny crack in a weld or fitting on a mast, or an elongated hole which should be round; but these little details might save your mast, or even your life.

If the mast is lowered for the winter, the above maintenance can be done more searchingly and with relative ease. Spars should be washed with warm, fresh water to remove salt deposits. For preference, use soap. If detergent is used, traces may react with the alloy, so ensure that the spar is thoroughly rinsed. When completely dry, the spar can be cleaned with liquid wax polish and a soft (old) plastic pan scourer, then finally buffed with a cloth. Lightly oil all moving fittings.

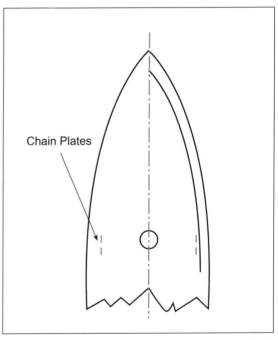

Fig. 17(4) Narrower sheeting angles for headsails require the chain plates to be set inboard from the deck edge, thereby narrowing the angle which a shroud makes with the mast aloft.

17.2 STANDING RIGGING

17.2.1 THE REQUIREMENTS

Standing rigging is intended to hold the mast straight and upright, or to control its required bend in the case of racing yachts. The rigging wires which hold the mast in the athwartships direction (sideways) are called shrouds; those which hold it fore-and-aft are stays.

The athwartships distance between shroud chainplates, together with the height of the mast, determines what angle a shroud will make to the mast at its point of attachment. In order that the shroud may provide sufficient athwartships pull, this angle needs to be as large as can be arranged; otherwise the shroud tension must be increased, which puts undue compression on the mast. A mast is essentially a strut in compression and under well established mechanical laws it will buckle at a certain load depending on its length, the moment of inertia (or strength) of its cross-section, the material, and how it is stepped (on the keel or on deck). The problem is exacerbated by the modern tendency to reduce the sheeting angle of headsails, making it necessary to set the chain plates inboard from the deck edge, see Fig. 17(4).

Consequently it is necessary for shrouds which run to or near the masthead to be provided with spreaders in order to increase the angle which they make to the mast. In Fig. 17(5) it is evident that the tension of the shroud bearing against

the end of the spreader is forcing the mast in the direction of the arrow.

Hence, in order to keep the mast straight, a lower shroud has to be fitted at this point. In cruising yachts there are commonly two pairs of lower shrouds, one set leading to the deck slightly forward of the mast and the other set slightly aft of it. The alternative is a pair aft of the mast, with a central stay (also known as a babystay or inner forestay) forward.

Fig. 17(6) and Fig. 17(7) show typical rigging arrangements in cruising yachts, and the names of the various components. In Fig. 17(6) the mast has only one pair of spreaders, a suitable layout for a typical masthead sloop.

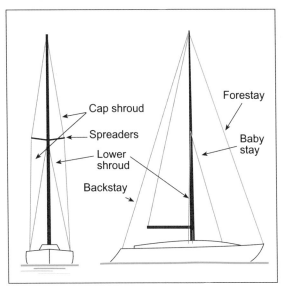

Fig. 17(6) Typical rigging for a masthead sloop.

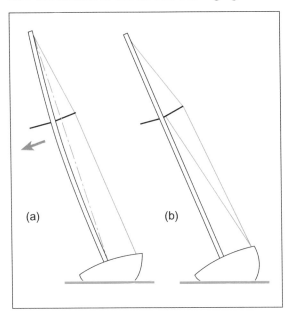

Fig. 17(5) In (a) the cap shroud bearing against the spreader bends the mast to leeward. The addition of a lower shroud (b), joining the mast at the spreaders, holds the mast up to windward at that point and keeps it straight.

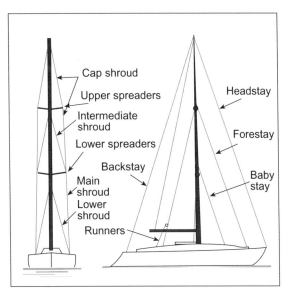

Fig. 17(7) Typical rigging suitable for a larger yacht, or one with cutter rig.

In Fig. 17(7) two pairs of spreaders are appropriate for a larger yacht, or one with cutter rig (two headsails). In special cases, particularly for racing yachts or larger vessels, more than two pairs of spreaders may be used. These two diagrams also show the stays which hold the mast fore-and-aft. With the sloop rig, this is done by the forestay and the backstay. The lower shrouds also help to steady the centre of the mast in the fore-and-aft plane, while an inner forestay (now usually referred to as a baby stay) may also be fitted at the height of the spreaders. The baby stay may be detachable, allowing it to be brought back to the mast in light conditions. This must be done with caution, as it is an essential part of the rig structure.

With a cutter rig some aft support must be provided to prevent the cutterstay from pulling the mast forward excessively. The most common options are jumper struts at the upper spreaders, aft intermediate stays (fixed) or running backstays. The first two options are usually preferred for cruising yachts, as they require no crew action. Running backstays (or runners) are lighter and less expensive, but must be set up in turn – the windward one being tensioned by a winch or lever, and the leeward one being slacked away clear of the boom and mainsail. Light runners (checkstays) are sometimes used on masthead rigs to prevent the mast pumping fore & aft when sailing to windward.

Racing yachts with in-line spreaders use runners for a different reason. Here, the windward runner actually holds the mast up; the backstay is only used to control mast bend.

On fractionally-rigged yachts with swept-back spreaders, the rig operates differently and runners are not recommended. The backstay is still used for bend control. The aft component of the cap shrouds' tension holds the mast up and tensions the forestay. Accept that the forestay will never be as tight as that on a masthead rig, or on a fractional racer with in-line spreaders and runners. The rig also keeps the foredeck clear, does not need runners and is forgiving – ideal for cruiser/racers. Importantly the cap shrouds also stabilise the middle of the mast, in the region of the spreaders. On the lee side the cap and aft lower shroud restrain the mast from describing an arc (wobbling) based on the windward rigging. The static tension in these shrouds must therefore be correct.

A few types of seagoing yacht have unstayed masts, eg those with modified Chinese lugsail (junk) rigs, and cat rigged yachts as in Fig. 17(38) with no headsails. These unsupported masts must necessarily be bigger and heavier, even though they are not subject to the compression loads which rigging imposes on an ordinary mast.

17.2.2   MATERIALS

The materials most commonly used for standing rigging are stainless steel rod and 1 x 19 wire rope. The 7 x 7 wire rope type is rarely used now. Cold drawn stainless steel rod is the simplest but most expensive type of standing rigging. It is usually circular in section, with threaded or specially formed bulb ends. Rod rigging has very little stretch for a given strength.and usually has less windage than wire rope types. But it does have some disadvantages, apart from its high cost. Because it is very rigid it must be laid out straight or carefully coiled in a big circle, and it is more prone to fatigue than other types of rigging. It is also brittle, and even minor damage to the surface can cause loss of strength. Trying to straighten a bent stainless steel fitting or rod rigging is likely to lead to early failure.

Wire rigging can be manufactured from galvanised wire or 316 specification stainless steel wire. Galvanised wire, which has a zinc coating, is much cheaper, rather stronger and more flexible than stainless steel wire. But it is not nearly so durable and does not look so nice.

Most yachts have standing rigging of 1 x 19 stainless steel wire, to specification AISI 316. Stainless steel can in fact stain under certain conditions, particularly if it is starved of atmospheric oxygen. A slight rusty-brown discolouration of the material itself is not serious, and can easily be removed. To avoid this, rigging screws (bottle screws) should **not** be taped over with adhesive tape. Rust inside a terminal or any sign of a broken strand indicate that the rope has reached the end of its life. Because it maintains a shiny appearance, stainless steel is likely to be ignored until a failure occurs. Galvanised wire will forewarn of failure by rusting first. Details of the construction and strength of wire ropes are given in 17.4.15 to 17.4.17.

17.2.3   WIRE RIGGING TERMINALS

Swaged and swageless terminals are amongst the various types of attachments to wire rigging, as discussed below:

Swaged terminals are the most commonly used type on stainless steel wire; see Fig. 17(8). They comprise a sleeve which fits closely over the end of the wire. With the wire inserted, the sleeve is squeezed on at very high pressure in a roll swage or rotary-hammer machine. If correctly done, the joint is as strong as the wire.

A well made swage should be straight, smooth sided and of constant diameter. If not perfectly formed, the swage (sleeve) may develop a hairline crack along the sides or at the end. Salt water or salt-laden air can cause corrosion here or at the grain boundaries of the

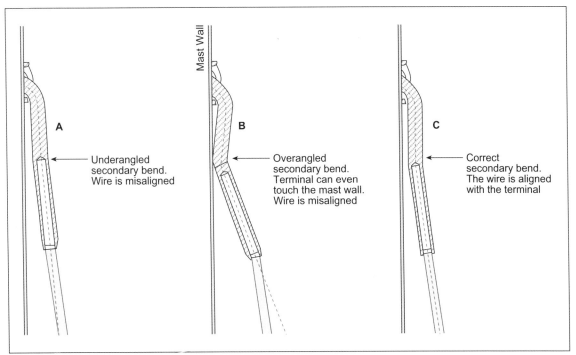

Fig. 17(8) Swaged terminals, showing misalignments which will lead to failure.

work-hardened stainless steel, which will lead to failure. Salty moisture may also settle in the minute spaces between the terminal and the wire, creating hidden pockets of corrosion. This is usually revealed by stains around the lip of the sleeve before they reach a critical stage. It is most important to examine such fittings very carefully, and at regular intervals. At the same time look closely at the wire rope for any signs of flattened and shiny strands adjacent to the swage, which indicate failure at this point.

Swageless screwed terminals, as made by Norseman and STALOK, are good alternatives to swaged terminals for stainless steel wire; see Fig. 17(9). They are attached to the wire without special tools or equipment, so they are ideal for use afloat, but are relatively expensive compared with swage terminals. The terminal can be routinely inspected by dismantling the assembly.

Emergency repairs to rigging can be done with bulldog grips, as shown in Fig. 17(10).

A seagoing yacht should carry a selection of these, in the correct sizes for the wire rope fitted. The grip consists of a U-shaped clamp, the two legs of the U being threaded. A drilled cross-piece fits over the legs of the U and is serrated on its inner edge to engage with the lay of the wire. The two lengths of wire within the U are compressed into the bend of the U by two nuts on the outside of the cross-piece. The short end of the wire should be against the U bend, and the longer standing part against the cross-piece.

Three grips, which must be the right size for the wire concerned, should be fitted alongside each other.

17.2.4 SHROUD ATTACHMENTS

At their upper ends, there are a number of methods by which shrouds are secured to the mast. They vary in strength, durability and cost.

External tangs are the traditional type, usually fitted to the mast with through bolts. The tang is usually a fork, and must be angled so that it is aligned with the associated shroud. If not aligned correctly, the cyclic load variation from the shroud will cause the tang to flex. Repeated flexing can lead to early fatigue failure. The shroud has a corresponding eye terminal/toggle, linked together with a clevis (cotter) pin.

The clevis pin, see Fig 17(11), must be a close fit within the toggle (or the fork end of a rigging screw) and the correct length, with the minimum longitudinal movement when secured in position by a good split pin. Split pins for such essential purposes should not be re-used after rigging has been removed for any reason, but should be replaced with new. A protective layer of tape reduces the possibility of sails or running rigging snagging on the ends of the split pin.

Propriety tangs are modern variants of External tangs. They are usually set into a specially shaped cutout, designed to optimise the transfer of shroud tension into the relatively thin mast wall. The top shroud terminal is usually an eye, which is permitted to self align.

Hook-in terminals (T-Terminal or T-Ball Terminal) are the most common current method

1. Place terminal body on the strand or rope as the case may be. Unlay the outer wires or strands from the centre strand.	2. Fit cone, with the centre strand protruding through the hole in the cone 1-1½ times the full diameter of the strand or rope.	3. Form the outer wires or strands back into position, evenly spaced around the cone.	4. Group all the protruding wires into the blind recess of the terminal end component (eye, fork, stud, etc). Offer the terminal body up to the end component and start mating the threads.	5. Complete the assembly turning the appropriate component in the direction of lay of the strand or rope, as shown in the sketch. Tighten until the resistance indicates that the cone is being compressed into the body of the terminal. DO NOT OVERTIGHTEN, as this is unnecessary and may damage the threads.
 1	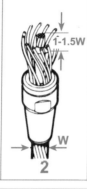 1-1.5W W 2	 3	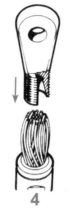 4	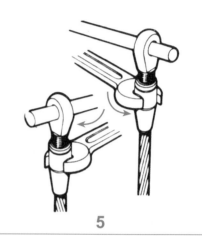 5

6. Unscrew to inspect and ensure wires are evenly spaced and neatly closed over the cone. Apply thread locking adhesive to the threads.	7. Apply non-corrosive marine adhesive sealant into the blind hole and assembly and screw up the assembly. Repeat if necessary until sealant oozes from the body end. Wipe clean. NB The wires and strands in a Norseman Swageless assembly have a progressive compression load upon them with the maximum at the top of the body taper. This minimises the 'working' of the stainless steel for longer and safer service.
 6	 7

Fig. 17(9) How to fit Norseman swageless terminals.

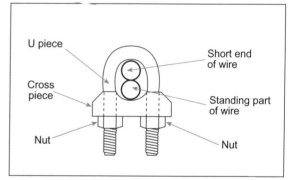

Fig. 17(10) Bulldog grip, for emergency repairs. The wires must be assembled as shown and described.

of shroud attachment for small and medium sized yachts. These articulate more freely than the traditional tang, but as they act like a crane hook, must be carefully designed, tested and manufactured. It is essential that the long swaged part of the terminal is in line with the wire. When the rigging is made, the manufacturer may have to adjust the terminal's secondary bend to achieve perfect alignment. This adjustment should be considered as part of the overall manufacturing process, and will enhance the terminal's fatigue life; see Fig. 17(8).

Stemball terminals are similar to hook-in types, but their hemispherical heads are contained within a matching fitting. Providing that they are able to articulate freely, allowing the long swaged part to align with the wire, they are as durable as any other type.

All such fittings aloft should be examined at regular intervals. To reduce windage and turbulence round the mast, racing yachts usually opt for a more sophistocated arrangement for shroud attachments.

Shrouds are tensioned at their lower ends by

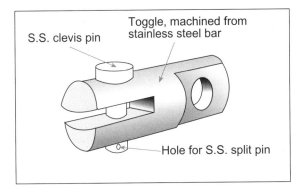

Fig. 17(11) Toggle terminal with clevis pin.

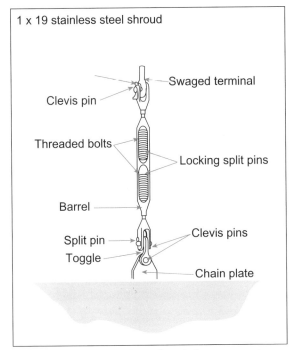

1 x 19 stainless steel shroud

Fig. 17(12) The wire shroud ends in a swaged terminal. This is connected by a clevis pin (secured by a split pin) to the upper fork end of the rigging screw. The lower fork end of the rigging screw is connected to the chain plate by a toggle, which allows freedom of movement in all directions.

rigging screws, which should be secured to the chainplates by toggles, as shown in Fig. 17(12).

The chainplates must be carefully designed and made, and securely fastened to the hull. They must be at the correct angle for the pull to be exerted on them. Like other rigging fittings, they are liable to wear and should be examined regularly.

A toggle, shown in Fig. 17(11), is a form of universal joint which allows the rigging screw to move in any direction – both to avoid damage to the rigging screw and also to minimise fatigue in the rigging wire where it enters the terminal

above the rigging screw. The clevis pins in toggles must of course be secured by split pins and inspected as for those in mast tangs referred to above. Forestays should be fitted with toggles at their upper and lower ends.

Rigging screws (also known as turnbuckles or bottle screws) are available to various designs, and in different materials, but basically they all consist of a central body which is threaded internally, right-handed at one end and left-handed at the other, Fig. 17(12). Into this central body are threaded bolts which have either eye, fork or stud ends – to match up with the rigging and with the toggle attached to the chainplate. Obviously, one of these bolts is threaded right-hand, and the other is threaded left-hand. When the central body is turned, the threaded ends protruding from it are either pulled together or pushed apart. Some means must be provided to prevent the rigging screw rotating under load. On open bodied rigging screws, this is often split pins, but modern options include propriety snap-on clips or even integral locking blocks. Closed body bottlescrews are usually secured with lock nuts.

In many sailing yachts the forestay is of fixed length (although some means may be provided for adjusting it, and hence the rake of the mast). The fore-and-aft tension of the rig is controlled by the permanent backstay. Modern rigs for racing yachts depend very much on proper control of backstay tension whereby mast bend, the shape of the mainsail and tension of the forestay (supporting the genoa) are correctly adjusted for optimum performance. Cruising yachts benefit from adequate forestay/backstay tension, particularly when fitted with a headsail furling gear. In smaller yachts the backstay may be controlled by a simple purchase or rigging screw, but more commonly tension is adjusted by a handwheel or lever operated tensioner.

More sophisticated are hydraulic backstay tensioners, with which even higher loadings can be achieved for larger yachts. It is important that such tensioners have some form of pre-set maximum load device, to avoid possible damage to the rig by overloading.

17.2.5 SETTING UP THE RIG

These notes are intended to give guidance on setting up the standing rigging for the average cruising yacht, so that it is safe and secure for any weather likely to be met, and allows the sails to set as well as possible. They do not apply to the more detailed tuning required for the mast of a racing yacht, which is a continuous process through the racing season.

The exact procedure depends on the type of rig, and every yacht needs somewhat different treatment according to the type of mast, how it is stepped, and details of the rigging plan. For our purpose we will assume that the yacht is a masthead sloop, and that the mast has a single pair of spreaders with two pairs of lower shrouds.

There is only one way that standing rigging can properly be set up, and that is under sail in smooth water in a breeze of about force 3 – 4.

Before reaching this stage, initial adjustments must be made in harbour. First, ensure that the rigging screw threads are clean and lubricated, and also that the boat is in normal trim – not down by the bow or stern. Adjust the mast fore-and-aft so that it stands with a slight rake aft. This can be judged by letting the main halyard hang down the aft side of the mast. In a l0m (33ft) LOA boat it lies about 200mm (8in) aft of the mast at deck level. This is only an initial setting, which may need adjusting later. Check, tighten and lock the forestay and backstay accordingly; they should be quite tight, because the forestay has to support the luff of the genoa when sailing.

Check that the mast is not leaning to port or starboard. To do this, take the main halyard's upper end down to the chainplates on each side in turn, and adjusting the cap shrouds until the two measurements are the same. Now tighten the upper (cap) shrouds equally each side, so that they both have almost the same tension as the forestay. Then adjust the lower shrouds each side so that they have similar tension to the cap shrouds, and that the mast is pulled forward slightly at the spreaders.

If the mast is keel-stepped, it should now be chocked in position at the partners (where it passes through the deck). The chocks can be special hard rubber pads, or similar. There should be unfilled gaps on either side of the mast, allowing some lateral movement. Shaped wooden wedges were commonly used, but can be unkind to thin walled aluminium masts.

Now the boat is ready to go sailing – as soon as conditions are suitable. Under full sail, beat to windward, and adjust the leeward cap shrouds on alternate tacks. The optimum is achieved when, at 18°-20° heel, the lee rigging just starts to slacken. Be careful to tighten both sides an equal amount by counting the turns of the rigging screws.

Next set up the lower shrouds in a similar way. The aim is to eliminate any lateral bend in the mast – which can be checked quite easily by squinting up the mainsail groove or mast track from a position underneath the gooseneck. When adjusting the lowers shrouds (and babystay), ensure that the prebend (forward deflection on the mast at the spreaders) is retained.

This can take some time to get right, and it is best to have one person doing the adjusting, another looking up the mast, while a third sails the boat. During this process check the balance of the boat on the helm. Mast rake is not the only cause of weather (or lee) helm, but it can be a major factor, and initial sailing trials may show that the masthead should be moved slightly forward or aft. Depending on the type of fitting, adjusting the forestay to achieve less or more rake may have to await return to harbour.

Rigs with two (or more) sets of spreaders are obviously more difficult to tune, since there are more variables, but the same basic principles apply. To facilitate adjustments it is best if all rigging screws are at deck level. The cap shrouds (which run to or near the masthead) must be fixed to the ends of the upper spreaders, but be free to run through the ends of the lower spreaders. If the intermediate shrouds are continuous from chainplate to mast attachment, they must be firmly fixed to the end of the lower spreaders. Some masts have discontinuous rigging, so the intermediates usually have a rigging screw at the tip of the lower spreaders. If the changes are large, the whole process under sail should be repeated.

When the best possible adjustments have been made, lock all rigging screws and tape over any exposed sharp items. The rigging of a new boat takes a little time to bed in, so after sailing a few times in medium strength winds, the rigging should be set up again.

17.2.6 MAINTENANCE

Routine inspections of the standing rigging aloft should be carried out at the same time as the inspection of other mast items, as described in 17.1.6. Standing rigging which can be inspected from deck level should be examined more frequently.

Inspection of standing rigging should cover:

1. The wires themselves for any signs of stranding or deterioration particularly with stainless steel wires adjacent to rigging terminals, where flattened strands with a shiny appearance indicate failure. Stainless steel wire requires no real maintenance, but galvanised wire will have a longer life if it is washed down periodically, and treated with boiled linseed oil. Any wire which is rusty or has broken strands should be condemned, and the condition of galvanised wire can also be judged by bending it to see how it reacts: if it stays bent, or straightens very slowly, it should be replaced.
2. Rigging terminals (swaged or swageless), for any signs of cracks, hole elongation, security of clevis pins and split pins.

3. Winches, tackles or other tensioning devices for backstays.
4. Chain plates, forestay fittings, backstay fittings – for general condition of securing arrangements, welds etc.

A portable, electronic non-destructive testing system is available for yacht rigging. It passes a very small current through the item on test (shrouds and stays) and measures the resistance at the terminal connection. This can detect faults not visible by eye; each fitting can be itemised and the resistance readings printed out for future comparison.

If the mast is unstepped for the winter, take the opportunity to examine thoroughly all the standing rigging. Ideally it should be labelled, removed from the mast, well washed and dried, and (for galvanised wire) treated with boiled linseed oil. Before storing away in the dry, examine each wire closely throughout its length, and bend it slightly where it enters the rigging terminals to check for any signs of broken strands.

The life of standing rigging depends somewhat on the use of the boat, but generally it is recommended that a cruiser's rigging be replaced after ten years use.

17.2.7 RIGGING FAILURES AND DISMASTING

In the event of a rigging failure the first action is to try to save the mast by minimizing the strain on it. For example, if a weather shroud parts, go about on the other tack; if the forestay carries away, run off before the wind. Then consider reducing sail, and either repairing the damage or rigging a jury shroud or stay. A genoa halyard can be set up as a temporary forestay, while the main halyard or even the topping lift might be utilised as a backstay. A halyard or the spinnaker pole lift can be pressed into service as a temporary shroud, sufficient to steady the mast on the leeward side while more permanent repairs are done.

Provided it can be reached, and this may be a problem, a parted wire can be repaired by using bulldog grips to form loops at the two broken ends, and then shackling a handy-billy between the two loops and setting it up tight. If a mast fitting fails it may be possible to pass a strop round the mast and over a spreader, to provide a temporary anchorage for a jury shroud.

Often however, when an item of standing rigging fails, the mast will break and/or go over the side. If a mast is actually falling it is better to bear away immediately, so that it drops into the sea rather than onto the deck and occupied cockpit.

The first priority is to try to recover the

Fig. 17(13) Jury rigged mast: Spinnaker pole lashed to stump of broken mast, and stayed by lines leading to the samson post, cleats etc.

wreckage from the sea, so that it does not damage the hull. If this is not possible it must be cut adrift, using bolt cutters. Salvage whatever is available for use as a jury rig; Fig 17(13). Do not start the engine until it is certain that all the rigging has been removed from the water, and there is no possibility of fouling the propeller.

The jury rig which can be devised depends very much on what gear, especially spars, is available. If the mast has been lost completely it should be possible to use the spinnaker pole or perhaps the main boom as a jury mast (set up with stays/shrouds rigged from sheets or warps), on which at least a small headsail can be set as a trysail.

17.3 RUNNING RIGGING

17.3.1 COMPONENTS AND FUNCTIONS

Running rigging comprises the numerous lines such as halyards, sheets, guys, lifts, downhauls, outhauls etc (together with their various snap shackles, blocks, cleats and the like) which hoist and control the set of the sails of a yacht. In a small boat these can be controlled by hand, or with simple tackles, but in larger yachts powerful winches and other mechanical devices have to be used.

Fig. 17(14) shows the principal running rigging of a modern masthead sloop. Some of the lesser items will be described separately.

Halyards

Halyards need to hold the luff in constant tension, often for long periods, so they should stretch as little as possible. Traditionally halyards were made from flexible wire, with a rope tail

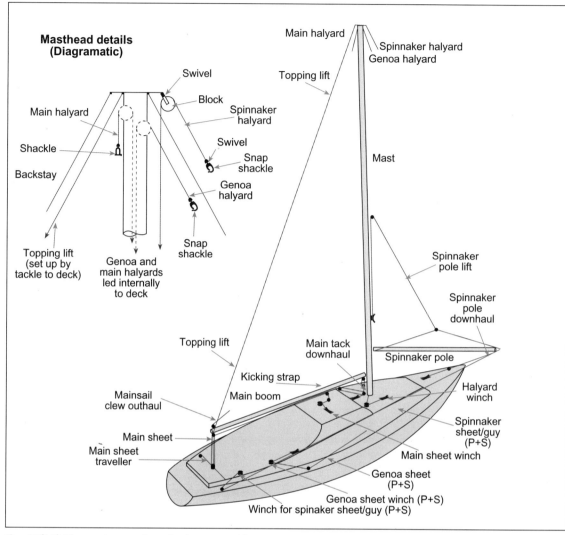

Fig. 17(14) The main running rigging on a 10m masthead sloop. For clarity the portside running rigging, all standing rigging and other details are omitted.

for easy handling. This wire rope had to be much more flexible than that used for standing rigging, because it had to pass over sheaves and around winches. Hence it had a larger number of smaller wires – typically 7 x 19 construction with a fibre core. Sheaves would have been 12 times the diameter of this type of halyard wire.

The handling problems of wire/rope halyards caused many yachtsmen to change to rope. Modern ropes are available in a multitude of specifications, and have virtually replaced flexible wire. Types of cordage and wire rope, together with their properties and strengths, and notes on their splicing, handling and maintenance, are described in 17.4.

Windage and noise generated by halyards are reduced by running them down inside the mast. The main halyard is shackled to the headboard

of the mainsail, whereas genoa and spinnaker halyards are normally fitted with snap shackles which need to be cleaned and lightly oiled from time to time to keep them free and secure.

Sheets

Sheets have to be frequently adjusted, and move continuously as the sail loads vary, so a slight amount of stretch is more acceptable. In any case they need to be easy to handle, so they must be made of rope, except for the largest yachts, where wire may still be used. Sheets are subject to chafe, so this should be minimised both for safety and economy. Blocks should be of sufficient size (with sheaves at least five times the diameter of the rope), and correctly aligned for the direction of pull. Chafe can be massively reduced by fitting plastic tubing or similar anti-chafe protection around shrouds, rigging screws and the like. It pays to buy sheets slightly overlength, because the points of wear can then be moved round to give a longer life.

The mainsheet must be powerful enough to control the mainsail in all foreseeable conditions, its large sheaved swivel blocks free to take up the necessary alignment according to the position of the boom. In modern yachts the lower block of the mainsheet is usually secured to a traveller, mounted on a track which runs athwartships.

The position of the traveller is controlled by tackles, and has a considerable influence on the set of the mainsail. Going to windward in moderate conditions the traveller should be about the middle of the track, but in stronger winds or when reaching it should be moved to leeward. In light airs the traveller may be brought up to windward, and the mainsheet eased, to give more fullness in the mainsail. The set of the mainsail is also controlled by the clew outhaul and the kicking strap (or boom vang).

The main clew outhaul controls the tension in the foot of the mainsail, which has a large effect on the shape of the whole sail. It may be a simple lashing, or a tackle which runs either along or inside the boom, or some kind of screw gear in older yachts. The clew outhaul should be tensioned as required before hoisting the mainsail, adjusted as necessary while under way, and always slacked off when the mainsail is lowered on return to harbour. More tension is required in the clew outhaul when sailing on the wind in a strong breeze, and less when sailing on the wind in lighter airs or when sailing with the wind free.

Tension on the luff of the mainsail is usually adjusted by the main boom gooseneck being moved up and down on a short track attached to the aft side of the mast, as controlled by a tackle rigged down to deck level. By taking down on this tackle the luff tension is increased, pulling the flow in the sail further forward. In some traditional yachts the halyard is used to tension the luff. A Cunningham luff (tackle) achieves the same aim.

Other running rigging

The function of the kicking strap (or boom vang) is to keep the boom down, and reduce the twist in the mainsail towards the head. In a small yacht it may also help to impart mast bend. Reducing twist mainly applies once the mainsheet is eased, ie when the boat is reaching. In most yachts the kicking strap consists of a tackle, leading from the underside of the boom forward to a position on the aft side of the mast at deck level, thence aft to the cockpit. A more sophisticated arrangement, is a gas spring (gas kicker) or hydraulically-operated strut which combines the functions of kicking strap and topping lift.

One other item of gear worthy of mention is the boom guy (or preventer). Its function is to steady the boom in a following wind and sea, and to prevent an accidental gybe. This is led from the outboard end of the boom, forward to a block near the bow, and back to the cockpit. On some yachts, the aft part of the preventer is permanently attached to the boom. Thus when you want to use the preventer, the inboard end is within easy reach and the preventer can readily be attached to it with a snap shackle. Because it is there, the preventer actually gets used.

Reefing systems for mainsails and headsails are given in detail under 'Sails' in 17.5.4 and 17.5.5.

Spinnaker gear

In smaller yachts the spinnaker sheets and guys are interchangeable, the windward one to the end of the spinnaker pole being called the guy and the leeward one to the clew of the spinnaker being the sheet. On the opposite gybe their roles are reversed. Larger yachts have separate guys and sheets. The sheets/guys are led outboard of all other rigging to blocks which are fitted right aft each side of the boat, and thence to winches.

The spinnaker pole is clipped to a traveller on a track secured to the forward side of the mast, so that the height of the heel of the pole can be adjusted according to the wind strength and the point of sailing. A topping lift and a downhaul control the height of the outer end of the spinnaker pole.

When the spinnaker pole is trimmed well forward, with the wind almost on the beam, the effective angle of pull of the guy is greatly reduced, making it difficult to pull the spinnaker pole aft. To improve control, a jockey pole is rigged athwartships at the mast, with a sheave at its outer end. This pushes the guy further outboard and increases its effective angle relative to the pole. The jockey pole also keeps the spinnaker guy clear of shrouds, guardrails and stanchions – avoiding mutual damage.

Fittings used with running rigging

More and more fittings are used with running rigging, all aimed to combine strength with lightness, and mechanical simplicity with ease of operation. For full details of what are currently on offer it is best to consult the illustrated catalogue of a good chandler, mail order company or manufacturer. Fig. 17(15) shows just a few of the more common items of gear. On many cruising yachts a variety of halyards, reefing lines and other control lines are led aft to the cockpit where they can be worked in safety without having to go forward to the mast. A line will typically exit the foot of the mast via a

Fig. 17(15) Items of gear for use with running rigging.

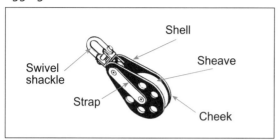

Single block with swivel. Typically made from glass fibre filled nylon, with stainless steel reinforcement and sheaves mounted on ball bearings.

Fiddle block with fixed eye. Since the sheaves are in the same plane, this type of block is less likely to twist than a double block, if the sheaves turn in the same direction.

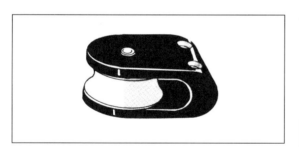

Turning block. The sheave runs on stainless steel ball bearings.

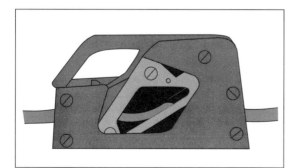

Rope clutch, released by the lever on top, even when under load. Jammers are used on larger boats where the greater load has to be taken up on a winch before the jammer can be released.

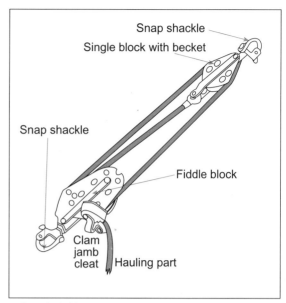

A handy-billy.

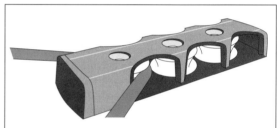

Deck organiser with triple sheaves.

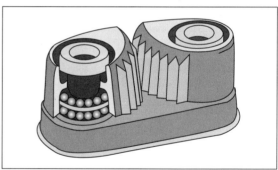

Cam cleat used to secure a fairly lightly loaded rope; it may be part of a mainsheet block.

Genoa sheet car, adjustable on deck-mounted track, gets the sheet as near the deck as possible.

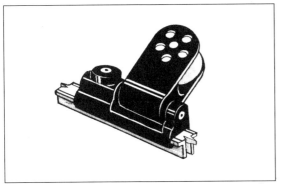

Double block with swivel and becket. Ensure that the sheave is wide enough for the rope, and that its diameter is at least five times the rope diameter, ie sufficient to allow the rope to render round it easily.

Snatch block with swivel. The shell is hinged so that one side can be opened to allow the bight of a rope to be inserted.

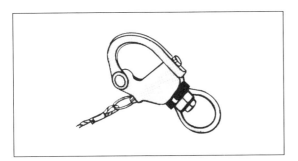

Snap shackle with swivel eye. A short lanyard is attached to the ring which releases the plunger.

General purpose cleat. All deck fittings must be through-bolted, with generous pad pieces and washers under the deck. A cleat should be secured so that its centreline is about 15° off the line of pull of the rope belayed to it.

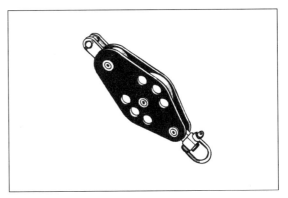

Fiddle block with swivel and becket. The standing part of the rope is made fast to the becket.

block, thence through a deck organiser (of up to six turning sheaves), and aft via a clutch, or stopper, to the winch. Clutches allow a tensioned line to be secured (and easily released), thus freeing the winch for other tasks.

A handy-billy (or luff tackle) can be used for various tasks. It is made up of a single block with a becket, to which is attached the standing part, and a fiddle block. That shown has a cam jamb cleat on the fiddle block. Snap shackles at each end allow the handy-billy to be used easily for a number of tasks. When rigged to advantage (with the single block fixed) the mechanical advantage is 4:1. When rigged to disadvantage (with the fiddle block fixed) it is 3:1.

17.3.2 MAINTENANCE

Chafe is the greatest enemy of running rigging, and it is easy to spot where the maximum wear is likely to occur in any particular rope. For example, a halyard suffers most where it bears on the masthead sheave, where it passes round an exit sheave on the mast, and where it is turned up on winch and cleat when the sail is hoisted. These areas are likely to fail long before the rest of the rope, unless this is crippled in some way by careless handling.

Where feasible, it pays to make up running rigging slightly over-length in the first place, so that its life can be extended by removing a worn end or equalising the wear along the rope. Some items of running rigging can be turned end for end to extend their life.

A yacht on an extended cruise should carry sufficient wire (carefully preserved) to make up a replacement halyard of the maximum length required, as well as spare cordage for other items such as sheets. All sheaves should be examined and lubricated at frequent intervals. If a sheave does not turn freely in a block it will soon damage the rope passing over it.

Fig. 17(16) A modern, 2 speed, self-tailing winch by Harken, showing the precision engineering, multiple roller bearings and rugged construction. Power ratios are 13:1 and 53:1.

When a halyard has to be removed from inside a mast, it should be replaced by a thin line known as a messenger (or mouse). If a halyard has parted inside a mast, a messenger will have to be passed through the mast ready for the replacement. This can be done by securing a short length of thin but flexible (bicycle) chain to a messenger. First set up all other internal halyards as tight as possible, to avoid twists in the halyard inside the mast. Then the messenger is passed over the masthead sheave, eased down inside the mast, and finally "fished" out of the lower exit by a wire hook.

17.3.3 WINCHES

Winches provide the power for hoisting and trimming sails, and for other tasks relating to a yacht's running rigging. The power which a winch develops is the ratio between the distance moved by the handle and the distance moved by the drum's surface. The power ratio of a simple direct action sheet winch in a small yacht might be 7:1. Power ratio is more meaningful than gear ratio, which is the number of turns of the handle for one turn of the drum; see Fig. 17(16).

Larger yachts need much more powerful winches to sheet home big genoas. But a winch with a power ratio of 46:1 would take a long time to take down the slack of a sheet before the higher power is really needed. So bigger sheet winches are two speed, or even three speed. A two speed winch might have power ratios of 7:1 and 30:1, obtained by rotating the handle in opposite directions. A three speed winch might give ratios of 5:1, 17:1 and 48:1, selected by a button on top of the winch drum, as well as reversing the direction of the handle.

Winches are accurately machined to close working tolerances, and for reliability they must be regularly dismantled, cleaned and greased, with special winch grease, according to the maker's instructions. It is sensible to have on board spare parts, including pawl springs which are notoriously easy to lose overboard.

Modern sheet winches are often 'self-tailing', ie the sheet is automatically kept taut on the winch drum and the winch can then be operated entirely by one person. A non-self tailer can be inexpensively converted to self-tailing with a 'Wincher', which is a strong rubber moulding fitted tightly over the top rim of the winch, so that it grips the sheet very effectively.

Winches normally turn clockwise, viewed from above, and the turns must be put on in that same direction. When pulling in a sheet or hauling a halyard first take in as much slack as possible by hand, then put on a single turn and continue to haul. Always keep your hands well away from the winch drum in case the rope takes charge and traps your fingers. As soon as any real strain comes on the rope put on a second turn, still hauling. Before winching in with the handle, ensure that at least three turns are on the drum. Putting on too many turns too soon encourages riding turns, as does pulling on the rope before it reaches the winch drum. Too few turns will allow the rope to slip on the drum.

Usually one person 'tails' the sheet or halyard, maintaining the tension of the rope round the drum, while another operates the winch handle. The lead of a rope to the drum must be such as to avoid the risk of a riding turn, ie when a turn rides up over the one above it and jams. Often a riding turn can only be cleared by taking the load off the winch. One way of doing this is by securing another line to the sheet with a rolling hitch, and then leading this line to another winch. Another method is by passing a stopper (see 17.4.8).

When winching is completed, cleat up the rope, remove and stow the winch handle. Often, halyards and reefing lines are led aft from the foot of the mast to winches in the cockpit, being rove through a clutch or stopper before reaching the winch. Thus when the rope is hard in, first engage the clutch or stopper, then take the rope off the winch, freeing it for other work.

When a sheet (say) which is under load around a winch is to be eased or let go, keep tension on the tail and uncleat it. Then, Fig. 17(17), reduce tension while carefully veering the turns around

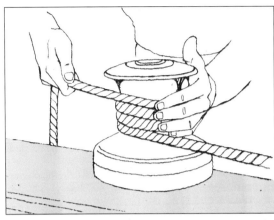

Fig. 17(17) Easing a sheet under load on a winch.

the drum with the palm of the hand (keeping fingers clear of possible danger). When tacking, once the load is off the sheet, the turns can be taken off the drum by twirling the tail from above.

The Editor acknowledges with Very Many Thanks the extensive technical help freely given by my former RN colleague, John Passmore of Selden Masts, in revising Sections 17.1 to 17.3 and 17.5.4 & 17.5.5.

17.4 ROPES

17.4.1   INTRODUCTION

Rope is a vital material for yachtsmen. Different types of rope are used for mooring, anchoring and, in sailing yachts, to hoist and trim their sails. Rope construction is fascinating, as are the many ways in which it can be used and knotted. A yachtsman should know how to use, handle and take care of rope; and to understand what type and size of rope is required for a given task.

Technical information on ropes has been supplied by BMIF, Technical Dept and by English Braids Ltd (Marine Division), Spring Lane, Malvern Link, Worcs WR14 1AL. Tel 01684 892222; Fax 01684 892111. info@english braids.com   www.english braids.com   The editor is grateful to both BMIF and English Braids for their kind assistance.

17.4.2   CONSTRUCTION

Traditionally most yacht ropes were made of three strands, and this form of construction is still used for mooring warps. Fibres are twisted in one direction to form yarns, and a bundle of yarns is twisted in the other direction to make a strand. Then three strands are twisted in the original direction to make a rope. This alternate twisting produces a rope of stable construction which does not tend to unravel, and where the load is distributed evenly. Three-strand rope is

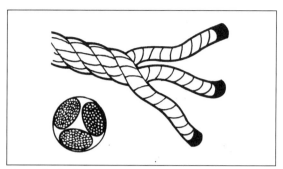

Fig. 17(18) Three-strand rope, hawser laid, ie three strands twisted together to form a rope, normally right-hand construction.

usually hawser-laid, which means that the strands are twisted together right-handed as in Fig. 17(18). Hawser-laid ropes are used in the fishing industry, on lorries and other economy applications. Cable-laid ropes look similar, but are constructed with an extra cabling stage and are laid-up left-handed; they are well suited to yachts' mooring warps, but have been replaced by braided ropes for most other applications.

Three-strand rope will kink unless properly coiled in the direction in which the strands are laid, clockwise for a right-handed rope. Plaited or braided ropes are used for sheets and other running rigging, however, because they work best in stoppers, clutches and jammers as fitted to cruising and racing yachts. They are made from inter-twined strands in various forms of construction, eg a three-strand rope encased in a braided cover, quite possibly of different materials. Double braided (or braid-on-braid) rope is made up of two single braided ropes, one inside as a core and the other forming a protective outer sheath, as illustrated in Fig. 17(19).

Or a low-stretch rope may have an outer braided polyester jacket, for example, with an inner braid around a core of parallel fibres, perhaps of polyester but increasingly of more exotic and expensive materials such as Dyneema or Spectra (see 17.4.3).

Braided ropes consist of 8 or 16 strands plaited together to form a close woven cord, with or

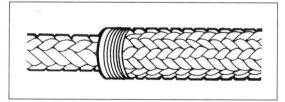

Fig. 17(19) Braid-on-braid – a double braided rope. A braided sheath and braided core combine to give very high strength.

without a central core depending on the application. In general, braided ropes have less stretch than laid ones of the same size, and are less prone to distortion. For some special applications a rope's cover can be 36-plait, giving a good feel to the rope and providing excellent protection against chafe.

Anchorbraid is a braided nylon rope made up of 8 strands, 4 laid up left-handed and the other 4 right-handed. The rope is open construction, therefore easy to splice to chain; it is strong, durable and stretchy.

17.4.3 MATERIALS

Almost all yacht ropes are made from synthetic fibres. **Nylon** is still the strongest rope in general use, though more exotic (and much dearer) materials have been developed for special applications in racing yachts. Nylon has excellent shock-absorbing properties, so is very suitable for anchor warps particularly in braided or plaited form. It is a soft rope, made from fine fibres, and is pleasant to handle; but it is too stretchy to be used for running rigging. In either three-strand or plaited form it is good for mooring warps.

Polyester (Terylene or Dacron) is the most common general purpose material for ropes; although slightly less strong it does not stretch as much as nylon. It has good resistance to wear, and is widely used for warps and cordage. Plaited or braided forms are very suitable for halyards and sheets. In small boats halyards may be entirely of pre-stretched polyester, which is heat set during manufacture to reduce stretch in service.

Polypropylene ropes are not as strong as nylon or polyester, but are lightweight and float. They are made in soft, multifilament form or in a hard monofilament or split film form. The latter is usually only used for water ski lines. In its three-strand form polypropylene can be used for mooring warps but should be slightly larger in size than polyester for the same purpose. Modern versions contain a UV inhibitor.

Kevlar is a trade name for an aramid (aromatic polyamide) fibre with low stretch, and about three times the strength of a polyester. But it is expensive and very vulnerable to ultra violet light, so it is usually used only as a core material. It is also brittle so that it must not be bent round small diameter sheaves, and it does not knot easily.

Kevlar in ropes has therefore been overtaken by HMPE (High Modulus Polyethylene) materials such as **Spectra** and **Dyneema**, made in the USA and the Netherlands respectively. These have the disadvantage of being slippery by nature, and care must be taken in construction to avoid the sheath slipping over the core. Also they tend to creep (extend) if left under load for long. However they are said to be ten times stronger than steel, and lighter than water. They knot well, are resistant to light, have good resistance to abrasion, and absorb very little water when wet.

Vectran and **PBO** are the latest exotic fibres with exceptional strength, low stretch and creep, but high cost; therefore only used on high-performance rigs.

Care of ropes

Although less prone to damage than natural cordage, synthetic ropes must be used and handled carefully to give long service. They are water and rot-proof, but should be stowed well away from any heat source. They can also be damaged by chemicals or dirt; even salt crystals can harm their internal structure, so ropes should be washed in clean, fresh water (no detergents) and dried naturally.

Sheaves which are too small in diameter, or too narrow, will damage ropes passing over them. A seized sheave can ruin a rope very quickly, so it is important to check and lubricate all sheaves regularly.

Most damage to ropes is usually caused by chafe, at fairleads for example in the case of mooring warps. Wherever a rope may be exposed to a rough surface it should be protected by parcelling or by a short length of plastic hose slipped over it.

When buying rope it pays to get slightly more than the minimum length required. It can then be moved around a little from time to time, to equalise the wear and extend the life. A rope can also be turned end for end for the same purpose.

With ordinary use polyester and nylon ropes acquire a slightly fluffy appearance, due to minor damage to the outer surface; this is not harmful to the main structure of the rope and in fact gives additional protection against abrasion.

Periodically the servings (bindings) should be removed from wire rope splices for inspection, since water can be trapped here. If the splice is sound and not corroded, regrease, parcel and serve.

17.4.4   RECOMMENDED SIZES OF ROPE

Rope size, or thickness, is measured by its diameter in millimetres, as opposed to the obsolete circumference in inches. Reminder: C = πD, where π = 3·142. Thus 8mm diameter has a circumference of 25mm or 1 inch. The following recommendations are only a general guide; other factors such as design, displacement, sail ratio, use etc may necessitate variations.

Halyards

Yacht LOA (m)	Main mm	Genoa mm	Spinnaker mm	Burgee mm
5	6	6	6	3
7	8	8	8	3
10	10	10	8	3
12	12	12	10	3
15 +	12	12	12	3

Sheets

Yacht LOA m	Main mm	Genoa mm	Spinnaker mm	Light spinnaker mm
5	10	10	8	6
7	10	10	10	6
10	10	12	12	8
12	12	14	14	8
15	12	16	16	10

Mooring warps

LOA (m)	Nylon mm	Polypropylene mm
5	8	10
7	12	14
10	14	14
12	16	20
15	18	22
17	20	24
20	24	28

Anchor cables (rope)

LOA (m)	Nylon mm	Polyester mm	Kedge warp mm (nylon)
7	12	14	8
8.5	14	16	8
10	16	18	10
12	18	20	10
15	20	22	10
17	20	22	10
20	24	–	12

Always use at least 5 metres of chain between the anchor and the rope, to add weight and reduce chafe on the seabed. See also Fig. 18(3) in Chapter 18.

17.4.5   YACHT ROPES - MINIMUM BREAKING LOADS (KG)

The figures in the table overleaf are of a general nature and are mainly intended for comparisons.

17.4.6   USEFUL KNOTS, BENDS AND HITCHES

A bend joins the ends of two ropes together, while a hitch makes a rope fast to some other object. A stopper knot is tied at the end of a rope to prevent unreeving, while a binding knot

Table of minimum breaking loads - see 17.4.5

Diam (mm)	Braided		Spectra	Nylon	Plaited dinghy ropes		Three-strand construction		
	Polyester	Nylon			Polyester matt finish	Muftifilament polypropylene	Polyester	Nylon	Polypropylene (all qualities)
4	–	–	–	–	–	180	295	320	250
5	–	–	–	–	225	225	400	500	350
6	690	950	1540	-	295	295	565	750	550
7	–	–	–	–	–	–	770	1020	740
8	1220	1450	2575	-	565	565	1020	1350	960
9	-	–	–	–	635	635	1270	1700	1150
10	1920	2725	3100	2080	905	905	1590	2080	1425
12	2780	3400	5750	3000	1360	1250	2270	3000	2030
14	3780	4300	7825	4100	–	–	3180	4100	2790
16	4950	5400	10350	5300	–	–	4060	5300	3500
18	6400	7700	13000	–	–	–	5080	6700	4450
20	–	–	–	–	–	–	6350	8300	5370
21	8720	9525	–	–	–	–	–	–	–
22	–	–	–	–	–	–	7620	10000	6500
24	11400	12700	–	–	–	–	9100	12000	7600

constricts a single object or holds two or more objects snugly together.

It is always important to use the appropriate knot, bend or hitch, first for security, and second so that it can be undone when required. Be aware that knots do reduce the breaking load of a rope, by up to 50%.

Some of the more useful knots and bends are listed below and illustrated in Fig. 17(20):

a. **Sheet bend**. A useful general purpose bend, which does not damage the rope, and unties readily. Often used to join ropes of different thicknesses. If used to join ropes of different materials, the ends should be seized or the bend may slip loose.

b. **Double sheet bend**. No stronger than the sheet bend, but more secure. If the rope is stiff and large, seize the eye and reeve the working end twice.

c. **Heaving line bend**. Used when bending a heaving line to a hawser.

d. **Figure of eight knot**. The normal stopper knot.

e. **Stevedore knot**. Another stopper knot, more suitable for synthetic rope than a figure of eight.

f. **Reef knot**. An admirable binding knot, as for reefing sails, but not as a bend. If tied with ends of unequal size, or if one is stiffer or smoother than the other, the knot is almost bound to come apart.

g. **Half hitch**. Usually the first stage in tying a more elaborate hitch, and should not be used on its own.

h. **Round turn and two half hitches**. Suitable for securing a rope to a bollard or pile. If employed aloft or in ground tackle, the working end should be seized to the standing part. It is easily untied.

j. **Clove hitch**. Often used as a binding knot, but it is not very secure for use afloat. Will unwind under a steady rotating pull.

k. **Rolling hitch**. Simple to tie, and the most reliable knot under a lengthwise pull in the direction of the round turn. When bending this knot to another rope, the round turns should be crossed.

l. **Fisherman's bend**. Useful as an anchor bend.

m. **Bowline**. A popular and versatile loop knot. If properly tied, this knot is unlikely to come undone before the breaking point of the rope is reached.

17.4.7 HANDLING ROPES
Some terminology

Fig. 17(21) illustrates various seamanlike terms referring to ropes and their different parts.

1. Rope coiled down right-handed (clockwise). The bitter end is the inboard end of a line. The working end is used for knotting etc. The standing part is the fixed (as opposed to hauling) part, or the part of a rope about which the working end is turned to make a knot or hitch. A bight is an open loop.

2. The end of a rope looped over the standing part (left) forms an overhand turn. When looped under the standing part (right) it forms an underhand turn.

3. When a rope is passed part way round an object, such as a bollard or a spar, it is said to form a turn. When it goes completely round the object it forms a round turn. However, the instruction 'Take a turn' (around a cleat or bollard, for example) normally implies taking a round turn.

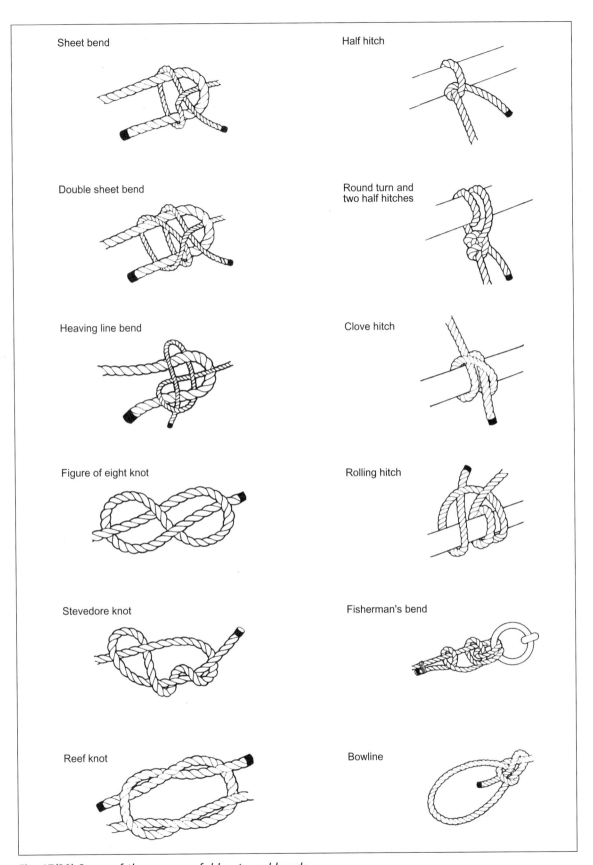

Sheet bend

Half hitch

Double sheet bend

Round turn and
two half hitches

Heaving line bend

Clove hitch

Figure of eight knot

Rolling hitch

Stevedore knot

Fisherman's bend

Reef knot

Bowline

Fig. 17(20) Some of the more useful knots and bends

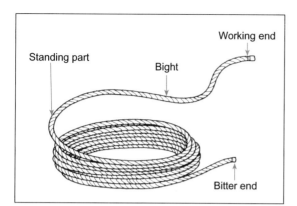

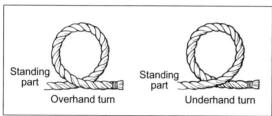

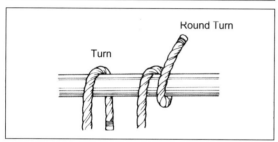

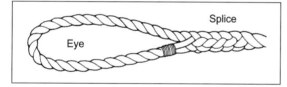

Fig. 17(21) Rope terms.

4. An eye is formed in rope when the working end is brought back and secured to the standing part, either temporarily by a hitch, or more permanently by splicing or seizing.

Ropes should always be stowed ready for immediate use. Three-strand rope is usually laid up right-handed, and should be coiled down right-handed (clockwise). Braided rope should be hanked up in a figure of eight, ensuring that subsequent turns cancel out the kinks caused by previous turns.

The tails of sheets or halyards, or the ends of warps, should be coiled so that the running part of the rope is on top, and not underneath or at the back of the coil. There are various ways of making up a halyard on a cleat, but one simple method is shown in Fig. 17(22).

When the halyard has been coiled the inner loop is pulled forward through the centre of the

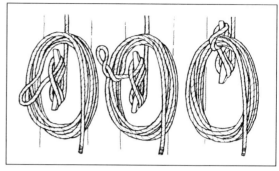

Fig. 17(22) Simple way of making up a halyard on a cleat.

coil, and twisted several times in a left-handed direction. The loop so formed is slipped over the top of the cleat, to hold the coil tight. There must be sufficient twists in the loop to allow it to slip over the cleat – just!

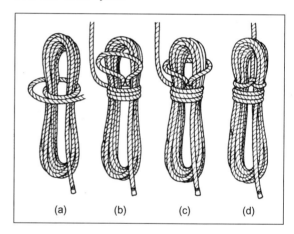

Fig. 17(23) Another way of making up a halyard or warp.

Fig. 17(23) illustrates another way of securing a halyard, suspended by its standing part. When it has been coiled down, a short length is brought from the back of the coil and turned three or four times round the coil, as in (a). Then

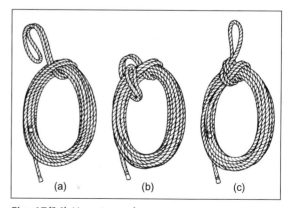

Fig. 17(24) How to make up a warp

524

a loop is brought out from the back of the coil, above the turns and slipped over the head of the coil, as in (b) and (c). The standing part is then pulled tight (d).

Warps should be coiled down ready for use, but the coil must be properly secured; in Fig. 17(24) at (a) the final coil of the rope is doubled to form a loop, which is passed over the head of the coil and then up, under its own part; (b) a turn is then taken with the end of the loop. Pull the turns tight, and the free end of the loop (c) can be hung over a hook.

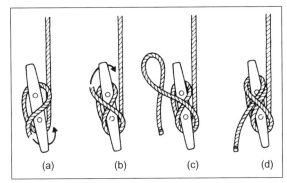

Fig. 17(27) Preparing to heave a line.

standing part to a cleat or similar fitting, and ensure that the line is long enough.

For any lengthy throw it is advisable to use a light (heaving) line as a messenger, in order to pass across a heavier warp. These instructions assume that the rope has a right-hand lay, and that the thrower is right-handed. Before heaving, transfer about half the coil to the right hand, Fig. 17(28).

Fig. 17(25) How to belay a line to a cleat.

When belaying a line to a cleat, Fig. 17(25), the first turn should be right round the base. (By convention this should be right-handed in case the line has to be handled by somebody else in the dark).

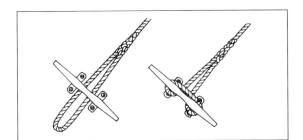

Fig. 17(28) Heaving a line.

Stand sideways to the direction of throw, bring the throwing arm well back, and swing it forwards with a round arm motion, or more overarm if a long throw is involved. Keep the coil in the other hand facing forward so that it can uncoil easily.

Fig. 17(26) A line with an eye splice in the end can be secured to an open-base cleat by passing the eye through the base; then put the loop over the horns.

The next turn is a figure of eight, as shown in (b). The final turn, (c) and (d), may be half-hitched for halyards or mooring warps. For sheets omit the half-hitch, and replace by a final turn round the base.

When heaving a line, Fig. 17(27), never rely on a previously coiled line being free of snags, but coil it down yourself into your left hand, in right-handed (clockwise) loops about l8in in diameter. Plaited or braided rope may fall into figures of eight. Before heaving the line secure the

17.4.8. PASSING A STOPPER

A stopper is used to relieve temporarily the strain on a rope, for example when a riding turn has to be cleared from a winch. The stopper should be a smaller rope, applied so that the

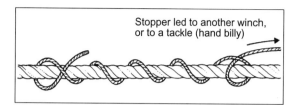

Fig. 17(29) Passing a single stopper.

direction in which it pulls is as near as possible the same as the direction of the rope which is to be relieved. If that is a laid rope a single stopper can be used, as shown in Fig. 17(29).

First half-hitch the stopper round the rope against the lay, then dog (wrap) it several times round the rope in the other direction so that the stopper lies closely into the lay of the rope; the end of the stopper can then be seized to the rope, or held against it by hand.

If the rope under load is plaited or braided, without any lay, a double stopper must be used. One end of the stopper is half-hitched round the rope as for a single stopper, above. The other end is then half-hitched alongside it, but in the opposite direction. The two ends are then criss-crossed in opposite directions round the rope several times, and the two ends either seized to the rope or held round it as before.

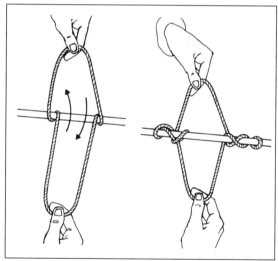

Fig. 17(30) An alternative method of passing a stopper.

Another way of passing a stopper is shown in Fig. 17(30), by using a loop of rope thinner than the rope to be relieved, and passing it round and round as illustrated. The relieving tackle should be shackled to both loops of the stopper.

17.4.9 WHIPPINGS
A rope end should always be neatly whipped, to stop it unravelling. A whipping is usually better than a back splice, which may snarl up when a

rope has to run through a block or fairlead.

When synthetic rope is first purchased the ends of the strands and the strands themselves can be stopped from unravelling by securing them temporarily with waterproof tape and fusing the ends with a match.

The three commonest whippings aboard a yacht are:

a. A sailor's whipping. Lay a short length of twine along the rope, and towards its end, as in Fig. 17(31).

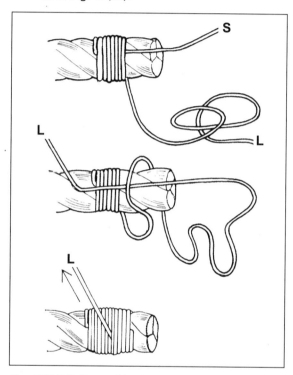

Fig. 17(31) Sailor's whipping.

Take about six tight turns round the rope and against its lay. Cut off the short length S. The longer length L is then laid back along the rope, and further turns are continued with the loop so formed. Finally L is drawn tight (a pair of fine-nosed pliers may be useful) and cut off close to the turns on the rope.

b. A common whipping, Fig. 17(32), is made by laying a loop along the rope and making a number of turns over it. The working end is put through this loop and pulled back out of sight. The two ends are then cut off short.

The length of either of the above whippings should be about the same as the diameter of the rope.

c. A sailmaker's whipping is the most secure, but it needs a palm and needle. The end of the twine is first anchored by stitching it through a strand, after which turns are

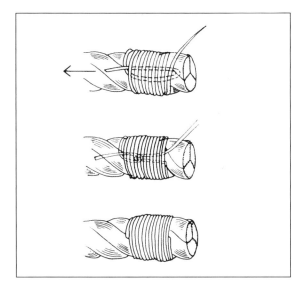

Fig. 17(32) Common whipping.

taken tightly round the rope – working towards the end and against the lay, as in Fig. 17(33).

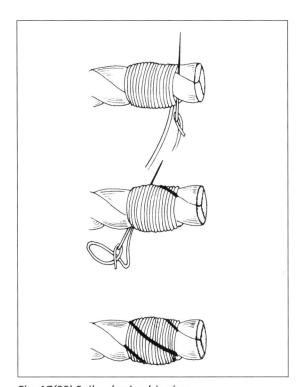

Fig. 17(33) Sailmaker's whipping.

The needle is then passed under a strand, and brought back along the groove between strands so that the turns of whipping are frapped tight. It is then stitched under the next strand, and the procedure repeated with each groove in turn. The end of the twine is then secured by stitching it through a strand, and the end cut off short.

17.4.10 EYE SPLICE IN THREE-STRAND ROPE

To make an eye splice in three-strand rope, first put a seizing on where the rope is to be unlaid. The amount of rope to be unlaid is 6 x the rope's circumference: eg an 8mm diameter rope (25mm in circumference) will require 150mm of rope to be unlaid. This will allow five full tucks to be taken in synthetic rope.

1. Secure the thimble, if one is required, in the bight of the rope. (The numbered instructions refer to the appropriate diagrams).

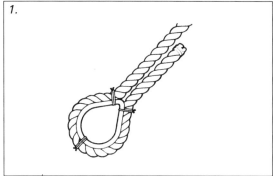

2. Unlay the rope back to the seizing, and whip each strand temporarily. The centre strand will be tucked first. The back of the thimble has been marked black, so that rotation of the work can be followed.

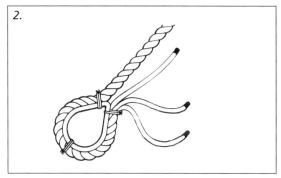

3. Insert the spike, with the lay of the rope, and open up the bight of the strand next to the one to be tucked; pass this strand through this bight from right to left – ie against its lay, looking back along the rope's length.

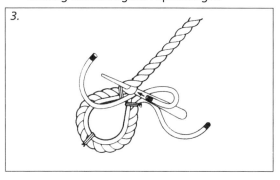

4. Pull the centre strand taut, insert the left hand strand underneath the next bight to the left, and pull taut.

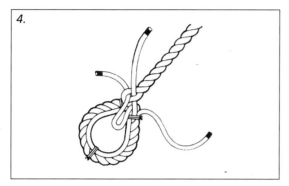

5. Turn the thimble over. Open up the remaining bight with the spike, and pass the remaining strand through, as indicated. All tucks are made from right to left, against the lay of the rope, keeping the lay of each strand correct and maintaining an even tension in the strands.

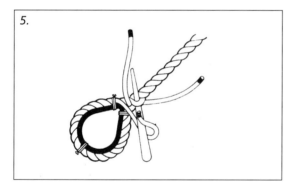

6. Turning the thimble over again, pull taut on each strand to ensure that the splice fits snugly at the toe of the thimble.

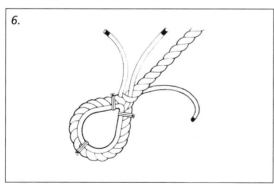

7. Each strand is now tucked over the strand to its left and under the next one. Continue tucking over and under with each strand in turn until five full tucks are completed.

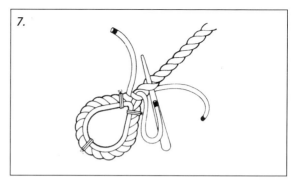

8. Then unlay each of the ends, and divide into two. Each half is matched with its partner of the next strand, and seized together over the intermediate strand. The surplus tails are cut off, and the ends fused together. The stops holding the thimble are removed, and the splice rolled in the hands to even it out.

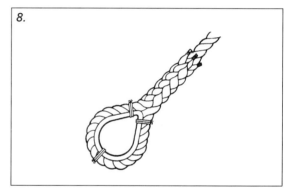

17.4.11 EYE SPLICE IN BRAIDED LINE
For splicing braided line a special fid and pusher are required. The fid must be the right size for the rope, eg size 10 for a 10mm rope.

Three marks must be made with a felt tip pen on the sheath, and three on the core, using the fid as a measure. One fid is the LOA of the fid; one short fid is the distance between the two marks on the fid and the hollow end.

During all stages of the splice ensure that any slack in the sheath is removed, particularly after extracting the core and when completing the splice. Braided line is a balanced rope, ie about half the strength is in the sheath and half in the core, so it is important that the tension is equally applied.

1. Marking the sheath (3 marks).
Tape the end of the sheath with adhesive tape, and cut off heat-sealed end, if applicable. Measure one fid length from end of rope, and mark (R). Form a loop and mark the size of eye required opposite the one fid length 'X', where the core is extracted. (See under 8 for

instructions on fitting a thimble). Measure about five fid lengths from core extraction point 'X' and secure to a cleat or similar. From R count ten double strands back towards the taped end, and mark all way round the rope 'T'. This is the crossover point.

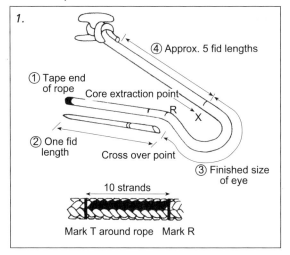

1.

④ Approx. 5 fid lengths

① Tape end of rope

Core extraction point

R

X

② One fid length

Cross over point

③ Finished size of eye

10 strands

Mark T around rope   Mark R

2.   Extract core and mark (3 marks).

Extract the core at 'X' by folding the rope and working the outer strands aside to expose the core. Pull out the core from the end of the rope, and tape the end. Holding the core, slide the sheath towards the knot and then smooth all of the slack of the sheath from the knot, back over the core. This ensures that all slack is removed from both core and sheath, and that tension is equal on both – most important. Mark the core where it comes out of the sheath (Mark 1). Slide the sheath back towards the knot and from mark 1 on the core measure towards the knot one short fid length (Mark 2). From mark 2 measure one full fid length plus a short fid length (Mark 3).

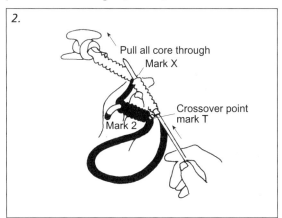

2.

Pull all core through Mark X

Crossover point mark T

Mark 2

3.   Insert sheath into core.

Lay the work out flat, and ensure the rope parts are not twisted. Place the fid into the core at mark 2, and carefully guide it through the centre and out at mark 3. Flatten the taped end of the sheath and fold it double; now place it in the hollow end of the fid, ensuring a smooth surface that will not catch the yarns as it is pushed through. Place the pusher into the hollow end of the fid, and slide the fid and sheath through the core. When the sheath protrudes at mark 3, remove the fid and pull the sheath through until mark 2 meets the crossover point (T).

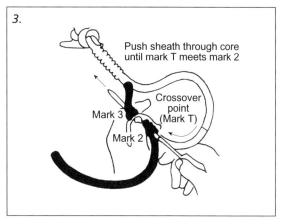

3.

Push sheath through core until mark T meets mark 2

Crossover point (Mark T)

Mark 3

Mark 2

4.   Insert core into sheath.

Place the fid into the sheath at the crossover point (T), along the centre and out of the same hole that the core was extracted from. Place the end of the core into the fid, and pass the fid and all of the core through the sheath. Remove the fid.

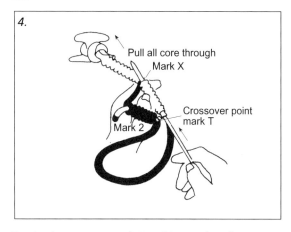

4.

Pull all core through Mark X

Crossover point mark T

Mark 2

5.   Lock crossover point and taper sheath.

Important: the core end must now be pulled, bunching the sheath back against the crossover point. Now pull the sheath end and bunch the core back to the crossover point, making sure that the crossover point is pulled tight. Take off the tape from the end of the sheath and unlay the sheath strands as far as possible. Take a quarter of the strands and cut off as far back as possible. Cut the next quarter of strands at two-thirds length, and the next quarter at one-third, leaving a quarter of strands at full length.

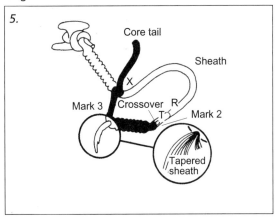

6. Smooth out the eye.

The slack parts of the rope are now smoothed out either side of the crossover point. Hold the crossover point as you do this making sure it does not slip. The tapered sheath will disappear into the core.

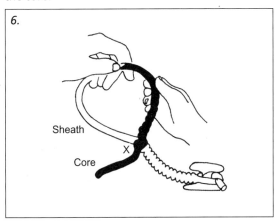

7. Bring back slack of sheath from knot.

Hold the core in the right hand and maintain tension against the knot. The left hand smooths the slack of the sheath from the knot, over the core and the crossover point. The right hand maintains tension on the core at all times, and it is necessary to slide the hand back as the sheath progresses. If you cannot get the sheath over the crossover point, slide the sheath back towards the knot, and smooth out the eye from the crossover point as in 6, and continue as above. Go over the rope several times from the knot to ensure that all of the sheath slack is removed. Marks X and R should now coincide.

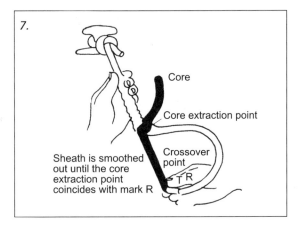

8. Finish the splice.

Smooth out the eye towards the core, and cut off the core leaving 6mm protruding; this is now tucked away into the throat of the splice. Fit thimble if required. Check once again that all of the sheath is smoothed out. Put a sailmaker's whipping on the neck of the splice, as near to the throat as practicable.

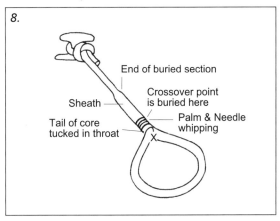

Note that the taped end of the sheath and core must fit neatly into the fid so that they do not catch yarns as they are pushed through. If it is difficult to place the taped end into the fid, several strands may be removed from the end, but do not cut off. If the sheath distorts or rucks during the splicing operations, this may be due to a joined strand. The strand ends at the join will be buried between the core and the sheath. Locate the join, and remove the strands by pulling out of the rope. Continue the splice. Smooth out the rucked area with the hands. When the splice is finished, bury the two join strands between the sheath and the core for a minimum distance of 125mm each way.

To fit a thimble in a braidline splice, first measure the size of eye around the thimble, as in 1 above, and continue the splice as instructed. Fit the thimble after cutting off the core. Carefully slide the sheath towards the knot just enough to insert the thimble. Now ensure that all of the slack is smoothed out towards the eye. Put a sailmaker's whipping at the neck of the splice. If slack remains in the sheath after the throat is tight on the thimble, this slack must be worked out through the tail of the rope after whipping, as instructed.

17.4.12 SPLICING USED BRAIDED ROPE
First soak the section of rope in water for several minutes, to lubricate and loosen the fibres. When extracting the core, as in (2) above, thoroughly loosen three to four sheath strands at point X, to obtain a large and flexible hole for the extraction.

Before burying the sheath at the crossover point, anchor the loop of slip knot to a firm object before starting to bury; both hands and weight of body can then be used to assist in burying sheath over core at crossover. Holding the crossover tightly, milk all the excess sheath from R to X. Cut off the core tail at X. Pull above crossover with one hand to reduce diameter of the crossover and core, then milk the sheath with the other hand. Use a small cord in a rolling hitch around the sheath to help the final burying process. Pulling on the hitch should be towards the eye until the sheath slackness is removed.

17.4.13 CENTRE EYE SPLICE
Measure the circumference of eye required, and mark the rope accordingly. Pierce the rope and pass rope end A through mark 2, and rope B through mark 1. The two rope intersections should be drawn as close together as possible. The eye will take a thimble if required.

17.4.14 SPLICING BRAIDED LINE TO WIRE
This splice is simple and quick, and extremely strong because it relies not only on the tucks for strength but also on the hollow braids gripping the wire as tension is applied. See illustrations 1. and 2.

If neatly made, little bulk is formed, and the lay of the wire is disturbed to a minimum. Measurements are not critical, providing enough wire is covered and the core tuck is made sufficiently deep to allow enough length for the sheath splice and length of tucks for working. In this case a 6mm diameter, 6 x 19 galvanised wire is spliced to a 10mm diameter polyester braided line. The numbered instructions refer to the diagrams.

3. The tools needed are a sharp knife, tape, and a hollow or Swedish fid to separate the wire strands. A braided line splicing fid helps, but is not essential.

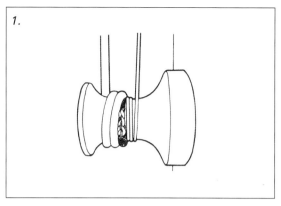

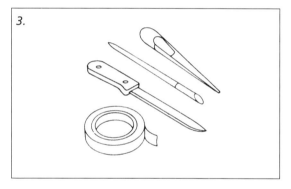

4. Tie a knot about two metres from the end of the braidline, securing it to a solid object. Bind the end of the wire with tape, and put a tape marker about 400mm along it. This amount of wire will be buried inside the rope. Lightly bind the rope about 25mm from the end and fray the strands out. Separating the core strands from the sheath, the sheath can be slid back along the core towards the knot, exposing about one metre of core.

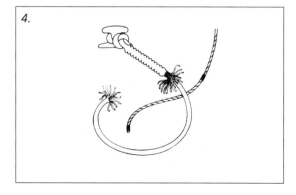

5. Bury the wire in the core, with the rope ends overlapping the marker tape.

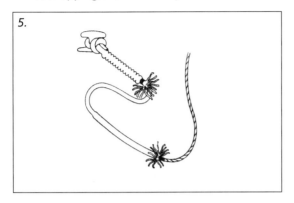

6. Tape the core firmly to the wire about 150mm from the wire marker, and carefully unlay the strands back to this tape.

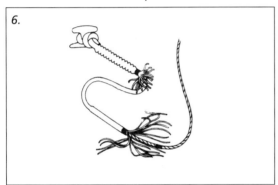

7. Neatly divide the loose strands into three, and bind each group together.

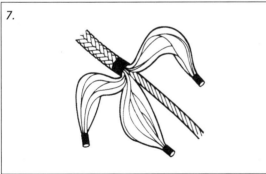

8. Pass the Swedish fid under two wire strands and tuck the first rope strand, making sure the strands lie flat and neat.

9. Follow round the wire taking the next two wire strands, and make the next tuck and the third the same.

10. 11. 12. 13. Continue until three full tucks are completed, and then cut off the loose ends of rope.

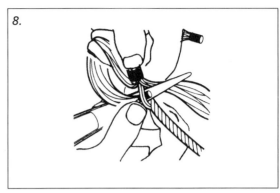

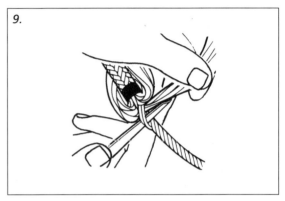

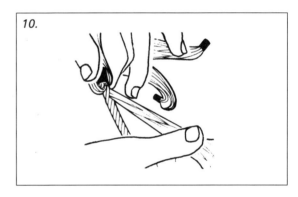

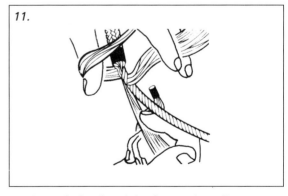

14. Smooth the sheath back over the splice, taking care not to ruck the cover over the wire, and ensure that all the slack sheath is worked back from the knot.

12.

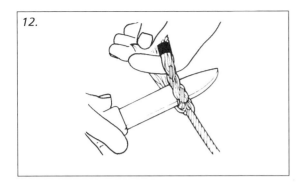

13.

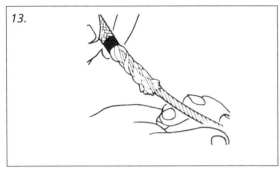

14.

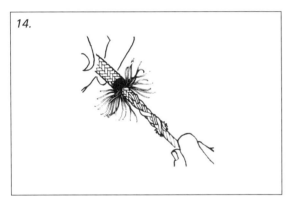

15. Tightly bind the sheath where the core splice finishes, unlay the rope strands and divide into three. Proceed as for the core splice, but add a fourth tuck, cutting out half of the strands to form a taper before tucking.

15.

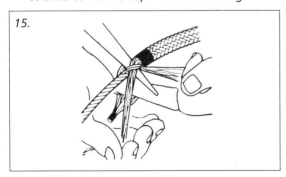

16. Binding the tucks is not essential, but it is a good idea to do so with waterproof tape. Keep the rope tucks neat and flat.

16.

17.4.15 WIRE ROPE – GENERAL

Wire is used for both standing and running rigging, but the requirements are different: Running rigging needs to be flexible; for standing rigging the prime requirement is minimum stretch for a given size.

The construction of wire rope is described by the number of strands and the number of wires in each strand. For example, Fig. 17(34) shows a 6 x 7 steel core rope: it has six strands over a steel core, and each strand consists of seven wires (six wires twisted round a central one).

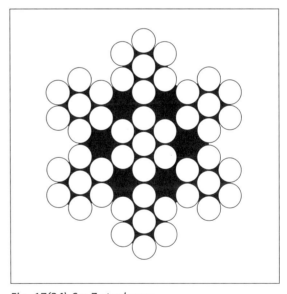

Fig. 17(34) 6 x 7 steel core.

17.4.16 WIRE STANDING RIGGING

The simplest, and most expensive, type of standing rigging is steel rod, which may be either round or lenticular (oval) in section. It has very little stretch, but is easily damaged.

More usual is single strand, 1 x 19, made up of six wires twisted round a central core with an outer layer of twelve further wires, as shown in Fig. 17(35).

Although more flexible than rod rigging, 1 x 19 can not be bent round a thimble for splicing,

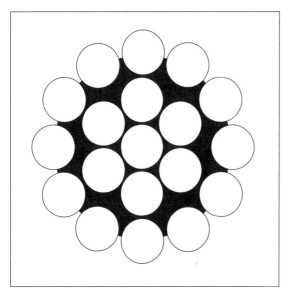

Fig. 17(35) 1 x 19 steel core.

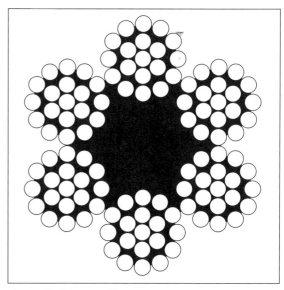

Fig. 17(36) 6 x 19 fibre core.

so special end fittings are required, see 17.2.2. This type of construction gives a smooth surface to reduce wind resistance, and allow sails and sheets to pass by easily with little chafing. 1 x 19 is made of stainless steel which lasts longer than galvanised wire, but is not so strong and is much more expensive. It needs to be handled carefully when stepping/unstepping the mast.

17.4.17   WIRE RUNNING RIGGING
Many types of ropes are used for running rigging. Wire rope is usually found in halyards because of its non-stretch properties, resistance to chafe, and small windage for a given strength. Its main disadvantages are that it can and does rust, and it does not like sharp bends. Obviously wire used for running rigging needs to be a lot more flexible than that used for standing

rigging, but even so sheaves over which it passes should be not less than 26 times the diameter of fast moving rope, or 12 times the diameter of wire used for halyards.

A typical wire rope used for running rigging is the 6 x 19 with fibre core, as illustrated in Fig. 17(36). This may be made of galvanised or stainless steel wire, the former being slightly stronger.

All wire rope needs to be examined regularly for any signs of corrosion or broken strands. If it is lightly oiled from time to time its life will be prolonged. With galvanised wire surface rust can be removed with a wire brush. If the rusting is serious, try bending the wire; if a strand breaks it should be discarded. Typical breaking loads of various sizes and types of wire rope are given in Fig. 17(37) below.

Size		Galvanised wire rope		Stainless steel wire rope		
		Standing rigging	Running rigging	Standing rigging		Running rigging
diam. (mm)	circumference approx (in)	6 x7 with Steel core	6 x 19 with fibre core	1 x 19	6 x7 with Steel core	6 x 19 with fibre core
2	$\frac{1}{4}$	0.28	–	–	0.24	–
3	$\frac{3}{8}$	0.63	0.50	0.72	0.55	0.43
4	$\frac{1}{2}$	1.12	0.88	1.28	0.97	0.77
5	$\frac{5}{8}$	1.75	1.38	2.00	1.51	1.20
6	$\frac{3}{4}$	2.52	1.99	2.88	2.18	1.73
7	$\frac{7}{8}$	3.43	2.71	–	–	–
8	1	4.48	3.54	–	3.87	–
9	$1\frac{1}{8}$	5.04	4.48	–	–	–
10	$1\frac{1}{4}$	7.00	–	–	–	–
12	$1\frac{1}{2}$	10.10	–	–	–	–

Fig. 17(37)   Minimum breaking loads (tonnes) of wire ropes.

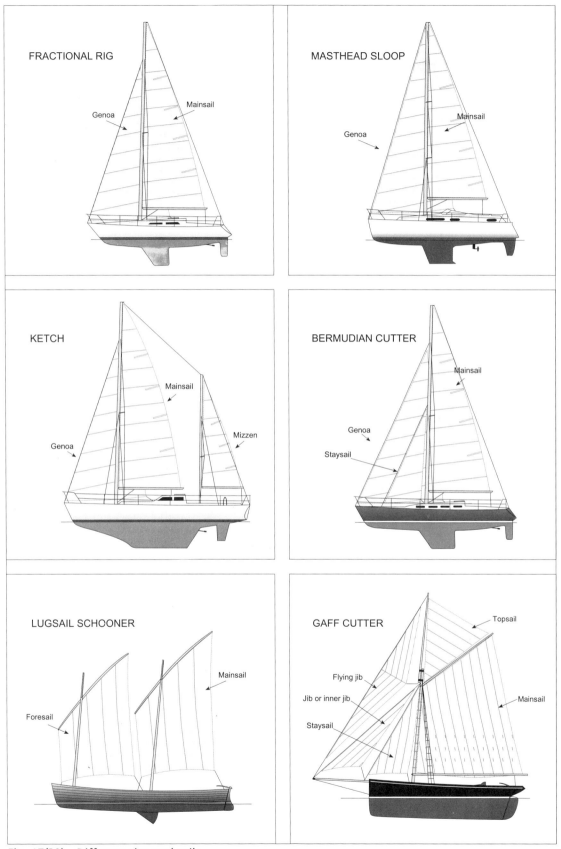

Fig. 17(38)   Different rigs and sails.

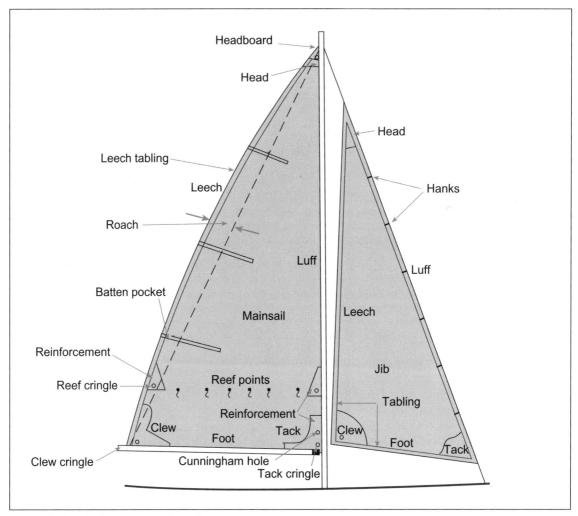

Fig. 17(39)   The basic parts of a sail.

17.5 SAILS

17.5.1 YOUR REQUIREMENTS

For any sailing yacht, cruiser or racer, it is important to have sails of the correct shape and design, built in the most suitable material. The essential starting point is therefore a dialogue with your sailmaker.

Tell him or her about your boat, where you sail and what sort of sailing you do. Is the boat traditional or a modern racer? Are you a pure cruising man or do you combine your cruising with a little club racing where performance needs to be enhanced? Or are you an out and out racing fanatic? Already a picture is emerging. Tell him next that you do not only sail in NW Europe, but plan a few seasons in the Med where for example UV protection for your sails is of great importance. Or that you will be away for three years on a global trip and are concerned about wear, chafe and durability. Armed with this information the sailmaker will

be able to offer one or more solutions – without it he can hardly proceed.

Racing and cruising yachts have undeniably different requirements, but not totally different. The former will sacrifice almost everything to speed, whilst the latter need sails which are more versatile (because fewer are carried), which are easy and safe to handle, have a long life and are not too expensive. But what a racing yacht was using five years or so ago may well be adopted by today's more performance-conscious cruising man. It is after all quite natural to want your boat to perform as well as possible, not just to win trophies, but to cover the ground efficiently and make longer passages a delight rather than a tedious slog.

The names of different rigs, the more common sails and the names of their various parts are shown in Figs 17(38) and (39).

17.5.2 SAILCLOTH

The efficiency of modern sails (which make boats ever more close-winded and faster in a wider range of conditions) depends on the chemical processes which have produced the materials now in use; on modern weaving techniques and heat treatment which provide tough and stable cloths; and on greater sophistication in both design and construction of sails.

So brush up your knowledge of sails; read articles in the magazines, attend lectures, visit sailmakers' websites which can be a mine of information. The design and building of a sail should not be a closed book, any more than sail trimming. As an aside, it is probably the case that many cruising yachtsmen know more about the workings of their 'auxiliary' engine than they do about their primary propulsion system, the sails.

Most fore-and-aft (as opposed to downwind) sails are now made from Terylene (Dacron), a product of the petro-chemical industry. Very fine filaments of polyester are formed by extruding a liquid at high pressure and temperature, and a number of these filaments make up the polyester fibre, which has several very desirable properties, ie good tensile strength, resistance to abrasion and the rot induced by moisture. The fact that the resulting cloth is hard can be a disadvantage, because stitches tend to stand proud of the surface and so wear more easily than if they bedded down into the material. Ultra violet light degrades Terylene, so it should be shielded as much as possible from bright sunlight, either with a UV sacrificial strip, a cover or even by lowering the sail.

Spinnakers are made from nylon, which has more stretch but is as strong and rot-resistant as Terylene. More recently other synthetic materials, ie Kevlar, Mylar and Pentex have been used for sails, but mostly in specialist racing applications.

Terylene, like other woven materials, is woven from threads at right angles to each other, the warp running lengthwise, and the weft across the length. A certain weight of cloth (Fig. 17(39)) may consist of heavier threads with rather an open weave or a larger number of thinner threads which are more compacted. The latter type of cloth, more closely woven, is more stable and durable; it also has less porosity, although this quality depends too on the dressing the cloth receives from fillers in the finishing stages.

While sailcloth will resist any deformation quite strongly if tension is applied uniformly along either the warp or the weft, it is a different matter if it is pulled on the bias, ie at an angle, say, of 45° to the warp and weft. What happens can be demonstrated by pulling two opposite corners of a handkerchief along the diagonal, when folds can be seen to appear close to the line of tension. This fact can be utilised in

sailmaking, as one way of getting the required shape into a sail. But if the stretch cannot be limited the sail will pull out of shape, so a certain minimum strength of cloth must be used for each application, and the stretch along the luff of a sail must be controlled by attaching the cloth to a rope or a tape.

Sailcloth is specified according to its weight per unit area. In Britain this is measured in ounces per square yard, but the Americans use a different unit which is ounces per yard of a cloth which is only 72cm wide. Fig. 17(40) shows comparative figures for cloths in British, American and metric weights.

British (oz/sq yard)	American (oz/yard, 285 in wide)	Metric (gram/sq metre)
1	0.8	34
2	1.6	68
3	2.4	102
4	3.2	136
5	4.0	170
6	4.8	203
7	5.6	237
8	6.4	271
9	7.2	305
10	8.0	339
11	8.8	373
12	9.6	407
13	10.4	441
14	18.2	475
15	12.0	508

Fig. 17(40) Equivalent sailcloth weights.

For racing sails exotic materials such as Kevlar are increasingly used. These are expensive and although they are very stretch-resistant they have a depressingly short effective life. More recently carbon fibre has appeared in the manufacture of sophisticated sailcloth. For more general purposes, laminates are being used in cruising sails, with films such as Mylar or Tedlar, used in conjunction with a Polyester or Pentex scrim, and sandwiched between Dacron to improve the stability of the cloth, which looks and feels like ordinary Dacron. Such cloth holds its shape better, but is more expensive. It can be transparent or white, and can be used for spinnakers and cruising chutes as well as for fore and aft sails.

17.5.3 DESIGN AND SAILMAKING

Although sailmaking can still be something of an art (based on experience), science plays an ever-larger part. Modern developments have been favourably influenced by computer assisted design (CAD), better cloths, and improvements in sail handling systems. Computers are now used extensively to analyse the loading on different parts of a sail in order to optimise the panel layout and the use of any special materials that may be included for extra strength along the lines of greatest stress. But, as in other applications, the computer is only as effective as its human operator.

Shape is designed into a mainsail by rounding the luff and the foot, so that when the sail is set on straight spars the surplus cloth is absorbed into the body of the sail; see Fig. 17(41). This can be clearly seen when the sail is spread out on a loft floor. The same applies to headsails, but here the designer must allow for the fact that the forestay sags somewhat, which in itself makes the sail fuller – so that the luff needs to be hollowed to allow for this. Fig. 17(41) also illustrates how tapering the seams puts fullness into a sail. This technique is of course used in conjunction with rounding the luff and foot.

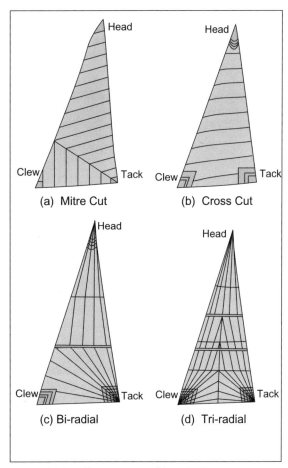

Fig. 17(42) Different cuts of headsails.
a. Mitre cut (traditional for headsails) but does not cope as well as radial cut with stress areas at head and clew.
b. Crosscut, or horizontal cut, (the most common cut for mainsails).
c. Bi-radial cut.
d. Tri-radial cut.

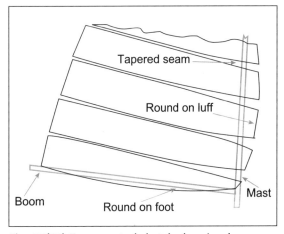

Fig. 17(41) Exaggerated sketch showing how fullness is worked into a mainsail by tapering the seams and rounding the luff and foot.

A striking development in recent years has been the increased popularity of fully battened mainsails. These sails do not flog, hold their shape well, and they are easy to trim. The mast track fittings at the forward ends of the battens need careful design, as they operate in compression. They must be free to articulate in all 3 axes, or the sail will be difficult to hoist and lower. Although the lack of flogging improves cloth life, the pockets are liable to chafe against the shrouds when the sail is squared off. Fully battened sails are usually combined with lazyjacks to facilitate lowering and reefing.

Fig. 17(42) shows various ways that a headsail can be cut (from a bolt of sailcloth) and assembled, thus combining the techniques mentioned briefly above with the properties of

the sailcloth, in order to produce the required shape. The luff is hollowed towards the head, so that it sets flat despite the sag in the forestay. Lower down the luff is rounded, to give the required flow to the sail. Similar cuts are also used for mainsails, but since there is no forestay to consider the mainsail luff has a slightly rounded convex curve.

17.5.4   MAINSAIL REEFING
There are various methods of reefing the mainsail:

1. *Roller Reefing*, where the sail is rolled around the boom, which is rotated by worm gear at the main gooseneck fitting or a handle, mounted on the mast forward face. The reefing procedure is simple, but the resulting sail shape may be

disappointing. With a mainsail, which has sliders on the luff, it is necessary to open the gate in the mast track and allow the slides to exit and roll with the luff around the boom. Roller reefing does have some disadvantages. The kicking strap has to be removed, and reattached by winding in a webbing strap as the rolls are taken in. Alternatively the kicking strap may be attached to a clawfitting on the boom, which must have an aft leading strop. Claw fittings are inclined to wear the sail. Roller reefing really requires a boom with a round section, which is not the best shape from other considerations.

2. *Point reefing* is the traditional method. It involves reeving reef pendants through special cringles on the luff and leech of the mainsail, and hauling them down to the level of the boom as the halyard is eased. Reef points in the sail are then tied (preferably passing between the sail and the boom, where possible) to bunch up the surplus sail; alternatively a reef lacing may be used. The kicking strap is not affected, and if the system is well laid out it is possible to get a better setting sail than with roller reefing, but the work involved is difficult when short-handed. Also, although there are usually two depths of reef, and sometimes three with mainsails of high aspect ratio, point reefing is not as flexible as roller reefing, where the reduction of sail can be adjusted roll by roll.

3. *Slab (or jiffy) reefing* is a variant of (2), using modern materials and equipment.

The procedure is to ease the kicking strap and main sheet, and set up the topping lift. Then slacken the main halyard until the luff cringle can be slipped over the hook at the gooseneck (it helps if the halyard is marked, so that it is slackened the right amount). Tighten the halyard again. Heave in on the reefing line so that the boom is pulled up to the leech cringle, and make fast. Ease the topping lift, tighten the mainsheet, and set up the kicking strap. The spare folds of the bottom of the mainsail can be gathered by a lacing passed through the eyelets in the sail for that purpose. The gear needs to be rugged and reliable, and it is important that the cheek blocks or line attachment eyes on the boom are properly positioned so that the sail is pulled down to the boom and also stretched along the foot to give the best sail shape.

4. *Single Line Slab Reefing* is another variation on slab reefing. It allows a slab reef to be taken in by using a single line from the cockpit, see Fig. 17(43).

As the reefline is pulled in, the tack and clew are simultaneously hauled down to the boom. There are numerous methods, with variations in hardware and technique. As all types introduce some form of purchase to give a really flat reefed sail, there will be more friction in lines when shaking out the reef. Good quality turning

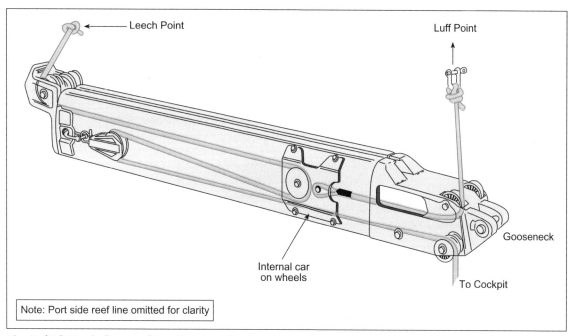

Note: Port side reef line omitted for clarity

Fig. 17(43) Single line reefing, showing the layout inside the boom. Only one reefing line is depicted; two are normally provided.

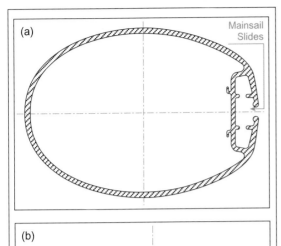

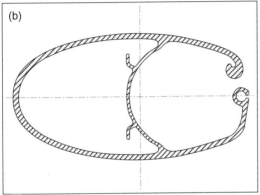

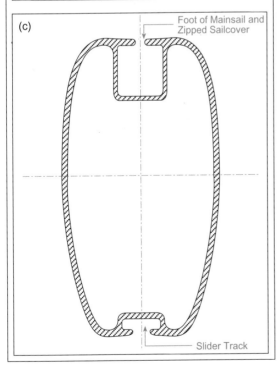

Fig. 17(44) Mast sections: (a) conventional and (b) for in-mast reefing. Boom section at (c). Note the booms's deep cross-section.

blocks and correctly aligned organisers for the reefing lines can significantly reduce friction.

5. *In-mast roller reefing* for mainsails is relatively new, but has rapidly developed into a popular option for medium and larger yachts with limited crew. There are two common methods: rolling on a luffspar inside the mast or onto an external luffspar.

An interior luffspar needs a special mast, see Fig. 17(44) or an additional casing, whereas an exterior roller is usually attached with a series of relatively small brackets. Operation can be manual or powered by electric or hydraulic motor. The sail can be partially rolled up for reefing or fully rolled for furling. Despite their undoubted popularity and ease of operation, in-mast systems have had certain disadvantages: loss of sail area, reduced performance, extra weight aloft when the sail is furled (compared to other methods), increased chafe in the cloth, and problems if something jams. Recent developments in sail construction have redressed some of the disadvantages by introducing vertical battens. These allow a sail with more area, yet still able to roll inside the mast.

6. *In-Boom roller furling* for mainsails is another comparatively recent development. This aims to combine the efficiency of a full-battened mainsail with the easy operation of an in-mast system. An added benefit is that the weight of the sail is lowered as it is reefed. When fully lowered, the sail is neatly stowed inside the boom. In-boom systems tend to be bulky, and require precise control to achieve a good furl. Operating friction can be high, and chafe of the lufftape is common where it enters the special mast track. Continued development is very likely, eventually, to overcome these undesirable features.

Reliability and Maintenance
Any reefing system must be reliable and available in an emergency and give the crew confidence. In-mast and in-boom roller furling must be operated and maintained in line with the manufacturer's instructions. It is unlikely that "the occasional bucket of fresh water" will suffice to keep bearings free of salt and rotating sweetly. With slab reefing the various pendants, reeflines and sheaves must be kept in good condition.

17.5.5   HEADSAIL FURLING AND REEFING
Traditionally, as the wind speed increased, sail area in the foretriangle of a yacht was reduced by changing to a smaller sail. Efficient and reliable roller furling/reefing gear means that a cruising yacht can readily set a genoa, progressively reef it, or totally furl it, without anybody going forward.

Headsail reefing gear is an integral part of the standing rigging, and also a very exposed but well designed rotating mechanism; see Fig. 17(45). The gear will rotate much more easily if the forestay

Fig. 17(45) Well designed roller reefing gear.

has adequate tension. The backstay provides this tension, which is relatively easy to adjust. If the headsail gear has an integral rigging screw, this should be treated purely as a length adjuster, for mast rake changes.

One very serious potential problem for headsail gears is halyard wrap. This occurs when the halyard is carried round the luffspar with the halyard slider. If a winch is used for the reefline at this stage, the halyard wrap can become very tight, causing serious damage to the luffspar or forestay. It is essential that some form of anti-halyard wrap device be fitted. As with mainsail roller furling, headsail gears require regular maintenance.

Roller reefing headsails are now often radial cut, either bi-radial with the panels radiating from the clew and head, or even tri-radial with panels radiating from all three corners; see . Radial cut sails, with modern cloths where the strongest fibres are aligned with the loading in the sail, hold their shape better with increasing wind speed. Although the sails themselves last well, the sacrificial strips along leech and foot need regular replacement. Opinion seems divided on the efficiency of treating Dacron to resist ultra violet light.

Various devices are used to eliminate the belly which can form in the body of the sail when furling. Some sails have a tapered foam insert fitted just behind the luff. An alternative is to have a device built into the headsail gear, which allows the tack attachment to lag behind as the gear starts to rotate, flattening the sail.

All furling headsails respond to careful adjustment of the sheet lead car. Large genoas have a nearly horizontal foot, so as the area is reduced, it is likely that the sheet car will require moving aft. Smaller sails with higher clews may not need this adjustment.

17.5.6 CHOOSING DOWNWIND SAILS
Cruising chute or spinnaker? that is the question for many cruising yachtsmen. For optimum efficiency a spinnaker is the answer, because the tack can be projected out on a pole from behind the mainsail on a broad reach or run. The drawback is that since the sail is larger than a cruising chute and only firmly attached at one corner (the head), it needs more care in hoisting, trimming, gybing and lowering (dowsing or handing). A cruising chute on the other hand is smaller and easier to manage, but less efficient when the wind comes further aft, because it is blanked by the mainsail.

For some the choice is one or the other, but one of each is another option: a 0·9oz spinnaker for racing and light wind running or broad reaching in cruising mode; plus a 1·5oz cruising chute. Not only can the chute be tacked to the stemhead in the normal way when cruising, but when flown from the pole as an asymmetric spinnaker it will double as a highly effective reaching kite in breezy conditions.

17.5.7 CRUISING CHUTES

Most sailmakers now provide asymmetrical cruising chutes, which are easier to handle than a spinnaker, especially when lightly crewed. With the wind well aft the chute is set on the opposite side to the mainsail, with or without a bearing-out spar. With the wind on or somewhat abaft the beam it can be set flying as a reaching headsail.

An economically-priced chute will probably be cross-cut, ideal for the smaller boat. A radial-cut chute will however hold its shape much better, especially in stronger winds, and is desirable in boats of more than 10m LOA.

The associated equipment is simple and minimal: a dedicated (if possible) halyard; a tack line led outside the pulpit and its working end led aft to the cockpit; and a pair of sheets, each about $2\frac{1}{2}$ times the boat's length. If, for absolute simplicity, you only rig one sheet, this means that you cannot gybe without first lowering and then re-hoisting the sail.

Before attaching these lines to the chute, check that the luff and leech are not twisted. Note that, unlike a spinnaker, the chute does actually have a definite luff and leech. Keep the chute in its bag, or a special turtle bag, or if you have neither, put it in 'stops', ie tied with weak cotton or elastic bands. Easiest of all is a snuffer or sock which like a sausage skin encases the whole sail and either unfurls or dowses it.

To hoist, put the boat on a broad reach so that the chute goes up in the lee of the main – but first roll the genoa – although opinions vary on this. Then hoist away. Adjust the tack line and get the sheet in so that the sail begins to draw. Thereafter trim the chute just as you would a large genoa. The closer you are to the wind the more the tack line will need to be hardened in, and conversely as the wind comes astern. When on a run, ease out the halyard, tack line and sheet so that the chute bellies out into a nice pulling shape on the opposite side to the main.

Gybing is straightforward, provided you first ease the tack line. This widens the gap between the chute's luff and the forestay, through which the rest of the sail will be pulled. Partially unrolling the genoa will fill the fore triangle and thus help to prevent the chute wrapping around the forestay. As the wind comes astern take up the slack on the lazy (new) sheet and keep a little tension on the old one so that the sail can be pulled across in a controlled fashion. Settle on the new course and re-trim.

To lower the chute, put it in the lee of the main, ie on a broad reach; trip the tack line shackle, then haul in on the sheet, whilst lowering the halyard, and pull the sail down into the companionway. Re-pack it ready for the next time.

17.5.8 SPINNAKERS

Different cuts, and hence shapes, of spinnaker are available for best performance on different points of sailing. Originally the spinnaker was essentially a running sail; now, using modern sailcloth and new cutting techniques, spinnakers can be carried with the apparent wind well forward of the beam. Three of the more common types of spinnaker and one cruising chute are shown in Fig. 17(46).

a. Radial head spinnaker. Broad-shouldered sail, with radial head and a flat, horizontally cut bottom; ideal for running, and broad reaching in light breezes.
b. Tri-radial spinnaker. Minimal distortion, stable shape and a narrower head are better for reaching.
c. Asymmetric spinnaker, ie clew higher than tack; looks like a cruising chute, but flies

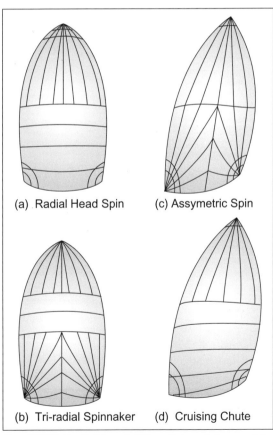

(a) Radial Head Spin   (c) Assymetric Spin

(b) Tri-radial Spinnaker   (d) Cruising Chute

Fig. 17(46) Radial head, Tri-radial and Assymetric spinnakers; plus a Cruising chute.

from a pole for optimum reaching performance; tri-radial construction.

d. Cruising chute. Radial head for more stable shape in stronger winds; versatile in most conditions.

Since a spinnaker must support itself in the air, the lightest possible material should be used, consistent with strength and resistance to stretch. Nylon cloth is normally used, typically about 1·5oz/sq yard, reinforced to discourage it from ripping. Reaching spinnakers are made of slightly heavier cloth so that they retain their shape. It is important not to carry a spinnaker in wind speeds greater than that for which it is designed. The maximum apparent wind speeds suggested in Fig. 17(47), are rather lower than might be expected.

Nylon weight	Boat LOA	Run	Broad reach	Beam reach	Close reach
0.5oz	< 9m	6	6	5	–
	> 9m	5	5	4	–
0.75oz	< 9m	22	17	14	12
	9 - 12m	16	13	12	11
	> 12m	13	12	11	9
1.5oz	< 9m	30	26	22	15
	> 9m	26	23	17	13

Fig. 17(47) Suggested maximum apparent wind speeds in knots for different weights of spinnaker cloth and on different points of sailing.

For easier hoisting, gybing and handing of cruising spinnakers, most sailmakers offer snuffers, a long nylon sleeve with a GRP bellmouth at the bottom end. The sleeve with the spinnaker packed inside is hoisted on the spinnaker halyard, like a long sausage. To unfurl, pull an uphaul, attached to the bellmouth, so that the sail is steadily unpeeled from the bottom up. While the spinnaker is flying, the bellmouth and bunched up sleeve remain at the masthead. To furl the spinnaker release the uphaul and pull the downhaul, so that the bellmouth and sleeve progressively smother and house the sail as the sheet is eased. The sleeve can then be lowered, with the spinnaker inside it. For gybing, the sail can be temporarily furled inside the sleeve, while the mainsail and spinnaker pole etc are moved across, and then unfurled on the new gybe.

17.5.9 SAIL CARE
The owner of a new sail should appreciate that much thought and skilled workmanship has gone into it. He should therefore look after and preserve this latest addition to his inventory.

Careless handling and bad practices can so easily spoil a sail. Any sail, but particularly a light nylon spinnaker, will rip on sharp objects such as split pins which are not taped over, so all rigging, spreader ends, guardrails etc should be checked regularly.

A sail will only set as well as the mast and rigging allow, and notes on setting up the rig are given in 17.2.5. To avoid creases and unfair strains, a mainsail must fit the mast and boom properly, with clew and tack cringles correctly positioned for the pins which are to hold them. The sailmaker should have taken detailed measurements on board. Headsails are easier to fit, but the tack fitting must be aligned with the forestay and the sail should avoid excessive chafe on the pulpit.

Even though a Terylene sail is reasonably robust, it should first be set in light conditions to ensure a good fit and reduce flogging; it should not be reefed during this period. A sail should always be hoisted or lowered by pulling on the luff, never along the leech. When a mainsail is hoisted or lowered the weight of the boom should be taken on the topping lift or kicker (or by hand in a small boat), to avoid stretching the leech, which is particularly vulnerable to maltreatment. For this reason, when sails are hung up to dry they should be hoisted by the head and the tack, not by the clew. Sails should not be allowed to flap needlessly, since this damages the cloth structure, particularly in the leech area where the flutter is greatest.

A mainsail should be hoisted and the foot tensioned just enough to to take up its designed shape. Avoid over-tensioning. In light to moderate winds tension the halyard enough to remove any horizontal creases, and adjust the outhaul so that sufficient flow is given to the lower part of the sail. In stronger breezes they should both be tensioned more, so that little folds appear close to the luff and foot when the sail is up. In strong winds maximum tension is needed to flatten the sail. To keep the flow in the sail well forward, apply extra luff tension by taking down on the Cunningham hole.

Headsails should be treated similarly. Before hoisting check that the halyard is clear aloft and that the sail is correctly hanked on or aligned with the luff foil. With roller reefing many a headsail on cruising yachts will be hoisted at the start of the season and lowered at the end. Make the effort in between times to check the luff tension regularly; the halyard and luff will both stretch and performance, especially to windward will suffer. It is also important to see that the sheeting positions are correct each side. Do not sheet the sail in before it is fully hoisted.

Headsails which have a wire luff rope, or a wire on which the luff can slide, need to have the halyard set up tight, so that the luff is as straight as possible. Headsails with a stretchy luff should have the halyard adjusted harder in heavy winds and less in lighter winds. If fitted, it is important not to overtighten a sail's leech line.

While sailing, do not allow the topping lift or any running backstay to flap against the lee side of the mainsail, nor allow the sail to press needlessly against the lee rigging or spreaders when running off the wind – this damages the cloth and the stitching. Reefing should not damage a sail but if (for example when unreefing) the full weight is taken by reef points or the reef lacing, instead of by the reef pendants at luff and leech, the sail may be seriously distorted.

On return to harbour, release the tension on the mainsail's clew outhaul, flake the sail down over the boom, secure it with ties and put the sail cover on (even if it is only overnight – it keeps the sail clean and dry, and protects it from the sun). If the mainsail is taken off the boom, flake it down carefully to the foot then roll it up from tack to clew; or flake it to the luff, then roll it to the head. When flaking a sail avoid putting a crease across a window, and flaking to the same creases every time; see Figs. 17(48) and 17(49). Sails should be bagged so that the tacks are on top ready for instant use. Sail bags should be roomy, to avoid sails being unduly crushed or creased. Sails left lying around on deck only get damaged by being walked on, or made damp from spray.

Modern sails with a hard finish should be rolled up from head to foot, and stowed in a long sausage bag without folding or flaking. Try to keep the bag as straight as possible, when stowing the sail or moving it from place to place.

When drying sails do not allow them to flap in the wind, as this causes chafe and damages the structure of the cloth. If sails are wet it is better to leave them spread out in the boat, if it is impossible to dry them on deck. Do not leave wet nylon sails bagged up, since sometimes the colours will run.

Salt and dirt form an abrasive surface on sails, which damages the cloth and the stitching. This can be reduced by keeping the deck and rigging clean, as well as by regularly hosing down or washing the sails in fresh water.

At the end of the season, or if sails get really dirty, they should be washed properly in warm water (not more than about 120°F or 50°C) using ordinary soap or a mild liquid detergent, and scrubbing gently with a sponge or a soft brush. After washing, sails must be very well rinsed with fresh water, and dried carefully. Then they

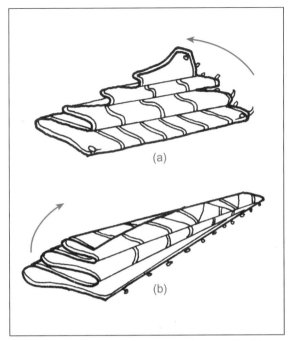

Fig. 17(48) Flake down a mainsail towards either the foot (a), or the luff as in (b).

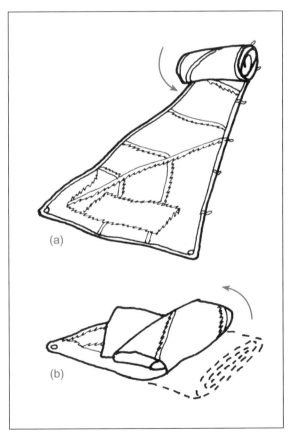

Fig. 17(49) Fold a headsail either by flaking down towards the foot, as for a mainsail; or roll the luff from head to tack as in (a), and then roll as in (b).

should be closely inspected for the smallest signs of damage before being stowed away. Check both sides of each sail, panel by panel, seam by seam, for any small holes in the cloth, broken stitches, wear on the roping or tabling, loose hanks on head sails, worn or damaged cringles at the corners, and defective slides or batten pockets on mainsails.

It is not easy to wash and inspect sails properly on board, and the work is better done if they can be spread out on a clean surface ashore. If this is not available, most sailmakers will wash, valet, repair and store your sails for the winter.

Certain stains on sails need speedy attention and special treatment. These notes refer to white sailcloth; coloured sails which need special cleaning are best treated professionally. Some of the solvents such as carbon tetrachloride are poisonous and others may involve a fire risk, so it is best if any cleaning is done in the open air and away from naked lights. After cleaning be sure to wash that area of the sail very thoroughly in order to remove all traces of the chemical used.

Oil or grease can usually be shifted by carbon tetrachloride or trichloroethylene as in proprietary stain removers like Thawpit; or by rubbing with Swarfega, then washing in warm water with a mild detergent.

Rust stains can be stubborn, but try a 5% solution of oxalic acid or 2% hydrochloric acid in warm water. Mix the solution in a plastic container, wear rubber gloves, and do not let the acid solution come into contact with metal fittings or the luff wire of a sail.

Tar or pitch stains can be treated with a solvent such as Polyclens, white spirit, trichloroethylene or carbon tetrachloride.

Paint or varnish should be removed with white spirit or turps substitute as soon as possible. Failing this, try Swarfega with a liquid detergent and warm water. Polyurethane varnish can be softened with chloroform, and ordinary varnish with surgical or methylated spirit. Never use alkali-based paint strippers on Terylene cloth.

Blood stains should be washed off immediately with plenty of cold water, and then with soap powder. A useful tip is to rub saliva into the stain to break it down. Old stains should be soaked in cold water with 0·15ltr (0·25pt) of ammonia to 2·2ltr (0·5 gal) of water. Residual stains can be treated with a 1% solution of pepsin in water with a few drops of hydrochloric acid.

Mildew is caused by dirt, a damp atmosphere and poor ventilation. On synthetic sailcloth it is more unsightly than harmful, but it can be brushed off with a stiff brush when dry, and then soaked in a solution of 1 part household bleach to 15 parts of cold water.

17.5.10 SAIL REPAIRS

Any yacht or motor sailer should carry needles, palm, thread and spare material, so that even a moderately torn sail can be repaired. Small holes or splits, which if left unattended would soon extend, can often be patched temporarily with self-adhesive material until a more permanent, professional repair can be made – and this is what a sailmaker would prefer, rather than having to undo amateur sewing. But at times a boat's safety may depend upon being able to re-stitch a seam, or rebuild a torn-out clew. Sails are expensive and regular inspection and prompt attention to minor defects will help to prolong their life.

A 'Sailmaker's Bag' for the average yacht should include:

a. Terylene thread, ranging from lightweight machine thread for spinnaker cloths to (say) 6lb thread for cloths of l2oz/sq yd. The upper limit depends upon the size of boat. The weight of thread needed is roughly half the weight of the cloth, ignoring units, eg a 3lb thread for a cloth of 6oz/sq yd.

b. Needles, appropriate for the weight of the cloth and the work to be done, can be bought individually or in pack of 5 assorted sizes, eg Nos 13 – 19. No. 13 is for very heavy cloth, No. 19 is a domestic size. Two No. 18 and two No. 16 should suit a smaller yacht. Large needles are needed to sew several thicknesses of cloth, but do not to use too large a needle, since it will weaken the cloth by making too large a hole. When repairing highly stressed parts of a sail such as head, tack or clew, use a heavier thread and a larger needle than the weight of cloth would otherwise require. The thread should normally be doubled, or sometimes even quadrupled, to give strength with the minimum number of stitches.

c. Beeswax is needed for treating the thread, partly for protection and partly to make it easier to work. Pull the thread through the beeswax three or four times. If no beeswax is available candlegrease is an acceptable substitute.

d. A sailmaker's palm is needed, with which to push the needle through the material.

e. Repair material, offcuts of sailcloth in different sizes and weights, can usually be obtained from your sailmaker. They are used for patches which give a stronger repair than a simple darn, see below.

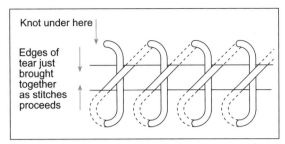

Fig. 17(50) Sailmaker's darn.

f. Special adhesive tape and material is useful for temporary sail repairs in light weather, and also for holding a patch or a tear together while it is being stitched or to await the sailmaker's attention.

g. A bench hook, with a line attached, is useful for tensioning the work while it is being stitched.

A sailmaker's darn pulls together the edges of a rip in a sail, using a type of herringbone stitch; Fig. 17(50).

The thread should be doubled and waxed, and the end knotted. First, working from the left, the needle is passed up through the cloth on the far side of the rip, and down through the cloth on the near side. It is then brought up through the gap, to the left of and over the top of the first stitch, and down under the cloth on the far side of the gap. Again pass it up through the cloth on the far side of the gap, and so on. The stitches should be about 5mm from the edges of the cloth each side of the rip, and spaced about that far apart or slightly closer. As each stitch is formed it should be tightened just enough to pull the edges of the tear together. When the end of the tear is reached, the repair is finished off with a couple of half-hitches, stitched over.

A sewn patch will produce a stronger repair than a straight-forward darn, but it involves correspondingly more work. The material for the patch should ideally be the same as the sail, both in weight and texture, but a near equivalent will suffice in emergency. The patch should overlap the tear by 50mm all round, and be orientated so that its weave (warp and weft) matches that of the sail. The warp runs the length of a roll of sailcloth, the weft across.

Unless the edges of the patch can be heat sealed to prevent them fraying (by using a hot knife, which is a specialist bit of sailmaking equipment), they will need to be turned under and secured with pins or tape for stitching.

A patch must be worked from one side of the sail so an overhand stitch is used as shown in Fig. 17(51).

Tie a knot in the end of the thread and push the needle down through the sail, and up

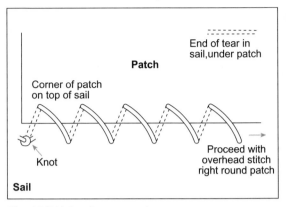

Fig. 17(51) Sewing a patch.

through the sail and the patch opposite as indicated. Then take a rather longer diagonal stitch, down through the sail outside the edge of the patch, and repeat. Spacing should be similar to a sailmaker's darn. Continue stitching right round the rectangular patch, from left to right, until the starting point is reached.

Then turn the sail over, and cut a rectangle around the tear with its sides parallel to the edges of the patch which have been stitched, and at least 40mm from them; see Fig. 17(52). At each corner of the rectangle hole, make a diagonal cut in the sail, about 20mm long towards the corner of the patch underneath. Tuck the four edges under, so that they are between the sail and the patch, and then stitch round the rectangle (securing the turned in edges of the sail to the patch) in the same way as the patch was originally stitched from the other side. Again work from left to right, and take care to keep the tension of the stitches uniform.

If part of a bolt rope has to be re-sewn to a sail*, first ensure that any twists are removed from the rope. If more than a very short length is to be re-stitched, it should be temporarily

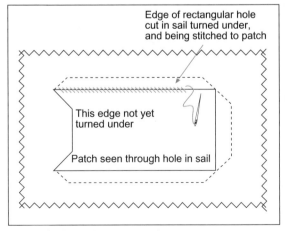

Fig. 17(52) Finishing a patch.

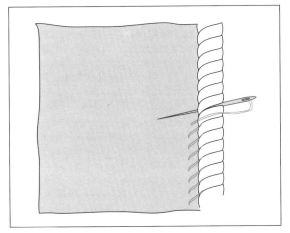

Fig. 17(53) Re-sewing a bolt rope to a sail.

attached about every foot, so that it is sewn on evenly. The stitch used is shown in Fig. 17(53), the needle being passed between the strands of the rope. To rope more than a short length properly takes experience if the correct tension is to be applied evenly.

*Modern sails normally have the bolt rope encased in sailcloth which is sewn to the sail.

17.6 WIND AND SAILS

17.6.1 TRUE AND APPARENT WIND

First, before trying to understand how a boat sails (particularly towards the wind direction), the difference between true and apparent wind must be understood. The true wind is what is felt when standing on the shore, or in a stationary boat on her mooring. But once the boat starts to move, whether under power or under sail, an observer experiences a different wind – the apparent wind, which is the resultant of the true

wind and the boat's velocity. This is shown in Fig. 17(54) where a boat is sailing with the wind abeam. RQ represents the true wind (V_T) in speed and direction. RP similarly represents the boat's velocity (V_s). From the vector triangle so established PQ gives the direction and strength of the apparent wind (V_A) as experienced by a person on board and more importantly by the boat's sails, or by a burgee or electronic wind indicator at the masthead.

A more obvious example of the effect of boat speed on the true wind is when the wind is dead astern. If the true wind speed is, say, 15 knots and the boat is sailing at 6 knots, the apparent wind speed affecting the sails is only 9 knots. But if you turn around, the apparent wind will go up to a brisk 21 knots.

A further example is shown in Fig. 17(55), where the boat is sailing more nearly into wind. Comparing the two diagrams, note that in both cases the boat's velocity pulls the apparent wind further ahead than the true wind. Also that when the wind is abaft the beam the apparent wind is less strong than the true wind, but that when the wind is ahead the apparent wind is stronger than the true wind – the former can induce a false sense of security, the latter can blow out sails.

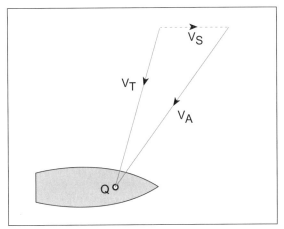

Fig. 17(55) When the wind is forward of the beam V_A is stronger than V_T.

A more extreme example of the effect of boat speed on the true wind is when the wind is dead astern. If the true wind speed is, say, 15 knots and the boat is sailing at 6 knots, the apparent wind speed affecting the sails is only 9 knots.

Today, given apparent wind and boat's course and speed, the true wind is quickly computed. This may be useful, for example, when prior to a course alteration it helps to know which gybe will apply or which sails to set. However, it is quite simple, more rewarding and certainly a lot cheaper to work this out graphically.

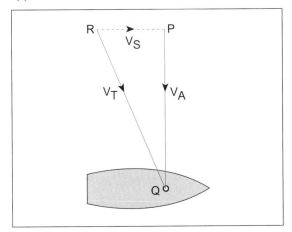

Fig. 17(54) Sails react only to the apparent wind, as shown above by V_A. V_A is always further ahead than the true wind V_T, due to the boat's velocity, V_s. In this example, with the wind aft, V_A is less in strength than V_T.

17.6.2 HOW SAILS WORK

It is easy to understand how a sailing yacht can blow away to leeward off the wind, but the mechanics of how a boat gets to windward are more complex; the following is only a brief and simple explanation. Fig. 17(56) shows how the air stream is deflected by a single sail when beating to windward. Along the lee side of the sail the air is speeded up and the pressure falls. Over the windward surface the air flow slows down and pressure rises. It is well established that the 'negative pressure' on the lee side has a greater effect on propelling the boat than the positive pressure on the windward side. The net effect is a resultant force in the horizontal plane indicated by the vector R_A. This can be regarded as having two components: L_A representing the lift from the aerofoil shape of the sail; and D_A the drag at right angles in the direction of the apparent wind, V_A. The major contribution to forward movement is derived from the first third of the sail aft from the luff, while the rest of the sail (increasingly towards the leech) only provides heeling and drag forces but this area cannot be dispensed with.

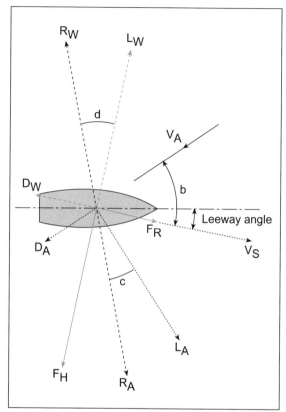

Fig. 17(57) The principal horizontal forces acting on a close-hauled upright yacht are shown as R_A due to the air (wind) and R_W due to the water.

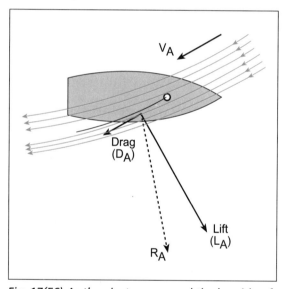

Fig. 17(56) As the air stream round the lee side of a sail is speeded up, the pressure drops. Over the windward side the air stream slows down, and pressure increases. The resultant effect R_A has a small forward component shown as lift L_A, whilst drag D_A acts along the line of the apparent wind.

When sailing the constant aim is to reduce D_A as much as possible and to maximise L_A. This is done by trimming the shape of the sail to suit the conditions, as described in 17.6.4 to 6.6. Maximum lift is obtained when the sail is set to deflect the wind as much as possible, while still maintaining a smooth air

flow. But as more curvature is put into the sail, not only is the forward drive increased but so too is the force pushing the boat sideways, to the point that the boat will heel over excessively and may even capsize. Hence as wind speed rises, the sail must be flattened to reduce the power.

Fig. 17(57) shows the principal horizontal forces on a boat sailing upright at a steady speed on the port tack. R_A has already been described, and is balanced by an equal and opposite force R_W which is the sum of the total hydrodynamic forces exerted by the hull and its appendages (principally the keel). Not only must R_W be equal and opposite to R_A, but both must pass through the same point or the boat would rotate, which is to say that the centre of effort of the rig must be over the centre of lateral resistance of the hull.

R_W has two component forces, D_W and L_W at right angles to each other. D_W is the drag of the hull and appendages, acting in the opposite direction to which the boat is moving. This is not along the centreline of the boat but slightly to leeward, as dictated by the leeway angle. Leeway is a necessary evil because it gives the keel the necessary angle of incidence to generate lift to counteract the sideways force of the rig, but with the minimum of drag and the smallest possible amount of leeway.

R_A is also resolved into two different components of more obvious application: one, a force F_R driving the boat ahead; the other F_H at right angles, pushes the hull sideways and heels the boat over. The angle c between R_A and L_A is called the (air) drag angle. If, for a given lift L_A, the drag and consequently the drag angle can be reduced, then R_A would be angled further ahead to increase F_R. Similarly the hydrodynamic drag angle d indicates the efficiency of the keel and hull to generate the necessary side force at the expense of minimum resistance and leeway. From the diagram it can be determined that c + d = b, which is the angle between the apparent wind and the course made good (including leeway). So in terms of heading ability the sum of the drag angles also needs to be as small as possible.

In the brief notes above the heeling forces acting on a boat due to her sails have been largely ignored. Heeling is resisted by the moment of the centre of gravity about the centre of buoyancy. In seeking from the sail plan a combination of maximum forward drive with minimum drag, the undesirable heeling effect of the rig is at the same time being reduced. This means that with an increasing wind optimum sail settings can be retained for longer before it is necessary to depower the rig.

Given the necessary finance, designers will go to extraordinary lengths to experiment with various appendages in full-scale yachts, as was seen in earlier America's Cup competitions in which the extravagant changing of keels was commonplace.

The ordinary yachtsman cannot change the keel of his boat every few races, but he can change the shape of the sails to suit the prevailing conditions and this requires constant attention, particularly when racing. Wind and sea conditions seldom stay the same for long, especially when sailing near the coast. Offshore conditions may be steadier, but even there the good sailor will have learned to detect quite small changes in wind speed or direction, or in the form and behaviour of the waves.

17.6.3 BOAT SPEED
Boat speed is of course vital when racing, but it is also highly desirable when cruising. Keeping a boat sailing at or near her optimum speed demands total concentration. Conditions are constantly changing with small shifts in wind direction, varying wind speed and different sea states. A helmsman will continuously be assessing these factors, and the crew will be trimming the sails accordingly.

Whether beating to windward or sailing off the wind, it is the correct angle of the sails to the apparent wind which results in good performance; that, and the actual shape (curvature) of each individual sail and its trim in relation to other sails. Sails must be set so that they generate the greatest lift or drive, together with the minimum drag and heeling effect.

In light winds it is important to ease the sheets a trifle, to have enough flow (fullness) in the sails. As the wind increases so the sheets are steadily hardened in to make the sails flatter.

In strong winds the boat must be kept on her feet and balanced on the helm, first by flattening the sails and then by reefing the headsail or mainsail (17.5.4/5). Most modern yachts are relatively beamy for their length, and do not perform well if heeled excessively.

Finally consider some extraneous factors: The boat's bottom must be clean, if boat speed is to be maximised. The best fore and aft trim must be determined, and weight should be kept out of the ends of the boat to reduce pitching which upsets the flow of air over the sails. The rig must be set up so that the mast is straight, and remains straight when the boat heels under pressure of sail, and the mast should have the correct fore and aft rake to give a nicely balanced helm.

17.7 SAIL TRIMMING

One ship sails East – another West,
On the selfsame wind that blows:
But it isn't the gales – it's the trim of the sails,
That determine the way she goes.

17.7.1 SAIL PARAMETERS
Given that in elevation fore and aft sails are triangular in shape – with a luff, leech and foot – there are subtle differences that can be built into the third dimension, ie how full or flat the sail is cut, and where the maximum draught (depth or fullness) occurs. The shape of a given sail can also be greatly adjusted by the different sail controls available. But first the terms used in Fig. 17(58) must be understood.

Draught is an important factor; it is expressed as a percentage of the chord, usually that at about half the height of the sail. So d/c in the diagram can vary from about 10 – 12% for a flat cut sail to 15 – 20% for a full one. The upper parts of a sail have rather more draught than at half height, and the lower parts have rather less. The position of maximum draught along the chord of the sail is another important factor, and typically a/c is about 45% but, like the maximum draught itself, this will depend upon the conditions.

So a sail can be set with an infinite number of shapes in terms of entry angle (that is, how close it will set to the wind), maximum draught, and the position of maximum draught. The aim is to get the right combination for both headsail and mainsail.

However, there is yet another complication – twist. Wind velocity increases with height above the water due to the reduction of friction. Thus higher up the sail the apparent wind moves aft. To maintain a constant angle of incidence the sail must be allowed to twist. Fig. 17(59) shows this in an exaggerated way to make the point.

When beating to windward, the correct trim of the headsail in relation to the mainsail is of considerable importance. The gap between the two sails forms a narrowing slot, and as the wind passes through this it speeds up, causing a drop in pressure (venturi effect) on the lee side of the mainsail. This negative pressure is the major force (L_A) that drives the boat on through the water (and allows aeroplanes to fly). The gap must therefore be high on the list of priorities.

17.7.2 HEADSAIL SHAPE

Headsail shape is controlled by luff tension, sheeting position, sheet tension and barber haulers (if fitted). Luff tension is set by the halyard and possibly also by a luff Cunningham near the tack. It affects the position of maximum draught in the sail. When fairly slack the draught will be further aft, and the angle of entry at the luff gives good pointing ability. As tension is increased for stronger winds the draught is moved forward, giving more power to the sail for going through waves but at the expense of pointing ability.

The fore and aft sheeting position is adjusted by

a car on a track, angled inboard from the deck edge toward the centreline; it affects not only the draught in the sail but also the twist. Moving the sheet lead forward reduces the twist (closes the leech). Bringing the lead aft increases the twist (opens the leech).

Barber haulers (also known as tweakers) are small tackles, or just a rope, snatched to the sheet and led aft via a block to a winch. They pull the sheet sideways (athwartships) and so help to place the clew in any desired position.

17.7.3 MAINSAIL SHAPE

There are even more ways of controlling mainsail shape: fore and aft mast bend, athwartships mast bend, luff tension, clew outhaul tension, mainsheet tension, mainsheet traveller position, kicking strap (gaskicker or boom vang) tension, clew Cunningham adjustments (where fitted), and leech line (where fitted).

In boats with relatively flexible masts, increasing the fore and aft bend flattens the mainsail and opens the leech, so depowering the sail. Athwartships bend, depending on its position, alters the flow in the mainsail and the position of maximum draught. If for example the lower part of the mast is allowed to fall slightly to leeward, that part of the mainsail becomes fuller and power increases. When the head of the mast falls off to leeward (a relatively common occurrence with increasing wind strength) the mainsail flattens, the draught moves forward, the leech opens and power is reduced – a desirable state of affairs.

The luff can be tensioned in various ways depending on the boat. Often it is by a sliding gooseneck, supplemented by a Cunningham hole a short distance above the tack. Increased luff tension pulls draught forward opening the leech.

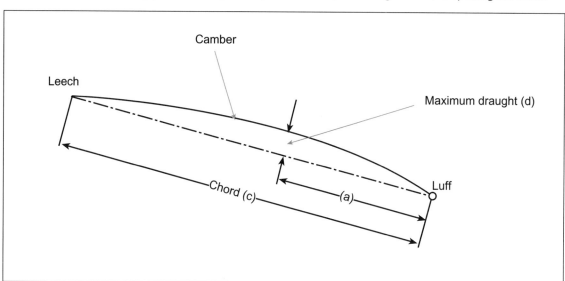

Fig. 17(58) Terms which describe a sail's shape.

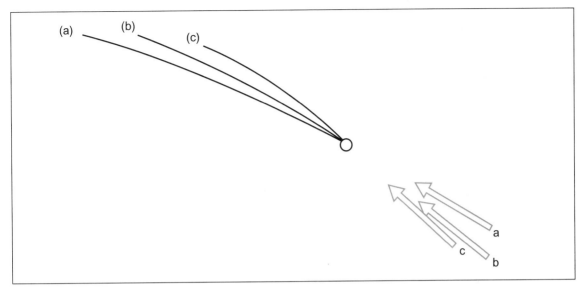

Fig. 17(59) How sail twist allows for the apparent wind's change in direction higher up the sail. (a) is the shape of the sail near the foot; (b) at half height; and (c) near the head. a, b and c show the corresponding directions of the apparent wind.

The clew outhaul also needs regular adjustment. Increased tension flattens the lower mainsail area, opens the lower leech, and moves the draught forward. It should always be slackened off when in harbour.

Mainsheet tension and the position of the traveller need to be considered together. Between them they control not only the sheeting angle of the mainsail but the important amount of twist in the sail. When on the wind a key indicator to mainsail trim is that the top batten should be parallel to the boom, and that the upper leech telltale (17.7.4) should be flying clear. To achieve this in light winds it may be necessary to haul the traveller up to windward of the centreline with less tension in the mainsheet, so that the leech is open. Conversely in strong winds the traveller is progressively let down to leeward, and sheet tension is increased to give a flat sail and a hard leech. For intermediate wind strengths many permutations are available, but only one setting will be just right!

The kicking strap (gaskicker or boom vang) plays an important role in controlling leech tension and mainsail twist once the boat comes off the wind. More tension is needed with increasing wind strength.

If fitted, a clew (or leech) Cunningham is an extra flattening device for strong winds, while a leech line can prevent flutter of the leech when sailing to windward, or stop battens falling to leeward in light airs.

All sail controls must be easy to adjust, ie ready to hand and powerful enough, with or without winches. Those most frequently used should be operable from either side of the boat to keep crew weight properly distributed.

17.7.4 TELLTALES

Telltales are essential for efficient sailing and good sail trimming and yet many cruising yachts do not have them. On a headsail there should be about four telltales, equally spaced along the luff and about 250mm aft of the luff in a small yacht, and slightly further aft in larger vessels. Various materials can be used, but tufts of wool about 200mm long on each side of the sail, put through the cloth with a needle and knotted in place each side, will suffice. In wet weather they can be coated with candlegrease to stop them sticking to the sail.

When sailing to windward with the sail trimmed correctly and the boat on a close-hauled course, the smooth airflow over both windward and leeward sides of the luff keeps both sets of telltales streaming steadily. If the boat is allowed to sail too close to the wind (or similarly if the genoa sheet is eased) the windward telltales will flutter as the airflow around that side of the sail starts to break down. If the boat bears away from a close-hauled course the leeward telltales will flutter as the airflow on the lee side is blanked. Hence the helmsman's aim is to keep both sets at rest, although in practice a slight upward flutter by the windward set gives the best results. Off the wind the helmsman steers the required course while the sail trimmer takes over the job of keeping the telltales quiet and maintaining the correct air flow over the headsail.

Headsail telltales also serve to determine the proper fore and aft sheeting position for the sail. When this is correct and the boat is slowly luffed above a close-hauled course, all the windward telltales should flutter simultaneously. If the top telltale flutters first, the sail has too much twist and the sheet lead must be moved forward. Conversely if the bottom telltale flutters first, the lead should be moved aft.

Mainsail telltales, usually made of ribbon, are equally spaced along the leech between the batten pockets. When they all stream smoothly aft most of the time, and the top batten is parallel to the boom, all is well and the mainsail twist is satisfactory. But if they flutter around the lee side of the sail, then it is not correctly sheeted. Often the top telltale gives the first such warning.

17.7.5   SPINNAKER HANDLING

Spinnakers call for a little more organisation and coordination than cruising chutes, but reward you with a far more satisfying offwind performance. And in a cruising yacht, which can, if need be, temporarily alter course while the spinnaker is hoisted or lowered, it should be perfectly easy to handle this sail with just a little foresight and practice. The basic spinnaker gear is described in 17.5.8 and illustrated in Fig. 17(14).

Preparation for hoisting

The key to this is preparation; the pole should be set up roughly at right angles to the apparent wind, at right angles to the mast and adjusted to the right height on the mast, so that the sail is well spread. A topping lift at the outboard end of the pole takes its weight and a downhaul resists the upward pull of the sail.

The spinnaker should be packed into a 'turtle', a rectangular bag secured to the side of the foredeck, rather than at the bow where a circular bag is used. This enables the hoist to be in the lee of the headsail. The two edges of the sail are usually coloured red and green (to avoid confusion when re-packing it). Get any twists out, and leave the two clews protruding at each side, ready for sheet and guy, with the head at the top to take the halyard's swivel shackle. The halyard routes outside the headsail and its sheets and over the guardrail. The guy runs from the tack outside everything, around the forestay, through the outboard end of the pole (jaws upwards) then via a turning block on the quarter to a suitable winch. The sheet simply goes from the clew to the quarter block and winch. Barber haulers may be used to adjust both the guy and the sheet. Both sheet and guy must be over the guardrails. Next ease the headsail from close hauled and bear away onto a broad reach. Pull the guy so that the tack is dragged out to the end of the pole; the sheet should be slack.

Hoisting

The headsail and main now provide a lee in which to hoist the spinnaker without it filling prematurely. Hoist smartly and secure the halyard. Aft the guy to

bring the pole back from the forestay, and trim with the sheet. Lower/roll the headsail.

Trimming

The basic rules are:

a. Adjust the outer end of the pole so that tack and clew are level. Keep the pole horizontal.

b. Trim the guy so the pole lies roughly in line with the main boom. Even on a close reach, never let the pole touch the forestay.

c. Ease the sheet until the luff curls, then trim it in – keep repeating the process.

d. If the top of the luff curls first, raise the outboard end of the pole. If the bottom breaks, lower it.

e. On a run, square the pole right aft so that the spinnaker flies clear of the main.

f. Keep the downhaul tight enough to stop the pole 'bouncing' in a seaway.

Gybing

This is not difficult in light winds, but get in practice before trying it in stronger winds. In boats up to about 36ft LOA you can usually end-to-end the pole in dinghy style. Start from a run with the pole squared right aft. As the helmsman gybes and the mainsail comes across, unclip the pole from the mast and attach that end to the new guy (which was the sheet). Release the old guy (now the sheet) from the other end, push the pole across to windward and clip this new inboard end to the mast. Meanwhile the trimmer has been tending the sheets and guys to keep the spinnaker drawing and ensure that it does not get wrapped around the forestay. Set up the barber haulers for the new gybe.

In larger yachts a dip-pole gybe is much better, even though it means a separate guy and sheet for each clew of the spinnaker, with all the extra rope entailed. The end of the pole is never detached from the mast, but is pushed as high as necessary up its track so that, when the old guy has been released from the outer end of the pole, the pole can be lowered on the topping lift and swung forward, dipping inside the forestay. At this point the lazy guy on the other side of the boat is snatched into the end of the pole and is winched aft to take the weight from the old sheet. With good crew co-ordination the spinnaker should be kept full throughout the gybe; this helps the procedure and avoids getting a wrap around the forestay.

Lowering

Lowering, or handing, the spinnaker is not difficult. Turn onto a broad reach and unroll (or hoist) the headsail, then sheet it in to provide a lee for lowering the spinnaker. Ease the guy so that the pole runs forward to the forestay. Haul in the sheet and as the halyard is gently eased away, pull the foot of the sail inboard abaft the shrouds on the lee side. Let the guy run through the pole end and bundle the sail down the companionway. Sort out the sail in the cabin and stow it in its turtle bag, ready for use. On a reach use the same basic procedure, but this can be more difficult because the headsail and mainsail do not provide such an effective lee. Snuffers are described in 17.5.8.

17.7.6   RUNNING IN STRONG WINDS

Downwind in strong winds it is best to use a narrow-shouldered, flat spinnaker, smaller than normal and of heavier cloth. The halyard should be hoisted close up, the pole should be lowered somewhat, and the sheet kept trimmed in more than usual, so that the sail is well stretched out and hence more stable.

Rig a preventer to the end of the boom. An efficient boom vang/gaskicker keeps the boom from lifting and eliminates undue twist near the head of the sail, which can push the masthead to windward and help induce rolling. Ideally the boom vang should be rove to the cockpit, so that it can be freed quickly if the boom dips in the sea, with a risk of breakage.

Broaching occurs for several reasons, and in bad conditions may cause the helmsman to lose control of the yacht. She then rounds up, beam on to wind and sea, and lies over on her side. The causes include:

a. carrying too much sail, creating excessive heel;
b. imbalance between the forward and aft immersed shapes of the hull, inducing a turning couple between the centre of lateral resistance and the centre of effort of the sail plan;
c. diminished rudder effectiveness as the boat heels;
d. diminished rudder effectiveness when the water flow over the rudder is reduced as a wave crest passes under the boat's stern;
e. the turning effect when the bow ploughs into the trough of a wave and the stern is swung round by the following crest, which is moving faster.

To counter a broach let the mainsheet run (if the boom is not already squared off), ease the boom vang to allow the mainboom to sky (thus spilling wind) and let go the spinnaker sheet. When the boat rights, get the spinnaker sheet and boom vang in again, so as to regain control of the boat.

When a cruising yacht is running downwind in bad conditions, instead of having to cope with a spinnaker especially if short-handed, it is more comfortable, sensible and safer (and not a lot slower) to goosewing the genoa, or perhaps a smaller headsail. Rig the spinnaker pole, with lift

and downhaul attached, and snatch the genoa sheet to the pole end. To stop the pole swinging about, rig a preventer.

Yachts intended for long downwind passages, as in the Trade winds, are often fitted with twin running headsails. This rig, with the main lowered, minimises chafe. But it can cause prolonged rolling, and if a man goes overboard, it takes time to hoist the mainsail and get back to windward.

In revising Sections 17.5, 17.6 and 17.7 the Editor acknowledges with thanks the technical assistance given by Rob Kemp of Kemp Sails Ltd, The Sail Loft, 2 Sandford Lane Industrial Estate, Wareham, Dorset BH20 4DY. Tel 01929 554803; Fax 554350. e-mail info@kempsails.com www.kempsails.com

17.8 BOOKS ABOUT RIGGING, ROPES AND SAILS

SPARS
Sailing Rigs & Spars Sheahan (Haynes)
Rigging Handbook Toss (Adlard Coles)
Sail and Rig Tuning Dedekam (Fernhurst)

ROPES AND KNOTS
Ashley Book of Knots Ashley (Doubleday)
The Colour Book of Knots Hin (Adlard Coles)
Nautical Knots & Lines Snyder (Adlard Coles)
Knots and Splices Day (Adlard Coles)
Book of Practical Knots Budworth (Adlard Coles)
RYA Book of Knots Owen (Adlard Coles)
Knots in Use Jarman (Adlard Coles, 2nd edn)
Alternative Knot Book Asher (Adlard Coles)
Splicing Handbook Merry & Darwin (Adlard Coles)
Complete Guide to Knots by Bigon & Regazzoni
Knots and Splices Judkins & Davison (Fernhurst)
The Handbook of Knots Pawson

SAILS
Nicolson on Sails Nicolson (Adlard Coles)
Sails Harvey (Adlard Coles)
Best of SAIL Trim Masson (Adlard Coles)
New Book of SAIL Trim Textor (Adlard Coles)
Practical Junk Rig Hasler & McLeod (Adlard Coles)
How to Trim Sails Schweer (Adlard Coles)
Sails for Cruising – Trim to Perfection Chisnell (Fernhurst)
Sail Power Smith & Preece (Fernhurst)
Sail Performance Marchaj (Adlard Coles)
Canvaswork and Sail repair Casey (Adlard Coles)

Chapter 18 Deck gear

CONTENTS

18.1 ANCHORS AND EQUIPMENT

18.1.1 TYPES OF ANCHOR

Anchors come in various shapes, each with its merits, but there is no 'best' shape. A genuine cruising yacht which anchors frequently needs at least three and preferably four anchors, of different types and sizes. Fig. 18(1) shows five main types of anchors: Fisherman, Danforth, CQR, Bruce and Delta.

a. The Fisherman (or stocked) anchor is the most traditional type. It is versatile and worth having, but it must be heavier than modern types for equal holding power and is rather awkward to haul aboard. It will hold well in any reasonable bottom, especially on rock, and will penetrate kelp and weed. With the stock unshipped it stows neatly and without the projections of the more modern shapes. A disadvantage is that the upper fluke may be fouled by the cable when the yacht swings (eg at the turn of the tide), possibly causing the anchor to drag. Holding performance is improved if the flukes are sharpened somewhat with a file and the exposed bare metal given a couple of coats of epoxy paint for protection. One of the common zinc-rich paints (such as Galvafroid) will preserve it excellently on deck, but they are rather soft and soon wear off if the anchor is used frequently. The stock should weigh about 20% of the total weight. The key which holds the stock in place must be securely fastened.

b. The Danforth dates from 1939. Its wide flukes can pivot about 30° either way, and have sharp points to dig into the bottom, while its long stock runs through the crown. It is a good general purpose anchor but, like the CQR below, it can skate over a weed-infested bottom rather than dig in. Once set it can be difficult to break out, so a tripping line may be needed. One of its attractions is that it can be lashed flat on deck.

The Fortress is a modern variant of the Danforth shape and is highly rated in the USA. It is made of a high tensile aluminium magnesium alloy which is strong and exceptionally light; the FX 16, suitable for a 10m boat, weighs 7 lbs (3kg). For the same holding power it is half the weight of a Danforth and hence is easier to handle, stow or take away in a dinghy as a kedge.

c. The CQR (ploughshare) anchor was designed in the 1930s for mooring flying boats. The ploughshare fluke is hinged at the crown so that it tries to dig into the bottom no matter

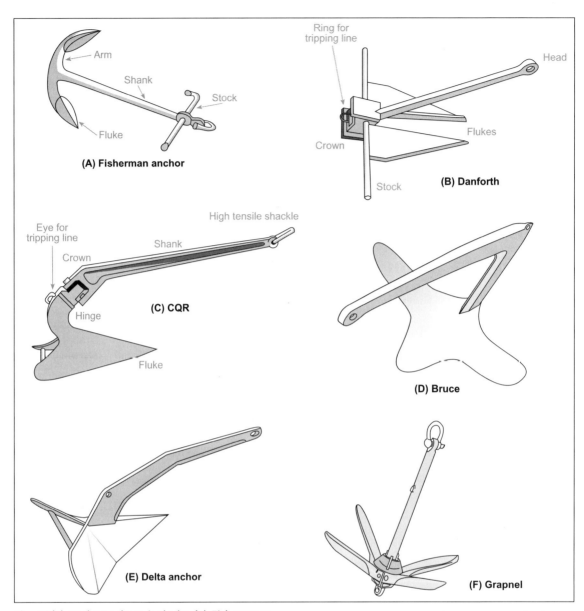

Fig. 18(1) Yacht anchors include: (a) Fisherman; (b) Danforth; (c) CQR; (d) Bruce; (e) Delta.

in what attitude it lands. The genuine CQR anchor is drop-forged for reliability and strength and is designated as 'High holding power' by Lloyd's. It weighs about the same as a Danforth of equal holding power. This good general purpose anchor is popular with yachtsmen and holds well on most bottoms except weed. But if it does drag it tends to reset better than most other types. It can be stowed neatly in the bow roller fittings; see Fig. 18(2).

Imitations of the Danforth and CQR can be found, the latter under the generic heading of 'plough' anchors. Although some are good, eg the Britany (sic) which is a Danforth look-

alike, others are not; if there are any doubts it pays to buy the genuine article.

d. The Bruce anchor originated for mooring oil rigs. Its rather clumsy claw-like shape is such that it will always lie with the weight on one of its three flukes. As the anchor then drags over the seabed this fluke digs in and turns the anchor so that the other flukes do likewise. It is awkward to stow on deck or below, but fits well into its own purpose-built bow fitting; see Fig. 18(2). It is claimed that for the same holding power it can be lighter than either a Danforth or CQR.

e. Since its introduction in 1990 the Delta has been much praised. It results from many years research and development into the merits of all known anchor types for different types of boat and seabeds and

f. The Grapnel folds conveniently and is ideal for use in an inflatable where it can do no harm. It is not made in sizes large enough for anchoring a yacht.

The Table overleaf, Fig. 18(3) suggests minimum sizes of anchors and cables for various boat lengths; anything larger is a bonus. The second, or kedge, anchor may be 70% of the weight of the main, or bower, anchor. A normal person can man-handle a 23kg (50lb) anchor without too much difficulty and a few people can manage up to maybe 34kg (75lb). Above that size a self-stowing anchor and a windlass, either manual or powered, become essential (18.1.3).

The chain should be clearly marked (with coloured paint or electrical cable ties) at intervals of about 3 - 6m, so that it is easy to veer the correct length of chain. The inboard end of the chain, known as the bitter end, should be secured, not shackled, with a lanyard to an eye or other secure point in the chain locker. If this is inaccessible, it is sensible to have the lanyard long enough for it to show through the chain pipe on deck. Thus, if the chain and anchor have to be abandoned in a hurry, it can be quickly cut (preferably after attaching a marker buoy and line to it). Lengths of chain are best joined with a proper chain joining link, available from chandlers, which is much stronger than using a shackle.

Chain cable which is to be used with a windlass (see 18.1.3.) must be calibrated chain which, when under tension, exactly fits the sprockets of the gypsy concerned. Regrettably there is no universal standard for the calibration of chain, so great care is needed when matching chain to gypsy, or vice versa, to avoid slippage and jamming. To ensure an exact fit you may have to buy chain, as well as the windlass, from the same manufacturer.

Anchor warp should be nylon because of its good elasticity; see also 17.4.4 for recommended rope sizes. Anchorplait is a proprietary brand which is tough, easily handled and ideal for a kedge. A 3 to 5m length of chain can readily be spliced between the warp and anchor. Flat webbing spools (Anchorline) are a good option for a kedge; they are conveniently mounted inside a pushpit and are usually tangle-free.

For anchoring techniques see Chapter 3.

18.1.2 STEMHEAD ROLLERS AND CHAIN STOPPERS

A roller fairlead very strongly bolted to the stemhead is essential except on very small boats. It keeps the chain or anchor warp in place when anchored, and allows it to be retrieved reasonably easily. The roller itself should be broad and free-running on its spindle. The jaws on each side should splay outward so that chain lies

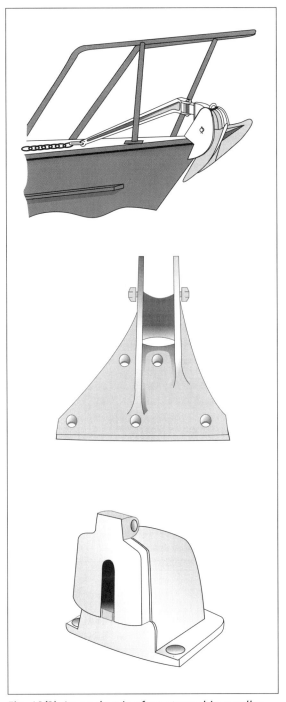

Fig. 18(2) An anchor is often stowed in a roller fairlead, as with this CQR (upper). A Bruce stows in a purpose-built fitting (centre). A chain pipe with hinged cover is below.

resembles a CQR. It is of one-piece rigid construction to give good performance under load and maximum strength. It is designed for easy self-launching and self-stowing, while the configuration gives quick setting once on the seabed, with the blade having a sharp point to improve penetration.

Minimum sizes for anchors and cable (based on craft of average displacement)												
Boat LOA m (ft)	6	(20)	7·3	(25)	9	(30)	11	(35)	12	(40)	14	(45)
Anchors kg (lb)												
Fisherman	12	(26)	14	(31)	18	(40)	23	(51)	32	(70)	41	(90)
Danforth	7	(15)	10	(22)	14	(30)	18	(40)	25	(55)	35	(77)
Fortress	2	(4)	2·7	(6)	3·2	(7)	3·2	(7)	6·3	(14)	8·6	(19)
Britany (sic)	8	(18)	10	(22)	12	(26)	20	(45)	25	(55)	35	(77)
CQR	6·8	(15)	9	(20)	11	(25)	16	(35)	20	(45)	27	(60)
Delta	6	(14)	6	(14)	10	(22)	10	(22)	16	(35)	25	(55)
Bruce	5	(11)	7·5	(16)	10	(22)	15	(33)	20	(45)	30	(66)
Chain, diam: mm (in)	6·5	(6)	8	($\frac{5}{16}$)	8	($\frac{5}{16}$)	8	($\frac{3}{8}$)	9·5	($\frac{7}{16}$)	11	($\frac{7}{16}$)
Chain weight: kg/m	1·1		1·5		1·5		1·5		2·2		2·8	
Nylon warp: mm (in)	10	($\frac{3}{8}$)	12	($\frac{1}{2}$)	16	($\frac{5}{8}$)	16	($\frac{5}{8}$)	18	($\frac{3}{4}$)	18	(7)

Fig. 18(3) Table of minimum anchor and chain sizes for different LOAs.

easily at any angle off the bow. A drophead pin will stop the chain jumping out of the jaws.

A stemhead roller with a pawl can be advantageous with chain. Fig. 18(4) shows one way of fitting the pawl; when lifted the chain can run out freely. When it is dropped the chain can be hauled in but cannot run out. This is useful on a sailing craft with no windlass, but even with one, a crewman can rest without making fast the chain, with the risk of jamming his fingers.

A chain stopper, separate from the the stemhead roller, serves a similar purpose to the above pawl. A modern version in stainless is available and works well in conjunction with a windlass.

A compressor is a rarely seen but useful item, particularly on large traditional craft when handling very heavy chain and anchors. It allows the foredeck man to check the run of the chain by leaning or pulling on a handle. He does not have to surge the chain round a bollard, which can be difficult; or worse still try standing on it! It may be hard to get, but can easily be made in a metal workshop.

A chain hook is a simple but very useful item. It is attached to a length of nylon rope and then hooked onto the anchor chain outboard of the roller fairlead. The nylon is secured on deck so as to take the weight off the anchor chain, thus silencing the overnight noise of chain working under load. It can also be used to help weigh anchor by taking a longer line aft to a sheet winch, if no windlass is fitted.

18.1.3 WINDLASSES

In a yacht context the word windlass is now taken to include capstans. The original distinction was that a windlass had a drum with a horizontal axis whilst the capstan's axis was vertical.

Windlasses now come with horizontal or vertical drums; see Fig. 18(5). They can handle chain and/or rope warp; and may be electrically, hydraulically or manually operated. A vertical drum axis, like that of a sheet winch, has advantages in that the lead to it can be taken from any angle. This is useful, especially when warping a boat into a berth. It can also double as an extra foredeck 'cleat', useful when rafted up with shore lines and other boats' warps to be secured.

Manual windlasses with a horizontal axis work by pumping a lever fore and aft. This may be single or double action, ie they may operate on only the aft stroke or on both, usually the latter. They may also have two speeds, eg high (14:1) for when the work is easy and the chain can come home quickly, and low (40:1) for when a real load is on the chain. The larger hand operated windlasses can be used for loads up to

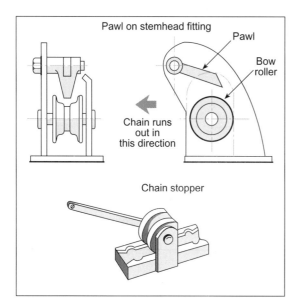

Fig. 18(4) A pawl at the bow roller helps when weighing anchor; a chain stopper serves a similar purpose.

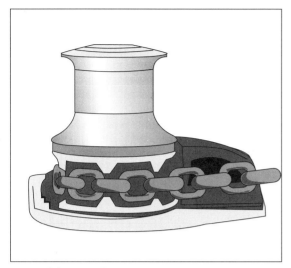

Fig. 18(5) Vertical windlass with rope drum.

450kg (1000lb) or more and are capable of handling chain up to 12mm (5in) diameter.

The gypsy (the drum at the side around which the cable runs) can accommodate chain only or chain and rope; this is useful where rope is the main anchor cable but is spliced to the anchor with a short length of chain. There is also normally a separate rope drum on the opposite side of the windlass from the chain gypsy. The rope drum and chain gypsy can operate independently of each other.

Electrical or hydraulic windlasses: Usually, the relatively small boats use electrical types but as craft get bigger with more elaborate engine arrangements, the tendency is to switch to the, perhaps, slightly more reliable and robust hydraulic types. This requires a hydraulic pump to be driven off the main engine or a generator (usually by belt) which transmits power via a hydraulic hose to another pump in the windlass itself; clearly it only works if the engine is running.

Typically, the electric windlass draws current, on a 12-volt system, as follows:

34 amps for a pull of 45kg (100lb); 69 amps for 135kg (300lb); and 100 amps for 225kg (500lb). For 24 volts the corresponding figures would be 20 amps, 33 amps and 44 amps; and 80 amps at 450kg (1000lb) pull.

These pull figures are a bit confusing but on smaller boats using up to 8mm (5/16in) chain, the maximum likely pull would be 135kg (300lb), while for those with 10mm (3/8in) chain the figure rises to 180kg (400lb), and on those that have 12mm ($\frac{1}{2}$in) chain the maximum likely is 225kg (500lb).

Most electric windlasses can be fitted with an overload protection unit which will trip if the windlass is overloaded other than briefly, and some are equipped with a gear change mechanism. To conserve battery power, an electric windlass should normally only be operated when the engine is running and the alternator is charging. Both hydraulic and electric types can normally be fitted with a lever for hand operation in an emergency. Some have an indicator which shows how much cable has been veered.

18.1.4 CHAIN LOCKERS

Allowing anchor chain to pile up in the bottom corner of an undrained chain locker is asking for trouble and unpleasant smells. It is easier to clean mud off the chain with a long-handled scrubber (milk churn brush from your nearest agricultural stockist) as it comes over the bow roller, rather than stowing filthy chain in the locker. The shape of some lockers stops the chain stowing itself evenly; instead it piles up into an ever taller pyramid which eventually blocks the navel pipe. A conical-shaped deflector may be devised or, in the short term, someone will have to go below to clear it. The locker should have a perforated tray in it on which the chain sits, and a good sized drain plug at the bottom. If the locker is not directly under the navel pipe, the chain should be led to the locker in a trough, not through a pipe in which it will inevitably jam. Chain lockers tend to be too far forward for best weight distribution. 70 metres of 5/16" chain, a suitable length for deeper water, weighs about 230lbs, the same as a large man.

18.2 DECK FITTINGS

18.2.1 PULPITS AND GUARDRAILS

A pulpit allows people to work round the forestay in safety and with reasonable ease. This means that a man must be able to get forward of the stay and be sustained in that position. If the pulpit does not extend far enough forward things may be difficult, and if it is too wide he may be flung from side to side in bad weather. There is more to the design of a pulpit than simply running a railing round the bow. Remember, too, that it will probably be necessary to haul the anchor on to the foredeck and this may be difficult if the lower rail is fixed at an inconvenient height. A pulpit must be at least 600mm (24in) high and its bases should be designed to take transverse loads as well as fore and aft.

Stanchions were discussed in 15.10.6 but it is worth repeating here that they too should be at least 600mm (24in) high (and are better if even more than that) and must be very securely through-bolted at their bases. Stanchions have a top wire (or rail in larger craft) and, lower down, a second wire at just above mid-height. The lead of these wires should be checked to see that they do not chafe. The wires themselves are probably best made of a plastic-covered stainless steel. Somewhere along their length they should be clipped to, rather than pass through, the

stanchions to make a gateway for getting aboard. Stanchions may be of stainless steel, aluminium alloy tube, or mild steel (epoxy-painted after fabrication).

18.2.2 MOORING CLEATS, BITTS AND BOLLARDS

An average sized yacht should have at least six large cleats on deck; two forward, two amidships and two aft. They should be as large as possible since they will often have to accept two or more warps. Normally the forward cleat will take a head rope and a spring, and the aft cleat a stern rope and a spring; the midships cleat may take a breast rope or springs although the latter are less effective in controlling the boat when secured amidships; see 3.3.2. Cleats should be very strongly bolted through stout backing plates glassed in over a generous area.

Fig. 18(6) shows attachment points more usually fitted on larger or more traditional craft; there is often little space for them on the foredeck of a modern yacht. A bitt has one vertical post with a horizontal bar (which can cause a nasty ankle injury) through it, and a bollard has two vertical posts. Either can accept several lines or the anchor chain or warp.

Many yachts lack an adequate attachment point for a tow rope, as the RNLI are only too well aware. Even the foot of a deck-stepped mast is rarely strong enough for the job, and a rope or bridle often has to be rigged right round the superstructure. A bridle can also be rigged to the main sheet winches which in turn can be backed up by lashings to other winches further aft. More traditional boats usually had a sampson post forward which was a stout timber post (ideally oak), stepped on the keel and emerging on the foredeck. This could take the immense strain of towing and is a desirable feature on today's cruising yachts. If fitting a windlass with vertical drum, this might serve as an attachment point for towing, as well as its main role, provided it is mounted as strongly as a sampson post.

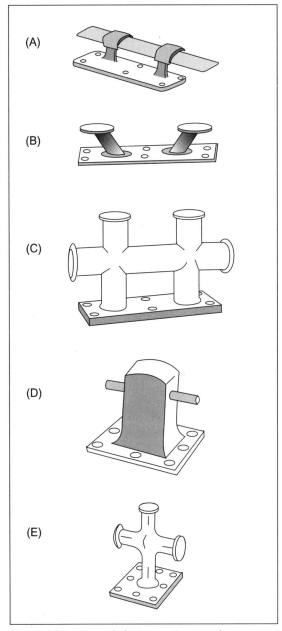

Fig. 18(6) Rope and chain require good attachment points, particularly on the foredeck. Typical fittings are (a) a mooring cleat; (b) a raked bollard; (c) crosshead bollard; (d) a mooring bitt; and (e) a better type of mooring bitt, or staghorn.

18.2.3 FAIRLEADS

Warps which are secured onboard to a cleat or similar point are lead outboard through a fairlead. This keeps the warp from chafing on toe rails and stanchions and allows it a clear lead ashore. The larger and better made the fairlead is, the less it will chafe the rope. Fairleads are made in various types, such as straight, handed, lipped, closed and roller, as in Fig. 18(7).

Handed types retain the warp quite well provided of course that they are fitted on the appropriate sides of the craft. The lipped type is similar; the warp needs to be slotted between

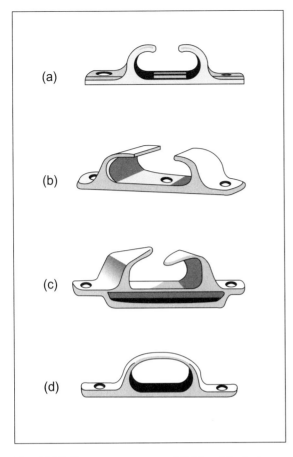

Fig. 18(7) Commoner types of fairlead include: (a) the straight type which may be mounted to port or starboard; (b) handed fairleads which must be fitted on the correct side; (c) a lipped type from which a rope is unlikely to be loosed accidentally; and (d) a closed (Panama) fairlead which is secure against a vertical pull.

the lips, but once in place it is not likely to jump out. A warp has to be threaded through closed fairleads, which may be a nuisance, but it can be guaranteed to stay in position; this is particularly useful if, for example, negotiating a deep lock where the warp might lead almost vertically upwards.

18.2.4 VENTILATORS

Very little attention is paid to natural ventilation on most small craft. An opening port or two, or sliding windows, plus a couple of hatches will provide a fair degree of ventilation if they could be left open, but in bad weather or when the craft is vacated openings are usually tight shut. This leads to a damp and unpleasant atmosphere which induces condensation below decks and, in a wooden boat, provides ideal conditions for the development of dry rot; nor is it good for humans. Ventilation should also be able to cope

with very high temperatures below deck in the tropics; see 19.7.6.

Properly there should be one air change every 20 minutes or so, and that is a reasonable figure on which to base calculations. If the cabin of a yacht were, say, 23 cu m (800 cu ft) in volume and the air inside could be evacuated at 1 knot (30m/min or l00ft/min) while she was closed up, the ventilators must be able to cope with 23/20 = 1.15 cu m (40cu ft) of air for there to be a change every 20 minutes. Using the 30m/min flow figure, then the cross-sectional area of the vents must be 1.15/30 = 0.038 sq m (0.4 sq ft). That would be achieved by two 75 mm (3in) diameter vents, plus two more same-sized vents to remove the old air.

The figure of 30m/min (l00ft/min) is a low one but the average yacht ventilator is so full of chokes and restrictions that it is probably realistic. In bad weather, although it may be blowing hard, some of the vents will probably be still be open and will have to cope with a wet and heavy-breathing crew below.

The classic type of vent is the Dorade, Fig. 18(8), where a cowl fits atop a box in which is a simple tube offset some little distance from the cowl. Any water getting in through the cowl will simply swill around the box, from which it can drain away, and will not find its way below unless so deep that it overflows the tube. It should be possible to remove a cowl from its spigot and snap on a watertight cap in its place.

The latest Dorade vents are in effect watertight, thanks to an integral damper which automatically closes in the event of very heavy rain or a particularly large wave, and reopens when the water has drained away from the base; it can also be manually operated.

Normal mushroom ventilators can be screwed shut or opened as far as is desirable. Cowl vents

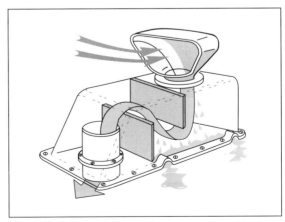

Fig. 18(8) The Dorade is virtually watertight. Any water entering the cowl drains out via holes in the base box.

are more efficient, as might be expected, but their height above deck makes them prone to being kicked or whisked overboard by errant feet, sheets or other lines.

The Aeolian is a special mushroom ventilator which allows air to pass while keeping out all but solid water. It is said to be able to move about 0.23 cu m (8 cu ft) per minute in even a light wind. The Solarvent has a solar-powered extractor fan, which will remove 0.3 cu m (11 cu ft) per minute even in still air.

18.2.5 BOARDING LADDERS
A rigid ladder is needed for boarding all but the smallest cruising boats, either from a tender or from a swim. (A rope ladder is hard to use without practice). The ladder may be of stainless steel, aluminium alloy, plastic or teak. It may be built into the yacht as rungs up the transom; or fold down from the transom into the water; or it may hook over a gunwhale or toe rail. The bottom rung should be at least 30mm (l2in) below the water level; it must be strong and demonstrably able to take the strains likely to be put on it.

A ladder is a mixed blessing in trying to recover a man overboard. A transom-hung ladder is potentially dangerous in that the man in the water can so easily be struck by the transom in even a slight sea state, or his feet may be perilously close to the propeller. A ladder over the boat's side may give the man overboard a chance to get himself aboard, if he is still physically able; or it may provide a footing from which a crew member can help him. Anyone who has been in the water for some time is likely to be too weak to pull himself over the deck edge. The important things are first to secure him with a line and secondly to lift him aboard as in 13.3.9.

18.2.6 TABERNACLES
The traditional tabernacle allows the mast to pivot aft or forward about a bolt through the cheeks of the tabernacle and the spar; the bolt can be through any of several holes in the tabernacle thus varying the height of the pivoting point, within limits. Thus the mast may lie horizontally when lowered aft over a doghouse, or have its truck no higher than the highest point of the yacht when lowered forward onto the pulpit. This ensures the minimum air draught when the craft has to pass under a low bridge. Unlike modern deck-stepped masts, the tabernacle also gives some control over the mast as it is being raised or lowered, since the cheeks extend a little way above the pivoting point and the spar is restrained within them.

In practice some of the load is taken off the bolt by driving a wedge under the heel of the

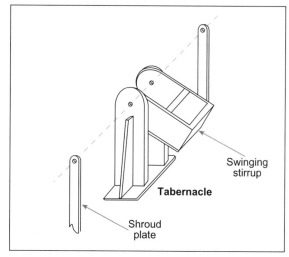

Fig. 18(9) A tabernacle allows a mast to be raised or lowered under reasonable control.

mast once it is raised, but this wedge sometimes jams while the bolt hole in the mast slowly becomes worn and elongated. Both factors make handling the mast more difficult than it should be.

A modern tabernacle is shown in Fig. 18(9) where the mast sits in a stirrup which swings about studs in the main structure. When lowered the mast can simply be slipped out of the stirrup. To ship it again, the stirrup is angled correctly and the mast slipped back. No awkward lining-up of bolt holes is needed.

Though not always possible, if a pair of shrouds can be arranged to be in the same plane as the mast, and if their connections at the chain plates are level with the pivoting studs, these shrouds can be kept tight when lowering or raising the mast and will thus prevent it oscillating laterally. But this set-up usually means extending the chain plates well above deck level.

18.2.7 GALLOWS
Like the tabernacle, boom gallows are out of fashion despite their usefulness. They can be made of timber and steel pipe and provide a good handhold if sited at the aft end of the superstructure. The boom is much more securely stowed in gallows than if supported by a topping lift and restrained only by the sheet. To keep the cockpit clear, the boom can be stowed to one side if the gallows has three slots.

Fig. 18(10) shows a type built from pipe frames (which drop into supports rather like deck stanchions) connected by a stout timber cross-piece. The frames can thus be unshipped and the cross-piece unbolted for stowage. The whole structure, of which there are many variations, should be robust and securely fixed.

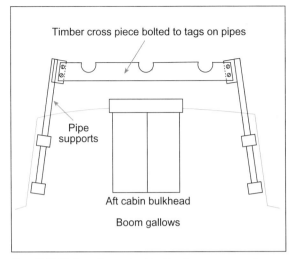

Fig. 18(10) A gallows holds the boom securely.

Timber cross piece bolted to tags on pipes

Pipe supports

Aft cabin bulkhead

Boom gallows

18.2.8 FENDERS

Fenders are needed to absorb any impact and spread the load; hence the larger the better. Modern air-filled types are very good and the cylindrical models which can be hung vertically or horizontally are the most versatile, augmented by large spherical fenders at bow and stern. When berthed against piles a short plank (fender board) is rigged outboard of a couple of fenders so as to bear against the piles. Fenders should always be brought aboard when under way. If left hanging they cause damage and spray, can be lost in rough water, and look untidy swinging about with the boat's motion.

18.2.9 AWNINGS

Whilst rarely needed in UK waters, a good awning is an important item in lower latitudes, certainly in the Mediterranean during summer and in the Caribbean, for example. If regularly used an awning must be easy and quick to erect, and this depends a good deal on the boat's configuration and cockpit layout. In a sloop or cutter athwartship spreaders are likely to be needed across the forward and aft ends of the cockpit, unless the layout allows for a hinged Bimini-type structure.

In the tropics some shelter must be provided at least for the helmsman when under way. This may be a small separate awning or part of the main structure. The latter should be designed for collecting rain water, and detachable sidescreens are a bonus when the sun is lower during longer spells in harbour. They can also preserve privacy when lying alongside a jetty.

Awnings need to be made of a fairly heavy, rotproof material which will resist penetration by the sun's rays and which will not flap about noisily. An awning is often needed on a day which is quite windy but where the sun is still beating down from a clear blue sky.

18.3 TENDERS

Today most cruising boats go to sea with an inflatable dinghy which despite its high cost and relatively short life, in comparison with a rigid dinghy, can at least be stowed on board all but the smallest vessels. It can thus be used as an improvised liferaft in emergencies and makes an adequate people and stores carrier. Rowing an inflatable is not always easy and it is a poor vehicle for laying out a kedge anchor.

Outboards are now the norm and are very much quieter, more efficient and more reliable than those of even twenty years ago. Nevertheless there is still much pleasure – not to mention useful and often strenuous exercise – to be had in rowing ashore through a quiet anchorage without disturbing the peace.

18.3.1 INFLATABLES

There is a wide range of inflatable dinghies on the market, most of which follow the same basic idea of multi-chamber inflatable tubes set on a fabric floor. There may also be an inflatable keel to reduce leeway and an inflatable floor, while wooden floorboards or slats are usually available. The transom may be timber to take an outboard, or a special bracket may be fitted. Built-in rowlocks are provided for the shortish oars. At the expensive end of the market buoyancy tubes are normally a hand-glued Hypalon/nylon material, but a bit lower down the price scale there are craft available with welded Dynalon tubes. Welding is cheaper than hand-glueing. The craft may be inflated by hand, foot or 12v electric powered pumps; these last being very effective. CO_2 inflation bottles are also available with some types, but are an expensive option.

A good quality inflatable is expensive and not to be confused with the toy boats that are blown off beaches complete with their young occupants. The materials used are of far better quality; there are separate buoyancy chambers so that springing a leak does not mean the collapse of the whole craft; and the whole dinghy is much more robustly built.

The British Standards specification for inflatables, MA 16, covers both materials and manufacture and requires, for example, that any ply used in the craft, such as for transoms and floorboards, should be to the marine ply specification BS1088.

Inflatables for use as tenders come in sizes ranging upwards from about 2.4m (8ft) to a maximum of roughly 3.6m (12ft). Much bigger types are also made for commercial applications.

All this excludes rigid bottom inflatables which are dealt with in 18.3.2. Some inflatables can be had with sailing gear. They make a very safe sailing dinghy which is unlikely to capsize under normal wind pressure alone. In fact one of the inflatable's advantages is that it is very stable. It requires deliberate action by the crew, or exceptional action by wind and waves, to turn one over. The tubes that surround the dinghy of course ensure a soft arrival when coming alongside the parent yacht.

Although an inflatable is not a liferaft (with the exception of the Henshaw models) some are offered with a canopy that can be lashed in place to give the occupants some protection against the elements. For a craft set on a lengthy cruise where the expense of a liferaft would be the straw that broke the proverbial camel's back, a canopied inflatable complete with sailing gear might be worth considering.

All reputable inflatable manufacturers supply a repair outfit with their craft and the instructions should be followed, but in an emergency a bicycle puncture repair kit will do a temporary job. The glue supplied with the manufacturer's outfits has a useable life of only about a year, after which it should be replaced. Bostik No. 3 is suitable and is available from many ironmongers or yacht chandlers. If a big tear has been made it is best first to sew the edges together using a herringbone stitch and a thin fishing line as the thread, before applying the patch.

If an inflatable is to be stored for any length of time, it should first be washed down in fresh water. If it can be stored partially inflated so much the better, but if it has to be put back in its valise fold it carefully and in the same manner as it was originally packed.

18.3.2   RIGID INFLATABLE BOATS (RIB)

The normal inflatable with its soft floor cannot make a very satisfactory motor boat because the bottom is all the wrong shape and changes what shape it has with every wave that passes under it. Thus the RIB was developed, where the buoyancy tubes are mounted on a GRP hull that stops at cockpit sole level. This level is above the waterline so that it can be made self-draining, and with the very buoyant tubes round the deck edge the result is a safe boat and one that can be driven as fast as any other high speed motor boat. The parent vessel should be big enough to sling a RIB in davits. It is widely used by the RNLI, the Royal Navy and many commercial companies as a rescue and patrol boat; it is also excellent for towing water skiers.

The fact that the bottom is rigid means that this type of craft loses the advantage the normal inflatable has of being capable of being folded

into a small package where it can be stowed on even quite small yachts. Hence it is not a substitute for the inflatable nor for the normal rigid dinghy. However there are types which can be sailed and rowed quite reasonably.

18.3.3   RIGID DINGHIES

A rigid dinghy's main advantage over an inflatable is that it is better for rowing; it is also drier inside due to a worthwhile depth of hull below the floorboards. Since it has more freeboard it can be rowed in worse weather without soaking the occupants and their gear, and it is a better than an inflatable for rowing out a kedge. With added buoyancy such as bags, slabs of foam or an inflatable collar around its gunwale, it can double as a makeshift liferaft.

Few small cruisers, however, can easily stow a dinghy on deck, and towing it may cause difficulties when manoeuvring in the confines of a marina. In any case a towed dinghy is always a potential source of trouble because in rough seas it may fill with water and break away. A proper cover, although a nuisance to fit, reduces this risk but does not totally eliminate it. Like reefing, a dinghy should always be hauled aboard in deteriorating weather as soon as you first think about it. Unless especially designed for it, a dinghy does not tow well behind a motor cruiser because the high speed causes it to sheer from side to side until eventually it starts to tow broad-side on, or capsizes.

Thus for most yachts (and especially those berthed in marinas) a rigid dinghy is not worth having unless it can be stowed on deck. Its occasional real advantages would be outweighed by its general drawbacks. A dinghy to stow on the deck of an average cruising yacht would have to be no more than 2m to 2.3m (6ft 6in to 7ft 6in) long. At that length it will not be a good rowing boat, but will be acceptable if it has been properly designed. A stem dinghy wastes much useful space forward, and either sheers away or capsizes if anyone is unwise enough to step aboard near the bow. A normal pram dinghy, with a transom at the bow as well as the stern, is better – while a hull of 'W' cross-section should be better still. With the latter, the hull's buoyancy is well outboard so that the boat will be more laterally stable; and, with in effect twin hulls, it will be more directionally stable for rowing and towing than a conventional pram.

The approximate minimum dimensions of a pram dinghy are given in Fig. 18(11); they demonstrate why the usual inflatable can never be rowed with much success – it is simply too shallow. In most small prams feet will be braced against the transom or a brace on the floorboards, with legs slightly flexed. The pram's

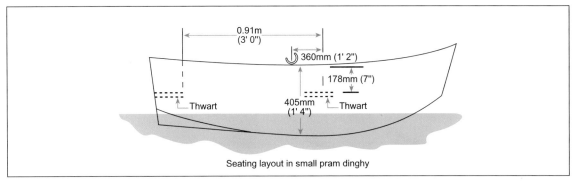

Seating layout in small pram dinghy

Fig. 18(11) Some minimum height and lengths for easy rowing in a small dinghy.

beam would be about 1.2m (4ft) and the oars as long as will stow inside. Thus 2m (6ft 6in) oars will fit neatly in a dinghy which is 2.l5m (7ft) long.

The rowing thwart should be adjustable in different slots, so that the boat is roughly balanced whether full of baggage forward or with two persons; two rowlock positions will also be needed. A notch in the transom is useful not only for sculling, but also for laying out a kedge, or its cable.

If the dinghy is regularly towed, it will tow better if a bridle is secured to two eyebolts at the lower outer corners of the forward transom. Attach the towing warp to the bridle's centre, or use twin warps.

There is no best material for building a dinghy. The lightest will probably be stitch-and-glue ply, and lightness is always a virtue in such craft.

18.3.4 COLLAPSIBLE AND FOLDING DINGHIES

Various collapsible boats appear on the market from time to time. Some have rigid sides that fold down flat on to the rigid bottom, so making a slender package; others fold up lengthways, concertina-wise. Some are made almost entirely of a flexible plastic; the thwarts and transom usually brace the sides apart. But these craft never seem to find much favour ...

18.3.5 EMBARKING TENDERS

At the lightweight end of the scale the popular 2 – 4 man inflatable is invariably manhandled in and out of the water by one or two men. It is then bagged or left partially inflated on deck. Some yachts carry it fully inflated across the transom, but this position blocks the view astern and could be unwise in any kind of following sea. Towing an inflatable is commonplace, but again needs to be done with a careful eye on the weather if it is not to become a liability.

Heavier dinghies can be lifted aboard via the main halyard, although it is a two-man operation; one fends the boat off the yacht's sides

and the other hoists. If floorboards and thwarts can easily be taken out, it will be lighter to hoist aboard, using stout eyebolts fore and aft. The main boom, a spinnaker boom or a stout jockey pole can also be used as a derrick, to swing the tender easily onto the foredeck or amidships. If a rigid dinghy is to be stowed upside down it is best to fix the lifting bridle to eye bolts on the outside of the stem and transom, so that it can be turned over in the air with the bridle still attached.

Many larger yachts and motor cruisers can carry a rigid dinghy at the stern on davits. These should be light, strong and fitted with efficient hoisting gear. Some types have extending arms which can be used to handle different sized tenders. A davit can also be used to sling an aft gangway into place.

18.4 WHEEL-STEERING GEAR

18.4.1 WIRE AND CABLE

The simplest and (generally) the cheapest form of steering gear is that where flexible wire cables are led back from the wheel via sheaves along the hull side to a quadrant on the rudder stock. The quadrant may be replaced by a tiller with a sliding collar attachment for the cables on an even cheaper system. The mechanical advantage can be varied by altering the size of the quadrant (or length of tiller) and the diameter of the wheel.

In its simplest form the wires may be attached to a drum on the wheel but a more usual arrangement is to fit a chain sprocket on the wheel. The wire cable is made fast to the ends of the chain and a typical layout is shown on Fig. 18(12).

A system like this is positive and if all the sheaves are carefully aligned and lubricated it is sensitive to pressures on the rudder. This is important on sailing vessels where 'feel' at the wheel makes for more responsive handling. The tension in the cables must be adjustable – even though everything is normally set up quite slack. Therefore rigging screws or tensioners are fitted at the quadrant or, alternatively, a similar device somewhere along the cable. Rudder stops are fitted to prevent shock loads to the rudder (as in a

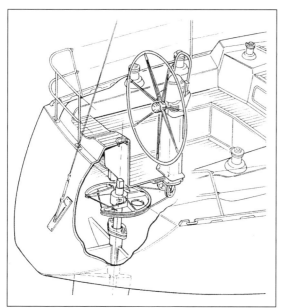

Fig. 18(12) A basic chain and wire wheel-steering system.

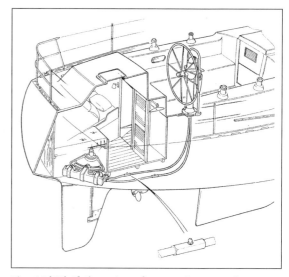

Fig. 18(13) If the wire of a steering gear is enclosed in a conduit, accurately aligned sheaves will no longer be required.

broach) being transmitted directly to the cables. Although the basic components in this system are comparatively inexpensive and there is very little to go wrong (and if it does it is easy to repair), the chain and cable gear may not be much cheaper than more sophisticated systems if installed professionally. This is simply because siting, aligning and bolting down the sheaves is quite a time-consuming business. Autopilots and dual steering positions can be arranged in the layout.

Many fishing boats and similar commercial craft used chain throughout. This was because nearly all the gear was on deck at the deck/bulwark edge and chain would last much longer than the wire then available.

18.4.2   CONDUIT WIRE CABLE GEAR
In this arrangement the wires are led to the quadrant in a conduit. At the quadrant is a special box designed to take the end of the conduit, and this box moves with the quadrant, transmitting the cable movement via sheaves. Autopilots and twin steering positions can be incorporated into the steering gear which is very quick to install since the conduit can follow any convenient path and needs no sheaves to guide it. A typical layout is shown in Fig. 18(13). Rudder stops are vital.

18.4.3   SINGLE CABLE STEERING
This type of steering moves the tiller through a single push-pull cable very similar to the Bowden cable used to operate gears and throttle on marine engines. The cable is contained in a conduit fastened at both ends, and is generally

actuated by a rack and pinion at the wheel. The system is positive in operation and simple to install. Maintenance requirements are low and consist of checking on the free-running of the cable and on lubrication of exposed moving parts, but there is virtually no 'feel' with such an arrangement and it is thus most suited to motor boats where it is widely used on craft up to about 15m (50ft) in length.

18.4.4   MECHANICAL STEERING
Mechanical steering is achieved through a gearbox and simple rod to the wheel as in Fig. 18(14). This is a very effective and comparatively low-cost system where the wheel is sited close to the rudder stock.

If greater distances are involved torque tubes are usually used. These transmit the rotary movement of the wheel to a helm unit which converts it to a back-and-forth movement of an arm linked to the tiller. The torque tubes themselves require bearings to support them if they are over about 2.4m (8ft) long but can change direction between bearings by the use of universal joints or, in more extreme cases, through angled transfer boxes. Various gear ratios are normally available in the bevel boxes below the steering wheel and in the final box at the aft end, so that different mechanical advantages can be obtained. In addition the number of turns of the wheel to achieve a hard-over helm can be selected.

Power assistance can be added, as well as autopilot gear and, if necessary, dual station steering. It is a strong and reliable system, and in many cases the various gearboxes are sealed and

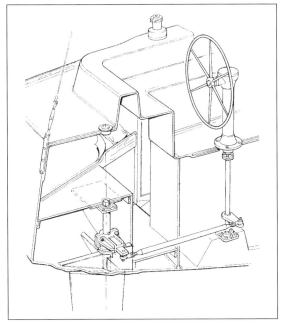

Fig. 18(14) The rotary motion of the wheel is converted by gearing into a push-pull movement of the connecting rod.

lubricated for life. The universal joints, bearings and ball joints need to be greased and clean but this is straightforward. Fig. 18(15) shows a layout.

Fig. 18(16) shows two types of rudder stop which prevent the gear from being damaged under duress, for example, a high-speed broach. Stops also prevent the rudder from assuming an extreme angle when going astern under power.

18.4.5 RACK AND PINION AND WORM GEARS

The two other types of wheel-steering gear in general use are: a. rack and pinion, and b. worm gear. In the former the pinion on the wheel drives the rack on a circular path pivoted about the line of the rudder pintles.

This movement can be transmitted directly to the rudder Fig. 18(17); or can be linked to a push-pull rod side mounted on the rudder, as shown in Fig. 18(18).

The system is smooth and normally has a fair amount of 'feel'. It is usually used in craft where the wheel and rudder are fairly close together, although universal joints may be employed to allow the wheel to be mounted out of line with the rudder pintles so that wheel angle may be adjusted.

Worm gears are best suited to motor boats or sailing yachts where 'feel' is less important than steadiness at the wheel. This might apply to a long-distance cruiser where the ultimate responsiveness could be sacrificed for a steering system where the wheel, on a well-balanced craft, can be left unattended for short periods in moderate conditions, without it being turned by the heaving of the boat. The gear tends to be heavy and very robust and usually requires more turns of the wheel from hard-over to hard-over than other types. Fig. 18(19) shows a typical installation.

18.4.6 HYDRAULIC STEERING

Various types of hydraulic steering are available with different features, but basically they all consist of a hydraulic pump near and directly actuated by the wheel, leading via hydraulic hoses to a ram near the rudder stock. Fig. 18(20) shows the basic layout.

Powered versions can be had for bigger craft and autopilots and dual station steering can easily be built into the layout. Hydraulic steering is quick to install since the hoses can follow any reasonable path and need no aligning. Maintenance requirements are low. For power craft this type of steering has the advantage that a locking valve prevents kick-back from the rudder, allowing it to be held in one position for considerable

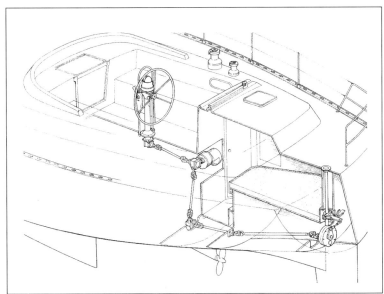

Fig. 18(15) A torque tube mechanical steering system. The torque tube runs directly to the helm unit near the wheel. If this cannot be achieved the line of the torque tube can be changed by the use of universal joints or angled transfer boxes between bearings.

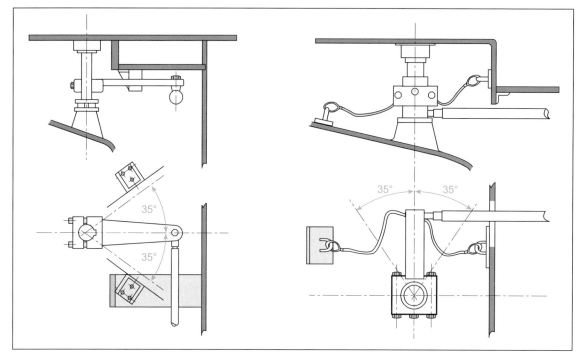

Fig. 18(16) Rudder stops are essential on virtually all steering gears.

periods with little attention since it cannot drive the wheel. This feature is undesirable on sailing craft where some feedback of pressure on the rudder is desirable.

There should be an emergency by-pass valve so that in the event of malfunction, tiller steering can be used.

18.4.7 EMERGENCY STEERING

However good and sound the basic wheel-steering system, there should always be some way of hand steering by tiller. This is best done by extending the rudder stock up to just short of the deck or cockpit sole level. A hole is cut in the deck or sole sufficiently large for an emergency tiller to be shipped over the end of the stock. The hole is covered by a watertight plate held down with thumb screws or wing nuts. It is helpful if the helmsman has a reasonable view, and is not confined to an aft cabin or has to steer with his head in a locker.

18.4.8 BOW THRUSTERS

Bow thrusters are popular on power boats and biggish sailing yachts and motor sailers. Basically a propeller is sited inside a transverse tube near the bow and below the waterline. The propeller is symmetrical, giving equal thrust whichever way it rotates. This transverse thrust, available well forward, enables quite precise manoeuvering – a boon when berthing in a tight spot or mooring stern-to, Mediterranean style.

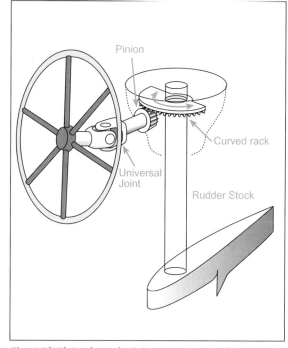

Fig. 18(17) Rack and pinion steering is direct and simple. With a universal joint on the shaft forward of the pinion, the wheel can be mounted at any reasonable angle.

The amount of thrust needed is not great, and small models developing some 45kg (l00lb) of push are normally adequate for craft up to 13·7m (45ft) LOA. Such power is usually supplied by an electric motor, but for larger boats hydraulic power is common.

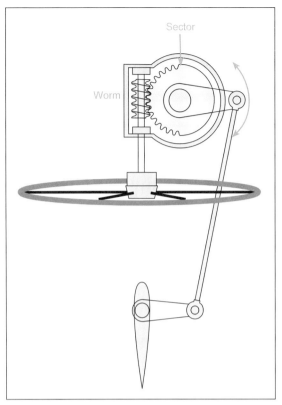

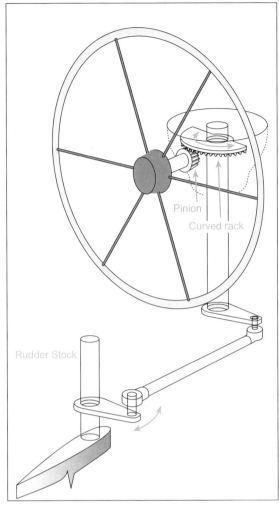

Fig. 18(18) Rack and pinion gear may be mounted at some distance from the rudder using a push-pull rod.

Fig. 18(19) The worm gear is robust but offers little 'feel' at the wheel.

Details vary between makes but a typical small bow thruster has a 3kW motor in an athwartships tube about 185mm (76in) in diameter.

Waterjet bow thrusters are less effective and more expensive, but minimise installation problems and unwanted drag when sailing due to the much smaller holes in the hull. Water is drawn in through an inlet valve and pumped to outlets port and starboard near the bow. The inlet valve can be anywhere convenient, and since the hoses are only about 30mm (l6in) diameter, the installation takes up very little space.

18.5 SELF STEERING

18.5.1 STEERING BY SAIL

A well-balanced yacht can be made to steer quite an accurate course with the rudder free – downwind, upwind or reaching – simply by easing or hardening the main and genoa sheets.

The mainsail tries to drive the boat's bows into the wind while the genoa has the opposite effect, and these opposing forces have to be balanced. This is normally achieved by sheeting in the genoa harder than would otherwise be desirable and freeing the main. This is a very basic form of self-steering, but worth experimenting with against the day that your rudder falls off. It also makes the point that unless a yacht's sails are properly trimmed and the boat is in balance, an unfair workload is imposed on any type of self-steering. Shades of Joshua Slocum ...

18.5.2 LINKING THE RUDDER AND SAILS

The next logical development was to link the main sheet to the tiller so that the sails can develop their full power; see Fig. 18(22).

Here the sheet leads through a block on the weather side of the boat and then back to the tiller. Under way the main tries to turn the yacht's head into wind, but is resisted by the rudder being pulled in the opposite direction. The harder the wind blows, the greater the pull on the sheet and thus on the rudder via the tiller.

The point at which the sheet joins the tiller is adjustable so that the leverage can be altered, and there is normally a length of shock cord made

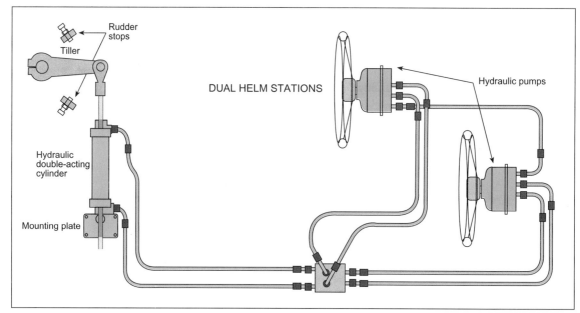

Fig. 18(20) Hydraulic steering gear.

fast on the opposite side, as shown, whose main function is to speed the return of the tiller to its correct angle. In practice two sheets are used with blocks on both quarters so that the system can be used on either tack. On most small yachts it works well enough when beating or close reaching, but not so satisfactorily on a run or with a quartering wind. Hence single or short-handed sailors may link their running sails (usually twin staysails or twin spinnakers) to the tiller as shown in Fig. 18(23).

If the yacht veers off course the pressure on one of the sails is increased and on the other, reduced. These pressures are transmitted back via lines and quarter blocks to the tiller, which then automatically heads the boat back on course where the pressure on both sails is the same. Running sails can be roller-reefed in the normal way.

18.5.3 SELF-STEERING BY VANE AND APPARENT WIND

Some form of windvane is needed to sense the wind which, so long as it remains reasonably steady in direction, will direct the course satisfactorily.

The windvane in Fig. 18(24) has a vertical axis, like the one on a church spire, and is free to point into wind; note that this will always be the *apparent* wind.

This is the wind felt on board and is the true wind (as felt when standing on the shore) modified by a boat's course and speed – and of course by any changes in the true wind itself. If a boat sails directly downwind at, say 6 knots in a 13-knot breeze, the apparent wind on deck

would be 13 – 6 = 7 knots and would still apparently come from dead astern. If, however, the boat beats to windward at 6 knots in a 13-knot breeze which is blowing at 45° to the boat's course, the apparent wind would be 17·7 knots at 33° to the boat's heading. In other words the apparent wind draws ahead and accelerates relative to the true wind. This is shown diagrammatically in Fig. 18(25) and 18.6.1 describes it in more detail.

This slightly theoretical vane would be connected by lines to the rudder. If the boat veers off course, the wind acts on one side or the other of the vane, and turns the vane (and hence the rudder) until the vane once again points into wind and pressure on both sides equalises. So much for basic theory.

18.5.4 MODERN WINDVANES

It is clear that the windvane is a vital sensor, but the vertical-axis vane, for a number of reasons, lacks the power to ensure effective results in the real world.

Horizontal axis vanes

The next development was to mount the windvane on a horizontal axis, so as to gain more power. The blade of a vane pointing directly into the apparent wind, with a counterbalancing weight below, will stand upright. If the boat changes course or the wind changes direction, the resulting breeze will blow on one side of the vane causing it to tilt quite forceably about its horizontal axis. This tilt can be translated into movement of the tiller lines and hence the rudder. The horizontal-axis vane is the sensor at the heart of nearly all modern vane-steering systems and can be clearly seen in Fig. 18(27).

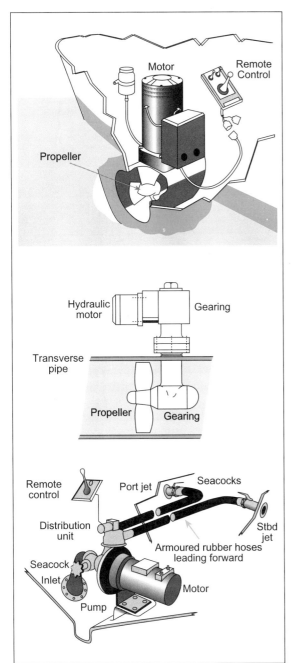

Fig. 18(21) Top, a typical arrangement for an electric bow thruster; middle, a hydraulic bow thruster; and bottom, a water jet bow thruster.

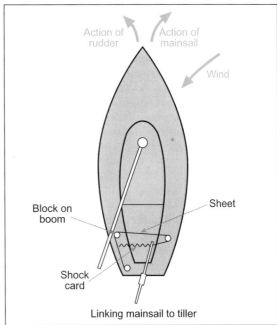

Fig. 18(22) The most basic form of positive self-steering is to link the mainsail sheet to the tiller via a quarter block.

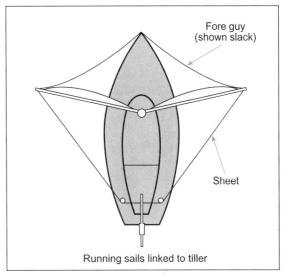

Fig. 18(23) Running sails may be linked to the tiller for downwind self-steering.

Having developed the sensor to its most efficient and powerful form, using air as the medium, waterpower was next utilised to provide the much greater power needed to move the yacht's main or auxiliary rudder.

Pendulum type
In the 1950s 'Blondie' Hasler, experimenting with a vertical-axis vane, developed an underwater

auxiliary rudder blade (or paddle) which worked in two ways:

a. Using the wind power of the vane, it could be turned in the water flow like any conventional rudder;
b. It could also swing (flip-flop) sideways on its fore and aft axis, like an athwartships pendulum.

So, when turned, the water swung it smartly sideways, generating substantial power in the

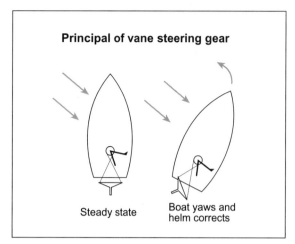

Principal of vane steering gear

Steady state

Boat yaws and helm corrects

Fig. 18(24) The principle of vane-steering.

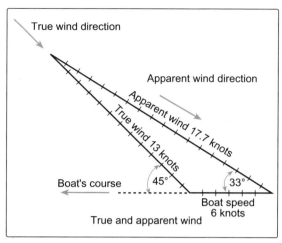

True wind direction

Apparent wind direction

Apparent wind 17.7 knots

True wind 13 knots

Boat's course

45°

33°

Boat speed 6 knots

True and apparent wind

Fig. 18(25) The difference between true and apparent wind with a yacht working to windward. The apparent wind is from further ahead and stronger than the true wind on this heading.

process; it had in effect become a true servo. This extra power could be used to operate lines fastened to the yacht's tiller and hence turn the rudder; see Fig. 18(26).

'Blondie' Hasler famously remarked that "the gear is the equivalent of at least one extra man, but with the advantage that most vane gears do not eat, answer back, or woo other people's girls in harbour".

Current vane gear

A good example of vane gear currently (2001) on the market is the Monitor Windvane from Scanmar International, 432 South 1st St, Richmond, California CA 94804. Tel +1 510 215 2010; Fax +1 510 215 5005. scanmar@selfsteer.com   www.selfsteer.com

The Monitor combines the principles of the servo-pendulum gear with a vane mounted on a near-horizontal axis as described previously; see Fig. 18(27). It has taken over the mantle from the similar Aries vane gear, which is now made in Denmark. Apart from the wind vane, made of marine ply, the rest of the structure is almost entirely stainless steel to minimise corrosion. Remote control of the wind vane setting is by stainless chain and sprocket drive. The pendulum is hinged in the middle to allow it to be swung up and out of the water when not in use. If necessary it can be locked in the central position and used for emergency steering. Maintenance-free roller and ball bearings are used to reduce friction between the wind vane and the servo-pendulum.

Any self-steering system needs feedback to prevent over-controlling; this is done via the master gearing which gradually neutralises the rotation of the pendulum blade as it swings outwards – bringing it back into alignment with the hull. Thus the water's force on the pendulum blade progressively reduces. The gear can be used for either tiller or wheel steering and in both

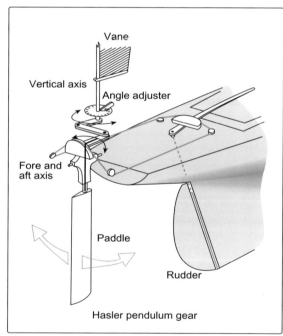

Vane

Vertical axis

Angle adjuster

Fore and aft axis

Paddle

Rudder

Hasler pendulum gear

Fig. 18(26) The Hasler pendulum gear translates the swing of a paddle about its fore and aft axis into a pull on rudder lines.

cases arrangements are made for quick disconnection if required.

There are at least eight other servo-pendulum models on the market made by companies in the UK, France, Germany, Denmark and the USA. The various means of steering the yacht, other than by turning the rudder itself (as already described), include: a slender auxiliary rudder blade, powered solely by the vane; a trim tab attached to the yacht's rudder; a trim tab on an auxiliary rudder; a double servo, ie a trim tab on the pendulum paddle; and a hydraulic actuator, powered by an impeller towed astern, which turns the rudder.

18.5.5 VANES IN GENERAL

The better balanced and easier to steer a boat is, the more chance a vane has of working well. To that end it is usually worth experimenting with shifting ballast, altering the rake of the mast and even, perhaps, trying different proportions of sail area ahead and astern of the mast to improve balance if the yacht is hard on the helm and good vane steering is a major requirement. Shifting ballast aft, for instance, will move the CLR aft by putting the stern deeper in the water and should reduce weather helm. Raking the mast aft, on the other hand, will shift the CE astern and may increase weather helm. A larger headsail and smaller main (adding up to the same working sail area) will move the CE forward and reduce weather helm.

Except for the servo-pendulum type, a wind vane can only produce a limited amount of power unless it is so large as to be cumbersome and a nuisance on board. Hence a balanced rudder (ie one with some blade area forward of the stock), which takes less power to turn than an unbalanced rudder, will be a good thing and bearings should be examined to make sure they are as friction-free as possible. The power required from the vane can be reduced if it is connected to an auxiliary rudder (if the yacht's rudder is forward, at the aft end of the keel), or to a trim tab if the rudder is transom-hung.

Many people have made their own vane systems with complete success. The criteria must always be to produce a robust structure with low friction, although the vertical axis vanes seem to be able to cope with friction better than the horizontal axis types. The vane gear must incorporate some method of disengagement that can be operated very quickly so that a helmsman can take over. And however good the design, it will probably not be too effective in really light winds; nor in big seas where the vane may be blanketed from time to time, nor where a big slop left over from a dying wind knocks the boat about to the extent that the breeze on the vane cannot control her. A vane will not usually work as well downwind as upwind (remember that the apparent wind is less than the true wind when running but is greater when going to windward) but on longer voyages the system is a great boon. It is not, however, a substitute for a man on deck keeping watch. It simply allows him to keep watch more efficiently since he does not have to bother about steering. The Amateur Yacht Research Society publish an excellent book on the subject, called *Self Steering*.

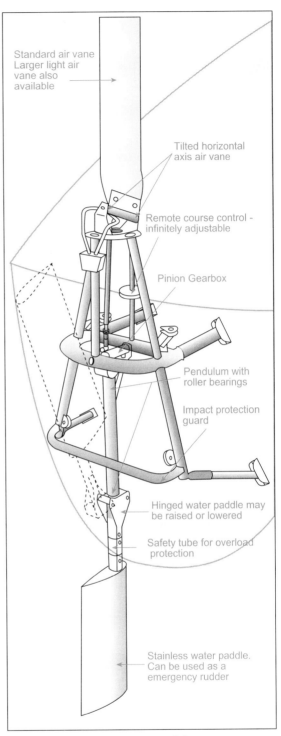

Standard air vane
Larger light air vane also available

Tilted horizontal axis air vane

Remote course control - infinitely adjustable

Pinion Gearbox

Pendulum with roller bearings

Impact protection guard

Hinged water paddle may be raised or lowered

Safety tube for overload protection

Stainless water paddle. Can be used as a emergency rudder

Fig. 18(27) Monitor servo-pendulum vane gear. The vane's near-horizontal pivot axis is evident.

18.5.6 AUTOPILOTS

The usual type of autopilot is a compass follower on which the desired course is set. The autopilot will then hold that course until it is changed, which can be done at any time and from anywhere on deck if a remote control lead is fitted.

A properly adjusted autopilot can steer a better course than the average helmsman, and keep doing it ad infinitum – provided the power supply lasts. But it does not relieve the person on watch from keeping a good lookout and a watchful eye on the autopilot to confirm that it is working properly. Fig. 18(28) shows the basic layout of an autopilot.

In principle it functions as follows: the desired heading is set on the course selector or the boat is steered to the required course and the autopilot engaged. The true heading is sensed by the course or error sensor (which usually has its own compass). The difference between the steered course and the set course – the course error – is calculated. Should the course error become greater than some pre-set value the drive of the autopilot operates the rudder sufficiently to bring the boat back on course. The drive motor may be a fractional horsepower electric type with an electro-magnetic clutch or an electrically driven hydraulic pump type which can be coupled directly into the boat's hydraulic steering system.

On some models there is a rudder feedback unit which monitors the rudder angle and passes the information back to the control unit, but in other models this information comes from the output of the control unit itself or from the drive of the steering motor.

On modern autopilots there are various refinements and additions. Thus, for instance, the amount of deadband (the angle through which the craft is allowed to veer off course before the rudder starts to correct) can be selected to take into account sea state and the general qualities of the boat.

The rudder control can act rather like a human helmsman in that it can react to course error and correct accordingly before it builds up sufficiently to require major rudder movement, while the rate at which the rudder is applied can be selected and automatically controlled.

Overswing may be automatically counteracted by applying counter rudder during course changing. The autopilot in some cases can be overridden in an emergency after which it will bring the craft back on the original course. Navigational systems (eg GPS) can be coupled to the autopilot so that the vessel will track from one position to another automatically rather than simply steering a selected course. Off-course alarms may be fitted as well as display units showing the rudder angle at any time (and so judge how hard it is having to work). The actual course, not just the selected one, may be shown as a further guide. Corrections for trim, weather helm and helm bias can be set to allow for the fact that most craft under sail or power

have a tendency to pull to one side or the other. Some makes of autopilot also incorporate wind vane steering.

Pilots for tiller steering work on the same principles as those for wheel steering, but are modified so that the mechanism is linked to the tiller.

The maintenance requirements on an autopilot are low, being mainly concerned with keeping all working parts of the steering gear free and eliminating backlash as far as possible. A radio transmitter close to the autopilot can cause uncontrolled course changing, and any magnetic objects close to the boat's compass or autopilot's sensing unit can lead to major trouble.

The failure rate of autopilots is quite high so back-up units are often carried on long voyages. Water ingress is one reason, which may be helped by silicon grease. Overstressing is another which can be minimised by good sail balance. Listen to the sound it is making. If it sounds distressed, it almost certainly is.

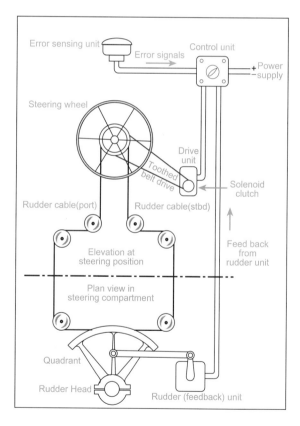

Fig. 18(28) The layout of a typical autopilot system. On some types certain functions may be incorporated in one unit and items such as the rudder feedback unit may be dispensed with; the information it supplies being gained from other sources.

Chapter 19 Below Decks

CONTENTS

19.1 ACCOMMODATING PEOPLE

19.1.1 HUMAN DIMENSIONS

Although human beings come in all shapes and sizes the sketches in Fig. 19(1) represent the space occupied by the average male, who is assumed to be about 1.8m (6ft) tall. From these, various ergonomic calculations can be made, for example, the proper height of a table or working surface; how much space needs to be left between obstructing items for an adequate passage between; the amount of foot room needed in front of a toilet and so on. They may also demonstrate why a settee wide enough to form a berth is much too wide for comfortable sitting, unless something is done to reduce the width when required.

19.1.2 COMPANIONWAY

The majority of small and medium size sailing craft use washboards rather than doors to close the entry between the cabin and the cockpit. These boards, which slide down channels each side of the entrance, are complemented by a sliding hatch to give headroom where it is required. The argument for washboards rather than doors is

that in bad weather only the lower board(s) need be in place, leaving a gap at the top for ventilation and through which the helmsman and those below can communicate. If the entrance is above a bridgedeck at the same height as the cockpit seats, or the entrance is cut at this height, the cockpit can be flooded to that depth before water starts to find its way below. Washboards are not in themselves watertight, although they will prevent anything more than a minor stream getting past them.

After the 1979 Fastnet Race, in which several boats foundered, the RORC recommended that washboards be permanently fastened to the parent vessel, so that they could not fall out if the yacht was rolled over (simple lanyards being the easiest method of achieving this), and that the hatch over the entrance should be lockable from both sides. In other words, it should be impossible to lock the hatch from one side without it being equally possible to unlock it from the other side.

An argument against washboards is that it takes time to remove or insert the individual boards, and though it is normally possible simply to slide back the hatch and climb over the boards in an

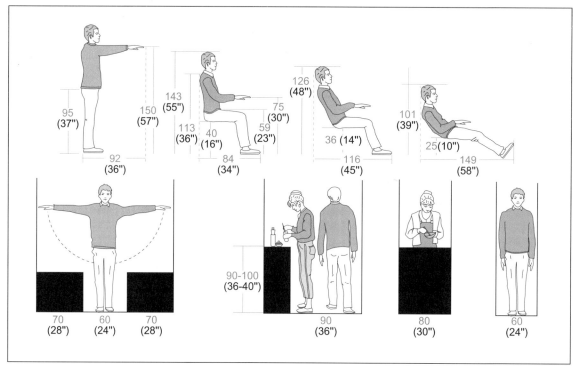

Fig. 19(1) Humans need a certain minimum space to move about comfortably on board. These are some typical limiting dimensions.

emergency, this may not be a sensible course in bad weather. An open hatch is an invitation to disaster. Washboards also have to be stowed away when not in use. A door can be operated and shut in a trice, and if properly and stoutly made is just as waterproof as washboards. If a stable door arrangement is used, ie a door opening in two halves, the bottom half can be left closed in bad weather to give ventilation and communication through the open top half. But the small size of the companionway on modern yachts and the arc through which a door swings may not be readily compatible.

Motor boats are generally not planned with bad weather in mind. Their cockpits are not intended to be watertight, and large doors for easy access are the order of the day.

19.1.3   WET LOCKERS
Fig. 19(2) shows the layout of a 8.5m (28ft) centreboard cutter. The boat is a 'one off' but will serve as a discussion vehicle for the various aspects of a below-decks layout.

Few production yachts have proper wet lockers in which to house soaking oilskins or even wet clothing when going below, but such a locker is essential if the interior is to be kept reasonably dry in bad weather. It should be tall enough to stow a full set of foul weather gear for each crew

member and should have a grating at the bottom draining into the bilges. Clothing will dry more quickly if draped over a plastic clothes hanger than if merely suspended from a hook, and so there should be a short rail in the locker. The door should have a louvred section to admit air. Alternatively ventilators, Fig. 19(3), should be fitted top and bottom. The locker should be immediately inside the companionway for best results.

19.1.4   CHART TABLES
The chart table should be conveniently close to the companionway. The navigator may need to talk to the helmsman, and if the skipper and the navigator are the same person quick access to the charts is important. On yachts the table should be sited so that the navigator sits fore and aft, but on motor boats the table can be orientated in any way to suit the layout. In both cases, though, the minimum size of the table is 0.76m x 0.55m (2ft 6in x 1ft 9in) which will take a folded Admiralty chart. Spread out, the chart occupies a space of about 1m x 0.76m (3ft 6in x 2ft 6in). The table should have a full-size but quite shallow drawer to hold ready-use charts, but if this is not possible a large net on a bulkhead is a reasonable substitute. Chart folios are often stowed under bunk mattresses where at least they stay flat.

A bookcase and a rack for stowing pencils, rubbers, pencil sharpeners, parallel rules etc should be next to the navigator. A red/white chart table

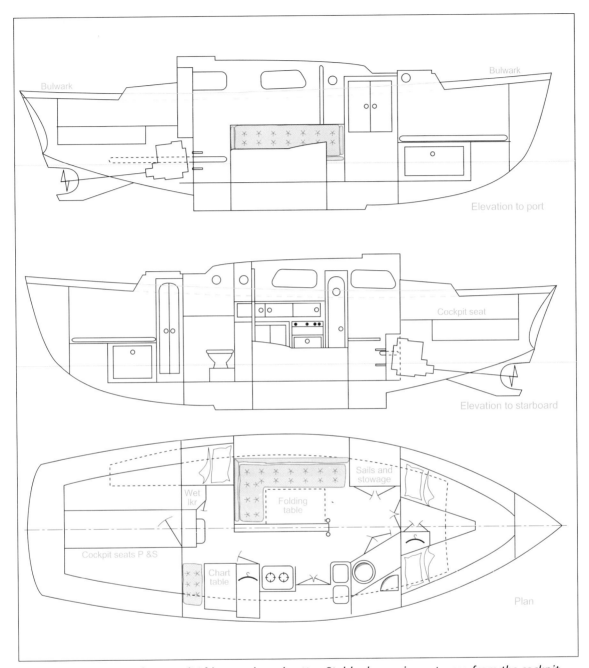

Fig. 19(2) The layout of a 8.5m (28ft) centreboard cutter. Stable doors give entrance from the cockpit above a bridgedeck formed by the engine box. A wet locker is sited close by the companionway and the back of the settee is removable to make it wide enough to double up as a berth when required.

light with a dimmer and a spot/flood option is essential. A more general deckhead light above the chart area is also useful, provided it does not dazzle the helmsman. Natural lighting through a port or window is always helpful. To the basic chart table set-up can be added as many instruments or their repeaters as the owner wants or can afford. Whatever is fitted should be visible and controllable by the navigator without his having to stretch or twist about too much.

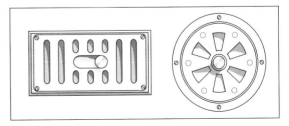

Fig. 19(3) Ventilators fitted to lockers in the accommodation allow a circulation of air.

19.1.5 BERTHS

Yacht berths should be at least l.9m (6ft 3in) and preferably 2m (6ft 6in) in length. They should not be too wide, 0.8m (2ft 6in) being a reasonable figure, but berths as narrow as 0.6m (2ft) are still perfectly useable. From that width at the shoulders they can taper down to about 0.5m (1ft 6in) at the foot if required. Bunk cushions or mattresses ought to be at least 100mm (4in) thick and preferably, if of a foam material, covered in cotton or some other fabric that does not sweat. Vinyl, for instance, is not very satisfactory. The bunk base on which the mattress lies should have holes drilled in it to allow air to get at the underside of the mattress or it will become damp. A flexible ventilation layer, marketed as Ventair, is sold in 1m wide rolls; the 15mm thickness is ideal for below mattresses and 10mm thickness is adequate for settees. Details from MMG Ltd, Tel 01553 617791.

Double bunks, which were once derided as being hopelessly non-seagoing, are increasingly used on yachts. They are perfectly satisfactory provided there are two mattresses and it is possible to divide them for use in rough weather. The division may be of canvas or solid wood and is, in effect, a leeboard.

Leeboards should be strong and simple to fit or stow. Traditionally, they are wooden and may be hinged to lie flat when not required, or they may slot in like washboards. Their height should be some 300mm (12in) above the top of the mattress. The object is to prevent the occupant of the berth from having to cling on in order to stay put or even to prevent him being pitched on to the cabin sole. A typical leecloth and leeboard are shown in Fig. 19(4).

Leecloths achieve the same object by stretching a canvas cloth, which is secured under the mattress, up towards the deckhead with lanyards. A leecloth is lighter and cheaper. It is also more comfortable to lie against than a leeboard (though the latter can be upholstered) but it tends to create rather a hot berth in warm weather. If used, a leecloth ought to extend at least 300mm (l2in) above the top of the mattress and the lanyards should be capable of being adjusted by the person in the bunk.

Fig. 19(4) This picture shows a pipecot, leecloth and leeboard.

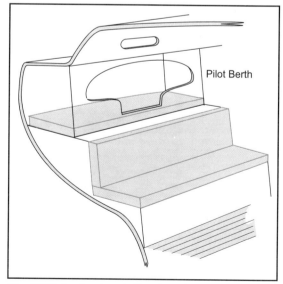

Fig. 19(5) A pilot berth fitted outboard of and above a settee makes a comfortable and secure bunk.

Quarter berths

When a bunk extends under some permanent part of the boat's structure, usually the cockpit seats, it is called a quarter berth, as shown on the port side, aft in Fig. 19(2). These berths are usually snug and comfortable since it is impossible to roll out, but a sleeping bag or duvet is needed, since there is no way the bunk can be made up in the conventional manner. A popular variation is a double bunk which in larger yachts may be of palatial size and only suitable for use in harbour.

Pilot berths

Another snug and comfortable bunk is the pilot berth which is built in outboard of and above a settee, usually in the saloon of more traditional boats. It can be entered through an oval cut in the bulkhead which otherwise shields it, Fig. 19(5).

Usually a curtain is arranged to draw across the entrance hole to give the occupant privacy and dark. There needs to be at least 0.55m of height (1ft 9in) above the top of the mattress to allow turning-over, but even that makes for a potentially very hot berth in warm weather and may be claustrophobic.

Fo'c'sle berths

In a forward cabin V-berths, joined at their feet, are fitted as in Fig. 19(2); a triangular insert at the aft end makes a comfortable double berth in harbour.

Alternatively, if there is plenty of height, two berths may be fitted, one above the other on different sides of the boat, Fig. 19(6).

Where the feet cross, the two berths should have about 300mm (12in) difference in height. This is a practical solution in many cases and may be preferred where strangers have to share the fo'c'sle. This arrangement is worth considering where headroom is 1.7m (5ft 6in) or more, but the shape of the boat will govern how low the lower bunk may be sited.

Pullman berths

This type of bunk is the backrest of a settee by day, but hinges up to form a berth at night. The angle to the horizontal which the berth makes when up must be adjustable, especially on sailing craft. Bedding can be stowed in the space behind the berth, when lowered.

Pipe cots

These are made of tubular steel or aluminium alloy frames with tightly stretched Terylene or similar material forming the base of the berth; see Fig. 19(4). Normally their outboard edges sit in U-shaped brackets fastened to the vessel's sides, while the inboard faces have lanyards secured to them which make fast to eyes on the deckhead, allowing their angle to be adjusted. Pipe cots are most often found in fo'c'sles where they are perfectly satisfactory and light in weight but need some sort of mattress to make them comfortable. The one trouble with berths like

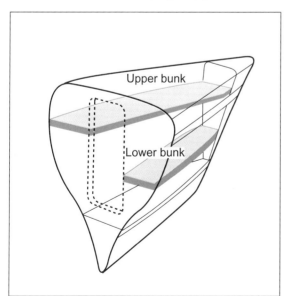

Fig. 19(6) In some craft it may be possible to install fo'csle berths one above the other with the feet crossing towards the bow.

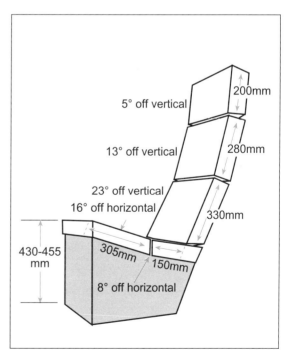

Fig. 19(7) If room is available for a comfortable seat that does not have to double up as a berth, this gives a suitable shape and is akin to airliner seating.

the pipe cot and pullman berth is that on yachts it is usually necessary to adjust their angle on each tack. This is a nuisance for the occupant. Leecloths can be fitted but cannot be tightened without the whole weight of the berth coming on their lashings which may be more than they can stand.

19.1.6 SETTEES

Whereas it is possible to sit for quite a few hours on a seat in an airliner without too much discomfort, the same cannot be said for the average yacht settee. The problem is that the settee, being used at different times for sitting, lounging and sleeping, cannot be designed to be really satisfactory in any of these roles.

If simple sitting comfort can be catered for, Fig. 19(7) shows the cross section through a suitable shape. The cushions should be about 75mm (3in) thick and of firm foam. The 100mm (4in) thickness recommended for bunks is too much for seats.

19.1.7 CABIN TABLES

At one time cabin tables were quite often gimballed so that they remained level whatever the heel of the boat. On a narrow table this is still a good idea, although the table needs to be ballasted with weights in a box well below the table top and its pivoting point. In addition it may be necessary to dampen the swing of the table. On high-class work this used to be done with a brake on the pivot, but shock cord can be substituted. With a wide table gimballing is not recommended since the table top will be up around the ears of the occupant on one side and hitting the knees of the person on the other side, Fig. 19(8).

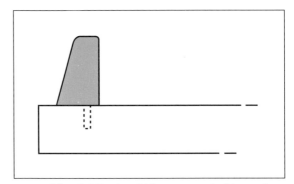

Fig. 19(9) A fiddle should have a vertical inner face and be some 65-75mm ($2\frac{1}{2}$-3in) high. If pegs in its bottom drop into holes in the surface it bounds, the fiddle can be made removable.

Most modern yachts have a fixed table bounded by fiddles. The shape of a proper fiddle is shown on Fig. 19(9). It should stop short of the corners of the table or work-top or wherever it is fitted so that crumbs and other debris can be swept clear. Alternatively it can be removable, in which case pegs in the bottom of the fiddle fit into holes in the surface it surrounds.

Someone wielding a knife and fork requires a width of at least 0.6m (2ft) and preferably a little more. This dimension governs how many people can sit round a table. If there are problems in arranging enough seating it is sometimes possible to have a passageway through a pair of tables which is closed with a hinged section for meals, Fig. 19(10).

The table on the cutter of Fig. 19(2) is hinged on the centreboard case so that it can be folded

Fig. 19(8) A wide gimballed table is not much use at big angles of heel.

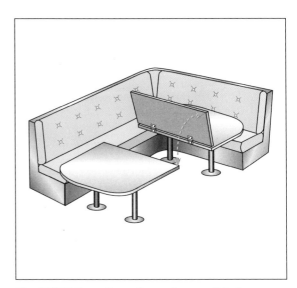

Fig. 19(10) Sometimes it may be possible to arrange a passageway through a table with a hinged flap filling the gap as required.

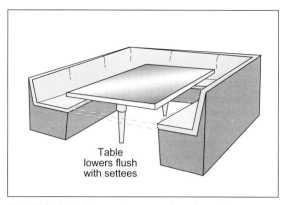

Fig. 19(11) A dinette is most often found in motor boats. With the table lowered a berth is formed.

Table lowers flush with settees

out of the way as required. A permanently wide table is always a nuisance on board a small yacht.

19.1.8   DINETTES
On motor boats in particular and some multihulls, a table set between athwartships seats can be lowered to be flush with those seats. The structure is then long enough for it to form a berth, Fig. 19(11). The result may be a single or double berth but the arrangement is not really suitable for sailing craft, where seating should run fore and aft to cater for the craft being well heeled over.

Such dinettes are space-savers since they combine the functions of eating, sitting and sleeping. The backs of the settees are usually removed to fit over the table when it is used as part of a berth. This multiplicity of rather inadequate berth cushions means that a dinette is not really very comfortable as a bunk. Nor is it ideal for lounging, since seats narrow enough to allow comfortable eating are too narrow for sprawling on.

19.1.9   THE HEADS
Fig. 19(1) showed the space needed for comfortable sitting with the implication that the distance between the back of the toilet itself and a bulkhead or other obstruction in front of it should be around 0.9m (3ft). This is a practical minimum and one to be exceeded wherever possible, but equally important is shoulder room. People have to be able to turn around, pull their trousers up and generally stretch in a minor manner. This means that the width of the compartment should not be less than 0.76m (2ft 6in). Ideally the toilet should be placed so that the user sits athwartships but this is not always possible, and since a toilet is used for only a few minutes a day some departures from the ideal can be accepted.

Washbasins are too often set under side decks where they are impossible to use effectively. Even if mounted clear of such obstructions but close to, say a bulkhead or cabin side they can be difficult unless at a good height above the sole; 0.8m (3ft) is normally right and reduces the need for the user to lean forward when washing. This height can be as much as 1m (3ft 4in) with advantage and at that even quite short people would have no problems.

There should be a fiddle at the basin surround and somewhere to stow washing things; preferably each crew member should have an individual space. Since there may be a fair amount of water splashing around, the sole should have a non-slippery surface or teak grating and the door sill should be reasonably high, especially if a shower is installed in the compartment. A 150mm (6in) sill is not excessive.

19.1.10   SAIL LOCKERS
Aboard small cruising yachts sails are often stowed in the cockpit lockers, along with warps, fenders and other paraphernalia. There is a good case for having them in the accommodation where they will stay drier and can be sorted out under more favourable conditions; there is usually space below the fore cabin bunks. If fitted, a sail locker should be convenient to the forehatch. It may take the form of a simple bin, but if a proper full-height locker is adapted the top half may be used for general stowage. Good stowage space on board is usually at a premium and fortuitously the almost universal roller reefing headsail has greatly reduced the sail wardrobe of a cruising yacht.

19.1.11   SAFETY AND CONVENIENCE
All the accommodation should lie on the same level. Some designers and builders succumb to the fact that going up a few inches from the cabin sole probably increases the available sole width quite dramatically; they therefore elevate dinettes or make the floor height in a sleeping cabin higher than elsewhere. Steps up or down are dangerous at sea and it is all too easy to trip over them in bad weather.

Keeping one's feet below is aided by handholds. These may take the form of grab handles, handrails under the deckhead or vertical pillars at strategic points. In Fig. 19(2) for example, a pair of pillars are at the forward end of the centreboard case, where they double as supports for the deck-stepped mast. Corners should be rounded as in the case of the two ends of the galley in the 8.5m (28ft) cutter.

There are many neat catches on the market which can be used on lockers and doors but old-fashioned barrel bolts and cabin hooks should not

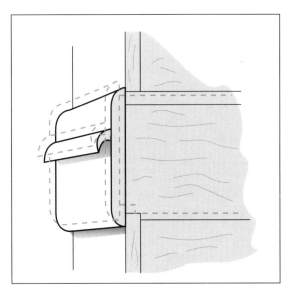

Fig. 19(12) A drawer has to be lifted to be opened, so will remain shut at almost any angle of heel.

be forgotten. They may not look as smart, but they are reliable and how they work is obvious to any newcomer on board. Hinging locker fronts should hinge along their bottom edges if possible. Drawers should be of the lift-out type, Fig. 19(12), and not have to rely on catches.

The sole should be laid in sections with inspection hatches inset, so that the inside of the hull bottom can quickly be inspected. The sole itself can be of timber in some form, but it might be considered a luxury for a family cruising boat to have carpet. As long as a wet locker is provided, and used, this is not as impractical as it may sound. The area of the sole to be covered will probably be quite small and a meagre offcut from the carpet shop will often suffice and leave enough over for a spare. So when the original becomes too dirty, use it as a pattern, then chuck it out and replace it with the spare. Provided the carpet was a good fit to begin with it will probably not need fastening down, but the edges will need binding.

19.2 GALLEYS

19.2.1 LAYOUT

In most smaller yachts the galley is arranged at the aft end of the accommodation, but there is really no best place for it; each position has its pros and cons. The motion is generally worse forward than amidships, but, if the galley is forward, the cook is less bothered by people wanting to get by and go on deck or into the cockpit. The draught through a boat is usually from aft to forward, so that with the forehatch

open a crack the sometimes hideous smells from the galley can escape overboard more rapidly – cooking smells do not much appeal to potentially seasick crewmembers. On the other hand the draught near, but to one side of the companionway, will be less fierce than that forward, so that in an aft galley there is less danger of the gas blowing out. Ultimately the galley will be where it is convenient for the designer to put it, and very good reasons will then be concocted for its position.

In any case since only one person at a time usually is in the galley, the floor space can be small; indeed, it is an advantage if everything is within easy reach. Since, especially on sailing boats, the motion may be wild and the vessel well heeled, it helps if the galley is shaped so that the cook can wedge his or herself in position aided by a strap to lean back against and a bar to prevent falling forward on to the stove. Hence the most practical galley configuration is either L or U shaped. In Fig. 19(2) the galley is U-shaped and there is only 0.6m (2ft) between the arms.

Cooking at sea is not quite like cooking at home, so the layout must be rather different. Sandwiches are frequently the main food in bad weather, so a good work surface is needed to prepare them. A draining board is not needed since everything would fall off it. Instead a rack above the sink will serve, or a second sink in which dirty dishes and pans can be placed until they can be washed. If space is really tight, the sink (which should be at least 200mm (8in) deep) can have a portable cover which doubles as a worktop. The outlet pipe from the sink should be as short and as near vertical as possible so that it gets rid of the water quickly.

Within these limitations the galley must be arranged around its equipment. A gimballed cooker needs to have its axis fore and aft so that it can swing as the boat rolls. Since gas piping (if gas is used) should be as short as possible, the cooker will be sited as close to the gas cylinder and locker as can be arranged. Refrigerator doors (but a top-opening lid is far better) must open into the centre of the vessel if they are to take advantage of the fact that many can accept quite fierce rolling without harm.

Work surfaces must be bounded by non-continuous fiddles to allow the mess to be swept off easily and all potentially harmful corners should be rounded. All locker shelves, even those behind doors, should have fiddles or a retaining bar to prevent the contents from raining out; a length of non-skid matting, such as is used for place-mats, is another solution. If gas is used, the supply tap (which should be closed every time the stove is not wanted and be quite separate from the main supply shut-off which is on the gas bottle itself) must be visible and easy to reach. Good natural light through a port or window is a desirable feature, as is proper artificial lighting. The cook should not operate constantly in his own shadow. A closable ventilator in the galley is desirable; if it remains open quite fierce draughts may blow out the gas. That is inconvenient at best and dangerous at worst.

The galleys of motor boats are not often arranged with seagoing cooking as a priority. The implication is that food will be prepared beforehand if a passage is to be made and proper cooking only undertaken in a sheltered berth. If that is the intention, then the normal motor boat galley will suffice but otherwise the same rules apply as to sailing craft. It is, however, worth mentioning that pre-cooking a meal and storing it in a large vacuum flask is a sensible way of going about things even under sail if only a short passage is to be made. This also applies to hot drinks or soup, but the flasks must be securely stowed.

Stowages

Unbreakable crockery and glasses are best on a boat and they too must be securely stowed. They should not simply be shoved in a locker from which they can avalanche if the door is opened on the wrong tack. There are many ingenious ways of devising neat stowages, the most basic being to stow the plates, for instance, between vertical dowels. These hold them in place but allow them to be easily extracted. Cutlery is best stowed in a drawer with high internal dividers.

If there is no refrigerator or other cooler, remember that the hull will be cooler below the waterline than some way up the topsides, so that vegetables and other perishables are best stowed low down and even in a suitable container in the bilges if this is feasible. If such perishables have to be kept in lockers around the galley, the doors should be louvred or ventilated to ensure a flow of air in the locker itself. Fresh fruit will keep longer if hung in netting from the deckhead. Airtight containers should be used for items like salt, sugar, flour and biscuits. A rubbish bin or container must be convenient for the cook but preferably stowed out of sight. Some household containers which hold disposable plastic bags can be fastened to a locker door. These are handy and, with a bag tied at the top, taking rubbish ashore is clean and easy. A dustpan and brush and damp cloth are essential and should be conveniently stowed. Cutting bread on board

spreads crumbs everywhere; sliced bread is less messy. A hand-held rechargeable vacuum cleaner is very useful.

19.2.2 COOKERS

Cookers in sailing yachts need to be gimballed and on all types of craft should have adjustable fiddle rails such that individual pots and pans can be clamped in position. Two burners and a grill are about the minimum requirements; an oven's versatility will enable slightly more advanced cooking to be tackled.

Fuel for cooking on board can be solid fuel, electricity, paraffin, methylated spirits or bottled gas. On larger, more traditional yachts the Aga, Esse or Rayburn type of solid fuel stove may be appropriate, especially if the background heating is appreciated. However such stoves should be backed up by something quicker, such as a couple of gas rings, for times when nearly instant meals are required. Microwave cookers can be used to back up the main cooker for really speedy work in bigger craft too, but having to run the generator even to boil a kettle is a nuisance for those aboard and in nearby boats. If the electrical supply fails, the crew will go hungry unless another form of cooking is available.

Paraffin pressure stoves such as the much revered Primuses were once just about the sole form of cooking aboard smallish cruising boats and they still have their merits. Paraffin is relatively easy to obtain in any part of the world (make sure you use the right word to obtain the correct liquid). Though paraffin burns, of course, it does not explode unlike mishandled gas. Its main drawback is that it is not as clean (the fine jet nozzle needs regular pricking) or as swift to start as a gas cooker. The paraffin has to be pre-heated either by methylated spirits in a cup below the burner or, on the latest models, by pumping up the pressure and lighting an auxiliary jet directed towards the main burner. In about a minute, either pre-heating method should allow the main burner to light safely. Failure to pre-heat properly can cause spectacular jets of burning paraffin to leap towards the deckhead. Provided the stove is turned off immediately, this is more alarming than dangerous, but it does tend to deposit oily soot about the place. It is not easy to get a really satisfactory oven for a paraffin pressure stove nor to turn the heat down sufficiently for gentle simmering (although an asbestos mat can be used).

Abroad, methylated spirit stoves are popular but they, too, need pre-heating and the smell of meths can upset squeamish stomachs. Meths in the UK is dear and not easily obtainable in any but small quantities. But it is safe and a fire can be put out with water.

The overwhelming majority of boat-owners in the UK choose bottled gas for cooking since it is convenient, readily available, easily stowed, clean and quick. It is however potentially dangerous if leaks occur or due care care is not exercised in handling it. It should be professionally installed and the piping should be as short as possible. Gas cookers should have a flame-failure shut-off device.

19.2.3   LIQUEFIED PETROLEUM GAS (LPG)

LPG is a generic term for bottled gases suitable for cooking aboard yachts; LPG has many other uses. Butane is predominantly used in the UK, France, the Mediterranean and tropical countries. Propane is more readily available world-wide and is the predominant form of LPG in Scandinavia, USA, Australia and New Zealand, and most countries south of 30°S.

Both propane and butane are heavier than air and present a fire/explosive danger unless properly handled. The safety aspects have already been discussed in Chapter 13 (13.3.5). Butane ceases to vapourise at about freezing point while propane can withstand temperatures of $-42°C$ ($-44°F$) before this happens, so that in a boat used all the year round propane may be preferable. On the other hand butane has a higher calorific value and is less highly pressurised in its container: 2.1kg/sq cm (30lb/sq in), compared with propane at about 7kg/sq cm (100lb/sq in). Thus butane is slightly safer should a fire break out. If butane is to be used in summer and propane in winter, then the 15kg (33lb) and 4.5kg (10lb) butane cylinders are the same size as the 13kg (29lb) and 3.9kg (8½lb) propane cylinders and will thus stow in the same lockers.

Calor Gas Ltd (Calor) is the leading UK supplier of butane and propane, in a range of cylinder sizes which are hired to the user. These cylinders may only be refilled by Calor Gas, and under no circumstances should any attempt be made to refill a Calor cylinder while abroad. Calor's main advice to traveller's abroad must be to ensure that if practicable, you take a large enough supply of Calor Gas with you to last the entire time away.

The following sizes of Calor cylinders are available in the UK. Butane (blue cylinders): 4.5kg, 7kg and 15kg. Propane (red cylinders): 3.9kg, 13kg, 19kg and 47kg. Cylinders may be connected singly, in pairs, or manifolded together. An automatic changeover valve is available for propane cylinders. Propane must never be filled into a butane cylinder because the setting of the pressure relief valve is unsuitable for propane's higher pressure.

All Calor propane cylinder valves have a female 'POL' connection with a 5/8" BSP female left hand thread. Calor 4.5kg butane cylinder valves have a 5/8" BSP male left hand thread on to which a hexagonal union nut screws. Calor 7kg and 15kg butane valves are quite different and are designed to take the 21mm 'Kosan Teknova Compact' system of connectors or regulators.

Camping Gaz International is also a major supplier of small butane cylinders in over 100 countries. But its largest cylinder 2.72kg (6lbs) is quite small so may need frequent changes depending on crew numbers and amount of cooking. A Camping Gaz/Calor adaptor (available from Calor dealers), allows a Camping Gaz cylinder to be connected to a Calor butane installation.

For safety reasons a LPG cylinder should never be filled to 100% capacity. In tropical or semi-tropical regions 70% capacity should not be exceeded, and in temperate regions 80%. Many small cylinders do not have relief valves, and if heated when overfilled could burst with disastrous results.

Cylinders usually have the 'tare weight' (the weight of the cylinder empty) stamped on an aluminium tare disc attached. Calor cylinders are tested and revalved every 15 years, and the next test date is stamped on the tare disc by the last two digits of the year. If you intend to have Calor cylinders for any length of time, obtain ones that will not require early testing. Also select smartly painted cylinders, lest depots will not handle cylinders said to be 'scruffy'.

Although butane and propane cylinders do not have the same connections, and their regulators are not interchangeable, the gases may safely be interchanged if certain precautions are taken. For appliances approved for butane use only, the butane regulator (28m bar) may be exchanged for a propane regulator (37m bar), as described below. The resulting performance may not be perfect, but it will be satisfactory and safe. Similarly, if butane appliances and a butane regulator are supplied with propane, they will work safely but the performance will be reduced, since the calorific content of propane by volume is less than that of butane. See below for solutions to problems with different cylinders and connections.

Advice for extended foreign cruising

Check each appliance in the boat to see if it is meant to use butane or propane. This can be determined from data on the appliance, from handbooks etc, from Calor dealers, or from the manufacturer. Ideally gas appliances should be approved for both butane and propane operation. Most boats built in the UK have a butane installation, but since propane is more universally available it may be wise to convert to propane before an extended cruise.

One solution to the problem of butane and propane connections not being interchangeable, and different cylinders in different countries having different connections, is to fix the regulator to a bulkhead (not directly to the cylinder) on which a 'wall-block manifold' is mounted. This can be obtained like all other Calor fittings from Calor Gas dealers and Peter Spreadborough, Southampton Calor Gas Centre, Third Avenue, Millbrook Trading Estate, Southampton SO15 0JX. Tel 023 8078 8155; Fax 023 8077 4768. southampton@socal.co.uk www.socal.co.uk

If you intend primarily to use propane, fit the appropriate propane regulator (such as Calor Gas 766P) to the wall-block manifold and take an equivalent butane regulator.

The bulkhead regulator must be connected by

high pressure LPG tubing to a propane cylinder via a male connector, or to butane via a female connector. It is most important to use 'High pressure type 2' tube to BS 3212/2 or equivalent, to avoid attack by propane or butane. The tube must be secured at each end by a stainless steel hose clip.

In Northern Ireland Calor 4.5kg refills are available, but the larger butane cylinders have a Kosan 'click-on' valve which is incompatible with Calor GB regulators. Propane 3.9kg and 13kg cylinders with standard (GB compatible) 'POL' connections are available.

In Eire LPG is provided by Kosan, a sister company of Calor Gas Ltd, in both butane and propane form. Calor cylinders can be exchanged for Kosan, but the latter are bigger and may not fit in a boat's gas locker. Kosan cylinders (butane or propane) are incompatible with Calor GB regulators.

In Spain Camping Gaz is universally obtainable.

For a lengthy cruise in Scandinavian waters it is best to use the Primus propane cylinders, available in the UK, although they are small (1.9kg) and have a unique connection.

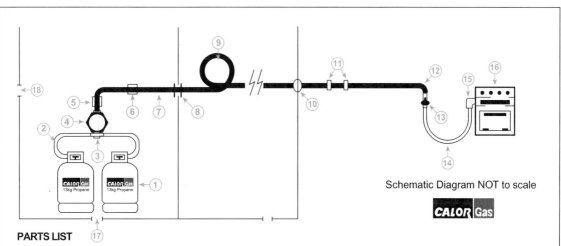

Schematic Diagram NOT to scale

PARTS LIST

1   Two calor propane 13kg cylinders each 630mm high x 330mm wide
2   High pressure hose to BS 3212 part 2 complete with end fittings from Calor, Part No. 342038.
3   Double Wall Block Manifold, propane, complete with non return valve and bracket, Part No. 300163.
4   766P37 propane regulator, Part No. 600845.
5   Shut-off valve kit complete with 12-volt switch in cabin.
6   'Alde 4071 -905' gas leak detector (bubbler device).
7   Copper pipe 8mm O.D up to the manual tap. Larger pipe size may be needed.
8   Bulkhead fitting with compression joints either side to give gas tight joint at pipe exit from cylinder locker.
9   Loop in copper pipe to allow for contraction/expansion (only on long straight pipe runs)
10 Plastic sleeve to protect pipe as it passes through bulkhead.

11 Pipe clips to support pipe at 150mm intervals.
12 Copper pipe 8mm O.D.
13 Manual tap with compression fittings pipe to pipe. (8mm OD) (3/8" O.D. also available).
14 Armoured hose to BS3212 with compression fittings at both ends, One metre length (for 8mm O.D. pipe) (also available in other lengths).
15 Elbow fitting between cooker and armoured hose.
16 Cooker with flame failure device on all burners ie. Plastimo Neptune 2000, Smev 7000. Force Ten Solent Taylors.
17 Gas vent to outside (not cockpit) at base of cylinder locker, Minimum internal diameter 20mm.
18 Gas vent to outside (not cockpit) at top of cylinder locker. Minimum internal diameter 20mm.

Note: All part numbers refer to items supplied by Calor.

Fig. 19(13) A 'Best Practice' LPG installation on a typical 40ft yacht going trans-Atlantic, but most of the fittings apply in principle world-wide.

BP Caravangas, which comes in a 7kg aluminium cylinder, is fairly generally available in Europe except in France and Italy. The cylinder does however have rather a large shroud, and as the name implies it is intended primarily for caravans.

For American waters note that UK and US 'POL' connections on propane cylinders are different, the US versions being slightly smaller in overall diameter, and usually with a smaller AF nut form. While it is usually possible, but not satisfactory, to connect a US 'POL' regulator into a UK 'POL' cylinder, it is physically impossible to get a UK 'POL' regulator into a US 'POL' cylinder; see Fig. 19(13), courtesy of Calor Gas Ltd.

For a lengthy cruise abroad it is advisable to take about 3 metres of high pressure LPG hose and some hose clips, for connecting local butane or propane cylinders to the boat's system. The ends of the tubing so used must be kept in good condition, and cut back as necessary, while it is important to tighten hose clips by just the right amount. Always check for gas leaks after installation with a little soapy water, and turn the gas off at the cylinder after use. Consider taking an additional regulator and a wall block manifold.

Any gas appliance must have adequate ventilation in order to avoid the generation of carbon monoxide, which is invisible, odourless and deadly poisonous.

For further information read the excellent booklet *"LPG (Bottled Gas) for Marine Use"* published annually and obtainable from Calor Gas Ltd, Athena Drive, Tachbrook Park, Warwick CV34 6RL. Tel 0845 7666 1111; Fax 01926 318706.

For other European countries contact the European Liquefied Petroleum Gas Association (AEGPL), 4 Avenue Hosche, 75008 Paris.

For further notes on LPG, see 13.3.5.

19.3 CABIN HEATING

19.3.1 CONDENSATION

In wooden boats condensation was/is rarely a serious problem, although the generally damp conditions on board might have led people to believe otherwise. But the comparatively thin skins of modern craft, built of materials such as GRP and steel, with far poorer insulating properties than timber, require active steps to be taken to reduce condensation. In some cases the use of an inner skin in the cabin area of GRP craft is quite effective, although the object of that skin is as much to give a smooth surface to the inside of the accommodation as it is to cut down condensation.

The first defence against damp is good ventilation. A flow of air works wonders. After this some form of insulating layer against the skin is valuable. On steel craft, for example, the plating between frames can be sprayed with a polyurethane foam up to the level of the frames, and then lined; this is excellent but rather expensive. A cheaper method is to use slabs of foam tailored to fit between those frames. The latter have timber battens fastened to them into which can be screwed the ply lining. Not quite as effective but good enough for most purposes is to stick a foam-backed vinyl direct to the steel, alloy or GRP shell. The thicker the foam, the better. Overheads can have battens glued, bonded or in some other way fastened in position; slabs of thin foam wedged between; and then tongue and groove planking screwed up to cover everything. This looks nice, and the combination of timber and foam has good insulating properties. This sort of approach is difficult on cabin sides where there are probably window or port cut-outs to contend with.

Dehumidifiers

Any boat which is occupied, and therefore heated, during the winter months is certain to suffer problems with condensation which the steps described above are unlikely to overcome completely. The warmer the air inside the boat, the more water vapour it can hold – until the temperature falls, say at night, when condensation streams down windows and other cool surfaces.

Gas heaters make the problem worse, because they actually produce water vapour.

The best way to reduce condensation afloat is to fit a dehumidifier. This type of machine, which works on a principle similar to that of a domestic refrigerator, has been in use ashore for some time, and on a larger scale has been used to preserve the insides of warships 'mothballed' for extended periods. But only recently have suitably 'marinised' units been available for yachts. Although they cost about £300, they are not particularly expensive to run, and can soon pay for themselves by reducing the deterioration of fittings, fabrics, furnishings, clothes, books etc which will otherwise occur, as well as providing healthier and more pleasant living conditions on board.

A dehumidifier, as illustrated in Fig. 19(14), has a larger cold coil (evaporator) than an ordinary refrigerator. Moisture-laden air from the accommodation is blown across this coil by a fan, so that the moisture condenses on the cold surface and is collected in a tank which can either be emptied manually or piped overboard. If ice

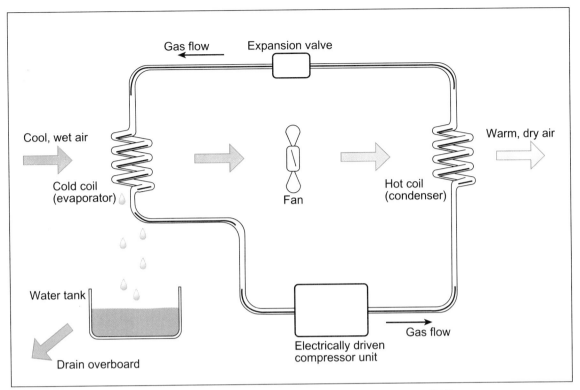

Gas flow   Expansion valve

Cool, wet air

Cold coil
(evaporator)

Fan

Hot coil
(condenser)

Warm, dry air

Water tank

Electrically driven
compressor unit

Gas flow

Drain overboard

Fig. 19(14) A dehumidifier has a gas flow similar to a domestic compressor-type refrigerator.

should form in the machine an automatic defrost sequence begins to operate. The air, now cooler and drier, then passes over the hot coil (condenser) of the machine, extracting heat from it and allowing the refrigeration cycle to continue.

The air, now both drier and warmer than it was originally, then passes back into the accommodation and the cycle is repeated. Gradually the humidity is reduced throughout the vessel. An automatic control can maintain the relative humidity (the percentage of water vapour contained in the air compared with the maximum amount that it could contain at a given temperature) at the required level, typically 55 to 60%.

Depending upon the temperature and relative humidity maintained, a dehumidifier can well extract 5 to $7\frac{1}{2}$ litres of water in 24 hours – a good indication of just how much moisture can be present in a boat. To obtain maximum efficiency from the unit, all ventilators and openings should be shut while the vessel is unoccupied, and used sensibly while people are on board. The water which is collected can be used for washing or for topping up batteries, but should only be drunk in emergency.

Machines are available which work on 12 volts DC, as well as models for 230 volts AC mains operation.

19.3.2   HOT AIR HEATING

Most hot air heaters (eg Eberspacher or Webasto) work in the same way. A glow plug lights an atomised diesel supply from the engine fuel tank; paraffin is also possible. (In an engineless boat or one with a petrol motor, a separate jerry-can or container can be installed and connected). Outside air passing around a heat exchanger is warmed by the heated air and is then blown into the cabin via up to four outlets, or is ducted to various parts of the boat. Safety devices are fitted so that the heater is turned off if it does not ignite, goes out unintentionally or starts to overheat. Most models are thermostatically controlled; see Fig. 19(15).

In some models the burner and heat exchanger are installed in a cockpit locker where fresh air is readily available; others can be fitted below decks where fresh air is trunked to them. Various sizes are available in 12 and 24v with heat outputs ranging from about 0.85 to 5 kilowatts; fuel consumption is modest, 0.2 to 0.4 litres (0.05 to 0.09 gallons) per hour. On start-up the current drawn is about 7 amps at 12v.

A different approach is the paraffin pressure burner or diesel drip-feed burner employed in cabin heaters built by Taylors. These bulkhead-mounted, traditional stainless steel models need no electrics and produce just over 2kW for a consumption of about 0·26 ltrs/hr. The Force 10

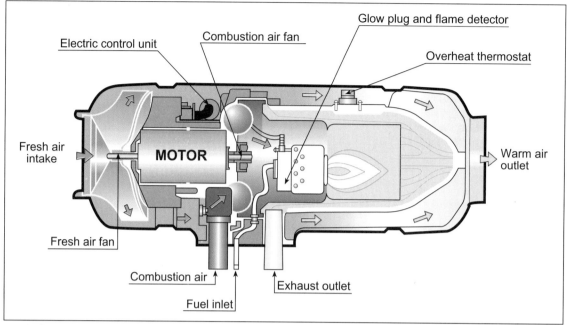

Fig. 19(15) A diesel-fired warm air heater is in principle a simple heat exchanger.

Cozy heater also runs off paraffin or diesel and a different version uses butane/propane.

19.3.3   HEATING BY HOT WATER

Hot water can heat radiators in various parts of the boat, and, of course, be used for washing as well. Water can be heated by:

   a. using the engine cooling water (see also 20.3.5).

   b. using the mains-powered immersion heater built into the calorifier.

   c. trunking hot air from a diesel heater through a heat exchanger with a water jacket. Fig. 19(16) is a diagram of a typical layout.

If required, the hot air heater could be used on its own, separate from the heat exchanger; or part of its output could heat the water and the other part still be employed in producing hot air. Such hybrid arrangements are available.

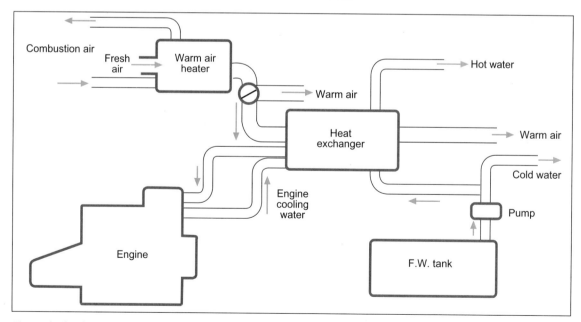

Fig. 19(16) A hot air blower can be used to heat water in a heat exchanger, and may also be used as a calorifier to extract waste heat from the engine cooling system.

A more conventional approach and one suitable for larger vessels is to fit what amounts to a miniature central heating boiler, such as the types made by Eberspacher (UK)Ltd. Models may be selected which produce from 1.6 to 35 Kw and operate on a variety of fuels. Hot water circulates through small bore piping to radiators or panel heaters. It may also be used, in a heat exchanger, to heat air. Heat exchangers also allow this circulating water to be used for domestic hot water supply. The Hydronic 10 model, suitable for boats up to 15 metres produces up to 9.5 Kw (32000 Btu) consuming up to 1.2 litres/hr; it weighs 6.5 kg and would be about 330mm long, 134mm wide, and 236mm deep.

In such a system bear in mind the need for frost protection while the boat is unattended during the winter. If the boat is alongside, the simplest solution is to install one or more electric heaters of the simple tubular type, run off shore power. These will protect the entire contents of the boat against both damp and frost. If this is not possible, all water systems must be drained down, but it is difficult to avoid small pockets of water remaining. A small bore central heating system can be protected by adding anti-freeze (ethylene glycol). A 25 per cent solution by volume will give protection down to –12°C (+ 10°F). Anti-freeze must not of course be added to water systems which form part of the domestic supply.

19.3.4   SOLID FUEL
Though infrequently seen these days, except on rather specialised craft such as canal boats, a solid fuel or bogie stove is a very good and quite convenient source of cabin heat. It circulates and dries air better than any other type and, on models where the fire can be seen through the doors, gives a cheerful glow guaranteed to lift the spirits after a cold watch on deck. It is quiet, undemanding and utterly low-tech. It takes no power to operate and the amount of heat given off is easily controlled.

There are several stoves made for yachts but, when choosing one, do ensure that there are draught controls both at the firebox and flue. It must be capable of being bolted down, and if it is fed through opening doors these must have a secure fastening. The flue pipe will get very hot on occasions. Thus it should either have an expanded metal or some other form of guard round it; or the flue should be a double one, with inner and outer pipes. With the latter arrangement the outer pipe is continued up through the level of the deckhead to obviate the danger of burning the structure. Where a guard only is used a water well should be fitted; this projects down through the

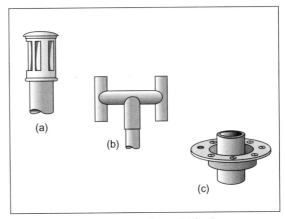

Fig. 19(17) The chimney of a solid fuel stove may have a Liverpool head (a) or a twin head (b). If the stove pipe passes through the deckhead without any form of outer casing, a water well (c) should be fitted.

deckhead and is filled with water to keep the surrounding area cool. The flue pipe fits over the lower projection of the water well and the chimney, or smoke head, over the upper. The Liverpool head type of chimney is normally quite effective under yacht conditions and is unobtrusive. If space is not at a premium in the deck area around the smoke head, the twin head type is excellent especially if it can be swivelled to suit wind direction. Both are shown in Fig. 19(17).

Solid fuel can range from the fruit of beachcombing to coal packed in standard 10kg (22lb) plastic bags. Using the latter a stove should be able to burn for at least eight hours without attention. Bulkheads and similar structures in way of a stove should be lined with a heat resistant and fireproof material while the cabin sole in the immediate vicinity should be similarly treated.

19.3.5   GAS HEATING
Modern gas heaters are made safe by flame failure cut-offs and atmospheric sensors. Thus if the flame goes out for any reason the gas supply is automatically cut off; likewise if the CO_2 level rises above a certain limit. It is strongly recommended that flued appliances are used wherever possible. Any gas appliance must have adequate ventilation in order to avoid the generation of carbon monoxide, which is invisible, odourless and deadly poisonous. There must always be some permanently open ventilator in any area heated by gas.

A catalytic heater burns gas without a flame and so does not give off carbon monoxide, but the heat output is only about 0·80 to 1·35kW.

The Force 10 Cozy cabin heater is available in a LPG version, in stainless steel, brass or bronze, and produces just under 2kW of dry heat.

Safety aspects of installing and using LPG are discussed in 13.3.5.

19.4 FRESH WATER SYSTEMS

19.4.1 MANUAL PUMPS

There is a wide range of manual and foot-operated galley pumps available, ranging from a toe-operated pump recessed in the galley sole, eg the Whale Tiptoe (useful if the galley slave has his or her hands fully occupied) – to the Whale Flipper pump operated by a little lever that is flipped backwards and forwards and mounted integrally with the tap; and others where the pump is a more conventional up-and-down affair. The Whale Gusher is a pedal operated diaphragm pump. All these have quite a modest output of somewhere between about 4.5 to 9 litres (1 to 2 gallons) per min. This is quite adequate for galley use and serves also to keep water consumption down.

However sophisticated the water pumping system fitted, there should always be a hand/foot pump at the galley sink for emergency use.

If long cruises are intended, a pump drawing up sea water is also useful for washing up, cleaning potatoes and cooking many vegetables.

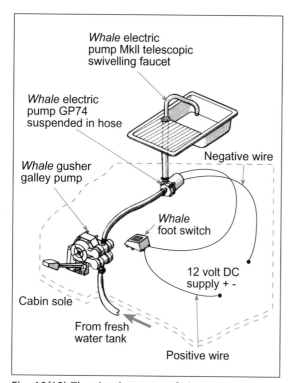

Fig. 19(18) The simplest type of electric water pump is incorporated into an existing system with a foot-operated pump.

19.4.2 PRESSURISED SYSTEMS

Be warned that water usage increases dramatically as soon as it is freely available through an electric pump; formerly ample water tanks soon become inadequate.

The simplest form of water pumping is to install an electric pump in an existing hand-operated system. Whale make a suitable model, light enough (220g or $\frac{1}{2}$lb) to be suspended from the water hoses, which eliminates mechanical vibration. This particular pump is not self-priming and in the absence of a gravity fed system has to be primed through the manual pump.

Fig. 19(18) shows a typical layout. In the event of it failing the hand pump will still operate, which is a considerable advantage. As will be seen the electric pump has to be switched on each time it is needed.

In contrast, much more sophisticated arrangements pressurise the whole system by a pump with automatic operation. When a tap is turned to allow water to flow out, the pressure is reduced and the pump cuts in to keep the water flowing, and to keep the pressure up to the required level. An accumulator tank in the system is an advantage since it holds a pressure reservoir of trapped air. This makes for a smooth flow of water and also means that the pump does not have to start every time an outlet is opened. This lengthens its life and reduces battery drain. These electric systems tend to be rather noisy but they do mean that showers and running hot water are available. Fig. 19(19) shows a typical layout which includes a calorifier to produce and store the hot water.

19.4.3 WATER HEATING

The three principal methods of heating water on board (apart from putting a kettle on) are to use an electric immersion heater in a tank; employ the engine cooling water to give up its heat in a calorifier (ie heat exchanger); or put a gas heater (like a geyser) in the system. The first two methods are usually combined by fitting an immersion heater in the calorifier. An immersion heater would lead to an impossible load on the battery, so it is normally only connected to a mains shore supply. On bigger yachts with ample generating capacity an immersion heater can be run without shore facilities.

A calorifier can only produce hot water in relation to the length of time the engine has been run. Typically, if the engine cooling water is at 82°C (180°F), 15 minutes running will give a modest-sized tankful of water at 60°C (140°F). If the tank is well lagged and the engine is run some time during the evening, the water next morning will still be hot enough for washing and washing up.

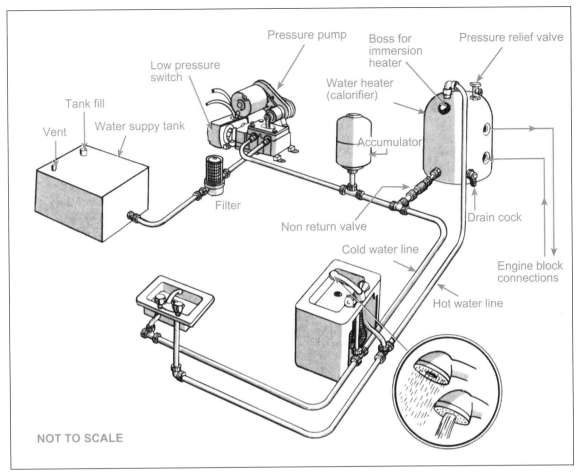

NOT TO SCALE

Fig. 19(19) A pressurised water system. A manual water pump should be added.

Standard calorifiers are available with capacities from about 22 litres (5 gallons) to 70 litres (15 gallons).

Like all gas appliances, gas water heaters are treated with some reserve and are probably best used on craft whose lives are spent mainly on tranquil waters. The heater should have a flame-failure shut-off device and an atmospheric sensor (see 19.2.3). Such a heater can, of course, supply hot water at any time in any quantity.

19.4.4   DESALINATION
Fresh water, or lack of, can limit the endurance of a cruising yacht, particularly in parts of the world where supplies of drinking water are hard to come by. The problem can be alleviated by fitting a desalination plant, operated by waste heat from the cooling system of the main engine or of an auxiliary generator.

The heat is employed to boil sea water in a vacuum, whereby the boiling point is considerably lowered and the amount of heat required is reduced. The resulting vapour is condensed in a distiller, cooled by sea water, and is then pumped away to a storage tank. The brine in the evaporator shell is discharged overboard by another pump. The purity of the made water is continually monitored by a salinometer, and any suspect water will automatically be diverted overboard.

Up to 13 litres (3 gallons) of fresh water per hour can be made from the waste heat of a 11kW (15hp) main engine or of a generator set developing 7.5kW.

Such plant should only be used in the open sea where there is no pollution, because the low boiling point of the sea water under vacuum is not enough to sterilise it from any bacteria which may be present.

Reverse osmosis
Desalination by reverse osmosis has been developed since the 1970s. The process of osmosis is defined as the property of a fluid of a given density, separated by a semi-permeable membrane from a fluid of lower density, to draw the less dense fluid through this membrane, in order to equalise the densities. The volume of the

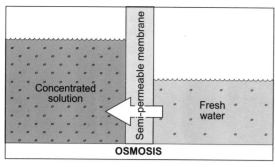

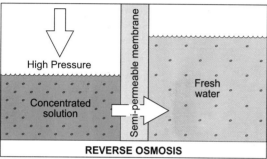

Fig. 19(20) The principle of a reverse osmosis desalination plant.

higher density fluid is increased and generates a pressure, if there is no escape behind the membrane. If fresh water is separated by a semi-permeable membrane from salty water, then pure water will permeate the membrane into the salty side.

However, if sufficient pressure, about 55 – 62 bar (800-900lb/sq in), is exerted on the salty water, and if a suitable membrane can physically resist such pressure, then pure water can be made to pass out of the salty water, through the membrane, and into the pure water side. This is the principle of reverse osmosis, as illustrated in Fig. 19(20). The process became a reality when a suitable synthetic membrane was developed.

In practical installations a reverse osmosis plant consists of a primer pump which delivers sea water to one or more filters to remove all silt and suspended matter. The (filtered) sea water then passes to a positive displacement pump which delivers it to a vessel containing the semi-permeable membrane, through which some fresh water passes. This is then led through a salinity sensor to a solenoid (dump) valve. Any impure water is dumped overboard, depending on the set value of the monitoring equipment, while pure water is filtered and sterilised before going to the storage tank.

The main advantage of a reverse osmosis plant is that it requires about 70 per cent less energy than the evaporator type of unit. Also the materials used do not have to withstand high temperatures, which permits the use of plastics,

glass fibre etc. to reduce weight and cost. It is also claimed that reverse osmosis plants are easier to maintain, and are more reliable.

A reverse osmosis plant for a yacht, producing 600 litres (130 gallons) of fresh water per day, can weigh less than 50kg (110lb) and will consume about 2kW of electricity when running, although the start-up load will be considerably higher. Alternatively the plant can be engine driven, using an electromagnetic clutch and pulley arrangement.

Solent Yacht Services at Shamrock Quay, William Street, Northam, Southampton SO14 5QL (Tel: 023 8033 5294) markets the range of Horizon and PUR desalinators, with outputs from 2 to 605 litres per hour. The smaller units, up to 80 litres per hour, are usually direct drive or AC powered.

An attractive package for the larger cruising yacht is a combined generator and reverse osmosis plant such as the Water-Gen provided by Sea-Fresh Desalinators Ltd, A4 Premier Centre, Abbey Park, Romsey, Hants SO51 9AQ. Tel 01794 830363; Fax 830385. This consists of a single-cylinder, four-stroke diesel which drives a marine alternator for AC services and battery charging and also the high pressure pump for a reverse osmosis Watermaker, giving 15.7 litres of fresh water per hour. With overall dimensions of about 760mm x 460mm x 530mm it is very compact, and weighs about 80kg (176lb) in toto. The firm also markets the Water-Gen-Plus which delivers 6kW 240v AC, and also provides fresh water, hot water, battery charging, compressor drive for refrigerator or freezer, hydraulic drive for bow thruster or windlass, plus a fire and bilge pump.

On a far smaller scale hand-operated watermakers are available which could be vital for survival in a liferaft. The Survivor 06 and the Survivor 35 are distributed in the UK by PUR Watermakers and cost between £540 and £1540. They are made feasible by a clever energy recovery system whereby the brine from the high pressure side of the membrane is directed to the reverse side of the piston, so that the force required to pressurise the incoming sea water is considerably reduced.

The Survivor 06 produces 1.1 litres (1.9 pints) per hour, weighs only 1.1kg (2.4lb) and is very compact. For optimum performance it needs a pump rate of 40 strokes per minute. The Survivor 35 is slightly larger and delivers 4.6 litres (8 pints) hourly.

For permanent installation onboard, an electrically operated version taking 4 amps at 12v DC is also available. A larger DC model, the PowerSurvivor 80 produces 12.5 litres (22 pints) per hour at 8 amps. For large yachts there are models able to produce up to 30 litres of fresh water per hour, but costing £3000-4000.

19.4.5   WATER STORAGE
Depending on the number of persons on board, the average cruising boat needs storage for at least 450 litres (100 gallons), and more often larger quantities, in at least two separate tanks. If your boat has only one permanent tank, and nowhere to fit a second, consider flexible tanks and/or containers to guard against contamination or loss of water. Boats which cruise far afield and in hot climes should arrange for collecting rainwater from awnings.

Water tanks made of GRP or stainless steel are quite satisfactory, if kept properly clean, but even short lengths of some types of clear plastic tubing, as commonly used in boats, can produce an unpleasant taste in the water. This is probably due to the added chlorine in the water reacting chemically with the material of the tubing, producing excessive levels of phenol. Black polythene tubing does not have this effect, and the opaque material also discourages the internal growth of mould and algae; so too does clear, blue or red food grade hose.

A useful palliative is to fit one of the types of water filter, such as the Jabsco Aqua Filta, which is charged with silver impregnated carbon in an easily replaceable cartridge. These will eliminate unpleasant tastes, but they will not completely remove bacteria, for which purpose water purification tablets are available.

19.5   BILGE PUMPING

19.5.1   HAND PUMPS
Diaphragm types dominate the market. They are tough, reliable and easily taken apart to clear blockages although, in fact, they will pass surprisingly large bits of debris. They range in capacity from about 22 litres (5 gallons) per minute to about 475 litres (105 gallons) per minute but at the top end of the scale these are capacities at maximum pumping rates which cannot be sustained for very long.

Diaphragm pumps are easier to work if over-length handles are used, and all pumps must be sited where the user is reasonably sheltered and comfortable at his work. Strum boxes or strainers should be fitted at the inlets, and the whole of the boat should be capable of being pumped dry. The most likely area of leaks is around an engine where the propeller shaft, sea water cooling inlet, exhaust outlet and so on go through the hull. If the yacht has a watertight bulkhead in its length, there should be a diverter valve close to the pump itself, such that either length can be pumped. Equally, if a sailing vessel has a wide, shallow bilge it may well be that when she is heeled, an inlet on the centreline will not pick up bilge water. That means there should be two suctions, again with a diverter valve. A combination of a shallow bilge and watertight bulkheads could therefore mean that two pumps are required. If so, so be it, for every boat, regardless of whether she also has electric or mechanical bilge pumps, should be capable of being cleared by hand.

On some form of marine toilets, such as the Lavac (Fig. 19(21)), the toilet pump, again with a diverter or change-over valve, can be used as a bilge pump, most suitably for the main cabin bilges.

Bilge pumps should exhaust directly overboard and not pump into a self-draining cockpit, for instance, for bilge water is often oily and a smear of oil left on the cockpit sole will make the going hazardous. A sea cock should be fitted at the outlet, unless it is well above the waterline and a swan neck curve can be made in the pipe before it reaches the outlet. This curve will have its highest point well above the skin fitting and so will reduce the chance of water flooding inboard, as could happen if the craft were heeled over and the outlet submerged. All curves in the piping should be gentle and smooth or there will be back pressure which will reduce the pump's capacity, and the inlet suction hose, in particular, should be of the reinforced type.

19.5.2   ELECTRICAL PUMPS
An electrical bilge pump is a valuable tool on board but just to emphasise the need for hand pumps as well, it will only function when the electrics are working and the battery has not been flooded. Current draw may in any case be a concern: As a guide, a small bilge pump with a capacity of around 270 gallons per hour will draw about 7 amps on 12v operation and 5 amps on 24v; while at 1140 gallons per hour a bigger pump will draw 9.5 amps on 12v and 7 amps on 24v. Electric bilge pumps for yachts are able to pump up to 3700 gallons per hour. They can be mounted high up, clear of likely bilge water and able to self-prime, or be submersible ie able to operate under water if required. They may be switched on manually or automatically when the bilge water reaches a certain height. Two types of automatic operation are available:

  i. a float mounted within the pump casing which is then installed at the required height.
  ii. the pump is mounted remotely with a hose and air bell reaching into the bilge.

The air bell transmits air pressure through a tube to a diaphragm switch, turning the motor on or off. Clearly, as the bilge water rises in the air bell, air pressure will increase.

On non-submersible electric pumps belt-drive types are generally recommended since they allow the motor to turn more slowly than a direct drive type, giving quieter running and a longer life.

19.5.3   MECHANICAL (CLUTCH) PUMPS

These are the giants of the bilge pumping brigade, and big versions will shift tremendous volumes of water. Mechanical or Clutch bilge pumps are belt-driven off the main engine or generator, and incorporate either a remotely controlled electro-magnetic clutch or a manual clutch. At 1500rpm and absorbing 1kW (or about 15hp) such a pump will discharge about 2640 gallons per hour which will cope with most leaks. By use of change-over cocks and a sea water inlet, pumps like this can double up as deck wash and fire pumps. They will continue to pump down to about 100rpm. Types capable of discharging nearly 4900 gallons per hour are available.

The dual pump is an interesting variation on the theme of bilge pumps since it combines the operations of the engine cooling water impeller with that of a bilge pump. It is shaft-driven off the engine and continuously pumps the bilges. When they are dry the bilge pump impeller is automatically lubricated by a bleed from the cooling pump chamber. A typical Jabsco dual pump, for example, can handle a flow rate of 2760 gallons per hour on the cooling side with a bilge pumping rate of 1200 gallons per hour. Smaller versions are available.

19.6 MARINE TOILETS

19.6.1   CONVENTIONAL MARINE TOILETS

There is a bewildering array of types and arrangements. All have inlets and outlets leading from/to the sea, but after that the situation changes. Some, like the SL400 and Lavac, require a single pump operation only. There are no levers to throw or wheels to turn or valves to open (apart from seacocks.) Some have a single pump with a lever to operate or a valve to open, whilst others have two pumps, one inlet and one outlet valve. Many can be converted to electric operation (ie the pumping is electrical rather than manual). All toilets from reputable manufacturers are reliable and if serviced according to their instructions will have a long life.

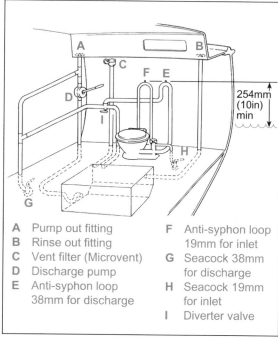

A Pump out fitting	**F** Anti-syphon loop
B Rinse out fitting	19mm for inlet
C Vent filter (Microvent)	**G** Seacock 38mm
D Discharge pump	for discharge
E Anti-syphon loop	**H** Seacock 19mm
38mm for discharge	for inlet
	I Diverter valve

Fig. 19(21) A Lavac toilet flushes the toilet and pumps overboard or to a pump-out connection on deck, or to a holding tank. It can also pump the bilge in emergency; a versatile layout.

Choice will ultimately depend on cost, size, weight and comfort. Some are really rather small for convenient sitting.

In the UK one of the leading suppliers of toilets and associated equipment is Lee Sanitation Ltd, Wharf Rd, Fenny Compton, Warwickshire CV33 0XE; Tel 01295 770000; Fax 01295 770022.

As the authorities become increasingly concerned over the discharge of raw sewage into the oceans of the world and especially into confined harbours and rivers, pumping overboard is often forbidden. Thus holding tanks have to be incorporated into the toilet systems. Such tanks can be bought commercially in small sizes with something like 22 litres (5 galls) to 45 litres (10 galls) capacity but most are fabricated by the boatbuilder.

Fig. 19(21) shows a typical arrangement allowing the toilet to discharge direct into the sea or into the holding tank from which it can be pumped either by the boat's own toilet pump or by an onshore facility. The system shown is based on the Lavac toilet since that has a separate pump normally sited above the toilet bowl, but other types can be similarly arranged.

The holding tank may also be used to collect waste (grey water) from basins, sinks and showers, and will have to be sized accordingly. A shower, for instance, will need about 3 gallons of water for each operation. If the tank connects only to the toilet, S = 1·5 (B x D). Where S is the minimum capacity in gallons; B is the number of berths; and D the number of days anticipated between pump-outs. Thus a five-berth yacht with an anticipated 14 days between pump-outs would ideally need a holding tank of 5 x 14 x 1.5 = 105 galls or 470 litres capacity. Such a hefty tank, when full, would weigh 450kg (l000lb) excluding the weight of the tank itself. Clearly on many small five-berthers this is not practicable, and pump-outs would have to be undertaken much more frequently.

The tank is usually made of GRP but aluminium alloy and stainless steel are very satisfactory, if more expensive. A large inspection hatch must be arranged in the top surface.

19.6.2   CHEMICAL TOILETS

Although much derided, chemical toilets are really not all bad, provided they can be fitted into a space where their distinctive smell may be isolated. Most types are in two parts: the top section holds the flushing water, while the bottom half holds the waste. A chemical is added to one or the other, depending on make. The two are separated by operating a sliding clamp device; the bottom can then be taken away for emptying. The jointing clamp is secure and a very basic, though quite effective, hooked catch keeps the whole toilet in place on board. In civilised surroundings the waste is emptied ashore. At sea it can be dumped overboard.

Chemical toilets are much preferable to the traditional bucket since they can be carried without fear of spillage and need not be emptied after every use. A full upper tank will give about 40 flushes, but the waste container in practice only lasts two people two or three days with normal use. A chemical toilet is cheap and needs no pipework or through-hull inlets and outlets. There are superior types available where the chemically treated flushing water is stored in a separate tank, and electrically recirculated. These models can usually also be had as a permanent installation with pump-out connections.

19.6.3   TOILET MAINTENANCE

Marine toilets need and deserve routine maintenance since this is the best way to avoid possible trouble, which can be inconvenient in the middle of a family cruise. Most of them have some perishable parts such as rubber seals, glands, washers, etc which, together with items like hose clips, need checking periodically and probably require renewal about every five years. Most manufacturers provide kits of these parts, and it is advisable to carry spares on board.

When the time comes to lay up, make sure that the whole system is well washed through, rinsed with disinfectant, and then drained out. If water is liable to be lingering somewhere, add a little anti-freeze. Chemical toilets must be emptied out and cleaned. Some of these units are sensitive to chemicals, so that use of the wrong materials can cause damage; it is best to stick to the maker's instructions.

At the start of the season, or whenever the boat is out of the water, clear the strainer on the sea water inlet and ensure that the seacocks are strongly fixed to the hull, in good condition and free to turn. The bronze tapered plug (Blakes) type of seacock is best; make certain that the plug is seating correctly, apply seacock grease and check that the gland is tight but not so tight as to be hard to operate. When a boat is unattended, it is a good rule to close all seacocks. Outlet pipes can become constricted by a hard deposit. If they are plastic pipes it may be easiest to replace them, but new 'odour-free' pipes are rarely easy to fit to the seacock: first bevel the inside of the pipe with a sharp knife; very hot water will soften the pipe; washing-up liquid is a good lubricant and, to get the pipe fully home, judicious use of a hot-air blower (hair dryer or paint stripper), coupled with muscle power will do the trick. If new pipes are unavailable, the old pipes can be removed and flexed or tapped with a mallet to shake out the deposit. Regular treatment with vinegar will help to keep pipes clear. Pump glands should be tight, and may need repacking. Clean the filter on recirculating toilets.

Properly treated, a marine toilet should be relatively trouble-free. Keep it clean at all times, and use only the recommended cleaning fluids and disinfectants. Above all, ensure that everybody who comes on board understands that no solid item of any kind may be put down the toilet – unless it has already been eaten.

19.7 REFRIGERATION

19.7.1   INTRODUCTION

Refrigerators aboard yachts are almost commonplace as manufacturers have successfully solved problems caused by the difficult operating conditions. Onboard, refrigerators are expected to work effectively, almost regardless of the angle of heel, while few small craft can provide truly adequate space for air to circulate around the cooling coils. Nevertheless in the UK's temperate climate they work satisfactorily most of the time, although their drain on batteries is serious, especially on yachts which are used only at weekends or which run their engines infrequently.

There is a widely-held belief that a top-opening refrigerator which readily retains cooled air is preferable on board; and that a front-opening door, which allows cooled air to flow out – because cold air is heavier than warm air – is wasteful of energy. But the arguments for and against front versus top loader are by no means as simple as that.

The top-opener may be awkward to site in the galley, and its horizontal lid doubles as a work surface which may be inconvenient. More importantly it is very much harder, and therefore time and energy-wasting, to stow and retrieve food and drink. 'Layers' of food packages lie on top of each other, whilst drinks are usually at the bottom if only to keep weight as low as possible. Tests have shown that a top-loader may be open 3 to 4 times longer than a front-loader. Top-loaders may be so deep that shorter users cannot reach items at the bottom; but at least the contents do not fall out, unless the boat turns turtle!

A front-opener on the other hand requires only that the door is opened, food removed and the door closed. The door (which may be full of heavy bottles) must be properly secured, especially in a seaway. Ventilating airflow over the compressor and heat exchanger which are at the back is at its most ineffectual. Insulation on a proprietary front-opener is always inadequate, and the box-shape is incompatible with the curvature of the hull and possibly the galley layout itself.

One key point: Any refrigerator is only as good as the box or cabinet which it is cooling. Really effective insulation is therefore essential, if the cooling ability of your installation is not to be squandered (see 19.7.5).

19.7.2 ELECTRO-MECHANICAL REFRIGERATORS

An electric motor, or belt drive from the engine, runs a rotary compressor (probably the ubiquitous and excellent Danfoss) which compresses a refrigerant gas such as Freon. This expands in coils (the evaporator) inside the cooling cabinet, extracting heat (ie lowering the temperature) as it does so. This heat is released when the gas is cooled in an external condenser, either by air or sea water.

Water, or keel, cooling is needed if the refrigerator is to work effectively in high ambient tropical or semi-tropical temperatures. An air-cooled condenser will start to give problems once the ambient temperature below deck climbs to 30°C (90°F) or more, with the compressor running almost continuously and causing a very big drain on battery capacity. Keel cooling is often chosen in UK waters because the equipment is smaller; no

airflow is required, hence no fans and no noise; and the plant runs cooler and at lower internal pressure thus extending its lifespan; see Fig. 19(22).

The length of time a refrigerator needs to run to maintain the selected temperature can be considerably reduced by the use of holdover plates in the cabinet. These plates contain a eutectic solution which freezes at a low temperature and, by virtue of its latent heat, stores coldness within the cabinet for several hours; so that the compressor need only run for an hour or so, twice a day. This is a considerable advantage. The plates themselves need to be installed vertically or horizontally near the top of the cabinet, but with at least 15mm clearance from the body of the cabinet to allow for proper air circulation. On bigger yachts a deep freeze compartment is quite common in addition to the normal refrigerator.

To avoid running the engine very frequently just for battery charging, consider installing a wind generator and/or solar cells (see 13.3.4); upgrading your battery charger and/or fitting larger, better batteries.

19.7.3 THERMO-ELECTRIC REFRIGERATORS

When a voltage is applied across the junction between two dissimilar metals, heat is removed from one of the metals and transferred to the other. This Peltier effect, so named after its originator, is the basis of thermo-electric cooling. In practice aluminium fins inside a cold chest absorb heat and transfer it through thermo-electric modules to heat-dissipating fins outside. A fan circulates the air in the cabinet and helps disperse the heat into the surrounding air. The fan is quiet in use and the only moving part. These units must be very well insulated if electrical demand is to be kept low and efficient operation achieved.

A portable cool box, such as is plugged into a car's lighter socket, suffices for short day cruises in a small yacht, but overnight a mains shore supply is almost essential. The unit draws about 4 amps at l2v when running, but is thermostatically controlled. Thus its overall current drain is around 3 amps when operating in a well-insulated, but small 3cu ft cabinet.

The initial cost is low, but running costs are high and continuous, about 3 times the battery drain of a similar sized unit driven by a Danfoss compressor.

19.7.4 INSULATION

Whether you already have a professionally installed refrigerator or are about to fit one yourself (a simple but painstaking DIY job), be

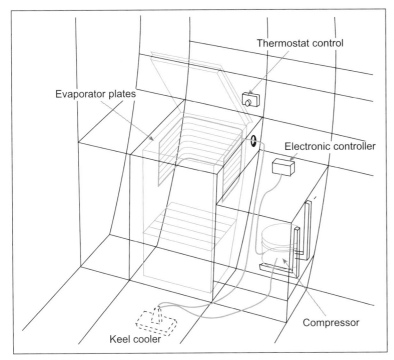

Thermostat control

Evaporator plates

Electronic controller

Compressor

Keel cooler

Fig. 19(22) Keel-cooled, compressor refrigerator.

aware of the very high standard of insulation required. Fig. 19(23) shows a professional installation utilising the hull side as one part of the structure.

Consider first the size of refrigerator best suited to your needs. A 6cu ft box may well be too large for a well-organised husband-wife team, for whom 4 cu ft might suffice. The larger the capacity the greater the power consumption and the harder to stow things.

The amateur may find it easiest to buy a GRP, welded pastic or stainless steel box around which the required thickness of polyurethane (closed cell) foam panels can be glued. (It is very difficult to make well fitting joints from Formica-faced plywood. There is a risk that condensate water with food particles etc will get into the ply and insulation. The rotting smell is unbelievable and difficult to eradicate).

For a 2 cu ft cabinet at least 50mm thick foam should be used and as cabinet capacity rises, so must the thickness of the foam at the rate of 12mm per 1 cu ft capacity. Thus a 6 cu ft box would need at least 100mm of foam insulation; these thicknesses should be regarded as the minimum. The foam panels must be a tight fit around the ply shell; to fill any existing air cavities, inject foam from an aerosol canister.

It is best not to fit a drain as this provides a thermal conduction path through the insulation. If the plug gets knocked out, battery power will in effect drain out continuously just as surely as

water. It is also a breeding ground for bacteria. A close-fitting, insulated lid should have a lip with double air-tight seals below.

19.7.5 USING A REFRIGERATOR AFLOAT

It goes without saying that a refrigerator must be scrupulously clean, both at the start of and throughout the cruise. If spillage occurs, wash it out thoroughly with fresh water and a mild cleaner, rinse it down and leave it open for several hours to get rid of any smell.

It helps if the temperature of the whole fridge can first be reduced by inserting a block or two of ice before loading proper begins. Ice cubes, as dispensed by machines at marinas, are of little or no use – except for G & T. Large blocks, which melt relatively slowly, may be obtained from the local ice plant if in a fishing harbour. These should completely cover the bottom of the ice box and form walls around the sides. The beer goes into the space in the middle. Ice is a precious commodity in some cruising areas.

Whatever the type of refrigerator used, thought is needed to get the best results. For example open the lid as infrequently and for as short a time as possible. Return cold items to the refrigerator as soon as possible, ie do not leave a milk carton standing in the sun gaining heat. If you have an icebox for making ice cubes, it may be worth partitioning it off so that its low temperature is not needlessly wasted on chilling the rest of the fridge. Subdivide the interior, so that different items cannot get mixed with (or possibly contaminate) others. Plastic bags and boxes are easily stored, economical with space and can be marked for quick identification; some boxes are colour coded. Or use a small portable container of the insulated 'picnic' variety, for ready-use items like milk, butter and cold drinks. Ideally you should never have to unload the entire refrigerator to find something at the bottom. Proponents of front-opening refrigerators argue that so much time is wasted looking for items in a top-opening fridge as to defeat the object of the exercise.

19.7.6 AIR CONDITIONING

In British waters the need is not so much for air conditioning, as for keeping warm; see 19.3. But in many cruising areas conditions can far exceed

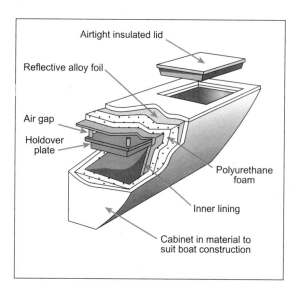

Fig. 19(23) Ice box or refrigerator construction using the hull side as one face of the box.

Labels on figure:
Airtight insulated lid
Reflective alloy foil
Air gap
Holdover plate
Polyurethane foam
Inner lining
Cabinet in material to suit boat construction

those in which human beings are reasonably comfortable: namely temperatures of around 18-21°C (65-70°F) and relative humidities of 40-65%.

Air conditioning is theoretically quite possible even in a small boat, but there are practical difficulties with the space occupied by the unit and, more notably, with the large amount of electric power consumed. The latter disadvantage can of course be overcome when the yacht is alongside and shore power is available.

Full air conditioning implies the delivery of air which can be cooled or warmed, and have its humidity either lowered or raised, to maintain a desirable internal atmosphere regardless of outside conditions. It should also include ways of removing dust, smells and bacteria from the air, and even the injection of beneficial elements. Enough oxygen must be provided, in the form of fresh air, for the crew to breathe. So the detailed design and control of the numerous fresh and recirculated air inlets and exhausts, are all very important factors. The design involves a detailed calculation of heat gained from outside the yacht (which depends on the efficiency of such insulation as may be fitted), from the fresh air admitted, from the occupants, and from internal sources of heat such as the galley, electrical appliances and machinery. Such a plant would only be found in the largest and most luxurious yachts. Units fitted in smaller craft normally only aim to reduce temperature and humidity to more acceptable levels, combined with some

form of air circulation and perhaps a dust filter.

Air conditioning sets in yachts are of the compressor type. In larger yachts a central refrigeration unit, probably sited in the engine room, distributes chilled water to air treatment units situated in the various spaces. Smaller yachts normally have individual air conditioning units in each cabin or space to be cooled, but since each unit has its own compressor and fan, they are more noisy.

An approximation to the cooling capacity per hour required is 14BTU per cu ft for cabins and spaces below deck level, and 17 BTU per cu ft above. Hence a cabin of 450 cu ft (13 cu m) might require a unit of about 6500 BTU/hr. (For conversion to metric units 1 BTU= 1055 Joules.) Such a unit would take about 1kW to run, but on first starting up the compressor might take a surge load of 3kW. These sorts of loads require an auxiliary generator, unless the yacht is connected to shore power.

As might be expected the American market caters more for air conditioning than the British. West Marine, PO Box 50070, Watsonville, California 95077 are a major distributor who offer an ordering service to UK customers on Freephone 0800 895473. Or e-mail catintl@westmarine.com or visit their Web site at www.westmarine.com

Most models operate on a 115v AC shore supply or from a suitable onboard generator. Manufacturers include Marine Air Systems who produce Cool Mate self-contained systems with outputs of 5000-16000Btu, suitable for boats in the 25-40ft LOA range; also portable units from Cruisair and Komfort Industries with outputs of 5000-6500Btu.

Good heat insulation of superstructure, deck and topsides reduces the demands on air conditioning units (and makes any non-air conditioned yacht more comfortable in hot or cold weather). Teak decks have good insulating properties (and benefit from being kept wet in hot weather), but even a wooden-hulled boat can be improved with an insulating lining. As already stated in 19.3.1, foam plastic is widely employed, although such materials are flammable and may give off toxic fumes in the event of fire. Large windows in the super-structure can make the interior very hot, and in warm climates it is sensible to have external screens which can be rigged in harbour, plus awnings to keep the decks cool and provide shade; a windscoop helps to channel the air through a fore hatch and below deck. See also 18.2.4 Ventilators.

Chapter 20 Engines

CONTENTS

20.1 DESIGN AND CONSTRUCTION

This chapter offers a simplified explanation of how the various types of yacht engines and their ancillary systems work and how they are constructed. A basic knowledge helps the owner to understand, operate and maintain his engine correctly. General advice is also given on maintenance; the maker's handbook will give more specific advice.

20.1.1 4-STROKE PETROL ENGINES

Many readers will already know how a petrol engine works. The main parts of a typical engine are shown in Fig. 20(1); Fig. 20(2) illustrates the 4 stroke cycle.

An air/petrol mixture from the carburettor or an injection pump is drawn into each cylinder in turn as the piston descends. On the upstroke the piston compresses this mixture which is ignited by a spark-plug near the top of the stroke. The burning mixture expands and pushes the piston down. Finally the piston re-ascends, pushing the exhaust gases out of the cylinder – and the 4 stroke cycle starts again.

The reciprocating movement of the pistons is converted to rotary motion by the connecting rods between pistons and crankshaft. A camshaft, driven at half engine speed, operates inlet and exhaust valves in the cylinder head, controlling the ingress of fresh mixture and the expulsion of exhaust gas. It also activates the spark plug at the right moment.

An engine's power output depends on the

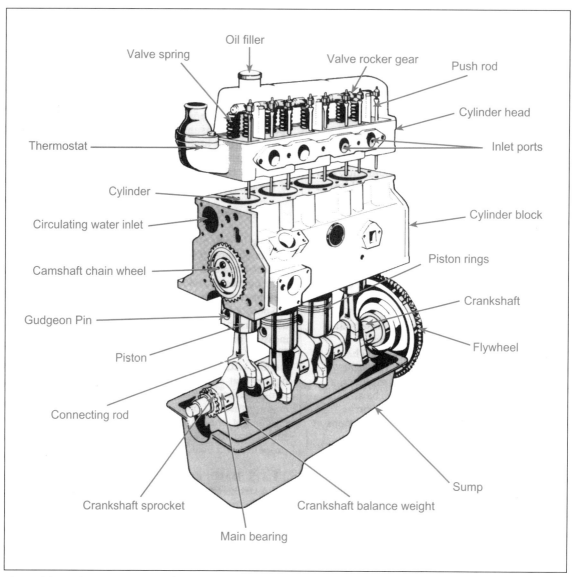

Fig. 20(1) Main components of an internal combustion engine.
1. Cylinder head; 2. Cylinder block; 3. Crankshaft; 4. Sump.

weight of air/fuel mixture that can be drawn into each cylinder, and how much it can be compressed. A typical compression ratio with ordinary petrol is 9:1. Too high a compression ratio causes uneven burning of the fuel (detonation), which is inefficient and can do damage. An extra air/fuel weight can be pushed into the cylinder by a supercharger, driven either off the engine or from a turbine operated by exhaust gases.

For 2-stroke petrol outboard engines, see 20.6.

20.1.2 DIESEL ENGINES
Outwardly, diesels resemble petrol engines, having a similar configuration and moving parts. The difference is in the method of igniting the fuel. Instead of a spark plug, each cylinder has a

fuel injector supplied by a high pressure pump. The pump meters very precise quantities of fuel at very high pressure and at just the right instant to the injectors.

On the induction stroke only air is drawn into the cylinder. This air is then compressed and thereby heated to a temperature which will spontaneously ignite a very fine (atomised) spray of diesel fuel from the injector. The burning fuel expands, producing the downward power stroke, followed by the ascending exhaust stroke – to complete the cycle.

Diesel engines have a higher compression ratio than petrol engines. They are therefore more robustly constructed and thus heavier for a given power. This factor is however diminishing in more modern engines due to improved design.

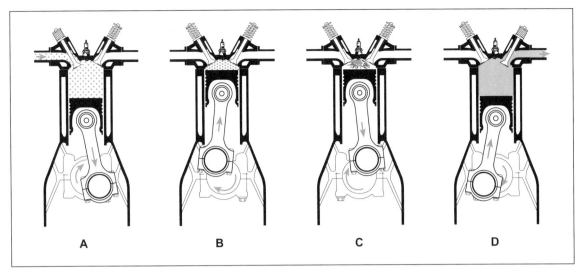

Fig. 20(2) ***Petrol*** *engine 4 – stroke cycle: a. Air/petrol mixture enters cylinder via inlet valve; b. Both valves shut, mixture compressed by rising piston; c. Near the top of the stroke the spark plug ignites the mixture and the piston is forced downwards; d. The exhaust valve opens and exhaust gas is expelled as the piston re-ascends.*

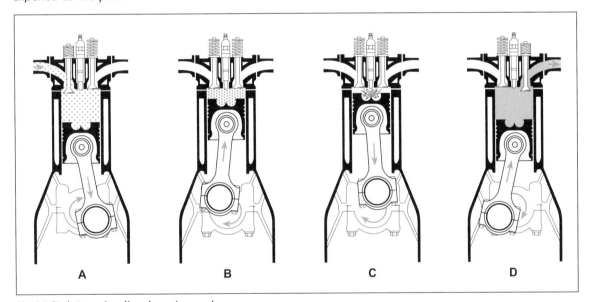

Fig 20 (2a) 4 stroke ***diesel*** *engine cycle.*
a. induction; b. compression; c. power; d. exhaust.

20.1.3 CHOICE OF ENGINES

The choice between a petrol and a diesel engine depends on the type of boat and the pattern of boat usage. The advantages and disadvantages of each type are summarised as:

Petrol

For	Against
Lower first cost	Higher fire risk
Better power/weight ratio	More prone to electrical faults

In general, inboard petrol engines are usually fitted to smaller yachts where weight and space are dominant factors. High speed motor boats are an exception, where the highest power/weight ratio is the over-riding requirement. Petrol out-board engines are very suitable for auxiliary pro-pulsion of tenders and light displacement yachts.

Diesel

For	Against
Safer	Higher first cost
More reliable	Heavier
Cheaper to run	Noisier

Medium and larger yachts are normally diesel powered. Diesel outboard motors are available, but their use is mainly confined to workboats where reliability is more important than weight.

20.1.4 POWER AND PERFORMANCE

Power is defined as the rate of doing work. It may be expressed in either horsepower or in kilowatts as follows:

1 horsepower	= 550 ft lbs/second
1 joule	= 1 Newton metre
(a Newton is a 1 kilogramme force)	
1 watt	= 1 joule/second
1 kilowatt	= 1.341 horsepower
1 horsepower	= 0.746 kilowatts

Engine power is measured on a test bed, using a dynamometer, or brake, which can measure the torque produced. Hence:

$$\text{Brake horsepower} = \frac{\text{Torque (ft Lb) x rpm}}{5252}$$

When all the various auxiliaries are fitted to the test engine, such as alternator, water pump, gearbox and exhaust system, the available power will be reduced. The power available for propulsion is called the shaft horsepower and is usually between 10 and 20% less than the brake horsepower.

Engine powers are sometimes quoted as both 'continuous' and as 'intermittent'. The latter is a higher output which can be used for short periods without damage or overheating.

An engine's technical information should include Power Curves. An example is shown at Fig. 20 (3).

The graph shows intermittent and continuous torque curves at the top, followed lower down by a similar pair of BHP curves. A typical 'propeller law' curve shows the horse power that the propeller can absorb at various rpm. In this example the propeller is matched to the engine at 2500rpm, when it will absorb the full BHP that the engine can deliver. This should correspond to the vessel's maximum speed. At lower (cruising) speeds (say 2000rpm, where the specific fuel consumption is least) the propeller can only absorb about half the power that the engine could theoretically deliver.

When comparing engines of similar power, the following factors should be considered:

Power to weight ratio;
Specific fuel consumption; and
Piston speed at similar rpm.

Specific fuel consumption is measured in lbs/bhp/hour or in grammes/kilowatt/hour. It is a measure of the engine's economy – or lack of. The internal combustion engine is not particularly efficient and only about 35% of the available energy in the fuel is transferred into useful propeller thrust. The rest is dissipated as waste heat to the cooling water, friction in engine, gearbox and shafting, radiant heat, exhaust pipe losses and propeller efficiency.

Piston speed is a useful measure of the likely life of an engine. Long-lasting diesels have piston speeds around 1500 ft/minute. Faster engines (usually with better power/weight ratios) may have figures of 2000 – 2500 ft/min. Petrol engines may exceed 3000 ft/min. The formulae for calculating piston speed are:

$$\text{Piston speed (ft/min)} = \frac{\text{Stroke (ins) x rpm}}{6}$$

or

$$\text{Piston speed (m/sec)} = \frac{\text{Stroke (cms) x rpm}}{6000}$$

20.1.5 BASIC ENGINE COMPONENTS

All 4-stroke engines, whether petrol or diesel, have similar structural and internal parts. The main items, eg cylinder head, cylinder block etc, are shown in Fig. 20 (1).

Cylinder head

The cylinder head is bolted to the top of the cylinder block. The joint between them, called the gasket, has to seal the joint face against leakage of combustion gases, cooling water and lubricating oil. It is made of a compressible fibre sandwiched between two layers of copper and can only be used once. A spare should be carried. The cylinder head contains on its underside the combustion chambers for each cylinder, at the sides the inlet and exhaust ports for each cylinder and on top the valve operating mechanism (rocker gear). The casting contains various cooling water galleries and passages, particularly around the combustion chambers and exhaust ports.

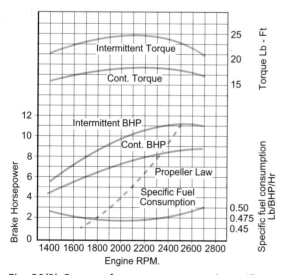

Fig. 20(3) Curves of torque, power and specific fuel consumption, plotted against engine rpm, for a small twin-cylinder diesel. Also shown (dotted) is a typical propeller law curve.

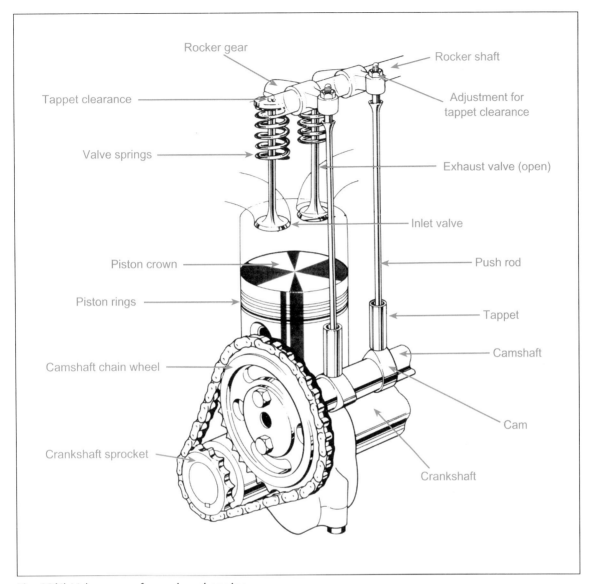

Fig. 20(4) Valve gear of a push-rod engine.

Valve gear

The valves are held onto their seats in the ports by valve springs, see Fig. 20(4).

Each valve is opened at the correct moment in the cycle by rocker arms which in turn are actuated by push rods from a camshaft. The cams actuate their push rod and rocker arm and force the valve open; further movement of the cam releases the pressure on the valve stem and the spring closes the valve. An adjustable gap is provided between the rocker arm and the valve stem to allow for wear and expansion. This "tappet clearance" must be periodically checked and adjusted.

Some higher performance engines have an overhead camshaft mounted on the top of the cylinder head in which case the push rods are not needed, making the valve gear lighter and simpler.

Cylinder Block

Contains the bores of the cylinders, usually in line, together with passages for water cooling and for lubrication. The cylinder walls are usually thin steel liners pressed into the cylinder block casting, so as to be replaceable if worn. The block also incorporates the crankcase housing the crankshaft, rotating in its main bearings. The sump is a rectangular pan-shaped casting or pressing bolted to the base of the block to act as a reservoir for the lubricating oil.

Pistons

The pistons have to transmit the forces of the burning, expanding gases in the cylinder to the connecting rods which produce rotary motion at the crankshaft. The pistons must also form a good seal within the cylinder, take away the heat from the piston crown, be strong enough to carry the

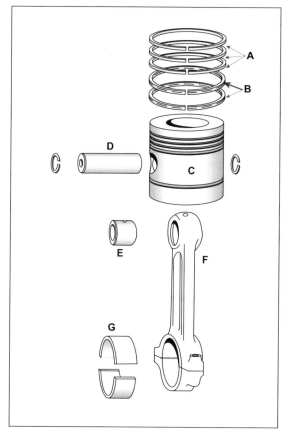

Fig. 20(5) Piston and connecting rod, showing:
a. Compression rings
b. Oil control (scraper) rings.
c. Piston.
d. Gudgeon pin and retaining circlips.
e. Small end bearing shell.
f. Connecting rod
g. Large end bearing shell.

small (upper) end bearing of the connecting rod and be able to suffer continual reversals of movement – about 80 times per second.

Pistons are therefore made of a light alloy which combines strength at high temperature with a low coefficient of expansion. The piston rings maintain a seal within the bore of the cylinder with minimum friction. There are usually 2 or 3 compression rings at the top and a scraper ring near the bottom of the piston skirt which removes excess oil from the bores on the downward stroke. Piston rings are subject to wear and may become gummed up by oil residues and combustion products. Poor starting from cold can be due to piston ring problems.

Connecting Rods

These are normally steel forgings, being one of the most highly stressed parts of an engine. The bottom end of the rod is split into two parts,

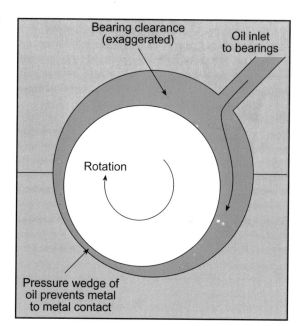

Fig. 20(6) Principle of lubrication of a typical big end bearing (enlarged).

bolted around the the crankpin of the crankshaft Fig. 20(7). This big end bearing housing contains a shell bearing lined with a suitable low friction alloy eg tin-aluminium. The bearing is lubricated via holes drilled in the crankshaft, fed from the oil pump; see Fig. 20(6).

Oil enters the bearing under pressure at a point of low bearing load – where there is maximum clearance between the journal and the bearing. As the journal (shaft) rotates inside the bearing it builds up a wedge of oil which is thinnest along the line of maximum bearing load, but which builds up sufficient internal pressure to prevent metal to metal contact. The oil also removes heat from the bearing. The small end bearing is fed with oil either via a hole drilled up the con rod or by splash (oil flung from the rotating crankshaft).

The general lubrication system of an engine is further discussed in 20.3.6.

20.1.6 TURBOCHARGERS

Turbochargers are fitted to boost the power output of an engine (typically by about 30%) by utilising the waste energy in the exhaust gases. The turbo-charger consists of a turbine disc attached to a rotor spindle. The turbine is rotated at high speed by the flow of the exhaust gas through it's vanes. See Fig. 20(8).

At the other end of the spindle is fitted a centrifugal compressor rotor which compresses the air supply to the engine manifold. If more air is thus provided, more fuel can be burnt efficiently and more power is produced.

Turbochargers rotate at extremely high

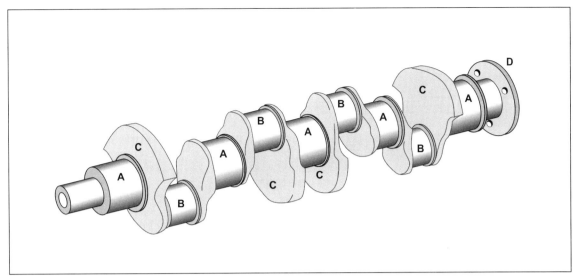

Fig. 20(7) Crankshaft: a. Main bearing journals; b. Crankpins which carry large end bearings of the connecting rods; c. Balance weights; d. Fly wheel flange.

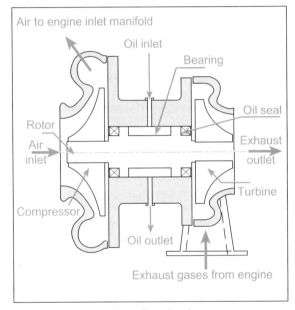

Fig. 20(8) A typical small turbocharger.

speeds (up to 100,000 rpm) and are very accurately made and assembled. The rotor bearings are fed with oil from the engine lubrication system and are fitted with oil seals to prevent oil leakage into the the turbine or the compressor, (some have unlubricated ceramic bearings). Most turbocharged engines are also fitted with an intercooler; the incoming air is heated up by compression and needs to be cooled down again to increase the density of the air charge into the cylinders to obtain better efficiency.

The performance of the turbocharger is monitored using the boost pressure gauge. A gradual fall in boost pressure at a given power indicates wear or fouling of the rotor blades. Reconditioned spare units can be obtained.

Maintenance requires regular changing of engine oil and of the turbocharger's own oil filter (if fitted); keeping the inlet air filter clean and occasionally checking that no oil is leaking from the bearings into the inlet manifold.

20.1.7 ENGINE CONFIGURATIONS

The simplest 4 stroke engine has one (usually vertical) cylinder and there are a few low-powered boat engines of this type. They are fitted with a relatively heavy flywheel to reduce the uneven torque from one power stroke every two revolutions and the out-of-balance reciprocating forces inherent in a single cylinder engine. Such engines can cause significant vibration.

Two cylinder engines have greatly improved balance of the moving parts and consequently much less vibration. Examples include: Volvo, Perkins and Yanmar. Three cylinder engines are also made, with the cranks set at 120°.

Four cylinder in-line engines, the most common configuration, give two power strokes per revolution. Most 30 – 80 HP units are 4 cylinder ones; see Fig. 20(9).

Six cylinder in-line engines, most common from 80 HP upwards, are smoother than four cylinders and have more main bearings supporting the crankshaft; such engines can develop 200 HP or more, with the emphasis on turbo-charged diesels at the top end of the range.

Engines with the cylinders arranged in V-formation are not common afloat, except for powerful V-6 and V-8 petrol engines, as fitted to larger outdrive units. A V-6 with a V-angle of 90°

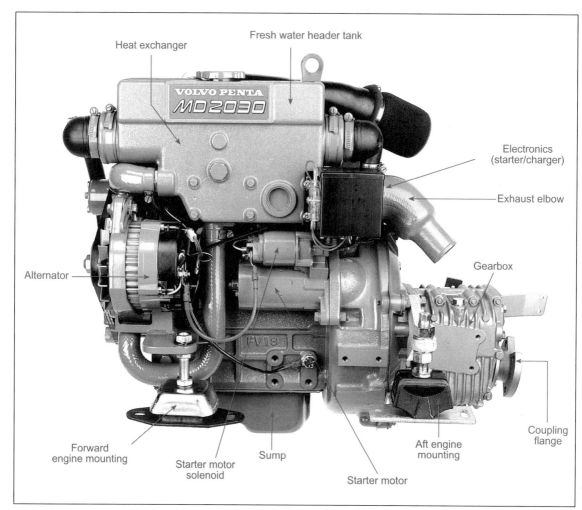

Fresh water header tank

Heat exchanger

VOLVO PENTA
MD2030

Electronics
(starter/charger)

Exhaust elbow

Gearbox

Alternator

Coupling
flange

Forward
engine mounting

Starter motor
solenoid

Sump

Aft engine
mounting

Starter motor

Fig. 20(9) Volvo Penta MD2030 marine diesel engine.

is slightly worse balanced than a straight six. A V-8 with a V of 90° is very well balanced and extremely smooth running. Some engines are now fitted with extra internal balance weights to reduce vibration yet further.

20.2 STERNGEAR

20.2.1 TRANSMISSION INSTALLATIONS

Six of the commoner installations, as shown in Fig. 20(10), are discussed below .

a. Most yachts have a conventional inboard engine installation where the power unit is mounted in the bottom of the boat and connected to a gearbox providing ahead/ neutral/astern operation. The propeller shaft is bolted to the output end of the gearbox and passes through a watertight gland in the hull to drive the propeller. This layout has several advantages: The weight of the unit is low down and roughly

amidships; if under the cockpit floor or wheelhouse, it does not occupy otherwise useful space and is protected from the elements; the propeller is immersed well below the waterline.

b. If for reasons of weight distribution or internal layout, the engine unit must be placed further aft it can be turned through 180° and the drive from the engine taken forward through a V-drive gearbox and back to a conventional propeller shaft.

c. Outdrives (also known as sterndrives) consist of the engine mounted on the forward side of the transom through which a short horizontal shaft runs to an external lifting leg, similar to that of an outboard, with bevel gears at top and bottom of the leg. The gears incorporate the reduction ratio and ahead/neutral/astern operation. To steer the boat, the leg swivels to direct the propeller thrust.

Outdrives are commonly fitted to smaller transom-hulled motor cruisers and have several advantages: the engine is mounted

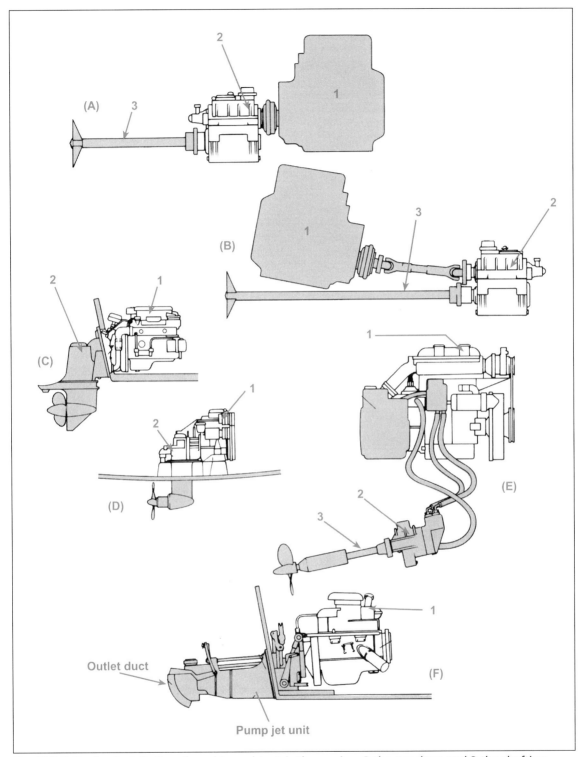

Fig. 20(10) Engine installations found in yachts: 1 is the engine; 2 the gearbox; and 3 the shafting.
a. *Conventional gearbox and shaft layout. The gearbox has drop centre transmission.*
b. *V-drive, with separately-mounted V-drive gearbox, and articulated shaft.*
c. *Outdrive power unit. Engine and transmission are installed as an integral unit.*
d. *Sail drive unit, with folding propeller.*
e. *Hydrostatic drive. An engine-mounted hydraulic pump is connected by flexible pipes to a hydraulic motor which drives the propeller shaft.*
f. *Water jet propulsion. An engine-driven pump (1) draws in water (2) and ejects it at high speed (3).*

inside the boat where it is protected and secure. Installation is simpler with no shaft alignment problems. The drive leg can be raised out of the water to take the ground or to gain access to the propeller. Larger units are fitted with a power tilting mechanism allowing the trim to be adjusted.

But there are disadvantages: some power is lost in the two sets of gearing; the propeller is not very deeply immersed; and handling at low speeds is difficult because there is no rudder.

d. Saildrives are similar in concept to outdrives, but with the power unit mounted low in the boat and the propeller projecting down through the hull. Intended for smaller yachts and motor cruisers, they are compact, easier to install and can be located where most convenient on the fore and aft line.

e. Instead of a normal gearbox, a hydraulic drive may be fitted between engine and propeller which allows the engine to be fitted anywhere within the hull. The engine drives a hydraulic pump. Power is transmitted via flexible high pressure oil pipes to a hydraulic motor connected to a short propeller shaft. It gives great flexibility of layout below and eliminates shaft alignment problems. However there is some loss of efficiency in the hydraulic system.

f. Water jet propulsion. This system eliminates the normal propeller and shafting. A pump, driven by the engine, takes in water from the bottom of the boat and forces it out astern. The resulting reaction force drives the boat forward. Steering and astern power are achieved by use of deflectors which re-direct the jet of water as required. Such installations are only found in specialist small craft designed for shoal waters, rescue work or water sports where the lack of a vulnerable and dangerous propeller is an advantage.

20.2.2 GEARBOX

All but the simplest boat engine require a gearbox to control its operation and provide reduction gearing so that the propeller revolves at about half engine speed, giving better propeller efficiency. But some small sailing cruisers have a sailing clutch which engages by centrifugal force when the engine speed is increased above idling. Others are fitted with a controllable pitch propeller which provides ahead/neutral/astern power by altering the angle of the propeller blades. In all other cases a gearbox is fitted.

There are two main types: layshaft and epicyclic.

Layshaft Gearbox

These have two sets of clutch plates, one for ahead propulsion the other for astern. In neutral,

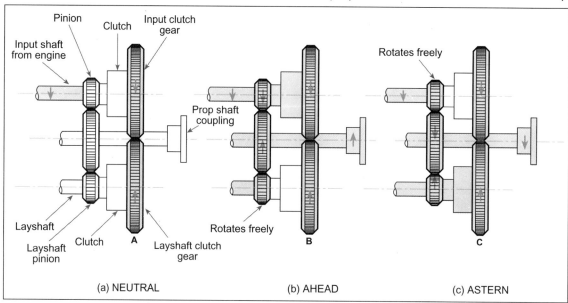

Fig. 20(11) A layshaft gearbox. The blue coloured components transmit the drive from the input shaft (top left).
a. Neutral: both clutches disengaged.
b. Ahead: input clutch gear engaged; power is transmitted via the clutch pinion to the output shaft.
c. Astern: layshaft clutch gear engaged, power is transmitted via the layshaft pinion to rotate the output shaft in the opposite direction.

both are disengaged. The clutches may be manually operated in small gearboxes by a direct lever system or more usually by hydraulic operation via the gearbox oil pump which also provides lubrication; see Fig. 20(11).

Epicyclic gearbox

In this type, astern operation is obtained by a brake band which locks the gear assembly, making the intermediate (planetary) gears rotate in the opposite direction; see Fig. 20(12).

It is important that the correct lubricant is used in gearboxes. Hydraulically operated boxes often specify automatic transmission fluid. Oil level should be checked regularly as described in the handbook.

Some gearboxes cannot be left to rotate (driven by the revolving prop shaft whilst under sail) for long periods with the engine stopped because the gearbox oil pump is driven from the engine input shaft. In such cases it may be necessary to fit a shaft brake together with some form of interlock so that the engine cannot be used with the shaft brake on.

Hydraulic gearboxes usually have a separate oil cooler and may be fitted with oil pressure and temperature gauges. In some models the gearbox can be manually locked in 'ahead' to get back to harbour in the event of clutch failure.

Never operate the ahead/astern control with the engine running at more than idling speed or damage may result.

20.2.3   PROPELLER SHAFTING

The propeller shaft transmits the drive from the gearbox to the propeller. The shaft passes through the stern tube of the hull where it is supported in bearings. In many designs there is a further support bearing (P-bracket) at the outboard end, just forward of the propeller. See Fig. 20(13) and (14).

Stern tube detail

The shaft is fitted with a flange at the inboard end which mates with the gearbox output flange. It is between these flanges that the alignment of the engine unit to the shaft can be checked by measuring the clearances between the flanges at 90° intervals before tightening the flange bolts.

The axial thrust of the propeller must be transferred to the hull. This is normally done using the gearbox output shaft bearing which transmits the thrust via the power unit to the hull. In larger vessels a separate thrust bearing may be fitted. The propeller is secured to the shaft by a tapered keyway backed by a propeller nut locked by a split pin.

One or sometimes two flexible couplings may be fitted between the gearbox and stern tube to make shaft alignment less critical and reduce vibration.

The shaft bearings in the stern tube may be of bearing metal or of cutless (fluted) rubber; the former are grease lubricated, normally from a remote screw-down greaser fitted above the water line. This is given a turn before start-up and then about every four hours while motoring. The fluted rubber type are lubricated by water which may be supplied by a salt water pipe from the engine cooling system or, in smaller sizes, by merely being underwater. See Fig. 20(13).

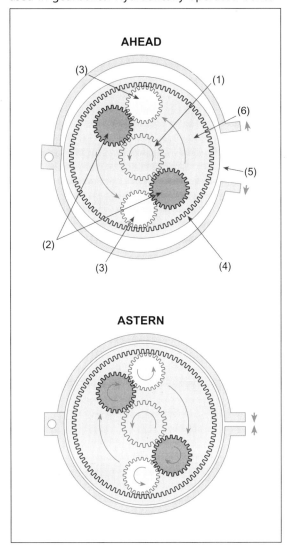

Fig. 20(12) Principle of operation of an epicyclic gearbox:
1. *Drive or sun gear.*
2. *Pinion gears.*
3. *Spur gears.*
4. *Annulus with internal gear teeth.*
5. *Brake band.*
6. *Assembly carrying the pinion and spur gears and connected to the output shafts.*

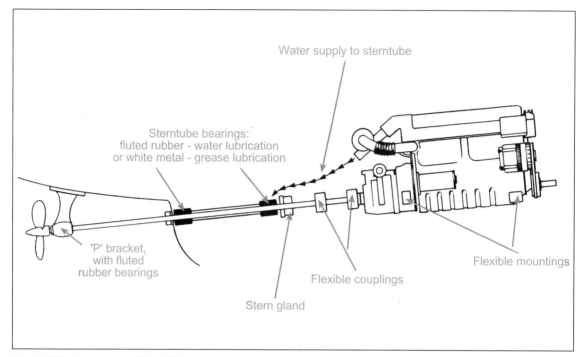

Fig. 20(13) Sterngear with rigid stern gland and bearings at each end of sterntube.

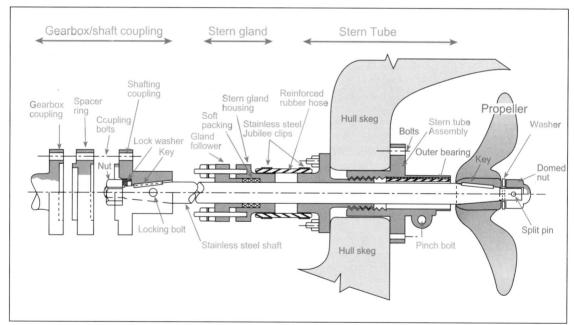

Fig. 20(14) Cross sectional details of a typical stern tube layout.

The stern gland, at the forward end of the stern tube, allows the shaft to rotate without sea water finding it's way into the boat. Several turns of soft packing are compressed by an adjustable gland follower. This must be tightened very carefully and evenly if the gland is leaking, until only the occasional drip appears, without the packing becoming overheated through excess friction. Eventually the packing is so compressed that no further adjustment is possible. The gland should then be repacked with the vessel ashore; in emergency it may be possible to add a further single turn of packing while aground at low tide but new soft packing is the only way to ensure that the shaft does not become worn, leading to persistent stern gland leakage.

Patent rotating seals are becoming more widely used. They rely on spring pressure to keep two annular seal faces (one rotating, one stationary) in contact. They require no adjustment but may be susceptible to dirt or misalignment.

20.2.4 PROPELLERS

It is the thrust from the propeller which drives the boat forward. It is essential that the correct size and shape of propeller is fitted to match the hull characteristics and the power/rpm available at the shaft. The main criteria which determine propeller shape are diameter, blade area, pitch and direction of rotation.

Diameter and blade area are related to the shaft horsepower available and propeller efficiency. Pitch is related to shaft rpm and boat speed; see Fig. 20(15).

Slip is the ratio between actual speed through the water and the speed calculated from propeller pitch multiplied by rpm.

Direction of rotation is defined as right-hand for a propeller which, when driving ahead, turns clockwise when viewed from astern.

Choosing a propeller/power unit combination for a boat is not as simple as it might seem and professional advice should be sought. Even then there is a certain mix of art and experience to selecting the correct propeller first time. If the diameter is too big, or the pitch too great, the engine will not reach its proper rpm and will become overloaded. In the opposite case the engine will overspeed without producing sufficient power.

Propellers are made of non-ferrous alloys, manganese bronze or similar. They are accurately machined and balanced; any minor blade

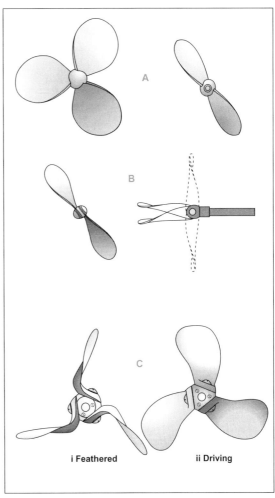

Fig. 20(16) Types of propeller:
a. Fixed bladed.
b. Folding. Blades unfold when power is applied.
c. Brunton Autoprop propeller. Blades adjust their pitch to suit the power applied and feather when the engine is stopped.

damage should be dressed to reduce vibration and bearing wear. Fig. 20(16) shows different types of propeller.

Several makes of folding/feathering propeller are now available which offer much reduced drag when under sail. A fairly recent development has been the Brunton Autoprop which has fully pivoting blades. Under sail they 'feather', like an aircraft propeller, so as to align with the water flow thus much reducing drag. Under power the pitch varies with rpm and boat speed, giving more efficient performance. In astern gear the blades automatically pivot through 180° so that, unlike a conventional propeller, the designed leading edge remains just that, giving better hydrodynamic efficiency and greater stopping power. There is also less prop

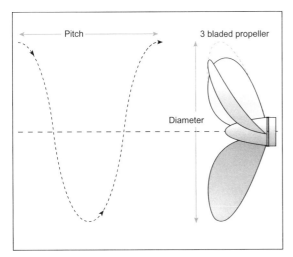

Fig. 20(15) Propeller pitch is the distance the propeller would move ahead in one revolution, if it did not slip in the water.

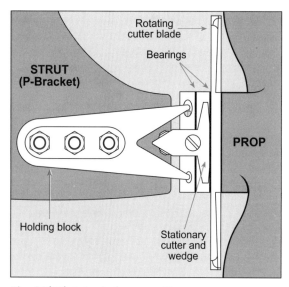

Fig. 20(17) A typical rope cutter.

Labels in figure:
- Rotating cutter blade
- Bearings
- STRUT (P-Bracket)
- PROP
- Holding block
- Stationary cutter and wedge

walk. They are of course more expensive than fixed blade propellers.

Propellers are liable to galvanic corrosion and should be protected by anodes. They may also suffer from erosion caused by cavitation which is more common in high powered motor boats.

A proprietary rope cutter can be fitted to the shaft just forward of the propeller. It will cut ropes within its capacity, thus avoiding a fouled propeller. A typical rope cutter is shown at Fig. 20(17). The original 'Spurs' cutter is sold by Harold Hayles Ltd, The Quay, Yarmouth, Isle of Wight PO41 0RS. Tel: 01983 760373. Fax: 01983 760666.

20.3 ENGINE SYSTEMS

20.3.1 PETROL FUEL SYSTEM

To aid stability and conserve space, fuel tanks are usually sited low in the boat. They need to be very firmly secured in place with bolted straps or lugs.

Petrol tanks are normally of galvanised, stainless or lead-coated steel, brass or copper (tinned on the inside). Tanks, unless very small, need surge baffles built into them. Ideally, a contents gauge should be fitted and a small sump placed at the bottom where dirt and water collect and can be drained periodically. If a flexible hose connects the deck connection to the tank, the two must be electrically bonded. Each tank must be fitted with an air escape/vent, ideally of greater diameter than the filling pipe and leading to a sheltered position on deck where vapour can disperse easily. The vent must be fitted with a gauze or spark arrestor.

The filling position, clearly marked, should be on deck so that any overflow will go directly overboard. With cars, any vapour from a leak or spill is easily dispersed; in a boat the vapour,

being heavier than air, can cause dangerous concentrations of explosive petrol/air mixture to accumulate in the bilges. A vapour detector/alarm is essential for a boat with inboard petrol engine and tank.

There MUST be a shut off cock where the fuel pipe leaves each tank and it MUST be operable from a remote position.

Fuel pipes should be made of copper, cupronickel or stainless tube with a minimum of joins and well clipped in place. The final length to the engine should be an approved flexible connection.

A coarse strainer/water separator should be fitted in this fuel pipe where access is easiest. Most petrol engines have a mechanically driven lift pump (with hand priming lever) which draws up fuel from the tank and delivers it via a fine filter to the carburettor.

The carburettor provides the correct petrol/air mixture to the engine. In principle, incoming air passes through a venturi where it's speed increases and it's pressure drops. This low pressure air sucks petrol from the float chamber through a jet, mixing atomised petrol with the air. The float chamber level is maintained by a float operated needle valve. A throttle (butterfly) valve controls the amount of mixture flowing to the engine. A choke device is fitted in the venturi aperture to reduce the airflow and thus give a richer mixture for cold starting.

Most carburettors have multiple jets and various refinements to promote efficiency and fuel economy. Many of the passageways inside the carburettor are very small; clean, water-free fuel is essential.

Carburettors are often replaced nowadays with petrol injection systems. Fuel is metered and pumped either to the inlet manifold or direct to each cylinder to give the correct air/fuel ratio under all conditions.

Grades and types of petrol

The grade of a petrol is generally defined by the octane number, ranging from about 94 octane up to around 98 octane for premium or super grade. There is no objection to using a higher octane fuel than specified, except price. But use of a lower octane fuel may provoke 'pinking'. Unleaded fuel is suitable for all modern engines including 2-strokes.

Leaded petrol was introduced in the 1920s to improve octane quality and hence prevent 'knocking' or 'pinking' under load. Environmental and health issues have ensured a progressive reduction in the amount of lead in petrol over the last 20 years and the use of lead is now being phased out completely, world-wide. The introduction of exhaust catalytic converters (which

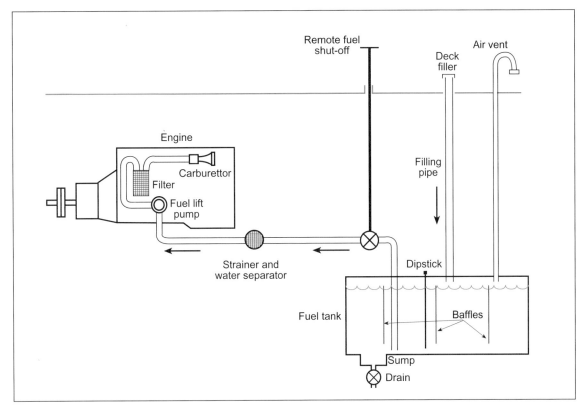

Remote fuel shut-off

Air vent

Deck filler

Engine

Carburettor

Filter

Fuel lift pump

Filling pipe

Strainer and water separator

Dipstick

Fuel tank

Baffles

Sump

Drain

Fig. 20(18) Petrol engine fuel system.

can reduce harmful emissions by a factor of 7 or 8) has hastened the demise of leaded petrol; catalysers are poisoned by lead in the exhaust gas. No alternative anti-knock agent has been discovered so unleaded fuels must have their octane quality made up by improved refining processes and/or by the use of oxygen-bearing additives.

Another key issue with older engines is to protect them from damage due to valve seat recession (VSR). If the valve seats are not designed with sufficient hardness they can suffer quite rapid wear when using unleaded petrol. (Leaded fuel did not produce this effect because the valve seats were protected by a thin film of lead compounds adhering to the valve and its seat. Hence they did not need to be very hard).

However, VSR is proportional to valve seat temperature which increases with the engine speed and the amount of power being developed. VSR is unlikely to be a problem in older engines unless they are highly stressed (eg too low powered for the boat).

If switching from lead replacement petrol to unleaded, VSR can be monitored by recording the valve tappet clearances at regular intervals. In the unlikely event that the wear rate exceeds about 0.002" (0.005mm) per 100 hours it may be necessary to change to harder valve seats or even consider an engine change.

Lead replacement petrol contains additives (usually based on sodium/potassium compounds) which help to reduce or even eliminate VSR. But it is not always stocked at marine fuel outlets.

Petrol tanks should be kept as full as possible to reduce the amount of airborne moisture condensing on the tank walls. But also note that petrol deteriorates in storage and modern petrols have a shorter shelf life.

20.3.2   IGNITION SYSTEM (PETROL ENGINE)

The petrol engine requires a high voltage spark to ignite the fuel/air mixture at the correct moment in the cycle. This spark may be provided at the sparking plug by either a magneto or by a high tension coil. The latter is more common, giving a better spark at low (starting) speed but the former allows the engine to be started by hand and is used in most small outboards.

For the coil ignition system, see Fig. 20(19).

A primary winding in the coil is energised by a 12 volt supply from the battery, creating a magnetic field in the iron core. The secondary winding is connected to the spark plugs via the distributor. When the primary circuit is broken by the contact breaker, the magnetic field in the secondary coil collapses, generating a very high voltage (up to 20kV) to create the spark at the plug. The contact breaker points must be clean, flat and adjusted to the correct gap, usually

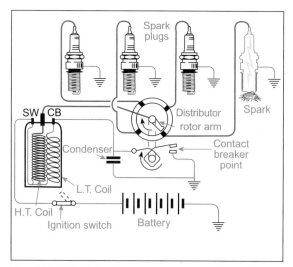

Fig. 20(19) Coil ignition system – petrol engine.

about 0·015"/0·4mm. A condenser is fitted across the contacts to reduce spark erosion.

The low tension contact breaker and the high tension distributor are combined in one unit driven off the engine camshaft. Angular adjustment can be made so that the timing of the spark can be correctly set (static timing). The distributor usually incorporates a centrifugal device which advances the ignition timing as the engine speeds up. A vacuum operated advance/retard mechanism is connected to the engine inlet manifold and alters the timing according to throttle opening (load).

Modern petrol engines, particularly outboards, are fitted with CD (capacitor discharge) or "electronic" ignition. See Fig. 20(20).

There are no contact breaker points to need adjustment and higher currents can be used to

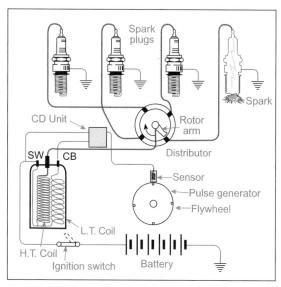

Fig. 20(20) CD ignition system – petrol engine.

provide a stronger spark. CD ignition is more resistant to damp and more sophisticated variable ignition timing can be arranged, giving lower exhaust emissions. The points are replaced by a triggering system actuated by a ferrite rod or a photo-electric cell on the flywheel (pulse generator). As this device passes the pre-set point it triggers an oscillator which switches a transistor so that the primary coil circuit is interrupted, inducing a high voltage in the secondary winding to produce the spark. CD ignition is not user maintainable.

Sparking plugs are vital components of the system and need regular maintenance. They must be of the correct type for the engine and need to be kept clean and the gap correctly set (usually about 0·025" – 0·030"/0·7 – 0·9mm). See 20.7.1 for further notes on spark-plug maintenance.

20.3.3   DIESEL FUEL SYSTEM

Tanks and filling arrangements for diesel fuel systems are similar to those for petrol engines but due to the properties of diesel fuel, tanks must not be of copper, brass or galvanised steel. Plain, stainless or lead coated steel are preferable, but glass fibre tanks are satisfactory if proper access for cleaning is available; they should not be adjacent to fresh water tanks.

Microbiological organisms pose a potential problem with diesel tanks. They can live and multiply at the interface between fuel and any water at the bottom of the tank. If water is regularly drained off and only 'clean' fuel embarked through a gauze funnel the problem should not arise. But if these organisms develop they can soon start to block filters. Biocides can be used to kill them but will not remove the resultant sludge. Serious infestation can only be tackled by steam cleaning the tanks and pipework. Tanks should be kept as full as possible to minimise condensation and possible airborne infection.

Pipelines can be of mild steel tube or the materials used for petrol systems. Nylon tubing of approved flameproof specification may also be used in low pressure parts of the system but should be agreed with the insurers; they are useful for detecting air leaks in the suction side.

The delivery side of the system is totally different to that of the petrol engine and is explained in detail. See Fig. 20(21).

Fuel is sucked from the tank(s) by an engine driven lift pump via a preliminary filter which removes water and sediment. Fig. 20(22) is a typical CAV 296 filter.

The fuel then passes through a fine filter to the fuel injection pump which delivers it at very high pressure to the injectors (also known as

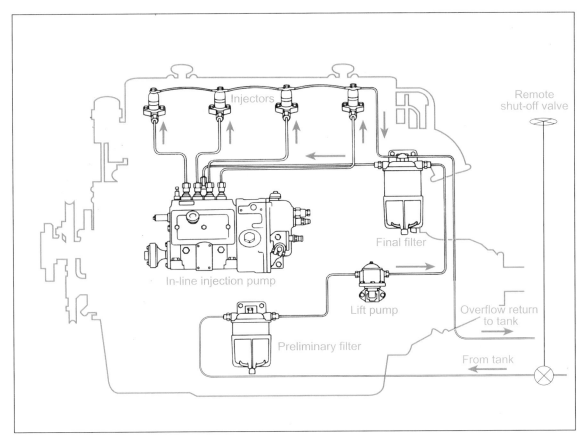

Fig. 20(21) Typical diesel fuel delivery system.

atomisers) mounted in each cylinder head. Surplus fuel from the injection pump and any leak-off from the injectors is returned to the suction side of the lift pump.

Both the injector pump and the injectors themselves have very fine clearances inside which can easily be damaged by dirt or water in the fuel. Good filtration is vital. The lift pump should have a hand-operated lever for use when bleeding through the system, eg after changing filters.

The fuel pump must deliver very small, accurately metered quantities of fuel to each cylinder in turn at exactly the right moment; see Fig. 20(23).

The pump plunger is cam operated, against a spring, by the engine-driven camshaft. As the plunger rises, fuel is forced at very high pressure through the delivery valve to the injector, and thence to the combustion chamber. The delivery valve acts as a non-return valve while the pump plunger is descending, gives a rapid build-up of pressure in the pipe to the injector, and provides a quick cut-off of fuel injection at the end of the pump stroke.

For each cylinder there is, within the pump, an individual pumping element, a close fitting plunger in a barrel; see Fig. 20(24).

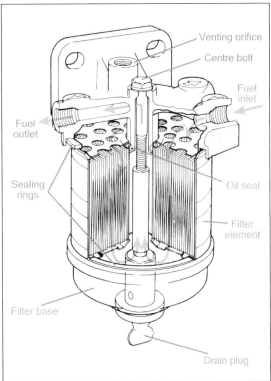

Fig. 20(22) A typical preliminary fuel filter of the CAV range, with three main parts: the filter head, the element and the base.

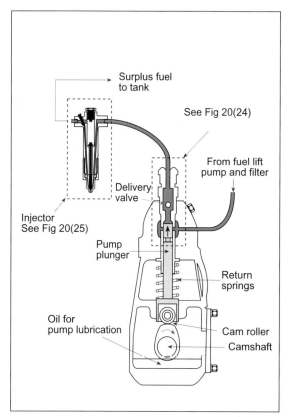

Fig. 20(23) A simplified diagram, showing a cross-section of a fuel injection pump, connected to one fuel injector.

The camshaft operates the plungers which are mounted in a line. The length of stroke of the plungers is constant but the working part of the stroke during which fuel is delivered, can be varied by rotating the plungers to allow helical grooves in them to uncover spill ports in the plungers and release the pressure. The plunger is shown at the bottom of its stroke. When it rises, and covers the inlet port, pumping starts. Pumping continues until the upper edge of the spill groove uncovers the spill port, allowing high pressure fuel above the plunger to pass down the central hole in the plunger and out through the spill port. The effective stroke of the plunger is determined by rotating the plunger in the barrel.

The plungers are rotated by a rack operated from the throttle, varying the amount of fuel delivered at each stroke. A governor mechanism in the pump controls maximum, minimum and set speed at any throttle setting.

Some engines are fitted with rotary distributor fuel pumps to feed the injectors. In which case there is only one pumping element, feeding via a distributor and non-return delivery valves to each injector in turn.

Maintenance or repair of fuel injection pumps must only be undertaken by authorised service

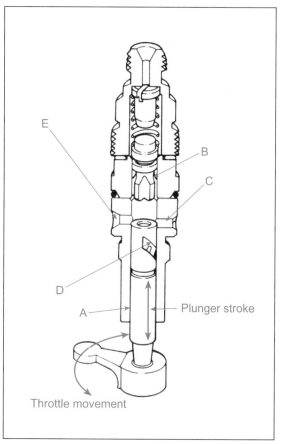

Fig. 20(24) A delivery valve within a diesel fuel injection pump; see Fig. 20(23). A: plunger; B: delivery valve; C: inlet port; D: helical spill groove in plunger; E: spill port.

agents with the necessary equipment and experience. The owner can keep the pump clean, leak free and supplied with clean fuel. Modern diesel fuel has less sulphur content than previously and also contains additives to promote cleaner combustion.

Direct injection

The volume of air in the cylinder before the piston ascends, compared to the volume remaining at top dead centre is called the compression ratio. In a direct injection engine, where the combustion chamber is wholly or partly formed in the piston crown, the CR is about 16:1. There are several jets in the injector nozzle to distribute the atomised fuel evenly. Direct injection engines start more easily and have better fuel economy.

Indirect injection

The fuel is injected into a small chamber in the cylinder head, connected to the cylinder itself. The compression ratio is higher, about 22:1. Air is forced into the pre-chamber to promote

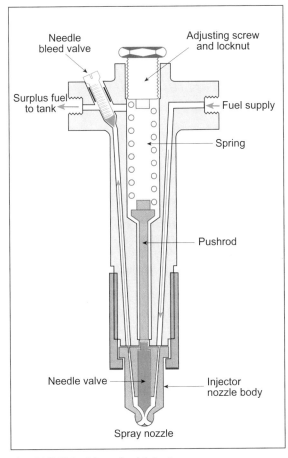

Fig. 20(25) Inside a fuel injector.

Labels on figure:
- Needle bleed valve
- Adjusting screw and locknut
- Surplus fuel to tank
- Fuel supply
- Spring
- Pushrod
- Needle valve
- Injector nozzle body
- Spray nozzle

turbulence. The injector is a single nozzle type, relying on the airflow to mix the atomised fuel. This type of engine can achieve higher rpm employing the rotary type of fuel pump with variable injection timing. It produces less emissions but is generally noisier than the direct injection type.

Fuel injectors

These supply fuel to the combustion chamber in a finely atomised spray. Injectors come in various sizes and types, specially designed for each engine model.

An injector is a spring loaded valve, operated by fuel supply pressure; see Fig. 20(25). When a certain pressure is reached the valve opens wide to produce the spray; when the pressure falls, the valve shuts cleanly without dribbling. Injectors must be cleaned professionally and re-set at stated intervals or when suspect. Loss of power, overheating, black exhaust smoke, difficult starting, cylinder knock and increased fuel consumption can all be signs of injector faults.

A single defective injector can be replaced with a spare. The defective one can be identified by running the engine at fast idle then slacking back the injector supply pipe union to each one in turn. Little or no change in engine revolutions indicates a faulty injector. After replacement, the engine can be started on the other cylinders while bleeding any air out of the supply pipe to the replaced injector. When liquid fuel flows without bubbles the union can be re-tightened. The injector must be fitted squarely into its recess with a new washer on a clean face; the clamping nuts must be tightened evenly to achieve a gas-tight joint.

20.3.4   AIR SUPPLY

For every pound of fuel supplied to it an engine needs about 15 lbs (6·8kg) of air for proper combustion. For example, an engine consuming one gallon (8·5 lb) of fuel per hour will require 127·5 lbs of air per hour, equivalent to 1,665 cu ft (47 cu mtrs) at normal temperature and pressure.

The engine compartment requires about the same amount again for removal of waste heat from the area; in total about 30 cubic feet per minute. Hence the air louvres around the engine casing need to be generously proportioned.

An air filter is fitted to the inlet manifold to remove harmful impurities and should be serviced regularly. Larger engine rooms have forced draught fans to help cool the space around the engine. Petrol engined boats need a spark-proof exhaust fan to suck from the bottom of the engine bay, discharging overboard through a gauze spark arrestor; this fan should be run for five minutes before start-up to remove any petrol vapour before the starter motor is energised.

20.3.5   COOLING SYSTEM

All engines need a cooling system to remove surplus heat. About one third of the total energy available from the fuel needs to be removed, just to prevent the engine overheating. Cars of course use radiators, boats are predominantly water cooled. (A few low-powered boat engines are air cooled; they tend to be bulkier and noisier than the water cooled).

Direct water cooling

Fig. 20(26) shows a typical direct cooling system.

Raw water is drawn in by an engine-driven pump via a seacock and a strainer. The water may go via an oil cooler, thence to the cylinder block and cylinder head and finally to the exhaust manifold before being discharged overboard. A thermostat controls engine temperature by adjusting a by-pass valve to allow more or less water to flow through the engine. Note that the engine-driven pump will supply

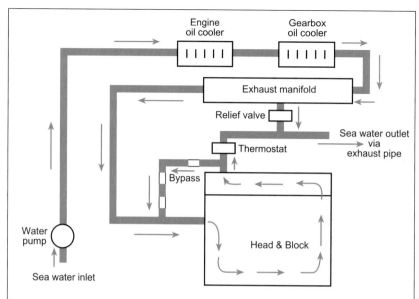

restricting the water flow just where it is most needed. The water ports into the exhaust manifold can be blocked by hard salt deposits, which should be removed every other year.

Indirect water cooling

A better arrangement is for the engine to be cooled by fresh water, pumped round it in a closed circuit and for this fresh water to be cooled by – but not mixed with – sea water, using a heat exchanger. A typical indirect water cooling system is shown at Fig. 20(27).

Fig. 20(26) Direct water cooling system.

more water as engine speed increases and more power is developed.

The direct system is simple but has disadvantages:

a. Corrosive sea water circulates through the engine. This is combated to some extent by fitting zinc anodes in the water passages within the engine. These need periodic renewal; and

b. Unless the engine is run at an unduly low temperature (which is inefficient) salt deposits will build up on internal surfaces,

Note that raw sea water is used for the gearbox and engine oil coolers (if fitted) before being pumped through the heat exchanger to the exhaust system and back overboard.

The fresh water is circulated by a separate pump, usually integral with the engine block and belt driven.

Keel cooling is a variation on fresh water cooling. The coolant is circulated through external pipes which run along the bottom of the boat and are cooled by the surrounding water. It is a very simple system but somewhat prone to underwater damage (eg grounding) and

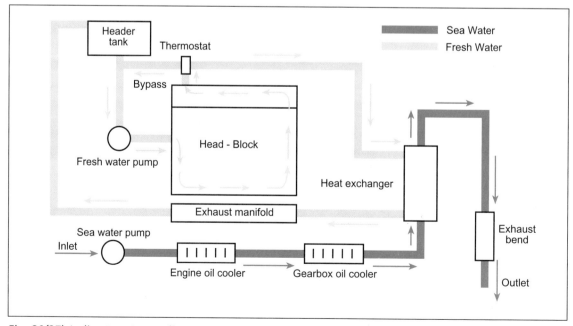

Fig. 20(27) Indirect water cooling system.

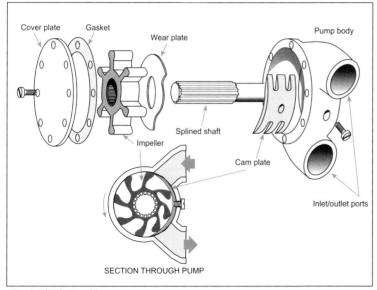

Cover plate Gasket
Wear plate
Pump body
Splined shaft
Impeller
Cam plate
Inlet/outlet ports

SECTION THROUGH PUMP

Fig. 20(28) Cooling water pump.

requires a dry exhaust system which needs good insulation and a silencer.

Cooling system maintenance involves cleaning inlet strainers and checking that there are no leaks in the system. In indirect systems the fresh water header tank must be kept topped up and the recommended amount of anti-freeze/corrosion inhibitor added from time to time, particularly in winter. Sea water pumps are liable to wear if operated in sandy or muddy water. A typical pump is shown at Fig. 20(28).

A spare impeller should be carried on board which an owner should be able to fit. Thermostats sometimes give trouble; if they stick open the engine will run too cool, if they stick shut the engine may overheat. A faulty thermostat can be removed in an emergency if no spare is available, but the engine temperature must be continually monitored.

Each time the engine is started, check that water is flowing correctly from the exhaust. Many engines have a temperature alarm; if not the temperature gauge should be checked regularly.

20.3.6 LUBRICATION SYSTEM
Bearings and their lubrication have been mentioned in 20.1.5. The lubrication of all 4-stroke engines, petrol or diesel, is basically similar. Most 2-stroke petrol outboards are lubricated differently; see 20.6.2. Fig. 20(29) shows a typical system for a 4-stroke engine.

The sump forms a reservoir for the oil which is pumped by an engine driven pump (usually fitted inside the sump) through an oil cooler and a filter to the various working parts. A relief valve controls the pressure, indicated by a gauge and/or warning light/alarm. The oil drains back to the sump by gravity.

Filters have a renewable element or are replaced in toto; change them at the recommended intervals and whenever the oil is changed.

Always check the oil level before starting the engine. Only top up the engine with the recommended type and grade of clean oil. Reserve oil must be kept in sealed containers to keep out dirt and moisture.

Modern oils are complex substances containing various additives to improve their performance. These additives improve detergency, oxidation resistance and dispersancy. Detergents clean the internal surfaces (particularly pistons and rings). Oxidation inhibitors reduce the tendency of hot oil to form lacquers or gummy substances. Dispersants keep combustion products in suspension in the oil, reducing sludge formation. Darkening of the oil in service shows that it is doing its job, but the additives are gradually used up; hence the need for regular oil changes.

Viscosity is measured by the time a certain quantity of oil takes to flow through a standard orifice at a specified temperature. A thin oil flows easily, has a low viscosity number and is suited to cold conditions; a thick oil with a high viscosity number is better in high temperatures. The SAE (Society of Automotive Engineers) system is used to classify oil viscosity. SAE 5W, 10W, 15W and 20W oils have a satisfactory viscosity at –18° C (0° F). "W" means suitable for winter use. SAE 20, 30, 40, or 50 indicate an oil that is satisfactory at 99° C (210° F), a normal operating temperature. Multigrade oils are satisfactory over a wider range of operating temperatures. For example the designation SAE 20W–50 spans the viscosity of a 20W oil at –18° C through to a SAE 50 oil at 99° C.

Choosing the correct viscosity oil is a compromise between good starting from cold and satisfactory load-bearing properties and oil consumption at high temperature. Additives help to maintain the viscosity as the oil temperature rises. NEVER neglect to change the oil at the specified intervals.

20.3.7 EXHAUST SYSTEM
The engine needs an efficient exhaust system to remove the hot waste gases as easily as possible, ie without undue back pressure, while minimising noise. Carbon monoxide in the exhaust gas is

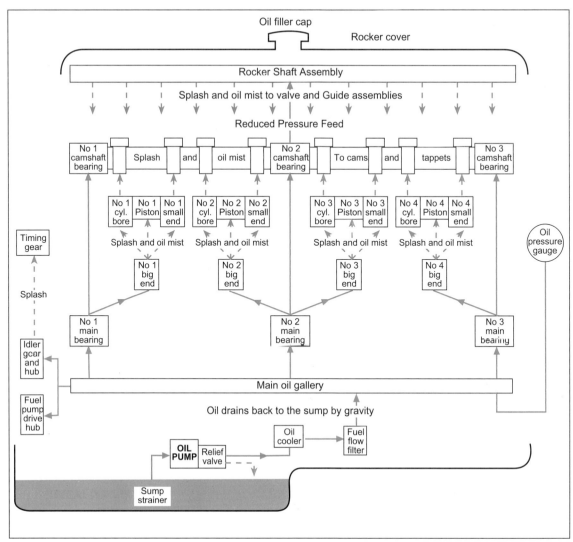

Fig. 20(29) Lubrication system for a typical four-cylinder 4-stroke engine (diesel or petrol).

poisonous and the exhaust gas itself is also corrosive. Hence use considerable care, and approved materials, when running exhaust pipework through the boat to the outlet.

Most engines have wet (water injected) exhausts which do not need bulky and expensive jacketing. Fig. 20(30) shows a typical layout.

Raw cooling water from the engine is injected into the exhaust piping immediately downstream of the exhaust manifold and thermostat, so as to quieten and cool the exhaust gases. The waterlock acts partly as a silencer and also traps water which may accumulate after prolonged cranking without the engine firing; it also traps water if no gooseneck is fitted. The silencer does just that, and the gooseneck ensures that water cannot flow back from the exhaust outlet and into the engine itself.

If the engine is below the waterline a gooseneck must be fitted, high enough to cope with all possible sea states, angles of heel and trim or boat loading. Where there is not much fall in the pipeline it is advisable to fit a shut-off valve at the outlet end which can be closed when the engine is not in use. A small air bleed may also be needed to prevent water back-siphoning into the engine. Fig. 20(31).

Exhaust piping can be of iron or galvanised steel. Copper or brass are suitable for petrol engines, but not for diesels. Approved flexible synthetic hose can be used for the wet part of the system; the best quality hose will not implode at high temperatures and block the pipe. A length of flexible pipe is needed near the engine to absorb vibration and expansion. An exhaust temperature alarm, if fitted in the wet part of the system, warns of cooling water failure and/or overheat.

Amendments to the Recreational Craft Directive are under review. They will affect both

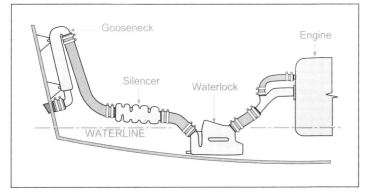

Fig. 20(30) Typical exhaust system, showing the waterlock, silencer and gooseneck fitting.

exhaust and sound emissions and are likely to be mandatory by the end of 2004 for all four-stroke internal combustion engines (diesel and petrol); and by the end of 2005 for two-stroke petrol engines. Exhaust emissions must not exceed the limits specified in EU Type Approvals. Sound emissions must not exceed the limits for engine sizes. For example 67dB for up to 10kW power; 72dB for 10–40kW; and 75dB for over 40kW. For twin and multi-engine craft these limits are increased by 3dB up to a maximum of 78dB.

20.3.8 CONTROLS AND INSTRUMENTS
See the Chapter 21 (Electrics), section 21.2, for a detailed explanation of the electrical circuitry which permits engine starting.

Controls for engine throttle and for the gearbox may be separate or combined into a single lever control. They must be fitted where they are within easy reach of the helmsman, but away from gangways, winches etc where they might inadvertently be moved.

The operating cables must be carefully installed to avoid sharp bends, accidental damage, heat and moving parts. The lever movements should be in the correct sense, ie forward for ahead, opposite way for astern and the throttle moving forward to increase speed. Engine stop controls (either key or stop lever) should be clearly marked.

Control linkages should be checked periodically to ensure that they work smoothly and are undamaged.

Instruments
The mimimum instrumentation for an inboard engine should comprise:
1. Oil pressure gauge/alarm
2. Water temperature gauge/alarm
3. Tachometer for rpm.
4. Ammeter indicating rate of charge/discharge.

Other optional instruments can give more information and hence better engine monitoring, for example:
5. Turbocharger boost pressure
6. Gearbox oil pressure and temperature
7. Exhaust temperature/alarm
8. Water cooling pump delivery pressure
9. Engine hours run meter

Get to know what all your instruments normally read at cruising speed and make a habit of checking the readings at least hourly on passage. It is useful to mark the dials at their normal reading so that any change is readily apparent. Your instruments can save you expensive repair bills.

Alarms
Most engines incorporate an audible alarm for low oil pressure and high cooling water temperature. When the engine is started the oil alarm will sound until pressure builds up. If either alarm sounds underway the engine should be stopped and carefully examined for signs of overheating or loss of oil pressure.

20.3.9 WORKING ON MACHINERY
It is all too easy to break things, shear off bolts and studs, crack castings or bend pipes, making it difficult or impossible to re-assemble them without shore help. When dismantling something, apply reasonable force but not too much

Fig. 20(31) Typical exhaust system, with engine mounted low down and anti-syphon tube.

until you gain confidence. Spanners are designed to be the correct length for their size; if they will not undo a nut, only apply increased leverage in a controlled and gradually increasing manner. Consider the use of penetrating oil or gentle heat (if safe to do so). A sharp hammer blow on the top of a bolt head may free the thread. Do not resort to hammer and cold chisel unless you have exhausted all other possibilities using the proper good quality tools. Do not rely on shifting spanners, mole grips, pipe wrenches etc. The proper tool is the answer. Make sure you have the correct size spanners etc to carry out the routine jobs, eg adjusting the stern gland or an alternator belt.

Safety is often forgotten in the heat of the moment, when accidents are most likely. If a problem arises and the solution is not obvious, pause for a cup of tea and some thought – if you are not on a lee shore. Always immobilise an engine by removing the start key before working on it. Never work on an engine when it is running. Always isolate the electrical supply to any equipment you are working on; even 12 volts can cause serious burns from arcing across terminals.

If working on sea water systems, make sure that the necessary valves have been shut to avoid uncontrolled flooding. Always have a thorough check around the work area for loose tools, rags etc before re-starting machinery.

Oils and greases

A vast number of lubricants are available, for many different purposes. It pays to use the right one. They include:

Penetrating oil. Frees rusted components by capillary action. It is not a lubricant.

WD 40. Useful thin oil, but evaporates quickly.

3 in 1. General purpose thin oil; available in spray cans.

Hydraulic transmission oil. Only use where specified, ie on certain types of gearbox, hydraulic circuits and some types of steering gear.

Gear oil. Very thick. For use in slow moving, heavily loaded applications such as steering gearboxes and windlasses.

Lithium grease. General purpose, with some water resistance.

High melting point grease. For ball and roller bearings.

Copper-bearing grease. For injector to cylinder head joints.

Silicone grease. For electrical connections, plugs etc.

Graphite grease. For high temperature components

20.3.10   ROUTINE ENGINE CHECKS

a.   Before start-up
FUEL – sufficient in tank and in reserve
FUEL/WATER TRAP – Clear
OIL LEVELS – Engine and gearbox; spare oil aboard
ENGINE BILGES – Clear, no leakages
COOLING WATER SEACOCK – Open
HEADER TANK LEVEL (fresh water cooling)
BATTERY ELECTROLYTE – topped up
BATTERY SWITCHES – ON
ENGINE BAY FAN – run for 5 minutes
THROTTLE/GEAR LEVER – Correctly set
NO ROPES – over the side or near propeller

b.   After start-up
OIL PRESSURE – Sufficient, within limits
COOLING WATER – flowing
GENERATOR – warning light out, charging rate
IDLING RPM – within limits
GEAR/THROTTLE – correct responses

c.   Running (at least hourly)
RPM – normal
OIL PRESSURE/TEMPERATURE – normal
AMMETER, OR CHARGING LIGHT – normal
COOLANT TEMPERATURE – normal
TURBOCHARGER BOOST PRESSURE – normal
GEARBOX OIL PRESSURE – normal
FUEL CONTENTS – sufficient
BILGE LEVEL – normal

d.   After shutdown
PETROL COCKS – shut (diesel systems stay open)
COOLING WATER SEACOCK – shut
STARTING BATTERY – switch off
ENGINE RUNNING HOURS – record in log
STERN GLAND & BILGE – no leaks, normal level

20.4 MAINTAINING INBOARDS

20.4.1   INTRODUCTION
If an engine is supplied with clean fuel, clean and regularly-changed lubricating oil, air for combustion and sufficient cooling water, nothing serious should go wrong. There are other items in the maker's handbook needing periodical attention, but if these are attended to regularly the engine should give reliable service without unexpected repair bills. Keep a record of engine hours so that maintenance routines are not forgotten.

20.4.2   TOOLS
Ensure that you have on board the necessary tools to carry out all maintenance tasks listed in the handbook.

A basic toolkit should include:

Set of open-ended and ring spanners; screwdrivers of various sizes and driving heads;

pliers, large and small; hammer, copper hammer/ mallet; files various, flat and round; allen key set; small hacksaw; socket spanners for spark plugs and other special jobs; Allen keys; hydrometer; volt/amp/ohm meter; hand/battery drill and bits. With experience this list can be added to as required.

20.4.3 SPARES

The quantity carried on board varies with the boat's intended usage, age/reliability of the engine and the owners skill.

A suggested list would normally include:

Set of drive belts (alternator etc); Set of hoses and clips; Fuel and oil filters; Thermostat; Water pump impeller and gasket; Spark plugs/injectors; Rocker box gasket; Fuel lift pump/spares kit; Points, plug lead, condenser, (petrol); Spare oil (gearbox, engine and Cold start device (diesel).

For extended cruising a larger range of spares might include: Alternator, fuel pump, cylinder head gasket, valve springs and gasket kits.

20.4.4 FUEL MANAGEMENT AND MAINTENANCE

Be sure to have sufficient fuel and a reserve for the voyage. Ensure that the dipstick or gauge is tolerably accurate and that you know what the fuel consumption rate is at cruising speed.If drain cocks are fitted to the tanks and/or filter, make sure that water/sediment is drained off regularly.

Keep the fuel pump, filters and system externally clean so that leaks are readily apparent. Fuel filters must be serviced at the intervals specified in the handbook, or more regularly if dirty fuel is suspected. Again, cleanliness is essential; all external dirt must be removed before dismantling the filter using clean, non-fluffy rag. See Fig. 20(32).

Clean off all external dirt, turn off the fuel supply if by gravity, and drain the base if the filter has a drain plug. Fig. 20(32a): Hold the base of the filter and unscrew the central bolt at the top. Twist and pull the base downwards. At this point observe exactly how the element and sealing rings are positioned, so that the filter is reassembled correctly.

Fig. 20(32b): Discard the used element, but keep the sealing rings if they are in good condition; otherwise renew them. Clean out the base and rinse with diesel fuel. Clean, refit and replace the drain plug, if present. Fig. 20(32c): Using a clean cloth (not a fluffy one) or a brush, wipe out the underside of the filter head including the groove for the sealing ring. Reassemble the filter with a new element, carefully rotating it slightly so that is slides easily over the small 'O' ring at the top. Do not

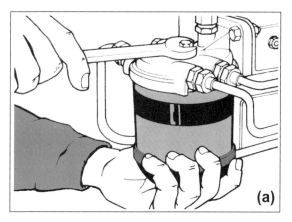

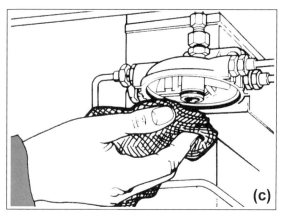

Fig. 20(32) Servicing a diesel fuel filter.

overtighten the bolt. Turn on the fuel, and bleed the system in accordance with the engine handbook.

20.4.5 BLEEDING THE FUEL SYSTEM

After servicing the filter (or running out of fuel!) the system must be "bled" to remove all traces of air. Procedures vary from engine to engine but are given in the handbook. Before starting, make sure that there is sufficient fuel in the tank and that all bleed screws have been cleaned off and that the right tools are available to open and close them. The general process is to bleed off all air from the system, moving down-stream from the lift pump and through to the injectors.

Slacken the bleed screw on the top of the filter and operate the lift pump by hand until all the air has been expelled; re-tighten the bleed screw. Repeat the process on the injection pump. Slack off the fuel pipe connections to at least two injectors; rotate the engine with the fuel lever at half-throttle until fuel issues from the slacked injector pipes. Re-tighten the injector pipes, reset the throttle to the normal start position and attempt to start up. The engine will probably run unevenly on one or two cylinders until air is expelled from everywhere in the system when it should run normally.

If the engine will not start, the bleeding process must be repeated. Particularly with rotary fuel pumps it may be necessary to rotate the engine for longer than expected which may give concern about the capacity of the starting battery. With the injector pipes slacked off and the air filter removed from the inlet manifold, place a flat piece of metal across the inlet orifice and crank the engine. Because no air enters the cylinders there is little or no compression and the engine can be cranked with little strain on the battery until fuel is flowing freely from the injector pipes.

Do not remove the piece of metal while cranking, only when the engine is stopped – or it may start suddenly and overspeed.

Bleeding the system is not an easy process and it is as well to have carried it out once before under ideal conditions (eg in the spring before launching) before tackling the job for the first time in earnest.

20.4.6   LUBRICATION SYSTEM

Always use an approved grade/make of oil for the engine and for the gearbox. Spare cans of oil must be kept clean with caps in place to prevent dirt/moisture ingress. Get to know how much oil your engine uses; all engines burn a small quantity of oil but the amount should remain steady; if it increases there must be a reason for it, usually a leak somewhere which should be located and rectified. Oil in the bilges is unpleasant and difficult to deal with without causing pollution for which there are now very severe penalties.

Always dispose of used oil and filters responsibly; most harbours have proper disposal facilities.

20.4.7   COOLING SYSTEM

With air cooled systems there is little to attend to provided that air intakes and vents are kept clean and free from obstruction.

In water cooled systems, overheating may be caused by a number of faults including:

a. Debris covering the intake	1. Stop; go astern; stop. 2. Disconnect inlet pipe and blow back through it.
b. Pump impeller failure	Change the impeller; if any vanes have broken off, retrieve them or they may cause a blockage elsewhere.
c. Thermostat failure	Replace thermostat.
d. Header tank low level	Allow engine to cool before adding warm water. Beware of scalding when opening the tank filler cap.

20.4.8   LAYING UP AN ENGINE

Any engine left idle for more than two or three weeks will begin to deteriorate. During the winter machinery must either be run regularly or be properly inhibited. Much more damage can be caused by one winter's neglect than by many summers of normal use.

Winter protection falls into two categories:

a. All internal working surfaces (bearing journals, cylinders, piston rings, fuel pumps and injectors) must be treated to prevent corrosion.

b. Water systems must be treated to prevent corrosion and be protected from frost damage.

When laying up, service the lubricating, fuel and water systems as follows:

1.   Lubrication system
Run the engine until warm. Stop. Pump/drain off all the oil. Fit new oil filter. Refill the engine with an inhibiting oil. Drain the gearbox; refill with normal transmission oil. Run the engine at fast idle for 15 minutes. Clean/replace the air filter.

2.   Fuel systems
Diesel: Drain clean and replace the fuel filter(s). Bleed the system until engine restarts satisfactorily. Stop. Disconnect the lift pump suction pipe and insert the pipe into a can of 2/3 diesel and 1/3 inhibiting oil. Run engine for ten minutes to allow preserving oil to reach the injectors. Stop. Reconnect lift pump suction. Fill the tank(s) completely with diesel to minimise condensation.

Petrol: NO SMOKING OR NAKED LIGHTS. Drain, clean and replace the filters. Drain and clean the carburettor and fuel pump. Drain and clean out the fuel tank(s), leave them empty.

Run the bilge blower to remove vapour on completion.

Petrol deteriorates quite quickly; do not keep it for next year.

3. Water system

Treat the fresh water system with anti freeze. Shut the cooling water seacock (if afloat) and drain the salt water system via the drain cocks provided. Remove the water pump impeller. If you can arrange to flush through the salt water system with fresh water this is preferable, but be careful not to overpressurise the system from the mains. A soluble rust inhibiting oil may be mixed with the flushing water for best results.

4. Other components

Remove the injectors (or spark plugs) and spray a little preserving oil into each cylinder. Rotate the engine a few times to oil the cylinder walls. Fit old injectors/plugs or suitable blanks.

Seal off the exhaust, inlet and any other openings with tape. Slack off any drive belts so that they do not become deformed. Spray any bare metal parts with oil. Grease any moving parts such as linkages. Clean off the exterior and touch up any defective paintwork.

Turn the engine half a revolution or so occasionally during the winter.

20.4.10   RE-COMMISSIONING

This is the reverse of the preservation process which was done in the autumn.

Pump/drain out the inhibiting oil and refill with the correct oil. (Inhibiting oil is not suitable for running an engine under load).

Remove all blanks, reconnect hoses, replace clips. Replace water pump impeller. Close all drain cocks. Tighten drive belts. Check and fit the batteries. Remove blanks and turn engine to expel excess oil from cylinders. Replace injectors/plugs.

Bleed the (diesel) fuel system. When afloat (or using a shore water supply) start the engine and check all round for leaks.

Remember to re-order all spares used and to ensure that the boat tools are all back on board.

20.5   FAULT FINDING

20.5.1   THE DIAGNOSIS

When a fault develops in an engine, take logical and progressive steps to find out what has gone wrong. Often the cause of the problem is obvious but where it is not, a calm and reasoned approach will identify the fault more certainly than an irrational guess.

The most obvious reasons for an engine to stop are:

a. Lack of fuel (empty tank, blockage or leak);
b. Overheating (blocked inlet or strainer)

If your engine stops or shows signs of distress, use all your senses to look for the trouble. Is there a hot smell somewhere? Was there an unusual noise or vibration? Did it stop abruptly or

splutter to a halt? What do the instruments tell you?

A few of the more common faults are discussed below. These are the ones where the remedy is fairly obvious and which the average yachtsman can rectify, even at sea if he has the necessary tools and spares. Other, more serious defects are less likely and are not covered here because they would require professional assistance ashore.

20.5.2   FAILURE TO START (DIESEL)

The first sign of trouble in marine diesels is often a reluctance to start from cold. The oil is thicker, and the engine more difficult to turn, hence there is more time for compression to be lost past the piston rings and for the heat of compression to be lost through the cold cylinder walls.

Most engines are fitted with some form of cold starting device, so first ascertain whether this device is working correctly. Usually it is a heater in the inlet manifold to warm up the incoming air. Remove the inlet filter and check that heat or smoke are produced when the heater is switched on.

If the engine can be turned by hand, an audible 'squeak' can be heard from the injectors at each firing stroke; if not, there may be insufficient fuel available at the injectors. Even the tiniest fuel leaks can cause this problem if the engine has been stopped for a while. Bleed the system if necessary.

Chronic and increasing difficulty in cold starting can of course mean that the engine needs an overhaul, but usually the cause is more prosaic. Ether-based aerosol starting aids should only be used as a last resort; they can damage cylinder head gaskets by the detonation they cause. Never use the cold starting heater and ether at the same time.

A summary of symptoms and possible remedies is at Fig. 20(33).

20.5.3   FAILURE TO START (PETROL)

Note: The two left-hand columns in Fig. 20(33) apply equally to petrol engines. The most probable causes of failure to start (assuming the engine can be cranked over at a satisfactory speed for starting) are:

a. The fuel supply or mixture strength; or
b. The ignition system.

A smell of petrol or a wet spark plug indicate that the engine is 'flooded,' ie the mixture is too rich. Let it stand for a few minutes with the throttle wide open, choke at 'run' and the plug removed. Then turn the engine slowly to expel surplus petrol. Dry and replace the plug and try again without the choke.

DIESEL ENGINE FAILS TO START

Engine does not turn	Engine only turns slowly	Engine rotates normally
In a few cases a switch prevents starting unless neutral gear is engaged; if so check accordingly.	A low cranking speed is a major cause of poor starting in diesel engines.	Check fuel tank contents, and filter clear of sediment.
		Check fuel tank on/off cock open.
A repeated clicking sound accompanied by a drop in voltmeter reading indicates a discharged battery.	Check battery state and electrical connections.	Check throttle setting.
	With twin engines, operate battery paralleling switch, if fitted.	Check stop control reset.
		Check decompression lever (if fitted).
Total silence is likely indication of a defective solenoid, or a fault in the starter switch circuit. In the latter case, try jumping out smaller cables leading from the switch to solenoid in order to operate solenoid.	Check gearbox in neutral.	Check solenoid-operated fuel shut-off (if fitted).
	Check air filter/air supply clear,	Check cold start aid works the correctly.
	Check correct grade of lubricating oil.	*If above are all found correct:*
	Apart from recharging battery, anything that will help warm up the engine will assist. A low cranking speed is particularly harmful in cold weather.	Slacken high pressure fuel pipes at injectors, put fuel setting to maximum and crank engine.
If a click is heard from starter, check battery state and that connections are clean and tight. If these are satisfactory, and still no rotation, starter is probably defective. Pinion may be jammed in engaged position.	(Note: The above also applies to petrol engines. But do not use any form of naked flame in attempting to warm a petrol engine.)	If fuel, free of air, is delivered, it indicates mechanical problems: Poor compression (see Note 1) Faulty injectors (see Note 2) Fuel pump timing (see Note 3)
If a click and a whirring sound is heard, starter pinion is failing to engage. Tap starter motor, or remove to clean the Bendix gear.		If no fuel is delivered, or there is air in the system, it is necessary to check back through fuel system to identify trouble: Open bleed screw(s) on fuel pump, operate lift pump and check flow. If this is satisfactory, fuel injection pump is suspect. If no flow, or air in system, go back to final fuel filter (renewing element if necessary) and so on through the system to lift pump (diaphragm and strainer), and preliminary filter or sedimenter.
(Note: The above symptoms and actions refer equally to petrol engines.)	*Notes:* (1) Poor compression may be overcome, sometimes, by injecting a small quantity of oil into air filter while cranking engine. This assists seal between rings and cylinder wall. (2) Fit spare injectors. (3) See engine handbook.	Having found blockage (or air leak or water) bleed the system thoroughly. Check for fuel leaks when the engine is running.

Fig. 20(33) Diesel engine fails to start. Fault-finding chart.

If on the other hand there appears to be a shortage of fuel, check the tank, shut-off cock, filter, fuel lift pump and then the carburettor.

If the engine still refuses to start, check the ignition.

Disconnect one sparkplug lead and attach it to a spare plug. Hold this plug in contact with the metal engine block with a pair of insulated pliers and turn the engine. A healthy spark should appear. If there is no spark, examine the contact breaker and work logically through the circuit.

Capacitor discharge ignition systems have no moving parts nor can they be serviced. A replacement is the only cure, but the failure rate is very low.

Other possibilities include a blocked jet or defective float valve in the carburettor.

20.5.4 ENGINE STOPS

Apart from a fuel solenoid valve inadvertently closing or rope around the propeller (or ignition failure in a petrol engine) it is rare for an engine to stop abruptly. Usually there is a brief indication of trouble either from the instruments or the alarms, a change of note or speed, a suspicious smell or ominous noise.

The most likely cause is fuel shortage which often causes a fluctuation of rpm as the lift pump loses and regains suction a few times before the engine stops. A petrol engine may behave similarly with spluttering popping noises from the carburettor.

20.5.5 OVERHEATING

This should first be detected by the instruments, then by an alarm. Steam comes out of the exhaust, the engine runs roughly, the oil pressure will decrease and hot smells are caused.

The engine may be extremely hot and care must be taken to avoid burns or scalding. Do not open the header tank filler cap until it has cooled down.

Possible causes include:

- Seacock not open; or inlet obstructed;
- Defective sea water pump;
- Defective thermostat;
- Broken fresh water pump belt;
- Water leak in the system; and
- Blocked heat exchanger.

20.5.6 FAILURE TO DEVELOP FULL POWER

The problem can conveniently be subdivided into two categories, gradual power loss and sudden power loss.

In an elderly engine where performance has gradually dropped, the most probable cause is overall mechanical deterioration. Poor compression due to worn rings/cylinder bores and/or poor condition of valves and valve seats can be assessed by having a compression test carried out. If this is inconclusive the fuel pump and injectors should be sent for testing and calibration. The turbocharger (if fitted) may be due for replacement; check the boost pressure at cruising speed.

But if the engine was running well, then suddenly loses power several less drastic items should be investigated. These include:

- restrictions in the fuel supply (valves not fully open?);
- Dirt in fuel system, filters becoming blocked;
- Defective throttle mechanism;
- Partially blocked air vent on fuel tank;

- Dirty air inlet cleaner;
- Incorrect injection or ignition timing;
- Restriction/back pressure in exhaust system; and
- Turbocharger failure due to seizure or fouling.

In a diesel engine the governor in the fuel pump may need attention. In a petrol engine the carburettor or fuel injection system may need cleaning, or the ignition system may be producing a weak spark.

20.5.7 MISFIRING

Identify whether this is limited to a particular cylinder by earthing each plug cap in turn (petrol engine) or by slackening the high pressure fuel pipe at each injector (diesel engine). If one particular cylinder is misfiring, investigate the items which affect only that cylinder; for example, spark plug and lead in a petrol engine, injector/fuel pump in a diesel. Another possible cause is a sticking valve; this may be corrected temporarily by a squirt of penetrating oil down the valve guide.

Misfiring on more than one cylinder points to more general problems, such as those already described under 20.5.6.

20.5.8 LOW OIL PRESSURE.

The most likely cause is a lack of oil in the sump – the reason for which must be found.

Possible reasons include:

- Failure to top up regularly;
- Oil leak into the bilge;
- Increase in oil consumption (blue exhaust smoke?) due to broken piston ring or cracked piston;
- Leaking oil cooler tube, allowing oil to be discharged overboard with the cooling water;
- Choked oil filter;
- Overheating;
- Defective pressure gauge/alarm;
- Wrong grade of oil being used;
- Defective oil pump; and
- Pressure relief valve stuck open.

A gradual drop in oil pressure over a period may indicate worn bearings.

20.5.9 EXHAUST SMOKE

The exhaust smoke can give some indication of the condition of an engine.

Blue smoke results from burning lubricating oil which has got past the piston rings or down the valve guides or past worn turbocharger oil seals. It usually indicates a worn engine but may be caused by a single defect.

White smoke is often seen when starting from cold. It is caused by a fog of partly burned fuel droplets and recondensing water vapour. It should become invisible as the engine warms up. If it persists, it may be due to water in the fuel, defective injectors or a coolant leak into the cylinder(s) usually from a defective cylinder head gasket.

Black smoke is carbon from partially unburned fuel. In diesel engines it usually indicates overloading, ie more fuel being delivered than can be burnt properly. Causes include:

- Dirty or incorrectly set injectors;
- Dirty air cleaner;
- Engine overloaded (hull fouling, towing);
- Wrong propeller (Diameter or pitch too great);
- Boat overloaded, floating below her designed water level.

20.6 OUTBOARD MOTORS

20.6.1 INTRODUCTION

Outboard motors are familiar to us all as power units for tenders and dinghies. They are also used to power small sailing boats and motor cruisers and as back-up motors on inboard-engined vessels. Very powerful outboards are used on larger RIBs and speedboats.

Outboards are self-contained power units with good power/weight ratio, easily portable (in the smaller sizes) and simple to install or move from boat to boat. Being fitted to the transom, the engine does not take up useful space. It can be tilted in shallow water. But since steering is effected by swivelling the engine, handling at low speeds can be awkward. Spare parts tend to be expensive. Outboards are very vulnerable to theft.

It is important to choose an outboard of the correct power and shaft length for the intended purpose. The power of outboards is rated according to tests laid down by the Boating Industry Association; these quote the power at the crankshaft and at a "sprint" rating, so tend to exaggerate the power available at the propeller.

20.6.2 TWO-STROKE OUTBOARDS

Until recently, all outboards were two-strokes but there is now a rapidly developing trend towards 4-strokes, even in the smaller sizes. This is because of progressive tightening of emission control parameters both in Europe, America and Japan.

2-strokes are never as "clean" as 4-strokes because oil has to be mixed with the fuel and therefore burnt during combustion. But modern designs use oil injection rather than pre-mixing and can run on as little as 100:1 fuel/oil mixtures.

They are heavy on petrol due to relatively poor combustion. Fig. 20(34) shows the combustion cycle of a typical two-stroke.

In (a) on the upstroke the piston draws a fresh charge of air/fuel into the crankcase. The previous charge is being compressed, and will be ignited by the spark-plug when the piston nears the top of its stroke.

In (b) the piston is on its power stroke; the reed valve is shut, and the next charge in the crankcase is being compressed as the piston descends.

In (c) the piston is more than half-way down its power stroke; the exhaust port is uncovering, through which the burnt gases are starting to flow; the transfer port is just opening, so that the next charge of air/fuel mixture is transferred from the crankcase to the cylinder.

In (d) the piston is at the bottom of its stroke, the fuel transfer is almost complete, and the cycle restarts.

Bearing in mind that outboards can attain high rpm, the design of the cylinder ports is critical in attaining proper scavenging of the exhaust gases and ingress of fresh mixture. Some engines are "loop charged", ie the ports are arranged to promote a swirling action to the incoming gases; others are of the "cross-flow" type where the ports are on opposite sides of the cylinder and the piston crown is shaped to improve gas flow.

New technology is developing lighter, smaller, cheaper and more reliable engines, incorporating CD ignition and fuel injection with electronic engine management systems, to give better fuel consumption and lower emissions.

It is important that the correct type of 2-stroke oil is used. Ordinary engine oil is not suitable. Specially formulated marine 2-stroke oils are available; type TCW 3 is usually specified.

20.6.3 FOUR-STROKE OUTBOARDS

4-stroke outboards are more efficient, economical and more enviromentally acceptable in terms of exhaust emissions.

The two most rigorous emission standards are the USA EPA2006 (enforceable by 2006) and the German Bodensee Step 1 regulations for inland waters. Most 4-stroke outboards now on sale now meet or exceed these standards. They all run on unleaded petrol, do not eject unburnt oil and are virtually smoke and smell free. They use up to 50% less petrol than a 2-stroke and no oil except for sump oil changes. The weight is similar to a 2-stroke in the smaller sizes (about 13kg). The higher initial cost is offset by the much lower running costs.

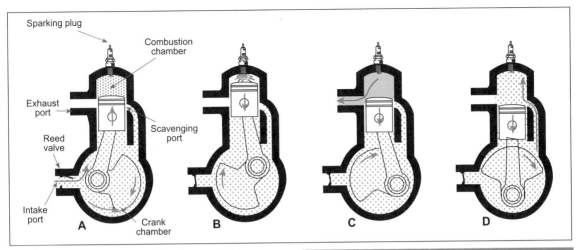

Fig. 20(34) Combustion cycle of a typical two-stroke petrol engine.

20.6.4 INSTALLATION

Outboard motors can be bought with long or short shafts. A 20 inch transom needs a long shaft, a 15 inch transom needs a short shaft. When the engine is fitted to the boat the cavitation plate above the propeller should be about level with the boat's bottom or slightly below it. The cooling water inlet should be well immersed. The tilt of the engine should be adjusted so that it is vertical when the boat is loaded and running at cruising speed.

Small engines are secured by clamps, larger ones are bolted to the transom. An anti theft device is essential and a clamped engine should also have a short strop secured to a fixed point to guard against accidental loss overboard; whilst shipping/unshipping an outboard, secure the strop to the yacht.

The direction of the propeller thrust can have a significant effect on fore and aft trim. In higher powered sportsboats the tilt of the engine can be adjusted under way to suit load, speed and sea conditions.

20.6.5 PROPELLERS

Most outboards are supplied with a standard propeller for the most likely applications of the engine. But propellers of different diameter and pitch are available for special purposes, eg trolling or water skiing.

Propellers are usually fitted to the shaft using a shear pin and secured by a split pin. The shear pin will break if the propeller hits an obstruction. Spare pins are normally carried in a holder attached to the motor. Larger engines may have a slipping clutch arrangemnt serving the same purpose.

20.7.1 INTRODUCTION

The comments in 20.4 about the maintenance of inboard engines apply, where applicable to outboards, but the latter have certain characteristics requiring special attention. Outboards are particularly exposed to the elements so it is important to keep them in good condition externally, to inspect regularly for damage which could lead to corrosion and to grease the various lubrication points indicated in the handbook.

The lower unit (bottom part, near propeller) needs special attention. Most units have a zinc anode here to protect against galvanic action. This should be kept clean and unpainted. Renew it when it is over half wasted away.

Check the oil level in the lower unit regularly and change it as specified, using the recommended oil. If the oil becomes emulsified, suspect a leak at the filler plug or the O-seal where the propeller shaft emerges.

2-stroke engines are sensitive to spark plug fouling at low power, so particular attention must be paid to plug maintenance. Plugs can be cleaned with a wire brush using a little petrol or white spirit. When setting the gap, bend the outer electrode never the centre one or the insulation may be damaged.

It is well worth having an outboard professionally serviced at the end of the season. This will prolong its life considerably.

20.7.2 STARTING AND STOPPING

Before using a new outboard, read the instruction book carefully and follow the suggested procedure. Always follow exactly the same procedure for cold and hot starting once you have established a succesful routine. Remember that most of the so familiar battles to start outboards are due to the simplest causes, ie:

- No fuel in tank
- Fuel cock shut
- Fuel vent shut
- Kill cord disconnected

When stopping after a trip, if possible close the fuel cock and allow the engine to run until the carburettor is empty. Hence it will be filled with fresh volatile petrol at the next start.

When carrying an outboard or laying it on a jetty after use, keep the propeller end below the engine so that water can not run into the engine and cause corrosion.

If the engine will not be used again in the near future it is good practice to run it in a fresh water tub to flush salt water out of the cooling system.

20.7.3 LAYING UP

As previously said, this should be done professionally nowadays due to the increased complexity of modern engines. However, should this not be possible, at least the following points should be attended to:

Flush out the cooling system by running the engine in fresh water for five minutes, then turning off the fuel to run the fuel system dry.

Remove the outer cover and carefully clean and dry the whole exterior of the engine. Remove the spark plug and put about a teaspoonful of engine oil into the cylinder; rotate the engine a few times to spread the oil over the cylinder walls; replace the plug.

Empty the fuel tank completely after washing it out with clean petrol to remove any dirt. Drain the lower unit. If there are signs of water ingress a new shaft seal or filler plug washer is needed. Refill with fresh oil of the correct grade.

Remove the propeller and store it in a safe place; grease the propeller shaft and wrap a cloth around it.

Grease the clamp screw threads, tilt and swivel bearings and replace the engine cover. Store the engine in a dry place, hanging on it's normal support, not standing on it's skeg.

20.7.4 RE-COMMISSIONING

Getting the engine ready to run is basically the reverse of the procedure in the previous paragraph:

Clean off the exterior surfaces. Check that there is the correct quantity of oil in the lower unit. Remove, clean and re-set the spark plug(s). Turn the engine over to expel any excess oil from the cylinders. Fit the plugs and connect the HT leads in the correct order (multi-cylinder engines). Replace the propeller.

Fill the fuel tank and the oil injection reservoir (if fitted). Place the engine on a boat or a test tank (never run an engine without cooling water). Turn on the fuel, choke the engine and start it. There may well be a cloud of blue smoke to start with as the excess oil in the cylinders is burnt off.

Check that cooling water is flowing properly. Try the engine ahead and astern.

20.7.5 SAVING AN IMMERSED OUTBOARD

If a motor should accidentally be immersed, it must be professionally stripped down as quickly as possible.

In the meantime, speedy first aid action will help to minimise internal damage.

Flush the whole engine liberally with fresh water to remove as much salt and dirt as possible. Remove the plug(s) and turn the engine over by hand while rotating the whole unit to get rid of water. If the engine will not turn over, do not use excessive force; if it was running when immersed, a connecting rod may be bent. Wash out the cylinders with paraffin or meths with a little light oil added via the plugholes and inlet manifold. Rotate the whole engine end for end to distribute the oil everywhere. Replace the plug(s).

It is now essential to take the engine to where it can be stripped down before corrosion attacks the bearing journals, ball races and cylinder walls. If this cannot be arranged within a few hours, fill the crankcase and cylinder with oil to exclude oxygen until strip-down begins.

20.8 BOOKS ABOUT MARINE ENGINES

RYA Book of Diesel Engines by Tim Bartlett (Adlard Coles).

How to install a new Diesel by Peter Cumberlidge (Adlard Coles).

The Care and Repair of Small Marine Diesels by Chris Thompson (Adlard Coles).

Boat Owner's Mechanical and Electrical Manual by Nigel Calder (Adlard Coles).

Marine Inboard Engines – Petrol and Diesel by Loris Goring (Adlard Coles).

Diesel Troubleshooter by Don Seddon (Fernhurst)

Boat Engines by Dick Hewitt (Fernhurst, 3rd edition).

Marine Diesel Engines by Nigel Calder (Ashford, Buchan & Enright).

Diesel Boat Engine Manual by Peter Bowyer (Haynes).

Propeller Handbook by Dave Gerr (Adlard Coles).

RYA Book of Outboard motors by Tim Bartlett (Adlard Coles).

The Outboard Motor Manual by Keith Henderson (Adlard Coles).

Outboard Troubleshooter by Peter White (Fernhurst)

Chapter 21 Electrics

CONTENTS

21.1 INTRODUCTION

At the start of the 21st century Electrics assume a more major role than ever before in the overall functioning of most boats, both sail and power. Yachtsmen need to be actively interested in marine electrical systems for many reasons: Today's yachts are designed and equipped to take advantage of the latest in electronic navigation and communications technology. Yachts now incorporate many of the comforts that are taken for granted at home, eg refrigerators, hot showers, television, microwave cookers and cabin heating. All this requires power, a comprehensive distribution system and almost certainly the ability to connect to AC shore power.

By the time this Handbook is published, hardly any modern marine engines will be built with a crank-handle for starting. Thus only the No 2 battery, assuming one is fitted, will be available for emergency starting. The life expectancy of the chart table (and paper charts) will be shortened as yacht designers give priority to computers, GPS and electronic chart plotters. These and similar trends are already changing attitudes towards marine electrics. Therefore a basic grounding in electrical theory and a knowledge of practical applications will stand the modern boat owner in good stead.

21.1.1 BASIC THEORY

First a recap on the principles of electrics, as taught at school, but possibly long since forgotten:

The materials that surround us in every day life are made up of atoms. Atoms are the building blocks of all substances and materials; models are used to help in understanding the atomic structure of materials. Such models are analogous to our planetary system, where the nucleus of the atom resembles the Sun and the electrons resemble the planets orbiting round the Sun. The nucleus is positively charged with protons and the orbiting electrons are negatively charged. The total number of protons and electrons make the atom electrically neutral. The ability of electrons to break free from their orbits and join the orbits of other atoms, determines whether the material in question is an electrical conductor or an insulator.

The movement of electrons, hopping from one atom to another, represents the motion of electrical current. Most electricians regard this flow of electrons as behaving like an abstract fluid and the flow rate of this imaginary fluid is called the electrical **current** and is measured in Amperes or Amps (A). Smaller currents are measured in milliamps, ie thousandths of an amp.

The current or electrons can not flow until acted upon or initiated by an electrical force or pressure. This electrical pressure is called **voltage** and is measured in Volts (V).

Any obstruction to the flow of current is termed as a **resistance** and is measured in Ohms (Ω).

Current, Voltage and Resistance are closely inter-related, such that any two of the three values will have a direct influence on the third; thus

i. for a given resistance, any increase in the electrical pressure (voltage) would increase the electrical flow of current by a proportional amount.

ii. for a given voltage, any increase in the resistance to the path of any current would decrease or impede the electrical flow of current by a proportional amount.

These relationships between the combination of voltage, current and resistance form the first basic fundamental law of electricity, namely Ohm's Law which can be simply stated as:

Voltage = Current x Resistance
or Volts = Amps x Ohms

Given any two values, then the third can easily be calculated.

The fourth and final element is **power** which can be defined as the rate at which energy is delivered or consumed; it is measured in Watts. In electrical terms, it follows therefore that, if amps represent the rate at which the current is delivered and volts represent the force or electrical pressure to deliver or generate this current, then the power can be defined as the product of both the voltage and current put together. Thus the second basic electrical relationship can be stated as:

Power = Voltage x Current
or Watts = volts x amps

From this relationship, a very important observation can be made which is highly relevant to boat electrics:

A 20 watt light bulb burning in a 240V household system will consume 0.0833 amps, or 83 milliamps, of current.

But a 20 watt light bulb of similar power burning in a boat's 12V domestic system will consume 1.6 amps, or 1666 milliamps, of current. Thus for the same power of bulb, but obviously differing bulb resistance, **the boat's electrics will be circulating a current 20 times that of the house.**

This highlights the misconception that 12V

systems in pleasure boats are safer than 240V household systems. Any mention of 240V immediately brings the fear of electric shock and its potential for endangering human life – correctly so. However, whilst an owner is of course relieved of this fear with a boat's 12V system, this false sense of security can blind him to the serious dangers resulting from the relatively high currents in the boat's electrical system.

Higher currents means that the electrons, hopping from atom to atom, are more agitated and moving faster within the walls of the conductor. Thus the electrons will suffer the effects of internal friction, thereby generating a considerable amount of heat. This analogy of internal friction is nothing more than resistance, perhaps in the form of unwelcome resistance in electrical feed wires. These effects are further increased when an intentional resistance, ie an electrical load, is introduced. Such resistance may be in the form of a wire whose small cross sectional area further confines the movement of the atoms so that their internal friction increases. Power through this small wire is obviously being lost to overcome this friction, and through not being able to go anywhere, this spent power is released in the form of heat.

This phenomenon is seen everyday in electrical bar heaters, cookers, kettles and even the simple light bulb. Here, under controlled conditions a current is deliberately passed through a fine resistance wire, such that the internal friction of the electrons will be so great, that it will produce copious amounts of heat; in the case of a light bulb, sufficient heat for the fine filament wire to glow white hot.

For conductor cables carrying electrical current, care is needed, for if the internal friction becomes too great and the production of heat is unchecked, then the insulation surrounding the electrical conductors would melt and catch fire.

Thus in marine 12V systems the sizes of currents and the calibre of cables that carry these currents must be carefully considered. Undersized cables, which by their nature offer resistance to current flow, will bring about a voltage drop along the length of the cable. Such voltage drops will deny the full battery voltage to all services or equipment down-stream.

Conversely, if conductor cables of ample cross-section size and negligible resistance supply a load of equally low resistance, then the current flow will increase to such an extent that the rate of flow will exceed the ability of the battery to maintain the system voltage or pressure. This is typical of an engine starter motor circuit: If the battery voltage is monitored as the engine is started, the voltmeter reading will be seen to fall from 12 to about 10·5 volts.

A firm grasp and clear understanding of the underlying laws and relationships associated with Voltage, Current, Resistance and Power, will get the average yachtsman most of the way to understanding the basics of all boat electrics.

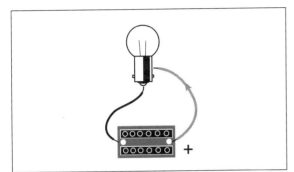

Fig. 21(1) A basic electrical circuit.

21.1.2 ELECTRICAL CIRCUITS

A very simple electrical circuit is shown in Fig. 21(1).

Here a battery distributes electrical current via two cables to a load or appliance (shown for simplicity as a light bulb). Note that the conventional direction of current flows out from the **+ve** battery terminal, through the circuit and back to the **-ve** battery terminal.

This lamp will of course possess a certain amount of resistance and it is interesting to see how the arrangement of multiple resistances in a circuit affects the behaviour of the voltages and currents within these electrical circuits.

A string of lamps or resistors in series offers a sizeable obstruction to the overall current flow in the circuit. Depending on its resistance, there will be a drop in the electrical pressure or voltage at every lamp, and the sum of all these voltage drops will equal the battery voltage. The current through each lamp is the same, indeed it is the same at any point in the circuit and the amount of current depends on the total resistance of all the lamps. Thus for every lamp that is added in series, the overall current in the circuit is reduced which in turn will reduce the brightness of all the lamps. This phenomenon can be likened to tying a series of knots along the length of a garden hose. Eventually, with a sufficient number of knots, all that will be left is a slight trickle of water at the end of the hose.

This seems rather straightforward and logical until the lamps are placed in parallel to one another; Fig. 21(2).

Here, the more lamps that are added in

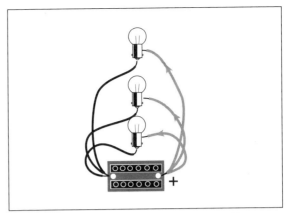

Fig. 21(2) An electrical circuit, lamps wired in parallel.

parallel to a circuit, then the overall current increases and the brightness of each lamp remains unchanged. At first glance this defies all logic and the difficulty appears to lie in appreciating why adding resistors in parallel should lower the resistance of the circuit which should then increase the load, but once explained it all begins to make sense.

Leave electricity at this point for one's familiar home. Consider the domestic water system, where a large water tank in the loft stores and maintains a head of water – this can be likened to a battery.

Imagine that a washbasin tap is opened a turn and the water is left to drain away – this can be likened to switching on a lamp. The water level in the loft tank will begin to fall slowly, enough to open the tank's ball-cock slightly and allow the water in the rising main to replenish the tank. Soon, a state of balance will exist. By opening another tap a turn, the water level in the loft tank will drop further and this time the water from the ball-cock will probably be heard entering the tank. Now run a bath as well and soon the hollow roar of the rising main will be heard, as the ball-cock by now will be fully open, allowing a full flow of the rising main water pressure to refill the tank. Thus it is clear that by opening various taps around the house, the resistance offered to the water flowing from the loft tank is reduced, and as a result the rising main works harder to maintain the head of water in the tank. If yet another tap were opened, then the demand might well exceed the supply, to a point where the rising main cannot replenish the tank fast enough to maintain the head of water. At this point the system could be said to have become overloaded.

Again this is relevant to a typical engine starter motor circuit: If you watch the battery voltage as the engine is started, the voltmeter will be seen to fall from 12V to about 10·5V. This is because, like the water system, the resistance of a starter motor is so small that the current flow will be elevated to such an extent that the rate of flow will exceed the ability of the battery to maintain the system voltage or pressure.

Household plumbing can broadly be described as a network of parallel circuits. The events described above very closely resemble what happens when resistors are added in parallel in an electrical circuit.

Turning this analogy into electrical practice and putting some quantitative values to the resistors, it can be demonstrated quite dramatically how placing resistors in parallel can affect the flow of electrical current: First place two identical resistors of equal value in series, and measure the circuit current. Then place the same two resistors in parallel, and the circuit current will have increased fourfold.

Nearly all the electrical circuits on a boat will be in parallel to the battery or bus bars. The reasons for this should be explained along with any exceptions to this rule. Christmas tree fairy lights provide a good example of why parallel circuits are needed. If there were twenty four 10V lamps, connected one after another in series and powered from a 240V supply, when one or more of these lamps fails, as happens, the whole chain of fairy lights is extinguished. However if connected in parallel, there would be twenty four individual lamp circuits at 240V each. The failure of one or more of these lamps would no longer affect the rest.

In a boat, this is far safer, more practical and therefore acceptable. So when several circuits are in parallel, each parallel arm is independent of the others. Although the currents in the various branches may be different, the potential difference or voltage between the common ends must be the same. That is to say, each branch is directly connected to the battery and each branch will receive the same equal voltage from the battery. The currents from each of the independent branches all join and add together to provide a sum of total current.

The general exception to the practice of paralleling is when Circuit Breakers, local switches and fuses are added to the system. Local switches placed in series to each of the parallel devices offers localised on/off switching without affecting other systems or circuits.

CBs or fuses on the other hand are usually placed in series to the overall paralleled network, so that any interruption here will, by deliberate design, remove power from the whole paralleled network.

21.1.3 MEASURING ELECTRICITY

The types of measuring instruments on the market are many and varied. First choose between analogue or digital display readouts – this hinges on ruggedness and personal preference. For example, a digital meter is much more rugged, whilst an analogue meter measures current and voltage without requiring a battery to do so. Fixed displays on distribution panels are dealt with later, but every boat owner should possess a portable meter which can measure amps, volts and ohms – hence often referred to as an AVO (meter). This instrument acts as a stethoscope for fault finding, Fig. 21(3), as well as reassuring owners that circuits are safe to work on.

To measure current (amps) the circuit must be broken at the point of measuring and the meter placed in series with the circuit. Breaking a circuit at a terminal point is a good accessible place to do it or an ammeter can be bridged across an open switch. The meter itself, when set to measure current, must offer the least possible resistance, if

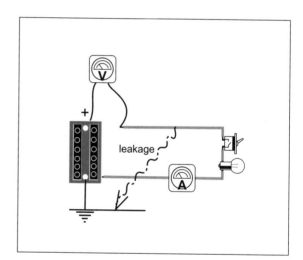

Fig. 21(3) Leakage or stray currents. If the connection at the +ve terminal of a 12V battery is interrupted, as shown, and a voltmeter is place across the break, and assuming the switch to the lamp is closed, the lamp will remain extinguished (since the high resistance of the voltmeter absorbs the full voltage drop); the voltmeter will register 12V and a very slight current will register at the ammeter.
With the lamp switch open, a null reading on both the voltmeter and the ammeter would be expected. However if a reading is apparent at the voltmeter, then current is leaking or straying from the battery source. If the meter at the battery happens to be a multi-meter, it could then be set to register current and thus establish the size of this current leakage.

not, then the meter itself would act as an obstruction to the current flow and register a completely false reading.

To measure voltage or voltage drop, the meter leads must straddle the component being measured. In contrast to measuring current, in the voltage mode the meter itself must offer the maximum possible resistance, since none of the current normally flowing through the component must pass into the meter, because this would register a false reading.

To measure the resistance of a circuit, the complete circuit must first be isolated from all power. Then identify the start and tail end of the circuit and connect these to the meter leads so as to close the circuit again. The meter injects a small current into the circuit and a measurement calibrated in ohms will be displayed. For portable AVO meters this injected current will usually come from a 1.5V pen battery.

A good AVO meter for a boat should be able to measure in the ranges: 0 to 10 Amps; 0 to 500V AC/DC; and 0 to infinity Ohms. For such a range of scales, AVOs come with a range switch to break down these ranges into manageable steps. To measure components – such as checking fuses – the item under test must often be disconnected from its neighbours to get a correct reading.

21.2 ENGINE ELECTRICS

Electrics for marine engines can be one of two, or three, basic types:

a. An insulated 2 wire system; or
b. An insulated ground return system; or
c. A combination of both.

The basic electrical circuit in Fig. 21(1) depicted a battery supplying electrical current via two cables to a load or appliance (shown here for simplicity as a light bulb). If a multitude of different loads is required from the battery, as in Fig. 21(2), they are best connected in parallel to ensure an equal voltage across each appliance. Now imagine a block of metal representing an engine and the light bulbs representing the engine's auxiliary appliances, ie gauge sensors, alternators, starter motors and solenoids etc. A circuit for these requirements is shown in Fig. 21(4), where each appliance is insulated from the engine block and fed by its own dedicated cabling.

This Figure represents the principles of an 'insulated 2 wire system' and is far and away the least common, although said to be theoretically preferred. However, this system is essential in steel or aluminium hulled boats where it is vital

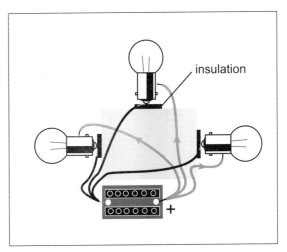

Fig. 21(4) An insulated 2 wire system

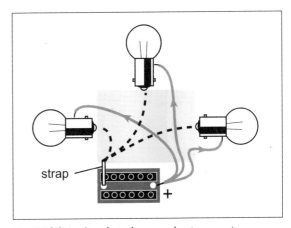

Fig. 21(5) An insulated ground return system.

that the engine block be insulated from the circuitry to prevent 'leakage currents' and the consequent ravages of electrolytic corrosion.

More commonly seen is the 'insulated ground return system' as shown in Fig. 21(5). Here, one of the terminals of each appliance is connected to the engine block, thereby using the conductive nature of the engine to form one side of the electrical circuit – usually the negative side. Obviously this requires only half the amount of cabling, is not only simpler and less vulnerable, but also clearly offers engine manufacturers and their customers some attractive cost saving. It is hardly surprising that most recreational marine engines employ this principle. The negative side of the battery is connected to the engine block by a single heavy duty cable called a 'Strap' and the engine block itself which acts like a sink of electrical current is usually called the 'Ground' or 'Earth'.

Note: The terms 'Ground' and 'Earth' are often loosely used, leading to possible confusion if not danger. For the sake of standardisation and to

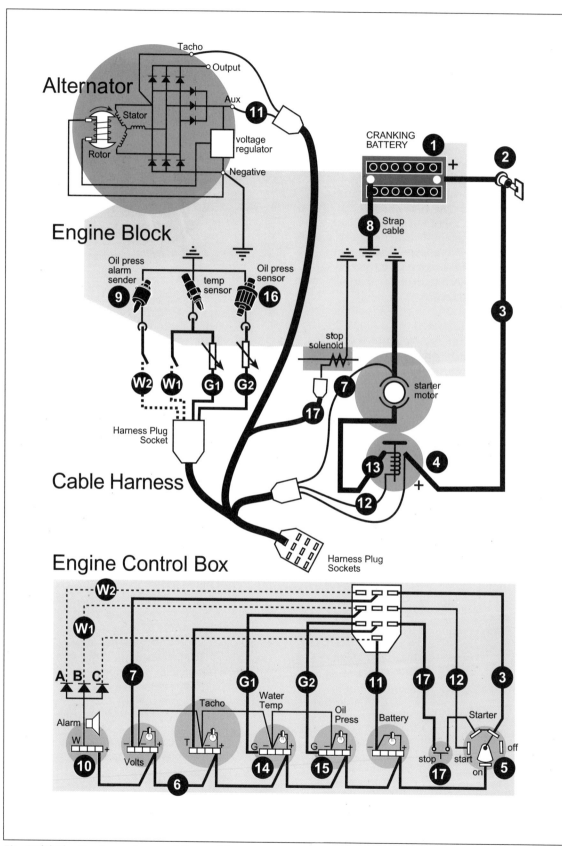

Fig. 21(6) The Engine system and Control Box system.

avoid misunderstanding, 'Ground' is used here in relation to DC circuits, and 'Earth' to AC circuits.

The 'insulated ground return system' is very similar to that in a car which is virtually the standard throughout the whole motor industry. Although some car manufacturers use the +ve polarity for the ground return, it is highly unlikely that a +ve ground return would be used in marine engines. This is because the engine block would become 'anodic' relative to everything else, making both external and internal parts of the engine sacrificial to the more 'cathodic' parts.

Basically all the engine's electrics are in two sections: the Engine System and the Control Box System, see Fig. 21(6), both usually supplied by the engine manufacturer.

Once installed the two sections are linked by a common 'loom' or 'harness' of cables with junction boxes at each end; each terminal or wire within the junction box is either coded or numbered.

21.2.1   ENGINE STARTING

The functioning of the complete system can be traced as the starter key is turned slowly past its several positions.

Starter key at 'Off'

With the key resting in the 'off' position, all the engine's circuits are dead. After stopping the engine, it is vital to return the key to this position, so as to avoid burning out the fuel pump solenoid; see the 'Engine Stop' position.

Starter key at 'On'

When the key is turned to the 'on' position, a light duty current (about 1 Amp) from the +ve terminal 1 of the Cranking Battery passes through the battery isolator switch 2, via line 3 to the +ve terminal of the starter solenoid 4. Thence through the ignition key 5 to power up the gauges 6 and their lamps where the needles of the gauges will be seen to flick over. The current from the gauge lamps is returned, via the various negative ground leads 7, to ground (usually at the negative terminal of the starter motor) where it is picked up by the negative terminal of the battery through the strap cable 8.

The currents from the temperature & pressure gauges, 14 and 15, are returned to ground along a parallel path through their respective sensing lines G1 and G2. The contacts of the oil pressure alarm sender are normally closed at engine standstill, so at this stage the sender 9 assumes an alarm condition. Thus the circuit in line W2 is closed, enabling the buzzer alarm 10 to sound since the positive current from the buzzer is made to ground via diode A.

Note: Sounding of this alarm annoys some people who get round this by installing an optional

timed alarm relay and a slight adjustment in the wiring. This arrangement delays the activation of the alarm condition and allows enough time for the engine to start up and build up its oil pressure to its running level. Leaving the alarm system as is, however, has the advantages of giving audible warning that the starter circuit is 'live' and also testing the oil pressure alarm every time the engine is started.

The 'Low/No battery charge' light and it's associated circuitry 11 play an important part by confirming that a charging current is flowing between the alternator and the battery (see Excitation, 21.3.2). But for the moment, in respect to the starter key, expect to see the 'charge' light come on. This circuit's return to ground is achieved via the alternator's voltage regulator.

Starter key at 'Start'

Turning the key to the next position 'start' causes a larger current of about 10 amps to flow down line 3 from the +ve terminal of the battery to the starter switch 5. Through this switch's position, the current is returned to ground via line 12, thus energizing the solenoid coil 13 of the starter solenoid 4. The energised coil closes the relay to bridge the heavy duty terminals of the starter solenoid; this allows heavy duty current to flow to ground via the starter motor and the strap cable 8. The current finally returns to the negative terminal of the battery.

The purpose of the starter solenoid relay is to relieve the Engine Control Box circuitry of the viciously high starting current which could be in the order of 400 Amps. The engine should now crank over and gradually pick up speed to the start throttle setting. Oil pressure will build up sufficiently to open the sender alarm 9 contacts which shut down the alarm circuitry W2 and alarm 10.

When the engine has taken over the start sequence and is running, the starter key 5 is released and springs back to the 'On' position. The starter solenoid relay 13 is now de-energised, opening the starter motor circuit and stopping the starter motor. Also in the 'On' position, all the gauges, sensors and alarm senders remain connected. Engine control panels with pressure and temperature gauges are more than likely to have only one common alarm shared amongst all the senders. So in the event of any alarm condition, a glance at the gauges is required to establish which is at fault. However, for a panel without pressure and temperature gauges, these gauges will be replaced by individual warning lights, viz 'High Water Temp', 'Low Oil Press' and 'Low/No battery charge', all still sharing a common buzzer alarm.

There may be occasions when despite a healthy

engine start an alarm condition is still present. This condition is most likely to be a 'Low/No battery charge' alarm and is merely a sign that the alternator has not yet developed a sufficient output voltage – probably due to the alternator not being sufficiently excited (see Excitation, 21.3.2). To resolve this, slowly increase engine rpm until the lamp and the buzzer go out, then throttle back to idle.

Starter key to 'Engine Stop' or pressing stop button

To stop the engine, press in the engine 'stop' button **17** and hold against its spring until the engine stops. This energises a solenoid (line **17**) on the fuel pump which pulls the fuel throttle rack to cut off fuel to the pumps. As the engine stops, the 'Oil press' sensor will cut in and sound the alarm, which is then silenced by turning the starter key to 'Off'. This also shuts off all the electrical circuitry to the engine.

Alternatively some engine panels have the engine stop sequence incorporated within the starter key **5**. Turn the starter key to 'engine stop' – a position midway between 'On' and 'Off'. This energises the fuel pump solenoid, as described above. When the engine has stopped, turn the starter key to 'Off'.

Note: A problem with this arrangement is that, despite the 'Oil press' alarm sounding, it is very easy to leave the key in the 'engine stop' position after the engine has stopped; eventually this will burn out the fuel pump solenoid.

21.2.2   ENGINE SENSORS AND ALARMS

Transducer is the correct technical name for a sensor, which is actually quite a simple device.

Some of the devices referred to in this and the previous section are shown in more detail in Fig. 21(10).

The cooling water temperature sensor, Fig. 21(7), usually located near the thermostat housing, uses a 'thermistor' pellet – a metal whose electrical resistance alters with variations in temperature, in this case of the surrounding water. If this sensor is connected to an electrical circuit, a gauge **14** indicates cooling water temperature.

Associated with cooling water temperature is the 'High temp' alarm which is activated by a bi-metallic switch. This switch contains a strip of two dissimilar metals, with different expansion rates, bonded together in a pre-set shape. With changes in temperature the different rates of expansion cause the strip to bend. If the strip is linked to an electrical circuit, this bending movement can act as an 'on/off' switch. Under normal engine running conditions these alarm contacts are open, but close when a

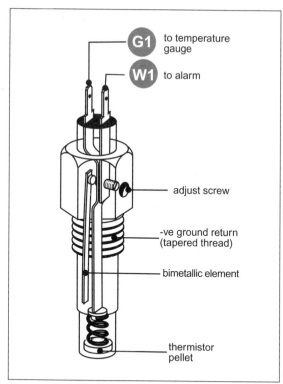

Fig. 21(7) The cooling water temperature sensor.

pre-set over-temperature condition is reached.

The 'Oil press' sensor, **16** and Fig. 21(8), is a hydraulically operated electrical device. Oil pressure within a chamber acts across a diaphragm. Any movement of the diaphragm is turned into a mechanical motion of levers whereby an electrical contact arm is swept across

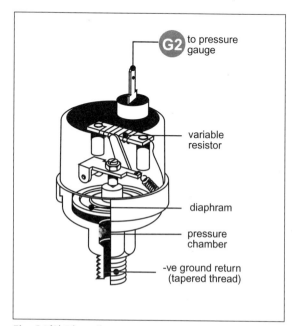

Fig. 21(8) The oil pressure sensor.

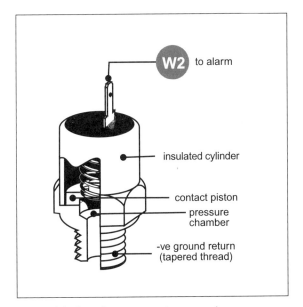

Fig. 21(9) The oil pressure alarm sender.

an electrical resistor coil, called a 'variable resistor' or 'rheostat'. Again, this device is connected to an electrical circuit and a gauge **15** to pickup any changes in the current as the rheostat alters its electrical resistance within the circuit.

The 'Oil press' alarm sender, Fig. 21(9) is an even simpler hydraulically operated electrical device. Oil pressure in a chamber lifts a very lightly spring-loaded piston. When the piston is lifted off its seat, an electrical contact opens. A complete loss of oil pressure (down to 0.1 bar) will re-seat the piston and close the contacts, causing the alarm to sound. Some engine manufacturers may combine the pressure sensor and alarm sender into one unit. This device will be similar to the oil pressure sensor, but with the low pressure alarm contacts incorporated within the mechanic linkage between the diaphram and the rheostat.

Sensing and sending devices have common ground terminals, ie their threaded bases which screw into the engine block. Their threads are deliberately and precisely tapered to ensure a tight seal and good electrical contact. Many boat owners have wound plumber's tape (PTFE) around the threaded bases, thinking thereby to provide a secure seal. Probably true, but they may wonder why there are no readings on the gauges and the alarms are a bit quiet? There is also a risk that the tape will tear and break-up on screwing in and may enter the oil system to block vital oil ways.

Should any of the three alarm sensing devices enter an alarm condition, say the water 'High temp', then the +ve current from line **6** is free to flow to ground through the buzzer, via its respective diode **B** and through the closed switch **W1**. The same principle applies for an 'Oil press' alarm, but the buzzer circuit flows instead via diode **A**.

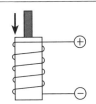

Solenoid

A wire coil wound around an insulated cylinder, within which a solid steel rod is able to move freely. Applying a current to the coil will, through electromagnetic influence, cause the steel rod to be drawn into the cylinder coil in a linear fashion. The inward pull on the rod does not depend upon the directional flow of current in the coil. Indeed, exactly the same inward pull upon the rod would occur if an AC current was applied to the coil.

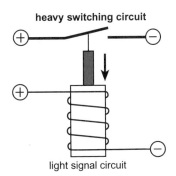

Relay

An extension to the solenoid, whereby the linear movement of the steel rod activates a switch either to open or close some separate circuit (often heavy duty, eg a starter) which is wholly independent of and separate from the solenoid coil.

Thermistor Pellet

A metal whose electrical resistance changes with variations in temperature. If this device is connected to an electrical circuit, a gauge can be incorporated to indicate any changes in the current flow as the thermistor alters its electrical resistance.

Bi-metallic Switch

This switch incorporates a strip of two dissimilar metals bonded together. With changes in temperature the different rates of expansion of these metals causes the strip to bend, either opening or closing a circuit, thus acting as an 'on-off' switch.

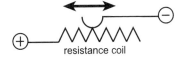

Rheostat/variable resistor

If this device is coupled to an electrical circuit, a gauge can be incorporated to pick up an changes in the current as the rheostat alters its electrical resistance within the circuit.

Fig. 21(10) Details of a solenoid, relay, thermistor pellet, bimetallic strip and a variable resistor.

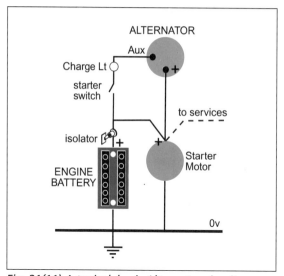

Fig. 21(11) A typical, basic Alternator circuit.

Note: A diode is an electrical non-return valve allowing current to flow in one direction but not the other. Here the three diodes prevent one alarm circuit from feeding back into another alarm circuit. Thus if alarm circuit A were to be energised, diodes B and C stop the circuit current from doubling back on itself and interfering with the other alarm circuits.

21.3 CHARGING SYSTEMS

21.3.1 THE ALTERNATOR

An alternator, or any other generating device for that matter, has two distinct functions in a boat's electrical system:

a. to charge and replenish the batteries; and
b. to supply electrical power to the boat's distribution system for general consumption.

Alternators initially produce a smooth sinusoidal pulse of electricity called alternating current (AC). To be of any use and compatible with the boat's DC system, AC must be converted (rectified) to DC. This is done through solid state electronics, namely diodes which are sensitive items and remarkably easy to destroy. The DC output voltage must then be controlled at the correct value, usually by limiting the amount of magnetic flux (which actually generates the alternator's output). This control is achieved by a voltage regulator, commonly mounted at the rear of the alternator as an integral part. Early regulators were of the electro-mechanical or thermal types. Today they are of the solid state electronic type, probably 'optimum fast charge devices' or 'smart' regulators.

Any voltage regulator senses the alternator's output either from the alternator's very own

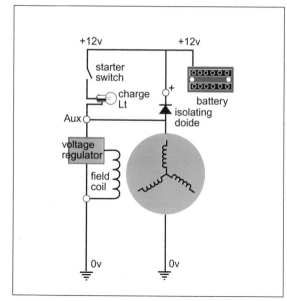

Fig. 21(12) An excitation circuit.

output ('machine-sensing'); or from the voltage at the battery ('battery-sensing') which the alternator is actually charging. The latter type can be identified by a fourth wire leading off to the battery.

An alternator can simply be regarded as a pump and as such needs to be incorporated into a system to achieve its distinct tasks. It is regulated to supply an output voltage of about 14V, giving it about a 2V potential head over and above the battery's 12V. The alternator will also have a current rating, usually between 50A and 120A, to ensure that it can fully handle its battery charging duties and also adequately supply the demand from domestic services.

The charging process requires the alternator to overcome the battery's own internal resistance, which rises with the battery voltage so that the charging current is reduced to a minimum well before a full charge is given. This is due to the irregular distribution of electrically charged ions within the electrolyte. Those near the battery plates are affected more readily, both when charging and discharging, than those in the body of the electrolyte. With a sudden discharge, as when starting the engine, only the ions in the electrolyte nearer the plates are affected in the short term, and these are soon restored when recharging begins. But with a slow discharge the whole of the electrolyte becomes affected; when recharging occurs the acid nearer the plates is more quickly restored, giving the regulator the false impression that the battery is recharged.

Thus for a battery subject to deep discharge over many hours – supplying lights, refrigerator, water pump, radio etc – the conventional regulator is unable to recharge the battery to full capacity and sulphation of the battery plates is likely. The battery may never be more than 65% to 70% charged.

To overcome this problem, a 'smart' regulator can be fitted which controls the alternator's charging voltage by continually sensing battery voltage and temperature. One such regulator is made by Adverc BM Ltd, 245 Trysull Road, Merry Hill, Wolverhampton WV3 7LG; Tel 01902 380494. This controls charging over alternate periods at high and low voltages, the latter being best regarded as rest periods to allow the battery counter-voltage to level off. This high/low charging sequence takes a couple of hours, after which there is a longer rest period to prevent gassing and overcharging. The cycle is then repeated as necessary until the battery is 95-100% charged in minimum engine running time. Indicator lights show when the boat is drawing more current than the alternator can supply, or if a fault develops. The regulator will function with up to four battery banks, and with one or two alternators. A smart regulator greatly improves alternator performance and hence battery charging; it can also be installed by any competent DIY layman.

Fig. 21(11) shows a typical alternator circuit, in its simplest form. This is a single battery unit, adequate for a small inshore cruiser, where the battery covers both engine start and domestic services. This is fine, provided the service demands are small and there is little risk of exhausting the battery. The main drawback to this system is that the domestic services will be subjected to large voltage drops when the heavy starter motor current is drawn from the battery. This is a tolerable inconvenience for the lights etc, as they dim momentarily, but may not be acceptable for sensitive navigational equipment.

The alternator output is usually taken to the heavy duty +ve terminal of the starter solenoid and this becomes the junction point, as it were, between the engine and the domestic services.

On some alternator circuits a fuse is located on the alternator output – the subject of some debate, because, if the fuse blows with the alternator running, the alternator becomes open circuited, thereby destroying its diodes. Many would argue that this is preferable to a short at the battery end, with all its attendant fire risks.

21.3.2   EXCITATION

By adjusting the current in the rotor field coil (called the field current) control of the alternator's output can be obtained, as required. Ingeniously, the current in the field coil is actually tapped off from the alternator's own DC output, thereby making it self-sufficient in generating its own magnetic field – and therefore, of course, its productive output.

The self-sufficiency of alternators raises an interesting 'chicken and egg' question, in that they will not generate an output without field current and there will not be any field current until it produces an output. So how does an alternator start from scratch? Fortunately the field coils are wound around soft iron cores which primarily helps to concentrate the magnetic flux over the generating coils in the stator. The secondary function of the soft iron is that the induced magnetism from the field coils remains in the cores after the alternator has stopped running. This phenomenon is called 'residual magnetism', ie it does not last for ever. Usually, through regular use, it is enough to generate an output which in turn will energise and excite the field coils and 'flash' the machine alive. An alternator that achieves this by itself is termed 'self-exciting'.

But if an alternator stands idle for too long, the residual magnetism can degrade to the point where self-excitation is impossible.

To guard against this, a branch feed, Fig. 21(12), called an excitation circuit, is tapped off the engine's ignition circuit, and conveniently has the secondary function of confirming that a charging current is flowing from the alternator to the battery through the charge light.

21.3.3   CHARGE LIGHT

When the starter switch is closed, the 12V charge light illuminates and brings the potential at the Aux terminal to just above 0V; indeed, leaving just about 100 mA of current from the cranking

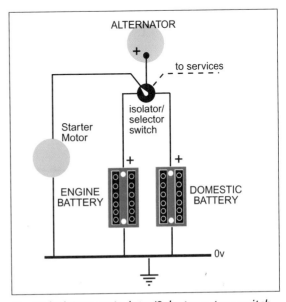

Fig. 21(13) Battery Isolator/Selector rotary switch.

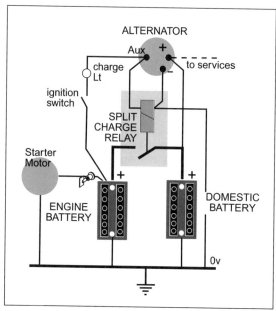

Fig. 21(14) Split charge relay in the Alternator circuit.

battery to energise the field coils and 'flash' up the alternator. Once the engine fires, the alternator starts generating, which in turn makes the voltage at the Aux terminal slightly higher than the battery voltage of 12V. With such a meagre potential difference across the 12V lamp, the light now goes out.

Where space permits, a pair of batteries offers two main advantages: usually one battery is reserved for engine starting, whilst the other (or possibly a bank of two or more batteries connected in parallel) serves the various domestic

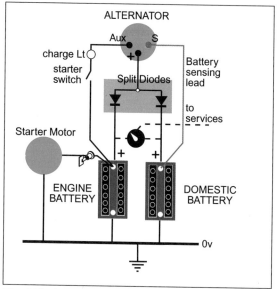

Fig. 21(15) Split charge diodes in an Alternator circuit.

and navigational equipments fitted to the boat. As there is no routine drain on the cranking battery, it should remain fully charged, thus offering the security of being able to start the engine at any time.

But multi-battery installations bring their own charging problems. Obviously, both batteries must be charged from the same source (the alternator), but if they remain connected together once the charging current has ceased, any imbalance in charge between them will tend to level out, with the least charged battery pulling down the other. If one of the batteries were to become defective, it could deplete the healthier one to the point where both could be useless.

This problem is overcome by being able to isolate the batteries from each other in one of three ways:

a. Combined Selector & Isolator Switch

These are rotary switches, Fig. 21(13), with 4 positions: **BATT 1**, **BATT 2**, **BOTH** and **OFF**. They offer the simplest and cheapest solution to battery management.

If, say, **BATT 1** is selected, then all starting and other electrical services will be drawn from it and only that battery will be charged. The same applies for the **BATT 2** and **BOTH** positions.

Of course these are entirely manual operations which require an owner to know and keep mental track of which battery is well up or well down in its state of charge. Also he must remember to switch to the engine battery before starting the engine and switch back to the service battery after the engine has been running for a while. This arrangement is inherently vulnerable to forgetfulness! Moreover, if the switch is absentmindedly selected to **OFF** with the engine running, the alternator diodes could blow. However many modern alternators have some defence in the form of an extra voltage-limiting snubber or surge-protection diode. Incidentally, good quality selector switches are of a make-before-break type, so that there is no battery disconnection when switching between them. It is not uncommon to see both batteries left accidentally paralleled under load so that both batteries are flattened, leaving the obvious problem of no power to start the engine – quite a dangerous oversight!

Another potential trap can occur if the engine proves difficult to start. After repeated cranking, the engine battery gives up the ghost. In desperation the switch is selected to **BOTH** to reinforce the engine battery – a bad move! Now a healthy battery is coupled to one which is seriously depleted. Current rushes from the good to the bad – almost tantamount to a short circuit between the two batteries. Both batteries risk damage if this treatment is repeated often enough. So, is there a better way?

b.   Split charge relays
Although rarely fitted nowadays, these devices, see Fig. 21(14), were once very common.

Usually wired into the engine ignition circuit, split charge relays isolate the batteries from each other when the alternator is not turning, but as soon as the engine starts, the relays connect the batteries together in parallel so that both may be charged.

There is a tale which claims that the batteries become paralleled as soon as the starter key is turned, and *before* the engine actually starts, thus running the risk of weaker batteries pulling the stronger batteries down. This tale is largely untrue. Consider Fig. 21(14): with the starter switch open there is no power to energise the relay. When the starter switch is closed, the 12V charge light illuminates, leaving a 0V potential at the alternator's Aux terminal. With a potential difference of 0V across the relay, it is still not energised, but at least the engine will be starting up. As soon as the engine is up to speed the alternator will develop an output of 12V at its Aux terminal. Now there is a 12V potential across the relay which will pull in the relay switch to parallel the two batteries. If however there was no charge light, then the afore-mentioned tale would hold true, because there is no lamp to absorb the initial 12V drop when the starter switch is closed.

Since there is a negligible voltage drop from the alternator to the batteries via this relay switch, then it is usual to find the alternator machine-sensed and therefore it has no cause to be interested in what is going on downstream of itself. However very small voltage drops could creep in due to underrated terminals, cables and negative path returns through the engine block.

c.   Split charge diodes
These are now almost common practice because of their simplicity and reliability, Fig. 21(15).

The pair of diodes lets the charging current flow freely to, but not between, both batteries. The battery with the lower charge will be charged first. Different battery sizes can be fitted within each system, so long as they have the same voltage. A manual selector switch can be wired into the battery circuit to allow the roles of the batteries to be changed or paralleled, if need be. This is a good system which offers flexibility and diversity and caters for most contingencies.

Nevertheless there is a down side: In consuming current in the forward direction there is an inherent voltage drop of about 0.7V across the diode which is independent of the current it carries. This is a nuisance in the case of marginal charging when the whole of the charging output would not be entering the battery. An alternator output of 14V would be lowered to 13.3V (14V – 0.7V) by the time it reaches the battery and the voltage head or potential might not be enough to charge the battery. A machine-sensing regulator would be totally unaware of this shortfall. Therefore it becomes essential for the alternator and its regulator to be battery-sensing so that any voltage drops are compensated for and the regulator will ensure that a full 14V reaches the battery. The domestic battery is usually the one chosen for sensing since it is generally the most used, whilst the cranking battery is almost permanently fully charged.

Regardless of the charging system, a battery-sensing regulator would be the best choice. Using the household water system analogy, the tank ball cock which 'regulates' the flow of water to the tank, is in a way sensing the tank water level, in the same way that a battery-sensing regulator senses the voltage level of the battery.

Diodes run hot and since they are sensitive to heat, they are usually mounted on a heat-sink with cooling fins. Diodes should be located in a well ventilated space with an adequate updraft of air. A common mistake is to mount the diodes with the cooling fins horizontal, which creates numerous thermal pockets within the heat-sink and rapidly shortens the life of the diodes through overheating. If diodes are mounted in the engine bay, it is wise to over-rate them so as to compensate for the heat.

21.3.4   BATTERY CHARGERS
Mains chargers step down 240V AC to 12V through a transformer and then rectify the output through a network of diodes to produce 12V DC. Some form of voltage control is built in, the sophistication of which largely depends on its cost.

The simplest units are the low cost type available in car accessory shops. These chargers are usually not regulated and should only be used as a temporary expedient to re-charge a flat battery. Although some are able to charge a smallish battery which is used solely for engine starting and is then promptly recharged, they can not deliver the progressive rate of charge required and may ultimately damage the battery. They simply can not cope with a large battery bank. Their loose leads and crocodile clips can easily lead to arcing and incorrect polarity.

If the power demand on your batteries is heavy, a large output charger permanently wired into the system, as in Figs. 21(22) and (23), may be the solution. Such chargers typically have outputs of 10A to 100A and can support more than one battery or bank of batteries. The charger's size should be matched to the batteries and the demand. A good rule of thumb is to have the charger's output rated at 20% of battery capacity. Thus for a 100Ah battery, a charging current of 20A would be ideal.

Chargers delivering higher rates of charge in 3 stages are the most sophisticated and will prevent overcharging – but are not cheap. An initial high charge rate at 14.4V is reduced during an equalisation phase (to limit gassing), and finally enters a float phase at about 13.8V.

Some chargers are specifically designed for, or can be adjusted, to suit lead-acid or gel type batteries. Other adjustments could include temperature compensation, as low ambient temperatures need higher charging voltages; in good chargers this will be an automatic feature. An equalising charge switch is fitted on some chargers; this is used at intervals to condition the batteries and clean the sulphate from the plates.

21.4 BATTERIES

21.4.1 BATTERY TYPES

Lead/acid batteries, usually 12V, are commonly fitted in boats, although there are advantages in using 24V, as in larger craft. Lead/acid batteries are of two main types:

a. The ordinary automotive type which is constructed internally to give a high current over a short period for starting the engine, and then to be promptly recharged once the engine is running. This type does not respond well to repeated cycles of deep discharge over several hours, followed by recharging.
b. The traction battery (as might be fitted in a milk float for example) is more suitable due to its heavier internal construction with fewer but thicker plates.

In recent years batteries with a gelled electrolyte have become popular because they need no maintenance, can be recharged at a higher rate, are not affected by large angles of heel, can tolerate a deeper discharge and can be left standing for longer. But they cost more. Some form of temperature sensor should be fitted to avoid overcharging and gassing.

Alkaline (nickel-cadmium) batteries are dearer still, but can retain their charge for long periods, and therefore do not require special attention during winter lay-ups. There are two basic types:

c. high-performance, for heavy discharge currents and hence particularly suited for engine starting; and
d. general service uses.

Discharge capacities of the high-performance batteries are quoted at a 2-hour rate, while those of the general use, normal resistance cells are given at a 5-hour rate. The specific gravity of the electrolyte in an alkaline battery does not vary with the state of charge, and is usually 1,200 at 20°C (68°F). This figure falls as the electrolyte deteriorates, indicating that it should be renewed.

Whatever type of battery is fitted, it must be securely mounted on a tray (for possible spillage) and in a lidless box or rack, to be readily accessible for maintenance. The compartment must be well ventilated, to remove explosive gases generated during charging and discharging. An extractor fan may be needed for large battery banks. Isolating switches must be fitted as discussed earlier.

21.4.2 BATTERY CAPACITY AND CHARGING

The capacity of a battery is measured in ampere-hours (Amp-hr or Ah), and is normally expressed as a 10-hour rating; for example a 150 amp-hour battery will give 15 amperes for 10 hours. At higher rates of discharge the capacity is reduced quite considerably. It is important that a battery with adequate capacity is fitted to allow for reduced performance with age, plus the likely fitting of more electrical items to the boat. The charge/discharge ratio of most batteries is about 1.4, which means that for every 100 amp-hours of discharge, 140 amp-hours of charging are needed to restore full capacity.

A battery should normally be charged at the 10-hour rate, but a higher rate of charge may be used if the battery is in good condition, provided that its temperature is kept below 43°C (110°F). The charging rate is automatically controlled in a properly fitted marine installation, allowing a higher rate of initial charge, then falling off as the battery voltage rises.

Lead/acid batteries must be charged regularly to keep them in good condition and available for use, particularly in warm weather; they must not be left standing idle for more than a month or two. The state of charge of a lead/acid battery is determined from the specific gravity of the electrolyte, as measured by a hydrometer. At 16°C (60°F) typical readings are: 1,280 = fully charged; 1,200 = half discharged; 1,115 = fully discharged.

The level of the electrolyte should be checked weekly, and distilled water added as necessary to keep the tops of the plates just covered. Sealed batteries obviously do not need this attention, even though in most of them the electrolyte is liquid. They need accurate re-charging, and a heavy discharge can mean a long re-charging time.

21.5 DC POWER DISTRIBUTION

A boat's DC electrical distribution system exists in a harsh environment, so it must be inherently robust. The wiring and the various devices must be electrically and mechanically sound, and also well protected so they remain reliable over a period of years.

Above all, the installation must be safe, for where there is electricity, there is also a fire risk. Many people think that because the voltage is low – usually 12V on all but the largest yachts – it must be safe. This is just not so. The lower the voltage, the higher the current (in amperes) must be to do a given amount of work. And it is lots of amps which can cause a component to overheat, perhaps igniting surrounding materials.

21.5.1 BUILDING FROM BASICS

Consider designing a typical boat circuit, Figs. 21(16) to (21), starting with the simplest possible arrangement:

Fig. 21(16) shows a battery supplying current to a single load or appliance, here represented by a light bulb. It is worth noting that the current flows out from the +ve battery terminal, through the circuit, and back to the negative terminal.

Where two or more appliances are being served, these are best connected in parallel, Fig. 21(17), so that each receives an equal voltage. But to wire a whole circuit that way would be both expensive and untidy.

Happily, we can start to economise by sharing some of the return leads, Fig. 21(18), connecting them together with the help of junction boxes. In this type of system the returning wire gets larger as the battery is approached. This is because it must handle the cumulative current of the various circuits feeding into it – like minor roads joining a motorway, adding to the overall traffic flow.

For safety, we need an isolator switch on the battery's positive side and fuses or circuit breakers (CBs) to protect the individual load circuits, Fig. 21(19).

By mounting the CBs on a common bus bar rail, we can use just one large cable to convey the power from the battery. This prevents cluttering

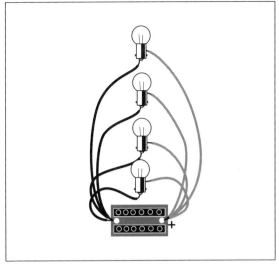

Fig. 21(17) Appliances connected in parallel.

up the battery +ve terminal and reduces the risk of any shorts across to the negative terminal.

For convenience, the bus bar and protection devices are often mounted behind a labelled panel, Fig. 21(20), from which the distribution system is controlled.

A bus bar is a metal junction strip from which individual circuits radiate out to serve the boat's appliances, each of which usually has its own on/off switch for local control.

Overall circuit protection is provided by placing an additional CB (or fuse) board between the battery and distribution panel – a very important requirement. As this is a sort of focal point where both the +ve and –ve sides of the primary circuit can be brought together, it also forms a convenient and ideal platform to add monitoring instruments,

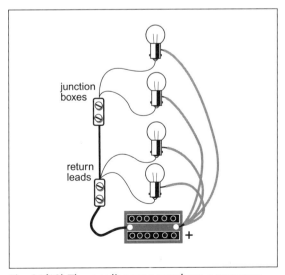

Fig. 21(18) The appliances now share a common return line ...

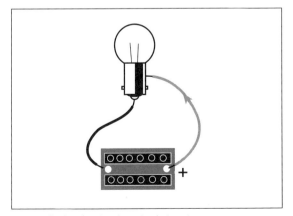

Fig. 21(16) A basic electrical circuit.

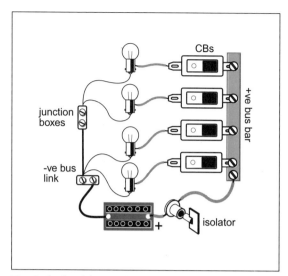

Fig. 21(19) Add an isolator switch, four CBs and a bus bar ...

such as a voltmeter and ammeter, the latter connected to a shunt. In a way this protection platform is the most important of all the system's protection devices, since it is the last line of defence against any over-current situation before reaching the batteries.

On leisure craft most batteries are 12V and the length of time that this voltage can be sustained to a given load depends on battery capacity, measured in ampere-hours. Capacity results from battery size and type (lead-acid, Ni-Cad etc) or from coupling up more batteries in parallel. This is known as a bank of batteries and, for all practical purposes, can be thought of as a single large battery having a capacity equal to the sum of them all.

Each battery should have its own isolator mounted as close as possible to its positive terminal, as this provides a means of reducing battery drainage caused by leakage currents from bad insulation or the damp atmosphere. If a fault should occur when the boat is left unattended, it will not result in a short circuit since the power that poses the potential danger has been isolated at source. All isolator keys must of course be able to carry the full starter motor load.

Isolators are of two kinds: key operated or a combined isolator/selector. The first of these will serve a single battery (or bank of them) and has the advantage that the key can be removed to disable that battery, thus depriving a would-be thief of any useful power to the boat. The isolator/selector type, as the name suggests, can choose between batteries, isolate them, or

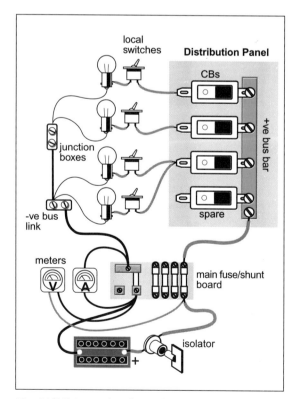

Fig. 21(20) Insert local switches, fuses, voltmeter and ammeter ...

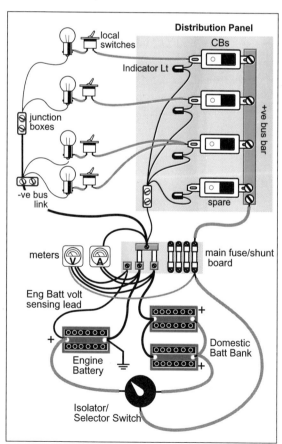

Fig. 21(21) The completed and much simplified boat system.

connect them together to combine their power – perhaps to start the engine as an emergency feature should the cranking battery be flat.

Whatever method of cross connection is adopted, there needs to be a common link between the negatives of the batteries. Note in Fig. 21(21) that the –ve leads from both the engine start and domestic batteries go to each arm of the horseshoe shunt, thereby coupling them together. (Note: A horseshoe shunt is two shunts placed side by side and joined at one end). The voltmeter and ammeter also take information from the shunt and, via selector switches (not shown) on the gauges, each system can be independently monitored. As a further refinement, indicator lights or LEDs have been added to the appliance circuits to show which CB is made and which appliances are live.

21.5.2   CIRCUIT BREAKERS VERSUS FUSES

Which is better? And if planning to change from one to t'other, could a 10A fuse be replaced with a CB of similar rating? The answers help to explain the fundamental differences between the two.

Some electrical loads, when first switched, take a large initial current, ie a surge. Generally a 10A 'slow-blow' fuse, say, is designed to carry its rated current, plus any surge peaks which may normally occur in a circuit. The degree of these surge currents is a product of both the current and the fuse's slow-blow time, eg: 5 seconds at 2.5 x rated current or within 1 second at 3.5 x rated current. Taking a fuse above its rated value, as in a surge, causes the fuse wire to burn and thereby weaken; if repeated frequently the fuse will blow. Thus, a 10A motor with a starting current of 50A, may require a fuse far exceeding its normal 10A rating to get over this problem. This would leave the motor's cabling dangerously vulnerable to higher overload currents and overheating.

A CB on the other hand can do the same as the fuse, but due to its robust design the time delays incorporated within a CB (to cope with surge current/overload) can be controlled – without damaging its own mechanisms. The 10A motor can therefore have a CB rated much nearer to 10A, whilst still able to carry the 50A starting surge. CBs and fuses are largely inter-changeable for normal, non-surging loads.

A common misconception about the function of fuses and CBs in the main circuits needs to be clarified. Such protection devices are there to protect the wiring, not the associated equipment. Thus any fuse/CB should be rated at a higher current than that expected to be drawn under steady, no-fault conditions. Beyond this rated current of the fuse/CB, the wire should most importantly be capable of carrying more current, without dangerous overheating. The equipment must be protected by a separate, locally sited fuse or by one built in by the manufacturer.

Fuses are made in 'quick-' and 'slow-blow' versions to suit different types of load. Fuses, due to their inherent simplicity, are cheaper than CBs but otherwise offer few advantages. One is that a blown fuse obliges you to check the circuit, otherwise the fuse will blow again! A real disadvantage is that fuses are open to abuse, ie it is tempting to replace a fuse which persistently blows with one of a higher rating than the design value – even with full knowledge of the consequences. Another problem is oxidisation of the sensitive fuse wire with age, causing it to break; remember this before checking the circuit.

CBs are a more expensive, longer term investment. The cost is slightly offset in that CBs can double as switches which must be separately fitted where fuses are used. CBs are more predictable and reliable and when tripped can be identified by feel in the dark. The two types most commonly used on boats are Thermal and Magnetic. A thermal CB passes the overload current through a wire element which heats up and operates a bimetallic strip to trip the CB open. A magnetic CB uses a solenoid working against a spring to activate the tripping mechanism.

21.6 AC POWER DISTRIBUTION

Having an AC supply at every marina berth is proving attractive to more and more yacht owners. Not only can many of the amenities they have at home be enjoyed, but whilst alongside, the boat's batteries should always be fully charged.

AC distribution on a boat falls into three categories:

a. a portable cable feeding a single appliance, most probably a battery charger;
b. a fixed installation, served through a distribution board and feeding multiple appliances; and
c. some combination of (a) and (b).

Consider their strengths and weaknesses:

a. *Portable power*

Fig. 21(22) shows an arrangement with which most boat owners will be familiar.

An extension lead is plugged into the pontoon supply and is used to power the battery charger. Thereafter the boat essentially runs on its 12V system, with the battery levels maintained by the charger.

The most worrying aspect of this set-up is that there is no polarity warning light (see 21.6.3). But, even if the polarity were correct, the degree of protection is meagre, relying as it does on fused plugs and sockets (sometimes) and the earth cable to shore.

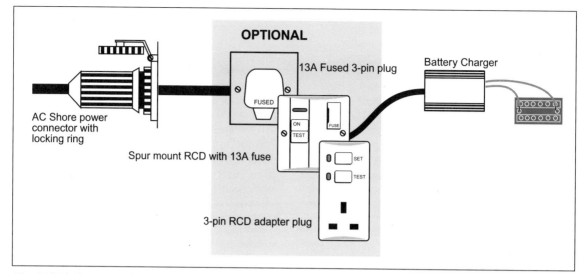

Fig. 21(22) Shore supply powering the battery charger via an RCD.

It is prudent to fit a Residual Current Device (RCD) (21.6.2), either a spur mounted RCD wired directly to the appliance, or an RCD adaptor plug between the ordinary plug and socket. Indeed, there is a powerful argument in favour of an RCD being the absolute minimum protection to be considered. They're not particularly expensive – typically £12 – yet offer considerably enhanced safety.

The connection with the marina pedestal can vary from place to place, but whatever arrangement is used must be be both watertight and lockable to ensure it is electrically and mechanically sound.

b. Fixed installation

In many ways, these are similar to a 12V DC distribution.

Thus in Fig. 21(23) each live wire from the distribution panel has its own lead direct to its respective appliance, and the neutral wire returns the current to a common neutral terminal. Even the CB indicator light adopts the same principles as its DC counterpart. AC distribution differs from DC, however, in that all cables leading to AC sockets must have a third cable to carry the earth.

Here it is worth stressing that only multi-strand 3-core cable should be used – not household-type single strand cable which can go brittle, and perhaps fail, due to the motion and shock to which all boats are subjected.

21.6.1 AC SAFETY DEVICES

Ensuring the safety of such systems calls for both earth leakage and over-current protection: a residual current device (RCD) and miniature circuit

breaker (MCB) respectively. There is much debate over which should precede the other, but many would say that it doesn't make a hoot of difference.

Today, most people would in any case install a residual current breaker overload (RCBO) device which combines an RCD and MCB into a single unit. A typical RCBO would trip on a residual current difference of 30mA in 30msecs or an overload of 16A. It is quite usual for such devices to be mounted on the boat's AC distribution panel – not exactly pleasing to look at but certainly convenient. Usually the panel will also have instrumentation and a polarity check light.

Although not shown, a refinement to this system is an Isolation Transformer (see 21.6.3) which would be electrically located between the shore power connector plug and the RCBO. This is a 1:1 transformer which neither raises nor lowers the voltage. Its purpose is to get the 240V supply to the boat without there being a direct connection to the shore – the transfer being achieved by induction between the transformer's coils. This isolation of the input from the output bestows two advantages:

a. it effectively brings the source of power to within the boat, so that the boat's earth can now be brought to the neutral point of the transformer. Any earth fault current in the boat's system now only has to travel to this point, making the system both safer and more efficient.

b. since the boat is electrically isolated from the shore, it becomes protected against leakage from the shore earth system, with all the electrolytic problems that any such failure could bring.

Isolation transformers affect the location of

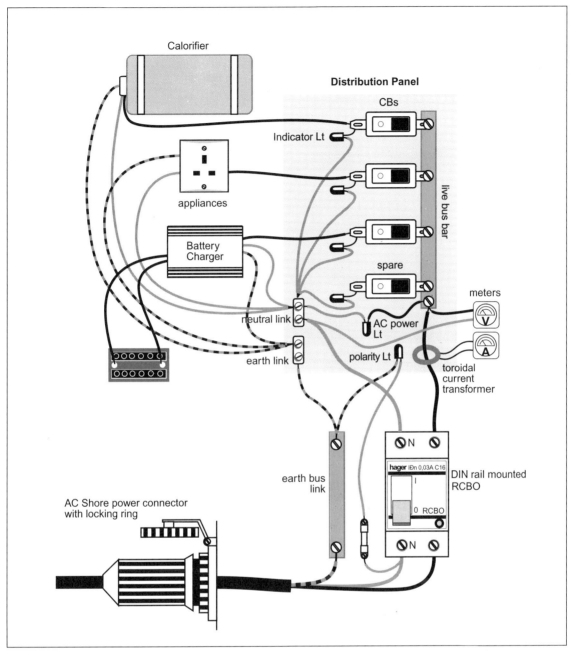

Fig. 21(23) An independently wired AC shore supply system, powering battery charger, immersion heater and other appliances via an RCBO.

protection devices. To detect earth leakage currents, RCBOs and RCDs must be downstream of the transformer. The location of MCBs relative to isolation transformers is debatable and therefore MCBs may be seen upstream or downstream of the transformer. A majority view seems to prefer MCBs downstream of the transformer since there is some concern that the transformer's impedance may restrict any fault current to the MCB.

21.6.2 RESIDUAL CURRENT DEVICE (RCD)

There are two sides to any electrical circuit: in DC there is the +ve side and the –ve side; in AC circuits there is the live and the neutral. With regard to AC, if 10A goes down the live wire, then 10A would be expected to return along the neutral wire; if it does not, there is a current leakage. Somewhere in the circuit the insulation has failed and as a consequence an appliance or broken insulated cable may be dangerously raised to live potential. Ideally the leakage, wherever it may be, would hopefully travel to ground via the earth wire and blow the fuse in the live wire. However, this may not happen if the ground/earth

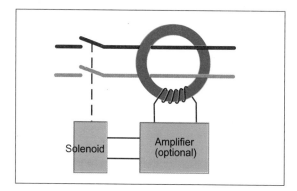

Fig. 21(24) A Residual Current Device (RCD).

resistance is high and the potential shock could still kill!

A faster, safer, and more sensitive piece of equipment like a Residual Current Device is needed; see Fig. 21(24).

In a RCD both the live and neutral wires pass through a circular iron ring. The incoming current from the live wire induces a magnetic field in the ring in one direction and the equal and opposite current from the neutral wire induces a magnetic field in the opposite direction. The net magnetic field detected at the sensing coil is therefore zero. Any difference in the two currents (resulting from a leakage somewhere) produces a net magnetic field which induces a current in the sensing coil wound around the ring. To enhance the sensitivity of these devices, the sensing signals may sometimes be amplified so as to activate a solenoid tripping mechanism, which disconnects both the live and neutral sides. To indicate their high degree of sensitivity, detected differences in current are measured in milliamps and the speed of activation is rated in fractions of a second.

21.6.3 POLARITY

The polarity light is one of the most important items on the distribution panel. It indicates whether a boat's wiring conforms with the shore power, ie live to live, neutral to neutral and earth to earth. Although the light itself is on the AC panel, its connections into the system must precede everything else.

When connecting a boat to shore power, always check that the polarity light shows an 'all clear', before letting power reach the various distribution circuits.

If the polarity were incorrect, the neutral would become live and the live neutral, as in Fig. 21(25a). If then a fault were to occur, the fuse, being now on the neutral side, would in effect be by-passed (and therefore useless); whilst the earth would carry the fault current back to the source and

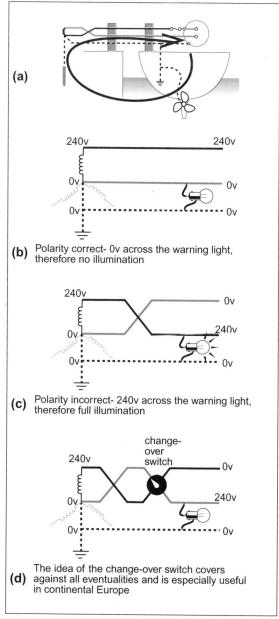

Fig. 21(25) A Polarity warning light. The yacht is alongside and connected to shore power.

along to the fault again – a very hazardous situation. Figs. 21 (25 b-d) illustrate correct and incorrect polarity and the use of a changeover switch. The 3-phase AC supply is at the left of each diagram.

It is vital to know whether an illuminated polarity light means that the polarity is correct or incorrect. The latter seems more logical, warning that all is not as it should be. Some panels have two lights which must be specifically checked to see which one is illuminated and indicating the polarity condition – a possible source of confusion.

WARNING: Beware when opening an AC distribution panel lest the cables feeding the polarity light are live, despite the main CBs being open. To be absolutely safe, before opening an AC panel, remove the shore power connection plug from the marina pedestal as well as opening the main CBs. Note: The cables to the polarity light are fused at the source, since they are upstream of the CB or RCBO protecting the whole boat.

If an isolation transformer is fitted, there is no need for this warning because a change in shore power polarity will have no effect on the transformer's output.

21.6.4   THE EARTH LOOP
Fig. 21(26a) shows a pair of yachts on a finger pontoon. Each is properly connected to the shore supply, and thus also connected to each other because all boats in the marina share the same common earth lead. Unfortunately there is now a galvanic relationship between the two vessels in which the one that is anodic to the other could suffer serious corrosion.

A device is needed which will permit a full AC earth fault current to pass through to ground, but will not allow small galvanic DC currents to leave or enter the boat.

The theoretical solution, Fig. 21(26b) is to install a Galvanic Isolator, in simplistic terms a pair of opposing diodes in parallel; this is small and cheap. Any AC can take either of the two routes through the diode circuit. As for any DC current, the reverse-biased diode will block any DC current outright and the forward-biased diode will block any DC current up to 0.7V; remember a diode in a forward direction has a small voltage drop, typically about 0.7V, to let current to pass in the forward direction. If a galvanic DC blockage of 0.7V is not enough then simply double up the diodes in series to total 1.4V.

In Fig. 21(26c) an isolation transformer (large, heavy and expensive) has been installed for maximum safety. This is a 1:1 transformer which neither steps up nor steps down the voltage; the input and output voltages therefore remain at 240V AC. By the nature of a transformer, the input and the output lines are not electrically connected to each other at all, and the communicating link or transfer between them is through magnetic flux. The Earth leads are also isolated since the Shore Earth terminates at the transformer shield core and is not carried on to the boat's distribution system. The boat's earth network is brought to the neutral point of the transformer output, so the boat is therefore isolated from any stray currents.

21.7   OTHER POWER SOURCES

In the serious cruising boat it is sensible to use any satisfactory means of generating 'free' electricity, thereby backing up the engine-driven alternator. Wind generators and solar cells both have their advantages and limitations.

Towed water generators and shaft generators no longer enjoy much appeal and are fitted to only 0.1% of the world's cruising yachts. Portable mechanical generators also have their uses and are considered first.

21.7.1   PORTABLE GENERATORS
These are now lighter, smaller, quieter and more truly portable than ever before. The smallest, single-cylinder two-stroke petrol generator has a dry weight of only 9kg (20lb) and a rated output of about 450 watts at 240V AC, or a DC output of about 6 amps at 12V. Sound levels are quoted as 58 decibels which at 7m equates to normal conversation. Larger and more powerful petrol generators are available.

Portable generators have two main uses:

a. to recharge the batteries, if they are discharged and unable to start the engine; or

b. to feed power tools, TV, video, computer or various domestic items requiring 240V AC in boats which otherwise only have AC when connected to a shore supply.

The disadvantages are the stowage space needed, and the need to carry petrol onboard –

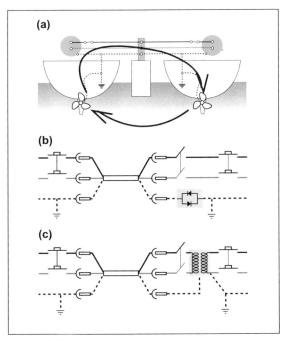

Fig. 21(26) The Earth Loop.

although some can be adapted to run on LPG. Larger and more powerful diesel-driven generators are available, but these are not strictly portable, and are better described as free-standing.

For safety (fuel and exhaust) all such units need to be run on deck and only in harbour, rather than at sea. They are not marinised, and great care is needed when using 240V AC in even slightly damp conditions.

21.7.2   WIND GENERATORS

Wind generators in the sometimes breezy climate of the UK and NW Europe may prove to be a worthwhile source of electrical power. They operate day and night, typically producing 4 amps in a 20 knot wind. This is adequate for replenishing current used in normal domestic activities, but too much for topping up or trickle charging of batteries when a boat is left unattended. Some form of regulation is therefore required to control the output in relation to the battery voltage.

The generator will be either a dynamo or something akin to an alternator type. Dynamos of course are DC motors working in reverse, so a diode on the output is essential; otherwise the battery that is supposed to be on charge will motorise the wind generator, providing an additional means of propulsion! The output of dynamos is usually double that of the alternator type, and the commutator wear often associated with dynamos is tolerable due to low rotational speeds. Alternator types resemble large bicycle generators, the generated current being either single or three phase before being rectified to DC through a nest of diodes.

One similarity between the dynamo and the alternator type is that neither have field coils, using instead permanent magnets to produce the fields. For much of the time a wind generator may be idling, and it is only when the wind gets up, that the output becomes excessive and it is essential to regulate the output. It is therefore considered wasteful and complex to use any form of field current control to regulate the output.

The most secure alternative means is a Shunt Regulator which works on similar lines to the transistorised voltage regulators in modern alternators. The transistors are mounted on a finned heat sink. A diode between the shunt and the battery guards against any fire risk. If however split charge diodes are in use they will conveniently take care of this problem.

The rated output of a wind generator must be carefully matched to the needs of the boat. The buyer must clearly understand what the rated output is against wind speed – a common source of ambiguity. Output values may be quoted as averages, peaks, maximums or even against specific wind speeds. Most generators will not produce an output below at least 7 knots wind speed. A quoted maximum output should be viewed with caution since it may not be achievable until a 30 knot wind is blowing. Realistically the buyer needs to know the output over a wind speed envelope of 10 to 20 knots. Do not experiment with the size, pitch and diameter of the blades; these are finely tuned and qualified advice should be sought.

Some larger generators have blades up to 0.9m (3ft) in diameter, which rotate at high speeds and are potentially lethal; they can also be quite noisy. Generators are best mounted on a strong metal pole above the pushpit, with the blades well clear of human heads.

21.7.3   SOLAR PANELS

Solar panels are a silent complement to wind generators, but quite a few panels are needed to obtain a worthwhile output. Some flexible panels can be permanently fixed on curved surfaces such as the coachroof. Others can be secured temporarily to guardrails, shrouds or booms, thus allowing them to be removed – for seagoing or for their own security in harbour.

Panels are expensive and the large outlay has to be weighed against the comparatively small output. In terms of output per units of money, solar panels deliver less than wind generators, and even thin cloud cover can reduce their efficiency by 70%. Their output is perhaps most useful for trickle charging on an unattended boat.

A panel consists of photovoltaic cells connected in series to provide 14V for a 12V system. A two square foot panel produces about 6 watts of power – not a lot! But a suitably sized panel on a sailing yacht will provide enough power to the battery for electronic navigational equipment, but not the autopilot.

All but the smallest panels need a regulator to prevent over-charging. In general, when the peak charge from the panel is less than 1.5% of the battery capacity in Ah, a charging regulator is not necessary. Some wind generator regulators will accept an input from solar panels, but the reverse is not usually possible. With multiple panels all the leads should be brought to a common junction box from which a feed lead is led to the batteries, via split diodes if desired. The ground return lead is led to the –ve link of the DC circuit breaker board.

21.8 MAINTENANCE

Marine electrical equipment operates, or fails to, in the most hostile of environments. Salt water and a salt-laden atmosphere corrode equipment and terminals both on deck and below. Masthead navigation lights are almost out of sight and probably out of mind. Deck connections for electrical wiring and aerial leads frequently cause a malfunction or complete failure. Batteries are tucked into an inaccessible and unventilated corner, covered in dirt and condensation, with unguarded, corroding terminals.

Keep equipment including batteries dry and clean; take portable items home in the winter. Clean battery terminals shiny bright, then grease them. Spray connectors and the inside of switch panels with WD40. Check alternator drive belt tension: when depressed by moderate finger pressure in the middle of its longest run, the belt should only give about 12mm (0·5in). Carry a spare belt.

Cherish your electrics as an infantryman cherishes his rifle – either could save your life.

21.9 BOOKS AND WEB SITES

21.9.1   BOOKS

The Marine electrics book by Geoffrey O'Connell/ Ashford, Buchan & Enright

Boat electrical systems by Dag Pike/Adlard Coles

Boat electrics by John Watney/David & Charles

Engine monitoring on yachts by Hans Donat

Simple Boat Electrics by John Myatt/Fernhurst

Reliable marine electrics by Chris Laming/Adlard Coles

Boat Owner's wiring manual by Charles Wing/ Adlard Coles

The Marine electrical and electronics Bible by John Payne/Adlard Coles

Boat Owner's mechanical & electrical manual by Nigel Calder/Adlard Coles

The 12V Doctor's handbook by Edgar Beyn

The 12V Doctor's troubleshooting book by Edgar Beyn

The 12V Bible for boats by Miner Botherton/ Waterline

Note: The last six books are from the United States and, although arguably the best books on the list, some of the practices and procedures differ from those in the UK and EU countries – especially with AC shore power.

21.9.2   WEB SITES

Most of the following sites contain excellent technical support and literature which can be freely downloaded:

www.heartinterface.com
www.power-store.com
www.balmar.net
www.victronenergie.com
www.adverc.co.uk
www.delphiauto.com
www.mastervolt.com
www.onboardpower.com

Index

T